Every Decker book is accompanied by a CD-ROM.

The disk appears in the front of each copy, in its own sealed jacket. Affixed to the front of the book is a distinctive BcD sticker **"Book *cum* disk."**

The disk contains the complete text and illustrations of the book in fully searchable PDF files. The book and disk are sold only as a package; neither is available independently, and no prices are available for the items individually.

BC Decker Inc is committed to providing high-quality electronic publications that complement traditional information and learning methods.

We trust you will find the book/CD package invaluable and invite your comments and suggestions.

Brian C. Decker
CEO and Publisher

Book No. **05021678**

CONTAINS 1 CD

Evidence-Based DIABETES CARE

Editors

Hertzel C. Gerstein, MD, MSc, FRCPC

Professor, Departments of Medicine,
Clinical Epidemiology, and Biostatistics
Director, Division of Endocrinology and Metabolism
McMaster University Faculty of Health Sciences
Hamilton, Ontario
Canada

R. Brian Haynes, MD, PhD, FRCPC, FACP

Professor of Clinical Epidemiology and Medicine
Chair, Department of Clinical Epidemiology and Biostatistics
McMaster University Faculty of Health Sciences
Hamilton, Ontario
Canada

2001
BC Decker Inc
Hamilton • London

BC Decker Inc
20 Hughson Street South
P.O. Box 620, L.C.D. 1
Hamilton, Ontario L8N 3K7
Tel: 905-522-7017; 1-800-568-7281
Fax: 905-522-7839; 1-800-311-4987
E-mail: info@bcdecker.com
www.bcdecker.com

02 03 04/ FP / 9 8 7 6 5 4 3 2

ISBN 1-55009-124-7

Printed in Canada

Sales and Distribution

United States
BC Decker Inc
P.O. Box 785
Lewiston, NY 14092-0785
Tel: 905-522-7017; 800-568-7281
Fax: 905-522-7839; 888-311-4987
E-mail: info@bcdecker.com
www.bcdecker.com

Canada
BC Decker Inc
20 Hughson Street South
P.O. Box 620, LCD 1
Hamilton, Ontario L8N 3K7
Tel: 905-522-7017; 800-568-7281
Fax: 905-522-7839; 888-311-4987
E-mail: info@bcdecker.com
www.bcdecker.com

Foreign Rights
John Scott & Company
International Publishers' Agency
P.O. Box 878
Kimberton, PA 19442
Tel: 610-827-1640
Fax: 610-827-1671
E-mail: jsco@voicenet.com

Japan
Igaku-Shoin Ltd.
Foreign Publications Department
3-24-17 Hongo
Bunkyo-ku, Tokyo, Japan 113-8719
Tel: 3 3817 5680
Fax: 3 3815 6776
E-mail: fd@igaku-shoin.co.jp

U.K., Europe, Scandinavia, Middle East
Elsevier Science
Customer Service Department
Foots Cray High Street
Sidcup, Kent
DA14 5HP, UK
Tel: 44 (0) 208 308 5760
Fax: 44 (0) 181 308 5702
E-mail: cservice@harcourt.com

Singapore, Malaysia,Thailand, Philippines, Indonesia, Vietnam, Pacific Rim, Korea
Elsevier Science Asia
583 Orchard Road
#09/01, Forum
Singapore 238884
Tel: 65-737-3593
Fax: 65-753-2145

Australia, New Zealand
Elsevier Science Australia
Customer Service Department
STM Division
Locked Bag 16
St. Peters, New South Wales, 2044
Australia
Tel: 61 02 9517-8999
Fax: 61 02 9517-2249
E-mail: stmp@harcourt.com.au
Web site: www.harcourt.com.au

Mexico and Central America
ETM SA de CV
Calle de Tula 59
Colonia Condesa
06140 Mexico DF, Mexico
Tel: 52-5-5553-6657
Fax: 52-5-5211-8468
E-mail: editoresdetextosmex@prodigy.net.mx

Argentina
CLM (Cuspide Libros Medicos)
Av. Córdoba 2067 - (1120)
Buenos Aires, Argentina
Tel: (5411) 4961-0042/(5411) 4964-0848
Fax: (5411) 4963-7988
E-mail: clm@cuspide.com

Brazil
Tecmedd
Av. Maurílio Biagi, 2850
City Ribeirão Preto – SP – CEP: 14021-000
Tel: 0800 992236
Fax: (16) 3993-9000
E-mail: tecmedd@tecmedd.com.br

Contributors

Michael A. Adams, PhD
Professor of Pharmacology and Toxicology
Queen's University
Kingston, Ontario

Sonia Anand, MD, MSc
Assistant Professor
McMaster University
Hamilton General Hospital
Hamilton, Ontario

Carolyn Beck, MD
Pediatrics Resident, Department of Pediatrics
University of Toronto
The Hospital for Sick Children
Toronto, Ontario

Iain S. Begg, MB, FRCS (Edin), FRCSC,
FRCOphth.
Associate Professor, Departments of
Ophthalmology and Medicine
University of British Columbia
Vancouver, British Columbia

Gillian L. Booth, MD, MSc, FRCPC
University of Toronto
Division of Endocrinology and Metabolism
St. Michael's Hospital
Toronto, Ontario

Sarah Capes, MD, FRCPC
Assistant Professor, Department of Medicine
McMaster University
Hamilton, Ontario

Alice Y. Y. Cheng, MD
Department of Medicine
University of Toronto
Toronto, Ontario

Jo-Anne Clarke, BSc
McMaster University
Hamilton, Ontario

Jacqueline Curtis, MD, FRCPC
Fellow, Pediatric Endocrinology
University of Toronto
The Hospital for Sick Children
Toronto, Ontario

Denis Daneman, MB, BCh, FRCPC
Professor, Department of Pediatrics
University of Toronto
Chief, Division of Endocrinology
The Hospital for Sick Children
Toronto, Ontario

Sean F. Dinneen, MD, FRCPI, FACP
Consultant Diabetologist
Addenbrookes Hospital
Cambridge, United Kingdom

Lisa Dolovich, PharmD
Department of Family Medicine
McMaster University
Centre for Evaluation of Medicines
St. Joseph's Hospital
Hamilton, Ontario
Faculty of Pharmacy
University of Toronto
Toronto, Ontario

John Dupre, MA, BSc, BMBCh, FRCP, FACP
Professor, Departments of Medicine and
Physiology
University of Western Ontario
London, Ontario

Marcia Frank, RN, MHSc, CDE
Clinical Nurse Specialist, Diabetes Team
The Hospital for Sick Children
Toronto, Ontario

Subhas C. Ganguli, MD, FRCPC
Clinical Scholar, Department of
Gastroenterology
McMaster Medical Centre
Hamilton, Ontario

Hertzel C. Gerstein, MD, MSc, FRCPC
Professor, Departments of Medicine
Clinical Epidemiology and Biostatistics
Director, Division of Endocrinology
and Metabolism
McMaster University Faculty of Health Sciences
Hamilton, Ontario

Russell E. Glasgow, PhD
Senior Scientist
AMC Cancer Research Center
Vashon, Washington

Jeannette M. Goguen, MD, FRCPC
Lecturer, University of Toronto
Department of Medicine
Staff Endocrinologist
St. Michael's Hospital
Toronto, Ontario

Gordon H. Guyatt, MD, MSc (Epid)
McMaster University
McMaster University Health Sciences Centre
Clinical Epidemiology and Biostatistics
Hamilton, Ontario

Jill Hamilton, MD, FRCPC
Assistant Professor, Department of Pediatrics
University of Toronto
The Hospital for Sick Children
Toronto, Ontario

Stewart B. Harris, MD, MPH, FCFP, FACPM
Associate Professor, Department of Family
Medicine
University of Western Ontario
London, Ontario

David T. Harvey, MD, FRCPC
Associate Professor of Medicine
Head, Division of PMTR
McMaster University
Hamilton Health Sciences – Henderson
Division
Hamilton, Ontario

R. Brian Haynes, MD, PhD, FRCPC, FACP
Professor of Clinical Epidemiology and Medicine
Chair, Department of Clinical Epidemiology
and Biostatistics
McMaster University Faculty of Health Sciences
Hamilton, Ontario

Jeremy P. W. Heaton, MD, FACS, FRCSC
Professor of Urology, Pharmacology and
Toxicology
Queen's University
Attending Staff, Kingston General Hospital
Kingston, Ontario

Anne M. Holbrook, MD, PharmD, MSc,
FRCPC
Associate Professor, Department of Medicine
McMaster University
McMaster University Medical Centre
Centre for Education of Medicines
St. Joseph's Hospital
Hamilton, Ontario

Dereck Hunt, MD, MSc, FRCPC
McMaster University
Hamilton Health Sciences Corporation
Hamilton, Ontario

Roman Jaeschke, MD, MSc
Associate Clinical Professor, Department of
Medicine
McMaster University
Hamilton, Ontario

Margaret L. Lawson, MD, MSc, FRCPC
Assistant Professor, Division of Endocrinology
and Metabolism
University of Ottawa
Department of Pediatrics
Children's Hospital of Eastern Ontario
Ottawa, Ontario

Lawrence A. Leiter, MD, FRCPC, FACP
Professor, Departments of Medicine and
Nutritional Sciences
Head, Division of Endocrinology and Metabolism
University of Toronto
St. Michael's Hospital
Toronto, Ontario

Mitchell A.H. Levine, MD, MSc, FRCPC
Associate Professor, Department of Clinical
Epidemiology and Biostatistics
McMaster University
Centre for Evaluation of Medicines
St. Joseph's Hospital
Hamilton, Ontario

Jeffrey Mahon, MD, MSc, FRCPC
Associate Professor, Departments of
Epidemiology and Medicine
University of Western Ontario
London, Ontario

Klas Malmberg, MD, PhD, FACC
Associate Professor, Department of Cardiology
Karolinska Hospital
Stockholm, Sweden

Finlay A. McAlister, MD, MSc
Assistant Professor, Division of General Internal
Medicine
University of Alberta
University of Alberta Hospital
Edmonton, Alberta

Graydon Meneilly, MD, FACP
Professor and Head Division of Geriatric
Medicine
University of British Columbia
Medical Director, Community and Specialty
Medicine
Vancouver Hospital
Vancouver, British Columbia

Laurie Mereu, MD
Assistant Professor, Department of Medicine
University of Alberta
University of Alberta Hospital
Edmonton, Alberta

Victor M. Montori, MD
Assistant Professor
Mayo Medical School
Fellow, Division of Endocrinology, Metabolism,
and Nutrition and Internal Medicine
Mayo Clinic
Rochester, Minnesota

Alvaro Morales, MD, FRCSC, FACS
Professor, Urology and Oncology
Queen's University
Attending Staff, Kingston General Hospital and
Hotel Dieu Hospitals
Kingston, Ontario

Sarah E. Muirhead, MD, FRCPC
Assistant Professor, Division of Endocrinology
Department of Pediatrics
University of Ottawa
Children's Hospital of Eastern Ontario
Ottawa, Ontario

John D. Piette, PhD
Department of Health Research and Policy
Center for Primary Care and Outcomes Research
Stanford University
Menco Park, California

Colette Raymond, BSc Pharm, PharmD student
Faculty of Pharmaceutical Sciences
University of British Columbia
Vancouver, British Columbia

Edmond A. Ryan, MD
Professor, Department of Medicine
University of Alberta
Capital Health Authority
Edmonton, Alberta

Michael Schulzer, MD, PhD
Professor, Departments of Medicine and Statistics
University of British Columbia
Vancouver, British Columbia

Andrew W. Steele, MD, FRCPC
Division of Nephrology
University of Toronto
St. Michael's Hospital
Toronto, Ontario
Lakeridge Health Corporation
Oshawa, Ontario

Sharon E. Straus, MD, FRCPC
Departments of Medicine and Geriatric Medicine
University of Toronto
Mount Sinai Hospital
Toronto, Ontario

Daniel Tessier, MD, MSc
Professor, Faculty of Medicine
Sherbrooke University
Clinician Researcher
Sherbrooke Geriatric University Institute
Sherbrooke, Québec

Gervais N. Tougas, MD, CM, FRCPC
Associate Professor, Division of
Gastroenterology
Director, Motility Laboratory
McMaster University
McMaster University Medical Centre
Hamilton, Ontario

Susan M. Webster-Bogaert, BSc(kin), MA
Research Associate, Department of Family
Medicine
University of Western Ontario
Centre for Studies in Family Medicine
London, Ontario

Rena R. Wing, PhD
Professor, Department of Psychiatry and
Human Behavior
Brown Medical School
Providence, Rhode Island

Jean-François Yale, MD, CSPQ
Associate Professor, McGill Nutrition Centre
McGill University
Director, Metabolic Day Centre
Royal Victoria Hospital
Montreal, Québec

Salim Yusuf, MBBS, DPhil, FRCPC, FRCP
(UK), FACC*
Professor of Medicine
Director, Division of Cardiology
Director, Population Health Research Institute
McMaster University
Hamilton, Ontario

Bernard Zinman, MDCM, FACP, FRCP
Department of Medicine
University of Toronto
Mount Sinai Hospital
Toronto, Ontario

Douglas W. Zochodne, MD, FRCPC
Professor, University of Calgary
Consultant in Neurology
Foothills Medical Center
Calgary, Alberta

*Dr. Yusuf is supported by a Senior Scientist Award of the Medical Research Council of Canada and a Heart and Stroke Foundation of Ontario Research Chair.

Preface

WHY EVIDENCE-BASED DIABETES CARE?

Diabetes is a common chronic condition that, in the year 2001, remains incurable. Although defined on the basis of elevated plasma glucose levels, it is clear that diabetes is characterized by many associated abnormalities related to both pancreatic beta-cell function and the effects and actions of insulin on fat, protein, and carbohydrate metabolism. These abnormalities can have an acute effect on quality of life and, in the case of Type 1 diabetes, can even lead to death if not appropriately identified and treated. More significantly, they predispose affected individuals to several serious chronic problems including, but not limited to, blindness, kidney failure, peripheral nerve damage, amputations, coronary heart disease, peripheral vascular disease, and cerebrovascular disease. Indeed, both diabetes and the related metabolic abnormalities that precede the rise of glucose levels into the diabetic range account for a substantial proportion of these problems in the developed world.

These depressing considerations are counterbalanced by a growing body of carefully collected evidence showing that many of these problems can be successfully treated, reduced, or even prevented by the application of emerging therapies and self-care behaviors. The major challenge is to communicate the advances identified by such research to health care practitioners, affected individuals, and the family of affected individuals. A related challenge is to identify these infrequent and sometimes "low-profile" research results that are most relevant to the day-to-day care of people affected by diabetes. Another is to distinguish these from the abundant genetic, cellular, physiologic, and preclinical scientific data that are published daily and that are often reported in the lay media.

The rationale for this textbook, then, is to highlight and document the evidence from applied clinical research regarding the diagnosis, prognosis, and therapy of diabetes-related medical problems. The work is designed for the clinician or researcher who asks questions such as "What is the evidence that laser therapy prevents blindness and how effective is it? What is the risk of diabetic nephropathy in people with microalbuminuria? Is the degree of hyperglycemia a risk factor for heart disease?" As such, much will be found describing analytic surveys of diagnostic tests, cohort studies relating risk factors to prognosis, and randomized trials of various therapies. Although every attempt has been made to be comprehensive, it is certain that the evidence described herein does not represent an exhaustive search of the literature; rather, it is a survey of much, if not most, of the relevant literature, often summarized in tabular form. Authors have been asked to identify relevant citations in support of their conclusions and to rank the quality of the evidence cited, so as to provide an indication of the strength of the conclusions, which are summarized at the end of every chapter.

In light of this, this textbook is not a comprehensive review of all of diabetes. Little will be found describing pathophysiology and biochemistry as there are many excellent reviews and textbooks covering these areas. Further, this is not a compendium of clinical practice guidelines and should not be used as one. Instead, it may be used as a resource either to assess guidelines or to help develop new ones, but the "evidence base" described herein represents only one ingredient in the guideline development process. Finally, since the content of this textbook spans the breadth of contemporary diabetes care, it will be clear to the reader that there are many "holes" in the evidence base that is currently available. Wherever possible, the absence of clear evidence has been identified and is reflected by low ratings of the cited evidence or by descriptions of empirical approaches to the topic being discussed.

This book is accompanied by a unique electronic database of abstracts of key studies on the cause, course, diagnosis, and therapy of diabetes, along with general descriptions of key information for patients. The Diabetes Mellitus Evidence Database has been collected and prepared by the Health Information Research Unit of McMaster University during the past 10 years, based on the same criteria used for the evidence-based journals and database prepared there, including *ACP Journal Club, Evidence-Based Medicine,* and *Best Evidence.* It provides details and summaries of key studies that are relevant to contemporary diabetes care.

We hope that our approach will help clarify the strengths and weaknesses of the evidence upon which current clinical practice is based, leading to the best match between evidence from research and patients' circumstances and wishes. We also hope that it will stimulate more research and inquiry into optimal diabetes care so that we can eventually reduce or eliminate the health burden associated with this all-too-common condition.

HCG
RBH
February 2001

Contents

DELIVERY OF CARE

CHAPTER 1

What Evidence?

R. Brian Haynes, MD, PhD, FRCPC, FACP, and
Hertzel C. Gerstein, MD, MSc, FRCPC

———————

ABSTRACT

The term "evidence-based medicine" refers to the explicit, conscientious, and judicious use of current best evidence from clinical care research in managing individual patients. This book applies these concepts to the care of people with diabetes. It focuses on discussing the clinical evidence that is available to support inferences related to the diagnosis, prognosis and risk evaluation, and management of people with diabetes. Key points are captured as "evidence-based messages" and assigned a level or strength of evidence, along with citations to support them. Combining this information with evidence obtained from clinical interaction with individual patients should lead to improved outcomes for people with diabetes.

———————

INTRODUCTION

Diabetes mellitus is an extremely common, complex, and serious chronic disease. It is also now recognized as a serious risk factor for other chronic diseases, often referred to as the chronic complications of diabetes, and represents a significant burden of illness in both the developed and developing world. The present and potential future impact of diabetes is thus sobering. The fact that there is a rapidly growing body of readily available applied clinical research, however, that can help reduce this impact, is exciting. This research needs to be highlighted, which this book sets out to do.

This chapter describes the rationale for the approach taken throughout this textbook, as well as the philosophy underlying it, questions:

1. What is "evidence-based medicine"?
2. Why focus on "evidence-based" diabetes care?
3. How was the evidence found and rated?

WHAT IS EVIDENCE-BASED MEDICINE?

Evidence from modern research has a lot to say about the management of diabetes mellitus. This book emphasizes the best evidence from health care research concerning the diagnosis, prognosis and risk, prevention, and treatment of Types 1 and 2 diabetes mellitus and their complications. "Health care research" refers to reports from applied clinical studies of prognosis, diagnosis, prevention, and therapy, rather than to the body of basic and preliminary clinical research on which these applied studies are based. This is not to denigrate the importance of basic research; applied research clearly and necessarily builds on relevant studies of biology, physiology, mechanisms, and pathophysiology. These basic studies may provide some support for clinical decisions, but they are not designed to reveal the benefits and hazards of using one diagnostic test over another, estimate the incidence and risk of a consequence of disease in an individual from the clinic or the general population, or estimate the effect of an intervention on clinically important outcomes in typical individuals in the clinic or community. Such knowledge can only be obtained from practical, clinical studies designed to answer these questions. It is knowledge derived from such applied studies that is highlighted throughout this book. Such studies support the practice of "evidence-based medicine," which is defined as "the conscientious and judicious use of current best evidence from clinical care research in the management of individual patients."[1]

WHY FOCUS ON EVIDENCE-BASED DIABETES CARE?

This book attempts to enhance the transfer of important evidence from clinical care research into the clinical practice domain. Such transfer promises to yield significant benefits for today's patients because, as landmark studies of the past two decades have documented, life-, morbidity-, and cost-sparing interventions of unprecedented benefit now exist for people with diabetes. Unfortunately, studies of the quality of diabetes care[2] reveal a large gap between what could be achieved with optimal use of current knowledge and the care that most people with diabetes actually receive. The reasons for this are numerous and complex[3,4] and are discussed further in Chapter 5. One of the most important barriers is the difficulty clinicians have in keeping up to date with advances in practical knowledge. Certainly, as described in this book, the care of patients with diabetes is complex, ranging from the preventive benefits of intensive glucose control, blood pressure lowering, and lipid control to effective treatments for diabetes-related complications, including cardiovascular, ophthalmic, neurologic, renal, and podiatric. Also, some treatment options for clinical problems and comorbid conditions conflict with the best care for diabetes (eg, drugs that raise blood sugar) or lead to adverse effects that may preclude their use in an individual. Clinicians and patients cannot be blamed for wondering how to come to grips with the current complexities of diabetes care and the new information being generated. Indeed, depending on how one's clinical practice is structured, it may be almost impossible to consistently follow every recommendation for care.

This book provides guidance. Authors were asked to assemble the current best evidence for diabetes care and to generate "evidence-based messages" summarizing the key points for clinical practice. These messages rate the strength of evidence on which they are based and explicitly identify supporting citations. Thus, readers have the option of independently judging the value of the diagnostic, prognostic, and therapeutic inferences made by the authors. Although this book is designed to be a useful reference for both the clinician and the clinician-researcher, it must be emphasized that highlighting and codifying the best evidence in clinically useful messages provides some, but only some, guidance for assessing and managing people with diabetes.

Evidence from research does not make decisions; clinicians and patients do. Real-life clinical assessment and decision-making must balance research evidence and recommendations with other important components, including assessment of the clinical circumstances of the patient and the patient's own preferences and wishes (Figure 1–1). In the clinical assessment of the patient, the practitioner applies his or her expertise to collect and interpret evidence from the history, physical examination, diagnostic tests, social and comorbid conditions, and other factors. The practitioner must also ensure that the patient's own wishes and preferences are determined and incorporated into the decision. No clinician involved in diabetes care will fail to appreciate that the patient has the last word, and decisions that do not take this into account will inevitably miss the mark. Thus, the term "evidence" may apply to both evidence from research ("external evidence") and evidence from the patient ("internal evidence").

HOW WAS THE EVIDENCE FOUND AND RATED?

It would be quite a feat to assemble all the evidence from research bearing on diabetes and its care. Indeed, if it were possible, such a feat would jeopardize the purpose of this book: to communicate the *best* current evidence from research that can help inform clinical assessments and decisions. Thus, the following chapters describe what authors judged to be the "best" evidence addressing important clinical questions relevant to determining the diagnosis, prognosis and risk, prevention, and treatment of people with diabetes mellitus and its chronic consequences.

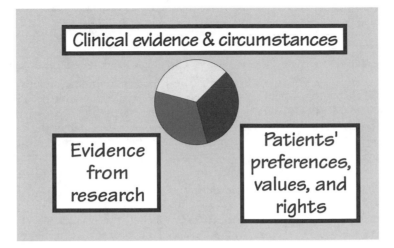

Figure 1–1 Clinical assessments and decisions.

In searching the literature, several authors accessed a database of summaries of studies meeting explicit criteria for scientific merit and clinical relevance.[5] The reader can also review these evidence summaries in the special database, *Evidence for Diabetes Care*, provided on the CD-ROM in the jacket of this book. This searchable database has been meticulously assembled over the past decade and provides special abstracts for the most important clinical studies in diabetes up to June 2000. Authors also searched MEDLINE and other appropriate databases and Web sites for additional studies, including those of the American Diabetes Association (*www.diabetes.org*), the Canadian Diabetes Association (*www.diabetes.ca*), and the National Institute of Diabetes and Digestive and Kidney Diseases (*www.niddk.nih.gov*).

Authors were also provided with criteria to rate the quality of research evidence supporting the evidence-based messages they developed. These criteria were based on the process developed for the Canadian Hypertension Society[6] and adopted by the Canadian Diabetes Association[7] in producing their regularly updated clinical practice guidelines. These criteria are listed in Table 1–1 and are described in more detail in the chapters that follow on prognosis, diagnosis, and treatment.

Readers who feel that our authors have missed or misconstrued important evidence, or that a given message is inappropriate, should contact the author and the editors. Finally, it is important to note that the purpose of this book can only be served transiently; knowledge that is relevant to diabetes care is quickly advancing and may supersede the evidence presented here. Web sites and other resources summarizing clinically relevant evidence and that are updated regularly (such as the one that contains the diabetes evidence database on the enclosed CD-ROM (*hiru.mcmaster.ca/dem*) are therefore important resources in this endeavor.

Table 1–1 Rating Evidence for Clinical Recommendations

The rating system used to categorize research articles focused on disease management, diagnosis, and prognosis/risk is described below.

Classification of Evidence for Management (Treatment or Prevention)

There are a number of proposed ways of assigning a level of evidence to a paper. These differ in specifics but are similar in that they assign higher levels to research that is least likely to be affected by bias and most likely to convince others of the validity of the conclusion. The levels are outlined below along with a brief description of the rationale.

Table 1–1 Rating Evidence for Clinical Recommendations — *(continued)*

Levels of Evidence

Level 1A   Systematic Overviews or Meta-Analyses of Multiple Randomized Controlled Trials

Systematic overviews are a structured approach to synthesizing the results of previous research by starting with a clear question, comprehensively searching the literature, retrieving, critically appraising, and analyzing the evidence, and synthesizing the results. Meta-analysis is a statistical technique used to numerically combine the results of a number of trials to generate a more precise estimate of the treatment effect and to detect useful treatments that did not yield statistically significant results in previous underpowered trials of low sample size.

Criteria for assignment of this level to an overview (so that it can be used to support a recommendation) include (1) comprehensive search for evidence, (2) avoidance of bias in selection of articles, (3) assessment of the validity of each article included, and (4) clear conclusions supported by the data and appropriate analyses demonstrating the efficacy of an intervention.

Because a properly conducted systematic overview of randomized controlled trials will incorporate the results of all of the included studies, a more robust estimate of the treatment effect is usually yielded.

Level 1A   Large Randomized Controlled Trial with Adequate Power to Answer the Question

A randomized, placebo-controlled trial (RCT) with a statistically significant positive result for a clinical endpoint that answers a specific question would be assigned this level. The result should also be of sufficient magnitude to be clinically important.

A negative RCT (one that does not support treating with a tested intervention) would also be assigned this level if it was large enough to exclude a clinically relevant effect of treatment (ie, if the type 2 error is small enough for the researcher to be confident that a negative result is not a false negative and really represents an estimate of the "true" result). The easiest way to assess this is to look at the confidence interval around the relative risk or relative risk reduction (calculated as 1–relative risk). If the trial was negative, the confidence interval around the relative risk (or odds ratio) will include "1." If the upper limit of the 95% confidence is < 1.20 or the lower limit is > 0.80 interval (if relative risk reduction is reported, the numbers are < 20% or > −20%, respectively), the trial would have been unlikely to miss a relative risk reduction (or increase) of 20% (with 95% confidence) and should be assigned a level of "1." This is admittedly an arbitrary and conservative cutoff. Although some may argue that relative risk reductions (or increases) of < 20% should not be missed, and therefore if the study can't detect them it should be ranked lower than "1," most current trials are not powered to detect differences much less than 15 to 20%.

Level 1B   Nonrandomized Clinical Trial or Cohort Study with Indisputable Results

This rare category would include studies in which *all* patients failed on the control therapy and some or all succeeded with the tested therapy (eg, amputation for gangrene).

Level 2   Randomized Controlled Trials or RCT Overviews that Do Not Meet Level 1 Criteria

An RCT that has insufficient power to exclude a clinically important result but that shows a trend toward a result would be assigned this level. An example could be prevention of coronary disease in Type 1 diabetes patients receiving intensified therapy (from the Diabetes Control and Complications Trial. Randomized trials with statistically significant results that are judged to be not clinically important or that are not reproducible may be included here as well.

Level 3   Nonrandomized Clinical Trial or Cohort Study

Studies in which the group receiving therapy was compared to a systematically selected contemporaneous group who did not receive therapy (but that was not excluded from therapy because of perceived unsuitability for the therapy) but were followed identically.

Table 1–1 Rating Evidence for Clinical Recommendations — *(continued)*

An example might be a study of the 5-year risk of myocardial infarction in diabetic smokers compared to diabetic ex-smokers.

Level 4	Other study designs and evidence, including consensus documents, etc.

Levels of Evidence for Studies of Diagnosis

Level 1	a. Independent interpretation of test result (without knowledge of the result of the diagnostic or gold standard)
	b. Independent interpretation of the diagnostic standard (without knowledge of the test result)
	c. Selection of patients who are suspected of having (but not known to have) the disorder
	d. Reproducible description of both the test and diagnostic standard
	e. At least 50 patients with and 50 patients without the disorder
Level 2	Meets 4 of the Level 1 criteria
Level 3	Meets 3 of the Level 1 criteria
Level 4	Meets 2 or less of the Level 1 criteria

Levels of Evidence for Studies of Prognosis or Risk

Level 1	a. Inception cohort of patients with the condition of interest (eg, microalbuminuria) but free of the outcome of interest (eg, nephropathy) has been assembled
	b. Reproducible inclusion/exclusion criteria
	c. Follow-up of at least 80% of subjects
	d. Statistical adjustment for extraneous prognostic factors (confounders)
	e. Reproducible description of outcome measures
Level 2	Criteria (a) above plus 3 of the 4 other criteria met
Level 3	Criteria (a) above plus 2 of the other criteria met
Level 4	Criteria (a) above plus 1 of the other criteria met

References

1. Sackett DL, Rosenberg WMC, Gray JA, et al. Evidence-based medicine: what it is and what it isn't. BMJ 1996;312:71–2.

2. Weiner JP, Parente ST, Garnick DW, et al. Variation in office-based quality. A claims-based profile of care provided to Medicare patients with diabetes. JAMA 1995;273:1503–8.

3. Haynes RB, Sackett DL, Gray JAM, et al. Transferring evidence from research into practice: 1. The role of clinical care research evidence in clinical decisions. ACP J Club 1996;125:A14–6; Evidence-Based Medicine 1996;1:196–8.

4. Haynes RB, Sackett DL, Guyatt GH, et al. Transferring evidence from research into practice: 4. Overcoming barriers to application. ACP J Club 1997;126:A14–6; Evidence-Based Medicine 1997; 2:68–70.

5. Purpose and procedure. ACPJ Club 1999;131:A15–6.

6. Feldman RD, Campbell N, Larochelle P, et al. Task Force for the Development of the 1999 Canadian Recommendations for the Management of Hypertension. Can Med Assoc J 1999;161:S1–21.

7. Meltzer S, Leiter L, Daneman D, et al. 1998 clinical practice guidelines for the management of diabetes in Canada. Can Med Assoc J 1998;159(Suppl 8):S1–29.

CHAPTER 2

What Is the Prognosis?

Sharon E. Straus, MD, FRCPC, and Finlay A. McAlister, MD, FRCPC

INTRODUCTION

Consider the clinical scenario of a 20-year-old woman who has recently been diagnosed with Type 1 diabetes mellitus. While searching on the Internet, she has found some material about diabetes and arrives at an outpatient appointment with several questions for her clinician about her target disorder and the potential complications that could arise. Her mother also has diabetes, has recently undergone laser surgery for retinopathy, and has been told she is developing renal failure; the patient wants to know if this will happen to her. Whether posed by patients, colleagues, or themselves, clinicians frequently need to consider questions about prognosis.

Prognosis refers to the possible outcomes of a target disorder and the probabilities that these outcomes might occur. It gives patients (and clinicians) an idea of what the future may hold and can provide guidance for making diagnostic and treatment decisions. For example, should a clinician screen for microalbuminuria in a patient with diabetes mellitus? Should a patient with microalbuminuria be treated with an angiotensin-converting enzyme inhibitor?

Several types of studies can provide information on the prognosis of a group of individuals with a defined problem or risk factor. Cohort studies (in which investigators follow one or more groups of individuals over time and monitor for the occurrence of the outcome(s) of interest) represent the best design for answering prognosis questions. Randomized clinical trials can also serve as a source of prognostic information (particularly since they usually include detailed documentation of baseline data), although trial participants may not be entirely representative of the population with a disorder. Case-control studies (in which investigators retrospectively determine prognostic factors by defining the exposures of cases who have already suffered the outcome of interest and controls who have not) are particularly useful when the outcome is rare or the required follow-up is long. However, the strength of inference that can be drawn from them is limited due to the potential for both selection and measurement bias.

Not infrequently, clinicians need to identify the prognosis for an individual patient. In the clinical literature, there are often reports describing one subgroup of patients that has a different prognosis from others with the same target disorder. Thus, the characteristics of an individual patient can sometimes be used to more accurately predict that patient's unique probability of developing certain clinical outcomes. For example, an individual with Type 2 diabetes and microalbuminuria has a high risk of developing future microvascular and macrovascular complications.[1,2]

PROGNOSTIC FACTORS

Prognostic factors are demographic (such as age, gender, or socioeconomic status), disease-specific (such as Type 1 or Type 2 diabetes mellitus), or comorbid (such as hypertension or hyperlipidemia in diabetic patients) variables that are associated with the outcome of interest. Outcomes can be favorable (such as survival) or unfavorable (such as the development of renal failure or blindness). Prognostic factors need not be causal—indeed, they often are not—but they must be strongly enough associated with the development of an outcome to predict its occurrence. For example, although mild hyponatremia does not cause death, serum sodium is an important prognostic marker in congestive heart failure (individuals with congestive heart failure and hyponatremia have higher mortality rates than heart failure patients with normal serum sodium).[3]

Risk factors are distinct from prognostic factors in that they are "an aspect of personal behaviour or life-style, an environmental exposure, or an inborn or inherited characteristic, which … is known to be associated with health-related conditions."[4] For example, smoking is an important risk factor for developing lung cancer, but tumor stage is the most important prognostic factor in individuals who have lung cancer.[5]

Risk factors may be continuous (eg, in hypertensive individuals, the risk of stroke is directly related to the degree of blood pressure elevation)[6] or discrete (hypertensive individuals with diabetes mellitus have a higher cardiovascular risk than nondiabetic hypertensives).[7] Risk factors may cluster together in certain individuals and exert a synergistic effect on the outcome(s) of interest. For instance, a high proportion of hypertensive individuals also have hyperlipidemia, impaired glucose tolerance, and are smokers.[8] Further, the risk of cardiovascular mortality increases with the number of risk factors. Hypertensive women in the Chicago Heart Association Detection Project had a relative risk (RR) for cardiac death of 2.2 if their only risk factor was their hypertension, while those with concomitant hyperlipidemia had an RR of 3.7, and those with hypertension and hyperlipidemia who also smoked had an RR of 8.9.[9] While some risk factors are nonmodifiable (such as age or gender), treatment of others can improve prognosis. For example, the lowering of blood pressure with antihypertensive drugs does reduce the incidence of stroke, myocardial infarction, or renal failure.[10]

Estimating an individual's risk is not an exact science. Thus, while several multivariate risk equations[11–13] have been developed that can discriminate between subgroups who are at high or low risk for cardiovascular events, these risk assessment tools cannot predict the exact risk for an individual with any degree of certainty.[14] However, as computer support technology and the understanding of the complex interplay between genetic makeup and environmental exposures continue to evolve, it is likely that the ability to predict risk for various outcomes in an individual will markedly improve. Until that time, it is important to critically evaluate risk assessment tools employing the principles outlined in this textbook.

ASSESSING EVIDENCE FROM STUDIES DESCRIBING THE PROGNOSIS FOR GROUPS OF PEOPLE

When questions about prognosis arise, where can the clinician find the answers? Traditionally, clinicians have sought answers from textbooks and local experts.[15] Traditional textbooks, however, are often already out of date at the time of publication[16] and therefore might not provide the most up-to-date evidence with which the clinician can answer the questions. However, a new generation of evidence-based textbooks (such as this one) that attempt to provide relevant answers to clinically important questions and that summarize and classify the evidence in support of the answer with corresponding levels of evidence are being developed. In the past, methodologists and clinicians have collaborated in the generation of levels of evidence for use in assessing and interpreting evidence on preventive[17] and therapeutic[18] interventions. These systems were created by identifying the specific scientific methods that maximize the validity of a study's conclusions and then creating a hierarchy of study types. Table 2–1 illustrates the levels of evidence used to describe articles about prognosis that are used throughout this textbook.

When assessing the evidence from individual prognosis studies, clinicians can use the same principles used in the development of the levels of evidence. Guides for assessing the validity, importance, and applicability of evidence about prognosis have been published elsewhere[5,19] but will be briefly summarized here (Table 2–2).

Was a Defined, Representative Sample of Patients Assembled at a Common Point in the Course of Their Disease?

Ideally, a prognosis study would include every patient who developed the target disorder, studied from the instant it developed. Unfortunately, this is impossible, and thus it is neces-

---

Table 2–1 Levels of Evidence for Articles about Prognosis

Level 1	A. Inception cohort of patients with the target disorder of interest but free of the outcome of interest has been assembled
	B. Reproducible inclusion and exclusion criteria
	C. Follow-up of at least 80% of subjects
	D. Statistical adjustment for extraneous prognostic factors (confounders)
	E. Reproducible description of outcome measures
Level 2	Criteria (A) above met plus 3 of the 4 other criteria
Level 3	Criteria (A) above met plus 2 of the other criteria
Level 4	Criteria (A) above met plus 1 of the other criteria

---

sary to determine how close to the ideal the report is with respect to how the target disorder was defined and how participants were assembled. If the individuals included in the study are representative of the underlying population (and reflect the spectrum of illness), it is reassuring.

From what point in the progress of the target disorder should patients be followed? The guide in Table 2–2 states "usually early," implying an inception cohort (a group of people who are assembled at an early point in their disease), but clinicians may want information about prognosis in later stages of disease. Thus, a study that assembled patients at any point in their disease may provide useful information. However, if observations are made at different points in the course of disease for various people in the cohort, the relative timing of outcome events would be difficult to interpret. For example, if a study designed to look at the development of retinopathy in patients with diabetes mellitus included (and analyzed together) patients who were newly diagnosed and those who had the disease for 10 years or more, the results would be difficult to interpret. The ideal cohort is one in which participants are all at a similar stage in the course of the same disease.

Was Patient Follow-up Sufficiently Long and Complete?

The ideal follow-up period for a study lasts until every patient recovers or has one of the other outcomes of interest, or until the elapsed time of observation is of clinical interest to clinicians or patients. If follow-up is short, it may be that too few study patients will have the outcome of interest, thus providing little information of use to a patient.

The more patients who are unavailable for follow-up, the less accurate the estimate of the risk of the outcome. Losses may occur because patients are too ill (or too well) to be followed or may have died, and the failure to document these losses threatens the validity of the study. Sometimes, however, losses to follow-up are unavoidable and unrelated to prognosis. Although an analysis showing that the baseline demographics of these patients are similar to those followed up provides some reassurance that certain types of participants were not selectively lost, such an analysis is limited by those characteristics that were measured at baseline. Investigators cannot control for unmeasured traits that may be important prognostically and that may have been more or less prevalent in the lost participants than in the followed-up participants. Therefore, most evidence-based journals of secondary publication require at least 80% follow-up for a prognosis study to be considered valid.

Were Outcome Criteria Applied in a "Blind Fashion?"

The application of explicit criteria for each outcome of interest, a discussion of how these criteria were applied, and evidence that they were applied without knowledge of the prognostic factors under consideration are key components of a study describing prognosis.

Table 2–2 Guides for Assessing Evidence about Prognosis

Is this evidence valid?

    Was a defined, representative sample of patients assembled at a common point (usually early) in the course of their disease?

    Was patient follow-up sufficiently long and complete?

    Were outcome criteria applied in a "blind fashion?"

    If subgroups with different prognosis are identified:

       • Was there adjustment for important prognostic factors?

       • Was there validation in an independent (test set) of patients?

Is this evidence important?

    How likely are the outcomes over time?

    How precise are the prognostic estimates?

Is this evidence applicable to the patient?

    Is the patient so different from the study patients that his or her outcome is expected to be so different that the study results would not be useful?

    Will this evidence make a clinically important impact on the clinician's conclusions about what to tell or offer the patient?

Blinding is crucial if any judgment is required to assess the outcome, because unblinded investigators may search more aggressively for outcomes in people with the characteristic(s) felt to be of prognostic importance than in other individuals. Blinding may be unnecessary if the assessments are preplanned for all patients and/or are unequivocal, such as total mortality; however, judging the underlying cause of death is difficult and requires blinding to the presence of the risk factor to ensure that it is unbiased.

If Subgroups with Different Prognoses Are Identified, Was There Adjustment for Important Prognostic Factors and Validation in an Independent Group of "Test Set" Patients?

If a study reports that one group of patients had a different prognosis than another, it is important to identify if there was any adjustment for known prognostic factors to ensure that the subgroup predictions are not being distorted by these known prognostic factors. Even if this is done, however, the identification of a prognostic factor for the first time could be the result of a chance difference in its distribution between patients with different prognoses. Therefore, the initial patient group in which the variable was identified as a prognostic factor may be considered to be a training set or a hypothesis-generation set. Indeed, if investigators were to search for multiple potential prognostic factors in the same data set, a few would be likely to emerge on the basis of chance alone. Ideally, therefore, data from a second independent patient group, or a "test set," would be required to confirm the importance of a prognostic factor. Although this degree of evidence has often not been collected in the past, an increasing number of reports are describing a second, independent study validating the predictive power of prognostic factors.

How Likely Are the Outcomes Over Time?

Once the validity of the evidence is established, it can be examined further to determine its importance (see Table 2–2). Typically, results of prognosis studies are reported in one of three ways: (1) as a percentage of the outcome of interest at a particular point in time (eg, 1-year survival rates), (2) as median time to the outcome (eg, the length of follow-up by which point

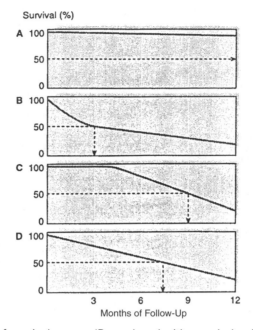

Figure 2–1 Examples of survival curves. (Reproduced with permission from Sackett DL, Straus SE, Richardson WS, et al. Evidence-based medicine: how to practice and teach it. London: Churchill Livingstone; 2000.)

50% of patients have died), or (3) as event curves (eg, survival curves) that illustrate, at each point in time, the proportion of the original study sample who have not yet had a specified outcome.

Examples of four different survival curves are shown in Figure 2–1. In Part A, very few patients have had events by the end of the study, which could mean that the prognosis is very good for this target disorder or that the study is too short (and thus not helpful). In Parts B, C, and D, the proportion of patients surviving to 1 year is the same in all three graphs. However, the median survival is very different: 3 months for B, 9 months for the disorder in C, and approximately 7.5 months in D. These examples highlight the importance of considering both the median survival and survival curves to fully inform patients about prognosis.

How Precise Are the Prognostic Estimates?

The precision of the estimate is best reflected in its 95% confidence interval, that is, the range of values within which we can be 95% sure that the population value lies: the narrower the confidence interval, the more precise is the estimate. If survival over time is the outcome of interest, earlier follow-up periods usually include results from more patients than later periods, so that survival curves are more precise (ie, have narrower confidence intervals) earlier in follow-up. If the article does not provide the confidence intervals, they can be calculated using the equations provided in Figure 2–2.

Is the Patient So Different from the Study Patients That the Study Would Not Be Useful?

Applicability of a study's results refers to whether or not they can be applied to an individual patient. Rather than considering if the study patients are similar to one's own patient (generalizability of the study), the question best considered is one of applicability: "Is my patient so different from those in the study that its results are not helpful?" For most differences, the answer to this question will be no.

$$\text{Standard error (SE)} = \sqrt{\frac{p(1-p)}{n}}$$

where 'p' is the proportion of people with the outcome of interest and 'n' is the sample size

95% confidence interval $= p \pm 1.96 \times \text{SE}$

Figure 2–2 Calculation of confidence intervals.

Will the Evidence Make a Clinically Important Impact on the Clinician's Conclusions?

Evidence regarding a person's prognosis is clearly useful in deciding whether or not to initiate therapy, in monitoring therapy that has been initiated, and in deciding which diagnostic tests to order. If, for example, a study demonstrated a good prognosis for patients with a particular target disorder who did not receive treatment, therapy probably would not be appropriate. In contrast, if the article showed that the prognosis is poor without treatment (and if there are treatments available that make an important difference), therapy would be offered.

WHAT IS THE PROGNOSIS IN AN INDIVIDUAL PATIENT?

Returning to the clinical scenario described at the beginning of this chapter, a 20-year-old female patient with Type 1 diabetes mellitus wants to know her risk of vision loss. PubMed (*http://www.ncbi.nlm.nih.gov/PubMed/clinical.html*) allows for searching of MEDLINE using search filters to help find the most clinically relevant papers. Using the search terms 'diabetes mellitus' and 'vision loss,' an article[20] is found that might provide an answer to this patient's questions. It describes the Wisconsin Epidemiologic Study of Diabetic Retinopathy, in which 10,135 patients with diabetes who were receiving care from primary care physicians in 1980 were assembled. Two subgroups of patients were identified from this group: those persons diagnosed with diabetes before 30 years of age (all of whom were taking insulin) and those persons diagnosed after 30 years of age (including patients taking insulin and those not taking it). While not all patients were assembled at a common point in their disease, the investigators attempted to correct for this by stratifying patients in the latter group by the duration of disease. After an initial assessment, patients received follow-up examinations at 4 and 10 years; at 10 years, however, only 76.8% of patients in the "younger-onset" group were available to be examined again.

Despite the less than 80% follow-up, few studies have assessed the incidence of vision loss in diabetes, and this study can provide useful information. From this study, the risk of blindness in the younger-onset group was 1.8% (95% confidence interval 0.9 to 2.7%) at 10 years (ie, the patient in question has a 1 in 55 likelihood of developing vision loss after 10 years). However, as noted previously, the presence or absence of prognostic factors can provide a prognosis that is specific to the individual patient. Several prognostic factors for developing vision loss were identified in this study, including duration of diabetes (>10 years) and glycosylated hemoglobin level. The patient has just recently been diagnosed with diabetes mellitus; however laboratory tests revealed that her glycosylated hemoglobin level was 0.075%. Therefore, her risk of vision loss is approximately 2.2% at 10 years (or a likelihood of 1 in 44); moreover, more intensive insulin management can reduce this risk.[21] This evidence can be used to provide the patient with encouragement in the management of her disease. Subsequent chapters provide information about the risk of developing nephropathy, retinopathy, and coronary artery disease in patients with diabetes mellitus. These may also be used to fully inform the patient of his or her prognosis.

REFERENCES

1. Gall MA, Borch-Johnsen K, Hougaard P, et al. Albuminuria and poor glycemic control predict mortality in NIDDM. Diabetes 1995;44:1303–9.

2. Ravid M, Savin H, Jutrin I, et al. Long-term stabilizing effect of angiotensin-converting enzyme inhibition on plasma creatinine and on proteinuria in normotensive Type 2 diabetic patients. Ann Intern Med 1993;118:577–81.

3. Mettauer B, Rouleau JL, Bichet D, et al. Sodium and water excretion abnormalities in congestive heart failure: determinant factors and clinical implications. Ann Intern Med 1986;105:161–7.

4. Last JM, editor. A dictionary of epidemiology. 3rd ed. Oxford: Oxford University Press; 1995.

5. Laupacis A, Wells G, Richardson WS, Tugwell P, for the Evidence-Based Medicine Working Group. Users' guide to the medical literature V. How to use an article about prognosis. JAMA 1994;272:234–7.

6. Rodgers A, MacMahon S, Gamble G, et al., for the United Kingdom Transient Ischemic Attack Collaborative Group. Blood pressure and risk of stroke in patients with cerebrovascular disease. BMJ 1996;313:147.

7. Peters AL, Hsueh W. Antihypertensive agents in diabetic patients. Great benefits, special risks. Arch Intern Med 1999;159:541–2.

8. MacDonald S, Joffres MR, Stachenko S, et al., for the Canadian Heart Health Surveys Research Group. Multiple cardiovascular disease risk factors in Canadian adults. Can Med Assoc J 1992;146:2021–9.

9. Lowe LP, Greenland P, Ruth KJ, et al. Impact of major cardiovascular disease risk factors, particularly in combination, on 22-year mortality in women and men. Arch Intern Med 1998;158:2007–14.

10. Collins R, Peto R, MacMahon S, et al. Blood pressure, stroke, and coronary heart disease. Part 2. Short-term reductions in blood pressure: overview of randomised drug trials in their epidemiological context. Lancet 1990;335:827–38.

11. Jackson R, Barham P, Bills J, et al. Management of raised blood pressure in New Zealand: a discussion document. BMJ 1993;307:107–10.

12. Wilson PWF, D'Agostino RB, Levy D, et al. Prediction of coronary heart disease using risk factor categories. Circulation 1998;97:1837–47.

13. Grover SA, Paquet S, Levinton C, et al. Estimating the benefits of modifying risk factors of cardiovascular disease: a comparison of primary vs. secondary prevention. Arch Intern Med 1998;158:655–62.

14. Grover S. Gambling with cardiovascular risk: picking the winners and losers. Lancet 1999;353:254.

15. McColl A, Smith H, White P, Field J. General practitioners' perceptions of the route to evidence based medicine: a questionnaire survey. BMJ 1998;316:361–5.

16. Antman EM, Lau J, Kupelnick B, et al. A comparison of results of meta-analyses of randomised control trials and recommendations of clinical experts. JAMA 1992;268:240–8.

17. Canadian Task Force on the Periodic Health Examination. The periodic health examination. Can Med Assoc J 1979;270:1193–254.

18. Cook DJ, Guyatt GH, Laupacis A, et al. Clinical recommendations using levels of evidence for antithrombotic agents. Chest 1995;108:227S–30S.

19. Sackett DL, Straus SE, Richardson WS, et al. Evidence-based medicine: how to practise and teach it. London: Churchill Livingstone; 2000.

20. Moss SE, Klein R, Klein BEK. Ten-year incidence of visual loss in a diabetic population. Ophthalmology 1994;101·1061–70.

21. Diabetes Control and Complications Trial Research Group (DCCT). The effect of intensive treatment of diabetes on the development and progression of long-term complications in insulin-dependent diabetes mellitus. N Engl J Med 1993;329:977–86.

CHAPTER 3

How Should Diagnostic Tests Be Chosen and Used?

Roman Jaeschke, MD, MSc, and Gordon H. Guyatt, MD, MSc (Epid)

INTRODUCTION

Any interaction with patients involves one or more tasks that may include establishing and communicating the prognosis of a particular condition, choosing, if available, an appropriate therapy or preventive strategy and supporting them during therapy. This chain of events clearly begins with a determination of what is happening, that is, establishing the diagnosis.

A rapidly growing literature describing the characteristics and usefulness of diagnostic tests and procedures provides information that can help clinicians make an accurate diagnosis. The concepts used in this literature (and the vocabulary used to describe them) are reviewed in this chapter. They will be introduced in the context of a clinical scenario describing the testing of a urine sample for the presence of microalbuminuria.

Recent guidelines for the management of diabetes recommend that patients have annual screening for proteinuria. The presence of even a small amount of protein in urine (microalbuminuria) has important prognostic and therapeutic implications. Twenty-four-hour urine collections for albumin remain the gold standard for detecting microalbuminuria, but since this is quite cumbersome, the need for a simpler, more convenient test is obvious. Determining the urinary albumin concentration (UAC), or the albumin:creatinine ratio (UACR), in a random urine sample is an appropriate option. This was assessed in a recent article[1] that described the diagnostic properties of a first morning urine sample using the concepts of criterion standard, receiver operating characteristics curve, and sensitivity and specificity. In this study, 95 diabetic patients collected 132 24-hour urine specimens for measurement of the urinary albumin excretion rate (UAER). When patients returned the 24-hour collection during a clinic visit, a random urine specimen was taken for determination of the UAC and UACR. The measurement of 24-hour UAER was considered adequate when creatinine measurement in the same sample was 700 to 1,500 mg/d for women and 1,000 to 1,800 mg/d for men. Nine samples were excluded based on this criterion. Thus, 123 pairs of 24-hour urine specimens and random urine specimens (RUS) were available to establish the diagnostic properties of the random sample.

Table 3–1 lists a set of criteria that can be used to help judge the value of the evidence provided by such a study. Such an assessment involves determining if the study provides valid

---

Table 3–1 Assessing Evidence Relating to the Use of Diagnostic Tests

How valid are the study's results, and what level of evidence does it provide?

What are the properties of the diagnostic test (ie, sensitivity, specificity, predictive value, likelihood ratios, and receiver operating characteristics)?

How applicable are study results and the diagnostic tests to different clinical settings?

information regarding the test and if it describes or allows the calculation of diagnostic test properties including likelihood ratios, sensitivity, specificity, and predictive values.

How Valid Are the Results of a Study Looking at Diagnostic Test Performance and What Level of Evidence Is Provided?

The validity or accuracy of a diagnostic test is best determined by comparing it to the "truth." Criteria that can help assess the validity of a study describing a diagnostic test are listed in Table 3–2. The extent to which an article about a diagnostic test adheres to these criteria determines the confidence we can have in its results. When dealing with diagnostic tests, the authors of chapters in this book will provide readers with an indication of this confidence by assigning a level of evidence to the reference (Table 3–3).

Table 3–2 Major Criteria for Determining the Validity of a Study Describing a Diagnostic Test

Has an appropriate reference standard, as well as the test under investigation, been applied to every patient?

Were the results of the new test and reference standard assessed independently? Did the results of the new test influence the decision to perform the reference standard?

Did the patient sample include an appropriate spectrum of patients in whom the diagnostic test will be applied in clinical practice?

Are reproducible descriptions of both the new test and reference standard provided?

Has an Appropriate Reference Standard Been Applied to Every Patient along with the Test Under Investigation?

Any new test must be compared to an appropriate reference standard such as biopsy, surgery, autopsy, or long-term follow-up. This standard, as well as the test under investigation, should be available for every study participant. In the study on microalbuminuria, in which both tests were biochemical assays, the issue of choosing this standard was arbitrary and related to the definition of microalbuminuria. In other situations (eg, stroke, myocardial infarction, urinary tract infection, or osteomyelitis), the choice of an appropriate reference standard (also called a gold standard, criterion standard, or diagnostic standard) may not be

Table 3–3 Levels of Evidence for Studies of Diagnosis

Level 1	A. Independent interpretation of test result (without knowledge of the result of diagnostic standard)
	B. Independent interpretation of the diagnostic standard (without knowledge of the test result)
	C. Selection of patients who are suspected (but not known to have) the disorder
	D. Reproducible description of both the test and diagnostic standard
	E. At least 50 patients with and 50 patients without the disorder
Level 2	Meets 4 of the Level 1 criteria
Level 3	Meets 3 of the Level 1 criteria
Level 4	Meets ≤ 2 of the Level 1 criteria

Table 3–4 Relationship between 24-Hour Urinary Albumin Excretion Rate (Gold Standard) and Urinary Albumin: Creatinine Ratio (Test): Three Levels of Test Results

	UAER	
UACR	> 28.8 mg/d	< 28.8 mg/d
> 26.8 mg/g	61	6
15–26.8 mg/g	8	8
< 15 mg/g	0	40
	69	54

UAER = 24-hour urinary albumin excretion rate; UACR = urinary albumin: creatinine ratio.

that clear. Any study of a diagnostic test that does not provide a reasonable criterion standard is unlikely to provide valid results.

Were the Results of the New Test and Reference Standard Assessed Independently?

To preclude the possibility that the results of the new diagnostic test are influenced by the results of the reference standard, it is important that the test results and the reference standard be assessed independently of each other (ie, by interpreters who were unaware of the results of the other investigation). Such independent comparison is not crucial when considering objective, biochemical tests. Its importance arises, however, when the interpretation of one test's results may be influenced by the knowledge of the other test's results. Examples include the assessment of funduscopy knowing angiography results, results of clinical examination for neuropathy knowing the EMG or nerve-conduction study results, interpretation of bone radiographs knowing bone-scan results, looking at chest radiographs knowing computed tomography (CT) scan results, conducting heart auscultation knowing echocardiogram results, etc. The more likely that the interpretation of a new test could be influenced by knowledge of the reference standard result (or vice versa), the more important it is that both tests be interpreted independently.

The second point may be illustrated by the situation where all patients with suspected peripheral neuropathy undergo nerve-conduction studies, but only those with abnormal velocities undergo a nerve biopsy. This situation, sometimes called "verification bias" or "work-up bias," was not a problem in the study under consideration, in which patients were given both tests.

Did the Patient Sample Include an Appropriate Spectrum of Patients?

The diagnostic test is useful only to the extent that it distinguishes between target states or disorders that might otherwise be confused. Almost any test can distinguish the healthy from the severely affected. The pragmatic value of a test is therefore established only in a study that closely resembles clinical practice. Testing the ability of UACR to distinguish between healthy volunteers and long-term diabetic patients with established nephropathy would not be useful in this regard (although if it was not working in those populations, it would not be useful in more challenging ones).

In the microalbuminuria article,[1] there is no full description of the process by which patients entered the study; it is not known how many were considered, how many were excluded, and why. It is only known that all patients classified at the time of the study (1997) as having Type 2 diabetes were eligible, that their ages ranged from 40 to 75 years (mean 61), that the mean duration of diabetes was 11 years (range 1 to 45 years), that the mean HbA_{1c} was 10.1% (range 6.9 to 15.6%), and that the median UAER was 18.3 µg/min (26 mg/d). It is therefore likely that the appropriate patient sample was chosen.

Table 3–5 Relationship between 24-Hour Urinary Albumin Excretion Rate (Gold Standard) and Urinary Albumin: Creatinine Ratio (Test): Two Levels of Test Results

	UAER	
UACR	> 28.8 mg/d	< 28.8 mg/d
> 26.8 mg/g	61	6
< 26.8 mg/g	8	48
	69	54

UAER = 24-hour urinary albumin excretion rate; UACR = urinary albumin: creatinine ratio.

Are Reproducible Descriptions of Both the New Test and Reference Standard Provided?

This point is important in that it helps the reader decide if the test being described is available in his or her setting and whether a generally accepted reference standard was used. As an illustration, all random urine specimens in the microalbuminuria study were collected as first morning urine samples after finishing the 24-hour collection. Whether the results can therefore be applied to a random urine sample collected at other times of the day is unknown.

WHAT ARE THE PROPERTIES OF THE DIAGNOSTIC TEST?

Sensitivity and Specificity

From the data provided by the authors of the microalbuminuria study,[1] one can construct Table 3–4, in which a UAER of over 28.8 mg/d (corresponding to excretion of 20 μg albumin/min) is considered abnormal. Sensitivity refers to the proportion of people with the target disorder in whom the test result is *positive*, and specificity refers to the proportion of people without the target disorder in whom the test result is *negative*. To use these concepts, the results can be divided into normal and abnormal; that is, a 2 × 2 table can be created. Table 3–4 (a 3 × 2 table) can be transformed into one of two possible 2 × 2 tables, depending on what we consider normal (negative) or abnormal (positive) test results. If one assumes that only UACR > 26.8 mg albumin/g of creatinine is abnormal (or positive), Table 3–5 can be constructed.

From Table 3–5, it is clear that 69 people had proven abnormal UAER and 61 of them had an abnormal test result. Thus, the sensitivity is 61 of 69, or 88%. Similarly, 48 of 54 people with a normal UAER had a normal UACR, yielding a specificity of 89%.

If the threshold of "positive" versus "negative" was set differently (ie, 15 mg/g instead of 26.8 mg/g), Table 3–6 would be generated. This analysis yields an improved sensitivity of 69 of 69, or 100%, but a poorer specificity of 40 of 54, or 74%. Thus, by increasing the ability to

Table 3–6 Relationship between 24-Hour: Urinary Albumin Excretion Rate (Gold Standard) and Urinary Albumin: Creatinine Ratio (Test): Two Levels of Test Results (Different Threshold)

	UAER	
UACR	> 28.8 mg/d	< 28.8 mg/d
> 15 mg/g	69	14
< 15 mg/g	0	40
	69	54

UAER = 24-hour urinary albumin excretion rate; UACR = urinary albumin: creatinine ratio.

Table 3–7 Relationship between Test Results and the True Situation

	Disease	
Test Result	Present	Absent
Positive	a (TP)	b (FP)
Negative	c (FN)	d (TN)
	a + c	b + d

TP = true positives; FP = false positives; FN = false negatives; TN = true negatives.

detect existing disease (in other words, increasing sensitivity, or the proportion of true-positives), some unaffected people are mislabeled as being target positive (ie, specificity is decreased, the proportion of false-positive cases is increased, and the proportion of true negative cases is decreased). This illustrates the fact that to use the concepts of sensitivity and specificity, one has to either throw away important information or recalculate sensitivity and specificity for every cutpoint. The use of likelihood ratios (discussed subsequently) presents a way of avoiding this problem.

Table 3–7 summarizes the above and other definitions. Using this table, the following calculations may be made: sensitivity = a/(a + c); specificity = d/(b + d); and accuracy (ability of a test to classify patients properly) = (a + d)/(a + b + c + d). Sensitivity is also sometimes referred to as the proportion of true positive cases and specificity as the proportion of true negative cases.

Receiver Operating Characteristic Curve

As noted above, different cutoffs defining positive and negative tests result in different sensitivities and specificities. One may create a graph where the vertical axis denotes sensitivity (or the true positive rate) for different cutoffs and the horizontal axis displays results of the formula "one minus specificity" (or the false-positive rate) for the same cutoffs. The curve established by connecting the points generated by using different diagnostic cutoffs is called a receiver operating characteristic (ROC) curve. For the data set under consideration, two points of this curve, on the basis of known sensitivities and specificities discussed above, are known. There could be a third read from the data provided in the article, representing 100% specificity at the expense of only 42% sensitivity. The resulting ROC curve, which represents modified ROC curve from the article, is presented in Figure 3–1.

Such ROC curves can be used to formally compare the value of different tests by examining the area under each curve; the better the test, the larger the area under the curve. Zelmanovitz and colleagues found that for the detection of abnormal protein secretion by UACR, the area under ROC curve was .9689 and that the area for another test (UAC) described in the same study was .9766. To put the discriminating abilities of those tests into perspective, one may consider that the area under ROC curve for ferritin in diagnosing iron deficiency anemia is about 0.95.[2]

Predictive Value

Predictive values represent another way of expressing the properties of a diagnostic test. In applying a given test to a patient, the vertical columns in Table 3–7 are of limited interest, because if one really knew the column the patient was in, the diagnostic test would not be required. The clinically relevant questions are embedded in the rows. For example (Table 3–6), what proportion of patients with UACR ratio > 15 mg/g have abnormal 24-hour urinary albumin secretion? In this study, the answer is 69 of 83 patients, or 83% (a proportion called the

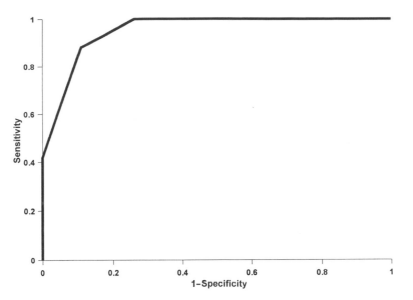

Figure 3–1 Receiver operating characteristics curve for UACR.

"positive predictive value," or PPV). For the same threshold, the probability that a patient with negative test results has no disease is 100% (40 of 40), a proportion called the "negative predictive value," or NPV. For the different threshold (26.8 mg/g), the respective values are 91% for PPV and 86% for NPV. Using the symbols in Table 3–7, PPV = a/(a + b) and NPV = d/(c + d).

The relationship between sensitivity and specificity, on the one hand, and predictive values, on the other, can be illustrated using a hypothetical example (Table 3–8), in which one assumes that a population has a smaller proportion of people with the disease of interest. In this example, the sensitivity (a/[a + c]) and specificity (2d/2[b + d] = d/[b + d]) are unchanged, but the PPV is reduced from a/(a + b) to a/(a + 2b), and the NPV has increased from d(c + d) to 2d/(c + 2d).

As a general rule, even though the sensitivity and specificity do not change, decreasing the disease prevalence decreases the PPV and increases the NPV. Similarly, it can be easily shown that maintaining test sensitivity and specificity but increasing the disease prevalence (2a and 2c) will increase the PPV and decrease the NPV. Therefore, predictive values reflect both the test characteristics and the disease prevalence in the population and are of limited value in populations different from that studied.

Occasionally, either sensitivity or specificity is so high that it can be used to rule in or out a target disorder. When a test has a very high sensitivity, a negative result rules *out* the diagnosis (a convenient mnemonic is sensitive-negative-out, or SnNout); this corresponds

Table 3–8 Relationship between Prevalence of Disease, Sensitivity, Specificity, and Predictive Values

Test Result	Disease	
	Present	Absent
Positive	a	2b
Negative	c	2d
	a + c	2(b + d)

to a very high NPV. When a test has a very high specificity, a positive test result rules *in* the diagnosis (specificity-positive-in, or SpPin); this corresponds to a very high PPV. Calling a test result positive or negative may be useful when the test has a good SpPin or SnNout, but for most tests, much information can be lost by creating this dichotomy.

There are clearly situations when it is important to maximize either sensitivity or specificity. The requirement for high sensitivity is obvious when a test is used as a screening tool. In this situation, it is important to identify all patients with a given condition in a population, not just part of them. This high sensitivity and associated high NPV, however, comes at a price of lower specificity, or an increased number of false-positives and an increased need for confirmatory (sometimes invasive) tests. Examples include mammography for breast cancer screening or prostate-specific antigen (PSA) tests for prostatic cancer screening. The opposite occurs when we require very high specificity (and a corresponding very high PPV), such as when establishing the diagnosis definitively has important therapeutic or prognostic implications.

Likelihood Ratios: Pre- and Post-test Probabilities

Despite the relative simplicity of the concepts described above, they are limited by the need to choose different thresholds for a test result, which can vary depending on the purpose of the test (ie, screening for, or confirming, disease). They also lump differing degrees of abnormality into a single category: either diabetic neuropathy is present or not, either ketoacidosis is present or not. Unfortunately, this distinction does not correspond to the clinical reality in which, for example, daily albumin secretions of 400 mg or 4 g, serum creatinine of 200 or 600 mmol/L, and serum glucose of 20 or 60 mmol/L are all abnormal but have clearly different clinical implications.

These distinctions are best captured by the concept of "likelihood ratios." This concept recognizes the fact that different patients have differing probabilities of having the disease of interest because of differing risk factors such as age and comorbidities. Therefore, the application of any test can be viewed as a way of either increasing or decreasing the probability that the patient has the disease of interest. That is, a test serves to modify the pretest probability of the disease and yields a new, post-test probability. The direction and magnitude of this change from pre- to post-test probability is determined by the test's properties, which are called the "likelihood ratios."

In the diagnostic process, one frequently proceeds through a series of different diagnostic tests (information from history-taking, physical examination, and laboratory or radiologic tests). If the properties of each of these pieces of information are known, one can move sequentially through them, incorporating each piece of information and continuously recalculating the probability of the target disorder. Clinicians implicitly proceed in this fashion, but because the properties of the individual items of history and physical examination are often not available, they must rely on clinical experience and intuition to arrive at the consecutive pretest probability that precedes ordering a diagnostic test.

The limited information regarding the properties of items of history and physical examination often results in widely varying estimates of pretest probabilities by clinicians. Potential solutions are to examine the literature, look at the prevalence of the target condition in populations similar to the one being considered, consult with other clinicians about their probability estimates (the consensus view is likely more accurate than individual intuition), or to assume the extreme plausible pretest probabilities and determine if this changes the clinical course of action.

Referring to the previously constructed Table 3–4 from the microalbuminuria article, there were 69 people with an abnormal albumin excretion and 54 people in whom the UAER was negative. One may now ask two questions: (1) How likely is a UACR above 26.8 mg/g among people who excrete >28.8 mg/d of albumin? Table 3–4 shows the answer to be 61 of 69, or 0.88. (2) How often is the same test result (UACR >26.8 mg/g) found among people who, although suspected of abnormal albuminuria, do not have it? The answer is 6 of 54, or 0.11. The ratio of these two likelihoods is called the likelihood ratio (LR), which for UACR > 26.8 mg/g is .88/.11, or 8.0. In other words, this particular test result is eight times as likely to occur in a patient with abnormal albuminuria compared to a patient without. In a similar fashion, the LR can be calculated for each level of the diagnostic test result. Each calculation involves answering two questions: first, how likely is it to get a given test result (eg, UACR between 15 and 26.8 mg/g) among people with the target disorder (abnormal albuminuria) and second, how likely is it to get *the same test result* (15 to 26.8 mg/g) among people without the target disorder (no abnormal albuminuria)? For this intermediate test result, these likelihoods are 8 of 69, or 0.12, and 8 of 54, or 0.15, and their ratio (the LR for this test result) is 0.8. To complete, the likelihood ratio for the UACR < 15 mg/g is 0 of 69 divided by 40 of 54, or 0.

The clinical utility of the LR is in its ability to indicate by how much a given diagnostic test result will raise or lower the pretest probability of the target disorder. An LR of 1 means that the post-test probability is exactly the same as the pretest probability. Likelihood ratios >1 increase the probability that the target disorder is present, and the higher the LR, the greater the increase in probability. Conversely, LRs < 1 decrease the probability of the target disorder, and the smaller the LR, the greater the decrease in probability and the smaller its final value. Likelihood ratios >10.0 or <0.1 generate large, often conclusive changes from pre- to post-test probability; LRs of 5.0 to 10.0 and 0.1 to 0.2 generate moderate shifts in pre- to post-test probability; LRs of 2.0 to 5.0 and 0.5 to 0.2 generate small (but sometimes important) changes in probability; and LRs of 1.0 to 2.0 and 0.5 to 1.0 alter probability to a small (and rarely important) degree.

Having determined the magnitude and significance of the LRs, how does one use them to go from pre- to post-test probability? Likelihood ratios cannot be combined directly; their formal use requires converting pretest probability to odds, multiplying the result by the LR, and converting the consequent post-test odds into a post-test probability. While not too difficult*, this calculation can be tedious and off-putting; fortunately, there is an easier way. The nomogram proposed by Fagan[3] (Figure 3–2) does all the conversions and facilitates the conversion from pre- to post-test probabilities. The first column of this nomogram represents the pretest probability, the second column represents the LR, and the third shows the post-test probability. One may obtain the post-test probability by anchoring a ruler at the pretest probability and rotating it until it lines up with the LR for the observed test result.

Thus, the LR incorporates the information that is usually used when arriving at a diagnosis: the specifics of a given clinical encounter (ie, the individual characteristics of a patient and one's clinical experience) and the external evidence coming from performing tests in a population of patients. The former determines the assessment of pretest probabilities, and the latter concerns the ability of the test's result to distinguish patients with and those without the condition of interest. These two elements are combined to establish estimates of whether the patient has the target disorder (post-test probabilities).

How Applicable Are Study Results and the Diagnostic Tests to Different Clinical Settings?

Is the Test Reproducible?

The value of any test depends on its ability to yield the same result when reapplied to stable patients in one's own clinical setting. Poor reproducibility can result from problems with the test itself (eg, variations in reagents in radioimmunoassay kits for determining hormone lev-

---

*The equation to convert probabilities into odds is probability/(1 – probability). This is equivalent to probability of having the target disorder/probability of not having the target disorder. Probability of .50 represent odds of 0.50 to 0.50, or 1 to 1; a probability of .80 represents odds of 0.80 to 0.20, or 4 to 1; a probability of 0.25 represents odds of 0.25 to 0.75, or 1 to 3, or 0.33. With the pretests odds known, the post-test odds are calculated by multiplying the pretest odds by the LR. The post-tests odds can be converted back into probabilities using the following formula: probability = odds /(odds + 1).

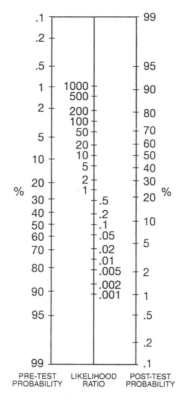

Figure 3–2 A likelihood ratio nomogram. (Adapted with permission from Fagan TJ. Nomogram for Bayes's theorem. N Engl J Med 1975;293:257.)

els). Different test results in stable patients may also arise whenever a test requires interpretation (eg, the extent of ST-segment elevation on an electrocardiogram). Ideally, an article about a diagnostic test will tell readers how reproducible the test results can be expected to be. This is especially important when expertise is required in performing or interpreting the test.

If the reproducibility of a test in the study setting is mediocre, disagreement between observers is common, and the test still discriminates well between those with and without the target condition, it is very useful. Under these circumstances, it is likely that the test can be readily applied in any clinical setting. If reproducibility of a diagnostic test is very high and observer variation very low, either the test is simple and unambigious or those interpreting it are highly skilled. If the latter applies, less skilled interpreters may not do as well.

Are the Results Applicable to One's Patients?

The issue here is whether the test will have the same accuracy among different populations of patients. Test properties may change with a different mix of disease severity or a different distribution of competing conditions. For example, the likelihood ratio for a given test result will tend to be higher if that value was derived from a study of patients who have severe disease; conversely, they will tend to be lower (ie, closer to 1) if the value was derived from a study of patients with only mild disease. As a second example, likelihood ratios will tend to be higher if few of the patients without the target disorder have competing conditions that lead to the "abnormal" test results seen in patients who do have the target disorder; they will tend to be closer to 1 if many of the unaffected patients have competing conditions that lead to a "false-positive" result.

The phenomenon of differing test properties in different subpopulations has been most strikingly demonstrated for exercise electrocardiography in the diagnosis of coronary artery disease. For instance, the more extensive the average severity of coronary artery disease in the studied population, the larger are the likelihood ratios of abnormal exercise electrocardiography for angiographic narrowing of the coronary arteries.[4] Another example comes from the diagnosis of venous thromboembolism, where compression ultrasound for proximal-vein thrombosis has proved more accurate in symptomatic outpatients than in asymptomatic postoperative patients.[5]

Occasionally, a test fails in just the patients one hopes it will serve best. The LR of a negative dipstick test for the rapid diagnosis of urinary tract infection is approximately 0.2 in patients with clear symptoms and thus a high probability of urinary tract infection but is > 0.5 in those with low probability,[6] rendering it of little help in ruling out infection in the latter, low-probability patients.

If one's practice is in a setting similar to that of the investigation and one's patient meets all the study inclusion criteria and does not violate any of the exclusion criteria, the results of the study are very likely applicable. If not, a judgment is required. As with therapeutic interventions, one should ask whether there are compelling reasons why the results should not be applied to given patients, either because the severity of disease patients, or the mix of competing conditions, is so different that generalization is unwarranted. The issue of generalizibility may be resolved if there is an overview that pools the results of a number of studies.[7,8]

Will the Results Change Management?

It is useful, in making, learning, teaching, and communicating management decisions, to link them explicitly to the probability of the target disorder. Thus, for any target disorder, there are probabilities below which a clinician would dismiss a diagnosis and not order further tests (a "test" threshold, also called a "no-test-no-treatment" threshold). Similarly, there are probabilities above which a clinician would consider the diagnosis confirmed and would stop testing and initiate treatment (a "treatment" threshold, also called the test-treatment threshold). When the probability of the target disorder lies between the test and treatment thresholds, further testing is mandated (Figure 3–3).[7] Thresholds obviously vary among diseases and individual patients.

Once it is decided what test and treatment thresholds are, post-test probabilities have direct treatment implications. If most patients have test results with LRs near 1.0, the test will not be very useful. Thus, the usefulness of a diagnostic test is strongly influenced by the proportion of patients suspected of having the target disorder whose test results have very high or very low LRs, so that the test result will move their probability of disease across a test or treatment threshold.

Referring again to Table 3–4, we can determine the proportion of patients (suspected of albuminuria) with extreme results (either over 26.8 or below 15 mg/g). The proportion can be calculated as 107 of 123, or 87%.

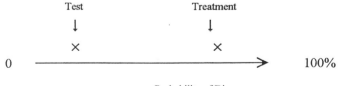

Figure 3–3 Diagnostic process: test and treatment thresholds.

One final comment concerns the use of sequential tests. Each item of history, or each finding on physical examination, laboratory test, or imaging procedure, represents a diagnostic test. Pretest probabilities are modified with each new finding. However, if two tests are very closely related, application of the second test may provide little or no information, and the sequential application of likelihood ratios will yield misleading results. For instance, once one has the results of the most powerful laboratory test for iron deficiency, serum ferritin, additional tests such as serum iron or transferrin saturation add no further information.[2]

Will Patients Be Better Off as a Result of the Test?

The ultimate criterion for the usefulness of a diagnostic test is whether it adds information beyond that otherwise available and whether this information leads to a change in management that is ultimately beneficial to the patient. The value of an accurate test will be undisputed when the target disorder, if left undiagnosed, is dangerous, the test has acceptable risks, and effective treatment exists.

In other clinical situations, tests may be accurate, and management may even change as a result of their application, but their impact on patient outcome may be far less certain. Examples include right heart catheterization for many critically ill patients or the incremental value of magnetic resonance imaging scanning over CT for a wide variety of problems.

CONCLUSION

The optimal use and interpretation of diagnostic test results remains a key part of diabetes management. The principles described in this chapter are relevant both for the diagnosis of diabetes and its type as well as for the presence or absence of concomitant problems such as cardiovascular disease, gastroparesis, erectile dysfunction, and renal insufficiency. They are also key considerations when interpreting published information regarding diagnostic tests and their properties.

REFERENCES

1. Zelmanovitz T, Gross JL, Oliveira JR, et al. The receiver operating characteristics curve in the evaluation of random urine specimen as a screening test. Diabetes Care 1997;20:516–9.

2. Guyatt GH, Oxman A, Ali M. Diagnosis of iron deficiency. J Gen Intern Med 1992;7:145–53.

3. Fagan TJ. Nomogram for Bayes's theorem (C). N Engl J Med 1975;293:257.

4. Hlatky MA, Pryor DB, Harrell FE. Factors affecting sensitivity and specificity of exercise electrocardiography. Am J Med 1984;77:64–71.

5. Ginsberg JS, Caco CC, Brill-Edwards PA, et al. Venous thrombosis in patients who have undergone major hip or new surgery: detection with compression US and impedance plethysmography. Radiology 1991;181:651–4.

6. Lachs MS, Nachamkin I, Edelstein PH, et al. Spectrum bias in the evaluation of diagnostic tests: lessons from the rapid dipstick test for urinary tract infection. Ann Intern Med 1992;117:135–40.

7. Irwig L, Tosteson A, Gatsonis C, et al. Guidelines for meta-analyses evaluating diagnostic tests. Ann Intern Med 1999;120:667–76.

8. Walter SD, Irwig L, Glasziou PP. Meta-analysis of diagnostic tests with imperfect reference standards. J Clin Epidemiol 1999;52:943–51.

9. Sackett DL, Haynes RB, Guyatt GH, Tugwell P. 2nd ed. Clinical epidemiology, a basic science of clinical medicine. Boston/Toronto: Little, Brown and Company; 1991. p. 145–8.

CHAPTER 4

How Should a Particular Problem Be Managed? Incorporating Evidence about Therapies into Practice

Anne M. Holbrook, MD, PharmD, MSc, FRCPC, Jo-Anne Clarke, BSc, Colette Raymond, BSc PharmD, PharmD student, Lisa Dolovich, PharmD, and Mitchell A.H. Levine, MD, MSc

INTRODUCTION

To provide optimal patient care, a clinician must combine principles of disease management with clinical experience and patient preferences. The process of answering a clinical question has previously been described (Table 4–1).[1]

While this process can seem complex and somewhat overwhelming, several resources are available to assist in it. More and more, evidence-based resources in packages are becoming available for clinicians to use. Good-quality, evidence-based clinical practice guidelines, such as those recently published for the management of diabetes in Canada,[2] have already summarized and appraised the literature on many aspects of benefits and harms associated with treatment. Such guidelines can quickly lead the clinician to step 6 or 7 of the algorithm.

In this chapter, issues pertinent to patient assessment are addressed through the following questions:

1. What should be considered when balancing benefit, harm, and cost?
2. Where and how can useful information be found?
3 How valid is the information?
4. What outcomes are described by the evidence?
5. How does one translate clinical trial evidence into practice?
6. How does one apply the evidence to individual patients versus populations?

Table 4–1 Stepwise Approach to Evaluation of the Appropriateness of a Therapy

1. Define a clinical question
2. Search the literature
3. Critically appraise the literature using principles of evidence-based medicine
4. Assess the benefits associated with treatment alternatives
5. Assess the harms associated with treatment alternatives
6. Decide on the applicability of the evidence to the patient
7. Consider compliance
8. Anticipate barriers to care
9. Incorporate patient preferences
10. Consider the financial cost to the patient
11. Consider cost to the system as a whole

WHAT SHOULD BE CONSIDERED WHEN BALANCING BENEFIT, HARM, AND COST?

When faced with a particular problem and a range of possible therapies, clinicians must consider the benefit, harm, and cost associated with each therapeutic option. No simple formula or equation exists that allows clinicians to integrate these issues quickly and easily. Providing the best possible treatment for a particular patient while minimizing harm and cost associated with the therapy is a complex task, and both the physician and the patient must rely on a variety of resources to assist them in their decision-making (Table 4–2). Economic evaluation is a complex task on its own, and readers are referred to two articles for further information on issues related to costs.[3,4]

WHERE AND HOW CAN USEFUL INFORMATION BE FOUND?

In the practice of evidence-based medicine (EBM), it is crucial to know where and how to find relevant, valid, and current information to address patient-specific problems. Most of this information will be found in the primary medical literature. Although consulting tertiary references (such as textbooks), peers, or experts may be more convenient in identifying information (the latter two clearly can be invaluable on issues of applying evidence to individuals), these sources usually are not as current, unbiased, or as familiar with the details of multiple cases as the primary literature.[5] However, more than 10,000 medical journals exist, so becoming familiar with various indexing databases is essential to make EBM practical. Two very good indexing databases are MEDLINE and EMBASE.

MEDLINE

Produced by the US National Library of Medicine, MEDLINE is a computerized index of citations of articles in over 4,500 biomedical journals dating back to 1966.[5] Most of the journals are North American, but many important international journals are also included. However, like any database, it is not comprehensive. Limitations to MEDLINE may include incompleteness in the fields of psychology, medical sociology, and nonclinical pharmacol-

Table 4–2 Considerations When Balancing Benefits, Harm, and Cost

Consideration	Benefits	Harm	Costs
Question	Is this therapy more effective than placebo? Is this therapy more effective than current treatment?	What are the types and frequencies of harm associated with this treatment?	What is the cost: • to the individual, • to the provider, • to the system, and • to society as a whole?
Usual source of information	Randomized controlled trials Meta-analysis	Nonexperimental studies: • cohort • case control • database studies (cohort or case-control design) • pharmaceutical industry • postmarketing surveillance	Economic analyses Case-costing studies Third-party payers Government health care plans
Main limitations	Generalizability Surrogate outcomes Short time horizons for outcomes of interest	Bias Cannot control for all confounding factors Generalizability	Difficult to find; requires knowledge of local costs and utilization

ogy.[6] MEDLINE is available on CD-ROM and is free through the Internet at the PubMed site (*http://www.ncbi.nlm.nih.gov/PubMed/*).

EMBASE

The database EMBASE is another computerized index of journal articles available on CD-ROM and through modem access, produced by Elsevier Publishing Company in the Netherlands (*http:www.silverplatter.com/catalog/embx.htm*).[5] It encompasses more European literature than MEDLINE and provides access to a different database of information while still including many of the important international journals.[5] The overlap of journals in MEDLINE and EMBASE is reported to be approximately 34%, and use of both databases can improve the retrieval of relevant information.[7]

Searching Strategies for MEDLINE and EMBASE

One of the most efficient and comprehensive ways to search these databases is through use of index terms, or MeSH (*Medical Subject Headings*). These are terms already coded into the database that serve as standard descripters for related terms used in the medical literature (eg, "diabetes mellitus" captures "diabetes," "IDDM" [insulin-dependent diabetes mellitus], and "NIDDM" [non–insulin-dependent diabetes mellitus].[5,8] Use of MeSH terms decreases the likelihood of missing relevant articles because of different terminology, spelling, or abbreviations. Other useful tools include the "explode" and "focus" functions. Exploding the search term to encompass all related topics (eg, exploding diabetes mellitus will capture IDDM, NIDDM, diabetic nephropathies, neuropathies, ketoacidosis, pregnancy in diabetes, etc) will expand the breadth of the search. By focusing the search, only those articles that have diabetes mellitus as the main subject will be included. Text word searches are very useful for terms not available as MeSH headings (especially useful for new therapies). One way to refine a search is to make use of the Boolean operators (AND, OR, NOT) to combine various topics of interest. Limiting a search to specific publications (eg, randomized controlled trials (RCTs), controlled clinical trials, meta-analyses) can further specify search results.[5,8] PubMed, a free Internet-based interface to MEDLINE, offers a special search site entitled "Clinical Queries" that can filter a search according to research methodology for therapy, diagnosis, etiology, or prognosis.[8]

HOW VALID IS THE INFORMATION?

What Resources Are Available?

There are many resources that can help clinicians develop the skills to practice EBM. Many evidence-based systematic overviews and practice guidelines exist to guide clinical decision-making. Additionally, many commentaries about the literature have been published and can serve to help clinicians better interpret existing evidence.

The "Users' Guide to the Medical Literature" is a series of articles written by The Evidence-Based Medicine Working Group, coordinated from McMaster University and published in the *Journal of the American Medical Association* (JAMA). These articles explain how to interpret and apply the information found in articles with a specific focus, including therapy and prevention,[9,10] harm,[11] prognosis,[12] diagnosis,[13,14] overviews,[15] clinical decision analyses,[16,17] clinical practice guidelines,[18,19] and economic analysis.[3,4] The Unit for Evidence-Based Practice and Policy has created a similar series of articles, published in the *British Medical Journal*.

Several organizations have attempted to critically evaluate the evidence available on a wide variety of topics to develop useful evidence-based summaries or guidelines. The Cochrane Collaboration group is an international body that has produced the Cochrane Library, a collection of databases that includes the Database of Systematic Reviews.[20] Cochrane reviews will be indexed by MEDLINE in the year 2001. In these reviews, the best evidence, generally RCTs, is evaluated and quantitatively summarized according to defined, systematic methods.[21] The American College of Physicians (ACP) produces a bimonthly supplement to the journal *Annals of Internal Medicine* called the *ACP Journal Club* (*ACPJC*), which pairs a structured abstract of a high-quality clinical study relating to an internal medicine topic with expert commentary focused on applicability of the study to practice. *Evidence-Based Medicine* is a sister publication, which reviews high-quality evidence for a variety of clinical topics with broader clinical coverage than *ACPJC*. *Best Evidence* is the electronic database for *ACPJC* and *Evidence-Based Medicine*. Additionally, the United States Agency for Health Care Policy and Research (AHCPR) once developed evidence-based clinical guidelines and currently as the Agency for Healthcare Research and Quality (AHRQ) (*http://www.ahcpr.gov/*) produces evidence summary reports to provide the basis for guidelines, performance measures, educational materials, and other quality improvement programs on a variety of topics.[21,22]

What Are the Levels of Evidence and the Types of Studies on Which They Are Based?

Practicing EBM involves summarizing and applying the best available evidence to clinical decision-making. The highest quality evidence for therapeutic efficacy is derived from large, rigorously performed, double-blind RCTs with appropriate follow-up and clinically important outcomes.[9] However, not every clinical question will have been addressed in an RCT. Different types of questions will require different types of studies, each subject to a range of strengths and weaknesses that influence validity and generalizability of results (Table 4–3).[23–27] For the clinician to summarize the strength of evidence surrounding particular recommendations, levels of evidence have been created as a tool. However, it is important to note that levels of evidence describe only the methodologic quality of the study supporting the evidence; they do not describe treatment effect or relevance and have not themselves been validated.[23] Levels of evidence have been developed for studies of treatment or prevention,[9,23] harm,[11] diagnostic tests,[13,14] and prognosis,[12] although the levels of evidence may vary from source to source. They are generally based on the strengths and limitations of study designs. The levels of evidence employed in this chapter are Levels 1 through 5.

Meta-Analysis and Systematic Overview

In a systematic overview, an objective review of all primary studies relevant to a particular problem is conducted with clear, explicit criteria and reproducible methods.[27] It begins with a well-defined clinical question. It uses prospective methods and a comprehensive literature search in at least one, and preferably several, databases (such as MEDLINE, EMBASE, Cochrane Controlled Trials Register). In a systematic overview, the criteria used to include and exclude studies must be well defined and explicitly described. This serves to limit the bias of narrative reviews, where the author may selectively review articles of interest.

The systematic overview that also quantitatively summarizes the results of trials is called a "meta-analysis."[23] Meta-analyses pool results of trials, which serves to increase the power to detect a clinically important or statistically significant effect of an intervention. Meta-analysis is helpful when the number of patients included in the RCTs is small or when the event rates in the RCTs are small. Both systematic overviews and meta-analyses must be explicit, be reproducible, and employ valid, reliable methods.[27] Criteria for evaluating the quality of a systematic overview or meta-analysis have been developed.[15] Results of a meta-analysis or systematic overview are only as valid as the trials they include.

Randomized Controlled Trials

The most methodologically sound clinical trials are double-blind RCTs, which are considered to be the "gold standard" method of determining effects due to a particular therapy or intervention. In an RCT, subjects are randomly allocated to receive an intervention (often a novel therapy) or control (conventional treatment or placebo).[28]

Table 4–3 Benefits and Limitations Associated with Different Types of Evidence

Type	Strengths	Limitations
Meta-analysis/ systematic overview	Provides useful information on a treatment in the absence of large RCTs Increased statistical power as compared to many small RCTs Enhanced precision as compared to many RCTs May provide robust estimates of true treatment effect Can address questions not possible in individual trials (eg, harm)	Incorporates biases of the trials they include Heterogeneity of RCTs influences results Subject to publication or selection bias Secondary outcomes/harm/adverse events may not be fully addressed Laborious; requires attention to prospective methodology analogous to clinical trial
Randomized controlled trial	If sufficiently large, best source of estimates of clinical outcomes—both benefit and harm Proper randomization ensures groups are similar, except for intervention Bias minimized	Costly Limited generalizability in some cases May be unfeasible—physicians, patients may have own bias, will not participate May be unethical—difficult to randomized to answer some questions of harm Long study durations required to answer most important questions
Cohort study	Useful design when assessing harm Identify risk factors for disease that provide clues for etiology Can assemble large sample sizes quickly for some cohorts More representative of real-world clinical practice	Impossible to control for all potential confounders Unforeseen bias, including channeling bias Long follow-up sometimes required
Case-control study	Often used for questions involving rare outcomes Real practice Accommodates long follow-up readily since retrospective	Shows association, not causality Impossible to control for all potential confounders Unforeseen bias, including channeling bias Valid measurement of exposure and outcome difficult
Case reports	May be first indication of uncommon instances of harm, drug interactions (signal detection) Simplest form of study Can provide individual case details	Isolated cases—questionable generalizability No denominator to describe the risk (ie, how many patients were exposed?)

RCT = randomized controlled trial.
Data from Cook et al,[23] Lau et al,[24] Borzak et al,[25] Greenhalgh et al.[26, 27]

Several characteristics define the quality of an RCT (Table 4–4). When properly employed, these characteristics ensure that the results of the study are due only to the treatment effects, rather than to other factors that could influence the outcome. Random allocation promotes that each patient has an equal chance of being assigned to a particular treatment group and that baseline characteristics of the two patient groups are the same.[29] Blinding investigators (and clinicians) and patients (and caregivers) to treatment allocation sequence and the treatment preparation reduces bias in the study processes and measurement of outcomes.

Table 4–4 Characteristics Affecting the Validity of Evidence Provided by Randomized Controlled Trial

Characteristic	Questions To Help Assess the Characteristic	Why Is It Important to Assess This Characteristic?
Randomization	Were the patients randomly allocated to treatment groups?	Minimizes selection bias where there might be greater treatment effects in one group due to a baseline imbalance. Ensures groups are the same except for the treatment they receive
Follow-up	Was follow-up complete? Are all patients accounted for at the end of the study?	Reduces exclusion bias, where all patients who withdraw are removed from analysis. Includes patients who may have withdrawn for any reason
Double-blinding	Were both the patients and the investigators (clinician and outcome analyst) blind to the treatment the patient received?	Reduces performance bias, where knowledge of treatment may influence the interpretation of measures and outcomes
Intention to treat analysis	Were the patients analyzed in the groups to which they were assigned?	Ensures that treatment efficacy is not overestimated
Sample size	Was the sample size large enough to detect the outcome of interest?	Allows the detection of therapeutic effect where meaningful effect exists. If no effect is detected in the trial, an adequate sample size generates confidence that none actually exists (usually sample size is large enough to address only potential benefit, not risk).

Adapted from Guyatt et al,[9] UK Prospective Diabetes Study Group,[38] and UK Prospective Diabetes Study Group.[39]

One common criticism of RCTs points to their limited generalizability. Many RCTs have strict inclusion or exclusion criteria, which can limit applicability of results to the patient population studied (which may or may not be representative of the whole population with the disease). Groups that are commonly excluded from or under-represented in clinical trials include women, children and the elderly,[30] and persons with multiple comorbid conditions, including diabetes. Poor representation of these patient groups can have potentially serious consequences. For example, people with diabetes and elderly patients have been excluded from trials examining long-term use of beta-blockers following myocardial infarction (MI). As a result, the 1996 American College of Cardiology (ACC) and American Heart Association (AHA) guidelines for treatment of MI listed IDDM as relative contraindications to beta-blockers post-MI.[31] Cohort studies have since indicated that larger groups excluded from the RCTs, including people with diabetes, those ≥ 80 years of age, and those with a left ventricular ejection fraction (LVEF) < 20% derive benefit from beta-blocker therapy.[32,33] It was observed in a retrospective cohort study that people with diabetes prescribed a beta-blocker post-MI had a relative risk of death of 0.64 (95% confidence interval [CI] 0.60 to 0.69) compared to those who were not prescribed a beta-blocker post-MI.[33] Additionally, the higher mortality rates in these high-risk groups (elderly, those with diabetes, LVEF < 20%) meant that the absolute reduction in mortality due to beta-blockers was greater than the mortality reduction for patients with no specific risk factors. As a result of these studies, the 1999 ACC/AHA update to these guidelines states that "although relative contraindications once may have been thought to preclude the use of beta-blockers in some patients, new evidence suggests that the benefits of beta-blockers in reducing reinfarctions and mortality may actually outweigh the risks, even in patients with (1) asthma, (2) insulin-dependent diabetes mellitus, (3) chronic obstructive pulmonary disease, (4) severe peripheral vascular disease, (5) PR interval > 0.24 seconds, and (6) moderate left ventricular failure."[34]

The issue of how to interpret the results of a large RCT when it contradicts results of a meta-analysis of previously conducted smaller trials is a current topic of debate. LeLorier and colleagues[35] examined 19 meta-analyses of small trials about a range of clinical topics and compared the results to 12 subsequent large RCTs published in the corresponding clinical areas. Where meta-analysis was positive, 32% of the subsequent RCTs showed no effect, or the intervention was worse than control. In a similar study,[36] it was noted that disagreement could be attributable to different disease baseline risks, variable protocols, quality, and publication bias.

In summary, a meta-analysis that pools the results of many small trials is not the same as a large RCT that includes the same number of patients.[25] However, a meta-analysis of large, well-designed RCTs can provide a reliable estimate of a treatment effect.[37–39] Further, more advanced techniques such as meta-analysis using individual patient data, meta-regression, and prospective meta-analysis may provide better estimates and explain heterogeneity.[24,36,37]

Cohort Studies

Cohort studies select a group or "cohort" of patients at the same stage of their disease based on exposure or nonexposure to a particular risk factor. The cohort is then followed prospectively to determine how many in each group will develop the outcome of interest.[26] Cohort studies are used to identify risk factors for disease, which can provide clues to etiology. This design is useful when it is impossible to randomly assign patients to an exposure group, to follow the prognosis of specific groups receiving various therapies, or to follow the prognosis of patients with specific risk factors or conditions. Cohort designs are also useful when the outcome of interest is an uncommon event and an RCT would be unethical or not feasible.[11] As previously mentioned, people with diabetes have been excluded from post-MI RCTs, but clinicians have reasonable evidence from a cohort study that beta-blockers decrease mortality in this particular patient population.[33] When employing or interpreting studies with cohort designs, it becomes critical to ensure that all patient characteristics that may be pertinent to the outcome of interest are documented since prognostic factors may well be distributed unequally between the groups and thereby confound the result.[11]

Case-Control Studies

Case-control studies select a group of patients who have a disease or a particular outcome (cases) and match them with a similar group of individuals who do not have the disease (controls). The investigators then collect and examine retrospective data on the subjects to determine if any differences in exposure to particular risk factors exist between the two groups.[26] For example, the relationship between MI and glycemia, insulin, lipids, and glucose tolerance was assessed in a case-control study of 300 South Asian patients who had a first MI (cases) and 300 matched controls with no MI. Cases had a greater incidence of diabetes (odds ratio [OR] 5.49, 95% CI 3.34 to 9.01), impaired glucose tolerance (OR 4.08, 95% CI 2.31 to 7.20), or impaired fasting glucose (OR 3.22, 95% CI 1.51 to 6.85) than controls.[40] Often when studying rare conditions, an investigator is left with no other option than to employ the case-control design to facilitate a feasible study that can answer a clinical question in a reasonable amount of time.[11] As with cohort studies, it is important for investigators to ensure balance by matching among the groups to account for all measurable confounders.[11] Additionally, it is important to have an unbiased and precise definition of cases (vs controls) and exposure measurement, since misallocated subjects may substantially influence the results.[26] Limitations to this design, as with the cohort design, are the unmeasured confounders and unforeseen bias.[11] The case-control design can only show association between risk factors (exposures) and outcomes, not causality, due to the retrospective design and its potential for these unmeasured confounders.[26]

Assessing Benefits and Harms

Assessing Therapeutic Benefit

Once the validity of a trial has been assessed, the next step involves scrutinizing the results of the trial.[10] The United Kingdom Prospective Diabetes Study (UKPDS) will be used as an example.[41–44] The UKPDS was a large, randomized, double-blinded RCT involving newly diagnosed patients with Type 2 diabetes. The UKPDS 33 trial assessed whether intensive pharmacotherapy with sulfonylureas or insulin to achieve tight glucose control reduced cardiovascular and microvascular endpoints when compared to conventional therapy with diet and pharmacotherapy to achieve less tightly controlled blood glucose.[42] The trial also compared the various pharmacotherapies (sulfonylureas, metformin, and insulin) to see if there was a specific advantage to any one therapy.[41,42] Additionally, UKPDS 38 and 39 compared the effects of tight blood pressure control to less tight blood pressure control[44] and the effects of blood pressure control with beta-blockers compared to angiotensin converting enzyme (ACE) inhibitors[43] in terms of the incidence of cardiovascular and microvascular complications in hypertensive diabetic patients. The results of the UKPDS 38 trial, which assessed the effect of blood pressure control in 1,148 hypertensive, diabetic patients with a mean baseline blood pressure of 160/94 mm Hg, are outlined in Table 4–5.

The outcome "any diabetes-related endpoint" was defined as the time to occurrence of sudden death, death from hypo- or hyperglycemia, fatal or nonfatal myocardial infarction, angina, heart failure, stroke, renal failure, amputation (of at least one digit), vitreous hemorrhage, retinal photocoagulation, blindness in one eye, or cataract extraction.[44] Patients in the tightly controlled blood pressure group had a mean blood pressure of 144/82 mm Hg, while patients in the less tightly controlled group had a mean blood pressure of 154/87 mm Hg after a median follow-up of 8.4 years.[44] This trial meets the criteria of being valid[9] with respect to randomization, blinding, and baseline characteristics.[44] There is consistency across outcomes, with significant benefit or trend associated with tighter BP control. Around the time of publication of this trial, other trials also confirmed that BP lowering was highly beneficial in people with diabetes and suggested that BP targets should be lower than 150/85.

Table 4–5 Results of the United Kingdom Prospective Diabetes Study[38]

Endpoint	Tight Control (BP < 150/85 mm Hg) (N = 758) (%)	Less Tight Control (BP < 180/105 mm Hg) (N = 390) (%)	RR for Tight BP Control (95% CI)	p Value
Any diabetes-related endpoint	259 (34)	170 (44)	0.76 (0.62–0.92)	.0046
Diabetes-related death	82 (11)	62 (16)	0.68 (0.49–0.94)	.0190
All-cause mortality	134 (18)	83 (21)	0.82 (0.63–1.08)	.1700
Myocardial infarction	107 (14)	69 (17)	0.79 (0.59–1.07)	.1300
Stroke	38 (5)	34 (9)	0.56 (0.35–0.89)	.0130
Microvascular disease	68 (9)	54 (14)	0.63 (0.44–0.89)	.0092

BP = blood pressure; RR = relative risk.

Adapted from UK Prospective Diabetes Study Group. Tight blood pressure control and risk of macrovascular and microvascular complications in type 2 diabetes: UKPDS 38. BMJ 1998;317:703–13.

Assessing Harm

Whereas well-designed RCTs are frequently available to the clinician in assessing the benefits of a therapy, studies are rarely designed to rigorously assess the potential harm of a treatment. While an RCT may occasionally demonstrate a harmful outcome associated with a treatment, these adverse events are often infrequent and receive little attention in the published report. Studies are rarely statistically powered to show a difference between groups in terms of adverse events within an RCT. Since the greatest concern is often associated with serious adverse events that are rare and occur over prolonged periods, such events are impossible to assess in RCTs. In the UKPDS 38 example, the side effects section briefly describes no significant difference in incidence of hypoglycemia in the groups assigned to tight and less tight blood pressure control; incidences were 6.1% and 4.4%, respectively,[44] and there was a qualitative description provided of some increased adverse events (cold feet, intermittent claudication, bronchospasm, and weight gain) associated with atenolol.[43] Levels of evidence to assess reports of trials that describe harm have been developed.[11] In order to answer a question, a clinician usually must rely on studies with more methodologic limitations than RCTs, such as cohort, case-control studies, or case reports.[11]

The example of the association between metformin use and lactic acidosis illustrates the fact that often there are no RCTs, cohort, or case-control studies that assess the issue, and clinicians are left with assessing case reports. Lactic acidosis (LA) is defined as serum lactic acid concentration > 5 mmol/L (normal 0.5 to 2.2 mmol/L). It is a rare but serious metabolic disturbance that can be fatal in up to 50% of cases.[45] In 1976, phenformin, a biguanide similar to metformin, was removed from the worldwide market because of LA associated with its use, with an estimated incidence of 40 to 64 cases per 100,000 patient-years.[46]

Consider the following assessment of whether metformin is associated with LA:

- The FDA reports 66 cases of LA from May 1995 through June 1996 experienced by patients treated with metformin. Of these 66 patients, 19 did not meet the criteria for the diagnosis of metformin-associated LA. Of the remaining 47 cases, 43 had one or more risk factors for LA, including congestive heart failure (CHF) and renal insufficiency. The rate of LA was estimated to be 5 cases per 100,000.[45]
- In Sweden, 16 cases of LA were reported from1977 to 1991. Incidence decreased from 15 cases per 100,000 patient-years in 1977 to 1981 to 2.4 cases per 100,000 patient-years in 1987 to 1991.[47]
- 11 cases of metformin-associated LA have been reported to the Canadian Adverse Drug Reaction Monitoring Program since metformin was first marketed in Canada in 1972. In all cases, one or more predisposing risk factor was present.[48]
- An analysis of the Saskatchewan Health administrative databases between 1980 and 1995 found two cases of metformin-associated LA. The incidence rate was estimated to be 9 cases per 100,000 person-years (95% CI 0 to 21).[46]

Based on the available evidence, it is prudent to conclude that the incidence of metformin-associated LA is between 2 and 9 per 100,000 patient-years of exposure[45–48] and occurs mostly in patients with risk factors for LA such as CHF or renal insufficiency.[45] Clinicians should bear this in mind when prescribing metformin for patients with diabetes and inform patients of this risk along with the benefits.

How Is the Benefit and Harm of a Therapy Expressed?

Journals often use several different measures to express the effectiveness or harm of treatment. As long as the outcome of interest is a dichotomous variable, many of these measures such as relative risk (RR), odds ratio (OR), absolute risk reduction (ARR), and number needed to treat (NNT) can be derived from a 2 × 2 table. To express the magnitude of benefit derived from achieving tight blood pressure control for patients with Type 2 diabetes, a 2 × 2 table of the incidence of any diabetes-related endpoint that occurred in UKPDS 38 is outlined in Table 4–6. The formulae discussed in this section are displayed in Table 4–8.

Relative Risk.   Relative risk is a way to express the size of the treatment effect. It describes the ratio of the risk of an outcome in the treatment group as compared to the control group.[10,49] An RR of 0.5 means that the risk of experiencing the outcome is halved, and an RR of 2 means that the risk of experiencing the outcome is doubled when treatment is compared relative to the control group. Relative risk is calculated by dividing the risk of experiencing the outcome in the experimental group by the risk of experiencing the outcome in the control group. In UKPDS 38, the risk of experiencing any diabetes-related endpoint was 259 of 758 or 0.341 in the tightly controlled group and 170 of 390 or 0.436 in the less tightly controlled group. Thus, RR is 0.341/0.436 = 0.78. This means that the RR of experiencing any diabetes-related endpoint for diabetic patients with tight blood pressure control is 0.78 times that of diabetic patients with less tight blood pressure control.[44] Of note, this RR is slightly different from the RR reported in UKPDS 38.[44] This difference is likely due to the fact that the endpoints in UKPDS 38 were reported as hazard ratios (similar in principle to relative risks) based on a more sophisticated survival analysis of time to experiencing diabetes-related endpoints and not the actual numbers of diabetes-related endpoints as described here.[44] This "calculation gap" frequently occurs when studies use time-dependent analysis.

Odds Ratio.   The OR describes the odds of a patient in the treatment group experiencing an outcome relative to the odds of a patient in the control group experiencing that outcome.[49,50] Numerically, odds are expressed by dividing the number of patients who experience the outcome by the number of patients in that treatment group who do not experience that outcome. Using the UKPDS 38 example in Table 4–6, the odds of patients in the tightly controlled blood pressure group experiencing any diabetes-related endpoint are 259 of 499 = 0.519. The odds of a patient in the less tightly controlled group experiencing that same outcome are 170 of 220 = 0.773. The OR would therefore be expressed as 0.519/0.773 = 0.67. This means that the odds of a person in the tightly controlled blood pressure group experiencing any diabetes-related endpoint are 0.67 times as great as the odds of a patient in the less tightly controlled blood pressure group experiencing that outcome.[44]

While OR and RR express a similar measure of treatment effect, the OR is only a reasonable approximation of RR when the outcome of interest is relatively rare (ie, < 20%).[51]

Table 4–6 Incidence of Any Diabetes-Related Endpoint in the United Kingdom Prospective Diabetes Study[38]

	Any Diabetes-Related Endpoint (+)		No Diabetes-Related Endpoint (–)	Total
Tightly controlled blood pressure group (BP < 150/85 mm Hg)	259	a	b 499	758 (a + b)
Less tightly controlled blood pressure group (BP < 180/105 mm Hg)	c 170	d	220	390 (c + d)
Total	429 (a + c)		719 (b + d)	1,148

As the outcomes become more common, the difference between OR and RR increases.[51] When interpreting the OR for a frequent outcome, it is useful to keep in mind that the OR will underestimate the RR if the OR is < 1.0 and will overestimate the RR when the OR is > 1.0.[51] The OR is a useful indicator of treatment effect size in examples such as case-control studies that assess harm associated with treatment, as these outcomes are more rare (eg, risk of LA in patients treated with metformin). Unfortunately, OR has limited usefulness clinically, as it does not convert to numbers needed to treat (see below).

Relative Risk Reduction.   Relative risk reduction (RRR) expresses a proportional reduction in outcomes in the treatment group relative to the control group.[10,49] The RRR has been described as an estimate of the amount of baseline risk that is removed owing to the effects of treatment.[52] It is calculated by subtracting the risk of outcome in the treatment group from the risk of outcome in the control group and dividing the absolute difference by the risk of outcome in the control group. In the UKPDS 38 example, the RRR for any diabetes-related endpoint is ([259/758] − [170/390]) /(170/390) = 0.22. This means that the treatment (intensively controlled blood pressure) reduced the risk of any diabetes-related endpoint by 22% relative to that in the less tightly controlled group.[44] The RRR can also be calculated by subtracting the RR from 1; in the UKPDS 38 example, this corresponds with 1 − 0.78 = 0.22.

Absolute Risk Reduction and Number Needed to Treat.   The ARR describes the absolute change in risk of an outcome between treatment and control groups.[10,49] It is calculated by taking the absolute value of the difference in risk of the outcome in the treatment group as compared to the control group.[10] For the UKPDS 38 example, this would correlate with (259/758) − (170/390) = 0.094.[44] This means that the treatment (intensively controlled blood pressure) reduces the incidence of any diabetes-related endpoint by 9.4% compared to less tightly controlled blood pressure.

The NNT describes the number of patients needed to treat to prevent one outcome. It is defined as the reciprocal of the ARR, which in our example would be 1/0.094, or 11. (In fact, this number is actually 10.6, but NNT is rounded up to the closest whole number.[10]) This means that 11 patients with Type 2 diabetes must be treated for 8.4 years (median follow-up of the study) with pharmacotherapy to maintain blood pressure < 150/85 mm Hg in order to prevent one diabetes-related endpoint, relative to patients with blood pressure < 180/105 mm Hg. The UKPDS trial reports that the NNT to prevent any diabetes-related endpoint over 10 years is 6.1 (this would round to 7).[44] When questioned about this difference in the apparent NNT, the authors explained that the reported NNT was calculated using attributable risk based on events per 1,000 person-years follow-up.[52] Because the method to calculate NNT described in this chapter does not adjust for duration of follow-up, it may give a less accurate result when survival analysis is used in RCTs.[52] However, because NNT is quickly and easily generated in practice using the method described in this chapter, clinicians should simply be aware of the potential inaccuracy when calculating NNT for RCTs that use survival analysis. Additionally, authors should be encouraged to report NNTs if they are not easily calculated, as did the authors of UKPDS 38.[44] The NNT and the ARR will change if the baseline risk changes. Thus, if the risk for an event in a subgroup is higher, the ARR will be larger and the number needed to treat will be less. This is not the case for the RRR, which does not generally change with the underlying risk of the population.[10] Number needed to treat is arguably the most clinically relevant expression of outcome of trials. Where harm is well studied, NNT can be weighed against calculated "number needed to treat to harm" (NNH). For large complex trials with multiple outcomes, multiple NNTs and NNHs can be generated. Clinical experience dealing with NNT across a variety of interventions with patients is required to put these numbers into perspective, but we endorse their use in practice, in discussions with patients, and when considering economics of various therapies.

Confidence Intervals. Confidence intervals can be generated for each measure of effect size.[51]As the results of any experiment are only an estimate of the truth, the confidence intervals indicate how much greater or smaller the true effect could be.[50] For example, in the reported results of the UKPDS 38, the OR of any diabetes-related endpoint occurring in the tight versus less tight blood pressure control groups was 0.76, and the 95% confidence interval was 0.62 to 0.92.[44] This means that there is a 95% probability that the true OR of the effect of tight blood pressure control on the incidence of any diabetes-related endpoint as compared to patients with less tight blood pressure control would be between 0.62 and 0.92.

Applying Estimates of Benefits and Harm: Another Example. Another example of the calculations used for the measures of benefit of therapy is that of the Diabetes Control and Complications Trial (DCCT).[53] The DCCT was a prospective, randomized trial that assessed the effect of intensive versus conventional insulin therapy on the incidence of microvascular complications of diabetes (retinopathy, nephropathy, neuropathy) in 1,441 patients over a mean follow-up of 6.5 years. Intensive glucose control consisted of $\geq$ three insulin injections and $\geq$ four measurements of blood glucose daily and frequent contact with investigators. Less intensive glucose control consisted of one to two insulin injections daily, once-daily blood glucose assessments, and less frequent contact with investigators.[53] Randomization was stratified according to the presence of retinopathy at baseline, and the trial was analyzed according to this stratification for the first incidence and the secondary progression of retinopathy.[56] The results of the DCCT trial for primary prevention are presented in Table 4–7.[53]

The AR, OR, RRR, ARR, and NNT for a mean follow-up of 6.5 years with intensive insulin versus conventional insulin therapy in order to prevent one case of retinopathy in a group of patients with Type 1 diabetes with no evidence of retinopathy at baseline are presented in Table 4–8. The NNT is 6, suggesting a strong protective effect of intensive insulin.

Formulae are also available to calculate the confidence intervals, but these are more complex and would generally require the use of statistical computer software.

Note that the RRR, ARR, and NNT trial might be more accurately expressed as relative benefit increase (RBI), absolute benefit increase (ABI), and NNT when the experimental treatment increases the probability of a good outcome, and as relative risk increase (RRI), absolute risk increase (ARI), and NNH when the experimental treatment increases the probability of a bad outcome.[49]

WHAT OUTCOMES ARE DESCRIBED BY THE EVIDENCE?

What Are Surrogate Outcomes?

Surrogate outcomes are defined as laboratory measurements or physical signs used as substitutes for clinically important outcomes.[49] Clinically important outcomes are those that are important to the patient, such as health-related quality of life, functional status, and sentinel events such as stroke, MI, retinopathy, or mortality.[49] Examples of surrogate outcomes used as primary outcomes in RCTs include bone mineral density instead of osteoporotic fractures,

Table 4–7 Incidence of Retinopathy in the Diabetes Control and Complications Trial

Therapy	Retinopathy		No Retinopathy	Total
Primary prevention Intensive insulin therapy	23	a	b 325	348
Primary prevention Conventional insulin therapy	91	c	d 287	378

Table 4–8 Formulae for Expressing Benefit or Harm Using the Example of the United Kingdom Prospective Study 38 and the Diabetes Control and Complications Trial

Measure	Formula	UKPDS Example*	DCCT Example†
RR	(a/[a + b]) / (c/[c + d])	(259/758) / (170/390) = 0.78	(23/348) / (91/378) = 0.27
OR	(a/b) / (c/d) = ad / bc	(259/499) / (170/220) = 0.67	(23/325) / (91/287) = 0.22
RRR	(a/[a + b] − c/[c + d])/ c/(c + d)	([259/758] − [170/390])/ (170/390) = 0.22	([23/348] − [91/378]) / (91/378) = 0.73
ARR	(a/[a + b] − c/[c + d])	(259/758) − (170/390) = 0.094	(23/348) − (91/378) = 0.5
NNT	1 / ARR (rounded up to closest round number)	1 / 0.094 = 11	1 / 0.175 = 6

*Risk of any diabetes-related endpoint with tighter vs less tight blood pressure control in Type 2 diabetes mellitus.
†Risk of retinopathy with intensive vs conventional insulin in Type 1 diabetes mellitus without retinopathy at baseline. Data from UK Prospective Diabetes Study Group. Tight blood pressure control and risk of macrovascular and microvascular complications in type 2 diabetes: UKPDS 38. BMJ 1998;317:703–13; and The Diabetes Control and Complications Trial Research Group. The effect of intensive insulin treatment of diabetes on the development and progression of long term complications in insulin-dependent diabetes mellitus. N Engl J Med 1993;329:997–86.

serum lipids for cardiovascular morbidity and mortality, hemoglobin A_{1c} (HgbA$_{1c}$), and fasting or postprandial plasma glucose concentrations for diabetes-related morbidity and mortality. When surrogate outcomes are used in RCTs instead of clinically important outcomes, trials are of shorter duration, involve fewer patients, and are less expensive.[54] Ideally, a surrogate outcome correlates with, predicts, and fully captures the effect of treatment on the clinically meaningful outcome.[55] If ideal surrogate outcomes existed and were used as outcomes of interest for RCTs, rapid dissemination of information about new therapies could occur.[54] However, surrogates are never ideal. Often years and several trials measuring both surrogate and clinical outcomes are required to establish the usefulness and limitations of the surrogate outcome. This process shows the potential for either or both of the surrogate and the clinically important outcome to be mediated through unknown, unintended, or unanticipated mechanisms.[55] The impact of calcium channel blockers or doxazosin on blood pressure versus mortality is an excellent current example of this debate.[56,57]

Guidelines have been developed to assess the quality of evidence when surrogate outcomes are used in studies.[54] Studies are assessed according to the strength of the association between the surrogate outcome and the clinical outcome and evidence from other RCTs (with drugs in the same and different class) that indicate that an improvement in the surrogate outcome leads to improvement in the clinical outcome.[54] An example of a surrogate outcome that meets some of these criteria and can be used to predict diabetes-related morbidity and mortality is microalbuminuria.[58–60] Meta-analysis has shown a positive correlation between microalbuminuria and death, with a crude OR of 2.4 (95% CI 1.8 to 2.3) in patients with Type 2 diabetes.[59] In studies that adjusted for other risk factors, microalbuminuria remained a significant predictor of mortality.[59] More recently, it has been shown that microalbuminuria and gross proteinuria are associated with all-cause mortality as well as cardiovascular, cerebrovascular, and coronary heart disease death, independent of other cardiovascular risk factors and diabetes-related variables.[58] However, whether the benefits of ACE inhibitors in diabetes are mediated solely through the effect on microalbuminuria seems unlikely.[61] An example of a surrogate outcome that has not reliably met either of these criteria is HgbA$_{1c}$. In UKPDS 33, where intensive blood glucose control was compared to less intense blood glucose control, there was no statistically significant difference between the two groups in terms of the clinical outcome of macrovascular complications of diabetes (diabetes-related death, all-cause mortality, MI, stroke, amputation, or death from peripheral vascular disease).[42] This lack of difference was observed despite a statistically significant difference between the groups in the surrogate outcome of median HgbA$_{1c}$ over 10 years (7.0% vs 7.9%).[45] In a meta-analysis[62] that assessed the relationship between blood glucose level and mortality in Type 2 diabetes mellitus, it was found that 23 of 27 articles found a positive association, but only 15 showed a statistically significant association. The authors concluded that blood glucose shows a positive but weak correlation with mortality in patients with Type 2 diabetes, although they were limited by heterogeneity in assessment of blood glucose and HgbA$_{1c}$.[62] An example of another potential surrogate outcome for diabetes-related morbidity and mortality that is less well understood and not fully evaluated in the literature is serum homocysteine level.[63]

Extrapolating Results of Drug Studies to Other Drugs within the Same Drug Family

Drugs are generally assigned to a particular class because they share a similar chemical structure, pharmacologic effect, and mechanism of action.[64] Because of these similarities, members of a drug class are often assumed to have similar effects on clinical outcomes.[64] Unfortunately, few studies are carried out to address this issue properly. Further, there is no well-accepted definition of a class effect.[64] Clinicians often are faced with a choice of five or more drugs within a class (eg, statins, beta-blockers), each with claims of superiority or lower cost or wider reimbursement by drug plans. Levels of evidence for determining whether the benefit associated with a drug is a class effect have been developed.[64]

The best sources of evidence to determine if drugs within a class have similar effect on clinical outcomes are head-to-head RCTs examining clinically important outcomes.[64] These equivalence trials have unique methodologic issues that threaten validity, including the need for appropriate outcomes, large sample size, and the long follow-up often required to detect clinically important outcomes.[65] In the absence of head-to-head RCTs, the next level of evidence involves comparing different drugs across RCTs of those drugs as compared to placebo (indirect comparison). This type of comparison is complicated by potentially differing methods, baseline risk, endpoint definitions, and compliance rates.[64] After the validity of available evidence has been considered, other factors that must be taken into consideration include the number, size, duration of studies, and positioning of the drug.[64] For example, among the statin class of lipid-lowering agents, lovastatin,[66] pravastatin,[67–69] simvastatin,[70] and atorvastatin[71] have trials showing effect on the clinically important outcomes of cardiovascular morbidity and mortality. Does this mean that other statins that lower serum lipids in a similar fashion do not benefit clinical events or simply that the manufacturers of the other statins do not need these higher quality trials to get their product on the market?

When trying to determine if a class effect exists, it is especially important to assess the quality and source of available evidence. When one drug from a class is the first to show a beneficial effect, it is common to assume that all agents in that class will share that beneficial effect.[72] This may indeed be the case for ACE inhibitors. The combined endpoint of MI, stroke, and cardiovascular death was reduced by ramipril compared to placebo in diabetic patients (ramipril group 15.3% vs placebo group 19.8%, NNT = 22) in the Heart Outcomes Prevention Evaluation Trial.[61] In a recent meta-analysis using individual patient data, a class effect of ACE inhibitors overall was suggested.[73] It is somewhat puzzling, then, that potential for harm is not considered in the same way. If one agent is shown to cause harm, much effort is exerted by competitors to establish differences among members of that class.[72] For example, sulfonlyureas were associated with an increased incidence of death in combination with metformin in the UKPDS 34.[41] Thus, clinicians would be very concerned about a class effect. However, it has recently been suggested that neither experimental nor clinical data support a uniform effect of sulfonylureas; thus, the debate remains open.[74]

Another consideration when assessing whether a class effect exists is that of a channeling bias, a type of allocation bias, in nonrandomized trials.[75,76] This term is used to refer to the (expected) prescribing of specific drugs within a class based on prescribers' and patients' perceptions of benefit and risk.[76] This phenomenon may occur with sequential cohort studies or when several drugs within a class are competing for market share. The preferential prescription of one agent to a certain group of patients based on perceived effects of that drug in that population may lead to inaccurate representation of the true effects or harms caused by that drug in the general population.[76] For example, if a new sulfonylurea was promoted as associated with less hypoglycemia than other available sulfonylureas, those patients who were more unstable or had "brittle diabetes" might be preferentially prescribed that agent. Subsequent nonexperimental analysis might well conclude that the new agent was associated with more hypoglycemia than the older agents, but the results would be confounded because of this channeling bias.

Is the Change in Outcome Clinically Important?

A difference that is statistically significant may not always be judged to be clinically important by patients, clinicians, or policy makers. For example, in UKPDS 38 an absolute difference of 3.5% (NNT = 29) in the incidence of myocardial infarction is reported.[44] While many clinicians would find this impressive, a patient might decide that this difference is not worth the additional effort of tight blood pressure control. The minimum clinically important difference (MCID) is the smallest difference in the outcome of interest that patients perceive as beneficial and that would mandate, in the absence of troublesome side effects and excessive cost, a change in the patient's management.[77] If the confidence interval for a reported outcome does not exclude what would be considered a clinically important benefit or harm, then the results would fail to provide a conclusive answer regarding the outcome of interest. The process of reviewing a study is streamlined by a prior sense of a reasonable MCID.

HOW DOES ONE TRANSLATE CLINICAL TRIAL EVIDENCE INTO PRACTICE?

Often, the evidence alone is not sufficient to encourage changes in practice.[21] This may be due to barriers occurring at different levels: at the level of the health care system, clinician, patient, or society.[21]

Efficacy versus Effectiveness: Why Is this Distinction Important?

Efficacy trials look at the magnitude of an intervention effect, usually in a homogeneous, highly selected group of low-risk, responsive patients.[78] Effectiveness trials examine the effect of an intervention in a heterogeneous group of patients (all comers) to achieve a more accurate representation of the effect of the intervention in real life.[78] The results of the UKPDS studies[41–44] address the efficacy of intensive glucose control in patients with Type 2 diabetes. However, the application of intensive treatment (and therefore, its effectiveness) in actual practice may be much less than the efficacy of the treatment observed in rigorously controlled RCTs. The benefit observed in UKPDS 33 was attained with HbA_{1c} levels of 7.0% in the intensively treated group and 7.9% in the conventionally treated group.[42] Since 1996, the American Diabetes Association diabetes guidelines have recommended target levels of $HbA_{1c} < 7\%$. However, a cohort study of 8,668 patients with Type 2 diabetes initiating insulin therapy found that after 2 years, over 60% of patients still had HbA_{1c} levels $\geq 8\%$.[79] This a good example of the limitations to generalizability of RCTs and the effectiveness of treatments, because of our inability or unwillingness to apply trial evidence or the enabling factors within trials that improve compliance and outcomes. In another classic example, despite evidence that people with diabetes are at high risk for future events post-MI, a retrospective cohort of more than 200,000 patients showed that only 28.3% of the 59,445 patients receiving insulin and 33.1% of patients not receiving insulin got prescriptions for beta-blockers at hospital discharge post-MI.[33] This can be explained in part by the frequent exclusion of people with diabetes from MI trials (although trials suggest a more impressive NNT for people with diabetes compared to nondiabetic people) and previously promulgated concerns regarding adverse impact of beta-blockers on surrogate endpoints (eg, blood glucose). In the cohort study, people with diabetes receiving beta-blockers had a large reduction in risk of death (ARR, 9.6%, NNT 10) compared to those not receiving beta-blockers.

Gap between Evidence and Practice

Deficiencies exist in transferring evidence for diabetes care into clinical practice.[80] For example, the impact of the American Diabetes Associations's standards of care for patients with Type 2 diabetes on practice patterns of university-based endocrine physicians and fellows was assessed through a retrospective chart review of 790 patients.[80] Deficiencies were noted in all aspects of the diabetic patient encounter before guideline publication and did not improve significantly following publication of the guidelines, except in the areas of foot care, eye examination, and lipid screening. Major deficiencies were noted in areas of quality assurance and chart documentation, and these did not improve over time.[80]

Many factors have been proposed to explain why there is such a gap between evidence and clinical practice. Proposed barriers to the application of research findings to patients are outlined in Table 4–9 and include those that affect patient, practitioner, education, health care, and society.[81,82]

Barriers that affect the transfer of diabetes-related evidence into clinical practice include patient-specific factors such as lack of knowledge, obesity, denial, apathy, sedentary lifestyle, physician neglect, culture, and stress.[83,84] Additional factors that affect physicians include poor practice organization, lack of appreciation of importance of interventions, too little time, lack of monitoring and alerting tools, attitude, enthusiasm, culture, language, and lack of resources.[85,86]

Harm associated with therapy may prevent the transfer of evidence into clinical practice. The DCCT showed that intensive glucose control reduced the risk for the development and progression of microvascular complications of diabetes, as compared to conventional glucose control for patients with Type 1 diabetes.[53] However, intensive glucose control was also associated with an increase in the risk of becoming overweight; 12.7 cases per 100 patient-years in the intensive group versus 9.3 in the conventional therapy group.[53] In population-based samples of patients with Type 1 diabetes, it has been found that women and adolescents with Type 1 diabetes will often omit insulin injections for weight control, leaving them at risk for microvascular complications of diabetes.[87–89] Barriers to the implementation of such policies as intensive insulin regimens into clinical practice must be addressed and overcome to translate this evidence into patient-oriented outcomes.

Interventions to Improve Practice: Hierarchy of Effectiveness and How to Appraise

Interventions to promote change in the behavior of health professionals, for example, to encourage the adoption of guidelines into clinical practice, have been reviewed and assessed in terms of relative efficacy.[90,91] Effective interventions include educational outreach visits, reminders, and interventions that employ more than one strategy (Table 4–10).[90,91] Coordinated implementation, the process of bringing distilled research information to frontline clinicians and patients, is presently imperfect.[92]

The implementation of new evidence into clinical practice in the field of diabetes is an area that requires further research and interventions. For example, the impact of a 7-hour small-group workshop designed to improve family physicians' implementation of diabetes practice guidelines was assessed in terms of the effect of the workshop on the physicians' attitude, knowledge, and self-reported practice patterns at 1 month and 1 year post-seminar.[93] It was found that the 177 participants had improved attitude ($p < .001$), knowledge ($p = .04$), and self-reported practice patterns ($p < .002$) about diabetes as compared to 113 nonparticipant controls after 1 month, but not after 1 year.[93] Often self-reported practice patterns are more optimistic than actual, audited practice. For example, knowledge of proper drug use does not correlate well with performance in practice.[94]

Computer Decision Support Systems

As health care and health care information computerizes at an accelerating rate, computer decision support systems (CDSS) become an important vehicle of intervention.[95] In a systematic review of controlled clinical trials assessing the effects of CDSS in all areas of medicine, it was shown that CDSS had a beneficial effect on physician performance in 66% of 65 studies.[96] Of 14 studies that assessed the effect of CDSS on patient outcomes, 6 showed a benefit, although most of the remaining studies had insufficient sample size to show a difference.[96] Given the chronic progressive nature of the disease and the multiple monitoring points and interventions supported by evidence in diabetes, CDSS are a logical intervention in diabetes. However, issues of availability, useability, validity, and portability currently hamper CDSS expansion.

Table 4–9 Perceived Barriers to Implementation of Research Findings into Clinical Practice

Domain	Barrier
Practice	Time
	Organizational limitations
	Increased malpractice liability
Education	Availability limited
	Volume of information
	Lack of incentive
	Time
Health care system	Limited resources
	Mismatch between evidence and practice realities
	Lack of defined practices
	Health policies that promote inaccurate recommendations
	Limited access to information
Society	Media affects patients' perceptions and beliefs
	Access to care
Practitioner	Knowledge outdated
	Difficulty in acquiring new skills
	Time limited
	Lack of agreement with publications
	Influence of opinion leaders
	Attitudes, beliefs, values
	Lack of awareness
	Lack of outcome expectancy
Patient	Demand
	Perception
	Attitude, beliefs, values

Table 4–10 Interventions to Change Behaviors of Health Professionals

Effectiveness	*Intervention*
Relatively strong	Academic detailing/outreach visits
	Reminders (manual or computer)
	Multiple interventions (combination of audit and feedback, local consensus, marketing, reminders)
	Regulatory interventions
Moderately effective	Audit and feedback
	Opinion leaders
	Local consensus
	Patient interventions
Relatively weak	Didactic educational events
	Written material
	Mailed material

Adapted from Davis et al[90] and Bero et al.[91]

HOW DOES ONE APPLY THE EVIDENCE TO INDIVIDUAL PATIENTS VERSUS POPULATIONS?

Individual Baseline Risk

Several guidelines have been developed to determine whether available evidence applies to a particular patient.[97,98] If a patient meets inclusion criteria, the net benefit that a patient will experience from an intervention is easy to extrapolate from a particular study. When patients are different from study inclusion criteria, they tend to have quantitative, not qualitative, differences from the patients in the study.[97] For example, patients may have an increased baseline risk of an outcome occurring as compared to an RCT, but they do not generally have no risk at all.[97] Clinicians must then consider if there are reasons (based on pathophysiology, patient or provider compliance, comorbid conditions, or risk of adverse outcomes)[97] that expected treatment response may be altered. More specifically, the clinician is estimating how that patient's RRR, baseline risk for the outcome, and risk for harm differ from those of the patients in the RCT.[98] To generate or estimate patient-specific estimated baseline risks (patient's expected event rate = PEER) for outcome or harms, clinicians can look at risks in a subgroup of the RCT if presented, clinical prediction guidelines if published, or population-based cohort studies.[98] Numerically, the patient-specific NNT can be calculated with the following formula:

$$NNT = 1 / (PEER \times RRR)$$

where the RRR is that observed from the RCT as a whole.[98] Alternatively, in the absence of such data with which to estimate the PEER, the clinician can employ clinical judgment to estimate the patient's risk of the outcome event relative to the patients in the RCT (f_t).[98] This number would be greater than one if the patient were felt to be at an increased risk of a negative outcome.[98] The patient-specific NNT is calculated by dividing the overall NNT by the patient's risk; in this manner, NNT (patient specific) = NNT / f_t.[98]

Patient Preferences

Patient preferences, values, and attitudes are part of any decision-making process that involves therapy or harm. Quality of life, one of the surrogates for patient preferences, is used as an outcome in an increasing number of clinical trials, although the effect of various diabetes treatments on quality of life is not yet fully understood. For example, in one RCT that assessed the impact of diet and glipazide versus placebo on quality of life indicators over 12 weeks in patients with Type 2 diabetes, the glipazide group had improved symptom distress, general perceived health, and cognitive functioning as compared to placebo.[99] In another example, the DCCT trial conducted a separate analysis of the effect of intensive versus less intensive blood glucose control on quality of life for 1,441 patients aged 13 to 39 years with Type 1 diabetes.[100] Main outcome measures of quality of life, satisfaction with disease management, and functional status did not differ between the two groups at baseline or at study end (mean follow-up 6.5 years), and the authors concluded that quality of life was not adversely affected by intensive insulin therapy.[100] These patients were younger and more educated than the average patient with diabetes, so it becomes difficult to extrapolate these results to other patients with Type 1 diabetes.[101] It becomes even more difficult to extrapolate these results to patients with Type 2 diabetes who are generally older, may be less well educated, and suffer from a greater number of comorbid conditions than did the patients in the DCCT trial.[101] The true effect of intensive therapy for patients with Type 1 and Type 2 diabetes on quality of life is still an important area of research.

Measurement of patient preferences in diabetes remains an important area for research.

CONCLUSION

In summary, clinicians and patients have multiple types, levels, and topics of evidence to apply to diabetes. Increasingly, our role as clinicians is as information distillers and managers for our patients. Future gains in important diabetes outcomes will likely rely as much on the implementation of evidence in practice as on the production of evidence itself. In this chapter, we have attempted to summarize issues to consider when looking for and appraising evidence and applying evidence to an individual patient and practice.

REFERENCES

1. Ellrodt G, Cook DJ, Lee J, et al. Evidence-based disease management. JAMA 1997;278:1687–92.

2. Meltzer S, Lawrence L, Daneman D, et al. 1998 clinical practice guidelines for the management of diabetes mellitus in Canada. Can Med Assoc J 1998;159(Suppl 8):S1–29.

3. O'Brien BJ, Heyland D, Richardson WS, et al. Users' guides to the medical literature. XIII. How to use an article on economic analysis of clinical practice. B. What are the results and will they help me in caring for my patients? Evidence-Based Medicine Working Group. JAMA 1997;277:1802–6.

4. Drummond MF, Richardson WS, O'Brien BJ, et al. Users' guides to the medical literature. XIII. How to use an article on economic analysis of clinical practice. A. Are the results of the study valid? Evidence-Based Medicine Working Group. JAMA 1997;277:1552–7.

5. McKibbon K, Wilczynski N, Walker-Dilks C. How to search for and find evidence about therapy. Evidence-Based Medicine 1996;Mar–Apr:70–2.

6. Greenhalgh T. How to read a paper: the MEDLINE database. BMJ 1997;315:180–3

7. Woods D, Trewheellar K. MEDLINE and EMBASE complement each other in literature searches. BMJ 1998;316:1116.

8. Haynes RB, Wilczynski N, McKibbon K, et al. Developing optimal search strategies for detecting clinically sound studies in MEDLINE. J Am Med Inform Assoc 1994;1:447–58.

9. Guyatt GH, Sackett DL, Cook DJ. Users' guides to the medical literature. II. How to use an article about therapy or prevention. A. Are the results of the study valid? Evidence-Based Medicine Working Group. JAMA 1993;270:2598–601.

10. Guyatt GH, Sackett DL, Cook DJ. Users' guides to the medical literature. II. How to use an article about therapy or prevention. B. What were the results and will they help me in caring for my patients? Evidence-Based Medicine Working Group. JAMA 1994;271:59–63.

11. Levine M, Walter S, Lee H, et al. Users' guides to the medical literature. IV. How to use an article about harm. Evidence-Based Medicine Working Group. JAMA 1994;271:1615–9.

12. Laupacis A, Wells G, Richardson WS, Tugwell P. Users' guides to the medical literature. V. How to use an article about prognosis. Evidence-Based Medicine Working Group. JAMA 1994;272:234–7.

13. Jaeschke R, Guyatt G, Sackett DL. Users' guides to the medical literature. III. How to use an article about a diagnostic test. A. Are the results of the study valid? Evidence-Based Medicine Working Group. JAMA 1994;271:389–91.

14. Jaeschke R, Guyatt GH, Sackett DL. Users' guides to the medical literature. III. How to use an article about a diagnostic test. B. What are the results and will they help me in caring for my patients? Evidence-Based Medicine Working Group. JAMA 1994;271:703–7.

15. Oxman AD, Cook DJ, Guyatt GH. Users' guides to the medical literature. VI. How to use an overview. Evidence-Based Medicine Working Group JAMA 1994;272:1367–71.

16. Richardson WS, Detsky AS. Users' guides to the medical literature. VII. How to use a clinical decision analysis. A. Are the results of the study valid? Evidence-Based Medicine Working Group. JAMA 1995;273:1292–5.

17. Richardson WS, Detsky AS. Users' guides to the medical literature. VII. How to use a clinical decision analysis. B. What are the results and will they help me in caring for my patients? Evidence-Based Medicine Working Group. JAMA 1995;273:1610–3.

18. Hayward RS, Wilson MC, Tunis SR, et al. Users' guides to the medical literature. VIII. How to use clinical practice guidelines. A. Are the recommendations valid? Evidence-Based Medicine Working Group. JAMA 1995;274:570–4.

19. Wilson MC, Hayward RS, Tunis SR, et al. Users' guides to the medical literature. VIII. How to use clinical practice guidelines. B. What are the recommendations and will they help you in caring for your patients? Evidence-Based Medicine Working Group. JAMA 1995;274:1630–2.

20. Jadad AR, Haynes RB. The Cochrane Collaboration: advances and challenges in improving evidence-based decision-making. Med Decis Making 1998;18:2–9.

21. Glanville J, Haines M, Auston I. Getting research findings into practice: finding information on clinical effectiveness. BMJ 1998;317:200–3.

22. The Cochrane Library. Update software. Updated quarterly. Issue 3. Oxford: 2000.

23. Cook DJ, Guyatt G, Laupacis A, et al. Clinical recommendations using levels of evidence for antithrombotic agents. Chest 1995;108:227S–30S.

24. Lau J, Ioannidis JPA, Schmid CH. Summing up the evidence: one answer is not always enough. Lancet 1998;351:123–7.

25. Borzak S, Ridker PM. Discordance between meta-analysis and large-scale randomized, controlled trials. Ann Intern Med 1995;123:873–7.

26. Greenhalgh T. How to read a paper. Getting your bearings (deciding what the paper is about). BMJ 1997;315:243–6.

27. Greenhalgh T. How to read a paper. Papers that summarize other papers (systematic reviews and meta-analysis). BMJ 1997;315:672–5.

28. Jadad AR. Randomized controlled trials: the basics. In: Randomized controlled trials. London: BMJ Books; 1998. p. 1–9.

29. Roberts C, Togerson DJ. Understanding controlled trials. Baseline imbalance in randomized controlled trials. BMJ 1999;319:185.

30. Gurwitz JH, Col NF, Avorn J. The exclusion of the elderly and women from clinical trials in acute MI. JAMA 1992;368:1417–22.

31. Ryan TJ, Anderson JL, Antman EM, et al. ACC/AHA guidelines for the management of patients with acute myocardial infarction. A report of the American College of Cardiology/American Heart Association Task Force on Practice Guidelines (Committee on Management of Acute Myocardial Infarction). J Am Coll Cardiol 1996;28:1328–428.

32. Soumerai SB, McLaughlin TJ, Spiegleman D, et al. Adverse outcomes of underuse of beta blockers in elderly survivors of acute myocardial infarction. JAMA 1997;277:115–21.

33. Gottlieb SS. Effect of beta-blockade on mortality among high-risk and low-risk patients after myocardial infarction. N Engl J Med 1998;339:489–97.

34. Ryan TJ, Antman EM, Brooks NH, et al. 1999 update: ACC/AHA guidelines for the management of patients with acute myocardial infarction. A report of the American College of Cardiology/American Heart Association Task Force on Practice Guidelines (Committee on Management of Acute Myocardial Infarction). J Am Coll Cardiol 1999;34:890–911.

35. LeLorier J, Gregoire G, Benhaddad A, et al. Discrepancies between meta-analysis and subsequent large randomized controlled trials. N Engl J Med 1997;337:536–42.

36. Ioannidis JPA, Cappelleri JC, Lau J. Issues in comparisons between meta-analysis and large trials. JAMA 1998;279:1089–93.

37. Pogue J, Yusuf S. Overcoming the limitations of current meta-analysis of randomized controlled trials. Lancet 1998;351:47–52.

38. Sibbald B, Roland M. Understanding controlled trials: why are randomized controlled trials important? BMJ 1998;316:201.

39. Greenhalgh T. How to read a paper. Assessing the methodological quality of published papers. BMJ 1997;315:305–8.

40. Gerstein HC, Pais P, Pogue J, et al. Relationship of glucose and insulin levels to the risk of myocardial infarction: a case control study. J Am Coll Cardiol 1999;33:612–9.

41. UK Prospective Diabetes Study Group. Effect of intensive blood-glucose control with metformin on complications in overweight patients with type 2 diabetes (UKPDS 34). Lancet 1998;352:854–65.

42. UK Prospective Diabetes Study Group. Intensive blood-glucose control with sulphonylureas or insulin compared with conventional treatment and risk of complications in patients with type 2 diabetes (UKPDS 33). Lancet 1998;352:837–53.

43. UK Prospective Diabetes Study Group. Efficacy of atenolol and captopril in reducing risk of macrovascular and microvascular complications in type 2 diabetes: UKPDS 39. BMJ 1998;317:713–20.

44. UK Prospective Diabetes Study Group. Tight blood pressure control and risk of macrovascular and microvascular complications in type 2 diabetes: UKPDS 38. BMJ 1998;317:703–13.

45. Misbin RI, Green L, Stadel BV, et al. Lactic acidosis in patients with diabetes treated with metformin. N Engl J Med 1998;338:265–6.

46. Stang M, Wysowski DK, Butler-Jones D. Incidence of lactic acidosis in metformin users. Diabetes Care 1999;22:925–7.

47. Wilholm BE, Myrhed M. Metformin associated lactic acidosis in Sweden 1977–1991. Eur J Clin Pharmacol 1993;44:589–91.

48. Drugs Directorate, Health Canada. Canadian adverse drug reaction newsletter. Metformin: lactic acidosis. Can Med Assoc J 1996;154:1057–8.

49. Sackett DL, Haynes RB. Summarizing the effects of therapy: a new table and some more terms. ACP J Club 1997;126:A15–6.

50. Sackett DL. Down with odds ratios! Evidence-Based Medicine 1996;1:164.

51. Jaeschke R, Guyatt G, Shannon H, et al. Assessing the effects of treatment: measures of association. Can Med Assoc J 1995;152:351–7.

52. Groetsch SM, LaVan JT, Epling JW. Numbers needed to treat need to be clarified [letter]. BMJ 1999;318:666.

53. Diabetes Control and Complications Trial Research Group. The effect of intensive insulin treatment of diabetes on the development and progression of long term complications in insulin-dependent diabetes mellitus. N Engl J Med 1993;329:977–86.

54. Bucher HC, Guyatt GH, Cook DJ, et al. Users' guides to the medical literature: XIX. Applying clinical trial results. A. How to use an article measuring the effect of an intervention on surrogate end points. Evidence-Based Medicine Working Group. JAMA 1999;282:771–8.

55. Fleming TR, Demets DL. Surrogate endpoints in clinical trials: are we being misled? Ann Intern Med 1996;152:605–13.

56. Lasagna L. Diuretics vs alpha-blockers for treatment of hypertension: lessons from ALLHAT. Antihypertensive and Lipid-Lowering Treatment to Prevent Heart Attack Trial. JAMA 2000;283:2013–4.

57. Psaty BM, Heckbert SR, Koepsell TD, et al. The risk of myocardial infarction associated with antihypertensive drug therapies. JAMA 1995;274:620–5.

58. Valmadrid CT, Klein R, Moss SE, Klein BE. The risk of cardiovascular disease mortality associated with microalbuminuria and gross proteinuria in persons with older-onset diabetes mellitus. Arch Intern Med 2000;160:1093–100.

59. Dinneen SF, Gerstein HC. The association of microalbuminuria and mortality in non-insulin-dependent diabetes mellitus. Arch Intern Med 1997;157:1413–8.

60. Keane WF. Proteinuria: its clinical importance and role in progressive renal disease. Am J Kidney Dis 2000;35(Suppl 1):S97–105.

61. Heart Outcomes Prevention Evaluation (HOPE) Study Investigators. Effects of ramipril on cardiovascular and microvascular outcomes in people with diabetes mellitus: results of the HOPE study and MICRO-HOPE substudy. Lancet 2000;355:253–9.

62. Groeneveld Y, Petri H, Hermanst J, Springer MP. Relationship between blood glucose level and mortality in type 2 diabetes mellitus: a systematic review. Diabet Med 1999;16:2–13.

63. Stabler SP, Estacio R, Jeffers BW, et al. Total homocysteine is associated with nephropathy in non-insulin-dependent diabetes mellitus. Metabolism 1999;48:1096–101.

64. McAlister FA, Laupacis A, Wells GA, Sackett DL. Users' guides to the medical literature: XIX. Applying clinical trial results. B. Guidelines for determining whether a drug is exerting (more than) a class effect. JAMA 1999;282:1371–7.

65. Hatala R, Holbrook A, Goldsmith CH. Therapeutic equivalence: all studies are not created equal. Can J Pharmacol 1999;6:9–11.

66. Downs JR, Clearfield M, Weis S, et al, for the AFCAPS/TexCAPS Research Group. Primary prevention of acute coronary events with lovastatin in men and women with average cholesterol levels: results of AFCAPS/TexCAPS. JAMA 1998;279:1615–22.

67. Sheperd J, Cobbe SM, Ford I, et al, for the West of Scotland Coronary Prevention Study Groups. Prevention of coronary heart disease with pravastatin in men with hypercholesterolemia. N Engl J Med 1995;333:1301–7.

68. Sacks FM, Pfeffer MA, Moye LA, et al, for the Cholesterol and Recurrent Events Trial Investigators. The effect of pravastatin on coronary events after myocardial infarction in patients with average cholesterol. N Engl J Med 1996;335:1001–9.

69. The Long-term Intervention with Pravastatin in Ischemic Disease (LIPID) Study Groups. Prevention of cardiovascular events and death with pravastatin in patients with coronary heart disease and a broad range of initial cholesterol levels. N Engl J Med 1998;339:1349–57.

70. Scandinavian Simvistatin Survival Study Groups. Randomized trial of cholesterol lowering in 4,444 patients with coronary heart disease. Lancet 1994;344:1383–9.

71. Pitt B, Waters D, Brown WV, et al. Aggressive lipid-lowering therapy compared with angioplasty in stable coronary artery disease. Atorvastatin versus Revascularization Treatment Investigators. N Engl J Med 1999;341:70–6.

72. Furberg CD, Gerrington DM, Psaty BM. Are drugs within a class interchangable? Lancet 1999;354:1202–4.

73. Flather MD, Yusuf S, Kober L, et al. Long-term ACE-inhibitor therapy in patients with heart failure or left-ventricular dysfunction: a systematic overview of data from individual patients. ACE-Inhibitor Myocardial Infarction Collaborative Group. Lancet 2000;355:1575–81.

74. Wascher TC. Sulfonylureas and cardiovascular mortality in diabetes: a class effect? Circulation 1998:97:1427.

75. Joseph KS. The evolution of clinical practice and time trends in drug effects. J Clin Epidemiol 1994;47:593–8.

76. Petri H, Urquhart J. Channeling bias in the interpretation of drug effects. Stat Med 1991;10:577–81.

77. Jaeschke R, Singer J, Guyatt GH. Measurement of health status: ascertaining the minimal clinically important difference. Control Clin Trials 1989;10:407–15.

78. Yusuf S, Held P, Tesk K. Selection of patients for randomized controlled trials: implications for wide or narrow eligibility criteria. Stat Med 1990;9:73–86.

79. Hayward RA, Manning WG, Kaplan SH, et al. Starting insulin therapy in patients with type 2 diabetes: effectiveness, complications, and resource utilization. JAMA 1997;278:1663–9.

80. Stolar MW. Clinical management of the NIDDM patient. Impact of the American Diabetes Association practice guidelines, 1985–1993. Endocrine Fellows Foundation Study Group. Diabetes Care 1995;18:701–7.

81. Haines A, Donald A. Getting research findings into practice: making better use of research findings. BMJ 1998;317:72–5.

82. Cabana MD, Rand CS, Powe NR, et al. Why don't physicians follow clinical practice guidelines? A framework for improvement. JAMA 1999;282:1458–65.

83. Hiss, RG. Barriers to care in non-insulin-dependent diabetes mellitus. The Michigan experience. Ann Intern Med 1996;124(1 Pt 2):146–8.

84. Glasgow RE, Hampson SE, Strycker LA, Ruggiero L. Personal-model beliefs and social-environmental barriers related to diabetes self-management. Diabetes Care 1997;20:556–61.

85. Worrall G, Freake D, Kelland J, et al. Care of patients with type II diabetes: a study of family physicians' compliance with clinical practice guidelines. J Fam Pract 1997;44:374–81.

86. Kenny SJ, Smith PJ, Goldschmid MG, et al. Survey of physician practice behaviors related to diabetes mellitus in the US. Diabetes Care 1993;16:1507–10.

87. Rydall AC, Rodin GM, Olmsted MP, et al. Disordered eating behavior and microvascular complications in young women with insulin-dependent diabetes mellitus. N Engl J Med 1997;336:1846–54.

88. Rodin GM, Daneman D. Eating disorders and IDDM. A problematic association. Diabetes Care 1992;15:1402–12.

89. Polonsky WH, Anderson BJ, Lohrer PA, et al. Insulin omission in women with IDDM. Diabetes Care 1994;17:1178–85.

90. Davis DA, Taylor-Vaisey A. Translating guidelines into practice: a systematic review of theoretical concepts, practical experience and research evidence in the adoption of clinical practice guidelines. Can Med Assoc J 1997;157:408–16.

91. Bero LA, Grilli R, Grimshaw JM. Closing the gap between research and practice: an overview of systematic reviews of interventions to promote the implementation of research findings. BMJ 1998;317:465–8.

92. Lomas J. Retailing research: increasing the role of evidence in clinical services for childbirth. Milbank Q 1993:71:439–75.

93. Gerstein HC, Reddy SS, Dawson KG, et al. A controlled evaluation of a national continuing medical education programme designed to improve family physicians' implementation of diabetes-specific clinical practice guidelines. Diabet Med 1999;16:964–9.

94. Grad R, Tamblyn R, McLeod PJ, et al. Does knowledge of drug prescribing predict drug management of standardized patients in office practice? Med Educ 1997;31:132–7.

95. Holbrook AM, Sullivan S, Keshavjee K, Hunt DL, for COMPETE Project. Predictors of success in electronic decision support for prescribing. Can J Clin Pharmacol 2000;7:61.

96. Hunt DL, Haynes RB, Hanna SE, Smith K. Effects of computer-based clinical decision support systems on physician performance and patient outcomes. JAMA 1998;280:1339–46.

97. Dans AL, Dans LF, Guyatt GH, et al. User's guide to the medical literature. XIV. How to decide on the applicability of clinical trial results to your patient. JAMA 1998;279:545–9.

98. McAlister FA, Straus SE, Guyatt GH, et al. User's guide to the medical literature XX. Integrating research evidence with the care of the individual patient. JAMA 2000; in press.

99. Testa MA, Simonson DC. Health economic benefits and quality of life during improved glycemic control in patients with type 2 diabetes mellitus. JAMA 1998;280:1490–6.

100. Diabetes Control and Complications Trial Research Group. Influence of intensive diabetes treatment on quality-of-life outcomes in the Diabetes Control and Complications Trial. Diabetes Care 1996;19:195–203.

101. Casey DE. Commentary on: "Intensive diabetes therapy did not adversely effect quality of life." ACP J Club 1996;125:19. Comment in: Diabetes Control and Complications Trial Research Group. Influence of intense treatment in quality-of-life outcomes in the Diabetes Control and Complications Trial. Diabet Med 1996;19:195–203.

CHAPTER 5

Evidence-Based Clinical Practice Guidelines

Stewart B. Harris, MD, MPH, FCFP, FACPM, and
Susan M. Webster-Bogaert, BSc (kin), MA

ABSTRACT

Clinical practice guidelines represent systematically developed statements that are designed to facilitate practitioner and patient decisions for specific clinical circumstances. Guidelines may be developed using different processes, including expert opinion and the consensus of stakeholders. Evidence-based guidelines represent a newer, more transparent approach. Regardless of how guidelines are developed, they require both a dissemination and an implementation plan. Although there are many barriers that prevent or delay the implementation of well-developed guidelines, strategies to reduce these barriers are now being identified.

INTRODUCTION

Clinical practice has been inundated with a plethora of clinical practice guidelines (CPGs) over the last decade. In general, this has been in response to a perceived need to reduce variation in physician practice, to incorporate related research outcomes, and to assist in the management and control of health care costs.[1,2] It is believed that their incorporation into practice will help clinicians make better decisions that will ultimately improve the quality of health care for patients. Clinical practice guidelines for diabetes care have also proliferated during this period, both to establish standards for care and to reflect mounting evidence for the need for aggressive management of diabetes and related complications. But are CPGs having their intended effect? Research to date has demonstrated that guidelines are falling short of their objectives.[3] More attention must therefore be paid to guideline development, dissemination, and implementation. This chapter reviews the evolution of diabetes clinical practice guidelines, their impact on clinical practice, and the challenges of incorporating them into diabetes care, by answering the following questions:

1. What is the purpose of CPGs?
2. What factors affect the implementation of CPG recommendations?
3. What CPGs have been developed for diabetes mellitus?
4. What factors affect adherence to diabetes CPGs?
5. What are the challenges facing CPGs in the future?

WHAT IS THE PURPOSE OF CLINICAL PRACTICE GUIDELINES?

Definition of Clinical Practice Guidelines

Clinical practice guidelines are commonly defined as "systematically developed statements to assist practitioner and patient decisions about appropriate health care for specific clinical circumstances."[4]

Advantages and Limitations of Clinical Practice Guidelines

It is generally believed that by improving the consistency and quality of care through the use of CPGs, mortality and morbidity may be reduced. Benefits generally associated with CPGs include dissemination of evidence-based information related to practice, bridging medical

Table 5–1 Advantages and Limitations of Clinical Practice Guidelines

Advantages	Limitations
Standardization of clinical care	Generalizability to individual practitioners
Improved quality of care	Generalizability to individual patients
Dissemination of new evidence	"Expert opinion" vs evidence-based
Enhanced efficiency and reduced cost	Authorship bias
Influence health policy and planning	Multiple versions/conflicting recommendations

care and relevant research findings,[2] reduced variation in clinical practice, improved quality of care, and reduced health care costs.[1,5] Clinical practice guidelines may also act to initiate, focus, and support quality improvement initiatives and research.[2] There are, however, limitations to CPGs. Not all recommendations may apply to individual patients if the evidence is not generalizable to all patients.[2] Numerous organizations may produce their own versions of CPGs, which may lead to confusion for health care providers. Clinical practice guidelines may be a mechanism for heath care rationing.[6] Immediate cost of health care may increase as a result of the implementation of CPGs, which may serve as a disincentive for health care funding agencies. Finally, recommendations arising out of CPGs may not be implemented due to restrictions within the existing health care system (ie, organization of care). In fact, few guidelines to date have been proven to change patient outcomes.[3] Table 5–1 lists the proposed advantages and limitations of CPGs.

Consensus-Based Clinical Practice Guidelines

Clinical practice guidelines arose out of the effort to standardize and increase the quality of patient care. Originally, they represented consensus statements emerging from general agreement by a group of experts and published in a specialized professional journal. While relevant literature could be reviewed, expert opinion often varied considerably. This format also ran the risk of being biased by financial or political agendas. Most of the thousands of CPGs published around the world have been produced in this manner.

Table 5–2 Levels of Scientific Evidence

Level 1A	Systematic overviews or meta-analyses of multiple randomized controlled trials
	Large randomized controlled trial with adequate power to answer the question
	A randomized placebo-controlled trial with a statistically significant positive result for a clinical endpoint (clinically important) that answers the specific question
Level 1B	Evidence from at least one randomized controlled trial
Level 2A	Evidence from at least one controlled study without randomization
Level 2B	Evidence from at least one other type of quasi-experimental study
Level 3	Evidence from nonexperimental descriptive studies, such as comparative studies, correlation studies, and case-control studies
Level 4	Evidence from expert committee reports or opinions or clinical experience of respected authorities or both

Adapted from Shekelle PG, Woolf SH, Eccles M, Grimshaw J. Clinical guidelines: developing guidelines. BMJ 1999; 318:593–6.

Table 5–3 Strength of Recommendation

A Directly based on Level 1 evidence

B Directly based on Level 2 evidence or extrapolated recommendation from Level 1 evidence

C Directly based on Level 3 evidence or extrapolated recommendation from Level 1 or 2 evidence

D Directly based on Level 4 evidence or extrapolated recommendation from Level 1, 2, or 3 evidence

Adapted from Shekelle PG, Woolf SH, Eccles M, Grimshaw J. Clinical guidelines: developing guidelines. BMJ 1999; 318:593–6.

Evidence-Based Clinical Practice Guidelines

The need to standardize methodology for the development of CPGs supported the movement toward evidence-based CPGs.[2] In this context, even guidelines for developing guidelines have been developed and published, and organizations (ie, the Cochrane Collaboration),[7] Web sites,[8] manuals,[9] and articles[10–12] are now devoted to the development of evidence-based reviews and CPGs.

When CPGs are referred to as being evidence-based, the implication is that they are based on published research evidence that examined clinically important outcomes (where this evidence is available), and that the research itself is critically appraised according to established criteria. Typically, the body of scientific literature is gathered, critically appraised, and incorporated into a series of gradings and recommendations based on the strength of the published evidence. Table 5–2 describes the most widely accepted approach used to categorize the research evidence in support of therapeutic interventions (for evidence-based guidelines), which has been adopted by the Cochrane Collaboration; a somewhat simplified version of this scheme, and of levels of evidence for research dealing with prognosis and diagnosis, is used throughout this textbook (see Chapter 1). These levels are then used to generate a grade for the strength of the recommendations (Table 5–3).[10] Often, there is only a limited amount of evidence to substantiate specific recommendations resulting in consensus-based recommendations. Consequently, most guidelines are still a combination of evidence-based and consensus recommendations.

In addition to summarizing the research evidence in a clinically useful way, evidence-based guidelines also effectively demonstrate gaps in current knowledge. Ideally, the cycle of evidence-based review and research will continue as guidelines are updated periodically to reflect new evidence.

WHAT FACTORS AFFECT THE IMPLEMENTATION OF CLINICAL PRACTICE GUIDELINE RECOMMENDATIONS?

Guidelines can only be considered effective if they lead to improved patient care. However, a recent survey of CPGs concluded that there is little evidence that CPGs improve patient outcomes in primary care.[3] This likely reflects the fact that it is often difficult to bring clinical practice into line with scientific evidence on the basis of dissemination of guidelines alone. Knowledge of the guidelines is the initial step. However, knowledge is based on awareness, followed by acceptance, and then familiarity.[13] The attributes of the CPG, the physician, and the method of CPG dissemination affect the level of knowledge. Physician factors, patient factors, and contextual factors influence implementation. These factors, their interaction, and the extent to which they are facilitated[14] all determine whether or not a CPG recommendation is implemented for an individual patient. The main factors influencing the implementation of CPGs are identified in Table 5–4.

Table 5–4 Factors Influencing the Implementation of Clinical Practice Guidelines

Attributes of the Clinical Practice Guideline
  Recommendation action[15]
  Characteristics of the guideline[15]
  Effect on daily work[16]
  Attributes/goals of CPG developers

Attributes of the Physician
  Area of clinical practice[15]
  Attitude[17–19]
  Individual factors[16,20] (ie, age, teaching status)
  Previous habits[20] (ie, practice style)
  Optimal learning style[21]

Attributes of the Context[14]
  Health care system
  Practice organization[20]
  Clinical setting

Attributes of the Patient
  Concordance of the patient
  Concerns of the patient[22]

Attributes of the Method of Dissemination
  Peer-led, small group[23]
  Educational outreach[24]
  Method of teaching[21]
  Audit feedback[25–27]

Attributes of the Method of Implementation
  Prompting, reminder systems[27–29]
  Patient database/registry[30]
  Practice organization changes (CQI)[31]
  Shared care[32]

CPG – clinical practice guideline, CQI – continuous quality improvement.

Facilitating the dissemination and implementation process begins with identifying and reducing barriers. It has even been suggested that intervention trials studying adherence to CPGs should document barriers as a confounding factor to the intervention.[13] Barriers have been described as either internal or external to the physician.[33] Table 5–5 lists examples of barriers found in the literature.

WHAT CLINICAL PRACTICE GUIDELINES HAVE BEEN DEVELOPED FOR DIABETES MELLITUS?

In 1979, the National Diabetes Data Group (NDDG) in the United States published one of the first classification and diagnosis schemes for diabetes, in response to the medical community's need for a working classification of diabetes, which would include a uniform terminology.[40] The World Health Organization (WHO) Expert Committee on Diabetes[41] and later the WHO Study Group on Diabetes Mellitus[42] endorsed the majority of the recommendations

Table 5–5 Barriers to Implementation of Clinical Practice Guidelines

Barriers internal to the physician	Perceived limitations on clinical freedom or concerns about litigation[34]
	Physician distrust[35,36] or disagreement with CPG recommendations[13]
	Lack of clinical skills[22] due to educational barriers[35,36] (ie, poor access to best evidence, ineffectual CME programs[37])
	Practice organizational barriers (ie, time constraints,[38] patient load[38])
	Reimbursement[22,38]
Barriers external to the physician	Health system does not support chronic disease management[22,35–39]
	Administrative[35–37] or practice organizational barriers[22] (ie, time constraints,[35,36,38] patient load,[38] lack of effectual office-based computer systems[38])
	Lack of or poor access to quality educational opportunities[35–37]
	Lack of relevance of CPGs to practice settings[35,36]
	Disparate patient or clinical situations[35,36]
	Low patient adherence to treatment[37]

CPG = clinical practice guideline; CME = continuing medical education.

of the NDDG with the publication of their own document. These consensus CPGs were developed for diagnosis, assessment, complication prevention, and treatment of diabetes mellitus and were based on critical review and discussion of the published scientific evidence on diabetes. These diagnosis and classification recommendations were incorporated into the first wave of guideline publications published in the late 1980s and early 1990s (ie, American Diabetes Association [ADA] in 1989[43] and Canadian Diabetes Association [CDA] in 1992[44]). The process for development was based on a consensus of expert opinion. However, major long-term diabetes intervention trials such as the Diabetes Control and Complications Trial (DCCT) and the United Kingdom Prospective Diabetes Study (UKPDS) further elucidated the underlying etiology of diabetes and its related complications, necessitating the need for updating the classification and treatment of diabetes. This coincided with the evolution and maturation of the guideline development process and resulted in publication of new CPGs that better reflected the scientific literature and major breakthroughs in the understanding of the pathophysiology of diabetes and its related complications.

The ADA was among the first to revise its CPGs, publishing a comprehensive review of an expert committee's recommendations overhauling the existing CPG in 1997. This was followed by the publication of CPGs by numerous countries and expert committees around the world. The National Guideline Clearinghouse Web site[45] has 801 clinical practice guidelines, 379 of which are for diseases, with 25 guidelines for diabetes alone. All of these guidelines target health care professionals involved in the management of patients with diabetes, in particular, primary care practitioners. Indeed, the International Diabetes Federation is currently compiling an international listing of published guidelines into one directory.[46] To date, they have received 77 communications, each submitting 1 to 7 guidelines and a listing of 37 Web site addresses (Cara Mclaughlin, personal communication, 1999). To date, comprehensive diabetes CPGs developed according to a published, graded, systematic, evidenced-based review process have only been developed and published in Canada.[47] Table 5–6 lists major diabetes CPG Web sites.

WHAT FACTORS AFFECT ADHERENCE TO DIABETES CLINICAL PRACTICE GUIDELINES?

Clinical practice guidelines have traditionally been developed and published without effective dissemination or implementation strategies. Poor adherence is exacerbated in diabetes

Table 5–6 Major Diabetes Clinical Practice Guideline Web Sites

Name of Guideline or Organization	Source (Web Site)
ADA 2000 Clinical Practice Recommendations	http://journal.diabetes.org/CareSup1Jan00.htm
Centers for Disease Control Guide for Primary Care Practitioners for the Prevention and Treatment of Complications of Diabetes Mellitus	http://www.cdc.gov/diabetes/pubs/complications/index.htm
Diabetes Guidelines 1996	http://www.mds.qmw.ac.uk/gp/east.htm
AACE Clinical Practice Guidelinesfor the Management of Diabetes Mellitus	http://www.aace.com/clinguideindex.htm
Report of the Expert Committee on the Diagnosis and Classification of Diabetes Mellitus	http://www.ahcpr.gov
Management of Type II Diabetes Mellitus	http://www.ahcpr.gov
Veterans Health Administration Clinical Guidelines for Management of Patients with Diabetes Mellitus	http://www.va.gov/health/diabetes.index.cfm
NHS Centre for Reviews and Dissemination	http://www.york.ac.uk/inst/crd/welcome.htm
WHO diabetes	http://www.who.int/ncd/dia/index.htm
CMA InfoBase Clinical Practice Guidelines	http://www.cma.ca/cpgs/index.asp
Canadian Diabetes Association	http://www.diabetes.ca./
International Diabetes Federation	http://www.idf.org/
Australian Diabetes Society	http://www.racp.edu.au/ads/index.htm
New Zealand Guidelines Group	http://www.nzgg.org.nz/index.cfm

ADA = American Diabetes Association; AACE = American Association of Clinical Endocrinologists; NHS = National Health Service; WHO = World Health Organization; CMA = Canadian Medical Association.

as it is a complex, chronic, multisystem disease requiring consistent application of management approaches to reduce or prevent complications. Health care systems commonly are not structured to reward preventive surveillance for chronic diseases such as diabetes, particularly in the primary care domain.[39] It is not surprising, therefore, that the literature indicates only a limited adherence to diabetes CPGs.

There are numerous studies from the United States, United Kingdom, and Canada performed in specialist and primary care environments that document the wide range of levels of adherence to diabetes CPGs (Table 5–7). On average, only one half of the recommended procedures are performed annually. Certain aspects of the examination that have been systematized into practice organization, such as blood pressure measurement, have the best adherence rates. Others, such as foot examinations and testing for neuropathy, have not been

Table 5-7 Studies Measuring Adherence to Diabetes Clinical Practice Guidelines

Author	Study Type	Findings
Chesover et al,[30] 1991	Audit of charts 77 general practitioners; 378 patients with Type 2 diabetes	57% of the general practitioners providing good to moderate diabetes care Poor levels of management were found in testing for peripheral pulses, HbA$_{1c}$, peripheral sensation, and urea and electrolyte assessment
Kenny et al,[38] 1993	Survey (national) 1,434 primary care physicians	Self-reported examination of teeth, gums, and feet as well as laboratory procedures for urine testing were deficient
Tunbridge et al,[48] 1993	Audit of charts 4 urban primary care group practices that used structured diabetes care scheme (186 diabetes patients)	Low levels of recording of cholesterol and triglyceride levels Relatively high recording of other process measures HbA$_{1c}$ levels, blood pressure, and smoking status
Miller and Hirsch,[49] 1994	Audit of charts 157 diabetic patients' charts (27-month retrospective) University of Washington primary care clinics	48% of the patients had received an annual measurement of urinary protein 29% had HbA$_{1c}$ measurements taken as recommended in the guidelines
Stolar,[50] 1995	Audit of charts 42 university-based and hospital-based endocrinology clinical training programs (n = 790 patient charts) Comparisons were made 3 years prior to, the year of, and 3 years following publication of the CPGs	Improved foot care, eye examination, and lipid screening Deficiencies in all other aspects of diabetes management Particularly poor in the areas of quality assurance and chart documentation
Dunn and Bough,[51] 1996	Audit of charts Survey 37 primary care practices (2,804 diabetic patients)	56% of the patients had a foot examination Average HbA$_{1c}$ = 8.07% 26% treated for hypertension; 45% of treated remained with hypertension
Worrall et al,[52] 1997	Audit of charts Impact of the 1992 CDA CPGs Family physicians working in 10 family practice clinics in Newfoundland 118 Type 2 DM patients	100% had had blood pressure and weight measurements 53% had a HbA$_{1c}$ measurement taken; 37.4% foot examination Eye checks were recorded for only 28% 5.9 of 11 recommended procedures performed
Beckles et al,[53] 1998	Survey of patients Cross-sectional population-based study with a sample of participants in the 1994 Behavioural Risk Factor Surveillance System Asked about visits to the physician, self-monitoring, eye and foot examination; awareness of HbA$_{1c}$	70% insulin users 55% noninsulin users had an eye examination 3% of insulin users and 1% of noninsulin users had met all 5 ADA guideline criteria in the past year
Bernard et al,[54] 1999	Survey of internal medicine residents Audit of charts	The performance gap between the audit and the survey results ranged from 0 to 35%
Valle et al,[55] 1999	Audit of charts National sample	67% had HbA$_{1c}$; average HbA$_{1c}$ = 8.6% 50% had poor glycemic control

CDA = Canadian Diabetes Association; CPG = clinical practice guideline; ADA = American Diabetes Association; DM = diabetes mellitus.

Table 5–8 Dissemination and Implementation Initiatives

Small-group, interactive CME events

Peer-expert academic detailing

Audit feedback

Identification of patients

Reminder/tickler systems

Strategies of care/quality assurance initiatives

Diabetes day or mini-clinic

Access to Diabetes Education Centers

Shared-care approach with specialists

Combination; multifaceted approach

CME = continuing medical education.

incorporated into the regular clinical routine and consistently fared worse. Overall, due to the lack of systematic support for primary care providers, who are responsible for managing the majority of patients with diabetes, the incorporation of CPG recommendations into routine practice represents a formidable task.

Factors Improving Implementation of Diabetes Clinical Practice Guidelines

Research has clearly demonstrated that strict control of glycemia and blood pressure results in improved clinical outcomes in patients with diabetes.[56–62] Currently, the preponderance of (CME) programs focus on increasing physician knowledge of CPGs using traditional didactic presentation approaches. Evidence clearly suggests this has had limited impact on changing practice behavior.[63,64] However, implementation strategies that reinforce and enable target practice behavior changes have greater impact on improving patient outcomes[65] (Table 5–8). Thus, attempts to support enhanced management of diabetes should involve diverse, multifaceted approaches so as to influence the primary care physician's management of diabetes. Table 5–9 highlights diabetes intervention CME studies that have successfully demonstrated a significant effect.

WHAT ARE THE CHALLENGES FACING CLINICAL PRACTICE GUIDELINES IN THE FUTURE?

To develop evidence-based CPGs from inception to dissemination requires significant resources. This includes the necessary expertise to gather and review the relevant literature, grade the literature according to the strength of the evidence, and develop recommendations. Dissemination and implementation strategies should be developed concurrently. Unfortunately, the majority of CPGs lack this feature.

Growing numbers of health care service providers believe there are too many guidelines focusing on specific clinical conditions. Further, primary care physicians who manage most patients with diabetes in the general population have numerous CPGs to be aware of. These deal with a multitude of disease states, so that physicians are progressively becoming bewildered and discouraged by growth of the CPG industry.[66]

Table 5–9 Successful Implementation Strategies for Diabetes Clinical Practice Guidelines

Study/Design	Type of Intervention	Measures/N	Results	Level of Evidence
Chesover et al[30] Stratified sample	None	Patient care 77 physicians N = 378 patients	Organizational changes vs none: • 48% good care vs 24% good care $p < .05$ Diabetes Registry • 68% good care vs 52% good care $p = .058$	3
Hempel[7] Retrospective control intervention period	Use of a diabetes flow sheet for patient care and patient education clinic	Patient care N = 45 control N = 158 interventions	22 to 46% referral to ophthalmologist 58 to 77% urinalysis 36 to 61% lower extremity examination	2B
O'Connor et al[31] Pre/post controlled trial	Continuous quality improvement (CQI): • audit review; monthly meetings • trained diabetes resource nurses (standing orders)	Patient care 2 group sites N = 267	Control HbA$_{1c}$ 8.8% (SE = 0.17) Intervention HbA$_{1c}$ 7.9% (SE = 0.17) t = 4.13, $p < .001$ Analysis of covariance significant reduction in HbA$_{1c}$	2A
Gerstein et al[23] Controlled trial	Small-group interactive sessions	Physician survey N = 290	After 1 month significant difference in change in attitude ($p < .0001$); knowledge ($p = .04$); practice ($p < .002$). No difference after 1 year.	2A
Grebe et al[68] Pre/post controlled trial	Audit feedback and follow-up form (flow sheet)	Patient care 1 group site N = 156	Relative likelihood recorded post vs pre $p < .00001$: • HbA$_{1c}$ measured: 1.15 (1.06; 1.24) • smoking Hx: 3.13 (2.42; 4.06) • foot inspection: 3.00 (2.30; 3.91); serum cholesterol: 1.75 (1.40; 2.19)	2B
Feder et al[69] Randomized controlled trial	Educational outreach of locally developed CPGs disseminated by expert peer using small-group methods and stamp prompts	Patient care 24 group sites N = 390	Analysis of covariance showed a significant improvement in all patient care variables	1B
Deeb et al[70] Pre/post controlled trial	Liaison nurse coordinator CME sessions X days Quarterly consultation Education modules (patients)	Patient care 6 sites N = 636	Referral to ophthalmologist post intervention: • intervention 43%; control 33% ($p < .001$) Lower extremity examination post intervention • intervention 94%; control 41% ($p < .001$)	2A
Koperski[71] Pre/post	"Diabetes day" or mini-clinic	Patient care 1 group site N = 64	Significant improvement in HbA$_{1c}$ 10.52% pre to 9.71% post ($p < .0$; CI 0.19; 1.39)	2B
Hoskins et al[32] Randomized controlled trial	GP care vs "shared care" between GP and clinic vs conventional hospital clinic	Patient care N = 206	Metabolic and BP control improved significantly all groups ($p < .05$) Shared care equal to hospital clinic care	1B
Lobach et al[72] Pre/post randomized controlled trial	Family physicians using computerized registries to track and audit patient care	Patient care 30 physicians N = 359	Median percent compliance: • urine protein: intervention 73.3% vs control 3.9% $p = .01$ • cholesterol: intervention 43.7% vs control 13.4% $p = .02$	2B
Streja and Rabkin[20] Stratified sample	None	Patient care 22 physicians N = 519	Association of implementation of 1 recommendation with 2 others Fast practice style associated with lower implementation of CPG Physicians sited "oversight" for noncompliance	3

CME = continuing medical education; CI = confidence interval; CPG = clinical practice guideline; Hx = history.

The problem is not just one of numbers. The evidence behind the guidelines is constantly changing, resulting in the need for consistent review and update of CPGs. Clinical practice guideline developers must incorporate strategies to facilitate dissemination and implementation of revised CPGs. Thus, incorporating new research findings, grading CPG recommendations according to evidence, and improving dissemination strategies are all important challenges facing guideline developers in the future.

CONCLUSION

Clinical practice guidelines lacking concurrent dissemination and implementation strategies are doomed to fail. As the majority of organizations developing CPGs do not include a dissemination strategy beyond publication, increased efforts by these groups are needed to develop effective dissemination strategies that maximize CPG attributes so they are more likely to be implemented. Further, the acceptance of evidence-based CPGs with levels of evidence for each recommendation has raised the bar for guideline development groups. This undertaking, however, requires resources beyond the capabilities of many organizations and countries. An international template and dissemination program for diabetes CPGs would therefore support the effort to update CPGs reflecting new evidence, identify any important gaps in existing knowledge, and help identify needed research areas.

As the trend toward improved cost and efficiency in health care delivery continues, the need for CPGs will continue. Incorporation of the evidence-based approach reflects a maturation in CPG development that improves their quality and increases their application by health care providers. Established guideline dissemination techniques have demonstrated limited effectiveness in changing practice behavior.[38,48,50,62,73–76] Improved dissemination and implementation strategies, including facilitators and feedback to practice, require further effort and should be incorporated concurrently in the ongoing development of diabetes CPGs.

REFERENCES

1. Wall EM. Practice guidelines: promise or panacea [editorial]? J Fam Pract 1993;37:17–9.

2. Woolf SH, Grol R, Hutchinson A, et al. Clinical guidelines: potential benefits, limitations, and harms of clinical guidelines. BMJ 1999;318:527–30.

3. Worrall G, Chaulk P, Freake D. The effects of clinical practice guidelines on patient outcomes in primary care: a systematic review Can Med Assoc J 1997;156:1705–12.

4. Committee to Advise the Public Health Service on Clinical Practice Guidelines, Institute of Medicine. Clinical practice guidelines: directions of a new program. Washington (DC): National Academy Press; 1990.

5. Kerr CP. Improving outcomes in diabetes: a review of the outpatient care of NIDDM patients. J Fam Pract 1995;40:63–75.

6. Norheim OF. Healthcare rationing—are additional criteria needed for assessing evidence based clinical practice guidelines? BMJ 1999;319:1426–9.

7. Cochrane Collaboration; 2000. Available from: URL: http://www.update-software.com/ccweb/default.html.

8. New Zealand Guidelines Group; 2000. Available from: URL: http://www.nzgg.org.nz/index.cfm.

9. CMA workshop guideline implementation: making it happen. Implementing clinical practice guidelines: a handbook for practitioners. 1997. Ottawa: Canadian Medical Association; 1996.

10. Shekelle PG, Woolf SH, Eccles M, Grimshaw J. Clinical guidelines: developing guidelines. BMJ 1999;318:593–6.

11. Haines A, Feder G. Guidance on guidelines [editorial]. BMJ 1992;305:785–6.

12. Jackson R, Feder G. Guidelines for clinical guidelines [editorial]. BMJ 1998;317:427–8.

13. Cabana MD, Rand CS, Powe NR, et al. Why don't physicians follow clinical practice guidelines? A framework for improvement. JAMA 1999;282:1458–65.

14. Kitson A, Harvey G, McCormack B. Enabling the implementation of evidence based practice: a conceptual framework. Qual Health Care 1998;7:149–58.

15. Grilli R, Lomas J. Evaluating the message: the relationship between compliance rate and the subject of a practice guideline. Med Care 1994;32:202–13.

16. Grol R, Dalhuijsen J, Thomas S, et al. Attributes of clinical guidelines that influence use of guidelines in general practice: observational study. BMJ 1998;317:858–61.

17. Sibley JC, Sackett DL, Neufeld V, et al. A randomized trial of continuing medical education. N Engl J Med 1982;306:511–5.

18. Anderson RM. The challenge of translating scientific knowledge into improved diabetes care in the 1990s [editorial]. Diabetes Care 1991;14:418–21.

19. Weinberger M, Cohen SJ, Mazzuca SA. The role of physicians' knowledge and attitudes in effective diabetes management. Soc Sci Med 1984;19:965–9.

20. Streja DA, Rabkin SW. Factors associated with implementation of preventive care measures in patients with diabetes mellitus. Arch Intern Med 1999;159:294–302.

21. Onion CW, Bartzokas CA. Changing attitudes to infection management in primary care: a controlled trial of active versus passive guideline implementation strategies. Fam Pract 1998;15:99–104.

22. Peterson KA, Vinicor F. Strategies to improve diabetes care delivery. J Fam Pract 1998;47:S55–62.

23. Gerstein HC, Reddy SS, Dawson KG, et al. A controlled evaluation of a national continuing medical education programme designed to improve family physicians' implementation of diabetes-specific clinical practice guidelines. Diabet Med 1999;16:964–9.

24. Thomson O'Brien MA, Oxman AD, Davis DA, et al. Educational outreach visits: effects on professional practice and health care outcomes. The Cochrane Library (2). Oxford: Update Software; 1999.

25. Hux JE, Melady MP, DeBoer D. Confidential prescriber feedback and education to improve antibiotic use in primary care: a controlled trial. Can Med Assoc J 1999;161:388–92.

26. Thomson O'Brien MA, Oxman AD, Davis DA, et al. Audit and feedback: effects on professional practice and health care outcomes (Cochrane Review). The Cochrane Library (2). Oxford: Update Software; 1999.

27. Buntinx F, Winkens R, Grol R, Knottnerus JA. Influencing diagnostic and preventive performance in ambulatory care by feedback and reminders. A review. Fam Pract 1993;10:219–28.

28. Balas EA, Weingarten S, Garb CT, et al. Improving preventive care by prompting physicians. Arch Intern Med 2000;160:301–8.

29. Shea S, DuMouchel W, Bahamonde L. A meta-analysis of 16 randomized controlled trials to evaluate computer-based clinical reminder systems for preventive care in the ambulatory setting. J Am Med Inform Assoc 1996;3:399–409.

30. Chesover D, Tudor-Miles P, Hilton S. Survey and audit of diabetes care in general practice in south London. Br J Gen Pract 1991;41:282–5.

31. O'Connor PJ, Rush WA, Peterson J, et al. Continuous quality improvement can improve glycemic control for HMO patients with diabetes. Arch Fam Med 1996;5:502–6.

32. Hoskins PL, Fowler PM, Constantino M, et al. Sharing the care of diabetic patients between hospital and general practitioners: does it work? Diabet Med 1993;10:81–6.

33. Baker R, Hearnshaw H, Cheater F, et al. Tailored interventions to overcome identified barriers to change: effects on professional practice and health care outcomes (protocol for a Cochrane Review). The Cochrane Library (2). Oxford:Update Software; 1999.

34. Conroy M, Shannon W. Clinical guidelines: their implementation in general practice. Br J Gen Pract 1995;45:371–5.

35. Lomas J, Anderson GM, Domnick-Pierre K, et al. Do practice guidelines guide practice? The effect of a consensus statement on the practice of physicians. N Engl J Med 1989;321:1306–11.

36. Haynes RB. Some problems in applying evidence in clinical practice. Ann N Y Acad Sci 1993;703:210–24.

37. Haynes B, Haines A. Barriers and bridges to evidence based clinical practice. BMJ 1998;317:273–6.

38. Kenny SJ, Smith PJ, Goldschmid MG, et al. Survey of physician practice behaviors related to diabetes mellitus in the U.S. Physician adherence to consensus recommendations. Diabetes Care 1993;16:1507–10.

39. Hiss RG. Barriers to care in non-insulin-dependent diabetes mellitus. The Michigan experience. Ann Intern Med 1996;124:146–8.

40. National Diabetes Data Group. Classification and diagnosis of diabetes mellitus and other categories of glucose intolerance. Diabetes 1979;28:1039–57.

41. World Health Organization. Expert Committee on Diabetes Mellitus. Technical Report Series No. 646. World Health Organization; 1980.

42. World Health Organization. Diabetes mellitus: report of a WHO study group. Technical Report Series No. 727. World Health Organization; 1985.

43. Standards of medical care for patients with diabetes mellitus. Diabetes Care 1989;12:365–8.

44. Expert Committee of the Canadian Diabetes Advisory Board. Clinical practice guidelines for treatment of diabetes mellitus. Can Med Assoc J 1993;147:697–712.

45. Agency for Heath Care Policy and Research; American Medical Association; American Association of Health Plans. National guideline clearinghouse. Available from: URL: http://www.guideline.gov; 1999.

46. International Diabetes Federation. IDF directory of clinical practice guidelines. Available from: URL: http://www.idf.org/tools/publi1.html; 1999.

47. Meltzer S, Leiter L, Daneman D, et al. 1998 clinical practice guidelines for the management of diabetes in Canada. Canadian Diabetes Association. Can Med Assoc J 1998;159(Suppl 8):S1–29.

48. Tunbridge FK, Millar JP, Schofield PJ, et al. Diabetes care in general practice: an approach to audit of process and outcome. Br J Gen Pract 1993;43:291–5.

49. Miller KL, Hirsch IB. Physicians' practices in screening for the development of diabetic nephropathy and the use of glycosylated hemoglobin levels. Diabetes Care 1994;17:1495–7.

50. Stolar MW. Clinical management of the NIDDM patient. Impact of the American Diabetes Association practice guidelines, 1985–1993. Endocrine Fellows Foundation Study Group. Diabetes Care 1995;18:701–7.

51. Dunn NR, Bough P. Standards of care of diabetic patients in a typical English community. Br J Gen Pract 1996;46:401–5.

52. Worrall G, Freake D, Kelland J, et al. Care of patients with type II diabetes: a study of family physicians' compliance with clinical practice guidelines. J Fam Pract 1997;44:374–81.

53. Beckles GL, Engelgau MM, Narayan KM, et al. Population-based assessment of the level of care among adults with diabetes in the U.S. Diabetes Care 1998;21:1432–8.

54. Bernard AM, Anderson L, Cook CB, Phillips LS. What do internal medicine residents need to enhance their diabetes care? Diabetes Care 1999;22:661–6.

55. Valle T, Koivisto VA, Reunanen A, et al. Glycemic control in patients with diabetes in Finland. Diabetes Care 1999;22:575–9.

56. UK Prospective Diabetes Study (UKPDS) Group. Effect of intensive blood-glucose control with metformin on complications in overweight patients with type 2 diabetes (UKPDS 34) [published erratum appears in Lancet 1998;352:1557]. Lancet 1998;352:854–65.

57. UK Prospective Diabetes Study (UKPDS) Group. Intensive blood-glucose control with sulphonylureas or insulin compared with conventional treatment and risk of complications in patients with type 2 diabetes (UKPDS 33). Lancet 1998;352:837–53.

58. UK Prospective Diabetes Study Group. Efficacy of atenolol and captopril in reducing risk of macrovascular and microvascular complications in type 2 diabetes: UKPDS 39. BMJ 1998;317:713–20.

59. UK Prospective Diabetes Study Group. Tight blood pressure control and risk of macrovascular and microvascular complications in type 2 diabetes: UKPDS 38. BMJ 1998;317:703–13.

60. UK Prospective Diabetes Study Group. UKPDS 28: a randomized trial of efficacy of early addition of metformin in sulfonylurea-treated type 2 diabetes. Diabetes Care 1998;21:87–92.

61. Turner RC, Cull CA, Frighi V, Holman RR. Glycemic control with diet, sulfonylurea, metformin, or insulin in patients with type 2 diabetes mellitus: progressive requirement for multiple therapies (UKPDS 49). UK Prospective Diabetes Study (UKPDS) Group. JAMA 1999;281:2005–12.

62. Diabetes Control and Complications Trial Research Group. The effect of intensive treatment of diabetes on the development and progression of long-term complications in insulin-dependent diabetes mellitus. N Engl J Med 1993;329:977–86.

63. Davis D, O'Brien MA, Freemantle N, et al. Impact of formal continuing medical education: do conferences, workshops, rounds, and other traditional continuing education activities change physician behavior or health care outcomes? JAMA 1999;282:867–74.

64. Davis DA, Thomson MA, Oxman AD, Haynes RB. Changing physician performance. A systematic review of the effect of continuing medical education strategies. JAMA 1995;274:700–5.

65. Davis DA. The dissemination of information optimizing the effectiveness of continuing medical education. In: Dunn EV, Norton PG, Stewart M, et al., editors. Disseminating research/changing practice. Thousand Oaks (CA): Sage; 1996.

66. Hibble A, Kanka D, Pencheon D, Pooles F. Guidelines in general practice: the new Tower of Babel? BMJ 1998;317:862–3.

67. Hempel RJ. Physician documentation of diabetes care: use of a diabetes flow sheet and patient education clinic. South Med J 1990;83:1426–32.

68. Grebe SK, Smith RB. Clinical audit and standardised follow up improve quality of documentation in diabetes care. N Z Med J 1995;108:339–42.

69. Feder G, Griffiths C, Highton C, et al. Do clinical guidelines introduced with practice based education improve care of asthmatic and diabetic patients? A randomised controlled trial in general practices in east London. BMJ 1995;311:1473–8.

70. Deeb LC, Pettijohn FP, Shirah JK, Freeman G. Interventions among primary-care practitioners to improve care for preventable complications of diabetes. Diabetes Care 1988;11:275–80.

71. Koperski M. How effective is systematic care of diabetic patients? A study in one general practice. Br J Gen Pract 1992;42:508–11.

72. Lobach DF, Hammond WE. Computerized decision support based on a clinical practice guideline improves compliance with care standards. Am J Med 1997;102:89–98.

73. Selby JV, FitzSimmons SC, Newman JM, et al. The natural history and epidemiology of diabetic nephropathy. Implications for prevention and control. JAMA 1990;263:1954–60.

74. Bild DE, Selby JV, Sinnock P, et al. Lower-extremity amputation in people with diabetes. Epidemiology and prevention. Diabetes Care 1989;12:24–31.

75. Escalante DA, Davidson J, Garber AJ. Maximizing glycemic control. Clin Diabetes 1993;11:3–6.

76. Ohkubo Y, Kishikawa H, Araki E, et al. Intensive insulin therapy prevents the progression of diabetic microvascular complications in Japanese patients with non-insulin-dependent diabetes mellitus: a randomized prospective 6-year study. Diabetes Res Clin Pract 1995;28:103–17.

CHAPTER 6

What Is Diabetes?

Hertzel C. Gerstein, MD, MSc, FRCPC

ABSTRACT

Risk factors identify people at high risk for adverse health outcomes. Diabetes mellitus is, by definition, a risk factor for eye and kidney disease. It is also, on the basis of many epidemiologic studies, a risk factor for many other serious adverse health outcomes; the risk for all of these other outcomes may, however, not be confined just to the diabetic range of hyperglycemia. In people with diabetes mellitus, the plasma glucose level is a continuous risk factor for all of these diabetes-related chronic illnesses and has been shown to be a modifiable risk factor for most of them. Lesser degrees of hyperglycemia such as impaired glucose tolerance and impaired fasting glucose are risk factors for subsequent diabetes; the risk of these metabolic states for other health outcomes is currently being intensively studied.

INTRODUCTION

Most diseases are risk factors for adverse health outcomes that range from discomfort and disability to death. Some of these diseases cause clear signs and symptoms, whereas others (such as hypertension and diabetes) may be silent, despite conferring a high future risk. In addition, in people who have a disease, certain characteristics may increase the risk of poor health outcomes even further than the presence of the disease itself. The nature of a risk factor for poor health outcomes and the implications of these considerations for the definition of diabetes will be discussed below by answering the following questions:

1. What is a risk factor?
2. How were the plasma glucose cutoffs that define diabetes chosen?
3. What is the significance of plasma glucose levels below the diabetes cutoff?

WHAT IS A RISK FACTOR (TABLE 6–1)?

In epidemiologic studies, the term "risk factor" usually refers to some measured variable that is linked to, or associated with, a subsequent adverse clinical outcome. Variables are most reliably identified as risk factors on the basis of cohort studies, in which measurements are made in a group of individuals at some point in time, who are then assessed at periodic intervals to determine whether or not a clinical outcome of interest occurs. Any baseline measurement can therefore be identified as a risk factor. Examples include demographic measurements (such as age, gender, ethnicity, and family history); clinical measurements (such as weight, body mass index, waist circumference, blood pressure, and ear creases); biochemical measurements (such as cholesterol, triglycerides, anti-islet cell antibodies, and homocysteine); genetic measurements (such as the presence of a gene for cystic fibrosis); exposure to drugs or environmental factors (such as alcohol, thalidomide, smoking, ultraviolet light, ionizing radiation, latitude, climate and toxic fumes); and exposure to diseases (such as hypertension and lupus). Risk factors may be categoric (either present or absent) or continuous. For example, the presence or absence of hypertension represents the presence or absence of a categoric risk factor: hypertensive people have a higher risk of stroke than normotensive people. The actual systolic blood pressure measurement is a continuous risk factor: the higher the systolic blood pressure, the higher the risk of stroke.

Table 6–1 Examples of Risk Factors and Causal Factors

Term	Examples of Factor	Relevant Disease
Risk factor	Smoking*	Lung cancer
	Systolic blood pressure†	Stroke
	Waist circumference†	Myocardial infarction
	Carotid artery narrowing†	Myocardial infarction
Modifiable risk factor	Smoking	Lung cancer
	Systolic blood pressure	Stroke
	Waist circumference	Myocardial infarction
Causal factor	Smoking	Lung cancer

*Categoric risk factor (number of cigarettes smoked would be the comparable continuous risk factor).
†Continuous risk factor.

Modifiable Risk Factors

Many risk factors can be modified. For example, people who smoke or drink excessively can quit, and systolic blood pressure, triglycerides, and the urinary albumin excretion rate can be lowered with dietary changes or pharmacologic interventions. If the elimination of a categoric risk factor, or the reduction of a continuous risk factor, leads to the future reduction or prevention of the related clinical outcome, the risk factor may be considered to be a modifiable one. Although much attention is directed at modifiable risk factors, many risk factors (such as a previous environmental exposure) cannot be modified, and modification of others does not affect the outcome. Examples of risk factors that are not modifiable risk factors include skin color (bleaching the skin from dark to light has no effect on the risk of sickle cell disease) and carotid artery narrowing (ie, although the degree of carotid narrowing is clearly a continuous risk factor for myocardial infarction, endarterectomy will have no effect on the risk of myocardial infarction, even though it will decrease the risk of stroke). From the foregoing it is clear that whether or not a risk factor is modifiable depends on the clinical outcome of interest; a modifiable risk factor for stroke may not be a modifiable risk factor for myocardial infarction. It also is limited by how well the disease has been studied.

Modifiable Risk Factors versus Causal Factors

A risk factor that causes a disease is considered a causal factor; indeed, all causal factors are risk factors. However, the converse is often untrue, and the relationship between risk factors and causality is rarely certain, even when the risk factor is modifiable. For example, as noted in Chapters 22 and 24, albuminuria is a continuous modifiable risk factor for renal and cardiovascular outcomes in people with diabetes: reductions in the degree of albuminuria with (ACE) inhibitors, blood pressure reduction, and diet reduce the risk of diabetic nephropathy and myocardial infarction. Despite this relationship, urinary albumin does not appear to be the cause of renal or cardiovascular disease. The continuous relationship between abdominal obesity and cardiovascular disease is another example: although waist circumference is a modifiable cardiovascular risk factor, it clearly does not cause cardiovascular disease. The likelihood that it is linked to some metabolic abnormalities that may be the "true" culprit is merely a hypothesis (for which evidence is available) that is advanced to explain the observation; such hypotheses, however, are limited by current knowledge and paradigms. Other examples in which risk factors are considered to be causal risk factors may also prove to be false as knowledge and paradigms change.

Identification of a modifiable risk factor is therefore insufficient to demonstrate causality. Such a determination requires a large body of evidence that satisfies many tests.[1] For the purpose of practicing evidence-based medicine, whether or not a modifiable risk factor is actually causal is irrelevant; as long as there is strong evidence that reduction of the risk factor by some intervention is safe and effective, that intervention can be prescribed with confidence.

Independent Risk Factors

In epidemiologic terms, an independent risk factor is one that is associated with an increased risk for disease after controlling for the association of other variables with the disease. Multivariate analyses are used to determine whether or not a variable is an independent risk factor. These analyses are useful tools for explaining why a risk factor is associated with a disease and may provide some clues to the pathogenesis of the disease. They can also determine which of several variables are most strongly associated with the disease.

Key determinants of "independence" include the other variables included in the analysis and the degree to which they are associated with the risk factor in question and each other. For example, a cohort of 13,446 white and black individuals free of coronary heart disease was followed for 4 to 7 years after measurement of baseline metabolic variables[2]; after multivariate adjustment for demographic factors, the relative risk of diabetes as a risk factor for coronary heart disease (compared to people with clearly normal fasting glucose levels < 5.08 mmol/L) was statistically significant (3.5 in women and 2.36 in men). After further adjustment for factors closely associated with diabetes (body mass index, waist-to-hip ratio, fibrinogen, total and high-density lipoprotein (HDL) cholesterol, triglycerides, blood pressure, and use of antihypertensive medications), however, these relative risks fell to 1.57 and 1.44, respectively, and were no longer statistically significant. This does not rule out the possibility that diabetes is a modifiable risk factor for coronary heart disease. Indeed, one can imagine many examples of modifiable risk factors that are not independent risk factors after adjustment for closely related factors. For example, analysis of a data set might show that body mass index is not an independent risk factor for heart disease after adjustment for the waist-to-hip ratio; reducing the body mass index may, however, prove to be an effective intervention to decrease the risk of heart disease, possibly because weight reduction may also decrease the waist-to-hip ratio and other associated risk factors. Unfortunately, we often have limited insight into the degree to which different variables are measuring the same (or a closely related) underlying biologic process and the degree to which modifying one risk factor also modifies other associated risk factors.

Therefore, risk factors identify people at risk for disease. Even if it is not an independent risk factor after adjustment for closely associated risk factors in a multivariate analysis, it may still be a modifiable risk factor for disease — a hypothesis that can be tested by clinical trials or other intervention studies.

HOW WERE THE PLASMA GLUCOSE CUTOFFS THAT DEFINE DIABETES CHOSEN?

Numerous studies have shown that diabetes mellitus is clearly a strong risk factor for several chronic diseases and for premature mortality. As discussed throughout this book, it increases the risk of blindness, cataracts, renal failure, nerve damage, lower limb amputations, erectile dysfunction, and cardiovascular events. The health impact of diabetes accounts for the observation that the direct and indirect costs of diabetes care in the United States approached 100 billion dollars in 1997.[3]

Hyperglycemia can produce uncomfortable symptoms and recognizable clinical signs; nevertheless, these clinical criteria are not the basis of the diagnostic criteria used to define diabetes. In fact, the diagnostic plasma glucose cutoffs for diabetes were based on those glucose levels above which various cohorts of people followed prospectively had a high incidence of retinal lesions and proteinuria.[4] The glucose levels that differentiated people at risk from those not at risk were a 2-hour plasma glucose level ≥ 11.1 mmol/L following a 75-g oral glucose challenge. Subsequent studies have also established that a fasting plasma glucose level ≥ 7.0 mmol/L predicts a 2-hour post-load plasma glucose level of ≥ 11.1 mmol/L; indeed, it has almost 100% specificity for a diagnosis of diabetes when diabetes is diagnosed on the basis of a 2-hour glucose tolerance test.[5] It is important to note, however, that the fasting plasma glucose has low sensitivity; lower fasting plasma glucose levels do not rule out diabetes that is defined on the basis of an oral glucose tolerance test, and up to 50% of individuals without previous diabetes who have a fasting plasma glucose level below the diagnostic cutoff of 7.0 mmol/L may have 2-hour glucose levels ≥ 11.1 mmol/L.[5,6] Therefore, the fasting glucose cannot be used to definitively exclude diabetes.

In summary, diabetes mellitus is a metabolic disorder characterized by hyperglycemia, which is associated with a high subsequent risk of eye and kidney disease (Table 6–2). Although it is also associated with a high subsequent risk of neurologic, cardiovascular, and other adverse health outcomes, the glycemic thresholds and definition of diabetes are not based on risks for these other problems. There is therefore no a priori reason that the risk for these other outcomes should be limited to the diabetic range, and, indeed, the fact that elevated plasma glucose levels below the diabetic range have been clearly shown to be a risk factor for cardiovascular outcomes (but not for eye and kidney disease) has led this author to propose that a new term — dysglycemia — be used to describe people identified to be at high cardiovascular risk on the basis of nondiabetic plasma glucose elevation.[7–9] This issue is discussed in more detail in Chapter 24.

Notwithstanding this risk of nondiabetic elevated glucose levels, plasma glucose levels above the diabetic cutoff are also a continuous risk factor for microvascular disease (a term that clumps eye, kidney, and nerve disease together) and cardiovascular disease[10–13]: higher levels predict a higher risk. The plasma glucose is also clearly a modifiable risk factor for microvascular disease within the diabetic range: glucose lowering by various means reduces the risk of retinopathy, nephropathy, and neuropathy for patients with both Type 1 diabetes[14] and Type 2 diabetes.[15–17] As discussed in Chapter 24, the impact of glucose lowering on cardiovascular outcomes is less certain.

EVIDENCE-BASED MESSAGES

1. Diabetes mellitus is a metabolic disorder characterized by a fasting plasma glucose ≥ 7.0 mmol/l or a 2-hour plasma glucose level ≥ 11.1 mmol/L; these numbers clearly differentiate people at high and low risk for subsequent retinopathy and nephropathy (Level 1).[4]
2. In people with diabetes, higher glucose levels predict a higher risk of microvascular and macrovascular disease (Level 1).[10–12,14]

Table 6–2 Plasma Glucose Cutoffs for Different Degrees of Glucose Intolerance

	Fasting Plasma Glucose (mmol/L)	2-Hr Post 75g Glucose Load (mmol/L)	Plasma Glucose Cutoffs Are a Risk Factor for:
Diabetes mellitus	≥ 7.0	≥ 11.1	Eye, kidney, nerve, and cardiovascular diseases
Impaired glucose tolerance	< 7.0	7.8–11.0	Diabetes and cardiovascular diseases
Impaired fasting glucose	6.1–6.9	N/A	Not well studied
Normal mean*	5.1	5.4	
Normal 75th percentile†	5.4	6.8	

*No diabetes or impaired glucose tolerance by history or testing.[22]
†No history of diabetes.[22]

WHAT IS THE SIGNIFICANCE OF PLASMA GLUCOSE LEVELS BELOW THE DIABETES CUTOFF?

Impaired glucose tolerance is defined as a 2-hour plasma glucose value between 7.8 and 11.0 mmol/L with a fasting plasma glucose < 7.0 mmol/L.[4] These individuals have a much higher risk of subsequently developing diabetes than individuals with lower 2-hour plasma glucose levels.[18–20] Therefore, people with diabetes are at risk for eye and kidney disease, and people with impaired glucose tolerance are at risk for diabetes. Epidemiologic studies have shown that both groups are at risk for cardiovascular disease (see Table 6–2).

The diagnostic category of impaired fasting glucose was introduced by the American Diabetes Association in 1997[4] and endorsed by the Canadian Diabetes Association in 1998.[21] Patients with impaired fasting glucose are those people whose glucose levels are clearly not normal but are not high enough to be classified as diabetes — that is, fasting plasma glucose levels between 6.1 and 6.9 mmol/L. The category was introduced in order to distinguish people with clearly normal fasting plasma glucose levels from people with fasting plasma glucose levels that are clearly in the diabetic range. It was also introduced because it was recognized that glucose tolerance tests are done seldom if at all in many practice settings, but fasting plasma glucose levels of 6.1 and higher are clearly abnormal; indeed, the normal mean fasting plasma glucose is 5.1 mmol/L and the 75th percentile is 5.4 mmol/L.[22] Epidemiologic analyses of the clinical significance of impaired fasting glucose are now emerging, and several studies are now exploring the relationship between impaired glucose tolerance and impaired fasting glucose.[23]

CONCLUSION

Diabetes is both a disease that can cause significant signs and symptoms related to hyperglycemia and a risk factor for poor health outcomes and tremendous health care expenditures. The high, and growing, prevalence of diabetes and its health impact also suggest that it is a major public health problem that affects society, as well as a clinical problem that affects individuals. Both public health and clinical approaches to the problem are therefore likely to reduce the impact of diabetes in the future.

SUMMARY OF EVIDENCE-BASED MESSAGES

1. Diabetes mellitus is a metabolic disorder characterized by a fasting plasma glucose ≥ 7.0 mmol/L or a 2-hour plasma glucose level ≥ 11.1 mmol/L; these numbers clearly differentiate people at high and low risk for subsequent retinopathy and nephropathy (Level 1).[4]
2. In people with diabetes, higher glucose levels predict a higher risk of microvascular and macrovascular disease (Level 1).[10–12,14]

REFERENCES

1. Hennekens CH, Buring JE. Statistical association and cause-effect relationships. In: Mayrent SL, editor. Epidemiology in medicine. Boston: Little, Brown and Company; 1987. p. 30–53.

2. Folsom AR, Szklo M, Stevens J, et al. A prospective study of coronary heart disease in relation to fasting insulin, glucose, and diabetes. The Atherosclerosis Risk in Communities (ARIC) Study. Diabetes Care 1997;20:935–42.

3. Economic consequences of diabetes mellitus in the U.S. in 1997. American Diabetes Association. Diabetes Care 1998;21:296–309.

4. Expert Committee on the Diagnosis and Classification of Diabetes Mellitus. Report of the Expert Committee on the Diagnosis and Classification of Diabetes Mellitus. Diabetes Care 1997; 20:1183 97.

5. Harris MI, Eastman RC, Cowie CC, et al. Comparison of diabetes diagnostic categories in the U.S. population according to 1997 American Diabetes Association and 1980-1985 World Health Organization diagnostic criteria. Diabetes Care 1997;20:1859–62.

6. Will new diagnostic criteria for diabetes mellitus change phenotype of patients with diabetes? Reanalysis of European epidemiological data. DECODE Study Group on behalf of the European Diabetes Epidemiology Study Group. BMJ 1998;317:371–75.

7. Coutinho M, Gerstein HC, Wang Y, Yusuf S. The relationship between glucose and incident cardiovascular events. A metaregression analysis of published data from 20 studies of 95,783 individuals followed for 12.4 years. Diabetes Care 1999;22:233–40.

8. Gerstein HC. Is glucose a continuous risk factor for cardiovascular mortality? [editorial; comment]. Diabetes Care 1999;22:659–60.

9. Gerstein HC, Yusuf S. Dysglycaemia and risk of cardiovascular disease. Lancet 1996; 347:949–50.

10. Moss SE, Klein R, Klein BEK, Meuer SM. The association of glycemia and cause-specific mortality in a diabetic population. Arch Intern Med 1994;154:2473–9.

11. Andersson DKG, Svardsudd K. Long-term glycemic control relates to mortality in type 2 diabetes. Diabetes Care 1995;18:1534–43.

12. Kuusisto J, Mykkanen L, Pyorala K, Laakso M. NIDDM and its metabolic control predict coronary heart disease in elderly subjects. Diabetes 1994;43:960–7.

13. Gall M-A, Borch-Johnsen K, Hougaard P, et al. Albuminuria and poor glycemic control predict mortality in NIDDM. Diabetes 1995;44:1303–9.

14. Diabetes Control and Complications Trial Research Group. The effect of intensive treatment of diabetes on the development and progression of long-term complications in insulin-dependent diabetes mellitus. N Engl J Med 1993;329:977–86.

15. UK Prospective Diabetes Study (UKPDS) Group. Intensive blood-glucose control with sulphonylureas or insulin compared with conventional treatment and risk of complications in patients with type 2 diabetes (UKPDS 33). Lancet 1998;352:837–53.

16. UK Prospective Diabetes Study (UKPDS) Group. Effect of intensive blood glucose control with metformin on complications in overweight patients with type 2 diabetes (UKPDS 34). Lancet 1998;352:854–65.

17. Ohkubo Y, Kishikawa H, Araki E, et al. Intensive insulin therapy prevents the progression of diabetic microvascular complications in Japanese patients with non-insulin-dependent diabetes mellitus: a randomized prospective 6-year study. Diabetes Res Clin Pract 1995;28:103–17.

18. Edelstein SL, Knowler WC, Bain RP, et al. Predictors of progression from impaired glucose tolerance to NIDDM: an analysis of six prospective studies. Diabetes 1997;46:701–10.

19. Diabetes Prevention Program. Design and methods for a clinical trial in the prevention of type 2 diabetes. Diabetes Care 1999;22:623–34.

20. Shaw JE, Zimmet P, Hodge AM, et al. Impaired fasting glucose: how low should it go? Diabetes Care 2000;23:34–9.

21. Meltzer S, Leiter L, Daneman D, et al. 1998 Clinical practice guidelines for the management of diabetes in Canada. Can Med Assoc J 1998;159(Suppl 8): S1–29.

22. Cowie CC, Harris MI. Physical and metabolic characteristics of persons with diabetes. In: Harris MI, Cowie CC, Stern MS, et al. editors. Diabetes in America. NIH Publication No. 95–1468. National Institutes of Health; 1995. p. 117–64.

23. Consequences of the new diagnostic criteria for diabetes in older men and women. DECODE Study (Diabetes Epidemiology: Collaborative Analysis of Diagnostic Criteria in Europe). Diabetes Care 1999;22:1667–71.

CHAPTER 7

Short-Term Clinical Consequences of Diabetes in Adults

Gillian L. Booth, MD, MSc, FRCPC

———

ABSTRACT

Hyperglycemia has many short-term consequences. The aim of this chapter is to highlight the acute complications of hyperglycemia, focusing on symptoms at presentation, quality of life, hyperglycemic emergencies, and acute infections.

Virtually all patients with Type 1 diabetes present with symptoms of hyperglycemia (up to 97%); however, patients with Type 2 diabetes may remain asymptomatic for years. Up to three-quarters of adults can be correctly classified on the basis of age and body mass index. For the remainder, other clinical features or laboratory markers (C-peptide and autoantibodies) may help to predict subsequent insulin requirement.

Overall, quality of life (QOL) appears to be lower in patients with diabetes; however, the impact is far less for individuals who are free of complications. The premise that tight glycemic control should improve QOL is not supported in randomized controlled trials, possibly because of other aspects of intensive therapy (more work and more frequent hypoglycemia) that may diminish QOL. However, targeted education programs may have a beneficial effect on QOL.

Diabetic ketoacidosis (DKA) is a serious complication characterized by hyperglycemia, elevated serum ketones, and an anion-gap metabolic acidosis (pH < 7.3, bicarbonate < 15 meq/L). It primarily affects individuals with Type 1 diabetes but may occur in Type 2 diabetes in response to acute stress. Other risk factors include extremes of age, poor glycemic control, use of an insulin pump, and lower socioeconomic status. Diabetic ketoacidosis may be the first manifestation of diabetes (5 to 40% of cases), or it may be precipitated by insulin omission (30 to 60% of cases), infection (20 to 40% of cases), or other acute illnesses (10 to 20% of cases). Therapy consists of intravenous (IV) fluids (6 to 8 L), insulin (0.1 U/kg/h by IV infusion), and IV KCl (10 to 40 meq/L) administration, continued until the acid-base abnormality is corrected. With appropriate management, current mortality rates are < 3%.

The hyperosmolar nonketotic state (HNKS) is a rare but life-threatening condition, occurring predominantly in elderly patients with Type 2 diabetes. It is characterized by severe hyperglycemia (usually > 33 mmol/L), hyperosmolality (> 320 mOsm/L), volume contraction, and mental status impairment following a precipitating event. The cornerstone of therapy is IV fluid hydration (up to 12 L) and KCl adminstration. Insulin is not necessary but may be used in low doses. Mortality rates from HNKS are extremely high (up to 50%); advanced age and higher osmolality confer the greatest risk.

Diabetic individuals appear to be more susceptible to certain types of infection (such as cutaneous and urinary tract infections) and to specific infectious agents (such as *Staphylococcus aureus*). Some rare but potentially fatal infections occur almost exclusively in patients with diabetes. Poor glycemic control and other host factors (such as the presence of DKA or vascular disease) appear to increase the risk of infection.

———

INTRODUCTION

There are a number of immediate consequences associated with hyperglycemia. Acutely, elevations in blood glucose can cause a constellation of symptoms; most notably, increased thirst, polydipsia, polyuria, fatigue, and weight loss (known as classic symptoms of diabetes). Further, the continual demand of managing diabetes on a day-to-day basis may impair quality of life for individuals with this disease. Other acute complications have even more profound effects: severe metabolic decompensation (DKA and the HNKS) is a medical emergency that carries a significant risk of mortality. Also, patients with diabetes may succumb to a variety of infections, some of which can be potentially life threatening.

The following issues are addressed in this chapter:

1. What is the clinical presentation of diabetes and what are the diagnostic characteristics of various presentations and combinations of signs and symptoms?
2. What is the impact of a diagnosis of diabetes on quality of life in adults?
3. What and how common is diabetic ketoacidosis?
4. What and how common is the hyperosmolar nonketotic state?
5. Are patients with diabetes more prone to various infections (excluding foot infections due to neuropathy/vascular disease)?

WHAT IS THE CLINICAL PRESENTATION OF DIABETES?

What Is the Clinical Presentation of Type 1 Diabetes?

Typically, Type 1 diabetes occurs in young (usually under age 30),[1] lean individuals who present with symptoms of metabolic decompensation over a short period of time. However, the onset of Type 1 diabetes has been described in patients over 80 years of age.[1] At presentation, classic symptoms of hyperglycemia, including excessive thirst, polydipsia, polyuria, general fatigue, or weight loss are reported in virtually all patients (93–97%).[2,3] Compared with children, adults tend to have a longer duration of symptoms and higher C-peptide concentrations and are less likely to exhibit ketonuria or ketoacidosis (Table 7–1).[3,4] The prevalence of islet cell and insulin autoantibodies declines, while glutamic acid decarboxylase (GAD) antibodies become more common with increasing age of onset.[3] A significant percentage of new patients with Type 1 diabetes (up to 40 to 60%) experience a transient "honeymoon period" characterized by reduced insulin requirements; this lasts an average of 6 to 7 months.[5,6] During this period, insulin action is enhanced and C-peptide levels tend to be higher.[5,7] In one study, greater presenting bicarbonate levels, body mass index, and beta-cell

Table 7–1 Presentation of Type 1 Diabetes Based on Age

Characteristic	Children	Adults
Clinical feature		
Duration of symptoms	3–4 wk	7–8 wk
Classic symptoms	95%	96%
Ketonuria	86%	76%
DKA	25%	25%
C-peptide level	0.17 nmol/L	0.29 nmol/L
Autoantibodies		
IAA	62	35
ICA	83	66
GAD65	75	80

DKA = diabetic ketoacidosis; IAA = insulin autoantibodies; ICA = islet-cell antibodies; GAD = glutamic acid decarboxylase.
Data from Vandewalle et al[3] and Karjalainen et al.[4]

function increased the likelihood of a complete remission (lack of insulin requirement with normalization of HbA_{1c}) for a period of at least 1 month.[7]

What Is the Clinical Presentation of Type 2 Diabetes?

The onset of Type 2 diabetes is estimated to occur at least 4 to 7 years before clinical presentation, based on the frequent finding of retinopathy at diagnosis.[8] Many patients with Type 2 diabetes are asymptomatic at diagnosis; hyperglycemia is discovered as an incidental finding on routine laboratory testing. In the third National Health and Nutrition Examination Survey, undiagnosed diabetes was discovered in 2.7% of the general adult population and in about 6% of individuals over age 60.[9] Incidental hyperglycemia is also a common finding among patients admitted to medical and surgical services for nondiabetic causes. Levetan and colleagues[10] discovered previously undiagnosed hyperglycemia in over one-third of patients in their series.

At clinical presentation, symptoms may or may not be specific to diabetes. In a cross-sectional analysis of patients with newly diagnosed Type 2 diabetes entering the United Kingdom Prospective Diabetes Study (UKPDS) (n = 430), over two-thirds were symptomatic on direct questioning.[11] The most common symptoms were fatigue, nocturia, dry mouth, thirst, weakness, and blurred vision (Figure 7–1); few symptoms, however, were independently related to HbA_{1c} levels or fasting plasma glucose. Patient characteristics may determine the degree of symptomatology. In a retrospective, population-based study from Rochester, Minnesota, only one-quarter of all patients with Type 2 diabetes were symptomatic at diagnosis.[2] Of those patients who were symptomatic, obese individuals were less likely to present with the common symptoms described above than were lean individuals (70% of obese vs 87% of lean individuals); they were also less likely to present with weight loss (16% of obese

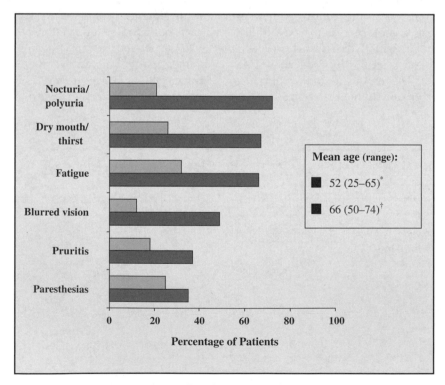

Figure 7–1 Presentation of Type 2 diabetes based on age.
(Adapted from *Bulpitt et al[11]; †Ruige et al.[14])

vs 49% of lean individuals). Similarly, in a small prospective study of patients with newly diagnosed Type 2 diabetes (n = 133), only 37% of men and 27% of women reported symptoms of thirst, polyuria, fatigue, and/or weight loss.[12] At baseline, symptomatic patients had higher glucose and lower insulin levels; however, their metabolic and clinical characteristics at 5 years were comparable to individuals who were initially asymptomatic.

It is estimated that nearly one-fifth of individuals over the age of 65 have diabetes.[9] Elderly patients, in particular, may present with atypical features, such as behavioral and personality changes or disordered mood.[13] Even if they occur, symptoms of hyperglycemia may be masked by the presence of coexisting medical complaints, such as urinary incontinence, prostate problems, or the use of diuretics.[13] In a cross-sectional analysis of middle-aged to elderly patients screened for diabetes by history and oral glucose tolerance testing, reports of fatigue (32%), pruritis (18%), polyuria (21%), frequent thirst (26%), or recent weight loss (15%) were relatively uncommon[14] (see Figure 7–1). Elderly patients with undiagnosed diabetes have similar self-perceived health ratings and few specific symptoms to nondiabetic individuals from the same population.[15]

Can Clinical or Laboratory Features at Presentation Predict Clinical Subtype?

Diagnostic Value of Clinical Characteristics

Patients who do not fit the classic picture of Type 1 or Type 2 diabetes pose a diagnostic dilemma. There have been several attempts to classify patients based on presenting features, such as age, weight, and presence of ketonuria. In a Finnish population-based study, Type 2 diabetes was relatively uncommon prior to age 40 (3% of cases), whereas Type 1 diabetes was less common over the age of 40 (< 10% of cases).[1] However, there was considerable overlap, particularly among young adults. For example, Type 2 diabetes accounted for 60% of all patients in the 30- to 34-year age group.[1] In a prospective study by Hother-Nielsen and colleagues,[16] 75% of adults with newly diagnosed diabetes were correctly classified as non-insulin-requiring or insulin-requiring based on age (above or below 40) and percent ideal body weight (IBW) (above or below 100%). In a retrospective analysis, MacIver and colleagues[17] discovered that symptom severity (polydipsia and/or polyuria), glucose levels, and the presence of ketonuria or glycosuria were directly related to treatment with insulin at 6 months, while increasing age and body mass index were negatively correlated. The prediction model had an accuracy of 72% when applied to a second cohort of patients. Hence, although clinical characteristics will usually discriminate between the two subtypes, up to one-quarter of patients will fall outside these traditional guidelines.

Diagnostic Value of C-Peptide Levels

C-Peptide is cosecreted with insulin in equimolar quantities and serves as a marker of endogenous insulin production. Several prospective studies have evaluated the ability of C-peptide levels to predict subsequent insulin requirement in patients with adult-onset diabetes. Low C-peptide levels are more likely in patients with an age of onset under 40 years and low body mass index (BMI), that is, individuals who fit the classic picture of Type 1 diabetes.[18] Irrespective of other characteristics, Hother-Nielsen and colleagues[16] found that fasting C-peptide levels above or below 0.3 nmol/L discriminated between insulin-requiring and non–insulin-requiring patients with an accuracy of 95% (sensitivity 97%, specificity 92%). In another study, glucagon-stimulated C-peptide levels under 0.6 nmol/L had a sensitivity of 94% and a specificity of 100% for predicting insulin requirement in newly diagnosed patients.[19] Basal and stimulated C-peptide levels were related to body weight among patients with Type 2 diabetes but not those with Type 1 diabetes.[19] Similarly, greater C-peptide responses to glucagon predicted the ability to discontinue insulin therapy in a small series of obese patients with questionable insulin dependency.[20]

Diagnostic Value of Autoantibodies

Specific autoantibodies to components of pancreatic islets (islet cell, insulin, and GAD65) occur in high concentrations in patients with Type 1 diabetes and in genetically predisposed individuals who are at risk of developing Type 1 diabetes. Conversely, low levels are found among non-predisposed individuals, including those with Type 2 diabetes. However, Groop and colleagues[21] described a subset of patients with presumed Type 2 diabetes (based on age) that had positive islet-cell antibodies and phenotypic characteristics of patients with Type 1 diabetes. These patients were leaner, demonstrated a progressive loss of beta-cell function, and were more likely to require insulin over 2 years of follow-up.[21] The term "latent autoimmune diabetes of the aged" (LADA) has been coined to describe this entity. Approximately 12 to 14% of patients initially diagnosed as having Type 2 diabetes are believed to have LADA.[22,23] Of patients with newly diagnosed Type 2 diabetes recruited to the UKPDS, those with islet cell or GAD antibodies (12% of the cohort) were younger, had a lower body mass index, higher HbA$_{1c}$ levels, and decreased beta-cell function.[23] In the UKPDS, GAD antibodies independently predicted the need for insulin therapy[23]; however, the magnitude was far greater for patients under age 45 (adjusted odds ratio [OR] 13.4 [5.28 to 34.0]) than for patients over age 45 (OR 5.62 [3.23 to 9.8]).[23] The sensitivity of GAD antibodies ranges from 51 to 76%[23-27] and may decline with increasing age.[23] In contrast, islet cell antibodies are less sensitive but generally more specific, particularly in the younger age range (specificity: 96 to 98%).[23] Hence, autoantibodies may be useful in identifying individuals who have a clinical profile compatible with Type 1 diabetes.

EVIDENCE-BASED MESSAGES

1. The vast majority of patients presenting under the age of 40 who have an ideal body weight (or less) have Type 1 diabetes. Patients over the age of 40 who are overweight (BMI greater than 100%) usually have Type 2 diabetes (Level 3).[16]
2. In patients with presumed Type 2 diabetes, anti-GAD and/or islet cell antibodies can help in predicting subsequent insulin requirement (Level 1).[23]
3. C-peptide assessments appear to have a greater sensitivity and specificity than either clinical features or the presence of autoantibodies in differentiating Type 1 and Type 2 diabetes (Level 3).[16]

WHAT IS THE IMPACT OF A DIAGNOSIS OF DIABETES ON QUALITY OF LIFE IN ADULTS?

What Is "Quality of Life" and How Is It Measured?

Health-related quality of life (QOL) describes the extent to which illness and medical treatment have an impact on an individual's perception of function and well-being. There is a growing emphasis on QOL as an outcome measure in clinical trials, necessitating the development of instruments to describe and quantify QOL in an objective and meaningful way. To capture different aspects of this complex phenomenon, multiple domains, such as physical, mental, emotional, and social functioning, are evaluated. Fundamental properties that need to be considered during the design of an instrument include validity (that it measures what it was intended to), reliability (that the measurement is consistent), feasibility, and the ease with which it can be administered. Instruments are designed with a specific population in mind. Generic QOL instruments are tailored to the general population, whereas disease-specific measures focus on aspects of QOL that are pertinent only to individuals with that disease. The advantages of the latter are that they may be more sensitive to clinically important aspects of a disease and are potentially more responsive to change. Quality of life instruments that have been validated in a diabetic population are discussed below.

How Does Diabetes Influence Quality of Life?

Theoretically, diabetes may have a greater impact on QOL than other chronic disease states. Diabetes management is an integral part of daily living and requires extensive education and lifestyle changes. Further, patients with diabetes may be at higher risk for developing psychological problems, including depression, anxiety, and eating disorders.[28–30] Psychiatric illness,[28] inadequate social support,[31] and certain sociodemographic characteristics (such as increasing age and low levels of income or education[31]) directly influence self-care behavior and have an adverse effect on QOL.[32–41] From cross-sectional data, there is an inverse relationship between QOL and the presence of both complications[32–35,42–45] and comorbid conditions.[33–36,46–51] Further, randomized trials have demonstrated improved QOL following the symptomatic relief of certain complications such as gastroparesis[52] and painful neuropathy.[53,54] Hence, both psychosocial and physical aspects of the disease contribute to QOL.

Is Quality of Life Different for Patients with Diabetes?

Cross-sectional analyses suggest that patients with diabetes have a lower QOL compared to nondiabetic individuals.[33,46–49] Referral bias may exaggerate any underlying differences, as diabetic patients from tertiary centers may be relatively more ill than those in the general population. However, even in a large population-based study that recruited patients from a primary care setting, QOL scores were lower for individuals with diabetes.[46] When analyzed separately, diabetic patients who are free of significant complications or comorbidity appear to have similar or only minimally reduced QOL compared to healthy controls.[47,48] For example, patients with Type 2 diabetes enrolled in the UKPDS had similar QOL scores to control subjects without diabetes, with the exception that diabetic individuals experienced reduced vigor and more specific symptoms.[45]

Few studies have accounted for the presence of comorbidity in their analysis. In the San Luis Valley Diabetes Study, patients with Type 2 diabetes reported a significantly lower perceived QOL, even after adjustment for comorbidity and other factors such as ethnicity, marital status, and social support.[33] Although QOL is impaired for patients with diabetic complications, ratings may be greater than for individuals with other chronic disease states, such as angina[47] or congestive heart failure.[49] In the absence of impaired vision or stroke, diabetes appears to have little additional impact on QOL for patients with severe underlying disease.[47] Thus, in general, QOL appears to be lower for patients with diabetes; however, the impact is largely related to the degree of morbidity.

Can Quality of Life Be Improved for People with Diabetes?

Effect of Improving Glycemic Control on Quality of Life

Several studies have noted a direct correlation between improved glycemic control and QOL outcomes,[47,55–61] particularly when a diabetes-specific measure is used. However, cross-sectional studies are unable to establish a causal relationship between lower HbA$_{1c}$ levels and QOL, and results of prospective studies are inconsistent.[55,60–63] In some studies, patients with Type 2 diabetes who are treated with insulin appear to have lower QOL ratings than those treated with oral agents or diet alone.[36,64] This difference persisted after adjustment for age, gender, BMI, and duration of diabetes.[64] However, failure to account for differences in comorbidity or complications may explain the findings of this[64] and other studies.[43,63] In contrast, UKPDS patients randomized to an intensive or conventional blood glucose policy demonstrated comparable QOL scores after 8 years of follow-up.[45] Moreover, the effect of different treatment modalities (insulin vs oral agents) was negligible.[45]

The Diabetes Quality of Life Measure[65] (DQOL) was designed to evaluate the relative burden of an intensive treatment regimen among patients with Type 1 diabetes enrolled in the Diabetes Control and Complications Trial[66] (DCCT). Deterioration in overall DQOL score of 12.5 points (out of 100) was determined a priori to represent a clinically significant endpoint.[67] This threshold was derived from evidence that individuals who have three microvascular complications have scores that are 25 points lower than those with no complications.[42] Further, QOL scores improve to a similar degree following kidney-pancreas transplantation.[68] During the DCCT, DQOL scores, functional health status, and psychological distress were similar between treatment groups. However, among intensively treated patients, symptoms of psychiatric distress rose with the frequency of hypoglycemic episodes.[67] There was a similar relationship between hypoglycemia and QOL observed among intensively treated patients in the UKPDS.[45]

Using QOL measures to study the impact of individual treatment regimens has a number of limitations. Quality of life measures may not capture important changes that are meaningful to patients. Further, the increased work involved in intensive care may offset the positive benefit of reducing hyperglycemic symptoms and gaining a sense of control over the disease. Certain complications of treatment, such as more frequent hypoglycemia and greater weight gain, may also negatively impact on QOL. Finally, these studies are not of sufficient duration to illustrate the effect that lower rates of long-term complications will have on QOL.

Other Effects of Therapy on Quality of Life

One of the potential advantages of using an ultra-short-acting insulin is the added flexibility with regard to meal planning. Kotsanos and colleagues[69] reported higher treatment flexibility and greater satisfaction among patients with Type 1 (but not Type 2) diabetes who were randomized to receive lispro rather than regular insulin before meals. However, overall QOL scores were comparable. In randomized[70–72] and nonrandomized[73] studies, insulin pump therapy was also associated with greater satisfaction and less disruption in daily life for patients with both Type 1[71–73] and Type 2 diabetes.[70] Whether improved ratings were due to an easier self-care regimen or other factors, such as less hypoglycemia or weight gain,[70] is unclear. In another study, using an insulin pen was reported to provide patients with a greater sense of freedom; however, concomitant changes in the insulin regimen and inadequate questionnaire validation render these findings inconclusive.[74] In summary, greater treatment flexibility may improve some aspects of QOL for patients with diabetes.

Education programs for both patients and health professionals may also improve QOL.[75,76] However, a study that randomized older patients with Type 2 diabetes to more or less frequent nurse contacts was unable to identify a significant effect on QOL.[77] Similar results were seen in a prospective, nonrandomized trial that provided support-group therapy to younger patients.[78] Targeted interventions may be of greater benefit. For example, coping-skills training resulted in greater QOL and general self-efficacy in a group of adolescents with Type 1 diabetes.[79] Similarly, an intervention that focused on strategies to improve patient decision-making and negotiation skills improved functional health status, health concern, and QOL.[80] Thus, education programs may influence QOL, depending on their scope and the target population.

EVIDENCE-BASED MESSAGES

1. Overall quality of life is impaired for patients with diabetes (Level 4),[33] although to a similar extent as patients with other chronic diseases (Level 4).[49]
2. In the short term, intensive therapy does not improve QOL for patients with Type 1 (Level 1)[67] or Type 2 diabetes (Level 1),[45] possibly because of adverse effects from hypoglycemia, weight gain, and a more challenging self-care regimen.
3. Therapy of some of the chronic complications of diabetes may improve QOL (Level 1).[52] Long-term improvements in glycemic control would also be expected to enhance QOL; however, such studies are lacking.
4. Targeted behavioral programs may improve QOL (Level 2).[79,80]

WHAT IS DIABETIC KETOACIDOSIS?

Diabetic ketoacidosis is an acute and potentially fatal complication of diabetes characterized by hyperglycemia, ketone body formation, and metabolic acidosis. Absolute or relative insulin deficiency in the presence of excess counter-regulatory hormones leads to a state of imbalance that provides the stimulus for ongoing metabolic disturbances. Hyperglycemia results from enhanced glucose production and impaired utilization by peripheral tissues. An osmotic diuresis ensues, leading to progressive urinary losses of fluid and electrolytes. Uncontrolled lipolysis provides free fatty acids that serve as substrates for hepatic ketone production through the process of β-oxidation. Ketoacids accumulate as the rate of production exceeds elimination, causing an anion-gap metabolic acidosis.

How Common Is Diabetic Ketoacidosis?

Several retrospective community-based studies have estimated the incidence of DKA from hospital-based registries. Between 1979 and 1980, DKA accounted for 1.6% of all acute admissions for patients with diabetes in Rhode Island, resulting in an incidence of 4.6 per 1,000 diabetic persons (both Type 1 and Type 2) per year.[81] During the same period, comparable rates were reported for patients in the Rochester Diabetes Project[82] and in Denmark.[83] However, the frequency of DKA appears to be increasing. According to the National Hospital Discharge Survey, the hospital discharge rate for DKA rose nearly 50% between 1980 and 1988, to a rate of 12.5 per 1,000 diabetic persons per year, well exceeding the rate of newly diagnosed diabetes.[84]

What Are the Risk Factors for Diabetic Ketoacidosis?

What Are the Common Precipitants of Diabetic Ketoacidosis?

The vast majority of reports describing the risk factors and precipitants of DKA derive from case series. Overall, therefore, the evidence is quite poor. In about one-quarter of cases reported in the literature, DKA was the first manifestation of diabetes (5 to 39%)[82,83,85–88] (Figure 7–2). Among known cases of diabetes, common precipitants include infection (20 to 38%)[81,82,85–87,89] and other intercurrent illnesses, among which myocardial infarction, abdominal crises (gastrointestinal bleeding, pancreatitis), and trauma are frequently described (10 to 20%).[83,85,86,90] Morris and colleagues[91] discovered that inadherence to prescribed insulin doses over the preceding year was associated with vastly greater odds of developing DKA (adjusted OR was 24.6 and 2.1 for the lowest two quartiles). In general, insulin omission or noncompliance is identified as being responsible for less than one-third of cases overall.[81,83,85–87] However, in areas of relative economic disparity in the United States, up to two-thirds of cases are associated with insulin omission.[92,93] Financial constraints[93] and alcohol or illicit drug abuse[92,94] were viewed as contributing factors in a large number of these cases.

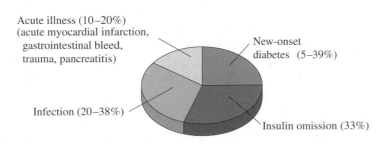

Figure 7–2 Precipitating factors in diabetic ketoacidosis.

Table 7–2 Risk Factors for Diabetic Ketoacidosis

Type 1 diabetes

Type 2 diabetes
  • during stress
  • ↑certain ethnic groups

Extremes of age

Socioeconomic status

Poor glycemic control

Noncompliance

Continuous subcutaneous insulin infusion

Noncompliance also places patients at risk for recurrent episodes.[81,95] Thus, in many cases, the development of DKA is potentially preventable by avoiding delays in diagnosis or errors in management. In fact, two prospective studies demonstrated a reduction in admissions for DKA following the institution of diabetes education programs.[95,96]

Which Patients Are Prone to Diabetic Ketoacidosis?

Risk factors for developing DKA are summarized in Table 7–2. Diabetic ketoacidosis principally affects patients with Type 1 diabetes. Although the majority of cases occur in young people, DKA can be a presenting feature of Type 1 diabetes at any age.[97] Patients at extremes of age appear to be most vulnerable.[81,85] Reports of higher rates among women have been inconsistent.[81,83,85,89,98] In the United States, hospitalization rates for DKA are higher in African-American compared to Caucasian males; however, economic issues may confound these analyses.[84] In a cohort of young patients with Type 1 diabetes from the Wisconsin Diabetes Registry, not being Caucasian and lacking private insurance were related to higher rates of hospitalization.[99] Other series have found an inverse relationship between socioeconomic status and DKA,[83,95] particularly in the absence of health insurance.[100,101]

Diabetic ketoacidosis was commonly reported among patients with Type 1 diabetes participating in the EURODIAB Study; 8.6% had had admissions for DKA in the previous 12 months.[102] Poor glycemic control is an independent predictor of hospitalization due to hyperglycemia,[99] including DKA.[102] However, the risk of DKA was similar between intensive and conventional treatment groups in the DCCT[103] (1.8 to 2 per 100 patient-years), despite lower HbA_{1c} levels achieved in the intensive group. Among patients treated intensively, rates were higher for patients using continuous subcutaneous insulin infusion compared to those on multiple injections (3.09 vs 1.39 per 100 patient-years, $p = .003$).[103] Similar findings were observed in a meta-analysis evaluating the effect of intensified insulin treatment on the risk of ketoacidosis.[104] Using data from 14 randomized trials (including the DCCT), the authors discovered that the overall risk of DKA was greater for patients treated with intensive versus conventional therapy (OR 1.74 [1.27 to 2.38]), largely due to the effect of continuous subcutaneous insulin infusion (OR 7.20 [2.95 to 17.58]). The OR for intensive therapy using only multiple daily injections (MDI) was 1.13 (0.15 to 8.35), and in trials offering a choice between MDI or pump therapy, the OR was 1.28 (0.90 to 1.83).

Table 7–3 Symptoms and Signs of Diabetic Ketoacidosis

Symptom

    Classic symptoms

    (↑thirst, polydipsia, polyuria, weight loss)

    Fatigue

    Nausea and vomiting

    Abdominal pain

Sign

    Dehydration

    Hypotension, tachycardia

    Kussmaul respiration

    Acetone odor on breath

    Impaired mental status (usually mild)

Endogenous insulin production is sufficient to prevent ketosis in the majority of patients with Type 2 diabetes. However, excessive catecholamine secretion during times of acute stress may severely suppress insulin release, precipitating ketoacidosis. In several large series, 9 to 26% of DKA episodes occurred in patients with Type 2 diabetes, as defined by the absence of prior insulin use or ketoacidosis.[83,85,88,89,97] Certain racial groups,[97] such as African-American and Hispanic patients with Type 2 diabetes, may be more prone to develop DKA.[92,93,105–109] In some cases, no precipitating factor could be identified.[109]

How Is Diabetic Ketoacidosis Diagnosed?

What Are the Presenting Features of Diabetic Ketoacidosis?

Symptoms of extreme thirst, polydipsia, polyuria, weight loss, and generalized weakness usually develop over several days[110] (Table 7–3). More rapid onset has been noted in cases associated with insulin pump failure.[111] Excessive ketones induce symptoms of nausea and vomiting in the majority of patients,[90,112] but abdominal pain occurs less frequently.[90] Persistent hyperglycemia eventually culminates in the clinical signs of dehydration and intravascular volume contraction. Tachycardia and mild hypotension are common; however, few present in frank hypovolemic shock.[85,110] Ketoacidosis causes deep and rapid respiration, known as Kussmaul's respiration, and the characteristic odor of acetone on the breath. Although many patients exhibit some degree of impaired mental status, only about 10 to 15% are severely obtunded or comatose.[81,113,114] When serum osmolality exceeds 340 mOsm/kg H₂0, stupor or coma is more likely to occur.[115]

What Criteria Are Used to Diagnose Diabetic Ketoacidosis?

Definitive criteria for the diagnosis of DKA have not been established. Most definitions include the presence of acidosis (pH < 7.3), low bicarbonate (< 15 meq/L), and raised serum ketones (Table 7–4).[116–118] Hyperglycemia is usually present (> 14 mmol/L or 250 mg/dL), but occasionally glucose levels are normal or only mildly elevated,[119] usually in association with food deprivation or excessive vomiting and continued insulin administration.[110,119] Accompanying laboratory abnormalities include moderate ketonuria and an increased anion gap (> 16 mmol/L).[116] Coexistent acid-base abnormalities are extremely common.[112,120,121]

Table 7–4 Criteria for Diagnosis of Diabetic Ketoacidosis

↓ pH (< 7.3)

↓ Serum bicarbonate (< 15 mmol/L)

↑ Serum ketones

↑ Blood glucose

↑ Anion gap (> 14 mmol/L)

↑ Urinary ketones

How Is Diabetic Ketoacidosis Treated?

How Should Patients with Diabetic Ketoacidosis Be Monitored?

The goals of treatment are to restore normal circulatory volume and tissue perfusion, decrease serum glucose, clear serum ketoacids, and correct electrolyte imbalances. Serum glucose and electrolytes should be monitored every 2 hours until resolution and then every 4 to 6 hours until full recovery.[118] Detailing the response of biochemical parameters to therapy in a flow sheet is useful.[118] An evaluation for underlying precipitating illnesses is essential, including bacterial cultures and an electrocardiogram to rule out infection or silent myocardial ischemia. No studies have specifically evaluated the effect of patient care setting on outcomes. Obtunded or comatose patients are best managed in an intensive care unit, whereas uncomplicated patients may be admitted to a stepdown unit.[118] Many authors are reluctant to admit moderate or severe cases of DKA to general hospital wards unless a protocol or written guidelines for insulin infusion are in place.[118] Other prerequisites include the ability of nurses to administer intravenous (IV) insulin infusions and monitor patients on an hourly basis and laboratory services with a sufficiently rapid turnaround time. Greater involvement of a diabetologist in the care of patients with DKA has been associated with a shorter time to onset of insulin therapy,[89] higher insulin doses,[89] and shorter lengths of stay.[89,122] In one study, the management of patients with DKA by an endocrinologist rather than by a generalist independently predicted lower hospital charges (primarily due to lower rates of procedures) and lower readmission rates over a 3½-year period.[122]

How Should Intravenous Fluids Be Administered?

Using central venous pressure measurements as a guide, one study reported that 3 to 9 liters of half-normal saline was required to restore normal volume.[123] Controversy exists regarding the optimal fluid regimen. Only one small randomized trial has evaluated the rate of IV fluid replacement in patients with DKA. Recovery was more rapid following lower rates of saline infusion (500 mL/h for 4 hours then 250 mL/h) than with rates that were twice as high.[124] However, no patients had shock or significant renal impairment. In the setting of hypotension, saline should be given more rapidly or be replaced by colloid solutions.[116] One compromise is to give normal saline (500 to 1,000 mL/h) for the first 1 to 2 hours to re-expand the intravascular space, followed by half-normal saline (200 to 500 mL/h), with the aim of replacing one half of the estimated fluid deficit in the first 12 hours.[118]

How Should Insulin Be Administered?

Insulin can be safely started at the same time as IV fluids, except in the presence of significant hypokalemia.[125] In two series, no complications were seen following IV fluid administration

Table 7–5 Randomized Trials of Insulin Therapy

Study	N	Group	Dose: Bolus	Maintenance	Time to ↓Glc* (h)	Time to ↓HCO₃† (h)	↓Glc (%)	↓K⁺ (%)
Kitabchi et al[127]	24	High	10–50 U IV & 15–50 U SQ	15–50 U/h SQ	4.5	11.6	25	29
	24	Low	0.1 U/lb IM	5 U/h IM	6.7	11.1	0	4
Heber et al[128]	7	High	25–150 U IV & SQ (each)	→ q 2h	3.9	—	0	—
	10	Low	6 U IV	6 U/h IV	3.1	—	10	—
Fisher et al[129]	15	IM	0.33 U/kg	7 U/h	4.9	12.2	0	—
	15	IV	0.33 U/kg	7 U/h	6.0‡	13.0‡	0	—
	15	SQ	0.33 U/kg	7 U/h	5.6	10.8	0	—
Sacks et al[130]	15	IM	0.44 U/kg (½ IV/½ IM)	7 U/h	4.5	14.1	0	33§
	15	IV	0.44 U/kg	7 U/h	4.3	17.9	0	33§

*Plasma glucose < 14 mmol/L (250 mg/dL).

†Serum bicarbonate < 15 meq/L.

‡The rate of decline of plasma glucose and ketone bodies in the first 2 h was greater with IV than IM or SC insulin.

§Mild hypokalemia (3.0 to 3.4 meq/L).

without insulin for a period of up to 20 hours.[123,126] However, IV fluids alone have no effect on serum ketones, bicarbonate, or pH.[126] Shorter time intervals to insulin administration are associated with faster recovery times and shorter lengths of hospital stay.[89] Prior to the 1970s, patients with DKA were conventionally treated with high doses of regular insulin. This practice was challenged once the efficacy of low-dose insulin was established. Two small nonblinded randomized trials[127,128] comparing high-dose (up to 50 to 150 U/h) and low-dose insulin (approximately 0.1 U/kg/h) found similar rates of biochemical recovery between the groups (Table 7–5). However, hypokalemia and hypoglycemia occurred more frequently,[127] and the decline in blood glucose was less predictable with high-dose therapy.[128] Two randomized trials compared different routes of insulin administration (intravenous vs intramuscular[129,130] or subcutaneous[129]) using equivalent doses (7 U/h). Intravenous insulin led to a faster initial decline in ketone and glucose levels,[130] yet the overall time to resolution was similar between groups.

No deaths occurred in any of the randomized studies. In a cohort of patients from the Rochester Epidemiology Project,[131] a trend toward more adverse events, defined as a combination of hypokalemia, hypoglycemia, or death, occurred in the group receiving bolus insulin injection (BII) compared to continuous insulin infusion (CII) (OR 2.1 [0.8 to 5.4]), despite a greater severity in infusion patients at presentation. However, the two comparison groups were not contemporaneous; all CII cases occurred between 1976 and 1992, while most BII cases occurred prior to 1976. Hence, overall differences in patient management strategies might have accounted for these observations.

The degree of hyperglycemia correlates poorly with the presence of ketoacidosis[132]; thus, glucose levels are not the best target for planning therapy. In two randomized studies, maintaining the insulin infusion rate at 5 to 10 U/h after glucose levels reached 10 mmol/L led to a more rapid clearance of serum ketones than regimens that decreased the infusion rate to 1.3 to 2.5 U/h.[133,134] Hypoglycemia was avoided by adding 5% dextrose (D_5W), whereas 10% dextrose ($D_{10}W$) led to higher glucose levels in the high insulin infusion group. Changes in anion gap were not reported in either study; however, bicarbonate, potassium, and pH levels were similar between groups. Hence, once glucose levels approach 10 to 14 mmol/L, IV D_5W or two-thirds dextrose should be started to prevent hypoglycemia, while the insulin infusion is maintained at its initial rate.

How Should Potassium Be Administered?

Despite total body potassium deficits in the range of 3 to 5 meq/kg body weight, most patients with DKA present with normal or increased serum potassium because of a shift of intracellular potassium to the extracellular compartment.[135,136] Potassium levels decline following the initiation of therapy because of insulin-mediated uptake into cells and the reversal of factors (such as pH) previously driving potassium out of cells. Both hyper- and hypokalemia are potentially life threatening to patients with DKA. In most series, addition of 20 to 40 meq/L of IV potassium to the second liter of saline successfully averted the development of hypokalemia.[118] Although severe hyperkalemia (greater than 6.5 meq/L) responds promptly to the institution of insulin and fluid replacement,[136] it may be prudent to delay potassium administration if levels are over 5.5 meq/L or in the presence of oliguria. Low potassium levels at presentation represent an even greater degree of depletion, necessitating immediate treatment with IV KCl (potassium chloride) (10 to 20 meq/h) to avoid life-threatening hypokalemia.[118,137,138] In summary, IV KCl should be added to the first liter of fluid when initial potassium levels are normal or low and to the second or subsequent liters when initial levels are elevated (Table 7–6).

What Is the Role of Bicarbonate Therapy?

The use of bicarbonate therapy to correct acidosis has been challenged because of the associated risk of hypokalemia[118,139] and possible worsening of cerebral edema.[118,140,141] Despite

Table 7–6 Summary of Management for Diabetic Ketoacidosis

Specific Therapy	Evidence	Study
ICU/step-down unit (depending on severity) Monitoring: • BG/electrolytes q 2h until resolution then q 4–6h until full recovery • Maintain flow sheet to record response to treatment Rule out underlying illness (bacterial cultures, ECG, etc)	Expert opinion	Kitabchi et al[118]

IV fluids:
• NS @ 500 to 1000 mL/h × 1–2 h, then
  $^1/_2$ NS @ 200 to 500 mL/h
• If hypotension, use higher rates and/or replace
  with colloid solutions
• Add D_5W or $^2/_3$ & $^1/_3$ once BG reaches 10 to 14 mmol/L
	Small RCT
	
	Small RCTs
		Adrogue et al[124]
		Wiaggam et al[133]
		Krentz et al[134]

IV insulin: 0.1–0.2 U/kg bolus IV then 0.1–0.2 U/kg/h by IV infusion* Maintain rate until 2 of the following are corrected: • $HCO_3 \geq 18$ meq/L • pH ≥ 7.3 • AG ≤ 14 meq/L	Small RCTs Small RCTs	Kitabachi et al[127] Heber et al[128] Fisher et al[129] Sachs et al[130] Wiggam et al[133] Krentz et al[134]
IV KCl: 10–40 meq/L Initial serum K^+: • low to (N): start immediately (first liter of saline) • 5.0 to 5.5: add KCl to second liter of saline • Over 5.5: add once serum K^+ is ≤ 5.5 and patient is passing urine	Expert opinion/ case series	Kitabchi et al[118] Fulop[136] Keller[137] Foster et al[138]
IV bicarbonate: • 44.8 to 133.8 meq IV • pH ≤ 6.85 or impending cardiovascular collapse (? potential benefit) • pH 6.85–7.2—no net benefit	Expert opinion Small RCTs	Kitabchi et al[118] Foster et al[138] Soler et al[139] Morris et al[142] Gamba et al[143] Hale et al[144]
IV phosphate: • Up to 200 mmol over 12 to 24 h • No net benefit	Small RCTs	Keller et al[148] Fisher et al[149]

*May substitute with IM or SQ insulin at same doses if IV infusion is unavailable.
BG = blood glucose; NS = normal saline; RCT = randomized controlled trial.

this evidence, bicarbonate is frequently promoted for use in patients with a pH < 6.9 to 7.1,[117,118,138] particularly in cases of impending cardiovascular collapse. However, individuals with severe acidosis (pH < 6.9) and those with hypotension were generally excluded from randomized trials; thus, the treatment of such patients is based empirically, rather than on evidence. If used, the recommended dose of sodium bicarbonate is between 44 and 100 meq as an isotonic solution, with 10 to 20 meq of added potassium.[118]

In four randomized trials[139,142-144] (three placebo controlled[139,143,144]), IV bicarbonate (44.8 to 133.8 meq) had no effect on the rate of metabolic recovery or amount of insulin and fluid replacement for patients with DKA and severe acidosis (pH in the range of 6.85 to 7.2). In fact, bicarbonate delayed the fall in ketones and lactate in one study[144] and resulted in lower potassium levels in another,[143] although potassium replacement had been greater in the placebo group. Hence, for patients with pH levels of > 6.9, there is no evidence to support the use of IV bicarbonate.

Concerns regarding bicarbonate therapy and the development of cerebral edema have not been substantiated. In one study,[143] mental status and mean arterial pressure remained the same between treatment groups. Similarly, in two retrospective cohort studies, patients who received bicarbonate had comparable rates of biochemical and neurologic recovery than those who did not.[145,146] Thus, bicarbonate therapy appears to have little impact on the development of clinically important cerebral edema (see section on cerebral edema, below).

What Is the Role of Phosphate Therapy?

Serum phosphate levels are raised in the majority of patients who present with DKA but tend to decline during therapy.[147,148] The potential risks of hypophosphatemia include the development of rhabdomyolysis, muscle weakness, impaired cardiac function, respiratory failure,[118,138] and reduced oxygen delivery to tissues through low 2,3-diphosphoglycerate levels[140] (2,3-DPG). The potential utility of adding phosphate to standard therapy for DKA was tested in three unblinded randomized trials.[147-149] Intravenous phosphate (15 to 204 mmol over 12 to 24 hours) resulted in higher serum phosphate and 2,3-DPG levels,[148,149] but did not affect the rate of metabolic recovery or clinical parameters (neurologic status, length of stay, or mortality).[147-149] Asymptomatic declines in serum calcium levels occurred more frequently in patients treated with phosphate,[149] but no other complications occurred. These results need to be viewed carefully in light of the fact that the studies were unblinded, included small numbers of patients, and only one included a placebo arm.[149] At this point, there is no clinical evidence supporting the use of phosphate therapy during the treatment of DKA.

When Can Therapy for Diabetic Ketoacidosis Be Stopped?

Although the criteria for resolution of DKA is variable, correction of at least two of three acid-base parameters (serum bicarbonate $\geq$ 18 meq/L, venous pH $\geq$ 7.3, anion gap $\leq$ 14 meq/L) is suggested as a target for therapy. Because the majority of patients develop a hyperchloremic metabolic acidosis within the first 8 hours of treatment, bicarbonate levels alone are insufficient.[121] Most standard assays for serum ketones, such as the nitroprusside reaction, measure acetoacetate and acetone, rather than β-hydroxybutyrate (βHB), the predominant ketone formed in DKA. Thus, ketone measurements become more strongly positive throughout therapy as βHB is converted to acetoacetate and then to acetone. This phenomenon prompted the development of a rapid, specific enzymatic test to measure β-hydroxybutyrate at the bedside. In one study, ketoacidosis, based on acid-base parameters, was cleared in all patients who had βHB levels < 0.5 mmol/L, whereas the nitroprusside reaction was still positive in over 50% of cases.[150] However, low βHB levels were noted in only three of eight patients who had normalization of biochemical indices.[151] Although βHB levels began to decline earlier, the overall time to resolution was similar for both βHB and acetoacetone measurements. Thus, although promising, there is insufficient evidence to recommend routine measurement of β-hydroxybutyrate levels for monitoring the response to therapy.

In summary, treatment for DKA consists primarily of adequate hydration (in the range of 6 to 8 L of normal or half-normal saline), low-dose insulin (0.1 U/kg/h by IV infusion), and IV KCl administration (see Table 7–6). The main target of insulin therapy is normalization of acid-base parameters rather than blood glucose level. Hence, IV insulin doses should be maintained at higher rates (5 to 10 U/h) until the acid-base abnormality is cor-

---

Table 7–7 Predictors of Mortality from Diabetic Ketoacidosis

Clinical Feature

↓Blood pressure (shock)

↓Level of consciousness

ARDS

Biochemical Feature

↓Serum bicarbonate

↑Blood glucose

↑Urea

↑Osmolality

ARDS = adult respiratory distress syndrome.

rected (at least two of the following achieved: serum bicarbonate ≥ 18 meq/L, venous pH ≥ 7.3, anion gap ≤ 14 meq/L). Insulin doses should be increased if there is no improvement in these parameters. Hypoglycemia can be avoided by adding IV D_5W or two-thirds dextrose once glucose levels reach ≤ 14 mmol/L.

What Is the Prognosis for Patients with Diabetic Ketoacidosis?

Are Adults with Diabetic Ketoacidosis at Risk for Cerebral Edema?

Cerebral edema is one of the most feared complications of DKA in children, as it carries a high risk of permanent neurologic sequelae or death.[152] Of confirmed cases of cerebral edema published in the literature, over 97% occurred in individuals under age 19.[152] In adults, symptomatic cerebral edema is a rare complication of DKA; however, transient and asymptomatic elevations in cerebraspinal fluid pressure have been noted using serial lumbar punctures[153] and echoencephalograms.[154] Treatment regimens for DKA have been implicated as a cause of cerebral edema. As DKA is treated, osmolality of the extracellular space falls, favoring movement of water into cells. Restoration of the sodium deficit contributes by increasing the hydrostatic pressure, which can then act as a driving force for entry of fluid into the interstitial space of the brain. There may be some evidence to support this theory in children; therefore, many authorities recommend gradual replacement of sodium and water deficits over 24 to 36 hours. Prevention of rapid declines in blood glucose has also been proposed. However, comparable rates of neurologic recovery for unconscious patients randomized to high- versus low-dose insulin therapy have been reported.[115] Hence, fluctuations in blood glucose levels may play a lesser role in the development of cerebral edema than previously thought.

What Is the Mortality Rate Associated with Diabetic Ketoacidosis?

Most deaths in patients with DKA are due to severe underlying disease such as pneumonia, sepsis, acute myocardial infarction, or pulmonary embolus.[87,155,156] Older series report mortality rates of up to 9%[81,83,85,87,154]; however, more recent rates range from 0.65 to 3.3%.[88,89,92,93,157] Mortality rates appear to be greater for patients who present with severe clinical shock[87,89,155] (or decreased level of consciousness[83,114,155]) or biochemical features (higher glucose, urea, or osmolality, and lower bicarbonate levels[87,89,114,158]) as well as certain complications such as adult respiratory distress syndrome[159] (Table 7–7). Increasing age is an independent predictor of mortality, even after adjustment for comorbid illnesses.[160] The occurrence of DKA may be associated with lower long-term survival. In the Rochester Epidemiology Study, patients surviving to 48 hours following the development of DKA had 15 to 20% lower survival rates at 5 years compared to controls without DKA who were matched for age and sex at diagnosis.[82] Individuals who experienced DKA were also more likely to develop microvascular complications of diabetes, possibly accounting for the higher mortality observed between the two groups.

Do Patients with Type 2 Diabetes Require Insulin if They Have Had Diabetic Ketoacidosis?

Patients with Type 2 diabetes may develop DKA in the setting of acute illness, yet many of these individuals will not require long-term treatment with insulin. In one study, a large percentage of obese African-American patients exhibited improved beta-cell function following resolution of DKA and were subsequently managed without insulin.[108] Aggressive treatment of hyperglycemia with oral agents may be sufficient to prevent episodes of DKA in this population. In a small randomized trial (n = 35), patients with presumed Type 2 diabetes treated with glyburide (1.25 to 2.5 mg/d) following an episode of DKA or hyperosmolar coma were less likely to experience recurrent hyperglycemia than patients treated with diet alone (p = .03).[161] No predictors of recurrence were identified. Hence, patients with Type 2 diabetes who develop DKA do not require insulin therapy at the time of discharge as long as other treatment modalities are able to provide optimal glucose control.

EVIDENCE-BASED MESSAGES

1. Among patients treated with intensive regimens, continuous subcutaneous insulin infusion is associated with a greater risk of DKA (Level 1A).[104]
2. The treatment of DKA includes IV fluids (normal saline: 500 mL/h for 4 hours, then 250 mL/h (Level 2)[124] or half-normal saline; higher rates in cases of hypotension, low-dose continuous insulin infusion (0.1 U regular insulin/kg bolus then 0.1 U/kg/h) (Level 2)[130] and adequate potassium replacement.
3. Bicarbonate therapy (Level 2)[143] and phosphate replacement (Level 2)[149] have no additional benefit, but IV bicarbonate may be considered for a pH ≤ 6.9 to 7.0.
4. Mortality from DKA ranges from 0.65 to 3.3% (Level 4),[89] with higher rates in older patients (Level 4).[160]

WHAT AND HOW COMMON IS THE HYPEROSMOLAR NONKETOTIC STATE?

Over the years, various terms have been used to describe this syndrome: hyperosmolar nonketotic state, diabetic coma, and diabetic hyperosmolar state. The constellation of severe hyperglycemia, dehydration, and hyperosmolarity, in the absence of severe ketosis, forms the hallmark of this syndrome. It classically occurs in older patients with Type 2 diabetes. Several hypotheses regarding the pathogenesis of this syndrome have been generated; however, the precise details are not yet understood. Mild volume depletion, such as occurs in the setting of acute illness, is thought to be the instigating factor. If water intake is insufficient to match water loss, then hyperosmolality occurs. Thus, individuals who have a diminished thirst sensation, or who have limited access to water (such as the elderly or debilitated), are at greatest risk. In a vicious cycle of worsening hyperglycemia and osmotic diuresis, progressive volume contraction and dehydration result. The clinical course is hastened by underlying renal insufficiency and consumption of fluids with a high glucose content. Although circulating insulin levels are low, they are sufficient to prevent lipolysis; thus, ketoacidosis is not a feature of this syndrome.

Since HNKS is a relatively rare condition, large-scale prospective studies are lacking. Figures from the National Hospital Discharge Survey (NHDS) revealed only 4,500 hospitalizations classified as being due to HNKS in the United States in 1990,[162] accounting for only

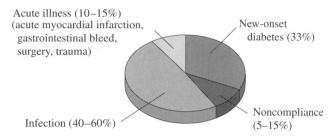

Figure 7–3 Precipitating factors in the hyperosmolar nonketotic state.

0.2% of all hospitalizations for patients with diabetes. However, this may be an underestimation, as unpublished data from the Rhode Island Department of Health identified a considerably higher rate—175 patients per 1 million population.[163]

What Are the Risk Factors for the Hyperosmolar Nonketotic State?

What Are the Common Precipitants of the Hyperosmolar Nonketotic State?

In many cases, HNKS is the first manifestation of a new diagnosis of diabetes (33% in the largest series)[164] (Figure 7–3). Other common precipitants are infection (40 to 60%),[164–167] insulin omission/noncompliance (5 to 15%),[166,168,169] and other acute illnesses, such as myocardial infarction, gastrointestinal bleeding, surgery, or trauma (10 to 15%).[165–168] In one series, 30% of patients developed HNKS after admission to hospital.[166] In another series,[170] 12 cases of HNKS occurred after cardiac surgery. Most cases went unnoticed for many days, with an average lag period between the onset of polyuria and diagnosis of 5.7 days. An association between HNKS and medications that exacerbate volume contraction or hyperglycemia has been reported; however, others[164] found a similar prevalence of diuretic, β-blocker, or corticosteriod use among patients with HNKS compared with age-matched diabetic controls.

Which Patients Are Prone to the Hyperosmolar Nonketotic State?

The majority of cases occur in the elderly; however, HNKS may develop at any age. The mean age is between 60 and 73 years, depending on the series.[155,164,165,167,168,171,172] In a case-control study, female gender, newly diagnosed diabetes, and presence of acute infection were identified as independent risk factors for the development of HNKS[164] (Table 7–8). Although patients with HNKS exhibited a high degree of comorbidity, rates were similar in the control population.

Table 7–8 Risk Factors for the Hyperosmolar Nonketotic State

Advanced age
Female gender
New-onset diabetes
Acute infection
Noncompliance
Acute illness

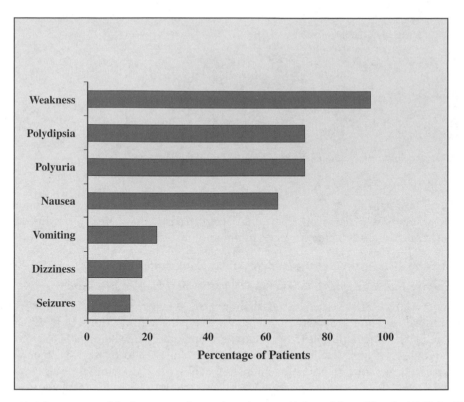

Figure 7–4 Symptoms of the hyperosmolar nonketotic state. (Adapted from Khardori R, Soler NG. Hyperosmolar hyperglycemic nonketotic syndrome: report of 22 cases and brief review. Am J Med 1984;77:899.)

What Are the Presenting Features of the Hyperosmolar Nonketotic State and How Is It Diagnosed?

Typical symptoms of hyperglycemia (increased thirst, polydipsia, polyuria, weakness, fatigue) usually follow a protracted course over several weeks[165,166,173] or even months[169] (Figure 7–4). Nausea and vomiting occur in < 50% of cases, and neurologic symptoms, such as dizziness or seizures, are not uncommon (10 to 20%).[165,166,168] Patients present clinically with signs of dehydration and occasionally hypovolemic shock.[165,166,169] Fever is present in approximately 50% of cases.[165] As a rule, mental status is impaired, ranging from confusion and lethargy (40 to 50%)[166,168,169] to stupor or coma (27 to 54%)[166–169] (Figure 7–5). A direct relationship between glucose or osmolality and level of consciousness has been observed.[167,168,174,175] An array of focal neurologic deficits may occur, occasionally mimicking an acute stroke.[165]

Table 7–9 Diagnosis of the Hyperosmolar Nonketotic State*

Diagnostic Factor

↑Blood glucose (> 33 mmol/L)

↑Serum osmolality (> 320 mOsm/L)

Absence of ketoacidosis

*No definitive criteria exist for the diagnosis of HNKS.

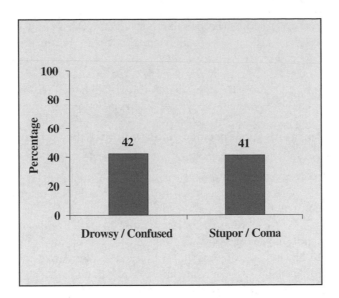

Figure 7–5 Level of consciousness in patients with the hyperosmolar nonketotic state. (Adapted from Gerich et al,[166] Khardori and Soler,[168] and Gale et al.[169])

Table 7–10 Summary of Management of the Hyperosmolar Nonketotic State

ICU:
- Attention to airway management, ventilation, and O_2 delivery
- Monitor vital signs q1–2 h

Monitoring:
  BG/electrolytes q 2–4h until resolution

Rule out underlying illness:
  (Bacterial cultures, CXR, ECG, etc)

Treatment*

IV fluids:
- NS @ 500 – 1,000 mL/h $\times$ 1–2 h, then $^1/_2$ NS @ 200–500 mL/h
- Lower rates in elderly, cardiac disease
- If hypotension use higher rates and/or replace with colloid solutions
- Add D_5W or $^2/_3$ & $^1/_3$ once BG reaches 10 to 15 mmol/L if on insulin drip

IV insulin:
- Optional
- If used: $\leq$ 0.1 U/kg IV bolus then $\leq$ 0.1 U/kg/h by IV infusion

IV KCl :
- 10–40 meq/L
- Initial serum K^+—low to (N): start immediately (first liter of saline)
              —5.0–5.5: add KCl to second liter of saline
              — >5.5: add once serum K^+ is $\leq$ 5.5 and patient is passing urine

*Evidence from case series.
CXR = chest radiography; ECG = electrocardiogram; BG = blood glucose.

No definitive criteria for the diagnosis of HNKS exist (Table 7–9). Glucose levels usually exceed 33 mmol/L (600 mg/dL) with serum osmolality > 320 mOsm/L.[163,168] The absence of acidosis (pH > 7.3, bicarbonate > 18 to 20 meq/L) or ketosis has been used as a criterion for discerning HNKS from DKA in many studies. However, mixed cases of hyperosmolar coma and ketoacidosis have been reported in up to one-third of all hyperglycemic emergencies, and other causes of an anion-gap metabolic acidosis can occur in patients with HNKS.[158,165,167,176]

How Should Patients with Hyperosmolar Nonketotic State Be Monitored?

How Is the Hyperosmolar Nonketotic State Treated?

Close attention to airway management, ventilation, and oxygen delivery is critical, particularly in unconscious patients. The severity of the condition at presentation dictates the degree of intervention required. In general, patients are best managed in an intensive care setting. Vital signs must be monitored frequently (every 1 to 2 hours),[177] and screening for underlying conditions such as infection or myocardial ischemia is essential.[163] Baseline laboratory investigation should include a complete blood count and differential, electrolytes, urea, creatinine, glucose, and osmolality[163] (or osmolality can be calculated). The majority of patients have elevated urea[163,165,166] and creatinine[163,165] levels. Electrolytes and glucose should be monitored on a frequent basis (every 2 to 4 hours) until resolution.

How Should Intravenous Fluids Be Administered?

Most treatment algorithms are based on data from retrospective case series or expert opinion. Because the primary derangement in HNKS is hypertonic dehydration, fluid and electrolyte replacement should be the primary goal of therapy. Most patients have lost approximately 25% of total body water. In five case series, an average of 4 to 12 liters were required to normalize biochemical parameters.[155,165–168] If patients present with hypotension, initial hydration should generally consist of normal saline at a rate of 1 L/h for 1 or 2 hours until the blood pressure is increased (or based on other parameters such as central venous pressure or pulmonary wedge pressure).[125,163] Although serum sodium can be high, normal, or low at presentation,[165,166,172,173] when dehydration is severe, hypernatremia invariably develops. Half-normal saline is usually the treatment of choice for further replacement (250 to 500 mL/h)[178] and can be used immediately if the blood pressure is normal at presentation.[165,166] One half of the water deficit should be corrected over the first 12 hours and then the remainder by 36 hours.[163,165,179] Rates of fluid replacement should be lower in elderly patients or those with known cardiac disease.

How Should Insulin Be Administered?

Patients can be treated successfully without insulin.[166] However, in the majority of published reports, patients with HNKS were treated with insulin at similar doses used in DKA. There are no prospective studies that have addressed this issue, and targets of insulin therapy are unknown. Precipitous drops in serum potassium and the development of hypovolemic shock were reported following the use of high-dose insulin therapy in patients with HNKS. Therefore, if used, low-dose insulin regimens are preferred (IV bolus 0.1 U/kg body weight, then 0.1 U/kg/h), and IV dextrose should be added when glucose levels approach 14 mmol/L or less.[117,163] Regardless of insulin dosage, if hydration is inadequate, glucose levels will fail to decline. Therefore, rehydration constitutes the single most important aspect of treatment for these patients (Table 7–10). Although unproven, insulin therapy may be helpful in low doses.

How Should Potassium Be Administered?

Potassium deficits are equivalent to or higher in HNKS than in DKA (300 to 500 meq).[178] Patients on diuretics are at particular risk of hypokalemia. Hypokalemia is exacerbated by

---

Table 7–11 Predictors of Mortality from the Hyperosmolar Nonketotic State

---

Clinical Features

    Advanced age*

    Hypotension

    Hypothermia

    Coma

    Greater insulin requirements

    Delay in therapy

Biochemical Features

    ↑Blood glucose

    ↑Urea*

    ↑Osmolality*

---

*Independent predictors on multivariate analysis.

insulin therapy (causing a shift of potassium into cells), IV fluid administration (dilution), and ongoing urinary losses. Therefore, IV KCl (10 to 40 meq/L) should be added to each liter of replacement fluid as soon as serum potassium levels are < 5.5 meq/L[163,177] (see Table 7–10).

What Is the Prognosis for Patients with the Hyperosmolar Nonketotic State?

Are Patients with the Hyperosmolar Nonketotic State at Risk for Specific Complications?

Complicating illnesses, such as pneumonia, gastrointestinal bleeding, renal failure, stroke, and pulmonary embolus, occur in up to 30% of hospitalizations for HNKS.[165] Suggested use of low-dose subcutaneous heparin for the prevention of thromboembolic events[163] has not been systematically evaluated in this population. In a cohort study, patients with HNKS (n = 16) who received prophylactic subcutaneous heparin had lower mortality rates than those who did not ($p < .05$).[180] However, no deaths were attributed to thromboembolic disease, and differences in other clinical factors (such as a lower level of consciousness) may have led to lower rates of heparin administration in patients who subsequently died.

    Mortality from HNKS is exceedingly high. Earlier series published mortality rates approaching 58%.[155,165] More recent studies report rates as low as 12 to 17%[156,158,164] but included patients with mixed DKA and hyperosmolality. About 50% of deaths occur in the first 48 to 72 hours. Severe metabolic abnormalities contribute to early mortality; however, the majority of deaths that occur after 48 hours are due to underlying acute illnesses.[168,169,172] There are a number of clinical features that may confer a higher risk for mortality. In univariate analyses, various measures of clinical severity (such as hypotension,[169,172,175] hypothermia, [169,172] coma,[169,172] higher urea or glucose levels,[169,172,175] greater insulin requirements,[169,172,175] and greater delays in therapy[165,170]) are related to mortality. However, only advanced age,[164] high osmolality,[164] and elevated urea levels[175] were independent predictors of mortality in a multivariate model (Table 7–11).

How Should Patients Be Treated following the Hyperosmolar Nonketotic State?

In three series, less than one-third of survivors remained on insulin following discharge; however, the length of follow-up was unavailable.[155,165,166] Factors that determine insulin requirements following HNKS have not been established. Due to the low incidence of HNKS, no studies have evaluated the role of prevention. Patient education and adherence to treatment may prove valuable in decreasing the risk of HNKS in patients with preexisting diabetes. Moreover, elderly patients, particularly those in nursing homes, should be monitored closely for hydration status and receive prompt treatment for infections. Since one-third of cases occur as an initial presentation of diabetes, more rigorous screening programs to identify individuals with Type 2 diabetes may have an impact on the incidence of HNKS.

EVIDENCE-BASED MESSAGES

1. Risk factors for HNKS include older age, female gender, previously undiagnosed diabetes, and the presence of acute infection (Level 4).[164]
2. The diagnosis is based on the presence of hyperglycemia (>33 mmol/L [600 mg/dL]) and hyperosmolality (> 320 mOsm/L) in the absence of ketoacidosis. Virtually all patients have impaired consciousness (Level 4).[169]
3. The mainstay of treatment is IV hydration (the usual deficit is 8 to 12 liters) (Level 4).[165]
4. Published mortality rates range from 12 to 58%; advanced age and higher serum osmolality and urea levels are poor predictors (Level 4).[164]

ARE PATIENTS WITH NEWLY DIAGNOSED DIABETES MORE PRONE TO INFECTION?

Patients with diabetes appear to be prone to a variety of infections, although few epidemiologic studies have carefully evaluated this relationship. Nevertheless, a host of immune defects have been described in both animal and in vitro models, from impaired neutrophil function (chemotaxis, phagocytosis, and bactericidal activity) to complement activation and cell-mediated immunity.[181,182] Humoral immunity appears to be intact, as evidenced by a normal response to immunization.[183]

Infections of the skin and soft tissue are particularly common in patients with diabetes[184–189] and may be the first manifestation of the disease.[189,190] In a large series, 21% of patients admitted to hospital with cellulitis, who had no prior history of diabetes, demonstrated abnormal glucose tolerance.[191] Previously undiagnosed diabetes was also more common among patients presenting to an emergency department with skin sepsis compared to controls; however, the numbers were too few to reach statistical significance.[191] Cutaneous fungal infections appear to be more common in patients with diabetes when compared with healthy young adults (26 to 32% vs 7 to 9%) but not in comparison to older patients with chronic disease.[185–187]

The genitourinary tract is another common site of infection for patients with diabetes. Asymptomatic bacteriuria occurs more frequently in patients with diabetes than in controls.[192] Because of the high propensity for upper urinary tract involvement and associated complications among diabetic individuals,[193] treatment of asymptomatic infection is recommended for this patient group.[192] Patients with diabetes are also susceptible to colonization of the urinary tract with *Candida*, although this is usually self-limited and does not require specific treatment.[194] In contrast, vaginal candidiasis is a common problem for women with diabetes, particularly among younger age groups. In one survey, up to 60% of diabetic women under age 40 reported episodes in the preceding year.[195]

From observational data, it appears that patients with diabetes have a heightened susceptibility to specific infectious agents. For example, diabetes is an independent risk factor for community-acquired adult group B streptococcal disease (OR 3.0 [1.9 to 4.7])[196] and for infection with *Salmonella enteritidis* (OR 3.1 [1.1 to 8.6]).[197] Patients with diabetes are also more likely to develop pneumonia due to atypical microorganisms, such as *Staphylococcus aureus*,[198] *Klebsiella pneumoniae*,[198] and *Legionella pneumophila* (legionnaires' disease: OR 1.89[199]). In contrast, the frequency of pneumococcal pneumonia is unaltered by the presence of diabetes, despite a higher rate of concomitant bacteremia.[200,201]

Table 7–12 Risk Factors for Infection in Diabetes

Site	Risk Factor	Study
Skin/soft tissue	Vascular disease/neuropathy	Bosshardt et al[219]
	Drug & alcohol abuse	Elliott et al[220]
	↓Immune function	Gupta et al[185]
UTI	Instrumentation	Patterson et al[192]
	Bladder dysfunction	
	Urinary tract obstruction	
Septic arthritis	Age > 80 y	Kaandorp et al[207]
	Joint disease/prosthesis	
	Skin infection	
Tuberculosis	↑Age	Pablos-Mendez et al[212]
	Ethnicity (Caucasian/Hispanic)	
	Poor glycemic control	
	Chronic renal insufficiency	
	HIV-positive	
	Drug & alcohol abuse	
ROCM	Poor glycemic control	Bosshardt et al[219]
	Ketoacidosis	Peterson et al[226]
	↓Immune function	
	Renal failure	
MOE	↑Age	Doroghazi et al[231]
	Travel to warm climate	Babiatzki et al[232]
	Hearing aid	
EPN	Poor glycemic control	Pontin et al[235]
	Ketoacidosis	Patel et al[236]
	Females	
	Urinary tract obstruction	
Emphysematous	Males	Landau et al[237]
Cholecystitis	Vascular disease	Roslyn et al[238]

UTI = urinary tract infection; ROCM = rhino-orbital-cerebral mucormycosis; MOE = malignant otitis externa; EPN = emphysematous pyelonephritis.

Several retrospective studies report higher rates of bacteremia[200–204] due to gram-positive (usually *S. aureus*[205,206]) or gram-negative organisms[204] among individuals with diabetes. Virtually any infection involving *S. aureus* (skin/soft tissue,[206] septic arthritis,[207] bursitis,[208] or vertebral osteomyelitis[209]) occurs more commonly in patients with diabetes. Other infectious agents may have a higher propensity for hematogenenous dissemination in patients with diabetes. For example, diabetes was the most frequent underlying disease in a series of patients with septic endophthalmitis and other complications associated with *K. pneumoniae* liver absess.[210] Studies suggest that diabetes is also a common cause of reactivation tuberculosis.[211] In the United States, Pablos-Mendez and colleagues discovered a strong association between diabetes and hospitalization for active tuberculosis among most ethnic groups (highest OR 2.95 [2.61 to 3.33]).[212]

Thus, overall, this evidence points to a higher rate of infections in diabetic than in nondiabetic individuals. Susceptibility varies depending on the site of infection and etiologic agent. Reasons for this selectivity are not clear. Patients with diabetes have higher rates of nasal colonization with *S. aureus*,[213] explaining their predisposition to staphylococcal infection. Other host factors likely play a role in determining the sensitivity to specific microorganisms.

What Are the Risk Factors for Infections?

Epidemiologic data have been unable to clearly establish a role for hyperglycemia in the development of routine infections. Moreover, glycemic control becomes unstable during times of infection, hindering any comparisons. In a retrospective study by Rayfield and colleagues,[214] preceding mean plasma glucose levels in patients with diabetes (during times when infection was not present) were significantly related to the subsequent development of acute infection. The results were not adjusted for possible risk factors; however, the frequency of infection was unrelated to age, duration of diabetes, or the presence of diabetic complications.[214] Other retrospective analyses suggest an association between elevated HbA_{1C} levels and the risk of mucocutaneous fungal infections,[184,195] whereas well-controlled patients are not at increased risk.[215] An association between *Mycobacterium tuberculosis* infection and glycemic control may also exist; patients with poor control or complications (identified through administrative data) faced significantly higher odds of being hospitalized for acute tuberculosis across all races, but the relationship is most marked among specific ethnic groups (OR 5.73 [4.78-6.87] for Hispanic Americans).[212] The most compelling evidence comes from prospective studies of glycemic control during coronary artery bypass surgery. Aggressive perioperative insulin therapy led to enhanced neutrophil function[216] and diminished the risk of postoperative wound infections.[217] Further, a retrospective analysis found that elevated glucose levels predicted the development of sternal wound infection.[218] These findings highly suggest a causal relationship between hyperglycemia and the development of infection.

Apart from glycemic control, there are a number of factors that may render patients with diabetes more prone to infection (Table 7–12). By altering both glucose levels and pH, DKA may provide an environment that favors the growth of specific microorganisms. Long-term complications, such as vascular disease and neuropathy, likely also play a role. The former may impede delivery of oxygen and inflammatory cells to the involved area, while the latter results in loss of function (such as bladder stasis in the case of diabetic uropathy, leading to higher rates of urinary tract infection).[192] In one study, vascular insufficiency, in addition to other characteristics (family history and use of immunosuppressive agents), independently predicted the risk of cutaneous infection.[185] Patients with diabetes also share common risk factors for infection as patients without diabetes, such as alcohol or parenteral drug abuse in the case of cellulitis and necrotizing fasciitis.[219,220] Hence, both diabetic and nondiabetic factors appear to increase the risk of infection.

Are There Infections That Are Unique to Patients with Diabetes?

Certain necrotizing infections occur almost exclusively in patients with diabetes. Rhino-orbital-cerebral mucormycosis (ROCM) is an uncommon but frequently fatal fungal infection that spreads from the nasal mucosa to surrounding structures (orbit, cavernous sinus, and brain). Lethargy, facial pain, and local swelling precede the development of progressive ocular findings. This infection occurs predominantly in patients with diabetes (72% of cases),[221–228] frequently in the setting of DKA. Mortality rates are lower for patients with diabetes than for other risk groups,[221,226] particularly with the use of combination amphotericin B and surgical débridement.[221]

Malignant otitis externa (MOE) is another necrotizing infection (usually caused by *Pseudomonus aeruginosa*) that involves the external ear canal and progresses to the mastoid air cells, temporal bone, or skull base. The clinical presentation is usually subacute, consisting of otalgia, otorrhea, fever, and local swelling and less commonly of cranial nerve palsies. Approximately 80 to 90% of cases occur in patients with diabetes; however, no clear relationship between glucose levels and MOE has been established.[229–234] Elderly patients are at increased risk (average age, 69 years); however, patients can develop MOE at any age (range 11 to 92 years). Occasionally, MOE is the first manifestation of diabetes.[231,232] With appropriate antibiotic therapy and surgical débridement, the mortality rate has fallen from as high as 46%[229] to < 15%.[231–233]

Emphysematous pyelonephritis is a rare gas-forming infection of the renal collecting system and surrounding tissues, occurring almost exclusively in patients with diabetes (92%).[235,236] The syndrome usually develops following a more typical urinary tract infection; however, the reason for progression is unknown. It occurs more frequently in women and in the setting of urinary tract obstruction (one-third of cases). Glycemic control may play a role. Many patients have elevated glucose levels at the time of admission (82%) or a history of poor glycemic control,[235,236] and many cases occur in the setting of DKA. In contrast, emphysematous cholecystitis, a similar type of infection involving the gallbladder, is more common in males, possibly due to a higher prevalence of vascular disease. Approximately 35% of cases involve patients with diabetes[237,238]; however, the influence of glycemic control is unknown.[181]

In summary, several severe, life-threatening infections are associated with diabetes and in some cases occur almost exclusively in this population. These infections tend to develop in the setting of poor glycemic control with or without concomitant ketoacidosis, suggesting a causative role for hyperglycemia and other local host factors.

EVIDENCE-BASED MESSAGES

1. Fungal and bacterial infections are more common in patients with diabetes (Level 4)[185,204] and may be a presenting feature (Level 4).[190]
2. Poor glycemic control appears to increase the risk of sporadic (Level 4)[214,235] and postoperative (Level 3)[217] infections.

CONCLUSION

The onset of Type 1 diabetes is heralded by progressive symptoms of hyperglycemia; however, patients with Type 2 diabetes may remain asymptomatic for years. Clinical features (age, BMI, presence of symptoms, or ketonuria) can discriminate between the two subtypes in the majority of cases. In atypical cases, other forms of testing (C-peptide and autoantibody measurements) may be useful in predicting the subsequent clinical course. In addition to symptoms, patients with diabetes may experience a lower QOL than nondiabetic individuals; albeit on a short-term basis, the effect of glycemic control on QOL appears to be negligible. Other acute manifestations of diabetes include DKA and the HNKS, both of which are potentially life threatening and require immediate medical attention. Patients with diabetes are susceptible to certain types of infections. Although not well studied, a portion of this risk may be directly attributed to hyperglycemia.

SUMMARY OF EVIDENCE-BASED MESSAGES

1. The vast majority of patients presenting under the age of 40 who have an ideal body weight (or less) have Type 1 diabetes. Patients over the age of 40 who are overweight (BMI greater than 100% of ideal) usually have Type 2 diabetes (Level 3).[16]
2. In patients with presumed Type 2 diabetes, anti-GAD and/or islet cell antibodies can help in predicting subsequent insulin requirement (Level 1).[23]
3. C-peptide assessments appear to have a greater sensitivity and specificity than clinical or other biochemical features in differentiating Type 1 and Type 2 diabetes (Level 3).[16]

4. Overall quality of life is impaired for patients with diabetes (Level 4),[33] although to a similar extent as patients with other chronic diseases (Level 4).[49]

5. In the short term, intensive therapy does not improve QOL for patients with Type 1 (Level 1)[67] or Type 2 diabetes (Level 1),[45] possibly because of adverse effects from hypoglycemia, weight gain, and a more challenging self-care regimen.

6. Therapy of some of the chronic complications of diabetes may improve QOL (Level 1).[52] Long-term improvements in glycemic control would be expected to enhance QOL; however, such trials are lacking.

7. Targeted behavioral programs may improve QOL (Level 2).[79,80]

8. Among patients treated with intensive regimens, continuous subcutaneous insulin infusion is associated with a greater risk of DKA (Level 1A).[104]

9. The treatment of DKA includes IV fluids (normal saline: 500 mL/h for 4 hours, then 250 mL/h (Level 2)[124] or half-normal saline; higher rates in cases of hypotension), low-dose continuous insulin infusion (0.1 U regular insulin/kg bolus then 0.1 U/kg/h) (Level 2),[130] and adequate potassium replacement.

10. Bicarbonate therapy (Level 2)[143] and phosphate replacement (Level 2)[149] have no additional benefit, but IV bicarbonate may be considered for a $pH \leq 6.9$ to 7.0.

11. Mortality from DKA ranges from 0.65 to 3.3% (Level 4),[89] with higher rates in older patients (Level 4).[160]

12. Risk factors for HNKS include older age, female gender, previously undiagnosed diabetes, and the presence of acute infection (Level 4).[164]

13. The diagnosis of HNKS is based on the presence of hyperglycemia (> 33 mmol/L [600 mg/dL]) and hyperosmolality (> 320 mOsm/L) in the absence of ketoacidosis. Virtually all patients have impaired consciousness (Level 4).[169]

14. The mainstay of treatment is IV hydration (the usual deficit is 8 to 12 liters [Level 4]).[165]

15. Published mortality rates range from 12 to 58%; advanced age and higher serum osmolality are poor predictors (Level 4).[164]

16. Fungal and bacterial infections are more common in patients with diabetes (Level 4)[185,204] and may be a presenting feature (Level 4).[190]

17. Poor glycemic control appears to increase the risk of sporadic (Level 4)[214,235] and postoperative (Level 3)[217] infections.

REFERENCES

1. Laakso M, Pyörälä K. Age of onset and type of diabetes. Diabetes Care 1985;8:114–7.

2. Melton JL III, Palumbo PJ, Chu C-P. Incidence of diabetes mellitus by clinical type. Diabetes Care 1983;6:75–86.

3. Vandewalle CL, Coeckelberghs MI, De Leeuw IH, et al. Epidemiology, clinical aspects, and biology of IDDM patients under age 40 years. Comparison of data from Antwerp with complete ascertainment with data from Belgium with 40% ascertainment. The Belgian Diabetes Registry. Diabetes Care 1997;20:1556–61.

4. Karjalainen J, Salmela P, Ilonen J, et al. A comparison of childhood and adult type 1 diabetes mellitus. N Engl J Med 1989;320:881–6.

5. Yki-Järvinen H, Koivisto VA. Natural course of insulin resistance in type 1 diabetes. N Engl J Med 1986;315:224–30.

6. Scholin A, Berne C, Schvarcz E, et al. Factors predicting clinical remission in adult patients with type 1 diabetes. J Intern Med 1999;245:155–62.

7. Martin S, Pawlowski B, Greulich B, et al. Natural course of remission in IDDM during 1st yr after diagnosis. Diabetes Care 1992;15:66–74.

8. Harris MI, Klein R, Welborn TA, Knuiman MW. Onset of NIDDM occurs at least 4-7 yr before clinical diagnosis. Diabetes Care 1992;15:815–9.

9. Harris MI, Flegal KM, Cowie CC, et al. Prevalence of diabetes, impaired fasting glucose, and impaired glucose tolerance in U.S. adults. The Third National Health and Nutrition Examination Survey, 1988–1994. Diabetes Care 1998;21:518–24.

10. Levetan CS, Passaro M, Jablonski K, et al. Unrecognized diabetes among hospitalized patients. Diabetes Care 1998;21:246–9.

11. Bulpitt CJ, Palmer AJ, Battersby C, Fletcher AE. Association of symptoms of type 2 diabetic patients with severity of disease, obesity, and blood pressure. Diabetes Care 1998;21:111–5.

12. Niskanen L, Siitonen O, Karjalainen J, Uusitupa M. Hyperglycaemic symptoms before diagnosis of non-insulin-dependent (type 2) diabetes mellitus in relation to 5-year outcome. J Intern Med 1992;231:397–402.

13. Gambert S. Atypical presentation of diabetes mellitus in the elderly. Clin Geriatr Med 1990;6:721–9.

14. Ruige JB, de Neeling JN, Kostense PJ, et al. Performance of an NIDDM screening questionnaire based on symptoms and risk factors. Diabetes Care 1997;20:491–6.

15. Hiltunen L, Keinanen-Kiukaanniemi S, Laara E, Kivela SL. Self-perceived health and symptoms of elderly persons with diabetes and impaired glucose tolerance. Age Ageing 1996;25:59–66.

16. Hother-Nielsen O, Faber O, Schwartz Sørensen N, Beck-Nielsen H. Classification of newly diagnosed diabetic patients as insulin-requiring or non-insulin-requiring based on clinical and biochemical variables. Diabetes Care 1988;11:531–7.

17. MacIver DH, McNally PG, Shaw DE, Hearnshaw JF. Predicting future treatment of diabetes mellitus from characteristics available at presentation. Diabet Med 1988;5:766–70.

18. Welborn TA, Garica-Webb P, Bonser AM. Basal C-peptide in the discrimination of type 1 from Type 2 diabetes. Diabetes Care 1981;4:616–9.

19. Koskinen P, Viikari J, Irjala K, Kaihola HL, Seppälä P. C-peptide determination in the choice of treatment in diabetes mellitus. Scand J Clin Lab Invest 1985;45:589–97.

20. Hoekstra JBL, van Rijn HJM, Thijssen JHH, Erkelens DW. C-peptide reactivity as a measure of insulin dependency in obese diabetic patients treated with insulin. Diabetes Care 1982;5:585–91.

21. Groop LC, Bottazzo GF, Doniach D. Islet cell antibodies identify latent type 1 diabetes in patients aged 35–75 years at diagnosis. Diabetes 1986;35:237–41.

22. Zimmet P, Turner R, McCarty D, et al. Crucial points at diagnosis. Type 2 diabetes or slow type 1 diabetes. Diabetes Care 1999;22(Suppl 2):B59–64.

23. Turner R, Stratton I, Horton V, et al. UKPDS 25: autoantibodies to islet-cell cytoplasm and glutamic acid decarboxylase for prediction of insulin requirement in type 2 diabetes. Lancet 1997;350:1288–93.

24. Tuomi T, Groop LC, Zimmet PZ, et al. Antibodies to glutamic acid decarboxylase reveal latent autoimmune diabetes mellitus in adults with a non-insulin-dependent onset of disease. Diabetes 1993;42:358–62.

25. Gottsäter A, Landin-Olsson M, Lernmark Å, et al. Glutamate decarboxylase antibody levels predict rate of β-cell decline in adult-onset diabetes. Diabetes Res Clin Pract 1995;27:133–40.

26. Hagopian WA, Karlsen AW, Gottsäter A, et al. Quantitative assay using recombinant human islet glutamic acid decarboxylase (GAD65) show that 65k autoantibody positivity at onset predicts diabetes type. J Clin Invest 1993;91:368–74.

27. Humphrey ARG, McCarty DJ, Mackay IR, et al. Autoantibodies to glutamic acid decarboxylase and phenotypic features associated with early insulin treatment in individuals with adult-onset diabetes mellitus. Diabet Med 1998;15:113–9.

28. Rubin RR, Peyrot M. Psychosocial problems and intervention in diabetes. Diabetes Care 1992;15:1640–57.

29. Wells KB, Golding JM, Burnam MA. Affective, substance use, and anxiety disorders in persons with arthritis, diabetes, heart disease, high blood pressure, or chronic lung conditions. Gen Hosp Psychiatry 1989;11:320–7.

30. Gavard JA, Lustman PJ, Clouse RE. Prevalence of depression in adults with diabetes: an epidemiologic evaluation. Diabetes Care 1993;16:1167–78.

31. Lloyd CE, Wing RR, Orchard TJ, Becker DJ. Psychosocial correlates of glycemic control: the Pittsburgh Epidemiology of Diabetes Complications (EDC) study. Diabetes Res Clin Pract 1993;21:187–95.

32. Trief PM, Grant W, Elbert K, Weinstock RS. Family environment, glycemic control, and the psychosocial adaptation of adults with diabetes. Diabetes Care 1998;21:241–5.

33. Caldwell EM, Baxter J, Mitchell CM, et al. The association of non-insulin-dependent diabetes mellitus with perceived quality of life in a biethnic population: the San Luis Valley Diabetes Study. Am J Public Health 1998;88:1225–9.

34. Lloyd CE, Matthew KA, Wing RR, Orchard TJ. Psychosocial factors and complications of IDDM. The Pittsburgh Epidemiology of Diabetes Complications Study. VIII. Diabetes Care 1992;15:166–72.

35. Parkerson GR Jr, Connis RT, Broadhead WE, et al. Disease-specific versus generic measurement of health-related quality of life in insulin-dependent diabetic patients. Med Care 1993;31:629–39.

36. Johnson JA, Nowatzki TE, Coons ST. Health-related quality of life of diabetic Pima Indians. Med Care 1996; 34:97–102.

37. Kohen D, Burgess AP, Catalán J, Lant A. The role of anxiety and depression in quality of life and symptom reporting in people with diabetes mellitus. Qual Life Res 1998;7:197–204.

38. Jacobson AM, deGroot M, Samson JA. The effects of psychiatric disorders and symptoms on quality of life in patients with Type 1 and Type 2 diabetes mellitus. Qual Life Res 1997;6:11–20.

39. Hanestad BR, Hörnquist JO, Albrektsen G. Self-assessed quality of life and metabolic control in persons with insulin-dependent diabetes mellitus (IDDM). Scand J Soc Med 1991;19:57–65.

40. Hanestad BR. Self-reported quality of life and the effect of different clinical and demographic characteristics in people with type 1 diabetes. Diabetes Res Clin Pract 1993;19:139–49.

41. Wikby, A, Hörnquist JO, Andersson PO. Background, quality of life and metabolic control in patients with insulin-dependent diabetes mellitus. Diabetes Res Clin Pract 1991;13:53–62.

42. Jacobson AM, DeGroot M, Samson JA. The evaluation of two measures of quality of life in patients with Type 1 and Type 2 diabetes. Diabetes Care 1994;17:267–74.

43. Anderson RM, Fitzgerald JT, Wisdom K, et al. A comparison of global versus disease-specific quality-of-life measures in patients with NIDDM. Diabetes Care 1997;20:299–305.

44. Benbow SJ, Wallymahmed ME, MacFarlane IA. Diabetic peripheral neuropathy and quality of life. QJM 1998; 91:733–7.

45. UK Prospective Diabetes Study Group. Quality of life in type 2 diabetic patients is affected by complications but not by intensive policies to improve blood glucose or blood pressure control (UKPDS 37). Diabetes Care 1999;22:1125–36.

46. Wändell PE, Brorsson B, Åberg H. Quality of life among diabetic patients in Swedish primary health care and in the general population: comparison between 1992 and 1995. Qual Life Res 1998;7:751–60.

47. Næss S, Midthjell K, Torbjøm M, et al. Diabetes mellitus and psychological well-being. Results of the Nord-Trøndelag health survey. Scand J Soc Med 1995;3:179–88.

48. Rose M, Burkert U, Scholler G, et al. Determinants of the quality of life of patients with diabetes under intensified insulin therapy. Diabetes Care 1998;21:1876–85.

49. Stewart AL, Greenfield S, Hays RD, et al. Functional status and well-being of patients with chronic conditions: results from the Medical Outcomes Study. JAMA 1989;262:907–13.

50. Wikblad K, Leksell J, Wibell L. Health-related quality of life in relation to metabolic control and late complications in patients with insulin dependent diabetes mellitus. Qual Life Res 1996;5:123–30.

51. Ahroni JH, Boyko EJ, Davignon DR, Pecoraro RE. The health and functional status of veterans with diabetes. Diabetes Care 1994;17:318–21.

52. Farup CE, Leidy NK, Murray M, et al. Effect of domperidone on the health-related quality of life of patients with symptoms of diabetic gastroparesis. Diabetes Care 1998;21:1699–706.

53. Harati Y, Gooch C, Swenson M, et al. Double-blind randomized trial of tramadol for the treatment of the pain of diabetic neuropathy. Neurology 1998;50:1842–6.

54. Backonja M, Beydoun A, Edwards KR, et al for the Gabapentin Diabetic Neuropathy Study Group. Gabapentin for the symptomatic treatment of painful neuropathy in patients with diabetes mellitus. JAMA 1998;21:1831–6.

55. Testa MA, Simonson CD. Health economic benefits and quality of life during improved glycemic control in patients with type 2 diabetes mellitus. JAMA 1998;280:1490–6.

56. Trief PM, Grant W, Elbert K, Weinstock RS. Family environment, glycemic control, and the psychosocial adaptation of adults with diabetes. Diabetes Care 1998;21:241–5.

57. Kaplan RM, Hartwell SL, Wilson DK, Wallace JP. Effects of diet and exercise interventions on control and quality of life in non-insulin-dependent diabetes mellitus. J Gen Intern Med 1987;2:220–8.

58. Mayou R, Bryant B, Turner R. Quality of life in non-insulin-dependent diabetes and a comparison with insulin-dependent diabetes. J Psychosom Res 1990;34:1–11.

59. Van der Does FEE, De Neeling JND, Snoek FJ, et al. Symptoms and well-being in relation to glycemic control in Type 2 diabetes. Diabetes Care 1996;19:204–10.

60. Klein R, Klein BEK. Relation of glycemic control to diabetic complications and health outcomes. Diabetes Care 1998;21(Suppl 3):C39–43.

61. Mazze RS, Lucido D, Shamoon H. Psychological and social correlates of glycemic control. Diabetes Care 1984;7:360–6.

62. Weinberger M, Kirkman S, Samsa GP, et al. The relationship between glycemic control and health-related quality of life in patients with non-insulin-dependent diabetes mellitus. Med Care 1994;32:1173–81.

63. de Sonnaville JJ, Snoek FJ, Colly LP, et al. Well-being and symptoms in relation to insulin therapy in type 2 diabetes. Diabetes Care 1998;21:919–24.

64. Petterson T, Lee P, Hollis S, et al. Well-being and treatment satisfaction in older people with diabetes. Diabetes Care 1998;21:930–5.

65. DCCT Research Group. Reliability and validity of a diabetes quality-of-life measure for the Diabetes Control and Complications Trial (DCCT). Diabetes Care 1988;11:725–32.

66. Diabetes Control and Complications Trial Research Group. The effect of intensive treatment of diabetes on the development and progression of long-term complications in insulin-dependent diabetes mellitus. N Engl J Med 1993;329:977–86.

67. DCCT Research Group. Influence of intensive diabetes treatment on quality-of-life outcomes in the diabetes control and complications trial. Diabetes Care 1996;19:195–203.

68. Nathan DM, Fogel N, Norman D, et al. Long-term metabolic and quality-of-life results with pancreatic/renal transplantation in insulin-dependent diabetes mellitus. Transplantation 1991;55:85–91.

69. Kotsanos JG, Vignati L, Huster W, et al. Health-related quality results from multinational clinical trials of insulin lispro. Assessing benefits of a new diabetes therapy. Diabetes Care 1997;20:948–58.

70. Saudek CD, Duckworth WC, Giobbie-Hurder A, et al. Department of Veterans Affairs Implantable Insulin Pump Study Group. Implantable insulin pump vs multiple-dose insulin for non-insulin-dependent diabetes mellitus: a randomized clinical trial. JAMA 1996;276:1322–7.

71. Bech P, Gudex C, Staehr Johansen K. The WHO (Ten) Well-Being Index: validation in diabetes. Psychother Psychosom 1996;65:183–90.

72. Haardt M-J, Selam J-L, Slama G, et al. A cost-benefit comparison of intensive diabetes management with implantable pumps versus multiple subcutaneous injections in patients with type 1 diabetes. Diabetes Care 1994;17:847–51.

73. Selam J-L, Micossi P, Dunn FL, Nathan DM, Implantable Insulin Pump Trial Study Group. Clinical trial of programmable implantable insulin pump for type 1 diabetes. Diabetes Care 1992;15:877–85.

74. Tallroth G, Karlson B, Nisson A, Agardh C-D. The influence of different insulin regimens on quality of life and metabolic control in insulin-dependent diabetics. Diabetes Res Clin Pract 1989;6:37–43.

75. Tilly KF, Belton AB, McLachlan JF. Continuous monitoring of health status outcomes: experience with a diabetes education program. Diabetes Educator 1995;21:413–9.

76. Kinmonth AL, Woodcock A, Griffin S, et al on behalf of The Diabetes Care From Diagnosis Research Team. Randomised controlled trial of patient centred care of diabetes in general practice: impact on current wellbeing and future disease risk. BMJ 1998;317:1202–8.

77. Weinberger M, Kirkman MS, Samsa GP, et al. A nurse-coordinated intervention for primary care patients with non-insulin-dependent diabetes mellitus: impact on glycemic control and health-related quality of life. J Gen Intern Med 1995;10:59–66.

78. Hanestad BR, Albrektsen G. The effects of participation in a support group on self assessed quality of life in people with insulin dependent diabetes mellitus (IDDM). Diabetes Res Clin Pract 1993;19:163–73.

79. Grey M, Boland EA, Davidson M, et al. Short-term effects of coping skills training as adjunct to intensive therapy in adolescents. Diabetes Care 1998;21:902–8.

80. Greenfield S, Kaplan SH, Ware JE, et al. Patients' participation in medical care: effects on blood sugar control and quality of life in diabetes. J Gen Intern Med 1988;3:448–57.

81. Faich GA, Fishbein HA, Ellis SE. The epidemiology of diabetic acidosis: a population-based study. Am J Epidemiol 1983;117:551–8.

82. Johnson DD, Palumbo PJ, Chu C-P. Diabetic ketoacidosis in a community-based population. Mayo Clin Proc 1980;55:83–88.

83. Ellemann K, Soerensen JN, Pedersen LJ, et al. Epidemiology and treatment of diabetic ketoacidosis in a community population. Diabetes Care 1984;7:528–32.

84. Wetterhall SF, Olson DR, De Stefano F, et al. Trends in diabetes and diabetic complications, 1980–87. Diabetes Care 1992;15:960–7.

85. Snorgaard O, Eskildsen PC, Vadstrup S, Nerup J. Diabetic ketoacidosis in Denmark: epidemiology, incidence rates, precipitating factors and mortality rates. J Intern Med 1989;226:223–8.

86. Gouin PE, Gossain VV, Rovner DR. Diabetic ketoacidosis: outcome in a community hospital. South Med J 1985;78:941–3.

87. Sheppard MC, Wright AD. The effect on mortality of low-dose insulin therapy for diabetic ketoacidosis. Diabetes Care 1982;5:111–3.

88. Bagg W, Sathu A, Streat S, Braatvedt GD. Diabetic ketoacidosis in adults at Auckland Hospital, 1988–1996. Aust N Z J Med 1998;28:604–8.

89. May ME, Young C, King J. Resource utilization in treatment of diabetic ketoacidosis in adults. Am J Med Sci 1993;306:287–94.

90. Faigel DG, Metz DC. Prevalence, etiology, and prognostic significance of upper gastrointestinal hemorrhage in diabetic ketoacidosis. Dig Dis Sci 1996;41:1–8.

91. Morris AD, Boyle DIR, McMahon AD, et al, for the DARTS/MEMO Collaboration. Adherence to insulin treatment, glycaemic control, and ketoacidosis in insulin-dependent diabetes mellitus. Lancet 1997;350:1505–10.

92. Umpierrez GE, Kelly JP, Navarrete JE, et al. Hyperglycemic crises in urban blacks. Arch Intern Med 1997;157:669–75.

93. Musey VC, Lee JK, Crawford R, et al. Diabetes in urban African-Americans. I. Cessation of insulin therapy is the major precipitating cause of diabetic ketoacidosis. Diabetes Care 1995;18:483–9.

94. Warner EA, Greene GS, Buchsbaum MS, et al. Diabetic ketoacidosis associated with cocaine use. Arch Intern Med 1998;158:1799–1802.

95. Fishbein HA. Precipitants of hospitalization in insulin-dependent diabetes mellitus (IDDM): a statewide perspective. Diabetes Care 1985;8(Suppl 1):61–4.

96. Müllhauser I, Bruckner I, Berger M, et al. Evaluation of an intensified insulin treatment and teaching program as routine management of type 1 (insulin-dependent) diabetes. Diabetologia 1987;30:681–90.

97. Westphal SA. The occurrence of diabetic ketoacidosis in non-insulin-dependent diabetes and newly diagnosed diabetic adults. Am J Med 1986;101:19–24.

98. Fulop M. Recurrent diabetic ketoacidosis. Am J Med 1985;78:54–60.

99. Palta M, LeCaire T, Daniels K, et al, for the Wisconsin Diabetes Registry. Risk factors for hospitalization in a cohort with type 1 diabetes. Am J Epidemiol 1997;146:627–36.

100. Wilson BE, Sharma A. Public cost and access to primary care for hyperglycemic emergencies, Clark County, Nevada. J Community Health 1995;20:249–56.

101. Javor KA, Kotsanos JG, McDonald RC, et al. Diabetic ketoacidosis charges relative to medical charges of adult patients with type 1 diabetes. Diabetes Care 1997;20:349–54.

102. Stephenson J, Fuller JH, on behalf of the EURODIAB IDDM Complications Study Group. Microvascular and acute complications in IDDM patients: the EURODIAB complications study. Diabetologia 1994;37:278–85.

103. Diabetes Control and Complications Trial Research Group. Adverse events and their association with treatment regimens in the Diabetes Control and Complications Trial. Diabetes Care 1995;18:1415–27.

104. Egger M, Davey Smith G, Stettler C, Diem P. Risk of adverse effects of intensified treatment in insulin-dependent diabetes mellitus: a meta-analysis. Diabet Med 1997;14:919–28.

105. Pinhas-Hamiel O, Donlan LM, Zeitler PS. Diabetic ketoacidosis among obese African-American adolescents with NIDDM. Diabetes Care 1997;20:484–6.

106. Banerji MA, Lebovitz HE. Remission in non-insulin-dependent diabetes mellitus: clinical characteristics of remission and relapse in black patients. Medicine 1990;69:176–85.

107. Banerji MA, Chaiken RL, Huey H, et al. GAD antibody negative NIDDM in adult black subjects with diabetic ketoacidosis and increased frequency of human leukocyte antigen DR3 and DR4. Flatbush diabetes. Diabetes 1994;43:741–5.

108. Umpierrez GE, Casals MMC, Gebhart SSP, et al. Diabetic ketoacidosis in obese African-Americans. Diabetes 1995;44:790–5.

109. Balasubramanyam A, Zern JW, Hyman DJ, Pavlik V. New profiles of diabetic ketoacidosis. Arch Intern Med 1999;159:2317–22.

110. Munro JF, Campbell IW, McCuish AC, Duncan LJP. Euglycaemic diabetic ketoacidosis. BMJ 1973;2:578–80.

111. Peden NR, Braaten JT, McKendry JBR. Diabetic ketoacidosis during long-term treatment with continuous subcutaneous insulin infusion. Diabetes Care 1984;7:1–5.

112. Paulson WD. Anion gap-bicarbonate relation in diabetic ketoacidosis. Am J Med 1986;81: 995–1000.

113. Fulop M, Tannenbaum H, Dreyer N. Ketotic hyperosmolar coma. Lancet 1973;2:635–9.

114. Soler NG, Fitzgerald MG, Bennett MA, Malins JM. Intensive care in the management of diabetic ketoacidosis. Lancet 1973;1:951–4.

115. Morris LR, Kitabchi AE. Efficacy of low-dose insulin therapy for severely obtunded patients in diabetic ketoacidosis. Diabetes Care 1980;3:53–6.

116. Lebovitz HE. Diabetic ketoacidosis. Lancet 1995;345:767–72.

117. Umpierrez GE, Khajavi M, Kitabchi AE. Review: diabetic ketoacidosis and hyperglycemic hyperosmolar nonketotic syndrome. Am J Med Sci 1996;311:225–33.

118. Kitabchi AE, Wall BM. Diabetic ketoacidosis. Med Clin North Am 1995;7:9–37.

119. Jenkins D, Close CF, Krentz AJ, et al. Euglycemic diabetic ketoacidosis: does it exist? Acta Diabetol 1993;30:251–3.

120. Elisaf MS, Tsatsoulis AA, Katopodis KP, Siamopoulos KC. Acid-base and electrolyte disturbances in patients with diabetic ketoacidosis. Diabetes Res Clin Pract 1996;34:23–7.

121. Adrogue HJ, Wilson H, Boyd III AE, et al. Plasma acid-base patterns in diabetic ketoacidosis. N Engl J Med 1982;307:1603–10.

122. Levetan CS, Jablonski KA, Passaro MD, Ratner RE. Effect of physician specialty on outcomes in diabetic ketoacidosis. Diabetes Care 1999;22:1790–5.

123. Waldhäusl W, Kleinberger G, Korn A, et al. Severe hyperglycemia: effects of rehydration on endocrine derangements and blood glucose concentration. Diabetes 1979;28:577–84.

124. Adrogue HJ, Barrero J, Eknoyan G. Salutary effects of modest fluid replacement in the treatment of adults with diabetic ketoacidosis. JAMA 1989;262:2108–13.

125. McCurdy DK. Hyperosmolar hyperglycemic nonketotic diabetic coma. Med Clin North Am 1970;54:683–99.

126. Owen OE, Licht JH, Sapir DG. Renal function and effects of partial rehydration during diabetic ketoacidosis. Diabetes 1981;30:510–8.

127. Kitabchi AE, Ayyagari V, Guerra SMO, and Medical House Staff. The efficacy of low dose versus conventional therapy of insulin for treatment of diabetic ketoacidosis. Ann Intern Med 1976;84:633–8.

128. Heber D, Molitch ME, Sperling MA. Low-dose continuous insulin therapy for diabetic ketoacidosis. Prospective comparison with "conventional" insulin therapy. Arch Intern Med 1977;137:1377–80.

129. Fisher JN, Shahshahani MN, Kitabchi AE. Diabetic ketoacidosis: low-dose insulin therapy by various routes. N Engl J Med 1977;297:238–41.

130. Sacks HS, Shahshahani M, Kitabchi AE, et al. Similar responsiveness of diabetic ketoacidosis and low-dose insulin by intramuscular injection and albumin-free infusion. Ann Intern Med 1979;90:36–42.

131. Butkiewicz EK, Leibson CL, O'Brien PC, et al. Insulin therapy for diabetic ketoacidosis. Bolus insulin injection versus continuous insulin infusion. Diabetes Care 1995;18:1187–90.

132. Brandt KR, Miles JM. Relationship between severity of hyperglycemia and metabolic acidosis in diabetic ketoacidosis. Mayo Clin Proc 1988;63:1071–4.

133. Wiggam MI, O'Kane MJ, Harper R, et al. Treatment of diabetic ketoacidosis using normalization of blood 3-hydroxybutyrate concentration as the endpoint of emergency management. Diabetes Care 1997;20:1347–52.

134. Krentz AJ, Hale PJ, Singh BM, Nattrass M. The effect of glucose and insulin infusion on the fall of ketone bodies during treatment of diabetic ketoacidosis. Diabet Med 1989;6:31–6.

135. Adrogue HF, Lederer ED, Suki WN, Eknoyan G. Determinants of plasma potassium levels in diabetic ketoacidosis. Medicine 1986;65:163–72.

136. Fulop M. Hyperkalemia in diabetic ketoacidosis. Am J Med Sci 1990;299:164–9.

137. Keller U. Diabetic ketoacidosis: current views on pathogenesis and treatment. Diabetologia 1986;29:71–7.

138. Foster DW, McGarry JD. The metabolic derangements and treatment of diabetic ketoacidosis. N Engl J Med 1983;309:159–69.

139. Soler NG, Bennet MA, Dixon K, et al. Potassium balance during treatment of diabetic ketoacidosis with special reference to the use of bicarbonate. Lancet 1972;2:665–7.

140. Kreisberg RA. Diabetic ketoacidosis: new concepts and trends in pathogenesis and treatment. Ann Intern Med 1978;88:681–95.

141. Matz R. Diabetic acidosis: rationale for not using bicarbonate. N Y State J Med 1976;76:1299–1303.

142. Morris LR, Murphy MB, Kitabchi AE. Bicarbonate therapy in severe diabetic ketoacidosis. Ann Intern Med 1986;105:836–40.

143. Gamba G, Oseguera J, Castrejon M, Gomez-Perez FJ. Bicarbonate therapy in severe diabetic ketoacidosis: a double blind, randomized placebo controlled trial. Rev Invest Clin 1991;43:234–48.

144. Hale PJ, Crase J, Nattrass M. Metabolic effects of bicarbonate in the treatment of diabetic ketoacidosis. BMJ 1984;289:1035–8.

145. Lever E, Jaspan JB. Sodium bicarbonate therapy in severe diabetic ketoacidosis. Am J Med 1983;75:263–8.

146. Viallon A, Zeni F, Lafond P, et al. Does bicarbonate therapy improve the management of severe diabetic ketoacidosis? Crit Care Med 1999;27:2690–3.

147. Wilson HK, Keuer SP, Lea AS, et al. Phosphate therapy in diabetic ketoacidosis. Arch Intern Med 1982;142:517–20.

148. Keller U, Berger W. Prevention of hypophosphatemia by phosphate infusion during treatment of diabetic ketoacidosis and hyperosmolar coma. Diabetes 1980;29:87–95.

149. Fisher JN, Kitabchi AE. A randomized study of phosphate therapy in the treatment of diabetic ketoacidosis. J Clin Endocrinol Metab 1983;57:177–80.

150. Umpierrez GE, Watts NB, Phillips LS. Clinical utility of β-hydroxybutyrate determined by reflectance meter in the management of diabetic ketoacidosis. Diabetes Care 1995;18:137–8.

151. Porter WH, Yao HH, Karounos DG. Laboratory and clinical evaluation of assays for β-hydroxybutyrate. Am J Clin Pathol 1997;107:353–8.

152. Rosenbloom AL. Intracerebral crises during treatment of diabetic ketoacidosis. Diabetes Care 1990;13:22–33.

153. Clements RS Jr, Blumenthal SA, Morrison AD, Winegrad AI. Increased cerebrospinal-fluid pressure during treatment of diabetic ketosis. Lancet 1971;2:657–61.

154. Fein IA, Rackow EC, Sprung CL, Grodman R. Relation of colloid osmotic pressure to arterial hypoxemia and cerebral edema during crystalloid volume loading of patients with diabetic ketoacidosis. Ann Intern Med 1982;96:570–5.

155. Beigelman PM. Severe diabetic ketoacidosis (diabetic "coma"). 482 episodes in 257 patients; experience of three years. Diabetes 1971;20:490–500.

156. Hamblin PS, Topliss DJ, Chosich N, et al. Deaths associated with diabetic ketoacidosis and hyperosmolar coma, 1973–1988; Med J Aust 1989;151:439–44.

157. Holman RC, Herron CA, Sinnock P. Epidemiologic characteristics of mortality from diabetes with acidosis or coma, United States, 1970-78. Am J Public Health 1983;73:1169–73.

158. Wachtel TJ, Tetu-Mouradjian LM, Goldman DL, et al. Hyperosmolarity and acidosis in diabetes mellitus: a three year experience in Rhode Island. J Gen Med 1991;6:495–502.

159. Carrol P, Matz R. Adult respiratory distress syndrome complicating severely uncontrolled diabetes mellitus: report of nine cases and a review of the literature. Diabetes Care 1982;5:574–80.

160. Malone ML, Gennis B, Goodwin JS. Characteristics of diabetic ketoacidosis in older versus younger adults. J Am Geriatr Soc 1992;40:1100–4.

161. Umpierrez GE, Clark WS, Steen MT. Sulfonylurea treatment prevents recurrence of hyperglycemia in obese African-American patients with a history of hyperglycemic crises. Diabetes Care 1997;20:479–83.

162. Fishbein HA. Acute metabolic complications in diabetes. In: Harris MI, Hamman RF, editors. Diabetes in America (National Diabetes Data Group). Washington (DC): Department of Health and Human Services; 1995. p.283–91.

163. Wachtel TJ. The diabetic hyperosmolar state. Clin Geriatr Med 1990;6:797–806.

164. Wachtel TJ, Silliman RA, Lamberton P. Predisposing factors for the diabetic hyperosmolar state. Arch Intern Med 1987;147:499–501.

165. Arieff AI, Carroll HJ. Nonketotic hyperosmolar coma with hyperglycemia: clinical features, pathophysiology, renal function, acid-base balance, plasma-cerebrospinal fluid equilibria and the effects of therapy in 37 cases. Medicine 1972;51:73–94.

166. Gerich JE, Martin MM, Recant LL. Clinical and metabolic characterisitics of hyperosmolar non-ketotic coma. Diabetes 1971;20:228–38.

167. Rimailho A, Riou B, Dadez E, et al. Prognostic factors in hyperglycemic hyperosmolar nonketotic sydrome. Crit Care Med 1986;14:552–4.

168. Khardori R, Soler NG. Hyperosmolar hyperglycemic nonketotic syndrome: report of 22 cases and brief review. Am J Med 1984;77:899–904.

169. Gale EAM, Dornan TL, Tattersall RB. Severely uncontrolled diabetes in the over-fifties. Diabetologia 1981;21:25–8.

170. Seki S. Clinical features of hyperosmolar hyperglycemic nonketotic diabetic coma associated with cardiac operations. J Thorac Cardiovasc Surg 1986;91:867–73.

171. Bendezu R, Wieland R, Furst B, et al. Experience with low-dose insulin infusion in diabetic ketoacidosis and diabetic hyperosmolarity. Arch Intern Med 1978;138:60–2.

172. Keller U, Berger W, Ritz R, Truog P. Course and prognosis of 86 episodes of diabetic coma: a five year experience with a uniform schedule of treatment. Diabetologia 1975;11:93–100.

173. Vinik A, Seftel H, Joffe BI. Metabolic findings in hyperosmolar, nonketotic diabetic stupor. Lancet 1970;2:797–9.

174. Fulop M, Rosenblatt A, Kreitzer SM, Gerstenhaber B. Hyperosmolar nature of diabetic coma. Diabetes 1975;24:594–9.

175. Piniés JA, Cairo G, Gaztambide S, Vazquez JA. Course and prognosis of 132 patients with diabetic non-ketotic hyperosmolar state. Diabetes Metab 1994;20:43–8.

176. Carrol P, Matz R. Uncontrolled diabetes mellitus in adults: experience in treating diabetic ketoacidosis and hyperosmolar nonketotic coma with low-dose insulin and a uniform treatment regimen. Diabetes Care 1983;6:579–85.

177. Braaten JT. Hyperosmolar nonketotic diabetic coma: diagnosis and management. Geriatrics 1987;42:83–92.

178. Gordon EE, Kabadi UM. The hyperglycemic hyperosmolar syndrome. Am J Med Sci 1976;271:253–68.

179. Cahill GF Jr. Hyperglycemic hyperosmolar coma: a syndrome almost unique to the elderly. J Am Geriatr Soc 1983;31:103–5.

180. Rolfe M, Ephraim GG, Lincoln DC, Huddle KRL. Hyperosmolar non-ketotic diabetic coma as a cause of emergency hyperglycaemic admission to Baragwanath Hospital. S Afr Med J 1995;85:173–6.

181. Smitherman KO. Peacock JE Jr. Infectious emergencies in patients with diabetes mellitus. Med Clin North Am 1995;79:53–77.

182. Joshi N, Caputo GM, Weitekamp MR, Karchmer AW. Primary care: infections in patients with diabetes mellitus. N Engl J Med 1999;25:1906–12.

183. Beam TJ Jr, Crigler ED, Goldman JK, et al. Antibody response to polyvalent pneumococcal polysaccharide vaccine in diabetics. JAMA 1980;244:2621–4.

184. Romano G, Moretti G, Di Benedetto A, et al. Skin lesions in diabetes mellitus: prevalence and clinical correlations. Diabetes Res Clin Pract 1998;39:101–6.

185. Gupta AK, Konnikov N, MacDonald P, et al. Prevalence and epidemiology of toenail onychomycosis in diabetic subjects: a multicentre survey. Br J Dermatol 1998;139:665–71.

186. Lugo-Somolinos A, Sanchez JL. Prevalence of dermatophytosis in patients with diabetes. J Am Acad Dermatol 1992;26:408–10.

187. Yosipovitch G, Hodak E, Vardi P, et al. The prevalence of cutaneous manifestations in IDDM patients and their association with diabetes risk factors and microvascular complications. Diabetes Care 1998;21:506–9.

188. Kour AK, Looi DP, Phone MH, Pho RWH. Hand infections in patients with diabetes. Clin Orthop 1996;331:238–44.

189. Patel MS. Bacterial infections among patients with diabetes in Papua New Guinea. Med J Aust 1989;150:25–8.

190. Harris RA, Hardman DT, Brown AR. Cellulitis and the occult diabetic. Aust N Z J Surg 1996;66:175–7.

191. Baynes C, Caplan S, Hames P, et al. The value of screening for diabetes in patients with skin sepsis. J R Soc Med 1993;86:148–51.

192. Patterson JE, Andriole VT. Bacterial urinary tract infections in diabetes. Infect Dis Clin North Am 1997;11:735–50.

193. Forland M, Thomas V, Shelokov A. Urinary tract infections in patients with diabetes mellitus: studies on antibody coating of bacteria. JAMA 1977;238:1924–6.

194. Rivett AG, Perry JA, Cohen J. Urinary candidiasis: a prospective study in hospital patients. Urol Res 1986;14:183–6.

195. Gibb D, Hockey S, Brown L, Lunt H. Vaginal symptoms and insulin dependent diabetes mellitus. N Z Med J 1995;108:252–3.

196. Jackson LA, Hilsdon R, Farley MM, et al. Risk factors for group B streptococcal disease in adults. Ann Intern Med 1995;123:415–20.

197. Telzak EE, Greenberg MSQ, Budnick LD, et al. Diabetes mellitus—a newly described risk factor for infection from Salmonella enteritidis. J Infect Dis 1991;164:538–41.

198. Wheat LJ. Infection and diabetes mellitus. Diabetes Care 1980;3:187–97.

199. Marston BJ, Lipman HB, Brieman RF. Surveillance for legionnaires' disease. Risk factors for morbidity and mortality. Arch Intern Med 1994;154:2417–22.

200. Lippman ML, Goldberg SK, Walkenstein MD, et al. Bacteremic pneumococcal pneumonia. A community hospital experience. Chest 1995;108:1608–13.

201. Watanakunakorn C, Bailey TA. Adult bacteremic pneumococcal pneumonia in a community teaching hospital, 1992–1996. A detailed analysis of 108 cases. Arch Intern Med 1997;157:1965–71.

202. Muñoz P, Llancaqueo A, Rodriguez-Créxems M, et al. Group B streptococcus bacteremia in nonpregnant adults. Arch Intern Med 1997;157:213–6.

203. Kristensen B, Schonheyder HC. A 13-year survey of bacteraemia due to beta-haemolytic streptococci in a Danish county. Clin Microbiol 1995;43:63 7.

204. Bryan CS, Reynolds KL, Metzger WT. Bacteremia in diabetic patients: comparison of incidence and mortality with nondiabetic patients. Diabetes Care 1985;8:244–9.

205. Cooper G, Platt R. Staphylococcus aureus bacteremia in diabetic patients. Endocarditis and mortality. Am J Med 1982;73:658–62.

206. Willcox PA, Rayner BL, Whitelaw DA. Community-acquired Staphylococcus aureus bacteraemia in patients who do not abuse intravenous drugs. QJM 1998;91:41–7.

207. Kaandorp CJE, van Schaardenburg D, Krijnen P, et al. Risk factors for septic arthritis in patients with joint disease. Arthritis Rheum 1995;38:1819–25.

208. Söderquist B, Hedström Å. Predisposing factors, bacteriology and antibiotic therapy in 35 cases of septic bursitis. Scand J Infect Dis 1986;18:305–11.

209. Colmenero JD, Jimenez-Mejias ME, Sanchez-Lora FJ, et al. Pyogenic, tuberculous, and brucellar vertebral osteomyelitis: a descriptive and comparative study of 219 cases. Ann Rheum Dis 1997;56:709–15.

210. Cheng D-L, Liu Y-C, Yen M-Y, et al. Septic metastatic lesions of pyogenic liver abscess. Their association with Klebsiella pneumoniae bacteremia in diabetic patients. Arch Intern Med 1991;151:1557–9.

211. Edsall J, Collins JG, Gran JAC. The reactivation of tuberculosis in New York City in 1967. Am Rev Respir Dis 1970;102:725–36.

212. Pablos-Mendez A, Blustein J, Knirsch CA. The role of diabetes mellitus in the higher prevalence of tuberculosis among Hispanics. Am J Public Health 1997;87:574–9.

213. Chandler PT, Chandler SD. Pathogenic carrier rate in diabetes mellitus. Am J Med Sci 1977; 273:259–65.

214. Rayfield EJ, Ault MJ, Keusch GT, et al. Infection and diabetes: the case for glucose control. Am J Med 1982;72:439–50.

215. Buxton PK, Milne LJ, Prescott RJ, et al. The prevalence of dermatophyte infection in well-controlled diabetics and the response to Trichophyton antigen. Br J Dermatol 1996;134:900–3.

216. Rassias AJ, Marrin CA, Arruda J, et al. Insulin infusion improves neutrophil function in diabetic cardiac surgery patients. Anesth Analg 1999;88:1011–6.

217. Furnary AP, Zerr KJ, Grunkemeier GL, Starr A. Continuous intravenous insulin infusion reduces the incidence of deep sternal wound infection in diabetic patients after cardiac surgical procedures. Ann Thorac Surg 1999;67:352–62.

218. Zerr KJ, Furnary AP, Grunkemeier GL, et al. Glucose control lowers the risk of wound infection in diabetics after open heart operations. Ann Thorac Surg 1997;63:356–61.

219. Bosshardt T, Henderson V, Organ CH Jr. Necrotizing soft-tissue infections. Arch Surg 1996;131:846–54.

220. Elliott DC, Kufera JA, Myers RAM. Necrotizing soft tissue infections. Risk factors for mortality and strategies for management. Ann Surg 1996;224:672–83.

221. Blitzer A, Lawson W, Meyers BR, Biller HF. Patient survival factors in paranasal sinus mucormycosis. Laryngoscope 1980;90:635–47.

222. Nussbaum ES, Hall WA. Rhinocerebral mucormycosis: changing patterns of disease. Surg Neurol 1994;41:152–6.

223. Parfrey NA. Improved diagnosis and prognosis of mucormycosis. A clinicopathologic study of 33 cases. Medicine 1986;65:113–23.

224. Yohai RA, Bullock JD, Aziz AA, Markert RJ. Survival factors in rhino-orbital-cerebral mucormycosis. Surv Ophthalmol 1994;39:3–22.

225. Abedi E, Sismani A, Choi K, Pastore P. Twenty-five years' experience treating cerebro-rhino-orbital mucormycosis. Laryngoscope 1984;94:1060–3.

226. Peterson KL, Wang M, Canalis RF, Abemayor E. Rhinocerebral mucormycosis: evolution of the disease and treatment options. Laryngoscope 1997;107:855–62.

227. Rangel-Guerra RA, Martínez HR, Sáenz C, et al. Rhinocerebral and systemic mucormycosis. Clinical experience with 36 cases. J Neurol Sci 1996;143:19–30.

228. Bodenstein NP, McIntosh WA, Vlantis AC, Urquhart AC. Clinical signs of orbital ischemia in rhinoorbito-cerebral mucormycosis. Laryngoscope 1993;103:1357–61.

229. Chandler JR. Malignant external otitis: further considerations. Ann Otol Rhinol Laryngol 1977;86:417–28.

230. Meyerhoff WL, Gates GA, Montalbo PJ. Pseudomonas mastoiditis. Laryngoscope 1977;87:483–92.

231. Doroghazi RM, Nadol JB Jr, Hyslop NE Jr, et al. Invasive external otitis. Report of 21 cases and review of the literature. Am J Med 1981;71:603–14.

232. Babiatzki A, Sade J. Malignant external otitis. J Laryngol Otol 1987;101:205–10.

233. Salit IE, McNeely DJ, Chait G. Invasive external otitis: review of 12 cases. Can Med Assoc J 1985;132:381–4.

234. Pedersen HB, Rosborg J. Necrotizing external otitis: aminoglycoside and beta-lactam antibiotic treatment combined with surgical treatment. Clin Otolaryngol All Sci 1997;22:271–4.

235. Pontin AR, Barnes RD, Joffe J, Kahn D. Emphysematous pyelonephritis in diabetic patients. Br J Urol 1995;75:71–4.

236. Patel NP, Lavengood RW, Fernandes M, et al. Gas-forming infections in genitourinary tract. Urology 1992;39:341–5.

237. Landau O, Deutsch AA, Kott I, et al. The risk of cholecystectomy for acute cholecystitis in diabetic patients. Hepatogastroenterology 1992;39:437–8.

238. Roslyn JJ, Thompson JE Jr, Darvin H, DenBesten L. Risk factors for gallbladder perforation. Am J Gastroenterol 1987;82:636–40.

CHAPTER 8

Diagnosis and Short-Term Clinical Consequences of Diabetes in Children and Adolescents

Jacqueline Curtis, MD, FRCPC, Jill Hamilton, MD, FRCPC,
Carolyn Beck, MD, Marcia Frank, RN, MHSc, CDE,
and Denis Daneman, MB, BCh, FRCPC

ABSTRACT

Diabetes mellitus is the most common endocrine disease of childhood and adolescence. The incidence of both Type 1 and Type 2 diabetes appears to be increasing and the age of onset decreasing. Diabetic ketoacidosis (DKA) is the leading cause of mortality and morbidity for children with diabetes. Diabetic ketoacidosis occurs in 10 to 83% of new-onset Type 1 and in 5 to 52% of new-onset Type 2 diabetes in children and adolescents. The readmission risk for DKA in established diabetes is 0.19 per patient-year in the first 4 years after diagnosis. Adolescence is a particularly vulnerable period for poor metabolic control due to a variety of physiologic and psychological factors. Adolescent females with diabetes are at increased risk of eating disorders; insulin omission is a key purging behavior. Diabetic ketoacidosis prevention strategies at new-onset diabetes include increasing public awareness and physician education and, in established diabetes, include psychosocial interventions and the provision of guidelines to manage alterations in metabolic control during sick days, including access to a 24-hour hotline telephone. During DKA treatment, a negative sodium trend and/or a decline in effective osmolality are predictors of clinically significant cerebral edema. Gradual rehydration with isotonic saline may reduce the risk of cerebral edema. Ambulatory care of the child with new-onset diabetes who is not metabolically unstable is both safe and more effective than inpatient care in terms of readmission rates, metabolic control, and direct and indirect costs.

INTRODUCTION

Diabetes mellitus is the most common endocrine disease and one of the most common chronic conditions in childhood and adolescence. A clear understanding of the presentation, acute complications, and therapy related to childhood/adolescent diabetes is crucial to the development of effective management approaches to these individuals. A discussion of these issues and of the pertinent available evidence is organized as responses to the following questions:

1. What is the incidence and classification of diabetes in children and adolescents?
2. How do children and adolescents present at the time of diagnosis of diabetes?
3. What key diabetes-related problems may occur in children and adolescents with previously diagnosed diabetes?
4. What strategies effectively treat diabetes and prevent diabetes-related problems in children and adolescents?

What Is the Incidence and Classification of Diabetes in Children and Adolescents?

Type I Diabetes

The incidence of Type 1 diabetes mellitus is rising with time and varies markedly in different parts of the world. The highest incidence is found in the Nordic countries (Finland in particular), and the lowest incidence is reported in Japan and China. Although national registries are not available in North America, the incidence in Canada and the United States lies between these two extremes.[1–4] The epidemiology of Type 1 diabetes is discussed in detail in Chapter 9.

Although Type 1 diabetes has always been recognized as a disease that often presents in childhood, the average age at diagnosis has been decreasing over time.[5] For example, in 1985, the incidence of Type 1 diabetes in English children was 18.6 cases in 100,000 children per year; this rose by 4% annually between 1985 and 1996. The increase was mainly due to a rapid rise in children aged 0 to 4 years, in whom there was an annual increase of 11% (95% confidence interval 6 to 15%, $p < .0001$). The annual increase in those aged 5 to 9 years was 4% (0 to 7%, $p = .05$) and in those aged 10 to 14 years was 1% (−2 to 4%, $p = .55$). Although the cause of the increase is unknown, environmental influences encountered before birth or in early postnatal life may be responsible.

Type II Diabetes

Until recently, the vast majority of children and adolescents were diagnosed as having Type 1 diabetes. New evidence, however, supports a rising incidence of Type 2 diabetes in the pediatric population, specifically among adolescents in high-risk groups, such as First Nations, Hispanics, African-Americans, and Asian-Americans. The true incidence of Type 2 diabetes remains uncertain, although an increased incidence in adolescents in the greater Cincinnati area from 0.7 in 100,000 in 1982 to 7.2 in 100,000 was reported in 1994.[6] In this study, the percentage of patients in their center with newly diagnosed Type 2 diabetes increased from 4 to 16% during this 12-year period. Of note, 33% of those in the 10- to 19-year age group were diagnosed with Type 2 diabetes. A similar trend in incidence was noted in Arkansas, where the number of children presenting to the Arkansas Children's Hospital with Type 2 diabetes increased 8.5-fold between 1988 and 1995.[7] The epidemiology of Type 2 diabetes is discussed in detail in Chapter 10.

Evidence-Based Message

> Although the most common type of diabetes in children and adolescents is Type 1 diabetes, a rapidly rising incidence of Type 2 diabetes has been recognized over the past decade (Level 3).[5,6]

How Do Children and Adolescents Present at the Time of Diagnosis of Diabetes?

Polydypsia, polyuria, lethargy, and weight loss are the classic symptoms of Type 1 diabetes. The frequency of presenting symptoms from two retrospective pediatric series is presented in Table 8–1.[8,9]

Estimates of the duration of symptoms prior to presentation are regionally variable and may relate to differences in the incidence of Type 1 diabetes. For example, in one study, the average duration of symptoms in children from a high-incidence area in Finland was 3.5 ± 3.9 weeks compared with 5.3 ± 8.8 weeks in children from an intermediate-incidence area in Canada.[10]

Prevalence of Diabetic Ketoacidosis in New-Onset Diabetes

Diabetic ketoacidosis (DKA) affects between 10 and 83% of new cases of Type 1 diabetes, depending on the geographic location. There is evidence that this frequency is lower in

Table 8–1 Frequency of Presenting Symptoms in Children and Adolescents with Diabetes

Symptom	Frequency, %
Polydypsia	93–97
Polyuria	93
Fatigue	68–89
Weight loss	52–72
Abdominal pain	22–45
Enuresis	38

regions with higher diabetes incidence[10] and can be significantly decreased with public and physician education programs[10,11] (see Chapter 14). For example, a comparison of disease features at onset in children from Oulu, Finland (with a very high incidence of Type 1 diabetes), and in children from Toronto, Canada (where the incidence was considerably lower), was published in 1990.[10] At that time, the frequency of DKA in new-onset children from Oulu and Toronto was 14 and 28%, respectively. Furthermore, in Oulu, patients from multiplex families were never diagnosed in DKA (compared with 17% of those from simplex families). These data suggest that a higher index of suspicion of diabetes may lead to detection of the disease before DKA can develop.

Although DKA is a very uncommon presenting feature of Type 2 diabetes in adults, several series in the pediatric population report DKA in 5 to 52.5% of adolescents with newly diagnosed Type 2 diabetes.[7,12–14]

EVIDENCE-BASED MESSAGES

1. The likelihood that children and adolescents will present with DKA at the time of initial diabetes onset varies by region; it is lower in areas where the incidence and, therefore, the index of suspicion of diabetes is high (Level 4).[10]
2. Children and adolescents with Type 2 diabetes may present with DKA (Level 4).[7,12–14]

WHAT KEY DIABETES-RELATED PROBLEMS MAY OCCUR IN CHILDREN AND ADOLESCENTS WITH PREVIOUSLY DIAGNOSED DIABETES?

Diabetic Ketoacidosis

Diabetic ketoacidosis is relatively common in children and adolescents with established diabetes. For example, in a large, prospective, population-based study from Oxford, UK, 14% of children with Type 1 diabetes developed DKA between 1 month and 1 year after diagnosis, 15% developed DKA within 2 years, and 22% developed DKA within 4 years. There were a total of 154 admissions in 197 patients; thus, the risk of DKA during the first 4 years of diabetes (excluding the time of onset) was 0.19 per patient-year.[15]

Although not all cases of DKA can be explained, it is clear that insulin omission is a frequent cause in teenagers. For example, a study from Dundee, Scotland, evaluated whether prescribed insulin was being picked up from pharmacies: 28% of 89 individuals under age 30 picked up less than their prescribed dose of insulin, with a deficit of up to 115 days per year.[16] Most interestingly, 90% of those experiencing DKA were in the insulin-omitting group. (For frequency of insulin omission, see below.)

Poor Metabolic Control During Adolescence

Metabolic control during adolescence is poorer than during childhood, and strategies to improve HbA$_{1c}$ are less effective than in adulthood.[17–20] In a recent large, multicentred, cross-sectional study, metabolic control and insulin therapy of almost 3,000 children in 18 countries were analyzed.[18] The mean HbA$_{1c}$ was 8.6%, with 41% of prepubertal children having HbA$_{1c}$ levels below 8.0%. In contrast, only 29% of adolescents (aged 12–18 years) had HbA$_{1c}$ values below 8%.[18,19] In a separate cross-sectional study of 884 diabetic children from Denmark, adolescent boys and girls had higher mean HbA$_{1c}$ levels (9.7%) than those in the prepubertal age range (8.9%) despite significantly higher dosages of insulin per kilogram of body weight.[17]

The Diabetes Control and Complications Trial enrolled 195 adolescents between the ages of 13 and 17 years.[20] Compared with adult subjects, HbA$_{1c}$ levels in these adolescents remained approximately 1% higher in both the conventional and intensive therapy groups despite increased insulin doses.

Adolescence-Related Factors Affecting Glycemic Control

The deterioration in metabolic control that may occur during adolescence can be attributed to both physiologic and psychosocial factors. These include increased insulin resistance during puberty, emergence of disordered eating patterns in this age group, increased independence in diabetes monitoring and insulin injection, adolescent experimentation behavior, and competing lifestyle demands that interfere with good self-care practices.[18,21–34]

Development of insulin resistance. Using the euglycemic-hyperinsulinemic clamp method, several studies in both diabetic and nondiabetic adolescents have shown that insulin sensitivity decreases by 20 to 30% during puberty.[23,30,33,35,36] In addition, in all age groups, people with Type 1 diabetes had significantly lower insulin sensitivity compared to their nondiabetic peers.[35] This physiologic change may explain, in part, the rising HbA$_{1c}$ despite increasing insulin dosages that is frequently observed during adolescence.

There is also direct and indirect evidence of differences in insulin sensitivity between male and female subjects. The best glucose clamp study showed a 43% decrease in insulin-mediated glucose use rate in 15 female adolescents with Type 1 diabetes as compared with 12 of their male counterparts matched for body mass index, pubertal stage, and glycemic control.[21] Two large population-based studies have revealed a higher insulin requirement in female children and adolescents, implying a decreased sensitivity to the effects of insulin.[29,37]

Psychosocial impact of chronic disease (diabetes). The psychosocial impact of Type 1 diabetes has been studied extensively in a 9-year longitudinal cohort study of 95 prepubertal children from disease onset.[27,38,39] Coping responses after diagnosis of diabetes were examined through interviews and psychometric testing and showed initial periods of depression, irritability, anxiety, and social withdrawal.[27] These complaints decreased within the first year after diagnosis of diabetes, and at 7-year follow-up, the children displayed positive self-esteem and low depression scores.[39] At 9-year follow-up, the group was assessed for medical noncompliance with diabetes management, and a significant association was found between poor metabolic control, recurrent hospital admissions, and noncompliance with significant aspects of the treatment regimen (insulin administration, glucose monitoring, or dietary management).[38] Pervasive adolescent noncompliance was significantly associated with a major psychiatric disorder (affective disorder, conduct/substance abuse disorder, or anxiety disorder) in early adulthood.[38]

A prospective 2-year study of children and adolescents newly diagnosed with diabetes showed an increased risk of depression at study end, as compared to a nondiabetic, age-matched, healthy control group.[24] Other cross-sectional studies have not detected a significant difference in psychological disturbance between teens with diabetes and their nondiabetic counterparts.[16,22,40–47]

Transition of care from parents: autonomy issues. As adolescents experience greater independence and assume more self-care, decreased compliance with insulin injections, glucose monitoring, and regular eating patterns often ensues. In a recent survey of 144 adolescent diabetic subjects, 25% admitted to missing insulin injections and fabricating blood glucose results.[46] In the pharmacy-based study assessing young adult adherence with prescribed insulin that was described above, there was a significant inverse association between a calculated adherence index and the HbA$_{1c}$ and also between this index and hospital admissions for DKA.[16] In a 9-year prospective study of newly diagnosed children, the cumulative rate of nonadherence was 0.45 over the study period; this problem first emerged in mid-adolescence and peaked in late adolescence.[39] Thus, poor adherence to insulin treatment in this age group appears to be the major factor contributing to long-term poor glycemic control.[16]

A recent critical review of the more than 30 studies on social support and health outcomes of adolescents with Type 1 diabetes found that supportive, cohesive families with low levels of conflict were more likely to have adolescents with strong adherence and good metabolic control than teens from families without such cohesion.[47] Although these are largely cross-sectional studies, there has been one 4-year longitudinal study that examined family milieu and diabetes control at various time points and also confirmed that strong family cohesion can help the young adolescent maintain good glycemic control in the first 4 years after diagnosis.[45]

Experimentation behaviors. Studies from the United Kingdom, Germany, and Australia using urinary cotinine measurements and structured interviews have found a prevalence of smoking among adolescents with diabetes between 7 and 48%.[22,26,31,48] Although these four studies did not find a significant association between smoking and HbA$_{1c}$, two of the studies examined albumin excretion rate and found a significantly higher rate in the smoking group independent of duration of diabetes and glycemic control.[22,26]

A survey of teens with diabetes found that 20% admitted to trying recreational drugs, with none admitting to frequent use. In addition, those who reported trying any drug other than alcohol had a significantly higher HbA$_{1c}$ (9.3%) compared to subjects that had not (8.1%).[25] Substance abuse disorders have been shown to be a risk factor for medical noncompliance with diabetes management.[38]

EVIDENCE-BASED MESSAGES

1. Adolescents who develop a psychological disturbance such as depression or anxiety are at risk for poor metabolic control (Level 2).[38]
2. Adolescents from families characterized by poor cohesion and high conflict levels are at risk for poor metabolic control (Level 2).[45]
3. Adolescents who smoke or use alcohol or drugs are at risk for poor metabolic control (Level 2).[22,25,26,31,38,48]

Eating Disorders in Girls

Prevalence of Eating Disorders

Whether eating disorders are more prevalent in diabetic girls compared to the general population is a question widely debated in the literature. The hypothesis for their increased risk is supported by the following factors: weight gain following the initiation of insulin treatment, dietary restraint as part of diabetes management, and the availability of insulin omission as a unique method of weight control.[49]

Eight studies evaluated eating disorders based on the *Diagnostic and Statistical Manual of Mental Disorders (DSM)* criteria and used standardized diagnostic interviews.[34,50–56] An increased prevalence of eating disorders in the diabetic girls interviewed was reported in four studies,[50,52–54] whereas the remainder concluded no significant difference when compared to the general population.[34,51,54,55] Importantly, sample sizes were small (n = 19–89) in all but one of the studies.[53] In the largest study, 10% of 356 diabetic girls fulfilled *DSM-IV* criteria for an eating disorder compared to 4% of the control population (ie, eating disorders were 2.2 times more frequent in the diabetic girls than in the nondiabetic girls).[53]

Consequences of Eating Disorders

The association of eating disorders with diabetes has striking medical implications. Studies consistently show poorer metabolic control, as evidenced by higher levels of HbA_{1c}, in girls with clinical and subclinical eating disorders as compared to those with no disordered eating behaviors.[51,52,55,57–59] Additionally, the HbA_{1c} increases with the severity of the eating disorder.[60]

In 1993, the Diabetes Control and Complications Trial[61] clearly demonstrated an association between poor metabolic control and the microvascular and neurologic complications of diabetes. The incidence of retinopathy is high in adolescent girls with diabetes and eating disorders[62] and appears to be directly correlated with the severity of the disordered eating behavior.[60] A less stringent investigation has also suggested an increased prevalence of neuropathy in this population.[63]

EVIDENCE-BASED MESSAGES

1. Eating disorders are more common in young females with Type 1 diabetes than in their nondiabetic peers (Level 1).[53] In these people, an eating disorder is a risk factor for a higher HbA_{1c} (Level 2).[51,52,55,57–60]
2. In young females with Type 1 diabetes, an eating disorder is a risk factor for diabetic retinopathy (Level 1).[60]

Insulin Omission as a Weight Control Strategy in Eating Disorders

In addition to traditional methods of weight loss such as fasting, bingeing/purging, and exercise, girls and young women with diabetes can manipulate their insulin therapy in an attempt to promote glucosuria and subsequent weight loss. Multiple studies examine, as a secondary outcome of their research, the prevalence of insulin manipulation, specifically insulin omission or underdosing, for the specific intent of weight control. This unique behavior is found to have a prevalence of between 11.4% and 39% among females with Type 1 diabetes.[51,53,54,57,64–67]

This finding is supported by a study that looks at insulin omission or underdosing as its primary outcome.[68] A total of 341 women with Type 1 diabetes were surveyed, 31% of whom misused insulin for the purpose of weight control. This frequency rose to 40% among 15 to 30 year olds, 15.9% of whom reported a high frequency of this behavior.

WHAT STRATEGIES EFFECTIVELY TREAT DIABETES AND PREVENT DIABETES-RELATED PROBLEMS IN CHILDREN AND ADOLESCENTS?

Management of Medically Stable Newly Diagnosed Children and Adolescents

The treatment of the child and adolescent with new-onset Type 1 diabetes varies enormously: some centers have been successfully practicing ambulatory management of most of these children for some time,[69–71] others have embraced this ambulatory philosophy more recently,[70–74] and still others steadfastly hold to an inpatient approach. In the United Kingdom in 1992, 96% of children with new-onset diabetes were admitted to hospital, and 42% were admitted for more than 1 week.[75] Interestingly, 90% of families expressed satisfaction with their program, irrespective of initial management.

A recent literature review of out- versus inpatient management of children with new-onset diabetes concluded that ambulatory care was a more cost-effective strategy.[76] However, a number of hypothetical disadvantages were listed, including (a) hypoglycemia early in the course in a family ill-equipped to deal with such an occurrence; (b) poor metabolic control early on to avoid hypoglycemia, which may contribute to long-term suboptimal control; (c) worsening or development of DKA while not under close supervision; (d) the need for 24-hour/day staff coverage to allow for ambulatory care; and (e) the resistance of health care payers to provide reimbursement for ambulatory services. Despite these theoretical disadvantages, no differences in the frequency of hypoglycemia or DKA episodes have been found, and HbA$_{1c}$ levels and readmission rates may be lower in children receiving ambulatory care.[76] Of note is that the outcome measures studied have generally not emphasized psychosocial indicators.

A randomized controlled trial comparing home care after initial diagnosis to hospitalization in 63 children with new-onset Type 1 diabetes found that home care resulted in reduced hospital days and improved health outcomes (specifically lower HbA$_{1c}$ levels). There were no significant differences in health care costs or in the psychosocial impact to the child and family.[77,78]

The benefits of ambulatory management are further supported by a recent report in which HbA$_{1c}$ levels, frequency of hypoglycemia and DKA, and hospital readmissions in children with new-onset diabetes treated at the Hospital for Sick Children, Toronto, were analyzed during three phases: 1988 to 1989, when all children were admitted to hospital for 5 to 10 days for stabilization and family education ("inpatient"; mean length of stay 7.8 days); 1993 to 1994, when children were admitted for a brief period ("short stay"; mean length 3.1 days); and 1995 to 1996, when we introduced an ambulatory approach ("no admit"), unless the child presented in DKA or psychosocial issues (eg, language difficulties or living far from our hospital) demanded admission (mean length for those admitted 2.8 days).[79] The three groups did not differ with respect to the frequency of hospital readmissions, episodes of DKA, or hypoglycemic episodes. There was a significant improvement in HbA$_{1c}$ levels over the 10-year period of observation. This was felt to be due in part to two factors: (1) the changing approach to blood glucose targets in children and adolescents with diabetes and (2) the introduction of three daily injections in the "no admit" group.

Initial ambulatory management may also reduce costs. Indeed, two American studies reported that the average costs of a 3- to 5-day hospital stay were US $2,500 to $3,000 per patient, with a reduction to US $550 to $625 per patient for outpatient management.[80,81] This represents a cost saving of about 80%.

EVIDENCE-BASED MESSAGE

Children with new-onset diabetes who are metabolically stable and otherwise well have lower readmission rates, better metabolic control, and lower direct and indirect costs when managed in an outpatient setting compared to an inpatient setting (Level 1).[77,78]

Prevention of Diabetic Ketoacidosis in Children and Adolescents

Community Interventions

Recent data suggest that simple community interventions may prevent or reduce the incidence of DKA at the time of diagnosis of diabetes.[11] In a program in Parma, Italy, schools and doctors' offices were provided with colorful posters with practical messages about diabetes, and local pediatricians were instructed on the use of glucose meters. In the study area, the incidence of DKA in new-onset cases decreased from 78% from 1987 to 1991 to 12.5% from 1991 to 1997, with no cases in the last 4 years of the study. In the control region nearby in which the intervention was not carried out, 83% of new cases presented in DKA.

EVIDENCE-BASED MESSAGE

Appropriate education of school personnel and health care professionals may lead to earlier recognition of new-onset diabetes in children before it progresses to DKA (Level 2).[11]

Management of Intercurrent Illnesses

Intercurrent illnesses also increase the risk of DKA in children and adolescents with established diabetes. The stress of an illness can trigger a substantial counter-regulatory response in children and teens with Type 1 diabetes leading to the development of DKA unless appropriate measures are taken. At least two studies document the effectiveness of patient education and the availability of advice via a 24-hour telephone hotline in reducing the incidence of DKA associated with intercurrent illness.[82,83] Table 8–2 outlines the general principles of care of children during times of intercurrent illness.[84]

EVIDENCE-BASED MESSAGE

> The provision of guidelines to manage alterations in metabolic control during sick days, including a 24-hour hotline telephone number to call for advice, reduces the risk and severity of DKA (Level 4).[82,83]

Reduction of Insulin Omission

As noted, insulin omission represents an important cause of DKA. It may also be a preventable cause, at least in the adolescent population,[85] with the introduction of a hierarchical set of educational, supervisory, and psychosocial interventions aimed at determining the reason for the insulin omission and preventing its recurrence.

EVIDENCE-BASED MESSAGE

> An education- and supervision-based program reduces the risk of DKA due to insulin omission in adolescents with Type 1 diabetes (Level 4).[85]

Cerebral Edema in Children and Adolescents with Diabetic Ketoacidosis

Although early mortality is very low in children and teens with Type 1 diabetes, DKA accounts for up to 80% of all deaths.[86,87] Cerebral edema (CE) is the leading cause (30–62%) of these DKA-related deaths. An important observation has been that all episodes occurred in patients less than 16 years of age.[88,89] Cerebral edema case-fatality estimates range from 25 to 67%.[90–92] In the largest CE case series (N = 69), the outcome was death in 64%, severe disability in 13%, mild disability in 8.6%, and intact survival in only 14.5%.[90]

Several case reports suggest that subclinical CE may be a common occurrence both before and during DKA treatment.[93–96] Clinically significant edema may occasionally be present at the time of presentation of the child with DKA to the hospital, but CE generally develops 2 to 24 hours after initiation of DKA treatment.[90]

Table 8–2 Rules for Management of "Sick Days" to Prevent Diabetic Ketoacidosis

---

Principle 1: Family education including written guidelines

Monitor blood glucose and urinary ketones at least every 4 hours around the clock.

Never omit insulin; the dose may need to be adjusted depending on the results of blood glucose and urine ketone measurement.

Ensure that sufficient fluids and calories are provided to prevent dehydration and hypoglycemia.

Treat the underlying illness.

Ensure close supervision of the routines of insulin injection and monitoring.

Principle 2: Call the 24-hour telephone hotline if

Vomiting occurs more than twice over a 6- to 8-hour period.

Hyperglycemia and/or ketonuria persist.

Hypoglycemia persists.

Identification of Risk Factors for Cerebral Edema

The cause of CE remains unclear. Nevertheless, several clinical characteristics provide clues to the possibility that the DKA will be complicated by CE. These are discussed below.

Young age. Younger children may be at increased risk of CE. In a large epidemiologic study in Japan, the mean age of children with diabetic coma at initial presentation was significantly lower than in uncomplicated cases (6.2 years vs 8.3 years). The highest incidence was in children less than 1 year of age (44%), decreasing to 10.8% in the greater than 5 years age group.[97] Similarly, in the large CE case series, 68 of 69 episodes occurred in the less than 20 years age group. Of these, 23 (33%) were in the less than 5 years age group and 17 (25%) in the less than 3 years age group.[90]

Time of diabetes onset. Cerebral edema occurs at the time of the initial presentation of diabetes in 60 to 70% of cases.[90,98] In a review of diabetes-related deaths in children, 7 of 11 (64%) deaths caused by CE occurred at the initial presentation of diabetes.[86]

Biochemistry at presentation with diabetic ketoacidosis. There is no convincing evidence that initial acid-base status, glucose, electrolytes, or effective osmolality (Eosmol) are useful predictors of CE.[90,98–101] Therefore, all pediatric DKA patients should be presumed to be at risk, independent of initial biochemical parameters.

Prevention of Cerebral Edema

In contrast, a negative trend in serum sodium and a decrease in Eosmol that becomes apparent while treating DKA are associated with CE.[98–101] This association has implicated overzealous rehydration and hypotonic fluid use as possible contributing factors.[100–102] This remains a controversial area of DKA management in children. For example, in a retrospective review of 42 CE cases, a significant inverse correlation was noted between the time of onset of brain herniation and the overall rate of fluid administration. Ninety percent of subjects who developed CE had received fluid rates in excess of 4 L/m^2/day.[101] Conversely, another review of 40 published reports and 29 unpublished case records of CE from 1961 to 1987 found no correlation with rates of fluid administration and time of collapse. Serum sodium was < 130 mmol/L in 11 of 58 (19%) patients at the time of deterioration, and this was not correlated with the amount of sodium administered.[90]

Two multicenter studies[100,102] provide compelling evidence supporting a more conservative approach to rehydration and the use of more hypertonic solutions. The first was a retrospective analysis of 214 DKA cases treated with conventional fluid regimes in which 145 of 182 (79.7%) patients received an "uneven" rehydration (more than half the calculated rehydration fluid during less than half of the treatment period) and 150 of 182 (82.4%) patients received rehydration fluids containing less than 75 mmol/L of sodium. Sodium fell or failed to rise during the course of treatment in 60% of those who received uneven fluids compared with 32% of those with even fluids ($p < .01$). A negative sodium trend occurred in 59% of those who received solutions containing < 75 mmol/L compared with 31% who received solutions with > 75 mmol/L ($p < .01$).

Following these observations, new fluid guidelines based on more gradual and even rehydration with more hypertonic fluids were implemented and then prospectively analyzed in 231 children with DKA.[102] Only 3 of 209 children required more than 20 mL/kg to correct initial shock, and intravenous fluids were discontinued after 24 hours in 98% of cases. A comparison of outcomes between the old and new rehydration regimes is summarized in Table 8–3. It appears that more gradual rehydration with fluids of higher tonicity during DKA decreases the risk of death and neurologic morbidity from CE. Finally, it is important to note that there is no evidence to support theories that rapid rates of glucose decline or pH changes contribute to brain edema.[90,99–101]

EVIDENCE-BASED MESSAGES

1. Younger age and new-onset diabetes are risk factors for the development of clinically significant CE during DKA therapy (Level 4).[86,90,97]
2. A negative sodium trend and a decreasing Eosmol during DKA therapy are risk factors for the development of clinically significant CE (Level 4).[98–101]
3. More gradual rehydration with less hypotonic (ie, more isotonic) solutions may prevent clinically significant CE (Level 4).[100,102]

Improving Metabolic Control

Psychosocial Interventions

Psychosocial intervention studies to improve metabolic control in adolescents have been reported infrequently and tend to look at short-term outcomes, and the majority do not have a control group for comparison.[28,32,103] They have all been group intervention (either children with their parents, families together, or adolescents without parents) and have been based on weekly meetings over a period of a few months to discuss diabetes management, to trouble-shoot common problems, and to provide a forum for support and guidance. These studies do show a favorable short-term outcome, both in participants' perception of management of diabetes and also in improvement in HbA$_{1c}$. The best intervention study was of 18 months duration with peer group intervention (small groups of adolescents and small groups of parents meeting separately) to develop diabetes problem-solving skills.[104] A control group received individual education and advice from their health care team. A significant improvement in adherence and metabolic control was observed for the intervention group compared with the control group.

EVIDENCE-BASED MESSAGE

Small-group psychosocial intervention that addresses practical diabetes management issues and provides a forum for support and guidance improves both patient perception of diabetes management and glycemic control in short-term trials (Level 4).[28,32,103,104]

Treating or Preventing Eating Disorders

Few data exist on strategies for treatment or prevention of eating disorders among young diabetic females. A well-designed study of treatment evaluating six-session group psychoeducational therapy has found, in its interim analysis, a significant improvement in eating attitudes and behaviors as compared to a nontreatment group, but no change in HbA$_{1c}$ levels over a 6-month follow-up period.[105] Also of note is a case series examining cognitive behavioral treatment with minor modifications made for diabetes. This series showed improvements in the eating habits and glycemic control in patients with diabetes and bulimia nervosa.[106]

Table 8–3 Comparison of Negative Sodium (Na) Trends, Lowest Mean Eosmol, Neurologic Complications, and Death between the Conventional and New Rehydration Protocols

	Negative Na Trend	Lowest Mean Eosmol (mOsm/kg H$_2$O)	Acute Neurologic Complications (%)	Death (%)	Permanent Deficits (%)
Old protocol[100]	100/184 (54)	281.7 (n = 178)	20/219 (9.1)	3/20 (15)	3/17 (17.6)
New protocol[102]	23/231 (10)	285.8 (n = 230)	6/231 (2.5)	0	0

CONCLUSION

Children and adults differ with respect to prevalence and predominant type of diabetes. Moreover, important developmental differences, both physiologic and psychologic, exist that impact on the risk, consequence, and management of both acute and long-term complications. Of particular note is the relative paucity of high-level randomized clinical trials in the pediatric diabetes population. Ongoing research and care for children and adolescents with diabetes must take the developmental stages of this population into account.

SUMMARY OF EVIDENCE-BASED MESSAGES

1. Although the most common type of diabetes in children and adolescents is Type 1 diabetes, a rapidly rising incidence of Type 2 diabetes has recently been recognized (Level 3).[6]

2. The likelihood that children and adolescents will present with DKA at the time of initial diabetes onset varies by region; it is lower in areas where the incidence and, therefore, the index of suspicion of diabetes is high (Level 4).[10]

3. Children and adolescents with Type 2 diabetes may present with DKA (Level 4).[7,12–14]

4. Adolescents who develop a psychological disturbance such as depression or anxiety are at risk for poor metabolic control (Level 4).[38]

5. Adolescents from families characterized by poor cohesion and high conflict levels are at risk for poor metabolic control (Level 1).[45]

6. Adolescents who smoke or use alcohol or drugs are at risk for poor metabolic control (Level 4).[22,25,26,31,38,48]

7. Eating disorders are more common in young females with Type 1 diabetes than in their nondiabetic peers (Level 1).[53] In these people, an eating disorder is a risk factor for a higher HbA_{1c} (Level 2).[51,52,55,57–60]

8. In young females with Type 1 diabetes, an eating disorder is a risk factor for diabetic retinopathy (Level 1).[60]

9. Children with new-onset diabetes who are metabolically stable and otherwise well have lower readmission rates, better metabolic control, and lower direct and indirect costs when managed in an outpatient setting compared to an inpatient setting (Level 1).[77,78]

10. Appropriate education of school personnel and health care professionals may lead to earlier recognition of new-onset diabetes in children before it progresses to DKA (Level 2).[11]

11. The provision of guidelines to manage alterations in metabolic control during sick days, including a 24-hour hotline telephone number to call for advice, reduces the risk and severity of DKA (Level 4).[82,83]

12. An education- and supervision-based program reduces the risk of DKA due to insulin omission in adolescents with Type 1 diabetes (Level 2).[85]

13. Younger age and new-onset diabetes are risk factors for the development of clinically significant CE during DKA therapy (Level 4).[86,90,97]

14. A negative sodium trend and a decreasing Eosmol during DKA therapy are risk factors for the development of clinically significant CE (Level 4).[98–101]

15. More gradual rehydration with less hypotonic (ie, more isotonic) solutions may prevent the clinically significant CE (Level 4).[100,102]

16. Small-group psychosocial intervention that addresses practical diabetes management issues and provides a forum for support and guidance improves both patient perception of diabetes management and glycemic control in short-term trials (Level 4).[28,32,103,104]

REFERENCES

1. Blanchard JF, Dean H, Anderson K, et al. Incidence and prevalence of diabetes in children aged 0–14 years in Manitoba, Canada, 1985–1993. Diabetes Care 1997;20:512–5.

2. Ehrlich RM, Walsh LJ, Falk JA, Middleton PJ, Simpson NE. The incidence of type 1 (insulin-dependent) diabetes in Toronto. Diabetologia 1982;22:289–91.

3. Tan MH, Wornell CM. Diabetes mellitus in Canada. Diabetes Res Clin Pract 1991;14:S3–8.

4. West R, Belmonte MM, Colle E, et al. Epidemiologic survey of juvenile-onset diabetes in Montreal. Diabetes 1979;28:690–3.

5. Gardner SG, Bingley PJ, Sawtell PA, et al. Rising incidence of insulin dependent diabetes in children aged under 5 years in the Oxford region: time trend analysis. The Bart's-Oxford Study Group. BMJ 1997;315:713–7.

6. Pinhas-Hamiel O, Dolan LM, Daniels SR, et al. Increased incidence of non-insulin-dependent diabetes mellitus among adolescents. J Pediatr 1996;128:608–15.

7. Scott CR, Smith JM, Cradock MM, Pihoker C. Characteristics of youth-onset non-insulin-dependent diabetes mellitus and insulin-dependent diabetes mellitus at diagnosis. Pediatrics 1997;100:84–91.

8. Hamilton DV, Mundia SS, Lister J. Mode of presentation of juvenile diabetes. BMJ 1976;2:211–2.

9. Proos LA, Kobbah M, Tuvemo T. Clinical characteristics of insulin-dependent diabetes mellitus in children at diagnosis. Ups J Med Sci 1997;102:121–31.

10. Daneman D, Knip M, Kaar Ml, Sochett E. Comparison of children with type 1 (insulin-dependent) diabetes in northern Finland and southern Ontario: differences at disease onset. Diabetes Res 1990;14:123–6.

11. Vanelli M, Chiari G, Ghizzoni L, et al. Effectiveness of a prevention program for diabetic ketoacidosis in children. An 8-year study in schools and private practices. Diabetes Care 1999;22:7–9.

12. Onyemere K, Lipton R, Bauman E, et al. Onset features of insulin-treated atypical type 1 and early-onset type 2 diabetes in African-American and US Latino children. Diabetes 1998;47:A87.

13. Pinhas-Hamiel O, Dolan LM, Zeitler PS. Diabetic ketoacidosis among obese African-American adolescents with NIDDM. Diabetes Care 1997;10:484–6.

14. Neufeld ND, Raffel LJ, Landon C, et al. Early presentation of type 2 diabetes in Mexican-American youth. Diabetes Care 1998;21:89–96.

15. Pinkey JH, Bingley PJ, Sawtell PA, et al. Presentation and progress of childhood diabetes mellitus: a prospective population-based study. The Bart's-Oxford Study Group. Diabetologia 1994;37:70–4.

16. Morris AD, Boyle DI, McMahon A, et al. Adherence to insulin treatment, glycaemic control and ketoacidosis in insulin-dependent diabetes mellitus. Lancet 1997;350:1505–10.

17. Mortensen HB, Hartling SG, Petersen KE. A nation-wide cross-sectional study of glycosylated haemoglobin in Danish children with type 1 diabetes. Diabet Med 1988;5:871–6.

18. Mortensen HB, Hougaard P. Comparison of metabolic control in a cross-sectional study of 2,873 children and adolescents with IDDM from 18 countries. The Hvidore Study Group on Childhood Diabetes. Diabetes Care 1997;20:714–20.

19. Mortensen HB, Robertson KJ, Aanstoot JJ, et al. Insulin management and metabolic control of type 1 diabetes mellitus in childhood and adolescence in 18 countries. Hvidore Study Group on Childhood Diabetes. Diabet Med 1998;15:752–9.

20. Effect of intensive diabetes treatment on the development and progression of long-term complications in adolescents with insulin-dependent diabetes mellitus: Diabetes Control and Complications Trial. Diabetes Control and Complications Trial Research Group. J Pediatr 1994;125:177–88.

21. Arslanian SA, Heil BV, Becker DJ, Drash AL. Sexual dimorphism in insulin sensitivity in adolescents with insulin-dependent diabetes mellitus. J Clin Endocrinol Metab 1991;72:920–6.

22. Couper JJ, Staples AJ, Cocciolone R, et al. Relationship of smoking and albuminuria in children with diabetes. Diabet Med 1994;11:666–9.

23. Cook JS, Hoffman RP, Stene MA, Hansen JR. Effects of maturational stage on insulin sensitivity during puberty. J Clin Endocrinol Metab 1993;77:725–30.

24. Grey M, Cameron ME, Lipman TH, Thurber FW. Psychosocial status of children with diabetes in the first 2 years after diagnosis. Diabetes Care 1995;18:1330–6.

25. Glasgow AM, Tynan D, Schwartz R, et al. Alcohol and drug use in teenagers with diabetes mellitus. J Adolesc Health 1991;12:11–4.

26. Holl RW, Grabert M, Heinze E, Debatin KM. Objective assessment of smoking habits by urinary cotinine measurement in adolescents and young adults with type 1 diabetes. Reliability of cigarette consumption and relationship to urinary albumin excretion. Diabetes Care 1998;21:787–91.

27. Kovacs M, Brent D, Steinberg TF, et al. Children's self-reports of psychologic adjustment and coping strategies during first year of insulin-dependent diabetes mellitus. Diabetes Care 1986;9:472–9.

28. Kaplan RM, Chadwick MW, Schimmel LE. Social learning intervention to promote metabolic control in type I diabetes mellitus: pilot experiment results. Diabetes Care 1985;8:152–5.

29. Komulainen J, Akerblom HK, Lounamaa R, Knip M. Prepubertal girls with insulin-dependent diabetes mellitus have higher exogenous insulin requirement than boys. Childhood Diabetes in Finland Study Group. Eur J Pediatr 1998;157:708–11.

30. Leslie RD, Taylor R, Pozzilli P. The role of insulin resistance in the natural history of type 1 diabetes. Diabet Med 1997;14:327–31.

31. Masson EA, MacFarlane IA, Priestley JJ, et al. Failure to prevent nicotine addition in young people with diabetes. Arch Dis Child 1992;67:100–2.

32. Massouh SR, Steele TM, Alseth ER, Diekmann JM. The effect of social learning intervention on metabolic control of insulin-dependent diabetes mellitus in adolescents. Diabetes Educator 1989;15:518–21.

33. Moran A, Jacobs DR, Steinberger J, et al. Insulin resistance during puberty. Results from clamp studies in 357 children. Diabetes 1999;48:2039–44.

34. Robertson P, Rosenvinge JH. Insulin-dependent diabetes mellitus: a risk factor in anorexia nervosa or bulimia nervosa? An empirical study of 116 women. J Psychosom Res 1990;34:535–41.

35. Amiel SA, Sherwin RS, Simonson DC, et al. Impaired insulin action in puberty. A contributing factor to poor control in adolescents with diabetes. N Engl J Med 1986;315:215–9.

36. Bloch CA, Clemons P, Sperling MA. Puberty decreases insulin sensitivity. J Pediatr 1987;110:481–7.

37. Mortensen HB, Villumsen J, Volund A, et al. Relationship between insulin injection regimen and metabolic control in young Danish type 1 diabetic patients. The Danish Study Group of Diabetes in Childhood. Diabet Med 1992;9:834–9.

38. Kovacs M, Goldston D, Obrosky DS, Iyengar S. Prevalence and predictors of pervasive noncompliance with medical treatment among youths with insulin-dependent diabetes mellitus. J Am Acad Child Adolesc Psychiatry 1992;31:1112–9.

39. Kovacs M, Iyengar S, Goldston D, et al. Psychological functioning of children with insulin-dependent diabetes mellitus: a longitudinal study. J Pediatr Psychol 1990;15:619–32.

40. Jacobson AM, Hauser ST, Wertlieb D, et al. Psychological adjustment of children with recently diagnosed diabetes mellitus. Diabetes Care 1986;9:323–9.

41. Ireys HT, Gross SS, Werthamer-Larsson LA, Kolodner KB. Self-esteem of young adults with chronic health conditions: appraising effects of perceived impact. J Dev Behav Pediatr 1994;15:409–15.

42. Margalit M. Mothers' perceptions of anxiety of their diabetic children. J Dev Behav Pediatr 1986;7:27–30.

43. Simonds JF. Psychiatric status of diabetic youth matched with a control group. Diabetes 1977;26:921–5.

44. Hanson CL, Rodrigue JR, Henggeler SW, et al. The perceived self-competence of adolescents with insulin-dependent diabetes mellitus: deficit or strength? J Pediatr Psychol 1990;15:605–18.

45. Hauser ST, Jacobson AM, Lavori P, et al. Adherence among children and adolescents with insulin-dependent diabetes mellitus over a four-year longitudinal follow-up: II. Immediate and long-term linkages with the family milieu. J Pediatr Psychol 1990;15:527–42.

46. Weissberg-Benchell J, Glasgow AM, Tynan WD, et al. Adolescent diabetes management and mismanagement. Diabetes Care 1995;18:77–82.

47. Burroughs TE, Harris MA, Pontious Sl, Santiago JV. Research on social support in adolescents with IDDM: a critical review. Diabetes Educator 1997;23:438–48.

48. Hargrave DR, McMaster C, O'Hare MM, Carson DJ. Tobacco smoke exposure in children and adolescents with diabetes mellitus. Diabet Med 1999;16:31–34.

49. Daneman D, Olmsted M, Rydall A, et al. Eating disorders in young women with type 1 diabetes. Prevalence and prevention. Horm Res 1998;1:79–86.

50. Engstrom I, Kroon M, Arvidsson C-G, et al. Eating disorders in adolescent girls with insulin-dependent diabetes mellitus: a population-based case-control study. Acta Paediatr 1999;88:175–80.

51. Fairburn CG, Peveler RC, Davies B, et al. Eating disorders in young adults with insulin dependent diabetes mellitus: a controlled study. BMJ 1991;303:17–20.

52. Friedman S, Vila G, Timsit J, et al. Eating disorders and insulin-dependent diabetes mellitus (IDDM): relationships with glycaemic control and somatic complications. Acta Psychiatr Scand 1998;97:206–12.

53. Jones JM, Lawson ML, Daneman D, et al. Eating disorders in adolescent females with type 1 diabetes: a controlled three-site study. BMJ 2000;320:1563–166.

54. Peveler RC, Fairburn CG, Boller I, Dunger D. Eating disorders in adolescents with IDDM. A controlled study. Diabetes Care 1992;15:1356–60.

55. Rodin GM, Johnson LE, Garfinkel PE, et al. Eating disorders in female adolescents with insulin dependent diabetes mellitus. Int J Psychiatr Med 1986;16:49–57.

56. Striegel-Moore RH, Nicholson TJ, Tamborlane WV. Prevalence of eating disorder symptoms in preadolescent and adolescent girls with IDDM. Diabetes Care 1992;15:1361–8.

57. Rodin GM, Craven J, Littlefield C, et al. Eating disorders and intentional insulin undertreatment in adolescent females with diabetes. Psychosomatics 1991;32:171–6.

58. Wing RR, Nowalk MP, Marcus MD, et al. Subclinical eating disorders and glycemic control in adolescents with type I diabetes. Diabetes Care 1986;9:162–7.

59. Affenito SG, Lammi-Keefe CJ, Vogel S, et al. Women with insulin-dependent diabetes mellitus (IDDM) complicated by eating disorders are at risk for exacerbated alterations in lipid metabolism. Eur J Clin Nutr 1997;51:462–6.

60. Rydall AC, Rodin GM, Olmsted MP, et al. Disordered eating behavior and microvascular complications in young women with insulin-dependent diabetes mellitus. N Engl J Med 1997;336:1849–54.

61. The effect of intensive treatment of diabetes on the development and progression of long-term complications in insulin-dependent diabetes mellitus. The Diabetes Control and Complications Trial Research Group. N Engl J Med 1993;329:977–86.

62. Nielson S, Molbak AG. Eating disorder and type 1 diabetes: overview and summing-up. Eur Eat Disord Rev 1998;6:1–23.

63. Steel JM, Young RJ, Lloyd GG, Clarke BF. Clinically apparent eating disorders in young diabetic women with painful neuropathy and other complications. BMJ 1987;294:859–62.

64. Powers PS, Malone JI, Coovert DL, Schulman RG. Insulin-dependent diabetes mellitus and eating disorders: a prevalence study. Compr Psychiatry 1990;31:205–10.

65. Biggs MM, Basco MR, Patterson G, Raskin P. Insulin withholding for weight control in women with diabetes. Diabetes Care 1994;17:1186–9.

66. Khan Y, Montgomery AM. Eating attitudes in young females with diabetes: insulin omission identifies a vulnerable subgroup. Br J Med Psychol 1996;69:343–53.

67. Stancin T, Link DL, Reuter JM. Binge eating and purging in young women with IDDM. Diabetes Care 1989;12:601–3.

68. Polonsky WH, Anderson BJ, Lohrer PA, et al. Insulin omission in women with IDDM. Diabetes Care 1994;17:1178–85.

69. Wilson RM, Clarke P, Barkes H, et al. Starting insulin treatment as an outpatient. Report of 100 consecutive patients followed up for at least one year. JAMA 1986;256:877–80.

70. Swift PG, Hearnshaw JR, Botha JL, et al. A decade of diabetes: keeping children out of hospital. BMJ 1993;307:96–98.

71. Spaulding RH, Spaulding WB. The diabetes day-care unit. II. Comparison of patients and costs of initiating insulin therapy in the unit and a hospital. Can Med Assoc J 1973;114:780–3.

72. Schneider AJ. Starting insulin therapy in children with newly diagnosed diabetes. Am J Dis Child 1983;137:782–6.

73. Lee PD. An out-patient focused program for childhood diabetes: design, implementation, and effectiveness. Tex Med 1992;88:64–8.

74. Chase HP, Crews KR, Garg S, et al. Outpatient management vs in-hospital management of children with diabetes. Clin Pediatr 1992;31:450–6.

75. Lessing DN, Swift PG, Metcalfe MA, Baum JD. Newly diagnosed diabetes: a study of parental satisfaction. Arch Dis Child 1992;67:1011–3.

76. Charron-Prochownik D, Maihle T, Siminerio L, Songer T. Outpatient versus inpatient care of children newly diagnosed with IDDM. Diabetes Care 1997;20:657–60.

77. Dougherty G, Schiffrin A, White D, et al. Home-based management can achieve intensification cost-effectively in type 1 diabetes. Pediatrics 1999;103:122–8.

78. Dougherty GE, Soderstrom L, Schiffrin A. An economic evaluation of home care for children with newly diagnosed diabetes. Med Care 1998;36:586–98.

79. Daneman D, Frank M. Defining quality of care for children and adolescents with type 1 diabetes. Acta Paediatr Suppl 1998;425:11–9.

80. Banion C, Klingensmith G, Giardano B, Radcliffe J. Efficacy of outpatient management of new onset diabetes in children. Diabetes 1987;36(Suppl 1):118A.

81. Strock E, Spencer M, Sandell J, Hollander P. Reimbursement of an ambulatory insulin program. Diabetes 1987;36(Suppl 1):33A.

82. Hoffman WH, O'Neill P, Khoury C, Bernstein SS. Service and education for the insulin-dependent child. Diabetes Care 1978;1:285–8.

83. Glasgow AM, Weissberg-Benchell J, Tynan WD, et al. Readmissions of children with diabetes mellitus to a children's hospital. Pediatrics 1991;88:98–104.

84. Daneman D, Frank M, Perlman K. When a child has diabetes. Toronto: Key Porter Books; 1999.

85. Golden MP, Herrold AJ, Orr DP. An approach to the prevention of recurrent diabetic ketoacidosis in the pediatric population. J Pediatr 1985;107:195–200.

86. Scibilia J, Finegold D, Dorman J, et al. Why do children with diabetes die? Acta Endocrinol Suppl 1986;279:326–33.

87. Edge JA, Ford-Adams ME, Dunger DB. Causes of death in children with insulin dependent diabetes 1990–1996. Arch Dis Child 1999;81:318–23.

88. Fitzgerald M, O'Sullivan M, Mallins M. Fatal diabetic ketosis. BMJ 1961;1:247–50.

89. Young E, Bradley RF. Cerebral edema with irreversible coma in severe diabetic ketoacidosis. N Engl J Med 1967;276:665–9.

90. Rosenbloom AL. Intracerebral crises during treatment of diabetic ketoacidosis. Diabetes Care 1990;13:22–33.

91. Mel JM, Werther GA. Incidence and outcome of diabetic cerebral oedema in childhood: are there predictors? J Paediatr Child Health 1995;31:17–20.

92. Levitsky LL, Ekwo E, Goselink CA, et al. Death from diabetes in hospitalized children [abstract]. Pediatr Res 1991;29:195A.

93. Clements RS, Prockop LD, Winegrad AI. Acute cerebral oedema during the treatment of hyperglycemia: an experimental model. Lancet 1968;ii:384–6.

94. Durr JA, Hoffman WH, Sklar AH, et al. Correlates of brain edema in uncontrolled IDDM. Diabetes 1992;41:627–32.

95. Hoffman WH, Steinhart CM, el Gammal T, et al. Cranial CT in children and adolescents with diabetic ketoacidosis. AJNR Am J Neuroradiol 1988;9:733–9.

96. Krane EJ, Rockoff MA, Wallman JK, Wolfsdorf JI. Subclinical brain swelling in children during treatment of diabetic ketoacidosis. N Engl J Med 1985;312:1147–51.

97. Coma at the onset of young insulin-dependent diabetes in Japan. The results of a nationwide survey. Japan and Pittsburgh Childhood Diabetes Research Groups. Diabetes 1985;34:1241–6.

98. Bello FA, Sotos JF. Cerebral oedema in diabetic ketoacidosis in children. Lancet 1990;336:64.

99. Hale PM, Rezvani I, Braunstein AW, et al. Factors predicting cerebral edema in young children with diabetic ketoacidosis and new onset type I diabetes. Acta Paediatr 1997;86:626–31.

100. Harris GD, Fiordalisi I, Harris WL, et al. Minimizing the risk of brain herniation during treatment of diabetic ketoacidemia: a retrospective and prospective study. J Pediatr 1990;117:22–31.

101. Duck SC, Wyatt DT. Factors associated with brain herniation in the treatment of diabetic ketoacidosis. J Pediatr 1988;113:10–4.

102. Harris GD, Fiordalisi I. Physiologic management of diabetic ketoacidemia. A 5-year prospective pediatric experience in 231 episodes. Arch Pediatr Adolesc Med 1994;148:1046–52.

103. Satin W, La Greca AM, Zigo MA, Skyler JS. Diabetes in adolescence: effects of multifamily group intervention and parent simulation of diabetes. J Pediatr Psychol 1989;14:259–75.

104. Anderson BJ, Wolf FM, Burkhart MT, et al. Effects of peer-group intervention on metabolic control of adolescents with IDDM. Randomized outpatient study. Diabetes Care 1989;12:179–83.

105. Olmsted M, Rodin G, Rydall A, et al. Effect of psychoeducation on disordered eating attitudes and behaviors in young women with IDDM [abstract]. Diabetes 1997;46:88A.

106. Peveler RC, Fairburn CG. The treatment of bulimia nervosa in patients with diabetes mellitus. Int J Eat Disord 1992;11:45–53.

What Is Type 1 Diabetes?

Margaret L. Lawson, MD, MSc, FRCPC, and Sarah E. Muirhead, MD, FRCPC

ABSTRACT

Type 1 diabetes is a chronic disease characterized by hyperglycemia due to absolute deficiency of insulin secretion. It is caused by autoimmune destruction of the pancreatic beta cells. The autoimmune destruction is primarily T-cell mediated, and the balance between subsets of T-helper cells appears to be critical to the process. Evidence of autoimmunity is provided by the appearance of autoantibodies prior to the onset of clinical disease. Measurement of these autoantibodies (glutamic acid decarboxylase [GAD], insulin autoantibodies [IAA], and islet-cell antibodies [ICA512/IA-2]) along with subtle indicators of beta-cell dysfunction (first phase insulin release [FPIR]) can be used to identify those at risk of developing Type 1 diabetes.

INTRODUCTION

The etiology of Type 1 diabetes is multifactorial. The extremely wide geographic and racial variability in both the incidence and prevalence of Type 1 diabetes suggests that genetics plays a significant role in the etiology of the disease. The single most important genetic determinant in Type 1 diabetes is the histocompatability locus (HLA) on chromosome six, in particular HLA-DR and HLA-DQ alleles. However, Type 1 diabetes is a polygenic disorder, with at least 15 different genes contributing in varying degrees. Further, the discordance in development of Type 1 diabetes between identical twins (30%) indicates that the etiology is only partly genetic. Epidemiologic studies demonstrating seasonality for the incidence of Type 1 diabetes, as well as outbreaks and secular trends, provide further evidence of nongenetic environmental involvement in the pathogenesis of Type 1 diabetes. Risk factors for which evidence exists include dietary triggers (cow's milk, caffeine, and nitrites), enterovirus infections during childhood and perhaps during pregnancy, and possibly psychosocial events in early childhood. There is no evidence that immunizations have a causative or protective role in the development of Type 1 diabetes.

Type 1 diabetes is a chronic disease characterized by hyperglycemia due to absolute deficiency of insulin secretion. The clinical presentation ranges from mild nonspecific symptoms or no symptoms to coma. Although Type 1 diabetes usually develops before 30 years of age, it can occur at any age. At presentation, most patients are thin and have experienced weight loss, polyuria (including enuresis in children), polydipsia, and fatigue. Approximately 25% of individuals with Type 1 diabetes present with diabetic ketoacidosis.[1]

The etiology of Type 1 diabetes is multifactorial. Most individuals with Type 1 diabetes have immune-mediated disease. This form of diabetes is caused by cellular mediated autoimmune destruction of the insulin-producing beta cells of the pancreas. There is a smaller group of people with Type 1 diabetes who have no evidence of autoimmunity or other known etiology; this condition is termed "idiopathic Type 1 diabetes." These patients often have severe but varying levels of insulin deficiency and are prone to diabetic ketoacidosis. This chapter focuses on the more common immune-mediated Type 1 diabetes, answering the following questions:

1. How common is Type 1 diabetes, and what factors affect its incidence?
2. What are the genetic determinants of susceptibility to Type 1 diabetes mellitus?

3. What is the evidence for an autoimmune pathogenesis for Type 1 diabetes, and how can markers of autoimmunity (ie, autoantibodies) be used to identify those at increased risk for Type 1 diabetes or those in whom the process of autoimmune beta-cell destruction has begun?
4. Is diet (cow's milk, caffeine, nitrates) linked to the risk of Type 1 diabetes?
5. Do viral infections increase the risk of developing Type 1 diabetes?
6. Do immunizations affect the risk of developing Type 1 diabetes?
7. Does emotional stress increase the risk of developing Type 1 diabetes?

How Common Is Type 1 Diabetes, and What Factors Affect Its Incidence?

Prevalence refers to the number of people who actually have the disease at a *point* in time. It is usually expressed as the number of cases per 1,000 persons and is defined as:

$$\text{Prevalence} = \frac{\text{number of people with the disease}}{\text{number of people at risk}} \times 1,000$$

Incidence refers to the number of people who developed the disease during a *period* of time. It is usually expressed as the number of cases per 100,000 population per year:

$$\text{Incidence} = \frac{\text{number of new cases of the disease per year}}{\text{number of people at risk}} \times 100,000$$

Prevalence data are often less precise than incidence data, because they can be difficult to track the population of interest after the development of disease. On the other hand, incidence figures are only accurate if population-based registries exist or capture-recapture methods are used to track new cases.

There is extremely wide geographic and racial variability in the incidence of Type 1 diabetes, suggesting that genetics plays a significant role in the etiology of the disease (Figure 9–1). Incidence rates worldwide vary 40-fold, between 0.6 per 100,000 per year in Mexico and Korea to 35.3 per 100,000 per year in Finland.[2] Further, Type 1 diabetes is much more common in Caucasians than in Blacks, Asians, or Hispanics[2] (Table 9–1).

There is a large body of evidence supporting an environmental influence on the development of Type 1 diabetes, acting in addition to genetic factors. The incidence of Type 1 diabetes is much higher in northern than in southern hemispheres.[2] There has been a high positive correlation found between the incidence of Type 1 diabetes and latitude and a negative correlation between incidence and average yearly temperature[3] (Figure 9–2). Although these differences in incidence are partly explained by genetic differences between the populations of these countries, there are great variations even among countries such as Finland, Lithuania, and Estonia, which are genetically homogeneous and have a similar climate.[4] In addition, epidemiologic studies based on well-ascertained incidence registries have shown significant increases in incidence in certain countries over the last three decades, specifically in Scandinavia,[5] as well as outbreaks/epidemics within other countries[6–7] (Figure 9–3). These varying incidence rates strongly suggest environmental influences in the development of the disease.

Data on the prevalence of Type 1 diabetes are less readily available than incidence data due to the difficulty of tracking individuals after onset. Data from the 1960s to 1980s in the United States found the prevalence in children < 17 years of age to vary from 0.6 to 2.5 cases per 1,000, with most studies finding prevalence rates of 1.2 to 1.9 per 1,000 children[8] (Table 9–2).

Association between Incidence, Age of Onset, and Gender

Type 1 diabetes is rare before 6 months of age. After 9 months of age, the incidence rises sharply, peaking between ages 9 and 13 years, with a decline in incidence thereafter[8] (Figure 9–4). The reported incidence of Type 1 diabetes after age 30 varies depending on the diag-

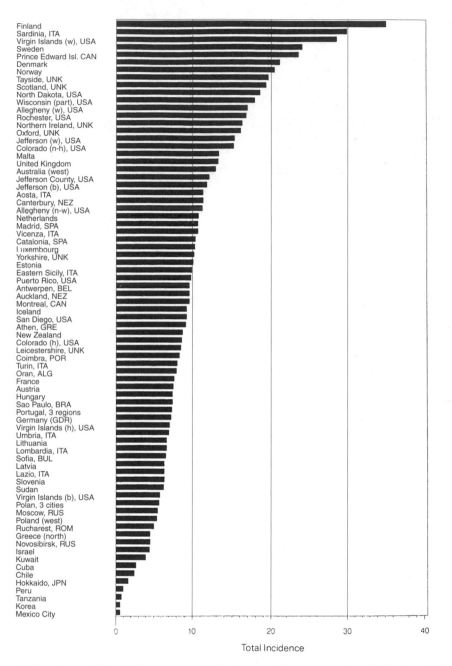

Figure 9–1 Incidence of Type 1 diabetes worldwide. Age-specific incidence (per 100,000 population) of Type 1 diabetes in age group under 15 years. Data for boys and girls have been pooled. The populations are arranged in ascending order according to incidence. w = White; n-w = non-White; b = Black; h = Hispanic; n-h = non-Hispanic. (Reproduced with permission from Karvonen M, Tuomilehto J, Libman I, et al. A review of the recent epidemiologic data on the worldwide incidence of Type 1 (insulin-dependent) diabetes mellitus. Diabetologica 1993;36:883–92.)

nostic criteria used. When Type 1 diabetes was diagnosed in all patients treated with insulin from onset, the incidence decreased from the second through the fourth decade but rose steadily after age 40, to a peak of 26.9 cases per 100,000 per year between ages 60 and 69 years.[9] In contrast, when stringent criteria were applied in a population-based study in Copenhagen, the incidence rate after age 30 was 9.6 per 100,000 per year.[10]

Table 9–1 Incidence of Type 1 Diabetes by Ethnic Group*

| Registry | Ethnic Groups | | | |
| | Non-Hispanic | | | Hispanic |
	White	Black	Oriental†	
United States				
Rochester, MN,	20.6			
1970–1979	13.9–29.5			
	(96%)			
North Dakota,	20.3			
1979–1983	17.2–24.0			
	(93%)			
Colorado,	16.4			9.7
1978–1983	15.0–17.8			7.4–12.4
	(82%)			(18%)
Allegheny County, PA,	16.2	11.8		
1978–1983	14.1–18.4	7.9–17.2		
	(84%)	(14%)		
Jefferson County, AL,	16.9	4.4		
1979–1983	13.4–21.4	2.3–7.5		
	(58%)	(40%)		
San Diego, CA,	13.8	3.3	6.4	4.1
1978–1980	9.8–18.9	0.4–11.9	1.3–18.7	1.3–9.6
	(53%)	(12%)	(10%)	(24%)
New Zealand				
Auckland,	14.3		4.4	
1982–1985	11.5–17.8		2.1–8.1	
	(70%)		(28%)	
Canterbury,	12.1		0.0	
1982–1985	8.7–16.6		0.0–20.5	
	(93%)		(4%)	

*Age-adjusted (0–14 y) incidence of Type 1 diabetes and 95% confidence intervals by ethnic group. Size of ethnic group is given in parentheses as percent of the total population 0–14 years old in area of registration.
†For New Zealand, data are for Maori and Polynesians.
Reprinted with permission from Diabetes Epidemiology Research International Group. Geographic patterns of childhood insulin-dependent diabetes mellitus. Diabetes 1988;37:1113–9.

Incidence rates in males and females are similar overall, although Type 1 diabetes is more common in males than in females < 7 years of age and more common in females than in males from 7 to 13 years of age, with similar rates for males and females thereafter.[8]

WHAT ARE THE GENETIC DETERMINANTS OF SUSCEPTIBILITY TO TYPE 1 DIABETES MELLITUS?

Empiric Risk to Family Members

Most cases of Type 1 diabetes are sporadic, given that only 10 to 15% of individuals report a family history of diabetes at the time of diagnosis. However, it is well known that the risk

Table 9–2 Prevalence Studies of Type 1 Diabetes

	Prevalence Estimate Year	Type of Study	Age Range (yr)	Overall Prevalence Rate/1,000
National health interview survey	1976	Interview	0–16	1.60
National health interview survey	1976	Interview	0–16	1.50
Allegheny County, PA	1976	Estimate from incidence data	5–17	1.73
Minnesota	1978	School survey	5–17	1.88
Rochester, MN	1976	Hospital/physician records	5–18	1.02
Michigan	1972	School survey	5–17	1.61
Pennsylvania	1975	School survey	5–17	1.71
Erie County, NY	1961	Hospital/physician records	0–16	0.6
Colorado	1981	School survey	< 15	1.7
Kentucky	1979	School survey	5–17	2.10
Rhode Island	1980	Random sample	< 15	2.50
Utah	1981	Random sample	< 15	1.20
North Dakota	1983	Outpatient records	< 18	1.30

Reprinted with permission from Cruickshanks KJ, La Porte RE, Dorman JS, et al. The epidemiology of insulin-dependent diabetes mellitus: etiology and prognosis. In: Ahmed PI, Ahmed N, editors. Coping with juvenile diabetes. Springfield (IL): Charles C. Thomas Publisher; 1985. p. 332–57.

of diabetes is increased in relatives of individuals with Type 1 diabetes. Approximately 5% of first-degree relatives of individuals with diabetes will develop the disease,[11] but this varies depending on the relationship to the proband. Table 9–3 contains a more detailed summary of the risk to family members.

Family studies have failed to identify any Mendelian pattern of inheritance of Type 1 diabetes, and its origin is thus considered to be polygenic. The main genetic determinant of diabetes risk is the histocompatibility locus (HLA) on chromosome 6 (labeled IDDM1). In recent years, several non–HLA-associated alleles have also been found to confer increased risk of diabetes (labeled IDDM2 to IDDM15).

Histocompatibility Locus Alleles

It has been estimated that the HLA loci provide approximately 60% of the influence that genetics has on the development of Type 1 diabetes.[12] Figure 9–5 shows a map of the major histocompatibility complex (MHC) loci on chromosome six, with its three groups of closely linked alleles. The class I loci (HLA-A, -B, and -C) encode the classic transplantation antigens. Class II loci (HLA-DR, -DQ, and -DP) encode proteins involved in the presentation of antigens to the T-helper lymphocytes. Class III loci encode other proteins, including those of the complement system. It is the class II loci, in particular DQ and DR, that are involved in susceptibility and resistance to Type 1 diabetes.

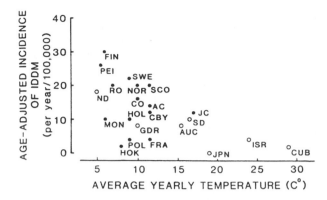

Figure 9–2 Incidence of Type 1 diabetes versus average yearly temperature. Correlation between age-adjusted incidence of Type 1 diabetes under age 15 years in various areas and average yearly temperature. FIN = Finland; PEI = Prince Edward Island, Canada; SWE = Sweden; RO = Rochester, MN; SCO = Tayside, Scotland; NOR = Norway; ND = North Dakota; CO = Colorado; AC = Allegheny County, PA; CBY = Canterbury, New Zealand; JC = Jefferson County, AL; HOL = The Netherlands; SD = San Diego, CA; MON = Montreal; AUC = Auckland, New Zealand; GDR = German Democratic Republic; POL = Wielkopolska, Poland; FRA = Rhone, France; ISR = Israel; CUB = Cuba; HOK = Hoddaido, Japan; JPN = Japan. IDDM = insulin-dependent diabetes mellitus. $r_s = -.55, p < .005$ for untransformed data. O = registries for which no ascertainment estimate was available. Ascertainment for Japan was 60%. (Reproduced with permission from Diabetes Epidemiology Research International Group. Geographic patterns of childhood insulin-dependent diabetes mellitus. Diabetes 1988;37:1113–9.)

HLA-DR Alleles

The HLA-DR3 and DR4 alleles confer susceptibility to Type 1 diabetes, especially if an individual has the DR3/DR4 haplotype (see Figure 9–5). In Caucasians, at least one of these alleles is present in 95% of those with diabetes and in 50% of the population without diabetes.[13,14] Nevertheless, only a minority of persons carrying the DR3 and/or DR4 haplotype will develop diabetes, underscoring the importance of other genetic and possibly non-

Table 9–3 Empiric Lifetime Risk of Type 1 Diabetes

Relation to Diabetic Proband	Risk (%)
General population	0.4
Sibling	5.0
Parent	5.0
Offspring of diabetic father	6.1
Offspring of diabetic mother	2.0
Offspring of diabetic mother and father	30.0
Monozygotic twin	30.0–50.0
Dizygotic twin	5.0
Sibling and offspring	30.0

Adapted from Eisenbarth GS, Ziegler AG, Colman PA. Pathogenesis of insulin-dependent (type 1) diabetes mellitus. In: Kahn CR, Weir GC, editors. Joslin's diabetes mellitus.13th ed. Philadelphia: Lea & Filbiger; 1994.

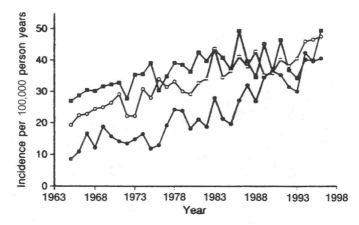

Figure 9–3 Rising incidence of Type 1 diabetes in Finland, 1965–1999. Age-specific annual incidence of Type 1 diabetes per 100,000 children in Finland, age 1–14 years, between 1965 and 1996. • 1–4 years, ○ 5–9 years, ■ 10–14 years. (Reproduced with permission from Tuomilehto J, Karvonen M, Pitkaniemi E, et al. Record-high incidence of Type 1 (insulin-dependent) diabetes mellitus in Finnish children. Diabetologia 1999;42:655–60.)

genetic factors. There are also protective DR alleles, notably DR2 and DR5, in Caucasians.[15] Diabetes does not develop in those with this allele, even in the presence of high titers of islet-cell antibodies or in those with high-risk DQ alleles (Figure 9–6).[16]

HLA-DQ Alleles

There is an even stronger association between DQ haplotypes and the risk of Type 1 diabetes. These haplotypes are estimated to contribute 30 to 40% in the development of diabetes.[17] Primary susceptibility haplotypes are DQB1*0302 and DQB1*0201, the DQB1*0302 /DQB1*0201 being at especially high risk. Other important susceptibility DQB1 alleles are shown in Table 9–4. These alleles (non–Asp-57) are notable for the absence of aspartic acid at position 57 of the DQB1 chain, which is the strongest single marker of susceptibility to Type 1 diabetes that has yet been identified.[18] Table 9–4 shows the relative frequencies of aspartic and nonaspartic

Table 9–4 HLA-DR and HLA-DQ Phenotype Frequencies in Type 1 Diabetes Cases and Healthy Controls

Phenotype	Diabetic (%)	Nondiabetic (%)	Odds Ratio
DR (serology)			
DR3/DR4	33	6	8.3
DR3/DR3	7	1	9.8
DR3/DRX	7	14	0.05
DR4/DR4	26	0	—
DR4/DRX	22	16	1.5
DRX/DRX	4	63	0.2
DQ (molecular probes)			
NA/NA	96	19	107.2
NA/A	4	46	0.04
A/A	0	34	0.0

HLA-DR and HLA-DQ = class II histocompatibility loci; NA = nonaspartic; A= aspartic.
Adapted from Sperling[22]; data from Morel P et al.[23]

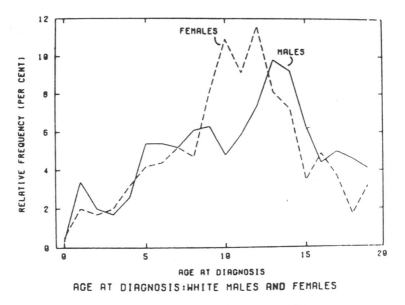

AGE AT DIAGNOSIS:WHITE MALES AND FEMALES

Figure 9–4 Incidence of Type 1 diabetes versus age of onset. Overall incidence rates for Type 1 diabetes in Allegheny County (PA). (Reproduced with permission from Cruickshanks KJ, La Porte RE, Dorman JS, et al. The epidemiology of insulin-dependent diabetes mellitus: etiology and prognosis. In: Ahmed PI, Ahmed PN, editors. Coping with juvenile diabetes. Springfield (IL): Charles C. Thomas Publisher; 1985. p. 332–57.)

acid residues in individuals with diabetes and in healthy controls. Of note, the population variation in the distribution of non–Asp-57 alleles may explain much of the geographic variation in insulin-dependent diabetes mellitus (IDDM) incidence.[19] The DQA1 alleles also influence susceptibility to Type 1 diabetes, with the presence of arginine at position 52 of the DQA1 chain conferring increased susceptibility.[20,21] Combining DQA1 and DQB1 typing helps in the risk assessment. Table 9–5 shows the influence of various HLA loci on susceptibility to diabetes, in estimated order of importance. It should be noted that certain HLA-DR and -DQ alleles tend to occur together because of linkage dissociation. Also, the correlation of specific loci with Type 1 diabetes depends on the ethnicity of the population studied.

CLASS II			CLASS III								CLASS I		
DP	**DQ**	**DR**	21B	C4B	21A	C4A	Bf	C2	HSP	TNF	B	C	A

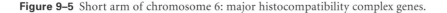

Figure 9–5 Short arm of chromosome 6: major histocompatibility complex genes.

Nonhistocompatibility Locus Alleles

The MHC on chromosome 17 (labeled IDDM1) is the major diabetogenic locus. It is necessary but not sufficient for the development of Type 1 diabetes. At least 16 non-HLA alleles have shown some association with diabetes susceptibility, suggesting that diabetes is a polygenic disorder.[25] Although individually none are as important as the MHC locus, collectively they are important and are necessary for disease development.

The second most important diabetes susceptibility gene is IDDM2,[26] located on the insulin (INS) gene on chromosome 11. The others are consecutively numbered from IDDM3 through IDDM15. Of these, there are four loci for which there is sufficient evidence from linkage and association studies[27] to suggest they are true susceptibility loci: IDDM4 (11q13),[28–31] IDDM5 (6q22),[28,31] IDDM8 (6q27),[28,31–33] and IDDM12 (2q33).[34] There are a number of genome-wide scans for linkage of chromosome regions to Type 1 diabetes underway.

Table 9–5 Relative Influence of Histocompatability Loci on Susceptibility to Type 1 Diabetes Mellitus

Relative Influence[†]	DQ Alleles	Associated HLA-DR	IDDM Influence
1	DQB1*0602, DQA1*0102	DR2 (DR15)	Protective (common allele)
2	DQB1*0301, DQA1*0501	DR5	Protective
3	DQB1*0302, DQA1*0301	DR4	Susceptible
4	DQB1*0201, DQA1*0501	DR3	Susceptible
5	DQB1*0501, DQA1*0101	DR1	Susceptible
	DQB1*0201, DQA1*0301	DR7	Susceptible (African Americans)
	DQB1*0502, DQA1*0102	DR2 (DR16)	Susceptible (common in Sardinia)
	DQB1*0303, DQA1*0301	DR4	Susceptible (Japanese)
	DQB1*0303, DQA1*0301	DR9	Susceptible (Japanese)
	DQB1*0600[‡]	DR6	Neutral
	DQB1*0201, DQA1*0201	DR7	Neutral
	DQB1*0303, DQA1*0301	DR4	Neutral
6	DQB1*0301, DQA1*0301	DR4	Neutral

[†]Grouped in descending order, from most to least influential.
[‡]Specific DQB1 and DQA1 alleles not specified.
Adapted from Winter et al[24]; adapted from Nepom.[15]

In the future, a combination of data from these scans should provide a clearer picture of the genetics of this condition.

Summary of Genetic Determinants of Susceptibility to Type 1 Diabetes Mellitus

1. The discordance in development of Type 1 diabetes between identical twins (30%) suggests that the etiology is only partly genetic. Susceptibility genotypes are necessary but not sufficient to cause the disease.
2. Diabetes is a polygenic disorder with at least 16 different loci demonstrating linkage with the disease. The relative importance of each of these loci in the susceptibility to, and pathogenesis of, diabetes remains to be determined.
3. The single most important genetic determinant in Type 1 diabetes is the histocompatability locus (HLA) on chromosome 6, in particular, HLA-DR and HLA-DQ alleles. Primary susceptibility alleles are DQB1*0302 and DQB1*0201, whereas DQB1*0602 is dominantly protective. IDDM2 (located on the insulin gene) also demonstrates strong evidence of association and linkage in those with Type 1 diabetes.

WHAT IS THE EVIDENCE FOR AN AUTOIMMUNE PATHOGENESIS FOR TYPE 1 DIABETES?

There is little doubt that Type 1 diabetes is an autoimmune disorder. This is suggested by a number of factors, including (1) the presence of insulitis, (2) the presence of humoral and cellular autoimmune markers against beta cells, (3) the association with other autoimmune conditions, (4) the association with certain HLA haplotypes, (5) the effect of immunomodulation on the treatment or prevention of diabetes, and (6) passive transfer studies in

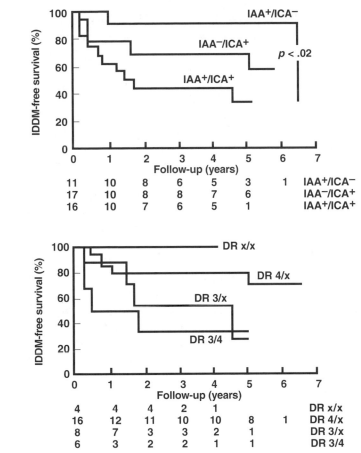

Figure 9–6 Life-table analysis of cumulative risk of Type 1 diabetes in antibody-positive first-degree relatives in relation to antibody status and HLA typing—(A) antibody status, (B) HLA-DR typing. (Reproduced with permission from Seidel D, Ziegler A-G. Prediction of Type 1 diabetes. Horm Res 1996;45[Suppl]:36–9.)

nonobese diabetic (NOD) mice whereby diabetes can be induced in the recipient mouse by the T cells of diabetic donor animals.[35–38]

Humoral immunity is conferred by B lymphocytes that express serum antibodies that react directly with antigens such as insulin. Cellular immunity involves T lymphocytes, which require antigens, or processed portions of proteins (peptides), to be presented to histocompatibility molecules on the surface of antigen-presenting cells such as macrophages or B lymphocytes. Activation of B and T lymphocytes against islet-cell antigens results in clonal expansion of these lymphocytes and the synthesis of various effector molecules, which results in islet-cell damage. The T cells are subdivided into helper (CD4+) and cytotoxic (CD8+) cells. The CD4+ cells further subdivide into Th1 and Th2 subsets; the balance between Th1 and Th2 subsets appears to be critical to the initiation of the autoimmune process.[39,40] The Th1 cells produce cytokines such as interleukin (IL)-2, interferon, and tumor necrosis factor, which mediate cellular immunity characterized by inflammation and cytotoxicity. These cells, in addition to macrophages, are the likely cause of the insulitis and beta-cell destruction, mediated at least in part by cytokines.[41] The Th2 cells secrete IL-2, IL-5, and IL-10, which appear to mediate a humoral- or antibody-mediated response and inhibit the Th1 cell inflammatory response.[42] Although T-cell mediated immunity is the primary cause of beta-cell damage, it has been difficult to study. The immunogenic markers primarily used are humoral markers or autoantibodies directed toward islet-cell antigens.

Hypothetical Stages in the Development of Type 1 Diabetes

As noted above, Type 1 diabetes is caused by autoimmune destruction of the pancreatic beta cells. The autoimmune destruction is primarily T-cell mediated, and the balance between subsets of T-helper cells appears to be critical to the process.

It is generally accepted that there are five stages in the development of autoimmune diabetes (Figure 9–7).[43] The genetically susceptible individual (stage 1) is exposed to an as yet unknown precipitating event that results in the development of autoantibodies toward beta-cell antigens and progressive beta-cell destruction (stage 2). This results in a progressive loss of insulin release, with normal glucose homeostasis on a day-to-day basis but subnormal release when the FPIR is measured during an intravenous glucose tolerance test (stage 3). Once the beta-cell mass is reduced to 20 to 30% of normal, overt diabetes develops (stage 4), although some residual endogenous insulin production remains. Eventually, the pancreas ceases all insulin production (stage 5), and the individual is entirely dependent on exogenous insulin. The prediabetes phase (stages 2 to 3) may last for months to years.

Predictive Value of Islet-Cell Antibodies for Type 1 Diabetes

Autoantibodies directed at the islet cell (ICA) were first described in 1974 by Bottazzo and colleagues in a cohort of patients with autoimmune polyendocrinopathy, including Type 1 diabetes.[44] This provided the first serologic evidence that autoimmunity is involved in the pathogenesis of Type 1 diabetes. It is now well established that autoantibodies are seen in the majority of individuals with Type 1 diabetes and that the presence of serum ICA is a predictive marker for the development of diabetes in first-degree relatives (FDR) and possibly in the general population. Highly sensitive prediction of diabetes in FDR of individuals with Type 1 diabetes is possible using ICA, provided that low titers are used as a cutoff. Islet-cell antibody positivity carries a 25 to 50% risk of diabetes in the next 5 years, but this is titer dependent. Titers are expressed as Juvenile Diabetes Foundation (JDF) units, which were standardized to improve comparability of results among laboratories. The higher the titer, the greater the risk of diabetes, as shown in Figure 9–8, which summarizes the results for the

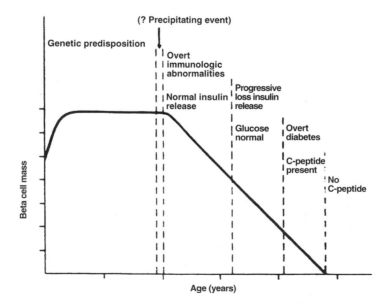

Figure 9–7 Hypothetical stages in the development of Type 1 diabetes. (Reproduced with permission from Eisenbarth G. Type 1 diabetes mellitus: a chronic autoimmune disease. N Engl J Med 1986;314:1360–8.)

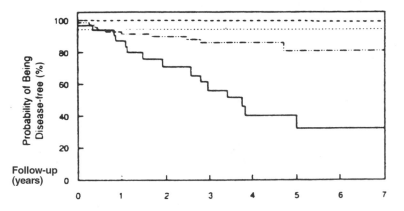

Figure 9–8 Probability of remaining free of Type 1 diabetes in four groups of relatives of probands with Type 1 diabetes, according to ICA status expressed as JDF units. (Reproduced with permission from Riley WJ, Maclaren NK, Krischer J, et al. A prospective study of the development of diabetes in relatives of patients with insulin-dependent diabetes. N Engl J Med 1990;323:1167–72.)
----- Antibody-negative relatives; ....relatives with titers of 10 JDF units; – ·· – ·· relatives with titers of 20 or 40 JDF units; —relatives with titers > 40 JDF units.

Barts-Windsor cohort.[45] Development of ICA positivity before the age of 10 years is an independent risk factor for the development of diabetes in first-degree relatives.[46]

Screening for ICA is the primary tool used in most screening programs and diabetes prevention trials. However, low cutoffs result in lowering of the specificity; therefore, screening for the presence of other autoantibodies and compromised FPIR have been added to the screening process to improve the accuracy of prediction and reduce the number of false-positive results.

Predictive Value of First-Phase Insulin Release for Type 1 Diabetes

The addition of FPIR (in response to glucose load) to autoantibody screening improves the prediction of risk for development of Type 1 diabetes,[47] with abnormalities indicating stage 3 of disease development. Figure 9–9 shows how the already increased risk of progression to diabetes in ICA-positive individuals is further increased if FPIR is reduced.

Predictive Value of Combinations of Autoantibodies for Type 1 Diabetes

The predictive value of insulin autoantibodies (IAA) alone is less than that of ICA. However, it is useful when used in combination with assessment of ICA and FPIR (see Figure 9–6). Insulin autoantibodies are the only antibodies that have been shown to correlate with younger age of onset of, and faster progression to, Type 1 diabetes.[48,49] In recent years, two additional autoantibodies have been identified that, when used in combination with IAA, appear to be better at predicting diabetes risk than ICA alone.[50,51] These include glutamic acid decarboxylase (GAD) autoantibodies and ICA512/IA-2 autoantibodies (the designations ICA512 and IA-2 are used interchangeably). Figure 9–10 shows how a progressive increase in the number of positive autoantibodies (IAA, GAD, and ICA512) increases the risk of developing Type 1 diabetes. Table 9–6 indicates the predictive characteristics of each of these autoantibodies.

Predictive Value of Other Autoantibodies for Type 1 Diabetes

There are several other candidate islet-cell autoantigens with low or controversial diagnostic sensitivity for Type 1 diabetes. These include ICA69Ab, carboxypeptidase H, heat shock protein (HSP), 38kDa jun-B, aromatic L-amino-acid decarboxylase (AADC), DNA topoisomerase II, glima 38, and imogen 38.[54] However, to date, none of these have been routinely used in the screening of those at risk.

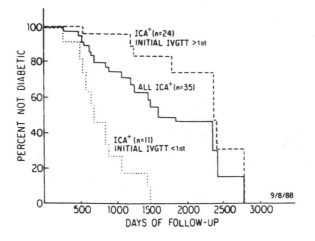

Figure 9–9 Life-table analysis of the development of overt diabetes in ICA-positive relatives based on first-phase insulin release (FPIR) on an intravenous glucose tolerance test (IVGTT). IVGTT 1+3 minute insulin ≥ 1st percentile (upper line) and < 1st percentile (lower line). Middle line is a life-table analysis for all patients combined. Elapsed days (x-axis) is from initial encounter with each patient. (Reproduced with permission from Vardi P, Crisa L, Jackson RA, et al. Predictive value of intravenous glucose tolerance test insulin secretion less than or greater than the first percentile in islet cell antibody positive relatives of Type 1 [insulin-dependent] diabetic patients. Diabetologia 1991;34:93–102.)

Summary of Predictive Value of Immune Markers for Type 1 Diabetes

Of those with high titer ICA, the risk of developing Type 1 diabetes is 8 to 10% per year, which is correlated with titer and age.[55] The addition of IAA and low FPIR increases the risk, such that ICA and IAA+ individuals have a risk of 85% within 5 years, ICA+ and low-FPIR individuals have a 95% risk within 5 years, and the combination of all three (ie, ICA+, IAA+, and low FPIR) confers a risk of 90% within only 3 years.[56–59] It should be noted that 10 to 20%

Table 9–6 Predictive Characteristics of Single Autoantibody Specificities and Antibody Combinations in the Development of Type 1 Diabetes Mellitus

Marker	Sensitivity (%)	Specificity (%)	Positive Predictive Value (%)	Negative Predictive Value (%)
ICA	81	95	43	96
IAA	25	97	29	97
GAD antibodies	69	96	42	99
IA-2 antibodies	69	98	55	99
GAD and/or IA-2 antibodies	81	98	41	99
One antibody	3	94	2	96
Two antibodies	9	99	25	96
Three or four antibodies	72	98	66	99

ICA = islet-cell antibodies; IAA = insulin autoantibodies; GAD = glutamic acid decarboxylase; IA-2 = a protein tyrosine-related protein.
Adapted from Knip[52]; data from Kulmata et al.[53]

of individuals who develop Type 1 diabetes have no detectable ICA or IAA at diagnosis. Newer antibodies are useful in refining the risk assessment, including ICA512 and GAD in combination with IAA.[50,51] Although individually these are less sensitive than ICA, they have a higher positive predictive value, especially when used in combination. The estimated 5-year risk of developing Type 1 diabetes in FDR with one of these antibodies is 15%, with two antibodies 44%, and with all three antibodies 100%.[51] Whether these estimates are valid for the general population remains to be seen. Table 9–7 summarizes the 3- and 5-year risks based on various autoantibody measurements.

EVIDENCE-BASED MESSAGES

1. The ICA assay has the highest sensitivity in detecting those at increased risk for Type 1 diabetes. Sensitivity for ICA is 81 to 95%, depending on the titer of ICA used, as compared with 25 to 69% for IAA, GAD, or ICA512/IA-2. Specificity for all antibodies is high at 95 to 99% (Level 1).[53]

2. The addition of evidence of subtle beta-cell failure through measurement of FPIR during an intravenous glucose tolerance test (IVGTT) can further identify those at high risk of Type 1 diabetes. In ICA-positive relatives, the incidence rate of progression to diabetes is 48% per year with FPIR < 1st percentile and 5% per year with FPIR > 1st percentile. The odds ratio for diabetes within the next 4 years for those with FPIR < 1st percentile is 36, and the positive and negative predictive values are 88% and 83%, respectively (Level 1).[47]

3. Identification of combinations of autoantibodies (GAD, IAA, and ICA512/IA-2) has a better positive predictive value for risk of diabetes than ICA alone. The estimated 5-year risk with zero, one, two, or three antibodies is < 0.5%, 15%, 44%, and > 90%, respectively (Level 1).[51]

Table 9–7 Prediction of the Development of Type 1 Diabetes in First-Degree Relatives: Use of Autoantibody Measurements

	Risk (%)	
Autoantibody	*3 Years*	*5 Years*
ICA (≥ 20 JDF units)	31	51
IAA	33	59
GAD AA	28	52
ICA 512 AA	40	81
Combinations of 2 positive AA		
GAD AA plus IAA	41	68
GAD AA plus ICA512 AA	45	86
IAA plus ICA512 AA	47	100
Effect of FPIR		
≥ 1 positive AA plus normal FPIR	16	21
≥ 1 positive AA plus low FPIR	79	100

ICA = islet-cell antibodies; JDF = Juvenile Diabetes Foundation; IAA = insulin autoantibodies; GAD AA = glutamic acid decarboxylase autoantibodies; FPIR = first-phase insulin release.
Adapted from Fantus[42]; data from Bingley.[50]

Do Environmental Factors Trigger Type 1 Diabetes?

There is strong evidence supporting the effect of nongenetic environmental factors in the pathogenesis of Type 1 diabetes. The incidence of Type 1 diabetes in Asian children who emigrated to Britain increased from 3.1 per 100,000 per year in 1978 to 1981 to 11.7 per 100,000 per year in 1988 to 1990, a rate similar to that seen in the indigenous British population.[60] Similarly, when Polynesians migrate from Western Samoa to New Zealand, their incidence rises from < 1 to 7 per 100,000 per year.[61] In addition, twin studies show significant discordance between identical twins for the development of Type 1 diabetes, indicating that nongenetically determined factors play a role in the etiology of the disease.[62] Further, epidemiologic studies demonstrating seasonality for the incidence of Type 1 diabetes, as well as outbreaks and secular trends, provide further evidence of nongenetic environmental involvement in the pathogenesis of Type 1 diabetes.[2] There have been numerous studies linking various environmental triggers with the subsequent development of Type 1 diabetes, although most attention has been focused on dietary triggers, viral infections, immunizations, and psychosocial stress.

Is Diet Linked to the Risk of Developing Type 1 Diabetes?

There is animal and laboratory evidence that early initiation of cow's milk-based products increases the risk of developing Type 1 diabetes.[62–64] Case-control studies in humans have found conflicting results, and there are no completed randomized controlled trials that have examined the role of cow's milk-based formula on the development of Type 1 diabetes. However, a systematic review of the literature that examined the available case-control studies found that patients with Type 1 diabetes were more likely to have been breastfed for less than 3 months (OR 1.37, 95% CI 1.22 to 1.53) and to have been exposed to cow's milk before 4 months of age (OR 1.57, 95% CI 1.19 to 2.07).[65] There is a randomized controlled trial of cow's milk-based versus non–cow's milk-based formulas in infants genetically at risk for the development of diabetes currently in progress. Early results indicate a higher rate of development of autoimmunity at 24 months of age in those with early exposure to cow's milk-based formulas compared to those without early exposure to cow's milk-based formulas (12.5% vs 1.9%, $p = .036$).[66] In addition, a recent prospective cohort study of siblings of children with Type 1 diabetes found that high milk consumption during childhood (> 2 8-oz glasses per day) was associated with an increased risk for development of autoantibodies (ICA, IAA, GAD, IA-2A) and a trend toward increased risk for development of diabetes.[67]

Other dietary triggers that have been examined include consumption of caffeine, dietary nitrite, nitrate, and nitrosamines (eg, smoked meat or fish); these last three were studied because consumption is common in the Scandinavian countries, which also have very high diabetes incidence. There has been a positive correlation found between per capita coffee consumption and the incidence of Type 1 diabetes.[68] It has also been suggested that during pregnancy, caffeine crosses the placenta and has a toxic effect on intrauterine pancreatic development. However, no association was found between maternal caffeine consumption during pregnancy, or by either parent during conception, and the subsequent development of diabetes in the offspring.[69] In contrast, increased caffeine consumption during childhood may lead to increased insulin secretion and additional stress on the beta cells, thus increasing the risk of developing Type 1 diabetes. In the Finnish population, an increased risk for Type 1 diabetes has been found in children who consume coffee or tea regularly.[69]

Toxic effects on animal pancreatic beta cells have been shown to result from consumption of N-nitroso compounds such as streptozotocin and N-nitrosomethylurea.[70,71] In a Swedish case-control study, a positive dose-response association between children's consumption of dietary nitrites, nitrates, or nitrosamines and the development of Type 1 diabetes was found.[72] Similarly, a Finnish study also found an association with maternal and children's consumption of nitrites but no association with dietary nitrates[73] (Table 9–8).

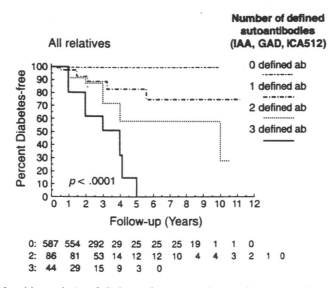

Figure 9–10 Life-table analysis of diabetes-free survival according to number of autoantibodies. (Reproduced with permission from Verge CF, Gianni R, Kawasaki E, et al. Prediction of type 1 diabetes in first-degree relatives using a combination of insulin, GAD, and ICA512/IA-2 autoantibodies. Diabetes 1996;45:926–33.)

Summary of the Link between Diet and Type 1 Diabetes

1. Early discontinuation of breastfeeding before 3 months of age and/or exposure to cow's milk formula before 4 months of age is associated with a 1.4- to 1.5-fold increased risk of developing Type 1 diabetes.[65]
2. Children (< 15 years of age) who consume one cup of tea or at least two cups of coffee daily have a twofold increased risk of developing Type 1 diabetes. [69]
3. Higher consumption of dietary nitrites during childhood is associated with a 2.3-fold increased risk of developing Type 1 diabetes. [73]

Evidence-Based Message

Children who have a sibling with diabetes *and* who drink more than two 8-oz glasses of cow's milk per day during childhood have a fourfold increased risk of developing diabetes-related autoantibodies (Level 2).[67]

Do Viral Infections Increase the Risk of Developing Type 1 Diabetes?

Congenital Rubella

There is strong evidence linking congenital rubella infection in the first trimester of pregnancy to the subsequent development of Type 1 diabetes in 20% of offspring during their childhood or young adult lives.[74] In contrast, postnatal rubella infection does not increase the risk of developing Type 1 diabetes. It has been suggested that transplacental passage of the rubella virus combined with chronic viral multiplication postnatally leads to ongoing beta-cell damage, most likely through molecular mimicry. Antibodies to ICA and other surface antigens are present in close to 80% of those with the congenital rubella syndrome who develop Type 1 diabetes, and these individuals usually have the high-risk HLA alleles DR3 or DR4.[75,76] However, congenital rubella-induced diabetes is rare and accounts for only a small percentage of all persons with Type 1 diabetes.

Table 9-8 Studies of the Association between Dietary Triggers and Type 1 Diabetes

Dietary Trigger (in Children)	Outcome	Study Design	Odds Ratio (95% CI)	Study	Grade of Evidence
Breastfeeding < 3 mo	Type 1 diabetes	Systematic review	1.37 (1.22–1.53)*	Gerstein[65]	N/A
Cow's milk before 4 mo	Type 1 diabetes	Systematic review	1.57 (1.19–2.07)*	Gerstein[65]	N/A
> 2 glasses cow's milk/d	Autoantibodies	Cohort study	3.97 (1.3–11.7)*	Virtanen et al[67]	2
> 2 glasses cow's milk/d	Type 1 diabetes	Cohort study	2.75 (0.9–8.4)	Virtanen et al[67]	2
> 1 cup of coffee/d	Type 1 diabetes	Case control	1.94 (1.08–3.47)*	Virtanen et al[69]	N/A
1 cup of tea/d	Type 1 diabetes	Case control	1.69 (1.21–2.37)*	Virtanen et al[69]	N/A
Dietary nitrates or nitrites	Type 1 diabetes	Case control	2.41 (1.64–3.54)*	Dahlquist et al[72]	N/A
Dietary nitrosamines	Type 1 diabetes	Case-control	2.56 (1.83–3.59)*	Dahlquist et al[72]	N/A
Dietary nitrites	Type 1 diabetes	Case-control	2.32 (1.67–3.24)*	Diabetes Epidemiology Research International Group[3]	N/A
Dietary nitrates	Type 1 diabetes	Case-control	0.94 (0.68–1.29)	Virtanen et al[73]	N/A

*Grades of evidence not applied to case-control studies.

Other Viruses

There are epidemiologic data to support the involvement of other viruses in the pathogenesis of Type 1 diabetes. It is unclear, however, whether viral infections initiate beta-cell destruction, participate in the progression from autoimmunity to diabetes, or are involved in both stages. The seasonal trends for diabetes onset could be due to an association with infections occurring more frequently during particular seasons. Several studies have found evidence of enteroviral infections at the time of diabetes diagnosis. In addition, case reports, case-control studies, and cohort studies have linked prior viral infection with subsequent development of Type 1 diabetes. However, serologic studies have found conflicting results, with varying reports of both high- and low-viral antibody titers in children developing Type 1 diabetes. It has also been suggested that higher antibody titers in children at risk of or in the course of developing diabetes may simply reflect a stimulated immune system or a predisposition to certain viral infections.[77] There have been very few studies that have used viral isolation techniques in individuals with new-onset diabetes. Further, there are methodologic problems with the available studies, such as the availability of adequate control subjects, the specimen source, and problems inherent in finding evidence of the viral infection that may have initiated the process of beta-cell destruction weeks to years prior to the onset of symptoms and diagnosis of Type 1 diabetes (Table 9–9).

The association between enteroviral infections and Type 1 diabetes has received the most attention among these viral studies. In a prospective cohort study of siblings of diabetic children, it was found that exposure to enteroviral infections, specifically coxsackie B as determined by antibodies to enteroviruses, was associated temporally with increases in autoimmunity and a subsequent increased risk of developing Type 1 diabetes.[78] However, levels of antibodies to control antigens were not measured, and it is not possible to exclude heightened immune response to enteroviruses among those children who were already going to develop diabetes. Unpublished observations from the prospective Diabetes Autoimmunity Study in the Young (DAISY) do not support any association between beta-cell autoimmunity and evidence of enteroviral infections.[77]

Two case-control studies of pregnant mothers whose children subsequently developed diabetes and control mothers whose children remained nondiabetic found significant elevations of enterovirus antibodies at the end of the first trimester[78] or at delivery[79] in those mothers whose children later developed diabetes. Neither study examined HLA genotypes of the mothers to rule out a possible confounding effect of this on the humoral response to enteroviral infections.

Many case-control studies of newly diagnosed children with Type 1 diabetes and nondiabetic controls have compared the prevalence of enteroviral antibodies in these children, with conflicting results.[77] The only study that tested for the presence of the virus found a much higher frequency of enterovirus RNA by polymerase chain reaction (PCR) (64% vs 4%) in children recently diagnosed with Type 1 diabetes compared to nondiabetic controls.[80] Taken together, review of the available evidence suggests that enteroviruses may increase the risk of developing Type 1 diabetes, but it is not clear whether enteroviruses play an etiologic role early in the initiation and acceleration of the autoimmune process or later in the final precipitation of the disease.

In a nationwide, incident case-control study, a questionnaire was used to examine the impact of early and recent infections on the risk of developing Type 1 diabetes.[81] The study found that children who developed diabetes had more infections in the year prior to diagnosis than other children but no more frequent infections in the first year of life. No specific infectious agents were identified, although lack of power may have contributed to this. There is, however, strong evidence that autoimmunity is usually present several years before onset of clinical disease.[55–59] Therefore, if these infections played an etiologic role in the development of diabetes in these children, it is most likely that the increased insulin required during these infections precipitated the onset of diabetes, rather than causing direct beta-cell

Table 9–9 Studies of the Association between Viral Infections and Type 1 Diabetes

Virus	Population	Outcome	Study Design	Odds Ratio (95% CI)	Study	Grade of Evidence
All infections						
during first year of life	New onset	Type 1 diabetes	Case control	0.64 (0.34–1.20)	Blom et al[81]	N/A
during year prior to diagnosis	IDDM	Type 1 diabetes	Case control	2.55 (1.44–4.52)*	Blom et al[81]	N/A
Enterovirus						
0.5–0.9 infections/yr	Siblings	Type 1 diabetes	Cohort	5.7 (0.7–48)*	Hyoty et al[78]	2
> 1.0 infections/yr	Siblings	Type 1 diabetes	Cohort	38.7 (4.0–370.0)*	Hyoty et al[78]	2
Materral enterovirus	New onset	DM onset < 15 y	Case control	3.19 (1.39–7.30)*	Dahlquist et al[79]	N/A
	IDDM	DM onset < 3 y	Case control	6.61 (1.86–23.52)*	Hyoty et al[78]	N/A

*Grades of evidence not applied to case-control studies.

IDDM = insulin-dependent diabetes mellitus; DM = diabetes mellitus; IAA = insulin autoantibodies; ICA = islet-cell antibodies; IA-2 = a protein tyrosine-related protein.

damage. In addition, it is possible that the altered immune status in these individuals developing diabetes resulted in increased susceptibility to infections.

Summary of the Link between Viruses and Type 1 Diabetes

1. Children with new-onset diabetes frequently have more infections than other children in the year prior to disease onset, but there is no evidence that these infections cause the development of diabetes.[81]
2. Enterovirus infections during pregnancy may be associated with an increased risk for later development of Type 1 diabetes in the offspring.[77]

EVIDENCE-BASED MESSAGE

Enterovirus infections during childhood, particularly coxsackie B, are associated with a high (5.7-fold increased) risk of developing Type 1 diabetes (Level 2).[78]

Do Immunizations Affect the Risk of Developing Type 1 Diabetes?

The possible association between viral infections and Type 1 diabetes has led investigators to examine whether immunizations increase or decrease the risk of developing Type 1 diabetes. The available evidence to date is restricted largely to case-control studies but indicates that immunizations do not increase the risk of developing Type 1 diabetes.[81, 83–85] Animal studies have suggested that bacille Calmette-Guérin (BCG) vaccination can prevent the development of diabetes.[86] However, human studies have shown no protective effect of BCG vaccine in the development of Type 1 diabetes.[81,87–88] Only one case-control study has suggested that measles vaccination might decrease the risk of Type 1 diabetes.[81] In combination with mumps and rubella, however, there is no protective effect of measles immunization[81,83] (Table 9–10).

Therefore, there is no evidence that any of the childhood immunizations increase the risk of developing Type 1 diabetes.[81] Indeed, measles immunization may have a slight protective effect.[81]

EVIDENCE-BASED MESSAGES

1. There is no relationship between BCG vaccination and the risk of developing Type 1 diabetes (Level 2).[87]
2. Pertussis immunization has no effect on the risk of developing Type 1 diabetes (Level 2).[84]
3. *Haemophilus influenzae* type b immunization has no effect on the risk of developing Type 1 diabetes (Level 2).[85]

Does Emotional Stress Increase the Risk of Developing Type 1 Diabetes?

Several retrospective case-control studies have examined the association between psychologic stress and the subsequent development of Type 1 diabetes. Clinical studies have found that psychological stress can affect immune function.[89] Further, emotional stress may result in secretion of counter-regulatory hormones, which may increase insulin requirements. As a result, it has been postulated that psychosocial stress may be a risk factor for the development of Type 1 diabetes.

In a population-based case-control study of 67 children with Type 1 diabetes and 61 healthy age-matched controls, negative life events in the first 2 years of life were associated with a twofold increased risk of developing Type 1 diabetes (OR 1.94, $p = .03$), although there was no association with stressful life events thereafter.[82] Similarly, a Swedish nationwide case-control questionnaire study of 338 children with Type 1 diabetes and 528 age- and sex-matched controls found that events related to actual or threatened severe losses within

Table 9-10 Studies of the Association between Vaccinations and Type 1 Diabetes

Vaccination	Outcome	Study Design	Odds Ratio (95% CI)	Study	Grade of Evidence
Smallpox	Type 1 diabetes	Case control	1.07 (0.77–1.49)	Blom et al[81]	N/A
BCG	Type 1 diabetes	Case-control	1.04 (0.77–1.40)	Blom et al[81]	N/A
	Type 1 diabetes	Cohort	1.09 (0.62–1.91)	Dahlquist et al[87]	
	Type 1 diabetes	Case control	1.26 (0.79–2.02)	Parent et al[88]	N/A
MMR	Type 1 diabetes	Case control	0.95 (0.71–1.28)	Blom et al[81]	N/A
	Autoantibodies	Cohort	0.72 (0.29–1.81)	Hummel et al[83]	2
Measles	Type 1 diabetes	Case control	0.74 (0.55–1.00)*	Blom et al[81]	N/A
Mumps	Type 1 diabetes	Case control	1.75 (0.54–5.70)	Blom et al[81]	N/A
Rubella	Type 1 diabetes	Case control	1.24 (0.41–3.73)	Blom et al[81]	N/A
Polio	Type 1 diabetes	Case control	1.04 (0.17–6.25)	Blom et al[81]	N/A
DPT	Type 1 diabetes	Case control	0.94 (0.70–1.28)	Blom et al[81]	N/A
Pertussis	Type 1 diabetes	Cohort	0.96 (0.68–1.37)	Heijbel et al[84]	2
Haemophilus influenzae type b	Type 1 diabetes	Cohort	1.13 (0.75–1.72)	Karvonen et al[85]	2

*Grades of evidence not applied to case-control studies.

BCG = bacille Calmette-Guérin; MMR = measles-mumps-rubella; DPT = diptheria-pertussis-tetanus.

the family were associated with an almost twofold increased risk of diabetes (OR 1.82, 95% CI 1.09 to 3.03).[83] These studies were retrospective, however, and subject to recall bias.

In summary, stressful life events in the first 2 years of life may increase the risk of developing Type 1 diabetes.[90] In older children, only severe psychosocial events (actual or threatened losses) are associated with an increased risk of diabetes.[91]

CONCLUSION

Type 1 diabetes is a chronic disease that is increasing in frequency with time and in certain geographic regions. In most affected people, it is caused by autoimmune destruction of the insulin-producing islet cells of the pancreas. There is also strong evidence implicating genetic as well as environmental determinants of this disease. Such evidence provides clues that may lead to subsequent preventive therapies.

SUMMARY OF EVIDENCE-BASED MESSAGES

1. The ICA assay has the highest sensitivity in detecting those at increased risk for Type 1 diabetes. Sensitivity for ICA is 81 to 95%, depending on the titer of ICA used, as compared with 25 to 69% for IAA, GAD, or ICA512/IA-2. Specificity for all antibodies is high at 95 to 99% (Level 1).[53]

2. The addition of evidence of subtle beta-cell failure through measurement of FPIR during an IVGTT can further identify those at high risk of Type 1 diabetes. In ICA-positive relatives, the incidence rate of progression to diabetes is 48% per year with FPIR < 1st percentile and 5% per year with FPIR > 1st percentile. The odds ratio for diabetes within the next 4 years for those with FPIR < 1st percentile is 36, and the positive and negative predictive values are 88% and 83%, respectively (Level 1).[47]

3. Identification of combinations of autoantibodies (GAD, IAA, and ICA512/IA-2) has a better positive predictive value for risk of diabetes than ICA alone. The estimated 5-year risk with zero, one, two, or three antibodies is < 0.5%, 15%, 44%, and > 90%, respectively (Level 1).[51]

4. Children who have a sibling with diabetes *and* who drink more than two 8-oz glasses of cow's milk per day during childhood have a fourfold increased risk of developing diabetes-related autoantibodies (Level 2).[67]

5. Enterovirus infections during childhood, particularly coxsackie B, are associated with a high (5.7-fold increased) risk of developing Type 1 diabetes (Level 2).[78]

6. There is no relationship between BCG vaccination and the risk of developing Type 1 diabetes (Level 2).[87]

7. Pertussis immunization has no effect on the risk of developing Type 1 diabetes (Level 2).[84]

8. *Haemophilus influenzae* type b immunization has no effect on the risk of developing Type 1 diabetes (Level 2).[85]

REFERENCES

1. Pinkey JH, Bingley PJ, Sawtell PA, et al. Presentation and progress of childhood diabetes mellitus: a prospective population-based study. The Bart's-Oxford Study Group. Diabetologia 1994;37:70–4.

2. Karvonen M, Tuomilehto J, Libman I, et al. A review of the recent epidemiologic data on the worldwide incidence of type 1 (insulin-dependent) diabetes mellitus. Diabetologica 1993;36:883–92.

3. Diabetes Epidemiology Research International Group. Geographic patterns of childhood insulin-dependent diabetes mellitus. Diabetes 1988;37:1113–9.

4. Padaiga Z, Tuomilehto J, Karvonen M, et al. Incidence trends in childhood onset IDDM in four countries around the Baltic sea during 1983–1992. Diabetologia 1997;40:187–92.

5. Tuomilehto J, Karvonen M, Pitkaniemi E, et al. Record-high incidence of type 1 (insulin-dependent) diabetes mellitus in Finnish children. Diabetologia 1999;42:655–60.

6. Rangasami JJ, Greenwood DC, McSporran B, et al. Rising incidence of type 1 diabetes in Scottish children, 1983–93. Arch Dis Child 1997;77:210–3.

7. Toth EL, Lee K-C, Couch RM, Martin LF. High incidence of IDDM over 6 years in Edmonton, Alberta, Canada. Diabetes Care 1997;20:311–3.

8. Cruickshanks KJ, La Porte RE, Dorman JS, et al. The epidemiology of insulin-dependent diabetes mellitus: etiology and prognosis. In: Ahmed PI, Ahmed N, editors. Coping with juvenile diabetes. Springfield (IL): Charles C. Thomas Publisher; 1985. p. 332–57.

9. Melton LJ III, Palumbo PJ, Chu C-P. Incidence of diabetes mellitus by clinical type. Diabetes Care 1983;6:75 86.

10. Christau B, Molbak AG. Incidence rates for type 1 (insulin-dependent) diabetes and insulin-treated diabetes in age groups over 30 years. Diabetologia 1982;23:160A.

11. Eisenbarth GS, Ziegler AG, Colman PA. Pathogenesis of insulin-dependent (type 1) diabetes mellitus. In: Kahn CR, Weir CG, editors. Joslin's diabetes mellitus. 13th ed. Philadelphia: Lea & Filbiger; 1994.

12. Rotter JI, Landlaw EM. Measuring the genetic contribution of a single locus to a multilocus disease. Clin Genet 1984;26:529–42.

13. Maclaren N, Riley W, Skordis N, et al. Inherited susceptibility to insulin-dependent diabetes is associated with HLA-DR1 while DR5 is protective. Autoimmunity 1988;1:197–205.

14. Todd JA, Bain SC. A practical approach to identification of susceptibility genes for IDDM. Diabetes 1992;41:1029–34.

15. Nepom GT. A unified hypothesis for the complex genetics of HLA associations with IDDM. Diabetes 1990;39:1153–7.

16. Seidel D, Ziegler A-G. Prediction of type 1 diabetes. Horm Res 1996;45(Suppl):36–9.

17. Todd JA. Genetic analysis of type 1 diabetes using whole genome approaches. Proc Natl Acad Sci U S A 1995;8560–5.

18. Todd JA, Bell JI, McDevitt HO. HLA-DQ beta gene contributes to susceptibility and resistance to insulin-dependent diabetes mellitus. Nature 1987;329:599–604.

19. Dorman JS, LaPorte RE, Stone RA, Trucco M. Worldwide differences in the incidence of type 1 diabetes are associated with amino acid variation in position 57 of the HLA-DQB chain. Proc Natl Acad Sci U S A 1990;87:7370–4.

20. Fletcher J, Mijovic C, Odugbesan O, et al. Transracial studies implicate HLA-DQ as a component of genetic susceptibility to type 1 (insulin-dependent) diabetes. Diabetologia 1988;31:864–70.

21. Guttierrez-Lopez MD, Bertera S, Chantres MT, et al. Susceptibility to type 1 (insulin-dependent) diabetes mellitus in Spanish patients correlates quantitatively with expression of HLA-DQ alpha Arg 52 and HLA-DQ beta non-Asp 57 alleles. Diabetologia 1992;35:583–8.

22. Sperling MA. Aspects of the etiology, prediction and prevention of insulin-dependent diabetes mellitus in childhood. Pediatr Clin North Am 1997;44:269–84.

23. Morel P, Dorman J, Todd J, et al. Aspartic acid at position 57 of the HLA-DQ chain protects against type 1 diabetes: a family study. Proc Natl Acad Sci U S A 1988;85:8111.

24. Winter WE, Chihara T, Schatz D. The genetic of autoimmune diabetes: approaching a solution to the problem. AJDC 1993;144:1282–90.

25. Pugliese A. Unravelling the genetics of insulin-dependent type 1A diabetes: the search must go on. Diabetes Rev 1999:39–54.

26. Bell GI, Horita S, Karam JH. A polymorphic locus near the human insulin gene is associated with insulin-dependent diabetes mellitus. Diabetes 1984;33:176–83.

27. Todd JA, Farrall M. Panning for gold: genome-wide scanning in type 1 diabetes. Diabetes Rev 1997;5:284–91.

28. Davies JL, Kawaguchi Y, Bennett ST, et al. A genome-wide search for human type 1 diabetes susceptibility genes. Nature 1994;371:130–6.

29. Field L, Tobias R, Magnus T. A locus on chromosome 15q26 (IDDM3) produces susceptibility to insulin-dependent diabetes mellitus. Nat Genet 1994;8:189–94.

30. Hashimoto L, Habita C, Beressi J, et al. Genetic mapping of susceptibility locus for insulin-dependent diabetes mellitus on chromosome 11q. Nature 1994;371:161–4.

31. Luo D-F, Buzetti R, Rotter JI, et al. Confirmation of three susceptibility genes to insulin-dependent diabetes mellitus: IDDM4, IDDM5, IDDM8. Hum Mol Genet 1996;5:693–8.

32. Davies JL, Cucca F, Goy JV, et al. Saturation multipoint linkage mapping of chromosome 6q in type 1 diabetes. Hum Mol Genet 1996;25:1071–4.

33. Luo D-F, Bui MM, Muir A, et al. Affected sibpair mapping of a novel susceptibility gene to insulin-dependent diabetes mellitus (IDDM8) on chromosome 6q25-q27. Am J Hum Genet 1995;57:911–9.

34. Nistico L, Buzetti R, Pritchard LE, et al. The CLTA-4 gene region of chromosome 2q33 is linked to, and associated with, type 1 diabetes. Hum Mol Genet 1996;5:1075–80.

35. Bendelac A, Carnaud C, Boitard C, Bach JF. Syngenic transfer of autoimmune diabetes from diabetic NOD mice to healthy neonates. Requirements for both L3T4+ AND Lyt-2+ T cells. J Exp Med 1987;166:823–32.

36. Haskins K, McDuffie M. Acceleration of diabetes in young NOD mice with a CD4+ islet-specific T cell clone. Science 1983;249:1433–6.

37. Shimizu J, Kanagawa O, Unanue ER. Presentation of beta-cell antigens to CD4+ and CD8+ T cells of non-obese diabetic mice. J Immunol 1993;151:1723–30.

38. Wicker LS, Miller BJ, Mullen Y. Transfer of autoimmune diabetes mellitus with splenocytes from nonobese diabetis (NOD) mice. Diabetes 1986;35:855–60.

39. Healey D, Ozegbe P, Arden S, et al. In vivo activity and in vitro specificity of CD4+ Th1 and Th2 cells derived from the spleens of diabetic NOD mice. J Clin Invest 1995;95:2979–85.

40. Katz JD, Benoist C, Mathis D. T helper subsets in insulin-dependent diabetes. Science 1995;268:1185–8.

41. Rabinovitch A. Roles of cytokines in IDDM pathogenesis and islet beta cell destruction. Diabetes Rev 1993;1:215–40.

42. Fantus IG, Delovitch TL, Dupre J. Prevention of diabetes mellitus: goal for the twenty-first century: part two. Can J Diabetes Care 1997;21:14–20.

43. Eisenbarth G. Type 1 diabetes mellitus: a chronic autoimmune disease. N Engl J Med 1986;314:1360–8.

44. Botazzo GF, Florin-Christensen A, Doniach D. Islet cell autoantibodies in diabetes mellitus with autoimmune polyendocrine deficiency. Lancet 1974;ii:1279–83.

45. Bonifacio E, Bingley PJ, Shattock M et al. Quantification of islet-cell antibodies and prediction of insulin-dependent diabetes. Lancet 1990;335:147–9.

46. Riley WJ, Maclaren NK, Krischer J, et al. A prospective study of the development of diabetes in relatives of patients with insulin-dependent diabetes. N Engl J Med 1990;323:1167–72.

47. Vardi P, Crisa L, Jackson RA, et al. Predictive value of intravenous glucose tolerance test insulin secretion less than or greater than the first percentile in islet cell antibody positive relatives of type 1 (insulin-dependent) diabetic patients. Diabetologia 1991;34:93–102.

48. Arslanian SA, Becker DJ, Rabin B, et al. Correlates of insulin antibodies in newly diagnosed children with insulin-dependent diabetes before insulin therapy. Diabetes 1988;84:926–30.

49. Eisenbarth G. Autoantibodies and autoantigens in type 1 diabetes: role in pathogenesis, prediction and prevention. Can J Diabetes Care 1999;23:59–65.

50. Bingley PJ, Christie MR, Bonifacio R, et al. Combined analysis of autoantibodies improves prediction of IDDM in islet cell antibody positive relatives. Diabetes 1994;43:1304–10.

51. Verge CF, Gianini R, Kawasaki E, et al. Prediction of type 1 diabetes in first-degree relatives using a combination of insulin, GAD, and ICA512/IA-2 autoantibodies. Diabetes 1996;45:926–33.

52. Knip M. Prediction and prevention of type 1 diabetes. Acta Paediatr 1998;425(Suppl):54–62.

53. Kulmala P, Savola K, Petersen JS, et al. Prediction of insulin-dependent diabetes mellitus in siblings of children with diabetes: a population-based study. J Clin Invest 1998;101:327–36.

54. Schranz DB, Lernmark Å. Immunology of diabetes: an update. Diabetes Metab Rev 1998;14:3–29.

55. Eisenbarth GS, Ziegler AG, Colman PA. Pathogenesis of insulin-dependent (type 1) diabetes mellitus. In: Kahn CR, Weir GC, editors. Joslin's diabetes mellitus. 13th ed. Philadelphia: Lea & Filbiger; 1994.

56. Karjalainen JK. Islet cell antibodies as predictive markers for IDDM in children with high background incidence of disease. Diabetes 1990;39:1144–50.

57. Krishner JP, Schatz D, Riley WJ, et al. Insulin and islet cell autoantibodies as time-dependent covariates in the development of insulin-dependent diabetes: a prospective study in relatives. J Clin Endocrinol Metab 1993;77:743–9.

58. Deschamps I, Boitard C, Hors J, et al. Life table analysis of the risk of type 1 (insulin-dependent) diabetes mellitus in siblings according to islet cell autoantibodies and HLA markers: an 8-year prospective study. Diabetologia 1992;35:951–7.

59. Ziegler AG, Baumgartl HJ, Standl E, Mehnert H. Risk of progression to diabetes of low titre ICA-positive first degree relatives of type 1 diabetics in southern Germany. J Autoimmun 1990;3:619–24.

60. Bodansky HJ, Staines A, Stephenson C, et al. Evidence for an environmental effect in the etiology of insulin-dependent diabetes in a transmigratory population. BMJ 1992;304:1020–2.

61. Elliott RB. Epidemiology of diabetes in Polynesia and New Zealand. Pediatr Adolesc Endocrinol 1992;21:66–71.

62. Kaprio J, Tuomilehto J, Koskenvuo M, et al. Concordance for type 1 (insulin-dependent) and type 2 (non-insulin-dependent) diabetes mellitus in a population-based cohort of twins in Finland. Diabetologia 1992;35:1060–2.

63. Scott FW, Daneman D, Martin JM. Evidence for a critical role of diet in the development of diabetes. Diabetes Res 1988;7:153–7.

64. Martin JM, Trink B, Daneman D, et al. Milk proteins in the etiology of diabetes. Ann Med 1991;23:447–52.

65. Gerstein HC. Cow's milk exposure and type 1 diabetes mellitus: a critical overview of the literature. Diabetes Care 1994;17:13–9.

66. Akerblom HK, Virtanen SM, Hamalainen A, et al. Emergence of diabetes associated autoantibodies in the nutritional prevention of IDDM (TRIGR Project). Diabetes 1999;48(Suppl 1):A45.

67. Virtanen SM, Hypponen E, Laara E, et al. Cow's milk consumption, disease-associated autoantibodies and type 1 diabetes: a follow-up study in siblings of diabetic children. Diabet Med 1998;15:730–8.

68. Tuomilehto J, Tuomilehto-Wolf E, Virtala E, LaPorte R. Coffee consumption as trigger for insulin dependent diabetes mellitus in childhood. BMJ 1990;300:642–3.

69. Virtanen SM, Rasanen L, Aro A, et al. Is children's or parents' coffee or tea consumption associated with the risk for type 1 diabetes mellitus in children? Eur J Clin Nutr 1994;48:279–85.

70. Rakieten N, Rakieten ML, Nadkarni MV. Studies on the diabetogenic action of streptozotocin. Cancer Chemother Rep 1963;29:91–8.

71. Wilander E, Gunnarsson R. Diabetogenic effects of the *N*-nitrosomethylurea in the Chinese hamster. Acta Pathol Microbiol Immunol Scand [A] 1975;83:206–12.

72. Dahlquist GG, Blom LG, Persson L-A, et al. Dietary factors and the risk of developing insulin dependent diabetes in childhood. BMJ 1990;300:1302–6.

73. Virtanen SM, Jaakkola L, Rasanen L, et al. Nitrate and nitrite intake and the risk for type 1 diabetes in Finnish children. Diabet Med 1994;11:656–62.

74. Menser MA, Forrest JM, Bransby RD. Rubella infection and diabetes mellitus. Lancet 1978;i:57–60.

75. Rubenstein P, Walker ME, Fedun N, et al. HLA system in congenital rubella patients with and without diabetes. Diabetes 1982;31:1088–91.

76. Ginsberg-Fellner F, Witt ME, Yaagihasi S, et al. Congenital rubella syndrome as a model for type 1 (insulin-dependent) diabetes mellitus: increased prevalence of islet cell surface antibodies. Diabetologia 1984;27(Suppl):87–9.

77. Graves PM, Norris JM, Pallansch MA, et al. The role of enteroviral infections in the development of IDDM: limitations of current approaches. Diabetes 1997;46:161–8.

78. Hyoty H, Hiltunen M, Knip M, et al. A prospective study of the role of coxsackie B and other enterovirus infections in the pathogenesis of IDDM. Diabetes 1995;44:652–7.

79. Dahlquist G, Frisk G, Ivarsson SA, et al. Indications that maternal coxsackie B virus infection during pregnancy is a risk factor for childhood-onset IDDM. Diabetologia 1995;38:1371–3.

80. Clements GB, Galbraith DN, Taylor KW. Coxsackie B virus infection and onset of childhood diabetes. Lancet 1995;346:221–3.

81. Blom L, Nystrom L, Dahlquist G. The Swedish childhood diabetes study: vaccinations and infections as risk determinants for diabetes in childhood. Diabetologia 1991;34:176–81.

82. Hummel M, Ziegler AG. Vaccines and the appearance of islet cell antibodies in offspring of diabetic parents. Results from the BABY-DIAB Study [letter]. Diabetes Care 1996;19:1456–7.

83. Heijbel H, Chen RT, Dahlquist G. Cumulative incidence of childhood-onset IDDM is unaffected by pertussis immunization. Diabetes Care 1997;20:173–5.

84. Karvonen M, Cepaitis Z, Tuomilehto J. Association between type 1 diabetes and Haemophilus influenzae type b vaccination: birth cohort study. BMJ 1999;318:1169–72.

85. Harada M, Kistimoto Y, Makino S. Prevention of overt diabetes and insulitis in NOD mice by a single BCG vaccination. Diabetes Res Clin Pract 1990;8:85–9.

86. Dahlquist G, Gothefors L. The cumulative incidence of childhood diabetes mellitus in Sweden unaffected by BCG vaccination [letter]. Diabetologia 1995;38:874–5.

87. Parent ME, Siemiatycki J, Menzies R, et al. Bacille Calmette-Guérin vaccination and incidence of IDDM in Montreal, Canada. Diabetes Care 1997;20:767–72.

88. Bateman A, Singh A, Kral T, Solomon S. The immune-hypothalamic-pituitary-adrenal axis. Endocr Rev 1989;10:92–112.

89. Thernlund GM, Dahlquist G, Hansson K, et al. Psychological stress and the onset of IDDM in children: a case-control study. Diabetes Care 1995;18:1323–9.

90. Hagglof B, Blom L, Dahlquist G, et al. The Swedish childhood diabetes study: indications of severe psychological stress as a risk factor for type 1 (insulin-dependent) diabetes mellitus in childhood. Diabetologia 1991;34:579–83.

CHAPTER 10

What Is Type 2 Diabetes?

Sarah Capes, MD, FRCPC, and Sonia Anand, MD, MSc

ABSTRACT

Type 2 diabetes currently affects more than 150 million people worldwide and is a leading cause of end-stage renal disease, blindness, limb amputation, and cardiovascular disease. The development of Type 2 diabetes depends on both hereditary and environmental factors, and the prevalence varies substantially among different ethnic groups. Individuals with Type 2 diabetes may have few or no classic symptoms of hyperglycemia; further, up to one half of all cases of Type 2 diabetes may be undiagnosed. Risk factors for Type 2 diabetes include advancing age, increased body mass index and central fat distribution, weight gain in adulthood, ethnicity, family history of diabetes, low birth weight, sedentary lifestyle, higher systolic blood pressure, impaired glucose tolerance, impaired fasting glucose, and history of gestational diabetes. High glycemic index diet and low cereal fiber intake may also increase the risk of Type 2 diabetes.

INTRODUCTION

Type 2 diabetes is a common disorder that currently affects more than 150 million people worldwide. The social and economic burden imposed by this disorder is highlighted by the observation that Type 2 diabetes is a major cause of end-stage renal disease, blindness, limb amputation, and cardiovascular disease. Despite the high prevalence and public health implications of Type 2 diabetes, researchers are only beginning to understand the complex interactions between genes and environment that lead to the clinical diagnosis of Type 2 diabetes. This chapter will answer the following questions:

1. What is the etiology and clinical presentation of Type 2 diabetes?
2. What is the prevalence and incidence of Type 2 diabetes?
3. What are the risk factors for Type 2 diabetes?

WHAT IS THE ETIOLOGY AND CLINICAL PRESENTATION OF TYPE 2 DIABETES?

Type 2 diabetes is a heterogeneous disorder with both genetic and environmental determinants. Twin studies, which show that concordance for Type 2 diabetes is twice as high in monozygotic twins as in dizygotic twins (34 to 80% vs 16 to 40%),[1] provide strong evidence for heritability. This is further supported by the finding that Type 2 diabetes is more common in certain ethnic groups and in offspring of parents with diabetes.[1] With the exception of rare forms of Type 2 diabetes (such as maturity-onset diabetes of the young [MODY] and diabetes-deafness syndromes), which account for < 1% of all cases of diabetes, the specific genetic defects implicated in most cases of diabetes are unknown.[2] Nevertheless, studies in nondiabetic relatives of individuals with Type 2 diabetes suggest that insulin resistance is a primary inherited defect that occurs early in the course of Type 2 diabetes.[3] Insulin secretion by the pancreatic beta cell is initially sufficient to compensate for insulin resistance, thereby maintaining normal blood glucose levels. However, in patients destined to develop Type 2 diabetes, insulin secretion eventually fails, leading to hyperglycemia and clinical diabetes.[4] Obesity contributes to the development of diabetes by further increasing insulin resistance; this effect may be particularly pronounced in people with a family history of diabetes.[4] Other environmental factors that may contribute to the development of Type 2 diabetes are discussed below (see "Risk Factors").

Classic symptoms of hyperglycemia are often absent in people with Type 2 diabetes. In a random sample of 2,364 middle-aged Dutch men and women who underwent an oral glucose tolerance test, frequent thirst was the only classic symptom of hyperglycemia reported significantly more often in people newly diagnosed with diabetes compared to people with normal glucose tolerance (25.7% vs 13.0%, OR [odds ratio] = 2.5 [95% confidence interval 1.5 to 3.9]). Other diabetes-related symptoms ("often tired," "often itching," "voiding large amounts of urine," "recent weight loss," "blurry vision from time to time") were not reported significantly more often in people with newly detected diabetes. However, those with newly detected diabetes were significantly more likely to report cardiovascular symptoms (such as pain during walking, with the need to slow down, and shortness of breath when walking with people of the same age); neurologic symptoms (including frequent numbness or tingling in the hands or feet); and ophthalmologic symptoms (including shortsightedness, farsightedness, and impairment of vision) than those without diabetes (Table 10–1).[5] In the 1989 US National Health Interview Survey, about one half of people with Type 2 diabetes reported that they had symptoms at the time of diagnosis of diabetes, while the remaining one half were diagnosed "by chance," usually during a routine physical examination or during treatment for another condition. Older patients were less likely to report symptoms at the time of diagnosis of diabetes than were younger patients.[6]

The lack of symptoms in many individuals with Type 2 diabetes may contribute to the high reported prevalence of undiagnosed diabetes in population-based surveys. For exam-

Table 10–1 Symptoms Associated with Newly Detected Diabetes in a Screening Study (N = 2,364)

Symptom	Prevalence in People with Newly Detected Diabetes (%)
Frequent thirst	25.7
Pain during walking	32.4
Pain in calf during walking	12.0
Pain during walking with need to slow down	20.6
Shortness of breath when:	
Washing/getting dressed	11.0
Walking with people of same age	20.2
Frequent numbness in hands or feet	19.3
Frequent tingling in hands or feet	24.8
Shortsightedness	15.5
Farsightedness	13.8
Impairment of vision	8.3

Adapted from Ruige JB, De Neeling JND, Kostense PJ, et al. Performance of an NIDDM screening questionnaire based on symptoms and risk factors. Diabetes Care 1997;20:491–6.

ple, in the Third National Health and Nutrition Examination Survey (NHANES III), 2.7% of the adult American population had undiagnosed diabetes. Indeed, one-third of all cases of diabetes in this survey (using the 1997 American Diabetes Association fasting plasma glucose criterion) were undiagnosed. Using the more sensitive World Health Organization (WHO) criteria, 44% of all cases of diabetes were undiagnosed.[7] In a similar survey in the United Kingdom, a prevalence of undiagnosed diabetes of 4.5% among people aged 40 to 65 years was found.[8]

EVIDENCE-BASED MESSAGE

Individuals with Type 2 diabetes may have few or no classic symptoms of hyperglycemia (Level 1).[5] Up to one half of all cases of Type 2 diabetes may be undiagnosed (Level 1).[7]

WHAT IS THE PREVALENCE AND INCIDENCE OF TYPE 2 DIABETES?

The prevalence of Type 2 diabetes varies substantially among different ethnic groups. The term "ethnic group" refers to a selected population with common cultural characteristics such as language, religion, and diet and some genetic characteristics.[9] The most accurate estimates of prevalence come from large population-based surveys of randomly selected individuals in which diabetes was diagnosed by plasma glucose levels 2 hours after a 75-g oral glucose load. Using these standardized criteria, striking differences in the prevalence of diabetes mellitus (DM) are observed between countries and ethnic groups.[10] In many traditional communities in the least industrialized countries, such as sub-Saharan Africa, rural China, and rural India, the prevalence of diabetes is extremely low (< 3%). There is moderate prevalence of DM (5 to 10%) observed among the people of Tunisia, Thailand, and among people of European origin who live in Europe and North America. There is a high prevalence (> 20%) of DM observed among migrant South Asians, Arab populations in the Middle East, and Chinese migrants living in Mauritius. Groups with extremely high rates of DM include aboriginal populations who have experienced marked changes in their energy consumption and physical activity patterns, such as the Pima and Papago Indians of Arizona (50%), the Micronesian Naurans (41%), Oji-Cree Aboriginals of Northern Canada (26%), and the Australian Aborigines (24%) (Table 10–2).

The effect that changes in lifestyle have on the prevalence of DM is also highlighted by intraethnic groups comparisons. For example, among people of South Asian origin, the relative prevalence of DM compared to the rural-dwelling South Asians (1.0) is three- to six-fold among urban South Asians in India and increases to six- to 12-fold among South Asians living in urban areas of Fiji. Similar increases in the relative prevalence of DM are observed among Chinese, black African, and Japanese migrants.

The projected rates of DM for the year 2025 demonstrate that marked increases in DM are expected, especially in developing countries. By 2025, WHO predicts that there will be 299,974,000 cases of non–insulin-dependent diabetes mellitus (NIDDM) worldwide (Figure 10–1).

Summary

The prevalence of Type 2 diabetes varies widely among different ethnic groups, ranging from < 3% in populations with traditional lifestyles in developing countries to > 20% in migrant Asians and aboriginal populations who have experienced marked changes in lifestyle. The worldwide incidence of Type 2 diabetes is expected to double in the next 25 years, with most of the increase occurring in developing countries.[10]

WHAT ARE THE RISK FACTORS FOR TYPE 2 DIABETES?

There are a number of clinical risk factors for Type 2 diabetes that have been identified in high-quality cohort studies (ie, studies with well-defined inclusion and exclusion criteria, in

Table 10–2 Age-Adjusted (30 to 64 Years) Prevalence Rates of Non–Insulin-Dependent Diabetes Mellitus in Selected Populations[10]

Ethnic Group	Men (%)	Women (%)
US Caucasians	5.0	5.0
US Hispanics	4.2	7.2
US Africans	5.9	7.8
South Asians in rural India	3.7	1.7
South Asians in urban India	11.8	11.2
South Asians in Fiji	24.0	20.3
Chinese in rural China	1.6	1.6
Chinese in Singapore	6.9	7.8
Chinese in Mauritius	16.0	10.3
Japanese in Osaka, Japan	7.3	5.6
Japanese in Brazil (first generation)	12.4	11.6
Black Africans in Cameroon		
Rural	1.1	0.5
Urban	1.0	2.8
Black Africans in West Indies	6.5	10.6
Black Africans in United Kingdom	15.3	14.0
Aboriginal populations		
Pima in the United States	49.4	51.1
Nauruans	40.6	42.0
Oji-Cree in Canada	24.2	28.0
Aborigines in Australia	24.0	21.0

Adapted from World Health Organization prevalence statistics. Available from: URL: http://www.who.int/ncd/dia/databases.htm.

which an inception cohort of subjects without diabetes at baseline was reported, follow-up was ≥ 80% complete, reproducible outcome measures were reported, and there was statistical adjustment for confounders). These are discussed below.

Age

In most populations, Type 2 diabetes is rare before age 30, but its incidence increases with age.[10] In 6,000 men enrolled in the Usual Care group of the Multiple Risk Factor Intervention Trial (MRFIT), the incidence of diabetes over 5 years follow-up increased by 30% for each 5-year increment in age.[11] In NHANES III, the prevalence of diabetes (diagnosed and undiagnosed) in the United States rose from 1 to 2% at ages 20 to 39 to 18 to 20% at ages 60 to 74, with a plateau after age 75.[7] Nevertheless, Type 2 diabetes has become more common in children and adolescents in the past decade. For example, among Pima Indian children, the prevalence of Type 2 diabetes more than doubled between 1967 and 1996 (to 1.4% of

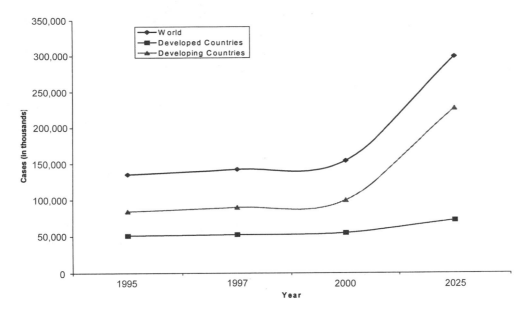

Figure 10–1 Global estimates of diabetes prevalence 1995–2025.

boys and 2.88% of girls aged 10 to 14, and 3.78% in boys and 5.31% in girls aged 15 to 19).[12] In a Canadian Aboriginal population, the prevalence of Type 2 diabetes was 0.53 per 1,000 children aged 7 to 14.[13] Among other ethnic minorities in North America, Type 2 diabetes accounts for an increasing proportion of diabetes diagnosed in children. In an American pediatric diabetes clinic, Type 2 diabetes represented 2 to 4% of all new cases of diabetes diagnosed in children under age 19 before 1992; by 1994, this proportion had risen to 16%, most of whom were African American.[14]

Obesity and Central Fat Distribution

Risk of Type 2 diabetes also increases with increasing body mass index (BMI, defined as weight in kilograms per height in meters squared) (Table 10–3). In men in the MRFIT Usual Care cohort, the risk of diabetes almost doubled for each 5 kg/m^2 increase in BMI.[11] The risk may extend into the "normal" range of BMI (20 to 25 kg/m^2); for women in the Nurses' Health Study, the risk of self-reported diabetes doubled for BMI 22 to 22.9 kg/m^2, tripled for BMI 23 to 23.9 kg/m^2, and was 5 times higher for BMI 25 to 26.9 kg/m^2, compared with BMI < 22 kg/m^2.[15] Central fat distribution further increases the risk of Type 2 diabetes for a given BMI.[16–18] In American men, waist circumference > 40 inches (101 cm) or waist-to-hip ratio > 0.99 were associated with a significantly increased risk of self-reported diabetes.[17] In American women, waist circumference > 29 inches (76 cm) or waist-to-hip ratio > .75 indicated an increased risk.[18] Weight gain in adulthood of > 10 kg after age 18 in women[15] or > 8 kg after age 21 in men[17] was also associated with an increased risk of clinical diabetes independent of BMI in early adulthood.

Ethnicity

As described above, the prevalence of Type 2 diabetes varies among different ethnic groups.

The reasons why selected populations appear "protected" from developing diabetes while others are at "high risk" are difficult to discern and are likely attributable to unique gene-environment interactions. Intergroup comparisons, as well as comparisons within ethnic groups, reveal that selected populations who have replaced a traditional lifestyle with an

Table 10-3 Weight-Related Risk Factors for Type 2 Diabetes Mellitus

Study	Study Population	F/U (yr)	Incidence of DM (%)	Risk Factor	RR (95% CI) of DM, Adjusted for Confounders
Shaten et al[11]	6,000 nondiabetic men aged 35–57 with cardiovascular risk factors	5	4	BMI (per 5 kg/m²)	1.56 (1.28, 1.90)*,†,‡,§,//,**,††,‡‡
Colditz et al[15]	113,861 nondiabetic female nurses aged 30–55	8	0.8	BMI (25–26.9 vs < 22 kg/m²); Wt gain after age 18 (10–20 kg vs < 3 kg)	5.2 (3.7, 7.5)‡‡,§§; 4.6 (3.4, 6.2)‡‡,////
Cassano et al[16]	1,972 nondiabetic men, mean age 41.9	18	12	BMI (> 26.9 vs < 24.6 kg/m²); Ratio of WC to hip breadth (> 2.61 vs < 2.48)	1.8 (1.1, 3.0)**,‡‡,##; 3.4 (1.9, 5.9)**,‡‡,***
Chan et al[17]	27,338 nondiabetic male health professionals aged 40–75	5	1.0	BMI (25–26.9 vs < 23 kg/m²); Wt gain after age 21 (8–9 vs < 2 kg); WHR (> 0.99 vs < 0.90); WC (> 101 vs < 87 cm)	1.9 (1.1, 3.3)§,**,‡‡,##; 3.5 (2.0, 6.3)§,**,‡‡; 1.7 (1.1, 2.7)§,**,‡‡,***; 3.5 (1.7, 7.0)§,**,‡‡,***
Carey et al[18]	42,492 nondiabetic female nurses aged 30–55	8	N/S	WHR (0.76–0.79 vs < 0.72); WC (76–81 vs < 71 cm)	1.9 (1.5, 2.4)§,**,‡‡,†††,‡‡‡,§§§; 2.7 (1.6, 4.6)§,**,‡‡,†††,‡‡‡,§§§
McPhillips et al[53]	1,847 nondiabetic men and women aged 40–79	12	12	BMI (per 3.3 kg/m²)	1.29 (1.01, 1.65) men‡‡; 1.54 (1.28, 1.85) women‡‡

*Race (Black vs non-Black).
†Fasting plasma glucose.
‡Plasma glucose 1 h after 75-g glucose load.
§Parental history of diabetes (yes/no).
//Systolic blood pressure.
#Alcohol use.
**Smoking.
††Biochemical variables: uric acid, triglycerides, HDL and LDL cholesterol.

‡‡Age.
§§Follow-up interval.
////BMI at age 18.
##WHR.
***BMI.
†††Exercise.
‡‡‡Diet: intakes of saturated fat, calcium, potassium, magnesium, and glycemic index.
§§§p for trend throughout the observed range of values < .0001.

F/U = follow-up; RR = relative risk; WHR = waist-to-hip ratio; WC = waist circumference; BMI = body mass index (weight over height squared); wt = weight; pt = patient; DM = Type 2 diabetes mellitus; N/S = not stated.

urban lifestyle constitute the "at-risk" population. The common factors associated with high-risk groups are decreased physical activity, increased energy consumption, and increased body weight, which occur in the setting of an urban environment. The "thrifty genotype" theory is one widely accepted paradigm, hypothesizing that populations who are exposed to periods of famine develop insulin resistance as a protective mechanism to use the least energy-expending mechanism to store energy as fat.[19] However, when exposed to an abundance of energy (as is found in urban environments), this once protective gene action becomes deleterious and results in increased abdominal obesity and DM.

Low Birth Weight

Low birth weight (< 2,500 g) has been associated with the development of Type 2 diabetes in adulthood in Pima Indians,[20] British men,[21] Swedish men,[22] and American men[23] and women[24] (Table 10–4). This association is further supported by the observation that in monozygotic twins discordant for diabetes, birth weight was significantly lower in the diabetic twin than in the nondiabetic individual.[25] While the mechanism of the association between diabetes and low birth weight is uncertain, a plausible hypothesis is that fetal undernutrition impairs pancreatic development, leading to inadequate beta-cell function in the face of dietary abundance later in life.[20] This theory, known as the "thrifty phenotype" hypothesis, also provides an alternative explanation for the high incidence of diabetes in migrants from underdeveloped countries to more affluent countries; however, it does not explain the low prevalence of diabetes in those populations who do not migrate and who maintain a traditional lifestyle. Another explanation that has been proposed for the increased incidence of Type 2 diabetes in people with low birth weight is that low birthweight infants who survive to adulthood have some genetic feature (such as a predisposition to insulin resistance) that allows them to survive but also predisposes to diabetes later in life.[20]

Among Pima Indians, high birth weight (> 4500 g) is also associated with the subsequent development of diabetes. This association is no longer significant, however, after controlling for maternal diabetes in pregnancy.[20] Further observations that offspring of Pima Indian women who were diabetic during pregnancy have a higher risk of diabetes than offspring of nondiabetic mothers or mothers who developed diabetes after pregnancy suggest that the diabetic environment in utero may itself be a risk factor for the subsequent development of diabetes.[26]

Family History of Diabetes

First-degree relatives of people with Type 2 diabetes have a twofold increased risk of diabetes.[27,28] In the United States, the prevalence of Type 2 diabetes in adults with one diabetic parent is four times as high as in adults without a parental history of diabetes (6.0% vs 1.5%); the risk is almost doubled again if both parents have diabetes.[1]

Impaired Glucose Tolerance, Impaired Fasting Glucose, and Gestational Diabetes

Impaired glucose tolerance (IGT, ie, plasma glucose level 2 hours after a 75-g oral glucose load ≥ 7.8 mmol/L but < 11.1 mmol/L)[29] and impaired fasting glucose (IFG, ie, fasting plasma glucose ≥ 6.1 but < 7.0 mmol/L)[29] strongly predict the subsequent development of Type 2 diabetes. In the Paris Prospective Study, subjects with IGT (defined as fasting glucose < 7.8 mmol/L and 2-hour glucose after a 75-g glucose load ≥ 7.8 and < 11.1 mmol/L) had a 9.6-fold increased risk of diabetes, while subjects with IFG (defined as fasting glucose > 6.1 and < 7.8 mmol/L and 2-hour glucose < 7.8 mmol/L) had a 5.6-fold increased risk of diabetes, compared with subjects with normal glucose tolerance.[30] In an analysis of six prospective studies, the risk of conversion from IGT to Type 2 diabetes ranged from 3.6% per year to 8.7% per year. Higher fasting plasma glucose (with a sharp increase in risk above 6.0 mmol/L), higher 2-hour post-challenge glucose, and increased BMI (> 27), waist circumference, and waist-to-hip ratio predicted conversion from IGT to diabetes.[31]

Table 10–4 Low Birth Weight and Risk of Type 2 Diabetes Mellitus

Study	Study Population	Prevalence of DM (%)	RR (95% CI) of DM Associated with Birth Weight < 2500 g* Compared to Reference Birth Weight	Reference Birth Weight (g)
McCance et al[20]	1,179 Pima Indians aged 20–39	18	3.81 (1.7, 8.52)[†,‡,§,//]	2,500–4,499
Curhan et al[23]	22,312 American male health professionals without DM at study entry, followed for 5 yr	1.9	1.7 (1.17, 2.48)[†,‡,#]	3,150–3,775
Rich-Edwards et al[24]	69,526 American female nurses without DM at study entry, followed for 16 yr	3.1	1.73 (1.47, 2.04)[†,‡]	3,160–3,820
Hales et al[21]	468 British men	7	6.6 (1.5, 28)**	> 4,309
Carlsson et al[22]	2,237 Swedish men	1.6	4.5 (1.9, 10.8)[†,‡,#]	≥ 3,601 g

*< 3,000 g for reference 22.
[†]Adjusted for age.
[‡]Adjusted for BMI.
[§]Adjusted for maternal diabetes during pregnancy.
[//]Adjusted for birth year.
[#]Adjusted for family history of diabetes.
**Odds ratio (95% CI) for IGT or DM adjusted for BMI.
RR = relative risk; DM = diabetes mellitus; BMI = body mass index; IGT = impaired glucose tolerance.

There is general consensus that a diagnosis of gestational diabetes mellitus (GDM) also predicts the development of Type 2 diabetes in women. The available case series of women with a history of GDM report a varying incidence of diabetes, ranging from 6 to 62% (due partly to variable diagnostic criteria for GDM and diabetes ascertainment),[32–34] and most fail to distinguish Type 1 from Type 2 diabetes.

Diet

The hypothesis that poor diet might lead to Type 2 diabetes was proposed centuries ago[1] and remains an attractive hypothesis, because diet is more easily modified than many other risk factors. Older studies of the association between diet and Type 2 diabetes showed contradictory results, with no relationship reported in several prospective studies.[35–37] Recently, however, two large prospective studies in American men and women found that a diet containing both a high glycemic load (ie, high in easily digestible carbohydrates, which produce a marked rise in blood glucose and insulin levels) and a low cereal fiber content increased the risk of self-reported Type 2 diabetes up to 2.5-fold.[38,39] Such a diet is thought to create a chronically high demand for insulin. Patients with a genetic predisposition to Type 2 diabetes may initially be able to produce enough insulin to meet these demands and maintain a normal blood glucose level. Diabetes may develop, however, if the ability of the pancreatic beta-cell to secrete these large amounts of insulin fails. Total energy and dietary fat intake were not significantly related to the risk of Type 2 diabetes in these studies after adjustment for age, BMI, physical activity, alcohol intake, smoking, and family history of diabetes. Interestingly, magnesium intake was inversely related to the risk of Type 2 diabetes. This is consistent with the observation that magnesium increases insulin sensitivity in vitro.[40] The effect of magnesium on glycemic control is discussed in Chapter 16.

In both of these studies, the risk of diabetes fell with increasing alcohol intake. Men with moderate alcohol intake (30 to 49.9 g/day) and women with alcohol intake of ≥ 15 g/d had about a 40% lower risk of diabetes than did nondrinkers.[41,42] In contrast, alcohol intake of > 176 g of alcohol per week (or > 25 g/d) significantly increased the risk of diabetes in men but not in women in the Rancho Bernardo study.[43] While the discrepancies between these studies remain to be resolved, increased insulin sensitivity has been demonstrated in moderate drinkers compared to abstainers,[44] which may partially explain the effect of moderate alcohol intake.

Sedentary Lifestyle

Sedentary lifestyle (ie, vigorous exercise less than once per week) increases the risk of Type 2 diabetes in men and women by 20 to 40% in both obese and nonobese individuals, independent of BMI.[45,46] The amount of daily physical activity appears to have a continuous inverse relationship with the risk of Type 2 diabetes, with a reduction in risk of 6% for each 500-kcal increase in leisure-time energy expenditure.[47,48] Exercise may be beneficial both by promoting weight loss and by increasing insulin sensitivity even in the absence of weight loss.[49]

Smoking

Cigarette smoking has been associated with an increased risk of diabetes in some cohort studies,[41,50] but others have failed to show this association.[47,51,52]

Hypertension and Other Cardiovascular Risk Factors

There has been a positive association noted between systolic blood pressure,[52–54] or use of antihypertensive drugs,[55,56] and the subsequent risk of diabetes in several prospective studies. High triglyceride,[53,54] low high-density lipoprotein (HDL) cholesterol,[51,56] and high very low-density lipoprotein (VLDL) cholesterol[56] levels have also been associated with an increased risk of diabetes in some studies.

EVIDENCE-BASED MESSAGES

Risk factors for Type 2 diabetes (Table 10–5) include increasing age (Level 1),[11] increasing BMI (Level 1),[11,15] weight gain in adulthood (Level 1),[15,17] central fat distribution (Level 1),[17,18] ethnicity, family history of diabetes (Level 1),[1,27,28] low birth weight (Level 1),[20–24] sedentary lifestyle (Level 1),[45–48] higher systolic blood pressure (Level 1),[52–54] and impaired glucose tolerance and impaired fasting glucose (Level 1).[30,31] Diet rich in easily digestible carbohydrates and low in cereal fiber may increase the risk of Type 2 diabetes (Level 1).[38,39] Gestational diabetes may also be a risk factor for Type 2 diabetes (Level 3).[32–34]

CONCLUSION

Type 2 diabetes is a complex disorder with potentially devastating consequences. The worldwide prevalence of Type 2 diabetes varies widely among ethnic groups and is expected to double in the next 25 years, with most of the increase occurring in developing countries. Control and prevention of Type 2 diabetes therefore constitutes a major public health challenge for the twenty-first century.

SUMMARY OF EVIDENCE-BASED MESSAGES

1. Individuals with Type 2 diabetes may have few or no classic symptoms of hyperglycemia (Level 1).[5] Up to one half of all cases of Type 2 diabetes may be undiagnosed (Level 1).[7]
2. Risk factors for Type 2 diabetes include increasing age (Level 1),[11] increasing BMI (Level 1),[11,15] weight gain in adulthood (Level 1),[15,17] central fat distribution (Level 1),[17,18] ethnicity, family history of diabetes (Level 1),[1,27,28] low birth weight (Level 1),[20–24] sedentary lifestyle (Level 1),[45–48] higher systolic blood pressure (Level 1),[52–54] and impaired glucose tolerance and impaired fasting glucose (Level 1).[30,31] Diet rich in easily digestible carbohydrates and low in cereal fiber may increase the risk of Type 2 diabetes (Level 1).[38,39] Gestational diabetes may also be a risk factor for Type 2 diabetes (Level 3).[32–34]

Table 10–5 Risk Factors for Type 2 Diabetes Mellitus

Definite risk factors

   Increasing age

   Obesity

   Central fat distribution

   Weight gain in adulthood

   Ethnicity

   Low birth weight

   Sedentary lifestyle

   Family history of diabetes

   Impaired glucose tolerance and impaired fasting glucose

   Hypertension

   Dyslipidemia (high triglyceride, low HDL cholesterol, high VLDL cholesterol levels)

Probable risk factors

   Gestational diabetes

   Diet: high glycemic load; low cereal fiber content

Possible risk factors

   Abstention from alcohol

   Cigarette smoking

REFERENCES

1. Rewers M, Hamman RF. Risk factors for non-insulin-dependent diabetes. In: National Diabetes Data Group, editors. Diabetes in America. 2nd ed. Bethesda (MD): National Institutes of Health/NIDDK; 1995. p. 179–220.

2. Kahn CR, Vicent D, Doria A. Genetics of non-insulin-dependent (Type 2) diabetes mellitus. Annu Rev Med 1996;47:509–31.

3. Eriksson J, Franssila-Kallunki A, Ekstrand A, et al. Early metabolic defects in persons at increased risk for non-insulin dependent diabetes mellitus. N Engl J Med 1989;321:337–43.

4. Warram JH, Martin BC, Krolewski AS, et al. Slow glucose removal rate and hyperinsulinemia precede the development of Type 2 diabetes in the offspring of diabetic parents. Ann Intern Med 1990;113:909–15.

5. Ruige JB, deNeeling JND, Kostense PJ, et al. Performance of an NIDDM screening questionnaire based on symptoms and risk factors. Diabetes Care 1997;20:491–6.

6. Harris MI. Classification, diagnostic criteria, and screening for diabetes. In: National Diabetes Data Group, editors. Diabetes in America. 2nd ed. Bethesda (MD): National Institutes of Health/NIDDK; 1995. p. 15–36.

7. Harris MI, Flegal KM, Cowie CC, et al. Prevalence of diabetes, impaired fasting glucose, and impaired glucose tolerance in U.S. adults. Diabetes Care 1998;21:518 24.

8. Williams DRR, Wareham NJ, Brown DC, et al. Undiagnosed glucose intolerance in the community: the Isle of Ely Diabetes Project. Diabetes Med 1995;12:30–5.

9. Anand S, Yusuf S. Ethnicity and vascular disease. In: Evidence Based Cardiology. Salim Y, editor. London: BMJ; 1998. p. 329–52.

10. World Health Organization prevalence statistics. Available from: URL: http://www.who.int/ncd/dia/databases.htm.

11. Shaten BJ, Davey Smith G, Kuller LH, Neaton JD. Risk factors for the development of Type 2 diabetes among men enrolled in the Usual Care group of the Multiple Risk Factor Intervention Trial. Diabetes Care 1993;16:1331–9.

12. Dabelea D, Hanson RL, Bennett PH, et al. Increasing prevalence of Type 2 diabetes in American Indian children. Diabetologia 1998;41:904–10.

13. Dean HJ, Mundy RL, Moffatt M. Non-insulin-dependent diabetes mellitus in Indian children in Manitoba. Can Med Assoc J 1992;147:52–7.

14. Pinhas-Hamiel O, Dolan LM, Daniels SR, et al. Increased incidence of non-insulin dependent diabetes mellitus among adolescents. J Pediatr 1996;128:608–15.

15. Colditz GA, Willett WC, Stampfer MJ, et al. Weight as a risk factor for clinical diabetes in women. Am J Epidemiol 1990;132:501–13.

16. Cassano PA, Rosner B, Vokonas PS, Weiss ST. Obesity and body fat distribution in relation to the incidence of non-insulin-dependent diabetes mellitus. Am J Epidemiol 1992;136:1474–86.

17. Chan JM, Rimm EB, Colditz GA, et al. Obesity, fat distribution, and weight gain as risk factors for clinical diabetes in men. Diabetes Care 1994;17:961–9.

18. Carey VJ, Walters EE, Colditz GA, et al. Body fat distribution and risk of non-insulin-dependent diabetes mellitus in women. Am J Epidemiol 1997;145:614–9.

19. Neel V. Diabetes mellitus: a thrifty genotype rendered detrimental by progress? Am J Hum Genet 1962;14:353–62.

20. McCance DR, Pettitt DJ, Hanson RL, et al. Birth weight and non-insulin-dependent diabetes: thrifty genotype, thrifty phenotype, or surviving small baby genotype? BMJ 1994;308:942–5.

21. Hales CN, Barker DJP, Clark PMS, et al. Fetal growth and impaired glucose tolerance at age 64. BMJ 1991;303:1019–22.

22. Carlsson S, Persson P-G, Alvarsson M, et al. Low birth weight, family history of diabetes, and glucose intolerance in Swedish middle-aged men. Diabetes Care 1999;22:1043–7.

23. Curhan GC, Willett WC, Rimm EB, et al. Birth weight and adult hypertension, diabetes mellitus, and obesity in US men. Circulation 1996;94:3246–50.

24. Rich-Edwards JW, Colditz GA, Stampfer MJ, et al. Birthweight and the risk for type 2 diabetes mellitus in adult women. Ann Intern Med 1999;130:278–84.

25. Poulsen P, Vaag AA, Moller Jensen D, Beck-Nielsen H. Low birth weight is associated with NIDDM in discordant monozygotic and dizygotic twin pairs. Diabetologia 1997;40:439–46.

26. Pettitt DJ, Aleck KA, Baird HR, et al. Congenital susceptibility to NIDDM: role of intrauterine environment. Diabetes 1988;37:622–8.

27. Ohson L-O, Larsson B, Björntorp P, et al. Risk factors for type 2 (non-insulin-dependent) diabetes mellitus. Thirteen and one-half years of follow-up of the participants in a study of Swedish men born in 1913. Diabetologia 1988;31:798–805.

28. Kawakami N, Takatsuka N, Shimizu H, Ishibashi H. Effects of smoking on the incidence of non-insulin-dependent diabetes mellitus. Am J Epidemiol 1997;145:103–9.

29. Report of The Expert Committee on the Diagnosis and Classification of Diabetes Mellitus. Diabetes Care 1997;20:1183–97.

30. Charles MA, Fontbonne A, Thibult N, et al. Risk factors for NIDDM in white population. Paris Prospective Study. Diabetes 1991;40:796–9.

31. Edelstein SL, Knowler WC, Bain RP, et al. Predictors of progression from impaired glucose tolerance to NIDDM. An analysis of six prospective studies. Diabetes 1997;46:701–10.

32. O'Sullivan JB. Diabetes mellitus after GDM. Diabetes 1991;29(Suppl 2):131–5.

33. Damm P, Kuhl C, Bertelsen A, Mølsted-Pedersen L. Predictive factors for the development of diabetes in women with previous gestational diabetes. Am J Obstet Gynecol 1992;167:607–16.

34. Henry OA, Beischer NA. Long-term implications of gestational diabetes for the mother. Bailleres Clin Obstet Gynaecol 1991;5:461–83.

35. Feskens EJM, Kromhout D. Cardiovascular risk factors and the 25-year incidence of diabetes mellitus in middle-aged men. Am J Epidemiol 1989;130:1101–8.

36. Lundgren H, Bengtsson C, Blohme G, et al. Dietary habits and incidence of noninsulin-dependent diabetes mellitus in a population study of women in Gothenburg, Sweden. Am J Clin Nutr 1989;49:708–12.

37. Medalie JH, Papier CM, Goldbourt U, Herman JB. Major factors in the development of diabetes mellitus in 10,000 men. Arch Intern Med 1975;135:811–7.

38. Salmerón J, Manson JE, Stampfer MJ, et al. Dietary fiber, glycemic load, and risk of non-insulin-dependent diabetes mellitus in women. JAMA 1997;277:472–7.

39. Salmerón J, Ascherio A, Rimm EB, et al. Dietary fiber, glycemic load, and risk of NIDDM in men. Diabetes Care 1997;20:545–50.

40. Resnick LM. Ionic basis of hypertension, insulin resistance, vascular disease, and related disorders: the mechanism of syndrome X. Am J Hypertens 1993;6:123S–34S.

41. Rimm EB, Chan J, Stampfer MJ, et al. Prospective study of cigarette smoking, alcohol use, and the risk of diabetes in men. BMJ 1995;310:555–9.

42. Stampfer MJ, Colditz GA, Willett WC, et al. A prospective study of moderate alcohol drinking and risk of diabetes in women. Am J Epidemiol 1988;128:549–58.

43. Holbrook TL, Barrett-Connor E, Wingard DL. A prospective population-based study of alcohol use and non-insulin-dependent diabetes mellitus. Am J Epidemiol 1990;132:902–9.

44. Facchini F, Chen Y-DI, Reaven GM. Light-to-moderate alcohol intake is associated with enhanced insulin sensitivity. Diabetes Care 1994;17:115–9.

45. Manson JE, Rimm EB, Stampfer MJ, et al. Physical activity and incidence of non-insulin-dependent diabetes mellitus in women. Lancet 1991;338:774–8.

46. Manson JE, Nathan DM, Krolewski AS, et al. A prospective study of exercise and incidence of diabetes among US male physicians. JAMA 1992;268:63–7.

47. Perry IJ, Wannamethee SG, Walker MK, et al. Prospective study of risk factors for development of non-insulin dependent diabetes in middle aged British men. BMJ 1995;310:560–4.

48. Helmrich SP, Ragland DR, Leung RW, Paffenbarger RS. Physical activity and reduced occurrence of non-insulin-dependent diabetes mellitus. N Engl J Med 1991;325:147–52.

49. Ruderman N, Apelian AZ, Schneider SH. Exercise in therapy and prevention of Type 2 diabetes: implications for blacks. Diabetes Care 1990;13(Suppl 4):1163–8.

50. Rimm EB, Manson JE, Stampfer MJ, et al. Cigarette smoking and the risk of diabetes in women. Am J Public Health 1993;83:211–4.

51. Njolstad I, Arnesen E, Lund-Larsen PG. Sex differences in risk factors for clinical diabetes mellitus in a general population: a 12-year follow-up of the Finnmark Study. Am J Epidemiol 1998;147:49–58.

52. Stolk RP, van Splunder IP, Schouten JSAG, et al. High blood pressure and the incidence of non-insulin dependent diabetes mellitus: findings in a 11.5 year follow-up study in the Netherlands. Eur J Epidemiol 1993;9:134–9.

53. McPhillips JB, Barrett-Connor E, Wingard DL. Cardiovascular disease risk factors prior to the diagnosis of impaired glucose tolerance and non-insulin-dependent diabetes mellitus in a community of older adults. Am J Epidemiol 1990;131:443–53.

54. Balkau B, King H, Zimmett P, Raper LR. Factors associated with the development of diabetes in the Micronesian population of Nauru. Am J Epidemiol 1985;122:594–605.

55. Skarfors ET, Selinus KI, Lithell HO. Risk factors for developing non-insulin dependent diabetes: a 10-year follow up of men in Uppsala. BMJ 1991;303:755–60.

56. Wilson PWF, Anderson KM, Kannel WB. Epidemiology of diabetes mellitus in the elderly. The Framingham Study. Am J Med 1986;80(Suppl 5A):3–9.

CHAPTER 11

What Is Gestational Diabetes?

Edmond A. Ryan, MD

ABSTRACT

Gestational diabetes mellitus (GDM) is any abnormal glucose tolerance first diagnosed during pregnancy. It occurs in 2 to 4% of the pregnant population and is due to a combination of the insulin resistance of pregnancy coupled with an insulin secretory defect. It is associated with neonatal macrosomia and hypoglycemia and, in the mother, a long-term risk for diabetes. It is best screened for with a 50-g oral glucose load followed by determination of plasma glucose 1 hour later. Values of 7.8 mM or greater indicate the need for an oral glucose tolerance test. There is no uniformity of criteria for diagnosing GDM. In Canada, levels to be met or exceeded at fasting and 1 and 2 hours are 5.3, 10.6, and 8.9 mM, respectively, before and after a 75-g challenge. In the United States, levels of 5.3, 10.0, and 8.6 mM are used for the same glucose load.

INTRODUCTION

Gestational diabetes is a common problem. Despite its high prevalence, issues relating to the diagnosis and management of the condition continue to be controversial. The evidence and debates surrounding these issues are summarized in this section, organized according to the following clinically important questions:

1. What is gestational diabetes mellitus (GDM)?
2. What is the etiology of GDM?
3. Who gets GDM?
4. What are the short- and long-term risks for the fetus when the mother has GDM?
5. What are the risks for the mother with GDM?
6. Should pregnant women be screened for GDM?
7. Who should be screened for GDM?
8. What screening test should be used for GDM?
9. How is GDM diagnosed?

WHAT IS GESTATIONAL DIABETES?

Gestational diabetes is defined as any abnormal carbohydrate intolerance first recognized during pregnancy.[1] It is associated with perinatal morbidity, and for the patient herself, there is an increased long-term risk of diabetes. Its pathophysiology of combined insulin resistance and insulin secretory defects coupled with the very high long-term risk of Type 2 diabetes all point to gestational diabetes being an early manifestation of Type 2 diabetes. Gestational diabetes is related to the insulin resistance of pregnancy and is thus typically found in later pregnancy. The diagnosis of gestational diabetes does not preclude the possibility that the carbohydrate intolerance may have been present previously and is simply being identified during the pregnancy. The occurrence of GDM in the first half of pregnancy should prompt consideration that glucose intolerance may in fact have predated the pregnancy and needs close observation postpartum.

Table 11–1 Risk Factors for Gestational Diabetes

Increasing age

Positive family history of diabetes

Increasing obesity, weight gain in early adulthood

Ethnicity

Cigarette smoking

WHAT IS THE ETIOLOGY OF GDM?

Pregnancy is associated with profound hormonal changes that have a direct effect on carbohydrate tolerance. In early pregnancy, progesterone and estrogen rise but counterbalance each other in terms of insulin action, in that progesterone causes insulin resistance and estrogen is protective.[2] Once the second trimester is entered, human placental lactogen (hPL), cortisol, and prolactin (but particularly hPL) all rise, causing decreased phosphorylation of insulin receptor substrate-1[3] and profound insulin resistance.[2,4] In most subjects, pancreatic insulin secretion rises to match this need,[5] but in those with underlying beta-cell defects, hyperglycemia ensues.[6–10] The insulin resistance of pregnancy is exaggerated in those with gestational diabetes, especially if fasting hyperglycemia is present,[11,12] and is related to additional defective tyrosine phosphorylation of the insulin receptor β-subunit.[3] It is the defect in insulin secretion that is likely the most critical in determining carbohydrate tolerance. Postpartum women with a history of gestational diabetes typically return to euglycemia, but defects in insulin secretion and action are still evident.[13–15] Thus, underlying defects in both insulin secretion and insulin action are likely present before pregnancy; if faced with the stress of insulin resistance induced by hormonal changes during gestation, GDM results.

WHO GETS GESTATIONAL DIABETES?

The overall incidence of GDM is 2 to 4% of the population,[16–20] but this rate is doubled in selected ethnic groups such as Aboriginal Canadians.[21] The major risk factors for GDM, as determined by a prospective cohort study,[22] are outlined in Table 11–1.

For each year gained after age 25, the relative risk (RR) of GDM increases by 4% (95% confidence interval [CI] 2 to 6%).[22] In general, the incidence of GDM under the age of 20 is < 1%, from 20 to 30 < 2%, and > 30 is 8 to 14%.[23,24] Why age is such a strong risk factor is unknown, aside from the general supposition that beta-cell function declines with age.

Family history is an important risk factor that has been confirmed in most, but not all, studies.[22,24] Positive family history confers an RR of 1.68 and is found in nearly one-quarter of women with GDM.[22] Interestingly, positive maternal history is more common than is paternal.[25] This suggests a preferred transmission along the maternal line, which is opposite that found for Type 1 diabetes[26,27] and raises the question as to the importance of the in utero environment.

Obesity is thought to increase the risk of GDM through its association with insulin resistance. The incidence of GDM is increased threefold in those with a body mass index (BMI) ≥ 30 kg/m[2] versus those with a BMI < 20 kg/m[2].[22] As expected, an increased waist-to-hip ratio increases the risk.[28,29]

The importance of ethnicity in the incidence of GDM is becoming increasingly recognized in multicultural societies.[30] The risk ratio for various races is profound, with some

Table 11–2 Gestational Diabetes Risk and Ethnicity

	Asians	Hispanics	African Americans	Aboriginals	Caucasians
Risk for GDM	5-fold	2.5-fold	2-fold	2–4-fold	1

GDM = gestational diabetes mellitus.

groups such as the Pima Indians being especially high. In the more general population, there are still dramatic differences, as shown in Table 11–2.[24,31–35]

Such a high prevalence of GDM in Asians is unexplained but is not simply related to the relatively large glucose load presented to a small body frame, as the risk persists even after adjustment for obesity.[33] Some groups of Aboriginal subjects have extremely high rates, approaching the unique situation of the Pima Indians, and the increased occurrence of Type 2 diabetes in Aboriginals supports the conclusion that a larger epidemic of Type 2 diabetes is occurring in North American Aboriginal people.[21]

Other classic risk factors for GDM, such as having had a large baby or poor obstetric history, primarily reflect probable missed glucose intolerance during a previous pregnancy and involve a much smaller group of people.

EVIDENCE-BASED MESSAGE

In a large prospective cohort study (N = 14,613, the Nurses Health Study II) using self-reporting of GDM (validated in a subset), an incidence of 4.9% was found. With multivariate analysis, the risk factors for GDM were increasing age, family history of diabetes (RR = 1.68), increasing obesity, weight gain in early adulthood (RR for a BMI $\geq$ 30 kg/m^2 = 2.9), ethnicity, and cigarette smoking (RR= 1.43) (Level 1).[22]

WHAT ARE THE RISKS FOR THE FETUS WHEN THE MOTHER HAS GESTATIONAL DIABETES?

The major short-term risks for the fetus as a consequence of the mother having GDM are shown in Table 11–3.

Macrosomia can be defined as a birth weight > 4,000 g.[36] Large for gestational age (LGA)—defined as a birth weight greater than the 90th percentile from an appropriate group—provides another measure of macrosomia. Macrosomia is found in as low as 6%[37] but more commonly between 18 to 29% of births of GDM women and is more prevalent if obesity is present.[38–41] An LGA baby is found in 29 to 32% of such births.[42,43] Macrosomia correlates weakly with degree of hyperglycemia. More important predictors of birth weight are gestational age, maternal weight gain, maternal pregravid weight, neonatal sex, and parity.[37,43–45] Hyperglycemia has a role but is of lesser importance, with insulin sensitivity accounting for only 7% of the variance in neonatal fat mass.[44] An elevated glucose, however, is the only variable controlling birth weight that can be readily modified. Tight glucose control does decrease the occurrence of macrosomia, cesarean section (C-section), and birth trauma in most[39,41,46–51] but not all studies.[52–54] Fat accumulation tends to be truncal, so that shoulder circumference is larger for a given weight. This leads to an increased risk of cephalopelvic disproportion and birth trauma.[48,55] The risk of Erb's palsy is increased, but

Table 11–3 Short-Term Risks for the Fetus When the Mother Has Gestational Diabetes

Macrosomia and possible birth trauma

Neonatal hypoglycemia

Jaundice

rarely are these injuries long term.[56–58] Macrosomia is related to fetal hyperinsulinemia, which, as Pederson hypothesized, is likely due to the increased transmission of substrates from the mother.[59] Even within the normal range of glucose levels for the mother, there is a confirmed relationship of higher glucose values with birth size.[60–62] Finally, in one report of a small number of subjects where the diagnosis of GDM, though made, was not acted on, there was a higher rate of macrosomia and shoulder dystocia in the neonates.[63]

Glucose levels in the neonatal stage are normally much lower than at other times, with a mean glucose of 2.6 ± 0.2 mM in neonates of nondiabetic mothers 2 hours after birth.[64] It is accepted that a level of < 1.7 mM needs to be attained before hypoglycemia can be diagnosed in the neonate.[65] Neonatal hypoglycemia is found in 3 to 38% of infants of GDM women.[39,40,48] Neonatal hypoglycemia is related to fetal pancreatic hyperplasia but shows the strongest correlation to maternal glucose levels during labor.[66] In Type 1 diabetes, a maternal glucose level > 5 mM during the last 4 hours of labor has been associated with neonatal hypoglycemia.[67] More recently, it was found that if these levels exceeded 10 mM, then all infants born to such mothers had neonatal hypoglycemia.[68] Neonatal hypoglycemia has also been directly related to amniotic fluid insulin level in the presence of macrosomia.[69,70] One prospective study looking at the long-term outlook for those who have suffered neonatal hypoglycemia showed no sequelae, but few would wish to see twitching from hypoglycemia in a baby.[71]

Jaundice also occurs more frequently in these infants, with an occurrence rate of about 16%.[38] It is usually mild and responds readily to phototherapy; it reflects an immaturity of the neonatal liver. Other, more rare, associations of GDM, such as hypocalcemia, polycythemia, and respiratory distress syndrome, still may be seen in the face of missed or untreated GDM, but this occurs infrequently with modern obstetric and diabetes care. Myocardial hypertrophy still occurs but rarely appears to be of clinical significance.[72] Stillbirths rarely occur,[73] but in large studies the presence of GDM is noted with increased frequency.[74] The setting is usually one of severe GDM that has been poorly controlled and is frequently not detected early.[74] There is an increased risk of C-section delivery in those mothers diagnosed with GDM (34.4% vs 22.4% in controls).[20] This rate is not explained by birth weight alone, and it appears that labeling someone with GDM does increase their chances of undergoing a C-section.[20,41]

Congenital malformations are reported in GDM series, but resolving whether this represents a subgroup who had preexisting Type 2 diabetes has been impossible.[75–79] As understood from the pathogenesis of GDM, hyperglycemia commonly occurs in the second and third trimesters, so that typical GDM is not associated with congenital malformations.[80] The occurrence of GDM in the first or early second trimester, or of very severe GDM in the late second trimester, is atypical, requiring fetal assessment for congenital malformations.

EVIDENCE-BASED MESSAGES

1. Several studies have documented that hyperglycemia is not the most important determinant of birth weight and that maternal obesity is much more closely related. However, intensive treatment of GDM in a large (N = 2,461 cases of GDM) prospective study (with randomization based on availability of glucose meters) showed lower macrosomia and neonatal hypoglycemia rates with better glucose control (Level 3).[48]

2. Below the threshold of GDM, higher glucose values are associated with higher incidences of macrosomia and C-section (large prospective cohort study, N = 3,637) (Level 1).[61]

ARE THERE LONG-TERM RISKS FOR THE OFFSPRING?

The infant of the subject with GDM inherits an increased susceptibility for glucose intolerance. As mentioned earlier, GDM itself predicts that the mother will likely progress to Type 2 diabetes, so that the child is likely to have a first-degree relative with Type 2 diabetes and is thus at higher risk. However, the in utero environment does appear to play a role. The elegant studies of Pettitt and colleagues of the Pima Indians have followed offspring of women who either had diabetes prior to pregnancy or developed diabetes after pregnancy.[81,82] Both groups thus passed on to their offspring a genetically based increased risk for diabetes. However, those with diabetes before pregnancy and those who develop diabetes postpartum will have either exposed the infants to increased glucose in utero or to normoglycemia, respectively. In those children and teenagers exposed to hyperglycemia in utero, the glucose level 2 hours postload was higher, and they were more obese. This pattern suggests an in utero role for later glucose intolerance. Two studies showed an increased insulin resistance in offspring of either Type 1 subjects or those who had GDM during puberty compared to offspring of nondiabetic women.[83,84] Animal studies also support this possibility, with the demonstration of either insulin resistance or some impairment of insulin secretion in offspring of diabetic dams.[85-88]

Obesity is also found more frequently in offspring of women with GDM.[81,82,89] Separation of hereditary effects from those of maternal glucose levels is difficult, as the mothers who have GDM are frequently obese. The studies of Pettitt and colleagues that separate, to a large extent, genetic versus environmental effects, indicate that obesity is a consequence of exposure to hyperglycemia in utero.[81,82] Other studies also support an increased risk of obesity in the offspring.[90,91]

WHAT ARE THE RISKS FOR THE MOTHER WITH GESTATIONAL DIABETES?

Rarely is the hyperglycemia in GDM severe enough to cause concern for the mother. Although there are reports of diabetic ketoacidosis and of retinopathy occurring in GDM, these are isolated case reports.[92-94] Many women attribute some of their symptoms of pregnancy, such as nocturia, to their diabetes, but the hyperglycemia is typically so mild that it is not likely a major factor in these symptoms.

Of more concern is the long-term risk of diabetes. The risk of diabetes is approximately 50% (Figure 11–1A) and as high as 75% for any impairment of glucose tolerance (Figure 11–1B).[95-101] The form of diabetes that is found is mainly Type 2. The foundation for this risk is in the underlying defect in these subjects in terms of insulin action and insulin secretion.[10,13-15,102-104] As subjects with GDM age, particularly if they gain weight, glucose intolerance and ultimately diabetes ensues. The risk factors for long-term diabetes as analyzed in studies using logistic regression are listed in Table 11–4.

There is a subgroup of women with gestational diabetes who are lean and frequently have islet-cell antibody titers that are positive.[115,116] These women are much more likely to go on to develop Type 1 diabetes. This involves about 5% of GDM women, and it is likely that the GDM findings reflect just a chance detection of Type 1 diabetes in evolution.[117-119]

EVIDENCE-BASED MESSAGE

Several retrospective studies have demonstrated that women with a history of GDM develop diabetes, typically Type 2. One large (N = 671) prospective study of Latino women with GDM found a 47% cumulative incidence of diabetes at 5 years postpartum,[111] and another prospective study found a 5% incidence of diabetes and 16% incidence of either impaired glucose tolerance or impaired fasting glucose at 3 to 6 months postpartum (Level 2).[111,120]

SHOULD PREGNANT WOMEN BE SCREENED FOR GESTATIONAL DIABETES?

Gestational diabetes is a mild condition, with virtually no symptoms, that increases the risk of perinatal morbidity and subsequent Type 2 diabetes in the mother.[95-101] Although some have argued against screening for GDM,[137,138] intensive therapy of diabetes does decrease the risk of macrosomia, resultant C-sections, and birth trauma.[48] In addition, control of glucose in labor lessens the chance of neonatal hypoglycemia.[66] Moreover, two studies have demonstrated that screening and treatment for gestational diabetes is cost effective.[139,140] Neverthe-

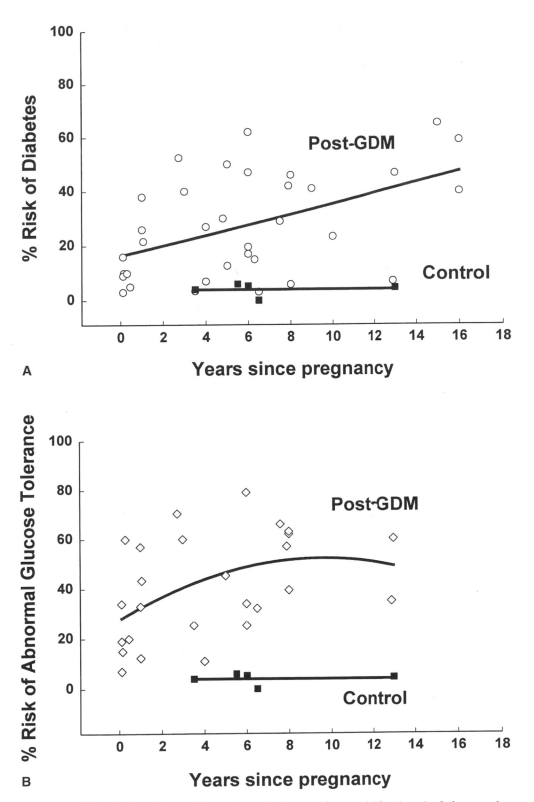

Figure 11–1 Risk of either diabetes (A) or abnormal glucose tolerance (either impaired glucose toler-ance or diabetes, B), post-GDM. Controls are shown as ■, occurrence of diabetes as O, and occurrence of abnormal glucose tolerance as ◇. Each point represents the report of one study. Lines represent regression curves.[78,95–102,104–112,114,118,120–136]

Table 11–4 Risk Factors for Progression to Diabetes in Women with a History of Gestational Diabetes

Increased prepregnancy BMI[98,105–109]

Severity of glucose intolerance during pregnancy

    Earlier gestational age of onset[105,110–112]

    Elevated fasting plasma glucose[98,105–107,111–113]

    Need for insulin[110,113,114]

    Presence of higher glucose values on postpartum OGTT[111,113]

OGGT = oral glucose tolerance test.
Data from Kaufmann et al,[98] Catalano et al,[105] Coustan et al,[106] Damm et al,[107] Henry et al,[108] Metzger et al,[109] Dacus et al,[110] Kjos et al,[111,112] Lam et al,[113] Greenberg et al.[114]

less, the value of identifying people at high risk for later diabetes, and whether anything can realistically be done to prevent it, is unknown. The negative aspect of screening is a labeling effect: once a patient is diagnosed with GDM, they are more likely to have a C-section, irrespective of fetal weight.[20,41] On balance, diagnosing GDM is cost effective but must be accompanied by education of caregivers so that a diagnosis of GDM will decrease the chance of a C-section rather than increase it.

EVIDENCE-BASED MESSAGES

1. When GDM is diagnosed, intensive treatment reduces macrosomia and neonatal hypoglycemia. This was shown in a large prospective study (N = 2,461 GDM cases) with randomization based on availability of glucose meters (Level 3).[48]
2. Diagnosis carries a labeling effect that increases the risk of a C-section, independent of birth weight, as evidenced by a large (N = 1,216 GDM cases) retrospective study and a prospective cohort study (N = 143 GDM cases) (Level 3).[20,41]

WHO SHOULD BE SCREENED FOR GESTATIONAL DIABETES?

Screening for gestational diabetes can be universal or based on risk factors.[141–143] Repeated studies have shown that limiting screening to risk factors alone will miss 50% of cases.[17,144–147] Thus, risk-factor screening that tests only those in a high-risk group is unsatisfactory. Results from one study indicate that the converse may be of value, that is, if someone has an absence of risk factors, then it may be unnecessary to screen them.[24] They also suggest using a variable diagnostic cutoff depending on the level of risk, but this has not been generally accepted.[142] Both the American Diabetes Association and the Canadian Diabetes Association[148,149] now recommend that all expectant mothers be screened for GDM except those falling into a very low-risk group as evidenced by *all* of the characteristics listed in Table 11–5.

The expected prevalence in such a restricted group as identified in Table 11–5 is < 1%,[24] and so is deemed not worth screening. Such a policy has not been uniformly endorsed and has been questioned by evidence showing that it will still miss 10% of all cases of GDM (of this group, 16% required insulin).[150]

WHAT SCREENING TEST SHOULD BE USED FOR GDM?

The best screening test consists of a 50-g glucose load followed by a plasma glucose sample take at 1 hour; a negative result is < 7.8 mM.[148,149] When performed between 24 to 28 weeks of gestation, the test has a sensitivity of 79% and a specificity of 87% at the 7.8-mM

Table 11–5 Necessary Characteristics for Omission of Gestational Diabetes Screening

Lean: prepregnancy BMI < 25 kg/m²

Young: age < 25 years

Absence of family history of diabetes

Not of an ethnic group predisposed to diabetes (ie, not Hispanic, African American, Aboriginal, Asian)

BMI = body mass index.

cutpoint.[151] For those at high risk (especially those who have had gestational diabetes in a previous pregnancy), the test should be administered when the patient is first seen. Disadvantages include the fact that it requires 1 hour of waiting, consumption of a glucose load, and the fact that its reproducibility is only moderate.[152] Indeed, some have argued for a lower cutoff value of 7.5 mM to improve sensitivity.[153] Other tests that have been proposed as well as their diagnostic properties are listed in Table 11–6. The formal recommendations of the American and Canadian Diabetes Associations[148,149] are to use the ≥ 7.8-mM cutoff for the 1-hour 50-g challenge. This is the level usually used, but some centers use the cutoff of 7.5 mM.[153]

Is the 50-Gram Screening Test Ever Diagnostic?

Early studies found that if the glucose level 1 hour after the 50-g screen was ≥ 10.0 mM, there was a 95% probability that GDM was present.[153] Others have set the level higher, at 12.2 mM,[160] but a more recent retrospective study using receiver operating characteristic (ROC) curves found that a glucose level of ≥ 10.3 mM was associated with GDM (96% specificity, 36% sensitivity).[161] This level has been accepted in Canada.[149]

Table 11–6 Screening Tests for Gestational Diabetes

Test	Specificity (%)	Sensitivity (%)
50-g 1-hour screen, 7.8-mM cutoff[151]	87.0	79.0
50-g 1-hour screen, 7.5-mM cutoff[153]	80.0	98.0
50-g 1-hour screen, 7.2-mM cutoff[141]	78.0	100.0
Random glucose > 6.4, > 2 h postprandial[154]	96.0	16.0
Urine glucose, first trimester[155]	98.5	7.1
Fasting glucose of 4.7 mM[156]	68.0	68.0
Fasting glucose of 4.9 mM[157]	40.0	80.0
Fructosamine[158]	77.0	79.0
Glycohemoglobin[159]	86.5	27.0

Data from Carr,[141] O'Sullivan et al,[151] Carpenter et al,[153] Nasrat et al,[154] Gribble et al,[155] Reichelt et al,[156] Sacks et al,[157] Hughes et al,[158] Shah et al.[159]

EVIDENCE-BASED MESSAGE

In a prospective study of 3,131 pregnant women, it was shown that a low-risk group, as defined by age ≤ 30, BMI ≤ 22, and Caucasian race, could be omitted for screening for GDM, knowing that the risk in this group is 0.9% (Level I).[24]

HOW IS GESTATIONAL DIABETES DIAGNOSED?

There is no area more controversial in the field of gestational diabetes than determining criteria for its diagnosis.[162,163] Table 11–7 shows a partial list of the multitude of criteria that are currently available on a worldwide basis.

The major problem in diagnosis is that evidence-based criteria are lacking. At what level of hyperglycemia do macrosomia, fetal trauma, neonatal hyperglycemia, and jaundice occur? The situation is compounded by the fact that causes of these problems in the fetus are multifactorial, not simply glucose driven. In the general field of diabetes, the level of glucose for diagnosis is based on the risk of microvascular disease.[149,174] In gestational diabetes, the original criteria of O'Sullivan and Mahan were based on the risk of future diabetes and only retrospectively applied to neonatal morbidity. In general diabetes, the problems are not just in hyperglycemia but are also in perturbations of lipids and proteins. So too in gestational diabetes—the derangements of lipids, especially free fatty acids and proteins, may actually be more important than glucose problems, but plasma glucose level is the only readily available marker of these abnormalities. The criteria used at the moment are arbitrary, but it is hoped that the current Hyperglycemia Adverse Pregnancy Outcome Study, due to a report in 2003, will answer some of these questions. The criteria currently in use in North America are listed in Table 11–8.

SUMMARY OF EVIDENCE-BASED MESSAGES

1. In a large prospective large cohort study (N = 14,613, the Nurses Health Study II) using self-reporting of GDM (validated in a subset), an incidence of 4.9% was found. With multivariate analysis, the risk factors for GDM were increasing age, family history of diabetes (RR = 1.68), increasing obesity, weight gain in early adulthood (RR for a BMI ≥ 30 = 2.9), ethnicity, and cigarette smoking (RR = 1.43) (Level 1).[22]

2. Several studies have documented that hyperglycemia is not the most important determinant of birth weight and that maternal obesity is much more closely related. However, intensive treatment of GDM in a large (N = 2,461 cases of GDM) prospective study (with randomization based on availability of glucose meters) showed lower macrosomia and neonatal hypoglycemia rates with better glucose control (Level 3).[48]

3. Below the threshold of GDM, higher glucose values are associated with higher incidences of macrosomia and C-section (Level 1).[61]

4. Several retrospective studies have demonstrated that women with a history of GDM develop diabetes, typically Type 2. One large (N = 671) prospective study of Latino women with GDM found a 47% cumulative incidence of diabetes at 5 years postpartum,[111] and another prospective study found a 5% incidence of diabetes and 16% incidence of either impaired glucose tolerance or impaired fasting glucose at 3 to 6 months postpartum (Level 2).[111,120]

5. When GDM is diagnosed, intensive treatment reduces macrosomia and neonatal hypoglycemia. This was shown in a large prospective study (N = 2,461 GDM cases) with randomization based on availability of glucose meters (Level 3).[48]

Table 11-7 Varying Criteria for Diagnosis of Gestational Diabetes

Criteria	Values To Be Met or Exceeded for Diagnosis (mM)				Number of Abnormal Values Required	Glucose Load (g)	Comment	Study
	0 h	1 h	2 h	3 h				
NDDG, O'Sullivan, and Mahan	5.8	10.6	9.2	8.1	2	100	Originally based on long-term risk of DM. Later showed fetal risks of GDM, based on whole blood determinations.	National Diabetes Data Group[164]; O'Sullivan et al[165,166]
ADA	5.3	10	8.6	7.8	2	75 or 100	Consensus from the Fourth International Workshop on GDM	Metzger et al[148]
Carpenter and Coustan	5.3	10	8.6	7.8	2	100	Based on O'Sullivan data but different conversion factor for whole blood to plasma than NDDG	Carpenter et al[153]
Langer	5.8	10.6	9.2	8.1	1	100	Based on one abnormal value on OGTT	Langer et al[167]
WHO DM IGT	7.8 7.8		11.1 7.8		1	75	Same cutoffs as nonpregnant population; treat IGT as abnormal	WHO Study Group[168]
UK Workgroup	8 6–8		11 9–11		1 (not formally stated)	75	Consensus statement form UK Workgroup	Brown et al[169]
Australia New Zealand	5.5 5.5		8.0 9.0		1	75	Consensus statement	Martin[170]; Hoffman et al[171]
Germany	5	10.6	8.9		2	75	Capillary blood	Fuchtenbusch[119]
Canada	5.3	10.6	8.9		2	75	Consensus based on references[172,173]	Meltzer et al[149]

ADA = American Diabetes Association; WHO = World Health Organization; DM = diabetes mellitus; IGT = impaired glucose tolerance; GDM = gestational diabetes mellitus; NDDG = National Diabetes Data Group; OGTT = oral glucose tolerance test.

Table 11–8 Current Criteria for Diagnosis of Gestational Diabetes in the United States and Canada*

United States[†]				Canada[‡]	
Glucose Load (g)				Glucose Load (g)	
Time (h)	75	100		Time (h)	75
0	5.3	5.3		0	5.3
1	10	10		1	10.6
2	8.6	8.6		2	8.9
3	7.8	7.8			

*Two or more values should be met or exceeded for the diagnosis of gestational diabetes. In Canada, if only one value is elevated, the term "impaired glucose tolerance of pregnancy" is used.
[†]75- or 100-g glucose load, with glucose levels (mM) at 0, 1, 2, and 3 hours.
[‡]75-g glucose load, with glucose levels (mM) at 0, 1, and 2 hours.

6.   Diagnosis carries a labeling effect that increases the risk of a C-section, independent of birth weight, as evidenced by a large (N = 1,216 GDM cases) retrospective study and a prospective cohort study (N = 143 GDM cases) (Level 3).[20,41]

7.   In a prospective study of 3,131 pregnant women, it was shown that a low-risk group, as defined by age ≤ 30, BMI ≤ 22, and Caucasian race, could be omitted for screening for GDM, knowing that the risk in this group is 0.9% (Level 1).[24]

REFERENCES

1.   American Diabetes Association. Gestational diabetes mellitus. Diabetes Care 1999;22(Suppl 1):S74–6.

2.   Ryan EA, Enns L. Role of gestational hormones in the induction of insulin resistance. J Clin Endocrinol Metab 1988;67:341–7.

3.   Friedman JE, Ishizuka T, Shao J, et al. Impaired glucose transport and insulin receptor tyrosine phosphorylation in skeletal muscle from obese women with gestational diabetes. Diabetes 1999;48:1807–14.

4.   Kühl C. Etiology and pathogenesis of gestational diabetes. Diabetes Care 1998;21:B19–26.

5.   Agardh C-D, Aberg A, Nordén NE. Glucose levels and insulin secretion during a 75-g glucose challenge test in normal pregnancy. J Intern Med 1996;240:303–9.

6.   Catalano PM, Tyzbir ED, Roman NM, et al. Longitudinal changes in insulin release and insulin resistance in nonobese pregnant women. Am J Obstet Gynecol 1991;165:1667–72.

7.   Catalano PM, Tyzbir ED, Wolfe RR, et al. Carbohydrate metabolism during pregnancy in control subjects and women with gestational diabetes. Am J Physiol 1993;264:E60–7.

8.   Nicholls JSD, Chan SP, Ali K, et al. Insulin secretion and sensitivity in women fulfilling WHO criteria for gestational diabetes. Diabet Med 1995;12:56–60.

9.   Bowes SB, Hennessy TR, Umpleby AM, et al. Measurement of glucose metabolism and insulin secretion during normal pregnancy and pregnancy complicated by gestational diabetes. Diabetologia 1996;39:976–83.

10. Kautzky-Willer A, Prager R, Waldhausl W, et al. Pronounced insulin resistance and inadequate β-cell secretion characterize lean gestational diabetes during and after pregnancy. Diabetes Care 1997;20:1717–23.

11. Ryan EA, O'Sullivan MJ, Skyler JS. Insulin action during pregnancy. Studies with the euglycemic clamp technique. Diabetes 1985;34:380–9.

12. Catalano PM, Huston L, Amini SB, et al. Longitudinal changes in glucose metabolism during pregnancy in obese women with normal glucose tolerance and gestational diabetes mellitus. Am J Obstet Gynecol 1999;180:903–16.

13. Ward WK, Johnston CL, Beard JC, et al. Insulin resistance and impaired insulin secretion in subjects with histories of gestational diabetes mellitus. Diabetes 1985;34:861–9.

14. Ward WK, Johnston CL, Beard JC, et al. Abnormalities of islet B-cell function, insulin action, and fat distribution in women with histories of gestational diabetes: relationship to obesity. J Clin Endocrinol Metab 1985;61:1039–45.

15. Ryan EA, Imes S, Liu D, et al. Defects in insulin secretion and action in women with a history of gestational diabetes. Diabetes 1995;44:506–12.

16. Forsbach G, Contreras Soto JJ, Fong G, et al. Prevalence of gestational diabetes and macrosomic newborns in a Mexican population. Diabetes Care 1988;11:235–8.

17. Coustan DR, Nelson C, Carpenter MW, et al. Maternal age and screening for gestational diabetes: a population-based study. Obstet Gynecol 1989;73:557–61.

18. Engelgau MM, Herman WH, Smith PJ, et al. The epidemiology of diabetes and pregnancy in the U.S., 1988. Diabetes Care 1995;18:1029–33.

19. Akhter J, Qureshi R, Rahim F, et al. Diabetes in pregnancy in Pakistani women: prevalence and complications in an indigenous South Asian community. Diabet Med 1996;13:189–91.

20. Remsberg KE, McKeown RE, McFarland KF, et al. Diabetes in pregnancy and cesarean delivery. Diabetes Care 1999;22:1567.

21. Harris SB, Caulfield LE, Sugamori ME, et al. The epidemiology of diabetes in pregnant native Canadians. Diabetes Care 1997;20:1422–5.

22. Solomon CG, Willett WC, Carey VJ, et al. A prospective study of pregravid determinants of gestational diabetes mellitus. JAMA 1997;278:1078–83.

23. McFarland KF, Case CA. The relationship of maternal age on gestational diabetes. Diabetes Care 1985;8:598–600.

24. Naylor CD, Sermer M, Chen E, et al. Selective screening for gestational diabetes mellitus. N Engl J Med 1997;337:1591–6.

25. Martin AO, Simpson JL, Ober C, et al. Frequency of diabetes mellitus in mothers of probands with gestational diabetes: possible maternal influence on the predisposition to gestational diabetes. Am J Obstet Gynecol 1985;151:471–5.

26. Vadheim CM, Rotter JI, Maclaren NK, et al. Preferential transmission of diabetic alleles within the HLA gene complex. N Engl J Med 1986;315:1314–8.

27. Warram JH, Krolewski AS, Kahn CR. Determinants of IDDM and perinatal mortality in children of diabetic mothers. Diabetes 1988;37:1328–34.

28. Zhang S, Folsom AR, Flack JM, et al. Body fat distribution before pregnancy and gestational diabetes: findings from coronary artery risk development in young adults (CARDIA) study. BMJ 1995;311:1139–40.

29. Branchtein L, Schmidt MI, Mengue SS, et al. Waist circumference and waist-to-hip ratio are related to gestational glucose tolerance. Diabetes Care 1997;20:509–11.

30. Beischer NA, Oats JN, Henry OA, et al. Incidence and severity of gestational diabetes mellitus according to country of birth in women living in Australia. Diabetes 1991;40(Suppl 2):35–8.

31. Hollingsworth DR, Vaucher Y, Yamamoto TR. Diabetes in pregnancy in Mexican Americans. Diabetes Care 1991;14:695–705.

32. Yue DK, Molyneaux LM, Ross GP, et al. Why does ethnicity affect prevalence of gestational diabetes? The underwater volcano theory. Diabet Med 1996;13:748–52.

33. Dornhorst A, Paterson CM, Nicholls JSD, et al. High prevalence of gestational diabetes in women from ethnic minority groups. Diabet Med 1992;9:820–5.

34. Dooley SL, Metzger BE, Cho NH. Gestational diabetes mellitus. Influence of race on disease prevalence and perinatal outcome in a U.S. population. Diabetes 1991;40(Suppl 2):25–9.

35. Rodrigues S, Robinson E, Gray-Donald K. Prevalence of gestational diabetes mellitus among James Bay Cree women in northern Quebec. Can Med Assoc J 1999;160:1293–7.

36. Schwartz R, Teramo KA. What is the significance of macrosomia? Diabetes Care 1999;22:1201–5.

37. Spellacy WN, Miller S, Winegar A, et al. Macrosomia—maternal characteristics and infant complications. Obstet Gynecol 1985;66:158–61.

38. Hod M, Merlob P, Friedman S, et al. Prevalence of congenital anomalies and neonatal complications in the offspring of diabetic mothers in Israel. Isr J Med Sci 1991;27:498–502.

39. Hod M, Rabinerson D, Kaplan B, et al. Perinatal complications following gestational diabetes mellitus how 'sweet' is ill? Acta Obstet Gynecol Scand 1995;75:809–15.

40. Stenninger E, Schollin J, Aman J. Neonatal macrosomia and hypoglycaemia in children of mothers with insulin-treated gestational diabetes mellitus. Acta Paediatr Scand 1991;80:1014–8.

41. Naylor CD, Sermer M, Chen E, et al. Cesarean delivery in relation to birth weight and gestational glucose tolerance: pathophysiology or practice style? JAMA 1996;275:1165–70.

42. Combs CA, Gunderson E, Kitzmiller JL, et al. Relationship of fetal macrosomia to maternal postprandial glucose control during pregnancy. Diabetes Care 1992;15:1251–7.

43. Jacobson JD, Cousins L. A population-based study of maternal and perinatal outcome in patients with gestational diabetes. Am J Obstet Gynecol 1989;161:981–6.

44. Catalano PM. Effect of maternal metabolism on fetal growth and body composition. Diabetes Care 1998;21:B85–90.

45. Breschi MC, Seghieri G, Bartolomei G, et al. Relation of birthweight to maternal plasma glucose and insulin concentrations during normal pregnancy. Diabetologia 1993;36:1315–21.

46. Leikin E, Jenkins JH, Graves WL. Prophylactic insulin in gestational diabetes. Obstet Gynecol 1987;70:587–92.

47. Buchanan TA, Gonzalez M, Kjos SL, et al. Use of fetal ultrasound to select metabolic therapy for pregnancies complicated by mild gestational diabetes. Diabetes Care 1994;17:275–83.

48. Langer O, Rodriguez DA, Xenakis EMJ, et al. Intensified versus conventional management of gestational diabetes. Am J Obstet Gynecol 1994;170:1036–47.

49. Thompson DM, Dansereau J, Creed M, et al. Tight glucose control results in normal perinatal outcome in 150 patients with gestational diabetes. Obstet Gynecol 1994;83:362–6.

50. Langer O, Mazze R. The relationship between large-for-gestational-age infants and glycemic control in women with gestational diabetes. Am J Obstet Gynecol 1988;159:1478–83.

51. al-Najashi SS. Control of gestational diabetes. Int J Gynecol Obstet 1995;49:131–5.

52. Garner P, Okun N, Keely E, et al. A randomized controlled trial of strict glycemic control and tertiary level obstetric care versus routine obstetric care in the management of gestational diabetes: a pilot study. Am J Obstet Gynecol 1997;177:190–5.

53. Miller JM. A reappraisal of "tight control" in diabetic pregnancies. Am J Obstet Gynecol 1983;147:158–62.

54. Nordlander E, Hanson U, Persson B. Factors influencing neonatal morbidity in gestational diabetic pregnancy. Br J Obstet Gynaecol 1989;96:671–8.

55. Gilbert WM, Nesbitt TS, Danielsen B. Associated factors in 1611 cases of brachial plexus injury. Obstet Gynecol 1999;93:536–40.

56. Parks GD, Zeil HK. Macrosomia. A proposed indication for primary cesarean section. Obstet Gynecol 1978;52:407–9.

57. Keller JD, Lopez-Zeno JA, Dooley SL, et al. Shoulder dystocia and birth trauma in gestational diabetes: a five-year experience. Am J Obstet Gynecol 1991;165:928–30.

58. Persson B, Hanson U. Neonatal morbidities in gestational diabetes mellitus. Diabetes Care 1998;21:B79–84.

59. Pedersen J. Weight and length at birth of infants of diabetic mothers. Acta Endocrinol 1954;16:330–41.

60. Moses RG, Calvert D. Pregnancy outcomes in women without gestational diabetes mellitus related to the maternal glucose level. Diabetes Care 1995;18:1527–33.

61. Sermer M, Naylor CD, Gare DJ, et al. Impact of increasing carbohydrate intolerance on maternal-fetal outcomes in 3637 women without gestational diabetes. Am J Obstet Gynecol 1995;173:146–56.

62. Tallarigo L, Giampietro O, Penno G, et al. Relation of glucose tolerance to complications of pregnancy in nondiabetic women. N Engl J Med 1986;315:989–92.

63. Adams KM, Li H, Nelson RL, et al. Sequelae of unrecognized gestational diabetes. Am J Obstet Gynecol 1998;178:1321–32.

64. Tanzer F, Yazar N, Yazar H, et al. Blood glucose levels and hypoglycaemia in full term neonates during the first 48 hours of life. J Trop Pediatr 1997;43:58–60.

65. Senior B. Neonatal hypoglycemia. N Engl J Med 1973;289:790–3.

66. Kenepp NB, Shelley WC, Gabbe SG, et al. Fetal and neonatal hazards of maternal hydration with 5% dextrose before caesarean section. Lancet 1982;1150–2.

67. Miodovnik M, Mimouni F, Tsang RC, et al. Management of the insulin-dependent diabetic during labor and delivery. Influences on neonatal outcome. Am J Perinatol 1987;4:106–14.

68. Carron Brown S, Kyne-Grzebalski D, Mwangi B, et al. Effect of management policy upon 120 Type 1 diabetic pregnancies: policy decisions in practice. Diabet Med 1999;16:573–8.

69. Fraser RB, Bruce C. Amniotic fluid insulin levels identify the fetus at risk of neonatal hypoglycaemia. Diabet Med 1999;16:568–72.

70. Heding LG, Persson B, Stangenberg M. B-cell function in newborn infants of diabetic mothers. Diabetologia 1980;19:427–32.

71. Greene MF, Hare JW, Krache M, et al. Prematurity among insulin-requiring diabetic gravid women. Am J Obstet Gynecol 1989;161:106–11.

72. Oberhoffer R, Högel J, Stoz F, et al. Cardiac and extracardiac complications in infants of diabetic mothers and their relation to parameters of carbohydrate metabolism. Eur J Pediatr 1997;156:262–5.

73. Åberg A, Rydhström H, Källén B, et al. Impaired glucose tolerance during pregnancy is associated with increased fetal mortality in preceding sibs. Acta Obstet Gynecol Scand 1997;76:212–7.

74. Beischer NA, Wein P, Sheedy MT, et al. Identification and treatment of women with hyperglycaemia diagnosed during pregnancy can significantly reduce perinatal mortality rates. Aust N Z J Obstet Gynaecol 1996;36:239–47.

75. Widness JA, Cowett RM, Coustan DR, et al. Neonatal morbidities in infants of mothers with glucose intolerance in pregnancy. Diabetes 1985;34(Suppl 2):61–5.

76. Becerra JE, Khoury MJ, Cordero JF, et al. Diabetes mellitus during pregnancy and the risks for specific birth defects: a population based case control study. Pediatrics 1990;85:1 9.

77. Adashi EY, Pinto H, Tyson JE. Impact of maternal euglycemia on fetal outcome in diabetic pregnancy. Am J Obstet Gynecol 1979;133:268–74.

78. Farrell J, Forrest JM, Storey GNB, et al. Gestational diabetes — infant malformations and subsequent maternal glucose tolerance. Aust N Z J Obstet Gynaecol 1986;26:11–6.

79. Martínez-Frías ML, Bermejo E, Rodríguez-Pinilla E, et al. Epidemiological analysis of outcomes of pregnancy in gestational diabetic mothers. Am J Med Genet 1998;78:140–5.

80. Mills JL. Malformations in infants of diabetic mothers. Teratology 1982;25:385–94.

81. Pettitt DJ, Bennett PH, Knowler WC, et al. Gestational diabetes mellitus and impaired glucose tolerance during pregnancy. Long-term effects on obesity and glucose tolerance in the offspring. Diabetes 1985;34(Suppl 2):119–22.

82. Pettitt DJ, Aleck KA, Baird HR, et al. Congenital susceptibility to NIDDM. Role of intrauterine environment. Diabetes 1988;37:622–8.

83. Silverman BL, Metzger BE, Cho NH, et al. Impaired glucose tolerance in adolescent offspring of diabetic mothers. Relationship to fetal hyperinsulinism. Diabetes Care 1995;18:611–7.

84. Plagemann A, Harder T, Kohlhoff R, et al. Glucose tolerance and insulin secretion in children of mothers with pregestational IDDM or gestational diabetes. Diabetologia 1997;40:1094–100.

85. Ryan EA, Liu D, Bell RC, et al. Long term consequences in offspring of diabetes in pregnancy: studies with syngeneic islet transplanted streptozotocin-diabetic rats. Endocrinology 1995;2:10–20.

86. Aerts L, Holemans K, Van Assche FA. Maternal diabetes during pregnancy: consequences for the offspring. Diabetes Metab Rev 1990;6:147–67.

87. Bihoreau MT, Ktorza A, Kinebanyan MF, et al. Impaired glucose homeostasis in adult rats from hyperglycemic mothers. Diabetes 1986;35:979–84.

88. Linn T, Loewk E, Schneider K, et al. Spontaneous glucose intolerance in the progeny of low dose streptozotocin-induced diabetic mice. Diabetologia 1993;36:1245–51.

89. Rodrigues S, Ferris AM, Peréz-Escamilla R, et al. Obesity among offspring of women with type 1 diabetes. Clin Invest Med 1998;21:258–66.

90. Vohr BR, McGarvey ST. Growth patterns of large-for-gestational-age and appropriate-for-gestational-age infants of gestational diabetic mothers and control mothers at age 1 year. Diabetes Care 1997;20:1066–72.

91. Vohr BR, McGarvey ST, Tucker R. Effects of maternal gestational diabetes on offspring adiposity at 4–7 years of age. Diabetes Care 1999;22:1284–91.

92. Pitteloud N, Binz K, Caulfield A, et al. Ketoacidosis during gestational diabetes. Diabetes Care 1998;21:1031–2.

93. Bedalov A, Balasubramanyam A. Glucocorticoid-induced ketoacidosis in gestational diabetes: sequela of the acute treatment of preterm labor. Diabetes Care 1997;20:922–4.

94. Hagay ZJ, Schachter M, Pollack A, et al. Development of proliferative retinopathy in a gestational diabetes patient following rapid metabolic control. Eur J Obstet Gynecol Reprod Biol 1994;57:211–3.

95. Buchanan TA, Xiang A, Kjos SL, et al. Gestational diabetes: antepartum characteristics that predict postpartum glucose intolerance and type 2 diabetes in Latino women. Diabetes 1998;47:1302–10.

96. Ali Z, Alexis SD. Occurrence of diabetes mellitus after gestational diabetes mellitus in Trinidad. Diabetes Care 1990;13:527–9.

97. Dornhorst A, Bailey PC, Anyaoku V, et al. Abnormalities of glucose tolerance following gestational diabetes. QJM 1990;77:1219–28.

98. Kaufmann RC, Schleyhahn FT, Huffman DG, et al. Gestational diabetes diagnostic criteria: long-term maternal follow-up. Am J Obstet Gynecol 1995;172:621–5.

99. Mestman JH, Anderson GV, Guadalupe F, et al. Follow-up study of 360 subjects with abnormal carbohydrate metabolism during pregnancy. Obstet Gynecol 1972;39:421–5.

100. O'Sullivan JB. Body weight and subsequent diabetes mellitus. JAMA 1982;248:949–52.

101. Steinhart JR, Sugarman JR, Connell FA. Gestational diabetes is a herald of NIDDM in Navajo women. Diabetes Care 1997;20:943–7.

102. Persson B, Hanson U, Hartling SG, et al. Follow-up of women with previous GDM: insulin, C-peptide, and proinsulin responses to oral glucose load. Diabetes 1991;40:136–41.

103. Catalano PM, Bernstein IM, Wolfe RR, et al. Subclinical abnormalities of glucose metabolism in subjects with previous gestational diabetes. Am J Obstet Gynecol 1986;155:1255–62.

104. Efendic S, Hanson U, Persson B, et al. Glucose tolerance, insulin release, and insulin sensitivity in normal-weight women with previous gestational diabetes mellitus. Diabetes 1987;36:413–9.

105. Catalano PM, Vargo KM, Bernstein IM, et al. Incidence and risk factors associated with abnormal postpartum glucose tolerance in women with gestational diabetes. Am J Obstet Gynecol 1991;165:914–9.

106. Coustan DR, Carpenter MW, O'Sullivan PS, et al. Gestational diabetes: predictors of subsequent disordered glucose metabolism. Am J Obstet Gynecol 1993;168:1139–45.

107. Damm P, Kuhl C, Bertelsen A, et al. Predictive factors for the development of diabetes in women with previous gestational diabetes mellitus. Am J Obstet Gynecol 1992;167:607–16.

108. Henry OA, Beischer NA. Long-term implications of gestational diabetes for the mother. Baillieres Clin Obstet Gynaecol 1991;5:461–83.

109. Metzger BE, Cho NH, Roston SM, et al. Prepregnancy weight and antepartum insulin secretion predict glucose tolerance five years after gestational diabetes mellitus. Diabetes Care 1993;16:1598–605.

110. Dacus JV, Meyer NL, Muram D, et al. Gestational diabetes: postpartum glucose tolerance testing. Am J Obstet Gynecol 1994;171:927–31.

111. Kjos SL, Peters RK, Ziang A, et al. Predicting future diabetes in Latino women with gestational diabetes. Utility of early postpartum glucose tolerance testing. Diabetes 1995;44:586–91.

112. Kjos SL, Buchanan TA, Greenspoon JS, et al. Gestational diabetes mellitus: the prevalence of glucose intolerance and diabetes mellitus in the first two months post partum. Am J Obstet Gynecol 1990;163:93–8.

113. Lam KSL, Li DF, Lauder IJ et al. Prediction of persistent carbohydrate intolerance in patients with gestational diabetes. Diabetes Res Clin Pract 1991;12:181–6.

114. Greenberg LR, Moore TR, Murphy H. Gestational diabetes mellitus: antenatal variables as predictors of postpartum glucose intolerance. Obstet Gynecol 1995;86:97–101.

115. Dozio N, Beretta A, Belloni C, et al. Low prevalence of islet autoantibodies in patients with gestational diabetes mellitus. Diabetes Care 1997;20:81–3.

116. Beischer NA, Wein P, Sheedy MT, et al. Prevalence of antibodies to gluctamic acid decarboxylase in women who have had gestational diabetes. Am J Obstet Gynecol 1995;173:1563–9.

117. Damm P, Kuhl C, Buschard K, et al. Prevalence and predictive value of islet cell antibodies and insulin autoantibodies in women with gestational diabetes. Diabet Med 1994;11:558–63.

118. Petersen JS, Dyrberg T, Damm P, et al. GAD65 autoantibodies in women with gestational or insulin dependent diabetes mellitus diagnosed during pregnancy. Diabetologia 1996;39:1329–33.

119. Fuchtenbusch M, Ferber K, Standl E, et al. Prediction of type 1 diabetes postpartum in patients with gestational diabetes mellitus by combined islet cell autoantibody screening. Diabetes 1997;46:1459–67.

120. Pallardo F, Herranz L, Garcia-Ingelmo T, et al. Early postpartum metabolic assessment in women with prior gestational diabetes. Diabetes Care 1999;22:1053–8.

121. Benjamin E, Winters D, Mayfield J, et al. Diabetes in pregnancy in Zuni Indian women. Diabetes Care 1993;16:1231–5.

122. Cocilovo G, Tomasi F, Guerra S, et al. Risk factors associated with persistence of glucose intolerance one year after gestational diabetes. Diabetes Metab 1990;16:187–90.

123. Fuhrmann K. Targets in oral glucose tolerance testing. In: Sutherland HW, Stowers JM, editors. Carbohydrate metabolism in pregnancy and the newborn. 4th ed. London: Springer Verlag; 1989. p. 227–37.

124. Hagbard L, Svanborg A. Prognosis of diabetes mellitus with onset during pregnancy: a clinical study of seventy-one cases. Diabetes 1960;9:296–302.

125. Hanson U, Persson B, Hartling SG, et al. Increased molar proinsulin-to-insulin ratio in women with previous gestational diabetes does not predict later impairment of glucose tolerance. Diabetes Care 1996;19:17–20.

126. Mestman JH. Outcome of diabetes screening in pregnancy and perinatal morbidity in infants of mothers with mild impairment in glucose tolerance. Diabetes Care 1980;3:447–52.

127. Metzger BE, Bybee DE, Freinkel N, et al. Gestational diabetes mellitus. Correlations between the phenotypic and genotypic characteristics of the mother and abnormal glucose tolerance during the first year postpartum. Diabetes 1985;34(Suppl 2):111–5.

128. Molsted-Pedersen L, Damm P, Buschard K. Diabetes diagnosed during pregnancy: follow-up studies. In: Sutherland HW, Stowers JM, Pearson DWM, editors. Carbohydrate metabolism in pregnancy and the newborn. 4th ed. London: Springer Verlag; 1989. p. 277–86.

129. O'Sullivan JB. Long-term follow up of gestational diabetics. In: Camerini-Davalos RA, Cole HS, editors. Early diabetes in early life. New York: Academic Press; 1975. p. 503–19.

130. O'Sullivan JB. Gestational diabetes. Unsuspected, asymptomatic diabetes in pregnancy. N Engl J Med 1961;264:1082–5.

131. Pettitt DJ, Venkat Narayan KM, Hanson RL, et al. Incidence of diabetes mellitus in women following impaired glucose tolerance in pregnancy is lower than following impaired glucose tolerance in the non-pregnant state. Diabetologia 1996;39:1334–7.

132. Wolff VC, Verlohren H-J, Arlt P, et al. Schicksal von gestationsdiabetikerinnen — klassifikation des gestationsdiabetes nach abschluß der gestation (p.g. klassifikation). Zentrabl Gynäkol 1987;109:88–97.

133. Mestman JH. Follow-up studies in women with gestational diabetes mellitus. The experience at Los Angeles Country/University of Southern California Medical Center. In: Weiss PAM, Coustan DR, editors. Gestational diabetes. New York: Springer-Verlag; 1988. p. 191–8.

134. Stowers JM, Sutherland HW, Kerridge DF. Long-range implications for the mother. The Aberdeen experience. Diabetes 1985;34(Suppl 2):106–10.

135. Kjos S, Buchanan TA, Montoro M, et al. Serum lipids within 36 mo of delivery in women with recent gestational diabetes. Diabetes 1996;40:142–6.

136. Kerényi Z, Stella P, Bosnyák Z, et al. Association between central adiposity and multimetabolic syndrome in a special cohort of women with prior gestational diabetes. Diabetes Care 1999;22:876–7.

137. Canadian Task Force on Periodic Health Examination. Periodic health examination, 1992 update: 1. Screening for gestational diabetes mellitus. Can Med Assoc J 1992;147:435–43.

138. Jarrett RJ. Should we screen for gestational diabetes? BMJ 1997;315:736–7.

139. Jovanovic-Peterson L, Bevier W, Peterson CM. The Santa Barbara county health care services program: birth weight change concomitant with screening for and treatment of glucose-intolerance of pregnancy: a potential cost-effective intervention? Am J Perinatol 1997;14:221–8.

140. Kitzmiller JL, Elixhauser A, Carr S, et al. Assessment of costs and benefits of management of gestational diabetes mellitus. Diabetes Care 1998;21:B123–30.

141. Carr SR. Screening for gestational diabetes mellitus. Diabetes Care 1998;21:B14–8.

142. Greene MF. Screening for gestational diabetes. N Engl J Med 1997;337:1625–6.

143. Coustan DR. Methods of screening for and diagnosing of gestational diabetes. Clin Perinatol 1993;20:593–602.

144. Macafee CA, Beischer NA. The relative value of the standard indications for performing a glucose tolerance test in pregnancy. Med J Aust 1974;1:911–4.

145. Gillmer MDG, Oakley NW, Beard RW, et al. Screening for diabetes during pregnancy. Br J Obstet Gynaecol 1980;87:377–82.

146. Lavin Jr JP. Screening of high-risk and general populations for gestational diabetes. Clinical application and cost analysis. Diabetes 1985;34(Suppl 2):24–7.

147. Jovanovic L, Peterson CM. Screening for gestational diabetes: optimum timing and criteria for retesting. Diabetes 1985;34:21–3.

148. Metzger BE, Coustan DR, The Organizing Committee. Summary and recommendations of the Fourth International Workshop-Conference on Gestational Diabetes Mellitus. Diabetes Care 1998;21:B161–7.

149. Meltzer S, Leiter L, Daneman D, et al. 1998 clinical practice guidelines for the management of diabetes in Canada. Can Med Assoc J 1998;159:S1–29.

150. Moses RG, Moses J, Davis WS. Gestational diabetes: do lean young Caucasian women need to be tested? Diabetes Care 1998;21:1803–6.

151. O'Sullivan JB, Mahan CM, Charles D, et al. Screening criteria for high-risk gestational diabetic patients. Am J Obstet Gynecol 1973;116:895—900.

152. Sacks DA, Abu-Fadil S, Greenspoon JS, et al. How reliable is the fifty-gram, one-hour glucose screening test? Am J Obstet Gynecol 1989;161:642–5.

153. Carpenter MW, Coustan DR. Criteria for screening tests for gestational diabetes. Am J Obstet Gynecol 1982;144:768–73.

154. Nasrat AA, Johnstone FD, Hasan SAM. Is random plasma glucose an efficient screening test for abnormal glucose tolerance in pregnancy? Br J Obstet Gynaecol 1988;95:855–60.

155. Gribble RK, Meier PR, Berg RL. The value of urine screening for glucose at each prenatal visit. Obstet Gynecol 1995;86:405–10.

156. Reichelt AJ, Spichler ER, Branchtein L, et al. Fasting plasma glucose is a useful test for the detection of gestational diabetes. Diabetes Care 1998;21:1246–9.

157. Sacks DA, Greenspoon JS, Fotheringham N. Could the fasting plasma glucose assay be used to screen for gestational diabetes? J Reprod Med 1992;37:907–9.

158. Hughes PF, Agarwal M, Newman P, et al. An evaluation of fructosamine estimation in screening for gestational diabetes mellitus. Diabet Med 1995;12:708–12.

159. Shah BD, Cohen AW, May C, et al. Comparison of glycohemoglobin determination and the one-hour oral glucose screen in the identification of gestational diabetes. Am J Obstet Gynecol 1982;144:774–7.

160. Bobrowski RA, Bottoms SF, Micallef J-A, et al. Is the 50-gram glucose screening test ever diagnostic? J Matern Fetal Med 1996;5:317–20.

161. Landy HJ, Gomez-Marin O, O'Sullivan MJ. Diagnosing gestational diabetes mellitus: use of a glucose screen without administering the glucose tolerance test. Obstet Gynecol 1996;87:395–400.

162. Glucose tolerance in pregnancy — the who and how of testing. Lancet 1988;ii:1173–4.

163. Dornhorst A, Chan SP. The elusive diagnosis of gestational diabetes. Diabet Med 1998;15:7–10.

164. National Diabetes Data Group. Classification and diagnosis of diabetes mellitus and other categories of glucose intolerance. Diabetes 1979;28:1039–57.

165. O'Sullivan JB, Mahan CM. Criteria for the oral glucose tolerance test in pregnancy. Diabetes 1964;13:278–85.

166. O'Sullivan JB, Gellis SS, Dandrow RV, et al. The potential diabetic and her treatment in pregnancy. Obstet Gynecol 1966;27:683–9.

167. Langer O, Brustman L, Anyaegbunam A, et al. The significance of one abnormal glucose tolerance test value on adverse outcome in pregnancy. Am J Obstet Gynecol 1987;157:758–63.

168. WHO Study Group. Definition, diagnosis and classification. Diabetes mellitus. Geneva: World Health Organization; 1985. p. 9–19.

169. Brown CJ, Dawson A, Dodds R, et al. Report of the pregnancy and neonatal care group. Diabet Med 1996;13:S43–53.

170. Martin FIR. The diagnosis of gestational diabetes. Med J Aust 1991;155:112.

171. Hoffman L, Nolan C, Wilson JD, et al. Gestational diabetes mellitus — management guidelines. Med J Aust 1998;168:93–7.

172. Sacks DA, Greenspoon JS, Abu-Fadil S, et al. Toward universal criteria for gestational diabetes: the 75-gram glucose tolerance test in pregnancy. Am J Obstet Gynecol 1995;172:607–14.

173. Lind T. A prospective multicentre study to determine the influence of pregnancy upon the 75-g oral glucose tolerance test (OGTT). In: Sutherland HW, Stowers JM, Pearson DWM, editors. Carbohydrate metabolism in pregnancy and the newborn. 4th ed. London: Springer Verlag; 1989. p. 209–26.

174. Expert Committee on the Diagnosis and Classification of Diabetes Mellitus. Report of the expert committee on the diagnosis and classification of diabetes mellitus. Diabetes Care 1997;20:1183–97.

Early Detection and Prevention of Diabetes Mellitus

Jeffrey Mahon, MD, MSc, FRCPC, and
John Dupre, MA, BSc, BMBCh, FRCP, FACP

ABSTRACT

Early detection and prevention of diabetes in nonpregnant adults is an attractive idea because it may make it possible to limit major, long-term metabolic and structural sequelae. Type 1 and Type 2 diabetes are well suited to early detection strategies because they are chronic processes that proceed through prolonged subclinical phases. These clinically silent phases can now be identified reliably through relatively simple, noninvasive testing procedures in selected high-risk populations.

High-quality randomized trials have identified several treatments that limit the impact of established Type 2 diabetes on major clinical endpoints. This and the fact that subclinical Type 2 diabetes is common and that many patients with newly recognized Type 2 diabetes have structural complications have made testing for subclinical Type 2 diabetes in selected groups a cost-effective activity worthy of routine clinical use.

Treatments that prevent onset of Type 1 and Type 2 diabetes are also theoretically possible. Clinical trials testing these treatments are currently under way, although to this point they have not identified efficacious, safe treatments to the extent that prediction and prevention of Type 1 and Type 2 diabetes can be deemed routine clinical activities.

INTRODUCTION

This chapter considers early detection of Type 2 diabetes in nonpregnant adults as well as prevention of Type 1 and Type 2 diabetes. These ideas are not new,[1–3] and each is based on the premise that asymptomatic persons with, or at risk for, diabetes can be identified through early detection tests and then given treatments that prevent more advanced disease states. This is an attractive premise when one is reminded of the failure of current treatments for Type 1 and 2 diabetes—which begin for most patients after onset of clinically apparent disease—to forestall metabolic and structural complications.

The chapter begins with a framework that underpins strategies of early detection and prevention of Type 1 and 2 diabetes. The methodologic approach toward assessing the efficacy of early detection tests is then discussed, with reference to direct and indirect randomized trials in the context of evidence-based schemes that rate the strength of such studies. Evidence is then reviewed that bears on why and how to undertake early detection for Type 2 diabetes. This is followed by a brief review of evidence related to prediction and prevention of Type 1 and Type 2 diabetes. An important message at present is that there is now sufficient evidence to justify early detection of Type 2 diabetes in selected populations in routine clinical practice but that prevention of diabetes is experimental. However, it will be indicated that this could change by drawing attention to ongoing randomized trials of prevention for both forms of diabetes.

The following questions are answered in this chapter:

1. What are the early detection tests for diabetes mellitus and how do they differ from other diagnostic and therapeutic strategies?

2. Why should persons be tested for subclinical Type 2 diabetes? What complications will be prevented in those who have subclinical Type 2 diabetes?
3. Who should be tested for subclinical Type 2 diabetes?
4. How should individuals be tested for subclinical Type 2 diabetes?
5. Can Type 1 or Type 2 diabetes be predicted?
6. Can diabetes be prevented?

WHAT ARE THE EARLY DETECTION TESTS FOR DIABETES MELLITUS AND HOW DO THEY DIFFER FROM OTHER DIAGNOSTIC AND THERAPEUTIC STRATEGIES?

"Early detection test" has been used here as a generic term for several different detection activities, which are listed in Table 12–1. In common to each is the aim of detecting and then treating individuals with a problem before they develop clinical manifestations. "Screening" occurs when the health care system solicits asymptomatic persons to undergo an early detection test; it is distinct from "case finding" or "opportunistic screening," in which the test is used in persons entering the health care system for another reason. Screening can be divided into "mass screening," in which the early detection test is used in an entire population, and "selective screening," in which the test is applied to a subset of high-risk individuals drawn from a larger population.

It can sometimes be difficult to discern the differences between screening, including mass and selective screening, and case finding. For example, recent recommendations by the American and Canadian Diabetes Associations that all persons over 45 years old be tested regularly for Type 2 diabetes[4,5] look very much like mass screening. However, this is selective screening as testing has not been recommended for the entire population but for a subset at higher risk for Type 2 diabetes due to their age. Similarly, the distinction between screening and case finding can be unclear, because both are usually prompted and operationalized by physicians on behalf of the health care system.[6]

The need for clinicians to appreciate the distinctions among these activities is less important than for them to understand three properties of early detection tests that distinguish them from the other main type of diagnostic encounter, for example, testing an asymptomatic 50-year-old woman for diabetes versus testing the same woman because she has symptoms suggestive of hyperglycemia. First, because an early detection test will lead to otherwise apparently well persons being told they have a problem, an important shift is created

Table 12–1 Types of Early Detection Tests

Test	Definition	Example
Screening	Use of early detection test prompted by the health care system or its representative in persons who otherwise have not entered the health care system	Public advertisements recommending that women undergo mammography for possible breast cancer
Mass	Early detection test used in an entire population	Testing all newborns for congenital hypothyroidism by serum thyrotropin-stimulating hormone levels
Selective	Early detection test used in a subset of a population	Testing women ≥ 50 years old for possible breast cancer by mammography
Case finding	Use of early detection test prompted by the health care system or its representative in persons who enter the health care system for another reason	Testing for Type 2 diabetes by fasting plasma glucose levels in all patients with acute myocardial infarctions

in the health care system's obligation to be particularly certain that testing will cause more good than harm in most people.[7] One can argue that this obligation always exists when clinicians diagnose and treat patients. However, the need to be even more certain about benefit during screening and case finding occurs because the process is initiated by the health care system or its representative and not by the individual undergoing the test.

There is a second, related difference between use of early detection tests versus diagnostic tests that are prompted by symptomatic individuals that reflects the potential for false-positive errors. These are, of course, an inevitable consequence of any diagnostic process. However, they are more difficult to accept when they lead to asymptomatic persons with no reason to suspect that they have a clinical problem being told incorrectly that they do and then being treated unnecessarily for that problem.

The third difference between use of an early detection test and diagnostic testing in symptomatic persons occurs because, for a given problem, the former is always used in larger numbers of persons relative to the latter. As a result, screening and case finding magnify the downstream economic costs and impact of negative consequences of the test relative to more restricted use of diagnostic tests in symptomatic persons. The costs of the program and the impact of these negative consequences to an individual (considered below) can seem minor when compared to the projected benefit and cost savings that follow early detection and prevention of a serious problem in many individuals. However, as a test is moved into the much larger population typical of case finding, selective screening, and, especially, mass screening, the absolute impact of even small negative individual effects and the total economic costs to implement the program accelerate sharply. Thus, although screening and case finding offer opportunities for greater benefit and cost savings relative to restricting use of diagnostic tests to persons with clinically apparent disease, they also carry the potential for considerably greater harm and resource consumption.

Opportunities for Early Detection and Prevention of Diabetes Mellitus

Type 1 and Type 2 diabetes are different diseases in many ways. Moreover, within each there is heterogeneity with respect to cause, pathogenesis, and clinical course. For example, the concept of slowly progressive, immune-mediated beta-cell loss as a cause of deteriorating glycemic control in roughly 10% of adults with phenotypic Type 2 diabetes is now established.[8] Similarly, persons with newly diagnosed Type 1 diabetes are not only insulin deficient but also have significant insulin resistance.[9] Nevertheless, patients with Type 1 and 2 diabetes share important similarities in respect to their general course, and it is these similarities that create opportunities for early detection and prevention (Figure 12–1, Table 12–2).

First, both types of diabetes are chronic processes lasting years that, in distinction to acute disease processes for which there is little time for early intervention, are well suited to early detection and treatment. Second, both diseases are identical in the narrow sense that they are defined by plasma glucose levels associated with an increased risk for diabetes-specific complications (≥ 7.0 mM and/or 2-hour PC glucose levels ≥ 11.1 mM). Third, both diseases can arise in persons with predisposing risk factors, where these are best defined through prospective cohort studies as variables having strong, often independent, associations with subsequent diabetic-range hyperglycemia. For example, risk factors for Type 2 diabetes include obesity and a past history of gestational diabetes and, for Type 1 diabetes, a first-degree relative with Type 1 diabetes as well as specific high-risk genotypes (eg, HLA-DQB1*0302, DQB1*0201).[10,11] Fourth, Type 1 and Type 2 diabetes are characterized by processses that can be divided into a series of transitions from nondiabetic but at-risk phases to "prediabetes" and then to definite diabetes, as defined by the plasma glucose levels noted above. In both types of diabetes, the prediabetic phases are marked by onset of the pathogenic mechanisms that eventually lead to definite diabetes. Over time within the prediabetic phases, progressive increases occur in glycemia that fall short of diabetes but that define impaired fasting glucose (IFG) and impaired glucose tolerance (IGT). Finally, there can be a further transition within the diabetes phase from asymptomatic or "subclinical diabetes" to clinically overt diabetes as a consequence of symptoms of hyperglycemia or structural complications.

There are also two differences between Type 1 and Type 2 diabetes worth emphasizing because they affect strategies for early detection and prevention and directly govern the design of clinical trials testing preventive therapies (see Table 12–2). First, the main pathogenic events that characterize pre-Type 1 and pre-Type 2 diabetes differ (respectively, immune-mediated beta-cell destruction and impaired insulin action with or without impaired insulin secretion). Efforts to detect and prevent Type 1 diabetes have therefore focused on recognizing and arresting immune-mediated beta-cell destruction, whereas the major focus in Type 2 diabetes has been on factors associated with insulin resistance. Second, IGT, IFG, and subclinical phases in Type 2 diabetes last considerably longer than they do in Type 1 diabetes. The prolonged phase of IFG/IGT in pre-Type 2 diabetes affords an opportunity for prevention that does not exist in Type 1 diabetes; it has also made the oral glucose tolerance test (OGTT) the main procedure by which to detect pre-Type 2 diabetes in clinical trials testing preventive therapies. The prolonged phase of subclinical Type 2 diabetes has also meant that structural complications are often present on diagnosis of Type 2 diabetes. This does not occur in Type 1 diabetes but, when linked to clear evidence of efficacious treatments to prevent progression of such complications, greatly strengthens the case for testing for subclinical Type 2 diabetes.

Primary, Secondary, and Tertiary Prevention of Diabetes

Three prevention levels—termed primary, secondary, and tertiary preventions—have been defined for diabetes, though in slightly different ways for the two different types (see Figure 12–1). In Type 1 diabetes, the prevention level is determined by the course of beta-cell

---

Table 12–2 Characteristics of Diabetes Types 1 and 2 That Affect Early Detection and Prevention

Similarities that justify early detection and prevention

    Chronic disease processes

    Prolonged clinically silent phases: nondiabetes → prodromal diabetes → subclinical diabetes

    Clinically silent phases can be identified through relatively noninvasive testing procedures

    Potential to modify disease course by therapies given before onset of clinically overt diabetes

    Current therapies, given after onset of clinically overt diabetes, do not always prevent complications

Differences that affect strategies of early detection and prevention

    Type 1 diabetes

        Main pathogenic mechanism: immune-mediated beta-cell loss

        Short subclinical phase and short duration of progressive hyperglycemia within prodromal phase limit value of glycemia-based screening tests

        Prediction strategies based on detecting markers of immune-mediated beta-cell loss in persons with, or who are predisposed to prodromal Type 1 diabetes

        Preventions directed toward altering onset and progression of abnormal immune response

    Type 2 diabetes

        Main pathogenic mechanisms: increased insulin resistance with or without impaired insulin secretion

        Prolonged subclinical phase, and prolonged duration of progressive hyperglycemia within prodromal phase enhance value of glycemia-based screening tests

        Prediction strategies directed toward factors associated with insulin resistance

        Preventions directed toward altering insulin resistance

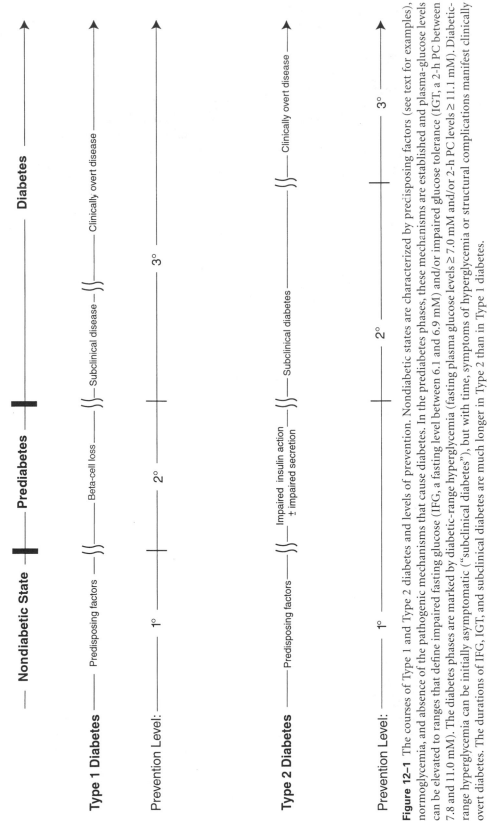

Figure 12–1 The courses of Type 1 and Type 2 diabetes and levels of prevention. Nondiabetic states are characterized by predisposing factors (see text for examples), normoglycemia, and absence of the pathogenic mechanisms that cause diabetes. In the prediabetes phases, these mechanisms are established and plasma-glucose levels can be elevated to ranges that define impaired fasting glucose (IFG, a fasting level between 6.1 and 6.9 mM) and/or impaired glucose tolerance (IGT, a 2-h PC between 7.8 and 11.0 mM). The diabetes phases are marked by diabetic-range hyperglycemia (fasting plasma glucose levels ≥ 7.0 mM and/or 2-h PC levels ≥ 11.1 mM). Diabetic-range hyperglycemia can be initially asymptomatic ("subclinical diabetes"), but with time, symptoms of hyperglycemia or structural complications manifest clinically overt diabetes. The durations of IFG, IGT, and subclinical diabetes are much longer in Type 2 than in Type 1 diabetes.

destruction: primary preventions are directed toward arresting onset of beta-cell autoimmunity and destruction, secondary preventions toward arresting established beta-cell destruction that is insufficient to cause diabetic-range hyperglycemia, and tertiary preventions toward preserving residual beta-cell function that exists in most persons at the time of diagnosis of Type 1 diabetes.[12] On the other hand, the prevention levels have been "right-shifted" in Type 2 diabetes because it has a much longer subclinical phase. Thus, primary prevention of Type 2 diabetes describes interventions directed toward everything short of onset of subclinical diabetes, including IGT and IFG, whereas secondary prevention focuses on subclinical Type 2 diabetes and tertiary prevention on limiting onset and progression of complications in persons with overt Type 2 diabetes.[13]

The concept of prevention levels for diabetes can be questioned, because it renders what are likely continuous processes into semiarbitrary steps. For example, there is probably no material difference in the risk for clinically important diabetic retinopathy between someone with two fasting plasma glucose levels of 7.0 mM versus someone with two values of 7.1 mM. Despite this, the concept is useful because it offers a convenient shorthand by which to describe clinical trials testing specific diabetes preventions. It also serves predictions about the prerequisites in terms of risks of therapies at each level of prevention and the anticipated benefits of those therapies.

For example, in the context of preventing Type 1 diabetes, less benefit can be anticipated as one moves from primary to tertiary preventions.[12] Thus, successful primary preventions will sustain a normal complement of beta cells and will therefore be most likely to prevent all negative consequences of Type 1 diabetes, including structural complications and the need for insulin treatment. Secondary preventions will preserve enough beta cells to forestall diabetic-range hyperglycemia, thereby preventing complications and, possibly, the need for daily full-dose insulin therapy. Tertiary preventions, because they verge on "too little, too late," may only be capable of allowing otherwise standard daily insulin therapy to maintain good long-term glycemic control, thereby reducing, though not necessarily eliminating, the risk of complications.

On the other hand, secondary preventions for Type 1 diabetes carry the additional problem of medicalizing apparently well individuals. This is because they depend on identifying at-risk individuals from a larger, healthy population. These "labeling" effects may negatively affect an individual's insurability, psychosocial behavior, and career choices. If strong, prompting them may be difficult to justify in the absence of highly effective, safe, secondary preventions. These effects do not occur in primary preventions that would be applied without regard to knowledge of an individual's risk for Type 1 diabetes (eg, the as-yet theoretical use of a diabetes vaccine for all infants),[14] nor are they an issue in tertiary preventions, as patients given these are already accorded the label "Type 1 diabetes."

Finally, because technologies to predict Type 1 diabetes will probably always carry the risk of some false-positive errors, primary and secondary preventions will inevitably result in persons being treated unnecessarily for future disease. Thus, a requirement for minimal to no toxicity is paramount for primary and secondary preventions, whereas higher risks may be acceptable in tertiary preventions, since there is no doubt that patients receiving them have Type 1 diabetes.

Importance of Carefully Assessing the Efficacy of Early Detection Tests

Judging the value of preventing complications in subclinical Type 2 diabetes, and of preventing Type 1 and Type 2 diabetes, is unavoidably linked to an assessment of the procedure by which it is determined that an asymptomatic person is at risk. For this reason, evidence-based schemes to assess these activities must also consider the early detection test itself.

There is a tendency to view early detection tests as diagnostic activities only. However, when one recognizes that they are interventions, and that the main purpose of an intervention is to cause a net improvement in health outcomes at an affordable economic cost, early detection tests must clear three hurdles before receiving widespread implementation: (1) they must be efficacious (ie, they must cause clinically important health gains in those being tested); (2) this benefit must exceed the negative effects of testing; and (3) the net benefit (total benefit less total harm) must justify the economic costs of testing and treatment (Table 12–3).[15] Of these hurdles, efficacy is foremost, simply because the other two do not matter in the absence of proof that the test is efficacious. This does not mean that the potential harm and costs of early detection tests should be ignored. Reservations about a screening test's benefit relative to its negative consequences and costs have created legitimate debates not only in diabetology[16] but in many other areas as well, for example, fecal occult blood testing to prevent colon cancer.[17] However, in all cases these debates are improved by valid data that establish or refute the early detection test's efficacy.

Evidence-Based Considerations in Assessing the Efficacy of Early Detection Tests

The efficacy of early detection tests can be assessed by observational or experimental (ie, randomized trials) methods. Observational studies are appealing because they are less expensive than randomized trials. They can assess outcomes at the level of populations (eg, national rates of cervical cancer deaths before and after implementation of Papanicolaou [Pap] smears) or individuals (eg, case-control or prospective cohort studies comparing rates of death from cervical cancer in women who did or did not receive Pap smears). However,

---

Table 12–3 Questions to Answer Before Implementation of an Early Detection Test

Is the test efficacious?

  Does the test cause clinically important health gains in those being tested?

    First question to be answered

    Randomized trials (direct or indirect: see Figure 12–2) provide the most reliable answers

    Observational methods can also be used but hold greater potential for bias and confounding

Does the benefit of using the test exceed the negative effects of testing?

  What are the potential negative effects of an early detection test?

    Direct adverse effects of the test and/or subsequent tests to confirm or refute the first test:

    Examples: • perforation during colonoscopy in persons with positive fecal occult blood tests

          • inconvenience and discomfort of 75-g OGTT for gestational diabetes mellitus

    Medicalizing otherwise healthy persons ("labeling" effects):

    Examples: • increased anxiety levels in women with positive mammograms

          • increased non–work-related absenteeism in persons with hypertension

          • loss of ability to obtain life or health insurance in persons with diabetes

    Negative consequences of false-positive and false-negative test results:

      False-positives: needless exposure to above risks and to the adverse effects of therapies for problems that were never going to occur in the first place

      False-negatives: failure to use therapies that prevent clinically important outcomes in persons who are at risk

Is the net benefit sufficient to justify the economic costs of using the test?

    Answer derived from economic evaluations that compare the costs of important immediate and long-term benefits and adverse effects as a consequence of using the test, relative to not using the test, from a specified perspective (eg, third-party payer)

this advantage of lower cost may be offset by uncertainty about whether an improvement in outcome associated with the early detection test is a true effect or a result of bias or confounding.

Bias, or systematic deviation from the truth, has many possible sources in observational studies of early detection tests. For example, there may be differences in the completeness by which the outcome of interest was ascertained between subjects who were and were not exposed to the screening test. In confounding, an unmeasured or unrecognized variable is present (the confounder) that is causally associated with the outcome of interest and is also associated with, but not caused by, the intervention. If the confounder is not accounted for, it is possible to falsely conclude that the intervention is efficacious. As discussed in Chapter 1, randomized trials offer the general advantage over observational studies of reducing bias. Randomization also more evenly balances confounders between treated and untreated subjects. This helps to control for known confounders and, most importantly, affords the only available way by which to control for unknown confounders.

When evaluating early detection tests, two types of randomized trial, termed "direct" and "indirect," may be employed (Figure 12–2).[15] In *direct trials*, subjects are randomized to receive the test or not. Those testing positive are treated, whereas negative persons are not, and all three groups (ie, positive, negative, and untested) are followed for the outcome of interest. For example, colon cancer mortality was reduced among individuals randomized to undergo regular fecal occult blood testing compared to those who were not.[18] In contrast, an *indirect trial* screens a population and then randomizes those who test positive to be treated or not. Thus, the efficacy of measuring low-density lipoprotein (LDL) cholesterol levels on primary prevention of atherosclerotic complications in high-risk individuals, of measuring blood pressure in middle-aged and older persons on preventing strokes, and of measuring bone mineral density by dual-energy x-ray absorptiometry (DXA) on preventing fractures in postmenopausal women were established in indirect trials.[19–21]

Compared to observational studies, direct and indirect randomized trials also provide better control on three specific biases that tend to overestimate the early detection test's efficacy. In *lead-time bias*, early detection of a disease or its risk factors followed by treatment may not delay the time to onset of the outcome but, rather, add to the time the individual has the disease.[7] *Length-time bias* occurs because of the fact that testing for a problem at a single time is more likely to find persons with longer, rather than shorter, subclinical prodromes: the former tend to have less aggressive disease and therefore do better than the latter.[7] Finally, *volunteer bias* occurs because persons who submit to screening or case-finding tests tend to be healthier and more compliant than those who do not and therefore do better.[7] Randomization serves to evenly distribute these characteristics between subjects receiving the early treatment compared to those who do not. The validity of conclusions within a direct or indirect trial about a particular early detection test's impact on clinical outcomes is thereby strengthened.

It is important to note that for a given early detection test, there can be differences between a direct and indirect trial in respect to when and in whom control for these biases occurs. As a result, discrepant conclusions about the test's efficacy become possible, that is, the indirect trial concludes that it is efficacious, but the direct trial does not, or vice versa. This is least likely to occur through volunteer bias, because both direct and indirect trials can only involve subjects who volunteer. It becomes a greater concern for lead- and length-time biases, especially when there are substantive differences between the two trials in the elapsed time between applying the early detection test and initiating therapy in positive subjects.

For this reason, schemes to formulate evidence-based recommendations on early detection tests have altered the strength of recommendations according to direct or indirect trial evidence. Thus, strong qualifiers such as "Level 1 Evidence" and "Grade A Recommendation" tend to be reserved for direct-trial evidence,[22] whereas results of indirect trials may not be sufficient to raise evidence levels and recommendations above weak qualifiers such as "Expert

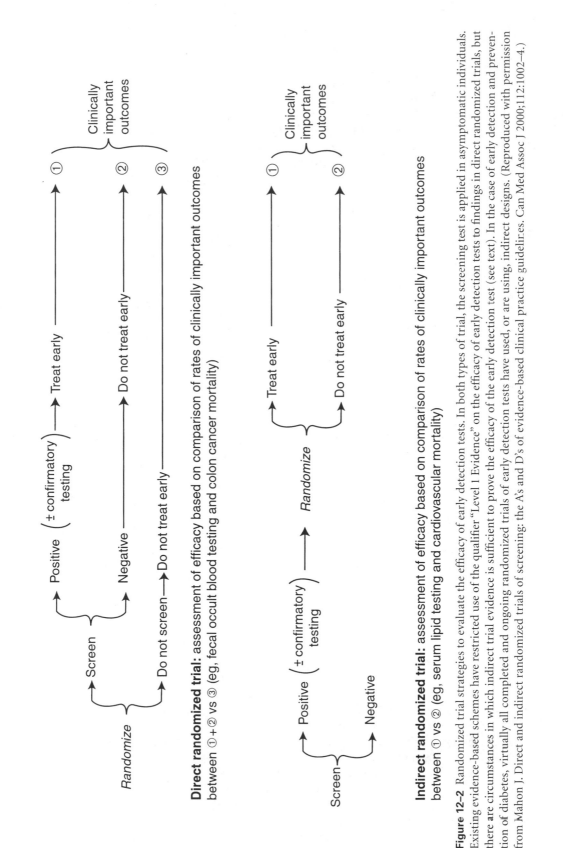

Direct randomized trial: assessment of efficacy based on comparison of rates of clinically important outcomes between ① + ② vs ③ (eg, fecal occult blood testing and colon cancer mortality)

Indirect randomized trial: assessment of efficacy based on comparison of rates of clinically important outcomes between ① vs ② (eg, serum lipid testing and cardiovascular mortality)

Figure 12–2 Randomized trial strategies to evaluate the efficacy of early detection tests. In both types of trial, the screening test is applied in asymptomatic individuals. Existing evidence-based schemes have restricted use of the qualifier "Level 1 Evidence" on the efficacy of early detection tests to findings in direct randomized trials, but there are circumstances in which indirect trial evidence is sufficient to prove the efficacy of the early detection test (see text). In the case of early detection and prevention of diabetes, virtually all completed and ongoing randomized trials of early detection tests have used, or are using, indirect designs. (Reproduced with permission from Mahon J. Direct and indirect randomized trials of screening: the A's and D's of evidence-based clinical practice guidelines. Can Med Assoc J 2000;112:1002–4.)

Consensus" or "Grade D."[5] The need to reserve stronger recommendations for direct trials occurs because such trials isolate the screening test as the experimental difference. Thus, there can be greater assurance that differences in outcomes—both good and bad—are explained by the act of testing. This is especially valuable if the screening test has the potential to cause the same outcome it prevents (eg, concern, since refuted, that irradiation during mammography causes breast cancer). As well, because direct trials assemble and concurrently follow an untested but randomized control group, the risk of other serious negative effects from the screening test or its sequelae (eg, colon perforation in patients with positive fecal occult blood tests who undergo colonoscopy)[17] can be more reliably determined. Because indirect trials lack these features, a conservative approach toward widespread endorsement of screening and case-finding activities is often justified in the absence of direct trials.

However, there can be indirect trials showing that a screening test is efficacious. Moreover, in some cases, there can be considerations that lead to the judgment that a subsequent direct trial of the same maneuver cannot be done. If the indirect trial uses the same screening test in similar populations and at similar points in their disease as would be used in the direct trial, the test and its sequelae are not expected to cause the outcome they are expected to prevent, there is consensus that the clinical importance of the outcomes prevented in the indirect trial exceeds the screening test's harm as measured in observational studies, and this net benefit justifies the test's economic costs, then the direct trial can become a difficult, if not unethical, proposition. This is because the direct trial leads to persons at risk for a clinically important outcome being randomized to the "no testing" group. They are therefore deprived of a therapy proven in the indirect trial to prevent an outcome judged to be of enough importance to justify the screening test's perceived risks and costs. It is largely because of this that, for example, direct trials of serum lipid or blood pressure measurements in asymptomatic middle-aged and older persons, or of DXA scanning in asymptomatic postmenopausal women, are unlikely to be undertaken.

This is precisely the situation that now exists with regard to judging the benefits of testing for subclinical Type 2 diabetes. Moreover, it is the evolving situation in testing preventions for Type 1 and 2 diabetes because, with one exception,[23] previous and current randomized trials of preventions for diabetes have used indirect designs[24-27] or are using them.[28-34] Any or all of the current prevention trials that use indirect designs may identify safe, effective preventions for diabetes. Thus, just as it has now become difficult to justify direct trials of screening for subclinical Type 2 diabetes in high-risk individuals, it may also become difficult to undertake a direct trial of an early detection test used to identify subjects similar to those who participated in a successful indirect trial.

Assigning Levels of Evidence to the Early Detection and Prevention Literature

Because prevention of diabetes remains experimental, the evidence-based messages have been limited to detection of subclinical (ie, undiagnosed) Type 2 diabetes. There are currently no evidence-based schemes to rate the efficacy of early detection tests that formally adjust recommendations according to indirect or direct randomized trial evidence. Rating evidence applicable to the efficacy of early detection of Type 2 diabetes for preventing future diabetes-related problems (ie, evaluating detection as an intervention strategy) has therefore been based on the traditional premise that Level 1 evidence can only be derived from a direct trial. However, such evidence does not exist because there have been no direct trials, yet many indirect trials have identified efficacious ways to prevent major diabetic complications. These indirect randomized controlled trials are classified as "Level 2" evidence in this chapter.

WHY SHOULD PERSONS BE TESTED FOR SUBCLINICAL TYPE 2 DIABETES?

In part, the decision to test for subclinical Type 2 diabetes is driven by observations that it is an extremely common problem and that structural complications are often present in persons with newly recognized Type 2 diabetes. For example, the Third National Health and

Nutrition Examination Survey (NHANES III) performed 75-g OGTTs in a large, probability-based sample of Americans between 40 and 74 years old and found that 6.7% had undiagnosed diabetes,[35] and the United Kingdom Prospective Diabetes Study (UKPDS) found that 36% of persons with newly diagnosed Type 2 diabetes had retinopathy.[36] However, it has been randomized trials over the last two decades identifying efficacious, generally safe ways to prevent onset and progression of complications in patients with Type 2 diabetes that have most strongly shifted the argument in favor of early detection.

Other chapters in this book have summarized the randomized trials in support of treatments for patients with Type 2 diabetes. Some of these trials also provide indirect, but strong, evidence to support the efficacy of testing for subclinical Type 2 diabetes; these will be briefly discussed here. The clinical importance of the benefits seen in these trials are highly likely to outweigh the potential negative effects of testing for subclinical Type 2 diabetes in high-risk persons. Moreover, economic evaluation (see below) has shown that the incremental cost effectiveness of testing for subclinical Type 2 diabetes is in a range that compares favorably to many other health care interventions now in routine clinical use. Thus, answers now exist to the questions in Table 12–3 seeking justification of testing for subclinical Type 2 diabetes in some individuals.

Microvascular Complications and Neuropathy

Three randomized trials—the UKPDS, the Kumamoto Study, and the Steno Type 2 Randomised Study—found that improving glycemic control in patients with Type 2 diabetes reduced the rate of progression of diabetic retinopathy, early diabetic nephropathy, and neuropathy.[36–39] Three randomized placebo-controlled trials tested the efficacy of angiotensin converting enzyme (ACE) inhibition on the course of nephropathy in patients with Type 2 diabetes. In a large diabetic substudy within the Heart Outcomes Prevention Evaluation study (HOPE),[40] ramipril was found to reduce the incidence of overt nephropathy (defined as albumin excretion rates [AER] > 300 mg/d). In two studies by Ravid and colleagues, enalapril reduced the incidence of incipient nephropathy (AER 30 to 300 mg/d) in normoalbuminuric patients[41] and the incidence of overt nephropathy in patients with incipient nephropathy.[42] In a randomized trial nested within the UKPDS, the effect of blood pressure control on structural complications in hypertensive patients with Type 2 diabetes was tested.[43] Onset and progression of retinopathy were reduced in those randomized to either captopril or atenolol versus untreated controls.[43] Finally, two randomized studies tested the efficacy of laser photocoagulation on the course of macular edema and proliferative retinopathy in patients with diabetes, including a large number with Type 2 diabetes, and found clinically important reductions in visual loss.[44,45]

There is a concern within the context of testing for subclinical Type 2 diabetes over whether the results of these trials can be generalized to asymptomatic patients found during screening or case finding who, because they are identified earlier in their disease, may have less advanced diabetes. Consequently, the benefit-to-risk ratio seen in the above trials may be overestimated for persons with subclinical Type 2 diabetes. However, the UKPDS[36] addressed this by including subjects with fasting plasma glucose (FPG) levels as low as 6.1 mM at entry. On a similar note, the clinical importance of the outcomes that were prevented in some of these trials can be debated. For example, in the trial by Ravid and colleagues testing the effect of enalapril on the development of incipient nephropathy,[41] the benefit relative to the risks of ACE inhibitor therapy could be questioned. Others have also questioned the clinical importance of the reduction in diabetic retinopathy observed among subjects randomized to obtain tighter glycemic control in the UKPDS.[16] However, these are just two trials from an impressive accumulation of high-quality randomized trials, including trials in Type 1 diabetes, that have shown repeatedly that the courses of diabetic microvascular and neuropathic complications can be materially improved through routinely available, generally safe therapies.[36–51] The consistency of these findings across so many trials therefore makes it improbable that they do not also apply to patients with relatively early disease who also have, or are at risk for, clinically silent complications.

Cardiovascular Complications

Several randomized trials have tested the effects of therapies on major cardiovascular outcomes in patients with Type 2 diabetes. Although none have shown that more normal glycemic control reduces macrovascular complications, at least three studies have shown that clinically important reductions in one or more of myocardial infarction (MI), stroke, cardiovascular death, diabetes-associated death, and all-cause mortality can be achieved through ACE inhibition and/or aggressive blood pressure control.

In the diabetic participants in the HOPE study, ramipril reduced the individual rates of MI, stroke, and cardiovascular death and also reduced all-cause mortality.[40] Although the latter was a secondary outcome, the validity of this finding is strong, because it was an a priori outcome of interest (in a subgroup defined a priori) and the significance level on the difference was very low ($p = .004$). In the Hypertension Optimal Treatment (HOT) study, participants with diabetes were identified as an important a priori subgroup, and those who were treated to a diastolic blood pressure goal of ≤ 80 mm Hg had a reduction in the primary outcome of combined rates of MI, stroke, and cardiovascular death relative to those treated to higher blood pressure targets.[52] The risk of cardiovascular death, specifically, was also lower among the more intensively treated diabetic patients. Again, though cardiovascular death was a secondary outcome in a subgroup analysis, the validity of the conclusion is strengthened by the significance level ($p = .016$) and the fact that the rate of cardiovascular death in patients with diabetes was an a priori question. The HOT findings are particularly relevant to testing for subclinical Type 2 diabetes, because the blood pressure targets associated with the benefit were lower than those that have generally defined hypertension (ie, 140/90 mm Hg). Thus, restricting testing for subclinical Type 2 diabetes to individuals with hypertension based on higher blood pressure levels will deprive some patients with diabetes from treatment who would benefit by it. Finally, in the UKPDS hypertension trial, tighter blood pressure control reduced the risk of stroke and diabetes-associated death (ie, death due to MI, sudden death, stroke, peripheral vascular disease, renal death, and hypo- or hyperglycemia).[43]

EVIDENCE-BASED MESSAGE

> Identifying persons with subclinical (ie, undiagnosed) Type 2 diabetes will lead to treatment strategies including laser photocoagulation, tighter glycemic control, tighter blood pressure control, and ACE inhibition that have been proven to prevent onset and progression of major diabetic complications (retinopathy, nephropathy, neuropathy, MIs, and strokes) and death (Level 2).[36–42,52]

WHO SHOULD BE TESTED FOR SUBCLINICAL TYPE 2 DIABETES?

National and international agencies have endorsed testing for subclinical Type 2 diabetes and have also provided guidance about who should be tested.[4,5,53–56] Because it remains unclear whether testing the entire population will be cost effective, no group has endorsed mass screening. Thus, existing guidelines share the common strategy of selective screening, and most have identified the criteria listed in Table 12–4 when choosing who to test.

Choosing who to test can be approached in two ways. These are not mutually exclusive strategies, but their relative merits may differ according to different estimates about their incremental cost effectiveness, that is, the amount of money spent to yield a beneficial effect—often expressed as a period of time adjusted for quality of life, such as the quality adjusted life year (QALY)—as a result of implementing versus not implementing the strategy. One strategy emphasizes a "prevalence-based" approach, because it attempts to find the largest number of individuals with subclinical disease irrespective of their risk for micro- and macrovascular complications. Therefore, choosing who to test is governed by factors that increase the probability for Type 2 diabetes. Examples in Table 12–4 include obesity, older age, and a history of gestational diabetes, impaired glucose tolerance (IGT), or impaired fasting glucose (IFG). These variables have been found to be associated with Type 2 diabetes in well-designed cross-sectional surveys.[10,57] Indirect, but strong, support for use of several of these criteria (eg., IGT and obesity) is also derived from high-quality prognosis studies showing that these criteria are associated with future Type 2 diabetes.[58]

However, the above prevalence-based approach may also identify many persons with milder disease who may be less likely to have, or go on to develop, clinically important complications. Thus, a second strategy focuses on finding persons with subclinical Type 2 diabetes who have, or are at higher risk for, those complications.[59,60] Because their risk is higher, the benefits of finding and treating them may be greater than an approach driven exclusively by disease prevalence. Examples of this in Table 12–4 include testing persons with hypertension or clinical or laboratory evidence of complications that are strongly associated with diabetes (eg, coronary artery disease or proteinuria).

Using Economic Evaluations to Assess the Benefits of Early Detection

The strengths and weaknesses of different strategies for identifying who to test can be illustrated by the uncertainty that currently surrounds estimates of the cost effectiveness of screening adults < 45 years old who have none of the risk factors listed in Table 12–4. Current guidelines do not endorse this approach, because the probability for disease in younger, risk-factor-free individuals is extremely low. Thus, there is doubt that the cost-savings and benefits of finding those few younger individuals with subclinical diabetes among the many without it will outweigh the costs and absolute impact of the negative effects that attend testing everyone. On the other hand, younger persons with diabetes are also at higher risk for microvascular complications relative to older persons, because they bear a greater, lifetime "glycemic burden." Because microvascular complications respond to improved glycemic control, the benefits of identifying younger persons with diabetes will be greater than doing so in older persons. Thus, one excellent economic evaluation has found that the incremental cost effectiveness of one-time opportunistic screening for diabetes irrespective of risk factors is lower in younger versus older individuals.[60]

However, two limitations of economic evaluations must be recognized before decisions can be made, both by policy-makers and by clinicians in their offices. First, they depend heavily on estimates about the absolute benefits derived from preventing diabetic structural complications, the impact of those complications on an individual's health-related quality of life

---

Table 12–4 Who to Test for Subclinical Type 2 Diabetes

Persons at higher risk for Type 2 diabetes

   Age 45 years or older

   Obesity

   History of diabetes in a first-degree relative

   Members of specific high-risk populations (eg, Aboriginal North Americans; Pacific Islanders; persons of African, Asian, or Hispanic descent)

   Past history of gestational diabetes including delivery of an infant over 4.0 kg

   Past history of impaired glucose tolerance or impaired fasting glucose

   Low HDL cholesterol (≤ 0.9 mM) or high fasting triglyceride (> 2.8 mM) levels

Persons at higher risk for complications of Type 2 diabetes

   Hypertension (BP $\geq 140/90$ mm Hg)

   Overt atherosclerosis (coronary artery, ischemic cerebrovascular, or peripheral vascular disease)

   Clinical or laboratory evidence suggestive or diabetic neuropathy, retinopathy, or nephropathy

(HRQOL), the negative impact of treatments to prevent those complications (eg, severe hypoglycemia as a consequence of aiming for tighter glycemic control), the negative impact of a false-positive test result for subclinical diabetes on HRQOL, and direct and indirect economic costs bearing on each of these parameters. In some instances, these estimates are based on high-quality evidence from randomized control trials (eg, the efficacy and risks of aiming for better glycemic control)[36,38,46,47] or prospective data from samples of patients with Type 2 diabetes (eg, the direct and indirect costs of treatments for diabetes and its complications[60–62]). In other cases, the data are less secure; thus, assumptions are required.[60–63] For example, the negative effects on HRQOL from disease labeling have not been determined in the setting of screening for Type 2 diabetes, yet these effects will reduce the cost effectiveness of early detection. On the other hand, although macrovascular disease is the largest contributor to the personal and societal burden of Type 2 diabetes, it remains unproven, but possible, that aggressive control of cardiovascular risk factors and tighter glycemic control in persons with early Type 2 diabetes will reduce macrovascular complications. Should such proof become available in future studies (eg, randomized trials testing the effect of glucose-lowering strategies and risk-factor modification on cardiovascular endpoints in persons with IGT),[28] it will greatly improve the cost-effectiveness ratio of screening for diabetes.

An additional, related limitation of economic evaluations is that they often derive estimates of benefits and risks of interventions from randomized trials conducted under "efficacy" ("ideal-world") rather than "effectiveness" ("real-world") conditions. Because the benefits and risks seen within efficacy trials may be, respectively, larger and smaller relative to use of the same intervention in the real world, economic evaluations based on efficacy data may not reflect the intervention's cost effectiveness in routine clinical practice. This is not an easy problem to resolve, because the sample sizes needed in randomized trials testing effectiveness questions are always larger (making such trials much less common) than trials testing efficacy. Economic evaluations that vary the assumptions about benefits and risks across plausible ranges (sensitivity analyses),[60–62] or that use inputs from health services research that assess outcomes under effectiveness conditions by observational methods, are useful alternatives in the absence of randomized trials of effectiveness.

Thus, conclusions drawn in economic evaluations about the cost effectiveness of testing for subclinical Type 2 diabetes according to who is tested are likely to be refined by evolving data, including data that more directly consider effectiveness. In the meantime, at least one high-quality economic evaluation has shown that early detection of Type 2 diabetes yields a cost-effectiveness ratio of $57,000 US per QALY gained, which is in the range of that achieved with many other interventions now in common use.[60]

How Should Individuals Be Tested for Subclinical Type 2 Diabetes?

Table 12–5 summarizes the strengths and weaknesses of the main options for testing for subclinical Type 2 diabetes. An interesting aspect of testing for subclinical diabetes relative to some other widely endorsed screening strategies is that the existing reference standard test of a 75-g OGGT for diabetes is relatively benign. For example, in the case of early detection for possible colonic neoplasia, the reference standard test is tissue obtained by endoscopic procedures such as colonoscopy or, in some cases, laparotomy. These are clearly more invasive procedures than an OGTT and therefore demand that simpler maneuvers such as fecal occult blood testing be done first. Moreover, because the OGTT is the reference standard for diabetes, it provides, in principle, perfect operating characteristics (100% sensitivity and specificity). One could therefore argue for the OGTT as the screening test of choice. However, this is not feasible because the demands and costs inherent to performing an OGTT in a single individual, although minor, make it an untenable option for screening large numbers of individuals. For this reason, a simpler measure is required, but accepting this strategy also means that one must accept unavoidable losses in sensitivity and specificity relative to that provided by the OGTT.

There has been general agreement that screening for diabetes by glycosuria is not a useful alternative because it is too insensitive to detect clinically important hyperglycemia. Therefore, current recommendations have focused on early detection strategies that directly measure glycemia. Unfortunately, there has not been uniform agreement on the measure or measures that, when applied in routine clinical practice, provide the best combination of high sensitivity and specificity, high acceptability to patients, and lowest cost. This uncertainty reflects an absence of studies that (1) assessed large numbers of subjects typical of those who should be offered testing for subclinical Type 2 diabetes; (2) ensured that each subject undergoes each screening test in addition to the current reference standard used to diagnosis diabetes (ie, a 75-g OGTT); (3) used current American Diabetes Association (ADA) and World Health Organization (WHO) cutpoints to define diabetes (fasting and 2-hour PC plasma glucoses of 7.0 mM and 11.1 mM, respectively); and (4) prospectively recorded the costs, negative effects, and acceptability to subjects of each screening procedure. Although data from a comprehensive study may be forthcoming, studies incorporating some of these design elements currently provide some guidance.[53,64]

The main choices for screening by glycemia include casual, fasting, and/or PC plasma glucose levels; capillary blood glucose levels; and glycated hemoglobin levels, including hemoglobin A_{1c} (HbA$_{1c}$).[4,5,53–56] Regardless of which of these is used, a positive screening test is not sufficient to diagnose diabetes in asymptomatic persons and must be confirmed by further testing on a different day.

Glucose Levels versus HbA$_{1c}$ Levels as an Early Detection Test

Casual plasma glucose levels are cheap, convenient, and acceptable to patients but have poorer operating characteristics than fasting or postglucose load levels. Similarly, the large coefficient of variation typical of a capillary whole blood glucose level measured by reflectance meters (even under optimal conditions) countermands its ease potential for wide implementation.

Table 12–5 Test Characteristics for Subclinical Type 2 Diabetes

Test	Convenience[*]	Cost[†]	Operating Characteristics[‡]	
			Sensitivity (%)	Specificity (%)
Random capillary glucose[*§]	++++	$	69	95
2-hr PC capillary glucose	+++	$$	69–90	93–98
Fasting plasma glucose	++	$$	44–65	93–99
2-hr PC plasma glucose	++	$$$	50	98
Hemoglobin A$_{1c}$	+++	$$$$	35–92	89–100

[*]More convenient for persons being screened (++++); less convenient for persons being screened (++).
[†]Estimates of cost based on Canadian figures ($ = least expensive; $$$$ = most expensive). The actual costs may vary in other jurisdictions, but the cost of one test relative to the others should not. Higher costs for PC glucose values reflect the need for glucose loading (eg, 75 g of oral glucose).
[‡]Sensitivities and specificities derived from selected studies.[53] For a given screening test, these characteristics are inversely related according to the cutpoint used to define "normal" and "abnormal." For example, the specificity of a fasting plasma glucose (FPG) level > 8.0 mM approaches 100% (ie, diabetes is virtually certain), but the sensitivity may not exceed 50% (ie, half of persons with subclinical Type 2 diabetes will have FPG levels below 8.0 mM), whereas sensitivity rises but specificity falls at a lower FPG cutpoint.
[§]Interpretation of random glucose values relative to possible diabetes in asymptomatic person made difficult by uncertainty regarding postprandial status.

Testing for subclinical Type 2 diabetes by HbA$_{1c}$ level has several strengths: it requires a single, nonfasting sample, it does not demand ingestion of oral glucose (which some patients find unpleasant), and (most importantly) it has been the primary measure of glycemia experimentally manipulated in the randomized trials proving that better control reduces microvascular diseases.[36–39,46,47] Thus, HbA$_{1c}$ level is the most convenient and best-validated marker for clinically important outcomes that respond to treatment. Unfortunately, difficulties and costs inherent in maintaining reliable HbA$_{1c}$ assays, and concern about wide biologic variability in HbA$_{1c}$ levels in normal persons, have made it less attractive than blood glucose levels for widespread screening.[65,66] Nevertheless, a recent study has shown that testing for subclinical Type 2 diabetes by an HbA$_{1c}$ assay that was rigorously standardized against that used in the Diabetes Control and Complications Trial (DCCT) across participating laboratories yielded excellent operating characteristics (sensitivity = 63% and specificity = 97% for an HbA$_{1c}$ level > 2 standard deviations above normal) relative to diagnosis of diabetes by a fasting plasma glucose level ≥ 7.0 mM.[66]

Until more evidence in support of using HbA$_{1c}$ levels is available, recommendations regarding how to test for undiagnosed diabetes have reflected consensus opinions[4,5,53–56] that attempt to balance optimized sensitivity and specificity, patient acceptability, cost, and local practice conditions. For example, the WHO chose not to make specific recommendations about screening, citing the example of the difficulty less affluent nations have in justifying the costs to maintain quality control programs for HbA$_{1c}$ assays.[64,67] In some cases, the guidelines have provided options from which clinicians can choose according to individual patient needs and local practice conditions. For example, the British Diabetes Association has advocated using fasting plasma or blood glucose levels or, alternatively, an unsupervised glucose load test in which blood or plasma glucose levels are determined 2 hours after ingestion of 75 g of glucose as timed by the patient.[54] On the other hand, the ADA and the Canadian Diabetes Association (CDA) have recommended fasting plasma glucose level as the screening test of first choice.[4,5] Other groups, such as the Australasian Working Party on Diagnositic Criteria, have not fully endorsed this strategy because it will miss some persons with diabetic-range postprandial hyperglycemia (2-hour PC plasma glucose levels ≥ 11.1 mM)[56]; the Australasian Group has therefore not abandoned the OGTT as a possible first option.

Frequency of Testing

How often individuals should be tested is dictated by their risk for diabetes. Thus, in the absence of any other risk factors beyond age alone, the ADA and CDA have advised testing once every 3 years, whereas yearly testing has been recommended for persons at higher risk (eg, a history of IGT, IFG, obesity, or a positive family history of diabetes).

Summary of Testing for Subclinical Type 2 Diabetes

Options for testing for subclinical Type 2 diabetes include fasting plasma glucose level, 2-hour postload glucose level, or HbA$_{1c}$ level (done in a laboratory that participates in quality control programs and that has been standardized against a high-quality assay such as that used in the DCCT); choosing how to test is best guided by local practice conditions and patient preference. One positive screening test is not sufficient to diagnose diabetes in asymptomatic persons and must be confirmed by further testing on a different day.

Can Type 1 or Type 2 Diabetes Be Predicted?

To prevent Type 2 diabetes and use primary and secondary preventions against Type 1 diabetes, technologies to predict future diabetes are required. Prediction studies are concerned with issues relevant to prognosis (see Chapter 2). The most useful diabetes prediction studies report long durations of follow-up in large numbers of at-risk people; as such, they identify more subjects developing diabetes and therefore provide more precise estimates of risk.

Based on studies of this nature, it has been possible to identify independent predictors with enough certainty to undertake large randomized prevention trials in Type 2 and Type 1 diabetes.[23–34]

Predicting Type 2 Diabetes

For Type 2 diabetes, associations have been found between future disease and one or more of obesity, older age, a family history of diabetes, selected ethnic groups (eg, Aboriginal North Americans), IGT, IFG, high serum insulin levels, gestational diabetes, and a high-normal HbA_{1c} level.[58,68,69] In general, IGT has emerged as the strongest independent predictor of future Type 2 diabetes, such that persons with IGT have an approximate risk of developing diabetes of 5% per year.[68,69] This risk is refinable according to presence or absence of other factors and, in particular, approaches 8% per year in persons who also have higher, but non-diabetic, FPG levels. The predictive value of IGT has made it the primary entry criterion for large trials testing preventions for Type 2 diabetes.[25,28,30,31]

Predicting Type 1 Diabetes

For Type 1 diabetes, prediction has been most thoroughly evaluated in persons with an immediate family history of the disease.[70–72] Prediction of Type 1 diabetes in the general population, where the majority (~ 80%) of cases occur, is also under evaluation.[73] However, unlike prediction in persons with a family history, prediction in the general population has yet to reach a level of certainty that can allow prevention trials to be undertaken. In general, Type 1 diabetes prediction is based mainly on detecting pancreatic autoantibodies in peripheral blood—including ICA, glutamic acid decarboxylase (GADA), the protein tyrosine phosphatase IA-2 (anti-IA-2), and insulin (IAA)—in persons with high-risk genotypes (eg, HLA-DQB1*0302, DQB1*0201); entry criteria for current prevention trials reflect this. In first-degree relatives, the risk for Type 1 diabetes depends directly on the number of positive autoantibodies. Thus, approximately 70% of those with at least two positive antibody tests and nearly 100% of those with three or more positive tests will become diabetic within 5 years.[72] Assays for GADA, anti-IA-2, and IAA may supplant the older ICA assay because it is semiquantitative, more labor intensive, and appears to offer no further capacity to refine the risk for Type 1 diabetes compared to the other three.[71] Absence of first-phase insulin response to intravenous glucose is also independently predictive of Type 1 diabetes and conveys a 3-year risk that approaches 100%.[70]

EVIDENCE-BASED MESSAGES

1. Although many risk factors have been identified, people with IGT and fasting hyperglycemia are at high risk for subsequent Type 2 diabetes (Level 1).[68,69]
2. A family history of Type 1 diabetes, serum pancreatic autoantibodies, and loss of first-phase insulin response are strong predictors of subsequent Type 1 diabetes (Level 1).[70–72]

CAN DIABETES BE PREVENTED?

Prevention of Type 2 Diabetes

Randomized trials of prevention of Type 2 diabetes have a much longer history than do those for Type 1 diabetes. Thus far, however, results have not been yielded that have changed clinical practice.[24–26,28–31] Older trials testing lifestyle modification and oral sulfonylureas did not show conclusive benefits.[24,26] More recently, a randomized trial from China using a cluster design (meaning that groups of people, rather than specific individuals, were randomized to different interventions, with the primary outcome expressed as the rate of diabetes per group) found that a program of diet and exercise reduced the incidence of Type 2 diabetes in persons with IGT.[25] Whether or not these results are generalizable to other populations requires confirmation. At present, there are four large trials randomizing individuals testing lifestyle interventions and oral agents (ie, metformin and acarbose) in persons with IGT or IFG.[28–31] Results from these studies should become available within 5 years.

Prevention of Type 1 Diabetes

Randomized trials of primary and secondary prevention for Type 1 diabetes have also been conducted[23,27] or are under way.[32–34,74] These trials were preceded by randomized trials of tertiary prevention showing that immunosuppressive drugs, including cyclosporine and azathioprine, could prevent further beta-cell loss.[75–77] These trials proved the immune-mediated basis for beta-cell loss in human Type 1 diabetes, but the observed benefits were insufficient to justify the risks of long-term immunosuppression.[12] Less toxic ways of protecting beta cells after onset of overt Type 1 diabetes, such as nicotinamide therapy,[78] have become attractive strategies that need to be tested over the long term. This is because of the causal relationship that is now established between better glycemic control and fewer microvascular complications, and the demonstration of a causal relationship in two tertiary prevention trials between preservation of residual beta-cell function and better glycemic control, at least in the short term.[74–76]

In an open, randomized cluster trial of secondary prevention, a reduction in Type 1 diabetes was found in children randomized to receive ICA testing followed by high-dose nicotinamide therapy in those testing positive.[23] The trial was necessarily open and, therefore, it was unclear whether the reduction in diabetes was because of nicotinamide, confounding, or an unrecognized bias such as incomplete ascertainment of diabetes in the control group. In a second randomized placebo-controlled trial of nicotinamide in ICA-positive children with a first-degree relative with Type 1 diabetes, no difference in the rates of diabetes was observed.[27] However, this trial could only detect an effect size of at least 80% and was therefore underpowered, given the benign nature of nicotinamide.[27] Currently, there are two other, very large randomized secondary prevention trials in ICA-positive relatives. One trial is testing nicotinamide[32] and the other oral or parenteral insulin according to low or high risk, respectively, for future Type 1 diabetes.[33] As well, a primary prevention trial based on avoidance of cow's milk protein is being planned.[34] As for prevention trials in Type 2 diabetes, results should begin to be available within 5 years.

EVIDENCE-BASED MESSAGE

> The risk of Type 2 diabetes in persons with IGT may be reduced by a program of diet and exercise (Level 2).[25]

CONCLUSION

There is strong justification for testing for subclinical Type 2 diabetes in certain high-risk populations as a routine clinical activity. Subclinical Type 2 diabetes is very common and is associated with clinically important complications at the time of diagnosis in many persons. Once identified, these persons can receive treatments including tighter glycemic control, tighter blood pressure control, and ACE inhibition, which have been proven to prevent retinopathy, nephropathy, neuropathy, myocardial infarction, stroke, and cardiovascular death.

Testing for subclinical Type 2 diabetes has been recommended for persons who are at higher risk for the disease and/or at higher risk for structural complications if they have diabetes. Variables that raise these risks include obesity; age > 45 years; an immediate family history of diabetes; a history of gestational diabetes, impaired glucose tolerance, or impaired fasting glucose; being a member of certain ethnic populations; high triglycerides and low high-density liproprotein (HDL) cholesterol levels; hypertension; and clinical or laboratory evidence of complications that are strongly associated with diabetes (eg, coronary artery disease, ischemic stroke, peripheral-sensory neuropathy, or proteinuria).

Although there is not uniform agreement on how to test for subclinical Type 2 diabetes, glycemic-based parameters are recommended. Testing options include FPG level, 2-hour PC plasma glucose level, and HbA$_{1c}$ level. If the HbA$_{1c}$ level is used, it must be done in a laboratory that participates in regular quality-control programs and that has been standardized against a high-quality assay such as that used in the DCCT. The decision about how to test must also bear in mind local practice conditions and patient preference. The frequency of testing depends on an individual's risk, with high-risk people requiring testing more frequently (eg, annually) than lower-risk people (eg, every 3 years). Diabetes cannot be diagnosed by a positive screening test alone in asymptomatic individuals and must be confirmed by further testing on a different day.

Future Type 1 and Type 2 diabetes can now be reliably predicted in some settings. However, safe, proven ways of preventing both types of diabetes do not exist. Thus, prediction and prevention of diabetes is an experimental activity. Clinical trials testing preventive therapies for Type 1 and Type 2 diabetes are in progress and should yield information within 5 years that can guide clinical practice.

SUMMARY OF EVIDENCE-BASED MESSAGES

1. Identifying persons with subclinical (ie, undiagnosed) Type 2 diabetes will lead to treatment strategies including laser photocoagulation, tighter glycemic control, tighter blood pressure control, and ACE inhibition that have been proven to prevent onset and progression of major diabetic complications (retinopathy, nephropathy, neuropathy, MIs, and strokes) and death (Level 2).[36–45,52]
2. Although many risk factors have been identified, people with IGT and fasting hyperglycemia are at high risk for subsequent Type 2 diabetes (Level 1).[68,69]
3. Family history of Type 1 diabetes, serum pancreatic autoantibodies, and loss of first-phase insulin response are strong predictors of subsequent Type 1 diabetes (Level 1).[70–72]
4. The risk of Type 2 diabetes in persons with IGT may be reduced by a program of diet and exercise (Level 2).[25]

REFERENCES

1. Haist RE, Cambell J, Best CH. The prevention of diabetes. N Engl J Med 1940;223:607–15.

2. Genuth SM, Houser HB, Carter JR, et al. Observations on the value of mass indiscriminate screening for diabetes mellitus based on a five-year follow-up. Diabetes 1978;27:377–83.

3. Jarrett RJ, Keen H, Fuller JH, McCartney M. Worsening to diabetes in men with impaired glucose intolerance ("borderline diabetes"). Diabetologia 1979;16:25–30.

4. American Diabetes Association. Screening for Type 2 diabetes (position statement). Diabetes Care 1999;22(Suppl 1):S20–3.

5. Meltzer S, Leiter L, Daneman D, et al. 1998 clinical practice guidelines for the management of diabetes in Canada. Can Med Assoc J 1998;159(Suppl 8):S1–29.

6. Meyer F, Fradet Y. Prostate cancer: 4. Screening. Can Med Assoc J 1998;159:968–72.

7. Sackett DL, Haynes RB, Guyatt GH, Tugwell P. Clinical epidemiology. A basic science for clinical medicine, 2nd ed. Boston, Toronto, London: Little, Brown, and Company; 1991.

8. Zimmet P, Rowley M, Turner R, et al. Crucial points at diagnosis. Type 2 diabetes or slow type 1 diabetes. Diabetes Care 1999;22(Suppl 2):B59–64.

9. Yki-Jarvinen H, Koivisto VA. Natural course of insulin resistance in Type 1 diabetes. N Engl J Med 1986;315:224–30.

10. Everhart JE, Knowler WC, Bennett PH. Incidence and risk factors for non-insulin dependent diabetes. In: National Diabetes Data Group. Diabetes in America. NIH Publication No: 85–1468. Washington (DC): US Government Printing Office; 1985.

11. Nepom GT. Immunogenetics and IDDM. Diabetes Rev 1993;1:93–103.

12. Mahon JL, Dupre J, Stiller CR. Lessons learned from use of cyclosporine for IDDM: the case for immunotherapy for insulin dependent diabetics having residual insulin secretion. Ann NY Acad Sci 1993;696:351–63.

13. Yki-Jarvinen H. The prediction and prevention of non-insulin-dependent diabetes mellitus. In: Pickup J, Williams G, editors. Textbook of diabetes. 2nd ed. London: Blackwell Science; 1997:83.1–13.

14. Sadelain MWJ, Qin H-Y, Lauzon J, Singh B. Prevention of type 1 diabetes in NOD mice by adjuvant immunotherapy. Diabetes 1990;39:583–9.

15. Mahon J. Direct and indirect randomized trials of screening: the A's and D's of evidence-based clinical practice guidelines. Can Med Assoc J 2000;162:1002–4.

16. Marshall KG. The folly of population screening for type 2 diabetes. Can Med Assoc J 1999;160: 1592–3.

17. Simon JB. Should all people over the age of 50 have regular fecal occult-blood tests? N Engl J Med 1998;338:1151–2.

18. Fletcher RH. Should all people over the age of 50 have regular fecal occult-blood tests? If it works, why not do it? N Engl J Med 1998;338:1153–4.

19. Shepard J, Cobbe SM, Ford I, et al. Prevention of coronary heart disease with pravastatin in men with hypercholesterolemia. N Engl J Med 1995;333:1301–7.

20. Ogilvie RI, Burgess ED, Cusson JR, et al. Report of the Canadian Hypertension Society Consensus Conference: 3. Pharmacologic treatment of essential hypertension. Can Med Assoc J 1993;149:575–84.

21. Karpf DB, Shapiro DR, Seeman E, et al. Prevention of nonvertebral fractures by alendronate. A meta-analysis. JAMA 1997;277:1159–64.

22. Woolf SH, Battista RN, Anderson GM, et al. Assessing the clinical effectiveness of preventive manoeuvres: analytic principles and sytematic methods in reviewing evidence and developing clinical practice recommendations. J Clin Epidemiol 1990;43:891–905.

23. Elliott RB, Pilcher CC, Fergusson DM, Stewart RW. A population-based strategy to prevent insulin-dependent diabetes using nicotinamide. J Pediatr Endocrinol Metab 1996;9:501–9.

24. Keen H, Jarrett RJ, McCartney P. The ten-year follow-up of the Bedford survey (1962–1972): glucose tolerance and diabetes. Diabetologia 1982;22:73–8.

25. Pan XR, Li GW, Hu YH, et al. Effects of diet and exercise in preventing NIDDM in people with impaired glucose tolerance: the Da Qing IGT and Diabetes Study. Diabetes Care 1997;20:537–44.

26. Sartor G, Schersten B, Carlstrom S, et al. Ten-year follow-up of subjects with impaired glucose tolerance: prevention of diabetes by tolbutamide and diet regulation. Diabetes 1980;29:41–9.

27. Lampeter EF, Klinghammer A, Scherbaum WA, et al. The Deutsche Nicotinamide Intervention Study. Diabetes 1998;47:980–4.

28. The Diabetes Prevention Program. Design and methods for a clinical trial in the prevention of type 2 diabetes. Diabetes Care 1999;22:623–34.

29. Chiasson JL, Gomis R, Hanefeld M, et al. The STOP-NIDDM Trial: an international study on the efficacy of an alpha-glucosidase inhibitor on development of type 2 diabetes in a population with impaired glucose tolerance: rationale, design, and preliminary screening data. Diabetes Care 1998;21:1720–5.

30. Dyson P, Hammersley M, Morris R, et al. The Fasting Hyperglycemia Study. II. Randomized controlled trial of reinforcing healthy-living advice in subjects with increased but not diabetic fasting plasma glucose. Metabolism 1997;12(Suppl 1):50–5.

31. Holman RR. Assessing the potential for alpha-glucosidase inhibitors in prediabetes. Diabetes Res Clin Pract 1998;40(Suppl):S21–5.

32. Gale EAM. Prevention studies in type 1 diabetes. Exp Clin Endocrinol Diabetes 1999;107(Suppl 3):S101.

33. The DPT-1 Study Group: The Diabetes Prevention Trial -Type 1 Diabetes (DPT-1): implementation of screening and staging of relatives. Transplant Proc 1995;27:3377.

34. Savilahati E, Tuomilehto J, Saukkonen TT, et al. Increased levels of cow's milk and beta-lactoglobulin antibodies in young children with newly diagnosed IDDM. Diabetes Care 1993;16:984–9.

35. Harris MI, Goldstein DE, Flegal KM, et al. Prevalence of diabetes, impaired fasting glucose, and impaired glucose tolerance in US adults. Diabetes Care 1998;21:518–24.

36. UK Prospective Diabetes Study (UKPDS) Group. Intensive blood-glucose control with sulphonylureas or insulin compared with conventional treatment and risk of complications in patients with type 2 diabetes (UKPDS 33). Lancet 1998;352:837–53.

37. UK Prospective Diabetes Study (UKPDS) Group. Effect of intensive blood-glucose control with metformin on complications in overweight patients with type 2 diabetes (UKPDS 34). Lancet 1998;352:854–65.

38. Gaede P, Vedel P, Parving H-H, Pedersen O. Intensified multifactorial intervention in patients with type 2 diabetes and microalbuminuria: the Steno type 2 randomised study. Lancet 1999;353:617–22.

39. Ohkubo Y, Kishikawa H, Araki E, et al. Intensive insulin therapy prevents the progression of diabetic microvascular complications in Japanese patients with non-insulin-dependent diabetes mellitus: a randomized prospective 6-year study. Diabetes Res Clin Pract 1995;28:103–17.

40. Heart Outcomes Prevention Evaluation (HOPE) Study Investigators. Effects of ramipril on cardiovascular and microvascular outcomes in people with diabetes mellitus: results of the HOPE and MICRO-HOPE substudy. Lancet 2000;355:253–9.

41. Ravid M, Brosh D, Levi Z, et al. Use of enalapril to attenuate decline in renal function in normotensive, normoalbuminuric patients with type 2 diabetes mellitus. A randomized, controlled trial. Ann Intern Med 1998;128:982–8.

42. Ravid M, Lang R, Rachmani R, Lishner M. Long-term renoprotective effect of angiotensin-converting enzyme inhibition in non-insulin-dependent diabetes mellitus. A 7 year follow-up study. Arch Intern Med 1996;156:286–9.

43. UK Prospective Diabetes Study Group. Tight blood pressure control and risk of macrovascular and microvascular complications in type 2 diabetes (UKPDS 38). BMJ 1998;317:703–13.

44. Early Treatment Diabetic Retinopathy Study Research Group. Photocoagulation for diabetic macular edema. ETDRS report 1. Arch Ophthalmol 1985;103:1796–806.

45. Diabetic Retinopathy Study Research Group. Photocoagulation treatment of proliferative diabetic retinopathy: the second report of Diabetic Retinopathy Study findings. Ophthalmology 1978;85:82–106.

46. Diabetes Control and Complications Trial Research Group (DCCT).The effect of intensive insulin treatment of diabetes on the development and progression of long-term complications in insulin-dependent diabetes mellitus. N Engl J Med 1993;329:977–86.

47. Reichard P, Nillson B-Y, Rosenqvist U. The effect of long-term intensified insulin treatment on the development of microvascular complications of diabetes mellitus. N Engl J Med 1993;329:304–9.

48. Vibarti G, Mogensen CE, Groop LC, Pauls JF for the European Microalbuminuria Captopril Study Group. Effect of captopril on progression to clinical proteinuria in patients with insulin-dependent diabetes mellitus and microalbuminuria. JAMA 1994;271:275–9.

49. Lewis EJ, Hunsicker LG, Bain RP, Rohde RD for the Collaborative Study Group. The effect of angiotensin-converting-enzyme inhibition on diabetic nephropathy. N Engl J Med 1993;329:1456–62.

50. Marre M, Chatellier G, Leblanc H, et al. Prevention of diabetic nephropathy with enalapril in normotensive diabetics with microalbuminuria. BMJ 1988;307:1092–5.

51. Mathiesen ER, Hommel E, Giese J, Parving H-H. Efficacy of captopril in postponing nephropathy in normotensive insulin dependent diabetic patients with microalbuminuria. BMJ 1991;303:81–7.

52. Hansson L, Zanchetti A, Carruthers GC, et al. Effects of intensive blood-pressure lowering and low-dose aspirin in patients with hypertension: principal results of the Hypertension Optimal Therapy (HOT) randomised trial. Lancet 1998;351:1755–62.

53. Engelgau MM, Aubert RE, Thompson TT, Herman WH. Screening for NIDDM in nonpregnant adults. A review of principles, screening tests, and recommendations. Diabetes Care 1995;18:1606–18.

54. Paterson KR for the Professional Advisory Committee of the British Diabetic Association. Population screening for diabetes mellitus. Diabet Med 1993;10:777–81.

55. Bonnici F, Hough S, Huddle K, et al. Guidelines for the management of Type 2 (non-insulin-dependent) diabetes mellitus at primary health care level in South Africa. S Afr Med J 1997;87: 497–512.

56. Colman PG, Thomas DW, Zimmet PZ, et al. New classification and criteria for diagnosis of diabetes mellitus. Med J Aust 1999;170:375–8.

57. Harris MI. Undiagnosed NIDDM: clinical and public health issues. Diabetes Care 1993;16:642–52.

58. Knowler WC, Narayan KMV, Hanson RL, et al. Preventing non-insulin-dependent diabetes mellitus. Diabetes 1995;44:483–8.

59. Goyder E, Irwig L. Screening for diabetes: what are we really doing? BMJ 1998;317:1644–6.

60. CDC Diabetes Cost-Effectiveness Study Group. The cost-effectiveness of screening for type 2 diabetes. JAMA 1998;280:1757–63.

61. Eastman RC, Garfield AS, Javitt JC, et al. Model of complications of NIDDM. I. Model construction and assumptions. Diabetes Care 1997;20:725–34.

62. Eastman RC, Dong F, Javitt JC, et al. Model of complications of NIDDM. II. Analysis of the heath benefits and cost-effectiveness of treating NIDDM with the goal of normoglycemia. Diabetes Care 1997;20:735–44.

63. Goyder E, Irwig L. Screening for type 2 diabetes. JAMA 1999;281:1986–7.

64. Rohlfing CL, Harris MI, Little RR, et al. Use of GHb (HbA$_{1c}$) in screening for undiagnosed diabetes in the U.S. population. Diabetes Care 2000;23:187–91.

65. Alberti KGMM, Zimmet PZ. New diagnostic criteria and classification of diabetes—again? Diabet Med 1998;15:535–6.

66. Kilpatrick ES, Maylor PW, Keevil BG. Biological variation of glycated hemoglocibin. Implications for diabetes screening and monitoring. Diabetes Care 1998;21:261–4.

67. Alberti KGMM, Zimmet PZ for the WHO Committee. Definition, diagnosis and classification of diabetes mellitus and its complications. Part 1: Diagnosis and classification of diabetes mellitus provisional report of a WHO consultation. Diabet Med 1998;15:539–53.

68. Narayan KMV, Bennett PH, Hanson RL, et al. A two-step strategy for identification of high-risk subjects for a clinical trial testing prevention of NIDDM. Diabetes Care 1996;19:972–8.

69. Edelstein SL, Knowler WC, Bain RP, et al. Predictors of progression from impaired glucose tolerance to NIDDM. An analysis of six prospective studies. Diabetes 1997;46:701–10.

70. Bingley PJ. Interactions of age, islet cell antibodies, insulin autoantibodies, and first-phase insulin response in predicting risk of progression to IDDM in ICA + relatives: the ICARUS data set. Diabetes 1996;45:1720–8.

71. Bingley PJ, Williams AJK, Gale EAM. Optimized autoantibody-based risk assessment in family members. Diabetes Care 1999;22:1796–801.

72. Verge CF, Kawasaki GR, Yu L, et al. Prediction of type 1 diabetes in first-degree relatives using a combination of insulin, GAD, and ICA512bdc/IA-2 autoantibodies. Diabetes 1996;45:926–33.

73. Bingley PJ, Bonifacio E, Williams AJ, et al. Prediction of IDDM in the general population: strategies based on combinations of autoantibody markers. Diabetes 1997;46:1701–10.

74. Mahon JL, Dupre J. The limitations of clinical trials of prevention for insulin dependent diabetes mellitus. Diabetes Care 1997;20:1027–33.

75. Feutren G, Papoz L, Assan R, et al. Cyclosporin increases the rate and length of remission in insulin-dependent diabetes of recent onset. Lancet 1986;2:119–23.

76. The Canadian-European Study Group. Cyclosporin-induced remission of IDDM after early intervention. Diabetes 1988;37:1574–82.

77. Silverstein J, Maclaren N, Riley W, et al. Immunosuppression with azathioprine and prednisone in recent-onset IDDM. N Engl J Med 1988;319:599–604.

78. Pozzilli P, Kolb H, Browne PD for the Nicotinamide Trialists. Meta-analysis of nicotinamide treatment in patients with recent-onset IDDM. Diabetes Care 1996;12:1357–63.

Education and Home Glucose Monitoring

John D. Piette, PhD, and Russell E. Glasgow, PhD

———•———

ABSTRACT

Recommendations promoting diabetes self-management education have become a standard component of most treatment guidelines. Because these services require a concerted investment of resources, it is important to weigh the evidence for specific interventions before they are mandated as part of standard care or certified as reimbursable. The objectives of this chapter are to review diabetes self-management education interventions, identify those that are effective, and suggest avenues of research that are necessary in order to identify evidence-based best practices. This review is based on empiric research published in English-language peer-reviewed journals. Emphasis is given to randomized trials that include either Type 1 or Type 2 adults and that measure either behavioral or health outcomes. Some key studies focusing on Type 1 diabetes in children are also noted.

The results of the review indicate that blood glucose self-monitoring (BGSM) may provide important feedback for both patients and providers. However, there is little evidence suggesting that frequent BGSM improves Type 1 patients' mean glycemic control more than less-frequent BGSM or urine testing. Moreover, there is no evidence that BGSM contributes to better glycemic control among Type 2 patients. This lack of impact on glycemic control could reflect patients' difficulty in obtaining accurate measures or reporting BGSM data to clinicians or clinicians' inability to respond effectively to BGSM data. Integrated treatment systems and more effective methods of linking BGSM to a patient and clinician response could increase its impact. The review also suggests that formal, structured skills training interventions can improve Type 1 patients' ability to perceive episodes of glucose dysregulation and may restore their epinephrine response to hypoglycemia. Foot care education is an effective means of improving patients' foot care behavior and can reduce the incidence of foot problems. Characteristics of effective foot care education are motivational counseling, skill-based training, and education and reminders delivered simultaneously to patients and physicians. Appropriate medication-taking can improve patients' health in the short-term and decrease their long-term risk of diabetic complications. Research suggests that computerized decision-support systems that inform insulin adjustments may improve some outcomes. Studies in nondiabetic populations indicate that simple devices and changes in practice (eg, medication alarm devices or simplifying the regimen) can assist patients in adhering to oral medication regimens. Some of the most innovative and effective self-management interventions address multiple dimensions of self-care simultaneously. These interventions usually have a patient-centered focus, actively engaging patients in managing their diabetes and are tailored to their preferences and social environment. Information technologies such as self-administered computerized assessments and automated telephone assessments between face-to-face clinical encounters can effectively supplement care and improve diabetes behavioral and health outcomes.

Common elements across the diverse interventions reviewed in this chapter are a patient-centered approach that individualizes self-management and goal setting, strategies for coping with barriers, and some form of follow-up that supports available primary care. Future research should focus on translating effective interventions into interventions that are feasible, efficacious, and cost effective in "real-world" treatment settings.

INTRODUCTION

What Is the Role of Self-Management Education in Diabetes Care?

Patients with diabetes and their families provide 95% of their care themselves,[1,2] and, as a consequence, educational efforts to improve self-management are central components of any effective treatment plan. The role of self-management behavior is clear, even in studies that address relationships between pharmacologic treatment and outcomes at the physiologic level. For example, both the Diabetes Control and Complications Trial[3] (DCCT) and the UK Prospective Diabetes Study[4] (UKPDS) required patients to adhere to complex and intensive treatments over long periods of time. As a consequence, these were as much studies of participants' ability to adhere to the intervention protocols as they were of the tight glycemic control that resulted. Self-management education may become increasingly important for the growing number of patients who find their access to clinicians curtailed in an era of cost containment.

Diabetes education cannot be delivered only at the time of diagnosis but must be provided continually to reinforce patients' learning and remain relevant, given patients' changing treatment goals, skill levels, and needs. For example, patients' need for BGSM may vary depending on fluctuations in their overall health, the severity of their glucose dysregulation, and their use of insulin or oral hypoglycemic medication. Self-care guidelines developed by health plans and professional organizations also change from year to year in light of emerging information about the effectiveness of new treatments. Diabetes education serves the function of making sense of these changes for patients.

Self-management education plays a major role in tailoring patients' care to the contextual realities within which that care takes place. Diabetes care, particularly among older patients, frequently occurs in conjunction with the management of other health problems such as cardiovascular disease, arthritis, or hypertension. Many patients receive services both from specialists and general practitioners who may give patients conflicting recommendations or simply too much advice for them to absorb. Depression and anxiety are common among patients with diabetes[5] and can lead to poor glycemic control.[6] Patients' mental health may be at least as important in determining their health-related quality of life and service use as diabetes per se.[7–9] Diabetes is disproportionately common among patients from ethnic minorities and low-income communities, many of whom have difficulty purchasing monitoring supplies or attending regular clinic appointments. Diabetes educators often have the primary responsibility for identifying patients' barriers to treatment and ways of surmounting those barriers or for developing more appropriate treatment plans.

Why Is a Reassessment of the Evidence Necessary?

Self-care education requires a concerted investment of resources, including staff time, clinical information system support, and self-care supplies. Changes in reimbursement policies and professional standards for diabetes self-management education reflect its growing acceptance as a means of preventing complications and lowering health care costs. In the years prior to 1998, the U.S. Health Care Financing Administration's Medicare Program covered blood glucose monitors and testing strips only for patients using insulin; in that year, coverage was expanded to include all patients with diabetes. Also in 1998, Medicare began paying for some diabetes education services, and more recent proposals have included expanding that coverage. One of the potentially most influential changes in professional standards for diabetes education is the planned inclusion of self-care management as part of the Diabetes Quality Improvement Project (DQIP) performance-monitoring process. The DQIP standards of care are sponsored by a number of prominent professional organizations in the United States, and meeting DQIP standards may soon be required by most large payers.

Inevitably, reimbursement policies and professional standards that promote diabetes self-management education reflect not only a belief in the general effectiveness of such services but the endorsement of specific types of interventions. Decisions such as these should

Table 13–1 Self-Management Activities

Self-monitoring

    Blood glucose self-monitoring

    Urine self-monitoring

    Monitoring for symptoms of glucose dysregulation

    Monitoring for symptoms of developing complications

Medication adherence

    Insulin (frequency and dose adjustment)

    Oral hypoglycemics

    Other medications such as antihypertensives and antilipidemics

Lifestyle changes

    Foot care

    Smoking cessation

    Healthy eating (eg, decreased fat and increased fiber)

    Physical activity

    Stress reduction

be based on evidence of effectiveness, since promoting ineffective but costly interventions could divert scarce funds from other activities that promote patients' health and well-being.[10] Conversely, it is important that effective self-management interventions be supported financially, since they may reduce the need for costly acute care services and lessen patients' dependence on the health care system more generally.

Types of Self-Management Activities

Diabetes self-management activities include self-monitoring, adherence to pharmacologic therapies, and lifestyle changes (Table 13–1). For many patients, monitoring glycemic control, whether by BGSM or other methods, is essential. Patients also must remain watchful for symptoms of hyperglycemia and hypoglycemia as well as emerging health crises, such as changes in visual acuity or the development of foot ulcers. Insulin-taking is a complex process that must be managed effectively if euglycemia is to be achieved. Patients who use oral hypoglycemic medications have a rapidly expanding number of treatment options, though most patients have some problems taking these medications as prescribed. Patients who use tobacco can decrease their risk of cardiovascular complications substantially if they quit smoking and remain abstinent.

Review of the Evidence

Data Sources

This review is based on empiric research published in English-language peer-reviewed journals. Emphasis was given to randomized trials that included either Type 1 or Type 2 adults and measured either behavioral or health outcomes.* Although our primary focus was on

---

*Because we identified no studies examining interventions to improve patients' adherence to oral hypoglycemic medications, we include in our review a discussion of medication adherence studies with nondiabetic samples.

Table 13–2 Functions of Blood Glucose Self-Monitoring

Increase patients' awareness of their typical glycemic control

Provide feedback on the impact that treatment and lifestyle have on glycemic control

Inform adjustments in insulin dose and injection frequency

Improve the information base for clinicians' treatment decisions

Alert patients to possibly life-threatening episodes of hyperglycemia

---

interventions targeted to adults, we also note some key studies focusing on Type 1 diabetes in children. Where appropriate, we alert readers to the availability of systematic review articles, if those reviews include an identifiable description of the methods used to identify and evaluate the studies described. Excellent, though somewhat outdated, reviews of the diabetes education literature are provided by Sharon Brown,[11–13] Steven Clement,[14] and Deborah Padgett.[15]

The literature pertinent to the area of self-management education is discussed by answering the following questions:

1. What is the role of blood glucose self-monitoring?
2. Can patients learn how to perceive episodes of glucose dysregulation?
3. Does foot care education prevent podiatric complications?
4. What interventions improve hypoglycemic medication compliance?
5. Is smoking cessation an important goal for diabetes education?
6. How effective are educational interventions with multiple outcome targets?
7. What is the role of clinicians in supporting effective self-care?
8. What are appropriate endpoints for evaluating self-care interventions?
9. What interventions exist that target patients with diabetes and other chronic diseases?
10. What are the directions for future research?

WHAT IS THE ROLE OF BLOOD GLUCOSE SELF-MONITORING?

Does Blood Glucose Self-Monitoring Improve Glycemic Control?

Blood glucose self-monitoring has been called an "essential component of the therapeutic regimen in diabetes management"[16] and a "key to the doctor-patient relationship."[17] It serves several functions (Table 13–2), including increasing patients' awareness of their average glycemic control, providing feedback about the impact that changes in treatment and lifestyle have on glycemic control, informing adjustments in insulin dose and injection frequency, improving the information base on which health care providers make treatment changes, and alerting Type 1 patients to possibly life-threatening episodes of hyperglycemia.

How Often Do Patients Self-Monitor Their Blood Glucose?

The frequency of BGSM varied considerably in a study of 2,500 adults with diabetes.[18] Among Type 1 patients, 40% monitored their blood glucose at least once per day, 39% monitored it less than once per day, and 21% never monitored their blood glucose at all. The frequency of Type 1 patients' BGSM increased with the number of daily insulin injections. Among Type 2 patients treated with insulin, 26% reported daily BGSM, while only 5% of those not treated with insulin monitored this frequently. Among both Type 1 and Type 2 patients, BGSM was substantially less frequent among older patients and patients with less formal education. Monitoring is associated with psychosocial factors such as patients' understanding of diabetes and its treatment, coping styles and stress levels, perceived barriers and benefits, family interactions, and the quality of patients' relationship with their health care providers.[19,20]

Although many self-management interventions focus at least in part on increasing the frequency of BGSM, relatively few studies report explicitly on changes in this behavior. Studies that have been reported suggest that a variety of interventions can be effective, including group educational sessions held in outpatient clinics[21-23] and patients' homes[24] (Table 13–3). In one study,[25] Type 1 adolescents received data-storing glucose meters or glucose meters plus a behavioral contract with a clinician. Investigators found that increases in BGSM frequency were more likely to be maintained when the contract was in place. Studies of other self-management interventions addressing multiple risk factors also suggest that at least some types of education can increase patients' use of BGSM.

What Are the Benefits of Blood Glucose Self-Monitoring?

Because BGSM among Type 1 patients is essential for identifying life-threatening hyperglycemic episodes, a randomized trial comparing BGSM to no BGSM in this population is ethically indefensible. However, a few noteworthy studies indicate that frequent monitoring may be only marginally effective as a means of improving Type 1 patients' *average* glycemic control as measured by tests such as HbA_{1c}.[29-31] In a double crossover study of Type 1 children,[29] participants were assigned either to urine glucose testing plus BGSM or to urine testing only. No significant between-group differences in HbA_{1c} were observed at the 6-month follow-up. In a second trial,[30] Type 1 patients were assigned to three 12-week periods varying in the frequency of prescribed BGSM: (a) 4-point profiles on 2 days per week, (b) 4-point profiles on 1 day per week, and (c) 2-point profiles every day. Results suggested no significant differences in mean blood glucose concentration, fructosamine, or HbA_{1c} associated with BGSM frequency. According to the authors, altering the frequency of BGSM had a "variable and uncertain influence" on the frequency with which patients' altered insulin doses. An observational prospective study of 92 Type 1 adults[31] identified no independent predictive association ($r^2 < .02$) between the frequency of BGSM and glycemic control measured either by HbA_{1c} or BGSM test results.

The effectiveness of BGSM as a means of improving glycemic control among Type 2 patients is addressed in reviews by Faas[32] and Gallichan.[33] Faas reviewed 11 studies regarding the relationship between BGSM and glycemic control, including 6 randomized trials,[22,34-38] with total sample sizes ranging from 27 to 208 patients and follow-up periods ranging from 12 to 62 weeks. Only one of these studies[36] identified any effect of BGSM on glycemic control. The results of that study are not definitive, since it included a strict clinician follow-up protocol applied only to intervention patients, which could explain the group differences. Observational studies described in the Gallichan review support the null findings of the remaining randomized trials. Two studies not covered in the Faas and Gallichan reviews also examined the potential benefits of BGSM. In a randomized trial,[35] investigators found no statistically significant differences in any measure of glycemic control between groups assigned to BGSM or urine glucose testing. As in the review by Gallichan, investigators noted that urine testing was the significantly less expensive option. In another study,[39] investigators reported that managed care patients who obtained free glucose testing supplies had similar HbA_{1c} levels to patients who did not obtain the supplies. Among those who obtained glucose testing strips, glycemic control was independent of the number of strips dispensed.

Even accurate BGSM reports to clinicians may not improve glycemic control, because they have little impact on provider or patient behavior. In two studies,[40,41] Type 1 patients used data storing glucose meters and brought these with them to regularly scheduled outpatient appointments. Monitoring data then were downloaded to a computer, analyzed, and summarized in brief reports for review by patients and their physicians during the visit. Both studies found that the BGSM reports had no impact on patients' BGSM behavior, self-reported insulin adjustments, or glycemic control. In a third study,[42] Marrero and colleagues investigated whether impacts on glycemic control would be increased if BGSM data were reported on a biweekly basis between clinic visits and followed-up by a nurse over the telephone. At the end of the 1-year study, intervention patients experienced a decrease in the

Table 13–3 Studies of Interventions Designed to Increase the Impact of Blood Glucose Self-Monitoring

Studies of Type 1 Patients

Investigator(s)	Sample Description	Intervention(s)	Control(s)	Follow-up and Outcomes	Intervention Effects*
Gordon et al (1991)[30]	25 clinic patients, mean age = 31, 9 females	BGSM 2× every day with measurement times varying each day. Balanced crossover study	1: BGSM 4× on any 2 nonconsecutive days per week; 2: BGSM 4× on any 1 day per week	f.u. = 12, 24, and 36 wk. HbA$_{1c}$, fructosamine, patient preference	No differences
Marrero et al (1989)[41]	57 children from outpatient clinics, mean age = 15, 39% female	Data storing glucose meter; BGSM data downloaded during clinic visits for review	Data storing glucose meter without clinic downloads of BGSM data	f.u. = 2 and 4 mo. HbA$_{1c}$, BGSM frequency, DM knowledge	IG showed greater improvements in DM knowledge; no other differences
Marrero et al (1995)[42]	106 children from DM specialty clinic, mean age = 13, 41% female	Data storing glucose meter; transmitted BGSM data by modem to the clinic; data reviewed by nurse who telephoned patients	Data storing glucose meter; BGSM data downloaded only during routine clinic visits	f.u. = 1 y. HbA$_{1c}$, health service use, psychosocial measures	No differences
Wolanski et al (1996)[26]	39 children and adolescents from a summer camp	Two one-on-one sessions on BGSM; group sessions with similar content	Group sessions only	f.u. = end of camp (time unspecified). BGSM technique	No differences

Studies of Type 2 Patients

Investigator(s)	Sample Description	Intervention(s)	Control(s)	Follow-up and Outcomes	Intervention Effects*
Allen et al (1990)[35]	54 male clinic patients, mean age = 58	Instructed to use BGSM only; instructed in monitoring technique	Instructed to self-monitor urine glucose only; instructed in monitoring technique	f.u. = monthly for 6 mo. HbA$_{1c}$, FPG, weight, cost	BGSM was more expensive than urine monitoring; no other differences

Table 13–3 Studies of Interventions Designed to Increase the Impact of Blood Glucose Self-Monitoring — *(continued)*

Studies of Type 2 Patients

Investigator(s)	Sample Description	Intervention(s)	Control(s)	Follow-up and Outcomes	Intervention Effects[*]
Estey et al (1990)[37]	53 clinic patients, mean age = 52, 54% female	BGSM education with postprogram review session, phone calls, and home visit by a nurse	BGSM education with one postprogram review session	f.u. = 3 mo HbA$_{1c}$, weight, BGSM frequency	IG had a higher frequency of BGSM; no other differences
Fontbonne et al (1989)[34]	164 patients from DM clinic, mean age = 55, 43% female	BGSM 2× every other day	1: self-monitored urine glucose 2× every other day 2: physician HbA$_{1c}$ monitoring only	f.u. = 6 mo HbA$_{1c}$ and weight	No differences
Gallichan (1994)[27]	20 patients from a general medicine clinic, mean age = 64, more women than men	Instructed to use BGSM only; instructed in monitoring techniques	Instructed to self-monitor urine glucose only; instructed in monitoring technique	f.u. = 6 mo Fructosamine	No differences
Rutten et al (1990)[36]	127 patients from outpatient clinics, mean age = 63, 65% female	Intensive BGSM education with structured follow-up physician visits	Usual care	f.u. = 1 y HbA$_{1c}$ and weight	HbA$_{1c}$ decreased in IG (−0.4%) but increased in CG (0.5%, $p < .05$); no change in weight
White et al (1986)[23]	32 male community volunteers, mean age = 62	BGSM education based on group interaction, goal setting, and mutual support	BGSM education based on lectures	f.u. = 3 and 6 mo HbA$_{1c}$, FPG, weight, DM knowledge	IG had lower mean FPG (161 mg/dL) than CG (243 mg/dL, $p < .05$); no other differences

Table 13–3 Studies of Interventions Designed to Increase the Impact of Blood Glucose Self-Monitoring — *(continued)*

Studies of Type 2 Patients

Investigator(s)	Sample Description	Intervention(s)	Control(s)	Follow-up and Outcomes	Intervention Effects
Wing et al (1986)[22]	50 patients from outpatient clinics, mean age = 54, 78% female	BGSM education focused on relationship between weight and blood glucose	Standard weight control program	f.u. = 12 and 62 wk Weight loss and loss maintenance, medication reduction, dietary compliance, mood	No differences

Studies of Both Type 1 and Type 2 Patients or Type Unspecified

Investigator(s)	Sample Description	Intervention(s)	Control(s)	Follow-up and Outcomes	Intervention Effects
Moorish et al (1989)[28]	18 hospital patients, mean age = 40, 7 females	Data storing glucose meter; BGSM data were downloaded during clinic visits Nonrandomized, matched control	Glucose meter without data storage	f.u. = 6 mo HbA_{1c}, fructosamine	No differences
Wysocki et al (1989)[25]	30 adolescents from children's hospital, mean age = 14, 13 females	Data storing glucose meter plus behavior contract with a clinician	Data storing glucose meter only	f.u. = 4, 8, 12, and 16 wk HbA_{1c}, FPG, serum glucose variability, BGSM frequency	IG had more frequent BGSM; no other differences

*Unless otherwise noted, intervention effects are measured as the difference between follow-up intervention and control group values. Unless otherwise noted in the "Intervention(s)" column, studies are randomized controlled trials.
BGSM = blood glucose self-monitoring; CG = control group; DM = diabetes mellitus; FPG = fasting plasma glucose; f.u. = follow-up; IG = intervention group.

amount of time nurses spent reviewing their glycemic control during clinic appointments as well as a decrease in patients' negative perceptions regarding BGSM. However, there was no improvement in patients' HbA$_{1c}$ levels, hospitalization rates, emergency room visits, or psychological measures such as self-esteem or perceived quality of life.

Why Might Interventions That Increase Blood Glucose Self-Monitoring Not Translate into Better Glycemic Control?

Wysocki conducted a comprehensive review of the factors that can interfere with the usefulness of BGSM.[43] Under ideal circumstances, BGSM data reflect only a sampling of information about the continual changes that occur in patients' glucose levels. For many Type 1 patients, true diurnal variability in glycemia is too great to be accurately reflected even by frequent checks.[44] Patients who monitor infrequently (eg, many Type 2 patients) obtain an even less accurate assessment of their mean glycemic levels, the periodic variation around their mean levels, or the frequency and magnitude of irregular spikes in their glycemic profiles. Poor BGSM techniques, such as the use of an inadequate amount of blood, delays in placing the blood on the meter, unclean equipment, and dropping or smearing the blood can all degrade the accuracy of BGSM readings.[45] Also, BGSM test strips[46] and glucose meters[47] vary in their reliability for measuring capillary glucose levels, and some have a systematic bias toward over- or underestimation.

The potential impact of BGSM also may be limited by what is done with the data. Patients may have difficulty remembering the complex pattern of glycemic changes that they observe in the weeks or months between outpatient encounters. Patients may also miss or misinterpret the precursors and consequences of atypical readings, especially when they receive little education from health care providers about how to use this information. Although glucose diaries can simplify this process, many patients have clinically significant errors in their records.[48] For example, Mazze and colleagues[49] found that 26% of logbook entries for a group of 19 Type 1 patients were different from values stored in the memory of their glucose meters.

The lack of evidence supporting BGSM among Type 2 patients has led some commentators to call for a reconsideration of when, how, and for whom BGSM should be used as a component of treatment. Faas and colleagues recommend "the use of [BGSM] only for patients with poor glycemic control despite optimal medication therapy." Gallichan takes a more extreme view that "the inappropriate use of BGSM is wasteful of [health care funds] and can cause psychological harm." He recommends the following decision rules: (1) patients not treated with insulin should test before breakfast and 2 hours after the main meal 1 to 2 days each week; (2) patients treated with insulin should test before meals and at bedtime 1 to 2 days each week, or test once per day, varying the time (eg, before breakfast one day, before lunch the next, etc.). He also notes that occasional tests at 2:00 to 3:00 am may be useful.

It is important, however, not to interpret the data in this area of research too strictly. As noted above, it can be difficult to standardize the frequency of patients' BGSM or clinicians' use of the information in the context of efficacy studies. Interventions that support coordinated care management may increase health systems' ability to deal effectively with glycemic control problems and therefore enhance the value of BGSM. Moreover, effective educational strategies that assist patients in responding effectively to BGSM data could also increase its importance. Blood glucose self-monitoring may be much more important for some patients than others, and the benefits can vary depending on factors such as whether the patient recently changed his or her treatment regimen or experienced a change in health status. In sum, clinicians should treat patients' situations as unique and develop BGSM regimens that are the least intensive possible while providing useful information to support each patient's self-care and treatment.

EVIDENCE-BASED MESSAGES

Based on available randomized trials, the following conclusions can be drawn about the effectiveness of BGSM:

1. Although it is essential that Type 1 patients monitor themselves for episodes of extreme hyperglycemia and hypoglycemia, there is little evidence suggesting that frequent BGSM (eg, 4 times/d) improves Type 1 patients' mean glycemic control more than less frequent BGSM or urine testing (Level 1A).[32]
2. There is no evidence that BGSM contributes to better glycemic control among Type 2 patients (Level 1A).[32,33]
3. Blood glucose self-monitoring may not affect glycemic control because of patients' difficulty obtaining accurate measures, difficulty reporting BGSM data to clinicians, or lack of an impact on clinicians' behavior. More efficient reporting of BGSM to clinicians appears to have no effect on patients' glycemic control (Level 2).[41,42]

CAN PATIENTS LEARN HOW TO PERCEIVE EPISODES OF GLUCOSE DYSREGULATION?

Hyperglycemic and hypoglycemic symptoms are among the most common complications of insulin therapy. Manifestations of glucose dysregulation (including mental confusion, bizarre behavior, and ultimately coma) mainly reflect impaired functioning of patients' central nervous systems and can limit their ability to take corrective measures to restore euglycemia.

Type 1 patients frequently are unable to estimate their glucose levels and make appropriate adjustments before cognitive symptoms develop. Many patients develop neurologic adaptations to chronic hyperglycemia and experience hypoglycemic symptoms above the usual range. Patients who are overtreated with insulin may be unaware of critically low levels of blood glucose because of a blunting of their epinephrine response owing to repeated episodes of hypoglycemia.[50] Patients' inability to identify and address poor glycemic control can have devastating consequences.[51,52] Some patients with Type 1 diabetes drive during periods when they are unaware that their cognitive abilities are dangerously impaired.[53] Neither duration of diabetes nor patients' demographic characteristics are helpful in identifying individuals who are most likely to miss signs of hypoglycemia and hyperglycemia.[54–57]

Interventions to Increase Awareness of Blood Glucose Level

Blood Glucose Awareness Training (BGAT) is a structured educational and skills training program developed by Daniel Cox and colleagues to improve the accuracy of Type 1 patients' perceptions regarding their glucose levels.[58] In a 1989 study (Table 13–4), they found that compared to matched controls, BGAT improved the accuracy with which patients estimated their blood glucose levels and improved their glycemic control.[59] In a follow-up randomized trial, investigators found that both standard and intensive BGAT improved patients' ability to detect hypoglycemia and hyperglycemia,[60] findings further supported by a multicenter evaluation using a repeated-baseline design.[61] In a 5-year follow-up, patients who received the training reported significantly fewer automobile crashes than did controls.[62] Another randomized trial evaluated the effects of BGAT on epinephrine and symptom responses.[63] At the 4-week follow-up, epinephrine response to hypoglycemia was greater among intervention patients than among controls, although there were no differences between groups in the frequency of hypoglycemia or in mean HbA_{1c} levels.

EVIDENCE-BASED MESSAGE

The available evidence indicates that a formal, structured, educational intervention can improve Type 1 patients' ability to identify episodes of hypoglycemia and hyperglycemia and may restore patients' epinephrine response to hypoglycemia (Level 2).[61,63]

DOES FOOT CARE EDUCATION PREVENT PODIATRIC COMPLICATIONS?

Effective foot care includes a variety of behaviors, such as appropriate foot washing, nail trimming, footwear, and, perhaps most importantly, vigilance for the signs and symptoms of abrasions, scrapes, and sores that can develop into infections that "threaten life and limb." Mayfield and colleagues provide a comprehensive review of the literature on preventive foot

Table 13–4 Studies of Blood Glucose Awareness Training among Type 1 Patients

Investigator(s)	Sample Description	Intervention(s)	Control(s)	Follow-up and Outcomes	Intervention Effects*
Cox et al (1989)[59]	22 community volunteers, mean age = 32, 14 females	7 weekly educational sessions on how to plot estimated blood glucose and BGSM results on an error grid and interpret them; homework included awareness exercises and discrimination training	7 weekly educational sessions discussing the effect of stress on metabolic control; homework included recording BGSM, insulin, diet, and stress levels in daily diaries	f.u. = 4 to 5 mo HbA₁c, blood glucose estimation accuracy	IG had a greater decrease in mean HbA$_{1c}$ (-1.4, $p = .04$); IG showed improvement in blood glucose estimation accuracy ($p < .001$), while CG did not ($p = .23$)
Cox et al (1991)[60]	39 community volunteers, mean age = 33, 14 females	1: inpatient manipulation of blood glucose via insulin infusion; participants rated symptom severity, estimated glucose levels, and received feedback about actual levels; post-discharge, 7 educational sessions using inpatient audiotapes to reinforce memory of blood glucose-related symptoms 2: inpatient manipulation of blood glucose via insulin infusion without feedback; 7 training sessions that included literature about symptoms of hypo- and hyperglycemia, factors influencing glycemic control, and glucose-level estimation	Group sessions on topics other than blood glucose awareness	f.u. = 8 wk HbA₁c, blood glucose estimation accuracy, fear of hypoglycemia, DM knowledge, BGSM frequency	Mean HbA$_{1c}$ for IG1 was lower (10.3%) than for CG (11.3%, $p < .002$); IG1 and IG2 improved blood glucose estimation accuracy relative to CG with no difference between IG1 and IG2; no other differences

Table 13–4 Studies of Blood Glucose Awareness Training among Type 1 Patients — *(continued)*

Investigator(s)	Sample Description	Intervention(s)	Control(s)	Follow-up and Outcomes	Intervention Effects*
Kinsley et al (1999)[53]	47 patients from a DM specialty clinic, mean age = 34, 24 females	8 outpatient blood glucose awareness training sessions	8 outpatient cholesterol education sessions	f.u. = 4 mo HbA_{1c}, blood glucose estimation accuracy, symptoms, counter-regulatory hormones	Epinephrine response in CG decreased while the response in IG was preserved ($p < .02$); no other differences

*Unless otherwise noted, intervention effects are measured as the difference between follow-up intervention and control group values. Unless otherwise noted in the "Intervention(s)" column, studies are randomized controlled trials.

BGSM = blood glucose self-monitoring; CG = control group; DM = diabetes mellitus; FPG = fasting plasma glucose; f.u. = follow-up; IG = intervention group.

care for patients with diabetes.[64] There is a detailed description of the epidemiology and medical treatment of diabetic foot disorders presented in Chapter 25.

Observational studies suggest that the absence of foot care education may contribute to a greater risk of foot problems. In a survey of patients who had developed foot ulcers,[65] only 29% previously considered themselves at risk for foot problems, while 59% of a comparison group without ulcers considered themselves at risk. Seventy percent of patients in both groups had not had their feet examined in the prior 10 years, and only 30% reported that they had received information about foot care from their health care providers. In a study of elderly men,[66] those who reported receiving no foot care education had a threefold increase in their risk of amputation.

Effectiveness of Foot Care Interventions

Most foot care education programs have been conducted as part of multifaceted self-management interventions, making it difficult to distinguish their impact from that of other intervention components. Nevertheless, studies suggest that foot care interventions that take advantage of health behavior change techniques, such as motivational counseling[67] or skill-based training,[68] have greater impacts on health behaviors than do didactic sessions[69] (Table 13–5). Patient-based education (eg, educational sessions reinforced with behavioral contracts) in conjunction with provider-based interventions (eg, education plus chart reminders) may be more effective than patient education alone. In one study combining patient and provider education,[70] intervention patients at 12 months were more likely than randomized controls to report that they engaged in appropriate foot care and had a 60% lower risk of ulcers and other serious foot lesions. In another study, primary care sites were randomized to usual care or group foot care education sessions provided by general practitioners[71] (see Table 13–9). After 6 months, fewer intervention patients had foot problems than controls, including fewer calluses (49% vs 82%), fewer minor skin problems (49% vs 65%), and less improper nail trimming (27% vs 92%).

Discussion

As noted at the beginning of this chapter, effective diabetes self-management education must be sensitive to contextual factors that can pose barriers to patients' self-care. This is certainly the case with regard to foot care. Foot care interventions need to take into account factors such as poor vision,[74] difficulty reaching toes, or problems responding appropriately to plantar lesions.[75] Policies to promote foot care must be developed in light of an understanding of patients' abilities, needs, and attitudes. For example, although specialized footwear can decrease ulcer recurrence rates by as much as 74%,[76] Medicare found in a 3-year evaluation of a footwear reimbursement benefit that only 3% of patients who were eligible took advantage of it.[77]

EVIDENCE-BASED MESSAGES

1. Foot care education is an effective means of improving patients' foot care behavior (Level 1A).[70]
2. Foot care education reduces the incidence of minor foot problems such as calluses, as well as major problems such as infections and amputations. (Level 1A).[70,76]
3. Foot care education can be more effective if it includes motivational counseling, skill-based training, and simultaneous education and reminders to physicians (Level 3).[70]

WHAT INTERVENTIONS IMPROVE HYPOGLYCEMIC MEDICATION COMPLIANCE?

Appropriate hypoglycemic medication-taking can improve patients' symptoms in the short term and decrease their long-term risk of diabetic complications. However, problems with medication-taking are a major cause of both hypoglycemia and hyperglycemia and have the potential to induce health crises. Nagasawa and colleagues conducted a review of the psy-

Table 13–5 Studies of Interventions to Improve Foot Self-Care

Studies of Type 2 Patients

Investigator(s)	Sample Description	Intervention(s)	Control(s)	Follow-up and Outcomes	Intervention Effects*
Barth et al (1990)[72]	62 patients from the community and from DM clinics, mean age = 59, 44% female	4 weekly group foot care education sessions including motivational techniques and monitored practice	Standard 3-d education session	f.u. = 1, 3, and 6 mo Foot care knowledge and behavior, podiatry visits, foot problems	IG had greater improvements in foot care knowledge and behavior; more IG patients had podiatry visits (17 of 26) at 1 mo than CG (7 of 25, $p = .008$); IG had fewer foot problems at 1 mo but not at 3 or 6 months
Litzelman et al (1993)[70]	352 general medicine patients, mean age = 60, 81% female	Foot care education and behavioral contract with f.u. contract reminders; providers given foot-care information and chart reminders	Usual care	f.u. = 1 yr Serious foot lesions, foot care behavior, number of foot exams, mention of foot problems in medical records	IG was less likely to have serious foot lesions than CG (odds ratio = 0.4, $p = .05$); IG reported more foot self-care and exams; IG providers were more likely to mention foot problems in medical records (24%) than CG providers (11%, $p < .01$)

Table 13–5 Studies of Interventions to Improve Foot Self-Care — *(continued)*

Studies of Both Type 1 and Type 2 Patients or Type Unspecified

Investigator(s)	Sample Description	Intervention(s)	Control(s)	Follow-up and Outcomes	Intervention Effects*
Uccioli et al (1995)[76]	69 patients from 2 teaching hospitals, mean age = 60, 38% female	Assigned to wear therapeutic shoes	Usual care	f.u. = monthly for 12 mo Recurrent foot ulcerations	Fewer IG patients (9 of 33) had recurrent foot ulcerations than CG (21 of 36, p = .009)
Malone et al (1989)[73]	182 patients with foot problems referred to podiatry or vascular surgery clinics	1-h lecture plus slide presentation on foot care	Usual care	mean f.u. = 13 mo (IG) and 9 mo (CG) foot and limb infections, ulcers, amputations	Fewer IG patients (5%) had foot and limb ulcerations than CG (15%, p = .005); fewer IG patients (4%) had amputations than CG (12%, p = .025); no other differences
Kruger et al (1992)[68]	30 patients from a DM treatment program	Foot-care lecture presentation and hands-on teaching session	Lecture presentation only	f.u. = 6 mo Foot care knowledge and pathology	No differences

*Unless otherwise noted, intervention effects are measured as the difference between follow-up intervention and control group values. Unless otherwise noted in the "Intervention(s)" column, studies are randomized controlled trials.

BGSM = blood glucose self-monitoring; CG = control group; DM = diabetes mellitus; FPG = fasting plasma glucose; f.u. = follow-up; IG = intervention group.

chosocial correlates of medication adherence among patients with diabetes.[19] The authors reviewed 26 studies and found that demographic factors were poor predictors of patients' adherence to medication, while emotional stability, perceived benefits, and supportive environments all improved adherence rates. Adherence to hypoglycemic medication schedules cannot be considered in isolation, since most elderly patients with diabetes take additional drugs that have their own dosing schedules, requirements regarding food intake, and side-effect profiles.

Interventions to Improve Insulin Adjustment

To achieve near-normal glycemic levels, patients taking insulin need to adjust their dosage in response to food intake, exercise, and changes in their health status. Frequent adjustments are recommended to achieve the reductions in complication rates demonstrated in the DCCT and UKPDS. However, these decisions are inherently complex, and many patients seek to avoid the hypoglycemic symptoms associated with taking insulin.[78,79] As a result, patients often select insulin doses high enough to avoid hypoglycemia and maintain a constant dosing regimen over weeks or months.

Several studies have evaluated computer programs to assist Type 1 patients in making decisions regarding insulin adjustments (Table 13–6). To assist Type 1 children, Brown and colleagues[80] evaluated a diabetes-education video game that patients were instructed to take home with them and use. Patients randomized to the control group received an entertaining video game with no diabetes educational content. At 3 and 6 months, parent-rated self-care and communication were improved, but there was no effect on diabetes-related knowledge or HbA_{1c}. Hand-held, computerized, decision-support systems have been developed to assist Type 1 patients in optimizing their glycemic control through more fine-tuned and effective insulin adjustment. Two systems that have been evaluated have shown some impact on daily variation in glucose levels but no impact on HbA_1/HbA_{1c} or insulin dosing.[81,82]

Interventions to Improve Adherence to Oral Medications

In an observational study, 32 Type 2 patients, all but one of whom were men, were given electronic medication event monitoring (MEMS) caps for their sulfonylurea pill bottles that recorded the number of times the bottles were opened as well as the actual timing of administration.[84] Investigators found that 47% of patients were nonadherent to some degree and that adherence rates were poorer among patients with more than once per day dosing. In a second study, adjudicated patient-level paid-claims data from the computer archive of the state of South Carolina's Medicaid program for the period of 1990 through 1994 were used to examine patients' adherence to sulfonylurea regimens.[85] Investigators found that only 18% of patients actually obtained a full year's supply of medication. Thirty-nine percent obtained a 6-month supply or less. Controlling for gender and race, patients who were < 40 years of age were twice as likely to obtain a supply of $\leq$ 6 months than patients aged 40 to 64 ($p = .0003$). Younger patients were 2.4 times as likely to obtain a supply of $\leq$ 10 months ($p = .0011$).

Because there are no randomized studies specifically addressing adherence to oral hypoglycemic medications, inferences must be drawn from a review of trials from other disease areas. There are a variety of simple, low-cost interventions that can improve oral medication adherence (Table 13–7). Adherence improves when a patient's regimen is simplified.[86] When the dosing and number of drugs cannot be reduced, adherence can be improved through the use of aids such as medication vials equipped with a digital timepiece display,[87] packaging that groups all medications required at each dosing event,[88] and medication alarm devices.[89] Automated telephone reminder calls have been shown to increase medication adherence.[90,91] Brief, one-time sessions with a nurse may be effective if they include advice regarding filling prescriptions, transportation, and returning for follow-up visits[92] or if they include concrete information, such as written medication schedules.[93] Brief discharge counseling by a pharmacist[94] or an educational videotape[95] may not be intensive enough to improve adherence.

Table 13–6 Studies of Interventions Designed to Increase the Effectiveness of Insulin Adjustment in Type 1 Patients

Investigator(s)	Sample Description	Intervention(s)	Control(s)	Follow-up and Outcomes	Intervention Effects*
Peterson et al (1986)[83]	16 community volunteers, mean age = 40, 8 females	Instruction from a small, interactive computer	Standard written algorithms for insulin adjustment	f.u. = 6 wk HbA$_{1c}$ serum glucose, hypoglycemic episodes	IG had lower mean HbA$_{1c}$ (6.2%) than CG (7.0%, $p = .06$); IG had lower mean serum glucose (121 mg/dL) than CG (148 mg/dL, $p < .01$); no difference in hypoglycemic episodes
Chiarelli et al (1990)[82]	20 children from DM clinics, mean age = 10, 10 females	Computerized device for insulin adjustment Nonrandomized, matched control	Manual insulin adjustment	3 8-wk periods HbA$_{1c}$, BGSM frequency, pre-meal glycemia, symptoms	No increase in IG symptoms (1.2 events/wk) but there was an increase in CG (1.1 to 2.3 events/wk, $p < .005$); no other differences
Peters et al (1991)[81]	42 patients from a DM education center, mean age = 33, 19 females	Wallet-sized computerized decision-support system	Usual care	f.u. = 32 d HbA$_{1c}$ serum glucose, hypoglycemic episodes	No differences
Brown et al (1997)[80]	59 children from DM clinics, ages 8 to 16	Home interactive DM educational video game	Home non–DM-related entertainment video game	f.u. = 6 mo HbA$_{1c}$, DM knowledge, self-efficacy, communication with parents about DM, self-care, DM-related urgent care visits	IG had a greater improvement in self-efficacy, parental communication, and self-care; IG had a greater decline in mean urgent care visits per patient (–0.43) than CG (0.04, $p = .08$); no other differences

*Unless otherwise noted, intervention effects are measured as the difference between follow-up intervention and control group values. Unless otherwise noted in the "Intervention(s)" column, studies are randomized controlled trials.

BGSM = blood glucose self-monitoring; CG = control group; DM = diabetes mellitus; FPG = fasting plasma glucose; f.u. = follow-up; IG = intervention group.

Table 13–7 Interventions That Can Improve Oral Medication Adherence

Intervention
Simplification of medication regimen
Medication vials with digital timepiece displays
Packaging that groups all medications required at each dosing event
Medication alarm devices
Automated telephone calls for patient reminding and counseling
Advice about obtaining transportation, filling prescriptions, and making follow-up appointments
Written medication schedules
Multidisciplinary teams
Patient education that includes peer support

Adherence has been shown to be increased by a multidisciplinary team approach,[96] and one study showed that patients might be more adherent when they have input into their medication schedule.[97] One study of asthma patients found that adherence improvements through patient education could be cost effective.[98]

EVIDENCE-BASED MESSAGES

Based on available studies, the following conclusions can be drawn about interventions to improve medication adherence:

1. Computerized decision-support systems to inform insulin adjustments may improve some outcomes (Level 2).[80,82]
2. Although studies specifically addressing adherence to oral hypoglycemic medications have not been conducted, studies in other disease areas indicate that there are a variety of simple devices and educational interventions to assist patients in adhering to oral medication regimens (Level 2).[87,90,96]

IS SMOKING CESSATION AN IMPORTANT GOAL FOR DIABETES EDUCATION?

The U.S. Agency for Health Care Research and Policy has published evidence-based guidelines for smoking cessation interventions that include a thorough literature review.[99] The role of smoking cessation in diabetes care was specifically addressed in a recent American Diabetes Association Technical Review.[100]

Using results of the U.S. Behavioral Risk Factor Surveillance System, the smoking behaviors of over 3,000 persons reporting diabetes were compared with those of 52,000 individuals without diabetes.[101] Similar percentages of smokers (26%), ex-smokers (26%), and never smokers (48%) were found in both populations. In a U.S. National Health Interview Survey, smoking prevalence was found to be approximately equal between persons with diabetes (27%) and those without diabetes (26%).[102] Smoking heightens diabetic patients' risk of coronary artery disease, stroke, and overall mortality.[103,104] Smoking is related to the development of complications[105,106] and increases the risk of microalbuminuria and nephropathy among both Type 1[106,107] and Type 2 patients.[108,109] Fortunately, patients who quit smoking improve their risk profile substantially.[110,111]

Smoking Cessation Interventions

Interventions delivered by any type of health care provider significantly increase smoking cessation rates relative to usual care (Table 13–8). However, cessation messages are most

Table 13–8 Components of Effective Smoking Cessation Interventions

Behavioral cessation counseling

Advice to quit from multiple sources

Proactive telephone hotline support

Nicotine replacement therapy (eg, nicotine gum, transdermal patches, and nasal sprays)
  when used with behavioral counseling

Bupropion, especially for smokers with mood disorders

effective when they are consistently and repeatedly delivered by as many providers as possible.[112–114] Mutual support groups and materials such as audiotapes, booklets, and telephone hotlines[115] increase cessation rates.[116] Even brief (3 to 10 minutes) counseling increases cessation rates, although longer interventions (eg, up to 1 hour) are more effective than shorter ones.[92,93]

Pharmacotherapy may increase the effectiveness of behavioral interventions for smoking cessation. Meta-analyses have found that nicotine gum significantly improves the likelihood that smokers will remain abstinent.[117,118] In one study, nicotine gum was found to improve 1-year cessation rates by 40 to 60%.[99] Transdermal nicotine (the nicotine patch) is also effective and may be more acceptable to patients than nicotine gum. Compared to a placebo patch, the nicotine patch doubles the likelihood of abstinence at 6 months, especially when used in conjunction with intensive behavioral change interventions.[119] Persons using nicotine nasal sprays may be more than twice as likely to achieve 12-month abstinence as placebo controls.[120] In a randomized trial of sustained-release bupropion, 1-year cessation rates of 12% among patients in the placebo group were found, 20% among patients receiving a 100-mg dosage and 23% among patients receiving ≥ 150 mg.[121] Bupropion may be especially effective for smokers with depression or other mood disorders.

The majority of publications about diabetes and smoking have extrapolated from the general primary care literature to include issues of particular pertinence to diabetes care.[111,122,123] The limited number of studies that have been conducted specifically among patients with diabetes are primarily descriptive in design[124] and report on small numbers of subjects.[125] Sawicki and colleagues conducted a prospective, randomized, controlled intervention study with 89 diabetic smokers that contrasted intensive behavior therapy over 10 weeks with 15 minutes of unstructured outpatient physician advice. Investigators found that the mean number of cigarettes decreased more in the behavior therapy group than in the control group. However, at the 6-month follow-up, cotinine-confirmed quit rates were 10% in both groups.[126]

EVIDENCE-BASED MESSAGES

Based on available literature, the following conclusions can be drawn about the effectiveness of smoking cessation interventions:

1. Interventions to help patients quit smoking increase cessation rates (Level 1A).[99,100]
2. There is no evidence that smoking cessation is more or less effective among patients with diabetes than among patients with other conditions (Level 3).[100,127]
3. Even brief advice to quit smoking produces increased quit rates, but behavioral counseling accompanied by pharmacologic therapy and ongoing support achieves the greatest reductions (Level 1A).[118,119]

How Effective Are Educational Interventions with Multiple Outcome Targets?

Psychosocial Support and Telephone Care

Some of the most innovative and effective self-management interventions have addressed multiple dimensions of self-care simultaneously. One of the earlier psychosocial intervention studies was conducted by Barbara Anderson and colleagues[128] among Type 1 adolescents and their family members. Adolescents randomized to the intervention group attended five group visits with peers, delivered as part of their usual medical visits, while their parents participated in concurrent group sessions. Meetings focused on problem-solving and using BGSM data for self-regulation. After 18 months, participants in the intervention group showed significantly greater reductions in HbA_{1c} (adjusted differences of about 1%) compared to those receiving usual care, and more of them (60% vs 33%) reported using BGSM information when they exercised. Not only did Anderson and colleagues recently report a replication and extension of these findings, they also reported that interventions such as these can decrease health care costs[129] (Table 13–9).

Robert Anderson and colleagues[130] have reported on the results of a training program for diabetes educators to help them learn empowerment strategies for working with their patients. They evaluated a 3-day skills-based workshop (these authors subsequently have developed shorter training programs) that included a simulated diabetes care regimen prior to the workshop training, demonstrations and practice in empowerment counseling skills, and a videotape review of the counseling sessions. Following training, participants in the workshop showed significant improvement over baseline in counseling skills (on both videotape simulations and audio recordings of actual counseling sessions) and in their attitudes toward supporting patient autonomy.[130] The empowerment approach has been demonstrated to produce better patient outcomes than usual care in a randomized trial.[131] More research on the empowerment model and related approaches, such as motivational interviewing, are needed, especially studies that evaluate the adoption (ie, who participates in such training), implementation, and maintenance of counseling skills.

An example of research using a patient-activation paradigm was reported by Greenfield and colleagues.[132] In this randomized trial, a research assistant met with patients for 20 minutes just prior to two quarterly office visits. During the meeting, patients' medical records were reviewed, medical decisions and self-management issues likely to arise during that visit were discussed, and negotiation and information-seeking skills were rehearsed. At their 12-week follow-up, patients receiving the intervention showed significant improvements in glucose control (adjusted differences of approximately 2% HbA_{1c}), days lost from work, and quality of life relative to controls.

The helpfulness of follow-up telephone support was demonstrated by Weinberger and colleagues.[133] In a randomized trial with elderly Type 2 men, these investigators found that relative to usual care, calls conducted an average of once per month significantly decreased HbA_{1c} levels (adjusted difference of 0.6%). In a more recent study of diabetes telephone care conducted in a managed care system, a 1.1% greater decrease in mean 12-month HbA_{1c} levels was achieved among intervention patients relative to randomized controls.[134] These studies are consistent with studies demonstrating the efficacy and cost effectiveness of telephone calls in enhancing and even serving as alternatives to office visits for nondiabetes health issues.[135–137]

Use of Information Technology

Information technology can serve several functions in improving diabetes management, from both the patient and provider perspective (Table 13–10). Two excellent reviews of the literature in this area are provided by Balas[152] and Krishna.[153] Conceptual discussions of the role of interactive technologies in behavioral medicine are provided by Noell and Glasgow,[154] Glasgow and colleagues,[155] and Street and colleagues.[156]

Table 13-9 Multiple Risk-Factor Intervention Studies

Studies of Type 1 Patients

Investigator(s)	Sample Description	Intervention(s)	Control(s)	Follow-up and Outcomes	Intervention Effects*
Anderson et al (1989)[128]	60 children from a pediatric DM clinic, mean age = 12, 53% female	Group educational session prior to scheduled clinic visits that focused on solving problems with BGSM	Usual care	f.u. = 18 mo HbA$_{1c}$	Fewer patients in IG (7 of 30) had increases in HbA$_{1c}$ than in CG (15 of 30, p = .04)
Anderson et al (1999)[129]	85 children from a pediatric DM clinic, mean age = 13, 50% female	4 sessions over 12 mo focusing on effects of growth and puberty on DM, coping with BGSM family conflicts, preventing conflicts about food, and parental support for exercise	1: 4 sessions over 12 mo focusing on telling others about diabetes, making healthy eating choices, and effects of exercise 2: usual care	f.u. = 12 and 24 mo HbA$_{1c}$, DM-related family conflict	More IG (68%) than CG1 + CG2 patients (47%) improved HbA$_{1c}$ (p < .07); no major deterioration in parental involvement in IG (0%) compared to 16% deterioration in CG1 + CG2 patients (p < .03); IG families reported significantly less conflict
Delamater et al (1990)[138]	36 children from a children's hospital, mean age = 9, 17 females	Self-management training (SMT) consisting of 7 outpatient sessions with a social worker during the first 4 mo after diagnosis and booster sessions at 6 and 12 mo	1: usual care 2: usual care + supportive counseling	f.u. = 12 and 24 mo HbA$_{1c}$	IG had lower mean HbA$_1$ (8.2%) than CG1 (9.8%, p < .05); IG had somewhat lower HbA$_{1c}$ (8.2%) than CG2 (9.1%; no p value given)

Table 13-9 Multiple Risk-Factor Intervention Studies — *(continued)*

Studies of Type 2 Patients

Investigator(s)	Sample Description	Intervention(s)	Control(s)	Follow-up and Outcomes	Intervention Effects[*]
Campbell et al (1996)[139]	238 patients from an outpatient DM education center, mean age = 59, 52% female	1: 2 initial 1-on-1 DM education sessions followed by 12 1-on-1 monthly sessions 2: 2 initial 1-on-1 DM education sessions plus a 3-d group course; 2 group follow-ups at 3 and 9 mo 3: 1-on-1 visits from a nurse educator using cognitive-behavioral strategies: at minimum, 3 in mo 1 and 1 each in mo 3, 6, and 12; phone calls from educator; emphasized cardiovascular risk and DM education topics	2, 1-on-1 sessions in the initial weeks of participation covering DM education topics, but in less depth	f.u. = 3, 6, and 12 mo for IG1-IG3; 3 and 6 mo for CG HbA$_{1c}$, BMI, lipid levels, blood pressure, health service use, cholesterol risk ratio (total cholesterol/HDLC), foot care, patient satisfaction, DM knowledge	IG3 had a greater reduction in mean diastolic blood pressure (−7.9 mm Hg) than IG1 (−5.0 mm Hg) and IG2 (−5.3 mm Hg, $p = .022$); IG3 had a greater reduction in mean cholesterol risk ratio over 3 mo (−1.13) than IG1 (−0.42), IG2 (−0.15), and CG (−0.29, $p = .011$); IG3 was more likely to have visited a podiatrist after 6 mo (65%) than IG1 (53%), IG2 (33%), or CG (27%, $p = .005$); IG3 reported greater satisfaction than other groups; IG2 and IG3 had greater improvements in DM knowledge than IG1 and CG; no other differences

Table 13-9 Multiple Risk-Factor Intervention Studies — *(continued)*

Studies of Type 2 Patients

Investigator(s)	Sample Description	Intervention(s)	Control(s)	Follow-up and Outcomes	Intervention Effects*
D'Eramo-Melkus et al (1992)[140]	49 community volunteers, mean age = 57, 22 females	1: 11 weekly cognitive behavioral group education and weight-reduction sessions; in week 4, patients received one individual session for content clarification 2: same intervention as IG1 plus 6 1-on-1 follow-up sessions	1 1-on-1 skill-based educational session	f.u. = 3 and 6 mo HbA$_{1c}$, FPG, weight	Greater decreases in mean HbA$_{1c}$ in IG1 (−1.55%) and IG2 (−2.89%) than CG (−0.40%, group by time interaction $p < .05$); greater decreases in mean FPG in IG1 (−2.14 mg/dL) and IG2 (−3.18 mg/dL) than CG (0.84 mg/dL, group by time interaction $p < .05$); no difference in weight
Glasgow et al (1992)[141]	102 community volunteers, mean age = 67, 63% female	DM education program (dietary and self-care behaviors) 10 group sessions, weekly for 8 wk followed by 2 meetings held at 2-wk intervals	Usual care	f.u. = 3 mo HbA$_{1c}$, percent of calories from fat, caloric consumption, weight	IG had a significant decrease in mean HbA$_{1c}$ (0.5%, $p < .05$) while CG did not; IG had a greater decrease in mean percentage of calories from fat (−3.6%) than CG (.3%, no p value given); IG had a greater decrease in mean daily caloric intake (−163.4 kcal) than CG (49.9 kcal, no p value given); IG had greater decrease in mean weight (−5.8 lb, $p < .05$) than CG (1.4 lb, not significant)

Table 13-9 Multiple Risk-Factor Intervention Studies — (continued)

Studies of Type 2 Patients

Investigator(s)	Sample Description	Intervention(s)	Control(s)	Follow-up and Outcomes	Intervention Effects*
Kirkman et al (1994)[142]	275 general medicine patients, mean age = 64, 1% female	1 or more monthly nurse telephone calls emphasizing regimen compliance and behavioral changes	Usual care	f.u. = 12 mo Weight, diet, exercise, lipid levels, smoking status, referrals	More IG patients had appropriate referrals; no other differences
Mazzuca et al (1986)[21]	275 patients from a general medicine clinic, mean age = 79, 79% female	Up to 7 modules of patient education (lecture, discussion, audiovisual, skill exercises, and behavior modification techniques), some patients' physicians received an educational program	Usual care	f.u. = 14 mo HbA_{1c}, FPG, serum creatinine, blood pressure, DM knowledge, weight, self-care, regimen compliance	IG had a greater decrease in mean HbA_{1c} (-0.43%) than CG (0.35%, $p < .05$), mean FPG (-27.5 mg/dL) than CG (-2.8 mg/dL, $p < .05$), serum creatinine levels (-0.05 mg/dL) than CG (0.06 mg/dL, $p < .05$), and blood pressure than CG ($p < .05$); IG had a greater increase in self-care and compliance; intervention effects were greater when physicians received DM education
Mulrow et al (1987)[143]	120 patients from DM clinics, mean age = 53, 55% female	1: 6 monthly education sessions with videotapes 2: 6 monthly education sessions without videotapes	Usual care	f.u. = 11 mo HbA_{1c} and weight	No differences

Table 13-9 Multiple Risk-Factor Intervention Studies — *(continued)*

Studies of Type 2 Patients

Investigator(s)	Sample Description	Intervention(s)	Control(s)	Follow-up and Outcomes	Intervention Effects*
Pieber et al (1995)[71]	94 general medicine patients, mean age = 65, 56% female	4 weekly group sessions on topics such as urine testing, diet, exercise, weight reduction, and foot care Nonrandomized controlled trial	Usual care	f.u. = 6 mo HbA_{1c}, oral hypoglycemic agent (OHG) treatment, BMI, blood pressure, lipid levels, foot problems, urine testing, DM-related knowledge, cost of care	IG had a greater decrease in mean HbA_{1c} (−1.61%) than CG (−0.23%, $p < .01$); IG rates of OHG treatment decreased from 38 to 45 ($p < .05$) while CG rates remained unchanged; IG had a greater mean decrease in BMI (−1.86) than CG (−.28, $p < .01$); IG had a greater mean diastolic blood pressure decrease (−10.9 mm Hg) than CG (−0.3 mm Hg, $p = .05$); IG had reduced lipid levels ($p < .006$) while CG lipid levels remained unchanged; IG had fewer calluses (49%) than CG (82%), foot skin problems (49%) than CG (65%), and nail trimming problems (27%) than CG (92%), (all $p < .05$); mean health care costs were reduced by UK£33 in IG, costs increased by £30 in CG
Weinberger et al (1995)[133]	275 general medicine patients, mean age = 64, 1% female	Monthly nurse-initiated phone calls focusing on patient education and health-status monitoring	Usual care	f.u. = 12 mo HbA_{1c}, FPG, symptoms, health-related quality of life	IG had lower mean HbA_{1c} (10.5%) than CG (11.1%, $p = .046$); IG had lower mean FPG (174.1 mg/dL) than CG (193.1 mg/dL, $p = .11$); no other differences

Table 13–9 Multiple Risk-Factor Intervention Studies — *(continued)*

Studies of Both Type 1 and Type 2 Patients or Type Unspecified

Investigator(s)	Sample Description	Intervention(s)	Control(s)	Follow-up and Outcomes	Intervention Effects*
Aubert et al (1998)[134]	100 patients, mean age = 53, 40% female	Nurse case management	Usual care	f.u. = 12 mo HbA$_{1c}$, FPG, weight, blood pressure, lipid levels, hypoglycemic symptoms, health service use, patient-perceived health status	IG had a greater decrease in mean HbA$_{1c}$ (−1.7%) than CG (−0.6%, $p < .001$); IG had a greater decrease in mean FPG (−43 mg/dL) than CG (−15 mg/dL, $p = .003$); IG patients had a better perception of their health status; no other differences
Bloomgarden et al (1987)[69]	226 patients from a DM specialty clinic, mean age = 58, 64% female	9 education sessions	Usual care	f.u. = 1.5 yr HbA$_{1c}$, FPG, blood pressure, foot lesions, lipid levels, health service use, BMI, DM knowledge and behavior	IG showed greater improvements in DM knowledge and behavior; no other differences
Gilden et al (1992)[144]	32 men from a DM clinic, mean age = 68	1: 6 weekly DM education sessions 2: same DM education program + 18 months of support group sessions Nonrandomized, matched control	Usual care	f.u. = 6 wk, 24 mo HbA$_{1c}$, FPG, DM knowledge, quality of life, depression	IG2 (6.6%) had lower mean HbA$_{1c}$ than CG (8.4%, $p < .05$) but no difference from IG1; IG2 had lower mean FPG (153 mg/dL) than CG (263 mg/dL, $p < .01$) but no difference from IG1; IG2 had higher DM knowledge and quality of life scores than IG1 and CG; IG2 had lower rates of depression than IG1 and CG

Table 13-9 Multiple Risk-Factor Intervention Studies — *(continued)*

Studies of Both Type 1 and Type 2 Patients or Type Unspecified

Investigator(s)	Sample Description	Intervention(s)	Control(s)	Follow-up and Outcomes	Intervention Effects[*]
Glasgow et al (1996)[157]	206 primary care clinic patients, mean age = 62, 62% female	Clinic-based touch-screen computer-assisted assessment providing patients and clinicians with reports about self-care problems, goals, and barriers; follow-up phone calls and take-home videos	Usual care	f.u. = 3 mo HbA$_{1c}$, serum cholesterol, dietary behavior, patient satisfaction	IG patients had a greater decrease in mean serum cholesterol (−9 mg/dL) than CG (8 mg/dL, $p < .001$); IG had greater improvements in dietary behavior and a greater increase in satisfaction; no other differences
Glasgow et al (1997)[158]	Same study as above	Same study as above	Same study as above	f.u. = 1 yr HbA$_{1c}$, serum cholesterol, dietary behavior, patient satisfaction	Effects on serum cholesterol, dietary behavior, and patient satisfaction maintained at 1 y
Greenfield et al (1988)[132]	59 patients from outpatient DM and general medicine clinics, mean age = 50, 51% female	Before physician visit, clinic assistant reviewed chart with patient and encouraged the patient to negotiate medical decisions with physician; intervention repeated at the next visit	Usual care	f.u. = 12 wk HbA$_{1c}$, patient participation in care measured via audiotape	More patients in IG had decreases in HbA$_{1c}$ (26 of 33) than in CG (8 of 26, $p < .01$); IG had greater participation in care
Korhonen et al (1983)[145]	77 community volunteers, mean age = 33, 46% female	Individual and small-group instruction from a team of physicians, nurses, and a dietitian	Two 30-min 1-on-1 sessions with a physician, one 1-on-1 session with a nurse, printed materials	f.u. = 6 mo and 18 mo post-intervention FPG, DM knowledge, diet, urine testing, urine glucose excretion	No differences

Table 13–9 Multiple Risk-Factor Intervention Studies — (continued)

Studies of Both Type 1 and Type 2 Patients or Type Unspecified

Investigator(s)	Sample Description	Intervention(s)	Control(s)	Follow-up and Outcomes	Intervention Effects*
Piette et al (2000)[63]	248 patients, mean age = 54, 59% female	Biweekly automated assessment and self-care education calls with telephone follow-up by a nurse educator	Usual care	f.u. = 12 mo HbA$_{1c}$, FPG, symptoms, self-care compliance	IG had somewhat lower mean HbA$_{1c}$ (8.1%) than CG (8.4%, $p = 0.1$); IG had a lower mean FPG (180 mg/dL) than CG (221 mg/dL, $p = .002$); IG had fewer mean symptoms (4.0) than CG (5.4, $p < .0001$); IG reported more frequent BGSM, foot care, and fewer medication compliance problems (all $p < .03$)
Piette et al (2000)[164]	Same study as above	Same study as above	Same study as above	f.u. = 12 mo Depressive symptoms, self-efficacy, satisfaction with care, days in bed due to illness, anxiety, health-related quality of life	IG reported fewer depressive symptoms, greater self-efficacy and satisfaction with care, and fewer days in bed due to illness (all $p < .05$); no other differences
Rettig et al (1986)[24]	373 inpatients, mean age = 52, 67% female	1 to 12 sessions of post-discharge individualized self-care instruction from a home health care nurse	Usual care	f.u. = 6 and 12 mo Foot problems, health care use, sick-days, self-care	IG had greater improvements in self-care than CG; no other differences

Table 13–9 Multiple Risk-Factor Intervention Studies — *(continued)*

Studies of Both Type 1 and Type 2 Patients or Type Unspecified

Investigator(s)	Sample Description	Intervention(s)	Control(s)	Follow-up and Outcomes	Intervention Effects*
Sadur et al (1999)[146]	142 HMO patients, mean age = 53, 42% female	Cluster outpatient DM management visits with a multidisciplinary team that included a nurse educator, psychologist, nutritionist, and pharmacist	Usual care	f.u. = 6 mo and health service use at 12 mo HbA_{1c} self-care, self-efficacy, satisfaction, health service use	IG had a greater decline in HbA_{1c} (-1.3%) than CG (-0.2%, $p < .0001$); IG had higher levels of self-care, self-efficacy, and satisfaction than CG; IG had fewer hospital stays and outpatient visits than CG (both $p = .04$)
Smith et al (1986)[147]	859 patients from general medicine clinics, mean age = 59, 74% female	Mailed information and intensive follow-up of visit failures	Usual care	f.u. = 12 mo Provider contacts	IG had a greater mean number of provider contacts (5.8) than CG (5.2, $p = .01$)
Tu et al (1993)[148]	27 hospitalized patients, mean age = 65, 18 females	Telephone educational intervention at 4 weeks post-discharge	Usual care	f.u. = 6 wk HbA_{1c}, DM self-care knowledge and behavior	IG had better DM self-care behavior; no other differences
de Weerdt et al (1989)[149]	516 outpatient clinic patients, mean age = 44, 50% female	1: 4 weekly group sessions on DM self-care led by a professional health care worker 2: 4 weekly group sessions led by a patient	Usual care	f.u. = 7 mo DM knowledge, locus of control, attitude, self-reported self-care	IG1 and IG2 had a greater increase in DM knowledge and locus of control; IG1 and IG2 had a somewhat greater improvement in attitude and self-care behavior

Table 13-9 Multiple Risk-Factor Intervention Studies — (continued)

Investigator(s)	Sample Description	Intervention(s)	Control(s)	Follow-up and Outcomes	Intervention Effects*
		Studies of Both Type 1 and Type 2 Patients or Type Unspecified			
Wise et al (1986)[150]	174 patients from a DM clinic, mean age = 50	1: 2 sessions with a computer-based, multiple-choice knowledge assessment program (KAP) 2: 2 KAP assessments with prescriptive feedback 3: 2 KAP assessments and 1 interactive computer teaching session including text and animated graphics	Usual care	f.u. = 2 mo HbA$_{1c}$ and diabetes knowledge	IG1–IG3 had greater mean decreases in HbA$_{1c}$ (0.9%, $p < .05$) than CG (0.2%, $p > 0.1$); IG1–IG3 had greater improvements in knowledge
Wood (1989)[151]	93 hospitalized patients, mean age = 60, 53% female	2 session inpatient DM education program	Usual care	f.u. = 1 and 4 mo FPG, insulin use, health service use, self-reported self-care behaviors	More IG patients (38 of 53) had a decrease in FPG than CG (23 of 40, $p = .10$); more IG patients (23 of 53) had reduced insulin use than CG (13 of 40, no p value given); fewer IG patients (2 of 53) had health service usage than CG (20 of 40, $p = .005$); IG had higher levels of compliance with self-care behaviors

*Unless otherwise noted, intervention effects are measured as the difference between follow-up intervention and control group values. Unless otherwise noted in the "Intervention(s)" column, studies are randomized controlled trials.

BGSM = blood glucose self-monitoring; CG = control group; DM = diabetes mellitus; FPG = fasting plasma glucose; f.u. = follow-up; IG = intervention group; HDLC = high-density lipoprotein cholesterol; BMI = body mass index; OHG = oral hypoglycemic agent.

Table 13–10 Potential Uses of Information Technology in Diabetes Care

For Patients	For Clinicians
Recommendations for preventive actions along with their rationale, ranked by risk-reduction potential and personal preferences	Prioritized summaries of patient health risk and health care problems for individual patients or for panels of patients with similar characteristics
Information to aid in self-care decision-making, tailored to patients' key concerns and level of information desired; reminders to assist in adherence to complex medication and self-examination schedules	Customized summaries of guidelines and recommended preventive services relevant to each patient; feedback reports on level of preventive services delivered across patients; point-of-service prompts and reminders to perform needed services
Information about active prescriptions, drug interactions, and other medication issues available 24 h/d	Lists of drugs prescribed by all clinicians; warnings for potential interactions; suggestions for cost-saving alternatives
Peer and health care team support; opportunities for sharing personal coping strategies	Remote consultations with colleagues and patients

Adapted from Glasgow RE, McKay HG, Boles SM, Vogt TM. Interactive computer technology, behavioral science, and family practice. J Fam Pract 1999;48:464–70.

In the technology-based approach to patient-centered self-management developed by Glasgow and colleagues, researchers focused on multiple dietary and cardiovascular risk factors.[157] The intervention centered around the use of a touch-screen computer located in the clinic waiting room and used by patients prior to scheduled outpatient visits. The intervention included the following components: (1) a 15-minute computerized assessment to help patients select a specific self-management goal and identify barriers to accomplishing this goal; (2) immediate scoring and printing of two tailored feedback reports summarizing the information (one for the patient and one for the physician); (3) a motivational message from the physician emphasizing the importance of the goal the patient had selected; (4) a 15- to 20-minute meeting with a health educator to review patients' goals and collaboratively develop barriers-based intervention strategies; and (5) two brief follow-up phone calls from the health educator to check on patients' progress. This sequence was repeated at a 3-month follow-up visit. Compared to a stringent, randomized control condition in which patients received the same computerized assessment (but no tailored feedback) and physician encouragement, the intervention improved outcomes for a variety of dietary behavior measures as well as serum cholesterol levels. Results were maintained at essentially the same level (eg, adjusted difference of 16 mg/dL in serum cholesterol) at a 12-month follow-up, and the intervention was found to be cost effective. On average, the annual incremental cost of the intervention was US$115 to $139 per patient and US$8.40 per unit reduction in serum cholesterol.[158]

Piette and colleagues evaluated the use of biweekly automated assessment and self-care education calls with follow-up over the telephone by a diabetes nurse educator.[159] They found that patients reported health and behavioral information using automated calls over an extended period,[160–161] that many patients used such calls to access self-care education, and that the information patients reported could be used to identify individuals at greatest risk for developing problems.[162] Outcomes measured at 12 months indicated that the intervention improved patients' self-care in the areas of BGSM, foot care, weight self-monitoring, and medication adherence.[163] The study also found decreases in HbA$_{1c}$ levels, serum glucose levels, and diabetes-related symptoms. Patients receiving the intervention were more satisfied with their health care than control patients, had greater confidence in their ability to perform self-care activities, and reported fewer symptoms of depression.[164] The intervention had no impact on health-related quality of life measured using a general instrument or a diabetes-specific instrument. Among subgroups of patients with the greatest need for preventive services (eye examinations and foot examinations), those receiving the intervention were more likely to be seen in appropriate specialty clinics during the follow-up year.

EVIDENCE-BASED MESSAGES

Based on the available literature, the following conclusions can be drawn about the effectiveness of educational interventions with multiple outcome targets:

1. Traditional knowledge-based diabetes education improves patient knowledge but is not sufficient to produce behavior change (Level 1A).[13,14]
2. Patient-centered interventions that are tailored to patient preferences and social environment and that actively engage patients in managing their diabetes through coping-skills training appear to be the most effective approaches to diabetes self-management (Level 2).[131,132,165]
3. Follow-up support is important to enhance maintenance of intervention effects (Level 2).[133]
4. The principles above have been successfully incorporated into practical clinical interventions, often coordinated by nurse case managers (Level 2).[134,146]
5. Information technologies can effectively supplement care and improve diabetes behavioral and health outcomes (Level 2).[157,163]

WHAT IS THE ROLE OF CLINICIANS IN SUPPORTING EFFECTIVE SELF-CARE?

Health systems and the clinicians they employ play vital roles as collaborators with patients in their self-management. In a 2-year longitudinal study, investigators found that patients' adherence to prescribed treatment was related to physicians' job satisfaction, the number of patients they saw per week, whether they scheduled a follow-up visit, their tendency to answer patients' questions, and the number of tests they ordered.[166] With regard to BGSM, clinicians can assist patients in interpreting their BGSM readings and recommend adjustments in their diet, exercise, or medication regimen. Often this process requires an ongoing dialogue so that barriers to glucose testing are addressed, observations are collected and recorded accurately, and BGSM data are communicated effectively to the care team. Blood glucose awareness training should also occur in conjunction with a concrete and explicit plan for communicating with clinicians about episodes of hyperglycemia and hypoglycemia. Foot care is an area where system-based clinician involvement may be particularly critical, because the interpretation of signs and symptoms of developing foot problems may be unclear while they are in early, reversible stages. Thus, providers play the dual role of supporting patients' ability to manage their foot care independently and alerting them to times when they may need to seek professional help. Many patients who fail to adhere to medication regimens do so knowingly because of cost concerns or to avoid perceived side effects or drug-drug reactions. Clinicians' input is essential in counseling such patients and, when appropriate, altering their treatment plans. It is also essential that providers be aware of patients' own self-management goals in areas such as diet and physical activity so that treatment plans can be coordinated across areas and among team members.

WHAT ARE APPROPRIATE ENDPOINTS FOR EVALUATING SELF-CARE INTERVENTIONS?

In the 1970s and 1980s, most evaluations of diabetes self-management education limited their focus to patient knowledge or HbA_{1c}.[167,168] We now know that outcomes of patient education are multidimensional and that evaluation measures should be as well.[168] Evaluating the process of implementing an intervention is important to understanding how it achieves, or fails to achieve, its intended effects. Behavior change outcomes are important in their own right, since they are the proximal targets of patient education, with several behaviors such as smoking cessation, physical activity, and nutritional habits being independent disease risk factors.[169] Health-related quality of life is considered by many to be the ultimate outcome of diabetes management and an important predictor of mortality, independent of physiologic factors.[170] In the current age of cost containment, the need for measures of impact on utilization and cost are self-evident, although almost none of the studies reviewed here discussed cost implications explicitly. Finally, we need to know much more about effectiveness results in practice settings, including the reach of and attrition rates produced by different interventions.[171]

WHAT INTERVENTIONS EXIST THAT TARGET PATIENTS WITH DIABETES AND OTHER CHRONIC DISEASES?

There is a recent trend in the research and delivery of disease-management services toward greater emphasis on interventions that can address the needs of patients with multiple chronic illnesses simultaneously. Such interventions can focus on "generic" disease-management issues, such as medication adherence, and also use systematic changes in the delivery of care to more efficiently address patients' disease-specific problems.

One innovative approach to redesigning the medical office visit has been employed with older chronically ill patients in the Denver Kaiser Permanente system. Rather than seeing patients in the usual 10- to 15-minute individual session, primary care is provided through monthly 90-minute group visits. These sessions, run by a physician and nurse coordinator, incorporate vital sign assessments, medication checks, and other elements of care into group sessions that also provide a forum for discussion of self-management topics and peer support. Beck and colleagues evaluated this approach relative to traditional physician-patient dyadic care in a 1-year randomized trial with 321 chronically ill seniors.[172] They found that the group visit participants had fewer emergency department visits, visits to subspecialists, and repeat hospitalizations. Both patients and physicians reported greater satisfaction with the group visits than usual care, and the cost of the group visits averaged US$15 per month less per member. Similar results, including encouraging effects on glycemic control, satisfaction, health care utilization, and costs of care, have been reported in a randomized trial by Sadur and colleagues,[146] using a combination of nurse care management and cluster visits similar to the program by Beck and colleagues.

One study of another promising intervention demonstrates that even novel disease management interventions can be ineffective in the absence of institutional support.[173] Elderly patients receiving the intervention participated in support groups as well as extended visits with physicians and pharmacists. After 2 years, there were no demonstrated impacts on outcomes of geriatric care such as incontinence, falls, or prescriptions to high-risk medications, suggesting that interventions such as this may be nullified if system-wide support for disease management is absent.

Lorig and colleagues have demonstrated repeatedly that chronic disease management services can be effective when provided by nonclinician peers. In their earlier studies, these investigators developed a peer-led arthritis self-management program and found it to be superior to usual care in randomized trials.[174] Recently, they have adapted their program for patients with diabetes and other chronic illnesses and conducted a study indicating lasting reductions in pain, physician visits, and cost relative to randomized controls.[175] In another community-based study, elderly patients received disability prevention and disease self-management education in a seniors center.[176] Individuals receiving the intervention had substantially less decline in physical function, greater levels of physical activity, and less reliance on psychoactive medications than randomized controls. Intervention patients also had fewer hospital admissions and days of hospital care.

Common elements across these diverse interventions seem to be a patient-centered approach that individualizes self-management and goal setting, provides strategies and models for coping with barriers, and, importantly, some form of follow-up support that either replaces or supplements that available through usual primary care.

WHAT ARE THE DIRECTIONS FOR FUTURE RESEARCH?

Tables 13–3, 13–5, 13–6, and 13–9 show clearly that most self-management education trials are small; many are underpowered for definitive conclusions. Rigorous application of quantitative meta-analytic techniques[177] should be applied to glean as much information as possible from studies that have been completed. Perhaps most importantly, investigators must pursue larger studies with longer-term follow-ups. These projects may be fostered through creative collaborations across research centers or between university-based investigators and health care provider organizations. Large behavioral studies are expensive, and greater funding for them by foundations and government agencies is encouraged.

Diabetes self-management intervention studies must be developed with an awareness of the factors increasing the likelihood that effective services will have a significant public health impact. For new interventions to be adopted, investigators must learn more about extant health care systems and the ways in which a new intervention fits within a given treatment framework. The issue of costs must be addressed either through demonstrating cost effects directly or using data from other research to estimate what those effects might be. Moreover, the applicability of novel treatments within ethnic minority and low-income groups should be demonstrated, ideally by including large enough samples of such patients for separate examination.

Finally, most intervention evaluations focus on efficacy only, that is, impacts within the relatively rarified confines of the randomized trial. Substantial changes in the lives of people with diabetes can only be achieved with a broader conceptual framework for defining "success." Specifically, investigators should consider additional factors such as the reach of the intervention, its adoption by provider organizations, the ways in which it is implemented in the "real world," and whether or not the intervention is maintained over time. Directions for future research are outlined in Table 13–11.

CONCLUSION

Because of the multiple intervention strategies and patient behaviors addressed, diabetes self-management education is a complex "treatment" to evaluate. Nevertheless, some general conclusions are possible based on the studies presented in this chapter.

It is clear that some types of interventions are effective while many have little or no impact on their target outcomes. Common themes among effective interventions are that they tend to include individually tailored interactions with patients and focus on increasing their involvement in active problem solving (Table 13–12). The "one-size-fits-all" strategy exemplified by the distribution of standard informational brochures or videotapes is unlikely to have any impact unless coupled with other approaches. Compared to one-time interventions delivered during an inpatient stay or outpatient education session, multiple follow-up sessions result in greater behavior change as well as the maintenance of changed behaviors. Another finding that may be less clinically intuitive is that group sessions can be at least as effective as one-to-one interactions between patients and clinicians. The effectiveness of groups is bolstered through the group dynamic itself, which includes mutual emotional support, identification with others' problems, and peer pressure to follow through with agreed-upon behavioral changes.

Interventions that include changing systems of care (eg, adding reminders to clinicians regarding foot examinations) tend to be more effective than interventions focused only on patients' behavior. System changes reflecting the belief that patients are key players in their diabetes management are probably the best approach. Such interventions will be most effective if they treat patients holistically by coordinating efforts at glycemic control with their other goals such as promoting smoking cessation and treatment for affective disorders. In the absence of true system-wide support, even creative and aggressive intervention efforts may not have a significant impact on patient outcomes.

Table 13–11 Directions for Future Research

Apply quantitative meta-analysis techniques to current studies

Pursue larger studies with longer follow-up times

Demonstrate economic impacts

Show applicability of novel strategies to ethnic minority and low-income groups

Broaden conception of success to include "real-world" feasibility, eg, adoption by providers and implementation by institutions

---

Table 13–12 Characteristics of Effective Diabetes Self-Management Education

Extensive use of behavior change theories

Communication styles that encourage patients to participate in setting treatment goals

Follow-up reinforcement at regular intervals

Hands-on demonstrations and monitored practice to augment didactic instructions

Linking patient education with provider reinforcement, eg, chart reminders and system delivery changes

Simplification of self-care regimens, eg, diet and medication regimens

Feedback to heighten awareness of hypo- and hyperglycemic symptoms

Use of computerized aids to augment the role of the diabetes educator and dietitian

Involvement of family and significant others

Peer support for goal achievement

SUMMARY OF EVIDENCE-BASED MESSAGES

There are a number of interventions that can assist patients with diabetes in improving their self-care. Interventions have been identified that improve glycemic control; decrease symptoms, complication rates, and use of acute care; and increase the appropriate use of preventive care. Interventions that promote BGSM have the least evidence of effectiveness, while there is strong evidence that foot self-care education can decrease podiatric problems. There are a variety of low-cost interventions that can improve patients' adherence to oral hypoglycemic medications; smoking cessation counseling is clearly important.

1. Although it is essential that Type 1 patients monitor themselves for episodes of extreme hyperglycemia and hypoglycemia, there is little evidence suggesting that frequent BGSM (eg, 4 times/d) improves Type 1 patients' mean glycemic control more than less frequent BGSM or urine testing (Level 1A).

2. There is no evidence that BGSM contributes to better glycemic control among Type 2 patients (Level 1A).

3. Blood glucose self-monitoring may not affect glycemic control because of patients' difficulty obtaining accurate measures, difficulty reporting BGSM data to clinicians, or lack of an impact on clinicians' behavior. More efficient reporting of BGSM to clinicians appears to have no effect on patients' glycemic control (Level 2).

4. Available evidence indicates that a formal, structured, educational intervention can improve Type 1 patients' ability to identify episodes of hypoglycemia and hyperglycemia and may restore patients' epinephrine response to hypoglycemia (Level 2).

5. Foot care education is an effective means of improving patients' foot care behavior (Level 1A).

6. Foot care education reduces the incidence of minor foot problems such as calluses as well as major problems such as infections and amputations (Level 1A).

7. Foot care education can be more effective if it includes motivational counseling, skill-based training, and simultaneous education and reminders to physicians (Level 3).

8. Computerized decision-support systems to inform insulin adjustments may improve some outcomes (Level 2).

9. Although studies specifically addressing adherence to oral hypoglycemic medications have not been conducted, studies in other disease areas indicate that there are a variety of simple devices and educational interventions to assist patients in adhering to oral medication regimens (Level 2).

10. Interventions to help patients quit smoking increase cessation rates (Level 1A).

11. There is no evidence that smoking cessation is more or less effective among patients with diabetes than among patients with other conditions (Level 3).

12. Even brief advice to quit smoking produces increased quit rates, but behavioral counseling accompanied by pharmacologic therapy and ongoing support achieves the greatest reductions (Level 1A).

13. Traditional knowledge-based diabetes education improves patient knowledge but is not sufficient to produce behavior change (Level 1A).

14. Patient-centered interventions that are tailored to patient preferences and social environment and that actively engage patients in managing their diabetes through coping-skills training appear to be the most effective approaches to diabetes self-management (Level 2).

15. Follow-up support is important to enhance maintenance of intervention effects (Level 2).

16. The principles above have been successfully incorporated into practical clinical interventions, often coordinated by nurse case managers (Level 2).

17. Information technologies can effectively supplement care and improve diabetes behavioral and health outcomes (Level 2).

REFERENCES

1. Glasgow RE, Anderson RM. In diabetes care, moving from compliance to adherence is not enough: something entirely different is needed. Diabetes Care 1999;22:2090–7.

2. Etzwiler DD. Chronic care: a need in search of a system. Diabetes Educ 1997;23:569–73.

3. Diabetes Control and Complications Trial Research Group. The effect of intensive treatment of diabetes on the development and progression of long-term complications in insulin-dependent diabetes mellitus. N Engl J Med 1993;329:977–86.

4. UK Prospective Diabetes Study (UKPDS) Group. Intensive blood-glucose control with sulphonylureas or insulin compared with conventional treatment and risk of complications in patients with type 2 diabetes (UKPDS 33). Lancet 1998;352:837–53.

5. Goodnick PJ, Henry JH, Buki VM. Treatment of depression in patients with diabetes mellitus. J Clin Psychiatry 1995;56:128–36.

6. Lernmark B, Persson B, Fisher L, Rydelius PA. Symptoms of depression are important to psychological adaptation and metabolic control in children with diabetes mellitus. Diabet Med 1999;16:14–22.

7. Kohen D, Burgess AP, Catalan J, Lant A. The role of anxiety and depression in quality of life and symptom reporting in people with diabetes. Qual Life Res 1998;7:197–204.

8. Davis WK, Hess GE, Hiss RG. Psychological correlates of survival in diabetes. Diabetes Care 1988;11:538–45.

9. Lustman PJ, Griffith LS, Freedland KE, et al. Cognitive behavior therapy for depression in type 2 diabetes mellitus. A randomized, controlled trial. Ann Intern Med 1998;129:613–21.

10. Kaplan RM, Davis WK. Evaluating the costs and benefits of outpatient diabetes education and nutrition counseling. Diabetes Care 1986;9:81–6.

11. Brown SA. Effects of educational interventions in diabetes care: a meta-analysis of findings. Nurs Res 1988;37:223–30.

12. Brown SA. Diabetes patient education interventions and outcomes: a meta-analysis revisited. Patient Educ Couns 1990;16:189–215.

13. Brown SA. Meta-analysis of diabetes patient education research: variations in intervention effects across studies. Res Nurs Health 1992;15:409–19.

14. Clement S. Diabetes self-management education. Diabetes Care 1995;18:1204–14.

15. Padgett D, Mumford E, Hynes M, Carter R. Meta-analysis of the effects of educational and psychosocial interventions on management of diabetes mellitus. J Clin Epidemiol 1988;41:1007–30.

16. Walker EA, Cypress ML. Self-monitoring: the patient-practitioner alliance. Nurse Pract Forum 1991;2:175–7.

17. Butler RN, Rubenstein AH, Gracia A-MG, Zweig SC. Type 2 diabetes: patient education and home blood glucose monitoring. Geriatrics 1998;53:62–7.

18. Harris MI, Cowie CC, Howie LJ. Self-monitoring of blood glucose by adults with diabetes in the United States population. Diabetes Care 1993;16:1116–23.

19. Nagasawa M, Smith MC, Barnes JH Jr. Meta-analysis of correlates of diabetes patients' compliance with prescribed medications. Diabetes Educ 1990;16:192–200.

20. Ruggiero L, Glasgow RE, Dryfous JM, et al. Diabetes self-management: self-reported recomendations and patterns in a large population. Diabetes Care 1997;20:568–78.

21. Mazzuca SA, Moorman NH, Wheeler ML, et al. The diabetes education study: a controlled trial of the effects of diabetes patient education. Diabetes Care 1986;9:1–10.

22. Wing RR, Epstein LH, Nowalk MP, et al. Does self-monitoring of blood glucose levels improve dietary compliance for obese patients with Type 2 diabetes? Am J Med 1986;81:830–6.

23. White N, Carnahan J, Nugent CA, et al. Management of obese patients with diabetes mellitus: comparison of advice education with group management. Diabetes Care 1986;9:490–6.

24. Rettig BA, Shrauger DG, Recher RR, et al. A randomized study of the effects of a home diabetes education program. Diabetes Care 1986;9:173–8.

25. Wysocki T, Green L, Huxtable K. Blood glucose monitoring by diabetic adolescents: compliance and metabolic control. Health Psychol 1989;8:267–84.

26. Wolanski R, Sigman T, Polychronakos C. Assessment of blood glucose self-monitoring skills in a camp for diabetic children: the effects of individualized feedback counselling. Patient Educ Couns 1996;29:5–11.

27. Gallichan MJ. Self-monitoring by patients receiving oral hypoglycaemic agents: a survey and a comparative trial. Practical Diabetes 1994;11(1):28–30.

28. Moorish NJ, Cohen DL, Hicks B, Keen H. A controlled study of the effect of computer-aided analysis of home blood glucose monitoring on blood glucose control. Diabet Med 1989;6:591–4.

29. Daneman D, Siminerio L, Transue D, et al. The role of self-monitoring of blood glucose in the routine management of children with insulin-dependent diabetes mellitus. Diabetes Care 1985;8:1–4.

30. Gordon D, Semple CG, Paterson KR. Do different frequencies of self-monitoring of blood glucose influence control in Type 1 diabetic patients? Diabet Med 1991;8:679–82.

31. Glasgow RE, McCaul KD, Schafer LC. Self-care behaviors and glycemic control in Type 1 diabetes. J Chron Dis 1987;40:399–412.

32. Faas A, Schellevis FG, Van Ejik JTM. The efficacy of self-monitoring of blood glucose in NIDDM subjects: a criteria-based literature review. Diabetes Care 1997;20:1482–6.

33. Gallichan M. Self monitoring of glucose by people with diabetes: evidence-based practice. BMJ 1997;314:964–7.

34. Fontbonne A, Billault B, Acosta M, et al. Is glucose self-monitoring beneficial in non-insulin-treated diabetic patients? Results of a randomized comparative trial. Diabetes Metab 1989;15:255–60.

35. Allen BT, DeLohng ER, Feussner JR. Impact of glucose self-monitoring on non-insulin-treated patients with Type 2 diabetes mellitus. Randomized controlled trial comparing blood and urine testing. Diabetes Care 1990;13:1044–50.

36. Rutten G, van Elijk J, de Nobel E, et al. Feasibility and effects of a diabetes type 2 protocol with blood glucose self-monitoring in general practice. J Fam Pract 1990;7:273–8.

37. Estey AL, Tan MH, Mann K. Follow-up intervention: its effect on compliance behavior to a diabetes regimen. Diabetes Educ 1990;16:291–5.

38. Gallichan MJ. Self-monitoring by patients receiving oral hypoglycemic agents: a survey and a comparative trial. Practical Diabetes 1994;11:28–30.

39. Rindone JP, Austin M, Luchese J. Effect of home blood glucose monitoring on the management of patients with non-insulin dependent diabetes mellitus in the primary care setting. Am J Managed Care 1997;3:1335–8.

40. Morrish NJ, Cohen DL, Hicks B, Keen H. A controlled study of the effect of computer-aided analysis of home blood glucose monitoring on blood glucose control. Diabet Med 1989;6:591–4.

41. Marrero DG, Kronz KK, Golden MP, et al. Clinical evaluation of a computer-assisted self-monitoring of blood glucose system. Diabetes Care 1989;12:345–50.

42. Marrero DG, Vandagriff JL, Kronz K, et al. Using telecommunication technology to manage children with diabetes: the computer-linked outpatient clinic (CLOC) study. Diabetes Educ 1995;21:313–9.

43. Wysocki T. Impact of blood glucose monitoring on diabetic control: obstacles and interventions. J Behav Med 1989;12:183–205.

44. Bolinder J, Ungerstedt U, Hagstrom-Toft E, Arner P. Self-monitoring of blood glucose in Type 1 diabetic patients: comparison with continuous microdialysis measurements of glucose in subcutaneous adipose tissue during ordinary life conditions. Diabetes Care 1997;20:64–70.

45. Campbell LV, Ashwell SM, Borkmarr M, Chisholm DJ. White coat hyperglycemia: disparity between diabetes clinic and home blood glucose concentrations. BMJ 1992;305:1194–6.

46. Ho SSM, Nakahiro RK, Okamoto MP. Comparison of two brands of test strips for self-monitoring of blood glucose. Am J Health Syst Pharm 1997;54:1058–62.

47. Chan JCN, Wong RYM, Cheung C-K, et al. Accuracy, precision and user-acceptability of self blood glucose monitoring machines. Diabetes Res Clin Pract 1997;36:91–104.

48. Gonder-Frederick LA, Julian DM, Cox DJ, et al. Self-measurement of blood glucose. Accuracy of self-reported data and adherence to recommended regimen. Diabetes Care 1988;11:579–85.

49. Mazze RS, Pasmantier R, Murphy JA, Shamoon H. Self-monitoring of capillary blood glucose: changing the performance of individuals with diabetes. Diabetes Care 1985;8:207–13.

50. Karam J. Diabetes mellitus & hypoglycemia. In: Tierney L, McPhee S, Papadakis M, editors. Current medical diagnosis & treatment. Stanford: Prentice Hall International; 1999. p. 1152–97.

51. Cox DJ, Gonder-Frederick L, Clarke W. Driving decrements in Type 1 diabetes during moderate hypoglycemia. Diabetes 1993;42:239–43.

52. Veneman TF. Diabetes mellitus and traffic incidents. Neth J Med 1996;48:24–8.

53. Clarke WL, Cox DJ, Gonder-Frederick LA, Kovatchev B. Hypoglycemia and the decision to drive a motor vehicle by persons with diabetes. JAMA 1999;282:750–4.

54. Clarke WL, Cox DJ, Gonder-Frederick LA, et al. Reduced awareness of hypoglycemia in adults with IDDM. A prospective study of hypoglycemic frequency and associated symptoms. Diabetes Care 1995;18:517–22.

55. Ruggiero L, Kairys S, Fritz G, Wood M. Accuracy of blood glucose estimates in adolescents with diabetes mellitus. J Adolesc Health 1991;12:101–6.

56. Cox DJ, Clarke WL, Gonder-Frederick L, et al. Accuracy of perceiving blood glucose in IDDM. Diabetes Care 1985;8:529–36.

57. Mokan M, Mitrakou A, Veneman T, et al. Hypoglycemia unawareness in IDDM. Diabetes Care 1994;17:1397–403.

58. Cox DJ, Gonder-Frederick L, Clarke WL. Helping patients reduce severe hypoglycemia. In: Anderson BJ, Rubin RR, editors. Practical psychology for diabetes clinicians. Alexandria (VA): American Diabetes Association; 1996. p. 93–104.

59. Cox DJ, Gonder-Frederick LA, Lee JH, et al. Effects and correlates of blood glucose awareness training among patients with IDDM. Diabetes Care 1989;12:313–8.

60. Cox DJ, Gonder-Frederick L, Julian D, et al. Intensive versus standard blood glucose awareness training (BGAT) with insulin-dependent diabetes: mechanisms and ancillary effects. Psychosom Med 1991;53:453–62.

61. Cox DC, Gonder-Frederick L, Polonsky W, et al. A multicenter evaluation of blood-glucose awareness training. II. Diabetes Care 1995;18:523–7.

62. Cox DJ, Gonder-Frederick L, Julian DM, Clarke W. Long-term follow-up evaluation of blood glucose awareness training. Diabetes Care 1994;17:1–5.

63. Kinsley BT, Weinger K, Bajaj M, et al. Blood glucose awareness training and epinephrine responses to hypoglycemia during intensive treatment in Type 1 diabetes. Diabetes Care 1999;22:1022–8.

64. Mayfield JA, Reiber GE, Sanders LJ. Preventative foot care in people with diabetes. Diabetes Care 1988;21:2161–77.

65. Masson EA, Angle S, Roseman P, et al. Diabetic foot ulcers: do patients know how to protect themselves? Practical Diabetes 1989;6:22–3.

66. Reiber GE, Pecoraro RE, Koepsell TD. Risk factors for amputation in patients with diabetes mellitus. Ann Intern Med 1992;117:97–105.

67. Barth R, Campbell LV, Allen S, et al. Intensive education improves knowledge, compliance, and foot problems in type 2 diabetes. Diabet Med 1991;111–7.

68. Kruger S, Guthrie D. Foot care: knowledge retention and self-care practices. Diabetes Educ 1992;18:487–90.

69. Bloomgarden ZT, Karmally W, Metzger MJ, et al. Randomized, controlled trial of diabetic patient education: improved knowledge without improved metabolic status. Diabetes Care 1987;10:263–72.

70. Litzelman DK, Slemenda CW, Langefeld CD, et al. Reduction of lower extremity clinical abnormalities in patients with non-insulin-dependent diabetes mellitus. Ann Intern Med 1993;119:36–41.

71. Pieber TR, Holler A, Stebenhofer A, et al. Evaluation of a structured teaching and treatment programme for type 2 diabetes in general practice in a rural area of Austria. Diabet Med 1995;12:349–54.

72. Barth R, Campbell LV, Allen S, et al. Intensive education improves knowledge, compliance, and foot problems in type 2 diabetes. Diabet Med 1991;8:111–7.

73. Malone JM, Snyder M, Anderson G, et al. Prevention of amputation by diabetic education. Am J Surg 1989;158:520–4.

74. Crausaz FM, Clavel S, Liniger C, et al. Additional factors associated with plantar ulcers in diabetic neuropathy. Diabet Med 1988;5:771–5.

75. Thomson FJ, Masson EA. Can elderly diabetic patients co-operate with routine foot care? Age Aging 1992;21:333–7.

76. Uccioli L, Faglia E, Monticone G, et al. Manufactured shoes in the prevention of diabetic foot ulcers. Diabetes Care 1995;18:1376–8.

77. Wooldridge J, Bergeron J, Thornton C. Preventing diabetic foot disease: lessons from the Medicare therapeutic shoe demonstration. Am J Public Health 1996;86:935–8.

78. Clarke WL, Gonder-Frederick A, Snyder AL, Cox DJ. Maternal fear of hypoglycemia in their children with insulin dependent diabetes mellitus. J Pediatr Endocrinol Metab 1998;11 (Suppl 1):189–94.

79. Marrero DG, Guare JC, Vandagriff JL, Fineberg NS. Fear of hypoglycemia in the parents of children and adolescents with diabetes: maladaptive or healthy response? Diabetes Educ 1997;23:281–6.

80. Brown SJ, Lieberman DA, Gemeny BA, et al. Educational video game for juvenile diabetes: results of a controlled trial. Med Inform 1997;22(1):77–89.

81. Peters A, Rubsmen M, Jacob U, et al. Clinical evaluation of a decision support system for insulin-dose adjustment in IDDM. Diabetes Care 1991;14:875–80.

82. Chiarelli F, Tumini S, Guido M, Albisser AM. Controlled study in diabetic children comparing insulin-dosage adjustment by manual and computer algorithms. Diabetes Care 1990;13:1080–4.

83. Peterson CM, Jovanovic L, Chanoch LH. Randomized trial of computer-assisted insulin delivery in patients with type 1 diabetes beginning pump therapy. Am J Med 1986;81:69–72.

84. Mason BJ, Matsuyama JR, Jue SG. Assessment of sulfonylurea adherence and metabolic control. Diabetes Educ 1995;21:52–7.

85. Sclar DA, Robinson LM, Skaer TL, et al. Sulfonylurea pharmacotherapy regimen adherence in a Medicaid population: influence of age, gender, and race. Diabetes Educ 1999;25:531–8.

86. Eisen SA, Miller DK, Woodward RS, et al. The effect of prescribed daily dose frequency on patient medication compliance. Arch Intern Med 1990;150:1881–4.

87. McKenney JM, Munroe WP, Wright JT Jr. Impact of an electronic medication compliance aid on long-term blood pressure control. J Clin Pharmacol 1992;32:277–83.

88. Murray MD, Birt JA, Manatunga AK, Darnell JC. Medication compliance in elderly outpatients using twice-daily dosing and unit-of-use packaging. Ann Pharmacother 1993;27:616–21.

89. Laster SF, Martin JL, Fleming JB. The effect of a medication alarm device on patient compliance with topical pilocarpine. J Am Optom Assoc 1996;67:654–8.

90. Friedman RH, Kazis LE, Jette A. A telecommunications system for monitoring and counseling patients with hypertension. Impact on medication adherence and blood pressure control. Am J Hypertens 1996;9(4 Pt 1):285–92.

91. Leirer VO, Morrow DG, Tanke ED, Pariante GM. Elders' nonadherence: its assessment and medication reminding by voice mail. Gerontologist 1991;31:514–20.

92. Azrin NG, Teichner G. Evaluation of an instructional program for improving medication compliance for chronically mentally ill patients. Behav Res Ther 1998;36:849–61.

93. Esposito L. The effects of medication education on adherence to medication regimens in an elderly population. J Adv Nurs 1995;21:935–43.

94. Williford SL, Johnson DF. Impact of pharmacist counseling on medication knowledge and compliance. Mil Med 1995;160:561–4.

95. Powell KM, Edgren B. Failure of educational videotapes to improve medication compliance in a health maintenance organization. Am J Health Syst Pharm 1995;52:2196–9.

96. Rich MW, Gray MB, Beckham V, et al. Effect of a multidisciplinary intervention on medication compliance in elderly patients with congestive heart failure. Am J Med 1996;101:270–6.

97. Myers E, Branthwaite A. Outpatient compliance with antidepressant medication. Br J Psychiatry 1992;160:83–6.

98. Windsor RA, Bailey WC, Richards JM Jr, et al. Evaluation of the efficacy and cost effectiveness of health education methods to increase medication adherence among adults with asthma. Am J Public Health 1990;80:1519–21.

99. Fiore M, Bailey W, Cohen S. Smoking cessation. Clinical practice guideline number 18. Rockville(MD): Department of Health and Human Services (US), Public Health Service, Agency for Health Care Policy and Research; 1996.

100. Haire-Joshu D, Glasgow RE, Tibbs TL. Technical review: smoking and diabetes. Diabetes Care 1999;22:1887–98.

101. Ford E, Newman J. Smoking and diabetes mellitus: findings from The 1988 Behavioral Risk Factor Surveillance System. Diabetes Care 1991;14:871–4.

102. Ford E, Malarcher A, Herman W, Aubert R. Diabetes mellitus and cigarette smoking: findings from the 1989 National Health Interview Survey. Diabetes Care 1994;17:688–92.

103. UKPDS Group. UK prospective diabetes study (UKPDS) VIII: study design, progress, and performance. Diabetologia 1991;34:877–90.

104. Yudkin J. How can we best prolong life? Benefits of coronary risk factor reduction in non-diabetic and diabetic subjects. BMJ 1993;306:1313–8.

105. Mulhauser I. Cigarette smoking and diabetes: an update. Diabet Med 1994;11:336–43.

106. Mulhauser I, Bender R, Bott U, et al. Cigarette smoking and progression of retinopathy and nephropathy in type 1 diabetes. Diabet Med 1996;13:536–43.

107. Chase H, Garg S, Marshall G. Cigarette smoking increases the risk of albuminuria among subjects with Type 1 diabetes. JAMA 1991;265:614–7.

108. Ikeda Y, Suehiro T, Takamatsu K, et al. Effect of smoking on the prevalence of albuminuria in Japanese men with non-insulin-dependent diabetes mellitus. Diabetes Res Clin Pract 1997;36:57–61.

109. Corradi L, Zoppi A, Tettamanti F, et al. Association between smoking and micro-albuminuria in hypertensive patients with type 2 diabetes mellitus. J Hypertens 1993;11(Suppl 5):S190–1.

110. Chaturverdi N, Stevens L, Fuller J. Which features of smoking determine mortality risk in former cigarette smokers with diabetes. Diabetes Care 1997;20:1266–72.

111. Haire-Joshu D. Smoking cessation and the diabetes health care team. Diabetes Educ 1993;17:54–67.

112. Kottke T, Solberg L, Brekke M, et al. A controlled trial to integrate smoking cessation advice into primary care practice: doctors helping smokers round III. J Fam Pract 1992;2:701–8.

113. Hollis J, Lichtenstein E, Vogt T, et al. Nurse-assisted counseling for smokers in primary care. Ann Intern Med 1993;118:521–5.

114. Pirie P, McBride C, Hellerstedt W. Smoking cessation in women concerned about weight. Am J Public Health 1992;82:1238–43.

115. Curry S. Self-help interventions for smoking cessation. J Consult Clin Psychol 1993;61:790–803.

116. Lichtenstein E, Glasgow RE, Lando HA, et al. Telephone counseling for smoking cessation: rationales and review of evidence. Health Educ Res 1996;11:243–57.

117. Cepeda-Benito A. A meta-analytic review of the efficacy of nicotine chewing gum in smoking treatment program. J Consult Clin Psychol 1993;61:822–30.

118. Tang J, Law M, Wald N. How effective is nicotine replacement therapy in helping people to stop smoking? BMJ 1994;308:21–6.

119. Fiore M, Smith S, Jorenby D, Baker T. The effectiveness of the nicotine patch for smoking cessation: a meta-analysis. JAMA 1994;271:1940–7.

120. Sutherland G, Stapleton J, Russell M. Randomised controlled trial of nasal nicotine spray in smoking cessation. Lancet 1992;340:324–9.

121. Hurt R, Sachs D, Glover E. A comparison of sustained-release bupropion and placebo for smoking cessation. N Engl J Med 1997;337:1195–1202.

122. Haire-Joshu D. Smoking and diabetes care: enhancing patient capacity for cessation. Diabetes Spectrum 1997;10:99–104.

123. MacFarlane I. The smoker with diabetes: a difficult challenge. Postgrad Med 1991;67:928–30.

124. Stacy R, Lloyd B. An investigation of beliefs about smoking among diabetes patients: information for improving cessation efforts. Patient Educ Couns 1990;15:181–9.

125. Fowler P, Hoskins P, McGill M, et al. Anti-smoking programme for diabetic patients: the agony and the ectasy. Diabet Med 1989;6:698–702.

126. Sawicki P, Didjurgeit U, Mulhauser I, Berger M. Behaviour therapy versus doctor's anti-smoking advice in diabetic patients. J Intern Med 1993;234:407–9.

127. US Department of Health and Human Services. The health benefits of smoking cessation: a report of the Surgeon General. Atlanta: Department of Health and Human Services (US), Public Health Service, Centers for Disease Control and Prevention, National Center for Chronic Disease Prevention and Health Promotion, Office on Smoking and Health; 1990.

128. Anderson BJ, Wolf FM, Burkart MT, et al. Effects of peer group intervention on metabolic control of adolescents with IDDM: randomized outpatient study. Diabetes Care 1989;12:179–83.

129. Anderson BJ, Brackett J, Ho J, Laffel LM. An office-based intervention to maintain parent-adolescent teamwork in diabetes management. Impact on parent involvement, family conflict, and subsequent glycemic control. Diabetes Care 1999;22:713–21.

130. Anderson RM, Funnell MM, Barr PA, et al. Learning to empower patients: results of a professional education program for diabetes educators. Diabetes Care 1991;14:584–90.

131. Anderson RM, Funnell MM, Butler PM, et al. Patient empowerment. Results of a randomized controlled trial. Diabetes Care 1995;18:943–9.

132. Greenfield S, Kaplan SH, Ware JE, et al. Patients' participation in medical care: effects on blood sugar control and quality of life in diabetes. J Gen Intern Med 1988;3:448–57.

133. Weinberger M, Kirkman MS, Samsa GP, et al. A nurse-coordinated intervention for primary care patients with non-insulin-dependent diabetes mellitus: impact on glycemic control and health-related quality of life. J Gen Intern Med 1995;10:59–66.

134. Aubert RE, Herman WH, Waters J, et al. Nurse case management to improve glycemic control in diabetic patients in a health maintenance organization: a randomized, controlled trial. Ann Intern Med 1998;129:605–12.

135. Weinberger M, Tierney WM, Booher P, Katz BP. Can the provision of information to patients with osteoarthritis improve functional status? A randomized, controlled trial. Arthritis Rheum 1989;32:1577–83.

136. Wasson J, Gaudette C, Whaley F, et al. Telephone care as a substitute for routine clinic follow-up. JAMA 1992;267:1788–93.

137. Debusk RF, Houston Miller N, Superko HR, et al. A case-management system for coronary risk factor modification after acute myocardial infarction. Ann Intern Med 1994;120:721–9.

138. Delamater AM, Bubb J, Davis SG, et al. Randomized prospective study of self-management training with newly diagnosed diabetic children. Diabetes Care 1990;13:492–8.

139. Campbell EM, Redman S, Moffitt PS, Sanson-Fisher RB. The relative effectiveness of educational and behavioral instruction programs for patients with NIDDM: a randomized trial. Diabetes Educ 1996;22:379–86.

140. D'Eramo-Melkus GA, Wylie-Rosett J, Hagan JA. Metabolic impact of education in NIDDM. Diabetes Care 1992;15:864–9.

141. Glasgow RE, Toobert DJ, Hampson SE, et al. Improving self-care among older patients with type 2 diabetes: the "Sixty Something…" study. Patient Educ Couns 1992;19:61–74.

142. Kirkman MS, Weinberger M, Landsman PB, et al. A telephone-delivered intervention for patients with NIDDM. Diabetes Care 1994;17:840–6.

143. Mulrow C, Bailey S, Sonksen PH, Slavin B. Evaluation of an audiovisual diabetes education program: negative results of a randomized trial of patients with non-insulin dependent diabetes mellitus. J Gen Intern Med 1987;2:215–20.

144. Gilden JL, Hendryx MS, Clar S, et al. Diabetes support groups improve health care of older diabetic patients. J Am Geriatr Soc 1992;40:147–50.

145. Korhonen T, Huttunen JK, Aro A, et al. A controlled trial on the effect of patient education in the treatment of insulin-dependent diabetes. Diabetes Care 1983;6:256–61.

146. Sadur C, Moline N, Costa M, et al. Diabetes management in a health maintenance organization: efficacy of care management using cluster visits. Diabetes Care 1999;22:2011–7.

147. Smith DM, Norton JA, Weingerger M, et al. Increasing prescribed office visits. A controlled trial in patients with diabetes mellitus. Med Care 1986;24:189–99.

148. Tu KS, McDaniel G, Templeton J. Diabetes self-care knowledge, behaviors, and metabolic control of older adults—the effect of a posteducational follow-up program. Diabetes Educ 1993;19:25–30.

149. de Weerdt I, Visser Ph A, Kok G, van der Veen EA. Randomized controlled evaluation of an education program for insulin treated patients with diabetes: effects on psychosocial variables. Patient Educ Couns 1989;14:191–215.

150. Wise PH, Dowlatshahi DC, Farrant S, et al. Effects of computer-based learning on diabetes knowledge and control. Diabetes Care 1986;9:504–8.

151. Wood ER. Evaluation of a hospital-based education program for patients with diabetes. J Am Diet Assoc 1989;89:354–8.

152. Balas EA, Austin SM, Mitchell JA, et al. The clinical value of computerized information services: a review of 98 randomized clinical trials. Arch Fam Med 1996;5:271–8.

153. Krishna S, Balas EA, Spencer DC, et al. Clinical trials of interactive computerized patient education: implications for family practice. J Fam Pract 1997;45:25–33.

154. Noell J, Glasgow RE. Interactive technology applications for behavioral counseling: issues and opportunities for health care settings. Am J Prev Med 1999;17:269–74.

155. Glasgow RE, McKay HG, Boles SM, Vogt TM. Interactive computer technology, behavioral science, and family practice. J Fam Pract 1999;48:464–70.

156. Street RL Jr, Gold WR, Manning TE. Health promotion and interactive technology: theoretical applications and future directions. London: Lawrence Erlbaum Associates; 1997.

157. Glasgow RE, Toobart DJ, Hampson SE. Effects of a brief office-based intervention to facilitate diabetes dietary self-management. Diabetes Care 1996;19:835–42.

158. Glasgow RE, La Chance PA, Toobert DJ, et al. Long-term effects and costs of brief behavioural dietary intervention for patients with diabetes delivered from the medical office. Patient Educ Couns 1997;32:175–84.

159. Piette JD. Moving diabetes management from clinic to community: development of a prototype based on automated voice messaging. Diabetes Educ 1997;23:672–9.

160. Piette JD, Mah CA. The feasibility of automated voice messaging as an adjunct to outpatient diabetes care. Diabetes Care 1997;20:15–21.

161. Piette JD, McPhee SJ, Weinberger M, et al. Use of automated telephone disease management calls in an ethnically diverse sample of low-income patients with diabetes. Diabetes Care 1999;22:1302–9.

162. Piette JD. Patient education via automated calls: a study of English- and Spanish-speakers with diabetes. Am J Prev Med 1999;17:138–41.

163. Piette JD, Weinberger M, McPhee SJ, et al. Do automated calls with nurse follow-up improve self-care and glycemic control among English- and Spanish-speaking patients with diabetes? A randomized controlled trial. Am J Med 2000;108:20–7.

164. Piette JD, Weinberger M, McPhee SJ. The effect of automated calls with telephone nurse follow-up on patient-centered outcomes of diabetes care (a randomized controlled trial). Med Care 2000;38:218–30.

165. Grey M, Kanner S, Lacey KO. Characteristics of the learner: children and adolescents. Diabetes Educ 1999;25(Suppl 6):25–33.

166. DiMatteo MR, Sherbourne CD, Hays RD, et al. Physicians' characteristics influence patients' adherence to medical treatment: results from the medical outcomes study. Health Psychol 1993;12:93–102.

167. Glasgow RE, Osteen VL. Evaluating diabetes education. Are we measuring the most important outcomes? Diabetes Care 1992;15:1423–32.

168. Glasgow RE. Outcomes of and for diabetes education research. Diabetes Educ 1999;25(Suppl 6):74–88.

169. Kaplan RM. Behavior as the central outcome in health care. Am Psychol 1990;45:1211–20.

170. Davis WK, Hess GE, Van Harrison R, Hiss RG. Psychosocial adjustment to and control of diabetes mellitus: differences by disease type and treatment. Health Psychol 1987;6:1–14.

171. Glasgow RE, McKay HG, Piette JD, Reynolds KD. The RE-AIM criteria for evaluating population-based interventions: what can they tell us about different chronic disease management strategies. Patient Educ Couns [In press].

172. Beck A, Scott J, Williams P. A randomized trial of group outpatient visits for chronically ill older HMO members: the cooperative health care clinic. J Am Geriatr Soc 1997;45:543–9.

173. Coleman EA, Grothaus LC, Sandu N, Wagner EH. Chronic care clinics: a randomized controlled trial of a new model of primary care for frail older adults. J Am Geriatr Soc 1999;47:775–83.

174. Lorig KR, Mazonson PD, Holman HR. Evidence suggesting that health education for self-management in patients with chronic arthritis has sustained health benefits while reducing health care costs. Arthritis Rheum 1993;36:439–46.

175. Lorig KR, Sobel DS, Stewart AL, et al. Evidence suggesting that a chronic disease self-management program can improve health status while reducing hospitalization: a randomized trial. Med Care 1999;37:5–14.

176. Leveille SG, Wagner EH, Davis C, et al. Preventing disability and managing chronic illness in frail older adults: a randomized trial of a community-based partnership with primary care. J Am Geriatr Soc 1998;46:1191–8.

177. Cook TD, Cooper H, Cordray DS, et al. Meta-analysis for explanation. A casebook. New York: Russell Sage Foundation; 1992.

CHAPTER 14

Weight Loss in the Management of Type 2 Diabetes

Rena R. Wing, PhD

ABSTRACT

Weight loss is considered an important aspect of the treatment of Type 2 diabetes. The present chapter reviews evidence on the relationship between weight loss and glycemic control to determine (1) the strength of the relationship between weight loss and improvements in glycemic control, (2) the magnitude of weight loss required for these improvements, (3) which patients are most responsive to weight loss therapy, and (4) what treatment components might maximize the benefits for Type 2 diabetic patients.

Studies reviewed in this chapter suggest that both weight loss and caloric restriction contribute to improving glycemic control in Type 2 diabetics. Large weight losses, as obtained with gastrointestinal surgery, produce large and long lasting improvements in glycemic control. More modest weight losses, as achieved with lifestyle interventions, produce more modest changes in blood glucose control. Weight losses of 5 to 10% of body weight improve glycemic control, but larger weight losses (closer to 20%) are needed to normalize glucose. Patients with higher fasting glucose levels and those who lose the most weight experience the greatest changes in glycemic control. The response to a short trial of weight reduction (ie, the response to a 2.5 to 5 kg loss) can be used to predict the response to larger weight loss. Very low-calorie diets deserve further attention as a way to improve glycemic control. Exercise alone produces very small weight losses and, when examined independent of weight loss, very small improvements in glycemic control. The benefits of exercise may be more in terms of improving maintenance of weight loss (and thereby improving control). Behavioral strategies including self-monitoring, stimulus control, social support, and continued contact may improve weight losses and consequently improve glycemic control.

INTRODUCTION

The association between obesity and Type 2 diabetes is well known. Approximately 80 to 90% of individuals with Type 2 diabetes are overweight. Obesity increases the risk of developing diabetes and complicates its medical treatment. The metabolic abnormalities associated with Type 2 diabetes, including hyperglycemia, hyperinsulinemia, and dyslipidemia, are all worsened by obesity. Obese individuals with diabetes also have higher mortality rates than thinner individuals with diabetes.[1]

Weight loss is recommended for obese individuals with diabetes because it reduces hyperglycemia by improving several of the physiologic defects associated with diabetes. Weight loss reduces hepatic glucose output, improves insulin resistance, and, in some patients, increases insulin secretion.[2] Weight loss may also reduce elevated triglyceride levels and low-density lipoprotein (LDL) cholesterol levels and, in longer duration studies, may increase levels of high-density lipoprotein (HDL) cholesterol. Positive effects of weight loss on blood pressure levels and body fat distribution have also been observed.[2] This constellation of benefits is of particular importance because of the association between diabetes and increased risk of coronary heart disease (CHD).

The purpose of this chapter is to examine the literature on the effects of weight loss on glycemic control in Type 2 diabetic patients. The focus is on longer studies, conducted in outpatient settings, that are most relevant to the clinical management of patients with diabetes.

The following questions are addressed in this chapter:

1. Are improvements in glycemic control due to weight loss or calorie restriction?
2. What is the evidence that long-term weight loss improves glycemic control?
3. How much weight loss is needed to improve glycemic control?
4. Who is most responsive to weight-loss intervention?
5. Do people with diabetes have greater difficulty losing weight than nondiabetic people?
6. What treatment components maximize benefits for Type 2 diabetic patients?

ARE IMPROVEMENTS IN GLYCEMIC CONTROL DUE TO WEIGHT LOSS OR TO CALORIE RESTRICTION?

The effects of dieting on glycemic control are observed very rapidly, typically within 7 to 10 days, raising the question of whether these effects are due to caloric restriction or weight loss. For example, in one study,[3] 30 obese patients with Type 2 diabetes were followed through 40 days of a 330 kcal/d diet. Subsequently, 12 of these subjects completed 40 days of gradual refeeding. Although weight loss occurred at a relatively constant rate over the 40 days of dieting, 87% of the reduction in fasting glucose occurred after 10 days on the diet. Similarly, when calories were increased during the refeeding period, glucose levels increased despite maintenance of virtually all of the initial weight loss. These data suggest that the level of calorie intake, rather than weight per se, is influencing glycemic control (Table 14–1).

This phenomenon was examined further in a sample of seven obese individuals with Type 2 diabetes.[4] Subjects were studied four times in a clinical research setting, as follows: phase I—7 days of calorie balance; phase II—7 days of 800-kcal intake; phase III—following 3 months of a weight-reducing diet that included 2 months of a very-low-calorie diet (VLCD) (400 kcal/d and then 4 weeks of gradual refeeding) and produced an average weight loss of 12.7 kg (and after 7 days of weight maintenance); phase IV—a final 7 days of calorie restriction (800 kcal/d). This study showed that the initial 7-day period of calorie restriction produced approximately 50% of the changes in fasting glucose and hepatic glucose production that would occur after the substantial weight loss. Likewise, most of the improvement in insulin sensitivity and insulin secretion occurred during the first 7 days of caloric restriction.

Another way to differentiate between the effects of caloric restriction and those of weight loss is to compare the improvements in glycemic control that occur after comparable weight loss produced by different degrees of caloric restriction. Overweight Type 2 diabetic patients who lost 11% of their body weight with a VLCD (400 kcal/d) achieved lower fasting glucose levels than subjects who had lost the same amount of weight using a 1,000 kcal/d diet.[5] When calories were increased in the 400-calorie group, these participants experienced worsening in glycemic control, despite further weight reduction.

Table 14–1 Effects of Caloric Restriction versus Weight Loss on Fasting Glucose Levels

Study	Baseline FPG mg/dL (mmol/L)	Period of Calorie Restriction (7–10 d)		Period of Weight Loss (40 d–12 w)	
		Weight Loss (kg)	FPG mg/dL (mmol/L)	Weight Loss (kg)	FPG mg/dL (mmol/L)
Henry et al[3]	297 (16.5)	−4.6	158 (8.8)	−10.5	138 (7.7)
Kelley et al[4]	223 (12.4)	−2.2	171 (9.5)	−12.7	125 (6.9)

FPG = fasting plasma glucose.

EVIDENCE-BASED MESSAGE

Both weight loss and calorie restriction contribute to the effect of dieting on glycemic control. There is rapid improvement in glycemic control with dieting that occurs before any real weight loss has occurred. This initial change reflects calorie restriction and accounts for 50% or more of the overall change that occurs after continued weight loss (Level 3).[3,4]

WHAT IS THE EVIDENCE THAT LONG-TERM WEIGHT LOSS IMPROVES GLYCEMIC CONTROL?

To determine the effects of weight loss rather than of calorie restriction, it is helpful to examine long-term weight loss interventions, where measures of glycemic control are obtained during maintenance rather than during the acute phase of weight loss. The strongest evidence supporting the effect of long-term weight loss on glycemic control comes from the surgical literature on obesity, since the magnitude of weight loss achieved with gastrointestinal surgery is larger than that achieved with other therapeutic approaches. In this section, we will review the surgical literature on the effects of weight loss on glycemic control and then discuss evidence from other types of therapy: weight loss medications and lifestyle interventions.

Effect of Gastrointestinal Surgery on Glycemic Control

To determine whether weight loss improves glycemic control in individuals with Type 2 diabetes, it is helpful to begin by assessing the effect of gastrointestinal surgery on this condition. Gastrointestinal surgery (vertical gastric banding) or gastric bypass (Roux-en-Y) can result in substantial weight losses that are sustained over time. Candidates for surgery are those with a body mass index (BMI) > 40 or a BMI of 35 to 40 and comorbid conditions. This procedure is discussed here because it provides evidence of the impact on diabetes of significant weight losses that are maintained long term.

The Swedish Obese Subjects (SOS) study consisted of a surgically treated group and a matched control group that received conventional weight loss treatments. Data from 767 surgical patients (who primarily received vertical banded gastroplasty) and 712 controls followed for 2 years have recently been reported.[6] Control patients lost 0.5 kg compared to 28 kg in surgical patients. For the 196 subjects with diabetes at baseline (glucose levels ≥ 120 mg/dL [≥ 6.7 mmol/L] or using hypoglycemic medications), the relative risk (RR) of recovering from diabetes (ie, reducing glucose levels to < 120 mg/dL, no drugs) was 3.7 (confidence interval [CI] of 2.3 to 6.0). The effect of weight loss on recovering from diabetes was stronger than that observed for recovery from hypertension (RR 2.0, CI 1.5 to 2.7), hypertriglyceridemia (RR 1.9, CI 1.5 to 2.4), or hypercholesterolemia (RR 1.2, CI 0.95 to 1.5).

Similar long-term results were reported after gastric bypass in 165 individuals with Type 2 diabetes.[7] Follow-up data were available for 146 of these individuals. Weights (given for the full cohort of 608 patients but not for the subset with diabetes) averaged 138 kg at baseline, 87 kg at 1 year, 93 kg at 5 years, and 93 kg at 14 years. At the 14-year follow-up, 82.9% of the patients with diabetes (121 of 146 patients) maintained normal blood glucose and glycosylated hemoglobin. Patients who failed to normalize their blood glucose levels were older (48.0 vs 40.7 years) and their diabetes was of longer duration (4.6 vs 1.6 years).

These investigators have also compared those diabetics who underwent gastric surgery to controls, who were evaluated for surgery but elected not to have the procedure.[8] Mean length of follow-up was 6 years in the control patients and 9 years in the surgical group. Fasting glucose in the surgery patients fell from 187 mg/dL (10.4 mmol/L) preoperatively to < 140 mg/dL (7.8 mmol/L) for up to 10 years of follow-up. The percent of control patients requiring oral hypoglycemics increased from 56 to 85%, whereas it decreased from 31 to 8% in surgery patients. The mortality rate was also decreased in surgical patients. The mortality rate was 28% in the control group and 9% in the surgical group. For every year of follow-up, control patients had a 4.5% chance of dying versus a 1% chance in surgical subjects.

EVIDENCE-BASED MESSAGE

Large weight losses, as obtained with surgical approaches, produce long-term improvements in glycemic control in Type 2 diabetic individuals (Level 2).[6–8]

Effect of Weight Loss Medications on Glycemic Control

There are currently two medications that have been approved by the Food and Drug Administration (FDA) for weight loss: orlistat and sibutramine. Both of these have been evaluated in year-long studies with Type 2 diabetic patients (Table 14–2).

Orlistat (Xenical) is a lipase inhibitor, which selectively inhibits the absorption of dietary fat. It was evaluated in a multicenter study in a cohort of 391 obese patients (BMI 28 to 40), aged > 18 years, with Type 2 diabetes treated with stable doses of oral sulfonylureas.[9] The study began with a 5-week single-blind placebo lead-in, during which all participants followed a mildly hypocaloric diet of approximately 30% fat. Three hundred and twenty-two patients completed the run-in and were randomly assigned to placebo (N = 159) or orlistat (N = 163) 120 mg tid for 52 weeks. The hypocaloric diet was maintained throughout the 1-year trial.

At 57 weeks, patients in the orlistat groups had lost 6.2 kg, versus 4.3 kg in placebo patients (intent-to-treat $p < .001$). An analysis of completers (115 placebo completers and 149 orlistat completers) yielded almost identical results. Moreover, 48.8% of orlistat patients lost 5% of their weight, versus 22.6% of placebo patients.

The greatest changes in fasting glucose and HbA_{1c} in both groups occurred during the run-in period (again indicating the effect of caloric restriction on initial improvements in glycemic control). There was a decrease in HbA_{1c} from 8.2 in placebo patients and 8.02 in orlistat patients to approximately 7.5 at the end of the run-in. At 52 weeks after randomization, orlistat patients had a further decrease in HbA_{1c} of 0.28, compared to a 0.18 increase in placebo ($p = .0019$). Improvements in HbA_{1c} were directly related to weight loss; subjects who lost 5 to 10% of their weight on placebo had the same HbA_{1c} benefits as those who lost 5 to 10% of their weight on orlistat. However, as noted above, few patients achieved such weight losses on placebo.

Findings for lipids were even more positive. Orlistat patients demonstrated greater improvements in LDL cholesterol, LDL-to-HDL ratio, and triglycerides than did placebo patients. At any given category of weight loss, orlistat patients experienced greater improvements in lipids than did placebo patients, indicating a specific drug effect (independent of weight loss) on these measures. It should be noted that the major side effects of orlistat are gastrointestinal (GI), as would be expected from its mode of action. Seven patients on orlistat withdrew due to GI side effects versus two on placebo. Mean vitamin E and betacarotene levels were lower in drug-treated patients and more patients received vitamin supplements.

Sibutramine (Meridia) is a serotonin and noradrenaline reuptake inhibitor that produces weight loss primarily through enhanced satiety. An abstract presented at the North Atlantic Association for the Study of Obesity (NAASO) meetings in November 1999[10] reported results for a 12-month study of sibutramine in the treatment of 236 obese (BMI ≥ 28 kg/m²) patients with Type 2 diabetes treated with diet only. This was a multicenter study, comparing 15-mg sibutramine versus placebo over 12 months. Both sibutramine and placebo were used with a 700-kcal/d deficit diet. Eighty-nine percent of subjects completed the study. Subjects on sibutramine experienced greater weight loss than did placebo patients (7.3% vs 2.4%, $p < .001$). Sixty-five percent of patients treated with sibutramine lost ≥ 5% of their weight, versus 17% of those on placebo ($p < .001$). There was no difference in HbA_{1c} decreases, however, for the two groups (–0.3% in sibutramine patients and –0.2% in placebo, NS). Sibutramine patients experienced greater decreases in triglycerides and increases in HDL cholesterol than did placebo patients. Given the marked differences in weight loss between sibutramine and placebo groups and the association between magni-

Table 14-2 Effect of Weight-Loss Medication: Changes in Weight and Glycemic Control (HbA$_{1c}$) in Type 2 Diabetic Patients

Medication	Diet	Subjects	Duration	Weight Loss (%)		Subjects Losing ≥ 5% Body Weight (%)		Change in HbA$_{1c}$ (%)	
				Drug	Placebo	Drug	Placebo	Drug	Placebo
Orlistat 120 mg tid[9]	Mildly hypocaloric 30% fat BMI 28–40	N = 391 Type 2 diabetics on oral hypoglycemic	12 mo	−6.2	−4.3*	48.8	26.6*	−0.28† −0.80‡	+0.18*† −0.52‡
Sibutramine 15 mg[10]	−700 kcal BMI > 28	N = 236 Type 2 diabetics on diet only	12 mo	−7.3	−2.4*	65	17*	−0.3	−0.2

*p < .05.

†Excludes changes seen during run-in.

‡Includes changes seen in run-in (data generated from information in text, but not actually provided and significance not reported).

Data from Hollander et al[9] and Rissanen et al.[10]

tude of weight loss and improvement in glycemic control seen in most of the studies reviewed in this chapter, the failure to find differences in HbA$_{1c}$ is surprising. The fact that all participants were diet controlled may have meant that their baseline glycemic control was quite good and that further improvements could not be observed. Additional analyses looking at patients divided by their baseline HbA$_{1c}$ levels might help interpret this finding. It should be noted that sibutramine appears to be well tolerated but may lead to increased heart rate and blood pressure. The medication must therefore be used cautiously in hypertensive patients and is not recommended for patients with coronary heart disease, arrhythmias, or stroke.

EVIDENCE-BASED MESSAGE

Weight loss medications used in combination with lifestyle changes may have a modest effect on weight loss through 1 year, compared to placebo Level 1.[9,10] To date, there have been no studies comparing the effects of weight loss medications to a strong lifestyle intervention including diet, exercise, and behavior modification.

Effect of the United Kingdom Diet Intervention on Glycemic Control

The United Kingdom Prospective Diabetes Study (UKPDS) provides the largest study of the response to weight loss of newly presenting Type 2 diabetic patients.[11] In total, 3,044 patients started the diet phase of the study. Baseline body weight averaged 130 lb ± 26% ideal body weight; thus, many participants were normal weight or below the level of obesity where weight loss is usually advocated. Participants averaged 52 years of age and had a mean fasting glucose of 218 ± 67 mg/dL (12.1 ± 3.7 mmol/L). Patients were seen monthly for 3 months for dietary counseling. They were advised to follow the British Diabetic Association recommendation for a diet of 50% carbohydrate, 30% fat, and 20% protein, with energy restriction tailored to the patient's weight and activity level. The mean prescribed diet was 1,361 kcal/d.

Fifteen percent of the participants (N = 447) were diet failures during the first 3 months (glucose ≥ 270 mg/dL [15 mmol] or symptoms of hyperglycemia). Dietary failures had higher fasting glucose at diagnosis, and a greater proportion were of normal weight (< 110% of ideal body weight) (Figure 14–1).

In the remaining 2,597 patients, who dieted for 3 months, percent overweight decreased from 130 to 123% (ie, 7% weight loss on average), and this weight loss was associated with a decrease in fasting glucose from 205 to 146 mg/dL (11.4 mmoL to 8.1 mmoL). Changes in both weight and glucose were greatest in the first month of therapy. Improvements in fasting glucose were related most strongly to initial glucose levels; patients with higher fasting glucose experienced the greatest decreases ($r = .76$; $p < .001$). Thirty-one percent of the variation in the improvement in fasting glucose over months 1 to 3 was explained by initial fasting plasma glucose; an additional 8% of the variation was explained by the magnitude of weight loss (initial body weight was not related to the improvement in fasting glucose). Of particular note is the fact that those centers with above average availability of dietary advice achieved the best weight losses and glycemic response.

Another way to examine outcome is to look at the characteristics of patients who achieved a normal glucose (< 108 mg/dL [< 6 mmol/L]) after weight loss. In the UKPDS, 16% of all patients (N = 482) achieved normal fasting glucose at 3 months. These individuals had a mean weight loss of 11% of ideal body weight (vs 7% in those who did not). However, a stronger predictor of the ability to achieve fasting glucose < 108 mg/dL (< 6 mmol/L) was initial fasting glucose; nearly 50% of individuals with an initial glucose of 108 to 144 mg/dL (6.0 to 8.0 mmol/L) were able to reduce their fasting glucose to < 108 mg/dL (< 6 mmol/L) at 3 months, versus 10% of those with an initial glucose of 288 to 396 mg/dL (16 to 22 mmol/L).

In the UKPDS, subjects who achieved an FBS < 108 mg/dL (< 6 mmol/L) at 3 months were maintained on diet therapy. The remainder were randomly assigned to various treat-

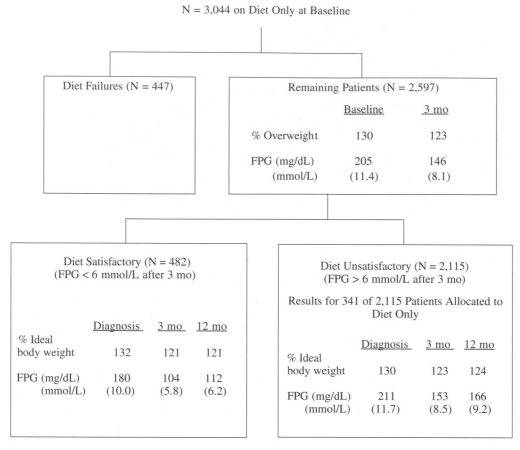

Figure 14–1 United Kingdom Prospective Diabetes Study results at 3 months and 12 months for patients on diet only. (Adapted from UK Prospective Diabetes Study Research Group. UK Prospective Diabetes Study 7: response of fasting plasma glucose to diet therapy in newly presenting type 2 diabetic patients. Metabolism 1990;39:905–12.)

ments, including, for some patients, randomization to further diet therapy. Figure 14–1 shows that both groups experienced worsening in glycemic control over the subsequent 12 months, despite fairly good maintenance of their weight loss. In fact, the follow-up at month 15 suggests that some degree of ongoing caloric restriction and continued weight reduction may be needed to maintain fasting plasma glucose levels < 108 mg/dL (< 6 mmol/L). Among the 482 subjects who achieved fasting glucose < 108 mg/dL (< 6 mmol/L) at 3 months, 54% maintained these levels at 15 months; these individuals had lost an additional 3% of their body weight over the latter 12 months. In contrast, the 46% of patients who initially achieved < 108 mg/dL (< 6 mmol/L) but at 15 months exceeded this level (glucose increased from 108 to 128 mg/dL or from 6 to 7.1 mmol/L) had regained 2% of their weight.

Effect of Behavioral and Lifestyle Interventions on Glycemic Control

The most systematic program of research on behavioral weight control for Type 2 diabetic patients has been conducted by Wing and associates.[12–18] In their initial study, a behavioral weight loss program was shown to be more effective than a nutritional education program with either weekly or monthly contact.[12] The behavioral program produced an average weight loss of 6.9 kg over 16 weeks, compared to 3.9 kg in the nutrition program given weekly contact, and 2.9 kg in the nutrition group seen only monthly. Later studies by these investigators (Table 14–3) produced far greater weight losses. For example, in the two most recent studies,[17,18] behavioral programs that included a low-calorie diet (LCD) (1,000 to 1,500 kcal/d) were compared to identical programs with VLCDs. Although in both studies, the VLCD group had larger initial weight losses (see discussion of VLCD later in this chapter), even the LCD group achieved weight losses of 10 to 13 kg at 6 months. In the 1991 study,[17] the behavioral program lasted 24 weeks; when subjects were re-examined 1 year later, they had maintained a weight loss of 6.8 kg. In the 1994 study,[18] the behavioral program was lengthened to 50 weeks. The LCD group now achieved weight losses of 13.5 kg at 6 months and 10.5 kg at 1 year.

Table 14–3 shows the changes in glycemic control that occurred in these studies. On average, patients in these studies had a 60 mg/dL (3.4 mmol/L) decrease in fasting glucose at 6 months and HbA_1 decreased by 1.67%. Since oral medication and/or insulin doses were adjusted as patients lost weight, it is somewhat difficult to interpret these changes in glycemic control. However, it is clear that studies with larger weight losses produced greater improvements in glycemic control. Also, in all studies, improvements in control were greater after 6 months than at 1-year follow-up. This may reflect the gradual weight regain that occurred during the year of follow-up. At 1-year follow-up, decreases in fasting glucose averaged 18.5 mg/dL (1.0 mmol/L) and HbA_{1c} decreases averaged 0.5%.

Weight losses obtained by this research group are far greater than those achieved by others when they reportedly apply a behavioral weight loss program (Table 14–4).[19–22] For example, in one study,[19] a conventional program with a 500 kcal/d deficit diet and bimonthly contacts for 24 months was compared to a comprehensive program, which included behavioral training and exercise in addition to the same diet counseling. Weight losses at the end of 6 months averaged 1.2 kg for the conventional group, compared to 2.9 kg for the comprehensive group ($p < .03$); weight losses at 2 years were 3.5 kg and 2.1 kg for comprehensive and conventional groups, respectively (NS). The comprehensive group had a greater decrease in HbA_{1c} after 6 months (median change of −1.0% vs −0.2%), but differences were not significant at 2 years (median changes of 0% vs +0.4% in comprehensive vs conventional).

Another study compared the effects of a combined diet and exercise intervention involving 12 weekly group sessions, 1 individual session, and 6 biweekly group sessions with usual care (1 class and 2 meetings) in the treatment of 64 overweight African-Americans with Type 2 diabetes. The intervention group lost 2 kg from baseline to 3 months (vs +.03 kg in controls) and −1.3 kg at 6 months (vs +1.1 kg in controls). Net changes in HbA_{1c} were greater than would be expected based on this weight loss (−1.6% and −2.4% at 3 and 6 months) and remained significantly different between groups, even after adjusting for weight loss.

Four weight-reduction strategies were evaluated in another report.[21] Diabetic subjects (N = 147) were randomly assigned to either *clinic*-based intervention (individual diet counseling at 6-week intervals for 6 months and then at 8-week intervals through 1 year); *standard behavior therapy* (biweekly meetings for 3 months and then meetings every 2 months through 1 year); *dexfenfluramine* (seen at the same frequency as clinic patients but prescribed 15 mg of dexfenfluramine twice per day for the first 3 months); or *home/clinic intervention* (seen at the same schedule as clinic-based patients but with two visits at their home). There was also a control group of 58 patients selected who received no diet advice. Weight changes were best in the dexfenfluramine group at 3 months. At 1 year, there were no significant differences in weight loss between treatment groups, although all maintained more weight loss than the controls. When re-examined at 4-year follow-up,[22] the dexfenfluramine group showed the best long-term weight losses (−2.6 kg). No significant differences between groups were seen for HbA_{1c} at 2 months, 1 year, or 4 years.

These studies are selected simply as examples. They illustrate the point that many behavioral weight-loss studies produce weight losses far less than those achieved by Wing and asso-

Table 14–3 Weight Loss and Changes in Glycemic Control in Selected Studies by Wing

Study	Baseline			End Treatment (4–6 mo)			1-Year Follow-up		
	WT (kg)	HbA$_{1c}$	FPG*	WT Δ (kg)	HbA$_{1c}$ Δ	FPG* Δ	WT Δ (kg)	HbA$_{1c}$ Δ	FPG* Δ
Wing et al[12]	96.4	9.3	178 (9.9)	−4.3	−0.4	−19 (−1.0)	−2.8	+0.3	−7 (−0.4)
Wing et al[13] WT	96.35	10.86	207.5 (11.5)	−6.8	−0.86	−16 (−0.9)	−8.2	−0.42	+2.7 (+0.1)
WT + SMBG	99.02	10.19	209.2 (11.6)	−5.8	−0.51	−12 (−0.7)	−4.1	0	+7.0 (+0.4)
Wing et al[14] Diet only	102.0	10.9	226 (12.5)	−5.6	−1.9	−61 (−3.4)	−3.8	−0.8	−14 (−0.7)
D + EX	106.9	10.7	214 (11.9)	−9.3†	−2.4	−58 (−3.2)	−7.9†	−1.4	−31 (−1.7)
Wing et al[15] BT + SMBG	95.1	10.54	233 (12.9)	−7.0	−2.1	−42 (−2.3)	−3.8	−0.79	—
BT + self-regulation	99.5	10.57	247 (13.7)	−5.1	−1.6	−71 (−3.9)	−3.6	+0.13	—

Table 14-3 Weight Loss and Changes in Glycemic Control in Selected Studies by Wing — *(continued)*

Study	Baseline			End Treatment (4–6 mo)			1-Year Follow-up		
	WT (kg)	HbA$_{1c}$	FPG*	WT Δ (kg)	HbA$_{1c}$ Δ	FPG* Δ	WT Δ (kg)	HbA$_{1c}$ Δ	FPG* Δ
Wing et al[16]									
Alone	103	10.3	226 (12.5)	−9.0	−2.1	−64 (−3.5)	−5.3	−0.7	−36 (−1.2)
Together	97	9.5	205 (11.4)	−8.6	−1.2	−50 (−2.8)	−3.2	−0.1	−11 (−0.6)
Wing et al[17]									
BT	104.5	10.4	229 (12.7)	−10.1†	−1.8†	−63† (−3.5†)	−6.8	+1.4†	+13† (+0.7†)
BT + VLCD	102.1	10.4	255 (14.1)	−18.6	−3.1	−117 (−6.5)	−8.6	−1.2	−68 (3.8)
Wing et al[18]									
LCD	107.7	10.5	220 (12.2)	−13.5	−1.7	−58 (−3.2)	−10.5†	−1.3	−43 (−2.4)
VLCD	105.8	10.3	220 (12.7)	−17.0	−2.0	−138 (−7.7)	−14.2	−2.3	−54 (−3.0)
Mean	101.18	8.88	220.74 (12.2)	−9.28	−1.67	−59.15 (−3.3)	−6.36	−.55	−18.56 (−1.0)

*FPG given as mg/dL and (mmol/L).

†Difference between groups is significant, $p < .05$.

WT = weight; FPG = fasting plasma glucose; SMBG = self-monitor bood glucose; D = diet; EX = exercise; BT = behavior therapy; VLCD = very-very-calorie diet; LCD = low-calorie diet.

Table 14–4 Selected Examples of Other Behavioral Weight-Loss Programs

Study	Short Term			Longer Term		
	Duration	Weight Δ (%)	HbA$_{1c}$ Δ (%)	Duration	Weight Δ (%)	HbA$_{1c}$ Δ (%)
Blonk[19]						
Conventional	6 mo	−1.2*	−0.2*	2 y	2.1	+.4
Comprehensive		−2.9	−1.0		3.5	0
Agurs-Collins[20]						
Usual care	3 mo	+0.3*	+0.06*	6 mo	+1.1*	+1.3*
Lifestyle		− 2	−1.5		−1.3*	−1.1*
Manning[21,22]						
Clinic	3 mo	−1.6	−3.6	1 y	−1.2	−.01
SBT		−1.2	−.05		−1.8	+.32
Dexfenfluramine		−3.4*	−.57		−2.8	+.51
Home + clinic		−1.7	−.34		−1.2	+.34
Controls			+.54		+1.2	+.96

*Significantly different from other conditions.
SBT = standard behavior therapy.

ciates. Despite the limited weight loss, significant changes in glycemic control are observed in some of these studies,[20] suggesting that other variables, perhaps changes in diabetes medication regimens or changes in adherence to these regimens, may be operative.

EVIDENCE-BASED MESSAGE

Lifestyle programs involving diet, exercise, and behavioral approaches vary in the weight loss obtained and the resulting glycemic changes. Programs that produce about a 7% decrease in body weight produce significant changes in FBS (approximately 200 mg/dL [11 mmol/L] at baseline to 150 mg/dL [8.3 mmol/L] after 3 to 6 months of weight loss) (Level 1).[11,17,18] However, some weight loss studies produce greater improvements in HbA$_{1c}$ than would be expected based on the weight losses, and some produce more modest improvements than anticipated.

HOW MUCH WEIGHT LOSS IS NEEDED TO IMPROVE GLYCEMIC CONTROL?

Improvements in glycemic control appear to be correlated with the magnitude of weight loss. Previous studies have reported correlations of $r = .55$, $p < .001$ between weight loss and HbA$_{1c}$ changes at 6 months[19]; and $r = .40$, $p < .001$[18], $r = .38$, $p < .05$,[14] and $r = .48$, $p < .001$[12] between weight losses and changes in HbA$_{1c}$ over the period of 12 to 16 months. As noted above, the UKPDS found that initial glucose level and weight change were related to improvements in glycemic control at 3 months.[11]

The long-term effect of weight loss on improvements in glycemic control appears weaker. For example, at 2-year follow-up, subjects who had been treated with behavior therapy plus a balanced low-calorie diet maintained a weight loss of 5.7 kg, but HbA$_{1c}$ was 0.24% above baseline levels.[18] Other studies[19] likewise find that weight loss and HbA$_{1c}$ changes at 2 years are no longer significantly correlated ($r = .25$, NS). Intervening changes in medication, gradual worsening in glycemic control over time, and the poor long-term maintenance of weight loss may make it difficult to detect the association between weight loss and improvements in glycemic control.

Table 14–5 Magnitude of Weight Changes and Improvements in Glycemic Control (HbA$_{1c}$) in Long-Term Diet Interventions

Study	Diet	Duration	Magnitude of Weight Loss	Associated Change in HbA$_{1c}$
Mancini[23]	400 kcal	3 yr f-u	< 5% body weight	Worsening
			> 5% body weight	Lasting improvements
Wing[24]	LCD	1 yr	2–4.9% body weight	+0.2%
			5–9.9% body weight	−0.6%
			> 10% body weight	−1.6%
Kanders[25]	VLCD	18 mo	< 10% body weight	30% have improvements
			10–19% body weight	55% have improvements
			> 20% body weight	70% have improvements
Wing[18]	VLCD	1 yr	< 5 kg*	−0.25%
	or		5–15 kg	−1.5%
	LCD		> 15 kg	−2.2%

*Since patients weighed 106 kg at baseline, this would equal an approximate 5% weight loss.
f-u = follow-up; VLCD = very-low-calorie diet; LCD = low-calorie diet.

Several studies provide data on long-term changes in glycemic control as a function of *magnitude* of weight loss.[18,23–25] These studies, reviewed in Table 14–5, suggest not only that there is a dose-response relationship between magnitude of weight loss and improvements in long-term glycemic control but begin to define the amount of weight loss needed to produce a significant long-term improvement in glycemic control. The studies suggest that modest weight losses of 5 to 10% body weight promote improvements in glycemic control through 1 year, but larger weight losses are associated with even better effects.

Another way to consider the benefit of weight loss is to ask how much weight loss is needed to "normalize" blood sugar levels. Table 14–6 presents data from the UKPDS[11] study showing the magnitude of weight loss needed to achieve a fasting glucose of < 6 mmol/L after 3 months of dieting. These data suggest that weight loss of approximately 20 kg was needed to normalize glucose. Larger weight losses were required in those with poorer initial levels of control.

EVIDENCE-BASED MESSAGE

The amount of improvement in glycemic control is related to the magnitude of weight loss. Weight losses of 5 to 10% of body weight improve glycemic control long term, but it may require weight losses of 20% of body weight to normalize glucose (Level 2).[11,18,23–25]

WHO IS MOST RESPONSIVE TO WEIGHT-LOSS INTERVENTION?

Given the variability in the glycemic response to weight loss noted in the UKPDS study, it would be helpful to determine baseline predictors of the effectiveness of weight loss. That is, for a given weight loss, what type of patient will exhibit the greatest improvements in blood sugar? The variables involved are considered below.

Duration of Diabetes

To determine the effect of duration of diabetes on outcome, 8 patients with long-duration diabetes (> 5 years) were compared to 10 patients with recent-onset diabetes (< 2 years).[26] After approximately 6 weeks of a 500 kcal/d diet, weight losses were comparable, but recent-onset patients had greater improvements in glucose level. This sample was unusual, however,

Table 14–6 Magnitude of Weight Loss (% of Ideal Body Weight Loss) that is Associated with Attaining Fasting Plasma Glucose < 6 mmol/L after 3 Months' Dieting

Obesity Categories at Diagnosis	Fasting Plasma Glucose (mmol/L) at Diagnosis				
	6–8	8–10	10–12	12–14	14+
< 110% ideal body weight (mean, 103%)	NS	13%	NS	NS	NS
110–130% ideal body weight (mean, 121%)	16%	16%	25%	36%	43%
130–150% ideal body weight (mean, 139%)	14%	23%	29%	29%	36%
> 150% ideal body weight (mean, 173%)	17%	27%	27%	34%	36%
All patient (mean, 121%)					
Weight loss intercept for FPG 6 mmol/L (% IBW)	16%	21%	28%	35%	41%
Weight loss intercept for FPG 6mmol/L	10 kg	13 kg	18 kg	22 kg	26 kg

FPG = fasting plasma glucose; IBW = ideal body weight; NS = not significant.
Reprinted from permission from UK Prospective Diabetes Study Research Group. UK Prospective Diabetes Study 7: response of fasting plasma glucose to diet therapy in newly presenting Type 2 diabetic patients. Metabolism 1990;39(9):905–12.

since the recent and longer-duration subjects were selected to be of equal body weight and glucose and all were treated with diet only.

Duration of diabetes was also analyzed in a sample of 155 Type 2 diabetics who had completed 12 to 20 weeks of a behavioral weight loss program (1,200 to 1,800 kcal/d diet and modest exercise).[24] Patients were treated with diet, oral medication, or insulin, and these medications were adjusted periodically during weight loss using a standard algorithm.

Recent-onset patients (N = 55, defined as < 2 years of diabetes) experienced decreases in fasting glucose that were comparable to long-duration patients (N = 88, defined as ≥ 5 years [31 vs 42 mg/dL]). Changes were also comparable at 1-year follow-up. Since the prior study[26] had examined only diet-treated subjects, these analyses were redone comparing diet-only treated subjects with recent-onset diabetes (N = 17) versus long-duration subjects (N = 8). The long-duration subjects had higher pretreatment fasting glucose (241 mg/dL vs 153 mg/dL [13.4 vs 8.5 mmol/L], $p < .02$) and experienced greater improvements in glycemic control from baseline to post-treatment (–82 vs –33 mg/dL [–4.5 vs –1.8 mmol/L], $p < .02$) and pretreatment to 1 year (–59 vs –7 mg/dL [–3.3 vs –0.4 mmol/L], $p < .02$). Recent and long-duration subjects had comparable short-term weight losses, but long-duration subjects maintained their weight losses better (–9.5 vs –2.7 kg, $p < .06$), partially explaining the differences in glycemic control.

Initial Fasting Glucose Level

As noted in the UKPDS study,[11] individuals with higher fasting glucose achieve greater *reductions* in glucose with weight loss. However, individuals with lower fasting glucoses (closer to normal) are more likely to normalize their glucose with weight loss.

Likewise, baseline fasting glucose level was found to be the strongest predictor of improvements in glycemic control (multiple r of .60) in a study with 155 Type 2 diabetic patients.[24] This effect was seen both at post-treatment and at 1-year follow-up. Patients whose blood sugar initially exceeded 200 mg/dL (11.1 mmol/L) experienced a 71 mg/dL (3.9 mmol/L) decrease in glucose from pretreatment to post-treatment, whereas subjects with FBS < 200 (11.1 mmol/L) experienced an 8 mg/dL (0.4 mmol/L) decrease. Similarly, changes from baseline to 1 year were –35 mg/dL versus +13 mg/dL (–1.9 vs +0.7 mmol/L) in subjects with FBS ≥ 200 or < 200 mg/dL (FBS ≥ 11.1 mmol/L or < 11.1 mmol/L). Initial fasting glucose levels were unrelated to weight loss. Similar analyses were done within treatment categories, that is, for diet only, oral medication, and insulin. In all three comparisons, subjects with higher fasting glucose at baseline experienced greater improvement in glucose over time. Other investigators[27] examined the number of patients who had to be restarted on diabetes medication because their glucose levels after 3 weeks of dieting remained > 250 mg/dL (13.9 mmol/L). Patients who had to be restarted on medication had higher initial fasting glucose levels but had similar changes in glucose from baseline to 3 weeks and similar weight losses. Thus, as in the UKPDS study, when a specific blood glucose criterion is used, those closer to the level at baseline are more likely to achieve the level with weight loss.

Diabetes Treatment Regimen

Although it is often assumed that patients on insulin have more difficulty losing weight, when the outcome of 155 Type 2 diabetics was analyzed according to their diabetic treatment regimen (diet, oral medication, insulin), there were no differences noted in initial or long-term weight loss.[24] In addition, after adjusting for initial glucose levels, there was no effect of diabetic treatment regimen on the glucose response to weight loss.[24]

Predicting Glucose Response to Weight Loss by Using an Initial Short-Term Weight Loss Trial

As noted above, there is a great deal of individual variation in the response of diabetic patients to weight loss. The best way to determine who is responsive to weight loss appears to be to examine the response to a short-term trial of weight reduction.[28] For example, in the UKPDS study,[11] only 8% of patients who did not achieve a fasting plasma glucose < 108 mg/dL (< 6 mmol/L) after an initial 3-month phase of weight reduction were able to achieve this level at 15 months. Similarly, the response to a 2.3 kg or 4.5 kg weight loss appears to distinguish "responders" (those who would achieve an FPG < 180 mg/dL [< 10 mmol/L]) from nonresponders.[28] When 135 Type 2 diabetics patients, all of whom had lost at least 9.1 kg, were studied,[28] fasting glucose was found to decrease from 281 to 246 mg/dL (15.6 to 13.7 mmol/L) after a 9.1 kg weight loss. However, there was a bimodel distribution of plasma glucose levels after weight loss. Forty-one percent of patients "responded" to weight loss (achieved FPG < 180 mg/dL or < 10 mmol/L) and 59% did not. The responders and nonresponders were comparable in age, sex, plasma glucose level, and body weight at the start of the study. (It is interesting, and somewhat surprising, that the baseline glucose level did not distinguish responders versus nonresponders, as it did in the UKPDS study.) However, responders could be identified by their response to a 2.3 kg weight loss. Among those who achieved FPG < 180 mg/dL (10 mmol/L) after losing 2.3 kg, 62% would achieve this level after a 9.1 kg weight loss; in those who did not achieve an FPG < 180 mg/dL (< 10 mmol/L) after losing 2.3 kg, only 25% would achieve this level even after losing 6.8 kg more. Even stronger positive predictive value (79%) and negative predictive value (77%) occurred after a 4.5 kg weight loss. In a more recent study,[27] it was also found that initial changes in glucose (week 0 to 3) predicted overall changes in fasting glucose (week 0 to 20), with an *r* value of .73.

EVIDENCE-BASED MESSAGE

The best predictors of the glycemic response to weight loss are initial fasting glucose level and the glycemic response to a short trial period of weight loss (Level 3).[24,28]

DO PEOPLE WITH DIABETES HAVE GREATER DIFFICULTY LOSING WEIGHT THAN NONDIABETIC PEOPLE?

Finally, it is important to note that several studies have suggested that Type 2 diabetics lose less weight than nondiabetics or regain their weight losses more rapidly (Table 14–7).[9,16,29–31] To study this phenomenon, weight losses in 12 diabetic patients (6 male, 6 female) and their nondiabetic spouses were compared. Patients and spouses were comparable in age, weight,

Table 14–7 Comparisons of Diabetic and Nondiabetic Subjects in Weight-Loss Studies

Study	N Diabetic	N Nondiabetic	Duration	Weight Loss Diabetic	Weight Loss Nondiabetic
Wing[16]	6	6	20 wk	7.5 kg	13.4 kg
Guare[31]	20	23	16 wk	7.4 kg	6.4 kg
	20	23	16 mo	2.0 kg	5.4 kg
Kahn[29]	19	19	12 mo	4.7 kg/m^2	7.9 kg/m^2
Hollander/Davidson[9,30]	322	892	12 mo	6.2 kg	8.7 kg (orlistat)
				4.3 kg	5.8 kg (placebo)

and percent overweight and were treated together in the same behavioral weight-loss program. Patients with diabetes lost significantly less weight than their nondiabetic partners. These differences in weight loss emerged by week 5 of the program and increased over time, such that by week 20, weight losses of the nondiabetic spouse were 13.4 kg, versus 7.5 kg in diabetics.

Since the nondiabetic spouses were enrolled in this program to "support" their diabetic partners, these individuals may have tried particularly hard to adhere to the regimen and thus model appropriate behaviors. To more directly compare diabetics and nondiabetics without this potential confound, 20 NIDDM and 23 nondiabetic women were recruited[31] to participate in a weight-loss program. Diabetic and nondiabetic subjects were matched for age and weight and treated together in a 16-week program. Weight losses at the end of 16 weeks were comparable (7.4 kg and 6.4 kg for diabetic and nondiabetic subjects, respectively). However, during 1-year follow-up, the diabetic subjects regained 5.4 kg, compared to 1.0 kg for nondiabetics ($p = .058$).

Using a retrospective cohort analysis, weight losses of 19 nondiabetic and 19 diabetic (7 diet controlled and 12 drug controlled) have also been compared.[29] All participants were treated with diet, exercise, behavior modification, and weight-loss medication. The nondiabetics had significantly greater weight loss (7.9 kg/m^2 vs 4.77 kg/m^2) after 12 months of therapy. Diabetics on drug treatment had smaller weight losses than those on diet only (5.92 vs 4.23 kg/m^2), a finding interpreted to reflect diabetes disease stage, not simply drug therapy.

Similar comparisons can be made *across* studies that utilize similar protocols. For example, it is interesting to compare the effect of orlistat on weight loss in Type 2 diabetics[9] with the results of a similar protocol in nondiabetics.[30] Although the starting weight of the diabetic and nondiabetic subjects was similar, the nondiabetics treated with orlistat had better weight losses at 1 year than diabetic patients on orlistat (8.76 vs 6.19 kg). Moreover, 65.7% of the nondiabetics lost > 5% of their weight on the drug, versus 49% of the diabetics. Interestingly, the same effect was seen in placebo patients; again, nondiabetics had better outcomes than diabetics. To date, there have been no studies examining the mechanism for this difference in weight loss; this difference may reflect metabolic differences or behavioral difference in level of adherence to the weight-loss intervention.

EVIDENCE-BASED MESSAGE

Further research is needed to confirm the finding that diabetics have more difficulty losing weight than nondiabetics and to identify the mechanisms accounting for this difference (Level 3).[29,31]

What Treatment Components Maximize Benefits for Patients with Type 2 Diabetes?

Treatment components that either increase the magnitude of weight loss and/or increase the glycemic response to a given weight loss would be particularly appropriate for Type 2 diabetics. To determine which interventions promote improvements in Type 2 diabetics, a meta-analysis of this literature has been performed.[32] This meta-analysis included 89 studies; 40% involved dietary interventions, 20% involved behavioral interventions, 10% were exercise, and the remaining 30% were medication, surgery, or a combination. Results from this meta-analysis are reported here; however, concern is raised about the differences between studies in methodologic rigor (72% of studies used one-group, pretest/post-test designs; these one group studies were noted to inflate outcome effects). In addition, most of the studies evaluated only short-term effects, with very few extending beyond 6 months.

The largest weight losses in this meta-analysis were obtained with surgery (–26 kg), followed by diet strategies (–9.1 kg) and behavior plus diet (approximately –8 kg).[32] For HbA_{1c}, the greatest decreases occurred for diet alone and behavioral strategies combined with diet and exercise (no data for surgery were presented). The effect of diet was due primarily to studies using VLCDs, the most commonly studied diet in this meta-analysis.

Evidence-Based Message

Dietary modification is an important component of a weight-loss program (Level 1).[32]

Very-Low-Calorie Diets

Very-low-calorie diets are diets of 400 to 600 kcal/d that typically are consumed as liquid formula. They are designed to maximize weight loss while sparing lean body mass. Consequently, these regimens usually include a minimum intake of 1 g of protein/kg ideal body weight. They have been shown to be effective for short-term weight loss, with weight losses averaging 20 kg in 12 weeks.[33,34] Very-low-calorie diets have been used in many of the studies documenting the benefits of weight loss for glycemic control and examining the physiologic mechanisms associated with these improvements.[35,36]

However, the problem with VLCDs is that the weight is usually rapidly regained when regular foods are reintroduced into the regimen.[37] Several investigators have tried to prevent or lessen this rapid regain by using VLCDs in combination with behavioral treatment.[17,37,38] Two studies with Type 2 diabetics have been conducted to assess the long-term effects of using a VLCD in combination with behavior modification (see Table 14–3), compared to using a more moderate, LCD.[17,18]

In the first study,[17] one half of the subjects were randomized to a 20-week behavioral weight-loss program that used a balanced, LCD of 1000 to 1500 kcal/d ([BT] + LCD). The other half of the subjects received a similar 20-week program but consumed a food-based VLCD (lean meat, fish, fowl) for 8 weeks of the program (weeks 5 to 12) and the 1,000 to 1,500 kcal/d diet at other times (BT + VLCD). At the end of the 20-week program, the BT + LCD condition had lost 10.1 kg, versus 18.6 kg in the BT + VLCD condition. There was no further treatment contact after the 20-week program. When patients were re-examined 1 year later, weight losses of the BT + VLCD and BT + LCD groups did not differ significantly from each other (8.6 vs 6.8 kg).

In contrast, the VLCD improved both short- and long-term glycemic control. Both conditions entered the study with HbA_{1c} averaging 10.4%. After 6 months in the program, HbA_{1c} averaged 8.6% for the BT + LCD group and 7.3% for BT + VLCD. At 1-year follow-up, the VLCD condition continued to have better HbA_{1c} levels (9.2% vs 11.8%), despite the failure to maintain weight loss. These data, which were not due to differences in hypoglycemic medication, appeared to suggest some type of long-term benefits of VLCDs on insulin secretion.[17]

In a follow-up study,[18] these investigators tried to increase the benefit of VLCDs by using two 12-week bouts of the VLCD diet (weeks 1 to 12 and 24 to 36) and providing weekly behavioral treatment for a full 50 weeks. The results for this BT + VLCD condition were again compared to a group given LCD (1,000 to 1,200 kcal/throughout). Subjects in the VLCD group achieved far greater weight loss than the LCD condition during the initial 12 weeks of the program (16.0 kg vs 11.1 kg) when the VLCD group was undergoing the first bout of VLCD. This initial weight loss was well maintained from weeks 12 to 24, but during the second VLCD bout, when the VLCD condition was prescribed a diet of only 400 kcal/d, both conditions experienced similar weight changes (−1.4 kg for VLCD vs + .74 for LCD). Poor adherence to the second VLCD was shown to be responsible for these poor weight losses.[39] At the end of the 50-week program, subjects in the VLCD group maintained a weight loss of 14.2 kg, versus 11.6 for the LCD group (p = .057).

Use of the VLCD increased the number of weeks that subjects were able to maintain a blood sugar < 240 mg/dL (13.3 mmol/L) without restarting medication. There was also evidence that the VLCD produced greater improvements in glycemic control and insulin sensitivity than the LCD after a comparable weight loss of 11% of body weight. However, when subjects on the 400-kcal diet increased their intake to 1,000 kcal, they experienced worsening in glycemic control despite continued weight loss. In contrast, the LCD group had further improvements in both blood glucose and insulin sensitivity with further weight loss. Consequently, at both 6 and 12 months, there were no differences between the VLCD and LCD groups in HbA$_{1c}$ or FBS. Both conditions experienced significant short- and long-term improvements on these measures, but the improvements were similar in LCD and VLCD. Thus, this study again shows that both caloric restriction and weight loss have independent effects on glycemic control, but it provides less support for use of VLCDs as part of a long-term weight-loss regimen. Given the limited benefits of the VLCD and the costs involved, their use (especially a second bout of the diet) is difficult to justify.

Another approach to using VLCDs may be to use these diets for only 1 day per week or 5 consecutive days every 5 weeks. One recent study[27] suggested that such use of VLCDs improved weight losses at the end of a 20-week treatment program; the 5-day group lost 10.4 kg, the 1-day group lost 9.6 kg, and the control group (which consumed 1,500 to 1,800 kcal/d throughout) lost 5.4 kg (p = .04). Although there were no differences between groups for changes in HbA$_{1c}$ or fasting glucose over the 20-week program, the 5-day approach increased the percentage of patients who achieved normal glucose levels.

EVIDENCE-BASED MESSAGE

The degree of calorie restriction involved in VLCDs appears to improve initial weight loss and glycemic control. However, even when VLCDs are used in combination with behavioral treatment, weight losses have not been maintained long term (Level 1).[17,18,37,38] Research on new ways to use VLCDs to promote long-term weight loss and glycemic control is warranted.

Exercise

Exercise is a key component of a behavioral weight-loss program. In this section, we will address several questions regarding exercise: (1) Does exercise alone improve glycemic control in Type 2 diabetics? (2) Does exercise alone or in combination with diet promote weight loss? (3) What are the outcomes for Type 2 diabetics treated with diet plus exercise versus diet alone?

Does Exercise Alone Improve Glycemic Control in Type 2 Diabetic Patients?

Although exercise clearly improves insulin sensitivity,[40,41] the effect of exercise on glycemic control in Type 2 diabetics is less clear (Table 14–8).[40,42–51] Table 14–8 reports results of several studies that used one-group pretest/post-test designs or randomized designs to analyze the effect of exercise. The one-group pretest/post-test studies do not control for the effects

Table 14–8 Effect of Exercise on Glycemic Control

Study	N	Duration	Condition	HbA$_{1c}$ Pre	HbA$_{1c}$ Post	FBS* Pre		FBS* Post	
Schneider[41]	20	6 wk	EX	12.2	10.7[†]	178	(9.9)	173	(9.6)
Trovati[43]	5	6 wk	EX	9.5	8.0[†]	157	(8.7)	142[†]	(7.9[†])
Rönnemaa[44]	25	16 wk	EX	9.6	8.6[†]	212	(11.8)	189	(10.5)
			C	10	9.9	205	(11.4)	202	(11.2)
Reitman[65]	6	6 wk	EX	—	—	142	(7.9)	108[†]	(6.0[†])
Leon[45]	48	12 wk	EX	NS		153	(8.5)	156	(8.6)
Ruderman[46]	6	24 wk	EX	—	—	149	(8.3)	145	(8.0)
Skarfors[47]	16	24 mo	EX	—	—	198	(11.0)	173	(9.6)
			C			153	(8.5)	123	(6.8)
Hartwell[48]	76	6 mo	EX[‡]	NS		191	(10.6)	207	(11.5)
			C			191	(10.6)	175	(9.7)
Ligtenberg[49]	51	26 wk	EX	8.9	8.7	—		—	
		Supervised	C	8.8	9.0	—		—	
Raz[50]	38	12 wk	EX	12.5	11.7[†]	205	(11.4)	184	(10.2)
			C	12.4	12.9	212	(11.8)	221	(12.3)
Khan[51]	39	15 wk	EX	8.7	8.4	191	(10.6)	215	(11.9)
			C	7.7	7.6	169	(9.4)	172	(9.5)

*FBS given as mg/dL and (mmol/L).
[†]Difference significant, $p < .05$.
[‡]Subjects were randomized to diet, exercise, diet plus exercise, or control. Results are presented here only for exercise vs control.
FBS = fasting blood sugar; EX = exercise; C = control; NS = not significant.

of being in a study and receiving high levels of treatment contact, which may independently improve glycemic control. Two of the six randomized studies in Table 14–8 reported significant benefits of exercise compared to control groups. One of these studies[44] reported small weight losses in the exercise condition, which may contribute to the effect on glycemic control. Improvements in glycemic control with exercise occur primarily in patients with less severe hyperglycemia (< 200 mg/dL [11.1 mmol/L][40] or < 234 mg/dL [13 mmol/L][44]).

Does Exercise Alone or in Combination with Diet Increase Weight Loss or Improve Maintenance?

There have been numerous studies comparing the weight-reducing effects of diet, exercise, and the combination of diet plus exercise in nondiabetic samples. These studies were reviewed[52] as part of a recent consensus conference conducted by the American College of Sports Medicine and are discussed in detail in the Clinical Guidelines on the Identification, Evaluation, and Treatment of Overweight and Obesity in Adults.[53] Exercise alone was shown to produce very modest weight losses (1 to 2 kg). Similarly, adding exercise to a diet program increased short-term weight loss only slightly compared to diet alone. Of 15 studies comparing short-term weight loss for diet only versus diet plus exercise, only 2 found significant differences (favoring diet plus exercise), but almost all pointed in that direction.[52] Six studies were identified[52] that compared long-term effects (1 year or longer) of diet versus diet plus exercise. Two of the six studies found a significantly greater weight loss at follow-up in diet plus exercise than in diet only; the other four studies indicated no significant difference. In all studies, however, the direction of the difference favored diet plus exercise. Stronger evidence of the benefit of exercise for long-term weight loss maintenance comes from correlational studies, which consistently show that individuals who maintain high levels of physical activity are most likely to maintain their weight loss.[54]

Does Diet Plus Exercise Improve Glycemic Control Compared to Diet Only?

Four studies were identified that compared diet only versus diet plus exercise in Type 2 diabetic participants (Table 14–9).[14,55–57] Only one of these studies[14] found significant effects. In this study, the effect of diet only was compared to diet plus exercise in a sample of 30 patients with Type 2 diabetes. Both groups received standard training in behavioral strategies and were placed on a 1,000 kcal/d deficit diet. The diet-only group was encouraged to maintain their current level of exercise, while the diet plus exercise group was asked to exercise three times per week as a group and once per week on their own, walking a 3-mile route at each session. Diet plus exercise led to better weight losses than diet only, both at the end of the 10-week program (−9.3 kg vs −5.6 kg, $p < .001$) and at 1-year follow-up (−7.9 kg vs −3.8 kg, $p < .001$). Both groups had similar improvements in HbA_{1c}, but the diet plus exercise group had larger and more frequent reductions in hypoglycemic medications. Analyses collapsing across condition showed a strong association between exercise at 1 year and both improvements in HbA_{1c} ($r = -.54$, $p < .001$) and weight loss ($r = -.57$, $p < .001$). The effects of exercise on improvements in HbA_{1c} levels remained significant ($r = -.44$, $p < .05$) even after adjusting for weight loss.

EVIDENCE-BASED MESSAGE

Studies comparing the effect of exercise versus no exercise suggest that exercise produces small effects on glycemic control. This benefit occurs primarily in milder diabetics (Level 1).[40,44] Similarly, exercise alone produces small amounts of weight loss (Level 1).[52,53] The

Table 14–9 Studies of Type 2 Diabetes Patients Comparing Diet versus Diet Plus Exercise

Study	N	Duration	Condition	Weight Δ (kg)	FBS Δ*	HbA$_{1c}$ Δ (%)
Hartwell[48,55]	76	6 mo	D	−3.5	−45 (−2.5)	NS
			D + EX	.24	−5 (−0.3)	
		18 mo	D	−1.7	—	−0.46
			D + EX	0	—	−1.48
Bogardus[56]	18	12 wk	D	9.9	−34 (−1.9)	—
			D + EX	11.1	−28 (−1.6)	—
Vanninen[57]	78	12 mo	D	+0.5 BMI units	−6 (−0.3)	−0.4
			D + EX	−0.7 BMI units	−4 (−0.2)	−0.5
Wing[14]	28	10 wk	D	−5.6	−61 (−3.4)	−1.9
			D+ EX	−9.3†	−58 (−3.2)	−2.4
		1 yr	D	−3.8	−14 (−0.7)	−0.8
			D + EX	−7.9†	−31 (−1.7)	−1.4

*FBS given as mg/dL and (mmol/L).
†Difference significant $p < .05$.
FBS = fasting blood sugar; D = diet; EX = exercise; BMI = body mass index; NS = not significant.

greatest benefit of exercise seems to be in the maintenance of weight loss. Randomized trials consistently show that diet plus exercise produces better maintenance of weight loss than diet only, although this difference is often not significant; these studies do not show significant differences in glycemic control (Level 2).[14,52] Since diet plus exercise is most commonly advocated for weight loss, further research evaluating its benefits for Type 2 diabetics would be useful.

Maximizing Weight Loss with Behavioral Strategies

Studies reviewed in this chapter show that the magnitude of improvement in glycemic control is related to the degree of weight loss achieved. Thus, strategies that have been shown to promote long-term weight loss in nondiabetic patients may well be useful in promoting weight loss in Type 2 diabetic patients, thereby improving glycemic control. Several important behavioral approaches to improving weight loss are described below (Table 14–10).

Self-Monitoring

Perhaps the most important behavioral strategy is self-monitoring. Typically, patients in behavioral weight-loss programs are instructed to record all of their intake and physical activity on a daily basis for the first 6 months of the program and 1 week per month thereafter. Participants often record calories and fat grams in each item they consume and either calories or minutes of exercise. Continuing to self-monitor has been related to weight loss outcome in Type 2 diabetics patients,[58] and a recent study[59] suggested that consistent self-monitoring may help reduce weight gain during high-risk periods of the year.

Stimulus Control

Patients in behavioral weight-loss programs are instructed to rearrange their home environment so that cues for healthy eating and physical activity are made more prominent and cues for unhealthy practices are removed. Recently, investigators have studied the effect of restructuring the home environment on patients. For example, providing food to patients in the portion sizes they should eat through weekly food distribution was found to promote weight loss through 18 months.[60] Similarly, putting treadmills in patients' homes improved exercise adherence and long-term weight loss.[61]

Social Support

Social support has been shown to be correlated with continued adherence to weight-loss prescription. To increase social support, several investigators have included spouses in the treatment program and taught them ways to help patients with their behavior change. Such approaches have had modest success.[62] In a study of spousal support of Type 2 diabetic patients,[16] no overall benefit was found; however, this approach did seem to benefit women in the program (and had an adverse impact on men). More recently, researchers have examined more general peer support.[63] Participants were asked to identify three friends to join the program with them. The program also included behavioral strategies to unite these friends into helpful support teams. Recruiting patients with friends and increasing social support within the program both seemed to help study retention and weight-loss maintenance.

Table 14–10 Key Behavioral Strategies for Weight Loss

Self-monitoring

Stimulus control

Social support

Continued contact

Exercise

Continued Contact

Increasing the length of treatment contact also appears to improve long-term outcome. Continuing to see patients biweekly during a year of follow-up markedly reduced weight regain.[64] Biweekly contact appears to be more effective than monthly contact; the frequency of these contacts may be more important than their content.

EVIDENCE-BASED MESSAGE

> Strategies that appear to improve long-term weight loss include self-monitoring, stimulus-control techniques, social support, and continued contact (Level 2).[16,58,60,64]

CONCLUSION

The overall conclusion to be drawn from this chapter is that weight loss improves glycemic control, with the magnitude of the improvement related to both the magnitude of weight loss and characteristics of the patient (particularly initial blood glucose levels). While the amount of weight loss required to "normalize" glucose is large, even modest weight losses produce improvements in glycemic control. The issue that must be addressed is how to improve weight loss, especially long-term weight loss, in Type 2 diabetic patients. Further research is needed to develop strategies to promote long-term changes in diet and exercise behavior and thereby produce long-term changes in body weight.

SUMMARY OF EVIDENCE-BASED MESSAGES

1. Both weight loss and calorie restriction contribute to the effect of dieting on glycemic control. There is rapid improvement in glycemic control with dieting that occurs before any real weight loss has occurred. This initial change reflects calorie restriction and accounts for 50% or more of the overall change that occurs after continued weight loss (Level 3).[3,4]

2. Large weight losses, as obtained with surgical approaches, produce long-term improvements in glycemic control in Type 2 diabetic individuals (Level 2).[6–8]

3. Weight loss medications used in combination with lifestyle changes may have a modest effect on weight loss through 1 year, compared to placebo Level 1.[9,10] To date, there have been no studies comparing the effects of weight loss medications to a strong lifestyle intervention including diet, exercise, and behavior modification.

4. Lifestyle programs involving diet, exercise, and behavioral approaches vary in the weight loss obtained and the resulting glycemic changes. Programs that produce about a 7% decrease in body weight produce significant changes in FBS (approximately 200 mg/dL [11 mmol/L] at baseline to 150 mg/dL [8.3 mmol/L] after 3 to 6 months of weight loss) (Level 1).[11,17,18] However, some weight loss studies produce greater improvements in HbA_{1c} than would be expected based on the weight losses, and some produce more modest improvements than anticipated.

5. The amount of improvement in glycemic control is related to the magnitude of weight loss. Weight losses of 5 to 10% of body weight improve glycemic control long term, but it may require weight losses of 20% of body weight to normalize glucose (Level 2).[11,18,23–25]

6. The best predictors of the glycemic response to weight loss are initial fasting glucose level and the glycemic response to a short trial period of weight loss (Level 3).[24,28]

7. Further research is needed to confirm the finding that diabetics have more difficulty losing weight than nondiabetics and to identify the mechanisms accounting for this difference (Level 3).[29,31]

8. Dietary modification is an important component of a weight-loss program (Level 1).[32]

9. The degree of calorie restriction involved in VLCDs appears to improve initial weight loss and glycemic control. However, even when VLCDs are used in combination with

behavioral treatment, weight losses have not been maintained long term (Level 1).[17,18,37,38] Research on new ways to use VLCDs to promote long-term weight loss and glycemic control is warranted.

10. Studies comparing the effect of exercise versus no exercise suggest that exercise produces small effects on glycemic control. This benefit occurs primarily in milder diabetics (Level 1).[40,44] Similarly, exercise alone produces small amounts of weight loss (Level 1).[52,53] The greatest benefit of exercise seems to be in the maintenance of weight loss. Randomized trials consistently show that diet plus exercise produces better maintenance of weight loss than diet only, although this difference is often not significant; these studies do not show significant differences in glycemic control (Level 2).[14,52] Since diet plus exercise is most commonly advocated for weight loss, further research evaluating its benefits for Type 2 diabetics would be useful.

11. Strategies that appear to improve long-term weight loss include self-monitoring, stimulus-control techniques, social support, and continued contact (Level 2).[16,58,60,64]

REFERENCES

1. Blackburn GL, Read JL. Benefits of reducing-revisted. Postgrad Med J 1984;60:13–8.

2. Maggio CA, Pi-Sunyer FX. The prevention and treatment of obesity: application to type 2 diabetes. Diabetes Care 1997;20:1744.

3. Henry RR, Scheaffer L, Olefsky JM. Glycemic effects of intensive caloric restriction and isocaloric refeeding in noninsulin-dependent diabetes mellitus. J Clin Endocrinol Metab 1985;61:917–25.

4. Kelley DE, Wing R, Buonocore C, et al. Relative effects of calorie restriction and weight loss in non-insulin dependent diabetes mellitus. J Clin Endocrinol Metab 1993;77:1287–93.

5. Wing RR, Blair EH, Bononi P, et al. Caloric restriction per se is a significant factor in improvements in glycemic control and insulin sensitivity during weight loss in obese NIDDM patients. Diabetes Care 1994;17:30–6.

6. Sjostrom C, Lissner L, Wedel H, Sjostrom L. Reduction in incidence of diabetes, hypertension and lipid disturbances after intentional weight loss induced by bariatric surgery: the SOS intervention study. Obes Res 1999;7:477–84.

7. Pories WJ, Swanson MS, MacDonald KG, et al. Who would have thought it? An operation proves to be the most effective therapy for adult-onset diabetes mellitus. Ann Surg 1995;222:339–52.

8. MacDonald KJ, Long S, Swanson M, et al. The gastric bypass operation reduces the progression and mortality of non-insulin dependent diabetes mellitus. J Gastrointest Surg 1997;1:213–20.

9. Hollander PA, Elbein SC, Hirsch IB, et al. Role of orlistat in the treatment of obese patients with type 2 diabetes: a 1-year randomized double-blind study. Diabetes Care 1998;21:1288.

10. Rissanen A, Pekkarinen T, Heinanen T, et al. Weight loss with sibutramine in obese patients with type 2 diabetes: a double-blind, placebo-controlled study [abstract]. Obes Res 1999;7(Suppl 1): 93S.

11. UK Prospective Diabetes Study Research Group. UK Prospective Diabetes Study 7: response of fasting plasma glucose to diet therapy in newly presenting Type 2 diabetic patients. Metabolism 1990;39:905–12.

12. Wing RR, Epstein LH, Nowalk MP, et al. Behavior change, weight loss and physiological improvements in Type 2 diabetic patients. J Consult Clin Psychol 1985;53:111–22.

13. Wing RR, Epstein LH, Nowalk MP, et al. Does self-monitoring of blood glucose levels improve dietary compliance for obese patients with Type 2 diabetes? Am J Med 1986;81:830–6.

14. Wing RR, Epstein LH, Paternostro-Bayles M, et al. Exercise in a behavioural weight control programme for obese patients with type 2 (non-insulin-dependent) diabetes. Diabetologia 1988;31:902–9.

15. Wing RR, Epstein LH, Nowalk MP, Scott N. Self-regulation in the treatment of Type 2 diabetes. Behav Ther 1988;19:11–23.

16. Wing RR, Marcus MD, Epstein LH, Jawad A. A "family-based" approach to the treatment of obese Type 2 diabetic patients. J Consult Clin Psychol 1991;59:156–62.

17. Wing RR, Marcus MD, Salata R, et al. Effects of a very-low-calorie diet on long-term glycemic control in obese type 2 diabetic subjects. Arch Intern Med 1991;151:1334–40.

18. Wing RR, Blair E, Marcus M, et al. Year-long weight loss treatment for obese patients with Type 2 diabetes: does inclusion of an intermittent very low calorie diet improve outcome? Am J Med 1994;97:354–62.

19. Blonk MC, Jacobs MAJM, Biesheuvel EHE, et al. Influences on weight loss in type 2 diabetic patients: little long-term benefit from group behaviour therapy and exercise training. Diabet Med 1994;11:449–57.

20. Agurs-Collins T, Kumanyika S, Ten Have T, Adams-Campbell L. A randomized controlled trial of weight reduction and exercise for diabetes management in older African-American subjects. Diabetes Care 1997;20:1503–11.

21. Manning R, Jung R, Leese G, Newton R. The comparison of four weight reduction strategies aimed at overweight diabetic patients. Diabet Med 1995;12:409–15.

22. Manning R, Jung R, Leese G, Newton R. The comparison of four weight reduction strategies aimed at overweight patients with diabetes mellitus: four-year follow-up. Diabet Med 1998;15:497–502.

23. Mancini M, DiDiase G, Contaldo F, et al. Medical complications of severe obesity: importance of treatment by very-low caloric diets: intermediate and long-term effects. Int J Obes 1981;5:341–52.

24. Wing RR, Shoemaker M, Marcus MD, et al. Variables associated with weight loss and improvements in glycemic control in Type 2 diabetic patients in behavioral weight control programs. Int J Obes 1990;14:495–503.

25. Kanders BS, Blackburn GL. Reducing primary risk factors by therapeutic weight loss. In: Wadden TA, Van Itallie TB, editors. Treatment of the seriously obese patient. New York: Guilford; 1992. p. 213–30.

26. Nagulesparan M, Savage PJ, Bennion LJ, et al. Diminished effect of caloric restriction on control of hyperglycemia with increasing known duration of Type 2 diabetes mellitus. J Clin Endocrinol Metab 1981;53:560–8.

27. Williams KV, Mullen ML, Kelley DE, Wing RR. The effect of short periods of caloric restriction on weight loss and glycemic control in type 2 diabetes. Diabetes Care 1998;21:2–8.

28. Watts NB, Spanheimer RG, DiGirolamo M, et al. Prediction of glucose response to weight loss in patients with non-insulin-dependent diabetes mellitus. Arch Intern Med 1990;150:803–6.

29. Khan M, St. Peter J, Breen G, et al. Diabetes disease stage predicts weight loss outcomes with long term appetite suppressants. Diabetes 1999;48(Suppl 1):A308.

30. Davidson MH, Hauptman J, DiGirolamo M, et al. Weight control and risk factor reduction in obese subjects treated for 2 years with orlistat: a randomized controlled trial. JAMA 1999;281:235–42.

31. Guare JC, Wing RR, Grant A. Comparison of obese NIDDM and nondiabetic women: short- and long-term weight loss. Obes Res 1995;3:329–35.

32. Brown S, Upchurch S, Anding R, et al. Promoting weight loss in Type 2 diabetes. Diabetes Care 1996;19:613–24.

33. Wadden TA, Stunkard AJ, Brownell KD. Very low calorie diets: their efficacy, safety, and future. Ann Intern Med 1983;99:675–84.

34. National Task Force on Prevention and Treatment of Obesity. Obesity NTFotPaTo: very low-calorie diets. JAMA 1993;270:967–74.

35. Amatruda JM, Richeson JF, Welle SL, et al. The safety and efficacy of a controlled low-energy (very-low calorie) diet in the treatment of non-insulin dependent diabetes and obesity. Arch Intern Med 1988;148:873–7.

36. Henry RR, Wiest-Kent TA, Scheaffer L, et al. Metabolic consequences of very low calorie diet therapy in obese non-insulin-dependent diabetic and nondiabetic subjects. Diabetes 1986;35:155–64.

37. Wadden TA, Stunkard AJ. Controlled trial of very low calorie diet, behavior therapy, and their combination in the treatment of obesity. J Consult Clin Psychol 1986;54:482–8.

38. Wadden TA, Foster GD, Letizia KA. One-year behavioral treatment of obesity: comparison of moderate and severe caloric restriction and the effects of weight maintenance therapy. J Consult Clin Psychol 1994;62:165–71.

39. Smith DE, Wing RR. Diminished weight loss and behavioral compliance during repeated diets in obese patients with Type 2 diabetes. Health Psychol 1991;10:378–83.

40. Schneider SH, Amorosa LF, Khachadurian AK, Ruderman NB. Studies on the mechanism of improved glucose control during regular exercise in type 2 (non-insulin-dependent) diabetes. Diabetologia 1984;26:355–60.

41. Kelley D, Goodpaster B. Effects of physical activities on insulin action and glucose tolerance in obesity. Med Sci Sports Exerc 1999;31:S619–23.

42. Reitman J, Vasquez B, Klimes I, Nagulesparan M. Improvement of glucose homeostasis after exercise training in non-insulin dependent diabetes. Diabetes Care 1984;7:434–41.42.

43. Trovati M, Carta Q, Cavalot F, et al. Influence of physical training on blood glucose control, glucose tolerance, insulin secretion, and insulin action in non-insulin-dependent diabetic patients. Diabetes Care 1984;7:416–20.

44. Rönnemaa T, Mattila K, Lehtonen A, Kallio V. A controlled randomized study on the effect of long-term physical exercise on the metabolic control in Type 2 diabetic patients. Acta Med Scand 1986;220:219–24.

45. Leon A, Conrad J, Casal D, et al. Exercise for diabetics: effects of conditioning at constant body weight. J Card Rehabil 1984;4:278–86.

46. Ruderman NB, Ganda OP, Johansen K. The effect of physical training on glucose tolerance and plasma lipids in maturity-onset diabetes. Diabetes 1979;28:89–92.

47. Skarfors ET, Wegener TA, Lithell H, Selinus I. Physical training as treatment for type 2 (non-insulin-dependent) diabetes in elderly men. A feasibility study over 2 years. Diabetologia 1987;30:930–3.

48. Hartwell SL, Kaplan RM, Wallace JP. Comparison of behavioral interventions for control of Type 2 diabetes mellitus. Behav Ther 1986;17:447–61.

49. Ligtenberg P, Hoekstra J, Zonderland M, Erkelens D. Effects of physical training on metabolic control in elderly type 2 diabetes mellitus patients. Clin Sci 1997;93:127–35.

50. Raz I, Hauser E, Bursztyn M. Moderate exercise improves glucose metabolism in uncontrolled elderly patients with non-insulin-dependent diabetes mellitus. Isr J Med Sci 1994;30:766–70.

51. Khan S, Rupp J. The effect of exercise conditioning, diet, and drug therapy on glycosylated hemoglobin levels in type 2 (NIDDM) diabetics. J Sports Med Phys Fitness 1995;35:281–8.

52. Wing R. Physical activity in the treatment of the adulthood overweight and obesity: current evidence and research issues. Med Sci Sports Exerc 1999;31:S547–52.

53. NHLBI Obesity Education Initiative Expert Panel on the Identification, Evaluation, and Treatment of Overweight and Obesity in Adults. Clinical guidelines on the identification, evaluation, and treatment of overweight and obesity in adults – the evidence report. Obes Res 1998;6(Suppl 3):51S–210S.

54. Pronk NP, Wing RR. Physical activity and long-term maintenance of weight loss. Obes Res 1994;2:587–99.

55. Kaplan R, Hartwell S, Wilson D, Wallace J. Effects of diet and exercise interventions on control and quality of life in non-insulin-dependent diabetes mellitus. J Gen Intern Med 1987;2:220–8.

56. Bogardus C, Ravussin E, Robbins DC, et al. Effects of physical training and diet therapy on carbohydrate metabolism in patients with glucose intolerance and non-insulin-dependent diabetes mellitus. Diabetes 1984;33:311–8.

57. Vanninen E, Uusitupa M, Siitonen O, et al. Habitual physical activity, aerobic capacity and metabolic control in patients with newly-diagnosed Type 2 (non-insulin-dependent) diabetes mellitus: effect of 1-year diet and exercise intervention. Diabetologia 1992;35:340–6.

58. Guare JC, Wing RR, Marcus MD, et al. Analysis of changes in eating behavior and weight loss in Type 2 diabetic patients. Diabetes Care 1989;12:500–3.

59. Boutelle K, Baker R, Kirschenbaum D, Mitchell M. How can obese weight controllers minimize weight gain during the high risk holiday season? By self-monitoring very consistently. Health Psychol 1999;18:364–8.

60. Jeffery RW, Wing RR, Thorson C, et al. Strengthening behavioral interventions for weight loss: a randomized trial of food provision and monetary incentives. J Consult Clin Psychol 1993;61:1038–45.

61. Jakicic J, Wing R, Winters C. Effects of intermittent exercise and use of home exercise equipment on adherence, weight loss, and fitness in overweight women. JAMA 1999;282:1554–60.

62. Black DR, Gleser LJ, Kooyers KJ. A meta-analytic evaluation of couples weight-loss programs. Health Psychol 1990;9:330–47.

63. Wing RR, Jeffery RW. Benefits of recruiting participants with friends and increasing social support for weight loss maintenance. J Consult Clin Psychol 1999;67:132–8.

64. Perri MG, Nezu AM, Viegener BJ. Improving the long-term management of obesity. New York: John Wiley & Sons; 1992.

CHAPTER 15

Currently Available Oral Hypoglycemic Agents for Type 2 Diabetes Mellitus

Victor M. Montori, MD, and Sean F. Dinneen, MD, FRCPI, FACP

ABSTRACT

When lifestyle modification fails to maintain adequate glycemic control in patients with Type 2 diabetes, an oral hypoglycemic agent is typically used to manage the disease. There are currently five classes of drug available, which differ in their mechanism of action, their side-effect profile, and the degree to which they lower blood sugar. The sulfonylureas and meglitinide analogues are insulin secretagogues; the biguanides and thiazolidinediones are insulin sensitizers, while the α-glucosidase inhibitors act by delaying carbohydrate absorption from the gut. The sulfonylureas and metformin can lower HbA_{1c} levels by up to 2%. The other classes are generally less potent. There is a paucity of evidence on the effects of these agents on mortality and cardiovascular outcomes. Only metformin has been clearly shown to reduce mortality in obese patients with Type 2 diabetes, and it is therefore the preferred first-line agent in this condition. More randomized controlled trials are needed to inform choice of agent decisions in patients with Type 2 diabetes and also to address the long-term effects of these drugs on vascular event rates.

INTRODUCTION

Proper management of patients with Type 2 diabetes must be based on an understanding of the pathophysiology of the disease as well as on clinical trial evidence that approved interventions do more good than harm. The diabetes literature has much more information on the abnormalities of glucose homeostasis in Type 2 diabetes than it does data from large-scale clinical trials. In a review of 280 MEDLINE citations of randomized controlled trials in Type 2 diabetes published between January 1991 and April 1995, it was revealed that major clinical endpoints such as myocardial infarction, stroke, or death were measured in only 4% of trials.[1] The past 3 to 4 years have seen an increase in the number of trials with major clinical endpoints, and, in particular, publication of the United Kingdom Prospective Diabetes Study (UKPDS) has helped address this lack of evidence. This chapter focuses on data from randomized controlled trials and discusses the various oral hypoglycemic agents used to treat the disease. It begins with a brief review of the pathophysiology of the disease; comprehensive reviews have recently been published.[2–4] The following questions are answered in this chapter:

1. What is the mechanism leading to hyperglycemia in people with Type 2 diabetes?
2. How effective are currently available oral agents (sulfonylureas, biguanides, α-glucosidase inhibitors, thiazolidinediones, and meglitinide analogues) in the treatment of hyperglycemia?

WHAT IS THE MECHANISM LEADING TO HYPERGLYCEMIA IN PEOPLE WITH TYPE 2 DIABETES?

Fasting and postprandial hyperglycemia are hallmarks of Type 2 diabetes. Elevated rates of hepatic glucose production, associated with elevated rates of gluconeogenesis, are largely responsible for fasting hyperglycemia. Following meal ingestion, altered rates of splanchnic glucose uptake have been shown to contribute to postprandial hyperglycemia.[5] Rates of hepatic glucose release do not suppress to a normal extent, and glucose uptake by insulin-sensitive tissues, including muscle and adipose tissue, is impaired.[6] Failure to adequately suppress glucagon levels, an impaired ability of glucose to modulate its own metabolism (glucose effectiveness), and elevated levels of free fatty acids are other potential contributors to hyperglycemia. In an individual patient, one or more of these abnormalities may dominate.

These metabolic defects result from altered beta-cell function and altered insulin action. Certain subtypes of diabetes, such as maturity-onset diabetes of youth (MODY), have been linked to genetic defects in specific cellular pathways (eg, glucokinase, the beta-cell glucose sensor, in the case of families with MODY 2). However, for the majority of patients with Type 2 diabetes, the underlying genetic defect(s) are not well understood. Most authorities believe that Type 2 diabetes represents a spectrum, from a predominant defect in insulin secretion to a predominant defect in insulin action. To date, only limited tools exist to determine, in an individual patient, which is the predominant abnormality.

The ideal treatment for Type 2 diabetes is one that corrects all of the underlying metabolic abnormalities, thereby eliminating hyperglycemia, and at the same time improves both duration and quality of life. As outlined in Chapter 14, lifestyle modification may be the closest thing we have to such a treatment. Because this proves to be so difficult to implement and/or maintain over the long term, clinicians frequently use pharmacologic therapy to help achieve glycemic goals. At present, five different classes of oral hypoglycemic agent are available for therapeutic use. These are outlined in Table 15–1 along with their main mechanism of action and common side effects. The remainder of this chapter comprises a detailed discussion of the evidence that these agents do more good than harm.

HOW EFFECTIVE ARE CURRENTLY AVAILABLE ORAL AGENTS IN THE TREATMENT OF HYPERGLYCEMIA?

Sulfonylureas

The sulfonylureas were introduced in the 1950s and, up until recently, have been the main oral agents used in treating Type 2 diabetes. They lower plasma glucose concentrations by stimulating endogenous insulin secretion. Their cellular mechanism of action involves binding of the drug to a specific sulfonylurea receptor on the membrane of the beta cell. Postreceptor signaling occurs independent of the prevailing glucose concentration. Because of this, the most common side effect associated with use of these agents is hypoglycemia. Cardiac myocytes also possess sulfonylurea receptors, and some investigators believe that binding of the drug with these receptors may result in potentially harmful cardiovascular effects.[7]

Newer second-generation agents, such as glipizide and glimepiride, have largely replaced first-generation sulfonylureas such as tolbutamide and chlorpropamide. Published trials evaluating these agents usually compare the glycemic response to the drug with that of placebo. In this setting, a difference in mean glycosylated hemoglobin lowering between groups in the order of 1.0 to 2.0% is typically seen.[8,9] Several studies have compared individual members of this class with each other and found little difference in effect.[10,11] Predictors of a poor initial response to sulfonylurea therapy include a relatively lean body weight, a low plasma insulin response to an oral glucose load, and the presence of antiglutamic acid decarboxylase (anti-GAD) autoantibodies at diagnosis of diabetes.[12,13] Taken together, these factors suggest that the patient has either occult Type 1 diabetes or a variant of Type 2 diabetes characterized by a predominant defect in insulin secretion. The term *primary failure* is used to describe the situation wherein sulfonylurea therapy fails to achieve glycemic goals when the drug is first introduced. Another problem, termed *secondary failure*, describes the inability of these drugs to maintain glycemic goals once they have initially been attained (Figure 15–1). While no study has been designed to determine the precise etiology of secondary failure, it most likely represents a progressive loss of beta-cell function as part of the natural

Table 15–1 Main Oral Agents for the Treatment of Type 2 Diabetes Mellitus

Class: Generic Name	Brand Name (available dosage forms)	Approved Daily Dosage (mg)	Duration of Action (hours or weeks)	Cost*	Metabolism	Elimination	Elimination Half-Life (hours)	Site of Action	Mechanism of Action	Effect on Glucose (mmol/L [mg/dL])	HbA$_{1c}$ Reduction (%)	Effect on Lipids	Effect on Weight	Adverse Effects
Sulfonylureas														
Tolbutamide	Orinase (250, 500)	500–3,000 (2,500)	6–12 h	17.35	Hepatic	Renal		Beta cell	↑Insulin secretion	↓FPG (3.3–3.9 [60–70]) and 24-h mean glucose	1–2%	↔	↑	Hypoglycemia, headache, dizziness, disulfiram-like reactions, hyponatremia
Chlorpropamide	Diabinese (100, 250)	100–500	> 48 h	14.69			30–42							
Tolazamide	Tolinase (100, 250, 500)	100–1,000	12–24 h	3.50			7							
Glipizide	Glucotrol (5–10)	2.5–40	12–18 h	2.79		Renal, intestinal	2–4							
	Glucotrol XL (5–10)	5–20	24 h	10.34										
Glyburide[7]	DiaBeta (1.25, 2.5, 5)	1.25–20	12–24h	15.17		Renal	6–10							
	Micronase (1.25, 2.5, 5)	1.25–20	12–24 h	24.30										
	Glynase (1.5, 3, 6)	0.75–2	12–24 h	17.61										
Glimepiride	Amaryl (1,2, 4)	1–8	24 h	7.34		Renal, intestinal	5–9							
Biguanides														
Metformin	Glucophage (500, 625, 750, 850, 1,000)	500–2,550	6–12h?	54.35	—	Renal	6	Liver, muscle	↓Hepatic glucose production; ↑muscle insulin sensitivity	↓FPG (3.3–3.9 [60–70])	1–2	↓LDL & Tg; ↑HDL	↓, ↔	GI 20–30% (diarrhea, nausea, metallic taste), lactic acidosis

Table 15–1 Main Oral Agents for the Treatment of Type 2 Diabetes Mellitus— *(continued)*

Class: Generic Name	Brand Name (available dosage forms)	Approved Daily Dosage (mg)	Duration of Action (hours or weeks)	Cost*	Metabolism	Elimination	Elimination Half-Life (hours)	Site of Action	Mechanism of Action	Effect on Glucose (mmol/L [mg/dL])	HbA₁c Reduction (%)	Effect on Lipids	Effect on Weight	Adverse Effects
α-Glucosidase inhibitors														
Acarbose	Precose (50, 100)	25–300	<4 h	46.54	Intestinal	Intestinal, renal	2	Small intestine	↓ GI absorption	↓ postprandial increase; ↓FPG (1.4–2 [25–36])	0.7–1.8 (monotherapy) / 0.2–1.4 (combination)	↔	↔	GI disturbances 30% (bloating, flatulence, diarrhea)
Miglitol	Glyset (25, 50, 100)	150–300		51.75										
Thiazolidinediones‡														
Troglitazone‡	Rezulin (200, 400)	200–600	>3 w	89.28	Hepatic	Intestinal, renal	16–34	Muscle, fat, liver	↓ Hepatic glucose production; ↑muscle insulin sensitivity	↓ FPG (1.9–2.2 [35–4(^{q})]) and post-prandial glucose	0.9–1.5	↑ LDL, HDL; ↓ Tg	↑	Hemodilution, edema, idiosyncratic hepatotoxicity, liver enzyme elevation
Rosiglitazone	Avandia (2,4)	2–8	>3–4 w	75.00	Hepatic	Renal, intestinal	3–4							Liver enzyme elevation
Pioglitazone	Actos (15, 30, 45)	15–45	>3–4 w	85.50	Hepatic	Renal, intestinal	3–24							Liver enzyme elevation, URI, edema
Meglitinide analogues														
Repaglinide	Prandin (0.5, 1, 2)	1–16	2–6 h	67.12	Hepatic	Intestinal	1	Beta cell	↑ Insulin secretion	↓ FPG (3.3–3.9 [60–70]) and postprandial glucose	1.5–1.7	↔	↑	Hypoglycemia, headache

*Cost per month to pharmacy based on wholesale price listings (August 1999 USD). Cost shown is of the brand form if a generic form is not available.

†Glyburide is known as glibenclamide in Europe; other sulfonylurea agents used in Europe include gliclazide and gliquidone.

‡Troglitazone is no longer approved for use.

↔ = no change; ↑ = increase; ↓ = decrease; FPG = fasting plasma glucose; Tg = triglycerides; GI = gastrointestinal; LDL = low-density lipoprotein; HDL = high-density lipoprotein.

Data from DeFrozo,[4] American Diabetes Association,[78] and *Physicians' Desk Reference.*[79]

progression of the disease.[14] In this context, secondary failure is not unique to sulfonylureas but has been seen with other oral hypoglycemic agents evaluated in long-term studies.[15,16]

The major side effects associated with use of sulfonylurea agents are hypoglycemia and weight gain (see Figure 15–1). Hypoglycemia is a particular problem in elderly patients and can lead to death in this age group (Table 15–2).[17,18] While individual second-generation sulfonylureas are claimed to have better safety profiles in the setting of renal or hepatic impairment, caution should be exercised when prescribing any of these drugs in the setting of altered drug clearance. Glimepiride is claimed to have a beneficial effect on insulin action in addition to its effect on insulin secretion.[19,20] Since any agent that lowers plasma glucose levels is going to have a beneficial effect on insulin action, this claim is tenuous at best. Hyperinsulinemic euglycemic clamp studies represent the optimal means of assessing insulin action and, when used to compare different hypoglycemic agents (including glimepiride), showed similar effects.[21,22] Weight gain associated with the use of sulfonylurea agents is not clearly understood. At least part of the explanation lies in conservation of calories previously excreted as glycosuria. However, additional factors are likely to be involved, and effects of endogenously secreted insulin on appetite and energy balance have been postulated. In the UKPDS trial, sulfonylurea use in the intensive policy arm was associated with a 2- to 3-kg weight gain.[23]

The outcomes that are most important to patients with Type 2 diabetes include mortality, cardiovascular event rate, and overall quality of life. Because these endpoints either require long periods of follow-up or are difficult to measure, very few trials have included them. The first trial to measure mortality was the controversial University Group Diabetes

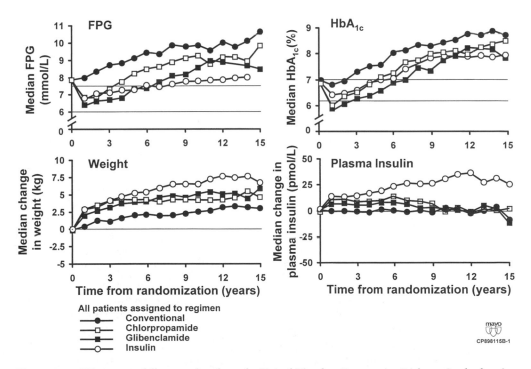

Figure 15–1 Fifteen-year follow-up data from the United Kingdom Prospective Diabetes Study showing the effects on fasting plasma glucose (FPG), glycosylated hemoglobin (HbA$_{1c}$), weight, and plasma-insulin concentration of an intensive versus a conventional glycemic-control policy. The sulfonylurea agents chlorpropamide and glibenclamide lead to similar decreases in FPG and HbA$_{1c}$ levels and similar increases in weight to that seen with exogenous insulin. There is a progressive deterioration in glycemic control seen with all three agents over time. (Reproduced with permission from Anonymous. Intensive blood-glucose control with sulphonylureas or insulin compared with conventional treatment and risk of complications in patients with Type 2 diabetes (UKPDS 33). Lancet 1998;352:837–53.)

Table 15–2 Incidence of Fatal Side Effects with Hypoglycemic Agents

Agent	Incidence of Mortality in 100,000 Persons Treated-Year	Mechanism of Fatal Side Effect	Study
Sulfonylurea	4.11		Cohort study, administrative database of 19,932 elderly subjects on sulfonylureas or insulin (1985–1989)[80]
Insulin	9.2	Hypoglycemia in elderly	
Sulfonylurea/insulin	11.3		
Metformin	9 (0–21)	Lactic acidosis in renal, hepatic, or circulatory insufficiency	Cohort study, administrative database, 11,797 users (1980–1995)[39]
Troglitazone	100	Idiosyncratic acute liver failure	FDA Office of Post-Marketing Risk Assessment[70]
	0.9–9.0		Parke-Davis[70,81]

Data from Stang et al,[39] Endocrinologic and Metabolic Drugs Advisory Committee,[70] Shorr et al,[80] and Miller.[81]

Program. Published in the early 1970s, this was the first large-scale clinical trial in Type 2 diabetes. The results showed a clear increased risk of death with use of tolbutamide compared to placebo or two different insulin regimens.[24] The trial design and analysis received a lot of criticism following publication.[25–28] Nevertheless, it raised serious questions about the long-term safety of these commonly used drugs.

The results of the UKPDS, published in 1998, demonstrated no increased risk of death, myocardial infarction, or other cardiovascular event in a large group of patients treated with sulfonylureas. The trial was not designed to directly compare one hypoglycemic agent with another but rather to compare a policy aimed at intensive glycemic control (fasting glucose values < 6.0 mmol/L) with a policy aimed at more conventional control (fasting glucose values < 15 mmol/L). The protocol called for patients to continue their initial randomly assigned treatment for as long as possible. This stipulation had to be modified during the trial to deal with the progressive deterioration in glycemic control observed with both policies (see Figure 15–1). Nevertheless, the overall results and subgroup analyses suggest that in the setting of newly diagnosed Type 2 diabetes, sulfonylureas appear to be safe. The agents used in UKPDS were chlorpropamide and glibenclamide. It has been suggested that the cardiovascular risk of participants in UKPDS was relatively low, given that they were recruited early in the course of their disease. The Diabetes Mellitus Insulin-Glucose Infusion in Acute Myocardial Infarction (DIGAMI) study assessed the effects of a glucose-insulin infusion followed by at least 3 months of subcutaneous insulin in Type 2 diabetic individuals undergoing treatment for acute myocardial infarction. The trial reported a 29% reduction in mortality among the insulin-treated group at 12 months follow-up.[29] Some investigators have claimed that the improvement in mortality seen in the insulin-treated group in DIGAMI may have resulted from cessation of prior sulfonylurea use in this group. This hypothesis requires further testing.

Measurement of quality of life in Type 2 diabetes has methodologic challenges. One recent randomized controlled trial found improved quality of life in association with use of a delayed release form of glipizide.[30] The UKPDS study included longitudinal and cross-sectional evaluations of quality of life. Although the intensive policy was associated with a reduced incidence of complications, the investigators reported no difference in measures of quality of life.[31] These observations need to be supported with further studies using validated quality-of-life instruments.

Sulfonylurea and Insulin Combination Therapy

Combining insulin with sulfonylurea therapy is a common approach in clinical practice. Many trials have evaluated this approach, but the current authors encountered several challenges to summarizing the existing evidence. Some trials included patients with sulfonylurea failure in whom insulin was added, while others studied patients already on insulin to whom sulfonylureas were added. Recently, three meta-analyses have been published. One meta-analysis[32] (published in 1991) of 8 randomized controlled trials and 14 crossover studies reported an improvement in glycosylated hemoglobin of 0.7% and in fasting plasma glucose of 2 mmol/L. The authors concluded that this difference in glycemic control was not clinically significant and recommended insulin monotherapy in patients with sulfonylurea failure. This meta-analysis included nonplacebo-controlled studies and studies of combination of insulin and metformin. Another meta-analysis published in 1992[33] concluded that combination therapy was beneficial; this conclusion was based mainly on lower insulin requirements and improvement in glycemic control. The most recent meta-analysis was published in 1996.[34] It is methodologically the most rigorous and included 16 randomized trials of insulin/placebo compared to insulin/sulfonylurea. The included trials used a variety of insulin regimens; however, in the majority, dose adjustment of insulin to achieve optimal glycemic control was not a feature. The insulin/sulfonylurea combination was associated with a decrease in fasting plasma glucose of 2.5 mmol/L (versus 0.6 mmol/L in insulin/placebo group) and a decreased HbA_{1c} of 1.1% (versus 0.25% in the insulin/placebo group), without any significant increase in weight. The dose of insulin was significantly smaller in the insulin/sulfonylurea arm than in the insulin/placebo arm. These findings were also observed in the crossover trials analyzed.

Randomized controlled trials of combination therapy continue to be published. However, variation in the design of their interventions remains a problem.[35,36] While the evidence does not clearly support a particular regimen, the commonly used approach of bedtime insulin and daytime sulfonylurea (BIDS) appears to be acceptable to patients, is popular with clinicians, and has a basis in pathophysiology (suppression of overnight hepatic glucose release by insulin and stimulation of postprandial insulin by sulfonylureas).

EVIDENCE-BASED MESSAGES

1. In patients with Type 2 diabetes, sulfonylureas decrease glycosylated hemoglobin by 1 to 2% (Level 1A).[8,9] The available sulfonylureas have similar glucose-lowering effect (Level 1A).[10,11]
2. Patients with Type 2 diabetes who are lean, have a low plasma insulin response to an oral glucose load, or have anti-GAD antibodies at diagnosis are less likely to respond to sulfonylureas (Level 1A).[12,13]
3. Patients with Type 2 diabetes who receive sulfonylureas will experience weight gain of approximately 2 to 3 kg (Level 1A).[23] Major hypoglycemic events occur in 1 to 2% of patients receiving sulfonylureas (Level 1A).[23]
4. Patients with Type 2 diabetes who receive sulfonylureas as part of an intensive policy of glycemic control are not at increased risk of death, myocardial infarction, or other cardiovascular event, compared to patients treated conventionally (Level 1A).[23]
5. In patients with Type 2 diabetes, combination therapy with insulin and sulfonylureas leads to a decrease in glycosylated hemoglobin of approximately 1%, with an associated increase in weight (Level 1A).[34]

Biguanides

The biguanides include metformin and phenformin, although the latter drug was withdrawn from the market in the 1970s because of an unacceptably high risk of fatal lactic acidosis. The precise mechanism of the glucose-lowering effect of metformin remains controversial. The drug is known to alter hepatic gluconeogenesis and lead to lower rates of hepatic glucose release.[37] Increased insulin-stimulated glucose uptake in muscle may be an indirect effect resulting from the lower prevailing glucose levels (see above). Unlike the sulfonylureas, metformin does not stimulate insulin secretion, is not associated with hypoglycemia, and does not cause weight gain. The most common side effect seen with the drug is gastrointestinal disturbance. This tends to be self-limiting and amenable to slow dose titration. The most serious side effect is lactic acidosis. In the initial 12-month period after reintroduction of the drug to the US market, 47 cases of lactic acidosis, leading to 20 deaths, were reported to the Food and Drug Administration (FDA).[38] An administrative database study revealed an incidence of lactic acidosis in patients dispensed metformin of 9 per 100,000 person-years (95%, CI 0 to 21)[39] (see Table 15–2). Careful analysis of these events revealed that in the majority of cases, the fatalities occurred in situations where the drug should not have been prescribed. If the prescribing information is strictly adhered to, the drug appears to be safe. Contraindications include renal impairment (creatinine above 124 μmol/L in women and 133 μmol/L in men) and clinical conditions associated with poor tissue perfusion (eg, cardiac failure, hypoxia, sepsis). Because of the risk of contrast-induced nephropathy associated with radiologic procedures, it has become common practice to stop metformin prior to any procedure involving administration of contrast and to resume it only when postprocedure renal function has been documented as normal.

The magnitude of the glucose-lowering effect associated with metformin monotherapy is similar to that seen with sulfonylureas[40–42] and averages between 1.0 to 2.0 percentage points drop in glycosylated hemoglobin levels, compared to placebo (Figure 15–2). Long-term follow-up data from UKPDS demonstrate that this effect is not maintained over time and that, if met-

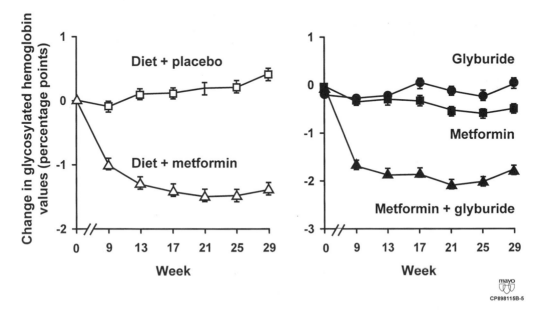

Figure 15–2 Twenty-nine-week follow-up data showing the effect of metformin on glycosylated hemoglobin values in patients with Type 2 diabetes previously treated with diet (left panel) and the effects of metformin monotherapy, glyburide monotherapy, and combination metformin/glyburide therapy (right panel). (Reproduced with permission from DeFronzo RA, Goodman AM. Efficacy of metformin in patients with non-insulin-dependent diabetes mellitus. The Multicenter Metformin Study Group. N Engl J Med 1995;333:541–9.)

formin is used as monotherapy, it frequently requires the addition of another agent to maintain glycemic goals.[15] The so-called pivotal trials of metformin use that led to re-introduction of the drug in the United States demonstrated a similar effect when metformin was used as monotherapy for diet failure or added to a sulfonylurea following secondary failure of that agent—1.5 versus 1.6 percentage points drop in glycosylated hemoglobin, respectively (see Figure 15–2).[43] In addition, use of the drug was associated with a beneficial effect on serum lipids.

Within UKPDS, a subset of overweight patients randomized to the intensive policy received metformin as their primary therapy. While glycemic control did not differ between this group and those assigned to receive chlorpropamide, glibenclamide, or insulin, weight change and cardiovascular outcomes did differ between groups. Patients who received metformin had significantly less weight gain and had a lower risk of any diabetes-related endpoint (a cumulative endpoint including sudden death, death from hyperglycemia or hypoglycemia, fatal or nonfatal myocardial infarction, angina, heart failure, stroke, renal failure, amputation, vitreous hemorrhage, retinopathy requiring photocoagulation, blindness in one eye, or cataract extraction), diabetes-related death, and myocardial infarction compared to the other treatment groups.[15] These data present compelling evidence to support the use of metformin as initial therapy in obese Type 2 diabetic patients. There is a cautionary note from UKPDS relating to the substudy in which patients, who developed secondary failure of sulfonylureas, were randomized either to addition of metformin or continued use of sulfonylurea alone. Within this substudy, individuals assigned to metformin had a significantly higher incidence of diabetes-related death. The number of events in this substudy was small and the overall conclusion of the investigators was that use of metformin in this setting needed further evaluation.

EVIDENCE-BASED MESSAGES

1. In patients with Type 2 diabetes, metformin use is associated with a 1 to 2% decrease in glycosylated hemoglobin (Level 1A),[40] similar to that for sulfonylureas (Level 1A).[41,42]
2. In overweight patients with Type 2 diabetes, an intensive glycemic control policy using metformin is associated with less weight gain and less hypoglycemia than an intensive policy using sulfonylureas or insulin therapy (Level 1A).[15]
3. In overweight patients with Type 2 diabetes, an intensive policy using metformin is associated with a reduced risk of all-cause mortality, any diabetes-related endpoints, and stroke, compared with results of a conventional policy (Level 1A).[15]

α-Glucosidase Inhibitors

There are two medications available in this class, acarbose and miglitol. Their mechanism of action is through inhibition of luminal intestinal brush border α-glucosidase activity. This leads to a delay in carbohydrate absorption and a blunting of the postprandial glucose level. Increased gut absorption of carbohydrate has not traditionally been viewed as a contributing factor in the pathophysiology of diabetes. However, recent studies suggest that the splanchnic response to meal ingestion may not be normal in Type 2 diabetes.[5,44] The α-glucosidase inhibitors may mitigate these abnormal responses. There is a clear dose-response effect: the more enzyme inhibition, the greater the glucose lowering.[45,46] The major side effects, bloating, flatulence, and diarrhea, are also related to α-glucosidase inhibition. Attempts to alleviate side effects through enzyme repletion have led to better tolerance but less efficacy.[47]

Acarbose, as monotherapy, reduces postprandial plasma glucose levels at 1 hour by 1.4 to 2 mmol/L.[48,49] Most trials of acarbose or miglitol have also demonstrated a decrease in fasting plasma glucose as well as a concomitant glycosylated hemoglobin decrease in the range of 0.7 to 1.8%, compared to placebo.[48–50] The majority of the larger trials have evaluated these drugs in the setting of combination therapy. In this setting, the HbA_{1c} lowering effect has ranged from 0.2 to 1.4% (Figure 15–3).[50–53] Studies of long duration report poor compliance due to flatulence and diarrhea.[51]

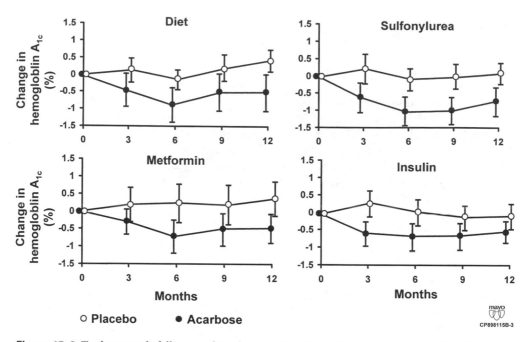

Figure 15–3 Twelve-month follow-up data showing the effects of acarbose compared to placebo on mean HbA_{1c} levels in patients with Type 2 diabetes mellitus previously treated with diet alone, sulfonylurea, metformin, and insulin. (Reproduced with permission from Chiasson J-L, Josse R, Hunt J, et al. The efficacy of acarbose in the treatment of patients with non-insulin dependent diabetes: a multicenter controlled clinical trial. Ann Intern Med 1994;121:928–35.)

EVIDENCE-BASED MESSAGES

1. In patients with Type 2 diabetes, α-glucosidase inhibitors decrease glycosylated hemoglobin by 0.7 to 1.8% (Level 1A).[48–50] In combination with other agents, α-glucosidase inhibitors decrease glycosylated hemoglobin by 0.2 to 1.4% without significant changes in body weight or hypoglycemia (Level 1A).[50–53]
2. Patients with Type 2 diabetes are poorly compliant with α-glucosidase inhibitors due to flatulence and diarrhea (Level 1A).[51]

Thiazolidinediones

This therapeutic class contains two agents currently approved for use, namely, rosiglitazone and pioglitazone, and one agent, troglitazone, that has been withdrawn from the market because of toxicity. All three agents bind to the nuclear receptor peroxisome proliferator-activated receptor-gamma (PPAR-γ)[54] and have been shown to improve insulin action.[55] Based on published data from randomized controlled trials, the glucose-lowering effect associated with use of troglitazone as monotherapy is not as great as that associated with the use of sulfonylureas or metformin. The thiazolidinediones need approximately 6 weeks to achieve their full glucose-lowering effect, and it is likely that monotherapy trials of relatively short duration and washout of previously used hypoglycemic agents[56,57] represent a minimal estimate of the drug's effect. Nevertheless, trials of longer duration with troglitazone monotherapy were still associated with, at best, a 0.9% reduction in HbA_{1c}.[58,59] Trials involving newer members of this class have shown a mean reduction in HbA_{1c} up to 1.5%.[60,61] Comparative studies within this class have not been published.

Each of these drugs has been approved for use in combination with other hypoglycemic agents, including insulin, sulfonylureas, and metformin. The trials studying combination therapy are not burdened with the same methodologic limitations as in monotherapy trials. One of the two pivotal trials of troglitazone/insulin focused on the ability of the drug to reduce the need for exogenous insulin.[62] There are no data to indicate that large doses of exogenous insulin are harmful; nevertheless, the concept of a drug with the potential to reduce or even eliminate the need for exogenous insulin remains appealing to patients and providers. The other pivotal trial addressed the glucose-lowering effect of troglitazone 600 mg/insulin therapy and reported a 1.5% reduction in HbA$_{1c}$, compared to insulin/placebo (Figure 15–4).[63] Other trials have assessed the combination of troglitazone/sulfonylurea[59,64,65] and troglitazone/metformin,[66] showing varying HbA$_{1c}$ reductions. These appeared to be dose related and ranged from 0.8 to 2.7% in the sulfonylurea trials and 1.2% in the metformin trial. Combination therapy using rosiglitazone with metformin led to a dose-dependent decrease in HbA$_{1c}$ of 1 to 1.2% and weight increase of 0.7 to 1.9 kg, compared with weight loss of 1.2 kg in the metformin group.[67] Results of other trials of combination therapy with rosiglitazone and pioglitazone are only available in preliminary publications, but these drugs appear to be as efficacious.[68,69]

Much has been written on the safety of the thiazolidinediones. The first agent of this class to be introduced in the US market, troglitazone, resulted in 43 cases of liver failure, including 7 liver transplants and 28 deaths.[70] This was recognized from postmarketing monitoring by the pharmaceutical company and the FDA. The company's estimated risk of liver failure leading to death or transplant in patients initiating the drug in 1997 was 1 in 36,000. This figure was later reduced (presumably by careful monitoring of liver enzymes) to 1 in 57,000.[70] In retrospect, preclinical data did suggest an effect of the drug on the liver.[71] This hepatotoxicity has not been noted in clinical trials of rosiglitazone and pioglitazone. Although there are not enough postmarketing data available at this time to judge their long-term safety, the newer agents appear to be safer than troglitazone. This realization resulted in the removal of troglitazone from the US market in March 2000.

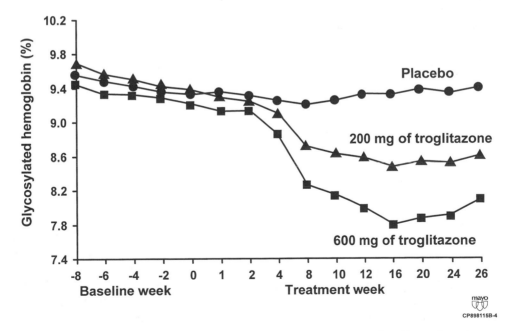

Figure 15–4 Data from a 26-week randomized controlled trial comparing the effects of troglitazone 200 mg and troglitazone 600 mg with placebo on glycosylated hemoglobin levels. (Reproduced with permission from Schwartz S, Raskin P, Fonseca F, Graveline JF. Effect of troglitazone in insulin-treated patients with Type 2 diabetes mellitus. Troglitazone and Exogenous Insulin Study Group. N Engl J Med 1998;338:861–6.)

EVIDENCE-BASED MESSAGES

1.   Patients with Type 2 diabetes treated with thiazolidinedione monotherapy can reduce their glycosylated hemoglobin by approximately 0.9 to 1.5% (Level 1A).[58–61]
2.   Patients with Type 2 diabetes treated with a combination of metformin and rosiglitazone can reduce their glycosylated hemoglobin by approximately 1 to 1.2% (Level 1A).[61]
3.   In patients with Type 2 diabetes, rosiglitazone, in combination with metformin, increases body weight by 0.7 to 1.9 kg in a dose-dependent manner and is not associated with hypoglycemia (Level 1A).[67]

Meglitinide Analogues

These meglitinide analogues, repaglinide and nateglinide, represent the newest class of hypoglycemic drugs to be approved for use in patients with Type 2 diabetes. They are nonsulfonylurea insulin secretagogues, and their cellular mechanism of action is related in part to stimulation of endogenous insulin secretion by a mechanism that does not involve binding to the sulfonylurea receptor on the beta cell. Their duration of action is short, and their recommended dosing is with meal ingestion.

Relatively few randomized controlled trials have been published on these agents. In a phase II trial of short duration using repaglinide, dose-related reductions in fasting plasma glucose of 3.4 mmol/L and in HbA_{1c} levels of 1.7% were shown.[72] Another brief phase II trial using nateglinide showed a dose-related decrease in fructosamine of up to 55 μmol/L, or an approximate 1.5% reduction in HbA_{1c}.[73] In a single published report evaluating the addition of repaglinide to patients treated with metformin, a reduction in HbA_{1c} of 1.4% at 3 months was shown.[74] In a multicenter, randomized, comparative study of glyburide and preprandial repaglinide with dose adjustment aimed at optimal glycemic control, both agents were shown to have similar efficacy; repaglinide, given in three 0.5- to 4.0-mg preprandial doses, decreased HbA_{1c} by 1.5% at 12 months in drug-naïve patients.[75] In a similar study enrolling a higher proportion of patients previously treated with sulfonylureas or metformin, no differences in HbA_{1c} in the repaglinide and glyburide groups were shown after 1 year.[76] This initial clinical trial experience suggests that these drugs are well tolerated.

EVIDENCE-BASED MESSAGES

1.   In patients with Type 2 diabetes, preprandial repaglinide may effectively decrease the glycosylated hemoglobin by 1 to 2% (Level 1A)[72,74]; this effect is not significantly different from that seen with sulfonylurea therapy (Level 1A).[75–76]
2.   Patients with Type 2 diabetes receiving repaglinide are at similar risk of hypoglycemia as patients receiving sulfonylureas (Level 1A).[76]

CONCLUSION

The past few years have seen a considerable increase in the availability of oral hypoglycemic agents. As outlined in this chapter, these drugs differ in their mechanism and duration of action, in their side-effect profile, and in their cost to the patient. These factors frequently contribute to the choice of agent used to manage the patient's hyperglycemia. There are some situations where the literature may support use of one type of oral agent over another. Thus, the use of metformin as the preferred oral agent in obese patients who have failed to maintain adequate glycemic control with lifestyle modification is supported by the literature and accepted by most as best practice. Unfortunately, most other treatment decisions are influenced more by individual provider preference, and there is a paucity of evidence to establish which management strategy is optimal. Additional randomized controlled trials assessing hard clinical endpoints to better inform the diabetes community on these issues were called for in a recent review article.[77]

SUMMARY OF EVIDENCE-BASED MESSAGES

1. In patients with Type 2 diabetes, sulfonylureas decrease glycosylated hemoglobin by 1 to 2% (Level 1A).[8,9] The available sulfonylureas have similar glucose-lowering effect (Level 1A).[10,11]

2. Patients with Type 2 diabetes who are lean, have a low plasma insulin response to an oral glucose load, or have anti-GAD antibodies at diagnosis are less likely to respond to sulfonylureas (Level 1A).[12,13]

3. Patients with Type 2 diabetes who receive sulfonylureas will experience weight gain of approximately 2 to 3 kg (Level 1A).[23] Major hypoglycemic events occur in 1 to 2% of patients receiving sulfonylureas (Level 1A).[23]

4. Patients with Type 2 diabetes who receive sulfonylureas as part of an intensive policy of glycemic control are not at increased risk of death, myocardial infarction, or other cardiovascular event, compared to patients treated conventionally (Level 1A).[23]

5. In patients with Type 2 diabetes, combination therapy with insulin and sulfonylureas leads to a decrease in glycosylated hemoglobin of approximately 1%, with an associated increase in weight (Level 1A).[34]

6. In patients with Type 2 diabetes, metformin use is associated with a 1 to 2% decrease in glycosylated hemoglobin (Level 1A),[40] similar to sulfonylureas (Level 1A).[41,42]

7. In overweight patients with Type 2 diabetes, an intensive glycemic control policy using metformin is associated with less weight gain and less hypoglycemia than an intensive policy using sulfonylureas or insulin therapy (Level 1A).[15]

8. In overweight patients with Type 2 diabetes, an intensive policy using metformin is associated with a reduced risk of all-cause mortality, any diabetes-related endpoints, and stroke compared to a conventional policy (Level 1A).[15]

9. In patients with Type 2 diabetes, α-glucosidase inhibitors decrease glycosylated hemoglobin by 0.7 to 1.8% (Level 1A).[48–50] In combination with other agents, α-glucosidase inhibitors decrease glycosylated hemoglobin by 0.2 to 1.4% without significant changes in body weight or hypoglycemia (Level 1A).[50–53]

10. Patients with Type 2 diabetes are poorly compliant with α-glucosidase inhibitors due to flatulence and diarrhea (Level 1A).[51]

11. Patients with Type 2 diabetes treated with thiazolidinedione monotherapy can reduce their glycosylated hemoglobin by approximately 0.9 to 1.5% (Level 1A).[58–61]

12. Patients with Type 2 diabetes treated with a combination of metformin and rosiglitazone can reduce their glycosylated hemoglobin by approximately 1 to 1.2% (Level 1A).[67]

13. In patients with Type 2 diabetes, rosiglitazone, in combination with metformin, increases body weight by 0.7 to 1.9 kg in a dose-dependent manner and is not associated with hypoglycemia (Level 1A).[67]

14. In patients with Type 2 diabetes, preprandial repaglinide may effectively decrease the glycosylated hemoglobin by 1 to 2% (Level 1A)[72,74]; this effect is not significantly different from that seen with sulfonylurea therapy (Level 1A).[75,76]

15. Patients with Type 2 diabetes receiving repaglinide are at similar risk of hypoglycemia as patients receiving sulfonylureas (Level 1A).[76]

REFERENCES

1. McIver B, Dinneen S. An overview of randomized controlled trials in non-insulin dependent diabetes mellitus. Diabetologia 1996;39(Suppl 1):A193.

2. Dinneen S, Gerich J, Rizza R. Carbohydrate metabolism in non-insulin-dependent diabetes mellitus. N Engl J Med 1992;327:707–13.

3. Draznin B, Rizza R, editors. Clinical research in diabetes and obesity. Totowa (NJ): Humana Press; 1997.

4. DeFronzo R, editor. Current therapy of diabetes mellitus. St. Louis: Mosby; 1998.

5. Ludvik B, Nolan JJ, Roberts A, et al. Evidence for decreased splanchnic glucose uptake after oral glucose administration in non-insulin-dependent diabetes mellitus. J Clin Invest 1997;100:2354–61.

6. Firth RG, Bell PM, Marsh HM, et al. Postprandial hyperglycemia in patients with noninsulin-dependent diabetes mellitus. Role of hepatic and extrahepatic tissues. J Clin Invest 1986;77:1525–32.

7. Brady P, Terzic A. The sulfonylurea controversy: more questions from the heart. J Am Coll Cardiol 1998;31:950–6.

8. Simonson DC, Kourides IA, Feinglos M, et al. Efficacy, safety, and dose-response characteristics of glipizide gastrointestinal therapeutic system on glycemic control and insulin secretion in NIDDM. Results of two multicenter, randomized, placebo-controlled clinical trials. The Glipizide Gastrointestinal Therapeutic System Study Group. Diabetes Care 1997;20:597–606.

9. Rosenstock J, Samols E, Muchmore DB, Schneider J. Glimepiride, a new once-daily sulfonylurea. A double-blind placebo-controlled study of NIDDM patients. Glimepiride Study Group. Diabetes Care 1996;19:1194–9.

10. Sonksen P, Lowy C, Perkins J, Lim H. Non-insulin-dependent diabetes: 10-year outcome in relation to initial response to diet and subsequent sulfonylurea therapy. Diabetes Care 1984; 7(Suppl 1):59–66.

11. Blohme G, Waldenstrom J. Glibenclamide and glipizide in maturity onset diabetes. A double-blind cross-over study. Acta Med Scand 1979;206:263–7.

12. Lyons T, Kennedy L, Atkinson A, et al. Predicting the need for insulin therapy in late onset (40–69 years) diabetes mellitus. Diabet Med 1984;1:105–7.

13. Turner R, Stratton I, Horton V, et al. UKPDS 25: autoantibodies to islet-cell cytoplasm and glutamic acid decarboxylase for prediction of insulin requirement in type 2 diabetes. Lancet 1997;350:1288–93.

14. Matthews D, Cull C, Stratton I, et al. UKPDS 26: sulphonylurea failure in non-insulin-dependent diabetic patients over six years. Diabet Med 1998;15:297–303.

15. Anonymous. Effect of intensive blood-glucose control with metformin on complications in overweight patients with type 2 diabetes (UKPDS 34). Lancet 1998;352:854–65.

16. Anonymous. Glycemic control with diet, sulfonylurea, metformin, or insulin in patients with type 2 diabetes mellitus. Progressive requirements for multiple therapies (UKPDS 49). JAMA 1999;281:2005–12.

17. Shorr RI, Ray WA, Daugherty J, Griffin M. Individual sulfonylureas and serious hypoglycemia in older people. J Am Geriatr Soc 1996;44:751–5.

18. Ben-Ami H, Nagachandran P, Mendelson A, Edoute Y. Drug-induced hypoglycemic coma in 102 diabetic patients. Arch Intern Med 1999;159:281–4.

19. Sato J, Ohsawa I, Oshida Y, et al. Effects of glimepiride on in vivo insulin action in normal and diabetic rats. Diabetes Res Clin Pract 1993;22:3–9.

20. Muller G, Wied S. The sulfonylurea drug, glimepiride, stimulates glucose transport, glucose transporter translocation, and dephosphorylation in insulin-resistant rat adiopocytes in vitro. Diabetes 1993;42:1852–67.

21. Clark H, Matthews D. The effect of glimepiride on pancreatic beta-cell function under hypergly-caemic clamp and hyperinsulinaemic, euglycaemic clamp conditions in non-insulin-dependent diabetes mellitus. Horm Metab Res 1996;28:445–50.

22. Firth R, Bell P, Rizza R. Effects of tolazamide and exogenous insulin on insulin action in patients with non-insulin-dependent diabetes mellitus. N Engl J Med 1986;314:1280–6.

23. Anonymous. Intensive blood-glucose control with sulphonylureas or insulin compared with conventional treatment and risk of complications in patients with type 2 diabetes (UKPDS 33). Lancet 1998;352:837–53.

24. Meinert C, Knatterud G, Prout T, Klimt C. A study of the effects of hypoglycemic agents on vascular complications in patients with adult-onset diabetes. II. Mortality results. Diabetes 1970;19 (Suppl):789–830.

25. Kilo C, Miller J, Williamson J. The Achilles heel of the University Group Diabetes Program. JAMA 1980;243:450–7.

26. Scott J, Poffenbarger P. Tolbutamide pharmacogenetics and the UGDP controversy. JAMA 1979;242:45–8.

27. O'Sullivan J, D'Agostino R. Decisive factors in the tolbutamide controversy. JAMA 1975;232:825–9.

28. Seltzer H. A summary of criticisms of the findings and conclusions of the University Group Diabetes Program (UGDP). Diabetes 1972;21:976–9.

29. Malmberg K. Prospective randomised study of intensive insulin treatment on long term survival after acute myocardial infarction in patients with diabetes mellitus. DIGAMI (Diabetes Mellitus, Insulin Glucose Infusion in Acute Myocardial Infarction) Study Group. BMJ 1997;314:1512–5.

30. Testa MA, Simonson DC. Health economic benefits and quality of life during improved glycemic control in patients with type 2 diabetes mellitus: a randomized, controlled, double-blind trial. JAMA 1998;280:1490–6.

31. Anonymous. Quality of life in type 2 diabetic patients is affected by complications but not by intensive policies to improve blood glucose or blood pressure control (UKPDS 37). Diabetes Care 1999;22:1125–36.

32. Peters A, Davidson M. Insulin plus a sulfonylurea agent for treating type 2 diabetes. Ann Intern Med 1991;115:45–53.

33. Pugh J, Wagner M, Sawyer J, et al. Is combination sulfonylurea and insulin therapy useful in NIDDM patients? A meta-analysis. Diabetes Care 1992;15:953–9.

34. Johnson JL, Wolf SL, Kabadi UM. Efficacy of insulin and sulfonylurea combination therapy in Type 2 diabetes. A meta-analysis of the randomized placebo-controlled trials. Arch Intern Med 1996;156:259–64.

35. Feinglos MN, Thacker CR, Lobaugh B, et al. Combination insulin and sulfonylurea therapy in insulin-requiring type 2 diabetes mellitus. Diabetes Res Clin Prac 1998;39:193–9.

36. Riddle MC, Schneider J. Beginning insulin treatment of obese patients with evening 70/30 insulin plus glimepiride versus insulin alone. Glimepiride Combination Group. Diabetes Care 1998;21:1052–7.

37. Cusi K, Consoli A, DeFronzo R. Metabolic effects of metformin on glucose and lactate metabolism in non-insulin dependent diabetes mellitus. J Clin Endocrinol Metab 1996;81:4059–67.

38. Misbin R, Green L, Stadel B, et al. Lactic acidosis in patients with diabetes treated with metformin. N Engl J Med 1998;338:265–6.

39. Stang M, Wysowski D, Butler-Jones D. Incidence of lactic acidosis in metformin users. Diabetes Care 1999;22:925–7.

40. Johansen K. Efficacy of metformin in the treatment of NIDDM—meta-analysis. Diabetes Care 1999;22(1):33–7.

41. Hermann LS, Schersten B, Bitzen PO, et al. Therapeutic comparison of metformin and sulfonylurea, alone and in various combinations. A double-blind controlled study. Diabetes Care 1994;17:1100–9.

42. Anonymous. UKPDS 13: relative efficacy of randomly allocated diet, sulfonylureas, insulin, or metformin in patients with newly diagnosed non-insulin dependent diabetes followed for three years. BMJ 1995;310:83–8.

43. DeFronzo RA, Goodman AM. Efficacy of metformin in patients with non-insulin-dependent diabetes mellitus. The Multicenter Metformin Study Group. N Engl J Med 1995;333:541–9.

44. Basu A, Basu R, Shah P, et al. Effects of type 2 diabetes on the ability of insulin and glucose to regulate splanchnic and muscle glucose metabolism. Evidence for a defect in hepatic glucokinase activity. Diabetes 2000;49:272–83.

45. Coniff R, Shapiro J, Robbins D, et al. Reduction of glycosylated hemoglobin and postprandial hyperglycemia by acarbose in patients with NIDDM. A placebo-controlled dose-comparison study. Diabetes Care 1995;18:817–24.

46. Fischer S, Hanefeld M, Spengler M, et al. European study on dose-response relationship of acarbose as a first-line drug in non-insulin-dependent diabetes mellitus: efficacy and safety of low and high doses. Acta Diabetol 1998;35(1):34–40.

47. Lettieri J, Dain B. Effects of Beano on the tolerability and pharmacodynamics of acarbose. Clin Ther 1998;20:497–504.

48. Chan JC, Chan KW, Ho LL, et al. An Asian multicenter clinical trial to assess the efficacy and tolerability of acarbose compared with placebo in type 2 diabetic patients previously treated with diet. Asian Acarbose Study Group. Diabetes Care 1998;21:1058–61.

49. Hoffmann J, Spengler M. Efficacy of 24-week monotherapy with acarbose, metformin, or placebo in dietary-treated NIDDM patients: the Essen-II Study. Am J Med 1997;103:483–90.

50. Johnston PS, Feig PU, Coniff RF, et al. Chronic treatment of African-American type 2 diabetic patients with alpha-glucosidase inhibition. Diabetes Care 1998;21:416–22.

51. Holman R, Cull C, Turner R. A randomized double-blind trial of acarbose in type 2 diabetes shows improved glycemic control over 3 years (UKPDS 44). Diabetes Care 1999;22:960–4.

52. Coniff R, Shapiro J, Seaton T, et al. A double-blind placebo-controlled trial evaluating the safety and efficacy of acarbose for the treatment of patients with insulin-requiring type 2 diabetes. Diabetes Care 1995;18:928–32.

53. Chiasson J-L, Josse R, Hunt J, et al. The efficacy of acarbose in the treatment of patients with non-insulin dependent diabetes mellitus: a multicenter controlled clinical trial. Ann Intern Med 1994;121:928–35.

54. Barroso I, Gurnell M, Crowley V, et al. Dominant negative mutations in human PPAR gamma associated with severe insulin resistance, diabetes mellitus and hypertension. Nature 1999;402:880–3.

55. Iwamoto Y, Kusuya T, Matsuda A, et al. Effect of new oral antidiabetic agent CS-045 on glucose tolerance and insulin secretion in patients with NIDDM. Diabetes Care 1991;14:1083–6.

56. Kumar S, Prange A, Schulze J, et al. Troglitazone, an insulin action enhancer, improves glycaemic control and insulin sensitivity in elderly type 2 diabetic patients. Diabet Med 1998;15:772–9.

57. Fonseca VA, Valiquett TR, Huang SM, et al. Troglitazone monotherapy improves glycemic control in patients with type 2 diabetes mellitus: a randomized, controlled study. The Troglitazone Study Group. J Clin Endocrinol Metab 1998;83:3169–76.

58. Maggs DG, Buchanan TA, Burant CF, et al. Metabolic effects of troglitazone monotherapy in type 2 diabetes mellitus. A randomized, double-blind, placebo-controlled trial. Ann Intern Med 1998;128:176–85.

59. Horton ES, Whitehouse F, Ghazzi MN, et al. Troglitazone in combination with sulfonylurea restores glycemic control in patients with type 2 diabetes. The Troglitazone Study Group. Diabetes Care 1998;21:1462–9.

60. Patel J, Anderson R, Rappaport E. Rosiglitazone monotherapy improves glycemic control in patients with type 2 diabetes: a twelve-week randomized placebo-controlled study. Diabetes Obes Metab 1999;1:165–72.

61. Grunberger G, Weston W, Patwardhan R, Rappaport E. Rosiglitazone once or twice daily improves glycemic control in patients with type 2 diabetes. Diabetes 1999;48(Suppl 1):A102.

62. Buse JB, Gumbiner B, Mathias NP, et al. Troglitazone use in insulin-treated type 2 diabetic patients. The Troglitazone Insulin Study Group. Diabetes Care 1998;21:1455–61.

63. Schwartz S, Raskin P, Fonseca V, Graveline JF. Effect of troglitazone in insulin-treated patients with Type 2 diabetes mellitus. Troglitazone and Exogenous Insulin Study Group. N Engl J Med 1998;338:861–6.

64. Iwamoto Y, Kosaka K, Kuzuya T, et al. Effect of combination therapy of troglitazone and sulphonylureas in patients with type 2 diabetes who were poorly controlled by sulphonylurea therapy alone. Diabet Med 1996;13:365–70.

65. Buysschaert M, Bobbioni E, Starkie M, Frith L. Troglitazone in combination with sulphonylurea improves glycaemic control in type 2 diabetic patients inadequately controlled by sulphonylurea therapy alone. Troglitazone Study Group. Diabet Med 1999;16:147–53.

66. Inzucchi SE, Maggs DG, Spollett GR, et al. Efficacy and metabolic effects of metformin and troglitazone in Type 2 diabetes mellitus. N Engl J Med 1998;338:867–72.

67. Fonseca V, Rosenstock J, Patwardhan R, Salzman A. Effect of metformin and rosiglitazone combination therapy in patients with type 2 diabetes mellitus. A randomized controlled trial. JAMA 2000;283:1695–702.

68. Charbonnel B, Lonnqvist F, Jones N, et al. Rosiglitazone is superior to glyburide in reducing fasting plasma glucose after one year of treatment in type 2 diabetic patients. Diabetes 1999;48 (Suppl 1):A114–5.

69. Actos—prescription information. Takeda Chemical Industries, Ltd. Available from: URL: http://www.actos.com/pi.htm.

70. Meeting 72. Endocrinologic and Metabolic Drugs Advisory Committee. Washington (DC): United States Food and Drug Administration. Available from: URL: http://www.fda.gov/ohrms/dockets/ac/99/transcpt/3499t1a.pdf 1999 Mar 26.

71. Watkins PB, Whitcomb RW. Hepatic dysfunction associated with troglitazone. N Engl J Med 1998;338:916–7.

72. Goldberg RB, Einhorn D, Lucas CP, et al. A randomized placebo-controlled trial of repaglinide in the treatment of type 2 diabetes. Diabetes Care 1998;21:1897–903.

73. Skillman C, Raskin P. A double-masked placebo-controlled trial assessing effects of various doses of BTS 67582, a novel insulinotropic agent, on fasting hyperglycemia in NIDDM patients. Diabetes Care 1997;20:591–6.

74. Moses R, Slobodniuk R, Boyages S, et al. Effect of repaglinide addition to metformin monotherapy on glycemic control in patients with type 2 diabetes. Diabetes Care 1999;22:119–24.

75. Marbury T, Huang W, Strange P, Lebovitz H. Repaglinide versus glyburide: a one-year comparison trial. Diabetes Res Clin Pract 1999;43:155–66.

76. Wolffenbuttel B, Landgraf R. A 1-year multicenter randomized double blind comparison of repaglinide and glyburide for the treatment of type 2 diabetes. Dutch and German Repaglinide Study Group. Diabetes Care 1999;22:463–7.

77. Richter B, Berger M. Randomized controlled trials remain fundamental to clinical decision making in Type 2 diabetes mellitus: a comment on the debate on randomized controlled trials. Diabetologia 2000;43:254–8.

78. ADA. Medical Management of type 2 diabetes. In: Kelly DE, editor. Clinical education series. Alexandria (VA): American Diabetes Association; 1998.

79. Physicians' Desk Reference. Oradell (NJ): Medical Economics Co.; 1999.

80. Shorr RI, Ray WA, Daugherty JR, Griffin MR. Incidence and risk factors for serious hypoglycemia in older persons using insulin or sulfonylureas. Arch Intern Med 1997;157:1681–6.

81. Miller J. Advisory panel hears contradictory evidence, backs keeping troglitazone on market. Am J Health Syst Pharm 1999;56:840–2.

CHAPTER 16

Alternative Therapy: The Role Of Selected Minerals, Vitamins, Fiber, and Herbs in Treating Hyperglycemia

Jeannette M. Goguen, MD, FRCPC, and
Lawrence A. Leiter, MD, FRCPC, FACP

ABSTRACT

Patients with diabetes mellitus frequently use alternative medicine. The purpose of this chapter is to critically review the evidence for the glycemic benefit of alternative therapies that are in common use as well as their toxicities. Several general issues are addressed first, including concerns with the literature relating to alternative medicine as a whole, the methodology of the studies, and the substances themselves. Subsequently, the following specific substances are examined in detail: several minerals (chromium, vanadium, magnesium), vitamins and/or antioxidants (vitamin C, vitamin E, coenzyme Q, biotin), fiber, fish oil, and ginseng.

There is evidence from reasonably well-conducted trials that some food and herbal substances may have beneficial effects on glycemia in patients with diabetes. This evidence is most notable for chromium, soluble fiber, and vitamin C. Fish oil is also beneficial, but only in Type 1 diabetes. There is less evidence for ginseng, vanadium, and biotin. Studies demonstrate that there is no impact on glycemia from the use of coenzyme Q. It is difficult to draw conclusions about magnesium and vitamin E due to the inconsistency of results among studies. More high-quality randomized controlled trials (RCTs) are required to establish the safety and efficacy of these substances.

INTRODUCTION

Alternative therapy, also known as complementary or unconventional medicine, can be defined as therapy that does not conform to the standards of the medical community, that is not taught widely in North American schools, and that is not available in North American hospitals.[1] It is commonly used by patients with diabetes (25% of 403 subjects with diabetes mellitus in one study[2]) for multiple reasons: (1) to improve glycemic control; (2) to improve other metabolic parameters (eg, lipid status); (3) in an effort to reduce oxidative stress (ie, to provide antioxidants) so that the risk of micro- and macrovascular disease may be reduced; and (4) for unrelated illnesses.

This chapter critically reviews the evidence for the glycemic benefit of alternative therapies that are in common use as well as their toxicities and for each agent discusses the following questions:

1. What is the rationale for its use?
2. What is its impact on glycemic control and other problems?
3. What doses are used?
4. What are its side effects?

IDENTIFICATION OF SUBSTANCES TO BE REVIEWED

Several endocrinologists, diabetes dietitians, diabetes nurse educators, pharmacists, and family physicians were surveyed to examine use of a reasonably comprehensive set of commonly used substances. Those substances that were identified by this process are reviewed here. This section does not provide an exhaustive review of every substance for which diabetes benefits have been claimed.

This process led to the identification of several minerals (chromium, vanadium, magnesium), vitamins and/or antioxidants (vitamin C, vitamin E, coenzyme Q, biotin), fiber, fish oil, and ginseng.

The medical literature was reviewed up to the end of November 1999 using OVID, PUBMED, the Cochrane Library, ALTMED, and the Health Information Research Unit (HIRU) databases. The following search terms were used: "meta-analysis," "randomized controlled trial," in combination with "diabetes mellitus," "insulin-dependent diabetes mellitus," "non–insulin-dependent diabetes mellitus," and the name for each of the substances reviewed. In cases where no articles were identified, the search was expanded to include literature of any study design.

It is useful to note that, as the databases were searched, several problems were encountered related to identification of the literature, design of the studies, and substances assessed.

LITERATURE REVIEW

Problems Related to Identification of the Literature

For most biomedical literature searches, fewer than 50% of the relevant articles are found using MEDLINE searches, as only 3,700 journals of a total of 16,000 biomedical journals are indexed.[3] This problem is magnified in searches of unconventional medical publications, as only 10% of such journals are identified using conventional search strategies.[3] As well, many of the alternative medicine journals are not readily available and provide no electronic abstracts. As in all searches for the evidence supporting a therapy, publication bias can lead to manuscripts being differentially submitted or accepted based on the direction or strength of the findings. Moreover, an additional language bias may affect some alternative medicine topics, as many articles are published in languages other than English.[3]

Problems Related to the Design of the Studies

As many alternative medicines have not traditionally been tested using principles of empirical research,[4] there is a paucity of evidence available in support of most of these therapies. Moreover, the fact that substances can be patented in the United States only when a new use is documented[4] has limited the funding available for the large studies necessary to evaluate all sorts of therapies. In the United States, the National Institutes of Health has an office of alternative medicine for just this purpose. To date, however, the trials funded have been modest and have not yet yielded positive results.

The following difficulties also limit the ability to interpret data from the studies that have been done: (1) lack of RCTs; (2) lack of placebo or blinding for some trials (eg, trials of acupuncture or relaxation therapy); (3) small numbers of subjects; (4) unique and highly selected patient populations that may not provide data that are generalizable; and (5) the fact that different studies have used different dosages of substances and different duration of therapy.

Problems Related to the Substances Assessed

There is much variability in the strength and purity of preparations of unconventional therapies that are used, and a variety of different preparations may be available under the same name. There is often little information regarding the toxicity of the substance and the toxicity of other substances that are added (such as heavy metals, prescription drugs, etc).[5] Finally, many unconventional therapies are used as one component of a general holistic approach; such an approach is generally missing when the substance is tested in isolation in the course of a clinical trial.

Method of Summarizing the Literature

The evidence supporting the use of minerals (chromium, vanadium, magnesium), vitamins/antioxidants (vitamin C, vitamin E, coenzyme Q, biotin), fiber, fish oil, and ginseng as glucose-modulating agents is described below. Acupuncture, relaxation techniques, and other herbal medicines are not discussed. Outcomes that were tabulated included HbA_{1c}, fasting plasma glucose (FPG), and lipids (where available). It should be recognized that the impact of any diabetes treatment is related to the pretreatment level of glycemic control (ie, glucose-lowering agents have a larger impact on glycemia when initial glucose control is poor compared to when it is less impaired).

A clinically important result was arbitrarily defined (before reviewing the data), using the US Food and Drug Administration criteria, as an absolute decrease in HbA_{1c} of $> 0.7\%$ or a decrease in FPG of > 1.7 mmol/L after therapy with the substance being reviewed. It was concluded that a substance was effective or ineffective when identified relevant studies were consistent with each other. If only some of the studies were positive and others were negative, and there were clear reasons why discrepancies may have existed, substances were identified as possibly being effective, and the word "may" was used. The questions asked for each of the reviewed substances are listed in Table 16–1.

CHROMIUM

What Is the Stated Rationale for the Use of Chromium?

Chromium intake is generally low in the United States,[6] and marginal dietary intake over decades can deplete chromium. As there is no established standard for assessing bodily stores of chromium (plasma levels do not reflect tissue levels or balance[7]), it can be difficult to document chromium deficiency in an individual.[8] Severe chromium deficiency results in insulin resistant diabetes mellitus that can be reversed with chromium administration. This was observed in patients treated with total parenteral nutrition early in the history of this therapy who initially were not given chromium and therefore were known to be deficient.[9] Chromium picolinate has also been shown to enhance insulin sensitivity in moderately obese nondiabetic subjects.[10] There is a putative molecular mechanism for this action of chromium: low-molecular weight chromium-binding substance has been isolated and shown to bind to the insulin receptor and increase insulin-stimulated kinase activity eightfold.[11] Therefore, the above data suggest that there may be a role for chromium in the treatment of patients with Type 2 diabetes.

What Is the Impact of Chromium on Glycemic Control?

Several RCTs examined the impact of chromium supplementation on glycemia in Type 2 diabetes.[6,8,12–18] As noted in Table 16–2, these studies enrolled small numbers of patients, were done in different populations with different chromium stores, and used different doses and formulations. For example, only three studies[6,8,12] used chromium picolinate—a compound that is associated with a higher absorption of chromium. Finally, only seven of these studies were done in people with diabetes, while the remainder were done in people with impaired glucose tolerance.

With the exception of one study, no effect of chromium on glycemic measures was observed. The one study that demonstrated a statistically and clinically significant effect[8] was

---

Table 16–1 Questions Addressed for Each Substance

What is the stated rationale for its use?

What is the impact on glycemic control? Is it clinically significant?

Are there other benefits to its use?

What dosage(s) was (were) used?

What are its possible side effects?

What conclusions can be drawn concerning its use?

Table 16–2 Effect of Chromium (Cr) on Glycemia

Study Design	Formulation; Dose	Sample	Time (mo)	HbA1c (%) Base	HbA1c (%) Change	FPG (mmol/L) Base	FPG (mmol/L) Change	Comments
RCT, DB, PC[6]	Cr picolinate; 924 µg/d	Non-DM = 32 IGT/IFG = 14	3	N/A	N/A	5.7	↔	No effect on glucose tolerance
RCT, DB, PC[8]	Cr picolinate; 1,000 µg/d	Type 2 DM = 180	4	9.3	↓1.2	10.2	↔	Data are read from bar graphs
RCT, DB, PC[8]	Cr picolinate; 1,000 µg/d	Type 2 DM = 180	4	9.3	↓ 2.1	9.8	↓1.7	Data are read from bar graphs; ↓ cholesterol
RCT, DB, C, PC[12]	Cr picolinate; 200 µg/d	Type 2 DM = 30	2/arm	6.4	↔	8.6	↔	>90%—no baseline detectable Cr; ↓ triglycerides
RCT, DB, PC[13]	Cr yeast; 160 µg/d	IGT = 26 men	6	5.4	↔	5.0	↔	No effect on glucose tolerance
RCT, DB, C, PC[14]	CrCl; 250 µ/d	Non-DM = 51 Type 2 DM = 25	7–16	N/A	N/A	9.7	↔	↓ Triglycerides
RCT, DB, C, PC[15]	Cr yeast or trivalent Cr; 150 µg/d	DM = 43 men	4/arm	N/A	N/A	11.3	↔	No effect on glucose tolerance
RCT, DB, C, PC[16]	trivalent Cr; 200 µg/d	Type 2 DM = 10	1.5	N/A	N/A	10.3	↔	No effect on glucose tolerance
RCT, DB, PC[17]	Cr yeast; 10.8 µg/d	Non-DM = 16 men DM = 8 men	2	N/A	N/A	5.6	↔	Improved glucose tolerance
RCT, DB, C, PC[18]	Trivalent Cr; 150 µg/d	Non-DM = 4 DM = 10 (all prisoners)	4/arm	N/A	N/A	6.4	↔	No effect on glucose tolerance

RCT = randomized controlled trial; DB = double blind; PC = placebo controlled; DM = diabetes mellitus; IGT = impaired glucose tolerance; IFG = impaired fasting glucose. ↔ = no statistically significant change; Ø = statistically significant decrease ($p < .05$).

the largest trial and showed the effect only with a high dose of chromium picolinate in a Chinese population that may have had chromium deficiency. All of the negative trials used smaller dosages of chromium and had significantly fewer subjects.

Are There Other Benefits to the Use of Chromium?

Two of the studies[12,14] reported a statistically significant decrease in triglycerides (17.4% and 11%, respectively) and one study[8] reported a decrease in total cholesterol (0.5 mmol/L).

What Dosage(s) Was (Were) Used?

The only study that reported a positive effect used a high dosage (1,000 µg/d) of chromium picolinate. It should be noted that this dosage is greater than the American estimated safe adequate daily dietary intake of 200 µg/d (equivalent to the recommended daily allowance).

What Are the Possible Side Effects of Chromium?

The potential for toxicity of chromium has been recently reviewed.[7] Chromium exists in two common forms: trivalent (in organic substances) and hexavalent. In the hexavalent form, chromium can accumulate in the liver, bind to DNA, and may be toxic and mutagenic due to the formation of reactive oxygen intermediates. The chromium used in the studies considered here is in the trivalent form. In vitro data assessing its potential for toxicity have been conflicting. Of a total of 209 studies, 161 found no evidence of toxicity. Chromium appears to be safe at high dosages in rats.[19] In clinical trials, 19 randomized studies (175 1,000 µg/d for 6 to 64 wk) did not document any toxicity.[7] Two case reports of renal disease following the use of high-dose chromium have been reported. Both cases had other possible mechanisms implicated.[7] It has therefore been suggested that the limit of the estimated safe adequate daily dietary intake of 200 µg/d should be used for unsupervised public use and that higher dosages be used only within clinical trials.[7]

What Conclusion Can Be Drawn Concerning the Use of Chromium?

Only one report found that high doses of chromium picolinate may improve glycemic control in people with Type 2 diabetes.[8] This trial was done in a population that was possibly deficient in chromium; thus, the generalizability of this finding is unknown.

EVIDENCE-BASED MESSAGE

Chromium picolinate may improve glycemic control in people with Type 2 diabetes (Level 2).[8]

VANADIUM

What Is the Stated Rationale For the Use of Vanadium?

In vitro data show that vanadium has insulinomimetic properties, including stimulation of glucose uptake, glycogen synthesis, and glucose oxidation.[20–22] Studies in many different rodent models have demonstrated improvement in glucose tolerance and insulin-mediated glucose disposal.[23] As well, studies in subjects with Type 2 diabetes also show an increase in insulin-mediated glucose uptake, glycogen synthesis, and inhibition of hepatic glucose production.[24]

What Is the Impact of Vanadium on Glycemic Control?

As noted in Table 16–3, the two identified placebo-controlled (but nonrandomized) trials did report a benefit of vanadium on FPG in patients with Type 2 diabetes that was both statistically and clinically significant.[25,26] Both were of short duration and had small sample sizes.

Are There Other Benefits to the Use of Vanadium?

No benefits other than the effect on glycemic control were reported in these studies.

Table 16–3 Effect of Vanadium on Glycemia

Study Design	Formulation; Dose	Sample	Time (wk)	HbA$_{1c}$ (%) Base	HbA$_{1c}$ (%) Change	FPG (mmol/L) Base	FPG (mmol/L) Change	Comments
Before/after SB, C, PC[25]	Vanadyl sulfate; 100 mg/d	Non-DM = 6 Type 2 DM = 7	3 (P) 3 (VS)	9.4	↓0.6	12.3	↓1.7	Change refers to the change with VS
Before/after SB, C, PC[26]	Vanadyl sulfate; 100 mg/d	Type 2 DM = 8	4 (VS) 4 (P)	N/A	N/A	9.3	↓1.9	Change refers to the change with VS

Before/after: two-phase trial design in which therapy in phase 2 is compared to phase 1; SB = single blind; C = crossover; PC = placebo controlled; DM = diabetes mellitus; P = placebo; VS = vanadyl sulfate, ↓ = statistically significant decrease ($p < .05$).

What Dosages Were Used?

Both studies used 50 mg bid of vanadyl sulfate.

What Are the Possible Side Effects of Vanadium?

In vitro studies showed that vanadium ions may promote genetic alterations and have mitogenic effects in cultured cells.[27,28] In animal studies, vanadium was deposited in bone but did not appear to affect bone strength or architecture.[29] Toxicity has been observed in animals at high dosages. One study reported increased weight loss and mortality in diabetic rats treated with vanadium;[30] however, it has been suggested that if the diabetic rats were polyuric, the taste of vanadium in the drinking water may have impaired their ability to drink sufficient water to avoid dehydration.[24] Another study[31] followed diabetic rats that were alive after treatment with vanadium for 1 year. In the two human trials, there were reports of gastrointestinal intolerance and a statistically significant drop in hematocrit with vanadium.

What Conclusion Can Be Drawn Concerning the Use of Vanadium?

There are no long-term data. Short-term data from nonrandomized trials suggest that vanadium may be effective.

EVIDENCE-BASED MESSAGE

Vanadium may improve glycemic control in patients with Type 2 diabetes (Level 3).[25,26]

MAGNESIUM

What Is the Stated Rationale for the Use of Magnesium?

Patients with poorly controlled Type 1 and Type 2 diabetes mellitus are often hypomagnesemic, likely due to renal losses of magnesium with glycosuria.[32–34] There is an association between magnesium depletion and insulin resistance.[35,36] Hypomagnesemia may also negatively affect insulin secretion.[37] It can be difficult to detect magnesium depletion in patients, as plasma magnesium is a specific but insensitive measurement of total body magnesium and intracellular magnesium measurement is not readily available.[38] Magnesium modulates glucose transport through the membranes and is a cofactor in several enzymatic systems involving glucose oxidation.[39]

In addition to its potential role in modifying glycemia, magnesium is an adenosinetriphosphatase allosteric effector involved in inositol transport; therefore, supplementation with magnesium may play a role in preventing the complications of diabetes.[40]

What Is the Impact of Magnesium on Glycemic Control?

Several RCTs assessed the impact of magnesium supplementation on glycemic control in Type 2 diabetes, as shown in Table 16–4.[41–45] Only one of the five trials showed that magnesium had a positive effect on glycemia: the largest trial to date demonstrated a statistically (and likely clinically) significant decrease in fructosamine in subjects receiving high-dose magnesium over 1 month[42] but no concomitant fall in FPG or HbA$_{1c}$. This trial was unique, in that one half of the subjects had a low plasma magnesium concentration at the start of the study. Further, the baseline glycemic control was worse than in the other negative trials, as reflected by the high HbA$_{1c}$. Although the other trials had smaller sample sizes compared to the positive study, most of these negative trials did report an adequate power.

Are There Other Benefits to the Use of Magnesium?

Two studies documented a potential beneficial impact of magnesium on blood pressure. In one trial, subjects with Type 1 diabetes had a drop in blood pressure.[43] In the second trial, there was a trend toward a decrease in diastolic blood pressure in Type 2 subjects.[41]

Table 16–4 Effect of Magnesium on Glycemia

Study Design	Formulation; Dose	Sample	Time (mo)	HbA1c (%) Base	HbA1c (%) Change	FPG (mmol/L) Base	FPG (mmol/L) Change	Comments
RCT, DB, PC[41]	Mg aspartate-HCl: 15 mmol/d	Type 2 DM = 50	3	8.7	↔	N/A	↔	Plasma Mg rose: no effect on lipids/blood pressure
RCT, DB, PC[42]	MgO: 20.7 mmol/d or 41.4 mmol/d	Type 2 DM = 128	1	9.6	↔	11.5	↔	48% had low initial plasma Mg; fructosamine in high-dose arm ↓9%, from 4.13–3.75 ($p < .05$)
RCT, DB, C[43] (Mg vs vitamin C)	Mg (anion); 25 mmol/d	Type 1 and Type 2 DM = 56	3/arm	9.2	↔	9.8	↔	Initial plasma Mg was 0.78 mmol/L; no effect on lipids
RCT, DB, PC[44]	Mg citrate; 30 mmol/d	Type 2 DM, low Mg = 40	3	7.2	↔	N/A	N/A	Initial plasma Mg was 0.72 mmol/L; normalized by 3 mo
RCT, DB, PC[45]	Mg lactate-citrate; 15 mmol/d	Type 2 DM = 56	4	7.3	↔	8.8	↔	Initial plasma Mg was "normal range"

RCT = randomized controlled trial; DB = double blind; PC = placebo controlled; DM = diabetes mellitus.

↔ = no statistically significant change.

What Dosage(s) Was (Were) Used?

The only trial that reported a positive effect used a high total amount of magnesium of 41 mmol (1,000 mg) daily, in three divided doses.

What Are the Possible Side Effects of Magnesium?

Diarrhea was reported in 12% of patients taking 41 mmol of magnesium daily.[42] Only one patient of 39 withdrew from the study due to this side effect. Long-term studies are required to assess the safety of magnesium.[46]

What Conclusions Can Be Drawn Concerning the Use of Magnesium?

There are no consistent data supporting the benefit of magnesium on glycemia.

EVIDENCE-BASED MESSAGE

Large studies do not support an effect of magnesium supplementation on glycemic control (Level 2).[41,43–45]

VITAMIN C

What Is the Stated Rationale for the Use of Vitamin C?

Metabolic control in patients with diabetes mellitus was inversely correlated with vitamin C concentrations in two studies.[47,48] The acute administration of antioxidants has been shown to improve insulin action in healthy subjects and in patients with Type 2 diabetes.[49] As well, a role for vitamin C in the prevention or treatment of the complications of diabetes can be postulated, as vitamin C and other antioxidants could reduce damage from free radicals that may contribute to the development of complications of diabetes.[50] Therefore, supplementation with vitamin C could improve metabolic control and reduce the complications of diabetes.

What Is the Impact of Vitamin C on Glycemic Control?

Three RCTs have examined the impact of vitamin C on glycemic control (Table 16–5).[43,50,51] Both of the two RCTs that were of longer duration, with larger sample sizes, and that were specifically designed to examine the impact of vitamin C on glycemia showed an absolute decrease in HbA_{1c} of 0.8% in patients with Type 2 diabetes treated with vitamin C, with no clinically significant change in FPG.[43,50]

Are There Other Benefits to the Use of Vitamin C?

Both studies that measured plasma lipids noted a small decrease in fasting triglycerides of 0.3 to 0.5 mmol/L,[43,50] and a fall in low-density lipoprotein (LDL) cholesterol of 26% occurred in one study.[50]

What Dosage(s) Was (Were) Used?

The two positive trials used dosages of 1 to 2 g of vitamin C daily in the treatment arms.

What Are the Possible Side Effects of Vitamin C?

No side effects were noted in the three studies. The American National Academy of Sciences has recently recommended 75 mg (women) to 90 mg (men) daily of vitamin C as the recommended daily allowance of vitamin C.[52] They set the upper limit at 2,000 mg daily, as higher dosages can result in diarrhea.

The ingestion of large doses is contraindicated in renal insufficiency, iron overload, and renal oxalate stone-formers.[53]

Table 16–5 Effect of Vitamin C on Glycemia

Study Design	Formulation; Dose	Sample	Time (mo)	HbA_{1c} (%) Base	Change	FPG (mmol/L) Base	Change	Comments
RCT, DB, C[43] (Mg vs vitamin C)	Vitamin C; 2 g/d	Type 1 DM = 29 Type 2 DM = 27	3/arm	9.3	↓0.8*	10.1	↓1.0	Triglycerides and cholesterol decreased in Type 2 participants
RCT, DB, PC (with tartaric acid)[51]	Vitamin C; 6 g/d	Type 1 DM = 24	1	8.9	↔	12.0	↔	
RCT, DB, C, PC[50]	Vitamin C; 1 g/d	Type 2 DM = 40	4/arm	8.0	↓0.8	8.8	↔	Triglycerides, total and LDL cholesterol decreased

RCT = randomized controlled trial; DB = double blind; PC = placebo controlled; DM = diabetes mellitus.

↔ = no statistically significant change; ↓ = statistically significant decrease ($p < .05$).

*Results are shown here for the participants with Type 2 DM only; there was no effect on glycemia for those with Type 1 DM.

EVIDENCE-BASED MESSAGE

Vitamin C may improve glycemia in patients with Type 2 diabetes (Level 2).[43,50]

VITAMIN E

What Is the Stated Rationale for the Use of Vitamin E?

Like vitamin C, vitamin E is an antioxidant, with theoretical benefits for the reduction of complications of diabetes. There is also a suggestion that it may have an impact on the progression of the disease itself: an increased risk of diabetes was noted at the 4-year follow-up of men with low initial vitamin E concentrations in one study.[54] As well, another trial demonstrated that vitamin E protected residual beta-cell function in subjects with recent onset of Type 1 diabetes.[55]

What Is the Impact of Vitamin E on Glycemic Control?

Six RCTs examined the impact of vitamin E supplementation on glycemic control, as detailed in Table 16–6.[56–61] Two of the six trials showed an improvement in glycemic control, with a decrease in HbA_{1c} of 0.8 to 0.9%.[59,60] The other four trials showed no impact on glycemia despite similar doses of vitamin E, similar duration of treatment, and equal or greater numbers of subjects, compared to the positive trials.

Are There Other Benefits to the Use of Vitamin E?

There was reversal of defective nerve conduction in 2 of 12 parameters in one study.[56] Variable and inconsistent effects on lipids were documented.

What Dosage(s) Was (Were) Used?

The two positive trials used 900 mg daily of vitamin E as *dl*-α-tocopheryl acetate or *d*-α-tocopherol.

What Are the Possible Side Effects of Vitamin E?

The recently revised American recommended daily allowance (RDA) for vitamin E is 15 mg. The upper level for daily consumption is 1,000 mg daily (which is equivalent to 1,100 IU *dl*-α-tocopherol [synthetic form] and 1,500 IU *d*-α-tocopherol [natural form]). Above this dosage, vitamin E acts as an anticoagulant,[52] and hence there are concerns of inducing a hemorrhagic stroke.

What Conclusions Can Be Drawn Concerning the Use of Vitamin E?

Although studies to date have been small, there are no consistent data supporting the benefit of vitamin E on glycemia.

EVIDENCE-BASED MESSAGE

Large studies do not support an effect of vitamin E supplementation on glycemic control (Level 2).[56–58,61]

BIOTIN

What Is the Stated Rationale for the Use of Biotin?

There are several lines of evidence for the potential role of the vitamin biotin in glucose homeostasis. The kk mouse model of Type 2 diabetes showed improvements in glycemia on oral glucose tolerance testing following ingestion of biotin.[62] In humans, patients with two skin diseases (psoriasis vulgaris and pustulosis palmaris et plantaris) have decreased plasma biotin concentrations and a high frequency of abnormal glucose tolerance (68%).[63] Biotin reduces excessive hepatic glucose output through increased synthesis of glucokinase[64,65] and repression of phospho*enol*pyruvate carboxykinase production (the rate-limiting enzyme for gluconeogenesis).[66]

Table 16–6 Effect of Vitamin E on Glycemia

Study Design	Formulation; Dose	Sample	Time (mo)	HbA$_{1c}$ (%)		FPG (mmol/L)		Comments
				Base	Change	Base	Change	
RCT, DB, PC[56]	Vitamin E: *dl*-α-tocopheryl acetate; 900 mg/d	Type 2 DM = 21	6	9.2	↔	7.4	↔	
RCT, DB, C, PC[57]	Vitamin E; 1,200 mg/d	Types 1 and 2 DM = 60	2/arm	11.9	↔	12.8	↔	No effect on fructosamine and lipids
RCT, DB, PC[58]	Vitamin E: *dl*-α-tocopherol; 1,500 mg/d	Type 2 DM = 21	2.5	7.2	↔	9.4	↔	
RCT, DB, C, PC[59]	Vitamin E: *dl*-α-tocopherol acetate; 900 mg/d	Type 2 DM = 15	4/arm	N/A	↓0.9	N/A	↓0.6	
RCT, DB, C, PC[60]	Vitamin E: *dl*-α-tocopherol; 900 mg/d	Type 2 DM = 25	3/arm	7.7	↓0.8	8.2	↓0.7	Decreased cholesterol, LDL, and triglycerides
RCT, DB, C, PC[61]	Vitamin E: *dl*-α-tocopherol nicotinate; 600 mg/d	Type 2 DM = 15	1.5	7.6	↔	5.8	↔	No effect on lipids

RCT = randomized controlled trial; DB = double blind; PC = placebo controlled; C = crossover; DM = diabetes mellitus.
↔ = no statistically significant change; ↓ = statistically significant decrease ($p < .05$).

What Is the Impact of Biotin on Glycemic Control?

In the only RCT found, 28 of 43 patients were selected for randomization to placebo versus biotin. After 1 month of therapy, FPG was significantly lower in the treatment arm, decreasing by 5.8 mmol/L[67] (Table 16–7).

Are There Other Benefits to the Use of Biotin?

No other benefits were noted.

What Dosage(s) Was (Were) Used?

The study used 3 mg tid of biotin plus Miya-BM 1 g tid. The latter is an antimicrobial agent given to discourage the degradation of biotin by gut flora.

What Are the Possible Side Effects of Biotin?

No side effects were documented during the trials, and no serious side effects were identified in a separate MEDLINE search.

What Conclusions Can Be Drawn Concerning the Use of Biotin?

The results from one small trial are encouraging. Preliminary results suggest that biotin may improve glycemic control in patients with Type 2 diabetes.

EVIDENCE-BASED MESSAGE

Biotin may improve glycemia in patients with Type 2 diabetes (Level 2).[67]

COENZYME Q

What Is the Stated Rationale for the Use of Coenzyme Q?

Mitochondrial respiratory activity is involved in glucose-stimulated insulin secretion, and its rate-limiting enzyme G3PD requires coenzyme Q_{10}.[68] There have been reports of patients with Type 1 diabetes developing hypoglycemia following intake of coenzyme Q.[69] Therefore, it is reasonable to postulate that suboptimal tissue levels of the vitamin could impair glycemia and that supplementation could improve glycemia.

What Is the Impact of Coenzyme Q on Glycemic Control?

Three RCTs examined the impact of coenzyme Q on glycemia (Table 16–8).[69–71] The studies looked at Type 1 or Type 2 diabetes. All three trials showed consistent results: coenzyme Q had no effect on glycemia by any parameter examined, over 3- to 6-month periods. As well, hypoglycemia was not observed. Although the duration of the trials was reasonable, the sample sizes were small; thus, the trials lacked power.

Are There Other Benefits to the Use of Coenzyme Q?

No other benefits were assessed in these trials. Other trials have examined a potential role for coenzyme Q in patients with maternally inherited diabetes and deafness due to a mitochondrial DNA mutation and found coenzyme Q to have an impact on progression of hearing loss[72] and neurologic impairment.[73]

What Dosage(s) Was (Were) Used?

The trials used 100 mg daily or 100 mg twice daily of coenzyme Q.

What Are the Possible Side Effects of Coenzyme Q?

No side effects were documented during the trials and no serious side effects were revealed in a MEDLINE search.

Table 16–7 Effect of Biotin on Glycemia

Study Design	Formulation; Dose	Sample	Time (mo)	HbA$_{1c}$ (%) Base	HbA$_{1c}$ (%) Change	FPG (mmol/L) Base	FPG (mmol/L) Change	Comments
RCT, SB, PC[67]	Biotin; 3 mg tid (+ antimicrobial)	Type 2 DM = 28	1	N/A	N/A	12.1	↓5.8	A subgroup of a larger study; insulin level was unchanged

RCT = randomized controlled trial; SB = single blind; PC = placebo controlled; DM = diabetes mellitus.
↓ = statistically significant decrease ($p < .05$).

Table 16–8 Effect of Coenzyme Q on Glycemia

Study Design	Formulation; Dose	Sample	Time (mo)	HbA$_{1c}$ (%) Base	HbA$_{1c}$ (%) Change	FPG (mmol/L) Base	FPG (mmol/L) Change	Comments
RCT, DE, PC[70]	CoQ10; 200 mg/d	Type 2 DM = 23	6	8.7	↔	11.7	↔	
RCT, DE, PC[69]	CoQ10; 100 mg/d	Type 1 DM = 34	3	N/A	↔	N/A	↔	No change in insulin dose or hypoglycemia
RCT, DE, PC[71]	CoQ10; 110 mg/d	Type 1 DM = 34	3	8.04	↔	N/A	N/A	No change in insulin dose, mean glucose, or hypoglycemia

RCT = randomized controlled trial; DB = double blind; PC = placebo controlled; DM = diabetes mellitus.
↔ = no statistically significant change ($p < .05$).

What Conclusions Can Be Drawn Concerning the Use of Coenzyme Q?

There are no data supporting the benefit of coenzyme Q on glycemia in Type 1 or Type 2 diabetes. It should be noted that all three studies examined were small and lacked power.

EVIDENCE-BASED MESSAGE

> Small studies do not support an effect of coenzyme Q supplementation on glycemic control in Type 1 or Type 2 diabetes (Level 2).[69–71]

SOLUBLE FIBER SUPPLEMENTATION

What Is the Stated Rationale for the Use of Soluble Fiber Supplement?

High-fiber and low-glycemic-index foods decrease postprandial plasma glucose excursions.[74,75] This effect is likely due to slowing the absorption of carbohydrates, as water-soluble fiber increases the viscosity of digesta in the gut,[76] delays gastric emptying, and increases satiety.[77] Soluble fiber supplements include Konjac-Mannan (the most effective), psyllium, guar gum, and fenugreek seeds. Their impact on glycemia when used long-term remains to be addressed.

What Is the Impact of Soluble Fiber Supplementation on Glycemic Control?

Twelve RCTs were identified that examined the role of soluble fiber supplements and glycemia, one in subjects with insulin resistance,[78] eight in Type 2 diabetes,[79–86] and three in Type 1 diabetes.[87–89] Overall, there were concerns about several of the studies, including: (1) several of the trials were of short duration and demonstrated changes in fructosamine but not in HbA_{1c}; (2) the sample sizes were small in most cases; (3) the HbA_{1c} or fructosamine levels were not always determined; and (4) the baseline fiber content of the diet was often not disclosed. All of these factors make comparisons among the trials more difficult.

Nonetheless, several consistent trends were noted. First, in patients with Type 2 diabetes (Table 16–9), five trials documented a statistically significant lowering of FPG or fructosamine with the use of Konjac-Mannan, psyllium, or guar gum,[79,81–84] with only two of the trials reaching the level of clinical significance stated as the minimum standard at the beginning of this chapter.[81,84] Unlike these five trials, three further trials were identified that demonstrated no impact on glycemia.[80,85,86] One of these used a smaller dose of psyllium and did describe reductions in postmeal glycemia on the metabolic ward, raising concerns about outpatient compliance.[80] Another negative trial used subjects with near-normal baseline FPG and post-meal glucose concentrations (interestingly, the average HbA_{1c} was higher than expected given the glucose levels).[86] Finally, the trial of longest duration[85] noted improved glycemia at 8 weeks, but no impact at 20 weeks. Therefore, it appears that *poorly controlled* diabetes responds best to soluble fiber supplementation, as trials with subjects whose initial glycemic control was good did not show any benefit with the addition of soluble fiber. An exception is the study using Konjac-Mannan, which demonstrated an improvement in fructosamine in subjects with impaired glucose tolerance after 3 weeks of soluble fiber supplementation.[78] It may be that this study was able to show this positive effect due to the fact that compared to other soluble fibers, Konjac-Mannan produces the most viscosity.

Three trials studied the impact of soluble fiber supplementation (guar gum or fenugreek seeds) in Type 1 diabetes (Table 16–10). Two demonstrated a clinically significant beneficial effect,[88,89] and one was negative.[87] Once again, the two positive trials differed from the negative one in a consistent manner, as initial glycemic control was poor in the positive trials and very good in the negative trial.

Are There Other Benefits to the Use of Soluble Fiber Supplement?

Across the studies, there was a consistent decrease in total cholesterol (range of 4 to 27%) and LDL cholesterol (8 to 33%). One study showed an improvement in high-density lipoprotein (HDL) cholesterol of 40%, and two studies showed a drop in triglyceride (12 to 20%).

Table 16–9 Effect of Soluble Fiber Supplements on Glycemia in Type 2 Diabetes

Study Design	Formulation; Dose	Sample	Time (wk)	HbA1c (%) Base	Change	FPG (mmol/L) Base	Change	Comments
RCT, DB, C, PC[78]	Konjac-Mannan; 8–13 g/d	IGT = 11	3/arm	N/A	N/A	6.7	N/A	Decreased fructosamine, LDL, and cholesterol
RCT, DB, C, PC[79]	Konjac-Mannan; 24–50 g/d	Type 2 DM = 11	3/arm	Men and women: 7.4 and 8.3	N/A	9.6	↔	Decreased fructosamine, total/HDL cholesterol, and systolic pressure
RCT, DB, PC[80]	Psyllium; 10.2 g/d	Type 2 DM = 34	8	7.3	↔	10.0	↔	Decreased post-lunch and all-day G 19.2% and 11%
RCT, DB, PC[81]	Plantago psyllium; 15 g/d	Type 2 DM = 125	6	N/A	N/A	9.7	↓2.2	Improved lipid profile
RCT, DB, C, PC[82]	Guar gum	Type 2 DM = 16	8/arm	7.9	↓0.3	10.6	↓1	63% subjects had side effects
RCT, DB, C, PC[83]	Guar gum 15 g/d	Type 2 DM = 9	4/arm	N/A	↔	10.6	↓1.6	All were on glibenclamide; cholesterol fell 11%
RCT, DB, C, PC[84]	Guar gum or metformin; 15 g/d or 1.5 g/d	Type 2 DM = 19	14/arm	N/A	N/A	10.9	↓1.9	
RCT, B, C, PC[85]	Guar gum; 10–15 g/d	Type 2 DM = 24	20	N/A	↔	10.1	↔	
RCT, DB, C, PC[86]	Guar gum; 15 g/d	Type 2 DM = 29	8/arm	8.0	↔	5.0	↔	LDL decreased 9%

RCT = randomized controlled trial; DB = double blind; C = crossover; PC = placebo controlled; DM = diabetes mellitus; G = glucose. ↔ = no statistically significant change; ↓ = statistically significant decrease ($p < .05$).

Table 16-10 Effect of Soluble Fiber Supplements on Glycemia in Type 1 Diabetes

Study Design	Formulation; Dose	Sample	Time (d)	HbA$_{1c}$ (%)		FPG (mmol/L)		Comments
				Base	Change	Base	Change	
RCT, C[87]	Guar gum; 15 g/d	Type 1 DM = 9	12/arm	5.8	N/A	6.0	↔	Decreased post-breakfast G
RCT, DB, C[88]	Guar gum 29 g or wheat bran 33 g ("placebo")	Type 1 DM = 28	98/arm	10.5	↓0.8	12.0	↔	Decreased post-meal G and total cholesterol
RCT, DB, C, PC[89]	Fenugreek seeds; 100 g	Type 1 DM = 10	10/arm	N/A	N/A	15.1	↓4.2	Improved lipid profile

RCT = randomized controlled trial; C = crossover; DM = diabetes mellitus; G = glucose; DB = double blind; PC = placebo controlled. ↔ = no statistically significant change; ↓ = statistically significant decrease ($p < .05$).

What Dosage(s) Was (Were) Used?

The dosages used were Konjac-Mannan 24 to 50 g daily (divided into three doses), psyllium 5 g tid, guar gum 5 g tid, and fenugreek seeds 50 g bid.

What Are the Possible Side Effects of Soluble Fiber Supplementation?

Gastrointestinal side effects are the most frequent complaint: diarrhea, flatulence, bloatedness, anorexia, and abdominal pain.[90] These complaints often subside with time, especially if the desired dosage is reached gradually. Rarely, fiber bezoars can cause intestinal obstruction.[91]

What Conclusions Can be Drawn Concerning the Use of Soluble Fiber Supplement?

The trials are fairly consistent in demonstrating that soluble fiber supplementation has a statistically significant positive effect on glycemic control in poorly controlled Type 1 and Type 2 diabetes mellitus. Fewer trials showed a clinically significant effect, often because HbA_{1c} was not tested. Glycemic control is also improved, as reflected by a fall in fructosamine in subjects with glucose intolerance using Konjac-Mannan, the most potent type of soluble fiber.[78]

EVIDENCE-BASED MESSAGE

> Soluble fiber may improve glycemia in patients with Type 1 and Type 2 diabetes (Level 2).[81,84,88,89]

FISH OIL

What Is the Stated Rationale for the Use of Fish Oil?

Glucose intolerance[92] and cardiovascular mortality[93,94] are less common in people who eat a diet rich in fish. Fish oil decreases plasma triglyceride levels by decreasing the hepatic production of very-low-density lipoprotein (VLDL) triglyceride.[95,96] This action may be of particular value to the patient with diabetes, as hyperglycemia is associated with elevated plasma triglyceride concentration. There are several reports of deterioration in glycemic control with the ingestion of fish oil.[97] The potential impact of fish oil on glycemia therefore needs to be addressed.

What Is the Impact of Fish Oil on Glycemic Control?

As shown in Table 16–11,[97–102] a meta-analysis[98] and four of five subsequent RCTs are consistent in demonstrating no impact of fish oil on HbA_{1c} in patients with Type 2 diabetes. These include one large trial with adequate power[99] and one study that used a very high dose of fish oil.[97] Interestingly, the one study that showed a negative impact of fish oil on glycemia actually had subjects consume one serving of fish daily.[100] The meta-analysis showed a trend toward higher FPG in Type 2 diabetes and a decrease in FPG in Type 1 diabetes, with no change in HbA_{1c} in either group.

Are There Other Benefits to the Use of Fish Oil?

The studies confirmed that fish oil induced a decrease in triglyceride levels, a slight increase in LDL cholesterol, and no effect on HDL cholesterol. In the meta-analysis, triglyceride concentration was lowered by 25 to 30% and LDL cholesterol increased by 5% in subjects with Type 2 diabetes.

What Dosage(s) Was (Were) Used?

The typical dose of fish oil was 3 g/d of ω-3 fatty acids.

What Are the Possible Side Effects of Fish Oil?

No side effects were documented in the studies. Concern has been raised about possible bleeding diathesis caused by inhibition of platelet action by n-3 polyunsaturated fatty acids,[103] although clinical trials have not documented any significant consequences.

Table 16–11 Effect of Fish Oil on Glycemia

Study Design	Formulation; Dose	Sample	Time (mo)	HbA$_{1c}$ (%) Base	HbA$_{1c}$ (%) Change	FPG (mmol/L) Base	FPG (mmol/L) Change	Comments
Meta-analysis of 26 studies[97]	N/A	425 subjects		N/A	↔	N/A	Type 2: ↑0.43 Type 1: ↓1.86	Decreased triglyceride and increased LDL were noted
RCT, DB, C, PC[98]	Fish oil; 6 g/d	Type 2 DM = 12	2/arm	8.8	↔	10.9	↔	Decreased triglyceride and Lp(a) were noted
RCT, DB, PC[99]	1–3 fatty acid ethyl esters: 3 g/d then low dose 2 g/d	Total = 935 Type 2 DM = 99	2 high, 4 low	7.2	↔	8.2	↔	Decreased triglyceride and increased LDL were noted
RCT, 4 parallel groups[100]	Daily fish; 3.6 g/d ω-3 vs no fish	Type 2 DM = 55	2	8.0	↑0.5	8.9	↑0.6	↑FPG and HbA$_{1c}$ were reversed by moderate exercise; decreased triglyceride and increased LDL were noted
RCT, DB, C, PC[101]	Fish oil; 3 g/d	Type 2 DM = 11	3/arm	5.8	↔	8.0	↔	Decreased triglyceride was noted
RCT, DB, PC[102]	Fish oil; 2.7 g/d then 1.7 g/d	Type 2 DM = 16	2 high, 4 low	N/A	↔	N/A	↔	Decreased triglyceride was noted

RCT = randomized controlled trial; DB = double blind; C = crossover; PC = placebo controlled; DM = diabetes mellitus.
↔ = no statistically significant change; ↓ or ↑ = statistically significant decrease or increase ($p < .05$).

What Conclusions Can Be Drawn Concerning the Use of Fish Oil?

There are consistent data supporting a neutral impact of fish oil on glycemic control in Type 2 diabetes[97–99,101,102] and a clinically significant decrease in FPG but not HgA$_{1C}$ in Type 1 diabetes, as shown in the meta-analysis.[98]

EVIDENCE-BASED MESSAGE

> Fish oil has no impact on glycemic control in Type 2 diabetes but reduces FPG in Type 1 diabetes (Level 1A).[97–99,101,102]

GINSENG

What Is the Stated Rationale for the Use of Ginseng?

There are several forms of ginseng that are in use for the treatment of depression and fatigue. Interestingly, animal studies show that ginseng improves glucose homeostasis and insulin sensitivity.[104,105] Possible mechanisms for this effect include neuronal modulation of digestion,[106] increased GLUT-2 in the liver,[107] and modulation of insulin secretion.[108] The latter two mechanisms may be mediated by nitric oxide.[109,110] It is therefore of relevance to examine the impact of ginseng on glycemic control in diabetes.

What Is the Impact of Ginseng on Glycemic Control?

The two RCTs that examined the impact of ginseng on glycemic control both documented a positive effect (Table 16–12). However, there are concerns with both studies. One trial quite rigorously demonstrated a fall in the glucose excursion during glucose-tolerance testing,[111] but it only examined the acute effects of a single dose of ginseng. The second trial had several design flaws,[112] and the impact on glycemia was statistically but not clinically significant (see Table 16–12).

Are There Other Benefits to the Use of Ginseng?

One study examined psychological issues, documenting a statistically significant improvement in mood, well-being, and vigor.[112]

What Dosage(s) Was (Were) Used?

The long-term trial used 100 to 200 mg daily. The acute trial used a single 3-g dose of North American ginseng.

What Are the Possible Side Effects of Ginseng?

None were noted during the trials. Multiple potential side effects have been reported, including the "ginseng-abuse syndrome." This may occur when ginseng is ingested together with caffeine or in high doses or for a prolonged period. This syndrome involves hypertension, diarrhea, restlessness, euphoria, insomnia, skin eruptions. As well, Stevens-Johnson syndrome, breast tenderness, and vaginal bleeding have been described in association with the use of ginseng.[113] Ginseng has known drug interactions with monoamine oxidase inhibitors (MAOIs), stimulants, and centrally acting drugs (eg, haloperidol, pentobarbital). Also, the effectiveness of warfarin may be decreased or increased and antihypertensive medications may be potentiated[113] with the use of ginseng.

EVIDENCE-BASED MESSAGE

> Preliminary evidence suggests that ginseng may have a beneficial impact on glycemia (Level 2).[111,112]

CONCLUSION

The scientific literature on the potential glycemic effects of alternative therapies is relatively limited, and many of the published studies have a variety of methodologic problems.

Table 16–12 Effect of Ginseng on Glycemia

Study Design	Formulation; Dose	Sample	Time	HbA$_{1c}$ (%)		FPG (mmol/L)		Comments
				Base	Change	Base	Change	
??RCT[111]	Ginseng, North American; 3 g/d	Type 2 DM = 10	4 doses	N/A	N/A	N/A	N/A	Improved G response to G load
RCT, B, PC[112]	Ginseng; 100 mg/200 mg	Type 2 DM = 36	8 wk	N/A	↓0.5	N/A	↓0.9	Type of ginseng was not indicated

RCT = randomized controlled trial; DM = diabetes mellitus; G = glucose; DB = double blind; PC = placebo controlled.
↓ = statistically significant decrease (*p* < .05).

Nonetheless, there is preliminary evidence from reasonably well-conducted trials that mega-doses of some food and herbal substances may have beneficial effects on glycemia in patients with diabetes. This evidence is most notable for chromium, soluble fiber, and vitamin C. Fish oil is also beneficial, but only in Type 1 diabetes. There is less evidence for ginseng, vanadium, and biotin. Studies demonstrate that there is no impact on glycemia from the use of coenzyme Q. It is difficult to draw conclusions about magnesium and vitamin E due to the inconsistency of results among studies. Clearly, more well-conducted RCTs are required to establish safety and efficacy of these substances. In the interim, clinicians should routinely inquire on the use of these substances by their patients.

SUMMARY OF EVIDENCE-BASED MESSAGES

1. Chromium picolinate may improve glycemic control in people with Type 2 diabetes (Level 2).[8]
2. Vanadium may improve glycemic control in patients with Type 2 diabetes (Level 3).[25,26]
3. Large studies do not support an effect of magnesium supplementation on glycemic control (Level 2).[41,43–45]
4. Vitamin C may improve glycemia in patients with Type 2 diabetes (Level 2).[43,50]
5. Large studies do not support an effect of vitamin E supplementation on glycemic control (Level 2).[56–58,61]
6. Biotin may improve glycemia in patients with Type 2 diabetes (Level 2).[67]
7. Small studies do not support an effect of coenzyme Q supplementation on glycemic control in Type 1 or Type 2 diabetes (Level 2).[69–71]
8. Soluble fiber may improve glycemia in patients with Type 1 and Type 2 diabetes (Level 2).[81,84,88,89]
9. Fish oil has no impact on glycemic control in Type 2 diabetes but reduces FPG in Type 1 diabetes (Level 1A).[97–99,101,102]
10. Preliminary evidence suggests that ginseng may have a beneficial impact on glycemia (Level 2).[111,112]

REFERENCES

1. Eisenberg DM, Kessler RC, Foster C, et al. Unconventional medicine in the United States: prevalence, cost and patterns of use. N Engl J Med 1993;328:246–52.

2. Ryan EA, Pick ME, Marceau C. Use of alternative therapies in diabetes mellitus. Diabetes 1999;48 (Suppl 1):A82.

3. Ezzo J, Berman BM, Vickers AJ, Linde K. Complementary medicine and the Cochrane collaboration. JAMA 1998;280:228–30.

4. Angel M, Kassirer JP. Alternative medicine: the risks of untested and unregulated remedies [editorial]. N Engl J Med 1998;339:839–41.

5. Ko RJ. Adulterants in Asian patent medicines. N Engl J Med 1998;339:847.

6. Joseph LJO, Farell PA, Davey, SL, et al. Effect of resistance training with or without chromium picolinate supplementation on glucose metabolism in older men and women. Metabolism 1999;48:546–53.

7. Jeejeebhoy KN. The role of chromium in nutrition and therapeutics and as a potential toxin. Nutr Rev 1999;57:329–35.

8. Anderson RA, Cheng N, Bryden NA, et al. Elevated intakes of supplemental chromium improve glucose and insulin variables in individuals with type 2 diabetes. Diabetes 1997;46:1786–91.

9. Jeejeebhoy KN, Chu RC, Marliss EB, et al. Chromium deficiency, glucose intolerance, and neuropathy reversed by chromium supplementation in a patient receiving long-term total parenteral nutrition. Am J Clin Nutr 1977;30:531–8.

10. Cefalu W, Bell-Farrow AD, Wang ZQ, et al. The effect of chromium supplementation on carbohydrate metabolism and body fat distribution. Diabetes 1997;46(Suppl 1):55A.

11. Davis CM, Vincent JB. Chromium oligopeptide activates insulin receptor tyrosine kinase activity. Biochemistry 1997;36:4382–5.

12. Lee NA, Reasner CA. Beneficial effect of chromium supplementation on serum triglyceride levels in NIDDM. Diabetes Care 1994;17:1449–52.

13. Uusitupa MJ, Mykkanen L, Siitonen O, et al. Chromium supplementation in impaired glucose tolerance of elderly: effects on blood glucose, plasma insulin, C-peptide and lipid levels. Br J Nutr 1992;68:209–16.

14. Abraham AS, Brooks BA, Eylath U. The effects of chromium supplementation on serum glucose and lipids in patients with and without non-insulin-dependent diabetes. Metabolism 1992;41:768–71.

15. Rabinowitz MB, Gonick HC, Levin SR, Davidson MB. Effects of chromium and yeast supplements on carbohydrate and lipid metabolism in diabetic men. Diabetes Care 1983;6:319–27.

16. Uusitupa MIJ, Kumpulainen JT, Voutilainen E, et al. Effect of inorganic chromium supplementation on glucose tolerance, insulin response, and serum lipids in noninsulin-dependent diabetics. Am J Clin Nutr 1983;38:404–10.

17. Offenbacher EG, Pi-Sunyer FX. Beneficial effect of chromium-rich yeast on glucose tolerance and blood lipids in elderly subjects. Diabetes 1980;29:919–25.

18. Sherman L, Glennon, JA, Brech WJ, et al. Failure of trivalent chromium to improve hyperglycemia in diabetes mellitus. Metabolism 1968;17:439–42.

19. Anderson RA, Bryden NA, Polansky MM. Lack of toxicity of chromium chloride and chromium picolinate in rats. J Am Coll Nutr 1997;16:273–9.

20. Dubyak GR, Kleinzeller G. The insulin-mimetic effects of vanadate in isolated rat adipocytes. J Biol Chem 1980;255:5306–12.

21. Shechter Y. Insulin-mimetic effects of vanadate: possible implications for future treatment of diabetes. Diabetes 1990;39:1–5.

22. Clausen T, Andersen TL, Sturup-Johansen M, Petkova O. The relationship between the transport of glucose and cations across cell membranes in isolated tissues: the effect of vanadate in ^{45}Ca-efflux and sugar transport in adipose tissue and in skeletal muscle. Biochem Biophys Acta 1981;646:261–7.

23. Rossetti L, Laughlin MR. Correction of chronic hyperglycemia with vanadate, but not with phlorizin, normalizes in vitro glycogen synthase activity in diabetic skeletal muscle. J Clin Invest 1989;84:892–9.

24. Cohen N, Halberstam M, Shlimovich P, et al. Oral vanadyl sulfate improves hepatic and peripheral insulin sensitivity in patients with non-insulin dependent diabetes mellitus. J Clin Invest 1995;95:2501–9.

25. Halberstam M, Cohen N, Shlimovich P, et al. Oral vandyl sulfate improves insulin sensitivity in NIDDM but not in obese nondiabetc subjects. Diabetes 1996;45:659–66.

26. Boden G, Chen X, Ruiz J, et al. Effects of vanadyl sulfate on carbohydrate and lipid metabolism in patients with non-insulin-dependent diabetes mellitus. Metabolism 1996;45:1130–5.

27. Owuso-Yaw J, Cohen SY, Wei CI. An assessment of the genotoxicity of vanadium. Toxicol Lett 1990;50:327–36.

28. Sabbioni E, Pozzi G, Pintar A, et al. Cellular retention, cytotoxicity and morphological transformation by vanadium (IV) and vanadium (V) in BALB/3T3 cell lines. Carcinogenesis 1991;12:47–52.

29. Poucheret P, Verma S, Grynpas MD, McNeill JH. Vanadium and diabetes. Mol Cell Biochem 1998;188:73–80.

30. Domingo JL, Gomez M, Llobet JM, et al. Oral vanadium administration to streptozotocin-diabetic rats has marked negative side-effects which are independent of the form of vanadium used. Toxicology 1991;66:279–87.

31. Dai S, Thompson H, McNeill JH. One-year treatment of streptozotocin-induced diabetic rats with vanadyl sulfate. Pharmacol Toxicol 1994;74:101–9.

32. Reznick LM, Altura BT, Gupta RK, et al. Intracellular and extracellular magnesium depletion in Type 2 (non-insulin-dependent) diabetes mellitus. Diabetologia 1993;36:767–70.

33. Mather HM, Nisbet JA, Burton GH, et al. Hypomagnesemia in diabetes. Clin Chim Acta 1979;95:235–42.

34. Fujii S, Tekemura T, Wada M, et al. Magnesium levels in plasma, erythrocyte and urine in patients with diabetes mellitus. Horm Metab Res 1982;14:161–2.

35. Paolisso G, Schenn A, d'Onofrio FD, LeFebvre PJ. Magnesium and glucose homeostasis. Diabetologia 1990;33:511–4.

36. Yajnik CS, Smith RF, Hockaday TDR, Ward NI. Fasting plasma magnesium concentrations and glucose disposal in diabetes. BMJ 1984;288:1032–4.

37. Paolisso G, Scheen A, Cozzolino D, et al. Changes in glucose turnover parameters and improvements in glucose oxidation after 4-week magnesium administration in elderly noninsulin-dependent (Type 2) diabetic patients. J Clin Endocrinol Metab 1994;76:1510–4.

38. Reinhart R, Marx J, Haas R, Desbiens N. Intracellular magnesium of mononuclear cells from venous blood of clinically healthy subjects. Clin Chim Acta 1987;167:187–95.

39. Mooradian A, Failla M, Hoogwerf B, et al. Selected vitamins and minerals in diabetes. Diabetes Care 1994;17:464–79.

40. Grafton G, Bunce C, Sheppard M, et al. Effects of Mg^{2+} on Na-dependent inositol transport. Diabetes 1992;91:35–9.

41. De Valk HW, Verkaaik R, van Rijn HJM, et al. Oral magnesium supplementation in insulin-requiring type 2 diabetic patients. Diabet Med 1998;15:503–7.

42. De Lourdes Lima M, Cruz T, Carreiro Pousada J, et al. The effect of magnesium supplementation in increasing doses on the control of type 2 diabetes. Diabetes Care 1998;21:682–6.

43. Eriksson J, Kohvakka A. Magnesium and ascorbic acid supplementation in diabetes mellitus. Ann Nutr Metab 1995;39:217–23.

44. Eibl NL, Kopp HP, Nowak HR, et al. Hypomagnesemia in Type 2 diabetes: effect of a 3-month replacement therapy. Diabetes Care 1995;18:188–92.

45. Gullestad L, Jacobsen T, Dolva L. Effect of magnesium treatment on glycemic control and metabolic parameters in NIDDM patients. Diabetes Care 1994;17:460–1.

46. American Diabetes Association. Consensus statement: magnesium supplementation in the treatment of diabetes. Diabetes Care 1992;15:1065–7.

47. Som S, Basu S, Mukherjee D, et al. Ascorbic acid metabolism in diabetes mellitus. Metabolism 1981;30:572–7.

48. Sinclair AJ, Girling AJ, Gray L, et al. Disturbed handling of ascorbic acid in diabetic patients with and without microangiopathy during high dose ascorbate supplementation. Diabetologia 1991;34:171–5.

49. Paolisso G, D'Amore A, Balbi V, et al. Plasma vitamin C affects glucose homeostasis in healthy subjects and non-insulin dependent diabetics. Am J Physiol 1994;266:E261–8.

50. Paolisso G, Balbi V, Volpe C, et al. Metabolic benefits deriving from chronic vitamin C supplementation in aged non-insulin dependent diabetics. J Am Coll Nutr 1995;14:387–92.

51. Klein F, Juhl B, Christiansen JS. Unchanged renal haemodynamics following high dose ascorbic acid administration in normoalbuminuric IDDM patients. Scand J Clin Lab Invest 1995;55:53–9.

52. Krinsky NI, for the Panel on Dietary Antioxidants and Related Compounds. Dietary reference intakes for vitamin C, vitamin E, selenium and carotenoids. Washington (DC): National Academy Press; 2000.

53. Rivers JM. Safety of high-level vitamin C ingestion. Int J Vitam Nutr Res Suppl 1989;30:95–102.

54. Salonen JT, Nyyssonen K, Tuomainen T-P, et al. Increased risk of non-insulin dependent diabetes mellitus at low plasma vitamin E concentrations: a four year follow up study in men. BMJ 1995;311:1124–7.

55. IMDIAB Study Group. Vitamin E and nicotinamide have similar effects in maintaining residual beta cell function in recent onset insulin-dependent diabetes (the IMDIAB IV study). Eur J Endocrinol 1997;137:234–9.

56. Tutuncu NB, Bayraktar M, Varli K. Reversal of defective nerve conduction with vitamin E supplementation in type 2 diabetes: a preliminary study. Diabetes Care 1998;21:1915–8.

57. Gomez-Perez FJ, Valles-Sanchez VE, Lopez-Alvarenga JC, et al. Vitamin E modifies neither fructosamine nor HbA$_{1c}$ levels in poorly controlled diabetes. Rev Invest Clin 1996;48:421–4.

58. Reaven PD, Herold DA, Barnett J, Edelman S. Effects of vitamin E on susceptibility of low-density lipoprotein and low-density lipoprotein subfractions to oxidation and on protein glycation in NIDDM. Diabetes Care 1995;18:807–16.

59. Paolisso G, D'Amore A, Giugliano D, et al. Pharmacological doses of vitamin E improve insulin action in healthy subjects and non-insulin-dependent diabetic patients. Am J Clin Nutr 1993;57:650–6.

60. Paolisso G, D'Amore A, Galzerano D, et al. Daily vitamin E supplements improve metabolic control but not insulin secretion in elderly Type 2 diabetic patients. Diabetes Care 1993;16:1433–7.

61. Wu H-P, Tai T-Y, Chuang L-M, et al. Effect of tocopherol on platelet aggregation in non-insulin-dependent diabetes mellitus: ex vivo and in vitro studies. J Formos Med Assoc 1992;91:270–5.

62. Raddi A, DeAngelis B, Frank O, et al. Biotin supplementation improves glucose and insulin tolerance in genetically diabetic kk mice. Life Sci 1988;42:1323–30.

63. Uehara M, Fujigaki T, Hayashi S. Glucose tolerance in pustulosis palmaris et plantaris. Arch Dermatol 1980;116:1275–6.

64. Dakshinamurti K, Cheah-Tan C. Biotin-mediated synthesis of hepatic glucokinase in the rat. Arch Biochem Biophys 1968;127:17–21.

65. Hsieh YTL, Mistry SP. Effect of biotin on the regulation of glucokinase in the intact rat. Nutr Res 1992;12:787–99.

66. Dakshinamurti K, Li W. Transcriptional regulation of liver phosphoenolpyruvate carboxykinase by biotin in diabetic rats. Mol Cell Biochem 1994;132:127–32.

67. Maebashi M, Makino Y, Furukawa Y, et al. Therapeutic evaluation of the effect of biotin on hyperglycemia in patients with non-insulin-dependent diabetes mellitus. J Clin Biochem Nutr 1993; 14:211–8.

68. McCarty MF. Can correction of sub-optimal coenzyme Q status improve β-cell function in Type 2 diabetics? Med Hypotheses 1999;52:397–400.

69. Henriksen JE, Bruun Andersen C, Hother-Nielsen O, et al. Impact of ubiquinone (coenzyme Q10) treatment on glycaemic control, insulin requirement and well-being in patients with type 1 diabetes mellitus. Diabet Med 1999;16:312–8.

70. Eriksson JG, Forsen TJ, Mortensen SA, Rohde M. The effect of coenzyme Q10 administration on metabolic control in patients with type 2 diabetes mellitus. Biofactors 1999;9:315–8.

71. Andersen CB, Henriksen JE, Hother-Nielsen O, et al. The effect of coenzyme Q10 on blood glucose and insulin requirement in patients with insulin dependent diabetes mellitus. Mol Aspects Med 1997;18:S307–9.

72. Suzuki S, Hinokio Y, Ohtomo M, et al. The effects of coenzyme Q10 treatment on maternally inherited diabetes mellitus and deafness, and mitochondrial DNA 3243 (A to G) mutation. Diabetologia 1998;41:584–8.

73. Suzuki Y, Kadowaki H, Atsumi Y, et al. A case of diabetic amyotrophy associated with 3243 mitochondrial tRNA (leu;UUR) mutation and successful therapy with coenzyme Q10. Endocr J 1995;42:141–5.

74. Wolever TM, Jenkins DJA, Vuksan V, et al. Beneficial effect of low-glycemic index diet in overweight NIDDM subjects. Diabetes Care 1992;15:562–4.

75. Jenkins DJ, Jenkins AL, Wolever TM, et al. Low glycemic-index: lente carbohydrates and physiological effects of altered food frequency. Am J Clin Nutr 1994;59:706S–9S.

76. Eastwood MA, Morris ER. Physical properties of dietary fiber that influence physiological function: a model for polymers along gastrointestinal tract. Am J Clin Nutr 1992;55:436–42.

77. Leeds AR. Dietary fiber: mechanisms of action. Int J Obes 1987;11(Suppl 1):3–7.

78. Vuksan V, Sievenpiper JL, Owen R, et al. Beneficial effects of viscous dietary fiber from Konjac-Mannan in subjects with the insulin resistance syndrome. Diabetes Care 2000;23:9–14.

79. Vuksan V, Jenkins DJA, Spadafora P, et al. Konjac-Mannan (Glucomannan) improves glycemia and other associated risk factors for coronary heart disease in type 2 diabetes. Diabetes Care 1999;22:913–9.

80. Anderson JW, Allgood LD, Turner J, et al. Effects of psyllium on glucose and serum lipid responses in men with type 2 diabetes and hypercholesterolemia. Am J Clin Nutr 1999;70:466–73.

81. Rodriguez-Moran M, Guerrero-Romero F, Lazcano-Burciago G. Lipid- and glucose-lowering efficacy of plantago psyllium in Type 2 diabetes. J Diabetes Complications 1998;12:273–8.

82. Chuang LM, Jou TS, Yang WS, et al. Therapeutic effect of guar gum in patients with non-insulin dependent diabetes mellitus. J Formos Med Asoc 1992;91:15–9.

83. Uusitupa M, Sodervik H, Silvasti M, Karttunen P. Effects of a gel forming dietary fiber, guar gum, on the absorption of glibenclamide and metabolic control and serum lipids in patients with non-insulin-dependent (type 2) diabetes. Int J Clin Pharmacol Ther Toxicol 1990;28:153–7.

84. Lalor BC, Bhatnagar D, Winocour PH, et al. Placebo-controlled trial of the effects of guar gum and metformin on fasting blood glucose and serum lipids in obese, type 2 diabetic patients. Diabet Med 1990;7:242–5.

85. Beattie VA, Edwards CA, Hosker JP, et al. Does adding fiber to a low energy, high carbohydrate, low fat diet confer any benefit to the management of newly diagnosed overweight Type 2 diabetics? BMJ 1988;296:1147–9.

86. Holman RR, Steemson J, Darling P, Turner RC. No glycemic benefit from guar gum administration in NIDDM. Diabetes Care 1987;10:68–71.

87. Lafrance L, Rabasa-Lhoret R, Poisson D, et al. Effects of different glycemic index foods and dietary fiber intake on glycaemic control in type 1 diabetic patients on intensive insulin therapy. Diabet Med 1998;15:972–8.

88. Vaaler S, Hanssen KF, Dahl-Jorgensen K, et al. Diabetic control is improved by guar gum and wheat bran supplementation. Diabet Med 1986;3:230–3.

89. Sharma RD, Raghuram TC, Sudhakar Rao N. Effect of fenugreek seeds on blood glucose and serum lipids in Type 1 diabetes. Eur J Clin Nutr 1990;44:301–6.

90. Cummings JH, Englyst HN. Fermentation in the human large intestine and the available substrates. Am J Clin Nutr 1987;45:1243–55.

91. Cooper SG, Tracey EJ. Small bowel obstruction caused by oat bran bezoar. N Engl J Med 1989;320:1148–9.

92. Feskens E, Bowles CH, Kromhout D. Inverse association between fish intake and risk of glucose intolerance in normoglycemic men and women. Diabetes Care 1991;14:935–41.

93. Kromhout D, Bosschieter EB, de Lezenne Coulander C. The inverse relation between fish consumption and 20-year mortality from coronary heart disease. N Engl J Med 1985;312:1205–9.

94. Norell SE, Ahlbom A, Feychting M, Pedersen NL. Fish consumption and mortality from coronary heart disease. BMJ 1986;293:426.

95. Nestel PJ, Connor WE, Reardon MF, et al. Suppression by diets rich in fish oil of very low density lipoprotein production in man. J Clin Invest 1984;74:82–9.

96. Harris WS, Connor WE, Illingworth R, et al. Effects of fish oil on VLDL triglyceride kinetics in humans. J Lipid Res 1990;31:1549–58.

97. Friedberg CE, Janssen MJFM, Heine RJ, Grobbee DE. Fish oil and glycemic control in diabetes: a meta-analysis. Diabetes Care 1998;21:494–500.

98. Luo J, Rizkalla SW, Vidal H, et al. Moderate intake of n-3 fatty acids for 2 months has no detrimental effect on glucose metabolism and could ameliorate the lipid profile in type 2 diabetic men. Diabetes Care 1998;21:717–24.

99. Sirtori CR, Paoletti R, Mancini M, et al, on behalf of the Italian Fish Oil Multicenter Study. n-3 Fatty acids do not lead to an increased diabetic risk in patients with hyperlipidemia and abnormal glucose tolerance. Am J Clin Nutr 1997;65:1874–81.

100. Dunstan DW, Mori TA, Puddey IB, et al. The independent and combined effects of aerobic exercise and dietary fish intake on serum lipids and glycemic control in NIDDM. Diabetes Care 1997;20:913–21.

101. McManus RM, Jumpson J, Finegood DT, et al. A comparison of the effects of n-3 fatty acids from linseed oil and fish oil in well-controlled type 2 diabetes. Diabetes Care 1996;19:463–7.

102. Rivellese AA, Maffettone A, Iovine C, et al. Long-term effects of fish oil on insulin resistance and plasma lipoproteins in NIDDM patients with hypertriglyceridemia. Diabetes Care 1996;19:1207–13.

103. Kristensen SD, Schmidt EB, Dyerberg J. Dietary supplementation with n-3 polyunsaturated fatty acids and human platelet function: a review with particular emphasis on implications for cardiovascular disease. J Intern Med Suppl 1989;225:141–50.

104. Oshima Y, Sato K, Hikino H. Isolation and hypoglycemic activity of quinquefolans A, B, and C, glycans of Panax quinquefolium roots. J Nat Prod 1987;50:188–90.

105. Martinez B, Staba EJ. The physiological effects of Aralia, Panax and Eleutherococcus on exercised rats. Jpn J Pharmacol 1984;35:79–85.

106. Yuan CS, Wu JA, Lowell T, Gu M. Gut and brain effects of American ginseng root on brainstem neuronal activities in rats. Am J Chin Med 1998;26:47–55.

107. Ohnishi Y, Takagi S, Miura T, et al. Effect of ginseng radix on GLUT2 protein content in mouse liver in normal and epinephrine-induced hyperglycemic mice. Biol Pharm Bull 1996;19:1238–40.

108. Kimura M, Waki I, Chujo T, et al. Effects of hypoglycemic components in ginseng radix on blood insulin level in alloxan diabetic mice and on insulin release from perfused rat pancreas. J Pharmacobiodyn 1981;4:410–7.

109. Roy D, Perrault M, Marette A. Insulin stimulation of glucose uptake in skeletal muscle and adipose tissue in vivo is NO dependent. Am J Physiol 1998;274:E692–9.

110. Spinas GA, Laffranchi R, Francoys I, et al. The early phase of glucose-stimulated insulin secretion requires nitric oxide. Diabetologia 1998;41:292–9.

111. Vuksan V, Koo VYY, Sievenpiper JL, et al. North American ginseng (Panax quinquefolius L.) reduces postprandial glycemia in nondiabetic and type 2 diabetic individuals. Arch Intern Med 2000;160:1009–13.

112. Sotaniemi EA, Haapakoski E, Rautio A. Ginseng therapy in non-insulin-dependent diabetic patients. Diabetes Care 1995;18:1373–5.

113. Martin JE. Help on herbals: weeding fact from fiction. Pharm Pract 1999;15:45–57.

CHAPTER 17

Insulin for Treating Type 1 and Type 2 Diabetes

Alice Y.Y. Cheng, MD, and Bernard Zinman, MDCM, FACP, FRCP

ABSTRACT

Insulin has been a fundamental component of diabetes management since its initial administration to humans in 1922. The major overall biologic action of insulin is to promote storage of ingested nutrients. Human insulins and, increasingly, analogues of human insulin are the main insulins in clinical use today. Insulin administration is targeted to normalize the glycemic response to meals and to replace basal requirements. The principal adverse effects of exogenous insulin are hypoglycemia and weight gain.

In Type 1 diabetes, insulin is an essential component of treatment. It is not only necessary for survival, but, as shown in the Diabetes Control and Complications Trial, when used with an intensive diabetes therapy regimen, it delays the onset and progression of microvascular complications. Intensive treatment with multiple daily injections (at least three/d) or continuous subcutaneous insulin infusion with basal insulin and boluses at mealtimes achieves the best glycemic control. With appropriate patient education, support, and counseling, most people with Type 1 diabetes can successfully use intensive treatment.

In Type 2 diabetes, insulin is used when diet, exercise, and oral agents are unable to provide adequate glycemic control. The United Kingdom Prospective Diabetes Study showed that improving glycemic control in Type 2 diabetes also reduces microvascular and all diabetes-related complications.

The specific insulin regimen and the insulin delivery system used depends on patient preference and the expertise of the diabetes treatment team. The benefits and risks of various treatment options have been evaluated in controlled clinical trials. It is evident that continued research is required to improve insulin therapy to ultimately achieve physiologic insulin replacement and thus optimize glycemic control.

INTRODUCTION

Insulin has been a fundamental component of diabetes treatment since its discovery and first clinical use in 1922. It represents one of the great success stories of contemporary medicine. Insulin is absolutely indicated in the treatment of Type 1 diabetes and may be necessary in the treatment of many patients with Type 2 diabetes. To treat Type 1 or Type 2 diabetes effectively with insulin, the following questions must be answered:

1. What are the major actions of insulin in humans?
2. What are the different types of insulin available?
3. What are the benefits and risks of using insulin for treating Type 1 and Type 2 diabetes?
4. What degree of glucose lowering leads to the best outcome when treating Type 1 and Type 2 diabetes? What are the risks?
5. Which insulin is most appropriate for mealtime insulin and for basal insulin?
6. What are the advantages and disadvantages of the various insulin delivery systems (syringe vs pen vs pump)?
7. What insulin regimens will achieve target glycemic levels for Type 1 diabetes and Type 2 diabetes?

8.   What are the emerging insulin delivery systems?
9.   What are the issues surrounding pancreas transplantation?

What Are the Major Actions of Insulin?

Insulin is a protein consisting of 51 amino acids within 2 peptide chains. Secreted by the pancreas, insulin actions are widespread and directly or indirectly affect the function of almost every tissue in the body.[1] The major function of insulin is to promote storage of ingested nutrients.[1] The effects of insulin on liver, muscle, and adipose tissue are crucial for energy storage. Table 17–1 provides a brief overview of these effects.

Metabolic Effects of Insulin

Insulin affects fundamental metabolic pathways in the liver, muscle, and adipose tissue. Insulin increases energy stores and anabolic pathways by promoting synthesis of glycogen, triglyceride, cholesterol, very-low-density lipoprotein (VLDL), and protein in the liver. It also inhibits the breakdown of hepatic glycogen and gluconeogenesis, thus controlling overnight hepatic glucose production.

In muscle, insulin increases amino acid transport and stimulates ribosomal protein synthesis, thereby promoting protein synthesis. It also increases glucose transport into muscle, enhances activity of glycogen synthetase, and inhibits activity of glycogen phosphorylase. These actions promote glycogen synthesis in muscle.

In adipose tissue, triglyceride is the most efficient means of energy storage. Insulin promotes triglyceride storage in adipocytes. It increases glucose transport into fat cells, enhances lipoprotein lipase activity, and inhibits lipolysis.

All of the above effects combine to perform one of insulin's major functions, promoting storage of ingested nutrients. In addition to storage, insulin also has important effects on growth and on other anabolic pathways.

Table 17–1 Insulin Effects on Liver, Muscle, and Adipocytes

Effects on liver
  Promotes:
            glycogen synthesis
            triglyceride, cholesterol, VLDL synthesis
            protein synthesis
  Inhibits:
            glycogenolysis
            ketogenesis
            gluconeogenesis

Effects on muscle
  Promotes:
            protein synthesis
            glycogen synthesis

Effects on adipocytes
  Promotes:
            triglyceride storage
  Inhibits:
            intracellular lipolysis

VLDL = very-low-density lipoprotein.
Adapted from Karam JH. Pancreatic hormones and diabetes mellitus. In: Greenspan FS, Strewler GJ, editors. Basic and clinical endocrinology. 5th ed. Norwalk: Appleton and Lange; 1997. p. 595–663.

WHAT ARE THE DIFFERENT TYPES OF INSULIN AVAILABLE?

For the first 50 years of the insulin era, insulin was only available in bovine or porcine preparations.[2] The limitations of animal insulin and the worldwide availability of human insulin since the early 1980s have made animal insulins essentially obsolete. Human insulins and newer insulin analogues are now the main insulins used in the treatment of diabetes. Human insulins are available in short-, intermediate-, long-, and very-rapid-acting preparations.[3] The onset, peak, and duration of action after subcutaneous injection are the most relevant pharmacologic parameters for insulin; these are shown in Table 17–2. However, there is wide variability in the reported time-action profiles of the insulins depending on the method used to measure it, patient-selection criteria, insulin doses, methods of insulin administration, and injection sites.[4,5] The different time-action profiles allow one to try to simulate natural insulin secretion, as shown in Figure 17–1. Insulin replacement should be thought of in the context of bolus or basal insulins. The bolus insulins are very rapid- and short-acting insulins. They simulate the higher levels of insulin after ingestion of a meal. The basal insulins are intermediate- and long-acting insulins. They simulate the basal level of insulin occurring between meals, through the night, and with fasting.

Very-Rapid-Acting Insulin Analogues

Insulin in solution tends to self-associate and form larger aggregates called hexamers. These large aggregates need to dissociate after injection before absorption can occur.[2] Therefore, researchers have developed analogues of human insulin that can dissociate from hexamers to monomers more quickly, thus allowing faster absorption and onset of action.[2,3] Insulin lispro is a new human analogue and is the first rapidly acting insulin approved for human administration.[4,6] It is absorbed more rapidly than regular insulin. Lispro begins acting within 15 minutes, reaches peak between 60 to 90 minutes, and has a duration of action of 4 to 5 hours. Lispro has been shown to lower postprandial glucose levels and decrease rates of hypoglycemia compared to regular insulin.[7–11] The impact of lispro compared with regular insulin on HbA_{1c}, has been variable.[12–17]

Table 17–2 Approximate Pharmacokinetic Parameters of Human Insulin Following Subcutaneous Injection

Insulin	Onset of Action	Peak of Action	Duration of Action	Blood Glucose Targets
Lispro	10–15 min	1–1.5 h	4–5 h	Postprandial
Regular	15–60 min	2–4 h	5–8 h	Postprandial Prior to next meal
NPH	2.5–3.0 h	5–7 h	13–16 h	Mid-afternoon (for morning NPH) Fasting glucose next morning (for bedtime NPH)
Lente	2.5–3.0 h	7–12 h	Up to 18 h	Similar to NPH
Ultralente	3–4 h	8–10 h	Up to 20 h	Similar to NPH

NPH = neutral protamine hagedorn.
Adapted from Heinneman L, Richter B. Clinical pharmacology of human insulin. Diabetes Care 1993; 16(Suppl 3):90–101.

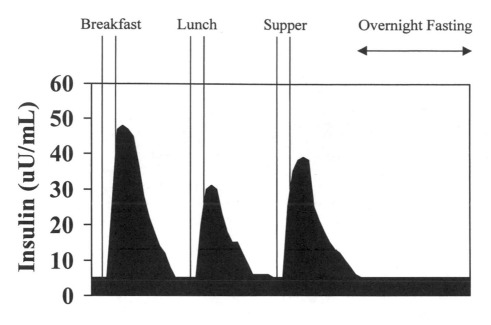

Figure 17–1 Normal insulin secretion in relation to meals and the overnight fasting state. (Adapted from Schade D, Santiago J, Skyler J, Rizza R. Intensive insulin therapy. Amsterdam: Excerpta Medica; 1983. p. 24.)

Another very-rapid-acting insulin analogue is insulin aspart. It is also absorbed more rapidly after subcutaneous injection, resulting in higher peak concentrations compared with regular insulin.[18] Randomized, 6-month, open-label trials comparing insulin aspart and regular insulin in patients with Type 1 diabetes show significantly reduced HbA$_{1c}$ for insulin aspart, with no difference in the frequency of hypoglycemia.[19–21] However, a randomized, 6-month, open-label trial comparing insulin aspart and regular insulin in patients with Type 2 diabetes showed no significant difference in HbA$_{1c}$ or hypoglycemia between the groups.[22] Insulin aspart is a newer insulin analogue and various clinical trials are still under way.

Short-Acting Human Insulin: Regular

Subcutaneously injected regular insulin is unable to mimic physiologic meal insulin secretion because of its slow rate of absorption from the subcutaneous space. Regular insulin has an onset of action 15 to 60 minutes after injection, a peak effect 2 to 4 hours after injection, and duration of action ranging from 5 to 8 hours.[2] Given the "short-acting" nature of regular insulin, it is used primarily to deal with acute rises in serum glucose, such as occurs with meals. Therefore, regular insulin should be administered approximately 30 to 45 minutes prior to a meal.[2]

Intermediate-Acting Human Insulin: NPH and Lente

First developed in 1946, Neutral Protamine Hagedorn (NPH) insulin has a longer duration of action than regular insulin.[4] Its onset of action is within 2.5 to 3 hours of injection, its peak action 5 to 7 hours after injection, and its duration of action between 13 to 16 hours.[4] The other intermediate-acting insulin is Lente. Its onset of action is similar to NPH at 2.5

hours, its peak action is at 7 to 12 hours after injection, and its duration of action is up to 18 hours.[4] Given the more prolonged action of NPH and Lente insulin, they are not ideal for controlling postprandial serum glucose levels. When given at appropriate times, they are effective in lowering fasting plasma glucose and lowering pre-dinner plasma glucose.[2]

Long-Acting Human Insulin: Ultralente

The goal of long-acting insulin (Ultralente) is to achieve more appropriate basal insulin coverage. Its onset of action is 4 hours after injection, peak action at 8 to 10 hours, and duration of action up to 20 hours.[4] In clinical practice, its biologic action appears to be similar to that of intermediate-acting insulin.

Long-Acting Insulin Analogue: Glargine

The insulin preparation glargine is a long-acting insulin analogue that attempts to provide a more constant level of insulin compared with the human long-acting insulin preparations.[3,23,24] Unlike the human long-acting insulin preparations, there are no pronounced insulin peaks with glargine, there is less nocturnal hypoglycemia, and there is slower absorption.[23,24] It has a higher isoelectric point than human insulin, which gives it its prolonged duration of action.[3,23,24] Its lower pH precludes it from being mixed with other insulins. This preparation is expected to soon be available clinically.

WHAT ARE THE BENEFITS AND RISKS OF USING INSULIN FOR TREATING TYPE 1 AND TYPE 2 DIABETES?

Benefits in Type 1 Diabetes

Insulin absence is the hallmark of Type 1 diabetes. Therefore, insulin is essential for life in people with Type 1 diabetes to avoid a constant catabolic state and ketosis. When used appropriately, it can effectively lower serum glucose concentrations, prevent symptoms of hyperglycemia, and promote normal growth and development. In addition, it has been shown that the use of insulin in intensive treatment regimens, with the goal of achieving near-normal plasma glucose concentrations, delays the onset and slows progression of microvascular complications in patients with Type 1 diabetes.[25,26] The Diabetes Control and Complications Trial (DCCT) was a multicenter randomized controlled trial comparing multiple daily injection therapy or continuous subcutaneous insulin infusion (intensive therapy) to one to two injections per day (conventional therapy). The intensive therapy group, who achieved significantly lower HbA_{1c} levels, had a relative risk reduction of 76% (95% confidence interval [CI] 62 to 85%) for developing retinopathy and a 54% relative risk reduction (95% CI 39 to 66%) for progression of retinopathy.[25] The intensive therapy also had a 39% relative risk reduction (95% CI 21 to 52%) for developing microalbuminuria and a 54% relative risk reduction (95% CI 19 to 74%) for progressing to albuminuria.[25] There was a relative risk reduction of 64% (95% CI 34 to 87%) for developing or progressing neuropathy in the intensive therapy group.[27] There was also a relative risk reduction of 40% (95% CI 6 to 61%) for developing elevated low-density lipoprotein (LDL) cholesterol levels in the intensive therapy group.[28] However, benefit for macrovascular complications was less clear.[29] In a recent review and meta-analysis of this subject, intensive therapy was shown to decrease the number of macrovascular events (odds ratio 0.55 [95% CI 0.35 to 0.88]), but no significant effect on the number of patients affected or on macrovascular mortality was shown.[29] The DCCT showed a 41% relative risk reduction (95% CI −10 to 68%) for macrovascular complications with intensive therapy, which was not statistically significant.[25] The need for insulin in Type 1 diabetes for survival is apparent. However, the appropriate use of insulin, with the goal of achieving near-normal serum glucose concentration, has benefits beyond those of mere survival and symptom relief.

EVIDENCE-BASED MESSAGES

1. Achieving near-normal serum glucose concentrations delays the onset and slows the progression of microvascular complications in Type 1 diabetes. Intensive insulin therapy reduces the risk for developing retinopathy by 76%, progressing in retinopathy by 54%, developing microalbuminuria by 39%, progressing to albuminuria by 54%, and developing neuropathy by 60% (Level 1A).[25]
2. Intensive insulin therapy seems to reduce the number of macrovascular complications in Type 1 diabetes but not the number of patients affected or macrovascular mortality (Level 1A).[29]

Benefits in Type 2 Diabetes

The initial treatment for Type 2 diabetes does not include insulin. Diet, exercise, weight loss, and oral hypoglycemic agents are initially adequate therapies to achieve glycemic control. However, insulin is indicated for patients who are unable to maintain glycemic control with a combination of oral agents, diet, and exercise.[30] The benefits of insulin in Type 2 diabetes result from improved glycemic control.[31–34] The United Kingdom Prospective Diabetes Study (UKPDS) was a multicenter randomized controlled study designed to establish whether intensive blood glucose control reduced the risk of macrovascular and microvascular complications in patients with Type 2 diabetes.[32] There was a 12% reduction in diabetes-related endpoints and a 25% risk reduction (95% CI 7 to 40%) in microvascular endpoints for the intensive therapy group.[32] There was no significant difference within the intensive therapy group (ie, no difference between insulin and sulfonylureas). In a smaller Japanese study,[33] significant reductions in microvascular complications with improved HbA_{1c} were shown (Table 17–3). With respect to macrovascular complications, the UKPDS showed a nonstatistically significant 16% risk reduction ($p = .052$) in macrovascular complications with intensive therapy.[32]

The Diabetes Insulin-Glucose in Acute Myocardial Infarction (DIGAMI) trial showed that insulin therapy in patients after an acute myocardial infarction significantly decreases mortality.[35,36] The use of insulin-glucose infusion for at least 24 hours after an acute myocardial infarction, followed by intensive insulin therapy, reduced in-hospital all-cause mortality by 58% ($p < .05$) and 1-year all-cause mortality by 52% ($p < .02$).[35] When the patients were followed for a mean of 3.4 years, the relative risk of all-cause mortality for the insulin-treated group was 0.72 (95% CI 0.55 to 0.92).[36] The effect was most apparent in patients who had not previously received insulin treatment and who were at a low cardiovascular risk.[35,36]

Table 17–3 Relative Risk Reduction for Diabetic Retinopathy, Nephropathy, and Neuropathy*

	DCCT (%) (95% CI)	Okhubo Study (%) (95% CI)	UKPDS[†] (%)
Retinopathy	63 (52–71)	62 (26–84)	27
Nephropathy	54 (19–74)	68 (22–87)	9
Neuropathy	60 (38–74)	Data not given[‡]	Data not given[‡]

*In the intensive therapy groups of the DCCT[25] In Type 1 diabetes, Okhubo study[33] in Type 2 diabetes, and UKPDS[32] in Type 2 diabetes.
[†]95% confidence intervals were not provided in the published data.
[‡]Data not published.
DCCT = Diabetes Control and Complications Study; UKPDS = United Kingdom Prospective Diabetes Study.
Data from the Diabetes Control and Complications Trial Research Group,[25] United Kingdom Prospective Diabetes Study Group,[32] and Okhubo et al.[33]

EVIDENCE-BASED MESSAGES

1. Achieving near-normal glucose concentrations irrespective of therapy used reduces diabetes-related endpoints by 12% and reduces the risk of microvascular complications in Type 2 diabetes by 25% (Level 1A).[32]
2. There was a trend toward reducing macrovascular complications in the intensive therapy group.[32] Use of insulin-glucose infusion for at least 24 hours in patients with diabetes and acute myocardial infarction, followed by intensive insulin therapy, reduced in-hospital all-cause mortality by 58% and 1-year all-cause mortality by 52%. The benefit continues for at least 3.5 years, with a relative risk of all-cause mortality of 0.72 (Level 1A).[35,36]

Risks in Type 1 Diabetes

The risks of insulin use are similar in both Type 1 and Type 2 diabetes. The two major adverse effects of insulin use are hypoglycemia and weight gain.[37,38] Other minor risks include insulin allergy and infection at the site of injection.[2]

Hypoglycemia is the most feared complication of insulin treatment, with potentially serious sequelae.[37] Inappropriate timing of mealtimes, exercise, and insulin treatment can lead to hypoglycemia.[38] Hypoglycemic unawareness or previous episodes of repeated severe hypoglycemia requiring assistance are risk factors for hypoglycemia.[38] In the DCCT, there was a threefold increase in frequency of severe hypoglycemia in the intensive-therapy group.[38] The risk of severe hypoglycemia was inversely related to HbA_{1c} levels.[25]

Weight gain is another potential adverse effect of insulin use. In the DCCT, the incidence of becoming overweight, defined as body mass index (BMI) ≥ 27.8 kg/m^2 for men and BMI ≥ 27.3 kg/m^2 for women, during the median 6.5 years of follow-up was 41.5% in the intensive therapy group compared to only 26.9% in the conventional group ($p < .001$).[38] Other studies have also shown more weight gain with intensive use of insulin in people with Type 1 diabetes.[26]

There is a rare risk of insulin allergy in insulin use. Human insulin is far less immunogenic than the animal insulins, but this adverse outcome can still occur.[2] Allergic reactions range from local hypersensitivity manifesting as a cutaneous wheal to systemic allergic reaction manifesting as anaphylaxis or urticaria.[2] Desensitization protocols have been developed for both local and systemic insulin hypersensitivity.[2]

EVIDENCE-BASED MESSAGES

1. The risks and adverse effects of insulin therapy in Type 1 diabetes are hypoglycemia, weight gain, and, rarely, allergy and infection. In the DCCT, the risk of hypoglycemia was threefold in the intensive therapy group (Level 1A).[38]
2. The risk of hypoglycemia is inversely related to the HbA_{1c} level achieved (Level 1A).[25]

Risks in Type 2 Diabetes

The risks of insulin use in Type 2 diabetes are similar to those for Type 1 diabetes, including hypoglycemia, weight gain, allergy, and infection. However, the rates of hypoglycemia in Type 2 diabetes are much less than in Type 1 diabetes.[32–34,39] In the UKPDS, the frequency of major hypoglycemic episodes was 1.8% per year in the insulin-treated group.[32] In the Okhubo study,[33] no major hypoglycemic episodes occurred with insulin-mediated intensive control over 7 years of follow-up (Table 17–4). However, the same general principle applies in Type 2 diabetes, namely, the risk of hypoglycemia is inversely related to the HbA_{1c}.[31]

The risk of weight gain with insulin use in Type 2 diabetes has also been well documented.[32,33,39,40] In the UKPDS, a mean weight gain of 4.0 kg was found in the insulin group ($p < .001$) as compared to conventional therapy.[32] Other studies had similar results.[33,39–41]

Table 17–4 Frequency of Hypoglycemia in Type 2 Diabetes Treated with Insulin to Achieve Tight Control

Study	HbA$_{1C}$(%)	Severe Hypoglycemia (%/y)	Any Hypoglycemia (%/y)
UKPDS[32]	7.1	1.8	28
Okhubo[33]	7.1	0	1.9
VACSDM[34]	7.3	3%	41
DIGAMI[36]	7.0	Same as control	N/A

Adapted from Gerstein HC, Capes S. Advantages and perceived disadvantages of insulin therapy for patients with Type 2 diabetes. Can J Diabetes Care 1999;23(Suppl 2):91–4.
UKPDS = United Kingdom Prospective Diabetes Study; VACSDM = Veterans Affairs Cooperative Study on Diabetes Mellitus; DIGAMI = Diabetes Insulin-Glucose in Acute Myocardial Infarction Trial.

There has been a concern for a number of years that insulin promotes and accelerates atherosclerosis, thereby increasing risk of macrovascular complications. Some studies have shown an association between high endogenous insulin levels and macrovascular disease.[42–48] Others have shown that hyperinsulinemia itself is not an independent risk factor for macrovascular disease.[49–53] It has been suggested that the direct effects of insulin do not promote atherosclerosis. Instead, it is the insulin resistance that hyperinsulinemia mirrors that is closely associated with other risk factors for macrovascular disease.[44,45,49–53] There is no evidence that exogenous insulin use is related to macrovascular disease, and its appropriate administration should not be discouraged.[54] The UKPDS showed that there was no increase in cardiovascular events or death in either the insulin or sulfonylurea group compared to the conventional group—despite the fact that these two groups had higher plasma insulin levels than did the conventionally treated patients.[32] As a consequence, one can safely conclude that exogenous insulin is not a risk factor for atherosclerosis.

Risk of insulin allergy and infection at the injection site is the same as in Type 1 diabetes.

EVIDENCE-BASED MESSAGE

The risks and adverse effects of insulin therapy in Type 2 diabetes are hypoglycemia, weight gain, and, rarely, allergy and infection. Hypoglycemia in Type 2 diabetes occurs less frequently than in Type 1 diabetes (Level 1A).[31,39] There is no increase in macrovascular disease risk when using exogenous insulin to treat Type 2 diabetes.[32]

WHAT DEGREE OF GLUCOSE LOWERING LEADS TO THE BEST OUTCOME?

Type 1 Diabetes

In Type 1 diabetes, insulin is an essential component of treatment. The degree of glucose lowering depends on many factors, including the dose and regimen of insulin used. It has been clearly shown that lowering HbA$_{1c}$ levels to near normal delays the onset and slows progression of microvascular complications.[25,26] In the DCCT, the mean HbA$_{1c}$ achieved by the intensive therapy group was approximately 7.0%.[25] The conventional therapy group had a mean HbA$_{1c}$ of 9.0%.[25] Clearly, an optimal HbA$_{1c}$ would be < 7.0%, or as close to normal as possible. However, one must consider the risks of hypoglycemia when aiming for a low HbA$_{1c}$. The latest clinical practice guidelines from the Canadian Diabetes Association state that an optimal HbA$_{1c}$ is < 7.0%, suboptimal 7.0 to 8.4%, and inadequate > 8.4%.[12]

EVIDENCE-BASED MESSAGE

An HbA_{1c} < 7.0% prevents or delays microvascular complications such as retinopathy, nephropathy, and neuropathy in people with Type 1 diabetes (Level 1A).[25]

Type 2 Diabetes

In Type 2 diabetes, insulin may need to be introduced later in therapy when diet, exercise, and oral agents are insufficient to achieve adequate glycemic control. Adding insulin to oral hypoglycemic agents or switching entirely to insulin can significantly improve HbA_{1c} levels in patients with Type 2 diabetes.[30,41] The UKPDS showed a significant reduction in microvascular complication risk in the intensive-therapy group, who achieved a median HbA_{1c} of 7.0%.[32] The conventional group achieved a median HbA_{1c} of 7.9%.[32] The Okhubo study[33] showed significant complication risk reduction, with a reduction in HbA_{1c} from 9.4 to 7.1%. Therefore, the target HbA_{1c} in people with Type 2 diabetes should be < 7.0%, or as close to normal as possible. However, one must always consider the risk of hypoglycemia when aiming for a low HbA_{1c} level.

EVIDENCE-BASED MESSAGE

An HbA_{1c} < 7.0%, or as close to normal as possible, prevents or delays microvascular complications such as retinopathy, nephropathy, and neuropathy in people with Type 2 diabetes (Level 1A).[32]

WHICH INSULIN IS MOST APPROPRIATE FOR MEALTIME INSULIN AND FOR BASAL INSULIN?

Mealtime (Bolus) Insulins

Lispro is an insulin analogue that has a faster onset of action, shorter time to peak action, and shorter duration of effect as compared to regular insulin.[3] It lowers postprandial glucose levels and has lower rates of hypoglycemia compared with regular insulin.[7-11] Also, lispro provides more flexibility for patients with inconsistent mealtimes, because it does not need to be administered 30 minutes prior to a meal. For these reasons, lispro is the insulin of choice for use before meals in multiple daily injection therapy.[7-11,13-15,17] It is the preferred insulin for continuous subcutaneous insulin infusion (CSII), as both a reduction in HbA_{1c} and hypoglycemic rates have been documented in a randomized double-blind controlled trial.[55] Some studies have shown that the use of lispro instead of regular insulin can improve HbA_{1c} if appropriate basal insulin regimen adjustments are made.[13,14,16,17] However, there are limitations to the use of lispro insulin. It must be used with caution in patients with gastroparesis because of its rapid onset of action. Pregnancy in a person with Type 1 or Type 2 diabetes or gestational diabetes is not a labeled indication for the use of lispro.[12]

Basal Insulin

The use of basal insulin is necessary for adequate glycemic control in Type 1 and Type 2 diabetes. Two commonly used basal insulins are NPH and Ultralente. The time-action profiles of these two insulins were described earlier. Human Ultralente has a slightly longer time-action profile than NPH, but they are similar. For a multiple daily injection regimen with lispro as the mealtime insulin, NPH and Ultralente provide similar glycemic control.[56] However, NPH showed a slightly better daily glycemic profile.[56] It is important to note that only NPH insulin is available for the pen delivery system.

Pre-Mixed versus Patient-Mixed Insulin

Mixing rapid-acting insulin with an intermediate or long-acting insulin before injection has become common because it reduces the number of injections per day. Patients can mix the insulins themselves or use pre-mixed insulin preparations. Patient-mixed insulin allows for flexibility in dosage; however, there are limitations. Patients must be well educated about proper mixing technique to avoid contamination. Regular insulin should only be mixed with NPH insulin, because mixing with Lente or Ultralente can cause retardation of the action of regular insulin.[2] Pre-mixed insulins are now available in a wide range of short- to intermediate-acting ratios, from 10:90 to 50:50.[2] Pre-mixed insulins are preferred by elderly patients and those with visual or fine motor impairment.[57] However, pre-mixed insulins do not allow for easy adjusting of meal and basal insulin doses. Several factors play a role in deciding which system to use in a particular patient, and individual circumstances must frequently be considered.

EVIDENCE-BASED MESSAGE

> When used as a mealtime (bolus) insulin treatment, Lispro is associated with less hypoglycemia, better postprandial glucose, and increased mealtime flexibility. It may offer improved glycemic control compared with regular insulin if basal insulin is appropriately adjusted (Level 1A).[17] Patient-mixed insulin allows for more flexible dosing but requires more skill than using pre-mixed insulin. Pre-mixed insulin is preferred for elderly patients and those with visual or fine motor impairment (Level 1A).[57]

WHAT ARE THE ADVANTAGES AND DISADVANTAGES OF THE VARIOUS INSULIN DELIVERY SYSTEMS?

There are several insulin delivery systems commonly used. Which delivery system one chooses should be based on personal preferences and needs.

Syringe and Needle

Syringe and needle is the traditional delivery system. The length and gauge of the needles have changed significantly over the years to decrease the pain of injecting. The syringe and needle system has the advantage of flexibility. Dosages can be readily adjusted and insulins can be mixed for fewer injections per day. However, the proper use of this delivery system requires good eyesight and fine motor skills to ensure that appropriate doses of insulin are drawn and administered. The vial, syringe, and needles need to be carried when going out, which some may find cumbersome.

Pen Devices

Pen-shaped devices have been available for a number of years. They use replaceable insulin cartridges containing 150 to 300 units of regular, lispro, NPH, or pre-mixed insulin. The insulin dose is dialed into the device, a fine needle is inserted, and the plunger is depressed to inject. The system is convenient, unobtrusive, and easy to carry. However, insulins cannot be mixed (unless using fixed pre-mixed ratios), so two injections are required for combined rapid-acting and intermediate-acting therapy.[58]

Continuous Subcutaneous Insulin Infusion

External insulin infusion pumps were first made available in the early 1980s. Short-acting insulin is infused through a catheter into a transcutaneous needle or Silastic infuser placed subcutaneously.[58] With CSII, a preprogrammed basal rate of insulin is delivered continuously. There is complete flexibility in meal timing since the basal rate maintains glycemic control and boluses are delivered before the meal. The disadvantages are that careful attention to self-care is necessary to avoid subcutaneous infection at the infusion site, the possibility of blocked catheter leading to rapid deterioration in control, and being "attached" to a device. With the newer pumps incorporating several safety alarms to indicate interrupted flow, the problem of glycemic deterioration is distinctly less. When used by a well-trained patient, CSII can be an effective method of providing near physiologic insulin replacement.

The greatest disadvantage, at this time, is the initial cost of the system and of its continued use.[58]

EVIDENCE-BASED MESSAGE

The choice of insulin delivery system depends on personal preferences and needs. The currently available delivery systems are syringe and needle, pen-devices, and external pumps for CSII (Level 4).[12]

WHICH INSULIN REGIMENS WILL ACHIEVE TARGET GLYCEMIC LEVELS?

The choice of an appropriate insulin regimen is influenced by the patient's lifestyle, age, motivation, general health, capacity for awareness of hypoglycemia, and self-management skills.[12] Interventions that facilitate insulin use include appropriate education and support regarding the care and use of insulin, recognition and treatment of hypoglycemia, management of sick days, and insulin adjustments for food intake and exercise.[12]

Type 1 Diabetes

In Type 1 diabetes, some of the commonly used insulin protocols are multiple daily injections (MDI), three-times-a-day dosing (tid), CSII, and twice-daily dosing (bid). The evidence from the DCCT clearly shows that intensive therapy with MDI or CSII achieves lower HbA$_{1c}$ levels and reduces the risk of microvascular complications.[25] Therefore, MDI or CSII should be the preferred therapy for all people with Type 1 diabetes. With appropriate education, counseling, and support, most people with Type 1 diabetes can successfully use these regimens. However, this may not always be possible, so the next less intensive insulin regimen that will achieve the best glycemic control should be chosen.

Multiple Daily Injections

Multiple daily injections, also known as the bolus-basal routine, involve at least three to four injections per day. Lispro insulin is the preferred insulin before each meal (bolus) because of its pharmacokinetic advantages over regular insulin. Basal insulin, classically at bedtime, is NPH or Ultralente, although different regimens have emerged. The short-acting insulin with each meal controls postprandial serum glucose concentrations, and the intermediate-acting insulin controls fasting or premeal serum glucose concentrations. There is greater risk of hypoglycemia with MDI, primarily because of the tighter glycemic targets and improved control achieved.[25] Therefore, patient education, self-monitoring, and hypoglycemia awareness are fundamental to this therapy. Changes to the MDI regimen can be made if necessary. Sometimes, the addition of a second injection of NPH or Ultralente before breakfast is required to provide basal insulin over the day and control predinner serum glucose concentration better. In a recent study comparing Ultralente and NPH as the bedtime basal insulin in MDI with lispro, similar glycemic control was shown, with 75% of individuals requiring only one basal insulin dose.[56] In those individuals requiring twice-daily intermediate-acting insulin, the use of NPH appeared superior, showing a trend toward lower HbA$_{1c}$ levels.[56] Other studies have shown that using NPH and lispro before each meal, with NPH at bedtime, provides even better glycemic control.[13–15,17] The actual doses of insulin used must be adjusted on an individual basis. Table 17–5 provides a rough empiric guide for choosing initial insulin doses for MDI. The approximate initial total daily insulin (TDI) requirements for an individual not on insulin is 0.5 u/kg. If the patient is already on insulin, then the TDI is the sum of all the current insulin doses. Approximately 40% of the estimated TDI should be given as the basal insulin (NPH or Ultralente) at bedtime. The remaining 60% should be rapid-acting insulin (eg, lispro), given before each meal. There are many different ways to implement intensive therapy. The goal is to optimize glycemic control in the context of the lowest HbA$_{1c}$ with the least hypoglycemia. Therefore, the regimen that can achieve this goal for a particular individual is the appropriate one for the given circumstance.

Table 17–5 Initiation of Multiple Daily Insulin Therapy*

	Before Breakfast	Before Lunch	Before Dinner	Bedtime
Total daily insulin (TDI): 0.5 u × weight (kg) (if patient is on insulin, then TDI = sum of all current insulin doses) eg, if patient is 80 kg, TDI = 0.5 × 80 = 40 u		Daytime dose = 60% of TDI eg, = 2/3 × 40 u = 24 u		Bedtime dose = 40% of TDI
NPH insulin	None	None	None	40% of TDI eg, = 40 × 40 u = 16 u
Mealtime insulin	1/3 of daytime dose eg, = 1/3 × 24 u = 8 u	1/3 of daytime dose eg, = 1/3 × 24 u = 8 u	1/3 of daytime dose eg, = 1/3 × 24 u = 8 u	None

*Four injections/d.
NPH = Neutral Protamine Hagedorn.

Three-Times-a-Day Dosing

Three-times-a-day dosing involves a mixture of lispro and NPH insulin administered before breakfast, lispro insulin at dinner, and NPH at bedtime. The lispro insulin controls postprandial serum glucose concentration with each meal. The NPH before breakfast controls lunch and predinner glucose levels, and the NPH at bedtime should control fasting glucose levels. The following is a rough guide for choosing initial insulin doses (Table 17–6): (1) two-thirds of the TDI should be administered before breakfast; two-thirds of that dose should be NPH and one-third lispro insulin; (2) the remaining one-third of the TDI should be

Table 17–6 Initiation of Three-Times-a-Day Insulin Therapy

	Before Breakfast	Before Dinner	Bedtime
Total daily insulin (TDI): 0.5 u × weight (kg) (if patient is on insulin, then TDI = sum of all current insulin doses) eg, if patient is 72 kg, TDI = 0.5 × 72 = 36 u	Breakfast dose = 2/3 of TDI eg, 2/3 × 36 u = 24 u		Evening dose = 1/3 of TDI eg, 1/3 × 36 u = 12 u
NPH insulin	2/3 of breakfast dose eg, = 2/3 × 24 u = 16 u	None	2/3 of evening dose eg, = 2/3 × 12 = 8 u
Mealtime insulin	1/3 of breakfast dose eg, = 1/3 × 24 u = 8 u	1/3 of evening dose eg, = 1/3 × 12 u = 4 u	None

NPH = Neutral Protamine Hagedorn.

administered in the evening; one-third of the evening dose should be lispro insulin given before dinner, and two-thirds of the evening dose should be bedtime NPH.

Titration of insulin doses need to be made on an individual basis and reassessed frequently. The bolus insulin given before each meal is reflected by the postprandial glucose and the glucose value before the next. The basal insulin given in the morning is reflected by the blood glucose in the middle of the afternoon, usually the blood glucose obtained before dinner. The basal insulin given at bedtime is reflected by the fasting blood glucose the following morning. Therefore, titration of insulin doses should be made based on the blood glucose levels at specific times of day (see Table 17–2).

Twice-Daily Dosing

Twice-daily injections are not recommended in Type 1 diabetes because they do not provide adequate opportunity for patient adjustments of insulin dose and result in less than optimal glycemic control.[25] It is important to note that NPH given before dinner increases the risk of hypoglycemia during the night.[2]

EVIDENCE-BASED MESSAGE

In Type 1 diabetes, intensive insulin therapy with MDI or CSII achieves lower HbA$_{1c}$ levels and significantly reduces risk of microvascular complications compared to once-daily or twice-daily injection regimens (Level 1A).[25]

Type 2 Diabetes

In Type 2 diabetes, there are many insulin regimens available to choose from. Insulin is indicated when adequate glycemic control cannot be achieved with diet, exercise, and multiple oral agents.[30,41] Insulin may be used in conjunction with oral hypoglycemic agents or alone. Oral hypoglycemic agents include biguanides, sulfonylureas, α-glucosidase inhibitors, thiazolidinediones, and meglitinides. Insulin-only regimens are equivalent to insulin plus oral agent regimens.[30,59,60] In fact, a recent study showed that adding metformin to insulin in poorly controlled Type 2 diabetes lowers glucose and lipids more effectively than does increasing the insulin dose alone.[60]

Different combinations of insulin and oral agents have been used to treat Type 2 diabetes. In 1992, a randomized controlled trial comparing the following five regimens was reported[30]: (1) oral agent plus morning NPH insulin; (2) oral agent plus bedtime NPH insulin; (3) NPH and regular insulin (30:70 ratio) given before breakfast and dinner; (4) NPH at bedtime, regular insulin before meals; and (5) oral agents alone (control group). All the insulin-treated groups had decreased HbA$_{1c}$ levels compared to controls, and there was no difference between insulin groups.[30] However, weight gain was significantly less (1.2 ± 0.5 kg) in the evening NPH plus oral agents group.[30] Combination therapy with bedtime NPH insulin and oral agents is therefore an effective means of achieving glucose control and minimizing weight gain.[30]

Recently, another randomized controlled trial compared the following four different bedtime insulin regimens[59]: (1) glyburide plus placebo plus bedtime NPH; (2) metformin plus placebo plus bedtime NPH; (3) glyburide plus metformin plus bedtime NPH; and (4) morning NPH plus bedtime NPH. Body weight remained unchanged in patients receiving bedtime insulin plus metformin (mean change 0.9 ± 1.2 kg, $p < .001$).[59] Moreover, the greatest decrease in HbA$_{1c}$ was observed in the bedtime insulin plus metformin group of -2.5% $\pm 0.4\%$ ($p < .05$).[59] The bedtime NPH group also had significantly fewer symptomatic and biochemical episodes of hypoglycemia ($p < .05$).[59] Combination therapy with bedtime NPH insulin and metformin seems superior to other bedtime insulin regimens with respect to glycemic control, frequency of hypoglycemia, and prevention of weight gain.[59]

Another class of oral antidiabetic medications, the thiazolidinedione class, has been studied in patients with Type 2 diabetes and is currently being used in several countries as monotherapy as well as in combination therapy.[61,62] These drugs target insulin resistance and are often referred to as insulin sensitizers. Insulin sensitizers improve glycemic control and reduce insulin requirements for patients with Type 2 diabetes who are on insulin.[61]

EVIDENCE-BASED MESSAGES

1. In Type 2 diabetes, the combination of oral hypoglycemic therapy with bedtime intermediate-acting insulin is as effective as insulin-only regimens, including MDI, but is more effective for controlling weight gain (Level 1A).[30]
2. The combination of metformin and bedtime NPH insulin is superior to other bedtime insulin regimens with respect to glycemic control (change in HbA_{1c} −2.5% ± 0.4%), hypoglycemia, and prevention of weight gain (Level 1A).[59]

WHAT ARE THE EMERGING INSULIN DELIVERY SYSTEMS?

Conventional subcutaneous injection of insulin can be painful, inconvenient, and delivers insulin slowly into the peripheral venous system.[58] There are other insulin delivery systems under development that are not generally available. These include the implantable insulin infusion pump (IIP), nasal insulin, inhaled insulin, oral insulin, islet-cell encapsulation, and closed-loop artificial pancreas.

For the IIP to be clinically meaningful, it must be safe and effective for a number of years without requiring further surgery. In 1990, trials were undertaken in individuals with Type 1 diabetes.[63] There has been one large multicenter randomized controlled trial comparing the safety and effectiveness of an IIP with multiple-dose insulin (intensive therapy) in Type 2 diabetes.[64] At the end of 1 year, there was no significant difference between groups for fasting plasma glucose and HbA_{1c} levels. The IIP was associated with less daily glycemic variation, less weight gain, fewer episodes of hypoglycemia, and better quality of life.[64] The greatest risk of IIP was underdelivery of insulin because of a blocked catheter. This study showed that the IIP is an effective system for achieving glycemic control but that there are disadvantages.

Research into nasal insulin demonstrated rapid absorption and good biologic activity.[65] However, bioavailability is low and significant fluctuations occur with minor changes in nasal mucosa, as in infections or nasal irritation.[58] Adjuvants used to enhance absorption were irritants to the nasal mucosa. These problems have made intranasal insulin impractical at the current time.

The vascularity, high surface area, and apparent lack of insulin receptors of pulmonary alveoli make the lungs an attractive alternative route for insulin delivery. Hypoglycemic effects of inhaled insulin have been demonstrated in both animal and human studies.[66,67] In a placebo-controlled pilot study, postprandial glucose levels were controlled by delivering 1.5 u/kg of insulin into the lungs 5 minutes before the ingestion of a meal.[68] These devices continue to be evaluated in large clinical trials.

Oral insulin is another attractive alternative route of delivery because of convenience and ease of administration from the patient's perspective. However, it has not been a feasible option to date. It would be necessary to circumvent the digestive process of the gut and provide adequate, precise, predictable bioavailability.[58] Much more research is required before this becomes a practical option.

Islet-cell transplantation is still experimental. The use of nonhuman islet cells encapsulated in a membrane that only allows glucose to enter and insulin to exit, avoiding immunologic reactions, would be ideal. Much more research is required to develop this into a clinical option.

The closed-loop artificial pancreas has been described as the "holy grail" of insulin-pump research.[58] In this system, a glucose sensor would drive an insulin-delivery system and achieve normal blood glucose homeostasis. At this time, a practical, continuous glucose sensor is not yet available. Research into the closed-loop approach continues.

WHAT ARE THE ISSUES SURROUNDING PANCREAS TRANSPLANTATION?

Simultaneous pancreas and kidney transplantation, pancreas transplantation after kidney transplantation, and isolated pancreas transplantation are options available at some centers.[69] Simultaneous pancreaticorenal transplants are performed far more frequently than pancreas-after-kidney transplantation or isolated pancreas transplantation. Pancreas transplantation was introduced in the mid 1960s. In 1984, the simultaneous pancreaticorenal transplant was introduced. By the end of 1996, 9,000 pancreas transplants had been reported to the International Pancreas Transplant Registry.[70] For 1994 to 1996, 1-year pancreas survival rates were 81% for simultaneous pancreas and kidney transplantation (n = 1,516), 71% for pancreas-after-kidney transplantation (n = 141), and 64% for isolated pancreas transplantation (n = 64).[70]

For potential cadaveric kidney recipients, the option of simultaneous pancreaticorenal transplantation should be considered. It is important to weigh the increased perioperative risk against the benefits of normoglycemia. Simultaneous pancreaticorenal transplants (SPR) are technically more difficult and require increased immunosuppression.[69] Complications involving the pancreas allograft include pancreas thrombosis, wound infection, periallograft abscess, urologic problems secondary to pancreatic drainage to bladder, pancreatitis, and anastomosis problems.[69] The increased immunosuppression carries risk of all complications secondary to immunosuppression. Major risk factors for poor outcome include age > 45 years, atherosclerotic vascular disease, congestive heart failure, obesity, and hepatitis C infection.[69]

The benefits of pancreas transplantation are secondary to the benefits of normo glycemia. Glycosylated hemoglobin and fasting serum glucose levels are normal in patients with functional grafts.[70] It is important to note that long-term data are limited. Pancreas transplantation has little demonstrated effect on established retinopathy.[70] Perhaps this is due to the fact that most people receiving transplants already have advanced eye disease. There does appear to be benefit for neuropathy. The progression of neuropathy was slowed in transplant recipients, and some even reported an improvement in neuropathy.[69,70] Moreover, the development of diabetic nephropathy in the allograft kidney in patients receiving SPR transplants is unlikely.[71] The effects of pancreas transplantation on the development and progression of macrovascular complications are uncertain. No studies are available to document the effect of prolonged pancreas allograft function on the risk of myocardial infarction, stroke, or amputations.[69,70] For the rare pancreas transplant recipient with little or no secondary diabetic complications, there is evidence that long-term normoglycemia may prevent and reverse early microvascular changes.[70] Finally, there is significant improvement in the quality of life of successful SPR recipients compared to kidney-alone recipients.[69]

EVIDENCE-BASED MESSAGES

1. Simultaneous pancreas and kidney transplantation, pancreas transplantation after kidney transplantation, and isolated pancreas transplantation are available options. However, simultaneous pancreas and kidney transplantations are performed more frequently and with greater success than the other options. The International Pancreas Registry data for 1994 to 1996 show 1-year pancreas survival rates of 81% for simultaneous pancreaticorenal transplants (n = 1,516), 71% for pancreas after kidney (n = 141), and 64% for pancreas transplantation alone (n = 64) (Level 3).[70]

2. Nonobese patients with Type 1 diabetes who are younger than age 45 and who have little or no atherosclerotic vascular disease and no congestive heart failure are good candidates for simultaneous pancreaticorenal transplantation (Level 4).[69] The surgical risks and immunosuppression risks of transplantation must be weighed against the potential benefits of normoglycemia.

Conclusion

Insulin is a fundamental component of diabetes management. The major actions of insulin, the different types of insulin available, evidence of benefits and risks of insulin use, evidence for the degree of glucose lowering leading to the best outcome and its associated risks, choice of insulin and delivery system, the different insulin regimens, emerging insulin delivery systems, and pancreas transplantation were reviewed.

The major function of insulin in the body is to promote storage of ingested nutrients, acting primarily on the liver, muscle, and fat, and to ensure normal growth and development. Human insulin and insulin analogues are the primary insulins being used today. They are available in short-, intermediate-, and long-acting preparations. The new insulin analogue lispro is a rapid-acting insulin that acts significantly faster than human regular insulin, simulating physiologic insulin secretion more closely. When used appropriately, contemporary insulin therapy effectively reduces morbidity in people with diabetes. The challenge for the future is to continue to simplify the use of insulin and achieve optimal glycemic control in all patients with diabetes.

Summary of Evidence-Based Messages

1. Achieving near-normal serum glucose concentrations delays the onset and slows the progression of microvascular complications in Type 1 diabetes. Intensive insulin therapy reduces the risk for developing retinopathy by 76%, progressing in retinopathy by 54%, developing microalbuminuria by 39%, progressing to albuminuria by 54%, and developing neuropathy by 60% (Level 1A).[25]

2. Intensive insulin therapy seems to reduce the number of macrovascular complications in Type 1 diabetes but not the number of patients affected or macrovascular mortality (Level 1A).[29]

3. Achieving near-normal glucose concentrations, irrespective of therapy used, reduces diabetes-related endpoints by 12% and reduces the risk of microvascular complications in Type 2 diabetes by 25% (Level 1A).[32]

4. There was a trend toward reducing macrovascular complications in the intensive therapy group.[32] Use of insulin-glucose infusion for at least 24 hours in patients with diabetes and acute myocardial infarction, followed by intensive insulin therapy, reduced in-hospital all-cause mortality by 58% and 1-year all-cause mortality by 52%, and the benefit continues for at least 3.5 years with a relative risk of all-cause mortality of 0.72 (Level 1A).[35,36]

5. The risks and adverse effects of insulin therapy in Type 1 diabetes are hypoglycemia, weight gain, and, rarely, allergy and infection. In the DCCT, risk of hypoglycemia was threefold in the intensive therapy group (Level 1A).[38]

6. The risk of hypoglycemia is inversely related to the HbA_{1c} level achieved (Level 1A).[25]

7. The risks and adverse effects of insulin therapy in Type 2 diabetes are hypoglycemia, weight gain, and, rarely, allergy and infection. Hypoglycemia in Type 2 diabetes occurs less frequently than in Type 1 diabetes (Level 1A).[31] There is no increase in macrovascular disease risk when using exogenous insulin to treat Type 2 diabetes.[32]

8. People with Type 1 diabetes should aim for optimal $HbA_{1c} < 7.0\%$ to prevent and delay microvascular complications such as retinopathy, nephropathy, and neuropathy (Level 1A).[25]

9. People with Type 2 diabetes should aim for HbA_{1c} levels $< 7.0\%$, or as close to normal as possible, to prevent and delay microvascular complications, such as retinopathy, nephropathy, and neuropathy (Level 1A).[32]

10. Lispro is the agent of choice for the mealtime (bolus) insulin in multiple daily injection therapy. Lispro offers less hypoglycemia, better postprandial glucose, and increased mealtime flexibility and may offer improved glycemic control compared to regular insulin if the appropriate basal insulin is used (Level 1A).[17] Patient-mixed insulin allows

for more flexible dosing but requires more skill than using pre-mixed insulin. Pre-mixed insulin is preferred by elderly patients and those with visual or fine motor impairment (Level 1A).[57]

11. The choice of insulin delivery system depends on personal preferences and needs. The currently available delivery systems are syringe and needle, pen-devices and external pumps for CSII (Level 4).[12]

12. In Type 1 diabetes, intensive insulin therapy with MDI or CSII achieves lower HbA_{1c} levels and significantly reduces risk of microvascular complications compared to once-daily or twice-daily injection regimens (Level 1A).[25]

13. In Type 2 diabetes, the combination of oral hypoglycemic therapy with bedtime intermediate-acting insulin is as effective as insulin-only regimens, including MDI, but is more effective for controlling weight gain (Level 1A).[30]

14. The combination of metformin and bedtime NPH insulin is superior to other bedtime insulin regimens with respect to glycemic control (change in HbA_{1c} −2.5% ± 0.4%), hypoglycemia, and prevention of weight gain (Level 1A).[59]

15. Simultaneous pancreas and kidney transplantation, pancreas-after-kidney transplantation, and isolated pancreas transplantations are available options; however, simultaneous pancreas and kidney transplantations are performed more frequently and with greater success than the other options. The International Pancreas Registry data for 1994 to 1996 show 1-year pancreas survival rates of 81% for simultaneous pancreaticorenal transplants (n = 1,516), 71% for pancreas after kidney (n = 141), and 64% for pancreas alone (n = 64) (Level 3).[70]

16. Nonobese patients with Type 1 diabetes, younger than age 45, with little or no atherosclerotic vascular disease and no congestive heart failure, are good candidates for simultaneous pancreaticorenal transplantation (Level 4).[69] The surgical risks and immunosuppression risks of transplantation must be weighed against the potential benefits of normoglycemia.

REFERENCES

1. Karam JH. Pancreatic hormones and diabetes mellitus. In: Greenspan FS, Strewler GJ, editors. Basic and clinical endocrinology. 5th ed. Norwalk: Appleton & Lange; 1997. p. 595–663.

2. Burge MR, Schade DS. Insulins. Endocrinol Metab Clin North Am 1997;26:575–98.

3. Lee WL, Zinman B. From insulin to insulin analogs: progress in the treatment of type 1 diabetes. Diabetes Rev 1998;6:73–88.

4. Heinemann L, Richter B. Clinical pharmacology of human insulin. Diabetes Care 1993; 16(Suppl 3):90–101.

5. Zinman B. The physiological replacement of insulin—an elusive goal. N Engl J Med 1989;321:363–70.

6. Howey DC, Bowsher RR, Brunelle R, Woodworth JR. (Lys [B28], Pro [B29]) – human insulin: a rapidly absorbed analogue of human insulin. Diabetes 1994;43:396–402.

7. Brunelle RL, Llewelyn J, Anderson JH, et al. Meta-analysis of the effect of insulin lispro on severe hypoglycemia in patients with type 1 diabetes. Diabetes Care 1998;21:1726–31.

8. Anderson JH Jr, Brunelle RL, Koivisto VA, et al. Reduction of postprandial hyperglycemia and frequency of hypoglycemia in IDDM patients on insulin analog treatment. Diabetes 1997;46:265–70.

9. Anderson JH Jr, Brunelle RL, Keohane P, et al. Mealtime treatment with insulin analogue improves postprandial hyperglycemia and hypoglycemia in NIDDM patients. Arch Intern Med 1997;157:1249–55.

10. Pfutzner A, Kustner E, Forst T, et al. Intensive insulin therapy with insulin lispro in patients with type 1 diabetes reduces the frequency of hypoglycemic episodes. Exp Clin Endocrinol 1996;104: 25–30.

11. Holleman F, Schmitt H, Rottiers R, et al. Reduced frequency of severe hypoglycemia and coma in well-controlled IDDM patients treated with insulin lispro. Diabetes Care 1997;20:1827–32.

12. Meltzer S, Leiter L, Daneman D, et al. 1998 clinical practice guidelines for the management of diabetes in Canada. Can Med Assoc J 1998;159(Suppl 8):S1–29.

13. Ciofetta M, Lalli C, Del Sindaco P, et al. Contribution of postprandial versus interprandial blood glucose to HbA$_{1c}$ in type 1 diabetes on physiologic intensive therapy with lispro insulin at mealtime. Diabetes Care 1999;22:795–800.

14. Colombel A, Murat A, Krempf M, et al. Improvement of blood glucose control in type 1 diabetic patients treated with lispro and multiple NPH injections. Diabet Med 1999;16:319–24.

15. Mohn A, Matyka KA, Harris DA, et al. Lispro or regular insulin for multiple injection therapy in adolescence—differences in free insulin and glucose levels overnight. Diabetes Care 1999;22:27–32.

16. Ebeling P, Jansoon P, Smith U, et al. Strategies toward improved control during insulin lispro therapy in IDDM. Diabetes Care 1997;20:1287–9.

17. Lalli C, Ciofetta M, Del Sindaco P, et al. Long-term intensive treatment of type 1 diabetes with the short-acting insulin analog lispro in variable combination with NPH insulin at mealtime. Diabetes Care 1999;22:468–77.

18. Mudaliar SR, Lindberg FA, Joyce M, et al. Insulin aspart: a fast acting analog of human insulin—absorption kinetics and action profile compared with regular human insulin in healthy non-diabetic subjects [abstract]. Diabetes 1999;48(Suppl 1):A108.

19. Home PD, Lindhom A, Riis AP, et al. Improved long-term blood glucose control with insulin aspart versus human insulin in people with type 1 diabetes [abstract]. Diabetes 1999;48(Suppl 1):A358.

20. Uwe B, Ebrahim S, Hirschberger S, et al. Effect of the rapid acting insulin analogue insulin aspart on quality-of-life and treatment satisfaction in type 1 diabetic patients [abstract]. Diabetes 1999;48(Suppl 1):A112.

21. Raskin P, Jovanovic L, Guthrie RA, et al. Insulin aspart (IAsp) improves glycemic control compared to human insulin (HI) for patients with type 1 diabetes [abstract]. Diabetes 1999;48(Suppl 1):A115.

22. Raskin P, McGill J, Kilo C, et al. Human insulin analog (insulin aspart) is comparable to human insulin in type 2 diabetes [abstract]. Diabetes 1999;48(Suppl 1):A355.

23. Rosskamp RH, Park G. Long-acting insulin analogs. Diabetes Care 1999;22(Suppl 2):B109–13.

24. Luzio SD, Owens D, Evans M, et al. Comparison of the sc absorption of HOE 901 and NPH human insulin in type 2 diabetic subjects [abstract]. Diabetes 1999;48(Suppl 1):A111.

25. Diabetes Control and Complications Trial Research Group. The effect of intensive treatment of diabetes on the development and progression of long-term complications in insulin-dependent diabetes mellitus. N Engl J Med 1993;329:977–86.

26. Reichard P, Britz A, Carlsson P, et al. Metabolic control and complications over 3 years in patients with insulin dependent diabetes (IDDM): the Stockholm Diabetes Intervention Study (SDIS). J Intern Med 1990;228:511–7.

27. The Diabetes Control and Complications Trial Research Group. The effect of intensive diabetes therapy on the development and progression of neuropathy. Ann Intern Med 1995;122:561–8.

28. Diabetes Control and Complications Trial Research Group. Effect of intensive diabetes management on macrovascular events and risk factor in the Diabetes Control and Complications Trial. Am J Cardiol 1995;75:894–903.

29. Lawson ML, Gerstein HC, Tsui E, Zinman B. Effect of intensive therapy on early macrovascular disease in young individuals with type 1 diabetes. Diabetes Care 1999;22(Suppl 2):B35–9.

30. Yki-Jarvinen H, Kauppila M, Kujansuu E, et al. Comparison of insulin regimens in patients with non-insulin-dependent diabetes mellitus. N Engl J Med 1992;327:1426–33.

31. Gaster B, Hirsch IB. The effects of improved glycemic control on complications in type 2 diabetes. Arch Intern Med 1998;158:134–40.

32. UK Prospective Diabetes Study (UKPDS) Group. Intensive blood-glucose control with sulphonylureas of insulin compared with conventional treatment and risk of complications in patients with type 2 diabetes (UKPDS 33). Lancet 1998;352:837–53.

33. Okhubo Y, Kishikawa H, Araki E, et al. Intensive insulin therapy prevents the progression of diabetic microvascular complications in Japanese patients with non-insulin-dependent diabetes mellitus: a randomized prospective 6-year study. Diabetes Res Clin Pract 1995;28:103–17.

34. Abraira C, Colwell JA, Nuttall FQ, et al. Veterans Affairs Cooperative Study on glycemic control and complications in Type 2 diabetes (VACSDM): results of the feasibility trial. Diabetes Care 1995;18:1113–23.

35. Malmberg K, Ryden L, Hamsten A, et al. Effects of insulin treatment on cause-specific one-year mortality and morbidity in diabetic patients with acute myocardial infaction—DIGAMI study group (Diabetes Insulin-Glucose in Acute Myocardial Infarction). Eur Heart J 1996;17:1298–301.

36. Malmberg K. Prospective randomised study of intensive insulin treatment on long term survival after acute myocardial infarction in patients with diabetes mellitus (DIGAMI). BMJ 1997;314:1512–5.

37. McCrimmon RJ, Frier BM. Hypoglycemia, the most feared complication of insulin therapy. Diabetes Metab 1994;20:503–12.

38. Diabetes Control and Complications Research Group. Adverse events and their association with treatment regimens in the Diabetes Control and Complications Trial. Diabetes Care 1995;18:1415–27.

39. Gerstein HC, Capes S. Advantages and perceived disadvantages of insulin therapy for patients with type 2 diabetes. Can J Diabetes Care 1999;23(Suppl 2):91–4.

40. Trischitta V, Italia S, Mazzarino S. Comparison of combined therapies in treatment of secondary failure to glyburide. Diabetes Care 1992;15:539–43.

41. Wolfenbuttel BH, Sels JJ, Rondas-Colbers GJ, et al. Comparison of different insulin regimens in elderly patients with NIDDM. Diabetes Care 1996;19:1326–32.

42. Welborn TA, Wearne K. Coronary heart disease incidence and cardiovascular mortality in Busselton with reference to glucose and insulin concentrations. Diabetes Care 1979;2:154–60.

43. Pyorala K, Savolainen E, Kaukola S, et al. Plasma insulin as a coronary heart disease risk factor: relationship to other risk factors and predictive value over 9.5 year follow-up of the Helsinki Policemen Study population. Acta Med Scand 1985;701:7–14.

44. Fontbonne A, Charles MA, Thibult N, et al. Hyperinsulinaemia as a predictor of coronary heart disease mortality in a healthy population: the Paris Prospective Study, 15-year follow-up. Diabetologia 1991;34:356–61.

45. Fontbonne AM, Eschwege EM. Insulin and cardiovascular disease: Paris prospective study. Diabetes Care 1991;14:431–69.

46. Nishimoto Y, Miyazaki Y, Toki Y, et al. Enhanced secretion of insulin plays a role in the development of atherosclerosis and restenosis of coronary arteries: elective percutaneous transluminal coronary angioplasty in patients with effort angina. J Am Coll Cardiol 1998;32:1642–9.

47. Fujiwara R, Kursumi Y, Hayashi T, et al. Relation of angiographically defined coronary artery disease and plasma concentrations of insulin, lipid, and apolipoprotein in normolipidemic subjects with varying degrees of glucose tolerance. Am J Cardiol 1995;75:122–6.

48. Kuusisto J, Mykkanen L, Pyorala K, et al. Hyperinsulinemic microalbuminuria: a new risk indicator for coronary heart disease. Circulation 1995;91:831–7.

49. Yudkin JS, Denver AE, Mohamed-Ali V, et al. The relationship of concentrations of insulin and proinsulin-like molecules with coronary heart disease prevalence and incidence. Diabetes Care 1997;20:1093–1100.

50. Folsom AR, Szklo M, Stevens J, et al. A prospective study of coronary heart disease in relation to fasting insulin, glucose, and diabetes. Diabetes Care 1997;20:935–42.

51. Mykkanen L, Laakso M, Pyorala K. High plasma insulin level associated with coronary heart disease in the elderly. Am J Epidemiol 1993;137:1190–1202.

52. Katz RJ, Ratner RE, Cohen RM, et al. Are insulin and proinsulin independent risk markers for premature coronary artery disease? Diabetes 1996;45:736–41.

53. Hauhan A, Foote J, Petch MC, et al. Hyperinsulinemia, coronary artery disease and syndrome X. J Am Coll Cardiol 1994;23:364–8.

54. American Diabetes Association. Implications of the United Kingdom Prospective Diabetes Study. Diabetes Care 1999;22(Suppl 1):S27–31.

55. Zinman B, Tildesley H, Chiasson JL, et al. Insulin lispro in CSII: results of a double-blind crossover study. Diabetes 1996;104:25–30.

56. Zinman B, Ross S, Campos RV, et al. Effectiveness of human ultralente versus NPH insulin in providing basal insulin replacement for an insulin lispro multiple daily injection regimen: a double-blind randomized prospective trial. Diabetes Care 1999;22:603–8.

57. Coscelli C, Calabrese G, Fedele D, et al. Use of premixed insulin among the elderly. Diabetes Care 1992;15:1628–30.

58. Saudek CD. Novel forms of insulin delivery. Endocrinol Metab Clin North Am 1997:26:599–610.

59. Yki-Jarvinen H, Ryysy L, Nikkila K, et al. Comparison of bedtime insulin regimens in patients with type 2 diabetes mellitus. Ann Intern Med 1999;130:389–96.

60. Relimpio F, Pumar A, Losada F, et al. Adding metformin versus insulin dose increase in insulin-treated but poorly controlled type 2 diabetes mellitus: an open-label randomized trial. Diabet Med 1998;15:997–1002.

61. Buse JB, Bumbiner B, Mathias NP, et al. Troglitazone use in insulin-treated type 2 diabetic patients. Diabetes Care 1998;21:1455–61.

62. Schwartz S, Raskin P, Fonsec V, et al. Effect of troglitazone in insulin-treated patients with Type 2 diabetes mellitus. N Engl J Med 1998;338:861–6.

63. Hanaire-Broutin H, Guerci B, Broussolle C, et al. The EVADIAC Study Group: feasibility of intraperitoneal insulin therapy with programmable implantable pumps in IDDM: a multicenter study. Diabetes Care 1995;18:388–92.

64. Saudek CD, Duckworth WC, Giobbie-Hurder A, et al, for the Department of Veterans Affairs Implantable Insulin Pump Study Group. Implantable insulin pump vs. multiple-dose insulin for non-insulin-dependent diabetes mellitus: a randomized clinical trial. JAMA 1996;276:1322–7.

65. Salzman R, Manson JE, Griffing GT, et al. Intranasal aerosolized insulin: mixed-meal studies and long-term use in type 1 diabetes. N Engl J Med 1985;312:1078–84.

66. Almer LO, Troedsson A, Arborelius M Jr, et al. Insulin inhalation—at last a breakthrough. Diabetes Res Clin Pract 1988:5(Suppl):S163.

67. Faube BI, Georgopoulos A, Adams GK. Preliminary study of the efficacy of insulin aerosol delivered by oral inhalation in diabetic patients. JAMA 1993;13:230–2.

68. Laube BL, Benedict W, Dobs AS. The lung as an alternative route of delivery for insulin in controlling postprandial glucose levels in patients with diabetes. Chest 1998;114:1735–9.

69. Manske CL. Risks and benefits of kidney and pancreas transplantation for diabetic patients. Diabetes Care 1999;22(Suppl 2):B114–20.

70. Dubernard JM, Tajra LC, Lefrancois N, et al. Pancreas transplantation: results and indications. Diabetes Metab 1998;24:95–9.

71. Fioretto P, Steffes MV, Sutherland DER, et al. Reversal of lesions of diabetic nephropathy after renal transplantation. N Engl J Med 1998;339:69–75.

CHAPTER 18

Diabetes Management During Pregnancy

Edmond A. Ryan, MD, and Laurie Mereu, MD

—————

ABSTRACT

Glycemic control is critical during pregnancy, and the benefits may result in a viable, healthy offspring. Microvascular complications of diabetes tend to progress if present before pregnancy. If no retinopathy is present, there is a 10% chance of eye changes occurring; if moderate retinopathy is present before pregnancy, then there is a 50% chance of progression. If macroproteinuria is present, then two-thirds of subjects develop nephrotic-range proteinuria during pregnancy. Glucose control before pregnancy and in the first trimester obviates the increased risk of congenital malformations for the fetus that occurs if the HbA_{1c} is higher than 6 SD above the mean. Maintenance of good glycemic control during the second and third trimesters reduces the risk of macrosomia and neonatal hypoglycemia. Careful management of diabetes during labor decreases the risk of neonatal hypoglycemia. The good glycemic control that is now attainable means it is possible for most women with Type 1 diabetes to have a good pregnancy outcome and a healthy baby. Management of gestational diabetes reduces the risk of neonatal macrosomia and hypoglycemia. The majority of patients respond to diet alone. Postpartum evaluation of glucose tolerance and appropriate counseling may help decrease the high risk of subsequent Type 2 diabetes in the long term.

—————

INTRODUCTION

Pregnancy and the preconception period are of particular importance to people with diabetes. Not only does the pregnancy itself pose challenges to the metabolic management of diabetes in the mother, it also increases the risk of other diabetes-related complications for the mother and the risk to the fetus of congenital anomalies and other neonatal problems. Whereas the former issue mainly concerns women with preconception diabetes, the latter affects the offspring of women with both preconception and gestational diabetes. The evidence that addresses these issues and some examples of a clinical approach to these issues are discussed as answers to the following questions:

1. What are the risks to the fetus and newborn?
2. What are the risks to the mother?
3. What degree of glucose control is required to optimize neonatal outcome?
4. How is preconception diabetes managed during pregnancy?
5. How is gestational diabetes managed during pregnancy?

WHAT ARE THE RISKS TO THE FETUS AND NEWBORN?

Maternal diabetes constitutes a risk factor for medical problems that can affect the fetus before birth and that can affect the newborn at the time of birth. Table 18–1 lists the risks faced by the infant of a woman whose diabetes was present before conception.

Congenital Malformations

Congenital malformations constitute a major cause of perinatal mortality in the offspring of diabetic subjects.[1–4] During embryogenesis, uncontrolled diabetes leads to abnormal fetal development. Although the mechanism for this is not fully understood, research from ani-

Table 18–1 Short-Term Risks for the Offspring of Women with Prepregnancy Diabetes

Congenital malformations

Macrosomia

Neonatal hyperglycemia

Jaundice

mal models suggests that gene dysregulation and oxygen free radicals may be involved.[5–9] The increased risk of congenital malformation can be completely abrogated by good glycemic control preconception,[10–17] and that preconception care is worthwhile.[18] Despite this, attendance at diabetes preconception clinics remains disappointingly low.[19,20] The major congenital malformations that occur are cardiac, renal, and neurologic.[1,21–23] For example, maternal preconception diabetes increases the risk of caudal regression more than 250 times compared to pregnancies in women with no diabetes. Despite this high relative risk, the fact that it occurs rarely (ie, has a low absolute risk in people both with and with no diabetes) means that defects in other major organ systems are more commonly seen.[1,24] These defects arise by the eighth week of pregnancy, 6 weeks from conception.[25]

Higher degrees of hyperglycemia are associated with a higher risk of congenital malformation. Moreover, this increased risk of congenital malformation can be eliminated by good glycemic control during organogenesis,[10–17] and good preconception care has been shown to be cost effective.[26,27] Several studies of the relationship between glycemic control as measured by the HbA_{1c} and the risk of congenital malformations[11,14,28–34] indicate that the increased risk is most apparent when the HbA_{1c} is several standard deviations above the mean (Table 18–2). Although most studies have suggested that a $HbA_{1c} < 6$ SD above the mean poses no significant risk, one recent prospective study of 488 women with 691 pregnancies raises the possibility that this interpretation may be too liberal and that a HbA_{1c} greater than 2 SD above the normal mean is associated with a threefold increased risk of congenital malformations.[20]

In contrast to the relationship between hyperglycemia and malformations, intermittent episodes of maternal hypoglycemia (a consequence of any intervention to tighten glycemic control) do not appear to be detrimental to the fetus.[35] These data have led to recommendations to target very tight glucose levels preconception as shown in Table 18–3.

Folic acid has been confirmed as helping to prevent neural tube defects in the general population,[36] but it is unknown if it has the same specific advantage for subjects with diabetes. Although pregnant women with diabetes also do not have any alterations of folic levels,[37] there is no reason to believe that they will not derive the same benefits from preconception folic acid supplements of 0.4 mg/d as their nondiabetic counterparts.[38]

Table 18–2 Risk of Congenital Abnormality Relative to the HbA_{1c}

	HbA_{1c}	Risk, %
Control population	Normal	< 2
Subjects with diabetes	< 3.5 SD above normal mean	< 2
	< 6 SD above normal mean	2
	10 SD above normal mean	4
	15 SD above normal mean	6

Table 18–3 Recommended Target Preconception Glucose Levels for Women with Diabetes

Fasting < 5.0 mM
Pre-meal < 6.0 mM
2 Hours postprandial < 7.0 mM

The foregoing is relevant to women with both Type 1 and Type 2 diabetes. The high frequency of Type 2 diabetes in women of child-bearing age from aboriginal and minority populations[39] raises the issue of whether using oral agents preconception has any negative consequences for the fetus.[40,41] Indeed, one study and several case reports[42,43] have suggested that oral hypoglycemic agents may be associated with congenital malformations, but in these reports, the HbA$_{1c}$ was raised; thus, it is unclear whether or not there is any teratogenicity from oral hypoglycemic agents. Of concern, however, is the fact that first-generation oral hypoglycemic agents cross the placenta[44]; insulin does not share this feature unless bound to antibodies.[45–48] On this basis alone, insulin appears to be a safer choice. Thus, anyone with Type 2 diabetes who is contemplating a pregnancy while on oral hypoglycemic agents should switch to insulin; if someone becomes pregnant on oral hypoglycemic agents, she should also be changed to insulin. If the HbA$_{1c}$ is acceptable, the patient can be reassured that the risk of congenital malformations is not increased.[21,43] Once pregnant, cessation of oral agents is also applicable to nondiabetic women with polycystic ovary syndrome who may be on metformin preconception.

EVIDENCE-BASED MESSAGES

1. Maternal Type 1 diabetes that is present preconception increases the risk of congenital malformations 10-fold (Level 1).[49]
2. The risk for congenital malformations is related to the degree of preconception glycemic control; good glycemic control preconception is associated with rates similar to those of nondiabetic women (Level 1).[10,14–16,20]

Macrosomia and Other Neonatal Problems

In the second and third trimesters, the risks to the baby are primarily macrosomia, neonatal hypoglycemia, and jaundice. The mechanisms for these abnormalities are believed to be similar to those for gestational diabetes (see Chapter 11). Macrosomia occurs in the offspring of approximately 30% of Type 1 diabetic subjects,[19,50–54] and neonatal hypoglycemia occurs in approximately 24%.[51,55–61] Jaundice also occurs more frequently in these neonates and likely reflects an immature liver in the face of diabetes.[51,62] Other complications, such as respiratory distress syndrome, hypocalcemia, and polycythemia, are now rare.[51,62–66] Just as in gestational diabetes, the occurrence of macrosomia is associated with increased risk for fetal trauma and injury to the birth canal.[67]

These problems and the issue of congenital abnormalities are together responsible for a high perinatal mortality rate in the offspring of women with Type 1 diabetes.[49,62,68,69]

EVIDENCE-BASED MESSAGES

1. Maternal Type 1 diabetes is a risk factor for neonatal macrosomia; this risk rises with the third-trimester nonfasting glucose levels (Level 1).[52]
2. Maternal Type 1 diabetes is a risk factor for neonatal hypoglycemia, hyperbilirubinemia, polycythemia, and respiratory distress (Level 1).[62]

WHAT ARE THE RISKS TO THE MOTHER?

Pregnancy has a profound impact on carbohydrate physiology, and unless the increasing insulin resistance is matched with more insulin, hyperglycemia ensues. Similarly, interventions to intensify glycemic control may increase the risk of hypoglycemia. Moreover, the physiologic changes associated with pregnancy may lead to a deterioration in some of the chronic complications of diabetes.

Retinopathy

Several studies have followed eye disease closely in pregnancy and report a worsening related to the pregnancy.[63,70–78] This deterioration is proportional to the initial status of the retinopathy and the glucose level. If virtually no eye disease is present, then there is about a 10% chance of some progression of the eye disease.[75] This very rarely gets to the stage of requiring photocoagulation. If more severe eye disease is present prepregnancy, then there is up to a 50% chance of progression,[74,75] and this deterioration is related to the occurrence of preeclampsia.[72] Clearly, with this risk, and given a starting point of moderate retinopathy, such a pregnancy may lead to the need for laser therapy. Why such deterioration occurs is unclear, but it could be related to either circulating growth factors or pressure change in the retinal circulation.[79,80] A further possibility is the sudden improved glucose control that is characteristic of pregnancy-related diabetes care,[76–78] but the changes appear to be independent of any changes in glycemic control.

EVIDENCE-BASED MESSAGE

1. Pregnancy increases the progression of diabetic retinopathy in women with Type 1 diabetes; the degree of progression is proportional to the prepregnancy ophthalmologic findings (no retinopathy to moderate-severe nonproliferative retinopathy) and the degree of glycemic control during pregnancy (Level 2).[75]

Nephropathy

The increased blood volume due to pregnancy puts tremendous pressure on the renal apparatus; how well the kidneys cope is related to the degree of diabetic injury prepregnancy.

Normal Prepregnancy Renal Function

If renal function is normal prepregnancy, then there is no significant deterioration of glomerular function, although microalbumin excretion increases fourfold and protein is found in 6% of cases.[81,82] The proteinuria rarely gets to the nephrotic range unless preeclamptic toxemia supervenes. Preeclamptic toxemia may occur,[81] but this is rare. Postpartum, the renal function returns to normal.

Prepregnancy Microalbuminuria

Microalbuminuria reflects underlying renal damage; it is also likely to reflect diffuse endothelial alterations. One-third of women with preconception microalbuminuria will develop nephrotic-range proteinuria during the course of the pregnancy.[81,82] Moreover, up to 60% of microalbuminuric women will develop preeclamptic toxemia.[83] These abnormalities usually resolve postpartum. Because it has not been shown to be safe during pregnancy, treatment with an angiotensin converting enzyme inhibitor for microalbuminuria should be stopped preconception.

Prepregnancy Macroproteinuria

Macroproteinuria reflects advanced renal disease and, as expected, is associated with a worse outcome. Two-thirds of women with a preconception urine protein excretion that exceeds 300 mg/d will develop nephrotic-range proteinuria during pregnancy,[84,85] up to three-quarters will develop preeclampsia,[86,87] and at least one-third will have significant changes in retinopathy.[85,88] These patients tend to have a difficult course and frequently require antihypertensive therapy during pregnancy.[84,85,87–89] Postpartum, the renal function returns to prepregnancy levels.

Creatinine Elevation

Once the serum creatinine is elevated, the pregnancy becomes more difficult. At this stage, there is usually significant macroproteinuria and often some vascular compromise. The latter factor accounts for the finding of small-for-gestational-age infants in these pregnancies. The birth weight is inversely proportional to the serum creatinine and renal dysfunction.[84–87,90] As expected, hypertension and edema are typically a problem in later pregnancy. There are conflicting reports as to whether pregnancy in this setting actually hastens the decline of renal function so that it is worse postpartum than prepregnancy. Some reports suggest that when prior renal function is significantly compromised, there is a worsening of renal function related to the pregnancy,[84,88] but others are less pessimistic.[90,91] Women contemplating pregnancy need to be fully cognizant of these risks before conception. If severe renal disease is present, consideration has to be given to the known risk of such a pregnancy versus deferring it until after kidney transplantation. Successful pregnancies have occurred post-renal transplantation, including diabetic subjects who also had a pancreas transplant.[92]

EVIDENCE-BASED MESSAGES

1. Preconception microalbuminuria increases the risk of preeclampsia in women with Type 1 diabetes during pregnancy (Level 1).[83]
2. Preconception proteinuria increases the risk of nephrotic-range proteinuria during pregnancy (Level 3).[84]

Vascular Disease

Fortunately, significant cardiovascular disease is rare in this population,[93] and if no vascular disease is present prepregnancy, then usually no problems are encountered. It must be recalled that in the presence of autonomic neuropathy, typical angina may not be present, and such patients should be evaluated more carefully. In the presence of preconception autonomic neuropathy or hyperlipidemia, exercise stress testing is worthwhile to ensure that the pregnancy can be embarked on safely. If vascular disease is present, caution for the pregnancy is required. A myocardial infarction during pregnancy—always ominous with a maternal mortality of 30%[94]—is even worse in the presence of diabetes with a maternal mortality of 60%.[95,96] If the subject has had a previous myocardial infarction, then the risk is dependent on the residual cardiac function, and successful pregnancy is possible.[97]

Neuropathy

Peripheral neuropathy tends not to change during pregnancy. Entrapment neuropathy such as carpal tunnel syndrome is more common, but, although troublesome, it usually resolves promptly postpartum. Autonomic neuropathy does not appear to deteriorate over the course of the pregnancy.[98] Gastroparesis diabeticorum makes good glucose control very difficult, particularly if morning sickness supervenes. Autonomic neuropathy may mask cardiovascular disease. Finally, genitourinary involvement increases the risk of pyelonephritis.

Hypoglycemia Unawareness

In patients with no problems with counter-regulation, hormonal responses appear to be normal, with the exception of the suppression of basal pituitary growth hormone levels.[99] If hypoglycemia unawareness is present, then nearly half of the subjects have a deficient epinephrine response to hypoglycemia, and there is an associated increased risk of macrosomia, likely related to the erratic glycemic control.[100] As the targets for glycemic control and pregnancy are very strict, the risk of severe hypoglycemia is substantially increased. Thus, targets for glycemic control during pregnancy clearly need to take each individual's risk for hypoglycemia unawareness into consideration.

Thyroid Disease

Women with Type 1 diabetes are at increased risk for autoimmune thyroid disease, and a thyroid-stimulating hormone (TSH) should be checked in anticipation of the pregnancy. Measuring thyroid antibodies will predict those who may encounter problems during the pregnancy.[101] Therapy of the hypothyroidism is essential, and it may be expected that the dose of L-thyroxine will increase during the pregnancy.

WHAT DEGREE OF GLUCOSE CONTROL IS REQUIRED TO OPTIMIZE NEONATAL OUTCOME?

As described above, preconception and pregnancy hyperglycemia is a continuous risk factor for neonatal morbidity; higher levels are related to higher risk, and a HbA_{1c} that is less than 6 SD above the normal mean (and ideally less than 3 SD[20]) is associated with the lowest risk of congenital anomalies (see Table 18–2). This strong epidemiologic relationship is supported by evidence that women in the Diabetes Control and Complications Trial who were randomized to intensive glycemic control had a much lower rate of neonatal congenital anomalies than those randomized to conventional control,[10] despite comparable levels during pregnancy. These data account for the lack of a definitive prospective, randomized study of two different levels of glycemic control during pregnancy; such a study would be deemed unethical. Whether the benefits of good diabetes control are due to the effects of glucose lowering alone or a change in some other related metabolite such as free fatty acids remains unclear.

Achieving Glycemic Control During Pregnancy

The degree of attainable glycemic control is only limited by the risk of hypoglycemia. With any tightening of glycemic control, the risk of severe hypoglycemia increases,[102] and this is also true in pregnancy.[103,104] The target glucose levels used in the author's clinic are 5 mM before breakfast, 6 mM before meals, and 7 mM 2 hours after meals and bedtime. If these can be obtained, the HbA_{1c} is usually acceptable. Occasionally, the HbA_{1c} stays elevated despite these levels; this may be due to hidden periods of hyperglycemia such as 1 hour postprandially and overnight or to patient misrepresentation of the true capillary values, which can be detected using a memory meter.[105]

Glucose monitoring a minimum of four times daily (pre-meals and bedtime) is required to attain this degree of glucose control. Nevertheless, there are many studies showing that a decrease in glucose is associated with less neonatal morbidity.[34,66,106–111] The intensive use of insulin has demonstrated benefit in pregnancy, and nearly all patients can achieve good glycemic control with such a regimen.[112,113] Continuous subcutaneous insulin infusions have the same advantages and disadvantages as in the nonpregnant states and facilitate attaining good glycemic control in some subjects.

Lispro insulin has a much shorter duration of action and is increasingly being used in general diabetes care. Although better glycemic control as evidenced by the HbA_{1c} is elusive, most patients find the same HbA_{1c} with less concerns about hypoglycemia. Lispro insulin has not been formally approved for use in pregnancy, but then neither has regular insulin. It does not appear to cross the placenta and thus is likely safe for pregnancy,[114] although one report of progression of retinopathy in three subjects with lispro insulin use indicates the need for continued caution.[115] The patient who has improved glycemic control on lispro insulin should continue this therapy with careful monitoring of retinopathy as it seems to be folly to transfer such a patient back to regular insulin and risk poorer glycemic control with its known adverse consequences compared with some theoretical risk that is low.

Subjects with Type 2 diabetes have the same need for glucose control and, as detailed above, should not be treated with oral hypoglycemic agents if diet alone is inadequate to achieve optimal glucose levels. Insulin is used as in Type 1 diabetes; because of a sustained endogenous insulin reserve, good glycemic control can easily be attained, and hypoglycemia is less of a problem for most patients. Because obesity is usually common in these patients, large doses of insulin are sometimes required.

EVIDENCE-BASED MESSAGES

1. Women with Type 1 diabetes who are receiving intensive glycemic therapy using three or more insulin injections or a pump and who conceive have a much lower incidence of neonatal congenital malformations than women receiving conventional glycemic therapy (Level 2).[10]

2. Many epidemiologic studies show that intensive glycemic control during pregnancy reduces the risk of neonatal morbidity (Level 3).[34,66,106–111]

3. In women with pregestational diabetes, an intensive glycemic therapy approach using four insulin injections daily leads to better glycemic control and a better neonatal outcome than a twice-daily regimen (Level 1).[113]

HOW IS PRECONCEPTION DIABETES MANAGED DURING PREGNANCY?

First Trimester

Monitoring the Mother

In the first 6 weeks during the period of organogenesis, weekly visits with the health care team of physician, nurse, and dietitian are warranted to review glucose records and insulin doses, reinforce dietary advice and recommendations for folic acid use, and deal with issues that can affect glycemic control such as morning sickness (for which doxylamine succinate [Diclectin®, Duchesnay Inc., Laval, QC, Canada] is safe to use). Some subjects have a decrement in insulin needs in the first trimester; in the second and third trimesters, insulin requirements rise about twofold from 0.83 ± 0.39 U/kg prepregnancy to 1.63 ± 0.65 U/kg.[116] In our practice, HbA_{1c} is measured monthly until normal and then every 2 months; 24-hour urine protein excretion is assessed with the same frequency. Ophthalmologic review is also arranged. The expected weight gain is 1 kg in the first trimester and then 1 kg every 2 weeks for the remainder of the pregnancy.

Monitoring the Fetus

The major concern at this time is to derive an accurate assessment of dates such that there will be no confusion at term. A detailed ultrasound is required at the end of the first trimester and early second trimester to assess any fetal damage.[117,118]

Second and Third Trimesters of Pregnancy

Monitoring the Mother

In our practice, the use of a flow sheet for each visit facilitates monitoring of the patient's weight, presence of edema, fundal height, blood pressure, fetal movements, total daily insulin dose, and results of dipstick urinalysis. Toward term, the increasing insulin requirements plateau and in one-third of subjects with Type 1 diabetes may actually decline.[119] Large decrements may not necessarily auger misfortune, but any decrease of 20% or more merits close observation of the baby. It is very rare that a decrease in insulin requirements of itself is an indication for induction, but it is an indication for increased fetal surveillance. If any other indicator suggests problems, then induction after confirmation of fetal lung maturity is advisable. If dexamethasone is used to advance fetal lung maturity, there is a marked increase in insulin requirements of about 20% that should be anticipated for 48 hours after the last dexamethasone dose.

Type 1 pregnant diabetic patients have a fourfold higher risk of pregnancy-induced hypertension (PIH).[120] Even in the second trimester, those destined to develop PIH appear to have higher night-time systolic values when assessed with ambulatory blood pressure monitoring.[120] If hypertension supervenes, methyldopa is the first-line drug with labetalol, pindolol, oxprenolol, and nifedipine as the second-line agents.[121–123]

Finally, women with Type 1 diabetes may develop diabetic ketoacidosis as a result of insulin omission or intercurrent illness. This may clearly jeopardize fetal viability but with intensive therapy need not be fatal for the fetus.[124]

Monitoring the Fetus

Fetal surveillance is recommended after 30 weeks of gestation[125] to detect fetal distress requiring intervention and to prevent premature delivery; unfortunately, no large randomized trial has assessed the benefit of fetal monitoring in diabetic pregnancies.

By the third trimester, the ultrasound is used to assess growth and risk of macrosomia.[126] Use of ultrasound monitoring and elective delivery of those infants over 4,250 g is associated with less shoulder dystocia and no significant increased use of operative delivery route.[127] In a large, prospective case series, 2,604 diabetic women with ultrasonographic estimated fetal weight ≥ 4,250 g underwent elective cesarean section. The rate of shoulder dystocia decreased from 2.4% to 1.1% (odds ratio 2.2). The cesarean section rate increased only slightly from 21.7 to 25.1% ($p < .04$). Ultrasound accurately determined the presence or absence of macrosomia in 87% of subjects.[127]

Maternal assessment of fetal movement is a simple indicator of fetal well-being. Perception of 10 distinctive movements within at least a 2-hour period is reassuring. In a prospective case series, 306 clinic patients started counting for 2 hours/d at 34 weeks gestation. Reassuring fetal movements were always followed by reactive nonstress tests (NSTs). The false-negative rate was < 1%. Alarming fetal activity was followed by a nonreactive NST 20% of the time.[128]

The NST has become one of the most popular tests to assess fetal viability. A reactive test is defined as a rise in fetal heart rate by 15 beats/min for 15 seconds, twice in a 20-minute period. A nonreactive test must be followed up with another NST or back-up test: the contraction stress test (CST) or Biophysical Profile (BPP). If the test remains abnormal, then early fetal intervention is warranted.

Monitoring with the NST may begin at 32 weeks and is done weekly or twice weekly until term, depending on glucose control and other clinical considerations. The test is imperfect as there have been published studies showing stillbirths within 1 week of a reactive NST.[129] Kjos et al studied prospectively 2,134 diabetic pregnant women. Antepartum monitoring with NST was performed twice per week, as well as an assessment of amniotic fluid. There were no stillbirths in the 1,501 deliveries that occurred within 4 days of a normal test.[130] If there is evidence of maternal vascular disease, intrauterine growth retardation, or uteroplacental insufficiency, then monitoring should start at 28 weeks and occur twice per week thereafter.[131] Both the American and Canadian professional obstetrics groups recommend routine surveillance.[132,133]

The CST was one of the first dynamic tests of fetal monitoring and measures fetal heart rate in response to uterine contractions. Approximately 1 to 11% of positive CST testing results in early delivery in the diabetic pregnancy. The incidence of false-positives is high at 40 to 60%.[134] In patients with good glycemic control, however, a negative CST predicts fetal well-being for the next week.[135] However, fetal heart rate pattern may not be as accurate in the presence of diabetes.[136]

The BPP is also used widely in antepartum fetal monitoring. First described by Manning et al in 1981, this test assesses four aspects of fetal well-being: fetal breathing movements, gross body movements, fetal tone, and amniotic fluid volume.[137] A score of 8/8 is normal. A score of < 6/8 is an indicator for early fetal intervention.[137] The BPP would appear to be a comparable test to the NST.[138] A modified BPP combines the NST with an assessment of amniotic fluid volume. A normal test has a reactive NST plus an amniotic fluid index of more than 5 cm.[139] Miller et al studied 3,364 diabetic women prospectively with the modified BPP. There were three stillbirths within 1 week of a normal test. The false-negative rate was 0.9 in 1,000 for diabetic pregnancies.[139] Doppler velocimetry has been shown to predict pregnancies at risk for placental vascular disease, which, in diabetes, would mainly be those with preexisting renal or vascular disease.[140]

If a question of delivery before 38 weeks gestation arises, then amniocentesis for fetal lung maturity should be considered. The lecithin-sphingomyelin ratio is measured. A value greater than 2.0 predicts normal lung function and no respiratory distress syndrome in the neonate. Acidic phospholipid phosphatidylglycerol is more accurate in the presence of diabetes and is the final marker of lung maturation.[134] Some have suggested that cord blood insulin levels may be the best predictor of diabetogenic fetopathy.[141] Weiss et al studied 213 neonates of insulin-dependent diabetic mothers and found an association between the degree of elevation of insulin levels in the cord blood and perinatal outcome.[141]

EVIDENCE-BASED MESSAGE

Epidemiologic studies suggest that fetal monitoring tests done weekly starting at 32 weeks and increased to twice weekly from 34 to 36 weeks, which include NSTs, BPPs, and other tests as needed, reduce the risk of neonatal mortality (Level 4).[130,132,133]

Labor

Maternal hyperglycemia during labor predicts neonatal hypoglycemia.[19,56–58,142] Indeed, if the maternal glucose exceeds 10 mM or the cord blood glucose is more than 7.8 mM, the infant's glucose is always low.[19,58] This and other observations have led to recommendations that glucose levels be kept below 6.5 mM during labor. This may be accomplished using several approaches, including subcutaneous insulin at a reduced dose,[56,60,143,144] combined insulin/glucose intravenous infusions,[55,145–147] or, most commonly, separate insulin and glucose infusions piggybacked into one IV.[57,59,61,148–151] There are no good prospective studies indicating which protocol is best, and so in our practice, subcutaneous insulin is used as long as the patient is eating and active labor has not commenced. Once dilation greater than 3 cm of the cervix and regular contractions are occurring, separate infusions of IV insulin and glucose are used. Hourly monitoring of glucose is maintained, and adjustments are made to the insulin according to a protocol developed by the authors and outlined in Table 18–4.

After delivery of the placenta, insulin needs drop dramatically, and the insulin infusion should be stopped. In our practice, the glucose is checked every 2 to 4 hours, and subcutaneous insulin is restarted when the glucose exceeds 10 mM at 80% of the prepregnancy requirements. Breastfeeding is clearly encouraged.[152,153]

EVIDENCE-BASED MESSAGES

1. Tight glucose control during labor reduces the risk of neonatal hypoglycemia (Level 3).[19,57]
2. Targeting maternal glucose levels of 4 to 7 mmol/L during labor leads to a lower risk of maternal hypoglycemia than targeting lower levels (Level 3).[19]

Postpartum

At the postpartum follow-up visit, an assessment of general diabetes complications—neuropathy, vascular disease, and retinopathy—is made together with laboratory determinations of lipids, HbA$_{1c}$, TSH, and microalbuminuria. A TSH is measured because of the increased

Table 18–4 Example of an Insulin Regimen During Labor for Patients with Type 1 Diabetes

Glucose infusion	IV dextrose	10% at 50 mL/hr with 10 mEq KCl/500 mL $D_{10}W$
Insulin infusion	IV insulin	50 U regular insulin in 500 mL NaCl (N), ie, 1 U = 10 mL
		Flush tubing and start at 10 mL/hr unless glucose < 4 mM
		If glucose < 4 mM, then just start with glucose infusion

Adjustments   Capillary glucose values are determined hourly
               At each hourly determination, the following scale is followed:

If glucose is   3.0 mM, stop the IV insulin for 1 hour and increase $D_{10}W$ to 100 mL/hr
             3.1–3.5 mM, decrease IV insulin by 10 mL/hr and increase $D_{10}W$ to 75 mL/hr
             3.6–4.0 mM, decrease IV insulin infusion by 5 mL/hr
             4.1–6.0 mM, leave at the same insulin infusion rate
             6.1–7.0 mM, increase IV insulin infusion by 5 mL/hr
             7.1–8.5 mM, increase IV insulin infusion by 10 mL/hr
             8.6–10.0 mM, increase IV insulin infusion by 15 mL/hr
             > 10 mM, increase IV insulin infusion by 20 mL/hr

If glucose falls > 2 mM in 1 hour and is > 5.1 mM, decrease IV insulin infusion rate to 10 mL/hr
                           ≤ 5.0 mM, stop insulin for an hour

If insulin is stopped and glucose rises above 4.5 mM, restart insulin at 5 mL/hr

Stop insulin after delivery of the placenta

risk of postpartum thyroiditis.[154] Finally, advice about any future pregnancy and, particularly, the need for good glycemic control preconception is reiterated.

HOW IS GESTATIONAL DIABETES MANAGED DURING PREGNANCY?

The first line of therapy for gestational diabetes is diet modification.[155] The current requirement of pregnancy is approximately 170 calories per day over and above the nonpregnant state from the twelfth week on.[156] If a person is obese, then some reduction can be used. The recommended weight gain for those of normal prepregnancy body mass index is 11.4 to 15.9 kg,[157] but this has been questioned.[158] Diet should also be modified in terms of the number of feedings and is best spread over three meals and three snacks. Diet alone is successful in attaining adequate glycemic control in two-thirds of patients. One review of the literature indicated that diet was useful at reducing the risk of large for gestational age infants but no benefit in terms of birth trauma.[159] Some have suggested more severe caloric restrictions, but these are typically associated with ketonuria.[160,161] Early reports raise the possibility that acetonuria was associated with some diminishment of IQ level attained in the offspring.[162,163] This has not been confirmed,[164] but elevated β-hydroxybutyrate levels in pregnancy are associated with subtle but statistically significant changes in sensitive psychological testing.[165–167] Monitoring urine ketones is simple and inexpensive and appears to be worth doing to detect the most blatant examples of starvation ketosis.

Glucose Monitoring Times

With the introduction of diet, the subject also needs some measure of glucose control. Self-monitoring of blood glucose is taught on the first visit, and the patient is instructed to monitor four times a day. Routine pre-meal glucose testing such as is used for Type 1 diabetic subjects is not suitable for those with mild gestational diabetes.[168] The timing should be pre-breakfast and then either 1 or 2 hours after meals. Both timings have proponents and have not been compared directly against each other. In our practice, typically 2-hour testing is performed unless the primary abnormality on the oral glucose tolerance test (OGTT) is an elevated glucose value at 1 hour, in which case, the subject is asked to monitor the glucose 1 hour after eating. The 2-hour target glucose value is less than 6.7 mM, and the determinations are typically checked just before the next snack.[169–174] The 1-hour testing target is less than 7.8 mM.[168,175,176] There is agreement that the fasting level should be less than 5.3 mM,[174] but some set the level lower or use a mean value to guide them.[173,177]

EVIDENCE-BASED MESSAGES

1. In women with gestational diabetes mellitus (GDM), adjusting insulin doses on the basis of postprandial versus preprandial capillary glucose values reduces the risk of large-for-gestational-age infants, cesarean sections, and neonatal hypoglycemia (Level 1).[168]
2. One-hour postprandial capillary glucose targets of < 7.8 mmol/L reduce neonatal morbidity associated with gestational diabetes (Level 1A).[168,178–180]
3. Two-hour postprandial capillary glucose values < 6.7 mmol/L eliminate the excess neonatal morbidity associated with gestational diabetes (Level 3).[181,182]
4. Intensive treatment of GDM targeting good glycemic control reduces the risk of macrosomia and neonatal hypoglycemia (Level 3).[181]

Use of Insulin in Gestational Diabetes Mellitus

Nearly one-third of patients require insulin for glucose control,[183] and if insulin is required, the simplest approach is to use multiple daily insulin injections targeting the insulin to the hyperglycemia[113]; the use of insulin pens facilitates the teaching and use of insulin therapy tremendously. The patient can be reassured that insulin does not cross the placenta.[47] If just after one meal the glucose is elevated, then short-acting insulin may be used prior to this meal. If the fasting glucose is elevated, then intermediate-acting insulin at bedtime may be used. We typically start with four units of each insulin component and instruct the subject on self-adjustment by two-unit increments for continued hyperglycemia. In this way, the insulin can be increased by up to eight units a day every 2 days, and high levels of insulin can be attained rapidly if necessary. Lispro insulin may have an advantage with its quicker onset of action, and early studies show that it does not cross the placenta.[114] At present, we reserve its use for those patients who have marked elevation of plasma glucose at 1 hour on the OGTT or evidence of delayed hypoglycemia on regular insulin.

EVIDENCE-BASED MESSAGE

In women with gestational diabetes, an intensive glycemic therapy approach using four insulin injections daily leads to better glycemic control and a better neonatal outcome than a twice-daily regimen (Level 1).[113]

Fetal Monitoring with Gestational Diabetes Mellitus

As the primary risks of GDM are macrosomia and neonatal hypoglycemia, and as physiologic glycemic control does not completely mitigate these risks, other markers for these outcomes, including macrosomia detected on ultrasound[184–186] and amniotic fluid insulin (AFI), have been proposed. Indeed, use of insulin therapy only in patients with elevated AFI has been proposed.[141,187,188] Further study of these options is required before they can be routinely recommended.

Given the high risk for these infants, systemic monitoring is presumably important[125]; however, there is little formal evidence to support such a position. Women with gestational

Table 18–5 Example of a Protocol for Glycemic Management During Labor for People with Gestational Diabetes Mellitus on Diet Alone or < 0.5 U/kg of Insulin

1.	Monitor the glucose every 1 to 2 hours
	If glucose < 5.5 mM, every 2 hours
	If glucose > 5.6 mM, every 1 hour
2.	If glucose > 6.5 mM, then use IV insulin as for a Type 1 diabetic subject

diabetes need monitoring proportional to the degree of metabolic abnormality. If they are diet controlled and stable, then no specific fetal monitoring is likely to be required. If they are on insulin, then more fetal surveillance is desirable. Maternal kick counts should start at 32 weeks gestation or earlier if the clinical situation dictates.[128] Nonstress test monitoring or modified BPP should start weekly at 32 weeks gestation for insulin-requiring gestational diabetic patients.[134]

EVIDENCE-BASED MESSAGE

Antepartum fetal monitoring with NSTs may not eliminate the neonatal risk in GDM (Level 4).[189]

Management of Labor

As in Type 1 diabetes, good glycemic control is required to prevent neonatal hypoglycemia. If the patient has been diet controlled or just requires a small amount of insulin (less than 0.5 U/kg), the work of labor, coupled with the minimal oral intake during labor, invariably results in normoglycemia, and all that is required is to monitor the glucose every 1 to 2 hours once active labor starts. If the glucose values rise above 6.5 mM, then some intervention is required (Table 18–5). Values above this level are usually due to either IV or oral glucose and are readily correctable. Persistent high values need IV insulin, and a protocol similar to that used for Type 1 diabetes is appropriate.

Postpartum Management

Postpartum, the insulin resistance abates within days if not hours,[190] glucose is usually normal, glucose monitoring can be discontinued, and a normal diet may be consumed; an OGTT should be booked for 6 weeks later. The largest prospective study of glucose tolerance in the early (3- to 6-month) postpartum stage reveals that 75% of subjects have normal glucose tolerance and 5% had diabetes.[191] Other studies showed similar results, with a risk of developing diabetes being 3 to 10%.[192–194]

As discussed in Chapter 3, the risk of long-term glucose intolerance in the mother is 60 to 70% at 15 years after the index pregnancy. A significant percentage of subjects have dia-

Table 18–6 Risk Factors for Progression to Diabetes in Women with a History of Gestational Diabetes Mellitus

Increased prepregnancy body mass index[192,196–200]

Severity of glucose intolerance during pregnancy

Earlier gestational age of onset[192–194,201]

Elevated fasting plasma glucose[192,194,196,197,199,201,202]

Need for insulin[193,202,203]

Presence of higher glucose values on postpartum OGTT[201,202]

Table 18–7 Issues for Review at the Postpartum Visit for Subjects Who Had Gestational Diabetes Mellitus

Increased risk of diabetes and its possible prevention by diet and exercise

Symptoms of diabetes, and, if they arise, a glucose level should be checked

Value of annual determination of fasting glucose level

For any future pregnancy, need to screen for diabetes preconception and for GDM during the pregnancy

betes within 5 years of the pregnancy.[191,195] The risk factors as determined by studies using logistic regression analysis are discussed in Chapter 3 (Table 18–6).

Islet cell antibodies are not common in GDM,[204] but the subgroup that is positive is likely to develop Type 1 diabetes.[205–209] These subjects have more insulinopenia.[210] Many of these subjects are thin, have more severe GDM, and typically require insulin for glucose control during pregnancy.

The postpartum OGTT can help clarify the short-term risks for diabetes. Because the history of GDM is such a strong risk factor, an annual fasting plasma glucose is a useful test to screen for diabetes in this group. Counseling regarding contraception should also take into account the possibility that some oral contraceptive agents increase insulin resistance,[211,212] possibly due to the progesterone content of the preparation[213,214]; avoidance of these preparations allows safer use of the contraceptive pill.[215] Finally, the risk of recurrent GDM with a future pregnancy is 30 to 70%.[216–220] It is likely related to the severity of the gestational diabetes in the index pregnancy, dietary practices, lack of weight loss between pregnancies, and changes in exercise patterns.[216,218,221] Thus, a preconception check of the glucose level and a careful check during a pregnancy are appropriate. Moreover, a 50-g screening test at the first visit that is repeated at 26 ± 2 weeks and again at 32 weeks is indicated, and if the index of suspicion is quite high (eg, if there were large insulin requirements in the last pregnancy), the fasting and 2-hour postprandial glucose levels can be checked on a monthly basis. Whether repeated episodes of gestational diabetes hasten the onset of Type 2 diabetes remains unclear; although one study suggested this possibility,[222] others showed that increasing parity up to four pregnancies contributes no increased risk of diabetes.[223–225]

CONCLUSION

Pregnancy combined with diabetes is one time when a patient can readily see the results of benefits as a consequence of glycemic control and attention to diabetes care. Although it requires a tremendous amount of work, the patient can be assured that, given no major complications to start with, the outcome in the pregnant diabetic subject who attains good glycemic control is equivalent to her nondiabetic counterpart. Although there can never be a guarantee of a healthy baby, this encouraging prognosis reflects a dramatic change over the last 20 years. For subjects with gestational diabetes, attaining good glycemic control lessens perinatal morbidity, and, hopefully, the interventions associated with diabetes in pregnancy will lead to dietary and exercise changes that may retard the development of Type 2 diabetes in later life (Table 18–7).

SUMMARY OF EVIDENCE-BASED MESSAGES

1. Maternal Type 1 diabetes that is present preconception increases the risk of congenital malformations 10-fold (Level 1).[49]
2. The risk for congenital malformations is related to the degree of preconception glycemic control; good glycemic control preconception is associated with rates similar to those of nondiabetic women (Level 1).[14–16,20]

3. Maternal Type 1 diabetes is a risk factor for neonatal macrosomia; this risk rises with the third-trimester nonfasting glucose levels (Level 1).[52]

4. Maternal Type 1 diabetes is a risk factor for neonatal hypoglycemia, hyperbilirubinemia, polycythemia, and respiratory distress (Level 1).[62]

5. Pregnancy increases the progression of diabetic retinopathy in women with Type 1 diabetes; the degree of progression is proportional to the prepregnancy ophthalmologic findings (no retinopathy to moderate-severe nonproliferative retinopathy) and the degree of glycemic control during pregnancy (Level 2).[75]

6. Preconception microalbuminuria increases the risk of preeclampsia in women with Type 1 diabetes during pregnancy (Level 1).[83]

7. Preconception proteinuria increases the risk of nephrotic-range proteinuria during pregnancy (Level 3).[84]

8. Women with Type 1 diabetes who are receiving intensive glycemic therapy using three or more insulin injections or a pump who conceive have a much lower incidence of neonatal congenital malformations than women receiving conventional glycemic therapy (Level 2).[10]

9. Many epidemiologic studies show that intensive glycemic control during pregnancy reduces the risk of neonatal morbidity (Level 3).[34,66,106–111]

10. In women with pregestational diabetes, an intensive glycemic therapy approach using four insulin injections daily leads to better glycemic control and a better neonatal outcome than a twice-daily regimen (Level 1).[113]

11. Epidemiologic studies suggest that twice-weekly fetal monitoring tests starting at 34 weeks, which include NSTs, BPPs, and other tests as needed, reduce the risk of neonatal mortality (Level 4).[130,132,133]

12. Tight glucose control during labor reduces the risk of neonatal hypoglycemia (Level 3).[19,57]

13. Targeting maternal glucose levels of 4 to 8 mmol/L during labor leads to a lower risk of maternal hypoglycemia than targeting lower levels (Level 3).[19]

14. In women with GDM, adjusting insulin doses on the basis of postprandial versus preprandial capillary glucose values reduces the risk of large-for-gestational-age infants, cesarean sections, and neonatal hypoglycemia (Level 1).[168]

15. One-hour postprandial capillary glucose targets < 7.8 mmol/L reduce neonatal morbidity associated with gestational diabetes (Level 1A).[168]

16. Two-hour postprandial capillary glucose values < 6.7 mmol/L eliminate the excess neonatal morbidity associated with gestational diabetes (Level 3).[181]

17. Intensive treatment of GDM targeting good glycemic control reduces the risk of macrosomia and neonatal hypoglycemia (Level 3).[181]

18. In women with gestational diabetes, an intensive glycemic therapy approach using four insulin injections daily leads to better glycemic control and a better neonatal outcome than a twice-daily regimen (Level 1).[113]

19. Antepartum fetal monitoring with NSTs may not eliminate the neonatal risk in GDM (Level 4).[189]

REFERENCES

1. Martinez-Frias ML. Epidemiological analysis of outcomes of pregnancy in diabetic mothers: identification of the most characteristic and most frequent congenital anomalies. Am J Med Genet 1994;51:108–13.

2. McFarland KF, Hemaya E. Neonatal mortality in infants of diabetic mothers. Diabetes Care 1985;8:333–6.

3. Miranda JA, Mozas J, Rojas R, et al. Strict glycemic control in women with pregestational insulin-dependent dabetes mellitus. Int J Gynecol Obstet 1994;47:223–7.

4. Francois R, Picaud JJ, Ruitton-Ugliengo A, et al. The newborn of diabetic mothers. Biol Neonate 1974;24:1–31.

5. Phelan SA, Ito M, Loeken MR. Neural tube defects in embryos of diabetic mice: role of the Pax-3 gene and apoptosis. Diabetes 1997;46:1189–97.

6. Cai J, Phelan SA, Hill AL, et al. Identification of *Dep-1*, a new gene regulated by the transcription factor pax-3, as a marker for altered embryonic gene expression during diabetic pregnancy. Diabetes 1998;47:1803–5.

7. Sakamaki H, Akazawa S, Ishibashi M, et al. Significance of glutathione-dependent antioxidant system in diabetes-induced embryonic malformations. Diabetes 1999;48:1138–44.

8. Wentzel P, Welsh N, Eriksson UJ. Developmental damage, increased lipid peroxidation, diminished cyclooxygenase-2 gene expression, and lowered prostaglandin E_2 levels in rat embryos exposed to a diabetic environment. Diabetes 1999;48:813–20.

9. Moley KH, Chi MM-Y, Knudson CM, et al. Hyperglycemia induces apoptosis in pre-implantation embryos through cell death effector pathways. Nat Med 1998;4:1421–4.

10. The Diabetes Control and Complications Trial Research Group. Pregnancy outcomes in the Diabetes Control and Complications Trial. Am J Obstet Gynecol 1996;174:1343–53.

11. Greene MF, Hare JW, Cloherty JP, et al. First-trimester hemoglobin A_1 and risk for major malformation and spontaneous abortion in diabetic pregnancy. Teratology 1989;39:225–31.

12. Fuhrmann K, Reiher H, Semmler K, et al. The effect of intensified conventional insulin therapy before and during pregnancy on the malformation rate in offspring of diabetic mothers. Exp Clin Endocrinol 1984;83:173–7.

13. Goldman JA, Dicker D, Feldberg D, et al. Pregnancy outcome in patients with insulin-dependent diabetes mellitus with preconceptional diabetic control: a comparative study. Am J Obstet Gynecol 1986;155:293–7.

14. Kitzmiller JL, Gavin LA, Gin GD, et al. Preconception care of diabetes. Glycemic control prevents congenital anomalies. JAMA 1991;265:731–6.

15. Rosenn B, Miodovnik M, Dignan PSJ, et al. Minor congenital malformations in infants of insulin-dependent diabetic women: association with poor glycemic control. Obstet Gynecol 1990;76:745–9.

16. Fuhrmann K, Reiher H, Semmler K, et al. Prevention of congenital malformations in infants of insulin-dependent diabetic mothers. Diabetes Care 1983;6:219–23.

17. Steel JM, Johnstone FD, Hepburn DA, et al. Can prepregnancy care of diabetic women reduce the risk of abnormal babies? BMJ 1990;301:1070–4.

18. Coustan DR. Debate: is preconception counseling for women with diabetes cost-effective? Diabetes Spectrum 1997;10:195–202.

19. Carron Brown S, Kyne-Grzebalski D, Mwangi B, et al. Effect of management policy upon 120 type 1 diabetic pregnancies: policy decisions in practice. Diabet Med 1999;16:573–8.

20. Suhonen L, Hiilesmaa V, Teramo K. Glycaemic control during early pregnancy and fetal malformations in women with type 1 diabetes mellitus. Diabetologia 2000;43:79–82.

21. Soler NG, Walsh CH, Malins JM. Congenital malformations in infants of diabetic mothers. QJM 1976;XLV:303–13.

22. Becerra JE, Khoury MJ, Cordero JF, et al. Diabetes mellitus during pregnancy and the risks for specific birth defects: a population-based case-control study. Pediatrics 1990;85:1–9.

23. Splitt M, Wright C, Sen D, et al. Left-isomerism sequence and maternal type-1 diabetes. Lancet 1999;354:305–6.

24. Mills JL. Malformations in infants of diabetic mothers. Teratology 1982;25:385–94.

25. Mills JL, Baker L, Goldman AS. Malformations in infants of diabetic mothers occur before the seventh gestational week—implications for treatment. Diabetes 1979;28:292–3.

26. Herman WH, Janz NK, Becker MP, et al. Diabetes and pregnancy: preconception care, pregnancy outcomes, resource utilization and costs. J Reprod Med 1999;44:33–8.

27. Willhoite MB, Bennert HW, Palomaki GE, et al. The impact of preconception counseling on pregnancy outcomes. The experience of the Maine Diabetes in Pregnancy Program. Diabetes Care 1993;16:450–5.

28. Hanson U, Persson B, Thunell S. Relationship between haemoglobin A_{1C} in early Type 1 (insulin-dependent) diabetic pregnancy and the occurrence of spontaneous abortion and fetal malformation in Sweden. Diabetologia 1990;33:100–4.

29. Ylinen K, Aula P, Stenman U-H, et al. Risk of minor and major fetal malformations in diabetics with high haemoglobin A1C values in early pregnancy. BMJ 1984;289:345–6.

30. Rosenn B, Miodovnik M, Combs CA, et al. Glycemic thresholds for spontaneous abortion and congenital malformations in insulin-dependent diabetes mellitus. Obstet Gynecol 1994;84:515–20.

31. Miller E, Hare JW, Cloherty JP, et al. Elevated maternal hemoglobin A_{1c} in early pregnancy and major congenital anomalies in infants of diabetic mothers. N Engl J Med 1981;304:1331–4.

32. Miodovnik M, Mimouni F, Dignan PSJ, et al. Major malformations in infants of IDDM women: vasculopathy and early first-trimester poor glycemic control. Diabetes Care 1988;11:713–8.

33. Mills JL, Knopp RH, Simpson JL, et al. Lack of relation of increased malformation rates in infants of diabetic mothers to glycemic control during organogenesis. N Engl J Med 1988;318:671–6.

34. Key TC, Giuffrida R, Moore TR. Predictive value of early pregnancy glycohemoglobin in the insulin-treated diabetic patient. Am J Obstet Gynecol 1987;156:1096–100.

35. Coustan DR, Berkowitz RL, Hobbins JC. Tight metabolic control of overt diabetes in pregnancy. Am J Med 1980;68:845–52.

36. Daly S, Mills JL, Molloy AM, et al. Minimum effective dose of folic acid for food fortification to prevent neural-tube defects. Lancet 1997;350:1666–9.

37. Kaplan JS, Iqbal S, England BG, et al. Is pregnancy in diabetic women associated with folate deficiency? Diabetes Care 1999;22:1017–21.

38. Whitehead R, Bates C. Recommendations on folate intake. Lancet 1997;350:1642–3.

39. Sellers E, Eisenbarth G, Young TK, et al. Diabetes-associated autoantibodies in aboriginal children. Lancet 2000;355:1156.

40. Towner D, Xiang A, Kjos SL, et al. Congenital malformations in pregnancies complicated by NIDDM. Increased risk from poor maternal metabolic control but not from exposure to sulfonylurea drugs. Diabetes Care 1995;18:1446–51.

41. Omori Y, Minei S, Testuo T, et al. Current status of pregnancy in diabetic women. A comparison of pregnancy in IDDM and NIDDM mothers. Diabetes Res Clin Pract 1994;24(Suppl):S273–8.

42. Piacquadio K, Hollingsworth DR, Murphy H. Effects of *in utero* exposure to oral hypoglycaemic drugs. Lancet 1991;338:866–9.

43. Hellmuth E, Damm P, Molsted-Pedersen L. Congenital malformations in offspring of diabetic women treated with oral hypoglycemic agents during embryogenesis. Diabet Med 1994;11:471–4.

44. Sivan E, Feldman B, Dolitzki M, et al. Glyburide crosses the placenta in vivo in pregnant rats. Diabetologia 1995;38:753–6.

45. Wolf H, Sabata V, Frerichs H, et al. Evidence for the impermeability of the human placenta for insulin. Horm Metab Res 1969;1:274–5.

46. Goodner CM, Freinkel N. Carbohydrate metabolism in pregnancy. IV. Studies on the permeability of the rat placenta to I^{131} insulin. Diabetes 1961;10:383–92.

47. Kalhan SC, Schwartz R, Adam PAJ. Placental barrier to human insulin-I^{125} in insulin-dependent diabetic mothers. J Clin Endocrinol Metab 1975;40:139–42.

48. Menon RK, Cohen RM, Sperling MA, et al. Transplacental passage of insulin in pregnant women with insulin-dependent diabetes mellitus. Its role in fetal macrosomia. N Engl J Med 1990;323:309–15.

49. Casson IF, Clarke CA, Howard CV, et al. Outcomes of pregnancy in insulin dependent diabetic women: results of a five year population cohort study. BMJ 1997;315:275–8.

50. Schwartz R, Brambilla D, Gruppuso PA, et al. Hyperinsulinemia and macrosomia in the fetus of the diabetic mother. Diabetes Care 1994;17:640–8.

51. Hod M, Merlob P, Friedman S, et al. Prevalence of congenital anomalies and neonatal complications in the offspring of diabetic mothers in Israel. Isr J Med Sci 1991;27:498–502.

52. Jovanovic-Peterson L, Peterson CM, Reed GF, et al. Maternal postprandial glucose levels and infant birth weight: the Diabetes in Early Pregnancy Study. The National Institute of Child Health and Human Development—Diabetes in Early Pregnancy Study. Am J Obstet Gynecol 1991;164:103–11.

53. Berk MA, Mimouni F, Miodovnik M, et al. Macrosomia in infants of insulin-dependent diabetic mothers. Pediatrics 1989;83:1029–34.

54. Small M, Cameron A, Lunan CB, et al. Macrosomia in pregnancy complicated by insulin-dependent diabetes mellitus. Diabetes Care 1987;10:594–9.

55. Yeast JD, Porreco RP, Ginsberg HN. The use of continuous insulin infusion for the peripartum management of pregnant diabetic women. Am J Obstet Gynecol 1978;131:861–4.

56. Soler NG, Malins JM. Diabetic pregnancy: management of diabetes on the day of delivery. Diabetologia 1978;15:441–6.

57. Miodovnik M, Mimouni F, Tsang RC, et al. Management of the insulin-dependent diabetic during labor and delivery. Influences on neonatal outcome. Am J Perinatol 1987;4:106–14.

58. Light IJ, Keenan WJ, Sutherland JM. Maternal intravenous glucose administration as a cause of hypoglycemia in the infant of the diabetic mother. Am J Obstet Gynecol 1972;113:345–50.

59. Lean MEJ, Pearson DWM, Sutherland HW. Insulin management during labour and delivery in mothers with diabetes. Diabet Med 1990;7:162–4.

60. Haigh SE, Tevaarwerk GJM, Harding PEG, et al. A method for maintaining normoglycemia during labour and delivery in insulin-dependent diabetic women. Can Med Assoc J 1982;126:487–90.

61. Golde SH, Good-Anderson B, Montoro M, et al. Insulin requirements during labor: a reappraisal. Am J Obstet Gynecol 1982;144:556–9.

62. Hanson U, Persson B. Outcome of pregnancies complicated by type 1 insulin-dependent diabetes in Sweden: acute pregnancy complications, neonatal mortality and morbidity. Am J Perinatol 1993;10:330–3.

63. Jervell J, Moe N, Skjaeraasen J, et al. Diabetes mellitus and pregnancy—management and results at Rikshospitalet, Oslo, 1970–1977. Diabetologia 1979;16:151–5.

64. Robert MF, Neff RK, Hubbell JP, et al. Association between maternal diabetes and the respiratory-distress syndrome in the newborn. N Engl J Med 1976;294:357–60.

65. Mimouni F, Miodovnik M, Whitsett JA, et al. Respiratory distress syndrome in infants of diabetic mothers in the 1980s: no direct adverse effect of maternal diabetes with modern management. Obstet Gynecol 1987;69:191–5.

66. Demarini S, Mimouni F, Tsang RC, et al. Impact of metabolic control of diabetes during pregnancy on neonatal hypocalcemia: a randomized study. Obstet Gynecol 1994;83:918–22.

67. Modanlou HD, Komatsu G, Dorchester W, et al. Large-for-gestational-age neonates: anthropometric reasons for shoulder dystocia. Obstet Gynecol 1982;60:417–23.

68. Hawthorne G, Robson S, Ryall EA, et al. Prospective population based survey of outcome of pregnancy in diabetic women: results of the Northern Diabetic Pregnancy Audit, 1994. BMJ 1997;315:279–81.

69. Gestation and Diabetes in France Study Group. Multicentre survey of diabetic pregnancy in France. Diabetes Care 1991;14:994–1000.

70. Soubrane G, Canivet J, Coscas G. Influence of pregnancy on the evolution of background retinopathy. Int Ophthalmol 1985;8:249–55.

71. Serup L. Influence of pregnancy on diabetic retinopathy. Acta Endocrinol 1986;277(Suppl):122–4.

72. Lovestam-Adrian M, Agardh C-D, Aberg A, et al. Pre-eclampsia is a potent risk factor for deterioration of retinopathy during pregnancy in type 1 diabetic patients. Diabet Med 1997;14:1059–65.

73. Klein BEK, Moss SE, Klein R. Effect of pregnancy on progression of diabetic retinopathy. Diabetes Care 1990;13:34–40.

74. Lauszus FF, Grøn PL, Klebe JG. Pregnancies complicated by diabetic proliferative retinopathy. Acta Obstet Gynecol Scand 1998;77:814–8.

75. Chew EY, Rand L, Mills JL, et al. Metabolic control and progression of retinopathy. The diabetes in early pregnancy study. Diabetes Care 1995;18:631–7.

76. Laatikainen L, Teramo K, Hieta-Heikurainen H, et al. A controlled study of the influence of continuous subcutaneous insulin infusion treatment on diabetic retinopathy during pregnancy. Acta Med Scand 1987;221:367–76.

77. Phelps RL, Sakol P, Metzger BE, et al. Changes in diabetic retinopathy during pregnancy. Correlations with regulation of hyperglycemia. Arch Ophthalmol 1986;104:1806–10.

78. Larinkari J, Laatikainen L, Ranta T, et al. Metabolic control and serum hormone levels in relation to retinopathy in diabetic pregnancy. Diabetologia 1982;22:327–32.

79. Hill DJ, Flyvbjerg A, Arany E, et al. Increased levels of serum fibroblast growth factor-2 in diabetic pregnant women with retinopathy. J Clin Endocrinol Metab 1997;82:1452–7.

80. Chen HC, Newsom RSB, Patel V, et al. Retinal blood flow changes during pregnancy in women with diabetes. Invest Ophthalmol Vis Sci 1994;35:3199–208.

81. Biesenbach G, Zazgornik J, Stoger H, et al. Abnormal increases in urinary albumin excretion during pregnancy in IDDM women with pre-existing microalbuminuria. Diabetologia 1994;37:905–10.

82. Biesenbach G, Zazgornik J. Incidence of transient nephrotic syndrome during pregnancy in diabetic women with and without pre-existing microalbuminuria. BMJ 1989;299:366–7.

83. Ekbom P. Pre-pregnancy microalbuminuria predicts pre-eclampsia in insulin-dependent diabetes mellitus. Lancet 1999;353:377.

84. Kitzmiller JL, Brown ER, Phillippe M, et al. Diabetic nephropathy and perinatal outcome. Am J Obstet Gynecol 1981;141:741–51.

85. Reece EA, Coustan DR, Hayslett JP, et al. Diabetic nephropathy: pregnancy performance and feto-maternal outcome. Am J Obstet Gynecol 1988;159:56–66.

86. Gordon M, Landon MB, Samuels P, et al. Perinatal outcome and long-term follow-up associated with modern management of diabetic nephropathy. Obstet Gynecol 1996;87:401–9.

87. Grenfell A, Brudenell JM, Doddridge MC, et al. Pregnancy in diabetic women who have proteinuria. QJM 1986;59:379–86.

88. Biesenbach G, Stoger H, Zazgornik J. Influence of pregnancy on progression of diabetic nephropathy and subsequent requirement of renal replacement therapy in female Type 1 diabetic patients with impaired renal function. Nephrol Dial Transplant 1992;7:105–9.

89. Combs CA, Rosenn B, Kitzmiller JL, et al. Early-pregnancy proteinuria in diabetes related to preeclampsia. Obstet Gynecol 1993;82:802–7.

90. Mackie ADR, Doddridge MC, Gamsu HR, et al. Outcome of pregnancy in patients with insulin-dependent diabetes mellitus and nephropathy with moderate renal impairment. Diabet Med 1996;13:90–6.

91. Miodovnik M, Rosenn BM, Khoury JC, et al. Does pregnancy increase the risk for development and progression of diabetic nephropathy? Am J Obstet Gynecol 1996;174:1180–91.

92. Van Winter JT, Ogburn PL, Ramin KD, et al. Pregnancy after pancreatic-renal transplantation because of diabetes. Mayo Clin Proc 1997;72:1044–7.

93. Hagay Z, Weissman A. Management of diabetic pregnancy complicated by coronary artery disease and neuropathy. Obstet Gynecol Clin North Am 1996;23:205–20.

94. Hankins GDV, Wendel GD Jr, Leveno KJ, et al. Myocardial infarction during pregnancy: a review. Obstet Gynecol 1985;65:139–46.

95. Gordon MC, Landon MB, Boyle J, et al. Coronary artery disease in insulin-dependent diabetes mellitus of pregnancy (Class H): a review of the literature. Obstet Gynecol Surv 1996;51:437–44.

96. Silfen SL, Wapner RJ, Gabbe SG. Maternal outcome in class H diabetes mellitus. Obstet Gynecol 1980;55:749–51.

97. Bagg W, Henley PG, Macpherson P, et al. Pregnancy in women with diabetes and ischaemic heart disease. Aust N Z J Obstet Gynaecol 1999;39:99–102.

98. Airaksinen KE, Salmela PI. Pregnancy is not a risk factor for a deterioration of autonomic nervous function in diabetic women. Diabet Med 1993;10:540–2.

99. Björklund A, Adamson U, Andréasson K, et al. Hormonal counterregulation and subjective symptoms during induced hypoglycemia in insulin-dependent diabetes mellitus patients during and after pregnancy. Acta Obstet Gynecol Scand 1998;77:625–34.

100. Rosenn BM, Miodovnik M, Khoury JC, et al. Deficient counterregulation: a possible risk factor for excessive fetal growth in IDDM pregnancies. Diabetes Care 1997;20:872–4.

101. Fernandez-Soto L, Gonzalez A, Lobon JA, et al. Thyroid peroxidase autoantibodies predict poor metabolic control and need for thyroid treatment in pregnant IDDM women. Diabetes Care 1997;20:1524–8.

102. Diabetes Control and Complications Trial Research Group. The effect of intensive treatment of diabetes on the development and progression of long-term complications in insulin-dependent diabetes mellitus. N Engl J Med 1993;329:977–86.

103. Farrag OA. Prospective study of 3 metabolic regimens in pregnant diabetics. Aust N Z J Obstet Gynaecol 1987;27:6–9.

104. Walkinshaw SA. Very tight versus tight control of diabetes in pregnancy. In: Enkin MW, Keirse MN, Renfrew MJ, et al, editors. Pregnancy and childbirth module of the Cochrane Database of Systematic Reviews. Oxford: The Cochrane Library; 1996.

105. Kyne-Grzebalski D, Wood L, Marshall SM, et al. Episodic hyperglycaemia in pregnant women with well-controlled type 1 diabetes mellitus: a major potential factor underlying macrosomia. Diabet Med 1999;16:702–6.

106. Nielsen GL, Sorensen HT, Nielsen PH, et al. Glycosylated hemoglobin as predictor of adverse fetal outcome in type 1 diabetic pregnancies. Acta Diabetol 1997;34:217–22.

107. Jovanovic L, Druzin M, Peterson CM. Effect of euglycemia on the outcome of pregnancy in insulin-dependent diabetic women as compared with normal control subjects. Am J Med 1981;71:921–7.

108. Adashi EY, Pinto H, Tyson JE. Impact of maternal euglycemia on fetal outcome in diabetic pregnancy. Am J Obstet Gynecol 1979;133:268–74.

109. Lufkin EG, Nelson RL, Hill LM, et al. An analysis of diabetic pregnancies at Mayo Clinic, 1950–79. Diabetes Care 1984;7:539–47.

110. Small M, Cassidy L, Leiper JM, et al. Outcome of pregnancy in insulin-dependent (type 1) diabetic women between 1971 and 1984. QJM 1986;61:1159–69.

111. Gyves MT, Rodman HM, Little AB, et al. A modern approach to management of pregnant diabetics: a two-year analysis of perinatal outcomes. Am J Obstet Gynecol 1977;128:606–16.

112. Gold AH, Reilly C, Walker JD. Transient improvement in glycemic control. The impact of pregnancy in women with IDDM. Diabetes Care 1998;21:374–8.

113. Nachum Z, Ben-Shlomo I, Weiner E, et al. Twice daily versus four times daily insulin dose regimens for diabetes in pregnancy: randomised controlled trial. BMJ 1999;319:1223–7.

114. Jovanovic L, Ilic S, Pettitt DJ, et al. Metabolic and immunologic effects of insulin lispro in gestational diabetes. Diabetes Care 1999;22:1422–7.

115. Kitzmiller JL, Main E, Ward B, et al. Insulin lispro and the development of proliferative diabetic retinopathy duing pregnancy. Diabetes Care 1999;22:874–6.

116. Steel JM, Johnstone FD, Hume R, et al. Insulin requirements during pregnancy in women with Type 1 diabetes. Obstet Gynecol 1994;83:253–8.

117. Brown ZA, Mills JL, Metzger BE, et al. Early sonographic evaluation for fetal growth delay and congenital malformations in pregnancies complicated by insulin-requiring diabetes. National Institute of Child Health and Human Development Diabetes in Early Pregnancy Study. Diabetes Care 1992;15:613–9.

118. Smith RS, Comstock CH, Lorenz RP, et al. Maternal diabetes mellitus: which views are essential for fetal echocardiography? Obstet Gynecol 1997;90:575–9.

119. McManus RM, Ryan EA. Insulin requirements in insulin-dependent and insulin-requiring GDM women during final month of pregnancy. Diabetes Care 1992;15:1323–7.

120. Flores L, Levy I, Aguilera E, et al. Usefulness of ambulatory blood pressure monitoring in pregnant women with type 1 diabetes. Diabetes Care 1999;22:1511.

121. Rey E, LeLorier J, Burgess E, et al. Report of the Canadian Hypertension Society consensus conference: 3. Pharmacologic treatment of hypertensive disorders in pregnancy. Can Med Assoc J 1997;157:1245–54.

122. Pearson DWM, Copland SA. The management of hypertension in a diabetic pregnancy. Diabetes Metab Res Rev 1999;15:146–51.

123. Koren G, Pastuszak A, Ito S. Drugs in pregnancy. N Engl J Med 1998;338:1128–37.

124. Hagay ZJ, Weissman A, Lurie S, et al. Reversal of fetal distress following intensive treatment of maternal diabetic ketoacidosis. Am J Perinatol 1994;11:430–2.

125. Harman CR, Menticoglou SM. Fetal surveillance in diabetic pregnancy. Curr Opin Obstet Gynecol 1997;9:83–90.

126. Rouse DJ, Owen J, Goldenberg RL, et al. The effectiveness and cost of elective cesarean delivery for fetal macrosomia diagnosed by ultrasound. JAMA 1996;276:1480–6.

127. Conway DL, Langer O. Elective delivery of infants with macrosomia in diabetic women: reduced shoulder dystocia versus increased cesarean deliveries. Am J Obstet Gynecol 1998;178:922–5.

128. Rayburn WF, McKean HE. Maternal perception of fetal movement and perinatal outcome. Obstet Gynecol 1980;56:161–4.

129. Barrett JM, Salyer SL, Boehm FH. The nonstress test: evaluation of 1000 patients. Am J Obstet Gynecol 1981;141:153–7.

130. Kjos SL, Leung A, Henry OA, et al. Antepartum surveillance in diabetic pregnancies: predictors of fetal distress in labor. Am J Obstet Gynecol 1995;173:1532–9.

131. Landon MB, Langer O, Gabbe SG, et al. Fetal surveillance in pregnancies complicated by insulin-dependent diabetes mellitus. Am J Obstet Gynecol 1992;167:617–21.

132. ACOG Committee on Practice Bulletins. Antepartum fetal surveillance. Int J Gynecol Obstet 2000;68:175–86.

133. Davies GAL. Antenatal fetal assessment. J Soc Obstet Gynecol Can 2000;22:456–62.

134. Landon MB, Gabbe SG. Fetal surveillance and timing of delivery in pregnancy complicated by diabetes mellitus. Obstet Gynecol Clin North Am 1996;23:109–23.

135. Gabbe SG, Mestman JH, Freeman RK, et al. Management and outcome of pregnancy in diabetes mellitus, classes B to R. Am J Obstet Gynecol 1977;129:723–9.

136. Weiner Z, Thaler I, Farmakides G, et al. Fetal heart rate patterns in pregnancies complicated by maternal diabetes. Eur J Obstet Gynecol Reprod Biol 1996;70:111–5.

137. Manning FA, Baskett TF, Morrison I, et al. Fetal biophysical profile scoring: a prospective study in 1184 high risk patients. Am J Obstet Gynecol 1981;140:289–94.

138. Golde SH, Montoro M, Good-Anderson B, et al. The role of non stress tests, fetal biophysical profile, and contraction stress tests in the outpatient management of insulin-requiring diabetic pregnancies. Am J Obstet Gynecol 1984;148:269–73.

139. Miller DA, Rabello YA, Paul RH. The modified biophysical profile: antepartum testing in the 1990s. Am J Obstet Gynecol 1996;174:812–7.

140. Reece EA, Hagay Z, Assimakopoulos E, et al. Diabetes mellitus in pregnancy and the assessment of umbilical artery waveforms using pulsed Doppler ultrasonography. J Ultrasound Med 1994;13:73–80.

141. Weiss PAM, Kainer F, Hass J. Cord blood insulin to assess the quality of treatment in diabetic pregnancies. Early Hum Dev 1998;51:187–95.

142. Kenepp NB, Shelley WC, Gabbe SG, et al. Fetal and neonatal hazards of maternal hydration with 5% dextrose before caesarean section. Lancet 1982;i:1150–2.

143. Hanson U, Moberg P, Efendic S. Dosage of insulin during delivery and the immediate post-partum period in pregnant diabetics. Acta Obstet Gynecol Scand 1981;60:183–6.

144. Pedersen J. The pregnant diabetic and her newborn: problems and management. 2nd Ed. Baltimore: Williams & Wilkins; 1977.

145. Njenga E, Lind T, Taylor R. Five year audit of peripartum blood glucose control in Type 1 diabetic patients. Diabet Med 1992;9:567–70.

146. Schneider JM, Huddleston JF, Curet LB, et al. Pregnancy complicating ambulatory patient management of diabetes. Diabetes Care 1980;3:77–81.

147. Tyson JE. Obstetrical management of the pregnancy diabetic. Med Clin North Am 1971;55:961–74.

148. Brudenell JM. Delivering the baby of the diabetic mother. J R Soc Med 1978;71:207–11.

149. Caplan RH, Pagliara AS, Beguin EA, et al. Constant intravenous insulin infusion during labor and delivery in diabetes mellitus. Diabetes Care 1982;5:6–10.

150. Nattrass M, Alberti KGMM, Dennis KJ, et al. A glucose-controlled insulin infusion system for diabetic women during labour. BMJ 1978;2:599–601.

151. West TET, Lowy C. Control of blood glucose during labour in diabetic women with combined glucose and low-dose insulin infusion. BMJ 1977;1:1252–4.

152. Gagne MP, Leff EW, Jefferis SC. The breast-feeding experience of women with type 1 diabetes. Health Care Women Int 1992;13:249–60.

153. Gerstein HC, VenderMuelen J. The relationship between cow's milk exposure and type 1 diabetes. Diabet Med 1996;13:23–9.

154. Alvarez-Marfany M, Roman SH, Drexler AJ, et al. Long-term prospective study of postpartum thyroid dysfunction in women with insulin dependent diabetes mellitus. J Clin Endocrinol Metab 1994;79:10–6.

155. Gunderson EP. Intensive nutrition therapy for gestational diabetes. Rationale and current issues. Diabetes Care 1997;20:221–6.

156. Durnin JVGA, Grant S, McKillop FM, et al. Energy requirements of pregnancy in Scotland. Lancet 1987;II:897–900.

157. Subcommittee on Nutritional Status and Weight Gain During Pregnancy. Summary. Nutrition during pregnancy. Washington, DC: National Academy Press; 1990. p. 1–23.

158. Feig DS, Naylor CD. Eating for two: are guidelines for weight gain during pregnancy too liberal? Lancet 1998;351:1054–5.

159. Walkinshaw SA. Dietary regulation in gestational diabetes does not reduce fetal and neonatal adverse outcomes. In: Enkin MW, Keirse MN, Renfrew MJ, et al, editors. Pregnancy and childbirth module of the Cochrane Database of Systematic Reviews. Oxford: The Cochrane Library; 1996.

160. Magee MS, Knopp RH, Benedetti TJ. Metabolic effects of 1200-kcal diet in obese pregnant women with gestational diabetes. Diabetes 1990;39:234–40.

161. Dornhorst A, Nicholls JSD, Probst F, et al. Calorie restriction for treatment of gestational diabetes. Diabetes 1991;40:161–4.

162. Churchill JA, Berendes HW, Nemore J. Neuropsychological deficits in children of diabetic mothers. A report from the Collaborative Study of Cerebral Palsy. Am J Obstet Gynecol 1969;105:257–68.

163. Stehbens JA, Baker GL, Kitchell M. Outcome at ages 1, 3, and 5 years of children born to diabetic women. Am J Obstet Gynecol 1977;127:408–13.

164. Persson B, Gentz J. Follow-up of children of insulin-dependent and gestational diabetic mothers. Neuropsychological outcome. Acta Paediatr Scand 1984;73:349–58.

165. Rizzo T, Metzger BE, Burns WJ, et al. Correlations between antepartum maternal metabolism and intelligence of offspring. N Engl J Med 1991;325:911–6.

166. Rizzo T, Freinkel N, Metzger BE, et al. Correlations between antepartum maternal metabolism and newborn behavior. Am J Obstet Gynecol 1990;163:1458–64.

167. Silverman BL, Rizzo T, Green OC, et al. Long-term prospective evaluation of offspring of diabetic mothers. Diabetes 1991;40(Suppl 2):121–5.

168. de Veciana M, Major CA, Morgan MA, et al. Postprandial versus preprandial blood glucose monitoring in women with gestational diabetes mellitus requiring insulin therapy. N Engl J Med 1995;333:1237–41.

169. Jang HC, Cho NH, Min Y-K, et al. Increased macrosomia and perinatal morbidity independent of maternal obesity and advanced age in Korean women with GDM. Diabetes Care 1997;20:1582–8.

170. Langer O, Berkus M, Brustman L, et al. Rationale for insulin management in gestational diabetes mellitus. Diabetes 1991;40:186–90.

171. Gyves MT, Schulman PK, Merkatz IR. Results of individualized intervention in gestational diabetes. Diabetes Care 1980;3:495–6.

172. Coustan DR, Imarah J. Prophylactic insulin treatment of gestational diabetes reduces the incidence of macrosomia, operative delivery, and birth trauma. Am J Obstet Gynecol 1984;150:836–42.

173. Langer O, Levy J, Brustman L, et al. Glycemic control in gestational diabetes mellitus—how tight is tight enough: small for gestational age versus large for gestational age? Am J Obstet Gynecol 1989;161:646–53.

174. American Diabetes Association. Gestational diabetes mellitus. Diabetes Care 1999;22 (Suppl 1):S74–6.

175. Combs CA, Gunderson E, Kitzmiller JL, et al. Relationship of fetal macrosomia to maternal postprandial glucose control during pregnancy. Diabetes Care 1992;15:1251–7.

176. Rey E, Monier D, Lemonnier M-C. Carbohydrate intolerance in pregnancy: incidence and neonatal outcomes. Clin Invest Med 1996;19:406–15.

177. al-Najashi SS. Control of gestational diabetes. Int J Gynecol Obstet 1995;49:131–5.

178. Jovanovic-Peterson L, Bevier W, Peterson CM. The Santa Barbara County Health Care Services Program: birth weight change concomitant with screening for and treatment of glucose-intolerance of pregnancy: a potential cost-effective intervention? Am J Perinatol 1997;14:221–8.

179. Drexel H, Bichler A, Sailer S, et al. Prevention of perinatal morbidity by tight metabolic control in gestational diabetes mellitus. Diabetes Care 1988;11:761–8.

180. Persson B, Stangenberg M, Hansson U, et al. Gestational diabetes mellitus (GDM). Comparative evaluation of two treatment regimens, diet versus insulin and diet. Diabetes 1985;34(Suppl 2):101–5.

181. Langer O, Rodriguez DA, Xenakis EMJ, et al. Intensified versus conventional management of gestational diabetes. Am J Obstet Gynecol 1994;170:1036–47.

182. Leikin E, Jenkins JH, Graves WL. Prophylactic insulin in gestational diabetes. Obstet Gynecol 1987;70:587–92.

183. Thompson DM, Dansereau J, Creed M, et al. Tight glucose control results in normal perinatal outcome in 150 patients with gestational diabetes. Obstet Gynecol 1994;83:362–6.

184. Buchanan TA, Gonzalez M, Kjos SL, et al. Use of fetal ultrasound to select metabolic therapy for pregnancies complicated by mild gestational diabetes. Diabetes Care 1994;17:275–83.

185. Buchanan TA, Kjos SL, Schafer U, et al. Utility of fetal measurements in the management of gestational diabetes mellitus. Diabetes Care 1998;21:B99–106.

186. Buchanan TA, Kjos SL. Gestational diabetes: risk or myth? J Clin Endocrinol Metab 1999;84:1854–7.

187. Weiss PAM, Hofmann HM, Kainer F, et al. Fetal outcome in gestational diabetes with elevated amniotic fluid insulin levels. Dietary versus insulin treatment. Diabetes Res Clin Pract 1988;5:1–7.

188. Fraser RB, Bruce C. Amniotic fluid insulin levels identify the fetus at risk of neonatal hypoglycaemia. Diabet Med 1999;16:568–72.

189. Girz BA, Divon MY, Merkatz IR. Sudden fetal death in women with well-controlled, intensively monitored gestational diabetes. J Perinatol 1992;12:229–33.

190. Ryan EA, O'Sullivan MJ, Skyler JS. Insulin action during pregnancy. Studies with the euglycemic clamp technique. Diabetes 1985;34:380–9.

191. Pallardo F, Herranz L, Garcia-Ingelmo T, et al. Early postpartum metabolic assessment in women with prior gestational diabetes. Diabetes Care 1999;22:1053–8.

192. Catalano PM, Vargo KM, Bernstein IM, et al. Incidence and risk factors associated with abnormal postpartum glucose tolerance in women with gestational diabetes. Am J Obstet Gynecol 1991;165:914–9.

193. Dacus JV, Meyer NL, Muram D, et al. Gestational diabetes: postpartum glucose tolerance testing. Am J Obstet Gynecol 1994;171:927–31.

194. Kjos SL, Buchanan TA, Greenspoon JS, et al. Gestational diabetes mellitus: the prevalence of glucose intolerance and diabetes mellitus in the first two months post partum. Am J Obstet Gynecol 1990;163:93–8.

195. Wolff VC, Verlohren H-J, Arlt P, et al. Schicksal von Gestationsdiabetikerinnen-klassifikation des Gestationsdiabetes nach abschluss der Gestation (p.g. Klassifikation). Zentrabl Gynakol 1987;109:88–97.

196. Coustan DR, Carpenter MW, O'Sullivan PS, et al. Gestational diabetes: predictors of subsequent disordered glucose metabolism. Am J Obstet Gynecol 1993;168:1139–45.

197. Damm P, Kuhl C, Bertelsen A, et al. Predictive factors for the development of diabetes in women with previous gestational diabetes mellitus. Am J Obstet Gynecol 1992;167:607–16.

198. Henry OA, Beischer NA. Long-term implications of gestational diabetes for the mother. Baillieres Clin Obstet Gynaecol 1991;5:461–83.

199. Kaufmann RC, Schleyhahn FT, Huffman DG, et al. Gestational diabetes diagnostic criteria: long-term maternal follow-up. Am J Obstet Gynecol 1995;172:621–5.

200. Metzger BE, Cho NH, Roston SM, et al. Prepregnancy weight and antepartum insulin secretion predict glucose tolerance five years after gestational diabetes mellitus. Diabetes Care 1993;16:1598–605.

201. Kjos SL, Peters RK, Ziang A, et al. Predicting future diabetes in Latino women with gestational diabetes. Utility of early postpartum glucose tolerance testing. Diabetes 1995;44:586–91.

202. Lam KSL, Li DF, Lauder IJ, et al. Prediction of persistent carbohydrate intolerance in patients with gestational diabetes. Diabetes Res Clin Pract 1991;12:181–6.

203. Greenberg LR, Moore TR, Murphy H. Gestational diabetes mellitus: antenatal variables as predictors of postpartum glucose intolerance. Obstet Gynecol 1995;86:97–101.

204. Dozio N, Beretta A, Belloni C, et al. Low prevalence of islet autoantibodies in patients with gestational diabetes mellitus. Diabetes Care 1997;20:81–3.

205. Ferber KM, Keller E, Albert ED, et al. Predictive value of human leukocyte antigen class II typing for the development of islet autoantibodies and insulin-dependent diabetes postpartum in women with gestational diabetes. J Clin Endocrinol Metab 1999;84:2342–8.

206. Beischer NA, Wein P, Sheedy MT, et al. Prevalence of antibodies to glutamic acid decarboxylase in women who have had gestational diabetes. Am J Obstet Gynecol 1995;173:1563–9.

207. Damm P, Kuhl C, Buschard K, et al. Prevalence and predictive value of islet cell antibodies and insulin autoantibodies in women with gestational diabetes. Diabet Med 1994;11:558–63.

208. Petersen JS, Dyrberg T, Damm P, et al. GAD65 autoantibodies in women with gestational or insulin dependent diabetes mellitus diagnosed during pregnancy. Diabetologia 1996;39:1329–33.

209. Fuchtenbusch M, Ferber K, Standl E, et al. Prediction of type 1 diabetes postpartum in patients with gestational diabetes mellitus by combined islet cell autoantibody screening. Diabetes 1997;46:1459–67.

210. Mauricio D, Corcoy R, Codina M, et al. Islet cell antibodies and beta-cell function in gestational diabetic women: comparison to first-degree relatives of Type 1 (insulin-dependent) diabetic subjects. Diabet Med 1995;12:1009–14.

211. Skouby SO, Andersen O, Saurbrey N, et al. Oral contraception and insulin sensitivity: in vivo assessment in normal women and women with previous gestational diabetes. J Clin Endocrinol Metab 1987;64:519–23.

212. Petersen KR, Skouby SO, Jespersen J. Contraception guidance in women with pre-existing disturbances in carbohydrate metabolism. Eur J Contracept Reprod Health Care 1996;1:53–9.

213. Molsted-Pedersen L, Skouby SO, Damm P. Preconception counseling and contraception after gestational diabetes. Diabetes 1991;40(Suppl 2):147–50.

214. Kjos SL, Peters RK, Xiang A, et al. Contraception and the risk of type 2 diabetes mellitus in Latina women with prior gestational diabetes mellitus. JAMA 1998;280:533–8.

215. Kjos SL, Peters RK, Xiang A, et al. Hormonal choices after gestational diabetes. Diabetes Care 1998;21:B50–7.

216. Major CA, deVeciana M, Weeks J, et al. Recurrence of gestational diabetes: who is at risk? Am J Obstet Gynecol 1998;179:1038–42.

217. McGuire V, Rauh MJ, Mueller BA, et al. The risk of diabetes in a subsequent pregnancy associated with prior history of gestational diabetes or macrosomic infant. Pediatr Perinatol Epidemiol 1996;10:64–72.

218. Gaudier FL, Hauth JC, Poist M, et al. Recurrence of gestational diabetes mellitus. Obstet Gynecol 1992;80:755–8.

219. Moses RG. The recurrence rate of gestational diabetes in subsequent pregnancies. Diabetes Care 1996;19:1348–50.

220. Philipson EH, Super DM. Gestational diabetes mellitus: does it recur in subsequent pregnancy? Am J Obstet Gynecol 1989;160:1324–31.

221. Moses RG, Shand JL, Tapsell LC. The recurrence of gestational diabetes: could dietary differences in fat intake be an explanation? Diabetes Care 1997;20:1647–50.

222. Peters RK, Kjos SL, Xiang A, et al. Long-term diabetogenic effect of single pregnancy in women with previous gestational diabetes mellitus. Lancet 1996;347:227–30.

223. Alderman BW, Marshall JA, Boyko EJ, et al. Reproductive history, glucose tolerance, and NIDDM in Hispanic and non-Hispanic white women. Diabetes Care 1993;16:1557–64.

224. Boyko EJ, Alderman BW, Keane EM, et al. Effects of childbearing on glucose tolerance and NIDDM prevalence. Diabetes Care 1990;13:848–54.

225. Kritz-Silverstein D, Barrett-Connor E, Wingard DL. The effect of parity on the later development of non-insulin-dependent diabetes mellitus or impaired glucose tolerance. N Engl J Med 1989;321:1214–9.

CHAPTER 19

Diabetes Management in the Elderly

Daniel Tessier, MD, MSc, and Graydon Meneilly, MD, FACP

ABSTRACT

Diabetes mellitus is a common disease in the older population. There are a number of factors, including the burden of diabetes complications, concomitant morbidity, and the comprehension of the disease process by the patient and his family, that make diabetes mellitus a challenging disease in the elderly. The vast majority of subjects have Type 2 diabetes, which means that the degree of hyperglycemia is variable and rarely results in ketosis. There is a body of literature suggesting that the pathophysiology and treatment of diabetes in the older population have particular characteristics that may require specific approaches in medical care. This chapter reviews current knowledge of the different aspects of diabetes mellitus management in the elderly.

INTRODUCTION

Diabetes is a common disease that increases in prevalence with age. Despite this fact, and the high prevalence in elderly populations, relatively little is known regarding differences between elderly and younger adult patients with diabetes with respect to their response to various management approaches. The literature specific to diabetes management in the elderly is reviewed in this chapter, according to the following outline:

1. Who are "the elderly" and how common is diabetes among them?
2. What is the optimal degree of glucose control in elderly people with diabetes and how should it be achieved?
3. How effective is management of traditional cardiovascular risk factors in elderly patients with diabetes ?
4. Which nonpharmacologic strategies may improve glycemic control in the elderly?
5. Is the pharmacologic approach to glycemic control different in the elderly?
6. What other problems may have an impact on diabetes care in the elderly?

WHO ARE "THE ELDERLY" AND HOW COMMON IS DIABETES AMONG THEM?

The definition of "elderly" varies from study to study. Some studies define elderly as being 60 years of age and older, whereas administrative guidelines frequently classify people over the age of 65 as elderly. Although there is no definitive definition of elderly, it is generally agreed that this is a concept that reflects an age continuum starting somewhere in the sixties and characterized by a slow progressive frailty that continues until the end of life. It is therefore important to note the age and health status of the population studied before generalizing the results of one study of the "elderly" to individuals of a particular age.

Diabetes is common in the elderly. The most recent Health and Nutrition Survey in the United States[1] demonstrated that the prevalence of diabetes approaches 20% in Caucasian patients over the age of 70 and may be as high as 50% in certain ethnic groups.[1] The importance of this high prevalence lies in the fact that people over 65 represent 12.7% of the total population in the year 2000. If the current demographic trend of "aging" persists, this group will likely represent around 20.5% of the population by 2020 (Statistics Canada). Consequently, there is likely to be a marked increase in the number of people with diabetes, particularly among the "elderly."

At least one half of elderly people with diabetes are unaware that they have the disease. Although the reasons for this are unclear, it may be related to a reluctance of physicians to diagnose diabetes in the elderly, a lack of awareness of the diagnostic criteria for diabetes, a lack of interaction with a physician, and/or the fact that elderly patients frequently do not manifest the classic symptoms of hyperglycemia until blood glucose levels are substantially elevated, possibly because the renal threshold for glucose increases with age. When patients do have symptoms, they are often nonspecific and may not always trigger the measurement of a plasma glucose level or attendance at a physician (eg, failure to thrive, low energy, confusion, nocturia with or without incontinence, urinary tract infection, etc). This phenomenon, along with the fact that identification and management of diabetes can relieve many of these symptoms, improve quality of life, and prevent or delay subsequent chronic illnesses, highlights the importance of screening for diabetes in these individuals. This may be accomplished by measuring fasting plasma glucose every 3 years, and more frequently in people with risk factors for the development of diabetes (such as obesity, hypertension, and a strong family history of diabetes).[2] As in younger people, diabetes is diagnosed by a fasting plasma glucose ≥ 7.0 mmol/L or ≥ 11.1 mmol/L 2 hours after a 75-g oral glucose load.[3] The lack of standardization of the hemoglobin (HbA_{1c}) across laboratories precludes its use as a test to detect diabetes.[2]

WHAT IS THE OPTIMAL DEGREE OF GLUCOSE CONTROL IN ELDERLY PEOPLE WITH DIABETES AND HOW SHOULD IT BE ACHIEVED?

The literature suggests that pathophysiology of Type 2 diabetes in the elderly has different characteristics than it does in the middle-aged population.[4] The older population is also more vulnerable to the side effects associated with antidiabetic medications, such as hypoglycemic reactions associated with the use of sulfonylureas.[5] However, current recommendations state that otherwise healthy elderly people should target the same glucose levels as younger people with diabetes.[2] This is discussed further below.

All clinicians agree that, at a minimum, blood glucose levels should be controlled sufficiently well to control the symptoms of hyperglycemia. There is less consensus regarding the optimal degree of glycemic control in the elderly. This is due in part to the fact that there are no randomized controlled trials in elderly subjects similar in scope to the Diabetes Control and Complications Trial (DCCT) or the United Kingdom Prospective Diabetes Study (UKPDS) that definitively assess whether tight glycemic control reduces the risk of disease and disability in this age group. The UKPDS data did demonstrate that improved glycemic control reduces the risk of micro- and perhaps macrovascular events in middle-aged patients (Level 1),[6] and it is reasonable to extrapolate these benefits to the elderly. Further, in observational studies of elderly subjects, improved glycemic control is associated with a reduced risk of macrovascular and microvascular complications (Level 2),[7–9] and small randomized trials have demonstrated improved cognitive function as well (Level 2).[10,11] Conversely, a recent study suggests that elderly subjects with baseline retinopathy who have their diabetes aggressively controlled with insulin have a more rapid progression of retinopathy during the first year of therapy (Level 2).[12] These data suggest that subgroups of elderly patients who will benefit from more stringent control need to be carefully defined in future studies.

Achieving optimal glycemic control in elderly persons with diabetes is challenging. These patients take multiple medications, have multiple comorbidities, and often have challenging social situations. Because of the complex nature of these patients and the need for lifestyle modifications, a team approach is essential. Structured diabetes teaching programs have been shown to improve glycemic control, compliance with therapy, and quality of life in older patients (Level 2).[13–15] Self-monitoring of glucose levels constitutes a key aspect of these interventions. Indeed, elderly patients and their caregivers can be taught to reliably self-monitor blood glucose values with no adverse effects on quality of life (Level 2).[16,17] Urine glucose testing is not a reliable measure of glycemic control in the elderly because renal threshold for glucose increases with age. Hemoglobin A_{1c} is the standard laboratory measure of long-term glycemic control in older individuals and should be assessed at least every 6 months to provide an index of glycemic control.[2] Two studies suggest that determination of serum fructosamine may eventually prove to be more reproducible in the elderly (Level 2).[18,19]

EVIDENCE-BASED MESSAGES

1. In elderly patients with diabetes, improved glycemic control is associated with a reduced risk of macrovascular and microvascular complications (Level 2).[7,8]
2. In elderly patients with diabetes, multidisciplinary interventions improve glycemic control, compliance with therapy, and quality of life (Level 2).[12–14]
3. Self-monitoring of blood glucose can be accomplished in the elderly without affecting their quality of life (Level 2).[16,17]

HOW EFFECTIVE IS MANAGEMENT OF TRADITIONAL CARDIOVASCULAR RISK FACTORS IN ELDERLY PATIENTS WITH DIABETES?

Traditional risk factors for cardiovascular disease, such as smoking, hypertension, and hyperlipidemia, are associated with an increased risk of diabetes-related complications in the elderly (Level 3).[20] Modification of these risk factors may reduce the risk of these complications.

Recent studies suggest that treatment of hypertension with thiazide diuretics and calcium channel blockers reduces mortality and the risk of macrovascular complications in the elderly (Level 1).[21,22] In the Systolic Hypertension in the Elderly Patient study (SHEP), patients with systolic hypertension and Type 2 diabetes whose treatment was initiated with a thiazide diuretic had a significantly lower incidence of major cardiovascular events than subjects receiving placebo (percentage of affected subjects over 5 years: 21.4 vs 31%, [RR] 0.45 to 0.94). The absolute risk reduction with active treatment compared with the placebo was twice as great for diabetic versus nondiabetic patients (101 of 1,000 vs 51 of 1,000 randomized participants at the 5-year follow-up) (Level 1).[22] In younger patients with diabetes,[23,24] angiotensin converting enzyme (ACE) inhibitors may be even more effective than the above drugs in reducing the risk of complications in patients with diabetes. The Systolic Hypertension in Europe Trial (SystEur) made a similar subgroup analysis of older patients with both systolic hypertension and Type 2 diabetes. Among the 4,203 nondiabetic participants who were started on the calcium channel blocker nitrendipine, a 55% reduction of mortality was observed compared to the placebo group (45.1 vs 26.4 deaths/1,000 patients, respectively). In the group receiving active treatment, reduction of overall mortality was significantly higher among the diabetic patients than among the nondiabetic patients ($p = .04$) (Level 1).[21] Pending further data, the choice of agent should be based on individual patient characteristics.

There are no data from randomized trials in the elderly to determine the benefits of treatment of hyperlipidemia. Subgroup analyses of middle-aged people with diabetes who were enrolled in both primary[25] and secondary[26] prevention trials of lipid-lowering drugs suggest that reduction of low-density lipoprotein (LDL) cholesterol can significantly decrease morbid events in this population.

Although no study has examined the effects of smoking cessation on the incidence of diabetes-related complications in the elderly, there is no reason to exclude smoking cessation from the list of risk-modifying interventions for this group of patients.[27]

EVIDENCE-BASED MESSAGES

1. Treatment of hypertension with diuretics and calcium channel blockers reduces mortality and risk of macrovascular complications in elderly patients with Type 2 diabetes (Level 1).[21,22]

2. Smoking cessation and dyslipidemia therapy may decrease the risk for cardiovascular disease in the elderly diabetic patient (Level 3).[27]

WHICH NONPHARMACOLOGIC STRATEGIES MAY IMPROVE GLYCEMIC CONTROL IN THE ELDERLY?

Exercise programs have been shown to improve the sense of well-being, glucose levels, and lipid levels in elderly patients with diabetes (Level 2).[28–32] Unfortunately, comorbid conditions often prevent elderly patients from participating in exercise programs, and activity levels may be difficult to achieve. Thus, exercise programs are of value in selected elderly patients.

Elderly patients with diabetes have diets that are too low in complex carbohydrates and too high in saturated fats, and they frequently do not comply with a diabetic diet (Level 3).[33] As noted above, multidisciplinary interventions have been shown to improve compliance with dietary therapy in the aged. In community-dwelling elderly subjects, weight-loss programs have been shown to result in substantial improvements in glycemic control (Level 3).[34] In contrast, in frail, elderly, nursing home residents, diabetic diets complicate and increase the cost of care for these patients and do not improve glycemic control (Level 3).[35]

Many elderly patients with diabetes have diets that are deficient in minerals and vitamins. Moreover, hyperglycemic stress results in an acute depletion of vitamin C and oxidation of glutathione in neutrophils in an older population with Type 2 diabetes (Level 3).[36] Magnesium, zinc, vitamin E, and vitamin C supplementation may improve glycemic control in selected elderly patients with diabetes.[37–41]

EVIDENCE-BASED MESSAGES

1. In elderly patients with diabetes, exercise programs improve well-being, glucose levels, and lipid levels (Level 2).[28–32]
2. In this population, weight-loss programs may result in improved glycemic control (Level 3).[34]
3. Vitamin and mineral supplementation may improve glycemic control in elderly patients with diabetes (Level 2).[37–41]

IS THE PHARMACOLOGIC APPROACH TO GLYCEMIC CONTROL DIFFERENT IN THE ELDERLY?

The principal metabolic defect in lean elderly patients with diabetes is profound impairment in glucose-induced insulin secretion (Level 3).[42] As a consequence, insulin secretagogues such as sulfonylureas are a good first choice for the treatment of diabetes in elderly patients not controlled with dietary therapy. The risk of severe or fatal hypoglycemia associated with the use of sulfonylureas increases exponentially with age (Level 2).[43,44] Chlorpropamide and glyburide are the sulfonylureas associated with the greatest risk of hypoglycemia in the elderly. Observational studies and small randomized controlled trials suggest that glipizide may be associated with a lower risk of hypoglycemia than glyburide.[44–46] Gliclazide has been shown to have a lower incidence of hypoglycemia than glyburide in the elderly (Level 2).[47] Pending the results of further studies, gliclazide and glipizide are the sulfonylureas of choice in the elderly. In general, initial doses of these drugs should be one half those for younger people, and the dose should be increased more slowly. The role of newer secretagogues such as repaglinide remains to be determined for the elderly. The low risk of hypoglycemia with these drugs, however, suggests that they may be a good choice for these patients.

The UKPDS suggests that metformin is an effective agent in obese middle-aged patients and may be more beneficial than sulfonylureas in reducing the risk of morbid events. The main effect of metformin is to reduce insulin resistance, and the principal metabolic defect in obese elderly patients is resistance to insulin-mediated glucose disposal (Level 3).[42] In addition, several small randomized studies suggest that this drug results in substantial improvements in glycemic control in obese elderly patients (Level 2).[48,49] Based on these data, metformin appears to be the ideal agent for the treatment of obese elderly patients. Age is not a risk factor for the development of lactic acidosis with metformin. However, metformin should not be given to patients with high creatinine values, chronic liver disease, or significant congestive heart failure. Patients should be started on 500 mg once a day and the dose should be increased by 500 mg weekly to a maximum of 2.5 g per day. Based on our clinical experience, approximately 20% of elderly patients who are poorly controlled on maximum doses of sulfonylureas can achieve optimal control with the addition of metformin. However, in the UKPDS, the early addition of metformin in sulfonylurea-treated patients was associated with an increased risk of diabetes-related death (96% increased risk; 95% CI 2–275%, $p = .039$). Therefore, pending the results of further studies, this combination should be used with caution in frail elderly patients.[50]

Because of their ability to improve insulin resistance, the thiazolidinediones may also be of value in obese elderly patients. To date, one randomized study has evaluated troglitazone in the elderly and found it to be safe and effective (Level 2).[51] However, as various drugs have increased hepatotoxicity in the elderly, this class of drugs is best reserved for obese elderly patients who are unable to tolerate metformin or have no response to the drug; when used, hepatic function should be carefully monitored. Most of this information comes from studies of troglitazone; at the present time, there are no studies on pioglitazone or rosiglitazone that have specifically looked at the elderly population with diabetes.

Alpha-glucosidase inhibitors interfere with the action of the enzymes responsible for the digestion of complex carbohydrates and disaccharides at the brush border of the intestine. Acarbose was the first of these drugs released for clinical use. Small randomized studies and a large post-marketing surveillance survey suggest that this drug is reasonably well tolerated in the elderly and can reliably reduce HbA$_{1c}$ by 1% alone or in combination with other oral agents or insulin (Level 2).[52–54] Further light on the safety and efficacy of this drug in the aged will be shed by a large randomized study of acarbose as monotherapy in the elderly that has recently been completed. Miglitol is a newer α-glucosidase inhibitor. Glyburide was compared with miglitol in elderly patients in a recent randomized study. Glycemic control was better with glyburide, but patients treated with miglitol had less weight gain, substantially fewer hypoglycemic events, and fewer adverse cardiovascular events (Level 2).[55] At present, acarbose may be best used as first-line therapy for lean elderly patients who have modest fasting hyperglycemia (FBS < 11 mmol/L), since these patients are at increased risk for hypoglycemia with sulfonylureas. It may also be appropriate for obese elderly patients in whom metformin is not tolerated or is ineffective and as combination therapy in patients reluctant to go on insulin. The starting dose of acarbose is 25 mg with the first bite of breakfast. This can be increased by 25 mg per week to a maximum daily dose of 150 mg. Doses above this level are generally not well tolerated in the aged and appear to have little added benefit.

Insulin therapy substantially improves glycemic control with no adverse effect on quality of life in patients who are inadequately controlled on oral agents (Level 2).[56] Elderly patients make substantial errors when trying to mix insulins on their own, and the accuracy of injections is improved by using premixed preparations (Level 2).[57–59] A comparative study in the older diabetic population between two premixed insulin preparations, 50/50 (50% neutral protamine hagedorn [NPH] human insulin and 50% regular human insulin) versus 70/30 (70% NPH human insulin and 30% regular human insulin) did not demonstrate any significant difference in effect on postprandial glycemia (Level 2).[60] Combination of a sulfonylurea with insulin is probably more effective than the same dose of insulin alone in the elderly (Level 2).[61] However, another study failed to show a difference from the efficacy point of view between two doses of insulin, one dose of insulin at bedtime plus oral agents, and one dose of insulin at breakfast plus oral agents (Level 2).[62] In this last study, weight gain was comparable between groups; however, one-third of those patients who were started on one dose of insulin daily needed a second injection to control glycemia.

In the elderly, awareness of hypoglycemic warning symptoms is greater with beef-pork insulin than with human insulin (Level 2).[63] For patients who have frequent hypoglycemic events or hypoglycemic unawareness in regard to human insulin, an animal insulin preparation should be considered if available.

EVIDENCE-BASED MESSAGES

1. Gliclazide and glipizide are the sulfonylureas associated with a lower risk of hypoglycemia in the elderly (Level 2).[44–47]
2. Metformin therapy in the elderly is associated with safe improvement in glycemic control (Level 2).[48–50]
3. Acarbose reduces HbA_{1c} by approximately 1% when used alone or in combination with other agents or insulin (Level 2).[48,53,54]
4. Insulin therapy should be used in elderly patients when there is inadequate glycemic control from other agents (Level 2).[56]
5. Insulin may be combined with sulfonylureas in the elderly (Level 2).[61]
6. Premixed preparations of insulin are associated with lower mixing errors and are therefore preferred to manually mixed preparations (Level 2).[57–59]

WHAT OTHER PROBLEMS MAY HAVE AN IMPACT ON THE DIABETES CARE IN THE ELDERLY?

Many elderly patients with diabetes are depressed. Fluoxetine has been demonstrated to improve glycemic control in obese elderly patients who are depressed, presumably because it results in weight loss (Level 2).[64]

SUMMARY OF EVIDENCE-BASED MESSAGES

1. In elderly patients with diabetes, improved glycemic control is associated with a reduced risk of macrovascular and microvascular complications (Level 2).[7,8]
2. In elderly patients with diabetes, multidisciplinary interventions improve glycemic control, compliance with therapy, and quality of life (Level 2).[12–14]
3. Self-monitoring of blood glucose can be accomplished in the elderly without affecting their quality of life (Level 2).[16,17]
4. Treatment of hypertension with diuretics and calcium channel blockers reduces mortality and risk of macrovascular complications in elderly patients with Type 2 diabetes (Level 1).[21,22]
5. Smoking cessation and therapy of dyslipidemia may decrease the risk for cardiovascular disease in the elderly diabetic patient (Level 3).[20]
6. In elderly patients with diabetes, exercise programs improve well-being, glucose levels, and lipid levels (Level 2).[28–32]
7. In elderly patients with diabetes, weight-loss programs may result in improved glycemic control (Level 3).[34]
8. Vitamin and mineral supplementation may improve glycemic control in elderly patients with diabetes (Level 2).[37–41]
9. Gliclazide and glipizide are the sulfonylureas associated with a lower risk of hypoglycemia in the elderly (Level 2).[44–47]
10. Metformin therapy in the elderly is associated with safe improvement in glycemic control (Level 2).[48–50]
11. Acarbose reduces HbA_{1c} by approximately 1%, when used alone or in combination with other agents or insulin (Level 2).[48,53,54]

12. Insulin therapy should be used in elderly patients when there is inadequate glycemic control from using other agents (Level 2).[56]

13. Insulin may be combined with sulfonylureas in the elderly (Level 2).[61]

14. Premixed preparations of insulin are associated with lower mixing errors and are therefore preferred to manually mixed preparations (Level 2).[57–59]

REFERENCES

1. Harris MI, Flegal KM, Cowie CC, et al. Prevalence of diabetes, impaired fasting glucose, and impaired glucose tolerance in U.S. adults. The Third National Health and Nutrition Examination Survey, 1988–1994. Diabetes Care 1998;21:518–24.

2. Meltzer S, Leiter L, Daneman D, Gerstein HC, et al. 1998 clinical practice guidelines for the management of diabetes in Canada. Can Med Assoc J 1998;159(Suppl 8):S1–29.

3. Expert Committee on the Diagnosis and Classification of Diabetes Mellitus. Diabetes Care 1997;20:1–15.

4. Meneilly GS, Elliott T, Tessier D et al. Metabolic alterations in middle-aged and elderly obese patients with type 2 diabetes. Diabetes Care 1999;22:112–8.

5. Asplund K, Wiholm BE, Lithner F. Glibenclamide associated hypoglycemia: a report on 57 cases. Diabetologia 1983;24:412–7.

6. Anonymous. Intensive blood glucose control with sulphonylureas or insulin compared with conventional treatment and risk of complications in patients with type 2 diabetes (UKPDS 33). UK Prospective Diabetes Study Group. Lancet 1998;352:837–53.

7. Kuusisto J, Mykkanen L, Pyorala K, et al. NIDDM and its metabolic control predict coronary heart disease in elderly subjects. Diabetes 1994;43:960–7.

8. Kuusisto J, Mykkanen L, Pyorala K, et al. Non-insulin-dependent diabetes and its metabolic control are important predictors of stroke in elderly subjects. Stroke 1994;25:1157–64.

9. Morisaki N, Watanabe S, Kobayashi J, et al. Diabetic control and progression of retinopathy in elderly patients: five-year follow-up study. J Am Geriatr Soc 1994;42:142–5.

10. Meneilly GS, Cheung E, Tessier D, et al. The effect of improved glycemic control on cognitive functions in the elderly patient with diabetes. J Gerontol 1993;48:M117–21.

11. Gradman TJ, Laws A, Thompson LW, et al. Verbal learning and/or memory improves with glycemic control in older subjects with non-insulin-dependent diabetes mellitus. J Am Geriatr Soc 1993;41:1305–12.

12. Tovi J, Ingemansson SO, Engfeldt P. Insulin treatment of elderly type 2 diabetic patients: effects on retinopathy. Diabetes Metab 1998;24:442–7.

13. Kronsbein P, Jorgens V, Venhaus A, et al. Evaluation of a structured treatment and teaching programme on non-insulin-dependent diabetes. Lancet 1988;2:1407–11.

14. Gilden JL, Hendryx M, Casia C, et al. The effectiveness of diabetes education programs for older patients and their spouses. J Am Geriatr Soc 1989;37:1023–30.

15. Wilson W, Pratt C. The impact of diabetes education and peer support upon weight and glycemic control of elderly persons with noninsulin dependent diabetes mellitus (NIDDM). Am J Public Health 1987;77:634–5.

16. Gilden JL, Casia C, Hendryx M, et al. Effects of self-monitoring of blood glucose on quality of life in elderly diabetic patients. J Am Geriatr Soc 1990;38:511–5.

17. Bernbaum M, Albert SG, McGinnis J, et al. The reliability of self blood glucose monitoring in elderly diabetic patients. J Am Geriatr Soc 1994;42:779–81.

18. Cefalu WT, Prather KL, Murphy WA, et al. Clinical evaluation of serum fructosamine in monitoring elderly outpatient diabetics. J Am Geriatr Soc 1989;37:833–7.

19. Negoro H, Morley JE, Rosenthal MJ. Utility of serum fructosamine as a measure of glycemia in young and old diabetic and non-diabetic subjects. Am J Med 1988;85:360–4.

20. Kannel WB, Garrison RJ, Wilson PW. Obesity and nutrition in elderly diabetic patients. Am J Med 1986;80(5A):22–30.

21. Tuomilehto J, Rastenyte D, Birkenhager WH, et al. Effects of calcium-channel blockade in older patients with diabetes and systolic hypertension. Systolic Hypertension in Europe Trial investigators. N Engl J Med 1999;340:677–84.

22. Curb JD, Pressel SL, Cutler J, et al. Effect of diuretic based antihypertensive treatment on cardiovascular risk in older diabetic patients with isolated systolic hypertension. J Am Med Assoc 1996;276:1886–92.

23. Tatti P, Pahor M, Byington RP, et al. Outcome results of the Fosinopril Amlodipine Cardiovascular Events Trial (FACET) in hypertensive patients with NIDDM. Diabetes Care 1998;21:597–603.

24. Estacio RO, Jefferes BW, Hiatt WR, et al. The effect of nisoldipine as compared with enalapril on cardiovascular events in patients with non-insulin-dependent diabetes and hypertension. N Engl J Med 1998;338:645–52.

25. Downs JR, Beere PA, Whitney E, et al. Design and rationale of the Air Force/Texas Coronary Atherosclerosis Prevention Study. Am J Cardiol 1997;80:287–93.

26. Pyorala K, Pedersen TR, Kjekshus J, et al. Cholesterol lowering with simvastatin improves prognosis of patients with coronary heart disease: a subgroup analysis of the Scandinavian Simvastatin Survival Study (4S). Diabetes Care 1997;20:614–20.

27. Haire-Joshu D, Glasgow RE, Tibbs TL. Smoking and diabetes. Diabetes Care 1999;22:1887–98.

28. Ligtenberg PC, Godaert GLR, Hillenaar EF, et al. Influence of a physical training program on psychological well-being in elderly type 2 diabetes patients. Diabetes Care 1998;21:2196–7.

29. Ligtenberg PC, Hoekstra JBL, Bol E, et al. Effects of physical training on metabolic control in elderly type 2 diabetes mellitus patients. Clin Sci 1997;93:127–35.

30. Agurs-Collins TD, Kumanyika SK, Ten Have TR, et al. A randomized controlled trial of weight reduction and exercise for diabetes management in older African-American subjects. Diabetes Care 1997;20:1503–11.

31. Raz I, Hauser E, Bursztyn M. Moderate exercise improves glucose metabolism in uncontrolled elderly patients with non insulin-dependent diabetes mellitus. Isr J Med Sci 1994;30:766–70.

32. Skarfors ET, Wegener TA, Lithell H, et al. Physical training as treatment for type 2 (non-insulin-dependent) diabetes in elderly men. A feasibility study over 2 years. Diabetologia. 1987;30:930–3.

33. Horwath CC, Worsley A. Dietary habits of elderly persons with diabetes. J Am Diet Assoc 1991;91:553–7.

34. Reaven GM, Staff of the Palo Alto GRECC Aging Study Unit. Beneficial effects of weight loss in older patients with NIDDM. J Am Geriatr Soc 1985;33:93–5.

35. Coulston AM, Mandelbaou D, Reaven GM. Dietary management of nursing home residents with non-insulin-dependent diabetes mellitus. Am J Clin Nutr 1990;51:67–71.

36. Tessier D, Khalil A, Fülöp T. Effects of an oral glucose challenge on free radicals/antioxidants balance in an older population with type 2 diabetes. J Gerontol A Biol Sci Med Sci 1999;54A: M541–5.

37. Song MK, Rosenthal MJ, Naliboff BD, et al. Effects of bovine prostate powder on zinc, glucose and insulin metabolism in old patients with non-insulin-dependent diabetes mellitus. Metabolism 1998;47:39–43.

38. Paolisso G, D'Amore A, Galzerano D, et al. Daily vitamin E supplements improve metabolic control but not insulin secretion in elderly Type 2 diabetic patients. Diabetes Care 1993;16:1433–7.

39. Paolisso G, Scheen A, Cozzolino D, et al. Changes in glucose turnover parameters and improvement of glucose oxidation after 4 week magnesium administration in elderly noninsulin-dependent (Type 2) diabetic patients. J Clin Endocrinol Metab 1994;78:1510–4.

40. Paolisso G, Passariello N, Pizza G, et al. Dietary magnesium supplements improve B-cell response to glucose and arginine in elderly non-insulin dependent diabetic subjects. Acta Endocrinol 1989;121:16–20.

41. Paolisso G, D'Amore A, Balbi V, et al. Plasma vitamin C affects glucose homeostasis in healthy subjects and in non-insulin-dependent diabetics. Am J Physiol 1994;266:E261–8.

42. Meneilly GS, Elliot T, Tessier D, et al. NIDDM in the elderly. Diabetes Care 1996;19:1320–5.

43. Shorr RI, Ray WA, Daugherty JR, et al. Individual sulfonylureas and serious hypoglycemia in older people. J Am Geriatr Soc 1996;44:751–5.

44. Rosenstock J, Corrao PJ, Goldberg RB, et al. Diabetes control in the elderly: a randomized comparative study of glyburide versus glipizide in non-insulin-dependent diabetes mellitus. Clin Ther 1993;15:1031–40.

45. Brodows RG. Benefits and risks with glyburide and glipizide in elderly NIDDM patients. Diabetes Care 1992;15:75–80.

46. Shorr RI, Ray WA, Daugherty JR, et al. Individual sulfonylureas and serious hypoglycemia in older people. J Am Geriatr Soc 1996;44:751–5.

47. Tessier D, Dawson K, Tetrault JP, et al. Glibenclamide vs gliclazide in type 2 diabetes of the elderly. Diabet Med 1994;11:974–80.

48. Josephkutty S, Potter JM. Comparison of tolbutamide and metformin in elderly diabetic patients. Diabet Med 1990;7:510–4.

49. Lalau JD, Vermersch A, Hary L, et al. Type 2 diabetes in the elderly: an assessment of metformin (metformin in the elderly). Int J Clin Pharmacol Ther Tox 1990;28:329–32.

50. UKPDS. Effect of intensive blood-glucose control with metformin on complications in overweight patients with type 2 diabetes (UKPDS 34). UKPDS Study Group. Lancet 1998;352:854–65.

51. Kumar S, Prange A, Schluze J, et al. Troglitazone, an insulin action enhancer, improves glycaemic control and insulin sensitivity in elderly type 2 diabetic patients. Diabet Med 1998;15:772–9.

52. Johansen K. Acarbose treatment of sulfonylurea-treated non-insulin dependent diabetics. Diabetes Metab 1984;10:219–23.

53. Orimo J, Akiguchi I, Shiraki M. Usefulness of acarbose in the management of non-insulin-dependent diabetes in the aged. In: Creutzfeld W, editor. Acarbose. Amsterdam: Excerpta Medica; 1982. p. 348–52.

54. Spengler M, Cagatay M. Evaluation of efficacy and tolerability of acarbose by postmarketing surveillance. Diab Stoffw 1992;1:218–22.

55. Johnston PS, Lebovitz HE, Coniff RF, et al. Advantages of alpha-glucosidase inhibition as monotherapy in elderly type 2 diabetic patients. J Clin Endocrinol Metab 1998;83:1515–22.

56. Tovi J, Engfeldt P. Well-being and symptoms in elderly type 2 diabetes patients with poor metabolic control: effect of insulin treatment. Practical Diabetes Int 1998;15:73–7.

57. Puxty JAH, Hunter DH, Burr WA. Accuracy of insulin injection in elderly patients. BMJ 1983;287:1762.

58. Kessor CM, Bailie GR. Do diabetic patients inject accurate doses of insulin? Diabetes Care 1981;4:333.

59. Coscelli C, Calabrese G, Fedele D, et al. Use of premixed insulin among the elderly. Diabetes Care 1996;15:1628–30.

60. Brodows R, Chessor R. A comparison of premixed insulin preparations in elderly patients. Diabetes Care 1995;18:855–7.

61. Kyllastinen M, Groop L. Combination of insulin and glibenclamide in the treatment of elderly non-insulin dependent (type 2) diabetic patients. Ann Clin Res 1985;17:100–4.

62. Wolffenbuttel BHR, Sels JPJE, Rondas-Colbers GJ, et al. Comparison of different insulin regimens in elderly patients with NIDDM. Diabetes Care 1996;19:1326–32.

63. Meneilly GS, Milberg WP, Tuokko H. Differential effects of human and animal insulin on the responses to hypoglycemia in elderly patients with NIDDM. Diabetes 1995;44:272–7.

64. Connolly VM, Gallagher A, Kesson CM. A study of fluoxetine in obese elderly patients with type 2 diabetes. Diabet Med 1995;12:416–8.

CHAPTER 20

Hypoglycemia

Jean-François Yale, MD, CSPQ

ABSTRACT

Hypoglycemia is the major obstacle to achieving the glycemic goals required to prevent the long-term complications of diabetes. In patients with Type 2 diabetes, insulin secretagogues and insulin injections increase the risk of hypoglycemia more than therapy with diet or other antihyperglycemic agents. The risk of hypoglycemia is especially important in patients with type 1 diabetes on intensive insulin therapy. The presence of frequent hypoglycemic episodes is a risk factor for hypoglycemia unawareness, and strict avoidance of hypoglycemic episodes improves the ability to perceive hypoglycemia. Hypoglycemia does not appear to cause neuropsychological impairment in adults, whereas it may in children. Acute treatment of hypoglycemia in a conscious individual should be with 15 to 20 g of oral glucose tablets or sucrose solution, whereas subcutaneous or intramuscular glucagon is efficacious in the unconscious individual.

INTRODUCTION

Hypoglycemia is the major obstacle to achieving the glycemic goals required to prevent the long-term complications of diabetes. The frequency of hypoglycemic episodes depends on the type of diabetes, the hypoglycemic therapy used, and individual risk factors. The severity of hypoglycemic episodes varies from annoying symptoms with a biochemically low glucose level to loss of consciousness. The brain is dependent on a continuous supply of glucose as its main energy source. When plasma glucose falls below a critical level, brain function is affected, leading to confusion, seizures, or coma. As it cannot synthesize glucose, the brain must continuously extract its main fuel from the circulation. Severe hypoglycemia, defined as a hypoglycemia requiring the help of others for reversal of the condition, is more common than ketoacidosis and potentially as dangerous. The immediate danger of this mental alteration limits the acceptable frequency of such episodes and often requires the glycemic goals to be increased (ie, relaxed).

Physiology of the Normal Response to Hypoglycemia

As plasma glucose levels decrease in people without diabetes, various physiologic responses occur in an effort to maintain a normal glucose level. The levels at which these responses occur vary between individuals, and the figures provided here are therefore approximations. At levels < 4.2 mmol/L, endogenous insulin secretion by the pancreas is suppressed. At levels of < 3.8 mmol/L, secretion of counter-regulatory hormones begins: glucagon, epinephrine, cortisol, and growth hormone (GH). At levels of < 3.2 mmol/L, this secretion of hormones causes the appearance of classic autonomic warning signals. Signs and symptoms of neuroglycopenia appear at levels of < 2.5 mmol/L (Table 20–1).

As discussed in this chapter, the levels at which these responses occur can be dramatically altered in people with diabetes, and these alterations greatly contribute to the morbidity of hypoglycemia. The problem of hypoglycemia in individuals with diabetes is addressed in this chapter by answering the following questions:

1. What is the definition of hypoglycemia?
2. How common is hypoglycemia with each available oral antihyperglycemic therapy?

Table 20–1 Symptoms and Signs of Hypoglycemia

Neurogenic (autonomic) (% incidence)	Neuroglycopenic (% incidence)
Trembling (32–78)	Difficulty concentrating (31–75)
Palpitations (8–62)	Confusion (13–53)
Sweating (47–84)	Weakness (28–71)
Anxiety (10–44)	Drowsiness (16–33)
Hunger (39–49)	Vision changes (24–60)
Nausea (5–20)	Difficulty speaking (7–41)
Tingling (10–39)	Headache (24–36)
	Dizziness (11–41)
	Tiredness (38–46)

Adapted from Hepburn DA. Symptoms of hypoglycemia. In: Frier BM, Fisher BM, editors. Hypoglycemia and diabetes. London: Edward Arnold; 1993. p. 93–103.

3. What are the risk factors for hypoglycemia in people treated with insulin?
4. What causes severe hypoglycemia and hypoglycemia unawareness?
5. How can severe hypoglycemia and hypoglycemia unawareness be prevented?
6. What are the long-term consequences of hypoglycemia?
7. How is hypoglycemia treated?

WHAT IS THE DEFINITION OF HYPOGLYCEMIA?

The presence of Whipple's triad is confirmatory of hypoglycemia. This triad consists of symptoms compatible with hypoglycemia, a low plasma glucose concentration, and relief of symptoms after plasma glucose is raised. The precise glucose level considered to be low remains the subject of debate. When a strict definition is required, levels of 2.8 mmol/L are often used. When the hypoglycemic episodes need to be quantified in studies, less strict criteria are usually set in order not to greatly underestimate the frequency of clinical hypoglycemia. Classic symptoms with relief with carbohydrates will sometimes be accepted as hypoglycemia. In clinical settings where one wants to minimize the risks, patients are often counseled to consider a value < 4 mmol/L as evidence of hypoglycemia and to treat with carbohydrates. The ambiguity of this definition is increased by the fact that glucose meters are most often used for the measurement of glucose levels in acute situations of hypoglycemia, and the accuracy of these devices at low glucose levels is not optimal.

Grades of Hypoglycemia

Precise terminology has been developed to grade the clinical severity of hypoglycemic episodes (Table 20–2). In a mild hypoglycemic episode, autonomic-mediated symptoms are present, and the patient is able to self-treat. In a moderate episode, neuroglycopenic symptoms occur (with or without autonomic-mediated symptoms), and the patient is still able to self-treat. Any hypoglycemic episode requiring assistance to treat, including cases involving confusion and/or loss of consciousness, is considered a severe hypoglycemic episode. Hypoglycemia unawareness occurs when the threshold for autonomic warning symptoms to appear becomes lower than the threshold for the neuroglycopenic symptoms, so that the first signs of hypoglycemia will often be confusion or loss of consciousness. Asymptomatic hypoglycemia is defined as the presence of a biochemically low glucose level without any symptoms and is said to occur frequently at night.

Table 20–2 Grades of Hypoglycemia

Grade	Primary Detection	Therapy
Asymptomatic	Laboratory or glucose meter	Adjust daily regimen
Mild	Autonomic symptoms	Oral CHO—self-therapy
Moderate	Neuroglycopenic ± autonomic symptoms	Oral CHO—self-therapy
Severe	Neuroglycopenic ± autonomic symptoms	Oral/parenteral CHO—assistance required
Unawareness	Coma, seizure, neuroglycopenic ± autonomic signs; first recognized by someone other than the patient	Oral/parenteral CHO—assistance required

CHO = carbohydrate.

How Common Is Hypoglycemia with Each Available Oral Antihyperglycemic Therapy?

Few large and randomized clinical trials have compared the rates of hypoglycemia between antihyperglycemic agents. Most of the data comes from randomized controlled trials comparing these agents to placebo (Table 20–3). The frequency of hypoglycemia can then vary depending on the HbA_{1c} at the start of the trial and on the glycemic goals during the study. In addition, the incidence of hypoglycemia in these trials is likely underestimated because of variable patient awareness of symptoms and under-reporting of episodes.

Sulfonylureas

The United Kingdom Prospective Diabetes Study (UKPDS) compared the effects of intensive blood glucose control with either sulfonylurea or insulin versus conventional treatment on the risk of microvascular and macrovascular complications in patients with Type 2 diabetes in a randomized controlled trial. Over the first 10 years, the mean proportion of patients per year with one or more major hypoglycemic episodes while taking their assigned treatment was 0.4% for chlorpropamide, 0.6% for glibenclamide, and 0.1% for diet. The corresponding rates for any hypoglycemic episodes were 11.0%, 17.7%, and 1.2%.[1] No statistical analysis comparing rates with different agents was provided.

Among other sulfonylureas, gliclazide has been associated with less hypoglycemia than glyburide in the elderly.[2]

Meglitinides

Repaglinide is a recently developed oral insulin secretagogue antihyperglycemic agent. It has a rapid onset and a shorter duration of action than other agents, and thus must be given before each meal. In a 1-year randomized double-blind study in patients with Type 2 diabetes, it was concluded that repaglinide and glyburide had similar potency and similar rates of hypoglycemia.[3] It was shown in a small study that when lunch is skipped, omitting the lunch repaglinide dose compared to taking the usual morning dose of glyburide resulted in less hypoglycemic events in the afternoon. Repaglinide may therefore have an advantage when the meal schedule is irregular.[4]

Biguanides

In the UKPDS, over 10 years of follow-up among patients taking therapy as allocated, the proportions of patients per year who had one or more major hypoglycemic attacks were 0.7% for the diet alone and 0.0% for the metformin group. For any hypoglycemic episode, the cor-

Table 20–3 Frequency of Hypoglycemia with Various Antihyperglycemic Therapies

	Study	*Severe Hypoglycemia* *(% patients/y)*	*Any Hypoglycemia* *(% patients/y)*
Type 2 diabetes			
Insulin secretagogues (sulfonylureas + meglitinides)			
Chlorpropamide	UK Prospective Diabetes Study Group[1]	0.4	16
Glibenclamide	UK Prospective Diabetes Study Group[1]	0.6	21
Biguanides			
Metformin	UK Prospective Diabetes Study Group[5]	0.0	4.2
	De Fronzo et al[6]	0.0	0.0–2.0
Thiazolidinediones			
Troglitazone	Iwamoto et al[7]	0.0	1.4
Rosiglitazone	Charbonnel et al[8]	0.0	< 2.0
Pioglitazone	Brockley et al[9]	0.0	< 3.0
Alpha-glucosidase inhibitors	Chiasson et al[10]	0.0	0.0
Insulin			
Regular insulin	UK Prospective Diabetes Study Group[1]	2.3	28
	Anderson et al[18]	2.2	
Lispro insulin	Anderson et al[18]	0.6	
Type 1 diabetes			
Conventional treatment	The DCCT Research Group[20]	5.4	
Intensive treatment	The DCCT Research Group[20]	10.0	
Regular insulin	Brunelle et al[15]	4.1	
Lispro insulin	Brunelle et al[15]	3.1	

responding proportions were 0.9% and 4.2%; no statistical analysis was provided.[5] In two randomized double-blind studies of metformin, symptomatic hypoglycemia occurred with monotherapy in ≤ 2.0% of patients.[6]

Thiazolidinediones

The frequency of hypoglycemia with thiazolidinediones has not been significantly different from placebo. No cases of severe hypoglycemia have been reported with monotherapy with these agents.[7–9]

Alpha-Glucosidase Inhibitors

Alpha-glucosidase inhibitors do not cause hypoglycemia.[10] However, if a patient has a hypoglycemic reaction (because of concomitant therapy with insulin for example), α-glucosidase inhibition may prevent sucrose or starch from being absorbed in a timely fashion for the treatment of hypoglycemia. Patients taking α-glucosidase inhibitors must therefore use glucose (dextrose tablets), grape juice, or honey to treat hypoglycemia.

EVIDENCE-BASED MESSAGE

In patients with Type 2 diabetes, therapy with sulfonylureas or meglitinides (ie, insulin secretagogues) increases the risk of hypoglycemia and severe hypoglycemia more than therapy with diet alone, biguanides, thiazolidinediones, or α-glucosidase inhibitors (Level 1A).[1–10]

WHAT ARE THE RISK FACTORS FOR HYPOGLYCEMIA IN PEOPLE TREATED WITH INSULIN?

Type of Diabetes

The UKPDS targeted a fasting plasma glucose of 6 mmol/L and a premeal glucose of 4 to 7 mmol/L in individuals with Type 2 diabetes allocated to a policy of intensive treatment. During the first 10 years, 2.3% of insulin-treated patients per year had one or more major hypoglycemic episodes (ie, 23% over 10 years), compared to an incidence of any hypoglycemic episode of 36.5% per year.[1]

The DCCT targeted premeal values between 3.9 and 6.7 mmol/L, postprandial values < 10 mmol/L, and 3:00 am values > 3.6 mmol/L in individuals with Type 1 diabetes allocated to intensified therapy. After an average of 6.5 years of follow-up, 65% of patients in the intensive group had at least one episode of severe hypoglycemia.[11]

Thus, although no direct comparisons are available, these data suggest that people with Type 1 diabetes have a greater frequency of severe hypoglycemic episodes with insulin therapy than those with Type 2 diabetes.

EVIDENCE-BASED MESSAGE

Intensive glycemic therapy with insulin increases the risk of severe hypoglycemia in people with Type 1 diabetes more than in people with Type 2 diabetes (Level 4).[1,11]

Degree of Glycemic Control

Intensive insulin therapy is an approach to therapy that targets euglycemia or near-normal glycemia using all available resources. This approach to glycemic control has only been carefully studied in people with Type 1 diabetes, in whom hypoglycemia is currently the greatest barrier to achieving euglycemia.

In the DCCT, the goals in the conventional group were the absence of symptoms of hyperglycemia using one or two daily insulin injections. By the end of the study, with an average of 6.5 years of follow-up, 65% of patients in the intensive group versus 35% in the conventional treatment group had had at least one episode of severe hypoglycemia.[11] The cumulative rates (episodes per 100 patient-years of follow-up) were 18.7 for the conventional approach and 61.2 for the intensive group, for a relative risk of 3.28 (95% CI 2.65 to 4.05, $p < .001$).[11] Adolescents were found to be at even greater absolute risk (conventional risk: 27.8 episodes per 100 patient-years; intensive: 85.7 episodes per 100 patient-years),[12] but the relative risk was of the same order: 2.96 (95% CI 1.90 to 4.62, $p < .001$). The event rate per 100 patient-years for severe hypoglycemia defined as coma or seizure was 5.4 in the conventional treatment group and 16.3 in the intensive treatment group, for a relative risk of 3.02 (95% CI 2.36 to 3.86, $p < .001$).[11]

In a 1997 meta-analysis of 14 randomized controlled trials with at least 6 months follow-up comparing intensive and conventional insulin treatment in Type 1 diabetes, the combined odds ratio for hypoglycemia was 2.99 (95% CI 2.45 to 3.64). The risk of severe hypoglycemia was determined by the degree of normalization of glycemia achieved ($p = .005$ for interaction term), with the results of the DCCT in line with other trials. The mode of intensified treatment was not predictive as soon as the reduction in glycosylated hemoglobin was included in the model,[13] suggesting that it is the glycemic goal and not the insulin regimen that determines the risk.

Hypoglycemia is therefore the most common adverse effect of intensive insulin therapy. All patients starting intensive insulin programs should be counseled regarding the risks of hypoglycemia and approaches to prevent its appearance. Self-monitoring of blood glucose should be performed frequently, and patients should receive appropriate instructions on how to adjust their insulin dosages in response to their glucose levels, food intake, and physical activity.

EVIDENCE-BASED MESSAGE

In people with Type 1 diabetes, intensified insulin therapy targeting euglycemia is associated with a threefold higher risk of hypoglycemia than is conventional insulin therapy targeting higher glucose levels (Level 1A).[13]

Source of Insulin

It was suggested in a review of 39 clinical studies and 12 epidemiologic reports comparing human insulin and porcine insulin that human and porcine insulin do not provoke different hormonal responses to or cause different symptoms of hypoglycemia and that the incidence of severe hypoglycemia with human insulin does not differ from that of porcine insulin.[14] It therefore can be concluded that patients switching from animal to human insulin do not require counseling about any change in frequency or perception of hypoglycemia.

Biochemical Structure of Insulin

In a meta-analysis of eight large multicenter clinical trials comparing insulin lispro (n = 2,327) with regular human insulin (n = 2,339) in patients with Type 1 diabetes, the frequency of severe hypoglycemia (defined as an episode resulting in coma or requiring intravenous glucose or intramuscular glucagon) was lower in patients with Type 1 diabetes taking lispro insulin (3.1%) than in those on regular insulin (4.4%). The relative risk of hypoglycemia with lispro compared to regular insulin was 0.703 (95% CI 0.518 to 0.956, $p = .024$). It should be noted that patients with a history of recurrent severe hypoglycemia were excluded from these trials, so the rate may be an underestimate. Nevertheless, the rate of severe hypoglycemia was 14.2 per 100 patient-years during insulin lispro and 18.2 during regular human insulin therapy. Of the eight studies, three had a parallel design, while five had a crossover design. Taking only the crossover studies into account to examine paired responses, the lower frequency with lispro insulin was confirmed ($p = .019$). There was no difference in HbA_{1c} between insulin lispro and regular insulin (8.15 ± 1.50% vs 8.14 ± 1.52%, $p = .370$),[15] suggesting that the effect on hypoglycemia was not due to differential levels of achieved glycemic control. In a large crossover study comparing lispro to human regular insulin as the premeal insulin, Anderson et al found a 12% reduction in total hypoglycemic episodes ($p < .001$), with the largest improvement being overnight.[16] In a smaller randomized double-blind crossover study (N = 90), another insulin analogue (insulin aspart) was also shown to result in significantly fewer major hypoglycemic episodes (20 episodes in 16 patients vs 44 episodes in 24 patients, $p < .002$).[17]

In Type 2 diabetes, a 6-month randomized open-label crossover study was performed in 722 patients comparing insulin lispro and human regular insulin as premeal insulin, with Humulin N or U as basal. The glycemic goals were a fasting glucose level below 7.8 mmol/L and a 2-hour level below 10 mmol/L. Whereas the HbA_{1c} levels were similar between treatments, the mean hypoglycemia rate during the study was less in the insulin lispro group than in the human regular insulin group (3.18 ± 0.16 vs 3.43 ± 0.19 episodes per 30 days, $p < .02$). The difference was particularly significant at nighttime (0h to 6h: 0.47 ± 0.05 vs 0.73 ± 0.07, *p* < .001). Severe hypoglycemia occurred at a low rate: 4 of 722 patients had an episode during the 3 months of regular insulin therapy (2.2 episodes per 100 patient-years), and 1 of 722 patients had an episode during lispro therapy (0.6 episodes per 100 patient-years).[18]

These data suggest that patients experiencing frequent hypoglycemic episodes on regular insulin should therefore be tried on lispro insulin.

EVIDENCE-BASED MESSAGE

In people with Type 1 and Type 2 diabetes, insulin therapy using rapid-acting analogues to achieve glycemic control is associated with a lower risk of hypoglycemia than is therapy with regular insulin (Level 1A).[15–18]

WHAT CAUSES SEVERE HYPOGLYCEMIA AND HYPOGLYCEMIA UNAWARENESS?

Severe hypoglycemic reactions are the main barrier to achieving optimal glucose control in people with Type 1 diabetes.[19] As discussed above, adrenergic symptoms usually occur before the onset of neuroglucopenic symptoms, allowing patients to treat their hypoglycemia in time. Severe hypoglycemic episodes occur mostly at night (39 to 55% during sleep)[20,21] or in the absence of hypoglycemia awareness that alerts patients to correct their glucose levels.[20] Of the daytime severe hypoglycemic events in the DCCT, 36% occurred with no warning, while symptoms were not recognized at the time of event in 51% of cases.[20]

Risk Factors for Severe Hypoglycemia

The important (and statistically significant) risk factors for severe hypoglycemia include a history of previous severe hypoglycemia (DCCT: adjusted relative risk estimate [RR] 2.54, 95% CI 1.67 to 3.88); a longer duration of diabetes (DCCT: RR 1.72, CI 1.07 to 2.77); a higher baseline HbA_{1c} (DCCT: RR 1.20 per 1%, CI 1.04 to 1.39); a lower most-recent HbA_{1c} (DCCT: RR 1.43 per 1%, CI 1.17 to 1.76); and a higher baseline insulin dose (DCCT: RR 1.11 per 0.1 u/kg higher, CI 1.03 to 1.19).[20] Hypoglycemia unawareness is another risk factor for severe hypoglycemia (RR = 5.6); it increased the risk from 50 to 280 episodes per 100 patient-years.[22] Finally, participants with low residual beta-cell secretory capacity were also shown to be at higher risk of severe hypoglycemia[11,23] (RR 4.35, CI 1.37 to 13.85).

Glucagon responses to hypoglycemia, normal at diagnosis of Type 1 diabetes, are blunted within a few years of diagnosis and eventually lost.[24] Patients are therefore dependent on sympathoadrenal responses for appropriate glucose counter-regulation and for hypoglycemia awareness. It is therefore not surprising that autonomic neuropathy (defined as defects in both heart rate and systolic blood pressure changes with standing) has also been shown to be an independent risk factor for severe hypoglycemia in people with Type 1 diabetes (RR 1.7, CI 1.3 to 2.2),[25] as those with autonomic neuropathy have further reduced epinephrine and norepinephrine responses to hypoglycemia.[26] However, autonomic neuropathy is not required for hypoglycemia unawareness to be present.

EVIDENCE-BASED MESSAGES

1. In people with Type 1 diabetes, important risk factors for severe hypoglycemia include the following: a previous episode; longer diabetes duration; higher baseline and lower recent HbA_{1c}; higher baseline insulin dose; a history of hypoglycemia unawareness; and low residual beta-call function (Level 1).[20–23]
2. In patients with Type 1 diabetes, evidence of autonomic neuropathy is a moderate risk factor for severe hypoglycemia (Level 1).[25]

Risk Factors for Hypoglycemia Unawareness

Prior hypoglycemic episodes are a crucial risk factor for hypoglycemia unawareness. On average, hypoglycemia has been reported to occur in people with Type 1 diabetes at a frequency of approximately two episodes per week. In one study, increasing the frequency of hypoglycemia by two episodes per week (ie, to four per week) resulted in a worsening in the defect of the hormonal responses to hypoglycemia (particularly epinephrine and pancreatic polypeptide).[27] This, in turn, could lead to a reduction in the self-detection of hypoglycemia (hypoglycemia unawareness) and in defective glucose counter-regulation. Defects in counter-regulatory responses have also been shown in patients with insulinomas.[28] It has been suggested that the brain adapts to recurrent hypoglycemia by maintaining glucose uptake despite hypoglycemia, preserving cerebral metabolism but reducing the responses of counter-regulatory hormones and awareness of hypoglycemia.[29]

Nocturnal hypoglycemia may be particularly important in this context because it occurs commonly (29 to 56% of nights), is frequently asymptomatic (49 to 67% of nocturnal hypoglycemia), and usually lasts > 1 hour (50 to 60%).[30–32] Deep sleep has been shown to impair the counter-regulatory hormone responses (particularly epinephrine, $p = .004$) to hypoglycemia in patients with diabetes as well as in normal subjects.[33]

HOW CAN SEVERE HYPOGLYCEMIA AND UNAWARENESS OF IT BE PREVENTED?

It is clear from the foregoing that identification of individuals at high risk for severe hypoglycemia on the basis of risk factors is the first step in reducing the frequency of this problem. Thus, adjusting insulin and other glucose-lowering therapy to reduce the frequency of all hypoglycemic episodes may be expected to also reduce the frequency of severe episodes and hypoglycemia unawareness. Further, to reduce the frequency of asymptomatic nocturnal hypoglycemia patients should periodically monitor their blood glucose levels at a time that corresponds with the peak action time of their bedtime insulin. Substituting a rapid-acting insulin analogue for human regular insulin at suppertime may prevent the delayed nighttime effect of regular insulin and reduce the risk of nocturnal hypoglycemia.

Evidence that the defects of hypoglycemia unawareness and defective glucose counter-regulation are potentially reversible by preventing any hypoglycemia derives from studies in patients with an insulinoma, in whom reversal occurs after removal of the insulinoma.[28] Moreover, in successful pancreas transplant patients, hypoglycemia-induced glucagon secretion and hepatic glucose production are normalized.[34] Many small before-after studies have explicitly tested the efficacy of avoidance of hypoglycemia for various lengths of time as a way of reducing hypoglycemia unawareness and/or improving the metabolic response to hypoglycemia. These have shown that strict avoidance of hypoglycemia for a period of 2 days to 3 years does indeed improve the recognition of severe hypoglycemia,[35,36] the counter-regulatory hormone responses,[37] or both[38–42] (Table 20–4). The most reproducible findings have been for the adrenergic symptoms. These data address the ability to detect hypoglycemia; unfortunately, there are no data on the impact of these measures on the frequency of severe hypoglycemia.

Blood glucose awareness training (BGAT) involves instruction in interpretation of physical symptoms, performance cues and moods, and feelings as internal cues to blood glucose awareness, as well as instructions on food, exercise, insulin dosage and action, time of day, and last blood glucose reading as external cues to estimate blood glucose level (see also Chapter 5 for a more detailed discussion of BGAT). Blood glucose awareness training has been shown to allow reduced-awareness subjects (these individuals, while having less awareness, did have some hypoglycemic symptoms) to detect a greater percentage of blood glucose levels < 3.9 mmol/L (from 35 to 45%, $p = .006$).[43] As above, these studies demonstrated an increased ability to detect hypoglycemia; the impact of BGAT in reducing the frequency of severe hypoglycemic events has not been reported.

The ingestion of caffeine has been shown to increase the sympathoadrenal and symptomatic responses during moderate hypoglycemia.[44] There are no data on the impact of caffeine consumption on the frequency of severe hypoglycemic episodes.

These data suggest that in patients with hypoglycemia unawareness, avoidance of hypoglycemic episodes by more frequent monitoring, a relaxation of glycemic goals, and novel approaches to patient education such as BGAT will restore hypoglycemia awareness and glucose

Table 20–4 Reversal of Counter-regulatory Defects and Symptom Unawareness by Avoidance of Hypoglycemia

Study	N	Duration	Glucagon Response	Epinephrine Response	Cortisol Response	Cognitive Dysfunction	Adrenergic Symptoms	Neuroglycopenic Symptoms
Fonelli et al[38]	21	6 mo	—	Y		Y	Y	Y
Dagogo-Jack et al[35]	12	3 d	—	—	—		Y*	Y
Dagogo-Jack et al[35]	12	3 wk	—	—	—		Y*	Y†
Dagogo-Jack et al[35]	12	3 mo	—	—	—		Y*	Y*
Fanelli et al[39]	16	2 wk	—	—	—	Y	—	—
Fanelli et al[39]	16	3 mo	Y	Y	Y	Y	Y	—
Fanelli et al[39]	16	1 y	Y	Y	Y	Y	Y	Y
Liu et al[40]	7	3 mo	—	Y	—	—	Y	Y
Davis et al[37]	5	3–5 mo		Y	—		—	
Lingenfelser et al[41]	16	2 d		Y	Y		Y	
Dagogo-Jack et al[36], Beregszaszi et al[31]	6	3 y post					Y	Y†
Fanelli et al[42]	8	2 wk	—	Y	Y	Y	—	—
Fanelli et al[42]	8	3 mo	Y	Y	Y	Y	Y	Y

*p < .01.
†p < .02.
Y = yes (p < .05); — = not significant; blank cells = not assessed.

counter-regulation. The unproven hope is that these approaches may result in a decreased frequency of severe hypoglycemic episodes and hypoglycemia unawareness.

EVIDENCE-BASED MESSAGES

1. In patients with Type 1 diabetes and hypoglycemia unawareness, strict avoidance of hypoglycemic episodes improves the ability to perceive hypoglycemia (Level 4).[35–42]
2. In patients with Type 1 diabetes and hypoglycemia unawareness, a program of blood glucose awareness training improves the ability to perceive hypoglycemia (Level 4).[43]

WHAT ARE THE LONG-TERM CONSEQUENCES OF HYPOGLYCEMIA?

The potential long-term complications of severe hypoglycemia, particularly the episodes with seizures or coma, have been a subject of concern. In addition to the transient reduction in cognitive function that can immediately affect performance during daily activities such as driving, the possibility of long-term brain damage has been feared in view of animal studies showing that such damage is possible.

Risk of Neuropsychologic Impairment in Adults

People with diabetes who have a history of severe hypoglycemia were found to have a decreased performance in various intellectual tests when compared to patients with diabetes without severe hypoglycemia and to subjects without diabetes. Patients with Type 1 diabetes with recurrent severe hypoglycemia scored lower than those without severe hypoglycemia in tests of motor ability,[45] short-term memory,[45,46] and performance intelligence quotient (IQ).[43,47,48] However, these retrospective studies could not differentiate between cause and effect.

Consequently, in the DCCT, neuropsychological assessments were done at baseline and at years 2, 5, 7 and at the end of the study. Intensive therapy, with its associated increase in the frequency of severe hypoglycemia, was not associated with neuropsychological impairments.[49] In a subanalysis in patients having had 1 to 5 episodes (n = 314) or > 5 episodes (n = 23) of coma or seizures, no difference compared to the group that had no episode of coma or seizure (n = 1,045) was revealed. These findings confirmed similar findings reported from the Stockholm Diabetes Intervention Study.[50]

These results are reassuring; nevertheless, the final answer will require longer-term studies. Efforts to minimize the occurrence of severe hypoglycemia should clearly be a priority in the intensive therapy of patients with diabetes.

EVIDENCE-BASED MESSAGE

In adult patients with Type 1 diabetes, intensified insulin therapy (and its associated higher frequency of hypoglycemia) does not appear to cause neuropsychological impairment (Level 2).[49,50]

Risk of Neuropsychological Impairment in Children

As for adults, the retrospective studies identified numerous defects in children or adolescents with diabetes, particularly those with early onset of diabetes. However, separating the effects of severe hypoglycemic episodes from the effects of diabetes per se is very difficult. Children with an early onset of diabetes (before 5 years of age) have been shown to have deficits in measures of intelligence, school achievement, visuospatial ability, memory, motor speed, and eye-hand coordination; however, no measurement of severe hypoglycemia was part of this study.[51] Some retrospective studies separated patients according to their past history of seizures. It was generally found that children with an early onset of diabetes with a history of seizures had worse deficits in visuospatial tests,[52] in psychomotor efficiency and attention,[53] on memory functioning,[54] and on verbal IQ.[55]

In a 1-year prospective study from diagnosis, lower scores in verbal ability were shown in those with an onset of diabetes before the age of 5, but no effect of severe hypoglycemia was found.[56] In a similar 2-year study, no changes were found after 3 months, but lower scores for general intelligence at 2 years were, particularly in those with an onset of the disease before the age of 5. Severe hypoglycemia was not assessed in this study.[57] In a 7-year prospective study on 16 subjects, children with hypoglycemic seizures had weaker perceptual-motor, attention, memory, and executive processing skills at the 7-year assessment. As this pattern was also seen in children with documented hippocampal damage, the authors suggested that hypoglycemia may cause damage in a specific way to the hippocampus. In this study, school achievement and sociobehavioral parameters were unaffected.[58] Finally, children at diagnosis were randomized to either intensive or conventional therapy and assessed an average of 2 years after diagnosis. Patients in the intensive group had three times more severe hypoglycemic events and exhibited a selective relative memory impairment, suggesting medial temporal dysfunction.[59]

These results have led to recommendations that extreme caution be exercised to avoid hypoglycemia in children (especially if < 5 years of age).

EVIDENCE-BASED MESSAGE

In children with Type 1 diabetes, intensified insulin therapy increases the risk of severe hypoglycemia and may cause neuropsychological impairment (Level 2).[59]

HOW IS HYPOGLYCEMIA TREATED?

The goals of hypoglycemia treatment are to detect and treat a low blood glucose level promptly by using an intervention that provides the fastest rise in blood glucose to a safe level, removing the risk of injury, and to relieve symptoms quickly while avoiding rebound hyperglycemia.

Therapy of an Acute Hypoglycemic Event in a Conscious Individual

Whereas 10 g of glucose administered at the time of an insulin reaction only briefly increases the blood glucose by 2 mmol/L, 20 g of glucose increases it by 3.6 mmol/L.[60] With 15 g of carbohydrate, the mean blood glucose levels 10 minutes after ingestion are similar with the use of tablets and the solutions of glucose, sucrose, or hydrolyzed polysaccharide. However, almost no increment is obtained at that time with the swallowed glucose gel (< 1 mmol/L) or the orange juice.[61] In another study, 20 g of milk were also shown to be insufficient compared to 20 g of carbohydrate as glucose tablets.[62]

Given these findings, it was recommended that patients with moderate hypoglycemia ingest 15 to 20 g of glucose as glucose tablets or sucrose solution and wait 20 minutes before retesting or electing to retreat themselves. If their blood glucose level has not by then increased by at least 1 mmol/L, patients should consider retreatment with another 20 g of glucose.[62]

Therapy of an Acute Hypoglycemic Event in an Unconscious Individual

For severe hypoglycemia with unconsciousness, 10 to 25 g of intravenous glucose over 1 to 3 minutes is the standard medical and paramedical treatment, despite the problems of intravenous access and risks of possible phlebitis.[63,64]

Glucagon 1 mg subcutaneously or intramuscularly will cause a prompt (in 15 minutes) increase in the blood glucose by 8.5 mmol/L, with a peak at 1 hour.[60] This should be the treatment of choice for the unconscious person in the home situation. In the home situation, support persons should be taught how to administer glucagon by injection.

Glucose gel must be swallowed to have an effect, and even then it is quite slow, with a < 1 mmol/L rise at 20 minutes. There is no evidence to support the practice of administering glucose gel buccally, since absorption through the mucosa is < 0.1 mg after a 15-g dose.[65]

Evidence-Based Messages

1. In a person with diabetes who has had a hypoglycemic reaction and is conscious, ingestion of 15 to 20 g of glucose tablets or sucrose solution increases blood glucose by 3.6 mmol/L (Level 4).[61,62]

2. In a person with diabetes who has had a hypoglycemic reaction and is unconscious, subcutaneous or intramuscular injection of 1 mg of glucagon increases blood glucose by 8.5 mmol/L (Level 4).[60]

Summary of Evidence-Based Messages

1. In patients with Type 2 diabetes, therapy with sulfonylureas or meglitinides (ie, insulin secretagogues) increases the risk of hypoglycemia and severe hypoglycemia more than therapy with diet alone, biguanides, thiazolidinediones, or α-glucosidase inhibitors (Level 1A).[1–10]

2. Intensive glycemic therapy with insulin increases the risk of severe hypoglycemia in people with Type 1 diabetes more than in people with Type 2 diabetes (Level 4).[11]

3. In people with Type 1 diabetes, intensified insulin therapy targeting euglycemia is associated with a threefold higher risk of hypoglycemia than is conventional insulin therapy targeting higher glucose levels (Level 1A).[13]

4. In people with Type 1 and Type 2 diabetes, insulin therapy using rapid-acting analogues to achieve glycemic control is associated with a lower risk of hypoglycemia than is therapy with regular insulin (Level 1A).[15–18]

5. In people with Type 1 diabetes, important risk factors for severe hypoglycemia include the following: a previous episode; longer diabetes duration; higher baseline and lower recent HbA_{1c}; higher baseline insulin dose; a history of hypoglycemia unawareness; and low residual beta-cell function (Level 1).[20–23]

6. In patients with Type 1 diabetes, evidence of autonomic neuropathy is a moderate risk factor for severe hypoglycemia (Level 1).[25]

7. In patients with Type 1 diabetes and hypoglycemia unawareness, strict avoidance of hypoglycemic episodes improves the ability to perceive hypoglycemia (Level 4).[35–42]

8. In patients with Type 1 diabetes and hypoglycemia unawareness, a program of blood glucose awareness training improves the ability to perceive hypoglycemia (Level 4).[43]

9. In adult patients with Type 1 diabetes, intensified insulin therapy (and its associated higher frequency of hypoglycemia) does not appear to cause neuropsychologic impairment (Level 2).[49,50]

10. In children with Type 1 diabetes, intensified insulin therapy increases the risk of severe hypoglycemia and may cause neuropsychological impairment (Level 2).[59]

11. In a person with diabetes who has had a hypoglycemic reaction and is conscious, ingestion of 15 to 20 g of glucose tablets or sucrose solution increases blood glucose by 3.6 mmol/L (Level 4).[61,62]

12. In a person with diabetes who has had a hypoglycemic reaction and is unconscious, subcutaneous or intramuscular injection of 1 mg of glucagon increases blood glucose by 8.5 mmol/L (Level 4).[60]

References

1. UK Prospective Diabetes Study Group. Intensive blood-glucose control with sulphonylureas or insulin compared with conventional treatment and risk of complications in patients with type 2 diabetes (UKPDS 33). Lancet 1998;352:837–53.

2. Tessier D, Dawson K, Tétralt JP, et al. Glibenclamide vs gliclazide in type 2 diabetes of the elderly. Diabet Med 1994;11:974–80.

3. Wofffenbuttel BHR, Landgraf R. A 1-year multicenter randomized double-blind comparison of repaglinide and glyburide for the treatment of type 2 diabetes. Diabetes Care 1999;22:463–7.

4. Damsbo P, Clauson P, Marbury TC, Windfeld K. A double-blind randomized comparison of meal-related glycemic control by repaglinide and glyburide in well-controlled type 2 diabetic patients. Diabetes Care 1999;22:789–94.

5. UK Prospective Diabetes Study (UKPDS) Group. Effect of intensive blood-glucose control with metformin on complications in overweight patients with type 2 diabetes (UKPDS 34). Lancet 1998;352:854–65.

6. De Fronzo RA, Goodman AM, and the Multicenter Metformin Study Group. Efficacy of metformin in patients with non-insulin-dependent diabetes mellitus. N Engl J Med 1995;333:541–9.

7. Iwamoto Y, Kosaka K, Kuzuya T, et al. Effects of troglitazone. A new hypoglycemic agent in patients with NIDDM poorly controlled by diet therapy. Diabetes Care 1996;19:151–6.

8. Charbonnel B, Lsnnqvist F, Jones NP, Abel MG. Rosiglitazone is superior to glyburide in reducing fasting plasma glucose after 1 year of treatment in type 2 diabetic patients. Diabetes 1999;48 (Suppl 1):A114.

9. Brockley MR, Schneider RL. The onset of blood glucose response in patients with type 2 diabetes treated with pioglitazone. Diabetes 2000;49 (Suppl 1):A99.

10. Chiasson JL, Josse RG, Hunt JA, et al. The efficacy of acarbose in the treatment of patients with non-insulin-dependent diabetes mellitus. Ann Intern Med 1994;121:928–35.

11. The DCCT Research Group. Hypoglycemia in the Diabetes Control and Complications Trial. Diabetes 1997;46:271–86.

12. Diabetes Control and Complications Trial Research Group. Effect of intensive diabetes treatment on the development and progression of long-term complications in adolescents with insulin-dependent diabetes mellitus: Diabetes Control and Complications Trial. J Pediatr 1994;125:177–88.

13. Egger M, Davey Smith G, Stettler C, Diem P. Risk of adverse effects of intensified treatment in insulin-dependent diabetes mellitus: a meta-analysis. Diabet Med 1997;14:919–28.

14. Nellemann Jorgensen L, Dejgaard A, Pramming SK. Human insulin and hypoglycemia: a literature survey. Diabet Med 1994;11:925–34.

15. Brunelle RL, Llewelyn J, Anderon JH, et al. Meta-analysis of the effect of insulin lispro on severe hypoglycemia in patients with type 1 diabetes. Diabetes Care 1998;21:1726–31.

16. Anderson JH, Brunelle RL, Koivisto VA, et al. Reduction of postprandial hyperglycemia and frequency of hypoglycemia in IDDM patients on insulin-analog treatment. Diabetes 1997;46:265–70.

17. Home PD, Lindholm A, Hylleberg B, Round P. Improved glycemic control with insulin aspart. Diabetes Care 1998;21:1904–9.

18. Anderson JH, Brunelle RL, Keohane P, et al. Mealtime treatment with insulin analog improves postprandial hyperglycemia and hypoglycemia in patients with non-insulin-dependent diabetes mellitus. Arch Intern Med 1997;157:1249–55.

19. Cryer PE. Banting lecture: hypoglycemia: the limiting factor in the management of IDDM. Diabetes 1994;43:1378–89.

20. The DCCT Research Group. Epidemiology of severe hypoglycemia in the diabetes control and complications trial. Am J Med 1991;90:450–9.

21. Daneman D, Frank M, Perlman K, et al. Severe hypoglycemia in children with insulin-dependent diabetes mellitus: frequency and predisposing factors. J Pediatr 1989;115:681–5.

22. Gold AE, MacLeod KM, Frier BM. Frequency of severe hypoglycemia in patients with type 1 diabetes with impaired awareness of hypoglycemia. Diabetes Care 1994;17:697–703.

23. Muhlhauser I, Overmann H, Bender R, et al. Risk factors of severe hypoglycemia in adult patients with Type 1 diabetes—a prospective population based study. Diabetologia 1998;41:1274–82.

24. Bolli G, De Feo P, Compagnucci P, et al. Abnormal glucose counterregulation in insulin-dependent diabetes mellitus. Interaction of anti-insulin antibodies and impaired glucagon and epinephrine secretion. Diabetes 1983;32:134–41.

25. Stephenson JM, Kempler P, Cavallo Perin P, et al. Is autonomic neuropathy a risk factor for severe hypoglycaemia ? The EURODIAB IDDM Complications Study. Diabetologia 1996;39:1372–6.

26. Meyer C, Grobmann R, Mitrakou A, et al. Effects of autonomic neuropathy on counterregulation and awareness of hypoglycemia in type 1 diabetic patients. Diabetes Care 1998;21:1960–6.

27. Ovalle F, Fanelli CG, Paramore DS, et al. Brief twice-weekly episodes of hypoglycemia reduce detection of clinical hypoglycemia in type 1 diabetes mellitus. Diabetes 1998;47:1472–9.

28. Mitrakou A, Fanelli C, Veneman T, et al. Reversibility of unawareness of hypoglycemia in patients with insulinomas. N Engl J Med 1993;329:834–9.

29. Boyle PJ, Kempers SF, O'Connor AM, Nagy RJ. Brain glucose uptake and unawareness of hypoglycemia in patients with insulin-dependent diabetes mellitus. N Engl J Med 1995;333:1726–31.

30. Vervoort G, Goldschmidt HMG, van Doorn LG. Nocturnal blood glucose profiles in patients with type 1 diabetes mellitus on multiple (≥ 4) daily insulin injection regimens. Diabet Med 1996;13:794–9.

31. Beregszaszi M, Tubiana-Rufi N, Benali K, et al. Nocturnal hypoglycemia in children and adolescents with insulin-dependent diabetes mellitus: prevalence and risk factors. J Pediatr 1997;131:27–33.

32. Gale EAM, Tattersall RB. Unrecognised nocturnal hypoglycaemia in insulin-treated diabetics. Lancet 1979:i:1049–52.

33. Jones TW, Porter P, Sherwin RS, et al. Decreased epinephrine responses to hypoglycemia during sleep. N Engl J Med 1998;338:1657–62.

34. Barrou Z, Seaquist ER, Robertson RP. Pancreas transplantation in diabetic humans normalizes hepatic glucose production during hypoglycemia. Diabetes 1994;43:661–6.

35. Dagogo-Jack S, Rattarasarn C, Cryer PE. Reversal of hypoglycemia unawareness, but not defective glucose counterregulation, in IDDM. Diabetes 1994;43:1426–34.

36. Dagogo-Jack S, Fanelli CG, Cryer PE. Durable reversal of hypoglycemia unawareness in type 1 diabetes. Diabetes Care 1999;22:866–7.

37. Davis M, Mellman M, Friedman S, et al. Recovery of epinephrine response but not hypoglycemic symptom threshold after intensive therapy in type 1 diabetes. Am J Med 1994;97:535–42.

38. Fanelli C, Pampanelli S, Lalli C, et al. Long-term intensive therapy of IDDM patients with clinically overt autonomic neuropathy. Effects on hypoglycemia unawareness and counterregulation. Diabetes 1997;46:1172–81.

39. Fanelli C, Pampanelli S, Epifano L, et al. Long-term recovery from unawareness, deficient counterregulation and lack of cognitive dysfunction during hypoglycaemia, following institution of rational, intensive insulin therapy in IDDM. Diabetologia 1994;37:1265–76.

40. Liu D, McManus RM, Ryan EA. Improved counter-regulatory hormonal and symptomatic responses to hypoglycemia in patients with insulin-dependent diabetes mellitus after 3 months of less strict glycemic control. Clin Invest Med 1996;19:71–82.

41. Lingenfelser T, Buettner U, Martin J, et al. Improvement of impaired counterregulatory hormone response and symptom perception by short-term avoidance of hypoglycemia in IDDM. Diabetes Care 1995;18:321–5.

42. Fanelli C, Epifano L, Rambotti AM, et al. Meticulous prevention of hypoglycemia normalizes the glycemic thresholds and magnitude of most of neuroendocrine responses to, symptoms of, and cognitive function during hypoglycemia in intensively treated patients with short-term IDDM. Diabetes 1993;42:1683–9.

43. Cox D, Gonder-Frederick L, Polonsky W, et al. A multicenter evaluation of blood glucose awareness training. II. Diabetes Care 1995;18:523–8.

44. Debrah K, Sherwin RS, Murphy J, Kerr D. Effect of caffeine on recognition of and physiological responses to hypoglycaemia in insulin-dependent diabetes. Lancet 1996;347:19–24.

45. Wredling R, Levander S, Adamson U, Lins PE. Permanent neuropsychological impairment after recurrent episodes of severe hypoglycaemia in man. Diabetologia 1990;33:152–7.

46. Sachon C, Grimaldi A, Digy JP, et al. Cognitive function, insulin-dependent diabetes and hypoglycaemia. J Intern Med 1992;231:471–5.

47. Langan SJ, Deary IJ, Hepburn DA, Frier BM. Cumulative cognitive impairment following recurrent severe hypoglycaemia in adult patients with insulin-treated diabetes mellitus. Diabetologia 1991;34:337–44.

48. Lincoln NB, Faleiro RM, Kelly C, et al. Effect of long-term glycemic control on cognitive function. Diabetes Care 1996;19:656–8.

49. The Diabetes Control and Complications Trial Research Group. Effects of intensive diabetes therapy on neuropsychological function in adults in the diabetes control and complications trial. Ann Intern Med 1996;124:379–88.

50. Reichard P, Pihl M. Mortality and treatment side-effects during long-term intensified conventional insulin treatment in the Stockholm Diabetes Intervention Study. Diabetes 1994;43:313–7.

51. Ryan C, Vega A, Drash A. Cognitive deficits in adolescents who developed diabetes early in life. Pediatrics 1985;5:921–7.

52. Rovet JF, Ehrlich RM, Hoppe M. Intellectual deficits associated with early onset of insulin-dependent diabetes mellitus in children. Diabetes Care 1987;10:510–5.

53. Bjorgaas M, Gimse R, Vik T, Sand T. Cognitive function in type 1 diabetic children with and without episodes of severe hypoglycaemia. Acta Pediatr 1997;86:148–53.

54. Hershey T, Craft S, Bhargava N, White NH. Memory and insulin dependent diabetes mellitus: effects of childhood onset and severe hypoglycemia. J Int Neuropsychol Soc 1997;3:509–20.

55. Rovet J, Alvarez M. Attentional functioning in children and adolescents with IDDM. Diabetes Care 1997;20:803–10.

56. Rovet JF, Ehrlich RM, Czuchta D. Intellectual characteristics of diabetic children at diagnosis and one year later. J Pediatr Psychol 1990;15:775–88.

57. Northam EA, Anderson PJ, Werther GA, et al. Neuropsychological complications of IDDM in children 2 years after disease onset. Diabetes Care 1998;21:379–84.

58. Rovet JF, Ehrlich RM. The effect of hypoglycemic seizures on cognitive function in children with diabetes: a 7-year prospective study. J Pediatr 1999;134:503–6.

59. Hershey T, Bhargava N, Sadler M, et al. Conventional versus intensive diabetes therapy in children with type 1 diabetes. Diabetes Care 1999;22:1318–24.

60. Wiethop BV, Cryer PE. Alanine and terbutaline in treatment of hypoglycemia in IDDM. Diabetes Care 1993;16:1131–6.

61. Slama G, Traynard PY, Desplanque N, et al. The search for an optimized treatment of hypoglycemia. Arch Intern Med 1990;150:589–93.

62. Brodows RG, Williams C, Amatruda JM. Treatment of insulin reactions in diabetics. JAMA 1984;252:3378–81.

63. MacCuish AC. Treatment of hypoglycemia. In: Hypoglycemia and diabetes. Frier BM, Fisher BM, editors. London: Edward Arnold; 1993. p. 212–21.

64. Weston C, Stephens M. Hypoglycaemic attacks treated by ambulance personnel with extended training. BMJ 1990;300:908–9.

65. Gunning RR, Garber AJ. Bioactivity of instant glucose. Failure of absorption through oral mucosa. JAMA 1978;240:1611–2.

66. Hepburn DA. Symptoms of hypoglycaemia. In: Hypoglycemia and diabetes. Frier BM, Fisher BM, editors. London: Edward Arnold; 1993. p. 93–103.

Eye Disease

Iain S. Begg, MB, FRCS (Edin), FRCS(C), FRCOphth,
and Michael Schulzer, MD, PhD

ABSTRACT

Diabetes mellitus is a risk factor for serious eye disease that can lead to blindness. Diabetic retinopathy (proliferative retinopathy and macular edema) accounts for 12.4% of all blindness in North America in the age group 20 to 74 years. Proliferative retinopathy affects 23% of patients with Type 1 diabetes, 14% of patients with Type 2 diabetes taking insulin, and 3% of people with Type 2 diabetes not taking insulin; macular edema occurs in 11%, 15%, and 4% of these groups, respectively. Intensive therapy of both elevated blood glucose and elevated blood pressure and the use of ACE inhibitors can reduce diabetic retinopathy progression. Blindness from proliferative diabetic retinopathy is largely preventable by scatter laser treatment and vitrectomy. The rate of moderate visual loss due to clinically significant macular edema is halved by focal/grid laser treatment, but blindness is only reduced by about one-third and significant visual improvement is infrequent, despite a resolution of retinal thickening. Although surgical interventions can improve the visual prognosis after significant eye disease develops, the fact that they are not effective in all patients emphasizes the importance of implementing known preventive interventions and testing new ones.

INTRODUCTION

Diabetes mellitus is a risk factor for other diseases, often termed "complications," that impose major health problems. Blindness, one of the long-term complications, is a very high burden to individuals with diabetes and to society in general, and is the most feared of all complications. Diabetes-associated eye diseases are listed in Table 21–1.

Table 21–1 Eye Diseases in Diabetes Mellitus

Microvascular	Macrovascular	Age-Related Conditions	Neuro-degenerative
Nonproliferative retinopathy	Nonarteritic anterior ischemic optic neuropathy[13,14]	Cataracts	Wolfram syndrome[25,26]
Macular edema		Reduced amplitude of accommodation[15,16]	
Proliferative retinopathy		Preretinal fibrosis[17]	
Iris neovascularization		Ocular hypertension[18]	
Neovascular glaucoma[9,10]		˙Primary open-angle glaucoma[18–23]	
Diabetic papillopathy[11]		Corneal disease[24]	
Ocular motor palsies[12]			

˙Evidence is conflicting.

Data from Nielson,[9] Sjolie,[10] Regillo et al,[11] Jacobson et al,[12] Hayreh et al,[13] Jacobson et al,[14] Moss et al,[15] Braun et al,[16] Mitchell et al,[17] Mitchell et al,[18] Klein et al,[19] Dielemans et al,[20] Kahn et al,[21] Leske et al,[22] Leske et al,[23] Sanchez-Thorin et al,[24] Kinsley et al,[25] Barrett et al.[26]

Diabetic retinopathy (proliferative retinopathy and macular edema) is a microvascular disease that is the commonest cause of new cases of legal blindness (12.49%) in North America in the age group 20 to 74 years.[1] Proliferative retinopathy affects 23% of patients with Type 1 diabetes, 14% of patients with Type 2 diabetes taking insulin, and 3% of people with Type 2 diabetes not taking insulin[2]; macular edema affects 11%, 15%, and 4% of these groups, respectively.[3] The incidence of proliferative retinopathy is greatest in people with Type 1 diabetes, whereas the incidence of macular edema is greatest in people with Type 2 diabetes.[4] The progression of retinopathy can be largely prevented by good blood glucose and blood pressure control,[5,6] ideally initiated as early as possible. Timely laser treatment of severe proliferative retinopathy and macular edema can stop or ameliorate progression to vision loss.[7,8]

Several schemes have been used to classify retinopathy. Nevertheless, the main outcome measures of retinopathy used in epidemiologic studies and controlled clinical trials have become the language for communication regarding retinopathy worldwide (Table 21–2). Moreover, progression, as defined by the Early Treatment Diabetic Retinopathy Study (ETDRS) scale of retinopathy severity (Table 21–3), is recognized by the scientific community as a clinically important outcome measure.

Evidence supporting conclusions related to the prognosis, diagnosis, prevention, and therapy of diabetes-related eye disease is presented below. Where appropriate, published data were used to calculate the clinical significance of therapeutic trials both in terms of relative risk reduction and absolute reduction or "number needed to treat" to prevent one event; these indices allow the clinician to compare the efficacy of therapeutic trials with similar outcome measures. Using this approach, the following questions are answered in this chapter:

1. What causes visual impairment in diabetes?
2. What is diabetic retinopathy?
3. How can eye disease (diabetic retinopathy) be screened for?
4. Does glycemic control prevent or delay the risk of eye disease?
5. What nonglycemic therapies can prevent/treat eye disease?
6. What is the efficacy of surgical therapy in diabetic retinopathy?

WHAT CAUSES VISUAL IMPAIRMENT IN DIABETES?

Retinopathy and cataract are complications of diabetes that may lead to visual impairment (visual acuity in the better eye ≤ 20/40) and blindness (visual acuity in the better eye ≤ 20/200). Whether or not the risk of chronic open-angle glaucoma is higher in people with diabetes than in nondiabetic people remains unclear.[18–23] Cataracts are the most common cause of severe visual loss in people with Type 2 diabetes and are second to proliferative retinopathy in Type 1 diabetes.[27] Loss of vision due to retinopathy is more likely to be associated with proliferative retinopathy in Type 1 diabetes and with macular edema in Type 2 diabetes.[27]

In proliferative diabetic retinopathy, new vessels and glial proliferation develop on the surface of the optic disc and retina between the internal limiting membrane and posterior vitreous cortex and into the posterior vitreous cortex. Any displacement of the vitreous cortex due to eye movement, trauma, or vitreous detachment transmits traction to the new blood vessels, which may result in sudden and severe visual loss from vitreous hemorrhage, distortion of the macula, cystic degeneration, traction retinoschisis, and traction retinal detachment.[28]

In macular edema, nonperfusion of capillaries and arterioles cause ischemia and breakdown of the blood retinal barrier, with leakage of macromolecules followed by influx of edema into the outer plexiform layer and, to a lesser degree, in the inner nuclear layer, due to osmotic effect.[29] As a result, there is necrosis of neuronal cells, proliferation of endothelial cells to form microaneurysms, edema accumulation that thickens the retina, and leakage deposit of lipoprotein that appears as hard exudate.[30] Loss of vision is caused by scattering of light by

Table 21–2 Main Outcome Measures of Retinopathy in Epidemiologic Studies and Clinical Trials

Outcome Measure	Definition
No retinopathy	
Any retinopathy	
Worsening of retinopathy	2 steps on ETDRS scale: single severity level per eye
	3 steps on expanded ETDRS scale (sustained at consecutive 6-month visits): overall retinopathy severity both eyes
Progression to proliferative retinopathy (PDR)	
High-risk proliferative retinopathy (HR-PDR)	NVD > ⅓ disk area with or without vitreous hemorrhage
	NVD < ⅓ disk area with vitreous hemorrhage
	NVE of moderate or greater severity with vitreous hemorrhage
Macular edema	Retinal thickening or hard exudate within 1-disk diameter of the center
Clinically significant macular edema (CSME)	One or more of the following: • retinal thickening at or within 500 microns of the centre of the macula
	• hard exudate at or within 500 microns of the center of the macula with adjacent retinal thickening
	• retinal thickening measuring 1-disk area or larger in extent, any part of which is within 1-disk diameter of the center of the macula
Visual acuity	Number of letters correctly identified on the ETDRS visual acuity scale at a standard distance, usually 4 meters
Moderate visual loss	Doubling of initial visual angle (3 lines [15 letters] on the ETDRS visual acuity chart)
Severe visual loss (SVL)	Visual acuity < 5/200 at 2 consecutively completed 4-month follow-up visits
Severe visual loss or vitrectomy	

ETDRS = Early Treatment Diabetic Retinopathy Study; NVD = new vessels on the optic disk; NVE = new vessels elsewhere.

the edematous cystic retina, surface wrinkling, and neuronal degeneration. When hard exudate accumulates as an opaque subretinal plaque within the fovea, blindness often results from neuronal degeneration and the development of a fibrovascular scar.[31,32]

Prevalence of Visual Impairment and Blindness

In the population-based study in Southern Wisconsin using standardized protocols for measuring visual acuity, the frequency of any visual impairment in people with diabetes was 7.8%. The prevalence of legal blindness was 3.6% in people with Type 1 diabetes and 1.6% in people with Type 2 diabetes.[27] Among people with Type 1 diabetes, 22% had visual impair-

Table 21–3 Abbreviated Early Treatment Diabetic Retinopathy Study Final Scale of Retinopathy Severity for Individual Eyes

Level	Severity	Definition
10	No retinopathy	Diabetic retinopathy absent
20	Very mild NPDR	Microaneurysms only
35	Mild NPDR	Microaneurysms plus hard exudates, soft exudates (cotton-wool spots), and/or mild retinal hemorrhages
43	Moderate NPDR	Microaneurysms plus mild IRMA or moderate retinal hemorrhages
47	Moderately severe NPDR	More extensive IRMA, severe retinal hemorrhages, or venous beading in 1 quadrant only
53 A–D	Severe NPDR	Severe retinal hemorrhages in 4 quadrants, or venous beading in at least 2 quadrants, or moderate-to-severe IRMA in at least 1 quadrant
53 E	Very severe NPDR	2 level 53 A–D characteristics
61	Mild PDR	NVE < $\frac{1}{2}$ disk area in 1 or more quadrants
65	Moderate PDR	NVE = $\frac{1}{2}$ disk area in 1 or more quadrants, or NVD = $\frac{1}{4}$–$\frac{1}{3}$ disk area
71,75	High-risk PDR	NVD > $\frac{1}{3}$ disk area with or without vitreous hemorrhage NVD < $\frac{1}{3}$ disk area with vitreous hemorrhage NVE of moderate or greater severity with vitreous hemorrhage
81, 85	Advanced PDR	Fundus partially obscured by vitreous hemorrhage and either new vessels ungradable or retina detached at the center of the macula

NPDR = nonproliferative diabetic retinopathy; PDR = proliferative diabetic retinopathy; IRMA = intraretinal microvascular abnormalities; NVE = new vessels elsewhere; NVD = new vessels on the optic disk.
Data from the Early Treatment Diabetic Retinopathy Study Research Group,[50] Davis, et al.[53]

ment after 30 or more years of diabetes, whereas among people with Type 2 diabetes, 30% were visually impaired and 7% were legally blind after 20 to 24 years of diabetes. Proliferative retinopathy and macular edema were partially or totally responsible for blindness in 80% of eyes in people with Type 1 diabetes and in 33% of eyes in people with Type 2 diabetes. In the latter, macular degeneration, cataract, and glaucoma were responsible in 49% of eyes.[27] By comparison, in the clinic-based EURODIAB IDDM Complications Study, 2.3% of 3,250 patients aged 15 to 60 years were blind.[33] In a sample of African-Americans with Type 1 diabetes obtained from hospital admissions in New Jersey, 11% were visually impaired and 3.1% of patients were legally blind, and diabetic retinopathy was responsible for 90.9% of the blindness.[34] The prevalence of blindness due to diabetic retinopathy was similar for African-Americans (5%) and Caucasians (6%) with Type 2 diabetes in the geographically defined population-based Baltimore Eye Study,[35] although the overall rate of visual impairment was higher in African-Americans.[36]

Table 21–4 Ten-Year Incidence of Vision Impairment and Blindness

	Type 1		Type 2 Taking Insulin		Type 2 Not Taking Insulin	
	No. at Risk	%	No. at Risk	%	No. at Risk	%
Moderate visual loss	880	9.2	472	32.8	494	21.4
Incidence of visual impairment*	832	9.4	423	37.2	454	23.9
Incidence of blindness	868	1.8	465	4.0	490	4.8

*20/40 or less in the better eye.

Data from Moss SE, Klein R, Klein BEK. Ten-year incidence of visual loss in a diabetic population. Ophthalmology 1994;101:106–70.

Incidence of Visual Impairment and Blindness

In the Wisconsin Epidemiologic Study Diabetic Retinopathy (WESDR), the estimated annual incidence rate of blindness due to diabetes was 3.3 per 100,000 population.[37] Table 21–4 shows the 10-year incidence.[38] The risk factors for the incidence of vision loss in the three groups were older age, poorer initial visual acuity, more severe retinopathy, and the presence of macular edema. In people with Type 1 diabetes and insulin-taking Type 2 diabetes, the risk factors were duration of diabetes, presence of proteinuria, and higher glycosylated hemoglobin.[37]

EVIDENCE-BASED MESSAGE

The risk of blindness due to diabetes is 3.3 per 100,000 population (Level 1).[37]

Does Diabetes Increase the Risk of Cataract?

Nuclear cataract, cortical spokes, and posterior subcapular cataracts occur in the diabetic and nondiabetic lens. Loss of vision is due to scattering and nonpenetrance of light. In two population-based studies, Framingham Eye Study and the US National Health and Nutrition Examination Survey, people with diabetes aged 50 to 65 years had higher rates of cataract or cataract extraction than those without diabetes (relative risk [RR] 4.2 and 2.97, respectively).[39] In people with Type 2 diabetes compared with people without diabetes in the Beaver Dam Study, there was increased risk of cortical opacity but not other types of lens opacities (odds ratio [OR] 1.72, 95% confidence interval [CI] 1.29 to 2.30) and increased frequency of cataract surgery (OR 2.01, 95% CI 1.43 to 2.82).[40] "Cortical only" opacities were significantly more common in Black diabetic persons, with increased frequency in people under age 60 than over age 60.[41] In the WESDR, the prevalence of cataract and surgical aphakia increased with age in both Type 1 and Type 2 diabetes and was higher in females than males.[42] The overall rate was 27% for Type 1 diabetes and 86% for Type 2 diabetes.[27] The risk for incident cortical and nuclear cataract increased with increasing age and increasing hemoglobin A_{1c} level.[43]

Cataract extraction is frequently performed in a diabetic population, as shown by the 10-year cumulative incidence in the WESDR (8.3%, 95% CI 6.2 to 10.8%) in people with Type 1 diabetes, and 24.9% (95% CI 21.3 to 28.5%) in Type 2 diabetes.[44] Compared with the nondiabetic population, cataract progressed to a level requiring surgery at an earlier age in each age group.[44,45] Risk factors for undergoing cataract extraction were age, retinopathy severity, and proteinuria in people with Type 1 diabetes, and age and use of insulin in those with Type 2 diabetes.[44] In the WESDR's baseline examination (1980 to 1982) the visual outcome of cataract surgery was poor: visual acuity was better than 20/40 in 44% of aphakic eyes in people with Type 1 diabetes and in 55% of aphakic eyes in people with Type 2 diabetes.[27] Endophthalmitis is uncommon (0.072%, 95% CI 0.043 to 0.12%) for 23,625 eyes undergoing extracapsular procedures but more frequent among diabetic patients (0.163%) compared with nondiabetic patients (0.055%).[46]

Does extracapsular cataract extraction (or phacoemulsification) with placement of posterior chamber lens contribute to the progression of nonproliferative diabetic retinopathy? In a prospective study on 223 treated eyes compared with unoperated fellow eyes, similar proportions of development and progression of retinopathy were shown and no adverse effect of capsular opening on retinopathy among eyes requiring Nd:YAG capsulotomy over 6 months.[47]

EVIDENCE-BASED MESSAGES

1. Diabetes and the level of hyperglycemia increase the risk of cataract (Level 1).[42,43]
2. Extracapsular cataract extraction has no significant adverse effects on retinopathy (Level 2).[47]

WHAT IS DIABETIC RETINOPATHY?

People with diabetes may develop several retinal lesions, primarily because hyperglycemia causes metabolic defects in capillary endothelium. When these are present and characteristically distributed in the posterior and midperipheral fundus, an individual is diagnosed with diabetic retinopathy. Table 21–5 provides a brief list of the characteristic lesions of diabetic retinopathy.

Classification of Diabetic Retinopathy

It is most important that a careful assessment of the severity of retinopathy be conducted to predict the visual prognosis of the patient. Studies of eyes assigned to deferral of photocoagulation in large clinical trials (Table 21–6) have documented the characteristics and natural history of diabetic retinopathy over long periods. Using an array of seven color stereoscopic fundus photographs as the gold standard,[48] lesions of retinopathy were graded separately and evaluated as risk factors for the progression of retinopathy, the occurrence of severe visual loss (SVL), and the combined outcome of SVL or vitrectomy.[48–53] These data were used to develop the ETDRS Retinopathy Severity Scale (see Table 21–3), which predicts the risk of progression to proliferative diabetic retinopathy (PDR) or high-risk PDR

Table 21–5 Principal Diabetic Retinopathy Lesions

Hemorrhages and/or microaneurysms

Hard exudates

Soft exudates

Intraretinal microvascular abnormalities (IRMAs)

Venous beading

New vessels on or within 1-disk diameter of the disk (NVD)

New vessels elsewhere (NVE)

Preretinal hemorrhage

Vitreous hemorrhage

Macular retinal thickening (edema)

Macular hard exudate rings

Macular confluent plaque of hard exudate, organized exudate, or subretinal scar

Clinically significant macular edema (CSME)

Table 21–6 Multicenter Controlled Clinical Trials

Study	Criteria for Enrolment	Endpoint
DRS	Severe nonproliferative retinopathy in both eyes or proliferative retinopathy in at least one eye	SVL
ETDRS	Mild to severe nonproliferative retinopathy or mild to moderate proliferative retinopathy	2-step progression SVL SVL plus vitrectomy Doubling of initial visual angle
	Mild NPDR with macular edema to moderate or severe NPDR or early PDR with or without macular edema	Mortality Cardiovascular disease HR-PDR Vitreous hemorrhage Cataract
DRVS	Recent nonclearing vitreous hemorrhage	VA ≥ 10/20 VA > 10/50 NLP
	Advanced active PDR	VA ≥ 10/20 VA < 5/200 NLP
DCCT	No retinopathy Very mild to moderate NPDR	≥ 3-step progression ≥ 3-step progression
UKPDS	No retinopathy Very mild to moderate NPDR	Microvascular disease Retinal photocoagulation Vitreous hemorrhage Blind in one eye Cataract extraction 2-step progression Doubling of initial visual angle

DRS = Diabetic Retinopathy Study; ETDRS = Early Treatment Diabetic Retinopathy Study; DRVS = Diabetic Retinopathy Vitrectomy Study; DCCT = Diabetes Control and Complications Trial; UKPDS = United Kingdom Prospective Diabetic Study; NPDR = nonproliferative diabetic retinopathy; PDR = proliferative diabetic retinopathy; SVL = severe visual loss; HR-PDR = high-risk proliferative retinopathy; VA = visual acuity; NLP = no light perception.

(HR-PDR).[48–50,54,55] For example, using this scale, the 1- and 3-year risk of HR-PDR increases with increasing severity category (Table 21–7). Moreover, when used to classify patients by overall retinopathy severity for both eyes, this scale predicts a clinically significant change in the severity of retinopathy (ie, three or more steps).[50]

The baseline severity of retinopathy strongly predicts the prognosis.[53,56–58] Characteristics of nonproliferative diabetic retinopathy on color fundus photographs that predicted progression to proliferative retinopathy were the severity of intraretinal microvascular abnormalities, hemorrhages and/or microaneurysms, and venous beading.[50,53] Hard exudates were not a significant risk factor for progression to PDR. Retinopathy risk factors for the 2-year risk of developing severe visual loss in untreated eyes are (1) presence of vitreous or pre-retinal hemorrhage, (2) presence of new vessels, (3) location of new vessels on or within 1-disk diameter of the optic disk, and (4) severity of new vessels (moderate or severe) as

Table 21–7 Progression to Proliferative Diabetic Retinopathy and High-Risk Diabetic Retinopathy by Baseline Retinopathy Severity

Severity Level ETDRS Scale	PDR 1 Year (% Eyes)	High-Risk PDR 1 Year (% Eyes)	High-Risk PDR 3 Year (% Eyes)
Mild NPDR	4.5	1.2	6.5
Moderate NPDR	12.2	3.6	13.3
Moderately severe NPDR	26.0	8.1	24.7
Severe NPDR	51.5	17.1	44.4
Mild PDR	—	21.5	52.8

ETDRS = Early Treatment Diabetic Retinopathy Study Research Group; NPDR = nonproliferative diabetic retinopathy; PDR = proliferative diabetic retinopathy.

Data from The Early Treatment Diabetic Retinopathy Study Research Group. Fundus photographic risk factors for progression of retinopathy. ETDRS Report No. 12. Ophthalmology 1991;98 (Suppl):823–33.

defined[51] (Table 21–8). Three or four of these risk factors defined eyes with high-risk characteristics for severe visual loss, of which the presence and extent of new vessels on the optic disk had the strongest association.[52] Untreated eyes with high-risk proliferative retinopathy are at very high risk of blindness. In the refined ETDRS Final Scale of Retinopathy Severity,

Table 21–8 Retinopathy Risk Factors for 2-Year Risk of Developing Severe Visual Loss

Hemorrhage Present?	New Vessels Present?	New Vessels on or Near Disk (NVD)?	New Vessels Moderate or Severe?	Number of Risk Factors	Rate (%)	Standard Error
☐	☐	☐	☐	0	3.6	1.3
■	☐	☐	☐	1	4.2	4.1
☐	■	☐	☐	1	6.8	2.2
■	■	☐	☐	2	6.4	6.2
☐	■	☐	■	2	6.9	2.2
■	■	☐	■	3	29.7	6.1
☐	■	■	☐	2	10.5	2.7
■	■	■	☐	3	25.6	5.9
☐	■	■	■	3	26.2	3.1
■	■	■	■	4	36.9	4.2

Risk Factors (■ = yes; ☐ = no) / 2-Year Incidence of Severe Visual Loss in Untreated Eyes

Data from The Diabetic Retinopathy Study Research Group. Four risk factors for severe visual loss in diabetic retinopathy. Arch Ophthalmol 1979;97:654–5.

the difference in cumulative annual incidence rates between steps 1 and 6 was approximately 60-fold at 1 year (0.8% and 48.5%, respectively).[53]

EVIDENCE-BASED MESSAGES

1. The ETDRS Final Scale of Retinopathy Severity in Table 21–3 clearly predicts progression to proliferative retinopathy and high-risk proliferative retinopathy and to the combined outcome of severe visual loss or vitrectomy (Level 1).[50,53]
2. The severity of intraretinal microvascular abnormalities, microaneurysms, and/or hemorrhages and venous beading predicts progression to proliferation (Level 1).[50,53]
3. Three or four retinopathy risk factors in Table 21–8 define eyes with high-risk characteristics for severe visual loss (Level 1).[51]

Rates of Any Diabetic Retinopathy

The WESDR carefully assembled the geographically defined cohort and followed it over time.[59] Seven-field stereo fundus photography was used to detect retinopathy. This study analyzed three cohorts: (1) people with diabetes developing before age 30 and taking insulin (defined as equivalent to Type 1 diabetes); (2) people with diabetes developing after age 30 and taking insulin (Type 2 diabetes); and (3) people with diabetes developing after age 30 and not on insulin (Type 2 diabetes). In people with Type 1 diabetes, the frequency of any retinopathy increased sharply from 2% in those who had had diabetes for < 3 years to 98% in those who had had it for ≥ 15 years.[60] In people with Type 2 diabetes, the distribution of retinopathy was different in the insulin-taking and non–insulin-taking groups (Table 21–9). In the former, the prevalence rose from 30% within 3 years of the diagnosis of diabetes to reach 84.5% at duration of 15 years. In the latter, the prevalence rose from 23 to 57.5% at duration of diabetes of 15 years.[61] The prevalence of moderate nonproliferative retinopathy or worse severity was greater in insulin users than in noninsulin users (Table 21–10).[4] The 10-year incidence is shown in Table 21–11.[56,63] The estimated annual incidence during the first 4 years and the next 6 years is shown in Table 21–12.[63]

Can duration of diabetes be used as a diagnostic tool for detecting the presence of retinopathy? We used WESDR data[60] to estimate the sensitivity and specificity of diagnosing the presence of any retinopathy in people with Type 1 diabetes on the basis of different cutpoints of duration of diabetes. The results are summarized graphically in the receiver operating characteristic (ROC) curve in Figure 21–1. The optimal cutoff for the presence of retinopathy appears to be at 10 years, where sensitivity is 77.4% (standard error [SE] 1.6%), while the false-positive rate is low at 11.3% (SE 1.8%). The further gain in specificity using a 15-year cutoff rather than a 10-year cutoff is quite minor (gain of 7%) and offset by considerable loss in sensitivity (loss of 21%).

Table 21–9 Prevalence of Retinopathy by Duration of Diabetes

	Any Retinopathy (%)		PDR (%)			CSME (%)	
			Duration of Diabetes				
	< 3y	15 y+	< 3y	15 y	20 y+	< 3 y	20 y
Type 1	2	98	0	26	53	0	12
Type 2 taking insulin	30	85	4	20	20	5	14
Type 2 not taking insulin	23	60	2.3	4	5	3	12

PDR = proliferative diabetic retinopathy; CSME = clinically significant macular edema.
Data from Klein et al.[60,61]

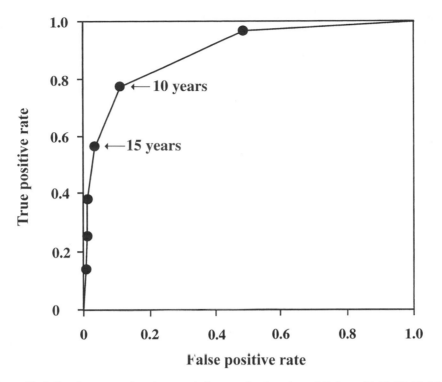

Figure 21–1 Receiver operating characteristic curve for duration of diabetes (5, 10, 15, 20, 25, 30 years) as a risk for retinopathy.

EVIDENCE-BASED MESSAGES

1. The duration of both Type 1 and Type 2 diabetes is a risk factor for diabetic retinopathy (Level 1).[60,61]
2. Diabetes duration of 10 years has 77.4% sensitivity for detecting the presence of retinopathy in Type 1 diabetes (Level 1).[60]

Rates of Proliferative Diabetic Retinopathy

In people with Type 1 diabetes, the frequency of proliferative retinopathy at 6, 10, 15, and 35 years was 0%, 4%, 26%, and 67%, respectively. After 15 years of diabetes, about 10% of people had HR-PDR, and an additional 10% had the most severe phase of retinopathy after 18 years.[60] In people with Type 2 diabetes, proliferative retinopathy was present early after the diagnosis of diabetes (see Table 21–9). In people with Type 2 diabetes taking insulin, the prevalence rose from 4% after diagnosis to reach 20% at duration of diabetes of 15 years.[61] In the non–insulin-taking group, the prevalence rose from 2.3 to 4.3% at duration of diabetes of 15 years. The prevalence of retinopathy by severity level is shown in Table 21–10.[4] The 10-year incidence is shown in Table 21–11.[56] The estimated annual incidence is shown in Table 21–12.[56] Although the highest 10-year incidence rates of retinopathy and proliferative retinopathy occur in people with Type 1 diabetes, the much higher frequency of Type 2 diabetes in the general population results in higher absolute numbers of people with Type 2 diabetes who are affected by diabetic retinopathy[62] (Level 1).

Prevalence and Incidence of Macular Edema in People with Diabetes Mellitus

The prevalence of clinically significant macular edema (CSME, defined in Table 21–2) is shown in Table 21–10.[4] In people with Type 2 diabetes, the overall prevalence rate of macular edema is 15% and in Type 1 diabetes 5.9%.[3] In all groups of diabetes, the frequency of

Table 21–10 Prevalence of Retinopathy by Severity Level

Retinopathy Severity	Type 1	Type 2 Taking Insulin	Type 2 Not Taking Insulin
None	29.3	29.9	61.3
Very mild and mild NPDR	30.4	30.6	27.3
Moderate-to-severe NPDR	17.6	25.7	8.5
Proliferative			
Mild to moderate	13.2	9.1	1.4
High risk	9.5	4.8	1.4
Clinically significant macular edema	5.9	11.6	3.7

NPDR = nonproliferative diabetic retinopathy.
Data from Klein R. Diabetic retinopathy. Annu Rev Public Health 1996;17:137–58.

macular edema increases with increasing duration of diabetes. In people with Type 1 diabetes, the prevalence rises from 0% in those with diabetes less than 5 years to 32% in persons with 22 to 24 years of diabetes. In people with Type 2 diabetes, macular edema is sometimes found during the first few years of diabetes. Macular edema was predominantly unilateral at the WESDR baseline examination, was more likely to be accompanied by PDR (65%) than in persons with Type 2 diabetes not using insulin (19%), and was less likely to be associated with hard exudates (2% versus 18%) and legal blindness (2% versus 9%).[3] The 10-year incidence of macular edema and CSME is shown in Table 21–11[63] and the estimated annual incidence in Table 21–12.[63]

EVIDENCE-BASED MESSAGE

People with Type 2 diabetes on insulin have a much higher risk of clinically significant macular edema than do people with Type 1 diabetes (Level 1).[63]

Table 21–11 Ten-Year Incidence of any Retinopathy, Progression of Retinopathy, Progression to Proliferative Retinopathy, Macular Edema, Clinically Significant Macular Edema

	Type 1		Type 2 Taking Insulin		Type 2 Not Taking Insulin	
	No. at Risk	%	No. at Risk	%	No. at Risk	%
Incidence of any retinopathy	261	89.3	146	79.2	301	66.9
Progression	712	75.8	417	68.7	487	52.9
Progression to proliferative retinopathy	712	29.8	417	23.6	487	9.7
Incidence of macular edema	688	20.1	329	25.4	444	13.9
Incidence of clinically significant macular edema	688	13.6	329	17.6	444	9.2

Data from Klein et al.[56,63]

Table 21–12 Estimates of Average Incidence, Progression to Proliferative Diabetic Retinopathy, and Progression to Macular Edema

	Type 1 (%)	Type 2 Taking Insulin (%)	Type 2 Not Taking Insulin (%)	Type 2 All (%)
Incidence per year				
First 4 y	20.0	14.8	10.2	—
Next 6 y	19.0	14.8	10.1	—
Progression to PDR				
First 4 y	2.7	2.0	0.6	—
Next 6 y	4.0	3.2	1.3	—
Progression to macular edema				
First 4 y	2.3	—	—	1.4
Next 6 y	2.0	—	—	2.4

PDR = progressive diabetic retinopathy.
Data from Klein et al.[56,63]

Prevalence of Diabetic Retinopathy in People with Undiagnosed Type 2 Diabetes

In Type 2 diabetes, retinopathy, including vision-threatening retinopathy, may be present within 3 years of the time of diagnosis (see Table 21–9). This is likely due to a long history of undiagnosed diabetes during which retinopathy develop,[64] and is highlighted by the fact that among people with newly diagnosed diabetes discovered by testing blood glucose in a recent cross-sectional screening study, the prevalence of retinopathy was 10.2%. Only 2% of people had CSME, and none had PDR; in the group with retinopathy, moderate nonproliferative retinopathy or worse degrees of retinopathy were present in 36%.[65] The fact that the prevalence of retinopathy is higher (21%) in people discovered to have Type 2 diabetes by their physician during a routine physical examination or when they attended with symptoms of diabetes,[61] further supports the conclusion that retinopathy is developing during the period of undiagnosed diabetes. The age-adjusted prevalence of retinopathy at diagnosis increases with the serum glucose level (see "Does Glycemic Control Prevent or Delay the Risk of Eye Disease?" below).[66–68] There is also a higher frequency of retinopathy found among people on insulin (30%) compared with those on oral agents or diet (23%).[61]

What Is the Prevalence of Lesions Typical of Diabetic Retinopathy in the Nondiabetic Population?

Two population-based studies have reported the presence of "diabetic retinopathy" in people with no evidence of diabetes.[68,69] In one of these studies, 7.8% of nondiabetic people had characteristic lesions including microaneurysms (5.1%), blot hemorrhages (1.5%), soft exudates, intraretinal microvascular abnormalities (IRMAs), or other lesions (1.1%).[69] In this population, 52% had increased blood pressure. Although the exact explanation for this finding is unclear, the 11.8% prevalence of systolic hypertension in the affected people suggests that it may be an important predisposing factor. The frequency of retinopathy among people with poorly controlled hypertension was 15%.

What Level of Fasting Plasma Glucose Best Predicts Diabetic Retinopathy?

Although plasma glucose concentrations are distributed over a continuum, a plasma glucose (PG) of 11.1 mmol/L 2 hours after a 75-g oral glucose load identifies people who are at substantially greater risk of microvascular complications than those with lower levels. The relationships of fasting plasma glucose (FPG) and 2hPG in the prediction of diabetic retinopathy were recently examined in three independent populations,[70,71] and the prevalence of retinopathy was noted to increase dramatically in the highest decile of FPG, 2hPG, and HBA_{1c}. Based on these data, the level of FPG > 7 mmol/L was chosen as the cutoff for a diagnosis of diabetes.

EVIDENCE-BASED MESSAGE

The new recommended diagnostic criteria for the diagnosis of diabetes (FPG ≥ 7 mmol/L) identifies people at high risk for diabetic retinopathy (Level 1).[70–72]

What Are the Risk Factors for Diabetic Retinopathy?

Data from epidemiologic studies suggest that important independent predictors of the progression of retinopathy are longer duration of diabetes, baseline severity of retinopathy, higher level of glycated hemoglobin, higher blood pressure, higher lipid levels, and, in Type 1 diabetes, pregnancy.[73–79] In those multivariate models that included accurate baseline retinopathy severity level and baseline glycosylated hemoglobin, duration of diabetes was not an independent risk factor for progression.[73,74,80] In Type 1 diabetes, the severity of diabetic retinopathy is also influenced by familial (possibly genetic) factors independent of metabolic control.[81] Risk factors for progression to high-risk proliferative retinopathy within 5 years include increased severity of retinopathy, decreased visual acuity (or increased extent of macular edema), higher glycated hemoglobin, history of diabetic neuropathy, lower hematocrit, elevated triglycerides, lower serum albumin, and younger age (or Type 1 diabetes).[53] These risk factors are discussed below.

Glycemic Control

Elevated glycated hemoglobin is strongly related to the incidence and progression of diabetic retinopathy,[5,73,74,80,82] up to and including severe nonproliferative and early proliferative stages.[53] In the WESDR, the cross-sectional baseline study revealed that people with higher glycated hemoglobin levels were more likely to have retinopathy.[60,61] In the 4- and 10-year follow-up studies, higher glycated hemoglobin levels at baseline were associated with a greater incidence and greater risk of progression of retinopathy, a greater progression to proliferative retinopathy,[73,74] and a higher incidence of macular edema (Table 21–13).[63,73,74,84] Over the 10-year period of the study, the risk rose from the lowest to the highest quartile of glycated hemoglobin; moreover, the risks (adjusted for duration and baseline severity of retinopathy) were similar for people with Type 1 diabetes, Type 2 diabetes taking insulin, and Type 2 diabetes not taking insulin.[74,84] Higher levels of glycemia also predicted a higher risk

Table 21–13 Independent Prediction of Increase in Retinopathy per One Percentage Point Increase in Baseline Glycated Hemoglobin

Group	Any Retinopathy OR (95% CI)	Progression of Retinopathy OR (95% CI)	Progression to Proliferation OR (95% CI)	Progression to Macular Edema OR (95% CI)
Type 1	1.6 (1.4–1.9)	1.7 (1.6–1.9)	1.9 (1.7–2.2)	1.6 (1.4–1.8)
Type 2 taking insulin	1.3 (1.0–1.6)	1.4 (1.2–1.6)	1.5 (1.2–1.9)	—
Type 2 not taking insulin	1.6 (1.4–1.8)	1.8 (1.5–2.0)	1.9 (1.5–2.5)	—
Type 2	—	—	—	1.6 (1.4–1.9)

OR = odds ratio; CI = confidence interval.
Data from Klein et al.[63,84]

of retinopathy in the Stockholm Diabetes Intervention Study (SDIS)[85] and the development of HR-PDR in the ETDRS (Table 21–14).[53]

As discussed in the section below entitled "Does Glycemic Control Prevent or Delay the Risk of Eye Disease?" the DCCT showed that glucose lowering reduces the risk of diabetic retinopathy; it also showed that hyperglycemia is a strong continuous and modifiable risk factor for both the incidence and progression of diabetic retinopathy. In this study, the total glycemic exposure (product of glycated hemoglobin and duration of exposure) was the principal risk factor for the progression of retinopathy.[83] There was a nonlinear relationship between the mean level of HbA_{1c} and the risk of progression of retinopathy; proportional rises in HbA_{1c} were accompanied by a proportional increase in the risk of complications (ie, there was a constant relative risk gradient). Also, although the absolute risk reduction decreased with proportional reductions in HbA_{1c}, there were still meaningful further reductions in risk as the HbA_{1c} level approached the normal range. There was no glycemic threshold for the effectiveness of intensive therapy, at least for the development of severe nonproliferative diabetic retinopathy (SNPDR).[86] The continuous relationship between the risk of diabetic retinopathy and degree of glycemia was also observed for people with Type 2 diabetes in the UKPDS.[82]

EVIDENCE-BASED MESSAGES

1. Elevated blood glucose measured by glycated hemoglobin is the strongest risk factor for predicting the incidence and progression of retinopathy, and progression to proliferative retinopathy, regardless of diabetes type (Level 1).[74]
2. The risk of developing HR-PDR increases with increasing level of glycated hemoglobin at baseline (Level 1).[53]
3. There is no glycemic threshold for the development of complications in Type 1 diabetes (Level 1).[86]

Race/Ethnicity

Information on race is important when applying the results of controlled clinical trials to different populations. Some studies found no racial associations after adjustments for the presence of other risk factors. For example, African-Americans with Type 1 diabetes had the same frequency of any retinopathy (63.9%) and proliferative retinopathy (18.9%) as Caucasians with Type 1 diabetes (69% and 23%, respectively).[34,60] In a clinic-based study of people with Type 1 diabetes (followed for an average of 4 years), the observed excess risk of PDR in African-Americans was accounted for by the presence of a worse risk-factor profile (espe-

Table 21–14 Development of High-Risk Proliferative Diabetic Retinopathy During 5 Years of Follow-Up

HbA_{1c} (%)	N	OR (95% CI)
< 8.3	677	1.00
8.3 – < 9.6	627	0.97 (0.78 – 1.20)
9.6 – < 11.0	675	1.18 (0.96 – 1.46)
11 – 12	341	1.55 (1.22 – 1.96)
> 12.0	334	1.59 (1.25 – 2.03)

OR = odds ratio.
Data from Davis MD, Fisher MR, Gangnon RE, et al. Risk factors for high-risk proliferative diabetic retinopathy and severe visual loss: Early Treatment Retinopathy Study Report No. 18. Invest Ophthalmol 1998;39:233–52.

cially poorer glycemic control), not race.[87] Conversely, in the Third National Health and Nutrition Examination Survey (NHANES III—a nationwide U.S. population-based study), diabetic retinopathy was identified by nonmydriatic one-field photography in 1,180 persons with previously diagnosed Type 2 diabetes aged ≥ 40 years. The prevalence was greater in non-Hispanic African-Americans (26.5%) and Mexican-Americans (33.4%) than in non-Hispanic Caucasians (18.2%),[88] and the risk of retinopathy in Mexican-Americans was twice that of non-Hispanic Caucasians (OR 2.15, 95% CI 1.15 to 4.04). Moreover, the prevalence of proliferative retinopathy was significantly higher in Mexican-Americans than in the other races; this excess risk could not be explained by an association with other risk factors. Such an excess risk for the presence and severity of retinopathy in Mexican-Americans compared with Caucasians was also found in the San Antonio study[89] but was not noted in the San Luis Valley Study.[90,91] Finally, in a small prospective study of persons with Type 2 diabetes age 40 to 69 years living in Baltimore (participation rate 65%), African-Americans were more likely to develop retinopathy than Caucasians after adjustment for other risk factors (OR 2.96, 95% CI 1.00 to 8.78).[92]

EVIDENCE-BASED MESSAGES

1. Racial/ethnic differences in the risk of diabetic retinopathy in Type 1 diabetes may be due to differences in glycemic control (Level 2).[87]
2. Racial/ethnic differences in the risk of diabetic retinopathy in Type 2 diabetes could not be explained by an association with other risk factors (Level 1).[88,89]

Duration of Diabetes and Age

The duration of diabetes is an important risk factor for the presence, severity, and progression of retinopathy, proliferative retinopathy, and macular edema as discussed above.[3,60,61] In Type 1 diabetes, the significant relationship between prevalence of retinopathy and age is probably due to the close association of age with duration of diabetes. Diabetic retinopathy is rare before the age of 10 years, regardless of the duration of diabetes. Vision-threatening retinopathy is not observed under age 15 and affects 2.5% of people aged 15 to 19.[93] Similarly, macular edema is not observed under age 15 and affects 2% of people aged 15 to 19 years and 26% of people aged 45 years or older.

Does puberty (which occurs at a median age of 13 years) affect the frequency of retinopathy? People older than age 13 years at diagnosis of diabetes are more likely to have retinopathy than those younger than age 13 years at diagnosis, even after controlling for the duration of diabetes.[94–96] More recently, however, prepubertal duration of diabetes was noted to be a risk factor for retinopathy.[97–100]

EVIDENCE-BASED MESSAGE

Both age and duration of diabetes are closely associated risk factors for retinopathy in people with Type 1 diabetes (Level 1).[3,60,93]

Elevated Blood Pressure

Most[78,101] but not all[102] studies report an association between hypertension and retinopathy. In the ABCD study of people with Type 2 diabetes, hypertension (sitting systolic ≥ 140 mm Hg, diastolic ≥ 80 mm Hg) did not predict progression of diabetic retinopathy after controlling for diabetes duration and glycated hemoglobin levels.[103] There was a continuous relationship between the risk of diabetic retinopathy and systolic blood pressure (> 130 mm Hg) observed in the UKPDS (with no evidence of a threshold).[6] In both the 4- and 10-year follow-up studies of the WESDR, increased systolic blood pressure (independent of other risk factors), predicted proliferative diabetic retinopathy in people with Type 1 but not Type 2 diabetes.[77] In both types of diabetes, elevated diastolic blood pressure was a risk factor for macular edema,[63,104] and elevated systolic blood pressure was a risk factor for loss of vision.[38] In a large cross-sectional study of Type 1 diabetes, blood pressure was linked to both the severity of retinopathy and the frequency of raised albumin excretion.[105]

EVIDENCE-BASED MESSAGE

Elevated blood pressure is an independent risk factor for any retinopathy, macular edema, and loss of vision in both Type 1 and Type 2 diabetes (Level 1)[38,63,78] and for proliferative retinopathy in Type 1 diabetes (Level 1).[77]

Lipids

The dyslipidemia of diabetes is characterized by decreased high-density lipoprotein (HDL) cholesterol, small low-density lipoprotein (LDL) particles, and elevated total and very low-density lipoprotein (VLDL) triglyceride levels.[106] Vascular damage in the macula leads to extravasation of serum with secondary development of edema (retinal thickening) and hard exudate in the extracellular space. In the DCCT conventional treatment group, patients with Type 1 diabetes in the higher quartile of baseline triglycerides had a twofold rate of progression of retinopathy compared with those in the lower quartile.[107] The severity of hard exudate was directly related to the risk of visual decrease, even after adjustment for retinal thickening. Elevated serum cholesterol > 6.2 mmol/L at baseline increased the risk of visual loss by 50% when compared with a low serum cholesterol level < 6.21 mmol/L.[76] In the ETDRS, the development and severity of retinal hard exudates in the macula were directly associated with elevations in serum total cholesterol[76,108,109] and LDL cholesterol.[76,109] Patients with total serum cholesterol ≥ 6.21 or triglycerides > 4.50 developed hard exudate approximately 50% faster than patients with serum cholesterol < 5.17 or triglycerides < 2.3.

EVIDENCE-BASED MESSAGE

Dyslipidemia is a risk factor for visual loss (Level 1).[76,108,109]

Pregnancy

Pregnancy predicts progression of retinopathy independently of glycemia and diastolic blood pressure[75]; moreover, the severity of diabetic retinopathy in the first trimester predicts adverse outcomes of delivery such as abortions, perinatal death, and severe congenital abnormalities.[110] In Type 1 diabetes, parity is not a risk factor for the progression of diabetes complications.[111,112] Independent risk factors for the progression of retinopathy during pregnancy are moderate or more severe nonproliferative retinopathy and elevated glycosylated hemoglobin at conception.[113] The magnitude of the decrease in hemoglobin A_{1c} from the first to second trimester, pregnancy-induced hypertension, chronic hypertension,[114] and preeclampsia[115] are all independent predictors of retinopathy progression. Patients with no retinopathy or microaneurysms only at conception are at low risk.

EVIDENCE-BASED MESSAGES

1. Pregnancy is an independent risk factor for progression of retinopathy (Level 1).[75]
2. Patients at greatest risk for retinopathy progression have the poorest control at baseline, largest improvement in glycemic control during early pregnancy, hypertension, and preeclampsia (Level 1).[114,115]
3. Adverse outcomes in delivery are predicted by the severity of diabetic retinopathy in the first trimester (Level 1).[110]

Cigarette Smoking

Cigarette smoking causes ischemic effects on vasculature. In the WESDR 10-year incidence study, neither smoking status nor total pack-years smoked showed significant associations with increased risk of retinopathy.[116]

EVIDENCE-BASED MESSAGE

Cigarette smoking is not a risk factor for retinopathy (Level 1).[116]

Alcohol

Alcohol, which has an effect on lipoprotein cholesterol, platelet aggregability, serum fibrinogen, blood glucose, and blood pressure, has the potential for positive and negative effects on retinopathy. In the WESDR 4-year incidence study, alcohol, consumed moderately, was not a risk factor for the incidence or progression of diabetic retinopathy.[117]

EVIDENCE-BASED MESSAGE

Alcohol is not a risk factor for retinopathy (Level 1).[117]

HOW CAN EYE DISEASE BE SCREENED FOR?

Screening refers to the identification among apparently healthy people of those at significant risk of having a specific disorder (such as sight-threatening retinopathy), sufficient to warrant diagnostic tests and treatment.[118] Table 21–15 lists several screening tests for diabetic retinopathy. Direct ophthalmoscopy with or without indirect ophthalmoscopy by *trained* examiners has close to 80% sensitivity and high specificity for proliferative retinopathy (Table 21–16).[119] Clinically significant macular edema is best detected by biomicroscopic examination with contact lens or stereo-photography.[120]

The probable yields from screening programs using tests with different sensitivities, conducted in populations with different rates of treatable retinopathy, can be estimated, along with their impact on the incidence of blindness.[121] When sensitivity falls below 40%, there is considerable reduction in predicted sight saved as well as a related decrease in federal budgetary savings.[122] The best screening protocols to identify patients with vision-threatening retinopathy are those based on assessing lesion severity in the posterior fundus according to precisely defined criteria.[123]

EVIDENCE-BASED MESSAGE

Direct ophthalmoscopy by skilled examiners detects the presence of proliferative diabetic retinopathy with a sensitivity of 79% and specificity of 99% (Level 1).[119]

DOES GLYCEMIC CONTROL PREVENT OR DELAY THE RISK OF EYE DISEASE?

Clinical trials have shown that intensive management and control of hyperglycemia prevents the development and progression of retinopathy in Type 1[5,107,124–126] and Type 2 diabetes.[82,127] The DCCT compared the effect of intensive therapy with conventional diabetes therapy on the

---

Table 21–15 Methods of Examination

Direct ophthalmoscopy

Indirect ophthalmoscopy

Biomicroscopy with diagnostic contact lens

Biomicroscopy with handheld lens

Nonmydriatic camera photography

7-standard field stereoscopic photography*

Digital camera photography

*Gold standard.

Table 21–16 Diagnostic Tests for Detection of Proliferative Diabetic Retinopathy

Screening Tests	Gold Standard	Sensitivity (%)	95% CI	Specificity (%)	95% CI
Dilated direct ± indirect ophthalmoscopy by ophthalmologist, trained ophthalmic technician, and optometrist	7-field stereoscopic color fundus photography using central reader	79	73–85	99	98–100

Data from Moss SE, Klein R, Kessler SD, Richie KA. Comparison between ophthalmoscopy and fundus photography in determining severity of diabetic retinopathy. Ophthalmology 1985;92:62–7.

development (primary prevention) and progression (secondary prevention) of early retinopathy in people with Type 1 diabetes. Over 9 years, an average difference of about 2% in glycosylated hemoglobin was maintained in both the primary and secondary prevention cohorts. The DCCT examined the relationship between allocated therapy and retinopathy by plotting the cumulative incidence of sustained progression of retinopathy (using the ETDRS Retinopathy Severity Scale) in the two cohorts, in subgroups of these cohorts by baseline covariates, and among clinics.[5]

In the primary prevention cohort, intensive therapy reduced the adjusted mean risk of retinopathy progression by three or more steps by 76% and in the secondary intervention cohort by 54% compared with conventional therapy. In the primary prevention cohort, progression rates were similar in both treatment groups until about 36 months, at which point the curves began to separate; in the secondary intervention cohort, the intensive therapy group had a higher rate of progression during the first year followed by a lower rate beginning at about 36 months, when the curves began to separate. In both cohorts, the risk reduction was consistent among subgroups and among clinics[5] (absolute risk reduction [ARR] 18%; number needed to treat [NNT] 6, 95% CI 4 to 7). Intensive insulin therapy reduced the risk of macular edema by only 29% and the risk of CSME by only 23% after 9 years.

The Stockholm Diabetes Intervention Study (SDIS) also evaluated the effect of intensified (mean glycated hemoglobin 7.1%) versus standard treatment (mean glycated hemoglobin 8.5%) in people with Type 1 diabetes. During 7.5 years of follow-up, intensified therapy reduced the risk of retinopathy by an absolute amount of 25% (95% CI 6 to 44%, $p = .01$).[124] The results of this trial and 5 other studies of more than 2 years duration were combined in a meta-analysis that confirmed that intensive therapy reduced progression of diabetic retinopathy in people with Type 1 diabetes (OR 0.49, 95% CI 0.28 to 0.85, $p = .011$).[126] More recently, the UKPDS study reported that intensive glycemic control reduced the risk of eye disease in people with Type 2 diabetes: the need for retinal photocoagulation was reduced by 19%; cataract extractions were reduced by 24%; progression of retinopathy was reduced by 21%; and "microvascular disease" (retinopathy requiring photocoagulation, vitreous hemorrhage, fatal or nonfatal renal failure) was reduced by 25%.[82] Post-trial follow-up studies confirm the durability of the beneficial microvascular effects of intensive therapy.[128,129]

Of interest, several but not all trials of intensive therapy in people with Type 1 diabetes reported a transient, early worsening of retinopathy (development of soft exudates and intraretinal microvascular abnormalities) during the first 12 months[130]; such a finding has not been reported with intensive treatment of people with Type 2 diabetes.[131]

EVIDENCE-BASED MESSAGES

1. Tight control of hyperglycemia using multiple daily injections, introduced as early as possible, prevents or delays the development and progression of retinopathy in people with Type 1 and Type 2 diabetes (Level 1A).[5,82,127]
2. Tight glycemic control using insulin or oral hypoglycemic therapy reduces the need for surgical interventions (laser treatment, vitrectomy, cataract extraction) in people with Type 2 diabetes (Level 1A).[82]

WHAT NONGLYCEMIC THERAPIES CAN BE USED TO PREVENT/TREAT EYE DISEASE?

Blood Pressure Lowering

In people with Type 2 diabetes and hypertension, a policy of tight blood pressure control (ie, a mean achieved blood pressure of 144/82 vs 154/87) reduced the rate of progression of retinopathy by 34% over 7.5 years. It also reduced deterioration in visual acuity (doubling of visual angle) by 47% and the risk of retinal photocoagulation by 35%.[6] The beneficial effect of tight blood pressure control was apparent earlier than the effect of tight blood glucose control. It was also unrelated to the initial drug used to lower blood pressure; the rate of retinopathy was similar for groups treated either with a β-blocker or an angiotensin converting enzyme (ACE) inhibitor and was independent of the glucose-lowering effect.[132]

EVIDENCE-BASED MESSAGE

Tight control of hypertension with either captopril or atenolol reduces progression of retinopathy, the need for laser treatment, and visual deterioration in people with Type 2 diabetes (Level 1A).[6]

Angiotensin Converting Enzyme Inhibition

Angiotensin converting enzyme is produced locally by retinal vascular endothelial cells. Because there is a link between ACE activity and vascular disease, ACE inhibition may have a beneficial effect on endothelium-dependent regulation of vasomotion.[133] The possibility that ACE inhibition may prevent eye disease was tested in the EUCLID study of normotensive, mostly normalbuminuric individuals with Type 1 diabetes. Participants were randomized to the ACE inhibitor lisinopril (10 mg) or placebo for 2 years; lisinopril independently reduced the risk of retinopathy progression (by at least one level of severity) by 50% (95% Cl 28 to 89%).[134] Consistent findings were reported in the Heart Outcomes Prevention Evaluation (HOPE) study of people at high risk of cardiovascular disease, in which ramipril reduced the combined outcome of overt nephropathy, self-reported use of laser therapy, or dialysis.[135]

EVIDENCE-BASED MESSAGE

Angiotensin converting enzyme inhibitors reduce the risk of progression of retinopathy (Level 2).[134]

Antiplatelet Agents

Platelet thromboemboli may be involved in the pathogenesis of diabetic microvascular disease. This led to randomized clinical trials in patients with early retinopathy using ticlopidine (500 mg daily for 3 years),[136] aspirin (330 mg 3 times daily for 3 years), and aspirin (330 mg 3 times daily) plus dipyridamole (75 mg 3 times daily for 3 years[137]; in patients with mild to severe nonproliferative retinopathy and early proliferative retinopathy, aspirin (650 mg daily) was used.[138] All three protocols significantly reduced microaneurysm formation in early retinopathy, although with ticlopidine the effect was limited to insulin users.[136,137]

In more severe retinopathy, aspirin did not prevent the development of high-risk proliferative retinopathy and did not reduce the risk of visual loss.[138] Of note, no adverse effect of aspirin was observed: vitrectomy rates were not higher in patients receiving aspirin versus those who were not,[139] and aspirin did not increase the risk or severity of vitreous hemorrhage.[138,140] Finally, aspirin had no effect on the development of cataracts.[141]

EVIDENCE-BASED MESSAGES

1. Although aspirin slows the development of microaneurysms,[137] it has no effect on mild NPDR or more severe retinopathy, including vitreous hemorrhage (Level 1A).[138]
2. Aspirin is not contraindicated in people with retinopathy when used to prevent macrovascular disease (Level 1A).[140]

Aldose Reductase Inhibitors

Excess polyol pathway activity in uncontrolled diabetes, driven by the enzyme aldose reductase, affects cell metabolism with potential for tissue damage as a consequence of polyol accumulation, altered *myo*-inositol and phosphoinositide metabolism, oxidative stress, and formation of advanced glycated products.[142] In none or very mild diabetic retinopathy, neither the aldose reductase inhibitor sorbinil (25 mg daily for median time of 41 months[143]) nor ponalrestat (600 mg daily for 18 months[144]) affected the rate of retinopathy progression.

EVIDENCE-BASED MESSAGE

Aldose reductase inhibitors do not slow progression of retinopathy (Level 1A).[143,144]

Antioxidants

Oxidative stress may potentially contribute to the pathogenesis of diabetic microvascular and macrovascular disease.[145] However, in a population-based study of Type 2 diabetes, examination of cross-sectional and longitudinal data on nutrient intake showed no protective effect of antioxidant vitamins C and E or β-carotene (both foods and supplements) on the prevalence and severity of diabetic retinopathy.[146]

EVIDENCE-BASED MESSAGE

Antioxidants (vitamins C and E and β-carotene) do not slow the progression of retinopathy in patients with Type 2 diabetes (Level 2).[146]

Multifactorial Therapy

Hypertension, obesity, dyslipidemia, and hyperglycemia are common comorbidities in Type 2 diabetes, and each is a risk factor for vascular complications that, if treated individually, reduce the complication rate. Multifactorial therapy is the standard of care in diabetes centers (stepwise pharmacologic therapy of each risk factor, low-fat diet, exercise, and prophylactic therapy, eg, vitamins C and E, angiotensin enzyme inhibitors, and aspirin). In a randomized open trial in patients with Type 2 diabetes and microalbuminuria, a 3.8-year mean period of intensive therapy significantly reduced the retinopathy progression (relative risk reduction [RRR] 40%, 95% Cl 6 to 63%) and blindness in one eye (RRR 85%, 95% Cl 11 to 98%) but not the development of any retinopathy, macular edema, or proliferative retinopathy[147] compared with standard treatment by general practitioners.

EVIDENCE-BASED MESSAGE

Intensified multifactorial therapy in patients with Type 2 diabetes reduces the progression of retinopathy (Level 2).[147]

WHAT IS THE EFFICACY OF SURGICAL THERAPY IN DIABETIC RETINOPATHY?

Efficacy of Surgery in Proliferative Retinopathy

Photocoagulation

The results of the Diabetic Retinopathy Study (DRS) and the Early Treatment Diabetic Retinopathy Study have shown that laser treatment is outstandingly effective. In fact, scatter laser treatment has become the standard of care for all eyes with high-risk proliferative diabetic retinopathy. The DRS enrolled eyes with PDR in at least one eye or SNPDR in both eyes. It demonstrated that both blue-green argon and xenon scatter photocoagulation reduced the risk of SVL by > 50% and reduced progression to more severe stages of retinopathy[7,148]; treated eyes with a visual acuity ≤ 5/200 were more likely to recover a better level of vision. After 2 years of follow-up, SVL developed in 16.3% of untreated eyes compared with 6.4% of treated eyes (ARR 9.5%, 95% CI 6.6 to 12.4%), that is, 11 eyes required therapy to prevent 1 eye from developing severe visual loss (95% CI 8 to 15). This relative risk reduction of > 50% was maintained for at least 6 years and was associated with regression of neovascularizaton.[149]

The adverse effects of argon laser treatment documented after 6 weeks included a 10% risk of visual acuity deterioration of one line; a 3% risk of visual acuity deterioration of ≥ two lines; and a 5% risk of modest constriction of peripheral visual fields.[150] Eyes with macular edema were twice as likely to lose two or more lines of visual acuity.[151] The risk of SVL decreased with increasing treatment density.[152]

The ETDRS studied the effects of photocoagulation in earlier stages of diabetic retinopathy (mild-to-severe nonproliferative retinopathy or mild PDR) and demonstrated only marginal benefit at 5 years: the risk of SVL or vitrectomy was reduced from 3.7% in deferred eyes to 2.6% in treated eyes ($p < .01$).[153] An analysis of the combined results of the DRS and ETDRS showed that scatter laser treatment and vitrectomy reduces SVL by 87% at 3 years, bilateral SVL by 97% at 3 years, and legal blindness by 90% at 5 years.[154] Early photocoagulation applied to SNPDR or mild PDR was most effective at reducing rates of HR-PDR, SVL, or vitrectomy in people with Type 2 diabetes and in people ≥ age 40.[155]

EVIDENCE-BASED MESSAGES

1. Scatter laser treatment for eyes with high-risk characteristics reduces the risk of severe vision loss by 50 to 60% over 6 years (Level 1A).[7]
2. There is no clear benefit of early scatter photocoagulation in eyes with mild-to-moderate NPDR, provided that follow-up can be maintained (Level 1A).[153]
3. In patients with Type 2 diabetes and in older (≥ 40 years) patients with SNPDR or mild PDR, early scatter laser treatment reduces the risk of HR-PDR, SVL, and combined SVL and vitrectomy by 50% (Level 1A).[155]

Vitreous Hemorrhage and the Role of Vitrectomy

The visual prognosis for eyes with very severe proliferation but without vitreous hemorrhage is related to baseline visual acuity and retinopathy stage.[156] During a 2-year study of 744 eyes, 45% of eyes with > four disk areas of new vessels and visual acuity < 20/40 at baseline deteriorated to a visual acuity < 5/200; 14% of eyes with traction retinal detachment not involving the center of the macula with a visual acuity < 20/40 deteriorated to a visual acuity < 5/200. The causes of visual acuity < 5/200 (recorded in 87% eyes) were retinal detachment (35%) and fresh vitreous hemorrhage (31%). In eyes with recent severe vitreous hemorrhage and visual acuity < 5/200 for at least 1 month, 15.2% had visual acuity 20/40 or better at 2 years, and 19.3% had no light perception.[157]

The possibility that vitrectomy may improve the prognosis of eyes with vitreous hemorrhage was assessed by randomizing eyes with nonclearing severe vitreous hemorrhage within 6 months to early vitrectomy (performed within days) or deferral of vitrectomy for 1 year. The visual acuity at enrolment was 5/200 to light perception at each of two baseline visits separated by 1 to 6 months. After 2 years of follow-up, 25% of the early vitrectomy group had a visual acuity 10/20 or better compared with 15% in the deferral vitrectomy group (ARR 9.35%, 95% CI 2.97 to 15.7%; $p = .01$); thus, 11 eyes needed to be treated to return vision in 1 to 10/20 or better (95% CI 6 to 34).[157,158] There was also an absolute risk reduction of 8.67% in the rate of persistent or recurrent hemorrhage in the early versus deferred vitrectomy eyes (95% CI, 1.75 to 15.59%) with an NNT to prevent 1 event of 12 (95% CI 6 to 57). The benefit of early vitrectomy was confined to people with Type 1 diabetes in whom the recovery of a visual acuity of 10/20 or better was 36% for early versus 12% for deferred vitrectomy. In people with Type 2 diabetes, there was no significant difference in recovery rates between groups, and the overall adverse event rate was significantly greater in the early vitrectomy group.

The role of early vitrectomy was also assessed in eyes with extensive active neovascular and fibrovascular proliferation and visual acuity $\geq$ 20/400 (Table 21–17). After 4 years, 44% of eyes randomized to early vitrectomy had a visual acuity $\geq$ 10/20, compared with 28% in the deferral group.[159,160] For the outcome of visual acuity 10/20 or better at 2-, 3-, and 4-year follow-up visits, the ARR (95% CI) was 10.6% (0.23 to 20.97%), 22.71% (12.15 to 33.27%), and 15.88% (4.79 to 26.97%), respectively; the corresponding NNT (95% CI) was 9.4 (4.8 to 434.8), 4.4 (3.0 to 8.2), and 6.3 (3.7 to 20.9), respectively.

EVIDENCE-BASED MESSAGES

1. Early vitrectomy for eyes with severe vitreous hemorrhage decreases the risk of SVL by 10% over 4 years in patients with Type 1 diabetes, whereas early vitrectomy has no benefit over deferral for 1 year in patients with Type 2 diabetes (Level 1A).[157,158]
2. In eyes with severe active neovascularization and useful vision, early vitrectomy decreases the risk of SVL by 16% over 4 years (Level 1A).[159]

Table 21–17 Early Vitrectomy versus Deferral in Type 1 and Type 2 Diabetes (2-Year Results)

	Type 1, Age Onset < 20 y		Type 2, Age Onset > 40 y	
	Early % Eyes	Deferral % Eyes	Early % Eyes	Deferral % Eyes
VA 10/20 or better	36	12*	16	18
Overall event rate†	34.5	41.0	43.9	24.5
Retinal detachment	9.5	26.5	14.0	11.8
Spontaneous clearing of vitreous hemorrhage		16.4		29.2

*$p = .0001$.
†$p = .004$ between types of diabetes.
VA = visual acuity.
Data from the Diabetic Vitrectomy Study Research Group. Early vitrectomy for severe vitreous hemorrhage in diabetic retinopathy. Two-year results of a randomized trial. Diabetic Retinopathy Vitrectomy Study Report No. 2. Arch Ophthalmol 1985;103:1644–52.

Efficacy of Surgery in Macular Edema

Photocoagulation

Clinically significant macular edema (CSME) is macular edema that involves or threatens the center of the macula, regardless of whether or not visual acuity is affected (see Table 21–2).[8] In the ETDRS, focal and grid photocoagulation of CSME was effective across a broad range of edema severity, visual acuity levels, and severity levels of nonproliferative retinopathy.[161–163] The benefits were apparent after 8 months, and by 3 years it had reduced the 3-year risk of moderate visual loss (see Table 21–2) from 33% in the control group to 13% in the treated group and significantly reduced the incidence of retinal thickening in the center of the macula from 54% in the control group to 24% in the treated group ($p < .0001$, 95% CI 20.7%, 40.9%; NNT 3.2, 95% CI 2.4, 4.8).[8,162] There was no beneficial effect in eyes with macular edema that were not classified as having CSME. Despite these benefits, < 3% of eyes improved by three lines of visual acuity.[8]

EVIDENCE-BASED MESSAGE

> Focal laser treatment for CSME in eyes with mild to moderate NPDR decreases the risk of moderate visual loss by 20% (Level 1A).[8]

CONCLUSION

There is a large body of epidemiologic and clinical trial evidence supporting the ocular benefits of aggressively managing hyperglycemia and hypertension and possibly using ACE inhibitors in people with diabetes. The evidence also supports the importance of regular eye examinations to detect eyes that may benefit from laser therapy.

SUMMARY OF EVIDENCE-BASED MESSAGES

1. The risk of blindness due to diabetes is 3.3 per 100,000 population (Level 1).[37]
2. Diabetes and the level of hyperglycemia increases the risk of cataract (Level 1).[42,43]
3. Extracapsular cataract extraction has no significant adverse effects on retinopathy (Level 2).[47]
4. The ETDRS final scale of retinopathy severity in Table 21–3 clearly predicts progression to proliferative retinopathy and high-risk proliferative retinopathy and to the combined outcome of severe visual loss or vitrectomy (Level 1).[50,53]
5. The severity of intraretinal microvascular abnormalities, microaneurysms, and/or hemorrhages and venous beading predicts progression to proliferation (Level 1).[50,53]
6. Three or four retinopathy risk factors in Table 21–8 define eyes with high-risk characteristics for severe visual loss (Level 1).[51]
7. The duration of both Type 1 and Type 2 diabetes is a risk factor for diabetic retinopathy (Level 1).[60,61]
8. Diabetes duration of 10 years has 77.4% sensitivity for detecting the presence of retinopathy (Level 1).[60]
9. People with Type 2 diabetes on insulin have a much higher risk of clinically significant macular edema than do people with Type 1 diabetes (Level 1).[63]
10. The new recommended diagnostic criteria for the diagnosis of diabetes (FPG ≥ 7 mmol/L) identifies people at high risk for diabetic retinopathy (Level 1).[70–72]
11. Elevated blood glucose measured by glycated hemoglobin is the strongest risk factor for predicting the incidence and progression of retinopathy and progression to proliferative retinopathy, regardless of diabetes type (Level 1).[74]
12. The risk of developing HR-PDR increases with increasing level of glycated hemoglobin at baseline (Level 1).[53]
13. There is no glycemic threshold for the development of complications in Type 1 diabetes (Level 1).[86]

14. Racial/ethnic differences in the risk of diabetic retinopathy in Type 1 diabetes may be due to differences in glycemic control (Level 2).[87]

15. Racial/ethnic differences in the risk of diabetic retinopathy in Type 2 diabetes could not be explained by an association with other risk factors (Level 1).[88,89]

16. Both age and duration of diabetes are closely associated risk factors for retinopathy in people with Type 1 diabetes (Level 1).[3,60,93]

17. Elevated blood pressure is an independent risk factor for any retinopathy, macular edema, and loss of vision in both Type 1 and Type 2 diabetes (Level 1)[138,63,78] and proliferative retinopathy in Type 1 diabetes (Level 1).[77]

18. Dyslipidemia is a risk factor for visual loss (Level 1).[76,108,109]

19. Pregnancy is an independent risk factor for progression of retinopathy (Level 1).[75]

20. Patients at greatest risk for retinopathy progression have the poorest control at baseline, largest improvement in glycemic control during early pregnancy, hypertension, and preeclampsia (Level 1).[114,115]

21. Adverse outcomes in delivery are predicted by the severity of diabetic retinopathy in the first trimester (Level 1).[110]

22. Cigarette smoking is not a risk factor for retinopathy (Level 1).[116]

23. Alcohol is not a risk factor for retinopathy (Level 1).[117]

24. Direct ophthalmoscopy by skilled examiners detects the presence of proliferative diabetic retinopathy with a sensitivity of 79% and specificity of 99% (Level 1).[119]

25. Tight control of hyperglycemia using multiple daily injections, introduced as early as possible, prevents or delays the development and progression of retinopathy in people with Type 1 and Type 2 diabetes (Level 1A).[5,82,127]

26. Tight glycemic control using insulin or oral hypoglycemic therapy reduces the need for surgical interventions (laser treatment, vitrectomy, cataract extraction) in people with Type 2 diabetes (Level 1A).[82]

27. Tight control of hypertension with either captopril or atenolol reduces progression of retinopathy, the need for laser treatment, and visual deterioration in people with Type 2 diabetes (Level 1A).[6]

28. Angiotensin converting enzyme inhibitors reduce the risk of progression of retinopathy (Level 2).[134]

29. Although aspirin slows the development of microaneurysms,[137] it has no effect on mild NPDR or more severe retinopathy, including vitreous hemorrhage (Level 1A).[138]

30. Aspirin is not contraindicated in people with retinopathy when used to prevent macrovascular disease (Level 1A).[140]

31. Aldose reductase inhibitors do not slow progression of retinopathy (Level 1A).[143,144]

32. Antioxidants (vitamins C and E and β-carotene) do not slow the progression of retinopathy in patients with Type 2 diabetes (Level 2).[146]

33. Intensified multifactorial therapy in patients with Type 2 diabetes reduces the progression of retinopathy (Level 2).[147]

34. Scatter laser treatment for eyes with high-risk characteristics reduces the risk of severe vision loss by 50 to 60% over 6 years (Level 1A).[7]

35. There is no clear benefit of early scatter photocoagulation in eyes with mild-to-moderate NPDR, provided that follow-up can be maintained (Level 1A).[153]

36. In patients with Type 2 diabetes and in older ($\geq$ 40 years) patients with SNPDR or mild PDR, early scatter laser treatment reduces the risk of HR-PDR, SVL, and combined SVL and vitrectomy by 50% (Level 1A).[155]

37. Early vitrectomy for eyes with severe vitreous hemorrhage decreases the risk of SVL by 10% over 4 years in patients with Type 1 diabetes, whereas early vitrectomy has no benefit over deferral for 1 year in patients with Type 2 diabetes (Level 1A).[157,158]

38. In eyes with severe active neovascularization and useful vision, early vitrectomy decreases the risk of SVL by 16% over 4 years (Level 1A).[159]

39. Focal laser treatment for CSME in eyes with mild-to-moderate NPDR decreases the risk of moderate visual loss by 20% (Level 1A).[8]

REFERENCES

1. Klein R, Klein BEK. Vision disorders in diabetes. In: Diabetes in America. 2nd ed. Washington: National Diabetes Data Group, National Institute of Diabetes and Digestive and Kidney Diseases, National Institutes of Health; 1995. p. 293–338.

2. Klein R, Klein BEK, Moss SE. Epidemiology of proliferative diabetic retinopathy. Diabetes Care 1992;15:1875–91.

3. Klein R, Klein BEK, Moss SE, et al. The Wisconsin Epidemiologic Study of Diabetic Retinopathy IV. Diabetic macular edema. Ophthalmology 1984;91:1464–74.

4. Klein R. Diabetic retinopathy. Annu Rev Public Health 1996;17:137–58.

5. The Diabetes Control and Complications Trial Research Group. The effect of intensive treatment of diabetes on the development and progression of long-term complications in insulin-dependent diabetes mellitus. N Engl J Med 1993;329:977–86.

6. UK Prospective Diabetes Study Group. Tight blood pressure control and risk of macrovascular and microvascular complications in type 2 diabetes. UKPDS 38. BMJ 1998;317:703–13.

7. The Diabetic Retinopathy Study Research Group. Photocoagulation treatment of proliferative diabetic retinopathy: the Second Report of Diabetic Retinopathy Study Findings. Ophthalmology 1978;85:82–106.

8. Early Treatment Diabetic Retinopathy Study Research Group. Photocoagulation for diabetic macular edema. Early Treatment Diabetic Retinopathy Study Report No. 1. Arch Ophthalmol 1985;103:1796–806.

9. Nielson NV. The prevalence of glaucoma and ocular hypertension in type 1 and type 2 diabetes mellitus. An epidemiologic study of diabetes mellitus on the Island of Falster, Denmark. Acta Ophthalmol (Copenh) 1983;61:662–72.

10. Sjolie AK. Ocular complications of insulin treated diabetes mellitus. An epidemiological study. Acta Ophthalmol (Copenh) 1985;63(Suppl 172).

11. Regillo CD, Brown GC, Savino PI, et al. Diabetic papillopathy. Patient characteristics and fundus findings. Arch Ophthalmol 1995;113:889–95.

12. Jacobson DM, McCanna TD, Layde PM. Risk factors of ischemic ocular motor nerve palsies. Arch Ophthalmol 1994;112:961–6.

13. Hayreh SS, Joos KM, Podhajsky PA et al. Systemic diseases associated with nonarteritic anterior ischemic optic neuropathy. Am J Ophthalmol 1994;118:766–80.

14. Jacobson DM, Vierkant RA, Belongia EA. Nonarteritic anterior ischemic optic neuropathy. A case-control study of potential risk factors. Arch Ophthalmol 1997;115:1403–7.

15. Moss SE, Klein R, Klein EK. Accommodative ability in younger-onset diabetes. Arch Ophthalmol 1987;105:508–12.

16. Braun CI, Benson WE, Ramaley NA. et al. Accommodative amplitudes in the Early Treatment Diabetic Retinopathy Study. ETDRS Report No. 21. Retina 1995;15:275–81.

17. Mitchell P, Smith W, Chey T, et al. Prevalence and associations of epiretinal membranes. The Blue Mountains Eye Study. Ophthalmology 1997;104:1033–40.

18. Mitchell P, Smith W, Chey T. Open-angle glaucoma and diabetes. The Blue Mountains Eye Study, Australia. Ophthalmology 1997;104:712–8.

19. Klein BEK, Klein R, Jensen SC. Open-angle glaucoma and older-onset diabetes. The Beaver Dam Eye Study. Ophthalmology 1994;101:1173–7.

20. Dielemans I, de Jong PT, Stolk R, et al. Primary open-angle glaucoma, intraocular pressure, and diabetes mellitus in the general elderly population. The Rotterdam Study. Ophthalmology 1996;103:1271–5.

21. Kahn HA, Milton RC. Alternative definitions of open-angle glaucoma. Effect on prevalence and associations in the Framingham Eye Study. Arch Ophthalmol 1980;98:2172–7.

22. Leske MC, Connell AM, Wu S-Y, et al. Risk factors for open-angle glaucoma. The Barbados Eye Study. Arch Ophthalmol 1995;113:918–24.

23. Tielsch JM, Katz J, Quigley HA, et al. Diabetes, intraocular pressure, and primary open-angle glaucoma in the Baltimore Eye Survey. Ophthalmology 1995;102:48–53.

24. Sanchez-Thorin JC. The cornea in diabetes mellitus. Int Ophthalmol Clin 1998;38:19–36.

25. Kinsley BT, Dumont RH, Swift M. Morbidity and mortality in the Wolfram Syndrome. Diabetes Care 1995;18:1566–70.

26. Barrett TG, Bundey SE, MacLeod AF. Neurodegeneration and diabetes: UK nationwide study of Wolfram (DIDMOAD) syndrome. Lancet 1995;346:1458–63.

27. Klein R, Klein BEK, Moss SE. Visual impairment in diabetes. Ophthalmology 1984;91:1–8.

28. Davis MD. Natural course of diabetic retinopathy. In: Kimura SJ, Caygill WM, editors. Vascular complications of diabetes mellitus. St. Louis: CV Mosby; 1967. p. 139–67.

29. Ferris FL III, Patz A. Macular edema. A complication of diabetic retinopathy. Surv Ophthalmol 1984; Suppl 28:452–61.

30. Green WR, Wilson DJ. Histopathology of diabetic retinopathy. In: Franklin RM, editor. Retina and vitreous. New Orleans Academy of Ophthalmology, New Orleans, LA. New York: Kugler Publications; 1993. p. 63–81.

31. Begg IS, Rootman J. Clinico-pathological study of an organized plaque in exudative diabetic maculopathy. Can J Ophthalmol 1976;11:197–202.

32. Sigurdson R, Begg IS. Organized macular plaques in exudative maculopathy. Br J Ophthalmol 1980;64:392–7.

33. Sjolie AK, Stephenson J, Aldington S, et al. Retinopathy and vision loss in insulin-dependent diabetes in Europe. The EURODIAB IDDM Complications Study. Ophthalmology 1997;104:252–60.

34. Roy MS. Diabetic retinopathy in African Americans with type 1 diabetes: The New Jersey 725. 1. Methodology, population, frequency of retinopathy and visual impairment. Arch Ophthalmol 2000;118:97–104.

35. Sommer A, Tielsch JM, Katz J, et al. Racial differences in the cause-specific prevalence of blindness in East Baltimore. N Engl J Med 1991;325:1412–7.

36. Tielsch JM, Sommer A, Witt K, et al, for the Baltimore Eye Survey Research Group. Blindness and visual impairment in an American urban population. Arch Ophthalmol 1990;108:286–90.

37. Moss SE, Klein R, Klein BEK. The incidence of vision loss in a diabetic population. Ophthalmology 1988;95:1340–8.

38. Moss SE, Klein R, Klein BEK. Ten-year incidence of visual loss in a diabetic population. Ophthalmology 1994;101:1061–70.

39. Ederer F, Hiller R, Taylor HR. Senile lens changes and diabetes in two population studies. Am J Ophthalmol 1981;91:381–95.

40. Klein BEK, Klein R, Wang Q, et al. Older-onset diabetes and lens opacities. The Beaver Dam Eye Study. Ophthalmic Epidemiol 1995;2:49–55.

41. Leske MC, Ma S-Y W, Hennis A, et al. The Barbados Eye Study Group. Diabetes, hypertension, and cortical opacity as cataract risk factors in a black population. Ophthalmology 1999;106:35–41.

42. Klein BEK, Klein R, Moss SE. Prevalence of cataracts in a population-based study of persons with diabetes mellitus. Ophthalmology 1985;92:1191–6.

43. Klein BEK, Klein R, Lee KE. Diabetes, cardiovascular disease, selected cardiovascular disease risk factors and the 5-year incidence of eye-related cataract and progression of lens opacities: The Beaver Dam Eye Study. Am J Ophthalmol 1998;126:782–90.

44. Klein BEK, Klein R, Moss SE. Incidence of cataract surgery in the Wisconsin Epidemiologic Study of Diabetic Retinopathy. Am J Ophthalmol 1995;119:295–300.

45. Klein BEK, Klein R, Linten KLP, et al. Cigarette smoking and lens opacities in the Beaver Dam Eye Study. Am J Prev Med 1993;9:27–30.

46. Kattan HM, Flynn Jr HW, Pflugfelder SC, et al. Nosocomial endophthalmitis survey. Current incidence of infection after intraocular surgery. Ophthalmology 1991;98:227–38.

47. Wagner T, Knaflic D, Rauber M, et al. Influence of cataract surgery on the diabetic eye: a prospective study. Ger J Ophthalmol 1996;5:79–83.

48. The Diabetic Retinopathy Study Research Group. A modification of the Airlie House classification of diabetic retinopathy. Report No. 7. Invest Ophthalmol Vis Sci 1981;21:210–26.

49. Early Treatment of Diabetic Retinopathy Study. Grading of diabetic retinopathy from stereoscopic fundus photographs—an extension of the Modified Airlie House classification. ETDRS Report No. 10. Ophthalmology 1991;98:786–806.

50. Early Treatment Diabetic Retinopathy Study Research Group. Fundus photographic risk factors for progression of diabetic retinopathy. ETDRS Report No. 12. Ophthalmology 1991; 98(Suppl):823–33.

51. The Diabetic Retinopathy Study Research Group. Four risk factors for severe visual loss in diabetic retinopathy. Arch Ophthalmol 1979;97:654–5.

52. Rand LI, Prudíhomme GJ, Ederer F, et al. Factors influencing the development of visual loss in advanced diabetic retinopathy. Diabetic Retinopathy Study (DRS) Report No. 10. Invest Ophthalmol Vis Sci 1985;26:983–91.

53. Davis MD, Fisher MR, Gangnon RE, et al. Risk factors for high-risk proliferative diabetic retinopathy and severe visual loss: Early Treatment Diabetic Retinopathy Study Report No. 18. Invest Ophthalmol 1998;39:233–52.

54. Klein BEK, Davis MD, Segal P, et al. Diabetic retinopathy. Assessment of severity and progression. Ophthalmology 1984;91:10–7.

55. Goldberg MF, Fine SL, editors. Symposium on the treatment of diabetic retinopathy. 1968 Sep 29–Oct 1; Airlie House, Warrenton, Virginia. Washington, DC: US Government Printing Office (PHS Publ. No. 1980); 1968. p. 569–92.

56. Klein R, Klein BEK, Moss SE, et al. The Wisconsin Epidemiologic Study of Diabetic Retinopathy XIV. Ten-year incidence and progression of diabetic retinopathy. Arch Ophthalmol 1994;112:1217–28.

57. Klein R, Klein BEK, Moss SE, et al. The Wisconsin Epidemiologic Study of Diabetic Retinopathy IX. Four-year incidence and progression of diabetic retinopathy when age at diagnosis is less than 30 years. Arch Ophthalmol 1989;107:237–43.

58. Klein R, Klein BEK, Moss SE, et al. The Wisconsin Epidemiologic Study of Diabetic Retinopathy X. Four-year incidence and progression of diabetic retinopathy when age at diagnosis is 30 years or more. Arch Ophthalmol 1989;107:244–9.

59. Klein R, Klein BEK, Moss SE, et al. Prevalence of diabetes mellitus in Southern Wisconsin. Am J Epidemiol 1984;119:54–61.

60. Klein R, Klein BEK, Moss SE, et al. The Wisconsin Epidemiologic Study of Diabetic Retinopathy II. Prevalence and risk of diabetic retinopathy when age at diagnosis is less than 30 years. Arch Ophthalmol 1984;102:520–6.

61. Klein, R, Klein, BEK, Moss SE, et al. The Wisconsin Epidemiologic Study of Diabetic Retinopathy III. Prevalence and risk of diabetic retinopathy when age at diagnosis is 30 or more years. Arch Ophthalmol 1984;102:527–32.

62. Kenny SJ, Aubert RE, Geiss LS. Prevalence and incidence of non-insulin dependent diabetes. In: Diabetes in America. 2nd ed. Washington, DC National Diabetes Data Group, National Institute of Diabetes and Digestive and Kidney Diseases, National Institutes of Health; 1995. p. 47–67.

63. Klein R, Klein BEK, Moss SE, et al. The Wisconsin Epidemiologic Study of Diabetic Retinopathy XV. The long-term incidence of macular edema. Ophthalmology 1995;102:7–16.

64. Harris MI, Klein R, Welborn TA, et al. Onset of NIDDM occurs at least 4–7 years before clinical diagnosis. Diabetes Care 1992;15:815–9.

65. Klein R, Klein BEK, Moss SE, et al. The Beaver Dam Eye Study. Retinopathy in adults with newly discovered and previously diagnosed diabetes mellitus. Ophthalmology 1992;99:58–62.

66. Stolk RP, Vingerling JR, de Jong PT, et al. Retinopathy, glucose and insulin in an elderly population. The Rotterdam Study. Diabetes 1995;44:1–11.

67. Kohner EM, Aldington SJ, Stratton IM, et al. United Kingdom Prospective Diabetes Study, 30. Diabetic retinopathy at diagnosis of non-insulin dependent diabetes mellitus and associated risk factors. Arch Ophthalmol 1998;116:297–303.

68. Rajala U, Laakso M, Qiao Q, et al. Prevalence of retinopathy in people with diabetes, impaired glucose tolerance and normal glucose tolerance. Diabetes Care 1998;21:1664–8.

69. Klein R. Retinopathy in a population-based study. Trans Am Ophthalmol Soc 1992;90:561–94.

70. McCance DR, Hanson RL, Charles M-A, et al. Comparison of tests for glycated hemoglobin and fasting and 2-hour plasma glucose concentrations as diagnostic methods for diabetes. BMJ 1994;308:1323–8.

71. Engelgau MM, Thompson TJ, Herman WH, et al. Comparison of fasting and 2-hour glucose and HbA$_{1c}$ levels for diagnosing diabetes. Diagnostic criteria and performance revised. Diabetes Care 1997;20:785–91.

72. The Expert Committee on the Diagnosis and Classification of Diabetes Mellitus. Report of the Expert Committee on the Diagnosis and Classification of Diabetes Mellitus. Diabetes Care 1997;20:1183–97.

73. Klein R, Klein BEK, Moss SE, et al. Glycosylated hemoglobin predicts the incidence and progression of diabetic retinopathy. JAMA 1988;260:2864–71.

74. Klein R, Klein BEK, Cruickshanks KJ. Relationship of hyperglycemia to the long-term incidence and progression of diabetic retinopathy. Arch Intern Med 1994;154:2169–78.

75. Klein BEK, Moss SE, Klein R. Effect of pregnancy on progression of diabetic retinopathy. Diabetes Care 1990;13:34–40.

76. Chew EY, Klein ML, Ferris FL, et al. Association of elevated serum lipid levels with retinal hard exudate in diabetic retinopathy. Early Treatment Diabetic Retinopathy Study Report No. 22. Arch Ophthalmol 1996;114:1079–84.

77. Klein BEK, Klein R, Moss SE, et al. A cohort study of the relationship of diabetic retinopathy and blood pressure. Arch Ophthalmol 1995;113:601–6.

78. Klein R, Klein BEK, Moss SE, et al. Is blood pressure a predictor of the incidence and progression of diabetic retinopathy? Arch Intern Med 1989;149:2427–32.

79. The Wisconsin Epidemiologic Study of Diabetic Retinopathy: XVII. The 14-year incidence and progression of diabetic retinopathy and associated risk factors in type 1 diabetes. Ophthalmology 1998;105:1801–15.

80. Lloyd CE, Klein R, Maser RE et al. The progression of retinopathy over 2 years: The Pittsburgh Epidemiology of Diabetes Complications (EDC) Study. J Diabetes Complications 1995;9:140–8.

81. Diabetes Control and Complications Trial Research Group. Clustering of long-term complications in families with diabetes in the Diabetes Control and Complications Trial. Diabetes 1997;46:1829–39.

82. UK Prospective Diabetes Study Group. Intensive blood glucose control with sulphonylureas or insulin compared with conventional treatment and risk of complications in patients with type 2 diabetes (UKPDS 33). Lancet 1998;352:837–53.

83. Diabetes Control and Complications Trial Research Group. The relationship of glycemic exposure (HbA$_{1c}$) to the risk of development and progression of retinopathy in the Diabetes Control and Complications Trial. Diabetes 1995;44:968–83.

84. Klein R, Klein BEK, Moss SE. Relation of glycemic control to diabetic microvascular complication in diabetes mellitus. Ann Intern Med 1996;124:90–6.

85. Reichard P. Risk factors for progression of microvascular complications in the Stockholm Diabetes Intervention Study (SDIS). Diabetes Res Clin Pract 1992;16:151–6.

86. Diabetes Control and Complications Trial Research Group. The absence of a glycemic threshold for the development of long-term complications: the perspective of the Diabetes Control and Complications Trial. Diabetes 1996;45:1289–98.

87. Arfken SL, Reno PL, Santiago JV, et al. Development of proliferative diabetic retinopathy in African-Americans and whites with type 1 diabetes. Diabetes Care 1998;21:792–5.

88. Harris MI, Klein R, Cowie CC, et al. Is the risk of diabetic retinopathy greater in non-Hispanic blacks and Mexican-Americans than in non-Hispanic whites with type 2 diabetes? A US population study. Diabetes Care 1998;21:1230–5.

89. Haffner SM, Fong D, Stern MP, et al. Diabetic retinopathy in Mexican-Americans and non-Hispanic whites. Diabetes 1988;37:878–84.

90. Hamman RF, Mayer EJ, Moo-Young GA, et al. Prevalence and risk factors of diabetic retinopathy in non-Hispanic whites and Hispanics with NIDDM. San Luis Valley Diabetes Study. Diabetes 1989;38:1231–7.

91. Tudor SM, Hamman RF, Baron A, et al. Incidence and progression of diabetic retinopathy in Hispanics and non-Hispanic whites with type 2 diabetes. San Luis Valley Diabetes Study, Colorado. Diabetes Care 1998;21:53–61.

92. Harris EL, Sherman SH, Georgopoulos A. Black-white differences in the risk of developing retinopathy among individuals with type 2 diabetes. Diabetes Care 1999;22:779–83.

93. Klein R, Klein BEK, Moss SE, et al. Severe retinopathy in insulin-taking children and young adults. Pediatr Adolesc Endocr 1988;17:146–52.

94. Kostraba JN, Dorman JS, Orchard TJ, et al. Contribution of diabetes duration before puberty to development of microvascular complications in IDDM subjects. Diabetes Care 1989;12:686–93.

95. Klein R, Klein BEK, Moss SE, et al. Retinopathy in young-onset diabetic patients. Diabetes Care 1985;8:311–5.

96. Roy MS. Diabetic retinopathy in African Americans with type 1 diabetes: The New Jersey 725. II. Risk factors. Arch Ophthalmol 2000;118:105–15.

97. Kokkonen J. Lautala D, Salmela P. Social maturation in juvenile onset diabetes. Acta Paediatr 1994;83:279–84.

98. Goldstein DE, Blinder KJ, De CH, et al. Glycemic control and development of retinopathy in youth-onset insulin-dependent diabetes mellitus. Ophthalmology 1993;100:1125–32.

99. McNally PG, Raymond NT, Swift PG, et al. Does the prepubertal duration of diabetes influence the onset of microvascular complications? Diabet Med 1993;10:906–8.

100. Donaghue KC, Fung AT, Hing S, et al. The effect of prepubital diabetes duration on diabetes. Microvascular complications in early and late adolescence. Diabetes Care 1997;20:77–80.

101. Teuscher A, Schnell H, Wilson PWF. Incidence of diabetic retinopathy and relationship to baseline plasma glucose and blood pressure. Diabetes Care 1988;11:246–51.

102. Arak A, Ho H, Hattori A, et al. Risk factors for the development of retinopathy in elderly Japanese patients with diabetes mellitus. Diabetes Care 1993;16:1184–6.

103. Estacio RO, Jeffers BW, Gifford N, et al. Effect of blood pressure control on diabetic microvascular complications in patients with hypertension and type 2 diabetes. Diabetes Care 2000;23:54–64.

104. Klein R, Moss SE, Klein BEK, et al. The Wisconsin Epidemiologic Study of Diabetic Retinopathy XI. The incidence of macular edema. Ophthalmology 1989;96:1501–10.

105. Stephenson JM, Fuller JH, Viberti GC, et al. Blood pressure, retinopathy and urinary albuminum excretion in IDDM: The EURODIAB IDDM Complications Study. Diabetologia 1995;38:599–603.

106. Laakso M. Epidemiology of diabetic dyslipidemia. Diabetes Rev 1995;3:408–22.

107. Diabetes Control and Complications Trial Research Group. Progression of retinopathy with intensive versus conventional treatment in the Diabetes Control and Complications Trial. Ophthalmology 1995;102:647–61.

108. Klein BEK, Moss SE, Klein R, et al. The Wisconsin Epidemiologic Study of Diabetic Retinopathy. XIII. Relationship of serum cholesterol to retinopathy and hard exudate. Ophthalmology 1991;98:1261–5.

109. Ferris FL, Chew EY, Hoogwerf BJ, and the Early Treatment Diabetic Retinopathy Study Research Group. Serum lipids and diabetic retinopathy. Diabetes Care 1996;19:1291–3.

110. Klein BEK, Klein R, Meuer SM, et al. Does the severity of diabetic retinopathy predict pregnancy outcome? J Diabetes Complications 1988;2:179–84.

111. Hemachandra A, Ellis D, Lloyd CE, et al. The influence of pregnancy on IDDM complications. Diabetes Care 1995;18:950–4.

112. Klein BEK, Klein R. Gravidity and diabetic retinopathy. Am J Epidemiol 1984;119:564–9.

113. Chew EY, Mills JL, Metzger BE, et al. Metabolic control and progression of retinopathy. The Diabetes in Early Pregnancy Study. Diabetes Care 1995;18:631–7.

114. Rosenn B, Miodovnik M, Kranias G, et al. Progression of diabetic retinopathy in pregnancy: association with hypertension in pregnancy. Am J Obstet Gynecol 1992;166:1214–8.

115. Lvestam-Adrian M, Agardh C-D, Berg A, et al. Pre-eclampsia is a potent risk factor for deterioration of retinopathy during pregnancy in type 1 diabetic patients. Diabet Med 1997;14:1059–65.

116. Moss SE, Klein R, Klein BEK. Cigarette smoking and ten-year progression of diabetic retinopathy. Ophthalmology 1996;103:1438–42.

117. Moss SE, Klein R, Klein BEK. The association of alcohol consumption with the incidence and progression of diabetic retinopathy. Ophthalmology 1994;101:1962–8.

118. Holland WW, Stewart S. Screening in health care: benefit or bane? Nuffield Provincial Hospital Trust; 1990.

119. Moss SE, Klein R, Kessler SD, Richie KA. Comparison between ophthalmoscopy and fundus photography in determining severity of diabetic retinopathy. Ophthalmology 1985;92:62–7.

120. Kinyoun J, Barton F, Fisher M, et al. Detection of diabetic macular edema. Ophthalmoscopy versus photography—Early Treatment Diabetic Retinopathy Study Report No. 5. Ophthalmology 1989;96:746–51.

121. Bachmann MO, Nelson SJ. Impact of diabetic retinopathy screening on a British district population: case detection and blindness prevention in an evidence-based model. J Epidemiol Community Health 1998;52:45–52.

122. Javitt JC, Aiello LP, Chiang Y, et al. Preventative eye care in people with diabetes is cost-saving to the federal government. Diabetes Care 1994;17:909–17.

123. Bresnick GH, Mukamel DB, Dickinson JC, et al. A screening approach to the surveillance of patients with diabetes for the presence of vision-threatening retinopathy. Ophthalmology 2000;107:19–24.

124. Reichard P, Nilson BY, Rosenquist U. The effect of long-term intensified insulin treatment on the development of microvascular complications of diabetes mellitus. N Engl J Med 1993;329:304–9.

125. Diabetes Control and Complications Trial Research Group. The effect of intensive diabetes treatment on the progression of diabetic retinopathy in insulin-dependent diabetes mellitus. Arch Ophthalmol 1995;113:36–49.

126. Wang PH, Lau J, Chalmers TC. Meta-analysis of effects of intensive blood glucose control on late complications of type 1 diabetes. Lancet 1993;341:1306–9.

127. Ohkubo Y, Kishikawa H, Araki E, et al. Intensive insulin therapy prevents the progression of diabetic microvascular complications in Japanese patients with non-insulin-dependent diabetes mellitus: a randomized prospective 6-year study. Diabetes Res Clin Pract 1995;28:103–17.

128. Shichiri M, Kishikawa H, Ohkubo Y. Long-term results of the Kumamoto study on optimal diabetes control in type 2 diabetic patients. Diabetes Care 2000;23:21–9.

129. Diabetes Control and Complications Trial/Epidemiology of Diabetes Interventions and Complications Research Group. Retinopathy and nephropathy in patients with type 1 diabetes four years after a trial of intensive therapy. N Engl J Med 2000;342:381–9.

130. Diabetes Control and Complications Trial Research Group. Early worsening of diabetic retinopathy in the Diabetes Control and Complications Trial. Arch Ophthalmol 1998;116:874–86.

131. Emanuele N, Klein R, Abraira C, et al. Evaluations of retinopathy in the VA Cooperative Study on glycemic control and complications in Type 2 diabetes (VA CSDM). Diabetes Care 1996;19:1375–81.

132. Efficacy of atenolol and captopril in reducing risk of macrovascular and microvascular complications in type 2 diabetes: UKPDS 39. BMJ 1998;317:713–20.

133. Rajagopalan S, Harrison DG. Reversing endothelial dysfunction with ACE inhibitors. A new trend. Circulation 1996;94:240–3.

134. Chaturvedi N, Sjolie A-K, Stephenson JM, et al. Effect of lisinopril on progression of retinopathy in normotensive people with type 1 diabetes. Lancet 1998;351:28–31.

135. Effects of ramipril on cardiovascular and microvascular outcomes in people with diabetes mellitus: results of the HOPE study and MICRO-HOPE substudy. Lancet 2000;355:253–9.

136. The TIMAD Study Group. Ticlopidine treatment reduces the progression of non-proliferative diabetic retinopathy. Arch Ophthalmol 1990;108:1577–83.

137. The DAMAD Study Group. Effect of aspirin alone and aspirin plus dipyridamole in early diabetic retinopathy. A multicentre randomized controlled clinical trial. Diabetes 1989;38:491–8.

138. Early Treatment Diabetic Retinopathy Study Research Group. Effects of aspirin treatment on diabetic retinopathy. ETDRS Report No.8. Ophthalmology 1991;98(Suppl);757–65.

139. Flynn HW Jr, Chew EY, Simons BD, et al. The Early Treatment Diabetic Retinopathy Study Research Group. Pars plana vitrectomy in the Early Treatment Diabetic Retinopathy Study: ETDRS Report No. 17. Ophthalmology 1992;99:1351–7.

140. Chew EY, Klein ML, Murphy RP et al. Effects of aspirin on vitreous/pre-retinal hemorrhage in patients with diabetes mellitus. Early Treatment Diabetic Retinopathy Study Report No. 20. Arch Ophthalmol 1995;113:52–5.

141. Chew EY, Williams GA, Burton TC, et al. Aspirin effects on the development of cataracts in patients with diabetes mellitus. Early Treatment Diabetic Retinopathy Study Report No. 16. Arch Ophthalmol 1992;110:339–42.

142. Boel E, Sehmer J, Flodgaard HJ. et al. Diabetic late complications: will aldose reductase inhibitors or inhibitors of advanced glycosylation end product formation hold promise? J Diabetes Complications 1995;9:104–29.

143. Sorbinil Retinopathy Trial Research Group. A randomized trial of Sorbinil, an aldose reductase inhibitor, in diabetic retinopathy. Arch Ophthalmol 1990;108:1234–44.

144. Arauz C, Ramirez L, Pruneda L et al. The effect of the aldose reductase inhibitor, Ponalrestat, on the progression of diabetic retinopathy. J Diabetes Complications 1992;6:131–7.

145. Bloomgarden ZT. Antioxidants and diabetes. Diabetes Care 1997;20:670–3.

146. Mayer-Davis EJ, Bell RA, Reboussin BA, et al. Antioxidant nutrient intake and diabetic retinopathy. The San Luis Valley Diabetes Study. Ophthalmology 1998;105:2264–70.

147. Gæde P, Vedel P, Parving H-H, et al. Intensified multifactorial intervention in patients with type 2 diabetes mellitus and micro-albuminuria: The Steno type 2 randomized study. Lancet 1999;353:617–22.

148. Diabetic Retinopathy Study Research Group. Preliminary report on effects of photocoagulation therapy. Am J Ophthalmol 1976;81:383–96.

149. Diabetic Retinopathy Study Research Group. Photocoagulation treatment of proliferative diabetic retinopathy. Clinical application of Diabetic Retinopathy Study (DRS) findings, DRS Report No. 8. Ophthalmology 1981;88:583–600.

150. Diabetic Retinopathy Study Research Group. Photocoagulation treatment of proliferative diabetic retinopathy: relationship of adverse treatment effects to retinopathy severity. Diabetic Retinopathy Study Report Number 5. Dev Ophthalmol 1981;2:248–61.

151. Ferris FL, Podgor MJ, Davis MD. The Diabetic Retinopathy Study Research Group: macular edema in Diabetic Retinopathy Study patients. Diabetic Retinopathy Study Report No. 12. Ophthalmology 1987;94:754–60.

152. Kaufman SC, Ferris FL, Seigel DG, et al, and the Diabetic Retinopathy Study Research Group. Factors associated with visual outcome after photocoagulation for diabetic retinopathy. Diabetic Retinopathy Study Report No. 13. Invest Ophthalmol Vis Sci 1989;30:23–8.

153. Early Treatment Diabetic Retinopathy Study Research Group. Early photocoagulation for diabetic retinopathy. ETDRS Report No. 9. Ophthalmology 1991;98:766–85.

154. Ferris FL. How effective are treatments for diabetic retinopathy? JAMA 1993;269:1290–1.

155. Ferris E. Early photocoagulation in patients with either type 1 or type 2 diabetes. Trans Am Ophthalmol Soc 1996;94:505–37.

156. Diabetic Retinopathy Vitrectomy Study Research Group. Two-year course of visual acuity in severe proliferative diabetic retinopathy with conventional management. Diabetic Retinopathy Vitrectomy Study (DRVS) Report No. 1. Ophthalmology 1985;92:492–502.

157. Diabetic Retinopathy Vitrectomy Study Research Group. Early vitrectomy for severe vitreous hemorrhage in diabetic retinopathy. Two-year results of a randomized trial. Diabetic Retinopathy Vitrectomy Study Report No. 2. Arch Ophthalmol 1985;103:1644–52.

158. Diabetic Retinopathy Vitrectomy Study Research Group. Early vitrectomy for severe vitreous hemorrhage in diabetic retinopathy. Four-year results of a randomized trial: Diabetic Retinopathy Vitrectomy Study Report No. 5. Arch Ophthalmol 1990;108:958–64.

159. Diabetic Retinopathy Vitrectomy Study Research Group. Early vitrectomy for severe proliferative diabetic retinopathy in eyes with useful vision. Results of a randomized trial. Diabetic Retinopathy Vitrectomy Study Report No. 3. Ophthalmology 1988;95:1307–20.

160. Diabetic Retinopathy Vitrectomy Study Research Group. Early vitrectomy for severe proliferative diabetic retinopathy in eyes with useful vision. Clinical application of results of a randomized trial. Diabetic Retinopathy Vitrectomy Study Report No. 4. Ophthalmology 1988;95:1321–34.

161. Early Treatment Diabetic Retinopathy Study Research Group. Treatment techniques and clinical guidelines for photocoagulation of diabetic macular edema. Early Treatment Diabetic Retinopathy Study Report No. 2. Ophthalmology 1987;94:761–74.

162. Early Treatment Diabetic Retinopathy Study Research Group. Photocoagulation for diabetic macular edema: Early Treatment Diabetic Retinopathy Study Report No. 4. Int Ophthalmol Clin 1987;27:265–72.

163. Early Treatment Diabetic Retinopathy Study Research Group. Focal photocoagulation treatment of diabetic macular edema. Relationship of treatment effect to fluorescein angiographic and other retinal characteristics at baseline: ETDRS Report No. 19. Arch Ophthalmol 1995;113:1144–55.

CHAPTER 22

Kidney Disease

Andrew W. Steele, MD, FRCPC

ABSTRACT

One of the most devastating manifestations of diabetes is end-stage renal disease (ESRD). Diabetes remains the leading cause of ESRD in North America, and the incidence of patients starting renal replacement programs due to diabetic kidney disease is rising. Diabetic nephropathy was previously thought to be a condition that occurred as a result of predetermined genetic factors. As such, early approaches to clinical management failed to address the risk factors for progression. In recent years, it has become apparent that the natural course of renal disease in diabetes can be altered. New goals of therapy relating to prevention of the progression of renal disease have emerged.

The clinical course of diabetic nephropathy is a stepwise progression from subclinical disease through incipient nephropathy (characterized by microalbuminuria—an albumin excretion rate of 30–300 mg/24 h) to overt nephropathy and macroscopic albuminuria (characterized by an excretion of > 300 mg albumin/24 h).[1] Once albuminuria develops, there is a considerable increase in the risk of cardiovascular morbidity and mortality, and many patients progress to eventual ESRD over a period of several years if they do not succumb to cardiovascular complications.[2–4]

Patients with diabetes and ESRD have a very high mortality, with an overall expected survival of approximately 3 years.[5,6] In addition, the financial costs of managing patients with renal replacement therapy are estimated between C$35,000 to C$88,000/y/patient in direct costs alone.[7,8] In North America, the costs of treatment of patients with ESRD in 1991 were in excess of $2 billion yearly.[9] With the increasing prevalence not only of diabetes but of ESRD attributed to diabetes, this becomes a major resource issue and one of vital public health importance. Consequently, the focus of management of the renal complications of diabetes is on prevention.

The earliest clinically recognizable sign of diabetic nephropathy is microalbuminuria.[10,11] Screening for this condition identifies individuals at high risk of progression. Numerous recent trials have shown that therapy at this stage, with improved metabolic and hemodynamic control, prevents the progression to overt diabetic nephropathy. Once diabetic nephropathy occurs, the glomerular filtration rate falls by 2 to 20 mL/min/y if no therapy is initiated.[12] In people with Type 1 diabetes, this results in ESRD developing in 50% of people over a 10-year period.[13,14] Therapy at this (late) stage, particularly with hypertension control and angiotensin converting enzyme (ACE) inhibitor use, is of considerable benefit in slowing the deterioration in renal function and delaying the time to dialysis or transplantation. The proportion of patients with Type 2 diabetes progressing to ESRD is smaller, presumably because of increased risk of dying from cardiovascular disease.[4,15] Despite the lower proportion of patients who progress, the much higher prevalence of Type 2 diabetes leads to the observation that over 50% of diabetic patients with ESRD entering dialysis programs have Type 2 diabetes.[16–18] After controlling for the duration of diabetes, the risk of nephropathy is the same in people with Type 2 and Type 1 diabetes.[12,19] Thus, as improvements in cardiovascular therapy occur and as patients with diabetes are living longer, an even higher proportion of patients with Type 2 diabetes may be expected to develop ESRD.

INTRODUCTION

This chapter deals with the definitions and diagnosis of the various stages of renal disease in diabetes. The focus is on early screening and intervention at the normoalbuminuric and microalbuminuric stages. Evidence relating to the plethora of recent clinical evidence is summarized. The chapter is divided into three broad sections dealing with (1) the prognosis and risk factors for diabetic nephropathy; (2) the diagnosis of the stages of diabetic nephropathy; and (3) the management of the stages of diabetic nephropathy. The following questions are addressed under each section:

Prognosis and Risk Factors

1. What are diabetic nephropathy and microalbuminuria?
2. What proportion of patients with Type 1 or Type 2 diabetes develop diabetic nephropathy and what is the timing?
3. What proportion of patients with Type 1 or Type 2 diabetic nephropathy develop renal failure?
4. What is the mortality in persons with diabetic nephropathy?
5. What is the pathogenesis of diabetic nephropathy?
6. What is the relationship of glucose levels and other risk factors to the risk of kidney disease?

Diagnosis

1. How is diabetic nephropathy diagnosed? What is the sensitivity and specificity of proteinuria compared to biopsy in Type 1 and Type 2 diabetes?
2. Can diabetic nephropathy be diagnosed early?
3. Can patients with diabetes be screened for hypertension alone rather than for microalbuminuria?

Management

1. Does glycemic control prevent or delay the progression of diabetic kidney disease?
2. What nonglycemic therapies can prevent or delay the progression of diabetic kidney disease?
3. What future treatment options are being studied to prevent the onset or progression of renal disease in patients with diabetes?

PROGNOSIS AND RISK FACTORS FOR DIABETIC KIDNEY DISEASE

What Are Diabetic Nephropathy and Microalbuminuria?

Diabetic nephropathy is defined as the presence of a persistently positive urine dipstick for albumin or > 0.3 g/d of albumin excretion (ie, clinical proteinuria) in a person with diabetes, in the absence of other renal disease.[20,21] By this definition, diabetic nephropathy is a late manifestation of diabetes; however, there are physiologic, pathologic, and clinical manifestations that occur before nephropathy is manifest. This has led some authors to suggest stages of renal disease in diabetes[1] (Table 22–1). These stages have been more clearly defined for patients with Type 1 diabetes than with Type 2 diabetes; nonetheless, it is clear that at least for the clinical stages, patients must pass through a period of microalbuminuria before they develop overt diabetic nephropathy. Microalbuminuria is the earliest clinically recognizable stage of diabetic nephropathy and is defined as increased excretion of albumin to between 30 and 300 mg/d (or 20 to 200 µg/minute).[11,22]

What Proportion of Patients with Type 1 or II Diabetes Develop Diabetic Nephropathy?

Unfortunately, most of the information regarding the progression of diabetic nephropathy comes from highly selected patient populations. The original studies were based on infor-

Table 22-1 Stages of Renal Disease in Type 1 and Type 2 Diabetes

	1	*2*	*3*	*4*	*5*
Description of Stage	*Renal Hypertrophy and Hyperfunction*	*Renal Lesions without Clinical Signs*	*Incipient Nephropathy— Microalbuminuria*	*Clinical Diabetic Nephropathy*	*End-stage Renal Failure*
Onset	At onset of DM	2–3 y duration of DM	7–15 y duration of DM	5–15 y after microalbuminuria	By 20–40 y duration of DM
			In Type 2 DM, up to 20% have microalbuminuria at diagnosis of DM	In Type 2 DM, up to 8% have diabetic nephropathy at diagnosis of DM	
Functional and structural abnormalities	Increased GFR and kidney size Increased glomerular volume and capillary surface area associated with increased glomerular capillary pressure	Glomerular and tubular basement membrane thickening and mesangial expansion with proteinaceous deposition; glomerulosclerosis begins with decreasing capillary filtration surface area. GFR is still elevated in most patients, as is glomerular capillary pressure.	Between 25–50% of patients with DM develop elevated rates of excretion of albumin (30–300 mg/d), undetectable on traditional urine dipstick. GFR begins to decline in this stage.	Widespread glomerulosclerosis and hyaline arteriolar sclerosis. Persistent proteinuria on urine dipstick, > 0.3 g/d of protein excretion associated with declining GFR, often hypertension and retinopathy (especially in Type 1 DM).	GFR continues to decline, requiring renal replacement therapy

DM = diabetes mellitus; GFR = glomerular filtration rate.
Data from Mogensen et al[1] and Selby et al.[45]

mation obtained from patients attending specialty clinics and therefore suffered from referral bias.[12,13] In addition, most of the epidemiologic evidence deals with nephropathy in patients with Type 1 diabetes. In patients with Type 2 diabetes, the date of onset of diabetes is often in question, and some authors have proposed that the average patient with Type 2 diabetes may have had diabetes for up to 8 years before the diagnosis is made.[23] Further, it has been postulated that the reason for a lower incidence of ESRD in patients with Type 2 diabetes and nephropathy is that these patients die as a result of excess cardiovascular events before ESRD is manifest.[12]

Prevalence Studies

The prevalence of diabetic nephropathy and microalbuminuria from various cross-sectional studies is outlined in Table 22–2.[14,24–29] Overall, the prevalence of microalbuminuria increases with age, duration of diabetes and level of glycemia and is associated with other cardiovascular risk factors such as hypertension, smoking, hyperlipidemia, male sex, and short stature.[24,30–40] The mean duration of progression from microalbuminuria to diabetic nephropathy was found to be 8 years in patients with Type 1 diabetes.[14]

Table 22–2 Prevalence of Microalbuminuria and Proteinuria in Cross-sectional Studies of Patients with Diabetes

Study	Location	Population	N	Normal (%)	Micro (%)	Macro (%)
					Albuminuria	
Klein et al[24]	Wisconsin	Type 1 DM Mean age 31	706	58	21	21
Parving et al[25]	Denmark	Type 1 DM	876	58	23	19
Orchard et al[26]	Pitsburgh	Type 1 DM Mean age 28 Mean duration of DM 20 y	627	51	22	27
Lloyd et al[27]	Europe	Type 1 DM Mean age 28 Mean duration of DM 18 y	1,215	63	25	12
Warram et al[14]	Boston	Type 1 DM Mean age 33 Duration 1–39 y	1,613	Postpubertal duration of DM: < 3 y of DM 10 y of DM 30 y of DM	6.4 17–18 25	0 2–3 27
Gall et al[28]	Denmark	Type 2 DM	507	58	28	14
Klein et al[29]	Wisconsin	Type 2 DM using insulin	435	50	29	19
Klein et al[29]	Wisconsin	Type 2 DM not using insulin	363	68	22	10

DM = diabetes mellitus.

Incidence Studies

Early studies of diabetic nephropathy in patients with Type 1 diabetes whose diabetes onset occurred in the 1930 to 1950s reported a cumulative incidence of diabetic nephropathy of 35 to 41% at 25 to 40 years duration of diabetes.[13,41] Although the proportion of patients who develop diabetic nephropathy has decreased recently, most studies still report cumulative incidence rates of diabetic nephropathy of 20 to 30% at 25 to 30 years duration of diabetes (Table 22–3).[13,14,16,37,41–46] In a population-based incidence study in Wisconsin among patients with

Table 22–3 Cumulative Incidence of Diabetic Nephropathy in Cross-sectional Studies of Patients with Diabetes

Study	Location	Population	N	Diabetic Nephropathy Cumulative Incidence (%)	Duration of DM
Andersen et al[41]	Denmark	Type 1 DM Onset of DM < 1953	1,475	41	> 25 y
Krolewski et al[13]	Boston	Type 1 DM Onset of DM 1930–59	292	35	40 y
Kofoed-Enevoldsen et al[43]	Denmark	Type 1 DM Onset of DM 1933–72	2,980	40.6 26.9	25 y (onset 1933–42) 25 y (onset 1953–62)
Bojestig et al[44]	Sweden	Type 1 DM Onset of DM 1961–80	213	30 8.9	25 y (onset 1961–65) 25 y (onset 1966–70)
Rossing et al[46]	Denmark	Type 1 DM Onset of DM 1961–80	356	18 20 16	15 y (onset 1965–69) 15 y (onset 1970–74) 15 y (onset 1975–79)
Warram et al[14]	Boston	Type 1 DM Onset of DM 1952–90	1,613	27	30 y
Tuomilehto et al[42]	Finland	Type 1 DM Onset of DM 1965–79	5,149	20	24 y
Klein et al[37]	Wisconsin	Type 1 DM (younger onset < 30)	666	28	10 y
Klein et al[37]	Wisconsin	Type 2 DM (older onset > 30)	376 418	40 33	10 y (insulin using) 10 y (non-insulin using)
Ballard et al[16]	Rochester, Minnesota	Type 2 DM Onset of DM 1945–69	1,031	24.6	20 y

DM = diabetes mellitus.

Type 1 and II diabetes, the incidence of proteinuria developing over a 10-year interval (beginning follow-up in 1984 to 1986) was 28% in the younger-onset group, 40% in the older-onset group taking insulin, and 33% in the older-onset group not taking insulin.[37]

In a population-based study of a cohort of mostly Caucasian patients whose Type 2 diabetes began in the years 1945 to 1969, it was revealed that 8.2% of patients had diabetic nephropathy within 6 months of the time their diabetes diagnosis was made. The cumulative incidence of diabetic nephropathy was 15.3/1000 patient-years, resulting in a cumulative incidence of diabetic nephropathy of 25% at 20 years.[16]

In a more recent population-based case-control study from the northeastern United States, persons with Type 1 and Type 2 diabetes were found to have a significantly increased risk of developing ESRD: the overall odds ratio (OR) was 11.1 (95% CI 7.2 to 16.9); the OR for Type 1 diabetes was 33.7 (95% CI 12.4 to 91.9); and the OR for Type 2 diabetes was 7.0 (95% CI 4.4 to 11.1).[18] In this study, the population-attributable risk for kidney failure due to diabetes was 42% overall (21% for Type 1 diabetes and 21% for Type 2 diabetes). Thus, of all cases of ESRD in this population, 42% could be ascribed to diabetes.

There has been a suggestion that there is a decline in the incidence of diabetic nephropathy. In a study from Sweden,[44] patients whose diabetes onset occurred from 1961 to 1965 were compared to those with onset occurring > 1965. The 25-year cumulative incidence of nephropathy decreased from 30 to 8.9%; however, this change in incidence has not been found in other recent studies (see Table 22–3). One reason for the difference may be the overall excellent glycemic control in the Swedish cohort, who had a mean glycosylated hemoglobin of 7 to 7.4% during the last 11 years in which it was measured.[44]

The largest study to date addressing the change in the incidence of diabetic nephropathy is based on a Finnish community-based register of over 5,100 patients with Type 1 diabetes.[42] This register has an ascertainment rate of > 95% and documented no change in the incidence of diabetic nephropathy over a 24-year period, with a cumulative incidence of diabetic nephropathy at 24 years of 20%. There was no significant difference in the cumulative incidence according to year of onset of diabetes. In this and other recent studies, the rate of diabetic nephropathy increases 8 to 10 years after the diagnosis and peaks at 2 to 3% annual incidence from 15 to 25 years after diagnosis.[42–44,46]

EVIDENCE-BASED MESSAGES

1. The population-attributable risk for kidney failure due to diabetes in a recent population-based case-control study from the northeastern United States was 42% overall (21% for Type 1 diabetes and 21% for Type 2 diabetes) (Level 1).[18]
2. Although lower than original reports, the cumulative incidence of diabetic nephropathy from European registry data appears to be stable over the last 20 years, with an incidence of 20% at 24 years (Level 1).[42]

What Proportion of Patients with Type 1 and Type 2 Diabetes Develop Renal Failure?

Clinical proteinuria is associated with a significant and persistent decline in renal function.[12,20,21,47–49] In patients whose Type 1 or Type 2 diabetes was diagnosed from the 1930 to 1970s and who had diabetic nephropathy, the median time from onset of proteinuria to the development of ESRD was between 7 and 10 years.[13,14,17] In the Joslin Clinic cohort, 50% of patients with Type 1 diabetes and proteinuria progressed to ESRD by 10 years; overall, 15% of all patients with diabetes developed ESRD, with a cumulative incidence by 30 years of 30%.[13]

The risk of renal failure in people with diabetes (regardless of nephropathy status) has also been reported. In the Wisconsin Epidemiologic Study of Diabetic Retinopathy (WESDR)—a population-based cohort of individuals with Type 1 diabetes followed from 1984 to 1986 and again from 1990 to 1992 and 1995 to 1996—the 10-year cumulative incidence of renal insufficiency or ESRD in patients with Type 1 diabetes was 14.4% (95% CI 12.8 to 17.0%) (Table 22–4).[50] In a retrospective population-based incidence cohort of 1,832 patients with Type 2 diabetes and 136 patients with Type 1 diabetes diagnosed between 1945 and 1979, the incidence of advanced renal failure (defined as a serum creatinine > 354 µg/L) or ESRD at 10 and 25 years was 0% and 8%, respectively, for patients with Type 1 diabetes and 0.8% and 6.2%, respectively, for patients with Type 2 diabetes.[17] In this study, 0.3% of patients with Type 2 diabetes without proteinuria at baseline developed ESRD within 10 years, compared to 8.4% in those with baseline proteinuria (hazard ratio 12.1 95% CI 4.3 to 34.0) and 10.7% in those who developed persistent proteinuria during the study.

Patients with diabetes account for the largest proportion of patients entering renal replacement programs in Canada and the United States.[5,6] In the United States Renal Data System (USRDS Annual Report 1999), the incidence of ESRD in patients with diabetes was 120 per million population, accounting for 33.2% of all patients with ESRD. The proportion of patients with ESRD attributed to diabetes is increasing annually. From 1988 to 1992, the annual increase was 14%, but this rate decreased to 9% between 1992 and 1997.[6] In patients registering with renal replacement programs, the proportion whose renal failure is ascribed to diabetes in Canada was 28%[5] and in the United States 41% in 1997.[6]

EVIDENCE-BASED MESSAGES

1. The 10-year cumulative incidence of renal insufficiency or ESRD in patients with Type 1 diabetes exceeds 14% (Level 1).[50]
2. Clinical proteinuria (overt nephropathy) is a strong risk factor for ESRD (Level 1).[13,17]

Table 22–4 The 10-Year Risk of Diabetic Nephropathy and Declining Renal Function as a Function of Baseline Glycosylated Hemoglobin[*]

10-Year Incidence of Creatinine Clearance Decline of ≥ 3 mL/min/1.73 m_2/y by Baseline Glucose Level

Glycosylated Hemoglobin	N in Subgroup	p Value	Relative Risk (95% CI)
5.4–8.7	160	< .0001	1.00
8.8–9.8	133	—	1.28 (0.94–1.75)
9.9–11.1	126	—	1.63 (1.22–2.17)
11.2–17.7	109	—	2.04 (1.55–2.68)

10-year Incidence of Renal Insufficiency[†] as a Function of Baseline Glycosylated Hemoglobin

Glycosylated Hemoglobin	N in Subgroup	p Value	Relative Risk (95% CI)
5.4–8.7	164	< .0001	1.00
8.8–9.8	138		2.84 (1.06–7.58)
9.9–11.1	131		4.00 (1.58–10.11)
11.2–17.7	120		11.99 (5.89–24.41)

[*]Data were taken from the WESRD population-based cohort of individuals with younger-onset diabetes. Patients were seen initially in 1984–86 (n = 891) and in follow-up during 1990–92 (n = 765) and during 1995–96 (n = 634).
[†]Renal insufficiency defined as serum creatinine ≥ 2.0 mg/dL (178 mmol/L) or receiving dialysis or a renal transplant. Data from Klein R, Klein BE, Moss SE, et al. The 10-year incidence of renal insufficiency in people with type 1 diabetes. Diabetes Care 1999;22:743–51.

What Is the Mortality in Persons with Diabetic Nephropathy?

Epidemiologic studies demonstrate a two- to threefold higher risk of cardiovascular mortality in male and three- to fivefold higher risk in female patients with diabetes compared to those without diabetes.[51–56] The highest risk occurs in those diabetic patients with proteinuria.[3,57,58] Patients with diabetes and renal involvement are at increased risk of cardiovascular (CV) morbidity and mortality and of total mortality.[4,56,59] This excess CV risk is more pronounced in females and occurs at all stages of renal involvement, from microalbuminuria to ESRD.

The mortality risk associated with microalbuminuria was recently summarized in a systematic overview of 11 cohorts involving 2,138 patients with Type 2 diabetes and microalbuminuria followed for > 6 years; it reported that compared to normoalbuminuric controls, the OR for total mortality was 2.4 (95% CI 1.8 to 3.1).[4] For CV morbidity and mortality, the OR was 2.0 (95% CI 1.4 to 2.7). These values were robust to sensitivity analyses. The mean unadjusted mortality rates were found to be 5.9% ± 2.0% and 2.7% ± 1.8% for those Type 2 patients with and without microalbuminuria, respectively. The positive association remained even after adjusting for other CV risk factors. In patients with Type 1 diabetes, a similar association has been found. In a matched case-control sample followed for 10 years, those patients with microalbuminuria had an eightfold increased incidence of coronary heart disease (CHD) (40% vs 5%) compared to patients without albuminuria.[57]

Patients with diabetic nephropathy have an even higher risk of CV mortality than those with microalbuminuria. In patients with Type 1 diabetes, the risk varies with sex and age, being higher for women than for men. Overall, the relative mortality from CV disease for diabetic patients with proteinuria was found to be 37 times that in the general population, whereas in patients with no proteinuria, the relative mortality was 4.2 times that in the general population.[3] The World Health Organization Multinational Study of Vascular Disease in Diabetes is a collection of 10 international cohorts of patients with Type 1 and Type 2 diabetes followed from 1975 to 1987. In this study, patients with diabetes and no proteinuria or hypertension had standardized mortality rates (SMRs) that were significantly increased (284 in men and 360 in women with Type 1 diabetes, 192 in men and 236 in women with Type 2 diabetes). In those patients with proteinuria, the SMRs were approximately 500 to 600 for Type 1 diabetes and 300 to 400 for Type 2 diabetes. In patients with both hypertension and proteinuria, the SMRs ranged between 1,100 for men and 1,800 for women with Type 1 diabetes and 500 for men and 800 for women with Type 2 diabetes.[56]

Patients with ESRD due to diabetes have the highest morbidity and mortality. In Canada, the 3- and 5-year survival rates for diabetes-related ESRD are 49% and 33%, respectively, values that are worse than colon and breast cancer survival rates.[5] The vast majority of this excess mortality is related to CV disease, with > 18% of these deaths occurring in patients < 45 years of age.[5]

EVIDENCE-BASED MESSAGE

Microalbuminuria, clinical proteinuria, and ESRD are progressively stronger risk factors for total and CV mortality in people with diabetes (Level 1).[3,4,5,56]

What Is the Pathogenesis of Diabetic Nephropathy?

The morphologic changes in diabetic nephropathy begin to develop before clinical albuminuria is present.[60–63] These early changes include thickening of the glomerular basement membrane (GBM) and thickening of the tubular basement membrane and Bowman's capsule. There is an increase in the volume of matrix proteins in the mesangium with mesangial expansion. In addition, there is accelerated hyalinosis of the afferent and efferent arterioles. Mesangial expansion leads to increased mesangial volume per glomerulus and decreased glomerular capillary surface area—thus, decreased glomerular filtration rate (GFR).[60,61,63–66] It is the mesangial expansion encroaching on the capillary surface area that correlates best with the clinical decline in renal function.[63,64,66,67] Ultimately, diffuse glomerulosclerosis may occur; however, the nodular sclerotic lesion first identified by Kimmelstiel and Wilson, which is the hallmark of diabetic glomerulosclerosis, is not present in 80% of cases of diabetic nephropathy.[68]

As these pathologic changes occur, there is decreasing filtration surface and decreased nephron mass, which leads to higher capillary flows in the remaining nephrons. This process is associated with increased intraglomerular hypertension, hyperfiltration, and progressive proteinuria, which is accelerated by changes in the permselectivity of the GBM.[69–71] This process is hastened by systemic hypertension, elevated angiotensin II levels leading to efferent arteriolar constriction, and high protein meals leading to renal vasodilation and increased glomerular hypertension.[69,72–75] Further, as renal function deteriorates, this leads to worsening systemic and glomerular hypertension—setting up a vicious cycle. Support for the hemodynamic theory of renal injury in diabetes comes from both animal and human experimental models demonstrating improvement in the above changes and declining proteinuria with ACE inhibitors, hypertension control, and avoidance of high-protein diets.[70,74,75]

Two main pathophysiologic mechanisms are responsible for the development of diabetic nephropathy: (1) the hemodynamic mechanism outlined above and (2) disturbances of the metabolic milieu, especially elevated glucose levels (glucotoxicity) and abnormal lipid profiles. Glucotoxicity and hemodynamic stressors lead to altered cellular functions that include increases in the polyol pathway through aldose reductase, resulting in increased intracellular sorbitol.[76,77] In addition, formation of advanced glycation end products (AGE) occurs proportionate to the concentration of glucose. These AGE products are known to alter the levels of cytokines and change the biologic activity of proteins and enzymes.[78–81] Other mechanisms include abnormal synthesis of glycosoaminoglycans, activation of protein kinase C isoforms, and increased production of transforming growth factor-beta and other growth factors. These mechanisms are thought to lead to alterations in the permselective filtration barrier and increase mesangial matrix deposition, hallmarks of diabetic nephropathy.

It should be noted that despite near-normalization of blood glucose in the Diabetes Control and Complications Trial (DCCT), a small number (2.2 per 100 patient-years of follow-up, or 16%) of patients with Type 1 diabetes did develop increasing microalbuminuria during the 9 years of follow-up.[82] These data indicate that subpopulations exist that have a remarkable, likely polygenic, predisposition to progressive diabetic nephropathy.[12,83–93] This and other epidemiologic evidence suggests that there is a subgroup of patients at high risk, irrespective of glycemic control. There is certainly a genetic component, accounting for the clustering of nephropathy in families and in high-risk populations such as Native Americans. Parental history of hypertension, diabetes, or CV disease appears to predispose to nephropathy in patients with diabetes.[92,94–96] The ACE gene insertion (I)/deletion (D) polymorphism has been studied extensively. This locus does not appear to be a strong risk marker for the development of nephropathy, but it does appear to have a role in progression of nephropathy and response to ACE inhibition, with II homozygotes being the most responsive and DD homozygotes the least.[88,97]

What Is the Relationship of Glucose Levels and Other Risk Factors to the Risk of Kidney Disease?

The level of glycemia is one of the strongest factors associated with the development of microalbuminuria. Data are now available from both observational and experimental studies indicating that higher levels of glucose are associated with the onset and progression of microalbuminuria. Further, data from interventional trials in patients with both Type 1 and Type 2 diabetes indicate that improving glucose control helps to prevent or delay the progression of microalbuminuria and prevents or delays the onset of diabetic nephropathy (see below).[82,98–100]

Higher glucose levels are also a risk factor for the progression from microalbuminuria to diabetic nephropathy. Both the DCCT investigators and the Joslin Diabetes Center reported a nonlinear relationship between glycated hemoglobin and risk of microalbuminuria and diabetic nephropathy.[30,102] The DCCT investigators, however, found no threshold value below which there is no further risk reduction from improved glycemic control.[30] In contrast, other authors, based on a retrospective study,[102] have suggested that a glycemic threshold for microalbuminuria and for retinopathy exists at an HbA_{1c} level of approximately 8%, below which there is no further appreciable reduction in risk. The latter authors have quantitated this risk in a recent prospective 4-year study (Table 22–5).[103]

Higher glucose levels also appear to predict renal insufficiency, and recent decision analyses suggest that by decreasing albuminuria and preventing or delaying the onset of diabetic nephropathy, improved glycemic control will prevent ESRD.[104–106] This is supported by epidemiologic evidence in both Type 1 and Type 2 diabetes that poor glycemic control is a risk factor for a poor renal outcome.[13,16] Moreover, in early clinical studies, patients in the highest glycemic quartile were at the greatest risk of proteinuria (relative risk [RR] = 4.52 vs first quartile),[94] and time to onset of proteinuria was shorter in those with poorest glycemic control.[107]

More recently, the relative risk for the development of a decline in renal function (defined as decrease in creatinine clearance of ≥ 3 mL/min/1.73 m^2/y) or the development of renal insufficiency (defined as serum creatinine ≥ 178 μmol/L or receiving dialysis or a renal transplant) with increasing levels of glycosylated hemoglobin has been analyzed (see Table 22–4).[50] After adjusting for other prognostic factors, the level of glycosylated hemoglobin was one of the most important determinants of progression of renal insufficiency. For every 1% increase in the glycosylated hemoglobin, the OR for fall in creatinine clearance ≥ 3 mL/min/1.73 m^2/y was 1.49 (95% CI 1.16 to 1.92). The OR for 10-year incidence of renal insufficiency for each 1% increase in glycosylated hemoglobin was 1.78 (95% CI 1.49 to 2.12).

Several cross-sectional and longitudinal studies (both retrospective and prospective) have analyzed other clinical variables linked to the development of progressive diabetic nephropathy. One of the most important risk factors for diabetic nephropathy is duration of diabetes.[12] There does not appear to be a difference in cumulative incidence of ESRD for a given duration of diabetes between Type 1 and Type 2 diabetes.[19,108] In the WESDR database of Type 1 diabetes, the nonglycemic variables associated with the incidence of renal insufficiency and declining creatinine clearance were higher systolic and diastolic blood pressure, male sex, duration of diabetes, and total cholesterol.[50] Several cross-sectional and prospective observational studies have documented these same risk factors in patients with Type 1 and II diabetes.[36,37,39,109–120] Other studies have found a strong association with smoking,[121–127]

Table 22–5 Relationship of HbA_{1c} to the Development of Diabetic Nephropathy in Patients with Microalbuminuria*

HbA_{1c} (%)	N	Rate of Progression to Proteinuria	Adjusted Effects of HbA_{1c} on Progression of Microalbuminuria to Proteinuria Odds Ratio (95% CI)
< 8.0	85	1.3/100 person-years	1.0
8.0–8.9	57	5.1/100 person-years	4.2 (1.2–14.4)
9.0–9.9	64	4.2/100 person-years	3.2 (0.9–11.2)
≥ 10	68	6.7/100 person-years	5.5 (1.6–18.7)

Data taken from 4-year prospective study in 279 patients who completed follow-up. Overall rate of progression was 4.1 per 100 person-years. The risk of progression rose rapidly between HbA_{1c} of 7.5 and 8.5%. Analysis adjusted for sex, age, duration of diabetes, antihypertensive treatment, and mean baseline albumin/creatinine ratio. Data from Warram JH, Scott LJ, Hanna LS, et al. Progression of microalbuminuria to proteinuria in Type 1 diabetes: nonlinear relationship with hyperglycemia. Diabetes 2000;49:94–100.

ethnicity (increased in black, Hispanic, and First Nations patients),[6,38,128–131] family history of renal disease,[92] parental hypertension,[94,95] and parental CV disease.[96] The association of renal disease with retinopathy is strong in univariate analyses but is not maintained in multivariate analyses; this association is therefore likely accounted for by the duration of diabetes and the level of glucose control.

Smoking has consistently been found to be a risk factor for the incidence and prevalence of albuminuria and progression of nephropathy in diabetes.[34,109–111,121,123,126,127,132–134] For example, one longitudinal study of 359 patients with Type 1 diabetes demonstrated that the prevalence of increased albumin excretion rates was 2.8 times higher in smokers than in nonsmokers; smoking remained a significant factor after multivariate analyses. Of interest, albuminuria decreased after subjects ceased smoking.[121] In another study of patients with Type 1 diabetes receiving intensified insulin and blood pressure control, smoking was the most important risk factor for progressive microalbuminuria and the development of diabetic nephropathy.[127] Moreover, the progression of nephropathy was less common in nonsmokers (11%) than in smokers (53%) and patients who had quit smoking (33%). This association was also found in a large prevalence study of 3,250 patients with Type 1 diabetes,[132] in which albuminuric people were approximately 1.5 times more likely to be smokers than were nonalbuminuric people. Finally, in patients with Type 2 diabetes enrolled in the Appropriate Blood Pressure Control in Diabetes Trial, a stepwise logistic regression demonstrated an independent association between smoking and diabetic nephropathy (OR = 1.61, 95% CI 1.01 to 2.58).[126]

EVIDENCE-BASED MESSAGES

1. The degree of glycemia, as measured by the glycated hemoglobin, is a strong independent risk factor for albuminuria and renal insufficiency (Level 1).[30,50,82,99–102]
2. Higher systolic and diastolic blood pressure, male sex, longer duration of diabetes, and higher total cholesterol are independent risk factors for renal insufficiency (Level 1).[50]
3. Smoking increases the risk of progression of nephropathy (Level 1).[121,127]

DIAGNOSIS OF DIABETIC KIDNEY DISEASE

How Is Diabetic Nephropathy Diagnosed?

Diabetic nephropathy is diagnosed on the basis of an elevated urinary albumin excretion (> 300 mg/d of albumin excretion or > 500 mg/d of proteinuria) in a patient with Type 1 or 2 diabetes.[20,21,131] Diabetic nephropathy is usually associated with hypertension in patients with Type 2 diabetes, which often precedes proteinuria by a number of years.[21,48,135] In patients with Type 1 diabetes, blood pressure is also often elevated but is usually still within the range of "normal" (< 140/90).[25,114] As outlined above, in patients with Type 1 diabetes it generally takes at least 5 years after diabetes is diagnosed before diabetic nephropathy is present, and usually 10 to 20 years of diabetes is required. In patients with Type 2 diabetes, nephropathy is often present earlier in the course, with up to 8% having proteinuria at the time their diabetes is diagnosed,[16] likely representing delayed diagnosis of diabetes.[23] Thus, the diagnosis of diabetic nephropathy is usually clinical, based on a patient with diabetes developing elevated UAE (> 300 mg/d) with the correct time course and the absence of features of other causes of renal disease.

Renal biopsy is not required to confirm the diagnosis for the majority of patients with diabetes and renal involvement. In patients with Type 1 diabetes who have an elevated UAE and more than 5 to 10 years of diabetes (especially when associated with retinopathy), the histologic changes of diabetic nephropathy are present in > 98% of all patients at the time of biopsy.[20,136,137] This is only slightly reduced, even in the absence of retinopathy, in patients with Type 1 diabetes; however, > 95% of all patients with Type 1 diabetes and nephropathy have retinopathy.[138]

The need for renal biopsy in people with Type 2 diabetes is a topic for debate. Studies of patients sent for renal biopsy to referral centers have reported that between 12% and 23% of such patients have nondiabetic causes of renal disease.[139–142] By contrast, other studies (including autopsy series) report that nondiabetic renal disease is rare in diabetes mellitus. For example, in a recent systematic overview of renal biopsy data in 580 patients with Type 2 diabetes, it was reported that only 12% of patients with Type 2 diabetes had nondiabetic reasons for their proteinuria.[141] This study suggests that there is a considerable bias in the literature toward including patients with nondiabetic renal disease in published studies, probably because many of the reports are generated from referral centers – places more likely to see the referred, nondiabetic cases (ie, they have a "referral bias"). Clues that nondiabetic renal disease may be present include a shorter duration of diabetes and the absence of retinopathy.[140,141] Diabetic retinopathy, however, is not as reliable a marker in Type 2 diabetes as it is in Type 1 diabetes. One recent report noted that it is present in 56% of patients with diabetic glomerulosclerosis and in 0% of patients with a nondiabetic glomerulopathy.[142] Thus, while it is not routinely indicated, the need for renal biopsy should be carefully considered when investigating patients with Type 2 diabetes and proteinuria.

EVIDENCE-BASED MESSAGE

Diabetic nephropathy is diagnosed clinically and not by renal biopsy; a urinary albumin excretion (UAE) > 300 mg/d and an appropriate time course in the absence of other obvious secondary causes of renal disease in diabetes defines diabetic nephropathy in Type 1 diabetes with near 100% specificity (Level 3).[136,137] In Type 2 diabetes, the specificity is reduced to 88% (Level 4).[141]

Can Diabetic Nephropathy Be Diagnosed Early?

What Is Microalbuminuria, How Is it Defined, and What Tests Are Available?

The earliest clinical marker of diabetic renal disease is microalbuminuria, or the presence of an increased albumin excretion rate (AER).[10,12,13,45,59,120,143–148] This degree of albuminuria (also called early or incipient diabetic nephropathy) has been detectable since the 1960s[144] and is (by definition) below the threshold detectable by dipstick urine tests. It predicts progression to more advanced renal disease and renal failure,[10,59,120,144–148] an observation that has led some authors to conclude that screening for microalbuminuria should be routinely performed on all diabetic patients on an annual basis.[22,23,90–96,148–151] Until recently, there was a lack of evidence regarding therapy of diabetic patients with microalbuminuria; thus, the recommendations to screen were perceived to be without benefit. However, over the past 3 years, several clinical trials have demonstrated a benefit to treating microalbuminuric diabetic patients using a two-pronged attack: addressing hemodynamic control (particularly with ACE inhibitors) and improved glycemic control (see "Management," below).

Diabetic nephropathy is a process that leads from normoalbuminuria to ESRD with the intervening steps of microalbuminuria and macroscopic albuminuria (overt proteinuria).[1] Indeed, for more advanced renal disease to develop, microalbuminuria must occur first.[10,12,59,120,144–147] Microalbuminuria may begin as early as 1 to 3 years after the onset of diabetes in up to 6.4% of patients with Type 1 diabetes and may be present in up to 18% of patients with Type 2 diabetes at the time their diabetes is diagnosed.[98,143]

The usual value taken to represent the boundary between normoalbuminuria and microalbuminuria is 30 mg/24 h (approximately 20 μg/min).[12,14] In a recent large trial, the 90th and 95th percentiles of normal (nondiabetic) albumin excretion rates were found to be 18 and 30 μg/min (approximately 25 mg and 45 mg/24 h) respectively.[14] Values of microalbuminuria greater than this predict progression to macroalbuminuria or overt diabetic nephropathy (see below). Although larger amounts of microalbuminuria are associated with higher relative risks of progression,[36,37,109–111,118,120,145–147] the likelihood ratios for progression at various levels of microalbuminuria and the optimal level at which to initate therapy to prevent progression have not been carefully defined. Therefore, at present, the most widely accepted definition of microalbuminuria is based on a statistical level of normal (the 95th percentile).

The gold standard test for microalbuminuria is the 24-hour AER as assessed by radio-immunoassay (RIA).[24,151–161] Microalbuminuria is defined as 30 to 300 mg/24 h or 20 to 200 µg/min of UAE. Timed collections need not be for 24 hours' duration, and some authors have reported overnight, 4-hour, and 12-hour UAE rates. There are a number of office-based qualitative dipstick tests for microalbumin that have been proposed in the literature, based on concentrations of albumin concentration.[152,156–159,161] Albumin concentration can also be measured on spot samples by standard assays such as RIA and nephelometry, and the concentration determined. When concentration of albumin is measured, microalbuminuria is defined as 30 to 300 mg/L (this assumes 1 L of urine output/d). To control for different urine volumes, the most widely accepted screening test for microalbuminuria is the albumin/creatinine ratio; the microalbuminuric range is defined as 2.0 to 25 mg/mmol in males and 3.0 to 30 mg/mmol in females (because females have lower creatinine excretion).[22]

What Is the Sensitivity and Specificity of the Testing Methods?

As noted in the foregoing, the urine dipstick is a very insensitive way of measuring albumin excretion rates above the 95th percentiles, generally not becoming positive until albumin excretion exceeds 300 mg/24 h (approximately 200 to 300 mg/L).[12,22,45,157,160] Thus, there is a considerable gap between the upper level of normal and the lower level of detection by routine urinalysis. In most patients with diabetes, microalbumin develops up to 10 years before diabetic nephropathy, and thus the inability to recognize this state of increased risk would result in lost treatment opportunities. To detect lower values of microalbumin excretion, more sensitive measures are required. These methods fall into two main categories: (1) quantitative or semiquantitative methods based on concentrations of albuminuria or (2) quantitative methods that assess either excretion of albumin per unit time or excretion per unit of creatinine excretion (which is fairly constant over time in a given patient). Although the gold standard test for microalbuminuria is the 24-hour AER as assessed by RIA[14,24,152–161] 4-hour and timed overnight AERs are extremely accurate (compared to the gold standard) and are used as alternative gold standards: correlation coefficients between measured 24-hour AER and AER determined from 4-hourly or overnight timed specimens are approximately 0.95.[153,159]

Because 24-hour and shorter timed collections are cumbersome and lead to poor compliance (eg, in one report only 59% of patients completed their 24-hour collections),[162] office-based qualitative dipstick tests for microalbumin have been proposed. These include the Micral-Test and Micral-Test II strips, MicroBumin, and AlbuSure. Each of these qualitative tests relies on a threshold concentration of albuminuria. A single urine sample, assayed by standard laboratory assays (RIA and nephelometry), has also been assessed as a method of screening for microalbuminuria. In studies using a timed AER as the gold standard, the overall sensitivity and specificity of this approach ranged from 60 to 97% and 77 to 97%, respectively (Table 22–6).[24,152,155–158,160,161] Depending on the prevalence of microalbuminuria, the positive and negative predictive values have been reported as low as 39% and 93%, respectively. Thus, although appealing because of simplicity, the performance characteristics of tests based on the measurement of albumin concentration are poor, and at present these tests cannot be recommended as the methods used to routinely screen diabetic patients for microalbuminuria. This is likely because methods based on albumin concentration will be affected by dilute urines, which will lead to falsely negative values.[155]

The most appealing method for the quantitation of microalbuminuria is the albumin/creatinine ratio (A/C ratio). This method is based on the fact that creatinine excretion is fairly constant throughout the day, so that a single spot ratio will approximate 24-hour

Table 22–6 Performance Characteristics of Various Microalbuminuria Screening Tests in Patients with Type 1 and II Diabetes Mellitus

Test	Population	Gold Standard	Level of Test	SN	SP	PPV	NPV	Study
Concentration based tests: office setting								
Albusure	N = 154 Type 1 NA/MA	24 h AER > 20 μg/min	Positive*	65.3	96.3	94	NR	Coonrod et al[152]
Micral-Test	N = 530 Type 1 NA/MA PMA = 16%	24 h AER > 20 μg/min	Positive* Pooled†	67% 78%	86% 77%	47% 39%	93% 95%	Webb et al[161]
Concentration based tests: laboratory setting								
Albumin concentration radioimmunoassay	N = 94 Type 1 NA/MA/ON PMA=29%	24 h AER > 30 mg/24 h	Random 20 mg/L First AM	89% 70%	85% 93%	NR NR	NR NR	Schwab et al[72]
Albumin concentration nephelometry	N = 363 Type 1 and 46 Type 2 NA/MA PMA~30%	Overnight AER > 15 μg/min	Type 1: 20 mg/L 10 mg/L Type 2: 20 mg/L 10 mg/L	70% 91% 60% 71%	97% 77% 97% 87%	NR NR NR NR	NR NR NR NR	Kouri et al[155]
Albumin concentration immunoturbidimetry	N = 104 Type 1 NA/MA PMA = 12.5%	Overnight AER > 20 μg/min	20 mg/L 17 mg/L	90 90	91 86	54 44	99 99	Shield et al[158]

Table 22-6 Performance Characteristics of Various Microalbuminuria Screening Tests in Patients with Type 1 and II Diabetes Mellitus — *(continued)*

Test	Population	Gold Standard	Level of Test	SN	SP	PPV	NPV	Study
Quantitative tests using albumin/creatinine ratio								
Albumin to creatinine ratio	N = 104 Type 1 NA/MA PMA = 12.5%	Overnight AER > 20 µg/min	> 2.0 mg/mmol[‡] > 2.5 mg/mmol	97% 94%	93% 94%	63% 66%	100% 99%	Shield et al[158]
Albumin to creatinine ratio	N = 261 Type 1 and II PMA=11.9%	Overnight AER > 30 µg/min	>3.0 mg/mmol[§]	97%	94%	68%	NR	Hutchison et al[160]
Albumin to creatinine ratio	N = 94 Type 2 PMA=36%	24 h AER > 30 mg/24h	>1.7 mg/mmol[||] >3.0 mg/mmol[||]	100% 89%	74% 89%	NR NR	NR NR	Zelmanovitz et al[163]

*Positive test refers to a positive quantitative test result as described by manufacturer.

†Pooled values represent the results of two separate tests.

‡Convert to standard units (mg/mL) by multiplying by 8.84 (eg, 2 mg/mmol = 17.7mg/g).

§Correlation coefficient for A/C ratio and 24-h AER was 0.921 in this study.

||Correlation coefficient for A/C ratio and 24-h AER was 0.92 in this study.

NA = normoalbuminuria; MA = microalbuminuria; ON = overt nephropathy (these refer to the spectrum of patients studied); PMA = prevalence on microalbuminuria; NR = not reported; AER = albumin excretion rate.

ratios. Indeed, this method is similar to fractional excretion of sodium in that it accounts for fluctuations in urine volumes of individual samples. The A/C ratio can be performed on a spot urine and thus avoids problems with patient compliance and timing issues related to timed urine collections. The performance characteristics of the A/C ratio are excellent, with sensitivity and specificity ranging from 93 to 100% and 93 to 99%, respectively.[153,154,159,163] Random A/C ratio and the 24-hour AER have correlation coefficients of 0.92 to 0.97.[14,154,159,163] One recent study validated the A/C ratio and reported the receiver operating characteristics (ROC) of random urine albumin:creatinine ratio (UACR) as a screening test for diabetic nephropathy,[163] using the 24-hour excretion measured by immunoturbidimetry as the gold standard. The area (± SE) under the ROC curve for the UACR was .9689 ± 0.014 (suggesting high diagnostic utility). Thus, random daytime urine sample assays for the A/C ratio are excellent screening tests for microalbuminuria.

The optimal cutoff value for the A/C ratio has been assessed. In one study of 218 healthy volunteers and 1,613 patients with Type 1 diabetes[14] who used a statistical definition of normal (the 95th percentile), the proposed cutoffs separating normoalbuminuria and microalbuminuria were 17 mg/g (1.92 mg/mmol) in men and 25 mg/g (2.83 mg/mmol) in women (as noted above, the gender-specific values differ due to different creatinine excretion rates). At least one prospective study assessed the cutoff that may predict progression to overt nephropathy. In 439 Pima Indians with Type 2 diabetes followed for 4 years,[164] a single initial A/C ratio of > 30 mg/g (compared to lower values) was independently associated with a relative risk of overt nephropathy of 9.2 (95% CI 4.4 to 21.4). These data have been used to support clinical practice guideline recommendations to use the A/C ratio to screen patients with diabetes for microalbuminuria.[150,151,165] Although the frequency of screening has not been studied prospectively, it is recommended annually, beginning 5 years after disease onset in people with Type 1 diabetes, and from the time of diagnosis in people with Type 2 diabetes. Screening threshold values for microalbuminuria of 2.0 mg/mmol in males and 2.8 mg/mmol in females are recommended.[165]

EVIDENCE-BASED MESSAGE

The A/C ratio is the best screening test for microalbuminuria, with high sensitivity and specificity for a cutoff of 2 to 3 mg/mmol (Level 1).[158,163]

What Proportion of Patients with Type 1 and Type 2 Diabetes and Microalbuminuria Develop Diabetic Nephropathy?

Initial retrospective and small studies of patients followed from the late 1960s and early 1970s reported that > 85% of people with microalbuminuria developed overt diabetic nephropathy during a 10- to 14-year period.[59,144,145] More recent studies have reported lower risks, with approximately 50% of such patients developing nephropathy over 7 to 9 years.[12,14,110,120,147] The annualized rate of progression of microalbuminuria to diabetic nephropathy from several studies in Type 1 and II diabetes[47,103,110,144,145,147,164,166–170] is outlined in Table 22–7. Calculating weighted values based on the numbers of participants in the studies, rates of progression from microalbuminuria to diabetic nephropathy are approximately 4% per year for Type 1 and 4.7% per year for Type 2 patients.

EVIDENCE-BASED MESSAGE

Microalbuminuria is an important risk factor for diabetic nephropathy; the rate of progression from microalbuminuria to diabetic nephropathy is approximately 4% per year (Level 1).[103,171]

Can Patients with Diabetes Be Screened for Hypertension Alone Rather than Microalbuminuria?

The presence of hypertension has been proposed by some as a screening tool for diabetic nephropathy, which obviates the need for microalbuminuria screening.[172,173] However,

Table 22–7 Annualized Rate of Progression from Microalbuminuria to Diabetic Nephropathy

Study	Year of Study Initiation	N with Microalbuminuria	Years of Follow-Up	Annualized Rate of Diabetic Nephropathy
Type 1 DM				
Viberti et al[145]	1966	8	14	6.3
Mogensen et al[144]	1969	14	10	8.2
Forsblom et al[147]	1980	18	10	2.8
Mathiesen et a[139]	1982	40	5	7.0
Almdal et al[110]	1985	118	5	3.8
Microalbumin Captopril Study Group[166]	1990	114	2	10.9
Warram et al[103]	1991	279	4	4.1
Type 2 DM				
Mogensen et al[144]	1973	76	9	2.5
Nelson et al[164]	1982	91*	4.2	12.8
Ravid et al[169]	1986	45	5	8.4
John et al[167]	1987	93	5	5.9
Lacourciere et al[168]	1988	12	3	5.6
Ahmad et al[170]	1989	51	5	4.7
Micro-Hope[171]	1993	1140	4.5	4.4

*Type 2 DM in a population of Pima Indians.
DM = diabetes mellitus.

most patients with Type 1 diabetes develop microalbuminuria before they develop hypertension.[22,144,145,147,174] Indeed, even with a very conservative definition of hypertension, such as that proposed by the American Diabetes Association of 130/85, most patients with Type 1 diabetes will not be hypertensive at the onset of microalbuminuria. The mean blood pressure does increase as incipient nephropathy develops, but generally to a mild degree.[174] In two recent randomized controlled trials of therapy in Type 1 diabetes patients with microalbuminuria, the mean arterial pressures of the 235 pooled patients was 92 mm Hg (approximately 120/80 mm Hg), despite a geometric mean AER of 57 μg/min, a value of albuminuria well within the pathologic level of early nephropathy.[166] Thus, the presence of hypertension is too insensitive a marker for the presence of incipient nephropathy in patients with Type 1 diabetes. The evidence is different for patients with Type 2 diabetes. Most of these individuals have hypertension before the onset of microalbuminuria.[11,12] Nonetheless, microalbuminuria identifies a subgroup of patients at particularly high risk for the development of CV morbidity and mortality[4,171] and for progressive renal disease.[36,37,39,111,113,115,116]

MANAGEMENT OF DIABETIC KIDNEY DISEASE

Does Glycemic Control Prevent or Delay the Progression of Diabetic Kidney Disease?

The best evidence supporting improved glycemic control in Type 1 diabetes comes from the DCCT.[100] The results of this landmark trial are also supported by several small trials and a methodologically sound meta-analysis.[101,107,175,176] The DCCT followed 1,441 Type 1 diabetic patients for a mean of 6.5 years (726 patients in a primary prevention group and 715 patients in a secondary prevention group) and achieved a hemoglobin A_{1c} in the conventional and intensive treatment groups of 9.1% and 7.2%, respectively. Intensive insulin therapy reduced the adjusted mean risk of the occurrence of microalbuminuria by 39% overall (34% [95% CI 2 to 56%] in the primary prevention group) and that of progression to albuminuria (> 300 mg/24 h) by 54% (95% CI 19 to 74%) (Table 22–8). The conventional therapy group experienced an average increase in AER of 6.5% per year versus no change in those receiving intensive therapy.[82] The DCCT and other trials also showed that intensified insulin therapy leads to a delay in the progression (as well as the development) of nephropathy.[82,100,101]

In patients with Type 2 diabetes, the United Kingdom Prospective Diabetes Study (UKPDS) demonstrated that a policy of tight glucose control led to a relative risk reduction (RRR) of 33% (95% CI 13 to 47%) in the development of microalbuminuria ($p = .000054$) and a 74% reduction in the number of patients who doubled their creatinine value over 12 years ($p = .0028$) (see Table 22–8).[98] These results were supported by another small randomized controlled trial (RCT) of intensified insulin therapy in Type 2 diabetes.[177] In this Japanese trial of 110 patients, lowering the HbA$_{1c}$ from a mean of 9.4 to 7.1% resulted in an absolute risk reduction for the development of diabetic nephropathy in microalbuminuric patients of 24% over 6 years.

EVIDENCE-BASED MESSAGES

1. In people with Type 1 diabetes, glucose lowering using intensive insulin therapy reduces the risk of microalbuminuria and the progression of albuminuria (Level 1A).[82]
2. In people with Type 2 diabetes, glucose lowering reduces the risk of microalbuminuria and renal insufficiency (Level 1A).[98]

What Nonglycemic Therapies Can Prevent or Delay the Progression of Diabetic Kidney Disease?

What Is the Effect of Hypertension Control and What Is the Optimal Blood Pressure?

Hypertension control is regarded as the most important measure in preventing both microvascular and macrovascular complications, particularly in patients with Type 2 diabetes. It has been almost 25 years since the original studies by Mogensen documented that hypertension treatment could slow the decline in renal function in patients with Type 1 diabetes and diabetic nephropathy.[178] As blood pressure fell from 162/103 mm Hg to 144/95 mm Hg in this study, the rate of decline in glomerlular filtration rate (GFR) was reduced from 1.23 mL/min/mo to 0.49 mL/min/mo.[179]

Table 22–8 Effect of Improved Glycemic Control on Diabetic Nephropathy in Patients with Type 1 and Type 2 Diabetes Mellitus

Study	Patient Description	Outcome	Active Rx	Control	RRR (CI)	NNT (CI)
Type 1 DM	Normo-albuminuria	Micro-albuminuria	Intensive therapy	Conventional therapy	34 (2–56)	83 (53–1000)
DCCT[100]	Existing microvascular disease	Diabetic nephropathy			56 (18–76)	125 (40–169)
Type 2 DM	Normo-albuminuria	Micro-albuminuria (at 12 y)	Intensive therapy	Conventional therapy	33 (14–47)	9 (4–13)
UKPDS[98]						
Ohkubo et al[177]	Normo-albuminuria	Micro-albuminuria	Intensive therapy	Conventional therapy	72	5

RRR = relative risk reduction; NNT = number needed to treat; CI = confidence interval; DM = diabetes mellitus.

Since these studies, overwhelming evidence has been presented (for both Type 1 and II diabetes) that blood pressure control, using ACE inhibitors as well as conventional agents, attenuates the decline in renal function.[180-185] Prior to more aggressive levels of hypertension control, the rate of loss of renal function was reported to be from 10 to 12 mL/min/y (approximately 1 mL/min/mo).[178,186] Over the last few decades, lower rates of decline in renal function have typically been reported in clinical trial settings, generally < 5 mL/min/y.[47,48,114,187-194] Certain high-risk populations, such as those with advanced nephropathy and hypertension, have still been reported to have rates of decline in GFR of > 1 mL/min/mo.[185,195] In a recent meta-analysis including 12 RCTs involving patients with diabetes and proteinuria, for each 10 mm Hg reduction in blood pressure, there was improvement in the relative decline in kidney function among diabetic patients with proteinuria (0.18 mL/min/mo, [95% CI 0.04 to 0.31 mL/min/mo]).[182] In this and other meta-analyses,[180-182] ACE inhibitors were associated with a greater improvement in proteinuria than were other classes of antihypertensive agents.

In the UKPDS trial of antihypertensive therapy, 1,148 participants (mean age 56 years) with untreated hypertension (whose systolic and/or diastolic blood pressure was ≥ 160 mm Hg or ≥ 90 mm Hg, respectively) or with treated hypertension (whose systolic and/or diastolic blood pressure was ≥ 150 mm or ≥ 85 mm, respectively) were allocated to a policy of intensive or conventional blood pressure control for a median period of 8.4 years.[196] The target for intensive control was a blood pressure < 150/85 and for conventional control was < 180/105; the mean blood pressure actually achieved in the intensive and conventional blood pressure groups was 144/82 and 154/87, respectively. This trial included patients with newly diagnosed diabetes, so the proportion of patients with renal events (which take many years to develop) was low; as such, < 8% of patients overall developed diabetic nephropathy and < 2% developed renal failure. Nevertheless, tight blood pressure control led to a 29% RRR in the development of microalbuminuria over 6 years ($p = .0085$), with an absolute risk reduction (ARR) of 8.2% and a number needed to treat (NNT) of 12; the effect was independent of the agent used.

Although the optimal blood pressure target is unknown, extrapolation to patients with other forms of renal injury and proteinuria[197] has suggested that a mean arterial pressure of 92 mm Hg (approximately 125/75 mm Hg) should be targeted in patients with diabetic nephropathy.[151,198,199] This target is supported by a trial of 129 patients with Type 1 diabetes and diabetic nephropathy randomly allocated to a mean arterial blood pressure (MAP) goal of 92 mm Hg or less (group I) or 100 to 107 mm Hg (group II); blood pressure targets were reached by prescribing escalating doses of ramipril as the primary therapeutic antihypertensive agent. After 2 years, the mean difference in MAP between groups was 6 mm Hg; there was no statistically significant difference in the rate of decline in renal function, but there was a significant difference in total urinary protein excretion of 535 mg/24 h (group I) and 1,723 mg/24 h (group II) ($p = .02$). In 32% of patients overall, a final total protein excretion < 500 mg/24 h was achieved.

EVIDENCE-BASED MESSAGE

Blood-pressure lowering reduces the decline in GFR and albuminuria (Level 1A).[182,196]

What Is the Effect of Using Angiotensin Converting Enzyme Inhibitors on the Progression of Renal Disease in Patients with Diabetes?

Angiotensin Converting Enzyme Inhibitors in Patients with Microalbuminuria. In addition to reducing blood pressure, ACE inhibitors decrease intraglomerular pressure and lead to reductions in proteinuria.[200-205] It has been suggested that ACE inhibitors may have beneficial effects in nephropathy independent of reductions in blood pressure, and this has led to numerous clinical trials in patients with diabetes. Angiotensin converting enzyme inhibitors have been studied extensively at the microalbuminuric stage[166,169-171,188,189,191,206-209] and also in patients with diabetic nephropathy.[185,210] From these clinical trials, it is still not entirely clear whether ACE inhibitors have a beneficial effect over and above their antihypertensive effect; nonetheless, they appear effective in delaying the progression of proteinuria in both Type 1 and Type 2 diabetes. In addition, ACE inhibitors lead to a lower rate of decline in GFR and prevent ESRD and death in patients with Type 1 diabetes and diabetic nephropathy.[185]

Angiotensin converting enzyme inhibitors decrease microalbuminuria and delay the progression of diabetic nephropathy in Type 1[166,171,211] and Type 2[168–170,188,191,207,208] diabetes following the onset of microalbuminuria (Table 22–9). The results from two randomized double-blind controlled trials[206,209] involving a total of 235 patients addressed this issue in normotensive patients with Type 1 diabetes; recently, the results from these trials have been pooled.[166] Captopril use caused a 69% RRR and a 15% ARR in the risk of progression to diabetic nephropathy (defined as an AER > 300 mg/24 h). There was also a progressive decline in GFR over the 24 months of study in the placebo group equal to 6.4 mL/min/1.73 m^2/y (95% CI 2.5 to 10.2) versus only 1.4 mL/min/1.73 m^2/y (95% CI 2.6 to 5.3) in the treatment group. In studies of patients with Type 2 diabetes and microalbuminuria,[169,170,207,212] ACE inhibitors led to similar risk reductions for progression to diabetic nephropathy and stabilization of the GFR (see Table 22–9).

Several meta-analyses of the effects of ACE inhibitors for diabetic microalbuminuria have been completed.[180,213,214] In one of these, the results of 11 clinical trials lasting 1 year or more using ACE inhibitors in patients with Type 1 and Type 2 diabetes were combined. This analysis found a reduction in albuminuria and progression to diabetic nephropathy but failed to show any difference in renal function between those treated and those untreated.[213] In a separate meta-analysis of 9 published and unpublished randomized, placebo-controlled, parallel trials of subjects with diabetic nephropathy and microalbuminuria[214] with at least 1 year of follow-up, the relative risk for developing macroalbuminuria was 0.35 (95% CI 0.24 to 0.53) for individuals treated with an ACE inhibitor compared with placebo (ARR = 16.3; 95% CI 11.7 to 24.7 NNT = 6, 95% CI 4 to 8).[214]

Finally, it is very important to note that changes in GFR would not be expected to occur in short-duration trials of people with microalbuminuria, as GFR does not begin to fall below the normal range until high levels of microalbuminuria or diabetic nephropathy (> 300 mg/d of UAE) develop. Thus, delaying the progression of diabetic nephropathy in patients with microalbuminuria is considered an important surrogate endpoint for the more clinically relevant decline in GFR and renal insufficiency.

Angiotensin Converting Enzyme Inhibitors in Patients with Diabetic Nephropathy.   The best data concerning the benefit of ACE inhibitors in people with diabetic nephropathy were collected in a trial of 409 patients with Type 1 diabetes and nephropathy who were randomized to captopril or placebo.[185] Captopril was associated with a 76% RRR and a 9% ARR (NNT = 11) of doubling serum creatinine over the 3.5-year study period and an improvement in overall renal and patient mortality. The mean (± standard deviation [SD]) rate of decline in creatinine clearance was 11 ± 21%/y in the captopril group and 17 ± 20%/y in the placebo group ($p = .03$). Hypertension control was not significantly different between the groups (difference between groups was consistently < 4 mm Hg), suggesting a specific protective effect of ACE inhibition.

There is a paucity of evidence concerning the use of ACE inhibitors in Type 2 diabetes patients with established diabetic nephropathy, although large clinical trials are nearing completion. Meta-analyses of trials of patients with both Type 1 and Type 2 diabetes,[181] or of patients with and without diabetes as the cause of renal disease,[214] suggest a similar treatment effect in patients with Type 2 diabetes. In seven trials of subjects with overt proteinuria and renal insufficiency from a variety of causes (30% diabetes, 70% nondiabetes), the relative risk for doubling of serum creatinine concentration or developing ESRD was 0.60 (95% CI 0.49 to 0.73) for individuals treated with an ACE inhibitor, compared with placebo.[214]

Table 22–9 Effect of Angiotensin Converting Enzyme Inhibitors in Patients with Type 1 and Type 2 Diabetes Mellitus and Microalbuminuria and Diabetic Nephropathy

Study	Stage of Renal Involvement	Outcome	Active Rx	Control	RRR (CI)	NNT (CI)	N
Type 1 DM							
Microalbuminuria Captopril Study Group[166]	Microalbuminuria	Progression to diabetic nephropathy	Captopril 50 mg bid	Placebo	69 (16–84)	15 (3–18)	225
Captopril Study, 1993	Diabetic nephropathy	Doubling serum creatinine		Usual HT Rx	43 (16–69)	11 (4–18)	409
		Combined ESRD, death, or transplantation	Captopril 25 mg tid		50 (18–70)	10 (4–14)	
Type 2 DM							
Ahmad et al[170]	Microalbuminuria	Progression to diabetic nephropathy	Enalapril 10 mg od	Placebo	67	15.8	103
Ravid et al,[169] 1993	Microalbuminuria	Progression to diabetic nephropathy	Enalapril 10 mg od	Placebo	71	3 (2–7)	94
*Micro-Hope[171]	Microalbuminuria	Progression to diabetic nephropathy	Ramipril 10 mg od	Placebo	24 (3–40)	51 (31–267)	3,577*

*In the Micro-Hope study, both patients with and without microalbuminuria were studied; 1,140 patients (32%) had microalbuminuria. Results presented here include those with and without microalbuminuria. The authors note that the treatment effect was preserved in both groups of patients. Patients with microalbuminuria had a higher rate of progression to diabetic nephropathy (RR = 14.0) (95% CI 10–19). Patients with microalbuminuria would be expected to have a higher ARR and thus a lower NNT, given the increased risk of progression. RRR = relative risk reduction; NNT = number needed to treat; CI = confidence interval; DM = diabetes mellitus; ESRD = end-stage renal disease; HT = hypertension.

EVIDENCE-BASED MESSAGES

1. Angiotensin converting enzyme inhibitors reduce the rate of diabetic nephropathy in patients with microalbuminuria (Level 1A).[214]
2. Angiotensin converting enzyme inhibitors reduce the rate of death, dialysis, or transplantation in patients with Type 1 diabetes, overt nephropathy, and impaired renal function (Level 1A).[185]

What Is the Effect of Protein Restriction on the Progression of Renal Disease in Patients with Diabetes?

During the last 20 years, there has been mounting experimental evidence that dietary protein restriction may delay progression of glomerular injury and ESRD.[215] High-protein diets are known to lead to hyperfiltration and increased intraglomerular pressure, which is associated with renal injury.[215] This finding has led to speculation that low-protein diets can reduce glomerular injury and delay renal failure in patients with glomerular disease. There have been a number of small trials in patients with diabetes that have looked at the effect of low-protein diets on the progression of diabetic nephropathy.[216–218]

In a recent meta-analysis of five clinical studies with a total of 108 patients, it was concluded that protein restriction reduced the risk for decline in the GFR and creatinine clearance with an RR of 0.56 (95% CI 0.4 to 0.77, $p < .001$).[217] In a separate systematic review, a similar conclusion was arrived at; however, the authors also focused attention on the short duration and small numbers of patients in these trials.[218] Finally, as the hemodynamic effect of ACE inhibitors is thought to act similarly to protein restriction, it is unclear if protein restriction offers additive benefit to patients receiving these agents. Nonetheless, it is recommended that a modest degree of protein restriction be followed (between 0.8 to 1.0 g/kg body weight/d).[217,218]

EVIDENCE-BASED MESSAGE

Protein restriction reduces the decline in the GFR and creatinine clearance (Level 1A).[217]

What Is the Effect of Cholesterol Lowering on the Progression of Renal Disease in Patients with Diabetes?

There is growing epidemiologic evidence that hyperlipemia is an important risk factor for the progression of renal disease.[219–231] In addition, patients with diabetic nephropathy often have more atherogenic lipoprotein profiles, which may be associated with increased CV risk in these patients.[232,233] Studies using animal models of diabetic nephropathy have demonstrated reduced glomerular injury and preserved GFR in those treated with statin agents (hydroxymethylglutaryl-CoA [HMG-CoA] reductase inhibitors).[219,221,227,228,234,235] This has led to interest in using statins in human subjects. One recent small double-blind crossover study involving 19 Type 2 diabetes patients with microalbuminuria reported reduction of UAE rate in patients receiving simvastatin compared to control over a 2-year period.[236] The UAE rate fell 25% (95% CI 16 to 40%) in those on simvastatin, with no reduction in controls.

Certainly, patients with diabetes (especially those with renal disease) are at very high risk for coronary artery disease (CAD). As such, aggressive reduction of lipid values has been recommended with targets for LDL-C of < 2.5 mmol/L, total cholesterol:HDL-C ratio < 4, and triglyceride level < 2.0 mmol/L.[237] Implementation of these lower lipid targets in clinical practice may therefore also lead to improved renal survival.

In a recent study, lipid reduction was used as part of a multifactorial intensified intervention in patients with Type 2 diabetes and microalbuminuria.[175] Intervention patients received intensified management of their lipid levels as well as hypertension and glucose control. Angiotensin converting enzyme inhibitors were prescribed irrespective of blood pressure control, and patients received behavior modification related to smoking cessation. The control group received standard diabetes care provided by family physicians. In this small but innovative clinical trial, intensified multifactorial treatment led to lower rates of progression to nephropathy, retinopathy, and autonomic neuropathy (RRR for nephropathy = 73%, 95% CI 25 to 90%; ARR=14%, 95% CI 5 to 17%), NNT = 7, 95% CI 6 to 20).

What Future Treatment Options Are Being Studied to Prevent the Onset or Progression of Renal Disease in Patients with Diabetes?

There are a number of newer therapeutic avenues being explored to treat and prevent diabetic nephropathy. Areas of clinical study include the use of angiotensin II receptor antagonists,[238,239] aldose reductase inhibitors (interfering with the polyol pathyway),[240,242] inhibition of AGE formation,[243–245] selective protein kinase-C inhibitors,[246–248] and selective growth factor inhibitors.[249,250] With the addition of novel agents to treat and prevent nephropathy, it will be interesting to see if the current trend of multifactorial intervention in patients with diabetes will lead to a greater clinical benefit.

SUMMARY OF EVIDENCE-BASED MESSAGES

Prognosis

1. The population-attributable risk for kidney failure due to diabetes in a recent population-based case-control study from the northeastern United States was 42% overall (21% for Type 1 diabetes and 21% for Type 2 diabetes) (Level 1).[18]
2. Although lower than original reports, the cumulative incidence of diabetic nephropathy from European registry data appears to be stable over the last 20 years, with an incidence of 20% at 24 years (Level 1).[42]
3. The 10-year cumulative incidence of renal insufficiency or ESRD in patients with Type 1 diabetes exceeds 14% (Level 1).[50]
4. Clinical proteinuria (overt nephropathy) is a strong risk factor for ESRD (Level 1).[13,17]
5. Microalbuminuria, clinical proteinuria, and ESRD are progressively stronger risk factors for total and CV mortality in people with diabetes (Level 1).[3,4,5,56]
6. The degree of glycemia, as measured by the glycated hemoglobin, is a strong independent risk factor for albuminuria and renal insufficiency (Level 1).[30,50,82,99–102]
7. Higher systolic and diastolic blood pressure, male sex, longer duration of diabetes, and higher total cholesterol are independent risk factors for renal insufficiency (Level 1).[50]
8. Smoking increases the risk of progression of nephropathy (Level 1).[121,127]

Diagnosis

1. Diabetic nephropathy is diagnosed clinically and not by renal biopsy; a UAE > 300 mg/d and an appropriate time course in the absence of other obvious secondary causes of renal disease in diabetes defines diabetic nephropathy in Type 1 diabetes with near 100% specificity (Level 3).[136,137] In Type 2 diabetes, the specificity is reduced to 88% (Level 4).[141]
2. The A/C ratio is the best screening test for microalbuminuria, with high sensitivity and specificity for a cutoff of 2 to 3 mg/mmol (Level 1).[158,163]
3. Microalbuminuria is an important risk factor for diabetic nephropathy; the rate of progression from microalbuminuria to diabetic nephropathy is approximately 4% per year (Level 1).[103,171]

Management

1. In people with Type 1 diabetes, glucose lowering using intensive insulin therapy reduces the risk of microalbuminuria and the progression of albuminuria (Level 1A).[82]
2. In people with Type 2 diabetes, glucose lowering reduces the risk of microalbuminuria and renal insufficiency (Level 1A).[98]

3. Blood-pressure lowering reduces the decline in GFR and albuminuria (Level 1A).[182,196]

4. Angiotensin converting enzyme inhibitors reduce the rate of diabetic nephropathy in patients with microalbuminuria (Level 1A).[214]

5. Angiotensin converting enzyme inhibitors reduce the rate of death, dialysis or transplantation in patients with Type 1 diabetes, overt nephropathy, and impaired renal function (Level 1A).[185]

6. Protein restriction reduces the decline in the GFR and creatinine clearance (Level 1A).[217]

REFERENCES

1. Mogensen CE, Christensen CK, Vittinghus E. The stages in diabetic renal disease. With emphasis on the stage of incipient diabetic nephropathy. Diabetes 1983;32(Suppl 2):64–78.

2. Borch-Johnsen K, Andersen PK, Deckert T. The effect of proteinuria on relative mortality in type 1 (insulin-dependent) diabetes mellitus. Diabetologia 1985;28:590–6.

3. Borch-Johnsen K, Kreiner S. Proteinuria: value as predictor of cardiovascular mortality in insulin dependent diabetes mellitus. BMJ 1987;294:1651–4.

4. Dinneen SF, Gerstein HC. The association of microalbuminuria and mortality in non-insulin-dependent diabetes mellitus. A systematic overview of the literature. Arch Intern Med 1997;157:1413-8.

5. Canadian Institutes for Health Information. Annual report 1999, Volume 1: Dialysis and renal transplantation. Canadian Organ Replacement Register. Ottawa (ON): Canadian Institutes for Health Information; 1999.

6. National Institutes of Health NIDDK. United States Renal Data System: USRDS Annual Report 1999. Kidney disease. Bethesda MA1, editor. Bethesda (MD): National Institutes of Health, National Institutes of Diabetes and Digestive and Kidney Disease; 1999.

7. Goeree R, Manalich J, Grootendorst P, et al. Cost analysis of dialysis treatments for end-stage renal disease (ESRD). Clin Invest Med 1995;18:455–64.

8. Anonymous. The economic cost of ESRD and Medicare spending for alternative modalities of treatment. Am J Kidney Dis 1999;34(Suppl 1):S124–39.

9. The economic cost of ESRD, vascular access procedures, and Medicare spending for alternative modalities of treatment. USRDS. United States Renal Data System. Am J Kidney Dis 1997;30 (Suppl 1):S160–77.

10. Mogensen CE. Prediction of clinical diabetic nephropathy in IDDM patients. Alternatives to microalbuminuria? Diabetes 1990;39:761–7.

11. Mogensen CE. Microalbuminuria, blood pressure and diabetic renal disease: origin and development of ideas. Diabetologia 1999;42:263–85.

12. Krolewski AS, Warram JH, Freire MB. Epidemiology of late diabetic complications. A basis for the development and evaluation of preventive programs. Endocrinol Metab Clin North Am 1996;25:217–42.

13. Krolewski AS, Warram JH, Christlieb AR, et al. The changing natural history of nephropathy in Type 1 diabetes. Am J Med 1985;78:785–94.

14. Warram JH, Gearin G, Laffel L, Krolewski AS. Effect of duration of Type 1 diabetes on the prevalence of stages of diabetic nephropathy defined by urinary albumin/creatinine ratio. J Am Soc Nephrol 1996;7:930–7.

15. Keller CK, Bergis KH, Fliser D, Ritz E. Renal findings in patients with short-term type 2 diabetes. J Am Soc Nephrol 1996;7(12):2627–35.

16. Ballard DJ, Humphrey LL, Melton LJ III, et al. Epidemiology of persistent proteinuria in Type 2 diabetes mellitus. Population-based study in Rochester, Minnesota. Diabetes 1988;37:405–12.

17. Humphrey LL, Ballard DJ, Frohnert PP, et al. Chronic renal failure in non-insulin-dependent diabetes mellitus. A population-based study in Rochester, Minnesota. Ann Intern Med 1989;111:788–96.

18. Perneger TV, Brancati FL, Whelton PK, Klag MJ. End-stage renal disease attributable to diabetes mellitus. Ann Intern Med 1994;121:912–8.

19. Pugh JA, Medina R, Ramirez M. Comparison of the course to end-stage renal disease of type 1 (insulin-dependent) and type 2 (non-insulin-dependent) diabetic nephropathy. Diabetologia 1993;36:1094–8.

20. Breyer JA. Diabetic nephropathy in insulin-dependent patients. Am J Kidney Dis 1992;20:533–47.

21. Ritz E, Stefanski A. Diabetic nephropathy in Type 2 diabetes. Am J Kidney Dis 1996;27:167–94.

22. Mogensen CE, Keane WF, Bennett PH, et al. Prevention of diabetic renal disease with special reference to microalbuminuria. Lancet 1995;346:1080–4.

23. Harris MI, Klein R, Welborn TA, Knuiman MW. Onset of NIDDM occurs at least 4–7 years before clinical diagnosis. Diabetes Care 1992;15:815–9.

24. Klein R, Klein BE, Linton KL, Moss SE. Microalbuminuria in a population-based study of diabetes. Arch Intern Med 1992;152:153–8.

25. Parving HH, Hommel E, Mathiesen E, et al. Prevalence of microalbuminuria, arterial hypertension, retinopathy and neuropathy in patients with insulin dependent diabetes. BMJ 1988; 296:156–60.

26. Orchard TJ, Dorman JS, Maser RE, et al. Prevalence of complications in IDDM by sex and duration. Pittsburgh Epidemiology of Diabetes Complications Study II. Diabetes 1990;39:1116–24.

27. Lloyd CE, Stephenson J, Fuller JH, Orchard TJ. A comparison of renal disease across two continents; the epidemiology of diabetes complications study and the EURODIAB IDDM Complications Study. Diabetes Care 1996;19:219–25.

28. Gall MA, Rossing P, Skott P, et al. Prevalence of micro- and macroalbuminuria, arterial hypertension, retinopathy and large vessel disease in European type 2 (non insulin dependent) diabetic patients. Diabetologia 1991;34:655 61.

29. Klein R, Klein BE, Moss SE. Prevalence of microalbuminuria in older-onset diabetes. Diabetes Care 1993;16:1325–30.

30. The absence of a glycemic threshold for the development of long-term complications: the perspective of the Diabetes Control and Complications Trial. Diabetes 1996;45:1289–98.

31. The Microalbuminuria Collaborative Study Group. Predictors of the development of microalbuminuria in patients with Type 1 diabetes mellitus: a seven-year prospective study. Diabet Med 1999;16:918–25.

32. Christiansen JS. Cigarette smoking and prevalence of microangiopathy in juvenile-onset insulin-dependent diabetes mellitus. Diabetes Care 1978;1:146–9.

33. Coonrod BA, Ellis D, Becker DJ, et al. Predictors of microalbuminuria in individuals with IDDM. Pittsburgh Epidemiology of Diabetes Complications Study. Diabetes Care 1993;16:1376–83.

34. Ekberg G, Grefberg N, Larsson LO. Cigarette smoking and urinary albumin excretion in insulin-treated diabetics without manifest nephropathy. J Intern Med 1991;230:435–42.

35. Forsblom CM, Groop PH, Ekstrand A, et al. Predictors of progression from normoalbuminuria to microalbuminuria in NIDDM. Diabetes Care 1998;21:1932–8.

36. Gall MA, Hougaard P, Borch-Johnsen K, Parving HH. Risk factors for development of incipient and overt diabetic nephropathy in patients with non-insulin dependent diabetes mellitus: prospective, observational study. BMJ 1997;314:783–8.

37. Klein R, Klein BE, Moss SE, Cruickshanks KJ. Ten-year incidence of gross proteinuria in people with diabetes. Diabetes 1995;44:916–23.

38. Nelson RG, Knowler WC, Pettitt DJ, et al. Incidence and determinants of elevated urinary albumin excretion in Pima Indians with NIDDM. Diabetes Care 1995;18:182–7.

39. Ravid M, Brosh D, Ravid-Safran D, et al. Main risk factors for nephropathy in type 2 diabetes mellitus are plasma cholesterol levels, mean blood pressure, and hyperglycemia. Arch Intern Med 1998;158:998–1004.

40. Savage S, Nagel NJ, Estacio RO, et al. Clinical factors associated with urinary albumin excretion in Type 2 diabetes. Am J Kidney Dis 1995;25:836–44.

41. Andersen AR, Christiansen JS, Andersen JK, et al. Diabetic nephropathy in Type 1 (insulin-dependent) diabetes: an epidemiological study. Diabetologia 1983;25:496–501.

42. Tuomilehto J, Borch-Johnsen K, Molarius A, et al. The unchanging incidence of hospitalization for diabetic nephropathy in a population-based cohort of IDDM patients in Finland [published erratum appears in Diabetes Care 1997; 20(:1802]. Diabetes Care 1997;20:1081–6.

43. Kofoed-Enevoldsen A, Borch-Johnsen K, Kreiner S, et al. Declining incidence of persistent proteinuria in Type 1 (insulin-dependent) diabetic patients in Denmark. Diabetes 1987;36:205–9.

44. Bojestig M, Arnqvist HJ, Hermansson G, et al. Declining incidence of nephropathy in insulin-dependent diabetes mellitus [published erratum appears in N Engl J Med 1994;330:584]. N Engl J Med 1994;330:15–8.

45. Selby JV, FitzSimmons SC, Newman JM, et al. The natural history and epidemiology of diabetic nephropathy. Implications for prevention and control. JAMA 1990;263:1954–60.

46. Rossing P, Rossing K, Jacobsen P, Parving HH. Unchanged incidence of diabetic nephropathy in IDDM patients. Diabetes 1995;44:739–43.

47. Mathiesen ER, Feldt-Rasmussen B, Hommel E, et al. Stable glomerular filtration rate in normotensive IDDM patients with stable microalbuminuria. A 5-year prospective study. Diabetes Care 1997;20:286–9.

48. Christensen PK, Rossing P, Nielsen FS, Parving HH. Natural course of kidney function in Type 2 diabetic patients with diabetic nephropathy. Diabet Med 1999;16:388–94.

49. Parving HH, Hommel E. Prognosis in diabetic nephropathy. BMJ 1989;299:230–3.

50. Klein R, Klein BE, Moss SE, et al. The 10-year incidence of renal insufficiency in people with type 1 diabetes. Diabetes Care 1999;22:743–51.

51. Barrett-Connor EL, Cohn BA, Wingard DL, Edelstein SL. Why is diabetes mellitus a stronger risk factor for fatal ischemic heart disease in women than in men? The Rancho Bernardo Study [published erratum appears in JAMA 1991;265:3249]. JAMA 1991;265:627–31.

52. Fuller JH, Shipley MJ, Rose G, et al. Mortality from coronary heart disease and stroke in relation to degree of glycaemia: the Whitehall study. BMJ 1983;287:867–70.

53. Kannel WB, McGee DL. Diabetes and cardiovascular disease. The Framingham study. JAMA 1979;241:2035–8.

54. Manson JE, Colditz GA, Stampfer MJ, et al. A prospective study of maturity-onset diabetes mellitus and risk of coronary heart disease and stroke in women. Arch Intern Med 1991;151:1141–7.

55. Stamler J, Vaccaro O, Neaton JD, Wentworth D. Diabetes, other risk factors, and 12-yr cardiovascular mortality for men screened in the Multiple Risk Factor Intervention Trial. Diabetes Care 1993;16:434–44.

56. Wang SL, Head J, Stevens L, Fuller JH. Excess mortality and its relation to hypertension and proteinuria in diabetic patients. The World Health Organization multinational study of vascular disease in diabetes. Diabetes Care 1996;19:305–12.

57. Jensen T, Borch-Johnsen K, Kofoed-Enevoldsen A, Deckert T. Coronary heart disease in young type 1 (insulin-dependent) diabetic patients with and without diabetic nephropathy: incidence and risk factors. Diabetologia 1987;30:144–8.

58. Rossing P, Hougaard P, Borch-Johnsen K, Parving HH. Predictors of mortality in insulin dependent diabetes: 10 year observational follow up study. BMJ 1996;313:779–84.

59. Mogensen CE. Microalbuminuria predicts clinical proteinuria and early mortality in maturity-onset diabetes. N Engl J Med 1984;310:356–60.

60. Chavers BM, Bilous RW, Ellis EN, et al. Glomerular lesions and urinary albumin excretion in Type 1 diabetes without overt proteinuria. N Engl J Med 1989;320:966–70.

61. Fioretto P, Steffes MW, Mauer M. Glomerular structure in nonproteinuric IDDM patients with various levels of albuminuria. Diabetes 1994;43:1358–64.

62. Osterby R, Gundersen HJ. Glomerular size and structure in diabetes mellitus. I. Early abnormalities. Diabetologia 1975;11:225–9.

63. Osterby R, Parving HH, Hommel E, et al. Glomerular structure and function in diabetic nephropathy. Early to advanced stages. Diabetes 1990;39:1057–63.

64. Ellis EN, Steffes MW, Goetz FC, et al. Glomerular filtration surface in Type 1 diabetes mellitus. Kidney Int 1986;29:889–94.

65. Fioretto P, Steffes MW, Sutherland DE, Mauer M. Sequential renal biopsies in insulin-dependent diabetic patients: structural factors associated with clinical progression. Kidney Int 1995;48:1929–35.

66. Mauer SM, Steffes MW, Ellis EN, et al. Structural-functional relationships in diabetic nephropathy. J Clin Invest 1984;74:1143–55.

67. Osterby R, Parving HH, Nyberg G, et al. A strong correlation between glomerular filtration rate and filtration surface in diabetic nephropathy. Diabetologia 1988;31:265–70.

68. Friedman EA. Renal syndromes in diabetes. Endocrinol Metab Clin North Am 1996; 25:293–324.

69. Brenner BM, Lawler EV, MacKenzie HS. The hyperfiltration theory: a paradigm shift in nephrology. Kidney Int 1996;49:1774–7.

70. Zatz R, Anderson S, Meyer TW, et al. Lowering of arterial blood pressure limits glomerular sclerosis in rats with renal ablation and in experimental diabetes. Kidney Int Suppl 1987;20:S123–9.

71. Zatz R, Brenner BM. Pathogenesis of diabetic microangiopathy. The hemodynamic view. Am J Med 1986;80:443–53.

72. Anderson S, Brenner BM. The role of intraglomerular pressure in the initiation and progression of renal disease. J Hypertens Suppl 1986;4:S236–8.

73. Meyer TW, Lawrence WE, Brenner BM. Dietary protein and the progression of renal disease. Kidney Int Suppl 1983;16:S243–7.

74. Neuringer JR, Brenner BM. Hemodynamic theory of progressive renal disease: a 10-year update in brief review. Am J Kidney Dis 1993;22:98–104.

75. O'Bryan GT, Hostetter TH. The renal hemodynamic basis of diabetic nephropathy. Semin Nephrol 1997;17:93–100.

76. Gabbay KH. The sorbitol pathway and the complications of diabetes. N Engl J Med 1973;288:831–6.

77. Greene DA, Lattimer SA, Sima AA. Sorbitol, phosphoinositides, and sodium-potassium-ATPase in the pathogenesis of diabetic complications. N Engl J Med 1987;316:599–606.

78. Brownlee M, Cerami A, Vlassara H. Advanced glycosylation end products in tissue and the biochemical basis of diabetic complications. N Engl J Med 1988;318:1315–21.

79. Friedman EA. Advanced glycosylated end products and hyperglycemia in the pathogenesis of diabetic complications. Diabetes Care 1999;22(Suppl 2):B65–71.

80. Larkins RG, Dunlop ME. The link between hyperglycaemia and diabetic nephropathy [published erratum appears in Diabetologia 1992;35:1100]. Diabetologia 1992;35:499–504.

81. Raj DS, Choudhury D, Welbourne TC, Levi M. Advanced glycation end products: a nephrologist's perspective. Am J Kidney Dis 2000;35:365–80.

82. Diabetes Control and Complications (DCCT) Trial Research Group. Effect of intensive therapy on the development and progression of diabetic nephropathy in the Diabetes Control and Complications Trial. Kidney Int 1995;47:1703–20.

83. Diabetes Control and Complications Trial Research Group. Clustering of long-term complications in families with diabetes in the Diabetes Control and Complications Trial. Diabetes 1997;46:1829–39.

84. Bain SC, Chowdhury TA. Genetics of diabetic nephropathy and microalbuminuria. J R Soc Med 2000;93:62–6.

85. Panagiotopoulos S, Smith TJ, Aldred GP, et al. Angiotensin-converting enzyme (ACE) gene polymorphism in Type 2 diabetic patients with increased albumin excretion rate. J Diabetes Complications 1995;9:272–6.

86. Parving HH, Jacobsen P, Tarnow L, et al. Effect of deletion polymorphism of angiotensin converting enzyme gene on progression of diabetic nephropathy during inhibition of angiotensin converting enzyme: observational follow up study. BMJ 1996;313:591–4.

87. Parving HH, Tarnow L, Rossing P. Genetics of diabetic nephropathy [editorial]. J Am Soc Nephrol 1996;7:2509–17.

88. Jacobsen P, Rossing K, Rossing P, et al. Angiotensin converting enzyme gene polymorphism and ACE inhibition in diabetic nephropathy. Kidney Int 1998;53:1002–6.

89. Nakajima S, Baba T, Yajima Y. Is ACE gene polymorphism a useful marker for diabetic albuminuria in Japanese NIDDM patients? Diabetes Care 1996;19:1420–2.

90. Penno G, Chaturvedi N, Talmud PJ, et al. Effect of angiotensin-converting enzyme (ACE) gene polymorphism on progression of renal disease and the influence of ACE inhibition in IDDM patients: findings from the EUCLID Randomized Controlled Trial. EURODIAB Controlled Trial of Lisinopril in IDDM. Diabetes 1998;47:1507–11.

91. Schmidt S, Schone N, Ritz E. Association of ACE gene polymorphism and diabetic nephropathy? The Diabetic Nephropathy Study Group [published erratum appears in Kidney Int 1995;48:915]. Kidney Int 1995;47:1176–81.

92. Seaquist ER, Goetz FC, Rich S, Barbosa J. Familial clustering of diabetic kidney disease. Evidence for genetic susceptibility to diabetic nephropathy. N Engl J Med 1989;320:1161–5.

93. Vleming LJ, van der Pijl JW, Lemkes HH, et al. The DD genotype of the ACE gene polymorphism is associated with progression of diabetic nephropathy to end stage renal failure in IDDM. Clin Nephrol 1999;51:133–40.

94. Krolewski AS, Canessa M, Warram JH, et al. Predisposition to hypertension and susceptibility to renal disease in insulin-dependent diabetes mellitus. N Engl J Med 1988;318:140–5.

95. Viberti GC, Keen H, Wiseman MJ. Raised arterial pressure in parents of proteinuric insulin dependent diabetics. BMJ 1987;295:515–7.

96. Earle K, Walker J, Hill C, Viberti G. Familial clustering of cardiovascular disease in patients with insulin-dependent diabetes and nephropathy. N Engl J Med 1992;326:673–7.

97. Tarnow L, Gluud C, Parving HH. Diabetic nephropathy and the insertion/deletion polymorphism of the angiotensin-converting enzyme gene. Nephrol Dial Transplant 1998;13:1125–30.

98. UK Prospective Diabetes Study (UKPDS) Group. Intensive blood-glucose control with sulphonylureas or insulin compared with conventional treatment and risk of complications in patients with type 2 diabetes (UKPDS 33) [published erratum appears in Lancet 1999;354:602]. Lancet 1998;352:837–53.

99. UK Prospective Diabetes Study (UKPDS) Gropu. Effect of intensive blood-glucose control with metformin on complications in overweight patients with type 2 diabetes (UKPDS 34). [published erratum appears in Lancet 1998;352:1557]. Lancet 1998;352:854–65.

100. Diabetes Control and Complications Trial Research Group. The effect of intensive treatment of diabetes on the development and progression of long-term complications in insulin-dependent diabetes mellitus. N Engl J Med 1993;329:977–86.

101. Wang PH, Lau J, Chalmers TC. Meta-analysis of effects of intensive blood-glucose control on late complications of Type 1 diabetes. Lancet 1993;341:1306–9.

102. Krolewski AS, Laffel LM, Krolewski M, et al. Glycosylated hemoglobin and the risk of microalbuminuria in patients with insulin-dependent diabetes mellitus. N Engl J Med 1995;332:1251–5.

103. Warram JH, Scott LJ, Hanna LS, et al. Progression of microalbuminuria to proteinuria in type 1 diabetes: nonlinear relationship with hyperglycemia. Diabetes 2000;49:94–100.

104. Diabetes Control and Complications Trial Research Group. Lifetime benefits and costs of intensive therapy as practiced in the diabetes control and complications trial. [published erratum appears in JAMA 1997;278:25]. JAMA 1996;276:1409–15.

105. Eastman RC, Javitt JC, Herman WH, et al. Model of complications of NIDDM. II. Analysis of the health benefits and cost-effectiveness of treating NIDDM with the goal of normoglycemia. Diabetes Care 1997;20:735–44.

106. Eastman RC, Javitt JC, Herman WH, et al. Model of complications of NIDDM. I. Model construction and assumptions. Diabetes Care 1997;20:725–34.

107. Hasslacher C, Ritz E. Effect of control of diabetes mellitus on progression of renal failure. Kidney Int Suppl 1987;22:S53–6.

108. Hasslacher C, Ritz E, Wahl P, Michael C. Similar risks of nephropathy in patients with Type 1 or Type 2 diabetes mellitus. Nephrol Dial Transplant 1989;4:859–63.

109. Microalbuminuria Collaborative Study Group, United Kingdom. Risk factors for development of microalbuminuria in insulin dependent diabetic patients: a cohort study. BMJ 1993;306:1235–9.

110. Almdal T, Norgaard K, Feldt-Rasmussen B, Deckert T. The predictive value of microalbuminuria in IDDM. A five-year follow-up study. Diabetes Care 1994;17:120–5.

111. Bruno G, Cavallo-Perin P, Bargero G, et al. Prevalence and risk factors for micro- and macroalbuminuria in an Italian population-base cohort of NIDDM subjects. Diabetes Care 1996;19:43–7.

112. Goetz FC, Jacobs DR Jr, Chavers B, et al. Risk factors for kidney damage in the adult population of Wadena, Minnesota. A prospective study. Am J Epidemiol 1997;145:91–102.

113. Hirata-Dulas CA, Rith-Najarian SJ, McIntyre MC, et al. Risk factors for nephropathy and cardiovascular disease in diabetic Northern Minnesota American Indians. Clin Nephrol 1996;46:92–98.

114. Jacobsen P, Rossing K, Tarnow L, et al. Progression of diabetic nephropathy in normotensive type 1 diabetic patients. Kidney Int Suppl 1999;71:S101–5.

115. Niskanen LK, Penttila I, Parviainen M, Uusitupa MI. Evolution, risk factors, and prognostic implications of albuminuria in NIDDM. Diabetes Care 1996;19:486–93.

116. Oue T, Namba M, Nakajima H, et al. Risk factors for the progression of microalbuminuria in Japanese type 2 diabetic patients—a 10 year follow-up study. Diabetes Res Clin Pract 1999;46:47–55.

117. Reichard P. Risk factors for progression of microvascular complications in the Stockholm Diabetes Intervention Study (SDIS). Diabetes Res Clin Pract 1992;16:151–6.

118. Strojek K, Grzeszczak W, Ritz E. Risk factors for development of diabetic nephropathy: a review. Nephrol Dial Transplant 1997;12(Suppl 2):24–6.

119. Yokota C, Kimura G, Inenaga T, et al. Risk factors for progression of diabetic nephropathy. Am J Nephrol 1995;15:488–92.

120. Mathiesen ER, Ronn B, Storm B, et al. The natural course of microalbuminuria in insulin-dependent diabetes: a 10-year prospective study. Diabet Med 1995;12:482–7.

121. Chase HP, Garg SK, Marshall G, et al. Cigarette smoking increases the risk of albuminuria among subjects with Type 1 diabetes. JAMA 1991;265:614–7.

122. Chaturvedi N, Stephenson JM, Fuller JH. The relationship between smoking and microvascular complications in the EURODIAB IDDM Complications Study. Diabetes Care 1995;18:785–92.

123. Corradi L, Zoppi A, Tettamanti F, et al. Association between smoking and micro-albuminuria in hypertensive patients with Type 2 diabetes mellitus. J Hypertens Suppl 1993;11(Suppl 5):S190–1.

124. Couper JJ, Staples AJ, Cocciolone R, et al. Relationship of smoking and albuminuria in children with insulin-dependent diabetes. Diabet Med 1994;11:666–9.

125. Ekberg G, Grefberg N, Larsson LO, Vaara I. Cigarette smoking and glomerular filtration rate in insulin-treated diabetics without manifest nephropathy. J Intern Med 1990;228(3):211–7.

126. Mehler PS, Jeffers BW, Biggerstaff SL, Schrier RW. Smoking as a risk factor for nephropathy in non-insulin-dependent diabetics. J Gen Intern Med 1998;13:842–5.

127. Sawicki PT, Didjurgeit U, Muhlhauser I, et al. Smoking is associated with progression of diabetic nephropathy. Diabetes Care 1994;17:126–31.

128. Cowie CC, Port FK, Wolfe RA, et al. Disparities in incidence of diabetic end-stage renal disease according to race and type of diabetes. N Engl J Med 1989;321:1074–9.

129. Friedman EA. Race and diabetic nephropathy. Transplant Proc 1987;19(Suppl 2):77–81.

130. Nelson RG, Bennett PH, Beck GJ, et al. Development and progression of renal disease in Pima Indians with non- insulin-dependent diabetes mellitus. Diabetic Renal Disease Study Group. N Engl J Med 1996;335:1636–42.

131. Nelson RG, Knowler WC, Pettitt DJ, et al. Diabetic kidney disease in Pima Indians. Diabetes Care 1993;16:335–41.

132. Chaturvedi N, Fuller JH. Glycosylated hemoglobin and the risk of microalbuminuria in insulin-dependent diabetes mellitus. EURODIAB IDDM Complications Study Group [letter; comment]. N Engl J Med 1995;333:940–1.

133. Ikeda Y, Suehiro T, Takamatsu K, et al. Effect of smoking on the prevalence of albuminuria in Japanese men with non-insulin-dependent diabetes mellitus. Diabetes Res Clin Pract 1997;36:57–61.

134. Muhlhauser I, Sawicki P, Berger M. Cigarette-smoking as a risk factor for macroproteinuria and proliferative retinopathy in type 1 (insulin-dependent) diabetes. Diabetologia 1986;29:500–2.

135. Ritz E, Orth SR. Nephropathy in patients with type 2 diabetes mellitus. N Engl J Med 1999;341:1127–33.

136. Mauer SM, Bilous RW, Ellis E, et al. Some lessons from the studies of renal biopsies in patients with insulin-dependent diabetes mellitus. J Diabet Complications 1988;2:197–202.

137. Mauer SM, Chavers BM, Steffes MW. Should there be an expanded role for kidney biopsy in the management of patients with Type 1 diabetes? Am J Kidney Dis 1990;16:96–100.

138. Kostraba JN, Klein R, Dorman JS, et al. The epidemiology of diabetes complications study. IV. Correlates of diabetic background and proliferative retinopathy. Am J Epidemiol 1991;133:381–91.

139. Kasinath BS, Mujais SK, Spargo BH, Katz AI. Nondiabetic renal disease in patients with diabetes mellitus. Am J Med 1983;75:613–7.

140. Lee EY, Chung CH, Choi SO. Non-diabetic renal disease in patients with non-insulin dependent diabetes mellitus. Yonsei Med J 1999;40:321–6.

141. Olsen S, Mogensen CE. How often is NIDDM complicated with non-diabetic renal disease? An analysis of renal biopsies and the literature. Diabetologia 1996;39:1638–45.

142. Parving HH, Gall MA, Skott P, et al. Prevalence and causes of albuminuria in non-insulin-dependent diabetic patients. Kidney Int 1992;41:758–62.

143. Stephenson JM, Fuller JH. Microalbuminuria is not rare before 5 years of IDDM. EURODIAB IDDM Complications Study Group and the WHO Multinational Study of Vascular Disease in Diabetes Study Group. J Diabetes Complications 1994;8:166–73.

144. Mogensen CE, Christensen CK. Predicting diabetic nephropathy in insulin-dependent patients. N Engl J Med 1984;311:89–93.

145. Viberti GC, Hill RD, Jarrett RJ, et al. Microalbuminuria as a predictor of clinical nephropathy in insulin-dependent diabetes mellitus. Lancet 1982;1:1430–2.

146. Messent JW, Elliott TG, Hill RD, et al. Prognostic significance of microalbuminuria in insulin-dependent diabetes mellitus: a twenty-three year follow-up study. Kidney Int 1992;41:836–9.

147. Forsblom CM, Groop PH, Ekstrand A, Groop LC. Predictive value of microalbuminuria in patients with insulin-dependent diabetes of long duration. BMJ 1992;305:1051–3.

148. Borch-Johnsen K, Wenzel H, Viberti GC, Mogensen CE. Is screening and intervention for microal-buminuria worthwhile in patients with insulin dependent diabetes? [published erratum appears in BMJ 1993;307:543]. BMJ 1993;306:1722–5.

149. Siegel JE, Krolewski AS, Warram JH, Weinstein MC. Cost-effectiveness of screening and early treatment of nephropathy in patients with insulin-dependent diabetes mellitus. J Am Soc Nephrol 1992;3(Suppl):S111–9.

150. Bennett PH, Haffner S, Kasiske BL, et al. Screening and management of microalbuminuria in patients with diabetes mellitus: recommendations to the Scientific Advisory Board of the National Kidney Foundation from an ad hoc committee of the Council on Diabetes Mellitus of the National Kidney Foundation. Am J Kidney Dis 1995;25:107–12.

151. American Diabetes Association: clinical practice recommendations 1999. Diabetes Care 1999;22 (Suppl 1):S1–114.

152. Coonrod BA, Ellis D, Becker DJ, et al. Assessment of AlbuSure and its usefulness in identifying IDDM subjects at increased risk for developing clinical diabetic nephropathy. Diabetes Care 1989;12:389–93.

153. Ellis D, Coonrod BA, Dorman JS, et al. Choice of urine sample predictive of microalbuminuria in patients with insulin-dependent diabetes mellitus. Am J Kidney Dis 1989;13:321–8.

154. Gatling W, Knight C, Mullee MA, Hill RD. Microalbuminuria in diabetes: a population study of the prevalence and an assessment of three screening tests. Diabet Med 1988;5:343–7.

155. Kouri TT, Viikari JS, Mattila KS, Irjala KM. Microalbuminuria. Invalidity of simple concentra-tion-based screening tests for early nephropathy due to urinary volumes of diabetic patients. Dia-betes Care 1991;14:591–3.

156. Poulsen PL, Hansen B, Amby T, et al. Evaluation of a dipstick test for microalbuminuria in three different clinical settings, including the correlation with urinary albumin excretion rate. Diabetes Metab 1992;18:395–400.

157. Schwab SJ, Dunn FL, Feinglos MN. Screening for microalbuminuria. A comparison of single sam-ple methods of collection and techniques of albumin analysis. Diabetes Care 1992;15:1581–4.

158. Shield JP, Hunt LP, Baum JD, Pennock CA. Screening for diabetic microalbuminuria in routine clinical care: which method? Arch Dis Child 1995;72:524–5.

159. Tiu SC, Lee SS, Cheng MW. Comparison of six commercial techniques in the measurement of microalbuminuria in diabetic patients. Diabetes Care 1993;16:616–20.

160. Hutchison AS, O'Reilly DS, MacCuish AC. Albumin excretion rate, albumin concentration, and albumin/creatinine ratio compared for screening diabetics for slight albuminuria. Clin Chem 1988;34:2019–21.

161. Webb DJ, Newman DJ, Chaturvedi N, Fuller JH. The use of the Micral-Test strip to identify the presence of microalbuminuria in people with insulin dependent diabetes mellitus (IDDM) par-ticipating in the EUCLID study. Diabetes Res Clin Pract 1996;31:93–102.

162. Gatling W, Knight C, Hill RD. Screening for early diabetic nephropathy: which sample to detect microalbuminuria? Diabet Med 1985;2:451–5.

163. Zelmanovitz T, Gross JL, Oliveira JR, et al. The receiver operating characteristics curve in the eval-uation of a random urine specimen as a screening test for diabetic nephropathy. Diabetes Care 1997;20:516–9.

164. Nelson RG, Knowler WC, Pettitt DJ, et al. Assessment of risk of overt nephropathy in diabetic patients from albumin excretion in untimed urine specimens. Arch Intern Med 1991;151:1761–5.

165. Meltzer S, Leiter L, Daneman D, et al. 1998 clinical practice guidelines for the management of diabetes in Canada. Canadian Diabetes Association. Can Med Assoc J 1998;159(Suppl 8):S1-29.

166. Captopril reduces the risk of nephropathy in IDDM patients with microalbuminuria. The Microalbuminuria Captopril Study Group. Diabetologia 1996;39:587–93.

167. John L, Rao PS, Kanagasabapathy AS. Rate of progression of albuminuria in Type 2 diabetes. Five-year prospective study from south India. Diabetes Care 1994;17:888–90.

168. Lacourciere Y, Nadeau A, Poirier L, Tancrede G. Captopril or conventional therapy in hypertensive Type 2 diabetics. Three-year analysis. Hypertension 1993;21(6 Pt 1):786–94.

169. Ravid M, Savin H, Jutrin I, et al. Long-term stabilizing effect of angiotensin-converting enzyme inhibition on plasma creatinine and on proteinuria in normotensive Type 2 diabetic patients. Ann Intern Med 1993;118:577–81.

170. Ahmad J, Siddiqui MA, Ahmad H. Effective postponement of diabetic nephropathy with enalapril in normotensive type 2 diabetic patients with microalbuminuria. Diabetes Care 1997;20:1576–81.

171. Effects of ramipril on cardiovascular and microvascular outcomes in people with diabetes mellitus: results of the HOPE study and MICRO-HOPE substudy. Heart Outcomes Prevention Evaluation Study Investigators. Lancet 2000;355:253–9.

172. Kiberd BA, Jindal KK. Routine treatment of insulin-dependent diabetic patients with ACE inhibitors to prevent renal failure: an economic evaluation. Am J Kidney Dis 1998;31:49–54.

173. Kiberd BA, Jindal KK. Screening to prevent renal failure in insulin dependent diabetic patients: an economic evaluation. BMJ 1995;311:1595–99.

174. Poulsen PL, Hansen KW, Mogensen CE. Ambulatory blood pressure in the transition from normo- to microalbuminuria. A longitudinal study in IDDM patients. Diabetes 1994;43:1248–53.

175. Gaede P, Vedel P, Parving HH, Pedersen O. Intensified multifactorial intervention in patients with type 2 diabetes mellitus and microalbuminuria: the Steno type 2 randomised study. Lancet 1999; 353:617–22.

176. Feldt-Rasmussen B, Mathiesen ER, Deckert T. Effect of two years of strict metabolic control on progression of incipient nephropathy in insulin-dependent diabetes. Lancet 1986;2:1300–4.

177. Ohkubo Y, Kishikawa H, Araki E, et al. Intensive insulin therapy prevents the progression of diabetic microvascular complications in Japanese patients with non-insulin-dependent diabetes mellitus: a randomized prospective 6-year study. Diabetes Res Clin Pract 1995;28:103–17.

178. Mogensen CE. High blood pressure as a factor in the progression of diabetic nephropathy. Acta Med Scand Suppl 1976; 602:29–32.

179. Mogensen CE. Long-term antihypertensive treatment inhibiting progression of diabetic nephropathy. BMJ 1982;285:685–8.

180. Weidmann P, Schneider M, Bohlen L. Therapeutic efficacy of different antihypertensive drugs in human diabetic nephropathy: an updated meta-analysis. Nephrol Dial Transplant 1995; 10(Suppl 9):39–45.

181. Kasiske BL, Kalil RS, Ma JZ, et al. Effect of antihypertensive therapy on the kidney in patients with diabetes: a meta-regression analysis. Ann Intern Med 1993;118:129–38.

182. Maki DD, Ma JZ, Louis TA, Kasiske BL. Long-term effects of antihypertensive agents on proteinuria and renal function. Arch Intern Med 1995;155:1073–80.

183. Breyer JA, Hunsicker LG, Bain RP, Lewis EJ. Angiotensin converting enzyme inhibition in diabetic nephropathy. The Collaborative Study Group. Kidney Int Suppl 1994;45:S156–60.

184. Lewis EJ. Therapeutic interventions in the progression of diabetic nephropathy. Am J Hypertens 1994;7(9 Pt 2):93S–5S.

185. Lewis EJ, Hunsicker LG, Bain RP, Rohde RD. The effect of angiotensin-converting-enzyme inhibition on diabetic nephropathy. The Collaborative Study Group [published erratum appears in N Engl J Med 1993;330:152]. N Engl J Med 1993;329:1456–62.

186. Parving HH, Smidt UM, Hommel E, et al. Effective antihypertensive treatment postpones renal insufficiency in diabetic nephropathy. Am J Kidney Dis 1993;22:188–95.

187. Gall MA, Nielsen FS, Smidt UM, Parving HH. The course of kidney function in type 2 (non-insulin-dependent) diabetic patients with diabetic nephropathy. Diabetologia 1993;36:1071–8.

188. Mathiesen ER, Hommel E, Giese J, Parving HH. Efficacy of captopril in postponing nephropathy in normotensive insulin dependent diabetic patients with microalbuminuria. BMJ 1991;303:81–7.

189. Mathiesen ER, Hommel E, Hansen HP, et al. Randomised controlled trial of long term efficacy of captopril on preservation of kidney function in normotensive patients with insulin dependent diabetes and microalbuminuria. BMJ 1999;319:24–5.

190. Nielsen FS, Rossing P, Gall MA, et al. Long-term effect of lisinopril and atenolol on kidney function in hypertensive NIDDM subjects with diabetic nephropathy. Diabetes 1997;46:1182–8.

191. Parving HH, Hommel E, Damkjaer NM, Giese J. Effect of captopril on blood pressure and kidney function in normotensive insulin dependent diabetics with nephropathy. BMJ 1989;299:533–6.

192. Parving HH. The impact of hypertension and antihypertensive treatment on the course and prognosis of diabetic nephropathy. J Hypertens Suppl 1990;8:S187–91.

193. Parving HH, Rossing P, Hommel E, Smidt UM. Angiotensin-converting enzyme inhibition in diabetic nephropathy: ten years' experience. Am J Kidney Dis 1995;26:99–107.

194. Bjorck S, Mulec H, Johnsen SA, et al. Renal protective effect of enalapril in diabetic nephropathy. BMJ 1992;304:339–43.

195. Parving HH. Diabetic hypertensive patients. Is this a group in need of particular care and attention? Diabetes Care 1999;22(Suppl 2):B76–9.

196. Tight blood pressure control and risk of macrovascular and microvascular complications in type 2 diabetes: UKPDS 38. UK Prospective Diabetes Study Group [published erratum appears in BMJ 1999;318:29]. BMJ 1998;317:703–13.

197. Peterson JC, Adler S, Burkart JM, et al. Blood pressure control, proteinuria, and the progression of renal disease. The Modification of Diet in Renal Disease Study. Ann Intern Med 1995;123:754–2.

198. Jacobson HR, Striker GE. Report on a workshop to develop management recommendations for the prevention of progression in chronic renal disease. Am J Kidney Dis 1995;25:103–6.

199. Feldman RD, Campbell N, Larochelle P, et al. 1999 Canadian recommendations for the management of hypertension. Task Force for the Development of the 1999 Canadian Recommendations for the Management of Hypertension. Can Med Assoc J 1999;161(Suppl 12):S1–17.

200. Hasslacher C, Kempe HP, Bostedt-Kiesel A. ACE inhibitors and diabetic nephropathy: clinical and experimental findings. Clin Invest 1993;71(Suppl):S20–4.

201. Kamper AL. Angiotensin converting enzyme (ACE) inhibitors and renal function. A review of the current status. Drug Saf 1991;6:361–70.

202. Mogensen CE. Renoprotective role of ACE inhibitors in diabetic nephropathy. Br Heart J 1994;72(Suppl):S38–45.

203. Molitch ME. ACE inhibitors and diabetic nephropathy. Diabetes Care 1994;17:756–60.

204. Parving HH. ACE inhibition in diabetic nephropathy. J Diabetes Complications 1990;4:86–7.

205. Ritz E. ACE inhibition and renal protection. Clin Physiol Biochem 1992;9:94–7.

206. Laffel LM, McGill JB, Gans DJ. The beneficial effect of angiotensin-converting enzyme inhibition with captopril on diabetic nephropathy in normotensive IDDM patients with microalbuminuria. North American Microalbuminuria Study Group. Am J Med 1995;99:497–504.

207. Sano T, Hotta N, Kawamura T, et al. Effects of long-term enalapril treatment on persistent microalbuminuria in normotensive type 2 diabetic patients: results of a 4-year, prospective, randomized study. Diabet Med 1996;13:120–4.

208. Sano T, Kawamura T, Matsumae H, et al. Effects of long-term enalapril treatment on persistent micro-albuminuria in well-controlled hypertensive and normotensive NIDDM patients. Diabetes Care 1994;17:420–4.

209. Viberti G, Mogensen CE, Groop LC, Pauls JF. Effect of captopril on progression to clinical proteinuria in patients with insulin-dependent diabetes mellitus and microalbuminuria. European Microalbuminuria Captopril Study Group. JAMA 1994;271:275–9.

210. Liou HH, Huang TP, Campese VM. Effect of long-term therapy with captopril on proteinuria and renal function in patients with non-insulin-dependent diabetes and with non-diabetic renal diseases. Nephron 1995;69(1):41–8.

211. Randomised placebo-controlled trial of lisinopril in normotensive patients with insulin-dependent diabetes and normoalbuminuria or microalbuminuria. The EUCLID Study Group. Lancet 1997;349:1787–92.

212. Ravid M, Lang R, Rachmani R, Lishner M. Long-term renoprotective effect of angiotensin-converting enzyme inhibition in non-insulin-dependent diabetes mellitus. A 7-year follow-up study. Arch Intern Med 1996;156:286–9.

213. Lovell HG. Angiotensin converting enzyme inhibitors in normotensive diabetic patients with microalbuminuria. Cochrane Database Syst Rev 2000;2:CD002183.

214. Kshirsagar AV, Joy MS, Hogan SL, et al. Effect of ACE inhibitors in diabetic and nondiabetic chronic renal disease: a systematic overview of randomized placebo-controlled trials. Am J Kidney Dis 2000;35:695–707.

215. Brenner BM, Meyer TW, Hostetter TH. Dietary protein intake and the progressive nature of kidney disease: the role of hemodynamically mediated glomerular injury in the pathogenesis of progressive glomerular sclerosis in aging, renal ablation, and intrinsic renal disease. N Engl J Med 1982;307:652–9.

216. Zeller K, Whittaker E, Sullivan L, et al. Effect of restricting dietary protein on the progression of renal failure in patients with insulin-dependent diabetes mellitus. N Engl J Med 1991;324:78–84.

217. Pedrini MT, Levey AS, Lau J, et al. The effect of dietary protein restriction on the progression of diabetic and nondiabetic renal diseases: a meta-analysis. Ann Intern Med 1996;124:627–32.

218. Waugh NR, Robertson AM. Protein restriction for diabetic renal disease. Cochrane Database Syst Rev 2000;2:CD002181.

219. Inman SR, Stowe NT, Cressman MD, et al. Lovastatin preserves renal function in experimental diabetes. Am J Med Sci 1999;317:215–221.

220. Keane WF, Kasiske BL, O'Donnell MP. Hyperlipidemia and the progression of renal disease. Am J Clin Nutr 1988;47:157–60.

221. Hommel E, Andersen P, Gall MA, et al. Plasma lipoproteins and renal function during simvastatin treatment in diabetic nephropathy. Diabetologia 1992;35:447–51.

222. Kasiske BL, O'Donnell MP, Schmitz PG, Keane WF. The role of lipid abnormalities in the pathogenesis of chronic, progressive renal disease. Adv Nephrol Necker Hosp 1991;20:109–125.

223. Keane WF. Lipids and the kidney. Kidney Int 1994;46:910–20.

224. Keane WF. Lipids and progressive renal disease: the cardio-renal link. Am J Kidney Dis 1999;34:xliii–xxlvi.

225. Keane WF, Kasiske BL, O'Donnell MP. Lipids and progressive glomerulosclerosis. A model analogous to atherosclerosis. Am J Nephrol 1988;8:261–71.

226. Keane WF, Kasiske BL, O'Donnell MP, Kim Y. The role of altered lipid metabolism in the progression of renal disease: experimental evidence. Am J Kidney Dis 1991;17(Suppl 1):38–42.

227. O'Donnell MP, Kasiske BL, Katz SA, et al. Lovastatin but not enalapril reduces glomerular injury in Dahl salt- sensitive rats. Hypertension 1992;20:651–8.

228. O'Donnell MP, Kasiske BL, Kim Y, et al. Lovastatin retards the progression of established glomerular disease in obese Zucker rats. Am J Kidney Dis 1993;22:83–89.

229. Oda H, Keane WF. Lipids in progression of renal disease. Kidney Int Suppl 1997;62:S36–8.

230. Schmitz PG, Kasiske BL, O'Donnell MP, Keane WF. Lipids and progressive renal injury. Semin Nephrol 1989;9:354–69.

231. Ravid M, Neumann L, Lishner M. Plasma lipids and the progression of nephropathy in diabetes mellitus Type 2: effect of ACE inhibitors. Kidney Int 1995;47:907–10.

232. Hirano H, Yamada Y, Otani H, et al. Evaluation of serum lipid abnormalities in chronic nephritis. Kidney Int Suppl 1999;71:S147–9.

233. Hirano T. Lipoprotein abnormalities in diabetic nephropathy. Kidney Int Suppl 1999;71:S22–4.

234. Kasiske BL, Velosa JA, Halstenson CE, et al. The effects of lovastatin in hyperlipidemic patients with the nephrotic syndrome. Am J Kidney Dis 1990;15:8–15.

235. Lam KS, Cheng IK, Janus ED, Pang RW. Cholesterol-lowering therapy may retard the progression of diabetic nephropathy. Diabetologia 1995;38:604–9.

236. Tonolo G, Ciccarese M, Brizzi P, et al. Reduction of albumin excretion rate in normotensive microalbuminuric type 2 diabetic patients during long-term simvastatin treatment. Diabetes Care 1997;20:1891–5.

237. Fodor JG, Frohlich JJ, Genest JJ Jr, McPherson PR. Recommendations for the management and treatment of dyslipidemia. Report of the Working Group on Hypercholesterolemia and Other Dyslipidemias Can Med Assoc J 2000;162:1441–7.

238. Andersen S, Tarnow L, Rossing P, et al. Renoprotective effects of angiotensin II receptor blockade in Type 1 diabetic patients with diabetic nephropathy. Kidney Int 2000;57:601–6.

239. Rodby RA, Rohde RD, Clarke WR, et al. The Irbesartan Type 2 diabetic nephropathy trial: study design and baseline patient characteristics. For the Collaborative Study Group. Nephrol Dial Transplant 2000;15:487–97.

240. McAuliffe AV, Brooks BA, Fisher EJ, et al. Administration of ascorbic acid and an aldose reductase inhibitor (tolrestat) in diabetes: effect on urinary albumin excretion. Nephron 1998;80:277–84.

241. Passariello N, Sepe J, Marrazzo G, et al. Effect of aldose reductase inhibitor (tolrestat) on urinary albumin excretion rate and glomerular filtration rate in IDDM subjects with nephropathy. Diabetes Care 1993;16:789–95.

242. Dedov I, Shestakova M, Vorontzov A, Palazzini E. A randomized, controlled study of sulodexide therapy for the treatment of diabetic nephropathy. Nephrol Dial Transplant 1997;12:2295–300.

243. Freedman BI, Wuerth JP, Cartwright K, et al. Design and baseline characteristics for the Aminoguanidine Clinical Trial in Overt Type 2 Diabetic Nephropathy (ACTION II). Control Clin Trials 1999;20:493–510.

244. Itakura M, Yoshikawa H, Bannai C, et al. Aminoguanidine decreases urinary albumin and high-molecular-weight proteins in diabetic rats. Life Sci 1991;49:889–97.

245. Soulis T, Cooper ME, Vranes D, et al. Effects of aminoguanidine in preventing experimental diabetic nephropathy are related to the duration of treatment. Kidney Int 1996;50:627–634.

246. Ha H, Kim KH. Pathogenesis of diabetic nephropathy: the role of oxidative stress and protein kinase C. Diabetes Res Clin Pract 1999;45:147–51.

247. Koya D, Haneda M, Nakagawa H, et al. Amelioration of accelerated diabetic mesangial expansion by treatment with a PKC beta inhibitor in diabetic db/db mice, a rodent model for Type 2 diabetes. FASEB J 2000;14:439–47.

248. Murphy M, McGinty A, Godson C. Protein kinases C: potential targets for intervention in diabetic nephropathy. Curr Opin Nephrol Hypertens 1998;7:563–70.

249. Bilous RW, Fioretto P, Czernichow P, Drummond K. Growth factors and diabetic nephropathy: kidney structure and therapeutic interventions. Diabetologia 1997;40(Suppl 3):B68–73.

250. Tsuchida K, Makita Z, Yamagishi S, et al. Suppression of transforming growth factor beta and vascular endothelial growth factor in diabetic nephropathy in rats by a novel advanced glycation end product inhibitor, OPB-9195. Diabetologia 1999;42:579–88.

CHAPTER 23

Peripheral Nerve Disease

Douglas W. Zochodne, MD, FRCPC

ABSTRACT

Neuropathies are important complications of diabetes mellitus and are associated with sensory loss, pain, and weakness. Among the neuropathies, focal entrapment neuropathies such as carpal tunnel syndrome and polyneuropathy, a diffuse disease of peripheral nerves, are the most common. While symptomatic polyneuropathy may occur in 13 to 15% of patients with diabetes mellitus, sensitive testing methods may identify features of polyneuropathy in the majority of diabetic patients. The incidence of polyneuropathy in diabetic subjects can be lessened with optimal control of hyperglycemia. Despite a number of clinical trials, no single agent or class of agents has yet to be unequivocally associated with stabilization or improvement of diabetic polyneuropathy. There are, however, several agents available for the treatment of pain and other symptoms associated with polyneuropathy.

INTRODUCTION

Diabetic neuropathies (disorders of peripheral nerves) comprise a group of disorders of the peripheral nervous system associated with Type 1 and Type 2 diabetes mellitus. They can be broadly classified into focal neuropathies (mononeuropathies) and generalized neuropathies or polyneuropathy. Focal entrapment neuropathy is often found in association with polyneuropathy. Most of this chapter, however, will deal with polyneuropathy, the condition usually referred to when discussing "diabetic neuropathy." Patients with diabetic polyneuropathy are also more likely to suffer from diabetic nephropathy or retinopathy,[1,2] although in clinical practice, there may be surprising discrepancies in the severity of individual complications. An overall classification of diabetic neuropathies is provided in Table 23–1. The care of these diabetes-related consequences is reviewed by answering the following questions:

Table 23–1 Classification of Diabetic Neuropathies

Focal neuropathies

   Entrapment neuropathies: carpal tunnel syndrome, ulnar neuropathy at the elbow, peroneal neuropathy at the fibular head, meralgia paresthetica

   Lumbosacral plexopathy (diabetic amyotrophy, Bruns-Garland syndrome)

   Oculomotor (cranial nerve III) neuropathy and abducens (cranial nerve VI) neuropathy

   Intercostal neuropathy

Polyneuropathy

   Predominantly sensory: large fiber, small fiber, or mixed

   Painful sensory

   Sensorimotor

   Autonomic

   Predominantly motor (controversial)

   Combinations of the above

---

1. What are the types of focal diabetic neuropathies and how are they managed?
2. What is diabetic polyneuropathy?
3. How is diabetic polyneuropathy diagnosed?
4. How is diabetic polyneuropathy managed?

WHAT ARE THE TYPES OF FOCAL DIABETIC NEUROPATHIES AND HOW ARE THEY MANAGED?

Focal Diabetic Neuropathies

Entrapment Neuropathies

Entrapment focal neuropathies are common in diabetes (Table 23–2). Diabetic patients may develop median-nerve entrapment at the wrist, or carpal tunnel syndrome. In the Rochester Diabetic Study, which examined a prospective cohort of diabetic subjects, asymptomatic carpal tunnel syndrome was found in 22% of those with Type 1 diabetes and 29% of those with Type 2, whereas symptomatic "definite" carpal tunnel entrapment was found in 2% of both types.[3] In a summary of eight studies[4] examining 2,652 diabetic patients, the overall prevalence of symptomatic carpal tunnel syndrome was 5.8%.

Carpal tunnel syndrome is identified by the presence of symptoms of numbness, tingling, prickling, or pain in the thumb, index, and middle fingers (or often the whole hand), prominent at night or with use. Clinical sensory examination with pinprick and light touch testing may identify abnormalities in the distal median nerve territory (eg, tips of the median innervated digits) or the whole median territory, or may detect no abnormality. There may be a Tinel's sign at the wrist, a symptom of typical tingling, or paresthesia, evoked by the examiner tapping over the nerve. The diagnosis is made using electrophysiologic testing, specifically nerve conduction studies. These identify selective slowing of sensory conduction across the carpal tunnel in early stages, later combined with motor slowing across the same segment and eventually evidence of axonal damage, or degeneration in the median nerve distal to the carpal tunnel. In these more advanced instances, there may be thenar muscle weakness, wasting, and denervation. Surgical decompression is of benefit in carpal tunnel syndrome,[5] but in diabetes surgery should be reserved for moderate to severe symptomatic involvement, where the electrophysiologic abnormalities at the site of entrapment by far exceed the generalized involvement (Level 4). There are no randomized controlled trials of carpal tunnel decompression in diabetic patients alone, but diabetic patients may have a less favorable outcome after surgical decompression, as diabetes slows nerve regeneration.[6,7]

Table 23–2 Entrapment Neuropathies in Diabetes and Their Prevalence

Neuropathy	Prevalence
Symptomatic carpal tunnel syndrome	5.8%[4]
Asymptomatic carpal tunnel syndrome	22% (Type 1 diabetes)[3]
	29% (Type 2 diabetes)[3]
Ulnar neuropathy at the elbow	2.1%[4]
Peroneal neuropathy at the fibular head[*]	?1.4–13%[4,169]
Lateral cutaneous nerve of the thigh (meralgia paresthetica)[*]	?0–1.0%[4,169]

[*]Figures are based on diabetic clinical series, nonpopulation based; higher numbers listed are from series that included nerve conduction studies.
Data from Dyck et al[3]; Wilbourn[4]; Fry et al.[169]

Diabetic patients may develop other types of entrapment neuropathy. Ulnar neuropathies may develop across the cubital tunnel at the elbow. Its estimated prevalence, based on four studies that included 756 diabetic patients, was 2.1%.[4] Ulnar neuropathy may present with tingling, numbness, and paresthesiae in the small finger and ring finger, radiating into the medial hand not more proximal than the wrist. Ulnar neuropathy can cause considerable disability when motor fibers are involved, since weakness of intrinsic hand muscles (sparing the median innervated thenar muscles) may be severe. Unlike carpal tunnel syndrome, there are no randomized controlled trials of surgical decompression, even in nondiabetic patients, to guide whether surgical decompression is warranted.

In the lower limb, peroneal neuropathy from entrapment at the fibular head, resulting in foot drop and paresthiae over the dorsum of the foot, may occur in diabetes. "Meralgia parasethetica" is an entrapment of the lateral cutaneous nerve of the thigh, with sensory loss and paresthesiae in the lateral thigh.

In patients with early polyneuropathy, electrophysiologic abnormalities may be particularly pronounced at "sites of entrapment," despite the absence of typical clinical symptoms or signs. In more advanced polyneuropathy, there may be clinical symptoms and electrophysiologic abnormalities that are pronounced at sites of entrapment but in the context of severe abnormalities of other territories. In neither instance is there evidence that decompressive surgery would be of benefit.

EVIDENCE-BASED MESSAGE

Surgical decompression may be helpful in improving symptom severity and functional status of the hand from carpal tunnel syndrome for up to 30 months after the procedure but is of unproven benefit in other entrapment neuropathies (Level 2).[5]

Lumbosacral Plexopathy

Lumbosacral plexopathy (Bruns-Garland syndrome, femoral neuropathy of diabetes, proximal diabetic neuropathy, diabetic amyotrophy) can be a severe and debilitating complication of even early diabetes. The reported prevalence is approximately 1% of diabetic subjects, but this figure may be high because it was based on a referral population.[8] Some instances paradoxically arise soon after insulin therapy is initiated. Classically, severe, deep-aching, unilateral thigh discomfort is followed over a few weeks by weakness and wasting of proximal thigh muscles and loss of the quadriceps reflex but relatively spared sensation. There may be associated weight loss or diabetic cachexia. There are variations of the classic description, with more distal or bilateral involvement, more sensory loss, or less prominent pain. Importantly, many instances have spontaneous recovery over several months.[9] Multiple small destructive lesions (interpreted as nerve infarcts), associated with an occluded interfascicular artery in the femoral and obturator nerves, were identified in serially sectioned nerves in a patient with non-insulin-dependent diabetes mellitus (NIDDM) who developed lumbosacral plexopathy 10 weeks before autopsy.[10]

Recently, there has been interest in the concept that lumbosacral plexopathy may be autoimmune and thus treatable with immunosuppressive therapy. Indeed, inflammatory lesions have been reported in biopsies of the intermediate cutaneous nerve of the thigh in patients with lumbosacral plexopathy.[11,12] Such patients had ischemic nerve lesions with "vasculitis-like" inflammatory infiltrates and infiltrating epineurial lymphocytes. Despite these findings, all patients improved spontaneously without immunosuppressive therapy. Although recent reports that have suggested immunomodulatory therapy (such as intravenous gamma globulin [IVIG]) is of benefit to patients with this condition,[13,14] randomized controlled trials are lacking.

Other Focal Neuropathies

Oculomotor (third cranial nerve) palsy, sparing the pupil, is a self-limited focal neuropathy that may develop in diabetic patients suddenly but that usually resolves over 3 to 4 months.

The single pathologic study of this condition suggested that centrofascicular ischemia of the third cranial nerve, with local demyelination at the level of the cavernous sinus, accounted for it.[15] It is likely that a similar lesion accounts for acute abducens (sixth cranial nerve) palsies in diabetic patients. Intercostal neuropathies, often of more than one sensory root level, may result in thoracic or abdominal pain, sometimes mistaken for cardiac, thoracic, or abdominal disease. There is often segmental sensory loss and tingling. Spontaneous recovery occurs, but there are no pathologic studies addressing its etiology.

WHAT IS DIABETIC POLYNEUROPATHY?

When Does Diabetes Polyneuropathy Occur and What Is Its Incidence, Prevalence, and Associated Risk Factors?

Contrary to widespread belief, polyneuropathy is not a "late" complication of diabetes but may occur, for example, in children early in the disease.[16] Poor control of diabetes is associated with a steeper rise in the incidence of polyneuropathy with the duration of diabetes.[17] In the Diabetes Control and Complications Trial (DCCT) (Level 1), 9.8% of patients developed "clinical neuropathy" after 5 years of study if they did not have preexisting retinopathy and were treated with conventional, not intensive, insulin therapy. Clinical neuropathy was defined as an abnormal neurologic examination consistent with peripheral sensorimotor polyneuropathy plus either abnormal nerve conduction in at least two peripheral nerves or unequivocally abnormal autonomic nerve testing.[1] In a secondary prevention cohort of patients with preexisting retinopathy, a 16.1% incidence of "clinical neuropathy" was found over 5 years in the trial. As will be discussed below, however, this definition may underestimate early diabetic polyneuropathy using stricter criteria (not requiring an unequivocally abnormal neurologic examination). In the San Luis Valley Diabetes Study, distal symmetric sensory polyneuropathy developed at the rate of 6.1 cases per 100 person-years in patients with NIDDM. Higher glycohemoglobin levels and lower C-peptide secretion were associated with a higher incidence of polyneuropathy but were not independent of the effect of diabetes duration. Insulin treatment, current smoking, and a history of myocardial infarction increased the risk of developing polyneuropathy. Height, weight, family history, peripheral vascular disease, hypertension, albuminuria, retinopathy, and ethanol use, however, did not.[18] Subclinical evidence (eg, prospective testing of nerve conduction or sensory thresholds) raises the proportion of patients with polyneuropathy to a majority.[19] The Rochester Diabetic Study (Level 1)[3] may provide the most useful prevalence data because it consists of a community-based study of 380 diabetic subjects who have volunteered to be followed longitudinally out of a total diabetic population of 870.[20] Results of both clinical assessments and laboratory evaluation were used to identify polyneuropathy (see below). In patients with insulin-dependent diabetes mellitus (IDDM) (n = 102), 66% had some form of neuropathy, whereas 54% had polyneuropathy. In patients with NIDDM (n = 278), 59% had some form of neuropathy and 45% had polyneuropathy. Overall, however, only a proportion of these patients had symptoms attributable to polyneuropathy—15% of IDDM and 13% of NIDDM patients. Polyneuropathy with particular involvement of the autonomic nervous system was diagnosed in 7% of patients with IDDM and 5% of patients with NIDDM. More severe symptomatic polyneuropathy (classed by the study as 2b), indicated by weakness of ankle dorsiflexion, was 6% in IDDM patients and 1% in NIDDM patients.

The prevalence of polyneuropathy in people with IDDM in the Pittsburgh Epidemiology of Diabetes Complications Study, defined using only clinical criteria, was 34% and correlated with diabetic control, retinopathy, nephropathy, diabetes duration, and smoking.[21] The prevalence of clinical neuropathy in NIDDM patients in the San Luis Valley Diabetes Study was 25.8% and correlated with age, duration of diabetes, male sex, and glycemic control.[22] Patients of Hispanic background did not have a different prevalence than Caucasians. Prevalence statistics are summarized in Table 23–3.

Table 23–3 Prevalence of Diabetic Polyneuropathy

Rochester Diabetic Study (n = 380)	Prevalence (%)
All patients with polyneuropathy	
Insulin-dependent diabetes	54
Non–insulin-dependent diabetes	45
Patients with symptomatic polyneuropathy only	
Insulin-dependent diabetes	15
Non–insulin-dependent diabetes	13
Neuropathy impairment scale + 7 abnormal tests (all diabetics)	20.5
Pittsburg Epidemiology of Diabetes Complications Study (n = 400)	
Insulin-dependent diabetes	34
San Luis Valley Diabetes Study (n = 279)	
Non–insulin-dependent diabetes	25.8

Data from Dyck et al[3,20]; Maser et al[21]; Franklin et al.[22]

EVIDENCE-BASED MESSAGES

1. In patients with Type 1 diabetes but without retinopathy, polyneuropathy develops in up to 10% of individuals within 5 years (Level 1).[1]
2. In patients with Type 1 diabetes who already have retinopathy, polyneuropathy develops in up to 16% of individuals within 5 years (Level 1).[1]
3. In patients with Type 2 diabetes, polyneuropathy may develop in 6.1% of individuals per year (Level 3).[18]
4. Risk factors for the development of polyneuropathy may include higher glycohemoglobin levels, lower C-peptide levels, insulin treatment, smoking, and a history of myocardial infarction (Level 3).[18]
5. Hyperglycemia is a risk factor for polyneuropathy in Type 1 diabetes (Level 1).[1]

What Are the Features of Polyneuropathy?

Polyneuropathy can be a disabling disorder, with associated sensory loss, neuropathic pain, autonomic insufficiency, and later motor weakness.[23,24] Some authors have subclassified types of polyneuropathy. These may include predominantly large-fiber involvement with ataxia, small-fiber involvement with prominent pain, autonomic neuropathy, polyneuropathy with prominent demyelination, acute axonal polyneuropathy with cachexia and poor control, acute axonal polyneuropathy following insulin therapy, and improved diabetes control.[25] Many of the subvarieties eventually have mixed involvement, although sensory involvement usually precedes and is much more severe than motor axon loss and weakness. Polyneuropathy is an important contributing factor in the development of lower limb ulceration.[26]

One of the most informative clinical descriptions of diabetic polyneuropathy was that of Rundles,[24] who provided detailed descriptions of 125 cases of diabetic neuropathy. Several important points in this older article remain worth emphasizing. These include the acute worsening in sensory symptoms that may accompany deteriorations in diabetes control due to infections, for example. Polyneuropathy appeared in younger patients, with the interval between diabetes diagnosis and the onset of symptomatic polyneuropathy as short as 2 to 6 months. Important symptoms were numbness, tingling, paresthesiae, cold feelings, aching and burning pains, shooting pains, and muscle aching. In Rundles' words, "The touch of bed-

Table 23–4 Clinical Features of Diabetic Polyneuropathy

Symptoms

Distal sensory loss (numbness): toes, feet, fingers

Distal paresthesiae (tingling, prickling, "pins and needles"): toes, feet, fingers

Pain (burning, aching, "charley horse," shooting pains, electrical-like sharp, worse at night): fingers, toes, arms, and legs

Weakness (clumsiness, loss of balance, dragging of the toes, falls): hands, legs

Loss of distal sweating, postprandial bloating, postural lightheadedness, constipation, diarrhea, hypoglycemic unawareness, impotence

Signs

Stocking and (or) glove sensory loss

Loss of ankle and other deep tendon reflexes

Distal weakness (later)

Foot ulcers

---

clothes was often unbearable, sleep and rest impossible." Findings on neurologic examination included diminished or absent stretch reflexes, particularly the ankle reflex (absent in 81% of patients), hypesthesia, anesthesia, and diminished vibratory sensibility. In a significant proportion of patients with diabetic polyneuropathy (37%), muscle tenderness was noted. Clinical features of diabetic polyneuropathy are listed in Table 23–4.

Autonomic dysfunction is an important feature of diabetic polyneuropathy and may be associated with an increased risk of mortality.[27–29] Symptoms include constipation, diarrhea, sweating abnormalities (distal loss of sweating or anhidrosis,[30] gustatory sweating, or inappropriate facial and upper-body sweating after eating[31]) hypoglycemic unawareness, postural dizziness, and impotence (see Table 23–4).

Why Does Diabetic Polyneuropathy Occur? Pathology and Pathogenesis

Pathologic abnormalities of human diabetic peripheral nerves have been detailed by a number of authors. In the sural sensory nerve, these changes include loss of myelinated and unmyelinated fibers, axonal degeneration, regenerative clusters, and segmental demyelination with remyelination.[32–39] In one study, loss of vibration sensation correlated with the loss of myelinated fibers on sural nerve biopsy.[40] Despite descriptions that "small fiber" neuropathy has a greater association with pain, sural nerve biopsies have not identified predominant small-diameter axon loss in patients with painful diabetic polyneuropathy.[41] Structural changes in microvessels of established human diabetic polyneuropathy have been well demonstrated in other studies of human diabetic patients and correlate with the clinical severity of polyneuropathy.[32,39,42–49] The changes include microvessel basement-membrane thickening, microvessel thrombosis or closure, endothelial cell reduplication, and smooth-muscle hypertrophy. The observation of a pattern of uneven, or multifocal, loss of myelinated fibers in transverse sections of diabetic nerves has been attributed to nerve ischemia by some, but not all, authors.[34,50] There have been relatively few studies of sensory dorsal root ganglia where the cell bodies of sensory axons reside. Targeted neuron loss in these ganglia in diabetes could account for selective sensory abnormalities in humans.[51] Dystrophic swollen-appearing axons within the dorsal root sensory ganglia have been described in patients with diabetes.[52]

The initial abnormalities that trigger the development of diabetic polyneuropathy are disputed. There is a metabolic hypothesis emphasizing that peripheral nerves (especially Schwann cells within them) accumulate excessive polyols, particularly sorbitol, by accelerated flux through the aldose-reductase pathway. There are associated depletions of nerve

Table 23–5 Diagnosis of Diabetic Polyneuropathy

History	Paresthesia, loss of sensation, pain (aching, lancinating, dysesthetic, electrical) starting in toes, feet
Clinical neurologic examination	Distal toe and foot (fingers) loss of sensation (stocking and glove later) to light touch (brush, cotton wool), pinprick, temperature, vibration, or Semmes-Weinstein monofilaments
	Loss of ankle reflexes (other reflexes later)
	Distal motor wasting and weakness (eg, loss of extensor digitorum brevis muscle bulk and toe dorsiflexion weakness)
	Neuropathy impairment score
Laboratory investigations	Nerve conduction studies, particularly sural sensory conduction and peroneal motor conduction
	Quantitative sensory testing: cold sensory threshold, heat as pain threshold, vibration threshold
	Autonomic function tests: cardiovascular testing (blood pressure, R-R EKG intervals), sudomotor (sweating) tests (QSART, sweat droplet implants, thermoregulatory sweat test), gastric motility studies, bladder urodynamics, sexual function in men, pupillary testing
	Nerve biopsy (generally not recommended)
	Skin biopsy or blister technique with epidermal fiber counting
Combinations	NIS + 7 (see text)

QSART = quantitative sudomotoraxon reflex test; NIS + 7 = neuropathy impairment scale plus 7 other abnormal tests.

myo-inositol, changes in protein kinase C subunits, and dysfunction of nerve Na^+/K^+ adenosinetriphosphatase (ATPase).[53–58] Increased axonal Na^+ content and later Na^+ channel migration out of nodes of Ranvier may account for early slowing of nerve conduction velocity in diabetes. The glycosylation hypothesis argues that nonspecific post-translational glycosylation of important structural nerve proteins accounts for polyneuropathy.[59–61]

The nerve microangiopathy hypothesis emphasizes the role of early nerve-trunk ischemia. While some groups have postulated that early reductions in nerve blood flow account for diabetic neuropathy,[62,63] others, including the current author, have not identified early ischemia in animal[64–72] or human diabetic polyneuropathy.[73] There is evidence for hypoxia in peripheral nerves (and ganglia) in models[63,69,70] of early diabetes and in human disease.[74] Hypoxia in nerve and ganglia may arise because of erythrocyte nondeformability and selective alterations in small-capillary erythrocyte (only) transit, hyperviscosity of blood, and defects in oxygen release locally (eg, reductions in 2,3-diphosphoglycerate [2,3-DPG]).[75]

Finally, the concept of deficient or "precarious" neurotrophic support in diabetic polyneuropathy is of uncertain relationship to the above mechanisms.[76–78] There may be inadequate target elaboration of the neurotrophins, reduced synthesis by Schwann cells, or less autocrine (self-support) and paracrine (neighbor support) activity within the ganglia themselves.[79–81] Further details regarding the pathophysiology of neuopathy have been reviewed elsewhere and are summarized in Table 23–6.[51,78,82]

How Is Diabetic Polyneuropathy Diagnosed?

Symptoms and Findings on Neurologic Examination

The history and clinical neurologic examination remain critical tools in the evaluation of diabetic polyneuropathy. Negative (numbness, loss of feeling) and positive sensory symptoms

Table 23–6 Proposed Mechanisms of Diabetic Polyneuropathy

Hypothesis	Comment
Excessive polyol flux in peripheral nerve: depleted nerve *myo*-inositol, elevated sorbitol, dysfunction of Na+/K+ ATPase	May explain conduction velocity slowing in diabetes; this pathway is approached using the aldose reductase inhibitors proposed for therapy
Nerve microangiopathy hypothesis: reductions in nerve blood flow and oxygen tension	Consistent with microvascular changes observed in nerve biopsies and multifocal loss of axons, but it is uncertain whether reductions in nerve blood flow trigger early changes of neuropathy; reductions were not observed in early human diabetic polyneuropathy, and results in experimental models are controversial
Nonspecific glycosylation of structural nerve proteins	May explain how diabetes targets different aspects of the peripheral nerve, such as microvessels, basement membranes, axons
Deficiency of specific trophic factors for nerve: impaired target tissue synthesis or nerve uptake or transport of nerve growth factor, other neurotrophins, insulin-like growth factors, insulin, and others	The experimental evidence for this has not been established. The recombinant nerve growth factor Phase III trial was negative.
Early targeting of sensory and autonomic neurons in ganglia: early loss or dysfunction of sensory or autonomic ganglia neurons, with inability to support their most distal terminals	Could explain early sensory and autonomic dysfunction in diabetic patients before motor axons are involved. Ganglia may be more vulnerable.
Others: excessive oxidative stress, nitric oxide toxicity, autoimmune attack (IDDM)	

ATPase = adenosine triphosphatase; IDDM = insulin-dependent diabetes mellitus.

(pain, paresthesia, tingling, prickling, "electric shocks") are important to elicit. Distal upper- and lower-limb motor symptoms (weakness, wasting) usually occur much later. Examination may disclose sensory loss or hypersensitivity in a stocking and glove distribution. In early polyneuropathy, sensory loss may be confined to the distal toes or may be absent. Sensory testing should include evaluation of light touch, pinprick perception, thermal sensitivity, and vibration perception (at 128 or 256 Hz). Both the extent (geographic territory) and severity (presence of anesthesia or analgesia, ie, complete loss of light touch and pinprick perception) should be sought. Use of a calibrated Von Frey hair (Semmes-Weinstein monofilament [SWM]) to detect light touch/pressure sensitivity on the soles of the feet is a useful adjunct but should not replace the standard examination. The chief value of the monofilament test (also discussed below) has been that of a rapid screening tool, with evidence (Level 3)[83–85] that it predicts which patients might develop foot ulceration, a consequence of more advanced polyneuropathy. Alone, however, the monofilament test lacks the rigor and sensitivity of other types of evaluation, such as NIS + 7 (see below). Loss of the ankle reflexes is an important early sign of polyneuropathy. Dyck and colleagues have combined features of the history and neurologic examination as the "neuropathy symptoms and change questionnaire" (NSC) and the "neuropathy impairment scale of the lower limbs" (NIS-LL).[86]

EVIDENCE-BASED MESSAGE

Clinical neurologic examination (CNE) and SWM are reasonably rapid screening tests for diabetic polyneuropathy (sensitivity for SWM 88 to 96%, specificity 61 to 46%; sen-

Table 23–7 Therapy for Painful Polyneuropathy

Level 1 evidence	Gabapentin 900–3,600 mg/d; 25% improvement compared to placebo[159]
	Tricyclic antidepressants: amitriptyline 105 mg/d 74% relief; desipramine 111 mg/d 61% relief; placebo 41% relief[151]
	Mexiletene: 675 mg/d; 35% improvement; 25% improvement in placebo[160]
	Other anticonvulsants: phenytoin 300 mg/d; carbamazepine 200–600 mg/d; 30–50% improvement in each over placebo[152]
Level 2 evidence	Capsaicin cream (only one of two studies showed benefit) 0.075% (n = 277 diabetics) 25 to 50% improvement compared to placebo[148,149]; 0.075% (n = 7 diabetics) no benefit[150]
Level 4 evidence	Opioid analgesics (morphine)
	Topical lidocaine or other local anesthetics
Not recommended	Selective serotonin reuptake inhibitors
	Surgical sympathectomy

Data from Backonja et al[159]; Oskarsson et al[160]; McQuay et al[152]; Donofrio et al (1991)[148]; Donofrio et al[149]; Low et al.[150]

sitivity for CNE 83 to 91%, specificity 61 to 63% compared to a "gold standard" of vibration perception. Both CNE and SWM miss milder polyneuropathy detected by more detailed alogorithms (Level 2).[84]

Laboratory Investigations

Laboratory testing for polyneuropathy may include nerve conduction studies (NCS), autonomic testing, quantitative computerized sensory threshold testing (QST), and cutaneous skin biopsy. There are four main reasons for considering these tests: (1) to shore up an uncertain diagnosis or detect entrapment neuropathy (NCS are probably the most useful here); (2) to measure the impact of therapy (if available); (3) to diagnose early polyneuropathy and follow it objectively in clinical trials of therapy for it; and (4) to predict which patients have a higher risk for the development of foot ulcers.[87] There is no established "gold standard" for the diagnosis of polyneuropathy because investigations have varied in which test batteries they have applied. Moreover, there are important relationships among different modes of testing for diabetic polyneuropathy. Examples are the relationships among ankle areflexia, nerve conduction abnormalities, elevated sensory thresholds, and changes on nerve biopsies.[88–93] In the Rochester Diabetic Study referred to above, the most sensitive indices for early polyneuropathy were changes in clinical symptoms and signs (NIS), NCS, and Valsalva autonomic testing, whereas QST was somewhat less sensitive.[94] Previous work by the same group established good reproducibility for NIS, NCS, and QST to vibration and cooling.[95] Finally, these investigators have suggested more recently that NIS + 7 (ie, the neuropathy impairment scale plus 7 other abnormal tests among NCS, QST, and autonomic tests[20]) should be the gold standard for diagnosing minimal criteria for diabetic neuropathy. This could be particularly important for new trials. Using these strict criteria, the overall prevalence of polyneuropathy in the Rochester Diabetic Study was 20.5% of all diabetic participants and 2.6% of age-matched nondiabetic healthy controls. Over 2 years, 15% of diabetic participants had a worsening in the NIS + 7. This approach, at the present time, provides the only gold standard for the diagnosis of polyneuropathy that amalgamates all currently available tests.

Nerve Conduction Studies

Nerve conduction studies, previously considered a gold standard diagnostic tool, may disclose abnormalities that include mild to moderate (10 to 20%) slowing of motor and sensory conduction velocity, mildly prolonged distal latencies (in the absence of entrapment, for example, at the carpal tunnel), prolonged F-wave latencies, absent tibial H-reflexes, and diminished amplitudes of compound sensory nerve action potentials (SNAPs).[4,96,97] With advanced disease, compound muscle action potentials, particularly in the feet, may disappear, and there may be distal denervation (fibrillations, positive sharp waves, and enlarged remodeled motor unit potentials from denervation with subsequent reinnervation) detected by needle electromyography. From clinical trials, sural-sensory conduction velocity and SNAP amplitude are probably the most sensitive indices of neuropathy in early disease.[98]

EVIDENCE-BASED MESSAGE

Nerve conduction studies are highly sensitive measures of abnormality in diabetes, with a sensitivity of 93% and specificity of 58%, compared to the NIS + 7 gold standard (Level 1).[20]

Sensory Threshold Tests

Quantitative sensory threshold testing (Level 1)[96] has been carried out using a variety of hardware and approaches. The CASE IV setup (WDR Medical, Minneapolis, MN) has been carefully standardized to large groups of age-matched control subjects. Sensory modalities tested include the cooling detection threshold, the warming detection threshold, heat-pain threshold, and vibratory threshold determination.[99] Using a different system, the following levels of sensitivity of QST in 81 diabetic subjects at a 90% specificity level have been described: warm (78%), cold (77%), vibration (88%), tactile pressure (using a Semmes-Weinstein series of monofilaments) (77%), and current perception threshold (250 Hz to 2000 Hz) (48 to 56%). The combination of thermal and vibratory perceptions gave optimum sensitivity (92 to 95%) and specificity (77 to 86%).[83]

EVIDENCE-BASED MESSAGE

Available quantitative sensory tests include cooling detection threshold, warming detection threshold, heat-as-pain threshold, and vibration-sensitivity threshold. Vibration testing has been the most carefully studied but is not as sensitive as other tests listed above (Level 1[20]; sensitivity of abnormal vibration on the toe was 17%, with a specificity of 96%, compared to NIS + 7 as the gold standard).

Autonomic Tests

There have been a variety of types of autonomic testing described (Level 1).[100] The Ewing battery of tests includes the heart rate (R-R interval) change with Valsalva, deep breathing, and standing blood pressure and the blood pressure change with standing or sustained handgrip.[101,102] In 543 patients with diabetes studied using the Ewing battery, 61% had at least one abnormal test and 43% had two abnormal tests.[101] Autonomic testing may be abnormal in diabetic patients within 2 years of onset, without specific symptoms.[103,104] Loss of the resting R-R interval variability may be an important early finding.[104] Orthostatic hypotension occurs somewhat later in 10 to 13% of diabetics.[105,106] Specific tests of abnormal sweating may include the Silastic imprint test, identifying reduced sweat-droplet size and density in diabetics, and the quantitative sudomotor axon reflex test (QSART), measuring quantitative sweat output and identifying reduced, absent, or abnormal "hung-up" responses.[107–109] Such abnormalities correlate, along with abnormal R-R intervals, to deep breathing or the Valsalva maneuver: up to 67% of 73 patients with diabetic neuropathy in one study had R-R interval abnormalities and 58% had abnormal foot QSART testing.[110] In the gastrointestinal (GI) tract, there may be dyspepsia, bloating, nausea, and vomiting from gastric stasis. Moreover, asymptomatic patients may have significant gastric stasis (gastroparesis) radiologically (22% in one series).[111] In the lower gut, diarrhea, often nocturnal, and constipation are problems, and fecal incontinence may occur.[24,112,113] Diabetic bladder involvement results from afferent sensory neuropathy, with a delay in the detrusor reflex and later areflexia.[114,115] Impotence is common in diabetic men, with a prevalence of 35% in one series.[116] Diabetes is associated with a reduction in the diameter of the pupil in the dark.[117,118]

EVIDENCE-BASED MESSAGE

Several autonomic tests are available in diabetic patients; R-R interval changes have been studied most carefully and have a sensitivity for the detection of polyneuropathy that is comparable to nerve conduction results (Level 1).[94]

Neuropathologic Abnormalities

Previous work has correlated the severity of neuropathologic abnormalities in the sural sensory nerve of diabetic patients with other clinical and laboratory tests of neuropathy.[32] Sural nerve biopsy, however, should generally not serve as a diagnostic tool (or a standard research tool) for diabetic polyneuropathy because of its invasiveness, its association with persistent discomfort and sensory loss, and the risk that it may not heal.[119]

There is a new and far less invasive technique offering significant diagnostic and staging possibilities through the quantitative assessment of epidermal nerve fibers using a 3-mm punch-skin biopsy or skin blister.[120,121] Kennedy and colleagues[120] studied 18 IDDM patients with polyneuropathy and 18 sex- and age-matched control subjects using skin biopsy and noted that diabetic subjects had considerably fewer epidermal fibers.

HOW IS DIABETIC POLYNEUROPATHY MANAGED?

Glycemia control reduces the incidence of new symptoms of diabetic neuropathy and retards the progression of neuropathy (Level 1).[1,122,123] This is the case for both Type 1[1,124] and Type 2 diabetes.[125] In the DCCT trial[1,122] of patients with Type 1 diabetes, the group without preexisting retinopathy had a reduction in the appearance of "clinical neuropathy" (see above) from 9.8 to 3.1% at 5 years with intensive therapy. The corresponding reduction in patients with preexisting retinopathy was from 16.1% down to 7.0%. In another study, successful pancreatic transplantation that achieved euglycemia halted the progression of diabetic neuropathy and slightly improved it, as assessed by clinical examination and neurophysiologic testing (nerve conduction and autonomic function testing) over 12 to 42 months of follow-up (Level 3).[126]

EVIDENCE-BASED MESSAGE

Strict control of hyperglycemia reduces the incidence of diabetic polyneuropathy (Level 1).[1,122-125]

What Glycemia Therapies Exist for Diabetic Polyneuropathy?

No pharmacologic approach directed at the underlying cause of diabetic polyneuropathy has been linked with definitive improvement in more than a single trial to date. There have been a relatively large number of trials using aldose-reductase inhibitors in diabetic neuropathy that have had mixed results, including tests of alrestat, sorbinil, tolrestat, ponalrestat, and others.[127-132] These agents reverse the accumulation of sorbitol in peripheral nerves and experimentally correct deficits of nerve conduction in diabetes (see above). Sorbinil was associated with unacceptable side effects. There have also been a number of reviews on the use of aldose-reductase inhibitors published.[128,133-142] More recent work has suggested some improvement with tolrestat,[129,143] but improvement has been mixed, and published trials had smaller numbers of patients. Results of larger Phase III trials with other aldose-reductase inhibitors have not been published. In a recent meta-analysis[131] of aldose-reductase inhibitor trials in human diabetic polyneuropathy published between 1981 and 1993, 13 randomized trials with placebo had mixed results. Overall, the authors concluded that there appeared to be benefits on motor-nerve conduction velocity, but there were no clear conclusions about any other forms of efficacy. Newer aldose-reductase inhibitors showing promise in early trials include epalrestat[130] and zenarestat (Phase III recently discontinued however).[144]

Recombinant human nerve growth factor (rhNGF) has been studied in a Phase II randomized controlled double-blinded trial,[145,146] in which it was given subcutaneously 3 times weekly for 6 months. There was an improvement in the cooling detection threshold (a quantitative sensory test), a borderline improvement in the perception of heat as pain, and trends toward an improved neurologic examination. Globally, patients felt better on the agent but blinding was incomplete because of discomfort upon injection of the active agent subcutaneously. Unfortunately, a subsequent Phase III randomized controlled multicenter double-blinded trial did not show any benefit from rhNGF (personal communication with Roche).

In a small randomized double-blinded placebo-controlled trial (22 patients) of gamma linolenic acid over 6 months, improvement in NCS and QST abnormalities of diabetic neuropathy was suggested (Level 2).[147]

Daily inspection of the feet in patients with polyneuropathy may detect lesions at risk for ulceration. Tight footwear and high-impact exercise should be avoided to prevent ulceration and Charcot joints.

Capsaicin cream is a simple, noninvasive approach to pain therapy in patients with prominent allodynia (pain evoked by an innocuous mechanical stimulus). While it was effective in one trial (Level 2),[148,149] a second smaller study of patients with neuropathic pain from a variety of causes showed no consistent benefit.[150] Other topical agents that may be tried are lidocaine 5% or a combination of lidocaine and prilocaine, either as a cream or occlusive dressing (EMLA Cream). Topical pastes of nonsteroidal anti-inflammatory agents have also been applied. Tricyclic antidepressants are helpful for chronic pain from diabetic polyneuropathy or lumbosacral plexopathy (Level 1).[151] Amitriptyline given in low doses in the evening may help patients who are unable to sleep because of pain. Nortriptyline and desipramine are alternatives with fewer sedative side effects but with a similar side-effect profile otherwise. Dosages may be titrated somewhat higher than with amitriptyline. Fluoxetine and other selective serotonin reuptake inhibitors (SSRIs) have not improved pain. Anticonvulsant agents may help neuropathic pain, particularly when it has a lancinating or electrical quality.[152] Phenytoin and carbamazepine are standard approaches (Level 1),[152–154] used in the same dosages as applied in epilepsy. Carbamazepine may be used in some patients in lower doses or on an as-needed basis. Other anticonvulsants may also be tried. Gabapentin is a newer anticonvulsant that may have some advantages over the above because of its favorable side-effect profile and near absence of interaction with other drugs (Level 1).[155–159] Mexiletine (Level 1)[160,161] administered up to a dosage of 675 mg daily was associated with a significant reduction of sleep disturbance and night pain in patients with painful diabetic neuropathy. Cardiac disease is a contraindication. Opioids, applied in standard dosages, should not be withheld from patients with severe neuropathic pain unresponsive to other approaches (Level 4); a concomitant bowel regimen to avoid constipation is recommended. Transcutaneous electrotherapy has been suggested for pain therapy, but the single randomized trial using it may have been difficult to blind (Level 2).[162]

Alpha-lipoic acid given as a 3-week intravenous infusion (600 mg/d) improved symptoms of pain, burning, paresthesia, and numbness in a multicenter randomized double-blinded placebo-controlled trial in 328 patients with symptomatic diabetic neuropathy (Level 1).[163,164]

For the treatment of orthostatic hypotension, sleeping with the head of the bed elevated, increasing the salt content of the diet, Jobst (pressure) stockings, and fludrocortisone are standard approaches. Erythropoietin may benefit orthostatic hypotension but has not been specifically tested in a series of diabetic patients (Level 2).[165] Midodrine, an alpha-agonist, improves blood pressure and orthostatic symptoms in patients with neurogenic orthostatic hypotension (Level 1)[166] but has not been separately tested in diabetes. Diabetic autonomic neuropathy resulting in gastric retention may be treated with cisapride (Level 2; but recently withdrawn from North America because of EKG side effects)[167] and has recently been reviewed.[168]

Patients with a Charcot joint at the ankle may benefit from input from an orthopedic surgeon for a possible stabilization procedure. Patients with early symptomatic carpal tunnel syndrome may benefit from the use of a wrist splint. Patients with a foot drop should be fitted for an ankle-foot orthosis to improve mobility and reduce the chance of falling. Patients with severe quadriceps weakness may benefit from a knee stabilization orthosis. If in doubt, consultation with a physiatrist is indicated. Physiotherapy may assist in the recovery of patients from focal neuropathies, particularly lumbosacral plexopathy. Physiotherapy consultation may help the patient with fixed or slowly progressive deficits develop a set of exercise activities to improve well-being and cardiovascular fitness. Consultation with an occupational therapist, and preferably a home visit, in patients with significant disabilities may allow the patient to make adjustments in their environment that allow them to cope more easily and avoid falls. Low-impact exercises are preferred in patients with loss of lower-limb sensation. Swimming or pool exercises or the use of a stationary bicycle may be a helpful choice in some patients.

EVIDENCE-BASED MESSAGES

1. No definitive pharmacologic therapy for reversing or stabilizing diabetic polyneuropathy has yet been clearly identified.
2. Painful diabetic polyneuropathy may be treated with amitriptyline, desipramine, phenytoin, carbamazepine, gabapentin, mexiletine, alpha-lipoic acid (Level 1),[151–161,163,164] or capsaicin cream (Level 2).[148,149]
3. Other therapies may benefit orthostatic hypotension and gastroparesis.

CONCLUSION

Diabetic neuropathies comprise several complications involving the peripheral nerve, including focal disorders such as entrapment neuropathy or lumbosacral plexopathy and generalized involvement or polyneuropathy. The cause(s) of diabetic polyneuropathy remain controversial, but its appearance and development closely depend on the degree of diabetic or hyperglycemic control. Polyneuropathy may be detected by clinical neurologic examination, but more sensitive approaches such as nerve conduction measurements, quantitative sensory testing, and autonomic nervous system testing can also be applied. Although no pharmacotherapy has yet been definitely linked with stabilization or improvement of polyneuropathy, evidence-based therapies for pain, postural hypotension, and gastroparesis are available.

SUMMARY OF EVIDENCE-BASED MESSAGES

1. Surgical decompression may be helpful in improving symptom severity and functional status of the hand from carpal tunnel syndrome for up to 30 months after the procedure but is of unproven benefit in other entrapment neuropathies (Level 2).[5]
2. In patients with Type 1 diabetes but without retinopathy, polyneuropathy develops in up to 10% of individuals within 5 years (Level 1).[1]
3. In patients with Type 1 diabetes who already have retinopathy, polyneuropathy develops in up to 16% of individuals within 5 years (Level 1).[1]
4. In patients with Type 2 diabetes, polyneuropathy may develop in 6.1% of individuals per year (Level 3).[18]
5. Risk factors for the development of polyneuropathy may include higher glycohemoglobin levels, lower C-peptide levels, insulin treatment, smoking, and a history of myocardial infarction (Level 3).[18]
6. Hyperglycemia is a risk factor for polyneuropathy in Type 1 diabetes (Level 1).[1]

7. Clinical neurologic examination (CNE) and SWM are reasonably rapid screening tests for diabetic polyneuropathy (sensitivity for SWM 88 to 96%, specificity 61 to 46%; sensitivity for CNE 83 to 91%, specificity 61 to 63% compared to a "gold standard" of vibration perception. Both CNE and SWM miss milder polyneuropathy detected by more detailed alogorithms (Level 2).[84]

8. Nerve conduction studies are highly sensitive measures of abnormality in diabetes, with a sensitivity of 93% and specificity of 58%, compared to the NIS + 7 gold standard (Level 1).[20]

9. Available quantitative sensory tests include cooling detection threshold, warming detection threshold, heat-as-pain threshold, and vibration-sensitivity threshold. Vibration testing has been the most carefully studied but is not as sensitive as other tests listed above (Level 1[20]; sensitivity of abnormal vibration on the toe was 17%, with a specificity of 96%, compared to NIS + 7 as the gold standard).

10. Several autonomic tests are available in diabetic patients; R-R interval changes have been studied most carefully and have a sensitivity for the detection of polyneuropathy that is comparable to nerve conduction results (Level 1).[94]

11. Strict control of hyperglycemia reduces the incidence of diabetic polyneuropathy (Level 1).[1,122–125]

12. No definitive pharmacologic therapy for reversing or stabilizing diabetic polyneuropathy has yet been clearly identified.

13. Painful diabetic polyneuropathy may be treated with amitriptyline, desipramine, phenytoin, carbamazepine, gabapentin, mexiletine, alpha-lipoic acid (Level 1),[151–161,163,164] or capsaicin cream (Level 2).[148,149]

14. Other therapies may benefit orthostatic hypotension and gastroparesis.

ACKNOWLEDGMENTS

Brenda Boake provided expert secretarial assistance. The author is a Medical Scholar of the Alberta Heritage Foundation for Medical Research. This work was supported by an operating grant from the Medical Research Council of Canada.

REFERENCES

1. Diabetes Control & Complications Trial Research Group. The effect of intensive treatment of diabetes on the development and progression of long-term complications in insulin-dependent diabetes mellitus. N Engl J Med 1993;329:977–86.

2. Pirart J. Diabetes mellitus and its degenerative complications: a prospective study of 4,400 patients observed between 1947 and 1973. Diabetes Metab 1977;3:97–107.

3. Dyck PJ, Kratz KM, Karnes JL, et al. The prevalence by staged severity of various types of diabetic neuropathy, retinopathy, and nephropathy in a population-based cohort: The Rochester Diabetic Neuropathy Study. Neurology 1993;43:817–24.

4. Wilbourn AJ. Diabetic entrapment and compression neuropathies. In: Dyck PJ, Thomas PK, editors. Diabetic neuropathy. 2nd ed. Toronto: WB Saunders; 1999. p. 481–508.

5. Katz JN, Keller RB, Simmons BP, et al. Maine Carpal Tunnel Study: outcomes of operative and nonoperative therapy for carpal tunnel syndrome in a community-based cohort. J Hand Surg [Am] 1998;23:697–710.

6. Bradley JL, Thomas PK, King RHM, et al. Myelinated nerve fibre regeneration in diabetic sensory polyneuropathy: correlation with type of diabetes. Acta Neuropathol 1995;90:403–10.

7. Ekstrom AR, Tomlinson DR. Impaired nerve regeneration in streptozotocin-diabetic rats: effects of treatment with an aldose reductase inhibitor. J Neurol Sci 1989;93:231–7.

8. Mulder DW, Lambert EH, Basdtron JA, et al. The neuropathies associated with diabetes mellitus. Neurology 1961;11:275–84.

9. Barohn RJ, Sahenk Z, Warmolts JR, et al. The Bruns-Garland Syndrome (diabetic amyotrophy) revisited 100 years later. Arch Neurol 1991;48:1130–5.

10. Raff MC, Sangalang V, Asbury AK. Ischemic mononeuropathy multiplex associated with diabetes mellitus. Arch Neurol 1968;18:487–99.

11. Said G, Elgrably F, Lacroix C, et al. Painful proximal diabetic neuropathy: inflammatory nerve lesions and spontaneous favorable outcome. Ann Neurol 1997;41:762–70.

12. Said G, Goulon-Goeau C, Lacroix C, et al. Nerve biopsy findings in different patterns of proximal diabetic neuropathy. Ann Neurol 1994;35:559–69.

13. Krendel DA, Costigan DA, Hopkins LC. Successful treatment of neuropathies in patients with diabetes mellitus. Arch Neurol 1995;52:1053–61.

14. Pascoe MK, Low PA, Windebank AJ, et al. Subacute diabetic proximal neuropathy. Mayo Clin Proc 1997;72:1123–32.

15. Asbury AK, Aldredge H, Hershberg R, et al. Oculomotor palsy in diabetes mellitus: a clinicopathological study. Brain 1970;93:555–66.

16. Solders G, Thalme B, Aguirre-Aquino M, et al. Nerve conduction and autonomic nerve function in diabetic children. A 10-year follow-up study. Acta Paediatr 1997;86:361–6.

17. Pirart J. Diabetes mellitus and its degenerative complications. Diabetes Care 1978;1:168.

18. Sands ML, Shetterly SM, Franklin GM, et al. Incidence of distal symmetric (sensory) neuropathy in NIDDM. The San Luis Valley Diabetes Study. Diabetes Care 1997;20:322–9.

19. Vinik AI, Holland MT, Le Beau JM, et al. Diabetic neuropathies. Diabetes Care 1992;15:1926–75.

20. Dyck JB, Dyck PJ. Diabetic polyneuropathy. In: Dyck PJ, Thomas PK, editors. Diabetic neuropathy. Toronto: WB Saunders; 1998. p. 255–78.

21. Maser RE, Steenkiste AR, Dorman JS, et al. Epidemiological correlates of diabetic neuropathy. Report from Pittsburgh Epidemiology of Diabetes Complications Study. Diabetes 1989;38:1456–61.

22. Franklin GM, Kahn LB, Baxter J, et al. Sensory neuropathy in non-insulin-dependent diabetes mellitus. The San Luis Valley Diabetes Study. Am J Epidemiol 1990;131:633–43.

23. Brown MJ, Asbury AK. Diabetic neuropathy. Ann Neurol 1984;15:2–12.

24. Rundles RW. Diabetic neuropathy—general review with report of 125 cases. Medicine 1945;24:111–60.

25. Bird SJ, Brown MJ. The clinical spectrum of diabetic neuropathy. Semin Neurol 1996;16:115–22.

26. McNeely MJ, Boyko EJ, Ahroni JH, et al. The independent contributions of diabetic neuropathy and vasculopathy in foot ulceration. How great are the risks? Diabetes Care 1995;18:216–9.

27. Ewing DJ, Boland O, Neilson JM, et al. Autonomic neuropathy, QT interval lengthening, and unexpected deaths in male diabetic patients. Diabetologia 1991;34:182–5.

28. Sampson MJ, Wilson S, Karagiannis P, et al. Progression of diabetic autonomic neuropathy over a decade in insulin-dependent diabetics. QJM 1990;75:635–46.

29. Low PA. Diabetic autonomic neuropathy. Semin Neurol 1996;16:143–51.

30. Goodman JI. Diabetic anhidrosis. Am J Med 1966;41:831–5.

31. Watkins PJ. Facial sweating after food: a new sign of diabetic autonomic neuropathy. BMJ 1973;1:583–7.

32. Dyck PJ, Giannini C. Pathologic alterations in the diabetic neuropathies of humans: a review. J Neuropathol Exp Neurol 1996;55:1181–93.

33. Dyck PJ, Karnes J, O'Brien P, et al. Spatial pattern of nerve fiber abnormality indicative of pathologic mechanism. Am J Pathol 1984;117:225–38.

34. Dyck PJ, Karnes JL, O'Brien P, et al. The spatial distribution of fiber loss in diabetic polyneuropathy suggests ischemia. Ann Neurol 1986;19:440–9.

35. Dyck PJ, Lais A, Karnes JL, et al. Fiber loss is primary and multifocal in sural nerves in diabetic polyneuropathy. Ann Neurol 1986;19:425–39.

36. Dyck PJ, Sherman WR, Hallcher LM, et al. Human diabetic endoneurial sorbitol, fructose, and myo-inositol related to sural nerve morphometry. Ann Neurol 1980;8:590–6.

37. Thomas PK, Lascelles RG. Schwann cell abnormalities in diabetic neuropathy. Lancet 1965;1:1355–6.

38. Thomas PK, Lascelles RG. The pathology of diabetic neuropathy. QJM 1966;35:489–509.

39. Yasuda H, Dyck PJ. Abnormalities of endoneurial microvessels and sural nerve pathology in diabetic neuropathy. Neurology 1987;37:20–8.

40. Llewelyn JG, Gilbey SG, Thomas PK, et al. Sural nerve morphometry in diabetic autonomic and painful sensory neuropathy. A clinicopathological study. Brain 1991;114(Pt 2):867–92.

41. Britland ST, Young RJ, Sharma AK, et al. Acute and remitting painful diabetic polyneuropathy: a comparison of peripheral nerve fibre pathology. Pain 1992;48:361–70.

42. Dyck PJ. Hypoxic neuropathy: does hypoxia play a role in diabetic neuropathy? The 1988 Robert Wartenberg lecture. Neurology 1989;39:111–8.

43. Johnson PC, Doll SC, Cromey DW. Pathogenesis of diabetic neuropathy. Ann Neurol 1986;19:450–7.

44. Malik RA, Newrick PG, Sharma AK, et al. Microangiopathy in human diabetic neuropathy: relationship between capillary abnormalities and the severity of neuropathy. Diabetologia 1989;32:92–102.

45. Malik RA, Veves A, Masson EA, et al. Endoneurial capillary abnormalities in mild human diabetic neuropathy. J Neurol Neurosurg Psychiatry 1992;55:557–61.

46. Malik RA, Tesfaye S, Thompson SD, et al. Endoneurial localisation of microvascular damage in human diabetic neuropathy. Diabetologia 1993;36:454–9.

47. Malik RA. The pathology of human diabetic neuropathy. Diabetes 1997;46:S50–3.

48. Timperley WR, Boulton AJ, Davies-Jones GA, et al. Small vessel disease in progressive diabetic neuropathy associated with good metabolic control. J Clin Pathol 1985;38:1030–8.

49. Williams E, Timperley WR, Ward JD, et al. Electron microscopical studies of vessels in diabetic peripheral neuropathy. J Clin Pathol 1980;33:462–70.

50. Llewelyn JG, Thomas PK, Gilbey SG, et al. Pattern of myelinated fibre loss in the sural nerve in neuropathy related to type 1 (insulin-dependent) diabetes. Diabetologia 1988;31:162–7.

51. Zochodne DW. Is early diabetic neuropathy a disorder of the dorsal root ganglion? A hypothesis and critique of some current ideas on the etiology of diabetic neuropathy. J Peripher Nerv Syst 1996;1:119–30.

52. Schmidt RE, Dorsey D, Parvin CA, et al. Dystrophic axonal swellings develop as a function of age and diabetes in human dorsal root ganglia. J Neuropathol Exp Neurol 1997;56:1028–43.

53. Borghini I, Ania-Lahuerta A, Regazzi R, et al. Alpha, beta I, beta II, delta, and epsilon protein kinase C isoforms and compound activity in the sciatic nerve of normal and diabetic rats. J Neurochem 1994;62:686–96.

54. Greene DA, Lattimer SA, Sima AA. Are disturbances of sorbitol, phosphoinositide, and Na$^+$K$^+$-ATPase regulation involved in pathogenesis of diabetic neuropathy? Diabetes 1988;37:688–93.

55. Greene DA, Sima AA, Stevens MJ, et al. Complications: neuropathy, pathogenetic considerations. Diabetes Care 1992;15:1902–25.

56. Lattimer SA, Sima AA, Greene DA. In vitro correction of impaired Na$^+$K$^+$ ATPase in diabetic nerve by protein kinase C agonists. Am J Physiol 1989;256:E264–9.

57. Roberts RE, McLean WG. Protein kinase C isozyme expression in sciatic nerves and spinal cords of experimentally diabetic rats. Brain Res 1997;754:147–56.

58. Sima AA, Thomas PK, Ishii D, et al. Diabetic neuropathies. Diabetologia 1997;40(Suppl 3):B74–7.

59. Cullum NA, Mahon J, Stringer K, et al. Glycation of rat sciatic nerve tubulin in experimental diabetes mellitus. Diabetologia 1991;34:387–9.

60. Ryle C, Leow CK, Donaghy M. Nonenzymatic glycation of peripheral and central nervous system proteins in experimental diabetes mellitus. Muscle Nerve 1997;20:577–84.

61. Vlassara H, Bucala R, Striker L. Pathogenic effects of advanced glycosylation: biochemical, biologic, and clinical implications for diabetes and aging. Lab Invest 1994;70:138–51.

62. Low PA, Lagerlund TD, McManis PG. Nerve blood flow and oxygen delivery in normal, diabetic, and ischemic neuropathy. Int Rev Neurobiol 1989;31:355–438.

63. Tuck RR, Schmelzer JD, Low PA. Endoneurial blood flow and oxygen tension in the sciatic nerves of rats with experimental diabetic neuropathy. Brain 1984;107(Pt 3):935–50.

64. Chang K, Ido Y, LeJeune W, et al. Increased sciatic nerve blood flow in diabetic rats: assessment by "molecular" vs. particulate microspheres. Am J Physiol 1997;273:E164–73.

65. Ido Y, Chang K, LeJeune W, et al. Diabetes impairs sciatic nerve hyperemia induced by surgical trauma: implications for diabetic neuropathy. Am J Physiol 1997;273(36):E174–84.

66. Pugliese G, Tilton RG, Speedy A, et al. Effects of very mild versus overt diabetes on vascular haemodynamics and barrier function in rats. Diabetologia 1989;32:845–57.

67. Tilton RG, Chang K, Nyengaard JR, et al. Inhibition of sorbitol dehydrogenase. Effects on vascular and neural dysfunction in streptozocin-induced diabetic rats. Diabetes 1995;44:234–42.

68. Zochodne DW, Cheng C, Sun H. Diabetes increases sciatic nerve susceptibility to endothelin-induced ischemia. Diabetes 1996;45:627–32.

69. Zochodne DW, Ho LT. Normal blood flow but lower oxygen tension in diabetes of young rats: microenvironment and the influence of sympathectomy. Can J Physiol Pharmacol 1992;70:651–9.

70. Zochodne DW, Ho LT. The influence of indomethacin and guanethidine on experimental streptozotocin diabetic neuropathy. Can J Neurol Sci 1992;19:433–41.

71. Zochodne DW, Ho LT. Diabetes mellitus prevents capsaicin from inducing hyperaemia in the rat sciatic nerve. Diabetologia 1993;36:493–6.

72. Zochodne DW, Ho LT. The influence of sulindac on experimental streptozotocin-induced diabetic neuropathy. Can J Neurol Sci 1994;21:194–202.

73. Theriault M, Dort J, Sutherland G, et al. Local human sural nerve blood flow in diabetic and other polyneuropathies. Brain 1997;120(Pt 7):1131–8.

74. Newrick PG, Wilson AJ, Jakubowski J, et al. Sural nerve oxygen tension in diabetes. Br Med J 1986;293:1053–4.

75. Nakamura J, Koh N, Sakakibara F, et al. Polyol pathway, 2,3-diphosphoglycerate in erythrocytes and diabetic neuropathy in rats. Eur J Pharmacol 1995;294:207–14.

76. Diemel LT, Brewster WJ, Fernyhough P, et al. Expression of neuropeptides in experimental diabetes; effects of treatment with nerve growth factor or brain-derived neurotrophic factor. Brain Res Mol Brain Res 1994;21:171–5.

77. Tomlinson DR, Fernyhough P, Diemel LT. Role of neurotrophins in diabetic neuropathy and treatment with nerve growth factors. Diabetes 1997;46:S43–9.

78. Zochodne DW. Neurotrophins and other growth factors in diabetic neuropathy. Semin Neurol 1996;16:153–61.

79. Sango K, Verdes JM, Hikawa N, et al. Nerve growth factor (NGF) restores depletions of calcitonin gene-related peptide and substance P in sensory neurons from diabetic mice in vitro. J Neurol Sci 1994;126:1–5.

80. Taniuchi M, Clark HB, Schweitzer JB, et al. Expression of nerve growth factor receptors by Schwann cells of axotomized peripheral nerves: ultrastructural location, suppression by axonal contact, and binding properties. J Neurosci 1988;8:664–81.

81. Apfel SC, Arezzo JC, Brownlee M, et al. Nerve growth factor administration protects against experimental diabetic sensory neuropathy. Brain Res 1994;634:7–12.

82. Zochodne DW. Diabetic neuropathies: features and mechanisms. Brain Pathol 1999;9:369–91.

83. Vinik AI, Suwanwalaikorn S, Stansberry KB, et al. Quantitative measurement of cutaneous perception in diabetic neuropathy. Muscle Nerve 1995;18:574–84.

84. Valk GD, de Sonnaville JJ, van Houtum WH, et al. The assessment of diabetic polyneuropathy in daily clinical practice: reproducibility and validity of Semmes Weinstein monofilaments examination and clinical neurological examination. Muscle Nerve 1997;20:116–8.

85. Klenerman L, McCabe C, Cogley D, et al. Screening for patients at risk of diabetic foot ulceration in a general diabetic outpatient clinic. Diabet Med 1996;13:561–3.

86. Grant IA, O'Brien P, Dyck PJ. Neuropathy tests and normative results. In: Dyck PJ, Thomas PK, editors. Diabetic neuropathy. Toronto: W.B. Saunders; 1999. p. 123–41.

87. Young MJ, Breddy JL, Veves A, et al. The prediction of diabetic neuropathic foot ulceration using vibration perception thresholds. A prospective study. Diabetes Care 1994;17:557–60.

88. Dyck PJ, Bushek W, Spring EM, et al. Vibratory and cooling detection thresholds compared with other tests in diagnosing and staging diabetic neuropathy. Diabetes Care 1987;10:432–40.

89. Dyck PJ, Karnes JL, Daube J, et al. Clinical and neuropathological criteria for the diagnosis and staging of diabetic polyneuropathy. Brain 1985;108:861–80.

90. Gregersen G. Vibratory perception threshold and motor conduction velocity in diabetics and non-diabetics. Acta Med Scand 1968;183(1–2):61–5.

91. Nielsen NV, Lund FS. Diabetic polyneuropathy. Corneal sensitivity, vibratory perception and Achilles tendon reflex in diabetics. Acta Neurol Scand 1979;59(1):15–22.

92. Russell JW, Karnes JL, Dyck PJ. Sural nerve myelinated fiber density differences associated with meaningful changes in clinical and electrophysiologic measurements. J Neurol Sci 1996;135:114–7.

93. Steiness IB. Vibratory perception in normal subjects: a biothesiometric study. Acta Med Scand 1957;158:137.

94. Dyck PJ, Karnes JL, O'Brien PC, et al. The Rochester Diabetic Neuropathy Study: reassessment of tests and criteria for diagnosis and staged severity. Neurology 1992;42:1164–70.

95. Dyck PJ, Kratz KM, Lehman KA, et al. The Rochester Diabetic Neuropathy Study: design, criteria for types of neuropathy, selection bias, and reproducibility of neuropathic tests. Neurology 1991;41:799–807.

96. Trojaborg W. The electrophysiologic profile of diabetic neuropathy. Semin Neurol 1996;16:123–8.

97. Wilbourn AJ. Diabetic neuropathies. In: Brown WF, Bolton CF, editors. Clinical electromyography. 2nd ed. Toronto: Butterworth Heinemann; 1993. p. 477–515.

98. Bril V, Ellison R, Ngo M, et al. Electrophysiological monitoring in clinical trials. Roche Neuropathy Study Group. Muscle Nerve 1998;21:1368–73.

99. Suarez GA, Dyck PJ. Quantitative sensory assessment. In: Dyck PJ, Thomas PK, editors. Diabetic neuropathy. 2nd ed. Toronto: W.B. Saunders; 1999. p. 151–69.

100. Zochodne DW, Kihara M. The autonomic nervous system. In: Brown WF, Bolton CF, editors. Clinical electromyography. 2nd ed. Toronto: Butterworth Heinemann; 1993. 149–73.

101. Ewing DJ. Which battery of cardiovascular autonomic function tests? Diabetologia 1990;33:180–1.

102. Ewing DJ, Martyn CN, Young RJ, et al. The value of cardiovascular autonomic function tests: 10 years experience in diabetes. Diabetes Care 1985;8:491–8.

103. Ewing DJ & Clarke BF. Diabetic autonomic neuropathy: present insights and future prospects. Diabetes Care 1986;9:648-65.

104. Pfeifer MA, Weinberg CR, Cook DL, et al. Autonomic neural dysfunction in recently diagnosed diabetic subjects. Diabetes Care 1984;7:447–53.

105. Krolewski AS, Warram JH, Cupples A, et al. Hypertension, orthostatic hypotension and the microvascular complications of diabetes. J Chronic Dis 1985;38:319–26.

106. O'Brien IA, O'Hare JP, Lewin IG, et al. The prevalence of autonomic neuropathy in insulin-dependent diabetes mellitus: a controlled study based on heart rate variability. QJM 1986;61:957–67.

107. Kennedy WR, Sakuta M, Sutherland D, et al. Quantitation of the sweating deficiency in diabetes mellitus. Ann Neurol 1984;15:482–8.

108. Low PA, Caskey PE, Tuck RR, et al. Quantitative sudomotor axon reflex test in normal and neuropathic subjects. Ann Neurol 1983;14:573–80.

109. Low PA. Autonomic neuropathy. Semin Neurol 1987;7:49–57.

110. Low PA, Zimmerman BR, Dyck PJ. Comparison of distal sympathetic with vagal function in diabetic neuropathy. Muscle Nerve 1986;9:592–6.

111. Kassander P. Asymptomatic gastric retention in diabetics (gastroparesis diabeticorum). Ann Intern Med 1958;48:797–812.

112. Bargen JA, Bollman JL, Depler EJ. The "diarrhea of diabetes" and steatorrhea of pancreatic insufficiency. Mayo Clin Proc 1936;11:737–42.

113. Feldman M, Schiller LR. Disorders of gastrointestinal motility associated with diabetes mellitus. Ann Intern Med 1983;98:378–84.

114. Bradley WE. Diagnosis of urinary bladder dysfunction in diabetes mellitus. Ann Intern Med 1980;92(2 Pt 2):323–6.

115. Bradley WE, Lin JT. Assessment of diabetic sexual dysfunction and cystopathy. In: Dyck PJ, Thomas PK, Asbury AK, et al, editors. Diabetic neuropathy. Philadelphia: WB Saunders; 1987. p. 146–61.

116. McCulloch DK, Campbell IW, Wu FC, et al. The prevalence of diabetic impotence. Diabetologia 1980;18:279–83.

117. Pfeifer MA, Cook D, Brodsky J, et al. Quantitative evaluation of sympathetic and parasympathetic control of iris function. Diabetes Care 1982;5:518–28.

118. Smith SA, Smith SE. Evidence for a neuropathic aetiology in the small pupil of diabetes mellitus. Br J Ophthalmol 1983;67:89–93.

119. Theriault M, Dort J, Sutherland G, et al. A prospective quantitative study of sensory deficits after whole sural nerve biopsies in diabetic and nondiabetic patients. Surgical approach and the role of collateral sprouting. Neurology 1998;50:480–4.

120. Kennedy WR, Nolano M, Wendelschafer-Crabb G, et al. A skin blister method to study epidermal nerves in peripheral nerve disease. Muscle Nerve 1999;22:360–71.

121. Kennedy WR, Wendelschafer-Crabb G, Johnson T. Quantitation of epidermal nerves in diabetic neuropathy. Neurology 1996;47:1042–8.

122. Anonymous. The effect of intensive diabetes therapy on the development and progression of neuropathy. Ann Intern Med 1995;122:561–8.

123. Reichard P, Nilsson BY, Rosenqvist U. The effect of long-term intensified insulin treatment on the development of microvascular complications of diabetes mellitus. N Engl J Med 1993;329:304–9.

124. Dahl-Jorgensen K, Brinchmann-Hansen O, Hanssen KF, et al. Effect of near normoglycaemia for two years on progression of early diabetic retinopathy, nephropathy, and neuropathy: the Oslo study. BMJ 1986;293:1195–9.

125. Ohkubo Y, Kishikawa H, Araki E, et al. Intensive insulin therapy prevents the progression of diabetic microvascular complications in Japanese patients with non-insulin-dependent diabetes mellitus: a randomized prospective 6-year study. Diabetes Res Clin Pract 1995;28:103–17.

126. Kennedy WR, Navarro X, Goetz FC, et al. Effects of pancreatic transplantation on diabetic neuropathy. N Engl J Med 1990;322:1031–7.

127. Judzewitsch RG, Jaspan JB, Polonsky KS, et al. Aldose reductase inhibition improves nerve conduction velocity in diabetic patients. N Engl J Med 1983;308:119–25.

128. Krans HM. Recent clinical experience with aldose reductase inhibitors. J Diabetes Complications 1992;6:39–44.

129. Sima AA, Greene DA, Brown MB, et al. Effect of hyperglycemia and the aldose reductase inhibitor tolrestat on sural nerve biochemistry and morphometry in advanced diabetic peripheral polyneuropathy. The Tolrestat Study Group. J Diabetes Complications 1993;7:157–69.

130. Uchida K, Kigoshi T, Nakano S, et al. Effect of 24 weeks of treatment with epalrestat, an aldose reductase inhibitor, on peripheral neuropathy in patients with non-insulin-dependent diabetes mellitus. Clin Ther 1995;17:460–6.

131. Nicolucci A, Carinci F, Cavaliere D, et al. A meta-analysis of trials on aldose reductase inhibitors in diabetic peripheral neuropathy. The Italian Study Group. The St. Vincent Declaration. Diabet Med 1996;13:1017–26.

132. Jaspan J, Maselli R, Herold K, et al. Treatment of severely painful diabetic neuropathy with an aldose reductase inhibitor: relief of pain and improved somatic and autonomic nerve function. Lancet 1983;2:758–62.

133. Greene DA. Effects of aldose reductase inhibitors on the progression of nerve fiber damage in diabetic neuropathy. J Diabetes Complications 1992;6:35–8.

134. Greene DA, Sima AA. Effects of aldose reductase inhibitors on the progression of nerve damage. Diabet Med 1993;10(Suppl 2):31S–2S.

135. Greene DA, Sima AA, Stevens MJ, et al. Aldose reductase inhibitors: an approach to the treatment of diabetic nerve damage. Diabetes Metab Rev 1993;9:189–217.

136. Masson EA, Boulton AJ. Aldose reductase inhibitors in the treatment of diabetic neuropathy. A review of the rationale and clinical evidence. Drugs 1990;39:190–202.

137. Pfeifer MA, Schumer MP, Gelber DA. Aldose reductase inhibitors: the end of an era or the need for different trial designs? Diabetes 1997;46(Suppl 2):S82–9.

138. Tomlinson DR, Stevens EJ, Diemel LT. Aldose reductase inhibitors and their potential for the treatment of diabetic complications. Trends Pharmacol Sci 1994;15:293–7.

139. Tomlinson DR, Willars GB, Carrington AL. Aldose reductase inhibitors and diabetic complications. Pharmacol Ther 1992;54:151–94.

140. Tsai SC, Burnakis TG. Aldose reductase inhibitors: an update. Ann Pharmacother 1993;27:751–4.

141. van Gerven JM, Tjon-A-Tsien AM. The efficacy of aldose reductase inhibitors in the management of diabetic complications. Comparison with intensive insulin treatment and pancreatic transplantation. Drugs Aging 1995;6(1):9–28.

142. Yue DK, Brooks B. The role of aldose reductase inhibitors in the treatment of diabetic peripheral neuropathy. Med J Aust 1993;159:76–8.

143. Giugliano D, Acampora R, Marfella R, et al. Tolrestat in the primary prevention of diabetic neuropathy. Diabetes Care 1995;18:536–41.

144. Greene DA, Arezzo JC, Brown MB. Effect of aldose reductase inhibition on nerve conduction and morphometry in diabetic neuropathy. Zenarestat Study Group. Neurology 1999;53:580–91.

145. Apfel SC, Kessler JA, Adornato BT, et al. Recombinant human nerve growth factor in the treatment of diabetic polyneuropathy. NGF Study Group. Neurology 1998;51:695–702.

146. Zochodne DW, Said G. Recombinant human nerve growth factor and diabetic polyneuropathy. Neurology 1998;51:662–3.

147. Keen H, Payan J, Allawi J, et al. Treatment of diabetic neuropathy with gamma-linolenic acid. The Gamma-Linolenic Acid Multicenter Trial Group. Diabetes Care 1993;16:8–15.

148. Donofrio P, Walker F, Hunt V, et al. Treatment of painful diabetic neuropathy with topical capsaicin. A multicenter, double-blind, vehicle-controlled study. The Capsaicin Study Group. Arch Intern Med 1991;151:2225–9.

149. Donofrio P, Walker F, Hunt V, et al. Effect of treatment with capsaicin on daily activities of patients with painful diabetic neuropathy. Capsaicin Study Group. Diabetes Care 1992;15:159–65.

150. Low PA, Opfer-Gehrking TL, Dyck PJ, et al. Double-blind, placebo-controlled study of the application of capsaicin cream in chronic distal painful polyneuropathy. Pain 1995;62:163–8.

151. Max MB, Lynch SA, Muir J, et al. Effects of desipramine, amitriptyline, and fluoxetine on pain in diabetic neuropathy. N Engl J Med 1992;326:1250–6.

152. McQuay H, Carroll D, Jadad AR, et al. Anticonvulsant drugs for management of pain: a systematic review. BMJ 1995;311:1047–52.

153. Rull J, Quibrera R, Gonzalez-Millan H, et al. Symptomatic treatment of peripheral diabetic neuropathy with carbamazepine: doubleblind crossover trial. Diabetologia 1969;5:215–8.

154. Chadda VS, Mathur MS. Double blind study of the effects of diphenylhydantoin sodium on diabetic neuropathy. J Assoc Physicians India 1978;26:403–6.

155. McCaffery M. Gabapentin for lancinating neuropathic pain. Am J Nurs 1998;98:12.

156. Rosenberg JM, Harrell C, Ristic H, et al. The effect of gabapentin on neuropathic pain. Clin J Pain 1997;13:251–5.

157. Rosner H, Rubin L, Kestenbaum A. Gabapentin adjunctive therapy in neuropathic pain states. Clin J Pain 1996;12:56–8.

158. Wetzel CH, Connelly JF. Use of gabapentin in pain management. Ann Pharmacother 1997;31:1082–3.

159. Backonja M, Beydoun A, Edwards KR, et al. Gabapentin for the symptomatic treatment of painful neuropathy in patients with diabetes mellits. A randomized controlled trial. JAMA 1998;280:1831–6.

160. Oskarsson P, Ljunggren JG, Lins PE. Efficacy and safety of mexiletine in the treatment of painful diabetic neuropathy. The Mexiletine Study Group. Diabetes Care 1997;20:1594–7.

161. Stracke H, Meyer UE, Schumacher HE, et al. Mexilitene in the treatment of diabetic neuropathy. Diabetes Care 1992;15:1550–5.

162. Kumar D, Marshall HJ. Diabetic peripheral neuropathy: amelioration of pain with transcutaneous electrostimulation. Diabetes Care 1997;20:1702–5.

163. Ziegler D, Gries FA. Alpha-lipoic acid in the treatment of diabetic peripheral and cardiac autonomic neuropathy. Diabetes 1997;46(Suppl 2):S62–6.

164. Ziegler D, Hanefeld M, Ruhnau KJ, et al. Treatment of symptomatic diabetic peripheral neuropathy with the anti-oxidant alpha-lipoic acid. A 3-week multicentre randomized controlled trial (ALADIN Study). Diabetologia 1995;38:1425–33.

165. Hoeldtke RD, Streeten DH. Treatment of orthostatic hypotension with erythropoietin. N Engl J Med 1993;329:611–5.

166. Wright RA, Kaufmann HC, Perera R, et al. A double-blind, dose-response study of midodrine in neurogenic orthostatic hypotension. Neurology 1998;51:120–4.

167. Camilleri M, Balm RK, Zinsmeister AR. Symptomatic improvement with one-year cisapride treatment in neuropathic chronic intestinal dysmotility. Aliment Pharmacol Ther 1996;10:403–9.

168. Champion MC. Management of idiopathic, diabetic and miscellaneous gastroparesis with cisapride. Scand J Gastroenterol Suppl 1989;165:44–52.

169. Fry IK, Hardwick C, Scott CW. Diabetic neuropathy: a survey and follow-up on 66 cases. Guys Hosp Rep 1962;111:113–29.

CHAPTER 24

Cardiovascular Diseases

Hertzel C. Gerstein, MD, MSc, FRCPC, Klas Malmberg, MD, PhD, FACC, Sarah Capes, MD, FRCPC, and Salim Yusuf, DPhil, FRCPC

ABSTRACT

Diabetes is a strong independent risk factor for cardiovascular (CV) disease, and CV diseases account for the largest burden of morbidity, mortality, and health care costs attributed to diabetes. The risk of CV events is clearly increased in the presence of other risk factors, including hyperglycemia, hypertension, high low-density lipoprotein (LDL) cholesterol, microalbuminuria, clinical proteinuria, diabetes-related eye diseases, insulin resistance, and previous CV events. When a CV event such as a myocardial infarction does occur, a lack of typical symptoms may delay the diagnosis. Whether or not intensive glycemic control delays or prevents cardiovascular disease remains uncertain, although several studies support the conclusion that it is beneficial. Preventive therapies for which there is strong supportive evidence include smoking cessation, blood-pressure lowering, angiotensin converting enzyme (ACE) inhibitors, aspirin, "statin" therapy for elevated LDL cholesterol, beta-blockers, and insulin infusion after an MI. New therapeutic approaches as well as novel ways of targeting both established and emerging risk factors are likely to yield more effective ways of reducing CV disease in people with diabetes.

INTRODUCTION

Diabetes has long been recognized as a strong, independent risk factor for cardiovascular (CV) disease—a problem that accounts for approximately 70% of all mortality in people with diabetes.[1] American population-based surveys have reported an age-adjusted prevalence of coronary heart disease in diabetic and nondiabetic Caucasian adults of approximately 45% and 25%, respectively; moreover, approximately 25% of Caucasian men and 10 to 15% of Caucasian women with diabetes have evidence of a previous myocardial infarction (MI), compared to approximately 12% and 2.5 to 10%, respectively, in nondiabetic individuals.[2] Finally, despite the fact that the incidence of heart disease is falling in the general population, the rate of fall is much smaller in patients with Type 2 diabetes and, in the case of women, may be rising.[3] This latter observation suggests that with time the relative importance of diabetes as a CV risk factor is likely to increase.

Concern over these statistics has stimulated much research regarding both the epidemiology of CV disease in people with diabetes and ways to delay, prevent, or treat CV disease in people with diabetes. In this chapter, the clinical issues of most relevance regarding CV disease in this population will be addressed by answering the following questions:

1. How does diabetes affect the risk and course of CV disease?
2. What are the clearly identified risk factors for CV disease in people with diabetes?
3. How can CV diseases be detected in a clinical setting?
4. Does glycemic control prevent or delay the risk of CV disease?
5. What nonglycemic therapies can prevent or delay CV disease?

Discussing the various forms of invasive and medical therapies for established coronary artery, cerebrovascular, and peripheral vascular disease in people with diabetes is beyond the scope of this textbook.

How Does Diabetes Affect the Risk and Course of Cardiovascular Disease?

Risk of Cardiovascular Events in People with Diabetes

Patients with both Type 1 and Type 2 diabetes are at very high risk for CV disease. Prospective studies clearly show that compared to their nondiabetic counterparts, the relative risk of CV mortality for men with diabetes is 2 to 3 and for women with diabetes is 3 to 4.[4–9] The annual risk of fatal and nonfatal CV events in middle-aged diabetic individuals is 2 to 5%.[4,10–13] This includes a four- and eightfold higher risk of congestive heart failure in young diabetic (compared to nondiabetic) men and women, respectively,[5] and an approximate threefold higher risk in elderly individuals.[14] The risk associated with diabetes is independent of the risk associated with other risk factors such as age, gender, body mass index, hypercholesterolemia, smoking, and hypertension in males.[4,14] The increased CV risk associated with diabetes is reflected in the observation that middle-aged individuals with diabetes have mortality and morbidity risks that are similar to nondiabetic individuals who have already suffered a CV event.[15,16]

EVIDENCE-BASED MESSAGE

> Diabetes is an independent risk factor for future CV events in the general population (Level 1).[4,5,14]

Risk of Cardiovascular Events in People with Diabetes and a Previous Cardiovascular Event

Prospective studies have also documented that diabetes predicts a poor prognosis following a CV event. For example, people with diabetes are up to two times more likely to die than those without diabetes after an MI[17–20] or after hospitalization for unstable angina or non-Q wave MI.[16,21] Moreover, a history of MI leads to a 1.5- to 3-fold increase in the risk of either mortality, CV mortality, MI, or stroke.[15,19,22–25] In the Heart Outcomes Prevention Evaluation (HOPE) trial[26] that compared the effect of ramipril on CV outcomes, volunteers with diabetes who were randomized to placebo and who had evidence of previous CV disease had an absolute rate of CV mortality, MI, or stroke of 23.9% during 4.5 years of follow-up; the rate in diabetic participants without previous CV disease but who had 1 or more CV risk factors was 9.9% (ie, a crude relative risk associated with previous CV disease of 2.4).

Diabetes also predicts a poorer prognosis following a diagnosis of asymptomatic heart failure[27] and coronary bypass surgery.[28] As in the epidemiologic studies of the risk of heart disease in the general population, the relative risk may be even higher in women than in men.[19]

EVIDENCE-BASED MESSAGE

> Diabetes is an independent risk factor for future CV events in people with previous CV disease. People with diabetes who have had a previous CV event or who have evidence of CV disease are two to three times more likely to have subsequent CV events than are diabetic people with no previous CV event (Level 1).[15–20,22,24–26]

What Are the Clearly Identified Risk Factors for Cardiovascular Disease in People with Diabetes?

What Are Risk Factors?

Risk factors are measured variables that predict a higher incidence of disease when they are present than when they are absent. Risk factors for CV events can be either categorical (ie, can be either present or absent, as exemplified by whether or not an individual smokes) or continuous (ie, associated with different grades of exposure, as exemplified by the number of cigarettes smoked or the number of years smoked). Whereas all causal factors are risk factors, the converse is seldom true; this is almost certainly because the identified risk factors are those variables that can be easily measured and are more likely to be associated with (or "confounded" with) both an underlying, hard-to-measure, or unrecognized causal factor (or other risk factor) as well as the outcome. For example, as noted below, there is strong evidence in support of the conclusion that microalbuminuria is a categorical risk factor for CV events and that the degree of urinary albumin excretion is a continuous risk factor; nevertheless, it is very unlikely that albumin in the urine causes CV events to occur. Albuminuria may, however, be a marker of subclinical CV disease—which is by itself a risk factor for a future CV event.

The following sections will discuss easily measured variables for which there is a large body of strong evidence supporting their inclusion as CV risk factors and that are specific or unique to diabetes. An exhaustive review of every postulated risk factor is beyond the scope of this text; for example, smoking and increasing age are not discussed separately, as the evidence supporting these variables as CV risk factors is well established from large studies of the general population.

Glucose

The fact that diabetes—a disease defined by the presence of hyperglycemia—is a risk factor for CV disease has been recognized for many years. Much less clear has been the relationship between different degrees of hyperglycemia and CV risk. Indeed, until recently, relatively little data examining whether or not higher levels of glucose predicted progressively higher risks of CV events were available. However, several recently published prospective epidemiologic studies have clearly demonstrated that such a relationship exists and that glucose is a continuous CV risk factor in people with both Type 1 and Type 2 diabetes.[22–24,29–34] These data are summarized in Table 24–1 and suggest that the risk of a CV event rises by about 10 to 30% for every 1% increase in HbA_{1c}. This is clearly supported by an analysis of the United Kingdom Prospective Diabetes Study (UKPDS) data, in which the incidence of MI rose 14% per 1% rise in HbA_{1c}.[35] Moreover, a growing body of evidence now exists demonstrating that this relationship between glucose and CV risk extends below the glucose thresholds that are required for a diagnosis of diabetes (ie, that identify people at risk for eye and kidney disease), and the glucose threshold below which people are not at increased risk for CV disease remains unknown.[36–42] These observations support the hypothesis that lowering the glucose to levels within the normal range may prevent CV disease.

EVIDENCE-BASED MESSAGE

The plasma glucose level is a continuous risk factor for CV events in people with Type 1 and Type 2 diabetes (Level 1).[22,23,29,30–35,43,44]

Low-Density Lipoprotein Cholesterol

More than 70% of people with Type 2 DM have low-density lipoprotein (LDL) levels > 3.4 mmol/L (130 mg/dL).[45] In the UKPDS study, the risk of either angina or an MI increased 1.57-fold for every 1 mmol/L (39 mg/dL) increase in LDL cholesterol (LDL-C).[23] Individuals with an LDL-C > 3.89 mmol/L (151 mg/dL) were 2.3 times more likely to develop angina or an MI than people with LDL-C < 3 mmol/L (117 mg/dL).[23] Total cholesterol and LDL-C levels are not higher in people with Type 2 diabetes mellitus (DM) than in people without DM[46] and do not vary with glycemic control.[45] However, the fact that in people with DM the LDL-C is more likely to be glycated and oxidized,[47] larger numbers of small, dense, atherogenic LDL-C particles are present, and higher triglyceride and lower HDL-C levels are present than in nondiabetic people (despite the same total and LDL-C)[45] accounts for some of the increased CV risk associated with DM.

EVIDENCE-BASED MESSAGE

Low-density lipoprotein cholesterol is a continuous risk factor for CV events in people with diabetes (Level 1).[23]

Table 24–1 Relationship between Glycemia and Risk of Cardiovascular Disease in Type 2 Diabetes Mellitus*

Study	N	Mean Age (y)	F/U (y)	Glycemia Comparison	Outcome	RR†	RR/1% ↑GHb‡
Type 2 DM							
Andersson et al[31]	411	66	7.4	CBG < 7.8 vs ≥ 7.8 mM	Death	1.4	N/A
Kuusisto et al[30]	229	68	3.5	GHb < 7 vs ≥ 7%	CHD death	4.3	N/A
				GHb < 7 vs ≥ 7%	All CHD	1.6	
Gall et al[32]	328	56	5.3	GHb ≥ 7.8 vs <7.8%	CV death	2.2	1.3
Agewall et al[33]	94	67	6.3	Across GHb range	CV death	N/A	1.54
Lehto et al[43]	1,059	58	7.2	GHb ≥ 10.7 vs < 10.7%	CHD death	1.4	N/A
Wei et al[22]	4,875	52	7.5	FPG 8–11.5 vs < 8 mM	CV death	2.9	N/A
Turner et al[23]	3,055	52	7.9	GHb > 7.5 vs < 6.2%	Fatal MI	1.72	N/A
					MI/angina	1.52	1.11
Moss et al[29]	1,265	66.6	8.3	Across GHb range	IHD death	N/A	1.10
					Stroke death	N/A	1.17
Fu et al[34]	479	61.2	4	GHb < 6.3 vs >8.4%	ECG MI/angina	1.5	1.17
Stratton et al[35]	3,642	53	10	Across GHb range	MI	N/A	1.14
					Stroke	N/A	1.12
					Heart failure	N/A	1.16
Type 1 DM							
Moss et al[29]	943	29.1	10	Across GHb range	IHD death	N/A	1.18
Lehto et al[44]	177	55.4	7.3	GHb > 10.4% vs ≤ 10.4%	All CHD	5.4	N/A
					CHD death	2.8	N/A

*Rates are either read from figures or text.
†RRs are either read or calculated for differences in rates.
‡The relative risk per 1% rise in GHb is reported in the respective paper.

F/U = follow-up; RR = relative risk; mM = mmol/L; GHb = glycated hemoglobin; CBG = capillary blood glucose; CHD = coronary heart disease; CV = cardiovascular; IHD = ischemic heart disease; ECG = electrocardiogram; N/A = not available; FPG = fasting plasma glucose; MI = myocardial infarction.

Blood Pressure

Up to 70% of adult patients with Type 2 diabetes have hypertension.[48] The relationship between blood pressure and CV events noted in prospective studies[4,22–24,32,49–51] is summarized in Table 24–2. Taken together, these studies suggest that an increase in systolic blood pressure (SBP) of 10 mm Hg is associated with an increased CV event risk of 20%. This is supported by an epidemiologic analysis of UKPDS data in which each 10 mm HG increase in systolic blood pressure increased the risk of MI by 11%.[51]

EVIDENCE-BASED MESSAGE

> Elevated blood pressure is a continuous risk factor for CV events in people with diabetes (Level 1).[4,22–24,32,49–51]

Microalbuminuria and Diabetic Nephropathy

Microalbuminuria (MA), defined as dipstick-negative albuminuria (and a urinary albumin excretion rate of 30 to 300 mg/d), is present in approximately 20 to 30% of middle-aged patients with DM. It is independently associated with hypertension, HbA_{1c}, age, abdominal obesity, smoking, and left ventricular hypertrophy (LVH).[52]

Several prospective epidemiologic studies have demonstrated that MA is an important risk factor for CV disease in patients with Type 2 diabetes. In a recent meta-analysis of these studies, it was shown that the presence of MA doubles the risk of CV morbidity or mortality as well as of total mortality.[53] This observation was confirmed in the HOPE study, in which 28.6% of diabetic participants with MA and 15.5% of diabetic participants with no MA who were randomized to placebo had an MI, stroke, or fatal CV event during 4.5 years of follow-up.[26] Other studies that included patients with higher degrees of albuminuria (macroalbuminuria) have noted an even higher relative risk of CV disease, in the range of 5 to 6.[33] It was reported in a recent 5-year prospective study that macroalbuminuric patients with type 2 DM had a 4.9-fold higher risk of all-cause mortality compared to normoalbuminuric patients[32]; the adjusted relative risk for CV mortality was 2.5 (95% confidence interval [CI] 1.1 to 5.8).

EVIDENCE-BASED MESSAGES

1. Microalbuminuria doubles the risk of CV events in people with diabetes (Level 1).[26,53]
2. Clinical proteinuria consistent with diabetic nephropathy increases the risk of CV events and total mortality greater than twofold (Level 1).[32,33]

Diabetes-Related Eye Disease

As discussed in Chapter 21, people with diabetes are at high risk for developing various eye diseases, including cataracts, retinopathy, and possibly glaucoma. In addition to increasing the risk of blindness and visual impairment, recent epidemiologic analyses have also shown that diabetes-related eye disease is a risk factor for death from ischemic heart disease and stroke. In this prospective study of 996 people with the clinical profile of Type 1 DM and 1,370 people with Type 2 DM (selected from a sample drawn from family practices), eye disease was assessed at baseline and mortality was measured during a median 16 years of follow-up for Type 1 DM and 8.5 years of follow-up for Type 2 DM.[54] Table 24–3 lists the relative hazards and 95% confidence intervals of CV events according to the presence of various ocular abnormalities. The fact that most of these risks became much less pronounced after controlling for other risk factors suggests that, to a large extent, eye disease reflects abnormalities linked to CV disease. Nevertheless, it also suggests that the presence of significant eye disease is a reliable marker for an increased CV risk.

Table 24–2 Relationship between Systolic Blood Pressure and Risk of Cardiovascular Disease in Type 2 Diabetes Mellitus

Study	N	Mean Age (y)	F/U (y)	BP	Outcome	RR	RR per 10 mm Hg↑ SBP
Stamler et al[4]	5,163 men	49.1	12	SBP 120–139 vs < 120	CV death	1.23	1.17
Gall et al[32]	328	56	5.3	N/A	CV death	N/A	1.2
Wei et al[22]	4,875	52	7.5	SBP > 140, DBP > 90 or on therapy	CV death	3.2	N/A
Turner et al[23]	3,055	52	7.5	SBP ≥ 142 vs < 125	Fatal MI	2.36	N/A
					Any MI/angina	1.82	1.15
Hadden et al[24]	432	55.8	10	N/A	Mortality	N/A	1.18
					MI		1.10
					Stroke		1.37
Mehler et al[49]	950	58	5.6	N/A	CV events or angina	1.39	N/A
Lehto et al[50]	1,059	58	7.2	SBP ≥ 160, DBP ≥ 95 or on therapy	Stroke	1.39	N/A
Adler et al[51]	3,642	53	10	Across SBP range	MI	N/A	1.11
					Stroke	N/A	1.19
					Heart failure	N/A	1.12

F/U = follow-up; BP = blood pressure; RR = relative risk; SBP = systolic blood pressure; CV = cardiovascular; N/A = not available; DBP = diastolic blood pressure; MI = myocardial infarction.

Table 24–3 Age and Sex-Adjusted Relative Risk (95% CI) of Cardiovascular Death in Diabetes Mellitus due to Eye Disease

Variable	Type 1 Diabetes Ischemic Heart Disease Mortality	Type 2 Diabetes Ischemic Heart Disease Mortality	Type 2 Diabetes Stroke Mortality
Proliferative retinopathy	11.02 (2.59–46.88)	2.07 (1.48–2.91)	2.32 (1.36–3.97)
Macular edema	1.82 (1.02–3.26)	1.57 (1.16–2.14)	1.39 (0.82–2.36)
Severe visual impairment	4.66 (2.47–8.78)	1.32 (0.68–2.57)	3.00 (1.50–5.99)
Cataract	2.51 (1.37–4.62)	1.65 (1.16–2.36)	1.37 (0.72–2.59)
Glaucoma	2.67 (1.45–4.91)	1.24 (0.88–1.75)	0.69 (0.35–1.35)

CI = confidence interval.

EVIDENCE-BASED MESSAGE

Proliferative retinopathy, macular edema, visual impairment, and cataracts are risk factors for ischemic heart disease mortality in people with Type 1 and Type 2 DM (Level 1).[55]

Insulin Resistance

Many individuals with both diabetes and lesser degrees of glucose intolerance show evidence of a reduced ability of insulin to mediate glucose uptake. Such an abnormality is referred to as insulin resistance (IR) and, depending on how it is measured, has been found quite commonly in individuals at risk for CV disease, including those with hypertension, abdominal obesity, hyperglycemia, and previous CV events. Several measures of IR have been reported. These include fasting insulin levels, measures derived from the insulin response to steady-state and bolus infusions of glucose (eg, using hyperglycemic "clamp" techniques and frequently sampled intravenous glucose tolerance tests, respectively), and measures based on mathematical models using fasting insulin and glucose levels (the HOMA, or homeostasis model assessment, technique). When the HOMA technique was applied to a population-based sample of diabetic and nondiabetic and impaired-glucose-tolerance individuals, IR was observed in 66% of people with impaired glucose tolerance and 84% of people with diabetes. This is compared to 27% of people with no glucose intolerance, dyslipidemia, hypertension, or hyperuricemia, and 43% of people in this subgroup whose body mass index (BMI) was > 25 kg/m^2.[56]

An association between IR and CV disease has been demonstrated using various measures. For example, some but not all prospective studies reported that hyperinsulinemia predicts the development of CV outcomes.[57] One meta-analysis of epidemiologic studies (not restricted to people with diabetes) demonstrated a weak relationship between hyperinsulinemia and CV disease[58]; this is supported by at least one study showing that hyperinsulinemia predicted future ischemic stroke.[59] Despite these observations, few prospective studies in nondiabetic people showing that a direct measure of IR predicts CV events have been published.[60] Although many of these studies were not done in individuals with diabetes, the fact that IR is a predictor of diabetes,[61,62] and the possibility that IR may be confounded with both diabetes and CV disease, strongly suggests that it is an important risk factor for CV disease.

Other Risk Factors

Several other traditional and emerging risk factors increase the risk of CV disease in people with diabetes. These include age, male gender, smoking,[23] advanced glycation end (AGE) products, obesity and abdominal obesity, elevated homocysteine and lipoprotein(a) levels, low birth weight, and low socioeconomic status. Many of these have not been studied exclusively in diabetic populations; nevertheless, accumulating evidence supports the general conclusion that CV risk factors are similar for diabetic and nondiabetic individuals.

How Can Cardiovascular Diseases Be Detected in a Clinical Setting?

As in all areas of clinical medicine, the history and physical examination provide important clues to the presence of CV disease. Although patients with diabetes may have a lower incidence of typical symptoms of angina than nondiabetic patients, they clearly may have typical symptoms and should be investigated accordingly. Moreover, because they have diabetes, the "index of suspicion" for CV disease and the intensity of inquiry should be higher than for nondiabetic patients. Indeed, as noted previously, the risk for serious CV events in diabetic people with no previous CV event is comparable to the risk in nondiabetic people with a previous event.[15,16]

This higher index of suspicion is also appropriate in the emergency department. This is illustrated in a recent report from a registry of 434,877 patients admitted to hospital with a confirmed MI in the United States, in which 33% did not have chest pain on presentation.[63] People with no chest pain were 1.21 times more likely to have diabetes than no diabetes (95% CI 1.19 to 1.23); other independent risk factors for a presentation with no chest pain included female gender (odds ratio [OR] = 1.06, 95% CI 1.04 to 1.08); non-white ethnicity (OR = 1.05, 95% CI 1.03 to 1.07); 10-year increment in age (OR = 1.28, 95% CI 1.26 to 1.30); prior stroke (OR = 1.43; 95% CI 1.40 to 1.47); and prior heart failure (OR = 1.77, 95% CI 1.74 to 1.81). Of most concern was the observation that these individuals had a 21% higher in-hospital mortality than those with chest pain (after adjustment for other risk factors), possibly due to differences in therapy provided in the absence of pain. Based on data reported in this article, in people with diabetes the sensitivity of chest pain for MI is only 62%.

Although several factors have been identified that may potentially affect the diagnostic properties of tests for CV disease in people with diabetes, there is no consistent evidence that these tests perform differently in this population. Thus, the approach used to diagnose CV disease in people with diabetes should be similar to that used in nondiabetic individuals.[64,65]

Evidence-Based Message

In patients with diabetes, a history of chest pain is an unreliable test for the presence of MI (Level 1).[63]

Does Glycemic Control Prevent or Delay Cardiovascular Disease?

As discussed above, several large prospective studies of people with diabetes have demonstrated that hyperglycemia is a continuous risk factor for CV events. That is, there is a progressive incremental relationship between glucose level (as measured by the HbA_{1c}) and the subsequent incidence of CV disease.[29–33] Although it is of key importance, this observation does not necessarily mean that hyperglycemia is a modifiable risk factor and that strategies that lower glucose levels in an individual or group of individuals will prevent or delay CV events. Such a conclusion can only be inferred with certainty from randomized controlled trials, in which the risk of CV events in those allocated or not allocated to optimal metabolic control is compared.

Trials in People at Relatively Low Risk for Cardiovascular Events

As discussed throughout this book, several trials of the effect of intensive glycemic control in individuals with either Type 1 or Type 2 diabetes who are at relatively low risk for CV events have now been published. Unfortunately, most of these trials tested the effect of glycemic control on eye and kidney disease; few were designed or powered to detect the effect of metabolic control on CV events. Nevertheless, CV events were measured as an additional outcome.

Studies of glycemic control in people with Type 1 diabetes have all been done in relatively young individuals, who are at low risk of CV events; thus, very large studies would be required to detect a clinically important benefit of glycemic control on CV events in this group. Although studies of sufficient size have not been done, the Diabetes Control and Complications Trial (DCCT) reported a nonsignificant reduction in the number of CV events in the group receiving intensified (0.5 events/100 person-years) versus conventional (0.8 events/100 person-years) insulin therapy.[66] When these results were meta-analyzed with the results from other trials in people with Type 1 diabetes (Table 24–4), intensified therapy was associated with a 45% reduction in the total number of CV events (OR = 0.55, 95% CI 0.35 to 0.88) and a nonsignificant 28% reduction (OR = 0.72, 95% CI 0.44 to 1.17) in the risk of a first event.[67]

The UKPDS was the first major trial to assess the effects on clinically important outcomes of a policy of intensive versus conventional glycemic control in people with Type 2 diabetes. Cardiovascular events were measured as a secondary outcome. In the main study of 3,867 individuals with newly diagnosed diabetes, a fasting plasma glucose < 6 mmol/L was targeted by initial therapy with either a sulfonylurea or insulin; other agents were added when needed. As a result, the intensive group achieved a median HbA$_{1c}$ of 7.0% over a 10-year period and the conventional group achieved a median HbA$_{1c}$ of 7.9% during this same period.[68] There was a strong trend toward a reduced risk of MI with an observed relative risk reduction (RRR) of 16% (95% CI 0 to 29%, $p = .052$). The results for the group initially randomized to insulin were similar to the results for the intensive group as a whole.

Unfortunately, the UKPDS investigators could not maintain stable degrees of glycemia: the median HbA$_{1c}$ in the intervention group was 6.6%, 7.5%, and 8.1% in the first, second, and third 5-year intervals, respectively. The median HbA$_{1c}$ in the conventional group during these 3 periods was 7.4%, 8.4%, and 8.7%, respectively. Therefore, the UKPDS essentially showed that delaying the rise in HbA$_{1c}$ by 5 years and maintaining good control for at least the first 5 years may reduce the risk of MI.

In a separate randomization of 1,704 obese participants in 15 UKPDS centers, 342 participants were allocated to intensive control with metformin, 951 to sulfonylureas or insulin, and 411 to conventional control.[69] The median HbA$_{1c}$ was 7.4% in the metformin and other intensive group and 8.0% in the conventional group during the first 10 years of follow-up. Despite a more modest separation in HbA$_{1c}$, the metformin group had a 39% risk reduction in MI (see Table 24–4). Of concern, however, was the observation that in another randomization the addition of metformin to sulfonylureas almost doubled the risk of diabetes-related death. Although this surprising observation was not apparent after a combined analysis with the "metformin-first" randomization and with epidemiologic analysis of the data, it remains unexplained and has led to uncertainty regarding the best treatment approach to prevent CV events.

Finally, the UKPDS reported the effect of the intervention on MI and not on a combined CV outcome, making it difficult to compare with other studies of CV protection. Moreover, in the main randomization of obese and nonobese individuals, the effect of the intervention on the risk of stroke and mortality was much more modest. Indeed, when a combined CV outcome of MI, stroke, or CV death is calculated from the data in the article (assuming that CV death accounted for 80% of all death), only an 8.8% reduction in CV events is noted. A similar calculation for the randomization of obese participants also yielded more modest results.

When these results are considered in the context of several other smaller trials of glycemic control in people with Type 2 DM (summarized in Table 24–4), no final conclusion regarding the CV benefits of glycemic control is possible. However, these studies provide strong support for the hypothesis that glucose lowering by a variety of therapies may prevent CV events and certainly does not increase them.

Table 24-4 Glucose Lowering Trials and Cardiovascular Disease in People with Diabetes Mellitus

Participants	F/U (y)	HbA$_{1c}$* (intense)	HbA$_{1c}$ (control)	Therapy	Outcome	RRR (% [95% CI])
Type 2 DM (UK Prospective Diabetes Study Group)[68]	10	7.0%	7.9%	Insulin/SU	MI	16% (0, 29)
Obese Type 2 DM (UK Prospective Diabetes Study Group)[69]	10.7	7.4%	8.0%	Metformin	MI	39% (11, 59)
Thin Type 2 DM (Ohkubo et al)[75]	6	7.1%	9.4%	Insulin	CV events	46% (N/A)
Type 2 DM (Abraira et al)[76]	2.3	7.1%	9.3%	Insulin/SU	CV events	−40% (5, −108)
Type 2 DM (Genuth)[77]	12.5	FPG 7.2–8.1 mmol/L	FPG 9.4–10.3 mmol/L	Insulin	CV deaths	9% (N/A)
Post MI Type 2 DM† (Malmberg et al)[71]	3	7.1%	7.9%	Insulin	Mortality	28% (8, 45)
Type 1 DM* (Lawson et al)[67]	2–7	7.6%	8.7%	Insulin	Any event	45% (22, 65)
Type 1 DM* (Lawson et al)[67]	2–7	7.6%	8.7%	Insulin	First event	28% (−17, 56)

*From a meta-analysis of all studies of tight control in Type 1 DM.
†From the variable insulin dose arm of the University Group Diabetes Program.
DM = diabetes mellitus; RRR = relative risk reduction; CI = confidence interval; MI = myocardial infarction; CV = cardiovascular; FPG = fasting plasma glucose; SU = sulfonylurea; N/A = data not available, but results described as not significant in the report.

Of note, however, is the fact that the benefits of tight glycemic control cannot be definitively established even in the setting of a very positive clinical trial. This is because it is very difficult to determine whether the positive result was due to the strategy (or drug) used to achieve the glycemic control or to the difference in glycemic control itself. Indeed, the differential effects of metformin and of insulin and sulfonylureas in obese people in the UKPDS have been cited to support the possibility that it was metformin and not glycemic control that was effective.[70] Such a dilemma may be resolved with further epidemiologic studies demonstrating a reduction in CV events with reduced HbA$_{1c}$ and by further clinical trials of the effects of glucose lowering. This dilemma is not restricted to assessments of glucose-lowering strategies; it occurs whenever a continuous risk factor is being targeted and measured as part of the response to therapy. Examples of risk factors that can be reduced by interventions that may also reduce CV events include LDL cholesterol, blood pressure, and the albumin excretion rate.

EVIDENCE-BASED MESSAGE

Randomized trials done to date only suggest (but do not prove) that intensified insulin therapy may reduce the risk of CV events in people with Type 1 diabetes (Level 2)[67] and that a policy of targeting intensive glycemic control with insulin or oral agents may reduce the risk of CV events in Type 2 diabetes (Level 2).[68,69]

Trials in People at Particularly High Risk for Cardiovascular Events

Only one clinical trial has assessed the benefit of glucose lowering in high-risk people with Type 2 diabetes (see Table 24–4). In this trial, 620 people with Type 2 diabetes were randomly assigned to either receive a 24-hour infusion of insulin followed by multiple daily injections of insulin for at least 3 months or to usual post-MI therapy.[71] After 1 year, total mortality in the treatment group was reduced by 29% (95% CI 4 to 51%, $p = .028$); this effect was maintained after 3.4 years[72] and was most pronounced in individuals without a previous history of insulin use. Moreover, by 3.4 years there was an absolute risk reduction of 11%: one life was saved for every 9 people treated. The results of this study were supported by a meta-analysis of the benefits of an infusion of glucose, insulin, and potassium on mortality after MI in mainly nondiabetic people[73] and by a subgroup analysis of a recent clinical trial.[74] Despite these promising results, it is important to note that despite the benefit regarding mortality, the intervention did not prevent recurrent MI; thus, the effect on CV events per se remains unclear.

EVIDENCE-BASED MESSAGE

Administration of a program of insulin infusion followed by ambulatory intensive insulin therapy after an MI reduces mortality by 30% in people with Type 2 diabetes (Level 1A).[71,72]

WHAT NONGLYCEMIC THERAPIES CAN PREVENT OR DELAY CARDIOVASCULAR DISEASE?

Several interventions may effectively prevent or delay CV events in the general population. These include smoking cessation, aspirin therapy, blood pressure and lipid therapy, weight loss, and exercise. When the effects of various therapies have been examined in diabetic and nondiabetic subgroups, similar benefits are generally observed; thus, it is reasonable to extrapolate observed benefits to people with diabetes, unless there is a specific reason not to do so. Evidence for the benefit of those interventions for which there are specific data in diabetes is reviewed below.

Blood Pressure Reduction

Recent clinical trials highlight the importance of blood pressure control[78–81,83] (Table 24–5) and clearly support the conclusion that tight blood pressure control will prevent CV disease in patients with DM. Moreover, a further analysis of the UKPDS (not yet published) showed that the effects of blood pressure control and glycemic control are independent.

Table 24-5 Blood Pressure Lowering Trials and Cardiovascular Disease in People with Type 2 Diabetes Mellitus

Study	Length (y)	BP in Rx	BP in Control	First Therapy	Outcome	RRR (crude, %)	RRR (paper, %)
UKPDS (UK Prospective Diabetes Study Group)[78]	9	144/82	154/87	Captopril or atenolol	CV events + S MI Stroke	29 20 42	N/A 21 44
SHEP (Curb et al)[79]	4.5	145/70	155/70	Chlorthalidone and atenolol	CV events Stroke	45 26	56 22
Syst-Eur (Tuomilehto et al)[80]	2	153/78	162/82	Nitrendipine	CV events Stroke	60 68	62 69
HOT (Hansson et al)[81]	3.8	140/81	144/85	Felodipine	CV events + S	51	52
ABCD (Estacio et al)[83]	5.3	138/86	132/78	Nisoldipine	Death	49	N/A
Cochrane (P) (Fuller et al)[84]	5	—	—	Various	CV mortality and morbidity	30 (95% CI 14, 42)	—
Cochrane (Sec) (Fuller et al)[84]	≥1	—	—	Various	CV mortality and morbidity	11 (95% CI –5, 26)	—

BP = blood pressure; RRR = relative risk reduction; CV = cardiovascular; MI = myocardial infarction; CI = confidence interval; P = primary, Sec = secondary prevention: S = stroke; SHEP = Systolic Hypertension in the Elderly Program; Syst-Eur = Systolic Hypertension in Europe Trial; HOT = Hypertension Optimal Treatment; ABCD = Appropriate Blood Pressure Control in Diabetes.

EVIDENCE-BASED MESSAGE

In people with diabetes, interventions with diuretics, beta-blockers, calcium-channel blockers, and angiotensin converting enzyme (ACE) inhibitors that decrease systolic blood pressure by 5 to 10 mm Hg result in a 20 to 30% RRR in CV events (Level 1A).[78–81,83,84]

Choice of Agent Used for Blood Pressure Reduction

Whether or not different classes of blood pressure lowering drugs have different effects on CV outcomes in people with DM has been addressed in several trials that reported outcomes in diabetic participants (Table 24–6). Angiotensin converting enzyme inhibitors were superior to calcium-channel blockers in the Fosinopril versus Amlodipine Cardiovascular Events Randomized Trial (FACET) and the Appropriate Blood Pressure Control in Diabetes (ABCD) trials.[82,85] They were also superior to diuretics and/or beta-blockers in the Captopril Primary Prevention Project (CAPPP), despite the fact that achieved blood pressures were slightly higher in the captopril group than in the diuretic/beta blocker group.[86] Conversely, the UKPDS study did not detect any difference between the effects of captopril and atenolol on CV outcomes.[87] A recent meta-analysis of the results of CAPPP, FACET, and ABCD reported that ACE inhibitors provided an overall benefit for MI (RR 0.37, 95% CI 0.24 to 0.57), CV events (RR 0.49, 95% CI 0.36 to 0.67), and all-cause death (RR 0.57, 95% CI 0.36 to 0.67). Inclusion of the UKPDS results did not substantially affect the conclusion, although they were not included in the final meta-analysis because of statistical heterogeneity.[86]

Although results specific to the diabetes subgroup were not reported, the Swedish Trial in Old Patients with Hypertension-2 (STOP-2) included 719 patients with diabetes and

Table 24–6 Trials That Compared Different Agents for Blood Pressure Lowering

	N (DM)	F/U (y)	Entry BP	Outcome	Therapies Tested	RR	p Value
UKPDS[87]	758	9	159/94	MI	Captopril vs atenolol	1.20	0.35
ABCD*[82]	470	5.6	156/98	MI	Enalapril vs nisoldipine	0.18	0.001
CAPPP[86]	572	6.1	163/97	MI/stroke/ CV death	Captopril vs diuretic/β-blockers	0.59	0.019
FACET[85]	380	2.5	170/95	MI/stroke/ Angina	Fosinopril vs amoldipine	0.49	0.03
STOP-2*[89]	719	5	194/98	CV death	ACE-I/CCB vs diuretic/ β-blockers	0.99	0.89
					ACE-I vs diuretic/ β-blockers	1.01	0.89
					CCB vs diuretic/β-blockers	0.97	0.72
					ACE-I vs CCB	1.04	0.67
ALLHAT[90]	8,664	3.3	145/84	CV events (see text)	Doxazosin vs chlorthalidone	1.24	0.001

*No difference was observed for the diabetes subgroup but actual numbers not published.

F/U = follow-up; RR = relative risk; MI = myocardial infarction; UKPDS = United Kingdom Prospective Diabetes Study; DM = diabetes mellitus; CCB = calcium-channel blocker; ACE-I = ACE inhibitor; ABCD = Appropriate Blood Pressure Control in Diabetes; CAPPP = Captopril Primary Prevention Project; FACET = Fosinopril vs Amoldipine Cardiovascular Events Randomized Trial; STOP-2 = Swedish Trial in Old Patients with Hypertension (no difference in blood pressure change was observed on therapy); ALLHAT = Antihypertensive and Lipid-Lowering Treatment to Prevent Heart Attack.

reported that results in the diabetic subgroup did not differ from the group as a whole. In this study, no difference in CV mortality was reported for patients randomized to either (1) diuretics and/or beta-blockers, (2) ACE inhibitors, or (3) calcium antagonists.[89] As this result clearly conflicts with the results from previous studies, any conclusions regarding the superiority of ACE inhibitors over other therapies need to be regarded as preliminary.

The Antihypertensive and Lipid-Lowering Treatment to Prevent Heart Attack (ALL-HAT) trial randomized participants aged 55 and older with hypertension and at least one other coronary heart disease risk factor to receive chlorthalidone, amlodipine, lisinopril, or doxazosin in a double-blind fashion; it is due to be finished in 2002. Recently, however, after 3.3 years of follow-up, the doxazosin arm was stopped on the recommendation of the external monitoring committee after an analysis of the 24,335 people in the doxazosin and chlorthalidone groups. This interim analysis revealed a higher risk of secondary outcomes, including stroke (RR = 1.19, 95% CI 1.01 to 1.40, $p = .04$) and either CV death, stroke, revascularization, angina, heart failure, or peripheral arterial disease (RR = 1.25, 95% CI 1.17 to 1.33; $p < .001$), the latter being due to a twofold higher risk of congestive heart failure (CHF) (RR = 2.04, 95% CI 1.79 to 2.32, $p < .001$); it also revealed higher risks for angina, coronary revascularization, and peripheral arterial disease.[90] In the 8,664 individuals with diabetes and hypertension, the RR for CV events was 1.24 (95% CI 1.12 to 1.38; $p < .001$).

EVIDENCE-BASED MESSAGES

1. Some[82,85,86] but not all[87,89] large trials suggest that ACE inhibitors may be superior to calcium-channel blockers when used to treat hypertension in people with DM (Level 1A).
2. When used as first-line therapy to treat hypertension in people with DM, alpha-blockers lead to a 20% higher risk of CV events than do diuretics (Level 1A).[90]

Low-Density Lipoprotein Reduction Using "Statins"

Despite the high risk of CVD in patients with Type 2 DM, few trials of lipid lowering explicitly included patients with diabetes. The best data are therefore from "post hoc" subanalyses of diabetic patients who were enrolled in these trials: unfortunately, the data from primary prevention are sparse and more are needed. Table 24–7 summarizes the results from the major primary and secondary prevention trials for which there are reported data on diabetic participants. Taken together, the data support recommendations to lower LDL.[91] They indicate that for patients who have had previous CHD, therapy with either simvastatin, pravastatin, or lovastatin reduces the risk of CV events by 20 to 30% for a 20 to 30% reduction in LDL; a more explicit analysis of the 4S study reported a 1.7% risk reduction for every 1% decrease in LDL-C.[92]

EVIDENCE-BASED MESSAGE

Although trials done specifically in patients with diabetes are lacking, subgroup analyses of the available trials suggest that in patients with DM and modestly elevated LDL levels, therapy with the "statin" class of agents reduces the risk of CV events by 20 to 30% (Level 2).[93–99]

Fibrates

Mean total and LDL cholesterol levels in individuals with diabetes are comparable to levels in nondiabetic individuals. Individuals with diabetes are nevertheless dyslipidemic. This dyslipidemia is characterized by high triglyceride levels and low HDL levels as well as high concentrations of small, dense LDL particles (detectable by a high apolipoprotein B level). This suggests that interventions that lower triglyceride and raise HDL levels may be particularly effective in individuals with diabetes. At least three large trials using fibrates—a group of medications that can target these levels—have now been reported, which include modest numbers of individuals with diabetes (Table 24–8).

Table 24–7 Low-Density Lipoprotein Lowering Trials with "Statins" and Cardiovascular Disease in People with Type 2 Diabetes Mellitus

Study	N (DM)	Mean Age (y)	F/U (y)	LDL (mmol/L) Baseline	LDL (mmol/L) Change (%)	Therapy	Outcome	RRR (%)
Primary prevention								
WOSCOPS (Shepherd et al)[93]	76	55	4.9	5.0	–26	Pravastatin	CHD death, nonfatal MI	N/A for DM
AFCAPS/TEXCAPS (Downs et al)[94]	155	58	5.2	3.9	–25	Lovastatin	CHD death, nonfatal MI, angina	37
Secondary prevention								
4S (Pyorala et al)[95]	202	60	5.5	4.8	–34	Simvastatin	CHD death, nonfatal MI	55
CARE (Sacks et al,[96] Goldberg et al)[97]	586	61	4.9	3.5	–27	Pravastatin	CHD death, nonfatal MI	13
LIPID (The Long-Term Intervention with Pravastatin in Ischaemic Disease Study Group)[98]	782	62	6.1	3.8	–25	Pravastatin	CHD death, nonfatal MI	19
Post-CABG (Hoogwerf et al)[99]	116	63	4.3	3.9	–38	Lovastatin (aggressive vs moderate)	CV death, MI, stroke, revascularized	47

F/U = follow-up; LDL = low-density lipoprotein; RRR = relative risk reduction; CHD = congenital heart disease; MI = myocardial infarction; WOSCOPS = West of Scotland Coronary Prevention Study; AFCAPS/TEXCAPS = Air Force/Texas Coronary Atherosclerosis Prevention Study; 4S = Scandinavian Simvastatin Survival Study; CARE = Cholesterol and Recurrent Events Trial; Post-CABG = Post-Coronary Artery Bypass Graft Trial.

Table 24–8 Recent Large Trials with "Fibrates" and Cardiovascular Disease in People with Type 2 Diabetes Mellitus

Study	N (DM)	Mean Age (y)	F/U (y)	Initial Level	Change (%) LDL	TG	HDL	Drug	Outcome	RRR (%)
Helsinki (P) (Koskinen et al;[100] Frick et al)[101]	135 men	49	5	LDL: 5.2	−10	−26	6	Gemfibrozil	CHD death, nonfatal MI	68
VA-HIT (Sec) (Rubins et al)[102]	627 men	64	5.1	LDL: 2.91 TG: 1.76 HDL: 0.83	0	−31	6	Gemfibrozil	CHD death, stroke, nonfatal MI	24
BIP (Sec)[103]	309 (90% men)	60	6.2	LDL: 3.85 TG: 1.64 HDL: 0.90	−6.5	−20.6	17.9	Bezafibrate	MI or sudden death	9*

*Risk reductions are for the group as a whole; diabetic subgroup results are not reported.

DM = diabetes mellitus; F/U = follow-up; LDL = low-density lipoprotein; TG = triglycerides; HDL = high-density lipoprotein; RRR = relative risk reduction; CHD = congenital heart disease; MI = myocardial infarction; Helsinki = Helsinki Heart Study; VA-HIT = Veterans Affairs HDL Cholesterol Intervention Trial; BIP = Bezafibrate Infarction Prevention Study; Sec = secondary prevention; p = primary prevention.

The Helsinki Heart Study was a primary prevention trial of the effect of fibrates on CV disease that included only 135 people with diabetes.[100,101] Participants were randomized to take either gemfibrozil or placebo and were followed for 5 years. Gemfibrozil-treated individuals experienced a lower LDL cholesterol and triglyceride level and a raised HDL cholesterol level compared to placebo-treated individuals; the results in the (small) diabetic subgroup were consistent with the overall results.[101] The Veterans Affairs HDL Cholesterol Intervention Trial (VA-HIT trial)[102] indicated that gemfibrozil reduced CV events by 24% in diabetic men with CHD and mean LDL cholesterol levels of 2.91 mmol/L. Conversely, the Bezafibrate Infarction Prevention Study (BIP) did not demonstrate a benefit of fibrates. Taken together, these trials support the hypothesis that fibrate-mediated triglyceride lowering and HDL raising can reduce the risk of CV events.

EVIDENCE-BASED MESSAGE

Although trials done specifically in patients with diabetes are lacking, subgroup analyses of the available trials suggest that in patients with DM, therapy with the "fibrate" class of agents may reduce the risk of CV events (Level 2).[100–103]

Angiotensin Converting Enzyme Inhibitors

There is a large body of biologic and epidemiologic evidence implicating the renin-angiotensin-kallikrein system and the effects of ACE in the etiology of CV disease. The possibility that ACE inhibitors may prevent CV events in people with diabetes was explicitly tested in the HOPE study, which randomized 9,541 people (age 55 or over) to the addition of the ACE inhibitor ramipril or placebo and followed them for 4.5 years.[104] This study included 3,654 people with diabetes and either previous CV disease or one or more CV risk factors; the effect of ramipril on the subgroup with diabetes was prespecified as a study question.[26] It was not a study of blood pressure lowering with ramipril; indeed, only 56% of diabetic participants were hypertensive at randomization, and the mean blood pressure at that time was 140/80.

The HOPE trial observed a clear 25% reduction in the combined aggregate outcome of MI, stroke, or CV death and clear reductions in each of the component outcomes (Table 24–9); moreover, this benefit could not be accounted for on the basis of the modest change in blood pressure that was observed. On the basis of this study, 15 high-risk middle-aged people with diabetes would have to be treated with ramipril for 4.5 years to prevent one significant CV event. This study clearly established the benefit of ACE inhibitors as a CV disease preventive therapy for high-risk people with diabetes.

EVIDENCE-BASED MESSAGE

The addition of ACE inhibitors to other effective therapies reduces the risk of CV events by 25% in high-risk people with diabetes (Level 1A).[26]

Acetylsalicylic Acid

Acetylsalicylic acid (ASA), or aspirin, has both antiplatelet and anti-inflammatory activity and has been shown to prevent CV events in a broad range of individuals when used in people with and without a history of CV disease. Although large trials restricted to people with DM have not been done, the effects of ASA in individuals with DM have been carefully summarized and show similar effects.[105] For example, the Physician's Health study[106]—a primary prevention trial using alternate-day therapy with 325 mg of ASA—demonstrated that ASA reduced MI by 44% ($p < .00001$). In a subgroup analysis of the 533 people with DM, it was shown that the diabetic subgroup experienced a 61% reduction in MI during 5 years of follow-up (an effect size that was statistically similar to the 40% reduction in the nondiabetic group). In a meta-analysis of all 145 secondary prevention trials in which the most commonly used dose was 75 to 325 mg/d,[107] the subgroup of people with DM had reductions in

Table 24–9 Results of the HOPE Study in Diabetic Participants

Outcome	Placebo Rate (%)	RRR (% [95% CI])	p Value
MI, stroke, or CV death	19.8	25 (12–36)	.0004
MI	12.9	22 (6–36)	.01
Stroke	6.1	33 (10–50)	.0074
CV death	9.7	37 (21–51)	.0001
Total death	14	24 (8–37)	.004

HOPE = Heart Outcomes Prevention Evaluation Study; RRR = relative risk reduction; CI = confidence interval; MI = myocardial infarction; CV = cardiovascular.

MI, stroke, or vascular deaths from aspirin that were similar to the group as a whole. These data therefore strongly support the conclusion that aspirin therapy prevents CV disease in people with DM. Based on these data, aspirin therapy is recommended for all high-risk people for prevention of CV events.[108]

Evidence-Based Message

> Although trials done specifically in patients with diabetes are lacking, aspirin therapy (75 to 325 mg/d) reduces the risk of CV events in high-risk people with DM (Level 1A).[106,107]

Beta-Blockers

It is now well established that beta-blockers will reduce mortality following an acute MI; they also reduce mortality in people with congestive heart failure.[109–115] The fact that beta-blockers shift myocardial substrate utilization from free fatty acids toward more oxygen-efficient glucose oxidation and also lower heart rate, may be of special importance in people with DM.

Despite these benefits, beta-blockers have traditionally been avoided in people with DM because of early fears (based on experiences with nonselective beta-blockers) that they would worsen metabolic control, mask early symptoms of hypoglycemia, and lead to serious hypoglycemic events due to suppression of counter-regulatory mechanisms.[116–121] These problems have been shown to be much less likely with beta-one selective agents.[120–122] Indeed, although trials have not been done exclusively in people with DM, analysis of the diabetic subgroups from large recent post-MI trials and epidemiologic studies have clearly shown that the benefit for people with DM is either equal to or greater than the benefit in nondiabetic people. Table 24–10 lists the results of the trials that reported outcomes in the diabetic participants.

Evidence-Based Message

> Although trials done specifically in patients with diabetes are lacking, subgroup analyses from available studies show a consistent mortality reduction due to beta-blockers of 30 to 40% in diabetic patients with established coronary artery disease (Level 2).[109–114]

Conclusion

Cardiovascular disease represents the most frequent diabetes-related complication. Based on recent therapy, up to 70% of people with diabetes will eventually die of CV disease,[1] compared to 49% of men in the general population.[123] There is now clear evidence based on clinical trials that new therapeutic approaches can clearly prevent or delay CV events in people with diabetes. The challenge for the future is to both ensure that these approaches are available and that new approaches continue to be studied and identified.

Table 24–10 Large Trials and Epidemiologic Studies (Post-Myocardial Infarction) of the Effect of Beta-Blockers on Mortality

	% DM	N (DM)	Follow-up (Mo)	Beta-Blocker	Estimated Risk Reduction
Acute therapy					
Gothenburg Metoprolol[111]	8.6	120	3	Metoprolol	0.41 (0.14–1.18)
MIAMI[111]	7.1	413	0.5	Metoprolol	0.5 (0.25–0.98)
ISIS-1[112]	6.0	958	0.25	Atenolol	0.76 (0.47–1.24)
Chronic therapy					
Norwegian Timolol[109]	5.5	99	17	Timolol	0.31 (0.12–0.82)
BHAT[110]	12.1	465	25	Propranolol	0.61 (0.35–1.08)

DM = diabetes mellitus; MIAMI = Metoprolol In Acute Myocardial Infarction Trial; ISIS-1 = First International Study of Infarct Survival; BHAT = Beta-blocker Heart Attack Trial.

SUMMARY OF EVIDENCE-BASED MESSAGES

1. Diabetes is an independent risk factor for future CV events in the general population (Level 1).[4,5,14]

2. Diabetes is an independent risk factor for future CV events in people with previous CV disease. People with diabetes who have had a previous CV event or who have evidence of CV disease are two to three times more likely to have subsequent CV events than are diabetic people with no previous CV event (Level 1).[15–19,20,22,24–26]

3. The plasma glucose level is a continuous risk factor for CV events in people with Type 1 and Type 2 diabetes (Level 1).[22,23,29–35,43,44]

4. Low-density lipoprotein cholesterol is a continuous risk factor for CV events in people with diabetes (Level 1).[23]

5. Elevated blood pressure is a continuous risk factor for CV events in people with diabetes (Level 1).[4,22–24,32,49–51]

6. Microalbuminuria doubles the risk of cardiovascular events in people with diabetes (Level 1).[26,53]

7. Clinical proteinuria consistent with diabetic nephropathy increases the risk of CV events and total mortality greater than twofold (Level 1).[32,33]

8. Proliferative retinopathy, macular edema, visual impairment, and cataracts are risk factors for ischemic heart disease mortality in people with Type 1 and Type 2 DM (Level 1).[55]

9. In patients with diabetes, a history of chest pain is an unreliable test for the presence of MI (Level 1).[63]

10. Randomized trials done to date only suggest (but do not prove) that intensified insulin therapy may reduce the risk of CV events in people with Type 1 diabetes (Level 2)[67] and that a policy of targeting intensive glycemic control with insulin or oral agents may reduce the risk of CV events in Type 2 diabetes (Level 2).[68,69]

11. Administration of a program of insulin infusion followed by ambulatory intensive insulin therapy after an MI reduces mortality by 30% in people with Type 2 diabetes (Level 1A).[71,72]

12. In people with diabetes, interventions with diuretics, beta-blockers, calcium-channel blockers, and ACE inhibitors that decrease systolic blood pressure by 5 to 10 mm Hg result in a 20 to 30% RRR in CV events (Level 1A).[78–81,84]

13. Some[82,85,86] but not all[87,89] large trials suggest that ACE inhibitors may be superior to calcium-channel blockers when used to treat hypertension in people with DM (Level 1A).

14. When used as first-line therapy to treat hypertension in people with DM, alpha-blockers lead to a 20% higher risk of CV events than do diuretics (Level 1A).[90]

15. Although trials done specifically in patients with diabetes are lacking, subgroup analyses of the available trials suggest that in patients with DM and modestly elevated LDL levels, therapy with the "statin" class of agents reduces the risk of CV events by 20 to 30% (Level 2).[93–99]

16. Although trials done specifically in patients with diabetes are lacking, subgroup analyses of the available trials suggest that in patients with DM, therapy with the "fibrate" class of agents may reduce the risk of CV events (Level 2).[100–103]

17. The addition of ACE inhibitors to other effective therapies reduces the risk of CV events by 25% in high-risk people with diabetes (Level 1A).[26]

18. Although trials done specifically in patients with diabetes are lacking, aspirin therapy (75 to 325 mg/d) reduces the risk of CV events in high-risk people with DM (Level 1A).[106,107]

19. Although trials done specifically in patients with diabetes are lacking, subgroup analyses from available studies show a consistent mortality reduction due to beta-blockers of 30 to 40% in diabetic patients with established coronary artery disease (Level 2).[109–114]

REFERENCES

1. Laakso M. Hyperglycemia and cardiovascular disease in type 2 diabetes. Diabetes 1999;48:937–42.

2. Wingard DL, Barrett-Connor E. Heart disease and diabetes. In: Harris MI, Cowie CC, Stern MS, et al, editors. Diabetes in America. Washington, DC: National Institutes of Health; 1995. p. 429–48.

3. Gu K, Cowie CC, Harris MI. Diabetes and decline in heart disease mortality in US adults. JAMA 1999;281:1291–7.

4. Stamler J, Vaccaro O, Neaton JD, Wentworth D. Diabetes, other risk factors, and 12-yr cardiovascular mortality for men screened in the Multiple Risk Factor Intervention Trial. Diabetes Care 1993;16:434–44.

5. Kannel WB, McGee DL. Diabetes and cardiovascular disease. The Framingham Study. JAMA 1979;241:2035–8.

6. Fuller JH, Shipley MJ, Rose G, et al. Mortality from coronary heart disease and stroke in relation to degree of glycemia: the Whitehall study. BMJ 1983;287:867–70.

7. Barrett-Connor E, Cohn BA, Wingard DL, Edelstein SL. Why is diabetes mellitus a stronger risk factor for fatal ischemic heart disease in women than in men? The Rancho Bernardo Study. JAMA 1991;265:627–31.

8. Goldbourt U, Yaari S, Medalie JH. Factors predictive of long-term coronary heart disease mortality among 10,059 male Israeli civil servants and municipal employees. A 23 year mortality follow-up in the Israeli Ischemic Heart Disease Study. Cardiology 1993;82:100–21.

9. Manson JE, Coldlitz GA, Stampfer MJ, et al. A prospective study of maturity-onset diabetes mellitus and risk of coronary heart disease and stroke in women. Arch Intern Med 1991;151:1141–7.

10. Morrish NJ, Stevens LK, Fuller JH, et al. Incidence of macrovascular disease in diabetes mellitus: the London follow-up to the WHO multinational study of vascular disease in diabetics. Diabetologia 1991;34:584–9.

11. ETDRS Investigators. Aspirin effects on mortality and morbidity in patients with diabetes mellitus. Early treatment of diabetic retinopathy study report 14. JAMA 1992;266:1292–300.

12. Damsgaard EM, Froland A, Jorgensen OD, Mogensen CE. Eight to nine year mortality in known non-insulin dependent diabetes and controls. Kidney Int 1992;42:731–5.

13. Neil A, Hawkins M, Potok M, et al. A prospective population-based study of microalbuminuria as a predictor of mortality in NIDDM. Diabetes Care 1993;16:996–1003.

14. Chen YT, Vaccarino V, Williams CS, et al. Risk factors for heart failure in the elderly: a prospective community-based study. Am J Med 1999;106:605–12.

15. Haffner SM, Lehto S, Ronnemaa T, et al. Mortality from coronary heart disease in subjects with type 2 diabetes and in nondiabetic subjects with and without prior myocardial infarction. N Engl J Med 1998;339:229–34.

16. Malmberg K, Yusuf S, Gerstein HC, et al. Impact of diabetes on long-term prognosis in patients with unstable angina and non-Q-wave myocardial infarction: results of the OASIS (Organization to Assess Strategies for Ischemic Syndromes) registry. Circulation 2000;102:1014–9.

17. Behar S, Boyko EJ, Reicher-Reiss H, Goldbourt U. Ten year survival after acute myocardial infarction: comparison of patients with and without diabetes. Am Heart J 1997;133:290–6.

18. Mak KH, Moliterno DJ, Granger CB, et al. Influence of diabetes mellitus on clinical outcome in the thrombolytic era of acute myocardial infarction. GUSTO-1 investigators. Global utilization of streptokinase and tissue plasminogen activator for occluded coronary arteries. J Am Coll Cardiol 1997;30:171–9.

19. Miettinen H, Lehto S, Salomaa V, et al. Impact of diabetes on mortality after the first myocardial infarction. Diabetes Care 1998;21:69–75.

20. Melchior T, Ber L, Madsen CR, et al. Accelerating impact of diabetes mellitus on mortality in the years following an acute myocardial infarction. Eur Heart J 1999;20:973–8.

21. Yusuf S, Flather M, Pogue J, et al. Variations between countries in invasive cardiac procedures and outcomes in patients with suspected unstable angina or myocardial infarction without initial ST elevation. OASIS (Organisation to Assess Strategies for Ischaemic Syndromes) Registry Investigators. Lancet 1998;352:507–14.

22. Wei M, Gaskill SP, Haffner SM, Stern MP. Effects of diabetes and level of glycemia on all-cause and cardiovascular mortality. The San Antonio Heart Study. Diabetes Care 1998;21:1167–72.

23. Turner RC, Millns H, Neil HAW, et al. Risk factors for coronary artery disease in non-insulin dependent diabetes mellitus: United Kingdom prospective diabetes study (UKPDS: 23). BMJ 1998;316:823–8.

24. Hadden DR, Patterson CC, Atkinson AB, et al. Macrovascular disease and hyperglycaemia: 10-year survival analysis in type 2 diabetes mellitus: the Belfast Diet Study. Diabet Med 1997;14:663–72.

25. Kuller LH, Velentgas P, Barzilay J, et al. Diabetes mellitus: subclinical cardiovascular disease and risk of incident cardiovascular disease and all-cause mortality. Arterioscler Thromb Vasc Biol 2000;20:823–9.

26. Heart Outcome Prevention Evaluation (HOPE) Study Investigators. Effects of ramipril on cardiovascular and microvascular outcomes in people with diabetes mellitus: results of the HOPE study and MICRO HOPE substudy. Lancet 2000;255:253–9.

27. Shindler DM, Kostis JB, Yusuf S, et al. Diabetes mellitus, a predictor of morbidity and mortality in the Studies of Left Ventricular Dysfunction (SOLVD) Trials and Registry. Am J Cardiol 1996;77:1017–20.

28. Thourani VH, Weintraub WS, Stein B, et al. Influence of diabetes mellitus on early and late outcome after coronary artery bypass grafting. Ann Thorac Surg 1999;67:1045–52.

29. Moss SE, Klein R, Klein BEK, Meuer SM. The association of glycemia and cause-specific mortality in a diabetic population. Arch Intern Med 1994;154:2473–9.

30. Kuusisto J, Mykkanen L, Pyorala K, Laakso M. NIDDM and its metabolic control predict coronary heart disease in elderly subjects. Diabetes 1994;43:960–7.

31. Andersson DKG, Svardsudd K. Long-term glycemic control relates to mortality in Type 2 diabetes. Diabetes Care 1995;18:1534–43.

32. Gall M-A, Borch-Johnsen K, Hougaard P, et al. Albuminuria and poor glycemic control predict mortality in NIDDM. Diabetes 1995;44:1303–9.

33. Agewall S, Wikstrand J, Ljungman S, Fagerberg B, Risk Factor Intervention Study Group. Usefulness of microalbuminuria in predicting cardiovascular mortality in treated hypertensive men with and without diabetes mellitus. Am J Cardiol 1997;80:164–9.

34. Fu CC, Chang CJ, Tseng CH, et al. Development of macrovascular diseases in NIDDM patients in northern Taiwan. A 4-yr follow-up study. Diabetes Care 1993;16:137–43.

35. Stratton IM, Adler AI, Neil HA, et al. Association of glycaemia with macrovascular and microvascular complications of type 2 diabetes (UKPDS 35): prospective observational study. BMJ 2000;321:405–12.

36. Coutinho M, Gerstein HC, Wang Y, Yusuf S. The relationship between glucose and incident cardiovascular events. A metaregression analysis of published data from 20 studies of 95,783 individuals followed for 12.4 years. Diabetes Care 1999;22:233–40.

37. Gerstein HC, Pais P, Pogue J, Yusuf S. Relationship of glucose and insulin levels to the risk of myocardial infarction: a case-control study. J Am Coll Cardiol 1999;33:612–9.

38. Gerstein HC, Yusuf S. Dysglycaemia and risk of cardiovascular disease. Lancet 1996;347: 949–50.

39. Gerstein HC. Glucose: a continuous risk factor for cardiovascular disease. Diabet Med 1997;14(Suppl 3):S25–31.

40. Balkau B, Shipley M, Jarrett RJ, et al. High blood glucose concentration is a risk factor for mortality in middle-aged nondiabetic men. Diabetes Care 1998;21:360–7.

41. Bjornholt JV, Erikssen G, Aaser E, J et al. Fasting blood glucose: an underestimated risk factor for cardiovascular death. Results from a 22-year follow-up of healthy nondiabetic men. Diabetes Care 1999;22:45–9.

42. Haffner SM. The importance of hyperglycemia in the nonfasting state to the development of cardiovascular disease. Endocr Rev 1998;19:583–92.

43. Lehto S, Ronnemaa T, Haffner SM, et al. Dyslipidemia and hyperglycemia predict coronary heart disease events in middle-aged patients with NIDDM. Diabetes 1997;46:1354–9.

44. Lehto S, Ronnemaa T, Pyorala K, Laakso M. Poor glycemic control predicts coronary heart disease events in patients with type 1 diabetes without nephropathy. Arterioscler Thromb Vasc Biol 1999;19:1014–9.

45. Mykkanen L, Kuusisto J, Pyorala K, Laakso M. Cardiovascular risk factors as predictors of type 2 (non-insulin-dependent) diabetes in elderly subjects. Diabetologia 1993;36:553–9.

46. Sempos CT, Cleeman JI, Carroll MD, et al. Prevalence of high blood cholesterol among US adults. An update based on guidelines from the second report of the National Cholesterol Education Program Adult Treatment Panel. JAMA 1993;269:3009–14.

47. Giugliano D, Ceriello A, Paolisso G. Oxidative stress and diabetic complications. Diabetes Care 1996;19:257–67.

48. Cowie CC, Harris MI. Physical and metabolic characteristics of persons with diabetes. In: Harris MI, Cowie CC, Stern MS, et al, editors. Diabetes in America. NIH Publication No. 95-1468. National Institutes of Health; 1995. p. 117–64.

49. Mehler PS, Jeffers BW, Estacio R, Schrier RW. Associations of hypertension and complications in non-insulin-dependent diabetes mellitus. Am J Hypertens 1997;10:152–61.

50. Lehto S, Ronnemaa T, Pyorala K, Laakso M. Predictors of stroke in middle-aged patients with non-insulin-dependent diabetes. Stroke 1996;27:63–8.

51. Adler AI, Stratton IM, Neil HA, et al. Association of systolic blood pressure with macrovascular and microvascular complications of type 2 diabetes (UKPDS 36): prospective observational study. BMJ 2000;321:412–9.

52. Gerstein HC, Mann JF, Pogue J, et al. Prevalence and determinants of microalbuminuria in high-risk diabetic and nondiabetic patients in the Heart Outcomes Prevention Evaluation Study. The HOPE Study Investigators. Diabetes Care 2000;23(Suppl 2):B35–9.

53. Dinneen SF, Gerstein HC. The association of microalbuminuria and mortality in non-insulin-dependent diabetes mellitus. Arch Intern Med 1997;157:1413–8.

54. Klein R, Klein BE, Moss SE, Cruickshanks KJ. Association of ocular disease and mortality in a diabetic population. Arch Ophthalmol 1999;117:1487–95.

55. Hennekens CH, Buring JE. Statistical association and cause-effect relationships. In: Mayrent SL, editor. Epidemiology in medicine. Boston: Little, Brown and Company; 1987:30–53.

56. Bonora E, Kiechl S, Willeit J, et al. Prevalence of insulin resistance in metabolic disorders: the Bruneck Study. Diabetes 1998;47:1643–9.

57. Haffner SM, Miettinen H. Insulin resistance implications for Type 2 diabetes mellitus and coronary heart disease. Am J Med 1997;103:152–62.

58. Ruige JB, Assendelft WJ, Dekker JM, et al. Insulin and risk of cardiovascular disease: a meta-analysis. Circulation 1998;97:996–1001.

59. Folsom AR, Rasmussen ML, Chambless LE, et al. Prospective associations of fasting insulin, body fat distribution, and diabetes with risk of ischemic stroke. The Atherosclerosis Risk in Communities (ARIC) study investigators. Diabetes Care 1999;22:1077–83.

60. Yip J, Facchini FS, Reaven GM. Resistance to insulin-mediated glucose disposal as a predictor of cardiovascular disease. J Clin Endocrinol Metab 1998;83:2773–6.

61. Haffner SM, Valdez RA, Hazuda HP, et al. Prospective analysis of the insulin-resistance syndrome (syndrome X). Diabetes 1992;41:715–22.

62. Haffner SM, Gonzalez C, Miettinen H, et al. A prospective analysis of the HOMA model. The Mexico City Diabetes Study. Diabetes Care 1996;19:1138–41.

63. Canto JG, Shlipak MG, Rogers WJ, et al. Prevalence, clinical characteristics, and mortality among patients with myocardial infarction presenting without chest pain. JAMA 2000;283:3223–9.

64. Nesto RW. Screening for asymptomatic coronary artery disease in diabetes. Diabetes Care 1999;22:1393–5.

65. American Diabetes Association. Consensus development conference on the diagnosis of coronary heart disease in people with diabetes. Diabetes Care 1998;21:1551–9.

66. Diabetes Control and Complications Trial Research Group. The effect of intensive treatment of diabetes on the development and progression of long-term complications in insulin-dependent diabetes mellitus. N Engl J Med 1993;329:977–86.

67. Lawson M, Gerstein HC, Tsui E, Zinman B. Effect of intensive therapy on early macrovascular disease in young individuals with type 1 diabetes. A systematic review and meta-analysis. Diabetes Care 1999;22(Suppl 2):B35–9.

68. UK Prospective Diabetes Study (UKPDS) Group. Intensive blood-glucose control with sulphonylureas or insulin compared with conventional treatment and risk of complications in patients with type 2 diabetes (UKPDS 33). Lancet 1998;352:837–53.

69. UK Prospective Diabetes Study (UKPDS) Group. Effect of intensive blood glucose control with metformin on complications in overweight patients with type 2 diabetes (UKPDS 34). Lancet 1998;352:854–65.

70. McCormack J, Greenhalgh T. Seeing what you want to see in randomised controlled trials: versions and perversions of UKPDS data. BMJ 2000;320:1720–3.

71. Malmberg K, Ryden L, Efendic S, et al. Randomized trial of insulin-glucose infusion followed by subcutaneous insulin treatment in diabetic patients with acute myocardial infarction (DIGAMI study): effects on mortality at 1 year. J Am Coll Cardiol 1995;26:57–65.

72. Malmberg K. Prospective randomised study of intensive insulin treatment on long term survival after acute myocardial infarction in patients with diabetes mellitus. DIGAMI (Diabetes Mellitus, Insulin Glucose Infusion in Acute Myocardial Infarction) Study Group. BMJ 1997;314:1512–5.

73. Fath-Ordoubadi F, Beatt KJ. Glucose-insulin-potassium therapy for treatment of acute myocardial infarction: an overview of randomized placebo-controlled trials. Circulation 1997;96:1152–6.

74. Diaz R, Paolasso EA, Piegas LS, et al. Metabolic modulation of acute myocardial infarction. The ECLA (Estudios Cardiologicos Latinoamerica) Collaborative Group. Circulation 1998;98:2227–34.

75. Ohkubo Y, Kishikawa H, Araki E, et al. Intensive insulin therapy prevents the progression of diabetic microvascular complications in Japanese patients with non-insulin-dependent diabetes mellitus: a randomized prospective 6-year study. Diabetes Res Clin Pract 1995;28:103–17.

76. Abraira C, Colwell JA, Nuttall F, et al. Cardiovascular events and correlates in the Veterans Affairs diabetes feasibility trial. Arch Intern Med 1997;157:181–8.

77. Genuth S. Exogenous insulin admininstration and cardiovascular risk in NIDDM and IDDM. Ann Intern Med 1996;124:104–9.

78. UK Prospective Diabetes Study (UKPDS) Group. Tight blood pressure control and risk of macrovascular and microvascular complications in type 2 diabetes: UKPDS 38. BMJ 1998;317:703–13.

79. Curb JD, Pressel SL, Cutler JA, et al. Effect of diuretic-based antihypertensive treatment on cardiovascular disease risk in older diabetic patients with isolated systolic hypertension. Systolic Hypertension in the Elderly Program Cooperative Research Group. JAMA 1996;276:1886–92.

80. Tuomilehto J, Rastenyte D, Birkenhager WH, et al. Effects of calcium-channel blockade in older patients with diabetes and systolic hypertension. Systolic Hypertension in Europe Trial investigators. N Engl J Med 1999;340:677–84.

81. Hansson L, Zanchetti A, Carruthers SG, et al. Effects of intensive blood-pressure lowering and low-dose aspirin in patients with hypertension: principal results of the Hypertension Optimal Treatment (HOT) randomized trial. Lancet 1998;351:1755–62.

82. Estacio RO, Jeffers BW, Hiatt WR, et al. The effect of nisoldipine as compared with enalapril on cardiovascular outcomes in patients with non-insulin-dependent diabetes and hypertension. N Engl J Med 1998;338:645–52.

83. Estacio RO, Jeffers BW, Gifford N, Schrier RW. Effect of blood pressure control on diabetic microvascular complications in patients with hypertension and type 2 diabetes. Diabetes Care 2000;23(Suppl 2):B54–64.

84. Fuller J, Stevens LK, Chaturvedi N, Holloway JF. Antihypertensive therapy in diabetes mellitus (Cochrane Review). The Cochrane Library, Issue 4. Oxford: Update Software; 1998.

85. Tatti P, Pahor M, Byington RP, et al. Outcome results of the Fosinopril versus Amlodipine Cardiovascular Events Trial (FACET) in patients with hypertension and NIDDM. Diabetes Care 1998;21:597–603.

86. Hansson L, Lindholm LH, Niskanen L, et al. Effect of angiotensin-converting-enzyme inhibition compared with conventional therapy on cardiovascular morbidity and mortality in hypertension: the Captopril Prevention Project (CAPPP) randomised trial. Lancet 1999;353:611–6.

87. UK Prospective Diabetes Study (UKPDS) Group. Efficacy of atenolol and captopril in reducing risk of macrovascular and microvascular complications in Type 2 diabetes: UKPDS 39. BMJ 1998;317:713–20.

88. Pahor M, Psaty BM, Alderman MH, et al. Therapeutic benefits of ACE inhibitors and other antihypertensive drugs in patients with type 2 diabetes. Diabetes Care 2000;23:888–92.

89. Hansson L, Lindholm LH, Ekbom T, et al. Randomised trial of old and new antihypertensive drugs in elderly patients: cardiovascular mortality and morbidity the Swedish Trial in Old Patients with Hypertension-2 study. Lancet 1999;354:1751–6.

90. Major cardiovascular events in hypertensive patients randomized to doxazosin vs chlorthalidone: the Antihypertensive and Lipid-Lowering Treatment to Prevent Heart Attack Trial (ALLHAT). ALLHAT Collaborative Research Group. JAMA 2000;283:1967–75.

91. Meltzer S, Leiter L, Daneman D, et al. 1998 Clinical practice guidelines for the management of diabetes in Canada. Can Med Assoc J 1998;159(Suppl 8):S1–29.

92. Pedersen TR, Olsson AG, Faergeman O, et al. Lipoprotein changes and reduction in the incidence of major coronary heart disease events in the Scandinavian Simvastatin Survival Study (4S). Circulation 1998;97:1453–60.

93. Shepherd J, Cobbe SM, Ford I, et al. Prevention of coronary heart disease with pravastatin in men with hypercholesterolemia. West of Scotland Coronary Prevention Study Group. N Engl J Med 1995;333:1301–7.

94. Downs JR, Clearfield M, Weis S, et al. Primary prevention of acute coronary events with lovastatin in men and women with average cholesterol levels: results of AFCAPS/TexCAPS. Air Force/Texas Coronary Atherosclerosis Prevention Study. JAMA 1998;279:1615–22.

95. Pyorala K, Pedersen TR, Kjekshus J, et al. Cholesterol lowering with simvastatin improves prognosis of diabetic patients with coronary heart disease. Diabetes Care 1997;20:614–20.

96. Sacks FM, Pfeffer MA, Moye LA, et al. The effect of pravastatin on coronary events after myocardial infarction in patients with average cholesterol levels. Cholesterol and Recurrent Events Trial investigators. N Engl J Med 1996;335:1001–9.

97. Goldberg RB, Mellies MJ, Sacks FM, et al. Cardiovascular events and their reduction with pravastatin in diabetic and glucose-intolerant myocardial infarction survivors with average cholesterol levels: subgroup analyses in the cholesterol and recurrent events (CARE) trial. The Care Investigators. Circulation 1998;98:2513–9.

98. Prevention of cardiovascular events and death with pravastatin in patients with coronary heart disease and a broad range of initial cholesterol levels. The Long-Term Intervention with Pravastatin in Ischaemic Disease (LIPID) Study Group. N Engl J Med 1998;339:1349–57.

99. Hoogwerf BJ, Waness A, Cressman M, et al. Effects of aggressive cholesterol lowering and low-dose anticoagulation on clinical and angiographic outcomes in patients with diabetes: the Post Coronary Artery Bypass Graft Trial. Diabetes 1999;48:1289–94.

100. Koskinen P, Manttari M, Manninen V, et al. Coronary heart disease incidence in NIDDM patients in the Helsinki Heart Study. Diabetes Care 1992;15:820–5.

101. Frick MH, Elo O, Haapa K, et al. Helsinki Heart Study: primary-prevention trial with gemfibrozil in middle-aged men with dyslipidemia. Safety of treatment, changes in risk factors, and incidence of coronary heart disease. N Engl J Med 1987;317:1237–45.

102. Rubins HB, Robins SJ, Collins D, et al. Gemfibrozil for the secondary prevention of coronary heart disease in men with low levels of high-density lipoprotein cholesterol. Veterans Affairs High-Density Lipoprotein Cholesterol Intervention Trial Study Group. N Engl J Med 1999;341:410–8.

103. Secondary prevention by raising HDL cholesterol and reducing triglycerides in patients with coronary artery disease: the Bezafibrate Infarction Prevention (BIP) study. Circulation 2000;102:21–7.

104. Effects of an angiotensin-converting-enzyme inhibitor, ramipril, on cardiovascular events in high-risk patients. N Engl J Med 2000 Jan 20;342:145–53.

105. Colwell JA. Aspirin therapy in diabetes. Diabetes Care 1997;20:1767–71.

106. Final report on the aspirin component of the ongoing Physicians' Health Study. Steering Committee of the Physicians' Health Study Research Group. N Engl J Med 1989;321:129–35.

107. Collaborative overview of randomised trials of antiplatelet therapy—I: Prevention of death, myocardial infarction, and stroke by prolonged antiplatelet therapy in various categories of patients. Antiplatelet Trialists' Collaboration [published erratum appears in BMJ 1994;308 :1540]. BMJ 1994;308:81–106.

108. American Diabetes Association. Aspirin therapy in diabetes. Diabetes Care 1997;20:1772–3.

109. Gundersen T, Kjekshus J. Timolol treatment after myocardial infarction in diabetic patients. Diabetes Care 1983;6:285–90.

110. A randomized trial of propranolol in patients with acute myocardial infarction. I. Mortality results. JAMA 1982;247:1707–14.

111. Malmberg K, Herlitz J, Hjalmarson A, Ryden L. Effects of metoprolol on mortality and late infarction in diabetics with suspected acute myocardial infarction. Retrospective data from two large studies. Eur Heart J 1989;10:423–8.

112. Randomised trial of intravenous atenolol among 16,027 cases of suspected acute myocardial infarction: ISIS-1. First International Study of Infarct Survival Collaborative Group. Lancet 1986;2:57–66.

113. Kjekshus J, Gilpin E, Cali G, et al. Diabetic patients and beta-blockers after acute myocardial infarction. Eur Heart J 1990;11:43–50.

114. Jonas M, Reicher-Reiss H, Boyko V, et al. Usefulness of beta-blocker therapy in patients with non-insulin-dependent diabetes mellitus and coronary artery disease. Bezafibrate Infarction Prevention (BIP) Study Group. Am J Cardiol 1996;77:1273–7.

115. Effect of metoprolol CR/XL in chronic heart failure: Metoprolol CR/XL Randomised Intervention Trial in Congestive Heart Failure (MERIT-HF). Lancet 1999;353:2001–7.

116. Helgeland A, Leren P, Foss OP, et al. Serum glucose levels during long-term observation of treated and untreated men with mild hypertension. The Oslo study. Am J Med 1984;76:802–5.

117. William-Olsson T, Fellenius E, Bjorntorp P, Smith U. Differences in metabolic responses to beta-adrenergic stimulation after propranolol or metoprolol administration. Acta Med Scand 1979;205:201–6.

118. Deacon SP, Karunanayake A, Barnett D. Acebutolol, atenolol, and propranolol and metabolic responses to acute hypoglycaemia in diabetics. BMJ 1977;2:1255–7.

119. Clausen-Sjobom N, Lins PE, Adamson U, et al. Effects of metoprolol on the counter-regulation and recognition of prolonged hypoglycemia in insulin-dependent diabetics. Acta Med Scand 1987;222:57–63.

120. Lager I, Blohme G, Smith U. Effect of cardioselective and non-selective beta-blockade on the hypoglycaemic response in insulin-dependent diabetics. Lancet 1979;1:458–62.

121. Abramson EA, Arky RA, Woeber KA. Effects of propranolol on the hormonal and metabolic responses to insulin-induced hypoglycaemia. Lancet 1966;2:1386–8.

122. Corrall RJ, Frier BM, Davidson NM, French EB. Hormonal and substrate responses during recovery from hypoglycaemia in man during beta 1-selective and non-selective beta-adrenergic blockade. Eur J Clin Invest 1981;11:279–83.

123. Lloyd-Jones DM, Larson MG, Beiser A, Levy D. Lifetime risk of developing coronary heart disease. Lancet 1999;353:89–92.

CHAPTER 25

Diseases of the Feet: Foot Ulcers and Amputations in People with Diabetes Mellitus

Dereck Hunt, MD, MSc, FRCPC

Abstract

Foot ulcers and amputations are common complications in people with diabetes mellitus. Patients with altered lower extremity sensation, foot deformities, or a history of previous ulceration or amputation are at especially high risk. Programs designed to identify these patients and provide focused foot-care education, podiatry, and protective foot wear, however, can prevent lower-extremity ulceration and amputation.

For patients who develop a noninfected neuropathic foot ulcer, pressure offloading using total contact casting had been shown to improve the rate of ulcer healing. New topically applied growth factors also appear to accelerate healing. Study findings, however, are heterogeneous. Oral antibiotic therapy does not appear to improve outcomes for patients with noninfected foot ulcers. For patients with more severe, infected foot ulcers, systemic hyperbaric therapy has been shown to decrease the rate of major amputations.

Introduction

Foot complications are common in people with diabetes mellitus. The annual incidence of foot ulcers is between 2 and 10%, while the annual incidence of amputation is between 0.2% and 2.0%.[1–10] While many factors contribute to this, including peripheral neuropathy, vascular disease, and infection, new evidence suggests that timely intervention can reduce the risk of these poor outcomes. Primary prevention of ulcers and amputation through identification of high-risk patients, coupled with education and close follow-up, is effective, as are secondary prevention interventions with people who have already had an ulcer or minor amputation. For people with established foot ulcers, several therapeutic interventions have been found to improve healing. This chapter reviews the risk factors for the development of diabetic foot ulceration and amputations and the effectiveness of different interventions designed to prevent these outcomes by answering the following questions:

1. What risk factors have been identified for foot ulceration and lower-extremity amputation?
2. What strategies have been shown to be effective for preventing foot ulceration and lower extremity amputation?
3. What strategies have been shown to be effective for treating established foot ulcers?

What Risk Factors Have Been Identified for Foot Ulceration and Lower-Extremity Amputation?

Risk factors for foot ulceration have been evaluated in several prospective studies (Table 25–1). After controlling for age, one study found that independent risk factors among patients with older-onset diabetes mellitus included duration of diabetes (odds ratio [OR] 1.5 per decade, 95% confidence interval [CI] 1.0 to 2.0), poor glycemic control (OR 1.6 per 2% increase in glycated hemoglobin, 95% CI 1.3 to 2.0), retinopathy status (OR 1.2 per 2-step increase in severity on an 11-step scale, 95% CI 1.0 to 1.4), and diabetic nephropathy

Table 25–1 Risk Factors for Foot Ulceration and Lower-Extremity Amputation

Risk Factor
Male sex
Duration of diabetes
Retinopathy or nephropathy
Poor glycemic control
Impaired lower-extremity sensation
Previous ulceration or amputation
Foot deformity

(OR 2.2, 95% CI 1.1 to 4.3). Male sex also increased the risk of foot ulceration (OR 1.6, 95% CI 1.0 to 2.7). Lower extremity sensation status, however, was not assessed in this study.[1] More recently, a large prospective study involving older men with Type 2 diabetes mellitus, who were being followed at a Veterans Affairs medical center, did assess lower-extremity sensory neuropathy as a risk factor for ulceration, along with a number of other patient characteristics.[2] Sensory neuropathy was defined as the inability to detect light touch sensation using the Semmes-Weinstein 5.07 monofilament. Independent predictors of ulceration during the 3.7 years of follow-up included sensory neuropathy (relative risk [RR] 2.2, 95% CI 1.5 to 3.1), previous foot ulceration (RR 1.6, 95% CI 1.2 to 2.3), previous amputation (RR 2.8, 95% CI 1.8 to 4.3), and foot deformity (RR 3.5, 95% CI 1.2 to 9.9). Insulin use, impaired vision, a reduced ankle-brachial index, elevated weight, and a reduced transcutaneous oxygen pressure were also independent risk factors.

Prospective studies have also identified risk factors for lower-extremity amputation.[3–10] The duration of diabetes (RR 1.6 to 4.0 per decade), male sex (RR 1.9 to 2.9), and the presence of retinopathy (RR 2.1 to 3.6) or nephropathy (RR 1.3 to 2.4), as well as poor glycemic control (OR 1.7 for every 2% rise in the baseline glycated hemoglobin value), all predict future amputation. Bedside physical examination maneuvers to detect altered lower-extremity sensation, using either the Semmes-Weinstein monofilament sensation status or vibration-perception status, identify patients at increased risk (RR 2.7 to 17). Patient history of previous foot ulceration or amputation also predicts future amputation (OR 3.3 to 122).

EVIDENCE-BASED MESSAGES

1. Patients with diabetes mellitus who have reduced monofilament sensation or vibration sensation in their feet or who have a history of a previous foot ulcer are at increased risk of foot ulceration and lower-extremity amputation (Level 2).[2,3]
2. Poor glycemic control and evidence of microvascular complications are associated with an increased risk of foot ulceration and amputation (Level 2).[1,9]

WHAT STRATEGIES HAVE BEEN SHOWN TO BE EFFECTIVE FOR PREVENTING FOOT ULCERATION AND LOWER-EXTREMITY AMPUTATION?

There have been a variety of strategies evaluated in prospective, controlled trials and found to be effective at preventing lower-extremity complications (Table 25–2).

Screening for Amputation Risk Factors Combined with High-Level Foot Care

One of the most effective approaches for preventing lower-extremity amputations is to screen patients to identify those who are at especially high risk and to subsequently refer these peo-

---

Table 25–2 Strategies for Preventing Foot Ulceration and Lower-Extremity Amputation

Screening for amputation risk factors combined with high-level foot care

Foot care education

Foot care reminders

Footwear

---

ple to a comprehensive foot care clinic. This strategy reduces the absolute risk for major amputations by 1%.[11] Patients (N = 2,001) attending a general diabetes care clinic were randomly allocated to either usual care or to a screening program. Patients in the screening arm were classified as high risk if they were found to have deficits in their pedal pulses, vibration sensation, or Semmes-Weinstein monofilament light-touch sensation on two separate occasions, as well as having a history of previous foot ulceration or the finding of a lower ankle-brachial index or foot deformities on physical examination. High-risk patients were referred to a foot care program that provided education, podiatry, and protective footwear. After 2 years, the major amputation rate in the usual care arm was 1.2%, whereas it was only 0.1% in the screening arm of the study (absolute risk difference 1.1%, 95% CI 0.4 to 1.9%).

Education and Reminders

Another approach is to educate and remind both patients and their health care practitioners about the importance of foot care.[12] Three hundred and fifty-two patients attending a general diabetes clinic participated in a randomized study evaluating this strategy. In the intervention arm, patients received foot care education and follow-up reminders, while their health care practitioners were reminded to examine people's feet and to discuss foot care during appointments. After 1 year, serious foot lesions developed significantly less often in the intervention arm than in the control arm (baseline prevalence 2.9%; relative risk reduction 0.6, 95% CI 0 to 0.8).

The value of patient education has also been evaluated for people who have recently been treated for a foot complication.[13] Two hundred and twenty-seven patients with diabetes who were initially referred because of a foot infection, a foot ulcer, or for assistance regarding management after amputation were allocated according to their social insurance number to either a control arm or to a 1-hour teaching session focusing on foot care and foot complications. Follow-up at 2 years demonstrated improved outcomes in the intervention arm. Foot ulcers recurred in 14.7% of control patients and only 4.5% of patients in the education arm (absolute risk difference 10.2%, 95% CI 3.8 to 16%). In the control arm, 10.2% of patients went on to have major amputations, compared with 2.8% in the intervention arm (absolute risk difference 7.3%, 95% CI 2.0 to 13%).

Footwear

Appropriate footwear is an intervention that is critical for people with a history of previous neuropathic foot ulceration. The potential for improved outcomes using this approach was demonstrated in a controlled trial by Uccioli and colleagues.[14] Sixty-nine people with a history of diabetic foot ulceration were alternately allocated to either a control group or a therapeutic footwear group. While all patients received education on the importance of foot care and footwear, the intervention arm patients were also provided with special shoes. These were made using soft thermoformable leather and were deep enough to accommodate both foot deformities and custom-molded insoles. After 1 year, the ulceration recurrence rate was 58% in the control arm, compared with 27% in the intervention arm (absolute risk difference 31%, 95% CI 7.1 to 55%).

Table 25–3 Treatment of Established Foot Ulcers

Total contact casting

Topical growth factors

Hyperbaric oxygen

EVIDENCE-BASED MESSAGES

1. In patients with diabetes mellitus who are at high risk for lower-extremity amputation, a foot care program that provides education, podiatry, and protective footwear clearly reduces the risk of amputation (Level 1A).[11]

2. In patients with previous neuropathic foot ulceration, using soft leather shoes that can accommodate custom insoles and foot deformities reduces the risk of recurrent ulceration (Level 2).[14]

3. Focused foot care education can reduce the risk of lower-extremity amputation in patients with recent foot complications (Level 2).[13]

WHAT STRATEGIES HAVE BEEN SHOWN TO BE EFFECTIVE FOR TREATING ESTABLISHED FOOT ULCERS?

While education and appropriate footwear are both important for prevention of foot complications, additional interventions are clearly necessary for patients who develop a foot ulcer (Table 25–3). Appropriate débridement and assessment for possible abscess formation or osteomyelitis is important, as is an evaluation of the vascular supply of the ulcerated foot. Broad-spectrum antibiotics are indicated if cellulitis or osteomyelitis are present, along with revascularization for patients with significant lower-extremity ischemia. For patients who are found to have noninfected, nonischemic neuropathic foot ulcers, additional interventions are available. These include total contact casting to relieve pressure from the ulcer site and the use of topical growth factors to hasten ulcer healing. For patients with more severe, infected foot ulcers, hyperbaric oxygen therapy may also have a role.

Total Contact Casting and Other Offloading Techniques for Patients with Noninfected Foot Ulcers

Complete pressure relief is an essential prerequisite for healing of chronic cutaneous ulcers. For patients with neuropathic foot ulcers, however, this can be difficult to achieve. In addition to lacking lower-extremity sensory feedback to indicate that excessive pressure is being applied to the ulcer site, the crutches, wheelchairs, and walkers that are often recommended can be difficult for patients to use, contributing to a reduced level of adherence. There are a number of alternate offloading devices that have been developed to specifically address this situation. These include the total contact cast, removable cast walkers, half-shoes, and felted foam.

Of these interventions, only the total contact cast has been evaluated in a prospective, controlled fashion to assess its effectiveness with respect to improving ulcer healing rates. In a study by Mueller and colleagues,[15] a group of 40 patients with noninfected, nongangrenous plantar foot ulcers were randomly allocated to either usual care or total contact casting. Usual care involved education, the provision of crutches or a walker, and accommodative footwear, as well as dressing changes two to three times daily. In contrast, the intervention arm participants had an initial total contact cast applied that was subsequently changed 5 to 7 days later, and then every 2 to 3 weeks until ulcer healing had occurred. Total contact casting involved the application of a layer of plaster over the foot and lower leg in such a way as to distribute pressure evenly over the entire plantar aspect of the foot. After a mean of 65 days, ulcer healing occurred in only 32% of the control arm patients. This compared with a heal-

Table 25–4 Effects of Cultured Human Dermis and Topical Growth Factors on Ulcer Healing

Agent	N	Ulcer Healing: Intervention Arm vs Control Arm	Absolute Difference in Healing Rates	Number Needed to Treat*
Cultured human dermis† (weekly for 8 weeks)[17]	50	50% vs 8%	42% (5–80%)	2
Cultured human dermis† (weekly for 8 weeks)[18]	281	39% vs 32%	7% (–6–20%)	14
Platelet-derived growth factor (30 μg/mL daily for 20 weeks)[19]	118	48% vs 25%	23% (5–41%)	4
Platelet-derived growth factor (30 μg/mL daily for 20 weeks)[20]	382	36% vs 35%	1%	100
Platelet-derived growth factor (100 μg/mL daily for 20 weeks)[20]	382	50% vs 35%	15% (2–28%)	7
Arginine-glycine-aspartic acid matrix (twice weekly for 10 weeks)[21]	65	35% vs 8%	27% (6–48%)	4
Thrombin-induced human platelet-derived factor (CT-102) applied twice weekly[22]	81	80% vs 29%	51% (19–84%)	2

*This is the number of people who required treatment for the period described in column 1 to heal one ulcer during that time period.
†Nonblinded studies.
Data from Gentzkow et al,[17] Naughton et al,[18] Steed et al,[19] Wieman et al,[20] Steed et al,[21] Holloway et al.[22]

ing rate of 91% for patients allocated to total contact casting, after a mean of only 42 days (absolute risk difference 59%, 95% CI 31 to 87%).

While other offloading approaches have not been evaluated for their effect on ulcer healing per se, the effect on the pressure applied to the ulcer site during ambulation has been investigated.[16] Fleischli and colleagues demonstrated that removable walking casts can be as effective as total contact casts in this respect. The same study demonstrated that while half-shoes and felted foam provided a degree of pressure offloading, this was significantly less than with the use of a walking cast.[16]

Topical Growth Factors for Patients with Noninfected Foot Ulcers

A new approach for treating foot ulcers is to apply a factor specifically designed to accelerate cellular growth and proliferation directly to the ulcer surface. Currently, four such factors have been developed and tested in moderately sized trials: neonatal cultured fibroblasts (cultured human dermis),[17,18] platelet-derived growth factors,[19,20] an arginine-glycine-aspartic acid matrix,[21] and thrombin-induced human platelet-derived factor.[22] Each of the randomized trials evaluating these agents enrolled hospital outpatients with chronic noninfected nonischemic diabetic foot ulcers. All participants received wound débridement and were encouraged to avoid weight bearing on the affected limb.

These trials (Table 25–4) demonstrated heterogeneous effects. For cultured human dermis, the healing rate was improved by 42% (95% CI 5 to 80%) in one trial and by only 7% (95% CI –6 to 20%) in another. Platelet-derived growth factors were found to improve healing by 23% (95% CI 5 to 41%) in one study. In a larger trial, no benefit was found when using the same concentration of platelet-derived growth factors, but a 15% (95% CI 2 to 28%) benefit in the healing rate was found with application of a higher concentration. Arginine-glycine-aspartic acid matrix and thrombin-induced human platelet-derived factor have each been assessed in a moderately sized trial to date. Healing rates were noted to improve by 27% (95% CI 6 to 48%) and 51% (95% CI 19 to 84%) in these trials, respectively.

Hyperbaric Oxygen for Patients with Severe, Infected Foot Ulcers

Total contact casting and topical growth factors clearly have no role in the management of patients with severe infected foot ulcers. Rather, débridement, intravenous antibiotic therapy, revascularization, and optimal glycemic control remain the primary components of treatment, short of amputation. In addition to these interventions, however, hyperbaric oxygen therapy also appears to have a potential role. Two randomized studies have evaluated the effectiveness of this intervention for hospitalized patients with infected diabetic foot ulcers.[23,24] One trial involved 70 patients and assessed the effects of daily 90-minutes sessions of systemic hyperbaric oxygen therapy at 2.2 to 2.5 atmospheres for patients with full, thickness gangrene or abscess or a large infected ulcer that had not healed for over 30 days. The major amputation rate for control patients after 10 weeks was 33%, compared with 8.6% for intervention arm patients (absolute risk difference 24%, 95% CI 4.4 to 45%). Results of a smaller study involving only 30 patients with chronic infected diabetic foot ulcers found a trend toward improved outcomes with the addition of four treatments of hyperbaric oxygen therapy over a 2-week period, in addition to usual care. The amputation rate was 13% for patients treated with hyperbaric oxygen therapy, compared with a rate of 46% for control patients (absolute risk difference 33%, 95% CI −1.6 to 68%).

Systemic Antibiotic Treatment for Patients with Noninfected Foot Ulcers

Oral antibiotic treatment is often considered for patients with neuropathic foot ulcers to improve healing. This approach, however, may not improve outcomes. One randomized controlled trial[25] that involved 44 patients evaluated the effect of providing patients who have neuropathic forefoot ulceration and no evidence of osteomyelitis or significant peripheral vascular disease with either amoxicillin combined with the β-lactamase inhibitor clavulinic acid or placebo. All participants were also treated with interventions to provide pressure relief as well as careful local wound care. After 20 days, ulcer healing occurred in 27% of patients treated with antibiotics, compared with 45% of patients who received placebo (absolute risk difference −18%, 95% CI −49 to +13%).

EVIDENCE-BASED MESSAGES

1. Total contact casting increases the rate of healing of chronic, noninfected neuropathic foot ulcers (Level 1A).[15]
2. Topical growth factors may improve neuropathic foot ulcer healing (Level 2).[17–22]
3. Systemic hyperbaric oxygen therapy reduces the risk of amputation for patients with severe infected foot ulcers (Level 2A).[23,24]
4. Antibiotic therapy does not improve healing of uncomplicated neuropathic foot ulcers (Level 2).[25]

CONCLUSION

Lower-extremity complications are common and devastating, affecting both individual quality of life and the cost associated with providing optimal diabetes health care. These poor outcomes, however, appear to be avoidable. Optimal foot care and education can make a difference for those diabetic patients at high risk for lower-extremity complications, as can aggressive management of people who develop ulceration of their feet. The challenge now is to ensure widespread implementation of these approaches.

Summary of Evidence-Based Messages

1. Patients with diabetes mellitus who have reduced monofilament sensation or vibration sensation in their feet or who have a history of a previous foot ulcer are at increased risk for foot ulceration and lower-extremity amputation (Level 2).[2,3]

2. Poor glycemic control and evidence of microvascular complications are associated with an increased risk of foot ulceration and amputation (Level 2).[1,9]

3. In patients with diabetes mellitus who are at high risk for lower-extremity amputation, a foot care program that provides education, podiatry, and protective footwear clearly reduces the risk of amputation (Level 1A).[11]

4. In patients with previous neuropathic foot ulceration, using soft leather shoes that can accommodate custom insoles and foot deformities reduces the risk of recurrent ulceration (Level 2).[14]

5. Focused foot care education can reduce the risk of lower-extremity amputation in patients with recent foot complication (Level 2).[13]

6. Total contact casting increases the rate of healing of chronic, noninfected neuropathic foot ulcers (Level 1A).[15]

7. Topical growth factors may improve neuropathic foot ulcer healing (Level 2).[17–22]

8. Systemic hyperbaric oxygen therapy reduces the risk of amputation for patients with severe infected foot ulcers (Level 2A).[23,24]

9. Antibiotic therapy does not improve healing of uncomplicated neuropathic foot ulcers (Level 2).[25]

References

1. Moss SE, Klein B. The prevalence and incidence of lower extremity amputation in a diabetic population. Arch Intern Med 1992;152:610–6.

2. Boyko ED, Ahroni JH, Stensel V, et al. A prospective study of risk factors for diabetic foot ulcer. The Seattle diabetic foot study. Diabetes Care 1999;22:1036–42.

3. Rith-Najarian SJ, Stolusky T, Gohdes DM. Identifying diabetic patients at high risk for lower-extremity amputation in a primary health care setting. Diabetes Care 1992;15:1386–9.

4. Veves A, Murray HJ, Young MJ, Boulton AJM. The risk of foot ulceration in diabetic patients with high foot pressure: a prospective study. Diabetologia 1992;35:660–3.

5. Young MJ, Breddy JL, Veves A, Boulton AJM. The prediction of diabetic neuropathic foot ulceration using vibration perception thresholds: a prospective study. Diabetes Care 1994;7:557–60.

6. Humphrey ARG, Dowse GK, Thoma K, Zimmet PZ. Diabetes and nontraumatic lower extremity amputations. Incidence, risk factors, and prevention—a 12 year follow-up study in Nauru. Diabetes Care 1996;19:710–4.

7. Lee JS, Lu M, Lee VS, et al. Lower-extremity amputation: incidence, risk factors, and mortality in the Oklahoma Indian diabetes study. Diabetes 1993;42:876–82.

8. Lehto S, Ronnemaa T, Pyorala K. Laakso M. Risk factors predicting lower extremity amputations in patients with NIDDM. Diabetes Care 1996;19:607–12.

9. Moss SE, Klein R, Klein B. Long-term incidence of lower-extremity amputations in a diabetic population. Arch Fam Med 1996;5:391–8.

10. Nelson RG, Gohdes DM, Everhart JE, et al. Lower-extremity amputations in NIDDM: 12 year follow-up study in Pima Indians. Diabetes Care 1988;11:8–16.

11. McCabe CJ, Stevenson RC, Dolan AM. Evaluation of a diabetic foot screening and protection programme. Diabet Med 1998;15:80–4.

12. Litzelman DK, Slemenda CW, Langefeld CD, et al. Reduction of lower extremity clinical abnormalities in patients with non-insulin-dependent diabetes mellitus. Ann Intern Med 1993;119:36–41.

13. Malone JM, Snyder M, Anderson G, et al. Prevention of amputation by diabetic education. Am J Surg 1989;158:520–4.

14. Uccioli L, Faglia E, Monticone G, et al. Manufactured shoes in the prevention of diabetic foot ulcers. Diabetes Care 1995;18:1376–8.

15. Mueller MJ, Diamond JE, Sinacore DR, et al. Total contact casting in treatment of diabetic plantar ulcers: controlled clinical trial. Diabetes Care 1989;12:384–8.

16. Fleischli JG, Lavery LA, Vela SA, et al. Comparison of strategies to reduce pressures at the site of neuropathic ulcers. J Am Podiatr Med Assoc 1997;87:466–72.

17. Gentzkow GD, Iwasaki SD, Hershon K, et al. Use of dermagraft, a cultured human dermis, to treat diabetic foot ulcers. Diabetes Care 1996;19:350–4.

18. Naughton G, Mansbridge J. Gentzkow G. A metabolically active human dermal replacement for the treatment of diabetic foot ulcers. Artificial Organs 1997;21:1203–10.

19. Steed DL, and the Diabetic Ulcer Study Group. Clinical evaluation of recombinant human platelet-derived growth factor for the treatment of lower extremity diabetic ulcers. J Vasc Surg 1995;21:71–81.

20. Wieman TJ, Smiell JM, Su Y. Efficacy and safety of a topical gel formulation of recombinant human platelet-derived growth factor-BB (Becaplermin) in patients with chronic neuropathic diabetic ulcers. Diabetes Care 1998;21:822–7.

21. Steed DL, Ricotta JJ, Prendergast JJ, et al. Promotion and acceleration of diabetic ulcer healing by arginine-glycine-aspartic acid (RGD) peptide matrix. Diabetes Care 1995;18:39–46.

22. Holloway G, Steed D, DeMarco M, et al. A randomized controlled dose response trial of activated platelet supernatant, topical CT-102 in chronic, non-healing diabetic wounds. Wounds 1993;5:198–206.

23. Faglia E, Favales F, Aldeghi A, et al. Adjunctive systemic hyperbaric oxygen therapy in treatment of severe prevalently ischemic diabetic foot ulcer. Diabetes Care 1996;19:1338–43.

24. Doctor N, Pandya S, Supe A. Hyperbaric Oxygen therapy in diabetic foot. J Postgrad Med 1992;38:112–4.

25. Chantelau E, Tanudjaja T, Altenhofet F, et al. Antibiotic treatment for uncomplicated neuropathic forefoot ulcers in diabetes: a controlled trial. Diabet Med 1996;13:156–9.

CHAPTER 26

Classification and Risk of Musculoskeletal Impairment Associated with Diabetes

David T. Harvey, MD, FRCPC

ABSTRACT

Neuropathy, retinopathy, nephropathy, and vasculopathy are common in diabetes and are usually discussed when complications of diabetes are considered. Musculoskeletal impairment is also very common in people with diabetes, although few large studies have been reported. Some of the musculoskeletal impairments seen in people with diabetes (such as Dupuytren's contracture) are common in the rest of the population, but some studies suggest that they may have a higher prevalence in people with diabetes. Other musculoskeletal impairments, such as limited joint mobility, appear to be unique to people with diabetes, as they occur with an extremely low prevalence in the general population.

This chapter describes the musculoskeletal impairments associated with diabetes, the prevalence of these conditions, and the association between the musculoskeletal findings and other complications of diabetes.

INTRODUCTION

People with diabetes have a higher prevalence of common musculoskeletal conditions than do nondiabetic individuals; they also develop some conditions that seem to be exclusive to diabetes (Table 26–1). Although the vascular and renal complications of diabetes are responsible for the highest morbidity and mortality, these musculoskeletal conditions may cause significant impairment in function. Indeed, validated measures of quality of life indicate that patients report concerns in the domains of physical function.[1–3] However, as these studies do not record the prevalence of musculoskeletal impairments, it is not possible to directly determine their specific impact on quality of life. Indeed, no reported studies have directly compared the impact of musculoskeletal impairment and classic diabetes-related complications. Nevertheless, both clinical experience and indirect evidence from the literature suggest that the impact of musculoskeletal problems on quality of life may exceed the impact of diabetes. For example, in a group of patients with hereditary hemochromatosis, arthropathy had a greater effect on quality of life than did cirrhosis or diabetes.[4] Similarly, a group of patients with shoulder pain had quality-of-life scores that did not differ from scores in patients with congestive heart failure, acute myocardial infarction, clinical depression, or diabetes.[5]

The musculoskeletal abnormalities associated with diabetes are reviewed in this chapter by answering the following questions:

1. Which common musculoskeletal conditions occur more commonly in people with diabetes?
2. Which rare musculoskeletal conditions are very common in people with diabetes?

WHICH COMMON MUSCULOSKELETAL CONDITIONS OCCUR MORE COMMONLY IN PEOPLE WITH DIABETES?

Bony Skeleton Abnormalities

Diffuse Idiopathic Skeletal Hyperostosis

Diffuse idiopathic skeletal hyperostosis (DISH) is usually an asymptomatic condition of unknown cause that is identified incidentally in radiography; it may also present with

Table 26–1 Musculoskeletal Problems in People with Diabetes

Conditions with higher prevalence in diabetes

  Bony skeleton

    Hyperostosis/DISH

    Osteopenia/osteoporosis

  Joints

    Neuropathic joints

    Osteoarthritis in Type 1 diabetes mellitus

    Arthropathy associated with hemochromatosis

  Periarticular tissues

    Adhesive capsulitis (shoulders)

    Dupuytren's contracture

    Flexor tenosynovitis of the fingers

Conditions specific to patients with diabetes

  Limited joint mobility of the hands.

  Forefoot osteolysis

DISH = diffuse idiopathic skeletal hyperostosis.

nonradicular pain in the thoracic/lumbar area. It is most frequent in the middle and lower portions of the thoracic spine and is rare in the upper portion of the thoracic spine. The anterior and lateral aspects of the vertebral bodies are selectively affected.

Approximately 8.5% of the general population are affected by DISH, and between 18 to 49% of people with diabetes. As diabetic individuals with either hyperuricemia or dyslipoproteinemia appear to be at highest risk for the development of DISH,[6] these other risk factors should be sought in affected individuals.

It is possible to clinically distinguish DISH from both degenerative arthritis and ankylosing spondylitis. Compared to degenerative arthritis, in DISH the disk spaces are not narrowed and osteophytes do not arise from the vertebral bodies themselves; the thoracic spine is favored, compared to the cervical and lumbar spine in degenerative spondylosis, and calcification develops near but not continuous with the margin of the vertebral body, whereas osteophytes of degenerative arthritis begin at the margin of the vertebral body. Compared to ankylosing spondylitis, DISH is usually asymptomatic (ankylosing spondylitis is symptomatic); calcification appears anteriorly and laterally, whereas in ankylosing spondylitis, the sacroiliac joints and posterior ligaments are affected; the calcifications are anterior and lateral, thick and irregular, and often not continuous with the vertebral body border, whereas in ankylosing spondylitis, the calcification is thin and vertically oriented and more likely to be posterior.[7]

Osteoporosis

The presence of insulin receptors in bone cells, evidence that insulin acts as a skeletal growth factor and encourages amino-acid uptake and collagen synthesis,[8,9] and differential effects of proinsulin and insulin growth factors on bone metabolism[10] suggest that diabetes may affect bone mineralization. Indeed, early studies in people with Type 1 diabetes (who are insulinopenic) do report modestly lower spine and appendicular bone density than in age-matched nondiabetic controls.[11,12] More recent studies have suggested that the reduced bone density may be specific to individuals with some renal involvement.[13] Conversely, a population-based study of 99 women of mean age 42 with Type 1 diabetes (median duration 27 years) showed no difference in bone mineral density compared with healthy volunteers.[14]

These data suggest that the risk of osteoporosis for people with Type 1 diabetes may be increased, but this remains unclear. This is of particular concern to adolescents who have not yet reached peak bone mass at the time of onset of their diabetes. Type 2 diabetes has not been linked to low bone mass or a higher incidence of fractures.[15]

Whether or not glycemic control affects bone density is also unclear. Of interest is the observation that glycemic control affects osteocalcin levels and other insulin growth factors, which may, in turn, affect bone density.[16–18]

Joint Abnormalities

Osteoarthritis

Whether or not diabetes is a risk factor for osteoarthritis is unclear. Population-based studies do not suggest an association for Type 2 diabetes,[19,20] and only a few early studies suggest increased osteoarthritis in young and middle-aged patients with Type 1 diabetes.[21,22]

Arthropathy Associated with Hemochromatosis

Up to 60% of people with hemochromatosis develop diabetes. Individuals with hemochromatosis also develop arthritic changes related to abnormal accumulation of iron. Typically, osteoarthritic-type changes are seen at the metacarpal phalangeal joints, with the development of carpal bone cysts, and patients present with pain and swelling of the second and third metacarpal phalangeal (MCP) joints. There are no data to suggest that diabetes control plays any role in the development of this arthropathy.

Periarticular Tissue Abnormalities

Adhesive Capsulitis (Frozen Shoulder)

Adhesive capsulitis is characterized by reduced range of movement, with pain and stiffness in the shoulder. Gradual onset, with progressive restriction in range of movement, without an identified injury is common. Women aged 40 to 60 years have the highest prevalence.

An association between adhesive capsulitis and diabetes was reported in a large cross-sectional study of 424 patients with Type 1 and Type 2 diabetes.[23] This study reported a prevalence of adhesive capsulitis in Type 1 diabetes of 10% and in Type 2 diabetes of 22%. It was associated with age and duration of diabetes, but not to the level of glycemic control. Of note, there was an association between adhesive capsulitis in both Type 1 and Type 2 diabetes and autonomic neuropathy (odds ratios of 4.1 and 1.6, respectively). There was also a strong association between adhesive capsulitis and myocardial infarction in Type 1 diabetes (odds ratio of 13.7). Reasons for such an association remain unclear; moreover, this relationship has not been examined prospectively.

The largest study of adhesive capsulitis is a case-control study of 900 people with Type 2 diabetes and 350 age- and sex-matched controls.[24] This study reported that 32% of people with Type 2 diabetes and 10% of controls had adhesive capsulitis.

Dupuytren's Disease

Dupuytren's disease (also called palmar fasciitis or palmar fibromatosis) is characterized by thickening and contracture of the palmar fascia. It involves the connective tissue in the palm of the hand as opposed to the tendon structures. It usually starts with one or several painless nodules in the palm, usually more prevalent in the distal palmar crease. Gradually, these nodules may thicken and contract, drawing the fingers into flexion. The fingers at the ulnar side of the hand are most commonly affected. As flexion contractures progress, they may create functional limitation for putting on gloves, placing the hand in a pocket, or opening the hand widely to grasp large objects.

Dupuytren's disease may be more common in people with diabetes and may predict future diabetes-related complications. For example, in one case-control study, a prevalence estimate of 28% was reported in diabetic patients and a prevalence of 8% in a nondiabetic age- and sex-matched control group.[25] In another study of 436 patients, 14% of patients with Type 1 diabetes and 14% of patients with Type 2 diabetes showed Dupuytren's disease. After controlling for age and duration of diabetes, Dupuytren's disease was independently associated with microalbuminuria in patients with Type 1 diabetes; it was not associated with the HbA_{1c} level.[26] An independent association with microalbuminuria (or any other diabetes-related problem) in people with Type 1 diabetes, after taking age and diabetes duration into account, was not confirmed in a 5-year prospective study of people with Type 1 diabetes.[27]

Flexor Tenosynovitis

Flexor tenosynovitis of the finger (which leads to "trigger" finger) is an inflammation of the flexor tendon sheath. It most commonly develops at the level of the MCP joint. Inflammation at this level and the development of a nodule within the tendon results in crepitation and sometimes catching or "triggering" of the finger, as the nodule passes underneath the flexor retinaculum. Patients report catching or sometimes a complete inability to extend the finger. Pain is common; palpation over the tendon sheath often reveals a painful nodule or a palpable crepitation as the tendon moves.

Cross-sectional studies suggest that flexor tenosynovitis affects 20% of individuals with Type 1 diabetes and that it is more common in females than in males.[28] In these studies, only the duration of diabetes has been independently associated with hand problems that included flexor tenosynovitis.

Treatment options include rest with the finger in extension for several days, use of non-steroidal anti-inflammatory drugs (NSAIDs), or injection of corticosteroid into the tendon sheaths. Although limited joint mobility of diabetes is considered a separate condition, flexor tenosynovitis may be a contributing factor in the development of the flexion contracture seen in limited joint mobility. This possibility is suggested by the observation that injection of corticosteroid into the flexor tendon sheaths reversed limited joint mobility in patients with limited joint mobility without clinical tenosynovitis.[29]

EVIDENCE-BASED MESSAGE

Corticosteroid injection into the flexor tendon sheaths reverses limited joint mobility in diabetic patients with and without clinical tenosynovitis (Level 4).[29]

WHICH RARE MUSCULOSKELETAL CONDITIONS ARE VERY COMMON IN PEOPLE WITH DIABETES?

Limited Joint Mobility

Limited joint mobility is a painless condition that has been best described in the hand; it has also been described in the foot and ankle. It is characterized by thickening and stiffening of the periarticular connective tissue and a consequent loss of range of movement; it is also associated with other limiting hand conditions including flexor tenosynovitis, peripheral nerve dysfunction, and Dupuytren's contracture.

Figure 26–1 shows a patient with long-standing Type 1 diabetes who has limited joint mobility. Compared to a normal individual (Figure 26–2), the classic "prayer" sign becomes evident, in which there is inability to close the fingers and fully extend the proximal interphalangeal joints as well as limited joint mobility at the wrist.[30] Figure 26–3 shows the same individual's hand as in Figure 26–1, compared with that of a nondiabetic patient of the same age and hand size. Note that the stiffness of the fingers has also resulted in a significant loss of the web space, with decreased ability to spread the fingers.

Several early cross-sectional studies have suggested that limited joint mobility increases the risk of diabetes-related complications.[31-34] This was not confirmed in prospective studies[35,37] despite evidence from at least one case-control study that there is a strong association between limited joint mobility and HbA_{1c}.[36]

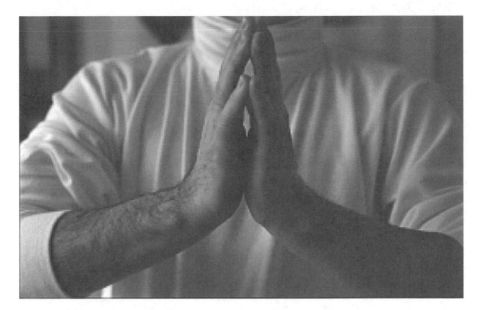

Figure 26–1 "Prayer" sign in a long-standing insulin-dependent diabetic.

Cause and Therapy of Limited Joint Mobility

It is thought that the cause of limited joint mobility is a change in the nature of the collagen in diabetic patients. "Browning of collagen" or "protein glycation" is thought to be the underlying mechanism related to the development of joint stiffness. This is consistent with electron microscopy studies of collagen showing structural alterations in diabetic rat collagen related to protein glycation.[38] It is also consistent with a report from the Diabetes Control and Complications Trial (DCCT), in which skin collagen glycation and crosslinking were lower in the intensive treatment group versus the conventional treatment group.[39] Thus, higher glucose levels were seen to lead to increased crosslinking and collagen glycation. Physical therapy was

Figure 26–2 Normal wrist and finger extension.

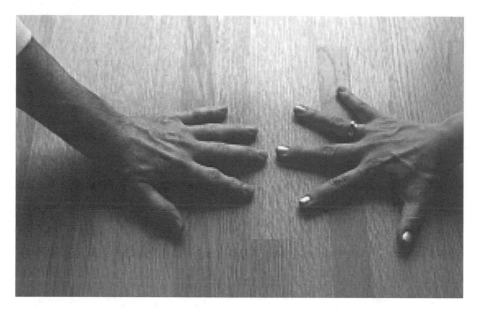

Figure 26–3 Reduced web space in an insulin-dependent diabetic compared to a non diabetic with normal web space.

shown to help limited joint mobility of the foot, but only temporarily, with no lasting benefit after therapy was stopped.[40]

EVIDENCE-BASED MESSAGE

Physical therapy may temporarily improve joint mobility in diabetes (Level 4).[40]

Forefoot Osteolysis

The diabetic foot is discussed in Chapter 25. In addition to neuropathy, ischemia, and infection, the foot in the diabetic patient is also affected by limited joint mobility—an abnormality that contributes to the risk of ulceration and infection.[41]

Forefoot osteolysis is a condition that seems to be unique to the diabetic foot. It is usually recognized as a generalized osteoporosis of the distal metatarsus and proximal phalanx and presents with pain, swelling, and erythema but no evidence of infection.[42] Although forefoot osteolysis has been described in case reports, its cause, association with other complications of diabetes, and association with diabetes control remain unclear.

CONCLUSION

Musculoskeletal abnormalities are common and appear to be more prevalent in people with diabetes. Moreover, certain abnormalities such as limited joint mobility and forefoot osteolysis appear to be specific to diabetes. Despite these observations, clear descriptions of risk factors for these abnormalities and strong evidence in support of their effective prevention or therapy are clearly needed.

SUMMARY OF EVIDENCE-BASED MESSAGES

1. Corticosteroid injection into the flexor tendon sheaths reverses limited joint mobility in diabetic patients with and without tenosynovitis (Level 4).[29]
2. Physical therapy may temporarily improve joint mobility in diabetes (Level 4).[40]

REFERENCES

1. Jacobson AM, de Groot M, Samson JA. The evaluation of two measures of quality of life in patients with Type 1 and Type 2 diabetes. Diabetes Care 1994;17:267–74.

2. Eiser C, Flynn M, Green E, et al. Quality of life in young adults with Type 1 diabetes in relation to demographic and disease variables. Diabet Med 1992;9:375–8.

3. Wredling R, Stalhammar J, Adamson U, et al. Well-being and treatment satisfaction in adults with diabetes: a Swedish population based study. Qual Life Res 1996:515–22.

4. Adams PC, Speechley M. The effect of arthritis on the quality of life in hereditary hemochromatosis. J Rheumatol 1996;26:707–10.

5. Gartsman G, Brinker M, Khan M, Karahan M. Self-assessment of general health status in patients with five common shoulder conditions. J Shoulder Elbow Surg 1998;7:228–37.

6. Vezyroglou G, Mitropoulous A, Kyriazis N, Antoniadis C. A metabolic syndrome in diffuse idiopathic skeletal hyperostosis. A controlled study. J Rheumatol 1996;23:672–6.

7. Tsukamoto Y, Onitsuka H, Lee K. Radiological aspects of diffuse idiopathic skeletal hyperostosis in the spine. AJR Am J Roentgenol 1977;129:913–8.

8. Bouillon R. Diabetic bone disease. Calcif Tissue Int 1991;49:155–60.

9. Rosen C. Endocrine disorders and osteoporosis. Curr Opin Rheumatol 1997;9:355–61.

10. Jehle P, Jehle D, Mohan S, Bohm B. Serum levels of insulin like growth factor system components and relationship to bone metabolism in Type 1 and Type 2 diabetics. J Endocrinol 1998;159:297–306.

11. Hui S, Epstein S, Johnston C. A prospective study of bone mass in patients with Type 1 insulin dependent diabetes mellitus. J Clin Endocrinol Metab 1985;60:74–80.

12. Mathiassin B, Nielsen S, Ditzel J. Long term bone loss in insulin dependent diabetes mellitus. J Intern Med 1990;227:325–7.

13. Clausen P, Feldt-Rasmussen B, Jacobsen P. Microalbuminuria as an early indicator of osteopenia in male insulin dependent diabetic patients. Diabet Med 1997;14:1038–43.

14. Lunt H, Florkowski C, Kundy T, et al. A population based study of bone mineral density in women with longstanding Type 1 (insulin-dependent) diabetes. Diabetes Res Clin Pract 1998;40:131–8.

15. Heath H. Bone mineral density in non-insulin dependent diabetes. Ann Intern Med 1996;125:253.

16. Sayinalp S, Gedic O, Corey Z. Increasing serum osteocalcin after glycemic control in diabetic men. Calcif Tissue Int 1995;57:422–5.

17. Rosato MT, Schneider SH, Shapses SA. Bone turnover and insulin like growth factor levels increase after improved glycemic control in non-insulin dependent diabetes mellitus. Calcif Tissue Int 1998;63:107–11.

18. Inaba M, Nishizawa Y, Mita K, et al. Poor glycemic control impairs the response of biochemical parameters of bone formation and resorption to exogenous 1,25+ dihydroxy vitamin D3 in patients with Type 2 diabetes. Osteoporos Int 1999;9:525–31.

19. Frey MI, Barrett-Connor E, Sledge PA, et al. The effect of non-insulin dependent diabetes mellitus on the prevalence of clinical osteoarthritis. A population based study. J Rheumatol 1996;23:716–22.

20. Bagge E, Bjelle A, Edon S, Spanborg A. Factors associated with radiography osteoarthritis: results from a population study of 70 year old people in Goteborg. J Rheumatol 1991;18:1218–22.

21. Crisp A, Heathcort J. Connective tissue abnormalities in diabetes mellitus. J Royal Coll Physicians Lond 1984;18:132–41.

22. Waine H, Nevinney D, Rosenthal J, Joffe IB. Association of osteoarthritis and diabetes mellitus. Tufts Folia Medica 1961;7:13–9.

23. Arkkila P, Kantola I, Viikari J, Ronnemaa T. Shoulder capsulitis in Type 1 and Type 2 diabetic patients: association with diabetic complications and related diseases. Ann Rheum Dis 1996;55:907–14.

24. Mavrikakis ME, Sfikakis PP, Kontoyannis SA, et al. Clinical and laboratory parameters in adult diabetics with and without calcific shoulder periarthritis. Calcif Tissue Int 1991;49:288–91.

25. Chammas M, Bousquet P, Renard E, et al. Dupuytren's disease, carpal tunnel syndrome, trigger finger and diabetes mellitus. J Hand Surg 1995;20:109–14.

26. Arkkila P, Kantola I, Viikari J. Dupuytren's disease: associated with chronic diabetic complications. J Rheumatol 1997;24:153–9.

27. Arkkila P, Kantola I, Viikari J, et al. Dupuytren's disease in Type 1 diabetic patients: a five year prospective study. Clin Exp Rheumatol 1996;14:59–65.

28. Gamstedt A, Holm-Glad J, Ohlson C, Sundstrom M. Hand abnormalities are strongly associated with the duration of diabetes mellitus. J Intern Med 1993;234:189–93.

29. Sibbitt WL Jr, Eaton RP. Corticosteroid response of tenosynovitis is a common pathway for limited joint mobility in the diabetic hand. J Rheumatol 1997;24:931–6.

30. Rosenbloom AL, Silverstein JH, Lezotte DC, et al. Limited joint mobility in childhood diabetes mellitus indicates increased risk for microvascular disease. N Engl J Med 1981;305:191–4.

31. Lawson PM, Maneschi F, Kohner EM. The relationship of hand abnormalities to diabetes and diabetic retinopathy. Diabetes Care 1983;6:140–3.

32. Rosenbloom AL, Silverstein JH, Lezotte DC, et al. Limited joint mobility in diabetes mellitus in childhood: natural history in relationship to growth impairment. J Pediatr 1982;101:874–8.

33. Kennedy L, Beacom R, Archer DB, et al. Limited joint mobility in Type 1 diabetes mellitus. Postgrad Med J 1982;58:481–4.

34. Starkman HS, Gleason RE, Rand LI, et al. Limited joint mobility of the hand in patients with diabetes mellitus relationship to chronic complications. Ann Rheum Dis 1986;45:130–5.

35. Arkkila P, Kantola I, Viikari J, et al. Limited joint mobility is associated with the presence but does not predict the development of microvascular complication in type 1 diabetes. Diabet Med 1996;13:828–33.

36. Silverstein J, Gordon D, Pollock B, Rosenbloom A. Long term glycemic control influences the onset of limited joint mobility in type 1 diabetes. J Pediatr 1998;132:944–7.

37. McCance D, Crowe G, Quinn M. Incidence of microvascular complications in type 1 diabetic subjects with limited joint mobility: a 10 year prospective study. Diabet Med 1993;10:807–10.

38. Odetti P, Aragno I, Rolandi R, et al. Scanning force microscopy reveals structural alternatives in diabetic rat collagen fibrils: role of protein glycation. Diabetes Metab Res Rev 2000;16:74–81.

39. Monnier VM, Bautista O, Kenny D, et al. Skin collagen glycation, glycoxidation and cross-linking are lower in subjects with long term intensive versus conventional therapy of type 1 diabetes: relevance of glycated collagen products versus hemoglobin A_{1C} as markers of diabetes complications. DCCT Skin Collagen Ancillary Study Group. Diabetes Control and Complications Trial. Diabetes 1999;48:870–80.

40. Dijs HM, Roofthooft JM, Driessens MF, et al. Effect of physical therapy on limited joint mobility in the diabetic foot: a pilot study. J Am Podiatr Med Assoc 2000;90:121–32.

41. Fernando DJ, Masson EA, Veves A, Boulton AJ. Relationship of limited joint mobility to abnormal foot pressures and diabetic foot ulceration. Diabetes Care 1991;14:8–11.

42. Crisp A, Heathcote J. Connective tissue abnormalities in diabetes mellitus. J Coll Physicians Lond 1984;18:132–41.

43. Arkkila PE, Kantola IM, Viikari JS. Limited joint mobility in diabetic patients. Correlation with other diabetic complications. J Intern Med 1994;236:215–23.

CHAPTER 27

Erectile Dysfunction

Jeremy P.W. Heaton, MD, FACS, FRCSC,
Alvaro Morales, MD, FRCSC, FACS, and Michael A. Adams, PhD

—————

ABSTRACT

Diabetes is a significant cause of erectile and sexual dysfunction. The pathologic processes in diabetes that particularly compromise the responsivity of vascular systems preferentially impact on the vulnerable vascular bed of the penis. About 36% of men with diabetes will experience some degree of erectile dysfunction. Unfortunately, this high-risk population is also difficult to treat. All of the pharmacologic therapies for erectile dysfunction have shown a decrease in efficacy in diabetic patients in comparison with non-diabetic patients. The many strategies for the treatment of erectile dysfunction share an important distinction from most other medical conditions in that the treatment is directed by the choice of the patient and partner. Alprostadil by intracavernous injection has been shown to benefit up to 94% of men with erectile dysfunction and diabetes. Sildenafil will restore the capacity for intercourse in >40% of diabetic patients. Other pharmacologic treatments are available and in development. Ultimately, penile rigidity may be created surgically if the sexual needs of the couple require it.

—————

INTRODUCTION

The last 5 years have been a momentous period of time for health care professionals and patients concerned with erectile dysfunction (ED). The understanding of the condition has progressed scientifically and socially, the pharmacotherapy has expanded dramatically, and the responsibility for care is shifting. Sexual function is an important component of the life of most people who anticipate keeping active into their later years, even in the face of chronic disease. It is now often possible to restore function medically in a large proportion of men. A remaining barrier is the unwillingness of many practicing physicians to take a lead in reviewing this with patients as a routine and relevant health issue. The essential feature of this recent surge of progress has been the introduction of new effective and safe medications that have each advanced the art substantially. The most recent step is the introduction of sildenafil (Viagra, Pfizer, NY) and its adoption by a wider range of patients and prescribers than could ever have been suspected even 3 years ago. The compounds currently under review, such as apomorphine SL and new (second) generation phosphodiesterase inhibitors, will further broaden the range of therapies and herald a phase of maturation of therapeutics in ED.

Erectile dysfunction is particularly frequent in men with diabetes, who constitute a prime population to benefit from single or multiple agents. Indeed, diabetes mellitus (DM) is one of the most common causes of ED. It constitutes a special subset of ED and one that is receiving increasing attention since the world is facing a pandemic of DM.

This chapter reviews the issues important to the management of ED and highlights special considerations for people with diabetes by answering the following questions:

1. What is erectile dysfunction?
2. How common is erectile dysfunction in men with diabetes?
3. Why does erectile dysfunction occur?
4. What are the risk factors for ED in men with diabetes?
5. How is ED assessed?
6. How is ED best managed?

WHAT IS ERECTILE DYSFUNCTION?

Erectile dysfunction is the preferred term for impotence as a result of the deliberations at the Consensus Conference in Impotence held by the US National Institutes of Health in 1992. The definition for ED provided as a result of this conference is "inability to attain and/or maintain penile erection sufficient for satisfactory sexual performance."[1] This term is less demeaning for patients than the term "impotence" and provides a framework for defining a diagnostic basis for identifying patients with ED. Still missing from this is the concept of time (continuous or for the last 3 months). Resolutions to this and many other issues are expected as a result of ongoing study.[2]

The subclassification of ED into clinically useful groups has not yet provided a basis for predicting therapy or outcomes, although much effort to this end has been expended.[3] In fact, useful subclassifications almost certainly will follow the development of a range of good therapies for ED. As long as therapeutic choice is restricted to one effective oral compound and patient preference, there is little need for a classification to help select therapy or predict success.

HOW COMMON IS ERECTILE DYSFUNCTION IN MEN WITH DIABETES?

There are few published sources of incidence data on erectile dysfunction, despite the many studies that have been designed to assess the epidemiology of ED in a number of countries. The general obstacles of proving a diagnosis of ED create difficulties in standardizing methodology, recruitment, question interpretation, and reporting accuracy. True incidence data can only be collected when the same group of patients is reassessed after a period of time has elapsed. Currently, the best estimate is that, in Caucasian men 40 to 69 years old, a rate of ED of 26 cases per 1,000 man-years can be expected.[4] This study also confirms all other studies in finding significant associations between age, diabetes, hypertension, cardiovascular disease, and ED. In this study, the age-adjusted relative risk (RR) of incident ED from diabetes was 1.83, which is higher than that documented for untreated heart disease or hypertension.

The best-accepted prevalence data derives from the Massachusetts Male Aging Study (MMAS), in which diabetes was again found to be a significant associated factor.[5] The Krimpen study, among others, also supports this finding, although only the data on benign prostatic hyperplasia have been published.[6] The basis for this close connection is likely due to the strong association of ED with vascular problems.

EVIDENCE-BASED MESSAGE

Diabetes inceases the risk of erectile dysfunction 1.5- to 2-fold; other risk factors include age, lower education, hypertension, and heart disease (Level 1).[4]

WHY DOES ERECTILE DYSFUNCTION OCCUR?

A brief review of the physiology of erections and the etiology of ED is provided below to facilitate understanding of the various therapeutic options.

Normal Physiology of Erections

Erections occur as a result of an orchestrated cascade of neural, cellular, and vascular events spanning brain initiation to penile rigidification. Reproductive systems have a very fundamental position in the survival of the species, and it is no surprise to discover the important role of ancient parts of the brain (the limbic system)[7] and the availability of multiple and overlapping pathways (redundancy).[8] These pathways balance proerectile and antierectile signals, with the central pathways providing overriding control and the spinal cord functional coordination and peripheral erectile reflex capability. Dopaminergic receptors have an important role in this signal transmission pathway[9] and provide an opportunity for centrally acting pharmacotherapy of erection, such as apomorphine.[10] Other neurotransmitters, such as serotonin and oxytocin, also play critical roles.[11] Spinal cord centers integrate central and local pelvic neural inputs, resulting in coordinated vasodilation (smooth muscle relaxation) in pelvic arteries, the cavernous arteries, and the smooth muscle of the penile trabecular tissue itself. In addition, there is some supportive somatic stimulation, and detumescence occurs through adrenergic signaling. The observation that reflex erections are possible, and may involve only spinal cord circuits, highlights the importance of reducing inhibition in these spinal cord centers as a means of causing an erection.

How this nerve traffic results in changes in penile rigidity was studied in the late 1980s and early 1990s. A major clarification came as a result of the discovery of the importance of the endothelium and nitric oxide (NO) in the physiology of erections.[12,13] This was the basis for the most important therapeutic developments of the past decade: sildenafil and the phosphodiesterase inhibitors.[14] Incoming nerve signals stimulate a rise in local NO, which diffuses into smooth muscle cells and activates guanylyl cyclase, which then generates cyclic guanylyl monophosphate (cGMP). This, in turn, activates cellular ion movement and smooth muscle relaxation.[15] An alternative pathway is the prostanoid pathway that works through similar and parallel mechanisms but involves cyclic adenylyl monophosphate (cAMP) production.[16] The end changes in ion flux and smooth muscle mechanics are similar for both pathways, although the protein kinases have important differences.[17] The cAMP pathway is the basis for the local action of prostaglandin E1—the first effective pharmacotherapy for ED to become available.

Smooth muscle relaxation on its own is insufficient to account for penile rigidity. The two other vital components are the availability of sufficient blood supply at adequate volume flow and pressure and functional structural mechanisms in the penis. Smooth muscle relaxation results in vasodilation, which permits an inrush of arterial blood. The inrush expands the spongy trabecular tissue of the corpora cavernosa, which, when sufficient, compresses the effluent veins lying between the trabecular tissue and the tough layers, containing fibrous tissue (the tunica), of the outside of the cavernous bodies. This compression of the veins traps the blood from escaping (veno-occlusion) and converts the high flow of the developing erection into the low flow of a rigid, fully erect penis. Detumescence occurs through active adrenergic constriction of the inflow arteries, which causes a decrease in inflow, a decrease in trabecular tissue pressure, and a consequent increase in runoff from the veins (decreasing the veno-occlusion), which empties the trabecular tissue.

Etiology of Erectile Dysfunction

From the foregoing, it is clear that any neural problems that affect the brain, midbrain, or spinal cord involved (eg, multiple sclerosis or spinal cord injury) may cause ED. Central biochemical disturbances or neurotransmitter disorders (eg, depression), surgical procedures to parts of the erectile system (pelvic nerves or penis), and diseases that directly affect the penis (cancer and Peyronie's disease) may all cause ED. Moreover, diseases of the vascular system, including hypertension and atherosclerosis, clearly increase the risk of ED. Finally, anatomic obliteration of smooth muscle in the cavernosa (or excess fibrosis) precludes achievement of normal erections. The fact that diabetes is a strong risk factor for many of these diseases likely accounts for the association of diabetes with ED.

Most men with ED have both functional impairment and structural damage.[18] For example, small defects in endothelial function, plus excessive adrenergic or renin angiotensin system (inhibitory) activity, may cause overwhelming vasoconstriction that is not reversed by normal proerectile signals. These considerations are the basis for the success of different pharmacotherapeutic approaches to treating ED.

Establishing the etiology of ED in an individual patient is based largely on the presentation and on clinical judgment. However, although risk factors may be identified, they are seldom the sole cause. Fortunately, effective therapy does not require identification of the cause; the clinical response to a drug and the choice of the patient ("goal-directed" therapy)[19] are the dominant factors in selecting therapy today.

What Are the Risk Factors for Erectile Dysfunction in Men with Diabetes?

The prevalence of ED in a large group of diabetic men has been estimated at about 36%. The percentage increased with age, the need for insulin, the historical quality of control, and the duration of diabetes.[20]

A recent Australian study focusing on diabetic men with ED found that the mean age at onset of ED was 48.4 and 58.4 years for those with Type 1 and Type 2 DM, respectively. In both groups, the majority had DM for over 5 years. Most men were overweight, and over one-third exhibited an abnormal lipid profile. Other factors associated with ED, and presumed contributors to erectile problems, included hypertension, ischemic heart disease, and peripheral vascular disease.[21] Studies of the arterial factors pertaining to ED in the diabetic patient have suggested that the incidence is similar in both Type 1 and Type 2 diabetes.[21]

Neurodegeneration[23] and neuropathic problems,[24] and even a possible "central neuropathy," may lead to ED in diabetic men.[25] Autonomic assessment may have a particular role in people with diabetes, although the consequences of the findings for changing or improving therapy have not been established. Evidence of peripheral neuropathy increases the likelihood of ED.[26]

More important is the finding that glycemic control, as determined by hemoglobin A_{1c}, is significantly associated with measures of the severity of ED.[27] There are no prospective data yet showing that changing glycemic control can change treatment or outcome, but the evidence in other vascular conditions is encouraging. Although there are clinical impressions that indicate that glycemic control may impact on the rate of onset of ED, there are as yet no data to support this.

How Is Erectile Dysfunction Assessed?

The best way of identifying ED is through a careful history and physical examination (Table 27–1). Because they are at high risk, men with diabetes should be routinely asked about ED. No accepted measurement (eg, blood test or imaging study) can determine the amount of erectile failure; specifically, the routine use of ultrasound, intracavernous injection, nocturnal testing, or any other invasive study in the primary assessment of the patient has no support in the literature. Although there are validated psychometric scales, such as the International Index of Erectile Function (or its short forms)[28] or the Brief Sexual Function Inventory,[29] these are best suited to trials, not to clinical practice. These instruments cannot replace an interactive clinical history. Erectile dysfunction should be clinically distinguished from premature ejaculation or desire disorders; there should be a thorough psychosexual history taken, and partner status needs to be evaluated. Erectile dysfunction risk factors such as diabetes should also be identified; the importance of a proper medication history is key, as various medications may cause ED (hydrochlorothiazide, beta-blockers, antiandrogens) and may have important drug interactions with potential therapies (eg, nitrates and phosphodiesterase inhibitors). The clinical assessment should clearly include the cardiovascular system (including heart rate and blood pressure); the genital exam should include the prostate.

Laboratory investigation is then guided by the presentation. For example, if there are no other known medical problems, a search for these and risk factors for vascular disease (such as

---

Table 27–1 Assessment of Patients with Erectile Dysfunction

History and physical examination

Education

Medication factors

Reversible factors

Lifestyle changes

Laboratory tests

hypertension, hyperlipidemia, and DM), is indicated. If there are known risk factors and ED is a new complaint, serum androgens (usually a bioavailable or free testosterone between 8:00 am and 10:00 am), serum prolactin, and a serum prostate-specific androgen may be indicated. It should be remembered that hypogonadism is difficult to diagnose in adults on a purely clinical basis and that biochemical confirmation is mandatory prior to onset of therapy.[30]

Neurologic testing may be useful in people with diabetes.[31] Nerve conduction studies may provide information regarding future therapeutic strategies, but a specific focus on these in the diabetic patient with ED is unlikely to change the approach to therapy.

How Is Erectile Dysfunction Best Managed?

Most men developing erectile dysfunction will experience a period where they will have significant fluctuation in their erectile ability. At such times, education, counseling, and stopping or altering any suspected drugs may be all that is required. If ineffective, medical therapy should be considered to avoid possible deterioration in self-esteem and the relationship.

Nonmedical Management

Current therapy of ED in people with diabetes is the same as it is in other individuals. This includes patient education, attention to medications, and cessation of any potentially causal agents including smoking, reversal of particular risk factors, and lifestyle modification (including regular exercise and dietary changes) where appropriate. Optimal therapy of diabetes together with any coexisting conditions (hypertension and dyslipidemia), should underlie any management of patients with ED.

Pharmacotherapy for Erectile Dysfunction

The natural state of the penis is detumescence (inhibitor dominance), and the opportunity for disruption of proerectile mechanisms is great. The many neural and biochemical pathways involved in an erection provide as many opportunities as do pathophysiologic vulnerabilities.

There are a number of current and proposed therapeutic strategies for treating ED, which can be classified according to their site and mode of action.[32] Table 27–2 provides a logical framework for comparing drugs and clinical trial results and may eventually be useful for clustering patients by the response within a therapeutic group. This classification allows clinicians to understand the differences and similarities between the new therapies in a practical way.

Central initiators with clinical data include apomorphine SL (TAP Pharmaceuticals Inc., Deerfield, IL),[33] other dopamine agonists, and melanocyte-stimulating hormone (MSH) analogues.[34] The central mode of action takes advantage of the natural amplification that occurs between the central nervous system (CNS) and the effector systems in the periphery.

Table 27–2 Current and Proposed Therapies for Erectile Dysfunction

	Initiator	Conditioner	Other
Centrally Acting	Apomorphine MSH analogues	Testosterone	
Peripherally Acting	PGE1, TT VIP/phen	Sildenafil, phen, PDEI, gene therapy	
			Prosthesis, VED

MSH = melanocyte-stimulating hormone; VIP = vasoactive intestinal polypeptide; PDEI = new phosphodiesterase inhibitors; phen = phentolamine; PGE1 = prostaglandin E1; TT = PGE1, phen, papaverine mix; VED = vacuum erection device.

Peripheral initiators cause vasodilation through direct action in vascular tissue. The penis is highly accessible to the direct introduction of agents, so almost anything that will cause vasodilation has been tested for intracavernous injection (ICI) or transdermal (penile skin) application. These vasoactive agents act directly on vascular smooth muscle cells or indirectly, leading to the release of vasoactive agents such as NO from vascular endothelial cells or neurons.[35] Currently, prostaglandin E1 (PGE1) is the basic component of the most common forms of peripheral initiator treatment. Other agents in this class or under consideration include triple therapy,[36] new forms of PGE1, SIN (3-morpholino-syndomimin)-1,[37] VIP (vasoactive intestinal polypeptide),[38] CGRP (calcitonin gene-related peptide),[39] and potassium-channel openers.[40]

Central conditioners that enable or enhance erectile function centrally may overlap with drugs that affect libido and orgasm. Testosterone[41] is the best example of such an agent, although it is not a primary therapy for ED. Peripheral conditioners increase the activity of peripheral systems that support or cause erections. They are best typified by the first of the type 5 phosphodiesterase inhibitors, sildenafil (Viagra, Pfizer, NY). Phentolamine (Vasomax, Schering-Plough, Madison, NJ), an α-adrenoceptor blocker, is another peripheral conditioner when prepared for use as a therapy for ED.

Agents for which there is some evidence of efficacy are discussed individually (vide infra). The outcomes of treatments for ED are uniquely complex to assess because of the subjective nature of sexual success and the participation by a partner of individual needs. This variability haunts the need for clear definitions of patient intake in clinical trials and clinical outcomes. The aforementioned psychometric instruments help considerably in achieving comparability, but there is still a wide variation in displaying the results of treatment, and the reader is cautioned to bear this in mind, particularly with reference to therapeutic trials not subject to regulatory authority guidance.

Sildenafil

Sildenafil is a peripheral conditioner. It acts as a type 5 phosphodiesterase inhibitor (inhibiting the degradation of cGMP by phosphodiesterase type 5 enzymes; Figure 27–1), thereby enhancing the availability of cGMP and promoting vasodilation; the specificity of action of sildenafil for erectile smooth muscle is based on the relative preponderance of type 5 phosphodiesterase isozymes in penile smooth muscle.

In the many published trials and in clinical use, sildenafil has shown a clear dose-response relationship and significant efficacy. The definitive article on sildenafil is the report of two studies published by Goldstein and colleagues.[42] At doses of 100 mg, 69% of patients indicated that sildenafil had improved their erections. A number of subsequent publications have confirmed the safety and efficacy of the drug in general and in specific ED populations.[43]

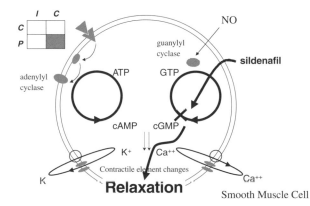

Figure 27–1 Simplified schematic showing the conceptual action of sildenafil in inhibiting the breakdown of cGMP thereby increasing its effect. The interacting vasodilator systems are included for context.

One published clinical trial also demonstrated efficacy in people with diabetes[44]; 268 patients took sildenafil citrate at 50 mg with the option to adjust the dose to 100 mg or 25 mg based on efficacy and tolerability for 12 weeks. Fifty-six percent of 131 evaluable patients in the sildenafil group reported improved erections (vs 10% in the placebo group, $p < .001$). Sixty-one percent of 117 evaluable patients taking sildenafil had at least one successful attempt at sexual intercourse (vs 22% taking placebo, $p < .001$). Adverse events related to treatment were reported for 16% of patients taking sildenafil (headache 11%, dyspepsia 9%, and respiratory tract disorder 6%, predominantly sinus congestion or drainage). The incidence of adverse cardiovascular events was comparable for both groups (3% sildenafil, 5% placebo).

The response rate in diabetic patients is less than in the general ED population but is typical of relative responses to pharmacotherapy in this population. Although publications frequently do not specify any possible relationship between the response to sildenafil and the severity of DM, an overall response of ~45% is generally acknowledged.[45]

The media has created a major issue surrounding the safety of sildenafil, which centers on cardiovascular and ocular toxicities.[46] The safety of the drug has been documented in extensive clinical trials and physicians should refer to the published literature for an understanding of the drugs they use, particularly sildenafil, and should not draw on or supply reports in the media for medical information. Naturally, the men in these trials have been carefully selected, and those taking nitrates were excluded. Since the drug became commercially available, further experience confirmed its cardiovascular safety when used under appropriate conditions.[47] There is similar information regarding potential detrimental effects to the retina.[48]

EVIDENCE-BASED MESSAGE

In > 40% of people with diabetes and ED, 25, 50, or 100 mg of sildenafil leads to successful intercourse (Level 1A).[44]

Apomorphine

Apomorphine HCl is the first centrally active agent ED drug; the sublingual tablet has been tested in phase III trials.[49] It is an aporphine (not an opiate) that acts as a dopaminergic agonist effective at nanogram concentrations, working in the midbrain (paraventricular and supraoptic nuclei).[50] Figure 27–2 depicts the essentials of the action of apomorphine in the brain. Since apomorphine acts centrally, any prosexual signaling is enhanced, and following the natural pathways, it generates an erectile response. The action on nuclei affecting erection is highly specific and sensitive, and there is little discernable direct action on cells outside the central nervous system at the doses used.

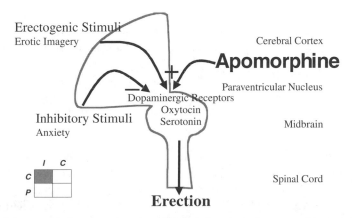

Figure 27–2 Conceptual diagram showing the site of action of apomorphine and its role in enhancing proerectile signaling in the midbrain.

In clinical trials,[51] in a representative patient population, the success rates (percentage of attempts resulting in an erection firm enough for intercourse based on all attempts) have been found to be 48 to 53% (placebo 35%; $p < .001$) resulted in actual intercourse in 45 to 51% of attempts (placebo 33%; $p < .001$). Data from the partners of patients almost exactly overlap these efficacy statistics. The response has been found to have a time to onset of 10 to 28 minutes (interquartile ranges), which is similar to untreated patients in the same measurement conditions, but with amorphine, the erections occur with greater frequency. The most commonly reported side effect was mild to moderate nausea, which occurred in up to 24% of patients at dose optimized to 2 to 4 mg. The frequency of nausea decreased after regular usage. Vasovagal syncope has occurred at a rate of about 0.6% in trials designed to model clinical usage. Apomorphine has been shown to be effective and safe in patients with hypertension, with cardiac disease, and in ED of all severities. Subgroup analysis of patients with diabetes has shown that apomorphine is effective at clinically and statistically relevant levels (40 to 48%),[52] a lower rate than for the general ED population as is appropriate for the increase in severity of ED in this group.

EVIDENCE-BASED MESSAGE

In > 40% of people with diabetes and ED, sublingual apomorphine leads to successful intercourse (Level 2).[52]

Phentolamine

Phentolamine mesylate is a peripheral conditioner delivered as Vasomax. It is an α-adrenoceptor blocker and acts to limit the vasoconstrictive effects of α-adrenoceptor activation as typified by stress response.[53] The preparation undergoing phase III trials is designed for oral administration at doses between 40 and 80 mg. Peak plasma levels are achieved within 60 minutes. At 40 and 80 mg, 55% and 59% of men, respectively, were able to achieve penetration at some time.[54] There are no data yet available on the specific efficacy of phentolamine on ED in diabetic patients.

EVIDENCE-BASED MESSAGE

There are no data regarding the efficacy on oral phentolamine in diabetic patients with ED, but penetration has been shown to be possible in up to 59% of ED patients in a clinical trial.

Yohimbine

There has been a continuing interest in the use of yohimbine in the treatment of ED.[55] Yohimbine is a presynaptic α-2 adrenoceptor agonist, although its precise mechanism and location of action in ED is not know. There are two meta-analyses that help dissect the difficult and vague primary literature relating to yohimbine. One points to the poor design of most studies,[56] and the other concludes that yohimbine may be considered as a reasonable therapeutic option with superiority over placebo (odds ratio 3.85, 95% confidence interval.[57] Yohimbine is not approved for use in ED, although sporadic ad hoc use continues.

EVIDENCE-BASED MESSAGE

Two meta-analyses suggest the superiority of yohimbine over placebo in various endpoints in the treatment of ED, although thera are no data regarding patients with diabetes.

Prostaglandin E1

Prostaglandin E1 for ED has been available since 1996 for intracavernous use (Caverject, Edex) and since 1998 as an intraurethral preparation (MUSE). Caverject has been assessed in an international multicenter study in diabetic men. Overall, 94% of men were able to find an effective dose (average 20 µg).[58] Direct application of powerful vasodilators has great appeal in the management of ED; however, the nonoral routes have proved to be a significant deterrent to widespread use. Nevertheless, the efficacy of intracavernous injections with PGE1 and the freedom to titrate doses to suit an individual have proven to be two persuasive factors in using it to treat people with diabetes.

EVIDENCE-BASED MESSAGE

Local application of alprostadil (PGE1) is an effective therapy for erectile dysfunction in men with diabetes (Level 1A).[58]

Vacuum Erection Devices

Vacuum erection devices (VED), create erections by drawing blood into the penis under negative pressure, where it is trapped by means of a customized rubber ring at the base of the penis.[53] These devices are well accepted by some patients and are a good example of the relevance of patient choice and good patient support. They are clumsy to use, however, and should be prescribed and supported by a knowledgeable team. Studies in diabetic men suggest that 75% of men may be able to have intercourse using the vacuum devices.[59]

EVIDENCE-BASED MESSAGE

Vacuum erection devices are an effective therapy for ED in men and 75% of men with ED and diabetes may achieve penetration (Level 3).[59]

Prostheses

People with diabetes constitute some of the most challenging populations for pharmacotherapy of ED. The insertion of penile prostheses avoids the need for functional cavernosal tissue and is therefore a universal, if invasive, option. Prosthesis implantation carries specific potential problems as well. Perioperative precautions regarding infectious disease need special attention although there is no increase in risk depending on the value of glycosylated hemoglobin.[60] Diabetic patients are more prone to develop wound infections,[61] and in the case of a prosthetic device, an infection may have devastating effects.[62] In a large-scale study, 13% of patients were diabetic, and overall , 87% had erections suitable for intercourse.[63]

EVIDENCE-BASED MESSAGE

Penile prostheses are an effective invasive therapy for erectile dysfunction in people with diabetes (Level 3).[63]

Testosterone

In diabetes, as in other chronic diseases, levels of testosterone and sex hormone-binding globulin may be decreased.[64] This phenomenon may theoretically result in an insufficient amount of bioavailable testosterone for sexual performance in some men. However, the efficacy of providing testosterone as a primary therapy of ED in mildly hypogonadal men is approximately 60%,[65] but when this condition is coincident with diabetes, there are no data to guide us. A recent meta-analysis of testosterone therapy for ED suggested an improvement over placebo, "implying a role for supplementation in select groups."[66] The issue is not clarified by reports of low testosterone levels in elderly men with Type 2 diabetes because in this population other comorbidities may contribute more than the mild diabetic condition.[67] In general, the use of testosterone ona speculative basis in the management of ED is attended by risks and discouraged in the absence of clear hormonal indications.

EVIDENCE-BASED MESSAGE

Testosterone therapy should be given as a response to documented androgen abnormalities (Level 4)[68] and cannot be considered as primary therapy of ED in diabetics.

New Agents

There are other new agents for ED in clinical trials, and developing specific preventive and management strategies for people with diabetes and ED is recognized as a priority. Most of the new drugs currently under consideration are phosphodiesterase inhibitors. Other interesting possibilities are being studied using endothelin-receptor antagonists, potassium-channel openers, and protein-kinase modulators.

Female Sexual Dysfunction

Female sexual dysfunction is justifiably receiving increasing attention.[69] It is clear that the anatomic and functional demands of sexual activity for men and women have both parallels and vital differences. It is also becoming clear that while much of the basic physiology of the penis and clitoris is equivalent, the actual nature of the problems women face in terms of sexual dysfunction cover a quite different spectrum of etiology and epidemiology.[70] There may be a subset of problems faced by women with diabetes, but, as for all women with sexual dysfunction, there is at present no established diagnostic or therapeutic framework.

CONCLUSION

Future generations of treatments for ED will incorporate a variety of mechanistic strategies, some of which may be especially suited to ED patients with diabetes. The field of hypertension has shown how improvements in pharmacotherapy naturally incorporate new classes of agents and variations within those classes. The therapy of ED will probably expand from monotherapy to combination therapy, and this should be based on suitable studies documenting real gains in efficacy, continuing safety, and better understanding of the characteristics of appropriate patient populations. Diabetic patients have been shown to be particularly susceptible to the development of ED and more resistant to the treatments that have found their way into clinical practice. For patients, rapid expansion of the therapy available for ED means that they now have a choice of effective medications; in the next 5 years, that choice will expand further. The medical choices and disease evaluation are now within the scope of a wide range of physicians, which will further enhance the management of this increasingly common problem. One would expect that prevention should be possible and that treatment, nearing the status of a cure, would eventually be available for many ED victims. For many people with diabetes, such a resolution may best be achieved in the form of successful management of the diabetes and prevention of the ED.

SUMMARY OF EVIDENCE-BASED MESSAGES

1. Diabetes increases the risk of ED 1.5- to 2-fold; other risk factors include age, lower education, hypertension, and heart disease (Level 1).[4]
2. In > 40% of people with diabetes and ED, 25, 50, or 100 mg of sildenafil leads to successful intercourse (Level 1A).[41]
3. In > 40% of attempts in men with diabetes and ED, sublingual apomorphine leads to successful intercourse (Level 2).[52]
4. There are no data regarding the efficacy of oral phentolamine in diabetic patients with ED, but penetration has been shown to be possible in up to 59% of ED patients in a clinical trial.
5. Two meta-analyses suggest superiority of yohimbine over placebo in various endpoints in the treatment of ED, although there are no data regarding patients with diabetes.
6. Local application of alprostadil (PGE1) is an effective therapy for ED in men with diabetes particularly when delivered by intracavernous injection where 94% will achieve an effective response (Level 1A).[58]

7. Vacuum erection devices are an effective therapy for ED in men and 75% of men with ED and diabetes may achieve penetration (Level 3).[59]

8. Penile prostheses are an effective invasive therapy for ED in people with diabetes (Level 3).[63]

9. Testosterone therapy should be given as a response to documented androgen abnormalities (Level 4).[71] and cannot be considered as primary therapy of ED in diabetes.

REFERENCES

1. NIH Consensus Development Panel on Impotence. JAMA 1993;270:83–90.

2. Jardin A, Wagner G, Khoury S, et al. editors. Erectile dysfunction. 1st International Consultation on Erectile Dysfunction. Paris:Health Publications;2000.

3. Lizza EF, Rosen RC. Definition and classification of erectile dysfunction: report of the Nomenclature Committee of the International Society of Impotence Research. Int J Impot Res 1999;11:141–3.

4. Johannes CB, Araujo AB, Feldman HA, et al. Incidence of erectile dysfunction in men 40–69 years old: longitudinal results from the Massachusetts Male Aging Study. J Urol 2000;163:460–3.

5. Feldman HA, Goldstein I, Hatzichristou DG, et al. Impotence and its medical and psychosocial correlates: results of the Massachusetts Male Aging Study. J Urol 1994;151:54–61.

6. Blanker MH, Groeneveld FP, Prins A, et al. Strong effects of definition and nonresponse bias on prevalence rates of clinical benign prostatic hyperplasia: the Krimpen study of male urogenital tract problems and general health status. Br J Urol Int 2000;85:665–71.

7. McKenna K. The brain is the master organ in sexual function: central nervous system control of male and female sexual function. Int J Impot Res 1999;11(Suppl 1):S48–55.

8. Adams MA, Banting JD, Maurice DH, et al. Vascular control mechanisms in penile erection: phylogeny and the inevitability of multiple and overlapping systems. Int J Impot Res 1997;9:85–91.

9. Argiolas A, Melis MR, Mauri A, Gessa GL. Paraventricular nucleus lesion prevents yawning and penile erection induced by apomorphine and oxytocin but not by ACTH in rats. Brain Res 1987;421:349–52.

10. Heaton JP, Morales A, Adams MA, et al. Recovery of erectile function by the oral administration of apomorphine. Urology 1995;45:200–6.

11. Maeda N, Matsuoka N, Yamaguchi I. Role of the dopaminergic, serotonergic and cholinergic link in the expression of penile erection in rats. Jpn J Pharmacol 1994;66:59–66.

12. Rajfer J, Aronson WJ, Bush PA, et al. Nitric oxide as a mediator of relaxation of the corpus cavernosum in response to nonadrenergic, noncholinergic neurotransmission. N Engl J Med 1992:9;326:90–4.

13. Argiolas A. Nitric oxide is a central mediator of penile erection. Neuropharmacology 1994;33:1339–44.

14. Goldstein I, Lue TF, Padma-Nathan H, et al. Oral sildenafil in the treatment of erectile dysfunction. Sildenafil Study Group. N Engl J Med 1998;14;338:1397–404.

15. Christ GJ, Moreno AP, Melman A, Spray DC. Gap junction-mediated intercellular diffusion of $Ca2^+$ in cultured human corporal smooth muscle cells. Am J Physiol 1992;263:C373–83.

16. Cahn D, Melman A, Valcic M, Christ GJ. Forskolin: a promising new adjunct to intracavernous pharmacotherapy. J Urol 1996;155:1789–94.

17. Hedlund P, Aszodi A, Pfeifer A, et al. Erectile dysfunction in cyclic GMP-dependent kinase I-deficient mice. Proc Natl Acad Sci U S A 2000;97:2349–54.

18. Pickard RS, King P, Zar MA, Powell PH. Corpus cavernosal relaxation in impotent men. Br J Urol 1994;74:485–91.

19. Lue TF. Impotence: a patient's goal-directed approach to treatment. World J Urol 1990;8:67–74.

20. Fedele D, Coscelli C, Santeusanio F, et al. Erectile dysfunction in diabetic subjects in Italy. Diabetics Care 1998;21:1973–7.

21. Kim CK, Bronwyn S, Earle C. Clinical profile of patients with diabetes mellitus treated for erectile dysfunction. Int J Impot Res 2000;12(Suppl 2):S29.

22. Metro MJ, Broderick GA. Diabetes and vascular impotence: does insulin dependence increase the relative severity? Int J Impot Res 1999;11:87–9.

23. Cellek S, Rodrigo J, Lobos E, et al. Selective nitrergic neurodegeneration in diabetes mellitus—a nitric oxide-dependent phenomenon. Br J Pharmacol 1999;128:1804–12.

24. Blanco R, Saenz de Tejada I, Goldstein I, et al. Dysfunctional penile cholinergic nerves in diabetic impotent men. J Urol 1990;144(2 Pt 1):278–80.

25. Nofzinger EA. Sexual dysfunction in patients with diabetes mellitus: the role of a "central" neuropathy. Semin Clin Neuropsychiatry 1997;2(1):31–9.

26. Wellmer A, Sharief MK, Knowles CH, et al. Quantitative sensory and autonomic testing in male diabetic patients with erectile dysfunction. Br J Urol Int 1999;83:66–70.

27. Romeo JH, Seftel AD, Madhun ZT, Aron DC. Sexual function in men with diabetes type 2: association with glycemic control. J Urol 2000;163:788–91.

28. Rosen RC, Riley A, Wagner G, et al. The international index of erectile function (IIEF): a multidimensional scale for assessment of erectile dysfunction. Urology 1997;49:822–30.

29. O'Leary MP, Fowler FJ, Lenderking WR, et al. A brief male sexual function inventory for urology. Urology 1995;46:697–706.

30. Buvat J, Lemaire A. Endocrine screening in 1,022 men with erectile dysfunction: clinical significance and cost-effective strategy. J Urol 1997;158:1764–7.

31. Morrissette DL, Goldstein MK, Raskin DB, Rowland DL. Finger and penile tactile sensitivity in sexually functional and dysfunctional diabetic men. Diabetologia 1999;42:336–42.

32. Heaton J. New classification system for erectile dysfunction therapies. J Androl 1998;19:399–404.

33. Heaton JPW, Morales A, Adams M, et al. Recovery of erectile function by the oral administration of apomorphine. Urology 1995;45:200–3.

34. Wessells H, Hansen JG, Fucciarelli K, et al. Melanotropic peptide for the treatment of psychogenic erectile dysfunction: Double blind placebo controlled crossover dosing study. J Urol 1997;157:201.

35. Rajfer J, Aronson WJ, Bush PA, et al. Nitric oxide as a mediator of relaxation of the corpus cavernosum in response to nonadrenergic, noncholinergic neurotransmission. N Engl J Med 1992;362:90–4.

36. Padma-Nathan H. The efficacy and synergy of polypharmacotherapy in primary and salvage therapy of vasculogenic erectile dysfunction. Int J Impot Res 1990;2(Suppl 2):257–8.

37. Stief CG, Holmquist F, Djamilian M, et al. Preliminary results with the nitric oxide donor linsidomine chlorhydrate in the treatment of human erectile dysfunction. J Urol 1992;148:1437–40.

38. Gerstenberg TC, Metz P, Ottesen B, Fahrenkrug J. Intracavernous self-injection with vasoactive intestinal polypeptide and phentolamine in the management of erectile failure. J Urol 1992;147:1277–9.

39. Stief CG, Wetterauer U, Schaebsdau FH, Jonas U. Calcitonin gene-related peptide: a possible role in human penile erection and its therapeutic application in impotent patients. J Urol 1991;146:1010–4.

40. Spektor M, Rosenbaum R, Melman A, Christ G. Further demonstration of the physiological relevance of potassium (K) channels to contraction of human corporal smooth muscle in vitro. J Urol 1997;157:4, 149.

41. Morales A, Johnston B, Heaton JPW, Lundie M. Testosterone supplementation for hypogonadal impotence: assessment of biochemical measures and therapeutic outcomes. J Urol 1997;157: 849–854.

42. Goldstein I, leu TF, Padma-Nathan H, et al. Oral sildenafil in the treatment of erectile dysfunction. N Engl J Med 1998;338: 1397–1459.

43. Morales A, Gingell C, Collins M, et al. Clinical safety of oral sildenafil citrate (Viagra) in the treatment of erectile dysfunction. Int J Impot Res 1998;10:69–74.

44. Rendell MS, Rajfer J, Wicker PA, Smith MD. Sildenafil for treatment of erectile dysfunction in men with diabetes: a randomized controlled trial. Sildenafil Diabetes Study Group. JAMA 1999;281:421–6.

45. Cummings MH, Alexander WD. Erectile dysfunction in patients with diabetes. Hosp Med 1999;60:638–44.

46. Herrmann HC, Chang G, Klugherz BD, Mahoney PD. Hemodynamic effects of sildenafil in men with severe coronary artery disease. N Engl J Med 2000;342:1622–6.

47. Kloner RA, Zusman RM. Cardiovascular effects of sildenafil citrate and recommendations for its use. Am J Cardiol 1999;84(5B):11N–17N.

48. Laties AM, Fraunfelder FT. Ocular safety of Viagra (sildenafil citrate). Trans Am Ophthalmol Soc 1999;97:115–25.

49. Padma-Nathan H, Fromm-Freeck S, Ruff DD, et al and the Apomorphine SL Study Group. Efficacy and safety of apomorphine SL vs placebo for male erectile dysfunction (MED). J Urol 1998;159:241.

50. Melis MR, Succu S, Argiolas A. Dopamine agonists increase nitric oxide production in the paraventricular nucleus of the hypothalamus: correlation with penile erection and yawning. Eur J Neurosc 1996;8:2056–63.

51. Dula E, Keating W, Siami PF, et al. Efficacy and safety of fixed-dose and dose-optimization regimens of sublingual apomorphine versus placebo in men with erectile dysfunction. Urology 2000;56:130–5.

52. Data on file, TAP Pharmaceuticals.

53. Porst H, Derouet H, Idzikowski M, et al. Oral phentolamine (Vasomax) in erectile dysfunction—results of a German Multicenter-Study in 177 patients. Int J Impot Res 1996;8:117.

54. Goldstein I, Oral phentolamin: an alpha-1, alpha-2 adrenergic antagonist for the treatment of erectile dysfunction. Int J Impot Res 2000;12(Suppl 1):S75–8.

55. Morales A. Yohimbine in erectiles dysfunction: the facts. Int J. Impot Res 12 2000;(Suppl 1):S70–74.

56. Carey MP, Johnson BT. Effectiveness of yohimbine in the treatment of erectile disorder: frou meta-analytic integrations. Arch Sex Behav 1996;25:341–60.

57. Ernst E, Pittler MH. Yohimbine for erectile dysfunction: a systematic review and meta-analysis of randomized clinical trials. J Urol 1998;159:433–6.

58. Heaton JPW, Lording D. Alprostadil for erectile dysfunction in diabetic men. Int J Impot Res. In press 2000.

59. Price DE, Cooksey G, Jehu D, et al. The management of impotence in diabetic men by vacuum tumescence therapy. Diabet Med 1991;8(10):964–7.

60. Wilson SK, Carson CC, Cleves MA, Delk JR 2nd. Quantifying risk of penile prosthesis infection with elevated glycosylated hemoglobin. J Urol 1998;159:1537–9.

61. Sentochnik DE. Deep soft-tissue infections in diabetic patients. Infe Dis Clin North Am 1995;9:53–64.

62. Carson CCC III. Penile prosthesis in the age of effective pharmacotherapy. In: Erectile dysfunction: issues in current pharmacotherapy. Morales A, editor. London: Martin Dunitz, 1998. p. 230–52.

63. Carson CC, Mulcahy JJ, Govier FE. Efficacy, safety and patient satisfaction outcomes of the amsw 700cx inflatable penile prosthesis: results of a long-term multicenter study. J Urol 2000;164: 376–38.

64. Barrett-Connor E, Khaw KT, Yen SS. Endogenous sex hormone levels in older adult men with diabetes mellitus. Am J Epidemiol 1990;132:895–901.

65. Morales A, Johnston B, Heaton JP, Lundie M. Testosterone supplementation for hypogonadal impotence: assessment of biochemical measures and therapeutic outcomes. J Urol 1997;157: 849–54.

66. Jain P, Rademaker AW. McVary KT. Testosterone supplementation for erectile dysfunction: results of a meta-analysis. J Urol 2000;164:371–375.

67. Andersson B, Bjorn P, Marin P, et al. Testosterone concentrations in women and men with NIDDM. Diabetes Care 1994;17:405–11.

68. Morales A, Bain J. Ruijs A, et al. Clinical practice guidelines for screening and monitoring male patients receiving testosterone supplementation therapy. Int J Impot Res 1996;8:95–7.

69. Enzlin P, Mathieu C, Vanderschueren D, Demyttenaere K. Diabetes mellitus and female sexuality: a review of 25 years' research. Diabet Med 1998;15:809–15.

70. Berman JR, Berman LA, Werbin TJ, Goldstein I. Female sexual dysfunction: anatomy, physiology, evaluation and treatment options. curr Opin Urol 1999;9:563–8.

71. Morales A, Bain J, Ruijs A, et al. Clinical practice guidelines for screening and monitoring male patients receiving testosterone supplementation therapy. Int J Impot Res 1996;8:95–7.

CHAPTER 28

Diabetes and the Gastrointestinal Tract

Subhas C. Ganguli, MD, FRCPC, and Gervais N. Tougas, MD, CM, FRCPC

ABSTRACT

Gastrointestinal symptoms are a common feature in patients with diabetes but in many instances are not causally related. Poor glycemic control and the development of autonomic neuropathy may predispose to gastrointestinal complications such as gastroparesis, diarrhea, and constipation, but the evidence is not strong. Esophageal symptoms, while common, are usually easily managed. Although often equated with nausea and vomiting, gastroparesis is often asymptomatic; conversely, the symptoms often present in its absence and are related to other factors such as glycemic control. Both pernicious anemia and celiac disease are more common in diabetics but are easy to diagnose, with a high index of suspicion. Whereas it is difficult to treat, "diabetic diarrhea" is rare. Constipation is probably the most common complaint in diabetics but will usually respond to a stepwise approach. Both pancreatic and hepatocellular carcinoma are more common in patients with diabetes, as are exocrine pancreatic insufficiency and gallstones.

INTRODUCTION

Diabetes has multiple effects at almost every level of the gastrointestinal (GI) tract. Manifestations may be secondary to either hyperglycemia (eg, transient impaired gastric emptying), *Candida* esophagitis, autonomic or enteric neuropathy (eg, gastroparesis, fecal incontinence), or a manifestation of autoimmunity (parietal-cell antibodies, celiac disease). This chapter discusses the clinical manifestations, diagnosis, and therapy of the GI manifestations of diabetes, along with the relevant pathophysiology. The following questions are answered:

1. How common are nonspecific GI symptoms in people with diabetes?
    2. How does diabetes affect the esophagus?
    3. How does diabetes affect the stomach?
    4. How does diabetes affect the small and large bowel?
    5. How does diabetes affect the exocrine pancreas?
    6. How does diabetes affect the liver?

HOW COMMON ARE NONSPECIFIC GASTROINTESTINAL SYMPTOMS IN PEOPLE WITH DIABETES?

Studies that examined the prevalence of GI symptoms in patients with diabetes[1–7] are reviewed below and listed in Table 28–1. Unfortunately, these studies used different definitions of symptoms, making comparisons between their respective findings difficult. Nevertheless, two of them[3,5] compared the prevalence of GI symptoms in people with diabetes and a healthy control population.[1,3]

In a review article,[4] 76% of 136 patients in a diabetic outpatient clinic had at least one GI symptom (which in most patients was chronic or recurrent). Constipation was particularly prevalent among those with neuropathy: 29% of individuals without neuropathy and

Table 28–1 Prevalence of Gastrointestinal Symptoms in Patients with Diabetes Mellitus

Symptom	1983 (%)	1989 (%)	1990 (%)	1991 (%)	1993 IDDM (%)	NIDDM (%)
Dysphagia	27	—	2	—	7	9
Nausea/vomiting	29	28	7	—	6/2	18/6
Abdominal pain	34	32	—	19	18	27
Diarrhea	22	21	0	5	1	10
Constipation	60	12	2	22	21	20
Fecal incontinence	20	—	1	—	—	—
No symptoms	24	32	—	—	—	—
Population (with DM)	N = 136	N = 114	N = 168	N = 200	N = 89	N = 481
Type 1/Type 2	Not noted	Equal	All Type 1	57:43	16	84

IDDM = insulin-dependent diabetes mellitus; NIDDM = non–insulin-dependent diabetes mellitus; DM = diabetes mellitus.
Data from Maxton et al,[1] Feldman et al,[4] Maser et al.[6]

88% with severe neuropathy complained of constipation. Diarrhea was also frequently reported in these patients (22%). Unfortunately, only limited information regarding the approach used to evaluate symptoms was provided, and there was no control group.

The association between GI symptoms, neuropathy (assessed through nerve conduction studies in all patients and autonomic testing in a subset of 30 consecutive patients), and psychiatric illness was retrospectively studied in 114 people with diabetes.[2] Sixty-one percent had peripheral neuropathy, 40% had autonomic neuropathy (AN), and 51% had a history of psychiatric illness (55% affective disorder, 19% anxiety disorder, 26% both); overall, 68% of subjects reported at least one GI symptom. Although no specific GI symptom or symptom group (upper GI, altered bowel habits, abdominal discomfort) was significantly associated with peripheral or autonomic neuropathy, psychiatric illness was significantly associated with nausea ($p = .001$), diarrhea ($p = .02$), abdominal pain ($p = .03$), or bloating ($p = .01$). Acknowledging that a causal relationship between psychiatric and GI abnormalities remains unproven, the authors speculated that psychiatric illness may precipitate physician-seeking behavior in this patient population.

The relationship between symptoms and autonomic neuropathy was studied in a cross-sectional study of 168 patients with Type 1 diabetes aged 25 to 34 years.[6] Although the overall prevalence of autonomic neuropathy was 37.5% (based on heart-rate response to multiple maneuvers), it was not associated with any specific GI symptoms. The fact that diarrhea was defined as > 20 bowel movements/d, however, suggests that mild symptoms may have been missed.

The relationship between symptoms of irritable bowel syndrome and autonomic neuropathy was also studied prospectively in 200 people with diabetes and in healthy controls.[1] Of the diabetic participants, 29.5% had evidence of AN; these people had more constipation (22.0%) than diabetic people without AN (9.2%; $p < .03$) or controls (6.8%; $p < .04$). Nevertheless, symptoms of pain, abdominal distension, diarrhea, and alternating bowel habits were not seen more commonly in people with diabetes than in controls.

In a more recent population-based study,[3] the prevalence of GI symptoms was assessed (using a postal survey) in 624 patients with diabetes aged 45 to 64 years (selected from a drug reimbursement register) and compared to that in 648 randomly selected nondiabetic controls. Subjects with diabetes were more likely than controls to experience dysphagia (28% vs 19%; $p < .05$), whereas women with Type 1 diabetes actually experienced less heartburn (48% vs 69%; $p < .05$) and regurgitation (35% vs 56%; $p < .05$) than controls. The rate of constipation was the same in all groups, but men with Type 1 or 2 diabetes (18% vs 13%, vs 2% for controls; $p < .01$) and women with Type 2 diabetes (21% vs 14% for controls; $p < .05$) were more likely to be taking laxatives at least once a month. There was a lower prevalence of gallstone disease in women with Type 1 diabetes (5% vs 19% for controls; $p < .05$) and a higher prevalence in women with Type 2 diabetes (29% vs 19% for controls; $p < .05$). It was concluded that the occurrence and spectrum of GI symptoms in middle-aged subjects with Type 1 and 2 diabetes is similar to that in the general population.

Finally, symptoms and objective evidence of peripheral and autonomic neuropathy were assessed in a population-based study of 380 patients with diabetes.[5] Although two-thirds of patients had some form of diabetic neuropathy on objective testing, only about 20% had experienced GI symptoms. The overall prevalence of symptomatic visceral autonomic neuropathy was 5.5% (GI and genitourinary), with gastroparesis in 0.8% and nocturnal diarrhea in 0.5% of diabetics. There was a significant association found between the occurrence of peripheral neuropathy and autonomic visceral neuropathy ($p = .04$).

In summary, the only consistent findings in two studies that examined the prevalence of multiple GI symptoms in both a diabetic and control population was an increased incidence of constipation, which could be controlled with laxatives.[1,3]

How Does Diabetes Affect the Esophagus?

Esophageal Symptoms in People with Diabetes

As noted above, no consistent relationship between most GI symptoms and diabetes has been established. For example, reports of the rate of dysphagia in diabetes have varied from 10%[3,6] to 27%.[4] Indeed, one study reported a lower prevalence of reflux symptoms (ie, heartburn, acid regurgitation, pain, eructation) in the presence of autonomic neuropathy than in unaffected individuals or healthy controls (40%, vs 62.5% and 69%, respectively; $p < .025$).[8]

Esophageal Motility

Several studies have assessed esophageal motility in diabetes and have found conflicting results. One study[9] reported a failure of peristalsis initiation after swallowing and an increased number of simultaneous (and thus ineffective) contractions. Decreased peristaltic velocity was found in association with peripheral neuropathy in one study[10] but not in another.[11] Similarly, a decreased peristaltic amplitude was noted in three studies[9,11,12] but was absent in two others.[10,13] Moreover, this was associated with the presence of peripheral and autonomic neuropathy in one study[12] but not in the other.[11] Decreased lower esophageal contractile pressures were noted in four of six studies[9–11,13–15] and peristaltic failure explained delayed emptying in one study.[16] Increased reflux or prolonged transit time has also been noted using nuclear scintigraphy[17] in 20 to 92% of people with diabetes,[8,13,18,19] particularly in those with peripheral or autonomic neuropathy.

Esophageal manometry, autonomic and peripheral neuropathy, symptoms, and psychiatric diagnoses were measured in an interesting study of 30 patients with Type 1 or Type 2 diabetes.[12] Fifty-three percent had motility abnormalities that were not related to demographics, type, or duration of diabetes or to glycosylated hemoglobin levels. Overall, 70% of patients were found to have one or more psychiatric diagnoses at some time in their life (most commonly depression, generalized anxiety disorder, or a simple phobia). There was a significantly higher rate of patients with psychiatric diagnoses found in the group with manometric abnormalities (93%) than in the group without manometric abnormalities (43%; $p < .05$). Surprisingly, psychiatric illness was predictive of abnormal manometry even if neuropathy (peripheral or autonomic) was also taken into account ($p < .001$). Conversely, neuropathy was not predictive of manometric abnormalities unless psychiatric illness was also included as a variable. More surprisingly, there was no association between esophageal symptoms and manometric abnormalities.

Reflux Disease

Gastroesophageal reflux disease (GERD) is equally prevalent in people with diabetes and healthy controls; indeed, the percentage of diabetic respondents stating they never had heartburn or acid regurgitation was 52% and 65%, respectively, in people with diabetes versus 31% and 44%, respectively, in controls ($p < .05$).[3] Moreover, although one study reported esophageal acid reflux in 45% of diabetic participants who had 24-hour pH monitoring,[13] only one-third had any symptoms of GERD, and an abnormal 24-hour pH study was not significantly associated with the presence of peripheral neuropathy or abnormal esophageal manometry.

Although the discrepancy between symptoms and objective evidence of reflux may be due to the selection of patients studied, it may also be explained by a diminished ability to sense acid reflux. For example, in a study of 24-hour pH measurements done in 50 asymptomatic patients with Type 1 diabetes with at least 5 years of disease, 28% had gastroesophageal reflux.[20] As this was significantly associated with abnormal cardiovascular autonomic reflexes, the authors hypothesized that the autonomic dysfunction of diabetes led to an increased frequency of transient lower esophageal sphincter relaxations that led to reflux. Subsequent studies have reported that diabetic patients with autonomic neuropathy also have altered sensory thresholds compared to healthy controls[21] and could thus have decreased visceral perception throughout the GI tract. This possibility should be taken into account when assessing individuals with diabetes for GI problems.[22]

Approach to Esophageal Symptoms in Patients with Diabetes

Dysphagia

Either a barium meal combined with swallowing a barium-coated marshmallow or an endoscopy can detect structural lesions. Endoscopy is preferred if there is odynophagia (painful swallowing) or heartburn to detect mucosal inflammation or injury.[23] Manometric investigations should be reserved for more severe cases who fail to respond to initial therapy with appropriate therapy. Such therapy consists of either acid reduction with a proton-pump inhibitor for reflux, prokinetic therapy for motor disorders, or antifungal therapy for candidiasis.

Heartburn

As symptoms are poor indicators of the severity of reflux disease, a high index of suspicion should accompany the common extraesophageal manifestations of reflux, including hoarseness, chronic cough, aspiration pneumonia, asthma, and worsening chronic obstructive pulmonary disease.[24] Unfortunately, their frequency in people with diabetes has not been assessed in well-designed studies.

If mild reflux is suspected, it is reasonable to empirically use acid suppression with proton-pump inhibitors; evidence from prospective trials in nondiabetic individuals suggests that a trial of omeprazole 40 mg/d for 2 weeks (ie, the omeprazole test)[25–28] is as useful as endoscopy or pH measurement in the diagnosis of reflux in patients with classic symptoms. In uninvestigated patients with chronic symptoms or those with alarm symptoms such as dysphagia, odynophagia, weight loss, or anemia, endoscopy should be done to exclude intestinal metaplasia in the distal esophagus (Barrett's esophagus), which has been associated with an increased risk of adenocarcinoma of the esophagus,[29] and to exclude adenocarcinoma itself.

EVIDENCE-BASED MESSAGE

Omeprazole administered in a short course is 80% sensitive for detecting reflux disase (Level 2).27

Candida Esophagitis

Although the actual risk has not been carefully studied, people with diabetes are considered to be at higher risk for *Candida* esophagitis than nondiabetic individuals; this has been noted most commonly in patients with poor glycemic control and is likely related to impaired phagocytosis.[30,31] The most common presenting symptom is painful swallowing (odynophagia, present in 63% of patients) or oral lesions (present in 37% of patients).[22] Patients with thrush may be treated empirically (with prompt endoscopy in 3 to 5 days if there is no improvement). Conversely, patients with odynophagia require upper endoscopy to exclude other infections such as herpes esophagitis or cytomegalovirus (CMV). Treatment of mild cases is with oral nystatin suspension or clotrimazole lozenges and of severe cases with oral fluconazole, or intravenous amphotericin B may be required.

HOW DOES DIABETES AFFECT THE STOMACH?

Gastroparesis

Impaired gastric emptying is probably the most serious GI complication of diabetes, for the following reasons: (1) it worsens the control of blood glucose levels because of unpredictable timing of oral drug absorption (including oral hypoglycemic agents) and of carbohydrate digestion and absorption; (2) it causes significant symptoms, including abdominal pain, nausea, vomiting, and early satiety; and (3) it is associated with nutritional deficiencies.[32]

It is critical to understand that hyperglycemia causes a transient, reversible impairment of gastric emptying,[33] which may be isolated or coexist with permanent gastroparesis (which is a complication of chronic diabetes). It is for this reason that the patient should be euglycemic when undergoing testing to assess for impaired gastric emptying.

Epidemiology of Gastroparesis

Symptoms suggestive of gastroparesis, such as nausea and vomiting, are an unreliable indication of this problem, as they may be due to other causes, including esophagitis, peptic ulcer disease, or gastritis.[34] More reliable estimates of the magnitude of the problem can be obtained from objective measures of gastric emptying. In 87 unselected ambulatory patients with Type 1 or Type 2 diabetes from a tertiary center, the prevalence of delayed gastric emptying and esophageal transit were 40% and 48%, respectively.[35] Of note, there was no correlation between delayed esophageal transit and slow solid gastric emptying ($r = .11$; $p =$ not significant [NS]), and only weak correlations between solid and liquid gastric emptying ($r = .32$; $p < .01$) and between delayed emptying of solids and autonomic dysfunction ($r = .35$; $p < .01$).

Pathophysiology of Gastroparesis

The mechanisms by which gastroparesis develops in patients with chronic diabetes are not fully understood, and data are frequently conflicting.[36] Impaired vagal function (with associated autonomic neuropathy) appears to be an important factor and has been identified in diabetics with, but also without, gastroparesis.[37,38] Antral hypomotility and dilation have also been found in diabetics with gastroparesis.[37,39-41] It is likely that vagal dysfunction is causally associated with its development. Increased pyloric activity and pylorospasm have been reported in diabetics with gastroparetic symptoms, both fasting and in the postprandial period.[40]

Hyperglycemia impairs gastric emptying, and its role in gastroparesis has been recently reviewed.[42] Unfortunately, the mechanism of action is unknown.[35] In an elegant study of eight healthy subjects and nine patients with Type 1 diabetes (without renal, peripheral nerve, or autonomic complications),[43] an insulin-glucose clamp was used to assess the effect of physiologic hyperglycemia on the gastric emptying of solids and liquids (measured by scintigraphy). Intragastric retention of the solid-meal component at 100 minutes was significantly increased at a glucose concentration of 8 mmol/L (146 mg/dL) compared to 4 mmol/L (73 mg/dL) in both healthy subjects (intragastric retention 55.2% vs 36.7% for glucose concentrations of 8 mmol/L and 4 mmol/L, respectively; $p = .004$) and in patients with Type 1 diabetes (44.2% vs 35.7%; $p = .04$). This effect was independent of either insulin levels or altered cholinergic activity (as assessed by levels of pancreatic polypeptide). In another study, gastric emptying was assessed during hyperglycemia (blood glucose concentration 16 to 20 mmol/L) and euglycemia (blood glucose concentration 4 to 8 mmol/L) in patients with Type 1 diabetes.[44] Hyperglycemia was associated with significant prolongation of the half-emptying time (141 vs 124 minutes during euglycemia; $p = .03$) and increased meal retention at 100 minutes (71% vs 61%; $p = .032$). No clear relationship could be established between gastric emptying and autonomic function, duration of diabetes, plasma creatinine, or presence of GI symptoms. These effects of hyperglycemia have been confirmed in healthy volunteers using antroduodenal manometry, showing a significant decrease in gastric (but not duodenal) motility with serum glucose concentrations > 6.6 mmol/L,[45] as well as in people with Type 2 diabetes, in whom plasma glucose was correlated to liquid ($r = .58$; $p < .01$) but not solid gastric emptying.[19] Conversely, other studies of patients with Type 1 diabetes have shown significant correlation between the degree of cardiac autonomic neuropathy and gastric emptying and no correlation between blood glucose or glycated hemoglobin levels and gastric emptying.[46]

Taken together, these data implicate both poor metabolic control and autonomic dysfunction as likely causes of delayed gastric emptying.

Clinical Presentation of Gastroparesis

Typical symptoms of gastroparesis classically include nausea, vomiting (especially if several hours after eating or consisting of food ingested many hours previously), early satiety, and abdominal pain.[47] Postprandial fullness and bloating may also be present.[36] However, none of these symptoms are either sensitive or specific markers of gastroparesis if the latter is defined on the basis of gastric emptying. When 28 consecutive patients diagnosed with gastroparesis at a tertiary care center (25% having Type 1 diabetes) were reviewed, the most common symptoms were found to be nausea and abdominal pain (Table 28–2).[48] The pain was localized in 76% of all patients, most commonly in the upper abdomen (36%). The nature of the pain varied; it was burning, vague, or crampy in 64% of patients, constant in 28%, and nocturnal in 80%. Meals worsened the pain in 60%, helped it in 15%, and had no impact in 8%. There was no correlation between the presence or absence of pain and findings on gastric emptying studies, electrogastrography, or endoscopy.

Physical examination in patients with gastroparesis is generally unremarkable. Complications of diabetes such as retinopathy or peripheral or autonomic neuropathy may be present.[36,49] The presence of a succussion splash implies retained gastric contents.

Finally, nutritional status should be assessed as part of the evaluation, as inadequate intake of vitamin C, folate, niacin, thiamine, calcium, magnesium, phosphorus, and zinc was associated with idiopathic gastroparesis in at least one case-control study.[31]

Table 28–2 Symptoms in 28 Patients with Gastroparesis

Symptom	Incidence (%)
Nausea	93
Abdominal pain	89
Early satiety	86
Fatigue	71
Vomiting	68
Weight loss	64
Postprandial pain	54
Heartburn	43

Adapted from Hoogerwerf WA, Pasricha PJ, Kalloo AN, Schuster MM. Pain: the overlooked symptom in gastroparesis. Am J Gastroenterol 1999;94:1029–33.

Evaluation and Diagnosis of Gastroparesis

As gastroparesis is defined by the presence of delayed gastric emptying in the absence of a structural cause, the major steps in the evaluation of diabetic individuals with symptoms suggestive of gastroparesis are to objectively measure gastric emptying and rule out structural or other causes for the symptoms.

There are many causes for delayed gastric emptying besides gastroparesis in diabetic subjects (Table 28–3). Upper endoscopy is necessary to rule out structural causes of impaired gastric emptying, such as gastric or duodenal ulcers, and to look for other complications, such as bezoars. The importance of endoscopy is highlighted by a retrospective study of findings on upper endoscopy of 20 diabetic patients with known gastroparesis who were hospitalized with refractory nausea and vomiting.[34] Over one half of examinations (55%) showed abnormalities (*Candida* esophagitis in three patients, erosive esophagitis in four patients, gastric ulcers in two patients, and duodenal erosions and bile reflux gastritis in one patient each), which all responded to specific therapy. Plain abdominal radiography during symptoms rules out obstruction; in selected patients (eg, with a history of past abdominal surgery, which could cause adhesions), a small bowel meal or enteroclysis may be appropriate. Other considerations in the differential diagnosis of gastroparesis include gastroesophageal reflux disease, chronic cholecystitis or pancreatitis, and metabolic abnormalities such as uremia, hypercalcemia, hypokalemia, hypocortisolemia, or hypothyroidism,[36] as well as lactose intolerance. Baseline evaluation usually includes the following tests: complete blood count, calcium, magnesium, electrolytes, urea, creatinine, thyroid-stimulating hormone (TSH), glucose, glycosylated hemoglobin, total protein, albumin, abdominal radiography, and an ultrasound of the abdomen.

Scintigraphy is considered the gold standard for the diagnosis of gastroparesis.[47,50] While some centers have advocated the use of a dual isotope technique to simultaneously assess liquid and solid gastric emptying,[35] most centers only use a solid meal. The technique and meal used varies widely between centers, making comparisons of results obtained in different centers difficult. The test meal should be palatable, representative of an ordinary meal, and should be 300 to 500 mL in volume.[47] The test is usually performed in the morning after an overnight fast. Agents that could alter gastric motility should be stopped 48 to 72 hours before testing. The radiation exposure due to testing is very low, approximately one-tenth of

Table 28–3 Causes of Gastroparesis

Causes of transient impaired gastric emptying

Metabolic: hyperglycemia, hypokalemia

Endocrine: hypothyroidism

Drugs: narcotics, anticholinergics, levodopa, β-adrenergic agonists, calcium-channel blockers, octreotide, vincristine, nicotine

Postoperative ileus

Infectious: acute viral gastroenteritis

Causes of chronic gastroparesis

Idiopathic: gastroparesis, chronic idiopathic intestinal pseudo-obstruction

Iatrogenic: postvagotomy, postirradiation

Endocrine: diabetes mellitus

Neoplastic: lung, pancreas, brain stem

Anorexia nervosa

Autoimmune: progressive systemic sclerosis, systemic lupus erythematosus

Amyloidosis

Neuromuscular: myotonic dystrophy, dermatomyositis, autonomic degeneration

Porphyria

Spinal cord injury

Atrophic gastritis/pernicious anemia

Data from Koch,[36] Horowitz et al,[47] Bingden et al.[51]

the dose from routine chest radiography.[42] Finally, it is useful to check the patient's glucose immediately prior to testing and to interpret results in light of the fact that glucose concentrations can affect emptying.

The definition of delayed gastric emptying depends on the exact testing protocol used and thus varies from center to center. In recent years, two separate multicenter studies have used standardized meals (liver, egg substitutes) and determined normal values in healthy control subjects of both sexes and over a broad age range. This now allows meaningful comparisons to be made using measurements at different institutions.[52,53] As it is much more palatable, easier to prepare, and better tolerated, the use of a low-fat meal using an egg substitute is preferable. Other promising technologies for assessing gastroparesis include electrogastrography[36] and breath testing with nonradioactive substances such as ^{13}C acetate[51] and ultrasonography. However, these techniques have yet to be extensively validated and remain experimental and confined to a few centers.

Nonpharmacologic Approaches to the Treatment of Diabetic Gastroparesis

The general management of diabetic gastroparesis involves dietary changes and drug therapy, with surgical intervention having little role.[49,54] The goals of treatment are (1) control of symptoms (nausea, vomiting, and early satiety), (2) improvement in glycemic control, and, (3) maintenance of adequate nutrition. Clearly, patients with refractory symptoms or who are dehydrated need hospital admission, gastric decompression with a nasogastric tube, and intravenous fluids and antiemetics, as well as optimization of glucose control.

Once treatable causes of gastroparesis are ruled out (see Table 28–3), a dietary approach[36] based on a low-fiber diet (since undigested food can contribute to bezoar formation) made up of multiple (5 to 6) small meals that can be easily digested and are low in fat (< 40 g/d)[54] can be instituted. One study proposes a three-step diet.[36] The initial step consists of electrolyte replacement fluids and dissolved bouillon cubes in multiple small servings (goal 1,000 to 1,500 cc/d), with avoidance of highly sweetened or acidic (citrus) drinks. If tolerated, the second step consists of soups with noodles or rice and crackers, with a goal of ~1,500 cal/d (with avoidance of creamy or milk-based drinks). The final step is the introduction of common foods the patients finds interesting. Noodles, pastas, potatoes, rice, and meats such as baked chicken breast and fish are best tolerated. At all steps, a daily multivitamin should also be taken. If necessary, food may be liquefied in a blender.[54]

Patients who fail repeated attempts at oral nutrition will need food delivered beyond the stomach. Usually, this is achieved by a surgically placed jejunostomy tube. Although these can be placed endoscopically, the procedure is complex, and tubes frequently malfunction.[54] It is recommended that a trial of nasojejunal feeding for 2 to 3 days be undertaken to assess patient tolerance (generally a rate of 60 to 80 mL nutrient/h is necessary to supply a patient's needs).[54] Patients are permitted to take fluids as tolerated per os once the feeding tube is surgically placed. In some patients with ongoing nausea and vomiting, a venting gastrostomy (which can be placed endoscopically) can provide significant relief.[54] Patients failing an enteral approach probably have an associated small bowel motility disorder and may need total parenteral nutrition.[54]

Gastric pacing may prove to be another appropriate intervention. In a recent study of nine patients with gastroparesis (five of whom had diabetes) refractory to medical therapy, the effect of gastric pacing by means of pacing wires placed at the time of laparoscopic jejunal feeding tube insertion was assessed.[55] Patients performed electrical stimulation (as outpatients) for 1 hour before and 3 hours after eating a meal, at least twice a day. The mean duration of outpatient pacing therapy was 49 days. Gastric emptying of solids by scintigraphy was assessed immediately after wire placement (with no pacing) and at the end of the study protocol (with pacing). There was also a daily symptom score calculated. At the end of the study, a significant decrease in gastric retention at 2 hours (77.0 to 56.6%; $p < .04$) and improvement in symptom score ($p < .05$) was noted. Although controlled trials still need to be performed, this initial study is very promising.

Prokinetic Agents in Treating Diabetic Gastroparesis

Cisapride. Cisapride is a serotonin (5-HT4) receptor agonist that enhances the physiologic release of acetylcholine at the myenteric plexus. It does not have direct cholinomimetic effects and therefore does not increase gastric acid secretion.[56] Cisapride increases esophageal peristalsis and lower esophageal sphincter pressure, thus decreasing gastroesophageal reflux. It also improves gastric and duodenal emptying and both small intestinal and colonic transit. However, its well-documented association with the induction of lethal ventricular arrythmias, including torsades de pointes and ventricular fibrillation (which can be precipitated by multiple coadministered medications, including antifungal drugs), have led to its use being severely restricted in most jurisdictions, including North America and Europe.

Domperidone. Domperidone is a peripheral dopamine (D2) receptor antagonist that does not readily cross the blood-brain barrier. It increases esophageal peristalsis and lower esophageal sphincter pressure, increases gastric motility and peristalsis, improves gastroduodenal coordination, and facilitates gastric emptying as well as decreasing small bowel transit time.[57] Although it does not have central effects, it can stimulate the chemoreceptor trigger zone situated outside the blood-brain barrier.[57] Domperidone also dose-dependently elevates serum prolactin levels, with galactorrhea being seen with high doses.[57] Side effects occur in < 7% of patients overall.[57] Those occurring in > 1% of patients include dry mouth and headaches/migraines. Elevation of prolactin, aspartate transaminase (AST), alanine transaminase (ALT), and cholesterol all occur in < 1% of patients.[57]

Erythromycin. Erythromycin is a macrolide antibiotic that also acts as a partial motilin agonist, binding to motilin receptors in the GI tract.[56] Erythromycin has been used in the setting of acute gastroparesis at dosages of up to 3 mg/kg IV every 8 hours[49] as well as orally (dosages of 250 to 500 mg qid) with follow-up of up to 8.4 months.[57] Erythromycin is contraindicated in persons with preexisting liver disease or in patients taking astemizole, terfenadine, or cisapride.[56] The most common side effects are gastrointestinal (eg, abdominal pain, cramping) and are dose related. Elevated transaminases (AST, ALT < 10%), cholestatic jaundice, and cholestatic hepatitis (2 to 4%) occur and are thought to be greater with the estolate and ethyl succinate salts and with increased duration and dose of therapy.[56]

Metoclopramide. Although the cellular mechanism of action of metoclopramide when acting as a prokinetic is not fully understood, it is known to be a dopamine antagonist that can cross the blood-brain barrier.[58] It is thought that this drug promotes the release of acetylcholine from myenteric neurons.[58] Its effect on the GI tract is to enhance the motility of smooth muscle from the esophagus to the small bowel[58] and to increase the resting tone of the lower esophageal sphincter.[59] This does not require intact vagal innervation but can be blocked by anticholinergic drugs. Administration results in decreased gastroesophageal reflux and accelerated transit of the stomach and small bowel. It has minimal effect on small bowel, gastric, biliary, or pancreatic secretion or colonic or biliary motility.[58,59] Its antinauseant effect (due to the antagonism of central and peripheral dopamine receptors) is associated with the side effect of hyperprolactinemia (which can lead to galactorrhea) and significant extrapyramidal symptoms, anxiety, and depression, especially at high doses.[58] The onset of action is 30 to 60 minutes after administration, and the duration of action is from 1 to 2 hours[59]; because of renal elimination, dose adjustment is required in renal failure. The drug is contraindicated in patients with pheochromocytoma (it may cause a hypertensive crisis) or those on monoamine oxidase inhibitors, and it should not be used in epileptic patients or those receiving other drugs that could cause extrapyramidal reactions. Metoclopramide is also contraindicated in patients with prolactin-producing pituitary tumors. Long-term use is restricted because of a reduction in efficacy and the high incidence of toxicity at dosages > 60 mg/d.[54]

Overall Efficacy of the Prokinetic Drugs. There has been a systematic overview of the efficacy of prokinetics in patients with gastroparesis recently published.[60] It examined 32 studies (involving 496 patients) published between 1980 and March 1998 that used scintigraphic assessment of gastric emptying and oral administration of cisapride, metoclopramide, domperidone, or erythromycin. Four of these studies measured the effects of two different prokinetics.[61–64] Variables assessed included characteristics of the study population, trial length, daily dosage of the drug, study design, main target variables, improvement in gastric emptying (percent of the initial value), and changes in the symptoms score as a percent of the initial score. The majority of the studies (18 of 32) included patients with diabetic gastroparesis, with the others examining mainly patients with idiopathic or postoperative gastroparesis. The median duration of treatment was 125 days (range 30 to 730 days). Symptomatic improvement was assessed in 352 patients; however, in 25 studies, no previously validated symptom score was used (only 1 study used a validated symptom assessment).[65] In the other studies, a symptom score based on different rankings (mean 5) of a mean of 6 symptoms was used. Study design was open trial in 18 studies (38% of all patients), double-blinded in 15 studies (54% of patients), and single-blinded in 3 studies (8% of patients).

Overall, the mean improvement in gastric emptying was significantly greater in the single-blind studies (40 ± 9.5%) than the double-blind studies (22.7 ± 12.7%) but similar to that of the open trials (31.9 ± 14.1%). Patients in open trail or single-blind studies showed a greater improvement in symptom score (52.1 ± 17.7% and 69 ± 8.5% improvement, respectively) than individuals in a double-blind trial (18.2 ± 25.8%; $p < .05$ for single vs double-blind trials). No correlation was found between the length of patient follow-up and improvement in gastric emptying or symptom score. Although there was a trend of symptomatic response overall, with erythromycin (50 ± 35.4%) > domperidone (47.7 ± 41%) > metoclopramide (40.5 ± 25.8%) > cisapride (30.8 ± 27.9%), this trend was not significant. The observed differences between different types of study design also make it difficult to compare these results.[65]

At present, therapy in patients with gastroparesis remains empiric at best. In the absence of symptoms, there is no evidence to suggest that treatment should be initiated. In those patients in whom symptoms compatible with delayed gastric emptying are present, a trial of prokinetic therapy certainly makes sense, although the evidence for efficacy is very limited. As cisapride is no longer available, metoclopramide (5–15 mg PO AC and HS) is the only available compound in many areas. However, its limited efficacy as a prokinetic and its narrow therapeutic windows combined with its frequent side effects somewhat limit enthusiasm for its use. Nevertheless, it is probably the best first option once optimal glycemic control has been achieved. Domperidone (10–20 mg PO AC and HS), where available, is easier to use and is associated with a lower frequency of side effects. In severe patients, erythromycin (250–500 mg PO AC and HS) will reliably improve gastric emptying but is not without side effects itself; in most instances, the improvement in gastric emptying is not necessarily associated with an equally impressive symptomatic improvement. Gastric pacing should be considered experimental for the time being.

Tolerability of the prokinetic agents.   Although few head-to-head comparisons have been reported, a recent randomized, double-blind trial assessed the 4-week effect of domperidone (20 mg qid PO) versus metoclopramide (10 mg qid PO) in 93 symptomatic ambulatory patients with type 1 diabetes of median age 39 years.[66] Symptoms and adverse drug reactions were assessed after 2 and 4 weeks. Although both drugs had the same benefit, more patients on metoclopramide suffered from somnolence (49% vs 29%) or a reduction in mental acuity (33% vs 20%) than did those on domperidone, and the severity of these side effects was greater with metoclopramide.

Effect of the prokinetic agents on glycemic control and quality of life.   Although improved glycemic control has been cited as a reason to treat gastroparesis, evidence supporting this is lacking. For example, in a well-designed, prospective, placebo-controlled, double-blind, crossover trial using cisapride (10 mg PO qid for 4 weeks), neither gastric emptying nor diabetes control was affected.[67]

In a large, double-blind prospective study, the effect of domperidone on symptom scores and health-related quality of life (HRQOL) in 269 symptomatic insulin-treated diabetic patients[68] who responded to an initial course of domperidone was examined; HRQOL was measured using the Medical Outcomes Study Short-Form 36 (SF 36).[69] After randomization, symptom severity increased in both groups, with significantly greater deterioration in the placebo group ($p < .05$). Moreover, domperidone therapy prevented the deterioration in HRQOL noted in the placebo group. Of interest, the effect of treatment on HRQOL was not related to the presence or absence of impaired gastric emptying.

Based on the above, the first drug to try should be domperidone, since this has the best side-effect profile. It is advantageous to combine prokinetics with antiemetic drugs such as diphenhydramine or trifluoperazine (which should not be used simultaneously with cisapride). If this is unsuccessful, metoclopramide may be tried in dosages of up to 60 mg/d, followed by either erythromycin or cisapride.

Bezoars

As impaired gastric motility is a risk factor for bezoar formation, bezoars may be more common in people with diabetes. Indeed, in a retrospective study of 3,247 upper endoscopies, bezoars were discovered in 14 patients (0.4%)[70]; 7 (50%) of these patients had diabetes, compared to 1 (3.6%) of 28 sex-matched controls ($p < .001$). Six of the seven diabetic patients with bezoars also had evidence of autonomic neuropathy.

The most common types of bezoar (phytobezoars) are made up of undigested cellulose and vegetable matter.[71] Symptoms include upper GI bleeding (57%), persistent nausea and vomiting (36%), and abdominal pain (29%). Therapies include the use of prokinetic agents, enzymatic therapy, endoscopic fragmentation, and surgery.[71,72]

Gastritis and Peptic Ulcer Disease

Helicobacter pylori is one of the most common human pathogens and is known to cause peptic ulcer disease. Fortunately, epidemiologic studies to date have not shown a higher prevalence in people with either diabetes or delayed gastric emptying. For example, in one cross-sectional study of 51 patients with symptoms of gastroparesis, *H. pylori* was found in 31% of patients with normal gastric emptying but in only 5% of those with delayed gastric emptying ($p < .05$). Moreover, this study and others reported that there was no evidence of an association between *H. pylori* and diabetes.[73,74]

Although it is not more common in people with diabetes, when it does occur, *H. pylori* infection may affect glycemic control. This possibility is supported by a recent study of 71 children with Type 1 diabetes[75] in which *H. pylori* infection was an independent predictor of a high HbA$_{1c}$ and increased insulin needs. *H. pylori* infection may also affect the risk of cardiovascular disease and has been detected up to 4 times more frequently in individuals with Type 1 or Type 2 diabetes and a history of coronary artery or cerebrovascular disease than in diabetic controls.[76]

As may be expected from the above, endoscopic studies in which diabetic individuals and matched nondiabetic controls with dyspeptic symptoms were investigated showed no association between diabetes and peptic ulcer disease.[77] Indeed, a review of the world literature noted a rate of peptic ulcers of 1.3% among 128,001 diabetic patients, which was lower than the incidence noted in the general population of 5 to 12%.[78]

Parietal Cell Antibodies and Pernicious Anemia

Pernicious anemia results from autoimmune destruction of the gastric parietal cells and is characterized by parietal cell antibodies (PCAs). As such, it is likely to be associated with other autoimmune diseases such as Type 1 diabetes. This was confirmed in a cross-sectional study of 497 unselected individuals with Type 1 diabetes,[76] in which PCAs were found in 20.9%, compared to 1.4 to 12% in nondiabetic individuals.[79] These individuals also had a greater incidence of atrophic gastritis (92.8% vs 56.3%; $p = .04$), pernicious anemia (10.5% vs 0.5%; $p < .0001$), higher levels of gastrin (194 vs 97 pg/mL; $p < .0001$), and a higher rate of hypochromic, microcytic anemia (15.4% vs 6.9%; $p < .01$). Such abnormalities are consistent with parietal-cell destruction leading to decreased gastric acid secretion and subsequent iron malabsorption. This hypothesis is supported by a longitudinal study of 371 Type 1 diabetics who were followed for up to 16 years with biannual blood counts as well as serum cobalamine, folate, thiamine, and pyridoxal levels.[80] Six patients were found to have a reduced serum cobalamine concentration, and one had mild anemia, giving an incidence of latent pernicious anemia and manifest disease of 11 cases per 1,000 and 3.9 cases per 1,000, respectively; this compares to an incidence of pernicious anemia of 1.27 per 1,000 in the general population. Earlier studies have also found an increased incidence of PCAs in people with Type 1 diabetes.[81,82] These results emphasize the importance of checking PCAs in patients with Type 1 diabetes and iron deficiency anemia, in whom initial evaluations do not reveal sources of blood loss.

EVIDENCE-BASED MESSAGE

Individuals with Type 1 diabetes have a higher risk of pernicious anemia than do non-diabetic individuals (Level 3).[80]

HOW DOES DIABETES AFFECT THE SMALL AND LARGE BOWEL?

"Diabetic Diarrhea"

Large population-based case-control studies have not detected a higher prevalence of diarrhea in diabetic individuals than in nondiabetic individuals.[3] Chronic diarrhea does, however, affect 3 to 4% of patients with diabetes,[83] approximately 30% of whom have "diabetic diarrhea." This condition is described as occurring in patients with long-standing (> 8 years) diabetes and consists of intermittent severe watery diarrhea, which may occur > 10 times per day, often at night, in association with fecal incontinence.[84] Although the cause is unclear, "diabetic diarrhea" is more common in patients with Type 1 diabetes than in those with type 2 diabetes (5.2% vs 0.4%; $p < .01$) and is characterized by a longer duration of diabetes (16.1 vs 11.3 years; $p < .01$) and a higher prevalence of autonomic neuropathy (100% vs 33.3%; $p < .01$).[83] One possible cause of "diabetic diarrhea" is bacterial overgrowth, which may cause deconjugation of bile salts, a secretory diarrhea in the colon, and impaired fat digestion.[85] Often, a trial of cholestyramine is used as a diagnostic test, without much data to support its use.

Fecal incontinence has been reported in up to 28% of diabetic patients with chronic diarrhea.[86] In a retrospective study of 33 patients with diarrhea of > 3 weeks duration (85% with Type 1 diabetes), the most common causes of fecal incontinence were bacterial overgrowth (24%), anorectal dysfunction (21%), and an intestinal motility or secretory disorder (21%).[84,87,88] Less common causes include celiac sprue and lactose intolerance.

The approach to "diabetic diarrhea" requires a careful history (Table 28–4), with attention to medications (eg, metformin, acarbose), relationship to milk products, travel, stool

---

Table 28–4 Causes of Diarrhea in Diabetics*

Medications
Bacterial overgrowth
Idiopathic, "diabetic diarrhea"
Irritable bowel syndrome
Dietary (eg, sorbitol)
Anorectal dysfunction
Celiac sprue
Parasitic infection
Lactose intolerance
Bile acid malabsorption
Inflammatory bowel disease
Pancreatic insufficiency

---

*In decreasing order of frequency.
Data from Lysy et al,[83] Valdovinos et al,[84] Falchuk et al.[89]

characteristics, symptoms of autonomic neuropathy (postural lightheadedness, blurred vision, abnormal sweating), and fecal incontinence (see section on colon). Physical examination should be directed at detecting autonomic neuropathy and ruling out celiac disease. Initial studies include markers of proximal bowel malabsorption (iron, complete blood count, calcium, folate); a decreased vitamin B_{12} plus elevated folate suggests bacterial overgrowth, and an elevated International Normalized Ratio reflects fat malabsorption (since vitamin K is fat soluble). Serology for celiac disease (see below) and stool samples for fat, bacteria, ova, parasites, and *Clostridium difficile* should be taken. If a spot stool sample shows excess fat, a 48- to 72-hour collection of stool should be made; although it is usually less than 7 g/d, it may rise to 14 g/d in the setting of diarrhea without implying impaired absorption.[90] Levels in excess of this suggest celiac disease, pancreatic insufficiency, or bacterial overgrowth.

Although no uniformly effective therapy has been identified for "diabetic diarrhea," the use of loperamide and anecdotal success with cholestyramine, clonidine, and octreotide have been reported.[91–96] Biofeedback has also been successfully used in small studies of fecal incontinence.[97,98]

Celiac Disease

Approximately 5% of patients with Type 1 diabetes have evidence of celiac disease,[99–102] and approximately 5% of patients with biopsy-proven celiac disease have Type 1 diabetes.[103] Older studies have shown that patients with both celiac disease and Type 1 diabetes often have a history of repeated hypoglycemia (especially in the setting of exacerbations of their diarrhea) and poor diabetic control.[104,105] When treated with a gluten-free diet, insulin requirements usually increase, and hypoglycemic episodes are less common.[104,105] Thus, celiac disease should be considered in Type 1 diabetics with diarrhea, recurrent hypoglycemia, and signs of malabsorption (anemia, iron deficiency, low serum folate, or albumin).[104] Some researchers have recommended the use of antibody screening for celiac disease in all Type 1 diabetics.[106] If this is done, it should be done with IgA endomysial antibody plus IgA and IgG antigliadin antibodies, if available[107]; at least one large study reported that the sensitivity and specificity of the IgA endomysial antibody assay in people with Type 1 diabetes were 96% and 100%, respectively.[108]

EVIDENCE-BASED MESSAGE

The IgA antiendomysial antibody assay has high sensitivity and specificity for the detection of celiac disease in people with Type 1 diabetes (Level 1).[108]

Constipation

As noted above, constipation is one of the most common GI symptoms reported by people with diabetes, with a prevalence of up to 60%[4]; indeed, in a population-based case-control study of 624 people with diabetes, the rate of laxative use in diabetic men was 6 to 9 times that in healthy controls.[3] Reasons for this discerned from case-control studies include pelvic-floor dysfunction or slow colonic transit[109] as well as loss of the gastrocolic reflex due to a neural abnormality.[110–112]

The diabetic patient with constipation should be screened for alarm features such as weight loss, blood in stool, or the onset of symptoms after the age of 50 years (which, if present, should lead to colonoscopy [especially since some epidemiologic studies suggest an increased risk of colorectal neoplasia in people with diabetes]).[113] Dietary and drug history focusing on fiber and fluid intake and drugs known to cause constipation (eg, tricyclic antidepressants, verapamil) should be taken. Biochemical testing can detect metabolic causes such as hypercalcemia and hypothyroidism, and a flat plate of the abdomen can detect obstruction. Initial therapy includes increasing fiber intake to at least 15 g/d (preferably by dietary means), ensuring an adequate fluid intake (6 to 8 glasses/d), and ensuring moderate physical activity. Second-line therapies include osmotic laxatives such as docusate, lactulose, or milk of magnesia (in patients without renal failure). Patients refractory to these measures should be referred to a gastroenterologist.

How Does Diabetes Affect the Exocrine Pancreas?

Although patients with both Type 1[111] and Type 2[112] diabetes may have impaired pancreatic exocrine function, the clinical significance of this abnormality is unclear. More important is the fact that diabetes has been linked to pancreatic cancer. Indeed, in a recent meta-analysis of 20 case-control and cohort studies, the pooled relative risk and 95% confidence interval (CI) of pancreatic cancer due to diabetes was 2.1 (95% CI 1.6 to 2.8). When just the 9 cohort studies were analyzed, a relative risk of 2.6 was obtained. The relationship of diabetes to subsequent pancreatic cancer was still significant when the analysis was restricted to studies in which the diagnosis of diabetes preceded the diagnosis of pancreatic malignancy by at least 5 years.[116] Reasons for this relationship remain unknown.

Evidence-Based Message

Newly diagnosed diabetes is a strong risk factor for subsequent pancreatic cancer, approximately doubling or tripling the risk compared to nondiabetic individuals (Level 1).[113]

How Does Diabetes Affect the Liver?

Biliary Tract Disease

The possibility that diabetes may be a risk factor for gallstones was investigated in a prospective population-based study[114] in which 1,962 subjects who were initially free of gallstones were followed by serial ultrasounds. In this study, individuals with diabetes were more than twice as likely (odds ratio [OR] 2.62, 95% CI 1.21 to 5.66) to develop gallstones than were nondiabetic individuals. This was confirmed in a cross-sectional prevalence study of 29,584 subjects using a questionnaire and ultrasonographic examination; a relative risk (on univariate analysis) of gallstone disease of 1.54 was found in men (95% CI 1.24 to 1.91) and of 1.92 in women (95% CI 1.60 to 2.31) with diabetes.[115]

Possible reasons for this increased risk include autonomic neuropathy, and, indeed, cross-sectional studies showed that those diabetic patients with autonomic neuropathy had significantly worse gallbladder emptying than those without autonomic neuropathy (40% vs 62%; $p < .05$).[116–118] The need for prophylactic cholecystectomy in asymptomatic individuals has been a topic of debate for many years and remains unresolved.[119–122] Conversely, symptomatic gallstone disease should result in prompt elective cholecystectomy.[123]

Evidence-Based Message

Diabetes increases the subsequent risk of gallstones two- to threefold (Level 1).[116]

Nonalcoholic Steatohepatitis

Nonalcoholic steatohepatitis (NASH) is a recently described clinical entity that has a prevalence of 7 to 9% among individuals undergoing liver biopsy.[124] It is strongly associated with obesity (in 69 to 100% of NASH patients), Type 2 diabetes (in 34 to 75% of NASH patients), and either increased triglycerides or cholesterol (in 20 to 81% of NASH patients).[124] Less common associations include total parenteral nutrition, jejunal bypass, Wilson's disease, and certain drugs (amiodarone, tamoxifen, glucocorticoids, estrogen).[124]

The pathogenesis of this disorder is a source of investigation.[125] Although NASH generally has an indolent course, approximately one half of patients develop progressive fibrosis, and up to one-sixth develop cirrhosis[124]; a retrospective study of 132 patients with NASH has shown that the presence on biopsy of ballooning degeneration, Mallory hyaline, or fibrosis is associated with the presence of cirrhosis.[126] Diabetes, obesity, age, and an AST/ALT ratio > 1 are independently associated with fibrosis.[127]

Clinically, patients with NASH are asymptomatic. Physical examination usually does not reveal stigmata of chronic liver disease, although patients may have hepatomegaly, and, biochemically, the transaminase levels are usually 2 to 3 times normal; alkaline phosphatase is elevated in fewer than one half of patients. Based on a series of patients assessed for other liver diseases, ultrasound has a sensitivity of 94% and a specificity of 84% in identifying steatosis.[128] Liver biopsy is the only way to definitively confirm the diagnosis and may also provide prognostic information. Currently there is no approved therapy for NASH, although a pilot study using ursodeoxycholic acid has shown promising results.[129]

Hepatocellular Carcinoma

It was reported in a recent, large, case-control study of 428 patients and 1,502 controls that diabetes was independently associated with hepatocellular carcinoma (wih an OR of 2), and that the association was strongest in patients with a body mass index > 25 kg/m^2, in whom the OR exceeded 3. It was concluded that diabetes explained 8% of cases of primary liver cancer in the population studies.[130] Reasons for this relationship remain unclear, although the possibility that NASH may underlie the relationship has been proposed.

Conclusion

Although common in people with diabetes, GI symptoms are poorly understood. This is not unique to people with diabetes, as the pathophysiology of several GI symptoms remains poorly understood in general. This is particularly true of functional and motility symptoms.

There is good evidence for an increased risk of both pancreatic and hepatocellular cancer in people with diabetes; this increased risk does not extend to other GI malignancies. Immune GI disorders such as pernicious anemia and celiac disease are also more common in people with diabetes. Exocrine pancreatic function is frequently altered in diabetes but is only uncommonly troublesome clinically.

Gastrointestinal problems clearly do affect people with diabetes. Gastroparesis continues to be poorly understood. It may well be only an epiphenomenon, although in some patients, its resolution is associated with improved symptoms. Good trials are urgently needed in this area. As it is often asymptomatic, gastroparesis should only be treated if the patient has symptoms. Similarly, symptoms such as nausea and vomiting often occur in the absence of gastroparesis and should not be interpreted as being synonymous. Diarrhea and constipation are the most common GI complaints in diabetic patients and should be carefully investigated, as their etiology is often multifactorial. Finally, a present aggressive glycemic control probably represents the best preventive measure against the development of most GI complications of diabetes.

Summary of Evidence-Based Messages

1. Omeprazole administered in a short course is 80% sensitive for detecting reflux disease (Level 2).[27]
2. Individuals with Type 1 diabetes have a higher risk of pernicious anemia than do nondiabetic individuals (Level 3).[80]
3. The IgA antiendomysial antibody assay has high sensitivity and specificity for the detection of celiac disease in people with Type 1 diabetes (Level 1).[97]
4. Newly diagnosed diabetes is a strong risk factor for subsequent pancreatic cancer, approximately doubling or tripling the risk compared to nondiabetic individuals (Level 1).[115]
5. Diabetes increases the subsequent risk of gallstones two- to threefold (Level 1).[116]

REFERENCES

1. Maxton DG, Whorwell PJ. Functional bowel symptoms in diabetes—the role of autonomic neuropathy. Postgrad Med J 1991;67:991–3.

2. Clouse RE, Lustman PJ. Gastrointestinal symptoms in diabetic patients: lack of association with neuropathy. Am J Gastroenterol 1989;84:868–72.

3. Janatuinen E, Pikkarainen P, Laakso M, Pyorala K. Gastrointestinal symptoms in middle-aged diabetic patients. Scand J Gastroenterol 1993;28:427–432.

4. Feldman M, Schiller LR. Disorders of gastrointestinal motility associated with diabetes mellitus. Ann Intern Med 1983;98:378–84.

5. Dyck PJ, Kratz KM, Karnes JL, et al. The prevalence by staged severity of various types of diabetic neuropathy, retinopathy, and nephropathy in a population-based cohort. Neurology 1993;43:817–24.

6. Maser RE, Pfeifer MA, Dorman JS, et al. Diabetic autonomic neuropathy and cardiovascular risk. Arch Intern Med 1990;150:1218–22.

7. Locke GR. Epidemiology of gastrointestinal complications of diabetes mellitus. Eur J Gastroenterol Hepatol 1995;7:711–6.

8. Channer KS, Jackson PC, O'Brien I, et al. Oesophageal function in diabetes mellitus and its association with autonomic neuropathy. Diabet Med 1985;2:378–82.

9. Mandelstam P, Siegel CI, Lieber A, Siegel M. The swallowing disorder in patients with diabetic neuropathy-gastroenteropathy. Gastroenterology 1969;56:1–12.

10. Hollis JB, Castell DO, Braddon RL. Esophageal function in diabetes mellitus and its relation to peripheral neuropathy. Gastroenterology 1977;73:1098–102.

11. Huppe D, Tegenthoff M, Faig J, et al. Esophageal dysfunction in diabetes mellitus: is there a relation to clinical manifestations of neuropathy? Clin Invest 1992;70:740–7.

12. Clouse RE, Lustman PJ, Reidel WL. Correlation of esophageal motility abnormalities with neuropsychiatric status in diabetics. Gastroenterology 1986;90:1146–54.

13. Murray FE, Lombard MG, Ashe J, et al. Esophageal function in diabetes mellitus with special reference to acid studies and relationships to peripheral neuropathy. Am J Gastroenterol 1987;82:840–3.

14. Stewart OM, Hosking DJ, Preston BJ, Atkinson M. Oesophageal motor changes in diabetes mellitus. Thorax 1976;31:278–83.

15. Vela AR, Balart LA. Esophageal motor manifestations in diabetes mellitus. Am J Surg 1970;119:21–6.

16. Holloway RH, Tippett MD, Horowitz M, et al. Relationship between esophageal motility and transit in patients with Type 1 diabetes mellitus. Am J Gastroenterol 1999;94:3150–7.

17. Sundkvist G, Hillarp B, Lilja B, Ekberg O. Esophageal motor functions evaluated by scintigraphy, video-radiography, and manometry in diabetic patients. Acta Radiol 1989;30:17–9.

18. Russell COH, Gannan FR, Coatsworth J, et al. Relationship among esophageal dysfunction, diabetic gastroenteropathy, and peripheral neuropathy. Dig Dis Sci 1983;28:289–93.

19. Horowitz M, Harding PE, Maddox AF, et al. Gastric and esophageal emptying in patients with Type 2 diabetes mellitus. Diabetologia 1989;32:151–9.

20. Lluch I, Ascaso JF, Mora F, et al. Gastroesophageal reflux in diabetes mellitus. Am J Gastroenterol 1999;94:919–24.

21. Kamath MV, Tougas G, Fitzpatrick D, et al. Assessment of the visceral afferent and autonomic pathways in response to esophageal stimulation in control subjects and in patients with diabetes. Clin Invest Med 1998;21:100–13.

22. Verne GN, Sninsky CA. Diabetes and the gastrointestinal tract. Gastroenterol Clin North Am 1998;27:861–74.

23. Cockeram AW. Canadian Association of Gastroenterology practice guidelines: evaluation of dysphagia. Can J Gastroenterol 1998;12:409–13.

24. DeVault KR, Castell DO. Updated guidelines for the diagnosis and treatment of gastroesophageal reflux disease. Am J Gastroenterol 1999;94:1434–42.

25. Bate CM, Riley SA, Chapman RWG, et al. Evaluation of omeprazole as a cost-effective diagnostic test for gastro-esophageal reflux disease. Aliment Pharmacol Ther 1999;13:59–66.

26. Fass R, Ofman JJ, Sampliner RE, et al. The omeprazole test is as sensitive as 24 h oesophageal pH monitoring in diagnosing gastro-oesophageal reflux disease in symptomatic patients with erosive oesophagitis. Aliment Pharmacol Ther 2000;14:389–96.

27. Fass R, Fennerty MB, Ofman JJ, et al. The clinical and economic value of a short course of omeprazole in patients with non-cardiac chest pain. Gastroenterology 1998;115:42–9.

28. Fass R, Ofman JJ, Gralnek IM, et al. Clinical and economic assessment of the omeprazole test in patients with symptoms suggestive of gastroesophageal reflux disease. Arch Intern Med 1999;159:2161–8.

29. Lagergren J, Bergstrom R, Lindgren A, Nyren O. Symptomatic gastroesophageal reflux as a risk factor for esophageal adenocarcinoma. N Engl J Med 1999;340:825–31.

30. Baehr PH, McDonald GB. Esophageal infections: risk factors, presentation, diagnosis, and treatment. Gastroenterology 1994;106:509–32.

31. Mathieson R, Dutta SK. Candida esophagitis. Dig Dis Sci 1983;28:365–70.

32. Ogorek CP, Davidson L, Fisher RS, Krevsky B. Idiopathic gastroparesis is associated with a multiplicity of severe dietary deficiencies. Am J Gastroenterol 1991;86:423–8.

33. Petrakis IE, Vrachassotakis N, Sciacca V, et al. Hyperglycemia attenuates erythromycin-induced acceleration of solid-phase gastric emptying in idiopathic and diabetic gastroparesis. Scand J Gastroenterol 1999;34:396–403.

34. Parkman HP, Schwartz S. Esophagitis and gastroduodenal disorders associated with diabetic gastroparesis. Arch Intern Med 1987;147:1477–80.

35. Horowitz M, Maddox AF, Wishart JM, et al. Relationships between oesophageal transit and solid and liquid gastric emptying in diabetes mellitus. Eur J Nucl Med 1991;18:229–34.

36. Koch KL. Diabetic gastropathy: gastric neuromuscular dysfunction in diabetes mellitus. A review of symptoms, pathophysiology, and treatment. Dig Dis Sci 1999;44:1061–75.

37. Undeland KA, Hausken T, Svebak S, et al. Wide gastric antrum and low vagal tone in patients with diabetes mellitus Type 1 compared to patients with functional dyspepsia and healthy individuals. Dig Dis Sci 1996;41:9–16.

38. Feldman M, Corbett DB, Ramsey EJ, et al. Abnormal gastric function in longstanding, insulin-dependent diabetic patients. Gastroenterology 1979;77:12–7.

39. Malagelada J-R, Rees WDW, Mazzotta LJ, Go VLW. Gastric motor abnormalities in diabetic and post-vagotomy gastroparesis: effect of metoclopramide and bethanechol. Gastroenterology 1980;78:286–93.

40. Mearin F, Camilleri M, Malagelada J-R. Pyloric dysfunction in diabetics with recurrent nausea and vomiting. Gastroenterology 1986;90:1919–25.

41. Camilleri M, Brown ML, Malagelada J-R. Relationship between impaired gastric emptying and abnormal gastrointestinal motility. Gastroenterology 1986;91:94–9.

42. Kong M-F, Horowitz M. Gastric emptying in diabetes mellitus: relationship to blood-glucose control. Clin Geriatr Med 1999;15:321–38.

43. Schvarcz E, Palmer M, Aman J, et al. Physiological hyperglycemia slows gastric emptying in normal subjects and patients with insulin-dependent diabetes mellitus. Gastroenterology 1997;113:60–6.

44. Fraser RJ, Horowitz M, Maddox AF, et al. Hyperglycemia slows gastric emptying in Type 1 (insulin-dependent) diabetes mellitus. Diabetologia 1990;33:675–80.

45. Barnett JL, Owyang C. Serum glucose concentration as a modulator of interdigestive gastric motility. Gastroenterology 1988;94:739–44.

46. Merio R, Festa A, Bergmenn H, et al. Slow gastric emptying in Type 1 diabetes: relation to autonomic and peripheral neuropathy, blood glucose, and glycemic control. Diabetes Care 1997;20:419–23.

47. Horowitz M, Fraser RJL. Gastoparesis: diagnosis and management. Scand J Gastroenterol 1995;30 (Suppl 213):7–16.

48. Hoogerwerf WA, Pasricha PJ, Kalloo AN, Schuster MM. Pain: the overlooked symptom in gastroparesis. Am J Gastroenterol 1999;94:1029–33.

49. Mearin F, Malagelada J-R. Gastroparesis and dyspepsia in patients with diabetes mellitus. Eur J Gastroenterol Hepatol 1995;7:717–23.

50. Braden B, Adams S, Duan L-P, et al. The 13C acetate breath test accurately reflects gastric emptying of liquids in both liquid and semisolid test meals. Gastroenterology 1995;108:1048–55.

51. Bingden O, Meunier F, Tollemar J, et al. Efficacy of amphotericin B encapsulated in liposomes (ambisome) in the treatment of invasive fungal infections in immunocompromised patients. J Antimicrob Chemother 1991;28(Suppl B):73–82.

52. Tougas G, Chen Y, Coates G, et al. Standardization of a simplified scintigraphic methodology for the assessment of gastric emptying in a multicenter setting. Am J Gastroenterol 2000;95:78–86.

53. Tougas G, Eaker EY, Abell T, et al. Assessment of gastric emptying using a low fat meal: establishment of international control values. Am J Gastroenterol 2000;95:1456–62.

54. Camilleri M. Appraisal of medium- and long-term treatment of gastroparesis and chronic intestinal dysmotility. Am J Gastroenterol 1994;89:1769–74.

55. McCallum RW, Chen JDZ, Lin Z, et al. Gastric pacing improves emptying and symptoms in patients with gastroparesis. Gastroenterology 1998;114:456–61.

56. Richards RD, Davenport K, McCallum RW. The treatment of idiopathic and diabetic gastroparesis with acute intravenous and chronic oral erythromycin. Am J Gastroenterol 1993;88:203–7.

57. CPS: Compendium of pharmaceuticals and specialties. Ottawa: Canadian Pharmacists Association; 1999.

58. Goodman & Gilman's The pharmacological basis of therapeutics. 9th ed. New York: McGraw-Hill; 1996.

59. Physician's desk reference. Montvale (NJ): Medical Economics Company; 1999. p. 2643–5.

60. Sturm A, Holtmann G, Goebell H, Gerken G. Prokinetics in patients with gastroparesis: a systematic analysis. Digestion 1999;60:422–7.

61. Corinaldesi R, Raiti C, Stanghellini V, et al. Comparative effects of oral cisapride and metoclopramide on gastric emptying of solids and symptoms in patients with functional dyspepsia and gastroparesis. Curr Ther Res 1987;42:428–35.

62. De Caestecker JS, Ewing DJ, Tothill P, et al. Evaluation of oral cisapride and metoclopramide in diabetic autonomic neuropathy: an eight-week double-blind crossover study. Aliment Pharmacol Ther 1989;3:69–81.

63. Champion MC, Braaten J, Gulechyn K. Domperidone compared to cisapride (prepulsid) in the management of gastroparesis. Am J Gastroenterol 1991;86:1309.

64. Erbas T, Varoglu E, Erbas B, Tastekin G. Comparison of metoclopramide and erythromycin in the treatment of diabetic gastroparesis. Diabetes Care 1993;16:1511–4.

65. Cooper T, Cutts T, Abell T, et al. Long-term cisapride therapy improves quality of life measures in patients with symptoms of gastroparesis. Gastroenterology 1991;100:A432.

66. Patterson D, Abell T, Rothstein R, et al. A double-blind multicenter comparison of domperidone and metoclopramide in the treatment of diabetic patients with symptoms of gastroparesis. Am J Gastroenterol 1999;94:1230–4.

67. Stacher G, Schernthaner G, Francesconi M, et al. Cisapride versus placebo for 8 weeks on glycemic control and gastric emptying in insulin-dependent diabetes: a double blind cross-over trial. J Clin Endocrinol Metab 1999;84:2357–62.

68. Farup CE, Leidy NK, Murray M, et al. Effect of domperidone on the health-related quality of life of patients with symptoms of diabetic gastroparesis. Diabetes Care 1998;21:1699–706.

69. Ware JE, Snow KK, Kosinski M, Gandek B. SF-36 health survey: manual and interpretation guide. Boston (MA): The Health Institute, New England Medical Center; 1993.

70. Ahm Y, Maturu P, Steinheber FU, Goldman JM. Association of diabetes mellitus with gastric bezoar formation. Arch Intern Med 1987;147:527–8.

71. Phillips MR, Zaheer S, Drugas GT. Gastric trichobezoar: case report and literature review. Mayo Clin Proc 1998;73:653–6.

72. Wang YG, Seitz U, Li ZL, et al. Endoscopic management of huge bezoars. Endoscopy 1998;30:371–4.

73. Barnett JL, Behler EM, Appelman HD, Elta GH. *Campylobacter pylori* is not associated with gastroparesis. Dig Dis Sci 1989;34:1677–80.

74. Salardi S, Cacciari E, Menegatti M, et al. *Helicobacter pylori* and type 1 diabetes mellitus in children. J Pediatr Gastroenterol Nutr 1999;28:307–9.

75. Begue RE, Mirza A, Compton T, et al. *Helicobacter pylori* infection and insulin requirement among children with type 1 diabetes mellitus. Pediatrics 1999;103:e83–6.

76. De Luis DA, Lahera M, Canton R, et al. Association of *Helicobacter pylori* infection with cardiovascular and cerebrovascular disease in diabetic patients. Diabetes Care 1998;21:1129–32.

77. Freeman JG, Cobden I, Shaw PJ, Terry G. Diabetes mellitus and duodenal ulceration. Br J Clin Pract 1986;40:508–9.

78. Forgacs S, Vertes L, Osvath J, Keri Z. Peptic ulcer and diabetes mellitus. Hepatogastroenterology 1980;27:500–4.

79. De Block CEM, De Leeuw IH, Van Gaal LF, The Belgian Diabetic Registry. High prevalence of manifestations of gastric autoimmunity in parietal cell antibody-positive type 1 (insulin-dependent) diabetic patients. J Clin Endocrinol Metabol 1999;84:4063–7.

80. Davis RE, McCann VJ, Stanton KG. Type 1 diabetes and latent pernicious anaemia. Med J Aust 1992;156:160–2.

81. Goldstein DE, Drash A, Gibbs J, Blizzard RM. Diabetes mellitus: the incidence of circulating antibodies against thyroid, gastric, and adrenal tissue. J Pediatr 1970;77:304–6.

82. Munichoodappa C, Kozak GP. Diabetes mellitus and pernicious anemia. Diabetes 1970;19:719–23.

83. Lysy J, Israeli E, Goldin E. The prevalence of chronic diarrhea among diabetic patients. Am J Gastroenterol 1999;94:2165–70.

84. Valdovinos MA, Camilleri M, Zimmerman BR. Chronic diarrhea in diabetes mellitus; mechanisms and an approach to diagnosis and treatment. Mayo Clin Proc 1993;68:691–702.

85. Camilleri M, Malagelada J-R. Abnormal intestinal motility in diabetics with the gastroparesis syndrome. Eur J Clin Invest 1984;14:420–7.

86. Scarpello JHB, Hague RV, Cullen DR, Sladen GE. The 14C-glycocholate test in diabetic diarrhea. BMJ 1976;2:673–5.

87. Le Marchand L, Wilkens LR, Kolonel LN, et al. Associations of sedentary lifestyle, obesity, smoking, alcohol use, and diabetes with the risk of colorectal cancer. Cancer Res 1997;57:4787–94.

88. Wald A. Incontinence and anorectal dysfunction in patients with diabetes mellitus. Eur J Gastroenterol Hepatol 1995;7:737–9.

89. Falchuk KR, Conlin D. The intestinal and liver complications of diabetes mellitus. Adv Intern Med 1993;38:269–86.

90. Fedorak RN, Field M, Chang EB. Treatment of diabetic diarrhea with clonidine. Ann Intern Med 1985;102:197–9.

91. Chang EB, Fedorak R, Field M. Experimental diabetic diarrhea in rats. Gastroenterology 1986;91:564–9.

92. Migliore A, Barone C, Manna R, Greco AV. Diabetic diarrhea and clonidine [letter]. Ann Intern Med 1988;109:170–1.

93. Walker JJ, Kaplan DS. Efficacy of the somatostatin analog octreotide in the treatment of two patients with refractory diabetic diarrhea. Am J Gastroenterol 1993;88:765–7.

94. Find KD, Fordtran JS. The effect of diarrhea on fecal fat excretion. Gastroenterology 1992;102:1936–9.

95. Schiller LR, Santa Ana CA, Schmulen C, et al. Pathogenesis of fecal incontinence in diabetes mellitus. N Engl J Med 1982;307:1666–71.

96. Marzuk PM. Biofeedback for gastrointestinal disorders: a review of the literature. Ann Intern Med 1985;103:240–4.

97. Acerini CL, Ahmed ML, Ross KM, et al. Coeliac disease in children and adolescents with IDDM: clinical characteristics and response to gluten-free diet. Diabet Med 1998;15:38–44.

98. Cronin CC, Feighery A, Ferriss JB, et al. High prevalence of celiac disease among patients with insulin-dependent (Type 1) diabetes mellitus. Am J Gastroenterol 1997;92:2210–2.

99. Talal AH, Murray JA, Goeken JASWI. Celiac disease in an adult population with insulin-dependent diabetes mellitus: use of endomysial antibody testing. Am J Gastroenterol 1997;92:1280–4.

100. Rossi TM, Albini CH, Kumar V. Incidence of celiac disease identified by the presence of serum endomysial antibodies in children with chronic diarrhea, short stature, or insulin-dependent diabetes mellitus. Pediatr 1993;123:262–4.

101. Collin P, Reunala T, Pukkala E, et al. Coeliac disease—associated disorders and survival. Gut 1994;35:1215–8.

102. Walsh CH, Cooper BT, Wright AD, et al. Diabetes mellitus and coeliac disease: a clinical study. QJM 1978;185:89–100.

103. Shanahan F, McKenna R, McCarthy CF, Drury MI. Coeliac disease and diabetes mellitus: a study of 24 patients with HLA typing. QJM 1982;203:329–35.

104. Maki M, Hallstrom O, Huupponen T, et al. Increased prevalence of coeliac disease in diabetes. Arch Dis Child 1984;59:739–42.

105. Gillett HR, Freeman HJ. Serological testing in screening for adult celiac disease. Can J Gastroenterol 1999;13:265–9.

106. Sategna-Guidetti C, Grosso S, Pulitano R, et al. Celiac disease and insulin-dependent diabetes mellitus. Screening in an adult population. Dig Dis Sci 1994;39:1633–7.

107. Maleki D, Camilleri M, Burton DD, et al. Pilot study of pathophysiology of constipation among community diabetics. Dig Dis Sci 1998;43:2373–8.

108. Battle WM, Snape WJ, Alavi A, et al. Colonic dysfunction in diabetes mellitus. Gastroenterology 1980;79:1217–21.

109. Sims MA, Hasler WL, Chey WD, et al. Hyperglycemia inhibits mechanoreceptor-mediated gastrocolonic responses and colonic peristaltic reflexes in healthy humans. Gastroenterology 1995;108:350–9.

110. Maleki D, Camilleri M, Zinsmeister AR, Rizza RA. Effect of acute hyperglycemia on colorectal motor and sensory function in humans. Am J Physiol 1997;273:G859–64.

111. Gorger G, Layer P. Exocrine pancreatic function in diabetic mellitus. Eur J Gastroenterol Hepatol 1995;7:740–6.

112. Newihi HE, Dooley CP, Saad C, et al. Impaired exocrine pancreatic function in diabetics with diarrhea and peripheral neuropathy. Dig Dis Sci 1988;33:705–10.

113. Everhart J, Wright D. Diabetes mellitus as a risk factor for pancreatic cancer. A meta-analysis. JAMA 1995;273:1605–9.

114. Misciagna G, Leoci C, Guerra V, et al. Epidemiology of cholelithiasis in southern Italy, part II: risk factors. Eur J Gastroenterol Hepatol 1996;8:585–93.

115. Attili AF, Capocaccia R, Carulli N, et al. Factors associated with gallstone disease in the MICOL experience. Hepatology 1997;26:809–18.

116. de Boer SY, Masclee AAM, Lam WF, et al. Effect of hyperglycaemia on gallbladder motility in type 1 (insulin-dependent) diabetes mellitus. Diabetologia 1994;37:75–81.

117. Stone BG, Gavaler JS, Belle SH, et al. Impairment of gallbladder emptying in diabetes mellitus. Gastroenterology 1988;95:170–8.

118. Hayes PC, Patrick A, Roulston JE, et al. Gallstones in diabetes mellitus: prevalence and risk factors. Eur J Gastroenterol Hepatol 1992;4:55–9.

119. Pellegrini CA. Asymptomatic gallstones: does diabetes make a difference? Gastroenterology 1986;91:245–6.

120. Sandler RS, Maule WF, Baltus ME. Factors associated with postoperative complications in diabetics after biliary tract surgery. Gastroenterology 1986;91:157–62.

121. Ransohoff DF, Miller GL, Forsythe SB, Hermann RE. Outcome of acute cholecystitis in patients with diabetes mellitus. Ann Intern Med 1987;106:829–32.

122. Aucott JN, Cooper GS, Bloom AD, Aron DC. Management of gallstones in diabetic patients. Arch Intern Med 1993;153:1053–8.

123. Strasberg SM. Cholelithiasis and acute cholecystitis. Baillieres Clin Gastroenterol 1997;11:643–61.

124. Sheth SG, Gordon FD, Chopra S. Nonalcoholic steatohepatitis. Ann Intern Med 1997;126:137–45.

125. Marchesini G, Brizi M, Morselli-Labate AM, et al. Association of nonalcoholic fatty liver disease with insulin resistance. Am J Med 1999;107:450–5.

126. Matteoni C, Younossi ZM, Gramlich T, et al. Nonalcoholic fatty liver disease: a spectrum of clinical and pathological severity. Gastroenterology 1999;116:1413–9.

127. Angulo P, Keach JC, Batts KP, Lindor KD. Independent predictors of liver fibrosis in patients with nonalcoholic steatohepatitis. Hepatology 1999;30:1356–62.

128. Saverymuttu SH, Joseph AE, Maxwell JD. Ultrasound scanning in the detection of hepatic fibrosis and steatosis. BMJ 1986;292:13–5.

129. Laurin J, Lindor KD, Crippin JS, et al. Ursodeoxycholic acid or clofibrate in the treatment of non-alcohol-induced steatohepatitis: a pilot study. Hepatology 1996;23:1464–7.

130. La Vecchia C, Negri E, Decarli A, Franceschi S. Diabetes mellitus and the risk of primary liver cancer. Int J Cancer 1997;73:204–7.

CHAPTER 29

Delivery of Diabetes Care

Dereck Hunt, MD, MSc, FRCPC

ABSTRACT

Providing optimal, well-coordinated care for patients with diabetes mellitus is complex. Patients need ongoing education and screening for complications, frequent blood pressure and glycemic control assessments, and regular adjustments to their therapeutic regimes. There may be a wide range of health care practitioners involved in the care of a person with diabetes mellitus—primary care practitioners and nurses, diabetes nurse educators, dietitians, endocrinologists, optometrists and ophthalmologists, foot care specialists, and others, including complication-specific specialists. Different approaches for delivering and coordinating diabetes care are also available. Many patients receive the majority of their diabetes-related care from their primary care practitioners. Alternatively, regional diabetes education centers may play a dominant role in ensuring optimal management and follow-up, along with patients' primary care physicians. Comprehensive hospital-based diabetes clinics, staffed by a group of endocrinologists, nurses, dietitians, and other specialists, provide another approach for delivering diabetes care.

Regardless of the model of care for a particular patient, a well-coordinated approach that includes a mechanism for ensuring ongoing reassessments and adjustments to therapeutic regimes is essential. Studies have demonstrated that diabetic patients who are free of significant complications can be cared for equally well by their primary care physicians, compared with hospital clinic-based care, as long as a prompting system is used. Without such prompting, the quality of diabetes care has been found to be less favorable in primary care settings. In view of the fact that many components of diabetes care need to be completed on a regular, predictable basis, computer-based reminder systems have also been evaluated and were found to have the potential to improve the quality of diabetes care.

INTRODUCTION

Diabetes mellitus is a common chronic condition that is associated with a range of complications, the majority of which can be prevented or delayed with timely intervention. Achieving this goal, however, requires well-organized and well-coordinated diabetes care. Patients require ongoing education and support to assist with daily self-management. Appropriate screening and intervention needs to be completed on a regular basis, along with assessments to evaluate the effectiveness of prescribed treatments and the need for changes or adjustments. There may be a wide range of health care specialists who, depending on a variety of factors, may be involved with the care of a person with diabetes, each assisting with different aspects of management and each being involved to varying degrees. Optimal care requires a well-organized approach that ensures ongoing and regular attention to key aspects of diabetes care and ensures a high level of communication among members of the diabetes health care team. This chapter reviews the different approaches available for delivering diabetes care. It also reviews the evidence supporting the need for a well-coordinated delivery system.

The questions to be addressed in this section include:

1. What approaches are available for organizing diabetes care?
2. Is there a need for a well-coordinated diabetes care delivery system that includes a mechanism for providing regular prompting for care?
3. Are computer-based reminder systems beneficial components of a diabetes care delivery system?

What Approaches are Available for Organizing Diabetes Care?

Optimal diabetes care requires the involvement of a range of individuals with expertise in different aspects of diabetes care.[1] These members form the diabetes health care team (Table 29–1). The person with diabetes is the central participant, while a variety of health care professionals are also involved. These may include the person's primary care physician and nurse, a diabetes nurse educator and dietitian, a diabetes specialist (such as an endocrinologist, ophthalmologist, or optometrist), a foot care specialist, and others, including specialists with expertise in managing the complications of diabetes. The degree to which these and other members are actively involved, however, can vary depending on how diabetes care is organized for a given person. Several different approaches are available, including a primary care-based approach and a hospital clinic-based approach (Table 29–2).

Models for Organizing the Delivery of Diabetes Care

The Primary Care Model

In the primary care model, an individual family physician or other primary care practitioner assumes the dominant role in coordinating all aspects of diabetes management. The primary care practitioner may request input from a diabetes educator or specialist or other member of the diabetes health care team but remains the principal person responsible for coordinating care and ensuring that key aspects of education and management are addressed. This remains the most common approach for delivering diabetes-related care. According to a survey completed in 1989, over 80% of diabetic patients are primarily followed by their primary care physicians for their diabetes.[2]

The Hospital Clinic Model

The primary care model contrasts with the hospital-based, comprehensive diabetes clinic model of care in which a group of endocrinologists, nurse educators, dietitians, foot care spe-

---

Table 29–1 The Diabetes Health Care Team

Person with diabetes mellitus

Relatives of the person with diabetes mellitus

Primary care physician and nurse

Diabetes nurse educator

Diabetes dietitian

Diabetes specialist (endocrinologist or general internist)

Ophthalmologist or optometrist

Foot care specialist (chiropodist or podiatrist)

Pharmacist

Other specialists (obstetricians, complication-specific specialists)

Visiting home nurse

Table 29–2 Models for Organizing the Delivery of Diabetes Care

Primary care model

Hospital clinic model

Mixed primary care/diabetes clinic model

Health service organization model

---

cialists, and others are assembled and assume the responsibility of assisting the person with diabetes in achieving optimal care. While the primary care practitioner continues to be involved, it is to a much lesser degree. Coordination of diabetes-related education and ongoing management is completed by the clinic itself while the primary care practitioner largely focuses on nondiabetes-related aspects.

The Mixed Primary Care/Diabetes Clinic Model

Other models of diabetes care delivery lie in between the primary care model and the hospital-based approach. These share certain characteristics with each system. Many diabetes education centers, for example, provide ongoing follow-up of patients, in addition to offering focused educational sessions. The diabetes educators at the center assume the responsibility of regularly assessing the level of glycemic control and blood pressure control, as well as screening for microvascular complications. In some cases, the educators may have the authority to adjust diabetes-related medication dosages or to make referrals to teaching programs available within the center. The primary care physician, however, continues to play an active role, being responsible for assessing the appropriateness of the treatment plan as well as deciding on the need to initiate new medications or to make referrals to specialists for more detailed complication-specific assessments. It is essential that there be a high degree of communication between the education center and the primary care physician in this approach.

The Health Service Organization Model

The health service organization provides another model for delivering diabetes care. Physicians participating in a health service organization have a roster of patients for whom they provide appropriate outpatient health care. They are remunerated according to the number of patients of different ages and gender in their practice. Preventive health care is a major focus of the health service organization mandate, and resources are generally provided for acquiring educators and dietitians within the clinic setting itself. This means that education and ongoing follow-up of patients with diabetes can occur almost entirely within the confines of the primary care physician's clinic and only require the involvement of "outside" specialists in more complicated cases.

Is There a Need for a Well-Coordinated Diabetes Care Delivery System That Includes a Mechanism for Providing Regular Prompting for Care?

Whereas many different approaches are available for organizing the delivery of care for people with diabetes mellitus, little evidence exists regarding the relative benefits of each model in terms of patient outcomes or satisfaction. Thus, the approach used for individual patients varies depending on a variety of factors, including local practice patterns, the availability of education centers or hospital-based clinics, the development of diabetes-related complications in individual patients, physician experience, and patient preferences.

Research does exist, however, regarding the importance of having a well-coordinated system that can prompt participants about the need for regular diabetes-related reassessments.

Specifically, the value of implementing a system that can prompt both patients and health care practitioners to complete necessary health care screening and glycemic control assessments has been evaluated in primary care settings. Several randomized studies have evaluated the effects of providing regular prompts to patients and primary care physicians. This approach has been compared with managing patients in hospital-based diabetes clinics in terms of quality of care.

These studies, including trials that compared primary care-based diabetes management in the absence of a prompting system with hospital-based clinic management, have been systematically reviewed.[3] Five randomized trials, with a total of 1,058 patients (mean age 58.4 years) who were free of significant diabetes-related complications or serious medical problems, were identified for inclusion in the review. Patients were followed for 2 years in three of the studies and for 1 and 5 years in the other two studies. Three of the five studies included prompting systems—a centralized computer system in two studies and a nurse-based prompting system in another study. Prompts were sent to both patients and physicians in all cases.

The studies in the systematic review demonstrated that primary care-based diabetes management, when coupled with a prompting system, can be as good as or better than hospital clinic-based care for people who do not have significant diabetes-related complications. There was no difference in mortality (odds ratio [OR] 1.1, 95% confidence interval [CI] 0.5 to 2.1), a trend toward superior glycemic control in the primary care arm by the end of the follow-up periods (difference in hemoglobin A_{1c} –0.3%, 95% CI –0.6 to 0.03%), and a lower rate of nonattendance for diabetes-related appointments (OR 0.4, 95% CI 0.2 to 0.6) among the patients randomized to primary care compared with those allocated to hospital clinic-based care (Table 29–3).

In contrast, the two studies that assessed primary care-based diabetes management in the absence of a prompting system found significantly worse outcomes for patients randomly allocated to primary care compared with the hospital clinic patients (see Table 29–3). For mortality, the odds ratio was 2.6 (95% CI 1.4 to 4.6); for hemoglobin A_{1c}, an increase of 0.3 was noted by the end of the study follow-up periods (95% CI –0.09 to 0.6); for nonattendance for diabetes-related appointments, the odds ratio was 28 (95% CI 16 to 49). These poor outcomes were noted despite the fact that steps were taken to facilitate optimal diabetes care in both studies. An administrative system for recalling patients was provided to physicians in one of the studies and a specialized diabetes record card was provided to physicians in the other study, along with copies of diabetes care guidelines.

EVIDENCE-BASED MESSAGES

1. Prompting patients and health care practitioners for diabetes-related assessments leads to a significant improvement in quality of care (Level 1A).[3]
2. For patients who are free of significant diabetes-related complications, primary care-based diabetes management can be as high quality as hospital-based clinic care, provided that an effective prompting system is in use (Level 1A).[3]

Table 29–3 Diabetes-Related Care and the Role of Prompting Systems: Primary Practice Compared with Hospital-Based Clinics

	Mortality (odds ratio)	Glycemic Control (primary care — hospital) (hemoglobin A_{1c})	Nonattendance for Diabetes-Related Visits (odds ratio)
Prompting system	1.1 (0.5–2.1)	–0.3 (–0.6–0.03)	0.4 (0.2–0.6)
No prompting system	2.6 (1.4–4.6)	0.3 (–0.09–0.6)	28 (16–49)

ARE COMPUTER-BASED REMINDER SYSTEMS BENEFICIAL COMPONENTS OF A DIABETES CARE DELIVERY SYSTEM?

While centralized prompting for diabetes care requires a high degree of cooperation between primary care practitioners, ophthalmologists, optometrists, and laboratories to be successful, it can be very effective. The use of a computer-based clinical decision support system (CDSS) to generate patient-specific reminders for diabetes care at individual clinics is a complementary approach that is gradually becoming more feasible with the introduction of electronic medical records. By matching patient-specific characteristics with an underlying knowledge base, computer systems can be used to provide patients and health care practitioners alike with reminders to complete necessary care or to begin appropriate treatments. In a recent systematic review,[4] 65 controlled trials that evaluated the effects on physician performance of using a CDSS were identified. Sixty-six percent of the studies found that providing decision support led to improved adherence with optimal care. Improvements were noted in preventive care, medication dosing, and many other aspects of clinical practice.

Three of the trials specifically evaluated the effect of using a CDSS on the quality of care that can be provided for patients with diabetes at academic primary care clinics. In a recent study,[5] general internal medicine residents were randomly allocated to an intervention or control group. All participants were provided with encounter forms developed to facilitate acquisition of information relevant to diabetes care. In addition, intervention-arm residents received computer-generated forms that summarized patients' current diabetes preventive health status and provided a list of upcoming or overdue preventive health activities. When the effect of the intervention was evaluated, compliance rates with recommended care were found to have improved significantly for both groups (36% at baseline vs 53% at follow-up). The adherence rates, however, were the same for participants in both the intervention and control arms of the study. The authors concluded that the encounter forms, rather than the reminders, contributed to the improved physician performance. In a study of a computer-based reminder system for diabetes care,[6] primary care providers, including both faculty members and residents, at a family medicine residency program clinic were randomly assigned to either receive or not receive patient-specific reminders generated using the clinic's electronic medical record system. During the 6-month trial period, compliance with recommendations among intervention physicians was 32% versus 16% among the control physicians ($p < .05$); another study[7] was less encouraging. Providing reminders significantly increased the number of prescriptions for home blood glucose monitoring but had no effect on other aspects of diabetes care.

EVIDENCE-BASED MESSAGES

1. Implementation of computer-based clinical decision support can lead to improvements in the delivery of preventive health care, drug dosing, and many other aspects of clinical practice (Level 1A).[5]
2. Computer-based clinical decision support can improve the quality of diabetes care in primary practice (Level 2).[6,7]

CONCLUSION

Providing optimal care for people with diabetes remains a complex task, with a host of factors contributing to this situation. New therapeutic approaches are constantly becoming available, and more aggressive treatment goals are being shown to have beneficial effects on patient outcomes. Resources for diabetes care and education vary from region to region. Individual patients have different preferences, personal circumstances, cultural attitudes, and beliefs. Individual and regional economic circumstances vary markedly. Approaches and interventions designed to improve the delivery of diabetes care need to recognize these considerations. Only by developing integrated approaches that address those factors most significant in a particular setting, while also incorporating our current understanding of optimal evidence-based diabetes care and the need to maintain ongoing regular assessments, can we hope to have a major impact on the long-term health outcomes for people with diabetes mellitus.

SUMMARY OF EVIDENCE-BASED MESSAGES

1. Prompting patients and health-care practitioners for diabetes-related assessments leads to a significant improvement in quality of care (Level 1A).[3]
2. For patients who are free of significant diabetes-related complications, primary care-based diabetes management can be as high quality as hospital-based clinic care, provided that an effective prompting system is in use (Level 1A).[3]
3. Implementation of computer-based clinical decision support can lead to improvements in the delivery of preventive health care, drug dosing, and many other aspects of clinical practice (Level 1A).[5]
4. Computer-based clinical decision support can improve the quality of diabetes care in primary practice (Level 2).[6,7]

REFERENCES

1. Meltzer S., Leiter L, Daneman D, et al. 1998 clinical practice guidelines for the management of diabetes in Canada. Can Med Assoc J 1998;159(Suppl 8):S1–29.

2. Harris MI. Medical care for patients with diabetes mellitus. Epidemiological aspects. Ann Intern Med 1996;124:117–22.

3. Griffin S, Kinmonth AL. Diabetes care: general practitioner or specialist? The effectiveness of systems for routine surveillance for people with diabetes. Cochrane Library. Oxford: Update Software; 1998.

4. Hunt DL, Haynes RB, Hanna SE, Smith K. Effects of computer-based clinical decision support systems on physician performance and patient outcomes. A systematic review. JAMA 1998;280:1339–46.

5. Nilasena DS, Lincoln MJ. A computer-generated reminder system improves physician compliance with diabetes preventive care guidelines. Proc Annu Symp Comput Appl Med Care 1995;640–5.

6. Lobach DF, Hammond WE. Development and evaluation of a computer-assisted management protocol (CAMP): improved compliance with care guidelines form diabetes mellitus. Proc Annu Symp Comput Appl Med Care 1994;787–91.

7. Mazzuca SA, Vinicor F, Einterz RM, et al. Effects of the clinical environment on physicians' response to postgraduate medical education. Am Educ Res J 1990;27:473–88.

Index